# Guide to

# 2002

# Distance Learning

# Programs

**PETERSON'S**

**THOMSON LEARNING**

Australia • Canada • Mexico • Singapore • Spain • United Kingdom • United States

PETERSON'S
™
THOMSON LEARNING

**About Peterson's**

Founded in 1966, Peterson's, a division of Thomson Learning, is the nation's largest and most respected provider of lifelong learning resources, both in print and online. The Education Supersite$^{SM}$ at www.petersons.com—the Internet's most heavily traveled education resource—has searchable databases and interactive tools for contacting U.S.-accredited institutions and programs. In addition, Peterson's delivers unmatched financial aid resources and test-preparation tools. Peterson's serves more than 100 million education consumers annually.

Peterson's is a division of Thomson Learning, one of the world's largest providers of lifelong learning. Thomson Learning serves the needs of individuals, learning institutions, and corporations with products and services for both traditional and distributed learning. Headquartered in Stamford, Connecticut, with offices worldwide, Thomson Learning is a division of The Thomson Corporation (www.thomson.com), one of the world's leading e-information and solutions companies in the business, professional, and education marketplaces. For more information, visit www.thomsonlearning.com.

For more information, contact Peterson's, 2000 Lenox Drive, Lawrenceville, NJ 08648; 800-338-3282; or find us on the World Wide Web at: www.petersons.com/about

ISBN 0-7689-0555-9

Printed in the United States of America

10  9  8  7  6  5  4  3  2  1     02  01

# TABLE OF CONTENTS

# HOW TO USE THIS GUIDE

## What's Inside

### INSTITUTION PROFILES

Here, in alphabetical order, you'll find nearly 1,100 institutions offering postsecondary education at a distance. For each institution, specific degree and certificate programs are listed, followed by a list of subjects for which individual courses are offered (undergraduate, graduate, and noncredit).

**Institutional Information.** The sections here describe overall characteristics of an institution and its distance learning offerings featuring key facts and figures about the institution, including the type of accreditation it has and the availability of financial aid and the person or office to contact for more information about the institution's distance learning courses.

**eCollege.com Information.** As a result of Peterson's partnership with eCollege.com, institutions that are members of eCollege.com are identified by a graphic in this section. This graphic includes a Web address (http://www.eCollege.com) that students can use to find exciting and up-to-date information about eCollege.com and its member institutions, Peterson's partnership with eCollege.com, and how to make education via distance learning more accessible and affordable.

**Degree and Certificate Programs.** This part of the profile lists each program leading to a degree or certificate that can be completed entirely at a distance. Programs are grouped by the level of award: associates degrees, baccalaureate degrees, graduate degrees, undergraduate certificates, and graduate certificates.

**Individual Course Subject Areas.** This part of the profile lists the general subject areas in which the institution offers courses at a distance. Subjects are divided into those offered for undergraduate credit, for graduate credit, and noncredit. (Note that this is not a listing of course titles; you will need to contact the institution for a detailed list of courses offered.)

### IN-DEPTH DESCRIPTIONS

Additional details on distance learning offerings are provided by participating institutions and consortia. Each two-page entry provides details on delivery media, programs of study, special programs, credit options, faculty, students, admission, tuition and fees, financial aid, and applying.

### CD

Peterson's *Guide to Distance Learning 2002* and the Distance Learning Channel on petersons.com comprise a fully integrated book and Web product that profiles accredited degree-granting institutions offering distance learning programs. In the back of this book, you'll find a CD that launches to the Distance Learning Channel on petersons.com (Internet access is required), where you can find additional program information and take a brief assessment on whether distance learning is the right avenue for your personal education goals.

## Finding What You Want

If you simply want to get a sense of the variety of programs being offered in distance learning, you may want to just browse through the **Institution Profiles** page by page.

If you are interested in locating a certificate or degree program in a specific field of study, refer to the **Index of Institutions Offering Degree and Certificate Programs.** Here you'll find institutions offering everything from Accounting to Theological & Ministerial Studies. There are more than 1,400 areas in all.

If it is individual courses you're looking for, the **Individual Courses Index** will guide you to institutions offering credit and noncredit courses at either the undergraduate or graduate level.

The **Geographic Index** lets you find programs that are offered by institutions that are located near you. Keep in mind that, most institution's offerings are available nationally, and sometimes internationally. See individual listings for details.

## How Colleges Get Into the Guide

This book profiles nearly 1,100 institutions of higher education currently offering courses or entire programs at a distance. To be included, all U.S. institutions must have full accreditation or candidate-for-accreditation (preaccreditation) status granted by an institutional or specialized accrediting body recognized by the U.S. Department of Education or the Council for Higher Education Accreditation.[1] Canadian institutions must be chartered and authorized to grant degrees by the provincial government, be affiliated with a chartered institution, or be accredited by a recognized U.S. accrediting body.

In the research for this guide, the following definition of "distance learning" was used: a planned teaching/learning experience in which teacher and students are separated by physical distance, and use any of a wide spectrum of media. This definition is based on the one developed by the University of Wisconsin Extension.

## RESEARCH PROCEDURES

The information provided in these profiles was collected during the summer of 2001 by way of a survey posted online for colleges and universities. With minor exceptions, all data included in this edition have been submitted by officials at the schools themselves. For a few schools that failed to respond to Peterson's web-based survey in time to meet the deadline, information was drawn from their Web sites. In addition, many of the institutions that submitted data were contacted directly by the Peterson's research staff to verify unusual figures, resolve discrepancies, and obtain additional data. All usable information received in time for publication has been included. The omission of any particular item from an index or profile listing signifies that the item is either not applicable to that institution or that data were not available. Although Peterson's has every reason to believe that the information presented in this guide is accurate, students should check with each college or university to verify such figures as tuition and fees, which may have changed since the publication of this volume.

---

[1] *The six U.S. regional accrediting associations are: the New England Association of Schools and Colleges, Middle States Association of Colleges and Schools, North Central Association of Colleges and Schools, Northwest Association of Schools and Colleges, Southern Association of Colleges and Schools, and Western Association of Schools and Colleges. Approval by state educational agencies is conferred separately on some distance education courses.*

# WHAT IS DISTANCE LEARNING?

One student is a professional who needs to update work-related skills. Another is a working mother who never finished her bachelor's degree and would love to have that diploma and get a better job. A third student attends a local community college but would like to get a degree offered by a four-year institution halfway across the country—without moving.

For this diverse group of students, disrupting family and work by commuting to sometimes distant on-campus classes on a rigid schedule is simply not a workable option. Many people, and perhaps you, are discovering that distance learning is a blessing—you can get the education you need, which might otherwise be difficult or impossible to obtain in the traditional manner.

*Broadly defined, distance learning is the delivery of educational programs to students who are off-site.*

In distance learning courses, the instructor is not in the same place as the student. The students may be widely separated by geography and time, and the instructor and students communicate with each other using various means, from the U.S. mail to the Internet. You can be a distance learner whether you live 300 miles from the university or across the street.

Distance learning courses are categorized according to the primary technologies they use to deliver instruction: print-based, audio-based, video-based, and Internet-based. The audio, video, and Internet courses all have variations that are synchronous—classes take place at specific times only—and asynchronous—classes occur at flexible times.

**PRINT-BASED** courses (correspondence courses) use print materials as the medium of instruction. Students receive the materials by mail at the start of the course and return completed assignments by mail. Sometimes fax machines speed up the delivery of assignments, and the telephone can be used if communication between instructor and student is necessary.

**AUDIO-BASED** courses may involve two-way communication, as in audio or phone conferencing; or they may involve one-way communication, including radio broadcast and prerecorded audiotapes sent to students. Audio technologies may be used to supplement the main technology used in the course. For example, in an Internet-based distance education course, students and professors may call one another periodically.

**VIDEO-BASED** technologies include two-way interactive videoconferencing, one-way video with two-way audio, one-way live video, and one-way prerecorded videotapes provided to students. Of these, two-way interactive video and prerecorded videotapes are the most popular.

**TWO-WAY INTERACTIVE VIDEO** courses take place simultaneously in two or more sites. The instructor is located in the home site with a group of students, and other students are located in satellite sites, often with a facilitator to help out. Each site has TV monitors or large screens on which the instructor and students can be viewed. The course is conducted as a lecture. When students speak in class, they press a button on an apparatus on their desks, which makes the camera point to them as they speak and allows their voices to be transmitted to the other location. Quizzes and exams are faxed to the satellite site and faxed back or mailed by an assistant when they are completed. Two-way interactive video bridges geographical distances but not time. Students must be in a particular place at a particular time to take the course.

**PRERECORDED VIDEO** courses are videotaped and mailed to off-site students. To supplement this, the course may have a Web site where notes and assignments are posted, or these may be mailed to the off-site students along with the tapes. If students have questions, they can call or e-mail the instructor after they view the tape.

**INTERNET-BASED** courses (also called online courses or e-learning) are offered over the Internet. Some online courses use synchronous, "real-time" instruction based primarily on interactive computer conferencing or chat rooms. However, most Internet-based courses use asynchronous instruction, making use of online course management systems, Web sites, e-mail, electronic mailing lists, newsgroups, bulletin boards, and messaging programs.

In asynchronous online courses, instructors post instructional material and assignments, including text, images, video, audio, and even interactive simulations, on the course Web site. Using messaging systems, newsgroups, or bulletin boards, they can start online discussions by posting a comment or question; students can log on using a password and join the discussion at their convenience. In some courses there may be periodic real-time interaction in chat rooms or interactive environments like MUDS (multiple-user dungeons) and MOOS (multiple-object orientations). Feedback and guidance to individual students can be done by e-mail or telephone. Note that most of the interaction in an online course is text-based; instructors and students communicate primarily through the keyboarded word.

Obviously, students must have a computer with the appropriate software and Internet access in order to take an Internet-based course. The cost of technology aside, online distance learning programs have considerable advantages. Because the course material stays on line for a period of time, students can log on at their own convenience.

To help ensure that students keep up, many instructors structure the learning environment by setting weekly deadlines for reading lectures and completing assignments, requiring group projects, and making participation in online discussions mandatory. In online courses with participation requirements, the amount of interaction between the faculty and students is far greater than in a large lecture class held on campus. There's no lying low in the back of the classroom in a well-run online course.

## Mixing the Technologies

Many courses combine technologies with print materials. For example, a course can begin with a videoconference, with the instructor introducing himself or herself and outlining the course requirements. A printed study guide with all assigned readings and activities is distributed to all participants at the first session. Students who cannot get to a videoconferencing site are sent a videocassette of the first session along with the study guide.

After the first session, the course moves on line. Using chat rooms, threaded discussions, and e-mail, participants do their assignments and group projects and interact on line. Assignments are snail-mailed to the faculty member. Finally, the class concludes with another synchronous videoconference or recorded videotape.

## Future Trends

Today, online instruction, two-way interactive video, and one-way prerecorded video are the most popular instructional technologies in distance education. According to the Department of Education's National Center for Education Statistics, colleges and universities are planning to increase their use of Internet-based instruction and two-way interactive video. Prerecorded video is likely to decrease in popularity.

The explosive growth in distance learning has come primarily from online courses, and that is likely to continue.

With better databases and other sources of information continuing to appear on the Internet, ease of access to reliable data will increase. As high bandwidth connections to the Internet start to replace phone connections, the capacity to quickly transmit large amounts of data will increase dramatically. For example, with a high-speed modem and phone connection, it can take several minutes to download a video snippet. Thus, most online courses today use text, images, and perhaps some animation, but they are limited in their video capabilities. Eventually, high bandwidth technologies will make individualized, customized, and live video interactions possible, with lengthy video programming available.

## Degree and Certificate Programs

Many institutions of higher learning simply offer a smorgasbord of distance education courses that can be taken for credit. An increasing number of institutions, however, have taken distance education to the next step; they have begun to offer undergraduate and graduate certificate and degree programs that can be completed entirely by distance education. For example, a student with an associate degree from a local community college can go on to earn a baccalaureate degree from a four-year institution by distance learning, without relocating. Or a working professional can earn a master's degree or professional certificate on a part-time basis through distance learning.

## Who Offers Distance Learning?

The better question might be, "Who doesn't?" With lifelong learning becoming commonplace and communications technologies improving rapidly, the demand for distance education has grown dramatically, and with it the number and variety of providers.

Peterson's *Guide to Distance Learning Programs 2002* lists more than 3,000 degree and certificate programs, representing a phenomenal increase in the last few years. The first group of providers consists of the traditional colleges, universities, graduate schools, community colleges, technical schools, and vocational schools. These providers range from schools only their neighbors have heard of to household names like Stanford, Virginia Tech, and the University of California.

The three most common subjects taught by distance education are social sciences, business, and education, followed closely by computer science and health. The challenges posed by distance education have forced colleges and universities to be creative in their approaches. Some schools have formed partnerships with cable companies, public broadcasting services, satellite broadcasters, and online education companies to deliver high-quality distance education. Colleges and universities also partner with corporations to deliver courses and degree programs to employees.

Finally, there are many online purveyors of noncredit distance education courses on subjects that range from candle making and beauty secrets to C++ programming and Spanish. These courses may be fun and even instructive, but they won't contribute to your formal educational credentials.

# Earn a respected degree
## in your own space...at your own pace.

*It's not always realistic to expect adults with family and job commitments to drop out of life to earn a degree.*

# WHAT CAN YOU STUDY VIA DISTANCE LEARNING?

If you are interested in pursuing your education by distance learning, you are not limited to a few specialized courses or degree programs. Actually, almost every course, certificate, and degree program that you can take on campus is also available in a distance learning format. There are exceptions, of course. Degree programs in subjects that require laboratory work or performance, for example, cannot usually be done completely at a distance. Still, distance education spans a wide range of offerings, from accredited graduate-level degree programs to self-help and hobby courses. Although some programs and courses are limited to residents of certain states or regions, many are available nationwide and internationally.

## Undergraduate Degree Programs

Today you can earn an associate or bachelor's degree entirely by distance learning. You also may be able to shorten the time it takes to earn a degree if you transfer college credits from other institutions of higher learning, earn credits through equivalency exams, or present a portfolio of your accomplishments. For adults, earning credits for past academic and other work can cut a year or more off the time it takes to earn an undergraduate degree. So don't be shy about negotiating for credits with the school in which you plan to enroll—the time and money you save may be considerable.

### ASSOCIATE DEGREE

Distance learning associate degrees are offered in a wide range of fields, including liberal arts, business, computer science, and health professions. Many students who have earned an associate degree go on to apply those credits toward a bachelor's degree.

### BACHELOR'S DEGREE

Distance learning bachelor's degrees are offered in many fields, including business, engineering, computer science, economics, English, history, nursing, psychology, and telecommunications. Some colleges and universities offer interdisciplinary degrees, such as environmental studies or arts management, and some permit students to design their own interdisciplinary program.

## Graduate Degree Programs

### MASTER'S DEGREE

Distance learning master's degree programs outnumbered other distance learning degree programs by a considerable margin. Most of these degree programs are professional in nature and are designed for working adults with experience in the field. If you are interested in a master's degree in library science, business, or education, you are in luck. These are fields in which there are many distance master's degree programs from which to choose. However, if you are looking for a distance learning master's degree program in an academic field, such as English language and literature, chemistry, or ethnic and cultural studies, your choices are far more limited. That's because most master's programs in academic fields are campus based.

Another type of master's degree that is offered via distance learning is the interdisciplinary degree. Some are offered in liberal studies or humanities and are granted for advanced study and a culminating project or thesis. Others combine academic and professional areas of study. Still others are offered in broad subject areas like environmental studies, in which students are expected to design their own course of study based on their particular interests.

### DOCTORAL DEGREE

Most distance learning doctoral programs, even those offered by virtual universities, have a brief residency requirement. There are far fewer distance learning doctoral programs than master's programs. However, you can find programs in a wide range of fields, although the number of programs within each field may be limited. You can earn a distance learning doctoral degree in fields as diverse as business, engineering, computer science, counseling psychology, instructional technology, education, human services, library science, English literature, management, pharmacy, and public policy. As with distance learning master's degrees, distance learning doctoral degrees tend to be professional rather than academic in orientation. Many of these degree programs are designed with the professional working adult in mind.

## Certificate Programs

Distance learning certificate programs can train you for a new career or give you a foundation in a new subject even if you've already earned a college degree in an entirely different field. Some schools now offer a portion of a master's or other degree as a certificate. This allows you to take part of the full degree curriculum and either stop at the certification level or proceed through for the entire degree. If this is an option that interests you, be sure to consider the admissions requirements carefully. If you think you may matriculate through to the entire degree, be sure you understand the admissions requirements for each program because they may differ.

## Professional Certificate Programs

To give you just a few examples of professional certificate programs offered via distance learning, within the engineering profession there are certificates in computer-integrated manufacturing, systems engineering, and fire-protection engineering. In business, there are distance learning certificate programs in information technology and health services management. In education, distance learning certificates include early reading instruction, children's literature, and English as a second language. In health care, certificates include medical assisting, home health nursing, and health-care administration. In law, distance learning certificates are offered in paralegal/legal assistant studies and legal issues for business professionals.

Professional certificate programs are often designed with the help of professional associations and licensing boards, and thus encompass real-world, practical knowledge. Many are designed to prepare students for professional certification or licensure. At the end of the program, the student sits for an exam and earns a state-recognized certificate from a certifying agency or licensing board. If this is your goal, you should make sure that the certification program you want to take meets the certifying agency or licensing board's requirements. That way, you won't waste your time or money completing a program that won't help you meet your ultimate professional goals.

## Certificate Programs in Academic Subjects

Less common, but still available via distance learning, are undergraduate and graduate certificate programs in many academic subjects. At the undergraduate level, you can earn a certificate in areas such as American studies, Chinese language and literature, English composition, creative writing, ethnic and cultural studies, general studies, humanities, and liberal arts and sciences. If you later enroll in an undergraduate degree program, you may be able to apply the credits earned in a certificate program toward your degree. At the graduate level, you can earn a certificate via distance learning in subjects like biology, English language and literature, geography, physiological psychology, religious studies, and statistics.

# WHAT IS A CONSORTIUM?

## Types of Consortia

Over the last few years, several types of consortia have emerged as the most successful and most popular distance education models. Among them are statewide consortia of public universities and colleges, statewide consortia of public and private institutions, regional consortia, consortia of peer institutions of higher education, and specialized consortia.

**Statewide Consortia of Public Colleges and Universities.** On the tightly focused side of the spectrum, a consortium may consist of the campuses of a single state university system. Students access the distance learning offerings of the various state colleges through a portal sometimes referred to as a virtual university.

A good example of a public statewide consortium is the University of Texas TeleCampus collaboration, which consists of fifteen UT campuses (www.telecampus.utsystem.edu). In collaborative degree plans offered via the TeleCampus, you may apply to one school, take courses from several partner institutions, use centralized support services, and receive a fully accredited degree from the "home" campus to which you originally applied. The TeleCampus serves as both a portal to distance education offerings in the Texas system and as a centralized point of service.

Many other states operate or develop consortia of their public colleges and universities, including Connecticut, Illinois, Kansas, Massachusetts, Michigan, New Jersey, New York, Ohio, Oklahoma, Oregon, South Dakota, and Tennessee. All have arrangements in place whereby students can take some transferable credits on line from more than one institution and apply them to a degree at their home institution.

**Statewide Consortia of Public and Private Colleges and Universities.** Broadening the scope a bit is the statewide consortium that includes both public and private institutions of higher education. Students in the state can use a single Web site to select distance education courses offered by member colleges and universities. If you are enrolled in a degree program at one member institution, you have access to distance learning courses given by other member institutions. Although the consortia members typically work together to maximize the transferability of credits from one college or university to another, it is still usually up to you to ensure that credits earned elsewhere can be applied to your home institution's degree.

For example, Kentucky Commonwealth Virtual University (KCVU) encompasses more than fifty institutions in the state of Kentucky, ranging from universities to technical colleges (www.kcvu.org). Each member institution charges its own tuition rates for in-state and out-of-state students. In addition to maintaining a centralized Internet directory of all distance learning courses offered in Kentucky, KCVU offers exceptional student support services. For example, you can fill out a common form to apply on line to any of the fifty member institutions. Once you are admitted to the KCVU system, you have centralized online access to every library book in the system as well as online access to the full text of 5,000 journals. If you wish to check out a book, it will be sent to the nearest public library, where you can pick it up free of charge. If there is no library nearby, the book will be sent by courier to your home or office. Your academic records will be maintained by each institution at which you take a course, but also by KCVU, which will keep your complete records from all institutions.

**Regional Consortia.** Regional consortia include institutions of higher education from more than one state. Such consortia may involve public institutions, private institutions, or a mix of both. The Southern Regional Education Board (SREB) launched the Southern Regional Electronic Campus (SREC) in 1998 and now offers more than 3,200 courses from 262 colleges and universities in sixteen states (www.electroniccampus.org). SREC attempts to guarantee a standard of quality in the courses it lists by reviewing them to make sure they are well set up and supported by adequate services. It does not judge curriculum (it leaves that to member institutions) nor does it list courses in their first year of instruction.

From the Electronic Campus Web site, you can identify distance learning programs and courses that are available from all member institutions. For more detailed information, you can search the site by college or university, discipline, level, and state, including course descriptions and how the programs and courses are delivered. You can also connect directly to a particular college or university to learn about registration, enrollment, and cost. To improve its student services, the Electronic Campus has formed a partnership with the University System of Georgia to create a new Web site known as Ways In (www.waysin.org). From that site, due to be operational in 2001–02, students will be able to apply for admission, register for classes, get information about and apply for financial aid, make payments, purchase textbooks, and use new online library services.

The SREC system is administratively decentralized. The acceptance of transfer credits and the use of credits for program requirements are determined by the college or university in which the student is enrolled. Likewise, all institutions set their own levels for in-state and out-of-state tuition, maintain individual student records, and determine policy with respect to access to their own student services. Therefore, if you take three classes from three different institutions you might have to be admitted to all three, pay three different tuition rates, and contact all three institutions for your academic records. A unique model of regional distance education collaboration, consisting of members from nineteen states, is Western Governors University (www.wgu.edu). Unlike most other virtual universities that serve as the hub of a consortium, WGU enrolls its own students and grants its own degrees by assessing students' knowledge through competency-based examinations. WGU does not teach its own courses, but it provides its students with access to courses from member institutions. WGU, established in 1998, is not yet regionally accredited, although it was awarded candidacy status in 2000 and hopes to be fully accredited in two to five years (see Chapter 5 for more on accreditation). Its unusual degree model and accreditation status may account for WGU's relatively low enrollment of about 200 degree-seeking students.

Other regional consortia include the National Universities Degree Consortium, a collaboration of ten accredited universities from across the United States (www.nudc.org); and the Canadian Virtual University, which includes seven universities across Canada (www.cvu-uvc.ca). Today, students can even choose to participate in a global consortium like CREAD, the Inter-American network of institutions throughout North, Central, and South America.

**Consortia of Peer Institutions of Higher Education.** Groups of institutions sometimes form consortia because they have a common orientation or complementary strengths from which students might benefit.

For example, the Jesuit Distance Education Network of the Association of Jesuit Colleges and Universities seeks to expand the array of learning options for students on its twenty-four campuses in nineteen states (www.jesuitnet.com). Administrators hope to develop the JesuitNET system so that a student enrolled at any member institution will be able to take fully transferable online courses at any other member institution. Tuition rates will be set by individual colleges and universities. Through its Web site, JesuitNET promotes these schools' online degree and certificate programs as well as individual courses.

Another, more recent private college and university consortium uses a "team teaching" approach to deliver courses to students on multiple campuses. Thirteen institutions in the Associated Colleges of the South have created a "virtual classics department," (www.sunoikisis.org). In this case, students must all log on at the same time in order to tune in to an online audio broadcast of a lecture. During the lecture students may pose questions and make comments in a live chat room. Classes are "team taught" in the sense that professors from several campuses may take responsibility for course material and all log on together with the students.

**Specialized Consortia.** Some consortia are formed by institutions that focus on a particular field. For example, National Technological University (NTU) is one of the oldest technology-based consortia (www.ntu.edu). A global university, NTU, arranges for its member colleges and universities across the country to deliver advanced technical education and training, usually to employees of corporate clients. Currently, more than 1,200 courses are available through NTU's participating universities, which provides fourteen master's degree programs. An unusual aspect of the NTU consortium is that the consortium itself, rather than the member institutions, is the degree-granting body.

NTU's focus is on technical education and training that is ready to use in the workforce. Its corporate customers typically have purchased the equipment necessary to receive the courses. Though students who are not employed by an NTU corporate client may take courses, they must pay an extra fee to have tapes or CD-ROMs of courses sent to them. NTU has also partnered with the Public Broadcasting System (PBS) to create the Business and Technology Network, a series of more than seventy-five engineering programs per year delivered directly to organizations via satellite.

## Pros and Cons of Consortia Learning Models

One obvious advantage of consortia is the pooling of resources. More university partners translates to more choices in curriculum, and often a shared expense in developing instructional design and technology. Consortia can offer a centralized database or course schedule that allows you to find members' courses easily rather than having to search many institutions' materials and Web sites for what you need. You may also have the chance to choose from among a group of respected faculty members from within the consortia, which allows you to find the teachers with expertise most closely suited to your academic and professional interests. This large sampling of faculty members tends to offer a more diverse worldview in the classroom. And, a consortium can often provide essential student services on a scale not fiscally achievable by a single university. For example, a dozen universities can pool resources for a much broader digital library than any single school could supply on its own.

However, from the student's point of view, consortia can have problems, many of which can be attributed to their relative newness. The most critical of these for students are problems with transferring credits. Other drawbacks may include large class sizes and problems in communication.

**Problems with Transferring Credits.** One problem that sometimes comes up for students trying to earn an entire degree, or part of a degree, on line is that their home institution may require a minimum number of "home" credits, yet it may not offer enough courses via distance learning for a student to meet that minimum. "I am concerned because [my home campus] offers a limited number of online classes," says Andrea Bessel, who is working toward a bachelor's degree in business administration with a concentration in finance. Bessel, who works full time and prefers the convenience of online to on-campus courses, has been taking classes from several institutions in the State University of New York (SUNY) Learning Network (www.sln.suny.edu). "It is great that other SUNY campuses offer more courses," continues Bessel, "but I am concerned about accumulating too many transfer credits—you are only allowed so many."

In the future, this problem is likely to arise less often for several reasons. First, as distance education degree programs become more common and well known, students are likely to search them out and apply directly to the institution that offers them. In contrast, like many other students, Bessel applied to her local state college campus and only later discovered that taking online courses within the statewide system was much more convenient than traveling to class. Second, individual institutions will continue to add to their distance education offerings, broadening the course choices for their "home" students. And third, some state systems and other consortia may eventually decide to liberalize their rules on transfer credit maximums within the consortium as the demand for distance degrees increases.

Indeed, some consortia have already succeeded in solving credit transfer problems, and others are addressing the challenge of reconciling differing credit transfer policies and logistics.

However, to ensure that any courses you take will successfully transfer from one institution to another (and ultimately toward your degree), you should secure an academic adviser at the start of your program and investigate the transferrability of credits before you register for courses at other institutions within the consortium. Serving as your own adviser brings the risk that some courses may ultimately not transfer toward your degree.

**Large Class Size.** Because so many students have access to courses in a consortium, online classes may reach an unmanageable size if limits are not placed on the student-to-teacher ratio. Many schools now adopt a ceiling on the number of students allowed in an online class, with teaching assistants or subsections of the course added for each additional set of students. This is vital to the processing of information and interaction required in the successful online course. Faculty members often find that a class of 25 students is quite manageable, but more may become problematic.

**Miscommunication.** Communication may be difficult in a consortium. The larger the consortium, the more likely that many universities or university systems are involved, and therefore you may need to communicate with several institutions that have differing policies and procedures. Additional communication snags can arise when you try to move your student records from one campus to the next. Some consortia have spent considerable time, effort, and money to make this tedious and laborious process appear seamless to you as a student. For those that have not, you should be prepared to take a proactive stance in helping to see that your records are successfully moved from one department, college, or university to another.

## COMPARING THE SINGLE UNIVERSITY TO THE CONSORTIUM

A student who is looking for a learning community with school pride and a great deal of local loyalty may find the multicampus environment of a consortium less desirable than the collegiality of the single university environment. In today's workplace and economy, however, many students opt for the flexibility and increased curriculum choices of a consortium over an individual school. Many consortia have succeeded in creating a sense of community for learners, and many more are attempting to do so. The high level of dialogue in the online environment can often build friendships, connections, and communities not achieved in a traditional environment. A single university can offer you the chance to immerse yourself in one department (of your major, for example), but a consortium can offer a wider variety of choices in mentors and philosophies. As a student, you should think about which you'd prefer.

# SELECTING THE RIGHT DISTANCE LEARNING PROGRAM TO FIT YOUR NEEDS

As a prospective distance learning student, you should evaluate programs as much as you would any campus-based, traditional program. The first question, of course, is: Does the curriculum meet your educational and professional goals? If it doesn't, there's not much point in looking into that program any further, however flexible and convenient it seems. If the program does seem to meet your educational needs, then the real work of evaluating it must begin. Distance education students need to be especially concerned about the quality of the programs they are considering for two main reasons.

First, with the proliferation of distance learning degree programs spurred by the Internet there are a lot of diploma mills out there. Second, you must be especially careful about quality because in many quarters, distance degrees are still considered the poor relations of degrees earned on campus.

Basically, you must do a lot of research by gathering information from the program, university, accrediting agencies, professional associations, faculty, current and former students, and colleagues. Only then can you make an informed decision about whether a program is good as well as right for you.

## Reputation

For many students, the reputation of the school is the paramount factor in selecting a program. Not only should you consider the reputation of a university in general, you should consider the reputation of a distance degree from a university in your field.

## Program Quality

If you are pursuing a graduate degree or know your field of interest as an undergraduate, it's important to separate the reputation of the program or department in which you are interested from the reputation of the university to which it belongs.

## Academic Quality

One way to assess the quality of a program is to find out whether or not it is accredited by a specialized agency—if that applies in your field (see the article on accreditation). But there are other ways to assess a program's academic quality. First, look at the curriculum. Does it cover what you need to learn? Is the syllabus up-to-date? Next, check some of the program's student data. For example, what percentage of students who enroll actually completes the degree? What percentage of students is employed in a field relating to their studies?

## Faculty

Check out the faculty members. What are their credentials? What are their areas of expertise? Are they well regarded in their field? If the program is professional in nature, look for faculty members with a blend of academic background and professional experience. If the program is academic, you should find out whether tenure-track professors with Ph.D.'s teach both the on-campus and distance courses or if distance courses are relegated to part-time adjunct faculty members and/or assistants.

## Experience with Adult Learners

Working adult students have different needs than full-time on-campus students, and assessing the degree to which a program takes those needs into account can help you decide whether or not a program is a good match for you.

## The Technology

Not only will you depend on your own computer, VCR, or television, but you will depend on the institution's technology, too. Ask current students what their experiences have been. Does the server often go down? Are there frequent problems with camera equipment or satellite transmissions?

Find out what technical support is offered to students. The best setup is free technical support accessed via a toll-free number 24 hours a day, seven days a week.

## Faculty-Student Interaction

Will you be expected to log on to an online course at specific times or at your convenience? Will you be expected to participate in online discussions a certain number of times during the course? Some programs do little to overcome the distance learner's social isolation; others rely on group work to forge a community of learning. Still others use a cohort format, in which a group of students enrolls in a program at the same time and proceeds through it together at the same pace. Pay particular attention to the faculty-student ratio in online courses. If there are more than 25 to 30 students per instructor, you're not likely to get much individual attention.

## Advising and Other Services

Academic advising is one of the most important student services for distance learners, especially if you are seeking to transfer credits or earn credits through examinations or from life experience to apply to a degree. Check what advising services are offered to distance learners, and see how easy they are to access. Advising is also of particular concern to students in a consortium. If you are interested in a program that is part of a consortium, find out if the consortium offers advising or mentoring to help you navigate among institutions and to guide your overall progress.

Has the institution kept up with an innovative degree program? For example, at many universities, distance learning courses and programs originate in a couple of departments eager to pursue new ways of educating. However, the university's centralized academic and administrative services may lag behind, leaving distance students to struggle with a system not designed for their needs.

## Time Frames

Check to see how much time you have to complete a certificate or degree program, and decide whether or not the time frame meets your needs. Some programs have a generous upper limit on the number of years you may take to complete a degree, which allows you to proceed at your own pace. Other programs may be structured on an accelerated or cohort model, with a timetable and lots of interim deadlines. If that's the case, make sure your own schedule can accommodate this.

## Cost

The cost of a distance education degree or certificate program is often the same for on-campus and distance students. However, there are some things you should look out for. If you enroll in a consortium, member institutions may charge tuition at different rates. If you enroll in a public university, you will probably be charged out-of-state tuition if you are not a state resident. Some institutions charge an extra technology fee to cover the costs associated with distance education.

# WHAT IS ACCREDITATION AND WHY IS IT IMPORTANT?

The accreditation status of a college, university, or program can give you an indication of its general quality and reputation. But just what does accreditation mean, and how does it affect distance learners?

In the United States, authority over postsecondary educational institutions is decentralized. The states, not the federal government, have the authority to regulate educational institutions within their borders, and as a consequence, standards and quality vary considerably for "state-approved" schools. You will find many state-approved schools that are not accredited and many that are. In order to ensure a basic level of quality, the practice of accrediting institutions arose. Private, nongovernmental educational agencies with a regional or national scope have adopted standards to evaluate whether or not colleges and universities provide educational programs at basic levels of quality.

Institutions that seek accreditation conduct an in-depth self-study to measure their performance against the standards. The accrediting agency then conducts an on-site evaluation and either awards accreditation or pre-accreditation status—or denies accreditation. Periodically the agency reevaluates each institution to make sure its continued accreditation is warranted. So accreditation is not a one-shot deal—an institution must maintain high standards or it runs the risk of jeopardizing its accreditation status as a result of one of the periodic evaluations.

Seeking accreditation is entirely voluntary on the part of the institution of higher education. The initial accreditation process takes a long time—as much as five or ten years—and it costs money. You can see that a very new school will not have been in operation long enough to be accredited. For example, Western Governors University, a virtual university established in 1998, was awarded accreditation candidacy status in 2000 and, if all goes well, will be fully accredited in two to five years. Of course, being awarded candidacy status does not ensure that an institution will eventually be fully accredited.

## Institutional and Specialized Accreditation

There are two basic types of accreditation: institutional accreditation and specialized accreditation. Institutional accreditation is awarded to an institution by one of six regional accrediting agencies and many national accrediting agencies, such as the Distance Education and Training Council. The regional accrediting agencies play the largest role in institutional accreditation (see the Appendix for a list of the regional accrediting agencies). If a college or university is regionally accredited, that means that the institution as a whole has met the accrediting agency's standards. Within the institution, particular programs and departments contribute to the institution's objectives at varying levels of quality.

## What Does Accreditation Mean to You?

There are several benefits of enrolling in a program at a regionally accredited college or university. You are assured of a basic level of quality education and services. Any credits you earn are more likely to be transferable to other regionally accredited institutions, although we've seen that each institution makes its own decisions on transfer credits on a case-by-case basis.

Any certificate or degree you earn is more likely to be recognized by other colleges and universities and by employers as a legitimate credential. You may qualify for federal loans and grants because regionally accredited institutions, like nationally accredited institutions, are eligible to participate in Title IV financial aid programs.

## What Is Specialized Accreditation?

In contrast to institutional accreditation, specialized accreditation usually applies to a single department, program, or school that is part of a larger institution of higher education. The accredited unit may be as big as a college within a university or as small as a curriculum within a field of study. Most specialized accrediting agencies review units within institutions that are regionally accredited, although some also accredit freestanding institutions. There are specialized accrediting agencies in almost fifty fields, including allied health, art and design, Bible college education, business, engineering, law, marriage and family therapy, nursing, psychology, and theology.

Specialized accreditation may or may not be a consideration for you when you evaluate distance education programs. That's because the role of specialized accreditation varies considerably depending on the field of study. In some professional fields, you must have a degree or certificate from a program with specialized accreditation in order to take qualifying exams or practice the profession. In other fields, specialized accreditation has little or no effect on your ability to work. Thus, it's especially important that you find out what role accreditation plays in your field since it may affect your professional future as well as the quality of your education.

## Checking on a School and Its Accreditors

It's important to find out what role accreditation plays in your field, since it may affect your professional future as well as the quality of your education. Since accreditation is awarded by private organizations, any group can hang out a shingle and proclaim itself an accrediting agency. Some diploma mills, for example, have been known to create their own accrediting agency and then proclaim themselves "accredited."

So how can you tell (1) if the school or college in which you are interested is regionally accredited, (2) if the program has the specialized accreditation you need, and (3) if the agencies that have accredited the school and program are legitimate?

Of course, you can simply ask the school or program, but since accreditation is so important, it's probably a lot wiser to check elsewhere. First, check with the regional accrediting agency that covers the state in which the school is located. Then check with any specialized accrediting agency that may assess the particular program in which you are interested. To find out if an accrediting agency is legitimate and nationally recognized, you can consult the Council for Higher Education Accreditation (CHEA), a private agency that accredits the accreditors (http://www.chea.org). Or you can check with the U.S. Department of Education (USDE). Their Web site has a complete list of institutional and specialized accrediting agencies recognized by the federal

government (http://www.ed.gov/offices/OPE/accreditation/natlagencies.html). This Web site will also tell you whether or not accreditation by a particular agency makes the school eligible to participate in federal financial aid programs.

## Checking on Canadian Institutions of Higher Education

In Canada, as in the United States, there is no centralized governmental accrediting agency. Instead, the provincial governments evaluate the quality of university programs in each province, with a few nationwide agencies evaluating professional programs. To check on a Canadian university, you can contact the appropriate provincial department of education. To get general information about accreditation in Canada, visit the Web site of the Council of Ministers of Education at http://www.cmec.ca. Their Web site also has contact information and links to the provincial departments of education.

## Checking on an Unaccredited Institution

As we've seen, seeking accreditation is a voluntary process, and some legitimate schools choose not to undertake it. In addition, the newer virtual universities may not have been around long enough to be accredited. So what can you do to make sure a school is legitimate if it is not accredited?

First, you can call the state agency with jurisdiction over higher education in the state in which the school is located. The agency can at least tell you whether or not the school is operating with a legitimate charter, and it may be able to tell you if any complaints have been lodged or legal action taken against it.

Second, you can call the school and ask why it is not accredited and whether the school has plans to seek accreditation. If the school tells you it has applied for accreditation, double-check its status with the agency it names.

Third, you can consult with people in your field about the school's reputation and the value of its degree. Remember, in some fields, a degree from an unaccredited school or program will bar you from professional licensure and practice. So, keep in mind that enrolling in an unaccredited school or program can be risky. If you can avoid it, do so.

## Accreditation Issues Relating to Distance Education

In the United States during the 1990s, controversy arose over the accreditation of online programs within traditional universities and the accreditation of completely virtual universities. On the one hand, many felt that online degree programs should be evaluated using the same criteria as other degree programs within institutions of higher education. Others thought that new standards were needed to properly evaluate distance education. Although this issue has not yet been settled, the six regional accrediting agencies have proposed uniform guidelines for evaluating distance education.

The impetus for this move is the fact that many distance education programs cross regional borders; the agencies want to ensure that similar standards are adopted across the country. Among the proposed criteria specific to accrediting distance education are faculty control of course content, technical and program support for both faculty members and students, and evaluation and assessment methods for measuring student learning. However, until these or other guidelines are accepted, distance education programs will continue to be evaluated using the same criteria as on-campus programs.

# Recognized Accrediting Bodies and Categories of Accreditation

Below is a list of all forms of accreditation awarded by accrediting bodies recognized by the U.S. Department of Education or the Council for Higher Education Accreditation.

## GENERAL ACCREDITATION

General accreditation applies to an institution as a whole and is not limited to institutions or programs in a particular field of specialization.

## REGIONAL

Regional accreditation denotes accreditation of an institution as a whole by one of the six regional associations of schools and colleges, each of which covers a specified portion of the United States and its territories as indicated in the following listings.

### Middle States

Degree-granting institutions that offer one or more post-secondary educational programs of at least one academic year in length in Delaware, the District of Columbia, Maryland, New Jersey, New York, Pennsylvania, Puerto Rico, and the Virgin Islands.

> Middle States Association of Colleges and Schools (MSA)
> Commission on Institutions of Higher Education (CIHE)
> 3624 Market Street
> Philadelphia, PA 19104-2680

Jean Avnet Morse, Executive Director
Telephone: 215-662-5606
Fax: 215-662-5501
E-mail: jmorse@msache.org
URL: http://www.msache.org

### New England

Institutions in Connecticut, Maine, Massachusetts, New Hampshire, Rhode Island, and Vermont.

Colleges and universities that offer programs leading to the baccalaureate or higher degrees and institutions that award only the associate degree but include in their offerings degree programs in liberal arts or general studies are covered by:

> New England Association of Schools and Colleges (NEASC)
> Commission on Institutions of Higher Education (CIHE)
> 209 Burlington Road
> Bedford, MA 01730-1433

> Dr. Charles M. Cook, Director
> Telephone: 781-271-0022
> Fax: 781-271-0950
> E-mail: CIHE@neasc.org
> URL: http://www.neasc.org/

Colleges and institutes that offer programs leading to the associate degree but do not offer programs leading to a degree in liberal arts or general studies are covered by:

> New England Association of Schools and Colleges (NEASC)
> Commission on Technical and Career Institutions (CTCI)
> 209 Burlington Road
> Bedford, MA 01730-1433
> Richard E. Mandeville, Director
> Telephone: 781-271-0022
> Fax: 781-271-0950
> E-mail: rmandeville@neasc.org
> URL: http://www.neasc.org/

### North Central

Institutions in Arizona, Arkansas, Colorado, Illinois, Indiana, Iowa, Kansas, Michigan, Minnesota, Missouri, Nebraska, New Mexico, North Dakota, Ohio, Oklahoma, South Dakota, West Virginia, Wisconsin, and Wyoming that offer at least one undergraduate program of two or more academic years in length or at least one graduate program of one or more academic years in length if no undergraduate programs are offered.

North Central Association of Colleges and Schools (NCA)
Higher Learning Commission
30 North LaSalle Street, Suite 2400
Chicago, IL 60602-2504

Dr. Steven D. Crow, Executive Director
Telephone: 312-263-0456
Fax: 312-263-7462
E-mail: scrow@hlcommission.org
URL: http://www.ncahigherlearningcommission.org

### Northwest

Postsecondary institutions with programs of at least one academic year in length in Alaska, Idaho, Montana, Nevada, Oregon, Utah, and Washington.

Northwest Association of Schools and Colleges (NASC)
Commission on Colleges
11130 Northeast 33rd Place, Suite 120
Bellevue, WA 98004

Sandra E. Elman, Executive Director
Telephone: 425-827-2005
Fax: 425-827-3395
E-mail: selman@cocnasc.org
URL: http://www.cocnasc.org

### Southern

Institutions in Alabama, Florida, Georgia, Kentucky, Louisiana, Mississippi, North Carolina, South Carolina, Tennessee, Texas, and Virginia.

Institutions that offer one or more degree programs of at least two academic years at the associate level, at least four academic years at the baccalaureate level, or at least one academic year at the postbaccalaureate level are covered by:

Southern Association of Colleges and Schools (SACS)
Commission on Colleges (CC)
1866 Southern Lane
Decatur, GA 30033-4097

Dr. James T. Rogers, Executive Director
Telephone: 404-679-4500
Fax: 404-679-4528
E-mail: jrogers@sacscoc.org
URL: http://www.sacscoc.org/

### Western

Institutions in American Samoa, California, Guam, Hawaii, the Trust Territory of the Pacific Islands, and the Commonwealth of the Northern Marianas.

Institutions that offer one or more educational programs of at least one academic year in length at the postsecondary level are covered by:

Western Association of Schools and Colleges (WASC)
Accrediting Commission for Community and Junior Colleges (ACCJC)
3402 Mendocino Avenue
Santa Rosa, CA 95403-2244

David B. Wolf, Executive Director
Telephone: 707-569-9177
Fax: 707-569-9179
E-mail: accjc@aol.com
URL: http://www.wascweb.org

Institutions that offer one or more educational programs of at least one academic year in length beyond the first two years of college are covered by:

Western Association of Schools and Colleges (WASC)
Accrediting Commission for Senior Colleges and Universities (ACSCU)
985 Atlantic Avenue, Suite 100
Alameda, CA 94501-1029

Ralph A. Wolff, Executive Director
Telephone: 510-748-9001
Fax: 510-748-9797
E-mail: rwolff@wascsenior.org
URL: http://www.wascweb.org

## State Program Registration

Registration of collegiate degree-granting programs or curricula offered by institutions of higher education and of credit-bearing certificate and diploma programs offered by degree-granting institutions of higher education.

New York State Board of Regents
New York State Education Department
89 Washington Avenue
Albany, NY 12234

Carl T. Hayden, Chancellor
Telephone: 518-474-5844
Fax: 518-473-4909
URL: http://www.regents.nysed.gov/

# PAYING FOR YOUR DISTANCE EDUCATION

Pursuing a certificate or degree can cost a lot of money, but it is usually money well spent. On average, people with undergraduate and graduate degrees make more money than those who do not have these credentials. Still, the question remains: How are you going to pay for school and support yourself (and perhaps your family) at the same time? Most adult distance learning students pay for their education by working full-time and attending school part-time.

## Federal Financial Aid

Most of your financial aid is likely to come from the federal government, which provides need-based aid in the form of grants, work-study programs, and loans. Up-to-date information about federal financial aid programs can be found at the U.S. Department of Education's Web site, http://www.ed.gov/studentaid, or by calling 800-4-FEDAID (toll-free).

## Are You Eligible for Federal Financial Aid?

Your financial need is just one criterion used to determine whether or not you are eligible to receive aid from the federal government. In addition, you must

- have a high school diploma or GED or pass a test approved by the Department of Education
- be enrolled in a degree or certificate program
- be enrolled in an eligible institution (see below)
- be a U.S. citizen or eligible noncitizen
- have a Social Security number
- register with the Selective Service if required
- maintain satisfactory academic progress once you are in school

## Institutional Eligibility: An Issue Pertinent to Distance Learners

In order to participate in federal financial aid programs, an institution of higher learning must fulfill the criteria estab-lished by Congress for the disbursement of Title IV funds, as federal student aid is officially known. There are many complex regulations that establish institutional eligibility. An institution's accreditation status affects its eligibility to participate in federal financial aid programs.

## The Distance Education Demonstration Program

The rules governing federal aid were originally promulgated to prevent fraud and to ensure that funds would be provided to students at schools that met certain standards. However, with the growth of distance education, these regulations are increasingly becoming obstacles to provide aid to students at legitimate but innovative institutions. Recognizing this, congress established the Distance Education Demonstration Program under the direction of the Department of Education.

## Determining the Eligibility Status of an Institution or Program

To make sure that the school and program in which you are interested are eligible to participate in federal financial aid programs, call them and ask. However, you can also do some double-checking on your own to confirm what the school tells you. If you plan to enroll in a regionally accredited traditional college or university, you can safely assume that the institution as a whole is eligible to participate in federal aid programs—since distance certificates and degrees are likely to be a very small proportion of its overall offerings. However, because institutions have the discretion to exclude specific programs, check to see if the school disperses federal aid to students enrolled in programs that interest you.

## Federal Aid Programs

Once you've established the eligibility of the institution and program in which you are interested, check the federal aid programs in which they participate. Not all schools participate in all the available programs. Below is a summary of the federal aid programs, but for more in-depth information about federal aid, check Peterson's Web site at www.petersons.com Schoolbook".

- **Pell Grants,** which do not have to be repaid, are awarded to undergraduate students on the basis of need, even if they are enrolled less than half-time.
- **Federal Supplemental Educational Opportunity Grants** are awards to undergraduates with exceptional financial need, even if they are enrolled less than half-time.
- **Federal Work-Study Program** provides part-time jobs in public and private nonprofit organizations to both undergraduate and graduate students who demonstrate financial need. The government pays up to 75 percent of your wages, and your employer pays the balance.
- **The Federal Family Education Loan (FFEL) Program and the William D. Ford Direct Loan Program,** commonly called Stafford Loans, are two loan programs sponsored by the federal government. You are eligible to borrow under these loan programs if you are enrolled at least half-time and have financial need remaining after your Estimated Family Contribution, Pell Grant eligibility, and aid from other sources are subtracted from your annual cost of attendance.
- **Perkins Loan Program** is available to both undergraduate and graduate students who demonstrate exceptional financial need, whether enrolled full-time or part-time.

## State Aid Programs

Some states offer financial aid to state residents who attend school in-state, some offer aid to state residents who attend school in-state or elsewhere, and some offer aid to students who attend school in their state regardless of their residency status. Contact your state scholarship office directly to find out what's available and whether you are eligible to apply.

## Private Sources of Financial Aid

### COLLEGES AND UNIVERSITIES

Second only to the federal government in the amount of financial aid disbursed yearly are colleges and universities. Many of these institutions award both need-based and merit-based aid to deserving students. To find out more about the types of aid that the school you are interested in disburses, contact the financial aid office.

### NATIONAL AND LOCAL ORGANIZATIONS

Foundations, nonprofit organizations, churches, service and fraternal organizations, professional associations, corporations, unions, and many other national and local organizations award grants to students of higher education.

## ALTERNATIVE LOAN PROGRAMS

In addition to the federal loan programs, there are many private alternative loan programs designed to help students. Most private loan programs disburse funds based on your creditworthiness rather than your financial need.

- **Home Equity Loans** A home equity loan or line of credit can be an attractive financing alternative to private loan programs. Some of these loans are offered at low rates and allow you to defer payment of the principal for years.
- **Credit Cards** Whatever you do, do not use your credit cards to borrow money for school on a long-term basis. The interest rates and finance charges will be high, and the balance will grow astronomically. Credit cards are useful to pay tuition and fees if you (1) can pay the balance in full, (2) expect a student loan to come through shortly, or (3) expect your employer to reimburse your costs. Otherwise, avoid them.
- **Internships and Cooperative Education Programs** Internships with organizations outside the university can provide money as well as practical experience in your field. As an intern, you are usually paid by the outside organization, and you may or may not get credit for the work you do.
- **Employer Reimbursement** If you work full-time and attend school part-time, you may be reimbursed for part or all of your tuition by your employer.

## Tax Benefits for Students

Whether or not you receive financial aid, there are many recently enacted tax benefits for adults who want to return to school. In effect, these tax cuts make the first two years of college universally available, and they give many more working adults the financial means to go back to school.

- **The HOPE Scholarship Tax Credit** Students whose adjusted gross income falls within certain limits receive a 100 percent tax credit for the first $1,000 of tuition and required fees and a 50 percent credit on the second $1,000.
- **The Lifetime Learning Tax Credit** A family may receive a 20 percent tax credit for the first $5,000 of tuition and required fees paid each year through 2002 and for the first $10,000 thereafter.
- **Individual Retirement Accounts** Taxpayers can withdraw funds from an IRA, without penalty for their own higher education expenses or those of their spouse, child, or even grandchild.
- **State Tuition Plans** When a family uses a qualified state-sponsored tuition plan to save for college, no tax is due in connection with the plan until the time of withdrawal.

- **Tax-Deductible Student Loan Interest** The new student loan interest deduction allows students or their families to take a tax deduction for interest paid in the first sixty months of repayment on student loans.

- **Tax-Deductible Employer Reimbursements** If you take undergraduate courses and your employer reimburses you for education-related expenses, you may be able to exclude up to $5,250 of employer-provided education benefits from your income.

- **Community Service Loan Forgiveness** This provision excludes from your income any student loan amounts forgiven by nonprofit, tax-exempt charitable, or educational institutions for borrowers who take community-service jobs that address unmet community needs.

# GLOSSARY

**accreditation**—In the United States, the process by which private, nongovernmental educational agencies with regional or national scope certify that colleges and universities provide educational programs at basic levels of quality

**ACT Assessment**—a standardized undergraduate admissions test that is based on the typical high school curriculum

**associate's degree**—a degree awarded upon the successful completion of a prebaccalaureate level program, usually consisting of two years of full-time study at the college level

**asynchronous**—not simultaneous or concurrent; for example, discussion groups in online courses are asynchronous because students can log on and post messages at any time

**audioconferencing**—electronic meeting in which participants in remote locations can communicate with one another using telephones or speakerphones

**bachelor's degree**—a degree awarded upon the successful completion of about four years of full-time college-level study

**bandwidth**—the width of frequencies required to transmit a communications signal without too much distortion. Video, animation, and sound require more bandwidth than text.

**broadband**—a high-speed, high-capacity transmission channel carried on coaxial or fiber-optic cable; it has a higher *bandwidth* than telephone lines and so can transmit more data more quickly than telephone lines

**broadcast radio and television**—radio and television programs sent out over the airwaves; one of the earliest distance learning technologies that is still used

**browser**—a computer program used to view, download, upload, or otherwise access documents (sites) on the World Wide Web

**bulletin board**—a site on the Internet where people can post messages

**cable television**—television programming transmitted over optical fiber, coaxial, or twisted pair (telephone) cables

**CD-ROM**—Compact disc, read-only memory; an optical storage technology that allows you to store and play back data

**certificate**—an educational credential awarded upon completion of a structured curriculum, typically including several courses but lasting for a period of less time than that required for a degree

**certification**—the awarding of a credential, usually by a professional or industry group, usually after a course of study and the passing of an exam

**chat room**—a site on the Internet in which people can communicate synchronously by typing messages to one another

**CLEP**—the College Level Examination Program, administered by the College Board, that tests students' subject knowledge in order to award college-level credit for noncollegiate learning

**common application form**—a standardized basic admissions application form, available on line, that is used by many colleges

**consortium**—a group of colleges and universities that pool resources to enable students to take courses as needed from all participating institutions

**continuing education unit**—10 contact hours of participation in an organized continuing education program; a nationwide, standardized measure of continuing education courses

**correspondence course**—individual or self-guided study by mail from a college or university for which credit is typically granted through written assignments and proctored examinations; also referred to as *independent study*

**correspondence school**—a school whose primary means of delivering instruction is via *correspondence courses*

**cost of attendance**—the total cost, including tuition, fees, living expenses, books, supplies, and miscellaneous expenses, of attending a particular school for an academic year

**CSS Profile**—the College Scholarship Service's Financial Aid Profile form, a standardized financial aid application form used by many colleges and universities

**DANTES Subject Standardized Tests**—a series of equivalency examinations used primarily by the U.S. Department of Defense but available to civilians as well

**distance learning**—the delivery of educational programs to students who are off site; also called *distance education*

**doctoral degree**—the highest degree awarded upon demonstrated mastery of a subject, including the ability to do scholarly research

# Glossary

**DVD**—digital video disc; an optical storage technology that allows you to store and retrieve audio and video data

**e-learning**—distance learning via the Internet

**electronic bulletin board**—an "area" of the Internet in which people can post messages

**e-mail**—text or other messages sent over the Internet; also called *electronic mail*

**enrollment status**—whether a student is enrolled full-time, three-quarter time, half-time, or less than half-time in a degree or certificate program

**equivalency examination**—an examination similar to the final exam of a college-level course; if you pass, you may be awarded college-level credit; for example, the CLEP and DANTES exams

**Expected Family Contribution (EFC)**—The amount a student and his or her family are expected to contribute to the cost of the student's education per academic year

**FAFSA**—the Free Application for Federal Student Aid, a form needed to apply for federal aid programs

**fax machine**—a telecopying device that transmits written or graphic material over telephone lines to produce a hard copy at a remote location; also called a *facsimile machine*

**Federal Supplemental Educational Opportunity Grant (FSEOG)**—a federal grant awarded to students that demonstrate the greatest financial need

**fellowship**—a gift, to be used for a student's education, that does not have to be repaid; also called a *grant* or *scholarship*

**financial need**—the amount of money a student needs to be given or loaned, or earn through work-study, in order to attend school for one year. It is calculated by subtracting Estimated Family Contribution from cost of attendance.

**first-professional degree**—a degree awarded upon the successful completion of a program of study for which a bachelor's degree is normally the prerequisite and that prepares a student for a specific profession

**GMAT**—the Graduate Management Admissions Test, a standardized test used by many graduate programs in business

**graduate degree**—a degree awarded upon the successful completion of a program of study at the postbaccalaureate level; usually a master's or doctoral degree

**grant**—a gift, to be used for a student's education, that does not have to be repaid; also called a *scholarship* or *fellowship*

**GRE General Test**—the Graduate Record Examinations General Test, which tests verbal, quantitative and analytical skills; usually taken by prospective graduate students

**GRE Subject Area Tests**—examinations that assess knowledge usually acquired in college-level courses

**instructional design**—the way course content is organized for the learner; it varies from one distance technology to another

**Internet**—the global computer "network of networks" that allows for the transmission of words, images, and sound to anyone with an Internet connection; it has become one of the major instructional delivery systems for distance learning

**Internet service provider (ISP)**—a company such as AOL or Earthlink that serves as a gateway to the Internet; by subscribing to its service, an individual can connect to the Internet

**life experience**—a basis for earning college credit, usually demonstrated by means of a portfolio

**LSAT**—the Law School Admissions Test, taken by law school applicants

**master's degree**—a degree awarded upon the successful completion of a program of study beyond the baccalaureate level, typically requires one or two years of full-time study

**MAT**—the Miller Analogies Test, a standardized admissions test used by some graduate programs

**MCAT**—the Medical College Admissions Test, taken by medical school applicants

**merit-based aid**—funding awarded on the basis of academic merit, regardless of financial need

**modem**—MOdulator DEModulator; a device that allows a computer to connect with other computers (and therefore the Internet) over telephone lines. The faster the modem speed, the faster data is transmitted.

**need-based aid**—financial aid awarded on the basis of financial need; it may take the form of grants, loans, or work-study

**online course**—a course offered primarily over the Internet

**online learning**—distance learning via the Internet; sometimes called *e-learning*

**Pell Grant**—a federal grant that is awarded to students on the basis of financial need

**Perkins Loan**—a loan offered by the federal government to students with exceptional financial need

**PowerPoint**—a software program that enables the user to prepare slides with text, graphics, and sound; often used by instructors in their class presentations

**Excelsior College Examinations**—a series of equivalency examinations administered by Excelsior College; formerly the Regents College Examinations

**SAT I**—the Scholastic Aptitude Test I, a standardized undergraduate admissions test

**SAT II**—subject area tests that assess high school level knowledge; used by some schools for undergraduate admissions

**satellite television**—programming beamed to an orbiting satellite, then retrieved by one or more ground-based satellite dishes

**scholarship**—a gift, to be used for a student's education, that does not have to be repaid; also called a *grant* or *fellowship*

**Stafford Loan**—a loan, either subsidized or unsubsidized, offered by the federal government

**streaming video**—high *bandwidth* video data transmission

**synchronous**—occurring simultaneously, in real time

**Title IV funds**—federal money disbursed to eligible students through eligible, accredited institutions of higher learning or directly from the government

**TOEFL**—the Test of English as a Foreign Language, taken by students who are not native speakers of English

**two-way interactive video**—two-way communication of video and audio signals so that people in remote locations can see and hear one another

**videoconferencing**—one-way video and two-way audio transmission, or two-way video transmission conducted via satellite; instructors and students can communicate among remote locations

**videotaped lecture**—recording of an on-campus lecture or class session; usually mailed to distance learners enrolled in the course

**virtual university**—a college or university that offers most or all of its instruction exclusively via technology and usually for a profit

**whiteboard**—a program that allows multiple users at their own computers to draw and write comments on the same document

**work-study award**—an amount a student earns through part-time work as part of the federal work-study program

# INSTITUTION PROFILES AND SPECIAL NOTES

This section contains factual profiles of institutions, with a focus on their Distance Learning programs. Each profile covers such items as accreditation information, availability of financial aid, degree and certificate programs offered, non-degree-related course topics offered, and whom to contact for program information. In addition, there are Special Notes from institutions about new programs or special events.

The profile information presented here was collected during the summer of 2002 via Peterson's on-line survey for Distance Learning Programs and is arranged alphabetically.

# ABILENE CHRISTIAN UNIVERSITY
*Instructional Technology*

1600 Campus Court, ACU Box 29201
Abilene, TX 79699-9201
**Contact:** Paul Pollard, Distance Learning Coordinator
**Phone:** 915-674-2553
**Fax:** 915-674-2834
**Web:** http://www.acu.edu/distanceeducation
**E-mail:** pollardp@acu.edu

**ACCREDITATION:** Southern Association of Colleges and Schools

**INSTITUTIONALLY ADMINISTERED FINANCIAL AID:** Yes

## DEGREE OR CERTIFICATE PROGRAMS OFFERED
**Programs offered do not lead to a degree or other formal award.**

## NON-DEGREE-RELATED COURSE TOPICS OFFERED
**Undergraduate**—communications, general; sociology.
**Graduate**—bible/biblical studies.

# ACADIA UNIVERSITY
*Division of Continuing and Distance Education*

38 Crowell Avenue
Wolfville, NS B0P 1X0, Canada
**Contact:** Continuing Education
**Phone:** 800-565-6568
**Fax:** 902-585-1068
**Web:** http://conted.acadiau.ca
**E-mail:** continuing.education@acadiau.ca

**ACCREDITATION:** Provincially Chartered

**INSTITUTIONALLY ADMINISTERED FINANCIAL AID:** Yes

## DEGREE OR CERTIFICATE PROGRAMS OFFERED
**Undergraduate**—*Certificate:* Business Administration; Computer Science. *Diploma:* Business Administration.

## NON-DEGREE-RELATED COURSE TOPICS OFFERED
**Undergraduate**—English language and literature, general; accounting; art history, criticism and conservation; astronomy; biology, general; business; chemistry; computer science; criminology; economics; education, general; foods and nutrition studies; geological and related sciences; history; physics; political science and government; psychology; sociology.
**Graduate**—education, other.
**Non-credit**—mathematics; music.

# ADAMS STATE COLLEGE
*Division of Extended Studies*

Alamosa, CO 81102
**Contact:** Judy Phillips, Director
**Phone:** 719-587-7671
**Fax:** 719-587-7974
**Web:** http://www.adams.edu/exstudies/

**E-mail:** ascextend@adams.edu
**ACCREDITATION:** North Central Association of Colleges and Schools
**INSTITUTIONALLY ADMINISTERED FINANCIAL AID:** No

## DEGREE OR CERTIFICATE PROGRAMS OFFERED
**Programs offered do not lead to a degree or other formal award.**

## NON-DEGREE-RELATED COURSE TOPICS OFFERED
**Undergraduate**—English composition; accounting; business; developmental and child psychology; environmental science/studies; finance, general; law and legal studies, other; management information systems and business data processing, general; mathematical statistics; radio and television broadcasting; sociology.
**Graduate**—education, general.

---

**Special Note**

Adams State College (ASC) is a coeducational, state-supported, comprehensive liberal arts college that awards degrees at the associate, baccalaureate, and master's levels and provides high-quality education with a personal touch. More than 30 areas of study, preprofessional programs, and guaranteed transfer programs are available through 4 undergraduate schools—Business; Education and Graduate Studies; Science, Mathematics, and Technology; and the Arts and Letters. A diverse population of 2,500 students, with a student-faculty ratio of 18:1, provides quality and value that has endured for three quarters of a century. ASC has been named one of the 100 best college buys in the U.S. by a publication that rates America's colleges and universities. ASC is located in south-central Colorado in Alamosa.

ASC Extended Studies is part of the Colorado Statewide Extended Campus. More than 18,000 students enroll for more than 400 sections of contract courses per semester, and for more than 45 independent study courses. More than 1,400 professionals have provided instruction for Extended Studies. These professionals are educational entrepreneurs that represent private and public institutions and form a strategic network of talent and experience. ASC Extended Studies aligns resources to deliver information and instruction globally, as if there were no barriers "connecting the DOTS" (Delivery of Transparent Systems). For more information, students should call 800-548-6679 (toll-free) or visit the Web site at http://www.adams.edu.

---

# ADIRONDACK COMMUNITY COLLEGE

640 Bay Road
Queensbury, NY 12804
**Contact:** Susan Trumpick, Director of Campus Technology
**Phone:** 518-743-2248
**Web:** http://www.sunyacc.edu/
**E-mail:** trumpics@acc.sunyacc.edu

**ACCREDITATION:** Middle States Association of Colleges and Schools

**INSTITUTIONALLY ADMINISTERED FINANCIAL AID:** Yes

## DEGREE OR CERTIFICATE PROGRAMS OFFERED
**Undergraduate**—*AAS:* Business Administration. *AS:* Criminal Justice (Police Science).

**NON-DEGREE-RELATED COURSE TOPICS OFFERED**

**Undergraduate**—English composition; English language and literature, general; English technical and business writing; accounting; business; business administration and management; business communications; criminal justice and corrections; developmental and child psychology; health professions and related sciences, other; history; mathematics; political science and government; psychology; sociology.

# ALASKA PACIFIC UNIVERSITY

*RANA (Rural Alaska Native Adult) Program*

4101 University Drive
Anchorage, AK 99508
**Contact:** Theresa Arevgaq John, Director of RANA Program
**Phone:** 907-564-8222 Ext. 8322
**Fax:** 907-564-8317
**Web:** http://www.alaskapacific.edu/
**E-mail:** tjohn@alaskapacific.edu

**ACCREDITATION:** Northwest Association of Schools and Colleges

**INSTITUTIONALLY ADMINISTERED FINANCIAL AID:** Yes

**DEGREE OR CERTIFICATE PROGRAMS OFFERED**

**Undergraduate**—*AA:* Accounting; Business; Education; Human Services; Liberal Studies. *BA:* Accounting; Business Administration; Education; Human Services; Liberal Studies.

# ALBANY COLLEGE OF PHARMACY OF UNION UNIVERSITY

Non-Traditional PharmD Program, 106 New Scotland Avenue
Albany, NY 12208
**Contact:** Cathy Shultes, Coordinator of Non-Traditional Pharm.D. Program
**Phone:** 518-445-7312
**Fax:** 518-445-7283
**Web:** http://www.acp.edu/
**E-mail:** ntpd@acp.edu

**ACCREDITATION:** Middle States Association of Colleges and Schools

**INSTITUTIONALLY ADMINISTERED FINANCIAL AID:** No

**DEGREE OR CERTIFICATE PROGRAMS OFFERED**

Programs offered do not lead to a degree or other formal award.

**NON-DEGREE-RELATED COURSE TOPICS OFFERED**

**Graduate**—pharmacy.

# ALBERTUS MAGNUS COLLEGE

Albertus Magnus College Library, 700 Prospect Street
New Haven, CT 06410
**Contact:** Dr. Samuel R. Brown, Director of Library and Information Services
**Phone:** 203-773-8595
**Fax:** 203-773-8588
**Web:** http://www.albertus.edu/

**E-mail:** brown@albertus.edu

**ACCREDITATION:** New England Association of Schools and Colleges

**INSTITUTIONALLY ADMINISTERED FINANCIAL AID:** Yes

**DEGREE OR CERTIFICATE PROGRAMS OFFERED**

Programs offered do not lead to a degree or other formal award.

**NON-DEGREE-RELATED COURSE TOPICS OFFERED**

**Undergraduate**—political science and government; sociology.

# ALBUQUERQUE TECHNICAL VOCATIONAL INSTITUTE

525 Buena Vista, SE
Albuquerque, NM 87106-4096
**Contact:** Chuck L. Baldonado, Dean of Learning Resources
**Phone:** 505-224-3292
**Fax:** 505-224-3293
**E-mail:** chuck@tvi.cc.nm.us

**ACCREDITATION:** North Central Association of Colleges and Schools

**INSTITUTIONALLY ADMINISTERED FINANCIAL AID:** Yes

**DEGREE OR CERTIFICATE PROGRAMS OFFERED**

Programs offered do not lead to a degree or other formal award.

**NON-DEGREE-RELATED COURSE TOPICS OFFERED**

**Undergraduate**—English composition; business; business administration and management; business and personal services marketing operations; business information and data processing services; business management and administrative services, other; communications, general; computer and information sciences, general; computer and information sciences, other; computer/information technology administration and management; criminal justice and corrections; culinary arts and related services; electrical and electronic engineering-related technology; health and medical laboratory technologies; mathematics; nursing; psychology.
**Non-credit**—English as a second language; English composition.

# ALEXANDRIA TECHNICAL COLLEGE

Alexandria, MN 56308
**Contact:** Jan Doebbert, Dean of Technology
**Web:** http://www.alextech.org/
**E-mail:** jand@alx.tec.mn.us

**ACCREDITATION:** North Central Association of Colleges and Schools

**INSTITUTIONALLY ADMINISTERED FINANCIAL AID:** Yes

**DEGREE OR CERTIFICATE PROGRAMS OFFERED**

**Undergraduate**—*Certificate:* AS400 Operations; AS400 Programming; Web Development and Management.

**NON-DEGREE-RELATED COURSE TOPICS OFFERED**

**Undergraduate**—English technical and business writing; accounting; administrative and secretarial services; computer science; drafting; electrical and electronic engineering-related technology; miscellaneous health professions; nursing; telecommunications; vehicle and mobile equipment mechanics and repairers.

**Non-credit**—English technical and business writing; computer science; engineering/industrial management; internet and world wide web; marketing management and research; miscellaneous health professions.

# ALLIANT INTERNATIONAL UNIVERSITY

10455 Pomerado Road
San Diego, CA 92131-1799
**See full description on page 290.**

# ALPENA COMMUNITY COLLEGE

666 Johnson Street
Alpena, MI 49707
**Contact:** Dr. Curtis G. Davis, Vice President of Instruction and Student/Community Services
**Phone:** 989-358-7233
**Fax:** 989-358-7561
**Web:** http://alpenacc.org
**E-mail:** davisc@alpena.cc.mi.us

**ACCREDITATION:** North Central Association of Colleges and Schools
**INSTITUTIONALLY ADMINISTERED FINANCIAL AID:** Yes

## DEGREE OR CERTIFICATE PROGRAMS OFFERED

**Programs offered do not lead to a degree or other formal award.**

## NON-DEGREE-RELATED COURSE TOPICS OFFERED

**Undergraduate**—computer systems networking and telecommunications; computer/information technology administration and management; criminal justice and corrections; philosophy.

# ALVIN COMMUNITY COLLEGE

*Instructional Services*

3110 Mustang Road
Alvin, TX 77511
**Contact:** Mr. Patrick M. Sanger, Director of Distance Education
**Phone:** 281-756-3728
**Fax:** 281-756-3880
**Web:** http://www.alvin.cc.tx.us/de
**E-mail:** psanger@alvin.cc.tx.us

**ACCREDITATION:** Southern Association of Colleges and Schools
**INSTITUTIONALLY ADMINISTERED FINANCIAL AID:** Yes

## DEGREE OR CERTIFICATE PROGRAMS OFFERED

**Programs offered do not lead to a degree or other formal award.**

## NON-DEGREE-RELATED COURSE TOPICS OFFERED

**Undergraduate**—American literature (United States); English composition; English creative writing; English language and literature, general; English language and literature/letters, other; administrative and secre-

tarial services; applied mathematics; biology, general; business; business administration and management; business communications; computer and information sciences, general; computer and information sciences, other; computer programming; computer science; computer/information technology administration and management; geography; history; internet and world wide web; liberal arts and sciences, general studies and humanities; mathematics; mathematics and computer science; mathematics, other; miscellaneous health professions; psychology; psychology, other.

# AMARILLO COLLEGE

PO Box 447
Amarillo, TX 79178
**Contact:** Mr. Tim McGee, Distance Education Coordinator
**Phone:** 806-371-5141
**Fax:** 806-371-5023
**Web:** http://www.actx.edu/
**E-mail:** mcgee-ti@actx.edu

**ACCREDITATION:** Southern Association of Colleges and Schools
**INSTITUTIONALLY ADMINISTERED FINANCIAL AID:** Yes

## DEGREE OR CERTIFICATE PROGRAMS OFFERED

**Programs offered do not lead to a degree or other formal award.**

## NON-DEGREE-RELATED COURSE TOPICS OFFERED

**Undergraduate**—American literature (United States); East and Southeast Asian languages and literatures; English composition; English language and literature, general; English technical and business writing; astronomy; biological and physical sciences; biology, general; child care and guidance workers and managers; communications, general; computer and information sciences, general; computer and information sciences, other; computer programming; computer science; fine arts and art studies; industrial equipment maintenance and repairers; mathematics; mathematics, other; miscellaneous health professions; music; nursing; real estate.

# AMBERTON UNIVERSITY

1700 Eastgate Drive
Garland, TX 75041
**Contact:** Dr. Jo Lynn Loyd, Vice President for Strategic Services
**Phone:** 972-279-6511 Ext. 126
**Fax:** 972-279-9773
**Web:** http://www.amberton.edu/
**E-mail:** jloyd@amberton.edu

**ACCREDITATION:** Southern Association of Colleges and Schools
**INSTITUTIONALLY ADMINISTERED FINANCIAL AID:** No

## DEGREE OR CERTIFICATE PROGRAMS OFFERED

**Undergraduate**—*BA:* Professional Development.
**Graduate**—*MA:* Professional Development.

# AMERICAN ACADEMY OF NUTRITION, COLLEGE OF NUTRITION

1204 Kenesaw Avenue
Knoxville, TN 37919

**Contact:** Cheryl Freeman, Student Services
**Phone:** 865-524-8079
**Fax:** 865-524-8339
**Web:** http://www.nutritioneducation.com/
**E-mail:** aantn@aol.com

**ACCREDITATION:** Distance Education and Training Council
**INSTITUTIONALLY ADMINISTERED FINANCIAL AID:** No

### DEGREE OR CERTIFICATE PROGRAMS OFFERED
**Undergraduate—AS:** Nutrition.

### NON-DEGREE-RELATED COURSE TOPICS OFFERED
**Undergraduate—**anatomy; biology, general; business marketing and marketing management; developmental and child psychology; environmental health; organic chemistry; physiology, human and animal. **Non-credit—**health professions and related sciences, other.

## THE AMERICAN COLLEGE

270 South Bryn Mawr Avenue
Bryn Mawr, PA 19010
**Contact:** Office of Student Services
**Phone:** 888-263-7265
**Fax:** 610-526-1465
**Web:** http://www.amercoll.edu/
**E-mail:** studentservices@amercoll.edu

**ACCREDITATION:** Middle States Association of Colleges and Schools
**INSTITUTIONALLY ADMINISTERED FINANCIAL AID:** No

### DEGREE OR CERTIFICATE PROGRAMS OFFERED
**Undergraduate—Certificate:** CFP(tm) Educational Curriculum; Financial Planning/Graduate School; LUTC Fellow Designation. **Diploma:** Chartered Financial Consultant (ChFC) Designation; Chartered Leadership Fellow (CLF) Designation; Chartered Life Underwriter (CLU) Designation; Registered Employee Benefits Consultant (REBC) Designation; Registered Health Underwriter (RHU) Designation.
**Graduate—Graduate Certificate:** Advanced Management; Asset Management; Business Succession Planning; Estate Planning and Taxation. **MSFS:** Financial Services.

### NON-DEGREE-RELATED COURSE TOPICS OFFERED
**Undergraduate—**business; business administration and management; finance, general; financial management and services; financial services marketing operations; human resources management; insurance and risk management; investments and securities.
**Graduate—**business; business administration and management; financial management and services; human resources management; insurance and risk management; investments and securities.

## AMERICAN COLLEGE OF COMPUTER & INFORMATION SCIENCES

2101 Magnolia Avenue
Birmingham, AL 32505
**Contact:** Natalie Nixon, Director of Admissions

**Phone:** 205-323-6191
**Fax:** 205-328-2229
**Web:** http://www.accis.edu/
**E-mail:** admiss@accis.edu
**ACCREDITATION:** Distance Education and Training Council
**INSTITUTIONALLY ADMINISTERED FINANCIAL AID:** No

### DEGREE OR CERTIFICATE PROGRAMS OFFERED
**Undergraduate—BS:** Computer Science; Information Systems.
**Graduate—MCS:** Computer Science.

### NON-DEGREE-RELATED COURSE TOPICS OFFERED
**Undergraduate—**English creative writing; accounting; applied mathematics; biology, general; business administration and management; communications, other; computer and information sciences, general; economics; educational psychology; history; mathematics and computer science; psychology; science, technology and society.
**See full description on page 292.**

## AMERICAN COLLEGE OF PREHOSPITAL MEDICINE

7552 Navarre Parkway, Suite 1
Navarre, FL 32566-7312
**Contact:** Dr. Richard A. Clinchy, III, Chairman and CEO
**Phone:** 850-939-0840
**Fax:** 850-939-7713
**Web:** http://www.acpm.edu/
**E-mail:** ceo@acpm.edu
**ACCREDITATION:** Distance Education and Training Council
**INSTITUTIONALLY ADMINISTERED FINANCIAL AID:** No

### DEGREE OR CERTIFICATE PROGRAMS OFFERED
**Undergraduate—AA:** Emergency Medical Services. **BA:** Emergency Medical Services.

### NON-DEGREE-RELATED COURSE TOPICS OFFERED
**Undergraduate—**biology, general.

## AMERICAN GRADUATE UNIVERSITY

733 North Dodsworth Avenue
Covina, CA 91724
**Contact:** Ms. Marie J. Sirney, Director of Administration
**Phone:** 626-966-4576
**Fax:** 626-915-1709
**Web:** http://www.agu.edu/
**E-mail:** mariesirney@agu.edu
**ACCREDITATION:** Distance Education and Training Council
**INSTITUTIONALLY ADMINISTERED FINANCIAL AID:** No

### DEGREE OR CERTIFICATE PROGRAMS OFFERED
**Graduate—MA:** Master of Acquisition Management; Master of Project Management.

### NON-DEGREE-RELATED COURSE TOPICS OFFERED
**Graduate—**accounting; business administration and management; business communications; business/managerial economics.

# AMERICAN INSTITUTE FOR PARALEGAL STUDIES, INC.

## Distance Education

17W705 Butterfield Road
Oakbrook Terrace, IL 60181
**Contact:** Ms. Annie Sacks, Director
**Phone:** 800-553-2420 Ext. 112
**Fax:** 810-771-8554
**Web:** http://www.aips.com
**E-mail:** annie.sacks@aips.com

**ACCREDITATION:** Accrediting Commission of Career Schools and Colleges of Technology

**INSTITUTIONALLY ADMINISTERED FINANCIAL AID:** No

### DEGREE OR CERTIFICATE PROGRAMS OFFERED

Programs offered do not lead to a degree or other formal award.

### NON-DEGREE-RELATED COURSE TOPICS OFFERED

Undergraduate—law and legal studies.

# AMERICAN INTERCONTINENTAL UNIVERSITY

## AIU Online Campus

2895 Greenspoint Parkway, Suite 400
Hoffman Estates, IL 60195
**Contact:** Jay Skiba, National Director of Admissions and Marketing
**Phone:** 877-701-3800 Ext. 3656
**Web:** http://www.aiu-online.com
**E-mail:** info@aiu-online.com

**ACCREDITATION:** Southern Association of Colleges and Schools
**INSTITUTIONALLY ADMINISTERED FINANCIAL AID:** Yes

### DEGREE OR CERTIFICATE PROGRAMS OFFERED

Programs offered do not lead to a degree or other formal award.
See full description on page 288.

# AMERICAN MILITARY UNIVERSITY

Student Service Center, 10648 Wakeman Court
Manassas , VA 20710
**Contact:** Mr. Bill Yamanaka, Public Relations Director
**Phone:** 703-330-5398 Ext. 131
**Fax:** 703-330-5109
**Web:** http://www.amunet.edu/
**E-mail:** byamanaka@amunet.edu

**ACCREDITATION:** Distance Education and Training Council
**INSTITUTIONALLY ADMINISTERED FINANCIAL AID:** Yes

### DEGREE OR CERTIFICATE PROGRAMS OFFERED

**Undergraduate—AA:** Military Studies. **BA:** Management; Marketing; Military History, Military Management, Intelligence Studies.
**Graduate—MA:** Military History, Military Management, Intelligence Studies; Military Studies. **MAM:** Management. **MBA/MPP:** Criminal Justice.

### NON-DEGREE-RELATED COURSE TOPICS OFFERED

**Undergraduate**—computer/information technology administration and management; criminology; health and medical administrative services; human resources management; international relations and affairs.
**Graduate**—business; criminal justice and corrections; ethnic and cultural studies; international relations and affairs; military studies; military technologies.
**See full description on page 294.**

# AMERICAN RIVER COLLEGE

## Open Learning

4700 College Oak Drive
Sacramento, CA 95841
**Contact:** Debby Ondricka, Administrative Assistant
**Phone:** 916-484-8456
**Fax:** 916-484-8018
**Web:** http://www.arc.losrios.cc.ca.us/learnres/distance.html
**E-mail:** ondricd@arc.losrios.cc.ca.us

**ACCREDITATION:** Western Association of Schools and Colleges
**INSTITUTIONALLY ADMINISTERED FINANCIAL AID:** Yes

### DEGREE OR CERTIFICATE PROGRAMS OFFERED

Programs offered do not lead to a degree or other formal award.

### NON-DEGREE-RELATED COURSE TOPICS OFFERED

**Undergraduate**—English composition; biology, general; business; business administration and management; business communications; business marketing and marketing management; business/managerial economics; computer and information sciences, general; computer software and media applications; entrepreneurship; gerontology; sociology; telecommunications.

# AMERICAN SCHOOL OF PROFESSIONAL PSYCHOLOGY, HAWAII CAMPUS

20 South Clark, 3rd Floor
Chicago, IL 60603
**Contact:** Ms. April Djakoniya, Coordinator of Online Services
**Phone:** 312-279-3839
**Fax:** 312-424-7282
**Web:** http://argosy.aspp.edu
**E-mail:** april@argosyeducation.com

**ACCREDITATION:** North Central Association of Colleges and Schools
**INSTITUTIONALLY ADMINISTERED FINANCIAL AID:** Yes

### DEGREE OR CERTIFICATE PROGRAMS OFFERED

Programs offered do not lead to a degree or other formal award.

**NON-DEGREE-RELATED COURSE TOPICS OFFERED**
Non-credit—psychology.

# AMERICAN SCHOOL OF PROFESSIONAL PSYCHOLOGY, SAN FRANCISCO BAY AREA CAMPUS

20 South Clark, 3rd Floor
Chicago, IL 60603
**Contact:** Ms. April Djakoniya, Coordinator of Online Services
**Phone:** 312-279-3839
**Fax:** 312-424-7282
**Web:** http://argosy.aspp.edu
**E-mail:** mpabst@argosyeducation.com

**ACCREDITATION:** North Central Association of Colleges and Schools

**INSTITUTIONALLY ADMINISTERED FINANCIAL AID:** Yes

**DEGREE OR CERTIFICATE PROGRAMS OFFERED**
Programs offered do not lead to a degree or other formal award.

**NON-DEGREE-RELATED COURSE TOPICS OFFERED**
Non-credit—psychology.

# AMERICAN SCHOOL OF PROFESSIONAL PSYCHOLOGY, VIRGINIA CAMPUS

20 South Clark, 3rd Floor
Chicago, IL 60603
**Contact:** Ms. April Djakoniya, Coordinator of Online Services
**Phone:** 312-279-3839
**Fax:** 312-424-7282
**Web:** http://www.aspp.edu/
**E-mail:** april@argosyeducation.com

**ACCREDITATION:** North Central Association of Colleges and Schools

**INSTITUTIONALLY ADMINISTERED FINANCIAL AID:** Yes

**DEGREE OR CERTIFICATE PROGRAMS OFFERED**
Programs offered do not lead to a degree or other formal award.

**NON-DEGREE-RELATED COURSE TOPICS OFFERED**
Graduate—psychology.
Non-credit—psychology.

# ANDREW COLLEGE

413 College Street
Cuthbert, GA 31740-1395
**Contact:** Dr. Jack Brodie Farris, Jr., Director Interactive Distance Learning
**Phone:** 229-732-5925
**Fax:** 229-732-5952

**Web:** http://www.andrewcollege.edu/
**E-mail:** jackfarris@andrewcollege.edu

**ACCREDITATION:** Southern Association of Colleges and Schools

**INSTITUTIONALLY ADMINISTERED FINANCIAL AID:** No

**DEGREE OR CERTIFICATE PROGRAMS OFFERED**
Programs offered do not lead to a degree or other formal award.

**NON-DEGREE-RELATED COURSE TOPICS OFFERED**
Undergraduate—English composition; accounting; business; computer and information sciences, general; economics; history; mathematics; political science and government; psychology.

# ANGELINA COLLEGE

*Continuing Education*
PO Box 1768
Lufkin, TX 75902-1768
**Contact:** Dr. Fred Kanke, Dean of Community Services and Development
**Phone:** 936-633-5204
**Fax:** 936-633-5478
**Web:** http://www.angelina.cc.tx.us
**E-mail:** fkanke@angelina.cc.tx..us

**ACCREDITATION:** Southern Association of Colleges and Schools

**INSTITUTIONALLY ADMINISTERED FINANCIAL AID:** Yes

**DEGREE OR CERTIFICATE PROGRAMS OFFERED**
Programs offered do not lead to a degree or other formal award.

**NON-DEGREE-RELATED COURSE TOPICS OFFERED**
Undergraduate—English composition; English literature (British and Commonwealth); criminal justice and corrections; medical basic sciences.
Non-credit—medical basic sciences.

# ANNE ARUNDEL COMMUNITY COLLEGE

*Distance Learning Center*
Arnold, MD 21012-1895
**Contact:** Mrs. Mary Barnes, Coordinator of Distance Learning Center
**Phone:** 410-777-2731
**Fax:** 410-777-4731
**Web:** http://www.aacc.cc.md.us/diseduc
**E-mail:** mabarnes@mail.aacc.cc.md.us

**ACCREDITATION:** Middle States Association of Colleges and Schools

**INSTITUTIONALLY ADMINISTERED FINANCIAL AID:** Yes

**DEGREE OR CERTIFICATE PROGRAMS OFFERED**
Undergraduate—*AA:* General Studies. *AAS:* Business Management. *AS:* Business Administration.

**NON-DEGREE-RELATED COURSE TOPICS OFFERED**
Undergraduate—American (United States) history; English composition; English creative writing; accounting; anthropology; biology, general;

business administration and management; business management and administrative services, other; business marketing and marketing management; business/managerial economics; computer and information sciences, general; computer science; developmental and child psychology; economics; finance, general; geography; health and physical education/fitness; history; law and legal studies, other; mathematical statistics; mathematics, other; oceanography; paralegal/legal assistant; social psychology; social sciences and history, other; sociology.

# ANTELOPE VALLEY COLLEGE

3041 West Avenue K
Lancaster, CA 93536-5426
**Contact:** Dr. Jackie Fisher, Vice President of Academic Affairs
**Phone:** 661-722-6304
**Fax:** 661-722-6324
**E-mail:** jfisher@avc.edu

**ACCREDITATION:** Western Association of Schools and Colleges
**INSTITUTIONALLY ADMINISTERED FINANCIAL AID:** Yes

## DEGREE OR CERTIFICATE PROGRAMS OFFERED
Programs offered do not lead to a degree or other formal award.

## NON-DEGREE-RELATED COURSE TOPICS OFFERED
**Undergraduate**—English composition; accounting; business management and administrative services, other; computer and information sciences, general; computer and information sciences, other; sociology.

# ANTIOCH UNIVERSITY MCGREGOR

*Individualized Master of Arts Programs*

800 Livermore Street
Yellow Springs, OH 45387
**Contact:** Ruth M. Paige, Associate Director of Admissions
**Phone:** 937-769-1825
**Fax:** 937-769-1805
**Web:** http://www.mcgregor.edu
**E-mail:** admiss@mcgregor.edu

**ACCREDITATION:** North Central Association of Colleges and Schools
**INSTITUTIONALLY ADMINISTERED FINANCIAL AID:** Yes

## DEGREE OR CERTIFICATE PROGRAMS OFFERED
**Graduate**—*MA:* Conflict Resolution; I. Individualized Liberal and Professional Studies; II. Individualized Liberal and Professional Studies; III. Individualized Liberal and Professional Studies; IV. Individualized Liberal and Professional Studies; IX. Individualized Liberal and Professional Studies; V. Individualized Liberal and Professional Studies; VI. Individualized Liberal and Professional Studies; VII. Individualized Liberal and Professional Studies; VIII. Individualized Liberal and Professional Studies; X. Individualized Liberal and Professional Studies; XI. Individualized Liberal and Professional Studies; XII. Individualized Liberal and Professional Studies.

## NON-DEGREE-RELATED COURSE TOPICS OFFERED
**Graduate**—area, ethnic and cultural studies, other; educational evaluation, research and statistics; peace and conflict studies.

# AQUINAS COLLEGE

*Learning and Technology*

1607 Robinson Road, SE
Grand Rapids, MI 49506-1799
**Contact:** Ms. Celee Mesler, Registrar
**Phone:** 616-459-8281 Ext. 5239
**Fax:** 616-732-4431
**Web:** http://www.aquinas.edu
**E-mail:** meslecec@aquinas.edu

**ACCREDITATION:** North Central Association of Colleges and Schools
**INSTITUTIONALLY ADMINISTERED FINANCIAL AID:** Yes

## DEGREE OR CERTIFICATE PROGRAMS OFFERED
Programs offered do not lead to a degree or other formal award.

## NON-DEGREE-RELATED COURSE TOPICS OFFERED
**Undergraduate**—business communications; ethnic and cultural studies; teacher education, specific academic and vocational programs; visual and performing arts.
**Graduate**—accounting; business management and administrative services, other; marketing management and research; psychology, other.

# ARCADIA UNIVERSITY

Glenside, PA 19038
**Contact:** Norah D. Peters-Davis, Dean of Undergraduate Studies and Faculty Development
**Web:** http://www.arcadia.edu
**E-mail:** peters@arcadia.edu

**ACCREDITATION:** Middle States Association of Colleges and Schools
**INSTITUTIONALLY ADMINISTERED FINANCIAL AID:** Yes

## DEGREE OR CERTIFICATE PROGRAMS OFFERED
Programs offered do not lead to a degree or other formal award.

# ARIZONA INSTITUTE OF BUSINESS & TECHNOLOGY

6049 North 43rd Avenue
Phoenix, AZ 85019
**Contact:** Ms. Mary Taylor, Distance Education Coordinator
**Phone:** 602-242-6265
**Fax:** 602-589-1365
**Web:** http://aibtonline.org
**E-mail:** mtaylor@aibt.edu

**ACCREDITATION:** Accrediting Council for Independent Colleges and Schools
**INSTITUTIONALLY ADMINISTERED FINANCIAL AID:** Yes

eCollege.com   *www.ecollege.com*

## DEGREE OR CERTIFICATE PROGRAMS OFFERED
**Undergraduate**—*AA:* Business Operations—Accounting; Business Operations—Business Technology; Health Technology Management—Medical Assis-

tant; Health Technology Management—Patient Care Technician; Justice Administration; Microcomputer Network Systems.

# ARIZONA SCHOOL OF PROFESSIONAL PSYCHOLOGY

2301 West Dunlap Avenue, Suite 211
Phoenix, AZ 85021
**Contact:** Ms. Gail Bartkovich, Director of Admissions
**Phone:** 866-216-2777 Ext. 209
**Fax:** 602-216-2601
**Web:** http://argosy.aspp.edu
**E-mail:** gbartkovich@azspp.edu

**ACCREDITATION:** North Central Association of Colleges and Schools
**INSTITUTIONALLY ADMINISTERED FINANCIAL AID:** Yes

## DEGREE OR CERTIFICATE PROGRAMS OFFERED
Programs offered do not lead to a degree or other formal award.

## NON-DEGREE-RELATED COURSE TOPICS OFFERED
Non-credit—psychology.

# ARIZONA STATE UNIVERSITY

*Distance Learning and Technology*
PO Box 870501
Tempe, AZ 85287-0501
**Contact:** Mr. Brent Woodhouse, Student Support Contact
**Phone:** 480-965-6738
**Fax:** 480-965-1371
**Web:** http://asuonline.asu.edu
**E-mail:** brent.woodhouse@asu.edu

**ACCREDITATION:** North Central Association of Colleges and Schools
**INSTITUTIONALLY ADMINISTERED FINANCIAL AID:** Yes

## DEGREE OR CERTIFICATE PROGRAMS OFFERED
**Undergraduate**—*BA:* History.
**Graduate**—*Graduate Certificate:* Gerontology. *ME:* Engineering. *MEngr:* Engineering. *MSE:* Electrical Engineering.

## NON-DEGREE-RELATED COURSE TOPICS OFFERED
**Undergraduate**—American literature (United States); English composition; English language and literature, general; English technical and business writing; accounting; advertising; botany; chemical engineering; city/urban, community and regional planning; computer science; computer systems networking and telecommunications; curriculum and instruction; drama/theater arts, general; dramatic/theater arts and stagecraft; educational/instructional media design; electrical and electronic engineering-related technology; family and community studies; fine arts and art studies; foreign languages and literatures; geography; history; horticulture science; housing studies; industrial/manufacturing engineering; journalism and mass communication, other; journalism and mass communications; law and legal studies; liberal arts and sciences, general studies and humanities; marketing management and research; mathematics; medieval and renaissance studies; peace and conflict studies; plant sciences; sociology; special education; tourism and travel services marketing operations; women's studies.

**Graduate**—aerospace, aeronautical and astronautical engineering; art history, criticism and conservation; chemical engineering; curriculum and instruction; educational psychology; electrical, electronics and communication engineering; engineering/industrial management; environmental/ environmental health engineering; industrial/manufacturing engineering; international business; mechanical engineering; medieval and renaissance studies.

# ARIZONA STATE UNIVERSITY EAST

*Distance Learning and Technology*
PO Box 870501
Tempe, AZ 85287-0501
**Contact:** Mr. Brent Woodhouse, Student Support Contact
**Phone:** 480-965-6738
**Fax:** 480-965-1371
**Web:** http://www.east.asu.edu/
**E-mail:** brent.woodhouse@asu.edu

**ACCREDITATION:** North Central Association of Colleges and Schools
**INSTITUTIONALLY ADMINISTERED FINANCIAL AID:** Yes

## DEGREE OR CERTIFICATE PROGRAMS OFFERED
**Graduate**—*MS:* Environmental Technology Management.

## NON-DEGREE-RELATED COURSE TOPICS OFFERED
**Undergraduate**—environmental control technologies; health and physical education/fitness.
**Graduate**—environmental control technologies.

# ARIZONA STATE UNIVERSITY WEST

*Office of Extended Instruction*
PO Box 870501
Tempe, AZ 85287-0501
**Contact:** Mr. Brent Woodhouse, Student Support Contact
**Phone:** 480-965-6738
**Fax:** 480-965-1371
**Web:** http://asuonline.asu.edu
**E-mail:** brent.woodhouse@asu.edu

**ACCREDITATION:** North Central Association of Colleges and Schools
**INSTITUTIONALLY ADMINISTERED FINANCIAL AID:** Yes

## DEGREE OR CERTIFICATE PROGRAMS OFFERED
**Graduate**—*Graduate Certificate:* Gerontology. *MBA:* Business Administration.

## NON-DEGREE-RELATED COURSE TOPICS OFFERED
**Undergraduate**—English technical and business writing; computer science; education, other; gerontology; law and legal studies; social work; special education; tourism and travel services marketing operations.
**Graduate**—computer science; education, other; educational/instructional media design; electrical and electronic engineering-related technology; gerontology; social work; special education; tourism and travel services marketing operations.

# ARIZONA WESTERN COLLEGE

PO Box 929
Yuma, AZ 85366
**Contact:** Brian Doak, Registrar
**Web:** http://www.awc.cc.az.us/
**E-mail:** bdoak@awc.cc.az.us

**ACCREDITATION:** North Central Association of Colleges and Schools
**INSTITUTIONALLY ADMINISTERED FINANCIAL AID:** Yes

## DEGREE OR CERTIFICATE PROGRAMS OFFERED

Undergraduate—*Certificate:* General Certificate.

## NON-DEGREE-RELATED COURSE TOPICS OFFERED

Undergraduate—English language and literature, general; accounting; business; computer and information sciences, general; criminal justice and corrections; fire protection; liberal arts and sciences, general studies and humanities.

# ARLINGTON BAPTIST COLLEGE

*Distance Education Department*

3001 West Division
Arlington, TX 76012
**Contact:** Janie Hall, Registrar
**Phone:** 817-461-8741 Ext. 105
**Fax:** 817-274-1138
**Web:** http://www.abconline.edu/

**ACCREDITATION:** Accrediting Association of Bible Colleges
**INSTITUTIONALLY ADMINISTERED FINANCIAL AID:** Yes

## DEGREE OR CERTIFICATE PROGRAMS OFFERED

Programs offered do not lead to a degree or other formal award.

## NON-DEGREE-RELATED COURSE TOPICS OFFERED

Undergraduate—bible/biblical studies.
Non-credit—bible/biblical studies.

# ARMSTRONG ATLANTIC STATE UNIVERSITY

*Academic Off-Campus Programs*

Savannah, GA 31419
**Contact:** Academic Off-Campus Programs
**Phone:** 912-921-5989
**Fax:** 912-961-3047
**Web:** http://www.armstrong.edu/distance.html
**E-mail:** admissions@mailgate.armstrong.edu

**ACCREDITATION:** Southern Association of Colleges and Schools
**INSTITUTIONALLY ADMINISTERED FINANCIAL AID:** Yes

## DEGREE OR CERTIFICATE PROGRAMS OFFERED

Programs offered do not lead to a degree or other formal award.

## NON-DEGREE-RELATED COURSE TOPICS OFFERED

Undergraduate—English composition; English literature (British and Commonwealth); English technical and business writing; computer and information sciences, general; education, general; miscellaneous health professions.
Graduate—general teacher education.

# THE ART INSTITUTES INTERNATIONAL

420 Boulevard of the Allies
Pittsburgh, PA 15219
**Contact:** Ms. Elizabeth A. Erickson, Vice President of Marketing and Director of Admissions
**Phone:** 303-680-6302
**Fax:** 303-766-8512
**Web:** http://www.aionline.edu
**E-mail:** ericksoe@aii.edu

**ACCREDITATION:** Accrediting Commission of Career Schools and Colleges of Technology
**INSTITUTIONALLY ADMINISTERED FINANCIAL AID:** Yes

## DEGREE OR CERTIFICATE PROGRAMS OFFERED

Undergraduate—*AS:* Graphic Design. *BS:* Graphic Design. *Diploma:* Digital Design.

## NON-DEGREE-RELATED COURSE TOPICS OFFERED

Non-credit—design and applied arts.

# ASHLAND COMMUNITY COLLEGE

1400 College Drive
Ashland, KY 41101
**Contact:** Dr. Carol M. Greene, Director of Library Services
**Phone:** 606-326-2142
**Fax:** 606-324-2186
**Web:** http://www.ashlandcc.org/
**E-mail:** carol.greene@kctcs.net

**ACCREDITATION:** Southern Association of Colleges and Schools
**INSTITUTIONALLY ADMINISTERED FINANCIAL AID:** Yes

## DEGREE OR CERTIFICATE PROGRAMS OFFERED

Programs offered do not lead to a degree or other formal award.

## NON-DEGREE-RELATED COURSE TOPICS OFFERED

Undergraduate—American literature (United States); English composition; English creative writing; English language and literature/letters, other; economics.

# ASSEMBLIES OF GOD THEOLOGICAL SEMINARY

*Office of Continuing Education*

1435 North Glenstone Avenue
Springfield, MO 65802

**Contact:** Randy C. Walls, Director
**Phone:** 800-467-2487 Ext. 1046
**Fax:** 417-268-1009
**Web:** http://www.agts.edu
**E-mail:** rwalls@agseminary.edu

**ACCREDITATION:** North Central Association of Colleges and Schools

**INSTITUTIONALLY ADMINISTERED FINANCIAL AID:** No

### DEGREE OR CERTIFICATE PROGRAMS OFFERED
Programs offered do not lead to a degree or other formal award.

### NON-DEGREE-RELATED COURSE TOPICS OFFERED
**Graduate**—bible/biblical studies; biblical and other theological languages and literatures; history; missions/missionary studies and missiology; pastoral counseling and specialized ministries; philosophy and religion; religion/religious studies; theological and ministerial studies; theological studies and religious vocations, other.

## ATHABASCA UNIVERSITY

1 University Drive
Athabasca, AB T9S 3A3, Canada
**Contact:** Information Centre
**Phone:** 800-788-9041
**Fax:** 780-675-6437
**Web:** http://www.athabascau.ca/
**E-mail:** auinfo@athabascau.ca

**ACCREDITATION:** Provincially Chartered

**INSTITUTIONALLY ADMINISTERED FINANCIAL AID:** Yes

### DEGREE OR CERTIFICATE PROGRAMS OFFERED
**Undergraduate**—*BA:* Bachelor of Arts (3 year); Bachelor of Arts (3 year) with Concentration; Bachelor of Arts (4 year) General or with Major. *BBA:* Bachelor of Administration (with Concentration); Bachelor of Administration Post Diploma (with Concentration). *BComm:* Bachelor of Commerce (4 year). *BGS:* Bachelor of General Studies with Designation (Arts/Science or Applied Studies). *BN:* Bachelor of Nursing—Post R.N.. *BPA:* Bachelor of Professional Arts with Major (4 year). *BS:* Bachelor of Science (4 year); Bachelor of Science—Post Diploma; Computing and Information Systems (4 year); Computing and Information Systems—Post Diploma; Human Science—Post Diploma; Human Science Major. *Certificate:* Accounting; Administration; Advanced Accounting; Career Development; Computers and Management Information Systems; Computing and Information Systems; Counseling Women; English Language Studies; French Language Proficiency; Health Development Administration; Home Health Nursing; Industrial Relations and Human Resources; Labour Studies; Public Administration. *Diploma:* Arts; Inclusive Education.
**Graduate**—*Advanced Graduate Diploma:* Advanced Nursing Practice; Distance Education Technology; Management. *MA:* Integrated Studies. *MBA:* Information Technology Management; Master of Business Administration. *MCH:* Master of Health Studies. *MDE:* Master of Distance Education. *MSIS:* Information Systems.
See full description on page 296.

## ATHENS TECHNICAL COLLEGE

800 US 29 North
Athens, GA 30601-1500

**Contact:** Ken Jarrett, Vice President for Academic Affairs
**Phone:** 706-355-5018
**Web:** http://www.aati.edu/
**E-mail:** jarrett@aati.edu

**ACCREDITATION:** Southern Association of Colleges and Schools

**INSTITUTIONALLY ADMINISTERED FINANCIAL AID:** Yes

### DEGREE OR CERTIFICATE PROGRAMS OFFERED
**Undergraduate**—*AS:* General Studies.

### NON-DEGREE-RELATED COURSE TOPICS OFFERED
**Undergraduate**—accounting; administrative and secretarial services; biological sciences/life sciences, other; business; business marketing and marketing management; child care and guidance workers and managers; computer and information sciences, other; health professions and related sciences, other; law and legal studies; marketing management and research; nursing; physical therapy.

## ATLANTIC CAPE COMMUNITY COLLEGE

*Academic Computing and Distance Education*
5100 Black Horse Pike
Mays Landing, NJ 08330
**Contact:** Dr. Michael A. Kolitsky, Dean
**Phone:** 609-343-4987
**Fax:** 609-343-5122
**Web:** http://www.atlantic.edu/distance_ed/
**E-mail:** mkolitsk@atlantic.edu

**ACCREDITATION:** Middle States Association of Colleges and Schools

**INSTITUTIONALLY ADMINISTERED FINANCIAL AID:** Yes

### DEGREE OR CERTIFICATE PROGRAMS OFFERED
**Undergraduate**—*AA:* History; Humanities; Liberal Arts; Literature; Psychology. *AS:* Business Administration; Computer Information Systems; General Studies.

### NON-DEGREE-RELATED COURSE TOPICS OFFERED
**Non-credit**—English technical and business writing; administrative and secretarial services; business communications; communications, other; computer software and media applications; hospitality and recreation marketing operations.

---

**Special Note**

Atlantic Cape Community College (ACCC), a public, 2-year, accredited institution in Mays Landing, New Jersey, offers 40 degree programs and 27 certificate programs to nearly 5,000 students. The College primarily draws its students from Atlantic and Cape May Counties and maintains extension centers in Atlantic City and Rio Grande in Cape May County.

ACCC is a leader in educational technology and offers 8 associate degrees through distance education. The programs are offered through online classes that are available via the Internet or as a combination of online and television courses. The degree programs available are the Associate of Science in general studies, the Associate of Arts in liberal arts, the Associate of Arts in history, the

Associate of Science in business administration, the Associate in Science in computer information systems, the Associate in Arts in psychology, the Associate in Arts in social science, and the Associate in Arts in humanities.

ACCC currently offers more than 80 online college-credit courses and more than 50 online continuing education courses. Students use a computer with a connection to an Internet Service Provider (ISP). Via e-mail, bulletin boards, and the World Wide Web, students and faculty members gather together in a true classroom without walls.

Students should have a Mac or Windows-based computer with a 28.8 or higher modem, connection to an ISP, and some knowledge of downloading and installing software. Students must be independent learners who can manage time effectively. ACCC uses conferencing software to help faculty members and students communicate with one another.

Online classes cost $80 per credit for all students. There are no additional fees. For more information about ACCC's online courses, students should contact the Admissions Office by telephone at 609-343-5000 or via e-mail at pionegro@atlantic.edu or visit the College's Web site at http://www.atlantic.edu.

# ATLANTIC UNIVERSITY

Building 3300, Suite 100, 397 Little Neck Road
Virginia Beach, VA 23452
**Contact:** Dr. Robert Danner, Director of Admissions
**Phone:** 757-631-8101 Ext. 202
**Fax:** 757-631-8096
**Web:** http://www.atlanticuniv.edu/
**E-mail:** info@atlanticuniv.edu

**ACCREDITATION:** Distance Education and Training Council
**INSTITUTIONALLY ADMINISTERED FINANCIAL AID:** No

## DEGREE OR CERTIFICATE PROGRAMS OFFERED
**Graduate—*MA:*** Transpersonal Studies.

## NON-DEGREE-RELATED COURSE TOPICS OFFERED
**Graduate**—English creative writing; art history, criticism and conservation; bible/biblical studies; education, other; fine arts and art studies; philosophy and religion; psychology, other; religion/religious studies; women's studies.
**Non-credit**—English creative writing; art history, criticism and conservation; bible/biblical studies; education, other; fine arts and art studies; philosophy and religion; psychology, other; religion/religious studies; women's studies.

# AUBURN UNIVERSITY
*Distance Learning/Outreach Technology*
Petrie Annex
Auburn University, AL 36849-5611
**Contact:** Mrs. Ernestine Morris-Stinson
**Phone:** 334-844-3114
**Fax:** 334-844-3125
**Web:** http://www.auburn.edu/outreach/dl

**E-mail:** morrier@auburn.edu
**ACCREDITATION:** Southern Association of Colleges and Schools
**INSTITUTIONALLY ADMINISTERED FINANCIAL AID:** No

## DEGREE OR CERTIFICATE PROGRAMS OFFERED
**Undergraduate—*Certificate:*** Academic Certificate Program in Community Employment Services; Dietary Management.
**Graduate—*Advanced Graduate Diploma:*** Rehabilitation Counseling. ***MAE:*** Aerospace Engineering. ***MBA:*** Business Administration. ***MCE:*** Chemical Engineering; Civil Engineering. ***MCSE:*** Computer Science and Engineering. ***MISE:*** Industrial and Systems Engineering. ***MME:*** Materials Engineering; Mechanical Engineering. ***MS:*** Aerospace Engineering; Chemical Engineering; Civil Engineering; Computer Science and Engineering; Hotel and Restaurant Management; Industrial and Systems Engineering; Materials Engineering; Mechanical Engineering.

## NON-DEGREE-RELATED COURSE TOPICS OFFERED
**Undergraduate**—animal sciences; educational evaluation, research and statistics; film/video and photographic arts.
**Non-credit**—foods and nutrition studies; hospitality services management.

See full description on page 298.

# AUSTIN PEAY STATE UNIVERSITY

PO Box 4678
Clarksville, TN 37044
**Contact:** Dr. Stanley Groppel, Dean of Extended and Distance Education
**Phone:** 931-221-7816
**Fax:** 931-221-7748
**Web:** http://www.apsu.edu/
**E-mail:** groppels@apsu.edu

**ACCREDITATION:** Southern Association of Colleges and Schools
**INSTITUTIONALLY ADMINISTERED FINANCIAL AID:** Yes

## DEGREE OR CERTIFICATE PROGRAMS OFFERED
**Undergraduate—*BPS:*** APSU Regents Online Degree Program; Organizational Leadership; Technology Studies.
**Graduate—*MA:*** Corporate Communication.

# AVILA COLLEGE

11901 Wornall Road
Kansas City, MO 64145
**Contact:** Mr. Norman Dexter, Assistant Vice President for Professional Education and Outreach
**Phone:** 816-501-2483
**Web:** http://www.avila.edu/
**E-mail:** dexternl@mail.avila.edu

**ACCREDITATION:** North Central Association of Colleges and Schools
**INSTITUTIONALLY ADMINISTERED FINANCIAL AID:** Yes

## DEGREE OR CERTIFICATE PROGRAMS OFFERED
Programs offered do not lead to a degree or other formal award.

## NON-DEGREE-RELATED COURSE TOPICS OFFERED

**Undergraduate**—business administration and management; economics; theological studies and religious vocations, other.

# AZUSA PACIFIC UNIVERSITY

901 East Alosta Avenue
Azusa, CA 91702-7000
**Contact:** Dr. Bruce Simmerok, Director of Distance Learning and Continuing Education
**Web:** http://online.apu.edu/
**E-mail:** bsimmerok@apu.edu

**ACCREDITATION:** Western Association of Schools and Colleges
**INSTITUTIONALLY ADMINISTERED FINANCIAL AID:** Yes

eCollege.com   www.ecollege.com

## DEGREE OR CERTIFICATE PROGRAMS OFFERED

**Undergraduate**—*Certificate:* Library Media Teaching.
**Graduate**—*MAE:* School Librarianship.

## NON-DEGREE-RELATED COURSE TOPICS OFFERED

**Undergraduate**—computer science; history; religion/religious studies.
**Graduate**—computer science; education administration and supervision; educational evaluation, research and statistics; educational/instructional media design; teacher education, specific academic and vocational programs; theological and ministerial studies.

# BAKER COLLEGE OF FLINT
*Baker College On-Line*
1116 West Bristol Road
Flint, MI 48507
**Contact:** Mr. Chuck J. Gurden, Director of Graduate and Online Admissions
**Phone:** 810-766-4390
**Fax:** 810-766-4399
**Web:** http://online.baker.edu
**E-mail:** gurden_c@corpfl.baker.edu

**ACCREDITATION:** North Central Association of Colleges and Schools
**INSTITUTIONALLY ADMINISTERED FINANCIAL AID:** Yes

## DEGREE OR CERTIFICATE PROGRAMS OFFERED

**Undergraduate**—*ABA:* Business Administration. *BBA:* Business Administration.
**Graduate**—*MBA:* Business Administration.

## NON-DEGREE-RELATED COURSE TOPICS OFFERED

**Undergraduate**—business administration and management; computer/information technology administration and management.
**See full description on page 300.**

# BAKERSFIELD COLLEGE
*Distance Learning*
1801 Panorama Drive
Bakersfield, CA 93305
**Contact:** Kathleen Loomis-Tubbesing, Distance Learning Coordinator
**Phone:** 661-395-4694
**Fax:** 661-395-4690
**Web:** http://www.bakersfieldcollege.org
**E-mail:** kloomis@bc.cc.ca.us

**ACCREDITATION:** Western Association of Schools and Colleges
**INSTITUTIONALLY ADMINISTERED FINANCIAL AID:** Yes

## DEGREE OR CERTIFICATE PROGRAMS OFFERED
Programs offered do not lead to a degree or other formal award.

## NON-DEGREE-RELATED COURSE TOPICS OFFERED

**Undergraduate**—English composition; accounting; astronomy; business; computer science; criminal justice and corrections; developmental and child psychology; finance, general; fire science/firefighting; mathematics.

# BALL STATE UNIVERSITY
*School of Continuing Education and Public Service*
Carmichael Hall, Room 200
Muncie, IN 47306
**Contact:** Ms. Diane K. Buck, Marketing Manager
**Phone:** 765-285-9042
**Fax:** 765-285-7161
**Web:** http://www.bsu.edu/distance
**E-mail:** dbuck@bsu.edu

**ACCREDITATION:** North Central Association of Colleges and Schools

## DEGREE OR CERTIFICATE PROGRAMS OFFERED
**Undergraduate**—*AA:* General Arts. *BSN:* Nursing.
**Graduate**—*MA:* Executive Development for Public Service. *MAE:* Educational Administration and Supervision; Elementary Education; Special Education. *MBA:* Business Administration. *MSN:* Nursing.

# BANK STREET COLLEGE OF EDUCATION
*Mathematics Learning Forums*
610 West 112th Street
New York, NY 10025
**Contact:** Linda Metnetsky, Senior Graduate Faculty and Director
**Phone:** 212-875-4557
**Fax:** 212-875-4753
**Web:** http://www.bankstreet.edu
**E-mail:** lmetnetsky@bnkst.edu

**ACCREDITATION:** Middle States Association of Colleges and Schools
**INSTITUTIONALLY ADMINISTERED FINANCIAL AID:** No

## DEGREE OR CERTIFICATE PROGRAMS OFFERED

Programs offered do not lead to a degree or other formal award.

## NON-DEGREE-RELATED COURSE TOPICS OFFERED

Graduate—education, other; mathematics; mathematics and computer science; mathematics, other.
Non-credit—education, other; mathematics; mathematics, other.

# THE BAPTIST COLLEGE OF FLORIDA

*Division of Distance Learning*
5400 College Drive
Graceville, FL 32440
**Contact:** Jerry E. Oswalt, Vice President of Academic Affairs
**Phone:** 850-263-3261 Ext. 412
**Fax:** 850-263-7506
**Web:** http://www.baptistcollege.edu/distance
**E-mail:** jeoswalt@baptistcollege.edu

**ACCREDITATION:** Southern Association of Colleges and Schools
**INSTITUTIONALLY ADMINISTERED FINANCIAL AID:** No

## DEGREE OR CERTIFICATE PROGRAMS OFFERED

Undergraduate—*BS:* Biblical Studies.

## NON-DEGREE-RELATED COURSE TOPICS OFFERED

Undergraduate—religious education; theological and ministerial studies.

# BARCLAY COLLEGE

*Home College Program*
607 North Kingman
Haviland, KS 67059-0288
**Contact:** Mrs. Elizabeth Griffin, Associate Dean for External Studies
**Phone:** 620-862-5252 Ext. 44
**Fax:** 620-862-5403
**Web:** http://barclaycollege.edu
**E-mail:** griel@barclaycollege.edu

**ACCREDITATION:** Accrediting Association of Bible Colleges
**INSTITUTIONALLY ADMINISTERED FINANCIAL AID:** Yes

## DEGREE OR CERTIFICATE PROGRAMS OFFERED

Undergraduate—*BS:* Business Management and Administration; Christian Ministry Leadership; Psychology/Family Counseling.

## NON-DEGREE-RELATED COURSE TOPICS OFFERED

Undergraduate—English composition; sociology.

# BARTON COLLEGE

*Lifelong Education and Summer Sessions*
PO Box 5364
Wilson, NC 27893
**Contact:** Teresa C. Parker, Assistant Professor, School of Business

**Phone:** 252-399-6421
**Fax:** 252-399-6575
**Web:** http://www.barton.edu
**E-mail:** tparker@barton.edu

**ACCREDITATION:** Southern Association of Colleges and Schools
**INSTITUTIONALLY ADMINISTERED FINANCIAL AID:** Yes

## DEGREE OR CERTIFICATE PROGRAMS OFFERED

Programs offered do not lead to a degree or other formal award.

## NON-DEGREE-RELATED COURSE TOPICS OFFERED

Undergraduate—internet and world wide web.

# BARTON COUNTY COMMUNITY COLLEGE

*Bartonline*
PO Box 2463
Fort Reilly, KS 66442
**Contact:** Mr. Wynn Butler, Director of Bartonline
**Phone:** 877-620-6606
**Fax:** 785-784-7542
**Web:** http://www.bartonline.org
**E-mail:** butlerw@barton.cc.ks.us

**ACCREDITATION:** North Central Association of Colleges and Schools
**INSTITUTIONALLY ADMINISTERED FINANCIAL AID:** Yes

> eCollege.com   *www.ecollege.com*

## DEGREE OR CERTIFICATE PROGRAMS OFFERED

Undergraduate—*AA:* General Studies. *AAS:* Business Military Management. *AGS:* General Studies; General and Military Studies. *AS:* General Studies. *Certificate:* Dietary Management; Hazardous Materials.

# BELLEVUE COMMUNITY COLLEGE

*Telecommunications Program–Distance Learning Department*
3000 Landerholm Circle, SE
Bellevue, WA 98007-6484
**Contact:** Thornton Perry, Director of Distance Learning
**Phone:** 425-564-2438
**Fax:** 425-564-6186
**Web:** http://distance-ed.bcc.ctc.edu
**E-mail:** tperry@bcc.ctc.edu

**ACCREDITATION:** Northwest Association of Schools and Colleges
**INSTITUTIONALLY ADMINISTERED FINANCIAL AID:** Yes

## DEGREE OR CERTIFICATE PROGRAMS OFFERED

Undergraduate—*AA:* General Studies; Web Authoring. *AAB:* Business. *AAS:* Transfer Degree. *Certificate of Achievement:* Web Authoring.

## NON-DEGREE-RELATED COURSE TOPICS OFFERED

Undergraduate—American studies/civilization; English composition; English creative writing; European history; accounting; adult and continuing teacher education; anthropology; art history, criticism and conservation; biology, general; environmental science/studies; film/cinema studies; geography; history and philosophy of science and technology; journalism and mass communication, other; law and legal studies, other; management information systems and business data processing, general; mathematical statistics; mathematics, other; oceanography; sociology.

# BELLEVUE UNIVERSITY
## Online Programs
1000 Galvin Road South
Bellevue, NE 68005
**Contact:** Online Programs
**Phone:** 800-756-7920
**Web:** http://www.bellevue.edu

**ACCREDITATION:** North Central Association of Colleges and Schools
**INSTITUTIONALLY ADMINISTERED FINANCIAL AID:** Yes

### DEGREE OR CERTIFICATE PROGRAMS OFFERED
**Undergraduate—*BS:*** Business Information Systems; Criminal Justice Administration; E-Business; Global Business Management; Management Information Systems; Management of Human Resources; Management. **Graduate—*MA:*** Leadership. ***MBA:*** Business Administration.
**See full description on page 302.**

# BELLINGHAM TECHNICAL COLLEGE
3028 Lindbergh Avenue
Bellingham, WA 98225-1599
**Web:** http://www.beltc.ctc.edu/
**E-mail:** beltcadm@beltc.ctc.edu

**ACCREDITATION:** Northwest Association of Schools and Colleges
**INSTITUTIONALLY ADMINISTERED FINANCIAL AID:** No

### DEGREE OR CERTIFICATE PROGRAMS OFFERED
Programs offered do not lead to a degree or other formal award.

# BELMONT UNIVERSITY
1900 Belmont Boulevard
Nashville, TN 37212
**Contact:** Ms. Lisa Hubbard, Associate Director of Admissions
**Phone:** 615-460-6000
**Web:** http://www.belmont.edu/
**E-mail:** hubbardl@mail.belmont.edu

**ACCREDITATION:** Southern Association of Colleges and Schools
**INSTITUTIONALLY ADMINISTERED FINANCIAL AID:** Yes

### DEGREE OR CERTIFICATE PROGRAMS OFFERED
**Graduate—*MSOT:*** Occupational Therapy, Post Professional Masters.

### NON-DEGREE-RELATED COURSE TOPICS OFFERED
**Undergraduate—**computer systems networking and telecommunications; philosophy.

# BEMIDJI STATE UNIVERSITY
## Center for Extended Learning
1500 Birchmont Drive, NE
Bemidji, MN 56601-2699
**Contact:** Robert J. Griggs, Dean of Distance Learning and Summer School
**Phone:** 218-755-2068
**Fax:** 218-755-4048
**Web:** http://www.bemidjistate.edu
**E-mail:** rjgriggs@bemidjistate.edu

**ACCREDITATION:** North Central Association of Colleges and Schools

### DEGREE OR CERTIFICATE PROGRAMS OFFERED
Programs offered do not lead to a degree or other formal award.

### NON-DEGREE-RELATED COURSE TOPICS OFFERED
**Undergraduate—**English composition; English creative writing; business administration and management; criminal justice and corrections; criminology; economics; general teacher education; geography; history; law and legal studies; philosophy; philosophy and religion; psychology; social work; sociology; teacher education, specific academic and vocational programs.
**Graduate—**education, general; educational/instructional media design.

# BENEDICT COLLEGE
1600 Harden Street
Columbia, SC 29204
**Contact:** Dr. Marcia Conston, Vice President of Institutional Effectiveness
**Phone:** 803-253-5662
**Fax:** 803-252-5215
**E-mail:** constonm@benedict.edu

**ACCREDITATION:** Southern Association of Colleges and Schools
**INSTITUTIONALLY ADMINISTERED FINANCIAL AID:** No

### DEGREE OR CERTIFICATE PROGRAMS OFFERED
Programs offered do not lead to a degree or other formal award.

# BERKELEY COLLEGE
3 East 43 Street
New York, NY 10017
**Contact:** Dr. Mildred Garcia, President
**Phone:** 212-986-4343
**Fax:** 212-986-8901
**Web:** http://www.berkeleycollege.edu/
**E-mail:** millieg@berkeleycollege.edu

**ACCREDITATION:** Middle States Association of Colleges and Schools

### DEGREE OR CERTIFICATE PROGRAMS OFFERED
Programs offered do not lead to a degree or other formal award.

### NON-DEGREE-RELATED COURSE TOPICS OFFERED
**Undergraduate—**business; business administration and management; business management and administrative services, other; business quan-

titative methods and management science; business/managerial economics; international business; marketing operations/marketing and distribution, other; psychology; social sciences and history, other.

# BERKELEY COLLEGE

44 Rifle Camp Road
West Paterson, NJ 07424
**Contact:** Dr. Mildred Garcia, President
**Phone:** 973-278-5400
**Fax:** 973-357-1678
**Web:** http://www.berkeleycollege.edu/
**E-mail:** millieg@berkeleycollege.edu
**ACCREDITATION:** Middle States Association of Colleges and Schools

## DEGREE OR CERTIFICATE PROGRAMS OFFERED
**Programs offered do not lead to a degree or other formal award.**

## NON-DEGREE-RELATED COURSE TOPICS OFFERED
**Undergraduate**—accounting; business administration and management; business management and administrative services, other; business quantitative methods and management science; business/managerial economics; international business; marketing operations/marketing and distribution, other; psychology; social sciences and history, other.
**See full description on page 304.**

# BERKELEY COLLEGE

99 Church Street
White Plains, NY 10601
**Contact:** Dr. Mildred Garcia, President
**Phone:** 914-694-1122
**Fax:** 914-328-9470
**Web:** http://www.berkeleycollege.edu/
**E-mail:** millieg@berkeleycollege.edu
**ACCREDITATION:** Middle States Association of Colleges and Schools

## DEGREE OR CERTIFICATE PROGRAMS OFFERED
**Programs offered do not lead to a degree or other formal award.**

## NON-DEGREE-RELATED COURSE TOPICS OFFERED
**Undergraduate**—accounting; business administration and management; business management and administrative services, other; business quantitative methods and management science; business/managerial economics; international business; marketing operations/marketing and distribution, other; psychology; social sciences and history, other.

# BERKSHIRE COMMUNITY COLLEGE

1350 West Street
Pittsfield, MA 01201-5786
**Contact:** Janet R. Kroboth, Assistant Dean of Academic Affairs
Business Division
**Phone:** 413-499-4660 Ext. 271
**Fax:** 413-447-7840

**Web:** http://cc.berkshire.org/
**E-mail:** jkroboth@cc.berkshire.org
**ACCREDITATION:** New England Association of Schools and Colleges
**INSTITUTIONALLY ADMINISTERED FINANCIAL AID:** Yes

## DEGREE OR CERTIFICATE PROGRAMS OFFERED
**Programs offered do not lead to a degree or other formal award.**

## NON-DEGREE-RELATED COURSE TOPICS OFFERED
**Undergraduate**—fire science/firefighting; law and legal studies, other; sociology.
**Non-credit**—English creative writing; business and personal services marketing operations; business communications; business management and administrative services, other; computer and information sciences, general; computer and information sciences, other; computer programming; computer software and media applications; financial management and services.

# BETHANY COLLEGE OF THE ASSEMBLIES OF GOD
*External Degree Program*
800 Bethany Drive
Scotts Valley, CA 95066
**Contact:** Mr. Wade Ryan Saari, External Degree Program Director
**Phone:** 831-438-3800 Ext. 1404
**Fax:** 831-430-0953
**Web:** http://www.bethany.edu
**E-mail:** wsaari@fc.bethany.edu
**ACCREDITATION:** Western Association of Schools and Colleges
**INSTITUTIONALLY ADMINISTERED FINANCIAL AID:** Yes

## DEGREE OR CERTIFICATE PROGRAMS OFFERED
**Undergraduate**—*AA:* Church Ministries; Early Child Development; General Studies. *BA:* Addiction Studies; Applied Professional Studies; Biblical and Theological Studies; Church Leadership; Early Child Development; General Ministries; Liberal Arts; Psychology; Social Science. *Certificate:* Certification Program in Addiction Counseling.

**Special Note**

Bethany College (BC), founded in 1919, has the distinction of being the oldest accredited Assemblies of God college in the world. Operating as the foremost leadership preparation school, BC, through its External Degree Program (EDP) offers more than 100 courses each semester that lead to a dozen AA and BA degrees in several concentrations. BC is regionally accredited, offering its students an excellent education, and has helped more than 200 students complete their BA degrees since 1992. The EDP is designed for busy adults who, because of work, family and church responsibilities, and geographic restrictions, are unable to attend classes in a traditional setting. The EDP curriculum is equivalent to the on-campus traditional program. Distance learners come to the campus for an initial orientation and return to the campus at the beginning of each semester for a progress review. During these visits, students register for classes, arrange for financial aid, receive academic advising, and meet with professors. Course work is completed at the student's home or office, with weekly contact with professors via e-mail or toll-free telephone access. EDP course delivery is achieved through the use of printed material, audiotapes, videotapes, electronic and hard copy faxing, and Web-based instruction. Students have online access to the BC library services, registration, and bookstore. For further information, students should contact EDP at 800-843-9410 (toll-free), fax: 831-843-9410, or e-mail: edp@bethany.edu or visit the Web site at http://www.bethany.edu.

# BEULAH HEIGHTS BIBLE COLLEGE

892 Berne Street, SE
Atlanta, GA 30316
**Contact:** Dr. Douglas M. Chatham, Sr., Director of Distance Learning
**Phone:** 404-627-2681 Ext. 251
**Fax:** 404-627-0702
**Web:** http://www.beulah.org/
**E-mail:** doug.chatham@beulah.org

**ACCREDITATION:** Transnational Association of Christian Colleges and Schools

**INSTITUTIONALLY ADMINISTERED FINANCIAL AID:** Yes

## DEGREE OR CERTIFICATE PROGRAMS OFFERED

**Undergraduate—BA:** Biblical Studies, Urban Ministry, Marketplace Leadership.

## NON-DEGREE-RELATED COURSE TOPICS OFFERED

**Undergraduate—**English language and literature, general; archaeology; bible/biblical studies; biblical and other theological languages and literatures; communications, general; computer science; ethnic and cultural studies; family and community studies; liberal arts and sciences, general studies and humanities; mathematics; pastoral counseling and specialized ministries; philosophy; religious education; urban affairs/studies.

# BEVILL STATE COMMUNITY COLLEGE

*Distance Learning Administration*
2631 Temple Avenue North
Fayette, AL 35555
**Contact:** Dr. Kandis R. Steele, Director of Instructional Services
**Phone:** 205-932-3221 Ext. 5606
**Fax:** 205-932-6974
**Web:** http://www.bevillst.cc.al.us
**E-mail:** ksteele@bevillst.cc.al.us

**ACCREDITATION:** Southern Association of Colleges and Schools
**INSTITUTIONALLY ADMINISTERED FINANCIAL AID:** Yes

## DEGREE OR CERTIFICATE PROGRAMS OFFERED

Programs offered do not lead to a degree or other formal award.

## NON-DEGREE-RELATED COURSE TOPICS OFFERED

**Undergraduate—**English composition; biological and physical sciences; business; business administration and management; business information and data processing services; chemistry; child care and guidance workers

and managers; computer and information sciences, general; fine arts and art studies; history; physical sciences, general; psychology.

# BISMARCK STATE COLLEGE

PO Box 5587
Bismarck, ND 58506-5587
**Contact:** Denise Lee Aberle, Director of Distance Education
**Phone:** 701-224-5414
**Fax:** 701-224-5552
**Web:** http://www.bismarckstate.com
**E-mail:** daberle@gwmail.nodak.edu

**ACCREDITATION:** North Central Association of Colleges and Schools

**INSTITUTIONALLY ADMINISTERED FINANCIAL AID:** Yes

eCollege.com   *www.ecollege.com*

## DEGREE OR CERTIFICATE PROGRAMS OFFERED

**Undergraduate—AA:** Criminal Justice. **AAS:** Power Plant Technology; Process Plant Technology. **Certificate of Completion:** Information Processing Specialist; Power Plant Technology; Process Plant Technology.

# BLACKHAWK TECHNICAL COLLEGE

6004 Prairie Road, PO Box 5009
Janesville, WI 53547
**Contact:** Connie Richards, Registration Supervisor
**Phone:** 608-757-7654
**Fax:** 608-743-4407
**Web:** http://www.blackhawktech.org
**E-mail:** crichard@mail.blackhawk.tec.wi.us

**ACCREDITATION:** North Central Association of Colleges and Schools
**INSTITUTIONALLY ADMINISTERED FINANCIAL AID:** Yes

## DEGREE OR CERTIFICATE PROGRAMS OFFERED

Programs offered do not lead to a degree or other formal award.

## NON-DEGREE-RELATED COURSE TOPICS OFFERED

**Undergraduate—**administrative and secretarial services; computer and information sciences, general; computer programming; computer systems networking and telecommunications.

# BLINN COLLEGE

*Distance Education Center*
PO Box 6030
Bryan, TX 77802
**Contact:** Candace Schaefer, Coordinator of Distance Learning
**Phone:** 979-821-0403
**Fax:** 979-821-0229
**Web:** http://www.blinncol.edu/disted/index.htm
**E-mail:** cschaefer@acmail.blinncol.edu

**ACCREDITATION:** Southern Association of Colleges and Schools
**INSTITUTIONALLY ADMINISTERED FINANCIAL AID:** Yes

## DEGREE OR CERTIFICATE PROGRAMS OFFERED

Programs offered do not lead to a degree or other formal award.

## NON-DEGREE-RELATED COURSE TOPICS OFFERED

Undergraduate—English composition; English language and literature, general; accounting; anthropology; art history, criticism and conservation; biology, general; business administration and management; business information and data processing services; computer and information sciences, general; computer programming; criminology; geography; history; law and legal studies, other; mathematics, other; philosophy; political science and government; psychology; sociology.

# BLOOMFIELD COLLEGE

Bloomfield, NJ 07003
**Contact:** Dr. Carole Carmody, Associate Vice President for Information Technology
**Phone:** 973-748-9000 Ext. 391
**Fax:** 973-743-3998
**Web:** http://www.bloomfield.edu/
**E-mail:** carole_carmody@bloomfield.edu

**ACCREDITATION:** Middle States Association of Colleges and Schools
**INSTITUTIONALLY ADMINISTERED FINANCIAL AID:** Yes

## DEGREE OR CERTIFICATE PROGRAMS OFFERED

Programs offered do not lead to a degree or other formal award.

## NON-DEGREE-RELATED COURSE TOPICS OFFERED

Undergraduate—business marketing and marketing management; computer and information sciences, general; nursing.

# BLUEFIELD STATE COLLEGE

*Instructional Technology Center/Center for Extended Learning*

219 Rock Street
Bluefield, WV 24701
**Contact:** Dr. Thomas Blevins, Director of the Institutional Technology Center and the Center for Extended Learning
**Phone:** 304-327-4059
**Fax:** 304-327-4106
**Web:** http://www.bluefield.wvnet.edu/
**E-mail:** tblevins@bluefield.wvnet.edu

**ACCREDITATION:** North Central Association of Colleges and Schools

## DEGREE OR CERTIFICATE PROGRAMS OFFERED

Programs offered do not lead to a degree or other formal award.

# BLUE RIDGE COMMUNITY COLLEGE

*Distance Learning Office*

PO Box 80
Weyers Cave, VA 24486

**Contact:** Mr. John Downey, Assistant to the Dean and Coordinator of Distance Learning
**Phone:** 540-234-9261 Ext. 2224
**Web:** http://www1.br.cc.va.us/cybercollege.htm
**E-mail:** brdownj@br.cc.va.us

**ACCREDITATION:** Southern Association of Colleges and Schools
**INSTITUTIONALLY ADMINISTERED FINANCIAL AID:** No

## DEGREE OR CERTIFICATE PROGRAMS OFFERED

Programs offered do not lead to a degree or other formal award.

# BLUE RIVER COMMUNITY COLLEGE

1501 West Jefferson Street
Blue Springs, MO 64015
**Contact:** Mr. Leo J. Hirner
**Phone:** 816-759-4489
**Web:** http://www.kcmetro.cc.mo.us/blueriver/brhome.html

**ACCREDITATION:** North Central Association of Colleges and Schools
**INSTITUTIONALLY ADMINISTERED FINANCIAL AID:** Yes

## DEGREE OR CERTIFICATE PROGRAMS OFFERED

Programs offered do not lead to a degree or other formal award.

## NON-DEGREE-RELATED COURSE TOPICS OFFERED

Undergraduate—English composition; accounting; biology, general; child care and guidance workers and managers; computer science; criminal justice and corrections; economics; education, general; engineering, general; environmental/environmental health engineering; fire protection; geography; heating, air conditioning and refrigeration mechanics and repairers; history; mathematics; philosophy; physical sciences, general; psychology; sociology.

# BOISE STATE UNIVERSITY

*Division of Extended Studies*

1910 University Drive, MS 1120
Boise, ID 83725-1120
**Contact:** Ms. Liz Ackerman, Coordinator of Distance Education Student Services
**Phone:** 208-426-4216
**Fax:** 208-426-3467
**Web:** http://www.boisestate.edu/extendedstudies/
**E-mail:** eackerma@boisestate.edu

**ACCREDITATION:** Northwest Association of Schools and Colleges
**INSTITUTIONALLY ADMINISTERED FINANCIAL AID:** Yes

## DEGREE OR CERTIFICATE PROGRAMS OFFERED

Graduate—*MS:* Instructional and Performance Technology. *MSE:* Educational Technology.

## NON-DEGREE-RELATED COURSE TOPICS OFFERED

Undergraduate—Spanish language and literature; accounting; business management and administrative services, other; business marketing and marketing management; curriculum and instruction; developmental and child psychology; drama/theater arts, general; educational/instructional media design; electrical, electronics and communication engineering; engineering, general; geography; health and medical administrative services; nursing; sociology; teacher education, specific academic and vocational programs.

**Graduate**—educational/instructional media design; health and medical administrative services.

# BOROUGH OF MANHATTAN COMMUNITY COLLEGE OF THE CITY UNIVERSITY OF NEW YORK

*Office of Academic Affairs*

199 Chambers Steet
New York, NY 10007
**Contact:** Mr. Peter Vida, Director of Admissions
**Phone:** 212-346-8101
**Web:** http://www.bmcc.cuny.edu
**E-mail:** pvida@bmcc.cuny.edu

**ACCREDITATION:** Middle States Association of Colleges and Schools

**INSTITUTIONALLY ADMINISTERED FINANCIAL AID:** Yes

**DEGREE OR CERTIFICATE PROGRAMS OFFERED**
Programs offered do not lead to a degree or other formal award.

**NON-DEGREE-RELATED COURSE TOPICS OFFERED**
Undergraduate—social sciences, general.
Non-credit—computer systems networking and telecommunications.

# BOSSIER PARISH COMMUNITY COLLEGE

*BPCC Distance Learning Program/Institutional Advancement*

2719 Airline Drive
Bossier City, LA 71111
**Contact:** Kathleen Gay, Director of Educational Technology
**Phone:** 318-741-7391
**Fax:** 318-741-7393
**Web:** http://www.bpcc.cc.la.us
**E-mail:** kgay@bpcc.cc.la.us

**ACCREDITATION:** Southern Association of Colleges and Schools
**INSTITUTIONALLY ADMINISTERED FINANCIAL AID:** Yes

**DEGREE OR CERTIFICATE PROGRAMS OFFERED**
Programs offered do not lead to a degree or other formal award.

**NON-DEGREE-RELATED COURSE TOPICS OFFERED**
Undergraduate—American (United States) history; English composition; European history; applied mathematics; art history, criticism and conservation; biological and physical sciences; biological sciences/life sciences, other; computer and information sciences, general; computer and information sciences, other; computer science; computer software and media applications; developmental and child psychology; education,

general; education, other; film/video and photographic arts; fire science/firefighting; food sciences and technology; health and medical assistants; mathematics, other; sociology.

# BOSTON ARCHITECTURAL CENTER

The Boston Architectural Center, 320 Newbury Street
Boston , MA 02115
**Contact:** Ms. Valerie Nichols, Director of Continuing Education
**Phone:** 617-585-0101
**Fax:** 617-585-0121
**Web:** http://www.the-bac.edu/
**E-mail:** ce@the-bac.edu

**ACCREDITATION:** New England Association of Schools and Colleges

**INSTITUTIONALLY ADMINISTERED FINANCIAL AID:** Yes

**DEGREE OR CERTIFICATE PROGRAMS OFFERED**
Programs offered do not lead to a degree or other formal award.

**NON-DEGREE-RELATED COURSE TOPICS OFFERED**
Undergraduate—architectural engineering; architecture; computer software and media applications.
Graduate—architectural engineering; architecture; computer software and media applications.
Non-credit—architectural engineering; architecture; computer software and media applications.

# BOSTON UNIVERSITY

*Department of Manufacturing Engineering*

Boston, MA 02215
**Contact:** Elizabeth Spencer-Dawes, Distance Learning Administrator
**Phone:** 617-353-2943
**Fax:** 617-353-5548
**Web:** http://www.bu.edu/mfg/dlp
**E-mail:** icv@bu.edu

**ACCREDITATION:** New England Association of Schools and Colleges

**INSTITUTIONALLY ADMINISTERED FINANCIAL AID:** No

**DEGREE OR CERTIFICATE PROGRAMS OFFERED**
Graduate—*MS:* Manufacturing Engineering.

**NON-DEGREE-RELATED COURSE TOPICS OFFERED**
Graduate—engineering/industrial management; industrial/manufacturing engineering.

See full description on page 306.

# BRADLEY UNIVERSITY

*Division of Continuing Education and Professional Development*

1501 West Bradley Avenue
Peoria, IL 61625

**Contact:** Susan Manley, Program Director
**Phone:** 309-677-2820
**Fax:** 309-677-3321
**Web:** http://www.bradley.edu/continue
**E-mail:** susank@bradley.edu

**ACCREDITATION:** North Central Association of Colleges and Schools
**INSTITUTIONALLY ADMINISTERED FINANCIAL AID:** Yes

## DEGREE OR CERTIFICATE PROGRAMS OFFERED

Graduate—*MSEE:* Electrical Engineering. *MSME:* Mechanical Engineering.

## NON-DEGREE-RELATED COURSE TOPICS OFFERED

Undergraduate—communications, general.
Graduate—electrical, electronics and communication engineering; mechanical engineering.

# BRENAU UNIVERSITY
*Department of Distance Learning*
1 Centennial Circle
Gainesville, GA 30501
**Contact:** Dr. Heather Snow Gibbons, Director of Online Education
**Phone:** 770-718-5327
**Fax:** 770-718-5329
**Web:** http://online.brenau.edu
**E-mail:** hgibbons@lib.brenau.edu

**ACCREDITATION:** Southern Association of Colleges and Schools
**INSTITUTIONALLY ADMINISTERED FINANCIAL AID:** Yes

## DEGREE OR CERTIFICATE PROGRAMS OFFERED

Undergraduate—*BSN:* RN-BSN Bridge Degree.
Graduate—*MBA:* Accounting; Leadership Development. *MEd:* Early Childhood Education.

## NON-DEGREE-RELATED COURSE TOPICS OFFERED

Undergraduate—accounting; business; communications, general; criminal justice and corrections; design and applied arts; education, general; foreign languages and literatures; general teacher education; history; human resources management; journalism and mass communications; law and legal studies; miscellaneous health professions; museology/museum studies; nursing; political science and government; psychology.
Graduate—accounting; business; business administration and management; business management and administrative services, other; education administration and supervision; education, general; education, other; educational evaluation, research and statistics; financial management and services; health and medical administrative services; health and medical diagnostic and treatment services; health professions and related sciences, other; international business; marketing management and research; marketing operations/marketing and distribution, other; miscellaneous health professions; nursing; rehabilitation/therapeutic services; taxation.

**See full description on page 308.**

# BREVARD COMMUNITY COLLEGE
*Distance Learning*
1519 Clearlake Road
Cocoa, FL 32955
**Contact:** Miss Elspeth McCulloch, Coordinator of Online Programs
**Phone:** 321-632-1111 Ext. 63727
**Fax:** 321-634-2487
**Web:** http://www.brevard.cc.fl.us
**E-mail:** mcculloche@brevard.cc.fl.us

**ACCREDITATION:** Southern Association of Colleges and Schools
**INSTITUTIONALLY ADMINISTERED FINANCIAL AID:** Yes

## DEGREE OR CERTIFICATE PROGRAMS OFFERED

Undergraduate—*AA:* General Studies. *AS:* Legal Studies.

## NON-DEGREE-RELATED COURSE TOPICS OFFERED

Undergraduate—accounting; advertising; biology, general; chemical engineering; developmental and child psychology; electrical, electronics and communication engineering; journalism; social psychology; sociology.

# BRIDGEWATER STATE COLLEGE
*Distance Learning and Technology Programs*
John Joseph Moakley Center for Technological Applications, Burrill Avenue
Bridgewater, MA 02325
**Contact:** Dr. Mary W. Fuller, Director of Distance Learning and Technology Programs
**Phone:** 508-531 6145
**Fax:** 508-531 6121
**Web:** http://www.bridgew.edu/DEPTS/MOAKLEY/distance
**E-mail:** mfuller@bridgew.edu

**ACCREDITATION:** New England Association of Schools and Colleges
**INSTITUTIONALLY ADMINISTERED FINANCIAL AID:** Yes

## DEGREE OR CERTIFICATE PROGRAMS OFFERED

**Programs offered do not lead to a degree or other formal award.**

## NON-DEGREE-RELATED COURSE TOPICS OFFERED

Undergraduate—English technical and business writing; anthropology; business communications; business/managerial economics; communication disorders sciences and services; communications, general; computer/information technology administration and management; criminology; curriculum and instruction; education administration and supervision; education, general; educational evaluation, research and statistics; entrepreneurship; ethnic and cultural studies; geography; music; political science and government; sociology; special education.
Graduate—education administration and supervision; special education.

# BRIERCREST BIBLE COLLEGE
*Briercrest Distance Learning*
510 College Drive
Caronport, SK S0H 0S0, Canada
**Contact:** Paul Wilder, Enrollment Coordinator

**Phone:** 800-667-5199
**Fax:** 306-756-7366
**Web:** http://www.briercrest.ca/bdl/
**E-mail:** distanceinfo@briercrest.ca

**ACCREDITATION:** Provincially Chartered

**INSTITUTIONALLY ADMINISTERED FINANCIAL AID:** Yes

### DEGREE OR CERTIFICATE PROGRAMS OFFERED

**Undergraduate—*AA:*** Christian Studies. ***BA:*** Christian Studies. ***Certificate:*** Bible.

### NON-DEGREE-RELATED COURSE TOPICS OFFERED

**Undergraduate**—English language and literature, general; bible/biblical studies; business administration and management; counseling psychology; history; missions/missionary studies and missiology; religion/religious studies; religious education; teaching English as a second language/foreign language; theological and ministerial studies; theological studies and religious vocations, other.

**Graduate**—bible/biblical studies; biblical and other theological languages and literatures; religion/religious studies; religious education; theological and ministerial studies; theological studies and religious vocations, other.

# BRIGHAM YOUNG UNIVERSITY

## *Independent Study*

206 Harman Building, PO Box 21514
Provo, UT 84606-1514
**Contact:** Registrar
**Phone:** 800-914-8931
**Fax:** 801-378-5817
**Web:** http://coned.byu.edu/is/
**E-mail:** indstudy@byu.edu

**ACCREDITATION:** Northwest Association of Schools and Colleges

**INSTITUTIONALLY ADMINISTERED FINANCIAL AID:** Yes

### DEGREE OR CERTIFICATE PROGRAMS OFFERED

**Programs offered do not lead to a degree or other formal award.**

### NON-DEGREE-RELATED COURSE TOPICS OFFERED

**Undergraduate**—American (United States) history; American literature (United States); English composition; European history; Germanic languages and literatures; Hebrew language and literature; Spanish language and literature; accounting; agriculture/agricultural sciences, other; anthropology; art history, criticism and conservation; astronomy; biology, general; botany; business administration and management; business marketing and marketing management; chemical engineering; chemistry; civil engineering; communication disorders sciences and services; communications, general; curriculum and instruction; dance; developmental and child psychology; drama/theater arts, general; economics; education administration and supervision; education, general; education, other; educational psychology; film/cinema studies; food sciences and technology; geography; geological and related sciences; health and physical education/fitness; history; information sciences and systems; liberal arts and sciences, general studies and humanities; mathematical statistics; mathematics, other; microbiology/bacteriology; music; nursing; organizational behavior studies; philosophy; philosophy and religion; physical sciences, general; physics; political science and government; psychology; religion/religious studies; religious education; social work; sociology; special

education; speech and rhetorical studies; technology education/industrial arts; visual and performing arts; zoology.

# BRISTOL COMMUNITY COLLEGE

## *Academic Computing and Distance Learning*

777 Elsbree Street
Fall River, MA 02720
**Contact:** Candy M. Center, Director of Distance Learning
**Phone:** 508-678-2811 Ext. 2850
**Fax:** 508-730-3270
**Web:** http://dl.mass.edu
**E-mail:** ccenter@bristol.mass.edu

**ACCREDITATION:** New England Association of Schools and Colleges

**INSTITUTIONALLY ADMINISTERED FINANCIAL AID:** Yes

### DEGREE OR CERTIFICATE PROGRAMS OFFERED

**Programs offered do not lead to a degree or other formal award.**

### NON-DEGREE-RELATED COURSE TOPICS OFFERED

**Undergraduate**—English composition; English literature (British and Commonwealth); English technical and business writing; European history; accounting; anthropology; business; business information and data processing services; computer and information sciences, general; computer and information sciences, other; computer programming; computer science; computer software and media applications; computer systems analysis; computer systems networking and telecommunications; computer/information technology administration and management; data entry/microcomputer applications; data processing technology; environmental science/studies; geography; history; information sciences and systems; mathematical statistics; mathematics; mathematics, other; psychology; psychology, other; social sciences and history, other; sociology.

**Non-credit**—accounting; administrative and secretarial services; business; business administration and management; business and personal services marketing operations; business communications; business information and data processing services; business management and administrative services, other; business quantitative methods and management science; communications, general; communications, other; computer and information sciences, general; computer and information sciences, other; computer engineering; computer programming; computer science; computer software and media applications; computer systems analysis; computer systems networking and telecommunications; computer/information technology administration and management; data entry/microcomputer applications; data processing technology; electrical and electronic engineering-related technology; electrical and electronics equipment installers and repairers; electrical and power transmission installers; electrical, electronics and communications engineering; electromechanical instrumentation and maintenance technology; engineering-related technologies, other; engineering/industrial management; human resources management; information sciences and systems; internet and world wide web; law and legal studies; marketing management and research; marketing operations/marketing and distribution, other; mathematics; mechanical engineering-related technologies; mechanics and repairers, other; miscellaneous engineering-related technologies; precision production trades, other; systems engineering; technology education/industrial arts; telecommunications; vehicle and equipment operators; vehicle and mobile equipment mechanics and repairers.

# BROCK UNIVERSITY

*Centre for Adult Studies and Distance Learning,
Faculty of Education*

St. Catharines, ON L2S 3A1, Canada

**Contact:** Sandra Plavinskis, Coordinator of B.Ed. in Adult
Education Degree and Certificate Programs

**Phone:** 905-688-5550 Ext. 4308

**Fax:** 905-688-0544

**Web:** http://adult.ed.brocku.ca

**E-mail:** sandra@ed.brocku.ca

**ACCREDITATION:** Provincially Chartered

**INSTITUTIONALLY ADMINISTERED FINANCIAL AID:** No

## DEGREE OR CERTIFICATE PROGRAMS OFFERED

Undergraduate—*BEd:* Adult Education. *Certificate:* Adult Education.

## NON-DEGREE-RELATED COURSE TOPICS OFFERED

Undergraduate—education, other.

# BROOME COMMUNITY COLLEGE

PO Box 1017

Binghamton, NY 13902

**Contact:** Will Corprew, Registrar

**Phone:** 607-778-1017

**Fax:** 607-778-5027

**Web:** http://www.sunybroome.edu/

**E-mail:** admissions@mail.sunybroome.edu

**ACCREDITATION:** Middle States Association of Colleges and Schools

## DEGREE OR CERTIFICATE PROGRAMS OFFERED

Undergraduate—*AS:* Engineering Science.

## NON-DEGREE-RELATED COURSE TOPICS OFFERED

Undergraduate—business; history; mathematics; psychology.

# BROWARD COMMUNITY COLLEGE

*Instructional Technology*

3501 Southwest Davie Road

Davie, FL 33314

**Contact:** Sharon Parker, Director of Extended Learning Services

**Phone:** 954-475-6564

**Fax:** 954-475-6959

**Web:** http://www.broward.cc.fl.us

**E-mail:** sparker@broward.cc.fl.us

**ACCREDITATION:** Southern Association of Colleges and Schools

**INSTITUTIONALLY ADMINISTERED FINANCIAL AID:** Yes

## DEGREE OR CERTIFICATE PROGRAMS OFFERED

Programs offered do not lead to a degree or other formal award.

## NON-DEGREE-RELATED COURSE TOPICS OFFERED

Undergraduate—American (United States) history; English composition; European history; Spanish language and literature; accounting; anthropology; biology, general; business; business marketing and marketing management; computer science; developmental and child psychology; economics; education, other; entrepreneurship; geography; geological and related sciences; health and physical education/fitness; law and legal studies, other; mathematical statistics; mathematics, other; nursing; philosophy; philosophy and religion; psychology; sociology.

---

### Special Note

Broward Community College (BCC) was founded in 1960 and serves students who reside in southeastern Florida. BCC offers an AA degree featuring 56 majors, an AS degree with 32 different majors, an AAS degree with 26 majors, and 39 different certificate programs. Portions of these degrees and certificates

can be completed through flexible learning courses offered through BCC's Open College Program. An AS degree with a concentration in nursing for paramedics transitioning to RN, LPN transitioning to RN, and RRT transitioning to RN can be earned entirely online, excluding clinical course work, which must be completed locally. Through BCC's Experiential Learning and CLEP Programs, students may earn credit for college-level knowledge and competencies they have acquired outside a classroom.

BCC's Open College Program began in 1978. In 2001, more than 50 different courses representing a range of subject areas were available through BCC's Open College. Open College courses use audiotapes, videotapes, television broadcasts, and/or the Internet to deliver course content. These courses require few on-campus meetings and are ideal for self-disciplined and self-motivated students who prefer not to attend traditional classes. Students can complete up to 95% of an AA degree through video-based telecourses at Broward Community College. Academic credit and content of Open College courses are equivalent to traditional classroom-based courses.

For information about distributed and distance learning courses at Broward Community College, students should contact the Extended Learning Services Department at 954-475-6564, send e-mail to sparker@broward.cc.fl.us, or visit BCC's Web site at http://www.broward.cc.fl.us/.

---

# BRUNSWICK COMMUNITY COLLEGE

PO Box 30

Supply, NC 28462

**Contact:** Ann Harrison, Distance Learning Coordinator

**Phone:** 910-755-7303

**Fax:** 910-754-6995

**Web:** http://www.brunswick.cc.nc.us/

**E-mail:** harrisona@mail.brunswick.cc.nc.us

**ACCREDITATION:** Southern Association of Colleges and Schools

**INSTITUTIONALLY ADMINISTERED FINANCIAL AID:** No

## DEGREE OR CERTIFICATE PROGRAMS OFFERED

Programs offered do not lead to a degree or other formal award.

## NON-DEGREE-RELATED COURSE TOPICS OFFERED

Undergraduate—administrative and secretarial services; agricultural business and production, other; chemistry; criminal justice and corrections; health professions and related sciences, other.

# BRYANT AND STRATTON ONLINE

1234 Abbott Road, Rear Building
Lackawanna, NY 14218
**Contact:** Ms. Jennifer Zukowski, Admissions
**Phone:** 716-821-5556 Ext. 242
**Fax:** 716-821-5518
**Web:** http://www.bryantstratton.edu
**E-mail:** online@bryantstratton.edu
**ACCREDITATION:** Accrediting Council for Independent Colleges and Schools

**INSTITUTIONALLY ADMINISTERED FINANCIAL AID:** Yes

## DEGREE OR CERTIFICATE PROGRAMS OFFERED
**Undergraduate—AD:** Business Online; Information Technology Online.

## NON-DEGREE-RELATED COURSE TOPICS OFFERED
**Undergraduate**—accounting; business; business administration and management; business communications; computer programming; computer software and media applications; computer systems networking and telecommunications; computer/information technology administration and management; internet and world wide web.

# BUCKS COUNTY COMMUNITY COLLEGE

## Distance Learning Office

275 Swamp Road
Newtown, PA 18940
**Contact:** Ms. Georglyn Davidson, Director of Distance Learning
**Phone:** 215-968-8052
**Fax:** 215-968-8148
**Web:** http://www.bucks.edu/distance
**E-mail:** learning@bucks.edu
**ACCREDITATION:** Middle States Association of Colleges and Schools
**INSTITUTIONALLY ADMINISTERED FINANCIAL AID:** Yes

## DEGREE OR CERTIFICATE PROGRAMS OFFERED
**Undergraduate—AA:** Business Administration; Liberal Arts; Management; Marketing; Science. **Certificate:** Entrepreneurship; Microsoft Office; Retailing; Supervision; Web Designer.

## NON-DEGREE-RELATED COURSE TOPICS OFFERED
**Undergraduate**—American (United States) history; English composition; European history; Spanish language and literature; accounting; art history, criticism and conservation; biology, general; business; business marketing and marketing management; computer and information sciences, general; developmental and child psychology; education, general; health and physical education/fitness; history; journalism and mass communications; law and legal studies, other; mathematical statistics; mathematics; music; philosophy and religion; social psychology; social sciences, general; sociology; teacher education, specific academic and vocational programs; women's studies.

# BUENA VISTA UNIVERSITY

## Centers

610 West 4th Street
Storm Lake, IA 50588

**Contact:** Peg Chown, Centers Office
**Phone:** 712-749-2250
**Fax:** 712-749-1470
**Web:** http://www.bvu.edu
**E-mail:** centers@bvu.edu

**ACCREDITATION:** North Central Association of Colleges and Schools
**INSTITUTIONALLY ADMINISTERED FINANCIAL AID:** Yes

## DEGREE OR CERTIFICATE PROGRAMS OFFERED
**Undergraduate—BA:** Business; Education; Social Sciences.
**Graduate—MS:** Educational Administration; School Guidance Counseling; Teaching Effectiveness.

## Special Note
Founded in 1891, Buena Vista University (BVU) is a leading New American College, preparing students for successful careers as well as leadership and service in their communities. With 1,381 undergraduate and graduate students on its main campus in Storm Lake and an additional 2,055 students at 17 branch sites throughout Iowa, BVU offers a balance between traditional learning and innovative experiential learning opportunities that require the practical application of knowledge.

This fall, Buena Vista University's eBVyou program equipped its nearly 2,000 full-time students and faculty members on the main campus with wireless Gateway notebook computers linked by a Lucent wireless network, creating the nation's first wireless notebook campus that provides students with anytime, anywhere access to the Internet and University resources.

Since 1975, BVU centers have made it possible for thousands of graduates to secure better jobs, achieve promotions, find personal satisfaction, continue their education, and pursue new opportunities in Iowa. BVU is working with area communities and community colleges to provide opportunities to a growing number of students each year.

Eighty-two percent of BVU center graduates remain in the state. They are making Iowa communities safer and more livable and improving the state's economic outlook by helping Iowa be more attractive to industry. As BVU's graduates are growing, changing, and learning, and so is BVU. BVU is adding more sites, developing more programs, and bringing more possibilities within reach.

For more information about Buena Vista University, students should contact Dr. John Phillips, Associate Vice President for External Programs and Marketing at 712-749-2250 or 800-383-2821 Ext. 2247 (toll-free) or via e-mail at centers@bvu.edu or the Web site at http://www.bvu.edu/centers.

# BURLINGTON COLLEGE

## Independent Degree Program (IDP)

95 North Avenue
Burlington, VT 05401
**Contact:** Kathy FitzGerald Collins, Director of Admissions and Public Relations
**Phone:** 802-862-9616
**Fax:** 802-660-4331
**Web:** http://www.burlingtoncollege.edu

**E-mail:** kcollins@burlcol.edu

**ACCREDITATION:** New England Association of Schools and Colleges

**INSTITUTIONALLY ADMINISTERED FINANCIAL AID:** Yes

## DEGREE OR CERTIFICATE PROGRAMS OFFERED

**Undergraduate—AA:** General Studies. **BA:** Cinema Studies and Film Production; Fine Arts; Human Services; Individualized Major/ Interdisciplinary Studies; Interdisciplinary Humanities; Psychology; Transpersonal Psychology; Writing and Literature.

## NON-DEGREE-RELATED COURSE TOPICS OFFERED

**Undergraduate—**English creative writing; comparative literature; counseling psychology; developmental and child psychology; educational psychology; ethnic and cultural studies; experimental psychology; family and community studies; fine arts and art studies; history; human services; liberal arts and sciences, general studies and humanities; multi/interdisciplinary studies, other; philosophy; psychology; sociology.

# BURLINGTON COUNTY COLLEGE
## Distance Learning Office

Route 530
Pemberton, NJ 08068
**Contact:** Sue Espenshade, Coordinator of Distance Learning
**Phone:** 609-894-9311 Ext. 7790
**Fax:** 609-894-4189
**Web:** http://www.bcc.edu/
**E-mail:** sespensh@bcc.edu

**ACCREDITATION:** Middle States Association of Colleges and Schools

**INSTITUTIONALLY ADMINISTERED FINANCIAL AID:** Yes

## DEGREE OR CERTIFICATE PROGRAMS OFFERED

**Undergraduate—AA:** Liberal Arts and Sciences. **AS:** Business Management.

## NON-DEGREE-RELATED COURSE TOPICS OFFERED

**Undergraduate—**American (United States) history; English composition; European history; French language and literature; Spanish language and literature; anthropology; art history, criticism and conservation; biology, general; business marketing and marketing management; developmental and child psychology; ecology; film/cinema studies; mathematical statistics; sociology.

## Special Note

Burlington County College (BCC) has been a leader in distance education since 1978. Last fall, 800 of its 5,900 for-credit students were enrolled in at least 1 distance learning course. The average BCC student is 28 years of age. The College's nontraditional programming overcomes obstacles of time and place for busy adults who seek college degrees, career training/retraining, and/or personal enrichment.

This fall, 16 of BCC's 69 for-credit distance learning courses are offered online. These courses add new flexibility for students who seek 2 distance degrees that were previously offered solely via telecourse through the nationally acclaimed Public Broadcasting System's (PBS) *Going the Distance* program.

Last spring, BCC added 87 online noncredit courses. These courses provide 24-hour, "anytime, anywhere" learning opportunities for students who seek personal or career growth in sought-after computer hardware, software, and networking applications; business communications; and business math. BCC is the only Microsoft Authorized Academic Training Program (AATP) in Burlington County.

BCC's membership in 3 distance learning consortiums greatly expands the alternative learning opportunities for BCC students. BCC President Dr. Robert Messina chairs the board of the Consortium of Distance Education (CODE). This association of colleges in New York, New Jersey, Pennsylvania, and Delaware helps BCC stay abreast of programming trends via regular contact with national producers and member providers of distance learning courses. The New Jersey Virtual Community College Consortium (NJVCCC, http://www.njvccc.cc.nj.us), launched in fall 1999, offers BCC students access to the shared distance learning resources among the state's 19 community colleges for one standardized tuition rate. The New Jersey Virtual University (http://www.njvu.org), created by former New Jersey Governor Christine Whitman in 1998, provides students with a user-friendly index of credit and noncredit courses and certificate and degree programs offered by participating colleges and universities in New Jersey.

# BUTTE COLLEGE
## Information Services and Technology

3536 Butte Campus Drive
Oroville, CA 95965
**Contact:** Jack Lemley, Media and Distance Learning Director
**Phone:** 530-895-2344
**Fax:** 530-895-2380
**Web:** http://www.butte.cc.ca.us
**E-mail:** lemleyja@butte.cc.ca.us

**ACCREDITATION:** Western Association of Schools and Colleges

**INSTITUTIONALLY ADMINISTERED FINANCIAL AID:** Yes

## DEGREE OR CERTIFICATE PROGRAMS OFFERED

Programs offered do not lead to a degree or other formal award.

## NON-DEGREE-RELATED COURSE TOPICS OFFERED

**Undergraduate—**English as a second language; English composition; agriculture/agricultural sciences; anthropology; applied mathematics; biology, general; business administration and management; developmental and child psychology; economics; film/video and photographic arts; foreign languages and literatures; history; multi/interdisciplinary studies, other; natural resources management and protective services; philosophy; plant sciences; psychology; radio and television broadcasting; social psychology; sociology.

# CABRINI COLLEGE
## Graduate Education Programs

610 King of Prussia Road
Radnor, PA 19087-3698
**Contact:** Beth Carey, Director of Marketing and Recruitment
**Phone:** 610-902-8500
**Fax:** 610-902-8522

**Web:** http://www.cabrini.edu/
**E-mail:** bcarey@cabrini.edu

**ACCREDITATION:** Middle States Association of Colleges and Schools

**INSTITUTIONALLY ADMINISTERED FINANCIAL AID:** Yes

eCollege.com www.ecollege.com

## DEGREE OR CERTIFICATE PROGRAMS OFFERED
Programs offered do not lead to a degree or other formal award.

## NON-DEGREE-RELATED COURSE TOPICS OFFERED
**Undergraduate**—computer science; education, general; family and community studies; history; liberal arts and sciences, general studies and humanities; sociology.
**Graduate**—education, general.

# CALDWELL COLLEGE
## Center for Continuing Education

9 Ryerson Avenue
Caldwell, NJ 07006
**Contact:** Mr. Jack Albalah, Adult Admissions
**Phone:** 973-618-3285
**Fax:** 973-618-3660
**Web:** http://www.caldwell.edu/adult-admissions/index.html
**E-mail:** jalbalah@caldwell.edu

**ACCREDITATION:** Middle States Association of Colleges and Schools

**INSTITUTIONALLY ADMINISTERED FINANCIAL AID:** Yes

## DEGREE OR CERTIFICATE PROGRAMS OFFERED
**Undergraduate**—*BA:* Communication Arts; Criminal Justice; English; Foreign Language; History; Political Science; Psychology; Sociology; Theology. *BS:* Accounting; Business; Computer Information Systems; International Business; Management; Marketing.

See full description on page 310.

# CALDWELL COMMUNITY COLLEGE AND TECHNICAL INSTITUTE

2855 Hickory Boulevard
Hudson, NC 28638-2397
**Contact:** Sherry Wilson, Director of Information Services
**Phone:** 828-726-2306
**Fax:** 828-726-2216
**Web:** http://www.caldwell.cc.nc.us
**E-mail:** swilson@caldwell.cc.nc.us

**ACCREDITATION:** Southern Association of Colleges and Schools

**INSTITUTIONALLY ADMINISTERED FINANCIAL AID:** Yes

## DEGREE OR CERTIFICATE PROGRAMS OFFERED
**Undergraduate**—*AA:* College Transfer. *AAS:* Emergency Preparedness Technology.

## NON-DEGREE-RELATED COURSE TOPICS OFFERED
**Undergraduate**—English composition; English language and literature, general; English technical and business writing; accounting; biological and physical sciences; biology, general; business administration and management; business communications; child care and guidance workers and managers; computer and information sciences, general; fine arts and art studies; fire protection; history; liberal arts and sciences, general studies and humanities; marketing management and research; mathematics; music; physical sciences, general; psychology; social sciences, general; sociology.
**Non-credit**—business administration and management; computer and information sciences, other; computer software and media applications.

# CALIFORNIA COLLEGE FOR HEALTH SCIENCES

2423 Hoover Avenue
National City, CA 91950
**Contact:** Gwen E. Fairley, Associate Director of Admissions
**Phone:** 619-477-4800
**Fax:** 619-477-4360
**Web:** http://www.cchs.edu/
**E-mail:** gfairley@cchs.edu

**ACCREDITATION:** Accrediting Commission of Career Schools and Colleges of Technology

**INSTITUTIONALLY ADMINISTERED FINANCIAL AID:** No

## DEGREE OR CERTIFICATE PROGRAMS OFFERED
**Undergraduate**—*AS:* Allied Health; EEG Technology; Early Childhood Education; Medical Transcription; Respiratory Therapy. *BS:* Health Science/Management; Health Services/Respiratory Care.
**Graduate**—*MBA:* Business. *MS:* Business; Health Care Administration; Health Services/Community Health; Health Services/Wellness Promotion; Public Health.

## NON-DEGREE-RELATED COURSE TOPICS OFFERED
**Undergraduate**—business; community health services; gerontology; health professions and related sciences, other; miscellaneous health professions.
**Non-credit**—miscellaneous health aides; miscellaneous health professions.

---

**Special Note**

Established in 1978, California College for Health Sciences (CCHS) offers proven, accredited distance education programs designed for working health-care professionals. CCHS offers master's degree programs in health services, health-care administration, public health, and business administration. Students can earn a bachelor's degree in business with a major in accounting, finance, general business, management, or marketing or a bachelor's degree in health services with a major in management or respiratory care. Associate degree programs are available in allied health, business, early childhood education, EEG technology, medical transcription, respiratory therapy, and advanced respiratory therapy. CCHS programs provide a combination of academically sound instruction with unparalleled convenience. All programs are developed by recognized leaders in their fields and require no on-campus attendance. All materials are shipped directly to students, who choose when and where to study, without having to commute or incur costs associated with living on campus. Although CCHS students study independently, they can rely on the support of faculty and student advisers, who can be contacted by telephone, fax, e-mail, or mail. CCHS is licensed as a degree-granting institution by the state of California's Bureau for Private Postsecondary and Vocational Education (BPPVE). CCHS is nationally accredited by the Accrediting Commission of the Distance Education and Training Council (DETC), which is listed by the U.S. Department of Education as a nationally recognized accrediting agency. California College for Health Sciences is a Harcourt Higher Learning Company, based in National City, California. For more information, students should contact CCHS at 800-774-7616 (toll-free) or visit the Web site at http://www.cchs.edu.

# CALIFORNIA LUTHERAN UNIVERSITY

Office of Continuing and Professional Education, 60 West Olsen Road
Thousand Oaks, CA 91360
**Contact:** Coordinator
**Phone:** 805-493-3130
**Web:** http://www.clunet.edu/

**ACCREDITATION:** Western Association of Schools and Colleges

## DEGREE OR CERTIFICATE PROGRAMS OFFERED

**Programs offered do not lead to a degree or other formal award.**

## NON-DEGREE-RELATED COURSE TOPICS OFFERED

Undergraduate—education, other; human resources management.

# CALIFORNIA NATIONAL UNIVERSITY FOR ADVANCED STUDIES

16909 Parthenia Street
North Hills, CA 91343
**Contact:** Dr. Lolly Horn, CEO/Vice President for Academic Affairs
**Phone:** 818-830-2411
**Fax:** 818-830-2418
**Web:** http://www.cnuas.edu/
**E-mail:** lhorn@mail.cnuas.edu

**ACCREDITATION:** Distance Education and Training Council
**INSTITUTIONALLY ADMINISTERED FINANCIAL AID:** Yes

## DEGREE OR CERTIFICATE PROGRAMS OFFERED

**Undergraduate—*AIS:*** Human Resource Management. ***BS:*** Business Administration; Computer Science; Engineering; Quality Assurance Science. ***Certificate:*** Human Resource Management Practice.
**Graduate—*MBA:*** Business Administration. ***MS:*** Engineering.

## NON-DEGREE-RELATED COURSE TOPICS OFFERED

Undergraduate—accounting; business administration and management; business communications; business marketing and marketing management; business/managerial economics; computer and information sci-

ences, general; economics; electrical, electronics and communication engineering; engineering, general; environmental/environmental health engineering; finance, general; human resources management; international business; management information systems and business data processing, general; mechanical engineering; organizational behavior studies; quality control and safety technologies.
**Graduate**—accounting; business administration and management; business marketing and marketing management; computer and information sciences, general; computer engineering; electrical, electronics and communication engineering; engineering, general; environmental/environmental health engineering; human resources management; management information systems and business data processing, general; mechanical engineering; organizational behavior studies.

# CALIFORNIA POLYTECHNIC STATE UNIVERSITY, SAN LUIS OBISPO

*Distance Education–Extended University Programs and Services*
1 Grand Avenue
San Luis Obispo, CA 93407
**Contact:** Ms. Patricia-Ann Stoneman, Director of Extended Education
**Phone:** 805-756-2053
**Fax:** 805-756-5933
**Web:** http://www.ExtendedEducation.calpoly.edu
**E-mail:** pstonema@calpoly.edu

**ACCREDITATION:** Western Association of Schools and Colleges
**INSTITUTIONALLY ADMINISTERED FINANCIAL AID:** No

## DEGREE OR CERTIFICATE PROGRAMS OFFERED

**Programs offered do not lead to a degree or other formal award.**

## NON-DEGREE-RELATED COURSE TOPICS OFFERED

Undergraduate—applied mathematics.
Graduate—education, general.
Non-credit—mathematics.

# CALIFORNIA STATE UNIVERSITY, BAKERSFIELD

*Extended University Division/CSU-Bakersfield, online degree programs*
9001 Stockdale Highway
Bakersfield, CA 93311
**Contact:** Marie Boucher, Student Services
**Phone:** 661-664-2463
**Fax:** 661-664-2049
**Web:** http://www.csub.edu/erm
**E-mail:** mboucher@csub.edu

**ACCREDITATION:** Western Association of Schools and Colleges
**INSTITUTIONALLY ADMINISTERED FINANCIAL AID:** Yes

## DEGREE OR CERTIFICATE PROGRAMS OFFERED

**Undergraduate—BS:** Environmental Resource Management. *Certificate:* Environmental Resource Management.

## NON-DEGREE-RELATED COURSE TOPICS OFFERED

**Undergraduate**—English language and literature, general; English technical and business writing; biology, general; environmental science/studies; geography; geological and related sciences; information sciences and systems; physical sciences, other; political science and government; public policy analysis.

# CALIFORNIA STATE UNIVERSITY, CHICO

*Center for Regional and Continuing Education*
Chico, CA 95929-0250
**Contact:** Mr. Jeffrey S. Layne, Program Director
**Phone:** 530-898-6105
**Fax:** 530-898-4020
**Web:** http://rce.csuchico.edu
**E-mail:** jlayne@csuchico.edu

**ACCREDITATION:** Western Association of Schools and Colleges
**INSTITUTIONALLY ADMINISTERED FINANCIAL AID:** Yes

## DEGREE OR CERTIFICATE PROGRAMS OFFERED

**Undergraduate—BA:** Jewish Studies; Liberal Studies; Social Sciences; Sociology. **BS:** Computer Science. **BSN:** Nursing.
**Graduate—MS:** Computer Science.

## NON-DEGREE-RELATED COURSE TOPICS OFFERED

**Undergraduate**—Jewish/Judaic studies; accounting; anthropology; area, ethnic and cultural studies, other; community health services; curriculum and instruction; dance; education, general; family and community studies; health and medical administrative services; history; liberal arts and sciences, general studies and humanities; music; nursing; psychology; social sciences, general; sociology.

# CALIFORNIA STATE UNIVERSITY, DOMINGUEZ HILLS

*Distance Learning*
1000 East Victoria Street
Carson, CA 90747
**Contact:** Registration Office
**Phone:** 877-GO-HILLS
**Web:** http://www.csudh.edu/dominguezonline
**E-mail:** eereg@csudh.edu

**ACCREDITATION:** Western Association of Schools and Colleges
**INSTITUTIONALLY ADMINISTERED FINANCIAL AID:** Yes

## DEGREE OR CERTIFICATE PROGRAMS OFFERED

**Undergraduate—BS:** Nursing, Completion Program. *Certificate of Completion:* Quality Assurance. *Certificate:* Assistive Technology; Production and Inventory Control; Purchasing.

**Graduate—MA:** Humanities; Negotiation and Conflict Management. **MS:** Nursing; Quality Assurance.
**See full description on page 312.**

# CALIFORNIA STATE UNIVERSITY, NORTHRIDGE

*Educational Technologies and Distance Learning*
College of Extended Learning,, 18111 Nordhoff Street, MS #8401
Northridge, CA 91311-8401
**Contact:** Distance Learning Program Coordinator
**Phone:** 818-677-6405
**Web:** http://www.csun.edu/exl/distance/
**E-mail:** distancelearning@csun.edu

**ACCREDITATION:** Western Association of Schools and Colleges
**INSTITUTIONALLY ADMINISTERED FINANCIAL AID:** Yes

## DEGREE OR CERTIFICATE PROGRAMS OFFERED

**Undergraduate—BS:** Engineering Management.
**Graduate—MS:** Electrical Engineering; Speech Pathology.

# CALIFORNIA STATE UNIVERSITY, SAN MARCOS

*Extended Studies*
San Marcos, CA 92096
**Contact:** Debby Hickman, Special Session Coordinator
**Web:** http://www.csusm.edu/es
**E-mail:** es@csusm.edu

**ACCREDITATION:** Western Association of Schools and Colleges
**INSTITUTIONALLY ADMINISTERED FINANCIAL AID:** No

## DEGREE OR CERTIFICATE PROGRAMS OFFERED

**Programs offered do not lead to a degree or other formal award.**

## NON-DEGREE-RELATED COURSE TOPICS OFFERED

**Undergraduate**—education, general; education, other; history; sociology.
**Non-credit**—business; law and legal studies; nursing.

# CALVARY BIBLE COLLEGE AND THEOLOGICAL SEMINARY

*Non-Traditional Studies*
15800 Calvary Road
Kansas City, MO 64147
**Contact:** Rev. Mike Piburn, Director of Non-Traditional Studies and Assistant Registrar
**Phone:** 800-326-3960 Ext. 1319
**Fax:** 816-331-4474
**Web:** http://www.calvary.edu

**E-mail:** nts@calvary.edu

**ACCREDITATION:** Accrediting Association of Bible Colleges

**INSTITUTIONALLY ADMINISTERED FINANCIAL AID:** Yes

## DEGREE OR CERTIFICATE PROGRAMS OFFERED

Programs offered do not lead to a degree or other formal award.

## NON-DEGREE-RELATED COURSE TOPICS OFFERED

**Undergraduate**—bible/biblical studies; biblical and other theological languages and literatures; counseling psychology; pastoral counseling and specialized ministries; religion/religious studies; theological and ministerial studies; theological studies and religious vocations, other.

**Graduate**—bible/biblical studies; biblical and other theological languages and literatures; counseling psychology; pastoral counseling and specialized ministries; religion/religious studies; theological and ministerial studies; theological studies and religious vocations, other.

# CALVIN COLLEGE

3201 Burton Street, SE
Grand Rapids, MI 49546

**Contact:** Shirley Roels, Dean for Academic Administration

**Phone:** 616-957-8557

**Web:** http://www.calvin.edu/

**E-mail:** roel@calvin.edu

**ACCREDITATION:** North Central Association of Colleges and Schools

**INSTITUTIONALLY ADMINISTERED FINANCIAL AID:** Yes

## DEGREE OR CERTIFICATE PROGRAMS OFFERED

Programs offered do not lead to a degree or other formal award.

## NON-DEGREE-RELATED COURSE TOPICS OFFERED

**Undergraduate**—American literature (United States); English language and literature, general; Germanic languages and literatures; accounting; animal sciences; anthropology; applied mathematics; architecture and related programs, other; astronomy; bible/biblical studies; biochemistry and biophysics; bioengineering and biomedical engineering; biological and physical sciences; biological sciences/life sciences, other; biology, general; botany; business; business administration and management; business management and administrative services, other; cell and molecular biology; chemical engineering; chemistry; civil engineering; communication disorders sciences and services; communications, general; computer and information sciences, general; computer programming; computer science; computer systems analysis; criminal justice and corrections; curriculum and instruction; dramatic/theater arts and stagecraft; economics; education administration and supervision; education, general; electrical and electronic engineering-related technology; electrical, electronics and communications engineering; engineering design; engineering mechanics; engineering, general; film/video and photographic arts; fine arts and art studies; foreign languages and literatures; general teacher education; geography; geological and related sciences; health and medical preparatory programs; health professions and related sciences, other; history; international business; journalism and mass communications; liberal arts and sciences, general studies and humanities; marketing management and research; mathematical statistics; mathematics; mathematics and computer science; mechanical engineering; medical basic sciences; microbiology/bacteriology; music; nursing; philosophy; philosophy and religion; physical sciences, general; physics; political science and government; psychology; religion/religious studies; religious/sacred music; romance languages and literatures; social psychology; social work; sociology; special education; teacher education, specific academic and vocational programs; theological and ministerial studies.

**Graduate**—education, general.

# CAMPBELLSVILLE UNIVERSITY

1 University Drive
Campbellsville, KY 42718-2799

**Contact:** Dr. Frank Cheatham, Vice President for Academic Affairs

**Phone:** 270-789-5231

**Fax:** 270-789-5550

**Web:** http://www.campbellsvil.edu/

**E-mail:** frank@campbellsvil.edu

**ACCREDITATION:** Southern Association of Colleges and Schools

eCollege.com   www.ecollege.com

## DEGREE OR CERTIFICATE PROGRAMS OFFERED

Programs offered do not lead to a degree or other formal award.

# CANADIAN BIBLE COLLEGE

4400 4th Avenue
Regina, SK S4T 0H8, Canada

**Contact:** Mrs. Eunice Emilson, Administrative Assistant for Extension Education

**Phone:** 306-545-1515 Ext. 203

**Fax:** 306-545-0210

**Web:** http://www.cbccts.ca/exted/extedhome.htm

**E-mail:** eemilson@cbccts.ca

**ACCREDITATION:** Provincially Chartered

**INSTITUTIONALLY ADMINISTERED FINANCIAL AID:** No

## DEGREE OR CERTIFICATE PROGRAMS OFFERED

Programs offered do not lead to a degree or other formal award.

## NON-DEGREE-RELATED COURSE TOPICS OFFERED

**Undergraduate**—bible/biblical studies; biblical and other theological languages and literatures; education, other; history; theological and ministerial studies.

**Graduate**—bible/biblical studies; biblical and other theological languages and literatures; education, other; history; theological and ministerial studies.

# CAPE COD COMMUNITY COLLEGE

*Distance and Learning Technology*

2240 Iyanough Road
West Barnstable, MA 02668

**Contact:** Dale Suffridge, Director of Distance Learning

**Phone:** 508-375-4040

**Fax:** 508-375-4041

**Web:** http://www.capecod.mass.edu/distancelearning

**E-mail:** dsuffrid@capecod.mass.edu

**ACCREDITATION:** New England Association of Schools and Colleges

### DEGREE OR CERTIFICATE PROGRAMS OFFERED
Programs offered do not lead to a degree or other formal award.

### NON-DEGREE-RELATED COURSE TOPICS OFFERED
**Undergraduate**—English composition; social psychology; sociology.

# CAPE FEAR COMMUNITY COLLEGE

411 North Front Street
Wilmington, NC 28401
**Contact:** Orangel Daniels, Dean of Arts and Sciences
**Phone:** 910-251-5629
**E-mail:** odaniels@capefear.cc.nc.us

**ACCREDITATION:** Southern Association of Colleges and Schools
**INSTITUTIONALLY ADMINISTERED FINANCIAL AID:** Yes

### DEGREE OR CERTIFICATE PROGRAMS OFFERED
Programs offered do not lead to a degree or other formal award.

### NON-DEGREE-RELATED COURSE TOPICS OFFERED
**Undergraduate**—English composition; English technical and business writing; accounting; business administration and management; chemistry; communications, general; fine arts and art studies; history; internet and world wide web; law and legal studies; marketing operations/marketing and distribution, other; mathematics; psychology; sociology. **Non-credit**—business; health and physical education/fitness.

# CAPELLA UNIVERSITY

222 South 9th Street, 20th Floor
Minneapolis, MN 55402
**Contact:** Admissions Center
**Phone:** 888-CAP-ELLA
**Web:** http://www.capellauniversity.edu/
**E-mail:** info@capella.edu

**ACCREDITATION:** North Central Association of Colleges and Schools

### DEGREE OR CERTIFICATE PROGRAMS OFFERED
Programs offered do not lead to a degree or other formal award.

### Special Note
Founded in 1993 and accredited by the North Central Association of Colleges and Schools, Capella University is one of the world's leading e-learning institutions. Its innovative, online course delivery format leverages the speed, convenience, and flexibility of the Internet to provide a quality education at a time and place most convenient for students. With more than 400 accredited online courses and degree programs, Capella University is dedicated to helping working adults integrate advanced education into their busy lives. The online curriculum enables students to learn at their own pace and schedule—while connecting them with an engaging, supportive community of expert faculty members and fellow learners around the world.

Capella University faculty members are not only respected academicians, they are real-world professionals with years of experience in their fields, ensuring an ideal balance of hands-on experience, academic theory, and expertise to help make the most of online learning.

Typical learners at Capella University are established and successful professionals. In the online classroom, they network with fellow students whose professional and personal experience spans all 50 states and 30 countries around the world.

Capella University programs are designed to be accessible from any Web browser anywhere, anytime, so learning can fit into students' professional and personal schedules. Capella University also helps students customize their program to achieve career and personal goals, and they receive a level of personal attention and individualized support not found in many traditional programs.

# CAPITAL COMMUNITY COLLEGE
*Distance Learning Class*
401 Flatbush Avenue
Hartford, CT 06106
**Contact:** Dr. John Mohammadi, Director of Institutional Research
**Phone:** 860-987-4882
**Fax:** 860-987-4822
**Web:** http://ccc.commnet.edu/
**E-mail:** mohammadi@commnet.edu

**ACCREDITATION:** New England Association of Schools and Colleges
**INSTITUTIONALLY ADMINISTERED FINANCIAL AID:** Yes

### DEGREE OR CERTIFICATE PROGRAMS OFFERED
**Undergraduate**—*AS:* Computer and Information Systems; General Studies.

### NON-DEGREE-RELATED COURSE TOPICS OFFERED
**Undergraduate**—English composition; English literature (British and Commonwealth); biological sciences/life sciences, other; biology, general; business; computer software and media applications; computer/information technology administration and management; foreign languages and literatures; internet and world wide web. **Non-credit**—computer and information sciences, general; computer software and media applications; computer systems networking and telecommunications; computer/information technology administration and management.

# CAPITOL COLLEGE

11301 Springfield Road
Laurel, MD 20708
**Contact:** Mr. Ken S. Crockett, Director of Graduate Admissions
**Phone:** 301-369-2800 Ext. 3044
**Fax:** 301-953-3876
**Web:** http://www.capitol-college.edu/academics/grad/

**E-mail:** gradschool@capitol-college.edu

**ACCREDITATION:** Middle States Association of Colleges and Schools

**INSTITUTIONALLY ADMINISTERED FINANCIAL AID:** Yes

## DEGREE OR CERTIFICATE PROGRAMS OFFERED

**Graduate—***MS:* Electronic Commerce Management; Information Architecture; Information and Telecommunication Systems Management; Network Security.

## NON-DEGREE-RELATED COURSE TOPICS OFFERED

**Undergraduate—**business quantitative methods and management science; computer and information sciences, general; computer and information sciences, other; computer programming; computer systems networking and telecommunications; computer/information technology administration and management; information sciences and systems; internet and world wide web; systems engineering; telecommunications.

**Graduate—**business quantitative methods and management science; computer and information sciences, general; computer and information sciences, other; computer systems networking and telecommunications; computer/information technology administration and management; information sciences and systems; internet and world wide web; management information systems and business data processing, general; systems engineering; systems science and theory; telecommunications.

# CARL ALBERT STATE COLLEGE

1507 South McKenna
Poteau, OK 74953
**Contact:** Dr. Ricky W. Streight, Vice President of Academic Affairs
**Phone:** 918-647-1230
**Fax:** 918-647-1201
**Web:** http://www.casc.cc.ok.us/
**E-mail:** rstreight@casc.cc.ok.us

**ACCREDITATION:** North Central Association of Colleges and Schools

**INSTITUTIONALLY ADMINISTERED FINANCIAL AID:** Yes

## DEGREE OR CERTIFICATE PROGRAMS OFFERED

Programs offered do not lead to a degree or other formal award.

## NON-DEGREE-RELATED COURSE TOPICS OFFERED

**Undergraduate—**English composition; accounting; administrative and secretarial services; business administration and management; business information and data processing services; computer and information sciences, general; criminal justice and corrections; data entry/microcomputer applications; health and physical education/fitness; history; mathematics; nursing; political science and government; psychology; telecommunications.

# CARLETON UNIVERSITY

*Instructional Television*

Robertson Hall, Room 303, 1125 Colonel By Drive
Ottawa, ON K1S 5B6, Canada
**Contact:** Shelly O'Hara, Liaison Officer for Instructional Television
**Phone:** 613-520-2600 Ext. 8905

**Fax:** 613-520-4456
**Web:** http://www.carleton.ca/itv/
**E-mail:** shelly_ohara@carleton.ca

**ACCREDITATION:** Provincially Chartered

**INSTITUTIONALLY ADMINISTERED FINANCIAL AID:** Yes

## DEGREE OR CERTIFICATE PROGRAMS OFFERED

Programs offered do not lead to a degree or other formal award.

## NON-DEGREE-RELATED COURSE TOPICS OFFERED

**Undergraduate—**Canadian studies; accounting; anthropology; biology, general; developmental and child psychology; earth and planetary sciences; finance, general; geography; philosophy and religion; social psychology; social work; sociology.

# CARNEGIE MELLON UNIVERSITY

*Software Engineering @ Carnegie Mellon,*
*Information Resource Management, MSIA*

5000 Forbes Avenue
Pittsburgh, PA 15213
**Contact:** Ms. Cheryl Aston, Administrative Associate
**Phone:** 412-268-1593
**Fax:** 412-268-5413
**Web:** http://www.distance.cmu.edu
**E-mail:** caston@cs.cmu.edu

**ACCREDITATION:** Middle States Association of Colleges and Schools

**INSTITUTIONALLY ADMINISTERED FINANCIAL AID:** No

## DEGREE OR CERTIFICATE PROGRAMS OFFERED

**Graduate—***MSE:* Software Engineering.

**See full description on page 314.**

# CARROLL COMMUNITY COLLEGE

1601 Washington Road
Westminster, MD 21157
**Contact:** Ms. Edie Hemingway, Coordinator of Admissions
**Phone:** 410-386-8405
**Fax:** 410-386-8446
**Web:** http://www.carrollcc.com
**E-mail:** ehemingway@carroll.cc.md.us

**ACCREDITATION:** Middle States Association of Colleges and Schools

**INSTITUTIONALLY ADMINISTERED FINANCIAL AID:** Yes

## DEGREE OR CERTIFICATE PROGRAMS OFFERED

Programs offered do not lead to a degree or other formal award.

## NON-DEGREE-RELATED COURSE TOPICS OFFERED

**Undergraduate—**English composition; English technical and business writing; astronomy; biology, general; business administration and management; computer and information sciences, general; computer systems networking and telecommunications; computer/information technology administration and management; criminal justice and corrections; economics; geography; history; marketing management and research; mathematical statistics; philosophy; psychology; social psychology; sociology.

Non-credit—English creative writing; English technical and business writing; administrative and secretarial services; business; business administration and management; computer software and media applications; financial management and services.

# CASPER COLLEGE

125 College Drive
Casper, WY 82601-4699
**Contact:** Dr. Gerald E. Nelson, Associate Dean of Academic Affairs
**Web:** http://www.cc.whecn.edu/
**E-mail:** gnelson@acad.cc.whecn.edu

**ACCREDITATION:** North Central Association of Colleges and Schools
**INSTITUTIONALLY ADMINISTERED FINANCIAL AID:** Yes

## DEGREE OR CERTIFICATE PROGRAMS OFFERED
Undergraduate—*AS:* Education.

## NON-DEGREE-RELATED COURSE TOPICS OFFERED
Undergraduate—English composition; accounting; biological and physical sciences; business administration and management; computer science; education, general; mathematical statistics; mathematics.

# CATAWBA VALLEY COMMUNITY COLLEGE

*Telecommunications Department*
2550 Highway 70 SE
Hickory, NC 28602
**Contact:** Dr. Linda Lutz, Dean of Education Support Services
**Phone:** 828-327-7000 Ext. 4130
**Fax:** 828-324-5130
**Web:** http://www.cvcc.cc.nc.us/specserv/lrc/distlear.htm
**E-mail:** llutz@cvcc.cc.nc.us

**ACCREDITATION:** Southern Association of Colleges and Schools
**INSTITUTIONALLY ADMINISTERED FINANCIAL AID:** Yes

## DEGREE OR CERTIFICATE PROGRAMS OFFERED
Undergraduate—*AAS:* Health Care Management Technology. *Certificate:* Business Administration; Health Care Management Technology.

## NON-DEGREE-RELATED COURSE TOPICS OFFERED
Undergraduate—English composition; English language and literature, general; accounting; advertising; bible/biblical studies; business; child care and guidance workers and managers; computer science; developmental and child psychology; economics; health and medical administrative services; health and physical education/fitness; history; horticulture services operations and management; mathematics; music; philosophy and religion; psychology; social psychology; sociology.
Non-credit—computer science.

# THE CATHOLIC DISTANCE UNIVERSITY

120 East Colonial Highway
Hamilton, VA 20158
**Contact:** Mr. Frank Degnan, Graduate Registrar
**Phone:** 540-338-2700
**Fax:** 540-338-4788
**Web:** http://www.cdu.edu/
**E-mail:** masters@cdu.edu

**ACCREDITATION:** Distance Education and Training Council
**INSTITUTIONALLY ADMINISTERED FINANCIAL AID:** No

## DEGREE OR CERTIFICATE PROGRAMS OFFERED
Graduate—*MA:* Religious Studies. *MBATM:* Religious Studies, MRS.

## NON-DEGREE-RELATED COURSE TOPICS OFFERED
Undergraduate—religion/religious studies.
Non-credit—religion/religious studies.

# CAYUGA COUNTY COMMUNITY COLLEGE

197 Franklin Street
Auburn, NY 13021
**Contact:** Ed Kowalski, Director of Evening and Special Programs
**Phone:** 315-255-1743
**Fax:** 315-255-2117
**Web:** http://www.cayuga-cc.edu/
**E-mail:** kowalskie@cayuga-cc.edu

**ACCREDITATION:** Middle States Association of Colleges and Schools
**INSTITUTIONALLY ADMINISTERED FINANCIAL AID:** Yes

## DEGREE OR CERTIFICATE PROGRAMS OFFERED
Undergraduate—*AA:* Business Administration; Liberal Arts and Humanities. *AS:* Business Administration.

## NON-DEGREE-RELATED COURSE TOPICS OFFERED
Undergraduate—English language and literature, general; biology, general; business; computer science; economics; health and physical education/fitness; history; mathematics; political science and government; psychology; telecommunications.

# CEDAR CREST COLLEGE

100 College Drive
Allentown, PA 18104
**Contact:** Ms. Nancy L. Hollinger, Director of Center for Lifelong Learning
**Phone:** 610-740-3770
**Fax:** 610-740-3786
**Web:** http://www.cedarcrest.edu/

**E-mail:** nlhollin@cedarcrest.edu

**ACCREDITATION:** Middle States Association of Colleges and Schools

**INSTITUTIONALLY ADMINISTERED FINANCIAL AID:** Yes

eCollege.com *www.ecollege.com*

### DEGREE OR CERTIFICATE PROGRAMS OFFERED

**Undergraduate—BS:** Business.

### NON-DEGREE-RELATED COURSE TOPICS OFFERED

**Undergraduate—**business; health and medical administrative services; information sciences and systems.

# CEDARVILLE UNIVERSITY

251 North Main Street
Cedarville, OH 45314
**Contact:** Chuck Allport, Assistant to the Academic Vice President
**Phone:** 937-766-7681
**Fax:** 937-766-3217
**Web:** http://www.cedarville.edu/
**E-mail:** chuckallport@cedarville.edu

**ACCREDITATION:** North Central Association of Colleges and Schools

**INSTITUTIONALLY ADMINISTERED FINANCIAL AID:** Yes

eCollege.com *www.ecollege.com*

### DEGREE OR CERTIFICATE PROGRAMS OFFERED

Programs offered do not lead to a degree or other formal award.

### NON-DEGREE-RELATED COURSE TOPICS OFFERED

**Undergraduate—**English composition; biology, general; social sciences, general; special education.

# CENTRAL ARIZONA COLLEGE

*Instructional Technology*

8470 North Overfield Road
Coolidge, AZ 85228
**Contact:** Registrar's Office
**Phone:** 800-237-9814
**Fax:** 520-426-4234
**Web:** http://www.cac.cc.az.us
**E-mail:** sandra_todd@python.cac.cc.az.us

**ACCREDITATION:** North Central Association of Colleges and Schools

**INSTITUTIONALLY ADMINISTERED FINANCIAL AID:** Yes

### DEGREE OR CERTIFICATE PROGRAMS OFFERED

Programs offered do not lead to a degree or other formal award.

### NON-DEGREE-RELATED COURSE TOPICS OFFERED

**Undergraduate—**American (United States) history; English composition; Spanish language and literature; anatomy; anthropology; art history, criticism and conservation; law and legal studies, other; mathematics; other; sociology.

# CENTRAL CAROLINA COMMUNITY COLLEGE

1105 Kelly Drive
Sanford, NC 27330
**Contact:** Ron Miriello, Vice President of Student Development Services
**Phone:** 919-718-7230
**Fax:** 919-718-7379
**Web:** http://www.ccarolina.cc.nc.us/
**E-mail:** rmiriello@gw.ccarolina.cc.nc.us

**ACCREDITATION:** Southern Association of Colleges and Schools

**INSTITUTIONALLY ADMINISTERED FINANCIAL AID:** Yes

### DEGREE OR CERTIFICATE PROGRAMS OFFERED

**Undergraduate—AA:** General.

### NON-DEGREE-RELATED COURSE TOPICS OFFERED

**Undergraduate—**English language and literature, general; accounting; business; computer programming; economics; history; library science, other; marketing management and research; mathematics; sociology.

# CENTRAL CAROLINA TECHNICAL COLLEGE

506 North Guignard Drive
Sumter, SC 29150
**Contact:** Ms. Ann A. Cooper, Vice President for Academic and Student Affairs
**Phone:** 803-778-6636
**Fax:** 803-778-7889
**Web:** http://www.sum.tec.sc.us/
**E-mail:** cooperaa@cctc.sum.tec.sc.us

**ACCREDITATION:** Southern Association of Colleges and Schools

**INSTITUTIONALLY ADMINISTERED FINANCIAL AID:** Yes

### DEGREE OR CERTIFICATE PROGRAMS OFFERED

**Undergraduate—Certificate:** Emergency Administration and Management.

### NON-DEGREE-RELATED COURSE TOPICS OFFERED

**Undergraduate—**English language and literature, general; accounting; administrative and secretarial services; agriculture/agricultural sciences; business administration and management; computer/information technology administration and management; criminal justice and corrections; data entry/microcomputer applications; economics; environmental/environmental health engineering; forestry and related sciences; law and legal studies; marketing management and research; natural resources conservation; nursing.

# CENTRAL COMMUNITY COLLEGE

PO Box 4903
Grand Island, NE 68802-4903
**Contact:** Mrs. Angela Pacheco, Admissions and Recruiting Director

**Phone:** 308-398-7406
**Fax:** 308-398-7398
**Web:** http://www.cccneb.edu/
**E-mail:** apacheco@cccneb.edu

**ACCREDITATION:** North Central Association of Colleges and Schools

**INSTITUTIONALLY ADMINISTERED FINANCIAL AID:** Yes

### DEGREE OR CERTIFICATE PROGRAMS OFFERED

Undergraduate—*AAS:* Business Administration; Industrial Technology.

### NON-DEGREE-RELATED COURSE TOPICS OFFERED

Undergraduate—English language and literature, general; accounting; administrative and secretarial services; agricultural business and production, other; biological sciences/life sciences, other; business management and administrative services, other; criminal justice and corrections; drafting; electrical and electronics equipment installers and repairers; family/consumer resource management; health and medical assistants; horticulture services operations and management; hospitality services management; human services; internet and world wide web; law and legal studies; mathematics, other; nursing; personal and miscellaneous services, other; psychology, other; social sciences, general.

## CENTRALIA COLLEGE

*Distance Learning*
600 West Locust
Centralia, WA 98531
**Contact:** Prof. Victor Freund, Director of Distance Learning
**Phone:** 360-736-9391 Ext. 253
**Fax:** 360-330-7502
**Web:** http://www.centralia.ctc.edu/
**E-mail:** vfreund@centralia.ctc.edu

**ACCREDITATION:** Northwest Association of Schools and Colleges

**INSTITUTIONALLY ADMINISTERED FINANCIAL AID:** Yes

### DEGREE OR CERTIFICATE PROGRAMS OFFERED

Programs offered do not lead to a degree or other formal award.

### NON-DEGREE-RELATED COURSE TOPICS OFFERED

Undergraduate—business and personal services marketing operations; business information and data processing services; computer and information sciences, general; computer software and media applications; computer systems analysis; data entry/microcomputer applications; internet and world wide web.
Non-credit—business and personal services marketing operations; business information and data processing services; computer and information sciences, general; computer programming; computer software and media applications; computer systems analysis; data entry/microcomputer applications; internet and world wide web.

## CENTRAL METHODIST COLLEGE

411 Central Methodist Square
Fayette, MO 65248
**Contact:** Rita Gulstad, Dean of Extended Learning
**Phone:** 660-248-6292
**Fax:** 660-248-6392

**Web:** http://www.cmc.edu/
**E-mail:** rgulstad@cmc.edu

**ACCREDITATION:** North Central Association of Colleges and Schools

**INSTITUTIONALLY ADMINISTERED FINANCIAL AID:** No

### DEGREE OR CERTIFICATE PROGRAMS OFFERED

Programs offered do not lead to a degree or other formal award.

### NON-DEGREE-RELATED COURSE TOPICS OFFERED

Undergraduate—American (United States) history; anatomy; biology, general; computer and information sciences, general; economics; educational psychology; mathematical statistics; mathematics, other; nursing; philosophy; physiology, human and animal.
Graduate—educational psychology; philosophy; sociology.
Non-credit—communications, general; communications, other; computer software and media applications; health professions and related sciences, other; nursing.

## CENTRAL MICHIGAN UNIVERSITY

*Distance/Distributed Learning*
College of Extended Learning
Mount Pleasant , MI 48859
**Contact:** Ms. Connie Detwiler, Distance Learning
**Phone:** 800-688-4268
**Fax:** 989-774-1822
**Web:** http://www.ddl.cmich.edu
**E-mail:** celinfo@mail.cel.cmich.edu

**ACCREDITATION:** North Central Association of Colleges and Schools

**INSTITUTIONALLY ADMINISTERED FINANCIAL AID:** Yes

### DEGREE OR CERTIFICATE PROGRAMS OFFERED

Undergraduate—*BAA:* Health Administration. *BS:* Community Development; Major in Administration.
Graduate—*Advanced Graduate Diploma:* Audiology. *MS:* General Administration.

### NON-DEGREE-RELATED COURSE TOPICS OFFERED

Undergraduate—Spanish language and literature; accounting; alcohol/drug abuse counseling; astronomy; business administration and management; business marketing and marketing management; communications, other; computer science; economics; environmental health; finance, general; geography; health system/health services administration; industrial and organizational psychology; international business; journalism; mathematical statistics; mathematics; music; organizational behavior studies; physics; psychology; religion/religious studies; social psychology; sociology; women's studies.
Graduate—alcohol/drug abuse counseling; business marketing and marketing management; medical genetics; organizational behavior studies.
See full description on page 316.

## CENTRAL MISSOURI STATE UNIVERSITY

*Extended Campus–Distance Learning*
403 Humphreys
Warrensburg, MO 64093

**Contact:** Debbie Bassore, Assistant Director for Distance Learning

**Phone:** 660-543-8480

**Fax:** 660-543-8333

**Web:** http://www.cmsu.edu/extcamp

**E-mail:** bassore@cmsu1.cmsu.edu

**ACCREDITATION:** North Central Association of Colleges and Schools

**INSTITUTIONALLY ADMINISTERED FINANCIAL AID:** Yes

### DEGREE OR CERTIFICATE PROGRAMS OFFERED

**Graduate—*MS:*** Criminal Justice; Industrial Management; Library Information Technology.

**Postgraduate and doctoral—*PhD:*** Technology Management.

### NON-DEGREE-RELATED COURSE TOPICS OFFERED

**Undergraduate**—English as a second language; business administration and management; computer science; criminal justice and corrections; curriculum and instruction; developmental and child psychology; electrical, electronics and communication engineering; engineering/industrial management; history; journalism and mass communication, other; library science, other; nursing; psychology; special education; technology education/industrial arts.

**Graduate**—English as a second language; construction and building finishers and managers; criminal justice and corrections; curriculum and instruction; developmental and child psychology; engineering/industrial management; journalism and mass communication, other; library science, other; mathematical statistics; nursing; psychology; special education; technology education/industrial arts.

**See full description on page 318.**

# CENTRAL OREGON COMMUNITY COLLEGE

*Open Campus Distance Learning Program*

2600 Northwest College Way

Bend, OR 97701

**Contact:** Dianne Reingold, Admissions Assistant

**Phone:** 541-383-7500

**Web:** http://www.cocc.edu/opencampus

**E-mail:** welcome@cocc.edu

**ACCREDITATION:** Northwest Association of Schools and Colleges

**INSTITUTIONALLY ADMINISTERED FINANCIAL AID:** Yes

### DEGREE OR CERTIFICATE PROGRAMS OFFERED

**Undergraduate—*AA:*** Oregon Transfer Degree.

### NON-DEGREE-RELATED COURSE TOPICS OFFERED

**Undergraduate**—biological and physical sciences; business administration and management; chemistry; communications, general; computer and information sciences, general; criminal justice and corrections; developmental and child psychology; foods and nutrition studies; geography; history; information sciences and systems; liberal arts and sciences, general studies and humanities; mathematics; psychology.

# CENTRAL TEXAS COLLEGE

*Distance Education and Educational Technology*

PO Box 1800

Killeen, TX 76540

**Contact:** S. Chapman, Director of Distance Education and Educational Technology

**Phone:** 254-526-1221

**Fax:** 254-526-0817

**Web:** http://disted.ctcd.cc.tx.us

**E-mail:** schapman@ctcd.cc.tx.us

**ACCREDITATION:** Southern Association of Colleges and Schools

### DEGREE OR CERTIFICATE PROGRAMS OFFERED

**Undergraduate—*AGS:*** General Studies.

### NON-DEGREE-RELATED COURSE TOPICS OFFERED

**Undergraduate**—American (United States) history; English composition; accounting; alcohol/drug abuse counseling; anthropology; art history, criticism and conservation; biology, general; law and legal studies, other; mathematics, other; sociology.

# CENTRAL VIRGINIA COMMUNITY COLLEGE

*Learning Resources*

3506 Wards Road

Lynchburg, VA 24502

**Contact:** Susan S. Beasley, Audiovisual Supervisor

**Phone:** 804-832-7742

**Fax:** 804-386-4531

**Web:** http://www.cv.cc.va.us/

**E-mail:** beasleys@cvcc.vccs.edu

**ACCREDITATION:** Southern Association of Colleges and Schools

**INSTITUTIONALLY ADMINISTERED FINANCIAL AID:** Yes

### DEGREE OR CERTIFICATE PROGRAMS OFFERED

**Undergraduate—*AAS:*** Medical Laboratory Technology.

### NON-DEGREE-RELATED COURSE TOPICS OFFERED

**Undergraduate**—English composition; English language and literature, general; English technical and business writing; administrative and secretarial services; applied mathematics; astronomy; biology, general; business marketing and marketing management; chemistry; computer and information sciences, general; criminal justice and corrections; economics; psychology; sociology.

# CENTRAL WASHINGTON UNIVERSITY

*Center for Learning Technologies*

Mitchell Hall, 400 East 8th Avenue

Ellensburg, WA 98926-7465

**Contact:** Tracy Schwindt, Associate Registrar

**Phone:** 509-963-3076

**Fax:** 509-963-3022

**Web:** http://www.cwu.edu/~media/noflash/
**E-mail:** schwindt@cwu.edu

**ACCREDITATION:** Northwest Association of Schools and Colleges
**INSTITUTIONALLY ADMINISTERED FINANCIAL AID:** Yes

## DEGREE OR CERTIFICATE PROGRAMS OFFERED
Programs offered do not lead to a degree or other formal award.

## NON-DEGREE-RELATED COURSE TOPICS OFFERED
**Undergraduate**—English language and literature, general; accounting; business administration and management; business information and data processing services; chemistry; communications, general; computer/information technology administration and management; criminal justice and corrections; economics; education administration and supervision; education, general; educational evaluation, research and statistics; electrical and electronic engineering-related technology; financial management and services; human resources management; industrial and organizational psychology; industrial production technologies; marketing operations/marketing and distribution, other; political science and government; psychology.
**Graduate**—industrial and organizational psychology; psychology.

# CENTRAL WYOMING COLLEGE
## Distance Education and Extended Studies
2660 Peck Avenue
Riverton, WY 82501
**Contact:** Mary Gores, Director of Admissions
**Phone:** 307-855-2231
**Fax:** 307-855-2231
**Web:** http://www.cwc.cc.wy.us
**E-mail:** mgores@cwc.cc.wy.us

**ACCREDITATION:** North Central Association of Colleges and Schools
**INSTITUTIONALLY ADMINISTERED FINANCIAL AID:** Yes

## DEGREE OR CERTIFICATE PROGRAMS OFFERED
**Undergraduate**—*AA:* General Studies.

## NON-DEGREE-RELATED COURSE TOPICS OFFERED
**Undergraduate**—English composition; accounting; anthropology; area, ethnic and cultural studies, other; biology, general; business; chemistry; computer and information sciences, general; criminal justice and corrections; economics; family and marriage counseling; foreign languages and literatures, other; geography; health and physical education/fitness; history; mathematics; political science and government; psychology; religion/religious studies; social sciences, general; sociology; teacher education, specific academic and vocational programs.

# CENTURY COMMUNITY AND TECHNICAL COLLEGE
## Customized Training Division
3300 Century Avenue, N
White Bear Lake, MN 55110
**Contact:** Patrick Thomas Gerkey, Director of Distance Learning
**Phone:** 651-439-7482

**Fax:** 651-779-5082
**Web:** http://www.century.cc.mn.us/
**E-mail:** p.gerkey@cctc.cc.mn.us

**ACCREDITATION:** North Central Association of Colleges and Schools
**INSTITUTIONALLY ADMINISTERED FINANCIAL AID:** No

## DEGREE OR CERTIFICATE PROGRAMS OFFERED
Programs offered do not lead to a degree or other formal award.

## NON-DEGREE-RELATED COURSE TOPICS OFFERED
**Non-credit**—English composition; accounting; anatomy; applied mathematics; business administration and management; communications, general; computer and information sciences, general; data entry/microcomputer applications; mathematics.

# CERRO COSO COMMUNITY COLLEGE
## Cerro Coso Online
Ridgecrest, CA 93555
**Contact:** Matt Hightower, Director
**Phone:** 888-537-6932
**Web:** http://www.cc.cc.ca.us/cconline/Default.htm
**E-mail:** mhightow@cc.cc.ca.us

**ACCREDITATION:** Western Association of Schools and Colleges

## DEGREE OR CERTIFICATE PROGRAMS OFFERED
**Undergraduate**—*Certificate:* Online Teaching.

## NON-DEGREE-RELATED COURSE TOPICS OFFERED
**Undergraduate**—East European languages and literatures; English language and literature, general; anthropology; computer programming; criminal justice and corrections; marketing operations/marketing and distribution, other; music; speech and rhetorical studies.

---

### Special Note
Cerro Coso (CC) Online currently offers courses leading to 12 different associate degrees that may be completed completely on line, with no campus attendance requirements. In addition, CC Online delivers complete online student services, including counseling, admission, registration, financial aid, and library services.

Cerro Coso offers a Practical Certificate in Online Teaching for faculty members interested in teaching online courses. The Practical Certificate in Online Teaching offers a unique opportunity to learn about online teaching in a practical, hands-on environment. The entire certificate can be completed in a typical semester. Unique to this certificate is the generation of a portfolio. This portfolio is created in the first course and developed as students progress through their course work. All courses are taught by experienced online instructors and presented in a consistent environment. Access to the Internet and a Windows or Macintosh computer with at least 100Mhz and multimedia capabilities is required for participation in the program. This program is specifically designed to assist faculty members in the development and delivery of online courses or course content. Cerro Coso Community College is a Service Member Opportunity College.

For more information, students should visit the College's Web site (http://www.cc.cc.ca.us/cconline) or call 888-537-6932 (toll-free).

# CHADRON STATE COLLEGE
## Extended Campus Programs
1000 Main Street
Chadron, NE 69337
**Contact:** Mr. Steve Taylor, Assistant Vice President for Extended Campus Programs
**Phone:** 308-432-6211
**Fax:** 308-432-6473
**Web:** http://www.csc.edu
**E-mail:** staylor@csc.edu

**ACCREDITATION:** North Central Association of Colleges and Schools
**INSTITUTIONALLY ADMINISTERED FINANCIAL AID:** Yes

### DEGREE OR CERTIFICATE PROGRAMS OFFERED
Programs offered do not lead to a degree or other formal award.

### NON-DEGREE-RELATED COURSE TOPICS OFFERED
**Undergraduate**—English composition; English literature (British and Commonwealth); English technical and business writing; accounting; biological and physical sciences; business; business administration and management; business and personal services marketing operations; business communications; business information and data processing services; business management and administrative services, other; business quantitative methods and management science; business/managerial economics; criminology; developmental and child psychology; economics; education, general; education, other; educational psychology; family and community studies; general retailing and wholesaling operations and skills; general teacher education; geography; history; home economics, general; home economics, other; housing studies; human resources management; human services; individual and family development studies; industrial and organizational psychology; information sciences and systems; law and legal studies; liberal arts and sciences, general studies and humanities; library science, other; marketing management and research; marketing operations/marketing and distribution, other; mathematical statistics; mathematics; mathematics and computer science; philosophy; philosophy and religion; physical sciences, general; physical sciences, other; psychology; psychology, other; real estate; social sciences and history, other; social sciences, general; social work; sociology; special education; teacher education, specific academic and vocational programs.
**Graduate**—English language and literature, general; accounting; business administration and management; business and personal services marketing operations; business information and data processing services; business management and administrative services, other; business quantitative methods and management science; business/managerial economics; counseling psychology; curriculum and instruction; education administration and supervision; education, general; education, other; educational evaluation, research and statistics; educational psychology; educational/instructional media design; history; human resources management; industrial and organizational psychology; marketing management and research; marketing operations/marketing and distribution, other; mathematical statistics; mathematics; mathematics and computer science; mathematics, other; psychology; psychology, other; school psychology; special education; teacher education, specific academic and vocational programs; technology education/industrial arts.

# CHAMINADE UNIVERSITY OF HONOLULU
3140 Waialae Avenue
Honolulu, HI 96816-1578
**Contact:** Skip Lee, Director Accelerated Undergraduate Program
**Phone:** 808-735-4851
**Fax:** 808-735-4766
**Web:** http://www.chaminade.edu/
**E-mail:** slee@chaminade.edu

**ACCREDITATION:** Western Association of Schools and Colleges
**INSTITUTIONALLY ADMINISTERED FINANCIAL AID:** No

### DEGREE OR CERTIFICATE PROGRAMS OFFERED
Programs offered do not lead to a degree or other formal award.

### NON-DEGREE-RELATED COURSE TOPICS OFFERED
**Undergraduate**—English composition; English creative writing; English language and literature, general; anthropology; business administration and management; communications, general; criminal justice and corrections; dramatic/theater arts and stagecraft; education, general; finance, general; history; mathematics; music; philosophy; philosophy and religion; physics; psychology; religion/religious studies.
**Graduate**—business administration and management; education, general.

# CHAMPLAIN COLLEGE
## Continuing Education Division
Champlain College OnLine, 163 South Willard Street
Burlington, VT 05401
**Contact:** Colleen Long, Associate Director
**Phone:** 802-865-6409
**Fax:** 802-865-6447
**Web:** http://www.champlain.edu/
**E-mail:** online@champlain.edu

**ACCREDITATION:** New England Association of Schools and Colleges
**INSTITUTIONALLY ADMINISTERED FINANCIAL AID:** Yes

### DEGREE OR CERTIFICATE PROGRAMS OFFERED
**Undergraduate**—*AS:* Accounting; Business; E-Business and Commerce; Global Networks and Telecommunications; International Business; Management; Software Development; Web Site Development and Management. *BS:* Computer Information Systems; Professional Studies; Software Engineering. *Certificate:* Accounting; Business; E-Business and Commerce; Global Networks and Telecommunications; International Business; Management; Software Development; Web Site Development and Management.

### NON-DEGREE-RELATED COURSE TOPICS OFFERED
**Undergraduate**—English composition; English creative writing; English language and literature, general; accounting; advertising; business; business administration and management; business communications; communications, general; communications, other; computer and information sciences, general; computer and information sciences, other; computer programming; computer software and media applications; computer systems networking and telecommunications; computer/information technology administration and management; economics; entrepreneurship;

financial management and services; geography; history; human resources management; international business; internet and world wide web; liberal arts and sciences, general studies and humanities; mathematics; mathematics and computer science; professional studies; psychology; sociology; telecommunications.

See full description on page 320.

# CHAPMAN UNIVERSITY
## Department of Distance Learning

1 University Drive
Orange, CA 92866
**Contact:** Dr. Gary A. Berg, Director of Extended Education
**Phone:** 714-532-6049
**Fax:** 714-532-6049
**Web:** http://www.chapman.edu
**E-mail:** gberg@chapman.edu

**ACCREDITATION:** Western Association of Schools and Colleges
**INSTITUTIONALLY ADMINISTERED FINANCIAL AID:** Yes

eCollege.com   www.ecollege.com

### DEGREE OR CERTIFICATE PROGRAMS OFFERED
Programs offered do not lead to a degree or other formal award.

### NON-DEGREE-RELATED COURSE TOPICS OFFERED
**Undergraduate**—film/video and photographic arts; history; mathematics.
**Non-credit**—business; computer science; education, general.

# CHARTER OAK STATE COLLEGE

55 Paul J. Manafort Drive
New Britain, CT 06053-2142
**Contact:** Susan Israel, Assistant Director of Academic Programs
**Phone:** 860-832-3800
**Fax:** 860-832-3999
**Web:** http://www.cosc.edu/
**E-mail:** sisrael@charteroak.edu

**ACCREDITATION:** New England Association of Schools and Colleges
**INSTITUTIONALLY ADMINISTERED FINANCIAL AID:** Yes

### DEGREE OR CERTIFICATE PROGRAMS OFFERED
**Undergraduate**—*AA:* General Studies. *AS:* General Studies. *BA:* General Studies. *BS:* General Studies.

### NON-DEGREE-RELATED COURSE TOPICS OFFERED
**Undergraduate**—English composition; English language and literature, general; anthropology; art history, criticism and conservation; biology, general; business; criminal justice and corrections; economics; film/video and photographic arts; geography; history; journalism and mass communication, other; mathematics; nursing; philosophy; political science and government; psychology; social sciences, general; sociology.
**Non-credit**—nursing.

See full description on page 322.

# CHATTANOOGA STATE TECHNICAL COMMUNITY COLLEGE
## Distance Learning Program

Amnicola Highway
Chattanooga, TN 37406-1097
**Contact:** Richard Seehuus, Associate Dean
**Phone:** 423-697-4408
**Fax:** 423-697-4479
**Web:** http://de.cstcc.cc.tn.us/
**E-mail:** seehuus@cstcc.cc.tn.us

**ACCREDITATION:** Southern Association of Colleges and Schools
**INSTITUTIONALLY ADMINISTERED FINANCIAL AID:** Yes

### DEGREE OR CERTIFICATE PROGRAMS OFFERED
Programs offered do not lead to a degree or other formal award.

### NON-DEGREE-RELATED COURSE TOPICS OFFERED
**Undergraduate**—English composition; English technical and business writing; biology, general; business; business administration and management; developmental and child psychology; fine arts and art studies; fire science/firefighting; geography; health and medical administrative services; health and medical assistants; health and medical preparatory programs; health professions and related sciences, other; history; liberal arts and sciences, general studies and humanities; mathematical statistics; mathematics; miscellaneous health professions; philosophy and religion; psychology; sociology; speech and rhetorical studies.

# CHESAPEAKE COLLEGE

1000 College Circle
Wye Mills, MD 21679
**Contact:** Mary Celeste Alexander, Coordinator
**Phone:** 410-822-5400 Ext. 263
**Fax:** 410-827-7057
**Web:** http://www.chesapeake.edu/
**E-mail:** mcalexander@chesapeake.edu

**ACCREDITATION:** Middle States Association of Colleges and Schools

### DEGREE OR CERTIFICATE PROGRAMS OFFERED
Programs offered do not lead to a degree or other formal award.

### NON-DEGREE-RELATED COURSE TOPICS OFFERED
**Undergraduate**—accounting; business; computer and information sciences, general; criminal justice and corrections; health and medical laboratory technologies; human services; nursing; tourism and travel services marketing operations.

# CHRISTOPHER NEWPORT UNIVERSITY
## CNU Online

Smith Libran
Newport News, VA 23606
**Contact:** Catherine Doyle, Director of CNU Online

Phone: 757-594-7130
Fax: 757-594-7717
Web: http://www.cnuonline.cnu.edu
E-mail: doyle@cnu.edu

ACCREDITATION: Southern Association of Colleges and Schools

## DEGREE OR CERTIFICATE PROGRAMS OFFERED

Undergraduate—*BA:* Philosophy and Religious Studies. *BS:* Governmental Administration.

## NON-DEGREE-RELATED COURSE TOPICS OFFERED

Undergraduate—English composition; law and legal studies, other; mathematical statistics; sociology.

# CINCINNATI BIBLE COLLEGE AND SEMINARY
*Correspondence Department*
2700 Glenway Avenue
Cincinnati, OH 45204-3200
Contact: Mrs. Joni Walker, Administrative Assistant to the Registrar
Phone: 513-244-8170
Fax: 513-244-8140
Web: http://www.cincybible.edu/
E-mail: joni.walker@cincybible.edu

ACCREDITATION: Accrediting Association of Bible Colleges
INSTITUTIONALLY ADMINISTERED FINANCIAL AID: Yes

## DEGREE OR CERTIFICATE PROGRAMS OFFERED

Programs offered do not lead to a degree or other formal award.

## NON-DEGREE-RELATED COURSE TOPICS OFFERED

Undergraduate—bible/biblical studies; psychology, other; theological studies and religious vocations, other.

# CINCINNATI STATE TECHNICAL AND COMMUNITY COLLEGE
3520 Central Parkway
Cincinnati, OH 45223
Contact: Mr. William Russell, Dean of Enrollment and Student Services
Phone: 513-569-1640
Fax: 513-569-1544
Web: http://www.cinstate.cc.oh.us/
E-mail: russellb@cinstate.cc.oh.us

ACCREDITATION: North Central Association of Colleges and Schools
INSTITUTIONALLY ADMINISTERED FINANCIAL AID: Yes

eCollege.com *www.ecollege.com*

## DEGREE OR CERTIFICATE PROGRAMS OFFERED

Programs offered do not lead to a degree or other formal award.

## NON-DEGREE-RELATED COURSE TOPICS OFFERED

Undergraduate—English composition; English language and literature, general; English technical and business writing; accounting; administrative and secretarial services; business; business administration and management; business information and data processing services; computer and information sciences, general; computer software and media applications; computer/information technology administration and management; data entry/microcomputer applications; data processing technology; environmental control technologies; foreign languages and literatures; health and medical administrative services; health and medical assistants; horticulture services operations and management; information sciences and systems; liberal arts and sciences, general studies and humanities; mechanical engineering-related technologies; miscellaneous health professions; psychology; sociology.

# CITRUS COLLEGE
*Distance Education*
1000 West Foothill Boulevard
Glendora, CA 91741-1899
Contact: Ms. Terry Adams, Distance Education Secretary
Phone: 626-914-8831
Fax: 626-852-8080
Web: http://www.citruscollege.com/ace
E-mail: online@citrus.cc.ca.us

ACCREDITATION: Western Association of Schools and Colleges
INSTITUTIONALLY ADMINISTERED FINANCIAL AID: Yes

## DEGREE OR CERTIFICATE PROGRAMS OFFERED

Undergraduate—*AA:* Liberal Arts.

## NON-DEGREE-RELATED COURSE TOPICS OFFERED

Undergraduate—English composition; anthropology; biological and physical sciences; communications, general; history; journalism and mass communications; liberal arts and sciences, general studies and humanities; mathematics; sociology.

# CITY UNIVERSITY
*Distance Learning Operations*
919 Southwest Grady Way
Renton, WA 98055
Contact: Distance Learning and Online Advisor
Phone: 800-422-4898
Fax: 425-277-2437
Web: http://www.cityu.edu

ACCREDITATION: Northwest Association of Schools and Colleges

## DEGREE OR CERTIFICATE PROGRAMS OFFERED

Programs offered do not lead to a degree or other formal award.
See full description on page 324.

# CLACKAMAS COMMUNITY COLLEGE
*Learning Resources*
19600 South Molalla Avenue
Oregon City, OR 97045

**Contact:** Cynthia R. Andrews, Director
**Phone:** 503-657-6958 Ext. 2417
**Fax:** 503-655-8925
**Web:** http://www.clackamas.cc.or.us
**E-mail:** cyndia@clackamas.cc.or.us

**ACCREDITATION:** Northwest Association of Schools and Colleges

**INSTITUTIONALLY ADMINISTERED FINANCIAL AID:** Yes

## DEGREE OR CERTIFICATE PROGRAMS OFFERED
Programs offered do not lead to a degree or other formal award.

## NON-DEGREE-RELATED COURSE TOPICS OFFERED
**Undergraduate**—American (United States) history; English as a second language; English composition; English technical and business writing; European history; accounting; administrative and secretarial services; adult and continuing teacher education; anthropology; biology, general; business; business administration and management; business and personal services marketing operations; business communications; business information and data processing services; business management and administrative services, other; chemistry; communications, other; computer and information sciences, other; computer software and media applications; criminal justice and corrections; criminology; drafting; environmental control technologies; family and community studies; fine arts and art studies; foods and nutrition studies; health and physical education/fitness; marketing management and research; mathematics; philosophy; psychology; sociology; speech and rhetorical studies.

# CLARION UNIVERSITY OF PENNSYLVANIA
*Extended Studies and Distance Learning Department*
840 Wood Street
Clarion, PA 16214
**Contact:** Mrs. Lynne Fleisher, Administrative Assistant
**Phone:** 814-393-2778
**Fax:** 814-393-2779
**Web:** http://www.clarion.edu/academic/distance/index.shtml
**E-mail:** fleisher@clarion.edu

**ACCREDITATION:** Middle States Association of Colleges and Schools

**INSTITUTIONALLY ADMINISTERED FINANCIAL AID:** Yes

## DEGREE OR CERTIFICATE PROGRAMS OFFERED
**Undergraduate**—*AA:* Arts and Sciences.
**Graduate**—*MLS:* Library Science. *MSN:* Family Nurse Practitioner.

## NON-DEGREE-RELATED COURSE TOPICS OFFERED
**Undergraduate**—communications, general; education, other; library science/librarianship; nursing; real estate.
**Graduate**—education, general; library science/librarianship.
**Non-credit**—real estate.

# CLARKE COLLEGE
1550 Clarke Drive
Dubuque, IA 52001

**Contact:** Shayne Labudda, Director of Adult Education and Time Saver Programs
**Phone:** 563-588-6354
**Fax:** 563-588-6789
**Web:** http://www.clarke.edu/
**E-mail:** info@clarke.edu

**ACCREDITATION:** North Central Association of Colleges and Schools

**INSTITUTIONALLY ADMINISTERED FINANCIAL AID:** Yes

## DEGREE OR CERTIFICATE PROGRAMS OFFERED
Programs offered do not lead to a degree or other formal award.

# CLARKSON COLLEGE
*Office of Distance Education*
101 South 42nd Street
Omaha, NE 68131
**Contact:** Admissions
**Phone:** 800-647-5500
**Fax:** 402-552-6019
**Web:** http://www.clarksoncollege.edu
**E-mail:** admiss@clarksoncollege.edu

**ACCREDITATION:** North Central Association of Colleges and Schools

**INSTITUTIONALLY ADMINISTERED FINANCIAL AID:** Yes

## DEGREE OR CERTIFICATE PROGRAMS OFFERED
**Undergraduate**—*BS:* Health Care Business; Medical Imaging. *BSN:* Nursing.
**Graduate**—*MSN:* Nursing, Major in Administration; Nursing, Major in Education; Nursing, Major in Family Nurse Practitioning. *PMC:* Family Nurse Practitioner.

## NON-DEGREE-RELATED COURSE TOPICS OFFERED
**Undergraduate**—English composition; accounting; business administration and management; developmental and child psychology; economics; fine arts and art studies; health professions and related sciences, other; liberal arts and sciences, general studies and humanities; mathematics; philosophy; political science and government; social psychology; sociology.
**Graduate**—business administration and management; health professions and related sciences, other; mathematics.

See full description on page 326.

# CLEMSON UNIVERSITY
*Office of Off-Campus, Distance, and Continuing Education*
PO Box 912
Clemson, SC 29633-0912
**Contact:** Dr. Barbara Hoskins, Assistant Vice Provost
**Phone:** 888-253-6766
**Fax:** 864-656-3997
**Web:** http://www.clemson.edu/odce

**E-mail:** barbara@clemson.edu

**ACCREDITATION:** Southern Association of Colleges and Schools

**INSTITUTIONALLY ADMINISTERED FINANCIAL AID:** Yes

### DEGREE OR CERTIFICATE PROGRAMS OFFERED

**Undergraduate—*BSN:*** Nursing.
**Graduate—*MCSM:*** Construction Science and Management. *MS:* Human Resource Development. *MSEE:* Electrical Engineering. *MSN:* Nursing.

### NON-DEGREE-RELATED COURSE TOPICS OFFERED

**Undergraduate—**forestry, general.
**Graduate—**education administration and supervision; foods and nutrition studies; special education.

# CLEVELAND COLLEGE OF JEWISH STUDIES

26500 Shaker Boulevard
Beachwood, OH 44122
**Contact:** Ms. Linda L. Rosen, Director of Student Services
**Phone:** 216-464-4050 Ext. 101
**Fax:** 216-464-5827
**Web:** http://www.ccjs.edu/
**E-mail:** lrosen@ccjs.edu

**ACCREDITATION:** North Central Association of Colleges and Schools

**INSTITUTIONALLY ADMINISTERED FINANCIAL AID:** No

### DEGREE OR CERTIFICATE PROGRAMS OFFERED

**Graduate—*MCP/MPH:*** Education Administration; Hebrew language and literature; Jewish Studies.

### NON-DEGREE-RELATED COURSE TOPICS OFFERED

**Undergraduate—**Hebrew language and literature; Jewish/Judaic studies.
**Graduate—**Hebrew language and literature; Jewish/Judaic studies.
**Non-credit—**Hebrew language and literature; Jewish/Judaic studies.

# CLEVELAND INSTITUTE OF ELECTRONICS

1776 East 7th Street
Cleveland, OH 44114
**Contact:** World College
**Phone:** 800-CIE-OHIO
**Web:** http://www.cie-wc.edu/WorldCollege/Main.html
**E-mail:** info@cie-wc.edu

**ACCREDITATION:** Distance Education and Training Council

### DEGREE OR CERTIFICATE PROGRAMS OFFERED

**Undergraduate—*BST:*** Electronics Engineering Technology.

### NON-DEGREE-RELATED COURSE TOPICS OFFERED

**Undergraduate—**communications, general; computer engineering; electrical and electronic engineering-related technology; engineering, general; social sciences and history, other.

# CLEVELAND STATE COMMUNITY COLLEGE

*Instructional Computer Technology Center of Emphasis*

3535 Adkisson Drive
Cleveland, TN 37312
**Contact:** Dr. David Watts, Dean of Planning and Computer Technology
**Phone:** 423-478-6204
**Fax:** 423-478-6255
**Web:** http://www.clscc.cc.tn.us
**E-mail:** dwatts@clscc.cc.tn.us

**ACCREDITATION:** Southern Association of Colleges and Schools

**INSTITUTIONALLY ADMINISTERED FINANCIAL AID:** Yes

### DEGREE OR CERTIFICATE PROGRAMS OFFERED

**Programs offered do not lead to a degree or other formal award.**

### NON-DEGREE-RELATED COURSE TOPICS OFFERED

**Undergraduate—**accounting; business; computer and information sciences, general; history; music; religion/religious studies; sociology; speech and rhetorical studies.

# CLOVIS COMMUNITY COLLEGE

417 Schepps Boulevard
Clovis, NM 88101
**Contact:** Ms. Susan M. Veronikas, Educational Technologist
**Phone:** 505-769-4903
**Web:** http://www.clovis.cc.nm.us/
**E-mail:** susan.veronikas@clovis.cc.nm.us

**ACCREDITATION:** North Central Association of Colleges and Schools

**INSTITUTIONALLY ADMINISTERED FINANCIAL AID:** Yes

eCollege.com  *www.ecollege.com*

### DEGREE OR CERTIFICATE PROGRAMS OFFERED

**Undergraduate—*AA:*** Liberal Arts. *AAS:* Criminal Justice.

### NON-DEGREE-RELATED COURSE TOPICS OFFERED

**Undergraduate—**American (United States) history; English composition; Spanish language and literature; art history, criticism and conservation; bible/biblical studies; biology, general; computer and information sciences, general; criminal justice and corrections; developmental and child psychology; economics; mathematics; mathematics, other; sociology.

# COASTAL CAROLINA COMMUNITY COLLEGE

444 Western Boulevard
Jacksonville, NC 28546
**Contact:** Mr. Michael R. Dodge, Dean of Information Resources
**Phone:** 910-938-6148
**Web:** http://www.coastal.cc.nc.us

**E-mail:** dodgem@coastal.cc.nc.us

**ACCREDITATION:** Southern Association of Colleges and Schools

**INSTITUTIONALLY ADMINISTERED FINANCIAL AID:** Yes

## DEGREE OR CERTIFICATE PROGRAMS OFFERED

**Programs offered do not lead to a degree or other formal award.**

## NON-DEGREE-RELATED COURSE TOPICS OFFERED

**Undergraduate**—English composition; business administration and management; fire services administration; information sciences and systems; marketing operations/marketing and distribution, other; psychology; sociology.

**Non-credit**—business; business information and data processing services; business management and administrative services, other; computer software and media applications; entrepreneurship; internet and world wide web.

# COASTLINE COMMUNITY COLLEGE

## *Distance Learning Department*

11460 Warner Avenue
Fountain Valley, CA 92708
**Contact:** Distance Learning Department
**Phone:** 714-241-6216
**Web:** http://pelican.ccc.cccd.edu/~dl
**E-mail:** itv@mail.ccc.cccd.edu

**ACCREDITATION:** Western Association of Schools and Colleges

**INSTITUTIONALLY ADMINISTERED FINANCIAL AID:** Yes

## DEGREE OR CERTIFICATE PROGRAMS OFFERED

**Undergraduate**—*AA:* Accounting; Business; Fine and Applied Arts; Humanities. *Certificate:* Cognitive Retraining.

## NON-DEGREE-RELATED COURSE TOPICS OFFERED

**Undergraduate**—American (United States) history; English composition; English language and literature, general; French language and literature; Spanish language and literature; administrative and secretarial services; anatomy; anthropology; astronomy; biological sciences/life sciences, other; biology, general; business; business administration and management; business and personal services marketing operations; business communications; business information and data processing services; chemistry; communications, general; communications, other; computer and information sciences, general; computer programming; computer software and media applications; construction/building technology; developmental and child psychology; ecology; economics; electrical and electronic engineering-related technology; foreign languages and literatures; foreign languages and literatures, other; gerontology; health and medical administrative services; history; human services; information sciences and systems; international business; internet and world wide web; journalism and mass communication, other; liberal arts and sciences, general studies and humanities; library science, other; marketing operations/marketing and distribution, other; mathematical statistics; mathematics; mathematics, other; oceanography; paralegal/legal assistant; philosophy; philosophy and religion; political science and government; psychology; social sciences and history, other; sociology; special education; visual and performing arts.

**Non-credit**—English as a second language.

# COLLEGE FOR FINANCIAL PLANNING

6161 South Syracuse Way
Greenwood Village , CO 80111
**Contact:** Ms. Debby Campbell, Marketing Coordinator
**Phone:** 303-220-4892
**Fax:** 303-220-4941
**Web:** http://www.fp.edu/
**E-mail:** debby.campbell@apollogrp.edu

**ACCREDITATION:** Distance Education and Training Council

**INSTITUTIONALLY ADMINISTERED FINANCIAL AID:** Yes

## DEGREE OR CERTIFICATE PROGRAMS OFFERED

**Graduate**—*MS:* Personal Financial Planning.

## NON-DEGREE-RELATED COURSE TOPICS OFFERED

**Undergraduate**—financial management and services; investments and securities.

**Graduate**—finance, general; financial management and services; investments and securities.

**Non-credit**—accounting; financial management and services.

# COLLEGE FOR PROFESSIONAL STUDIES

## *Distance Education*

College for Professional Studies, 1801 Clint Moore Road, Suite 215
Boca Raton, FL 33487
**Contact:** Ms. Linda Lee, Director of Admissions
**Phone:** 800-669-2555
**Fax:** 561-988-5559
**Web:** http://www.kaplancollege.edu
**E-mail:** infocps@kaplancollege.edu

**ACCREDITATION:** Distance Education and Training Council

**INSTITUTIONALLY ADMINISTERED FINANCIAL AID:** No

## DEGREE OR CERTIFICATE PROGRAMS OFFERED

**Undergraduate**—*AD:* Criminal Justice Specialized Associate Degree Program; Paralegal Specialized Associate Degree. *BS:* Criminal Justice; Paralegal Studies. *Certificate:* Law Office Management Specialty; Legal Research Specialty; Litigation Assistantship Specialty; Real Estate Law Specialty. *Diploma:* Criminal Justice Diploma Program; Legal Nurse Consultant Paralegal Diploma Program; Paralegal Diploma Program.

## NON-DEGREE-RELATED COURSE TOPICS OFFERED

**Undergraduate**—criminal justice and corrections; law and legal studies.

---

### Special Note

College for Professional Studies (CPS), founded in 1976, is a distance education institution offering diplomas, certificates, and degrees. CPS, Kaplan College, and Concord University School of Law, the nation's first online law school, comprise the Kaplan Colleges, the distance education division of Kaplan, Inc., a wholly owned subsidiary of the Washington Post Company. CPS is licensed by the State of Florida Board of Independent Colleges and Universities and Board of Nonpublic Career Education and is accredited by the Accrediting Commission of the Distance Education and Training Council. CPS consists of 3 academic divisions—the School of Paralegal Studies, the School of Criminal Justice, and the School of Legal Nurse Consulting.

Applicants may request an evaluation of their past academic, life, and work experience for the purpose of advanced placement in the degree programs. This evaluation is conducted free of charge and, based upon its outcome, applicants may be awarded both academic and tuition credit. The all-inclusive tuition, which includes all textbooks and materials for the degree programs prior to any appropriate reductions for transfer credit, is as follows: paralegal specialized associate degree, $7500; Bachelor of Science degree program in paralegal studies, $15,995; criminal justice specialized associate degree program, $8995; and Bachelor of Science degree program in criminal justice, $19,995. CPS provides flexible financing options and is approved by the US Department of Defense/DANTES and US Department of Veterans Affairs for all programs. For more information, students should contact Admissions at 800-669-2555 (toll-free), send e-mail to infocps@kaplancollege.edu, or visit the Web site at http://www.kaplancollege.edu.

# COLLEGE OF DUPAGE

## Alternative Learning Division

Center for Independent Learning, 425 22nd Street
Glen Ellyn, IL 60137-6599
**Contact:** Ron Schiesz, Counselor, Alternative Learning Program
**Phone:** 630-942-2130 Ext. 3326
**Fax:** 630-942-3749
**Web:** http://www.cod.edu/cil
**E-mail:** schiesz@cdnet.cod.edu

**ACCREDITATION:** North Central Association of Colleges and Schools
**INSTITUTIONALLY ADMINISTERED FINANCIAL AID:** Yes

### DEGREE OR CERTIFICATE PROGRAMS OFFERED
Programs offered do not lead to a degree or other formal award.

### NON-DEGREE-RELATED COURSE TOPICS OFFERED
**Undergraduate**—American (United States) history; English as a second language; English composition; Spanish language and literature; accounting; anthropology; biology, general; business administration and management; communications, general; computer programming; computer software and media applications; computer systems networking and telecommunications; criminal justice and corrections; developmental and child psychology; earth and planetary sciences; economics; educational psychology; history; journalism and mass communications; liberal arts and sciences, general studies and humanities; marketing operations/marketing and distribution, other; mathematics; music; philosophy and religion; physics; psychology; social psychology; social sciences and history, other; social sciences, general; sociology.

# COLLEGE OF MOUNT ST. JOSEPH

5701 Delhi Ave
Cincinnati, OH 45233

**Contact:** Ms. Peggy Minnich, Director of Admissions
**Phone:** 513-244-4814
**Web:** http://www.msj.edu/
**E-mail:** peggy_minnich@mail.msj.edu

**ACCREDITATION:** North Central Association of Colleges and Schools
**INSTITUTIONALLY ADMINISTERED FINANCIAL AID:** Yes

### DEGREE OR CERTIFICATE PROGRAMS OFFERED
Programs offered do not lead to a degree or other formal award.

### NON-DEGREE-RELATED COURSE TOPICS OFFERED
**Undergraduate**—biology, general; paralegal/legal assistant; religion/religious studies; social psychology.
**Non-credit**—religion/religious studies.
See full description on page 328.

# THE COLLEGE OF ST. SCHOLASTICA

## Graduate Studies

1200 Kenwood Avenue
Duluth, MN 55811
**Contact:** Mrs. Debra A. Bekkering, Graduate Studies Administrative Assistant
**Phone:** 218-723-6285
**Fax:** 218-723-5991
**Web:** http://www.css.edu/grad
**E-mail:** gradstudies@css.edu

**ACCREDITATION:** North Central Association of Colleges and Schools
**INSTITUTIONALLY ADMINISTERED FINANCIAL AID:** Yes

### DEGREE OR CERTIFICATE PROGRAMS OFFERED
**Graduate**—*MEd:* Curriculum and Instruction; Educational Media and Technology.

### NON-DEGREE-RELATED COURSE TOPICS OFFERED
**Undergraduate**—biology, general; economics; psychology.
**Graduate**—curriculum and instruction; educational/instructional media design; health and medical administrative services; nursing.

# COLLEGE OF SAN MATEO

1700 West Hillsdale Boulevard
San Mateo, CA 94402-3784
**Contact:** Gloria Bianchi, Distance Learning Coordinator
**Phone:** 650-524-6933
**Fax:** 650-574-6345
**Web:** http://gocsm.net
**E-mail:** bianchig@smccd.net

**ACCREDITATION:** Western Association of Schools and Colleges
**INSTITUTIONALLY ADMINISTERED FINANCIAL AID:** Yes

## DEGREE OR CERTIFICATE PROGRAMS OFFERED

**Undergraduate—AA:** Liberal Studies; Natural Sciences, Social Science, and Humanities.

## NON-DEGREE-RELATED COURSE TOPICS OFFERED

**Undergraduate—**Chinese language and literature; English as a second language; English composition; English creative writing; European history; French language and literature; Italian language and literature; Spanish language and literature; anthropology; business marketing and marketing management; family and marriage counseling; film/cinema studies; law and legal studies, other; philosophy and religion; social psychology; sociology.

# COLLEGE OF SOUTHERN MARYLAND

## Distance Learning Department

8730 Mitchell Road, PO Box 910
La Plata, MD 20646-0910
**Contact:** Paul Toscano, Distance Learning Coordinator
**Phone:** 301-934-2251
**Fax:** 301-934-7699
**Web:** http://www.csm.cc.md.us/
**E-mail:** pault@csm.cc.md.us

**ACCREDITATION:** Middle States Association of Colleges and Schools
**INSTITUTIONALLY ADMINISTERED FINANCIAL AID:** Yes

## DEGREE OR CERTIFICATE PROGRAMS OFFERED

**Undergraduate—AA:** Arts and Sciences; Arts and Sciences: Arts and Humanities; General Studies. **AAS:** Information Services Technology; Management Development. **AS:** Business Administration. **Certificate:** Accounting: Advanced; Accounting: Basic; Computer Skills for Managers; Information Services Technology; Web Developer.

## NON-DEGREE-RELATED COURSE TOPICS OFFERED

**Undergraduate—**English composition; English creative writing; English technical and business writing; Spanish language and literature; accounting; art history, criticism and conservation; astronomy; biology, general; business; business communications; business marketing and marketing management; child care and guidance workers and managers; communications, general; computer systems analysis; computer systems networking and telecommunications; criminal justice and corrections; economics; education, other; educational psychology; geography; health and physical education/fitness; history; human resources management; information sciences and systems; international business; law and legal studies, other; mathematical statistics; mathematics; mathematics, other; oceanography; philosophy; philosophy and religion; physics; political science and government; psychology; sociology.
**Non-credit—**computer/information technology administration and management; education, general; health professions and related sciences, other; nursing.

# COLLEGE OF THE ALBEMARLE

## Distance Education

PO Box 2327
Elizabeth City, NC 27906-2327

**Contact:** Jeff Zeigler, Distance Education Coordinator
**Phone:** 252-335-0821 Ext. 2313
**Fax:** 252-337-6710
**Web:** http://www.albemarle.cc.nc.us
**E-mail:** jzeigler@albemarle.cc.nc.us

**ACCREDITATION:** Southern Association of Colleges and Schools

## DEGREE OR CERTIFICATE PROGRAMS OFFERED

**Undergraduate—AAS:** Business Administration.

## NON-DEGREE-RELATED COURSE TOPICS OFFERED

**Undergraduate—**English creative writing; European history; accounting; advertising; art history, criticism and conservation; aviation and airway science; business marketing and marketing management; education, other; law and legal studies, other; mathematics, other; social psychology; sociology.

# COLLEGE OF THE CANYONS

## Learning Resources

26455 Rockwell Canyon Road
Santa Clarita, CA 91355
**Contact:** Ms. Renee Drake, Library and Media Technician II
**Phone:** 661-362-3600
**Fax:** 661-259-3421
**Web:** http://www.coc.cc.ca.us
**E-mail:** drake_r@mail.coc.cc.ca.us

**ACCREDITATION:** Western Association of Schools and Colleges
**INSTITUTIONALLY ADMINISTERED FINANCIAL AID:** Yes

## DEGREE OR CERTIFICATE PROGRAMS OFFERED

Programs offered do not lead to a degree or other formal award.

## NON-DEGREE-RELATED COURSE TOPICS OFFERED

**Undergraduate—**English composition; administrative and secretarial services; anthropology; astronomy; business communications; chemistry; computer and information sciences, general; computer programming; developmental and child psychology; economics; history; hospitality services management; music; philosophy; political science and government; psychology; sociology.

# COLLEGE OF THE SOUTHWEST

6610 Lovington Highway
Hobbs, NM 88240
**Contact:** Glenna Ohaver, Director of Educational Services
**Phone:** 505-392-6561
**Fax:** 505-392-6006
**Web:** http://www.csw.edu/
**E-mail:** gohaver@csw.edu

**ACCREDITATION:** North Central Association of Colleges and Schools
**INSTITUTIONALLY ADMINISTERED FINANCIAL AID:** Yes

## DEGREE OR CERTIFICATE PROGRAMS OFFERED

**Graduate—MSE:** Curriculum and Instruction; Educational Administration and Counseling.

## NON-DEGREE-RELATED COURSE TOPICS OFFERED

**Undergraduate**—English as a second language; English composition; English creative writing; accounting; advertising; biology, general; criminal justice and corrections; developmental and child psychology; educational psychology; industrial and organizational psychology; social psychology; sociology.

**Graduate**—educational psychology.

# COLORADO CHRISTIAN UNIVERSITY

## *Academic Technologies Group*

180 South Garrison Street
Lakewood, CO 80226
**Contact:** Jan Coombs, Technical Assistant
**Phone:** 303-963-3382
**Fax:** 303-963-3381
**Web:** http://www.ccuonline.org
**E-mail:** jcoombs@ccu.edu

**ACCREDITATION:** North Central Association of Colleges and Schools

**INSTITUTIONALLY ADMINISTERED FINANCIAL AID:** Yes

eCollege.com *www.ecollege.com*

## DEGREE OR CERTIFICATE PROGRAMS OFFERED

**Graduate**—*MBA:* Business Administration.

## NON-DEGREE-RELATED COURSE TOPICS OFFERED

**Undergraduate**—business administration and management; business communications; computer and information sciences, general; history; mathematics.

**Graduate**—accounting; business marketing and marketing management.

# COLORADO COMMUNITY COLLEGE ONLINE

## *CCC Online*

8880 East 10th Place
Denver, CO 80230
**Contact:** John Schmahl, Director of Student Services
**Phone:** 303-365-8807
**Fax:** 303-365-7616
**Web:** http://ccconline.org
**E-mail:** john.schmahl@heat.ccoes.edu

**ACCREDITATION:** Accreditation varies across member institutions

**INSTITUTIONALLY ADMINISTERED FINANCIAL AID:** Yes

eCollege.com *www.ecollege.com*

## DEGREE OR CERTIFICATE PROGRAMS OFFERED

**Undergraduate**—*AA:* General Education. *AAS:* Agricultural Business; Business; Computer Networking; Construction Technology—Construction Electrician emphasis; Convergent Technology; Emergency Management and Planning; Library Technician; Occupational Safety and Health Technology.

## NON-DEGREE-RELATED COURSE TOPICS OFFERED

**Undergraduate**—English composition; English creative writing; English language and literature, general; English technical and business writing; accounting; agricultural business and management; agricultural business and production, other; anthropology; astronomy; biological and physical sciences; biology, general; business; business marketing and marketing management; chemistry; communications technologies; comparative literature; computer and information sciences, general; computer science; computer systems networking and telecommunications; computer/information technology administration and management; construction/building technology; criminal justice and corrections; developmental and child psychology; fine arts and art studies; foreign languages and literatures; geography; history; human resources management; information sciences and systems; liberal arts and sciences, general studies and humanities; library assistant; library science, other; marketing management and research; mathematical statistics; mathematics; mathematics and computer science; mathematics, other; music; philosophy; physical sciences, general; physics; political science and government; psychology; public administration; quality control and safety technologies; social sciences and history, other; social sciences, general; sociology; speech and rhetorical studies; telecommunications; tourism and travel services marketing operations.

See full description on page 330.

# COLORADO ELECTRONIC COMMUNITY COLLEGE

9075 East Lowry Boulevard
Denver, CO 80230
**Contact:** John Schmahl, Director of Student Services
**Phone:** 303-365-8807
**Fax:** 303-365-7616
**Web:** http://www.ccconline.org
**E-mail:** john.schmahl@heat.cccoes.edu

**ACCREDITATION:** Accreditation varies across member institutions

**INSTITUTIONALLY ADMINISTERED FINANCIAL AID:** Yes

## DEGREE OR CERTIFICATE PROGRAMS OFFERED

**Undergraduate**—*AA:* Liberal Arts; Public Administration. *AAS:* Business; Construction Technology; Convergent Technologies; Library Technician. *AD:* Accounting; Computer Networking; Criminal Justice; Emergency Management; Occupational Safety and Health.

## NON-DEGREE-RELATED COURSE TOPICS OFFERED

**Undergraduate**—English composition; English language and literature, general; anthropology; biology, general; business; chemistry; computer and information sciences, general; computer science; computer systems networking and telecommunications; criminal justice and corrections; developmental and child psychology; foreign languages and literatures, other; geography; history; history and philosophy of science and technology; journalism and mass communication, other; library science, other; marketing management and research; mathematical statistics; mathematics; mathematics, other; philosophy; philosophy and religion; political science and government; sociology; speech and rhetorical studies.

**Non-credit**—tourism and travel services marketing operations.

# COLORADO NORTHWESTERN COMMUNITY COLLEGE

## Distance Learning Department

500 Kennedy Drive
Rangely, CO 81648
**Contact:** Ken Langston, Director of Distance Learning
**Phone:** 970-675-3273
**Fax:** 970-675-3291
**Web:** http://www.cncc.cccoes.edu
**E-mail:** ken.langston@cncc.cccoes.edu

**ACCREDITATION:** North Central Association of Colleges and Schools

**INSTITUTIONALLY ADMINISTERED FINANCIAL AID:** Yes

eCollege.com  www.ecollege.com

### DEGREE OR CERTIFICATE PROGRAMS OFFERED

Undergraduate—*AS:* Criminal Justice.

### NON-DEGREE-RELATED COURSE TOPICS OFFERED

**Undergraduate**—American (United States) history; English composition; Spanish language and literature; accounting; anthropology; art history, criticism and conservation; biology, general; developmental and child psychology; educational psychology; mathematical statistics; mathematics, other; sociology.

# COLORADO STATE UNIVERSITY

## Division of Educational Outreach

Spruce Hall
Ft Collins, CO 80523-1040
**Contact:** Cherilynn Castleman, Director of Marketing
**Phone:** 970-491-5288
**Fax:** 970-491-7886
**Web:** http://www.learn.colostate.edu
**E-mail:** ccastleman@learn.colostate.edu

**ACCREDITATION:** North Central Association of Colleges and Schools

**INSTITUTIONALLY ADMINISTERED FINANCIAL AID:** Yes

### DEGREE OR CERTIFICATE PROGRAMS OFFERED

**Undergraduate**—*BA:* Liberal Arts—Social Science. *BS:* Fire Science Management and Training. *Certificate:* Gerontology; Natural Resources and the Environment.
**Graduate**—*Graduate Certificate:* Post-Secondary Teaching. *MAg:* Agricultural Sciences. *MBA:* Business Administration. *ME:* Electrical and Computer Engineering. *MEd:* Education (Human Resource Development). *MS:* Bioresources and Agricultural Engineering; Civil Engineering; Computer Science; Electrical Engineering; Engineering Management; Environmental Engineering; Industrial Engineering; Mechanical Engineering; Statistics; Systems Engineering.
**Postgraduate and doctoral**—*PhD:* Electrical Engineering; Industrial Engineering; Mechanical Engineering; Systems Engineering.

### NON-DEGREE-RELATED COURSE TOPICS OFFERED

**Undergraduate**—agriculture/agricultural sciences; animal sciences; computer science; consumer and homemaking education; developmental and child psychology; economics; educational psychology; foods and nutrition studies; history; horticulture services operations and management; individual and family development studies; psychology; sociology.
**Graduate**—business marketing and marketing management; chemical engineering; electrical, electronics and communication engineering; engineering mechanics; engineering/industrial management; environmental/environmental health engineering; finance, general; industrial/manufacturing engineering; mechanical engineering.
**Non-credit**—accounting; business; computer programming; economics; law and legal studies; music; tourism and travel services marketing operations.

**See full description on page 332.**

# COLUMBIA BASIN COLLEGE

2600 North 20th Avenue
Pasco, WA 99301
**Contact:** Deborah Meadows, Dean for Business and Social Science
**Phone:** 509-547-0511 Ext. 2373
**Fax:** 509-546-0401
**Web:** http://www.cbc2.org
**E-mail:** dmeadows@ctc.edu

**ACCREDITATION:** Northwest Association of Schools and Colleges

**INSTITUTIONALLY ADMINISTERED FINANCIAL AID:** Yes

### DEGREE OR CERTIFICATE PROGRAMS OFFERED

Programs offered do not lead to a degree or other formal award.

### NON-DEGREE-RELATED COURSE TOPICS OFFERED

**Undergraduate**—English composition; English creative writing; accounting; anthropology; art history, criticism and conservation; business; business administration and management; computer and information sciences, other; computer programming; computer science; economics; film/cinema studies; geography; history; internet and world wide web; mathematics, other; psychology; sociology.
**Non-credit**—business; health professions and related sciences, other; real estate.

# COLUMBIA COLLEGE

## Evening College

1301 Columbia College Drive
Columbia, SC 29203
**Contact:** Dr. Anne M. McCulloch, Dean of the Evening College and Graduate School
**Phone:** 803-786-3788
**Fax:** 803-786-3393
**Web:** http://www.columbiacollegesc.edu
**E-mail:** amcculloch@colacoll.edu

**ACCREDITATION:** Southern Association of Colleges and Schools

**INSTITUTIONALLY ADMINISTERED FINANCIAL AID:** Yes

eCollege.com  www.ecollege.com

### DEGREE OR CERTIFICATE PROGRAMS OFFERED

Programs offered do not lead to a degree or other formal award.

## NON-DEGREE-RELATED COURSE TOPICS OFFERED

**Undergraduate**—English language and literature, general; art history, criticism and conservation; computer and information sciences, general; dance; health and physical education/fitness; history; law and legal studies; liberal arts and sciences, general studies and humanities; political science and government; religion/religious studies; women's studies.
**Graduate**—education, other; multi/interdisciplinary studies, other.

# COLUMBIA COLLEGE

Distance Education Department, 1001 Rogers Street
Columbia, MO 65216
**Contact:** Ms. Sara Farris, Operations Manager
**Phone:** 573-875-7459
**Fax:** 573-875-7444
**Web:** http://www.ccis.edu/departments/distanceeducation
**E-mail:** sbfarris@email.ccis.edu

**ACCREDITATION:** North Central Association of Colleges and Schools
**INSTITUTIONALLY ADMINISTERED FINANCIAL AID:** Yes

## DEGREE OR CERTIFICATE PROGRAMS OFFERED

Programs offered do not lead to a degree or other formal award.

## NON-DEGREE-RELATED COURSE TOPICS OFFERED

**Undergraduate**—American literature (United States); English literature (British and Commonwealth); accounting; biological sciences/life sciences, other; business administration and management; computer and information sciences, general; criminal justice and corrections; curriculum and instruction; education, general; enterprise management and operation; history; marketing operations/marketing and distribution, other; mathematics; mathematics and computer science; multi/interdisciplinary studies, other; philosophy and religion; political science and government; psychology; social sciences and history, other; social work; sociology.

# COLUMBIA INTERNATIONAL UNIVERSITY

*Columbia Extension*
PO Box 3122
Columbia, SC 29230-3122
**Contact:** Mrs. Joyce Burlingame, Secretary of Enrollment
**Phone:** 800-777-2227 Ext. 3710
**Fax:** 803-754-9119
**Web:** http://www.ciu.edu/
**E-mail:** extoff@ciu.edu

**ACCREDITATION:** Accrediting Association of Bible Colleges
**INSTITUTIONALLY ADMINISTERED FINANCIAL AID:** Yes

## DEGREE OR CERTIFICATE PROGRAMS OFFERED

Programs offered do not lead to a degree or other formal award.

## NON-DEGREE-RELATED COURSE TOPICS OFFERED

**Undergraduate**—bible/biblical studies; missions/missionary studies and missiology; theological and ministerial studies; theological studies and religious vocations, other.
**Graduate**—anthropology; bible/biblical studies; education, other; missions/missionary studies and missiology; religion/religious studies; theological and ministerial studies; theological studies and religious vocations, other.
**Non-credit**—anthropology; bible/biblical studies; educational psychology; missions/missionary studies and missiology; religion/religious studies; theological and ministerial studies; theological studies and religious vocations, other.

# COLUMBIA STATE COMMUNITY COLLEGE

*Division of Extended Services*
PO Box 1315
Columbia, TN 38402
**Contact:** Mike Shuler, Dean of Extended Services
**Phone:** 931-540-2750
**Fax:** 931-540-2796
**Web:** http://www.coscc.cc.tn.us
**E-mail:** shuler@coscc.cc.tn.us

**ACCREDITATION:** Southern Association of Colleges and Schools
**INSTITUTIONALLY ADMINISTERED FINANCIAL AID:** Yes

## DEGREE OR CERTIFICATE PROGRAMS OFFERED

**Undergraduate**—*AA:* General Studies (University Parallel). *AAS:* Information Technology. *AS:* General Studies (University Parallel).

## NON-DEGREE-RELATED COURSE TOPICS OFFERED

**Undergraduate**—English composition; English language and literature, general; business administration and management; data entry/microcomputer applications; economics; educational psychology; philosophy; psychology.

# COLUMBIA UNIVERSITY

*Columbia Video Network*
540 Mudd Building, MC 4719, 500 West 120th Street
New York, NY 10027
**Contact:** Kamal Hasan Basri, Associate Director
**Phone:** 212-854-6447
**Fax:** 212-854-2325
**Web:** http://www.cvn.columbia.edu
**E-mail:** info@cvn.columbia.edu

**ACCREDITATION:** Middle States Association of Colleges and Schools

## DEGREE OR CERTIFICATE PROGRAMS OFFERED

**Undergraduate**—*Certificate of Achievement:* Financial Engineering; Finite Element Method/Computational Fluid Dynamics; Genomic Engineering; Industrial Engineering; Information Systems; Intelligent Systems; Manufacturing Engineering; Materials Science and Engineering;

Multimedia Networking; Networking and Systems; New Media Engineering; Operations Research; Telecommunications; Wireless and Mobile Communications.
**Graduate—MS:** Computer Science; Earth and Environmental Engineering; Engineering and Management Systems; Materials Science and Engineering. **MSEE:** Electrical Engineering. **MSME:** Mechanical Engineering.
**Postgraduate and doctoral—PhD:** Computer Science; Electrical Engineering; Mechanical Engineering.

## NON-DEGREE-RELATED COURSE TOPICS OFFERED

**Undergraduate**—computer science.
**Graduate**—applied mathematics; business; civil engineering; computer science; electrical, electronics and communication engineering; engineering/industrial management; environmental/environmental health engineering; industrial/manufacturing engineering; journalism; materials science; mechanical engineering.
**Non-credit**—applied mathematics; business; civil engineering; computer science; electrical, electronics and communication engineering; engineering/industrial management; environmental/environmental health engineering; industrial/manufacturing engineering; journalism; materials science; mechanical engineering.

# COLUMBUS STATE COMMUNITY COLLEGE

*Department of Instructional Studies*
550 East Spring Street
Columbus, OH 43215
**Contact:** Department of Instructional Services
**Phone:** 800-621-6407
**Web:** http://www.cscc.edu/

**ACCREDITATION:** North Central Association of Colleges and Schools

## DEGREE OR CERTIFICATE PROGRAMS OFFERED

**Programs offered do not lead to a degree or other formal award.**

## Special Note

Columbus State Community College offers a variety of distance learning options through its Global Campus (http://global.cscc.edu), designed to meet the needs of working and nontraditional students. Global Campus utilizes a variety of technologies, including the Internet, electronic communication, computer technology, videoconferencing, and video-based programming. Global Campus enables students to choose from more than 140 Web-based courses, 25 interactive videoconferencing courses, and more than 40 video-based courses. Video-based courses are broadcast over local cable stations WOSU and Educable, or they can be rented for viewing at home by contacting the College bookstore (http://bookstore.cscc.edu). Proctored exams for out-of-state students can be arranged for most courses by notifying the instructor and contacting the College's Testing Center at 614-287-2478. Columbus State is a charter member of the Ohio Learning Network (OLN), a consortium of Ohio's colleges and universities that promotes the use of technology to enhance distance learning (http://www.oln.org). Columbus State is also a member of the Regional Learning Network (RLN), which is an agreement between Columbus State, Clark State, Edison State, and Southern State Community College to share the distance learning curriculum between institutions toward the completion of degree programs. For more information on Columbus State programs and services, contact 800-621-6407 (toll-free) or visit the Web site at http://www.cscc.edu.

# COLUMBUS STATE UNIVERSITY

*Instructional Technology Services*
4225 University Avenue
Columbus, GA 31907
**Contact:** Sandra K. Stratford, Instructional Technology Services Coordinator
**Phone:** 706-568-2043
**Fax:** 706-568-2459
**Web:** http://www.colstate.edu/
**E-mail:** stratford_sandra@colstate.edu

**ACCREDITATION:** Southern Association of Colleges and Schools

**INSTITUTIONALLY ADMINISTERED FINANCIAL AID:** Yes

eCollege.com  *www.ecollege.com*

## DEGREE OR CERTIFICATE PROGRAMS OFFERED

**Graduate—MS:** Applied Computer Science.

## NON-DEGREE-RELATED COURSE TOPICS OFFERED

**Undergraduate**—curriculum and instruction.
**Graduate**—curriculum and instruction; educational psychology.

# THE COMMUNITY COLLEGE OF BALTIMORE COUNTY

*Office of Distance/Extended Learning*
7201 Rossville Boulevard
Baltimore, MD 21237
**Contact:** Tinnie Banks, Senior Director of Distance Learning
**Phone:** 410-682-6000
**Web:** http://www.ccbc.cc.md.us/
**E-mail:** tbanks@ccbc.cc.md.us

**ACCREDITATION:** Middle States Association of Colleges and Schools
**INSTITUTIONALLY ADMINISTERED FINANCIAL AID:** Yes

## DEGREE OR CERTIFICATE PROGRAMS OFFERED

**Programs offered do not lead to a degree or other formal award.**

# COMMUNITY COLLEGE OF PHILADELPHIA

*Division of Community Services and Continuing Education*
Workforce Development Center, 1600 Callowhill Street
Philadelphia, PA 19130
**Contact:** Mr. Ted Campbell, Coordinator

**Phone:** 215-751-8370
**Web:** http://faculty.ccp.cc.pa.us/faculty/msaks/ccpde/
**E-mail:** tcampbell@ccp.cc.pa.us

**ACCREDITATION:** Middle States Association of Colleges and Schools

## DEGREE OR CERTIFICATE PROGRAMS OFFERED

Programs offered do not lead to a degree or other formal award.

## NON-DEGREE-RELATED COURSE TOPICS OFFERED

**Undergraduate**—English composition; English creative writing; administrative and secretarial services; anthropology; biology, general; chemistry; criminal justice and corrections; developmental and child psychology; economics; foreign languages and literatures; geography; history; law and legal studies; marketing management and research; mathematics; philosophy; political science and government; psychology; sociology.

# COMMUNITY COLLEGE OF RHODE ISLAND
*Instructional Technology and Distance Education*
Academic Affairs Office, 1 Hilton Street
Providence, RI 02905
**Contact:** Philip J. Sisson, Assistant Dean of Academic Affairs
**Phone:** 401-455-6113
**Fax:** 401-455-5190
**Web:** http://www.ribghe.org/waverider/ccriinst.htm
**E-mail:** pssison@ccri.cc.ri.us

**ACCREDITATION:** New England Association of Schools and Colleges

## DEGREE OR CERTIFICATE PROGRAMS OFFERED

Programs offered do not lead to a degree or other formal award.

## NON-DEGREE-RELATED COURSE TOPICS OFFERED

**Undergraduate**—English composition; business information and data processing services; computer and information sciences, general; computer programming; computer software and media applications; developmental and child psychology; liberal arts and sciences, general studies and humanities; nursing; sociology.

# COMMUNITY COLLEGE OF VERMONT
1197 Main Street, Suite 3
St. Johnsbury, VT 05819
**Contact:** John Christensen, Coordinator of Academic Services
**Phone:** 802-334-3387
**Fax:** 802-748-5014
**Web:** http://www.ccv.vsc.edu/
**E-mail:** christej@mail.ccv.vsc.edu

**ACCREDITATION:** New England Association of Schools and Colleges
**INSTITUTIONALLY ADMINISTERED FINANCIAL AID:** No

## DEGREE OR CERTIFICATE PROGRAMS OFFERED

Programs offered do not lead to a degree or other formal award.

## NON-DEGREE-RELATED COURSE TOPICS OFFERED

**Undergraduate**—American (United States) history; Jewish/Judaic studies; accounting; environmental science/studies; law and legal studies, other; philosophy and religion; sociology; women's studies.

# COMMUNITY HOSPITAL OF ROANOKE VALLEY–COLLEGE OF HEALTH SCIENCES
PO Box 13186
Roanoke, VA 24031
**Contact:** Bridget Moore, Director of Distance Learning
**Phone:** 540-985-4046
**Fax:** 540-985-9773
**Web:** http://www.chs.edu/
**E-mail:** bfranklin@health.chs.edu

**ACCREDITATION:** Southern Association of Colleges and Schools
**INSTITUTIONALLY ADMINISTERED FINANCIAL AID:** Yes

## DEGREE OR CERTIFICATE PROGRAMS OFFERED

Programs offered do not lead to a degree or other formal award.

## NON-DEGREE-RELATED COURSE TOPICS OFFERED

**Undergraduate**—English composition; English technical and business writing; anatomy; community health services; gerontology; health and medical diagnostic and treatment services; health and physical education/fitness; health professions and related sciences, other; human resources management; mathematical statistics; miscellaneous health professions; nursing; philosophy; psychology; public health; sociology.

# CONCORDIA COLLEGE
*CUENET (Concordia University Education Network)*
171 White Plains Road
Bronxville, NY 10708
**Contact:** Dr. David C. Jacobson, Provost
**Phone:** 914-337-9300 Ext. 2126
**Fax:** 914-395-4500
**Web:** http://www.concordia-ny.edu
**E-mail:** dcj@concordia-ny.edu

**ACCREDITATION:** Middle States Association of Colleges and Schools
**INSTITUTIONALLY ADMINISTERED FINANCIAL AID:** No

## DEGREE OR CERTIFICATE PROGRAMS OFFERED

Programs offered do not lead to a degree or other formal award.

## NON-DEGREE-RELATED COURSE TOPICS OFFERED

**Undergraduate**—business communications; psychology; sociology.

# CONCORDIA UNIVERSITY
## School of Human Services
275 Syndicate Street, N
Saint Paul, MN 55104
**Contact:** Gail Ann Wells, Marketing Coordinator
**Phone:** 800-211-3370 Ext. 6186
**Fax:** 651-603-6144
**Web:** http://www.cshs.csp.edu
**E-mail:** cshs@csp.edu

**ACCREDITATION:** North Central Association of Colleges and Schools
**INSTITUTIONALLY ADMINISTERED FINANCIAL AID:** Yes

### DEGREE OR CERTIFICATE PROGRAMS OFFERED
**Undergraduate—BA:** Child Development; Criminal Justice; Human Services; School Age Care; Youth Development.
**Graduate—MA:** Human Services—Family Studies; Human Services—Leadership. **MAE:** Early Childhood; Parish Education; School Age Care; Youth Development.

### NON-DEGREE-RELATED COURSE TOPICS OFFERED
**Undergraduate—**English composition; English creative writing; English language and literature, general; anthropology; biological sciences/life sciences, other; communications, general; community psychology; computer software and media applications; developmental and child psychology; economics; fine arts and art studies; history; individual and family development studies; mathematics and computer science; psychology; science, technology and society; sociology; systems science and theory.

# CONCORDIA UNIVERSITY
## Information Resources
Web: http://www.cui.edu

**ACCREDITATION:** Western Association of Schools and Colleges
**INSTITUTIONALLY ADMINISTERED FINANCIAL AID:** Yes

### DEGREE OR CERTIFICATE PROGRAMS OFFERED
Programs offered do not lead to a degree or other formal award.

### NON-DEGREE-RELATED COURSE TOPICS OFFERED
**Undergraduate—**liberal arts and sciences, general studies and humanities; social sciences and history, other.
**Graduate—**education administration and supervision; education, other; educational evaluation, research and statistics; educational psychology; general teacher education.

# CONCORDIA UNIVERSITY AT AUSTIN
## Center for Distance Education
3400 I.H. 35 North
Austin, TX 78705
**Contact:** Rev. Dr. David Kluth, Vice President Information and Technology Services
**Phone:** 512-486-1176
**Fax:** 512-302-5856

**Web:** http://www.concordia.edu
**E-mail:** kluthd@concordia.edu

**ACCREDITATION:** Southern Association of Colleges and Schools
**INSTITUTIONALLY ADMINISTERED FINANCIAL AID:** Yes

### DEGREE OR CERTIFICATE PROGRAMS OFFERED
Programs offered do not lead to a degree or other formal award.

### NON-DEGREE-RELATED COURSE TOPICS OFFERED
**Undergraduate—**American (United States) history; English language and literature/letters, other; biology, general; developmental and child psychology; mathematics; religion/religious studies; sociology.
**Non-credit—**American (United States) history; English language and literature/letters, other; biology, general; journalism and mass communication, other; mathematics; psychology; religion/religious studies; sociology.

# CONCORDIA UNIVERSITY WISCONSIN
## Continuing Education Division
12800 North Lake Shore Drive
Mequon, WI 53097
**Contact:** Sarah A. Weaver, Coordinator
**Phone:** 262-243-4257
**Fax:** 262-243-4459
**Web:** http://www.cuw.edu
**E-mail:** sarah.weaver@cuw.edu

**ACCREDITATION:** North Central Association of Colleges and Schools
**INSTITUTIONALLY ADMINISTERED FINANCIAL AID:** Yes

### DEGREE OR CERTIFICATE PROGRAMS OFFERED
**Graduate—MBA:** Business Administration. **MS:** Curriculum and Instruction; Education Administration; Education Counseling; Reading. **MSN:** Nursing.

### NON-DEGREE-RELATED COURSE TOPICS OFFERED
**Undergraduate—**English composition; European history; Spanish language and literature; anthropology; art history, criticism and conservation; earth and planetary sciences; geography.
**Graduate—**English composition; curriculum and instruction.

# CONNECTICUT STATE UNIVERSITY SYSTEM
## OnlineCSU
39 Woodland Street
Hartford, CT 06105-2337
**Contact:** OnlineCSU
**Phone:** 860-493-0000
**Web:** http://www.onlinecsu.ctstateu.edu

**E-mail:** onlinecsu@ctstateu.edu

**ACCREDITATION:** New England Association of Schools and Colleges

eCollege.com    www.ecollege.com

## DEGREE OR CERTIFICATE PROGRAMS OFFERED

Graduate—*MLS:* Library Science.

## NON-DEGREE-RELATED COURSE TOPICS OFFERED

**Undergraduate**—Asian studies; English composition; accounting; adult and continuing teacher education; anthropology; business marketing and marketing management; communications, general; computer science; criminal justice and corrections; curriculum and instruction; drama/theater arts, general; economics; information sciences and systems; management information systems and business data processing, general; mathematical statistics; mechanical engineering; nursing; organizational behavior studies; philosophy; sociology.

**Graduate**—Asian studies; English composition; accounting; adult and continuing teacher education; anthropology; business marketing and marketing management; computer systems networking and telecommunications; curriculum and instruction; educational/instructional media design; management information systems and business data processing, general; mathematical statistics; mechanical engineering; organizational behavior studies; social work; sociology.

**See full description on page 334.**

# CONNORS STATE COLLEGE

*Academics and Technology*

RR 1, Box 1000
Warner, OK 74469
**Contact:** Dr. Jo Lynn Autry Digranes, Vice President for Academics and Technology
**Phone:** 918-463-2931
**Fax:** 918-463-2233
**Web:** http://www.connors.cc.ok.us
**E-mail:** jdigranes@connors.cc.ok.us

**ACCREDITATION:** North Central Association of Colleges and Schools

**INSTITUTIONALLY ADMINISTERED FINANCIAL AID:** Yes

## DEGREE OR CERTIFICATE PROGRAMS OFFERED

Programs offered do not lead to a degree or other formal award.

## NON-DEGREE-RELATED COURSE TOPICS OFFERED

**Undergraduate**—Spanish language and literature; agricultural economics; art history, criticism and conservation; geography; mathematics; political science and government; sociology.

# CONTRA COSTA COLLEGE

2600 Mission Bell Drive
San Pablo, CA 94806
**Contact:** Linda Larence, Dean
**Phone:** 510-235-7800 Ext. 4268
**Fax:** 510-236 6768
**Web:** http://www.contracosta.cc.ca.us

**E-mail:** lschweid@contracosta.cc.ca.us

**ACCREDITATION:** Western Association of Schools and Colleges

**INSTITUTIONALLY ADMINISTERED FINANCIAL AID:** Yes

## DEGREE OR CERTIFICATE PROGRAMS OFFERED

Programs offered do not lead to a degree or other formal award.

## NON-DEGREE-RELATED COURSE TOPICS OFFERED

**Undergraduate**—English as a second language; English language and literature, general; library science, other.

# COPIAH-LINCOLN COMMUNITY COLLEGE

PO Box 649
Wesson, MS 39191
**Contact:** Dr. Paul D. Johnson, Dean of the College
**Phone:** 601-643-8306
**Fax:** 601-643-8213
**Web:** http://www.colin.cc.ms.us/
**E-mail:** paul.johnson@colin.cc.ms.us

**ACCREDITATION:** Southern Association of Colleges and Schools

**INSTITUTIONALLY ADMINISTERED FINANCIAL AID:** Yes

## DEGREE OR CERTIFICATE PROGRAMS OFFERED

Undergraduate—*AA:* General Studies.

## NON-DEGREE-RELATED COURSE TOPICS OFFERED

**Undergraduate**—English composition; biology, general; business; health and physical education/fitness; mathematics, other; social sciences and history, other.

# COPIAH-LINCOLN COMMUNITY COLLEGE–NATCHEZ CAMPUS

11 Co-Lin Circle
Natchez, MS 39120-8446
**Contact:** Mrs. Gwen S. McCalip, Director of Admissions and Records
**Phone:** 601-446-1224
**Fax:** 601-446-1222
**Web:** http://www.colin.cc.ms.us/
**E-mail:** gwen.mccalip@colin.cc.ms.us

**ACCREDITATION:** Southern Association of Colleges and Schools

**INSTITUTIONALLY ADMINISTERED FINANCIAL AID:** Yes

## DEGREE OR CERTIFICATE PROGRAMS OFFERED

Programs offered do not lead to a degree or other formal award.

## NON-DEGREE-RELATED COURSE TOPICS OFFERED

**Undergraduate**—American literature (United States); English composition; English literature (British and Commonwealth); accounting; administrative and secretarial services; biology, general; business; economics; geography; history; mathematics; psychology; sociology.

# CORNING COMMUNITY COLLEGE

*Open Learning Program*
1 Academic Drive
Corning, NY 14830
**Contact:** Barry Garrison, Director of Institutional Effectiveness
**Phone:** 607-962-9527
**Fax:** 607-962-9485
**Web:** http://corning-cc.edu/distancelearning
**E-mail:** garrisbb@coning-cc.edu

**ACCREDITATION:** Middle States Association of Colleges and Schools

**INSTITUTIONALLY ADMINISTERED FINANCIAL AID:** Yes

## DEGREE OR CERTIFICATE PROGRAMS OFFERED
Programs offered do not lead to a degree or other formal award.

## NON-DEGREE-RELATED COURSE TOPICS OFFERED
**Undergraduate**—English composition; accounting; business administration and management; business/managerial economics; computer systems networking and telecommunications; education, general; health and physical education/fitness; history; human services; journalism; philosophy; psychology; sociology.

# COSUMNES RIVER COLLEGE

*Media Resources Center*
8401 Center Parkway
Sacramento, CA 95823-5799
**Contact:** Distance Learning
**Phone:** 916-691-7289
**Web:** http://wserver.crc.losrios.cc.ca.us/dl.htm
**E-mail:** crc_pio@mail.crc.losrios.cc.ca.us

**ACCREDITATION:** Western Association of Schools and Colleges

## DEGREE OR CERTIFICATE PROGRAMS OFFERED
Programs offered do not lead to a degree or other formal award.

## NON-DEGREE-RELATED COURSE TOPICS OFFERED
**Undergraduate**—English composition; business; computer and information sciences, general; environmental control technologies; health and medical administrative services; mathematics.

# COUNTY COLLEGE OF MORRIS

*Professional Programs and Distance Education*
214 Center Grove Road
Randolph, NJ 07869-2086
**Contact:** Mrs. Millie Roman-Buday, Coordinator of Distance Education
**Phone:** 973-328-5184
**Fax:** 973-328-5082
**Web:** http://www.ccm.edu
**E-mail:** mroman@ccm.edu

**ACCREDITATION:** Middle States Association of Colleges and Schools

**INSTITUTIONALLY ADMINISTERED FINANCIAL AID:** Yes

## DEGREE OR CERTIFICATE PROGRAMS OFFERED
Programs offered do not lead to a degree or other formal award.

## NON-DEGREE-RELATED COURSE TOPICS OFFERED
**Undergraduate**—English composition; business; computer science; history; psychology; sociology.
**Non-credit**—English creative writing; computer and information sciences, general; computer systems networking and telecommunications; internet and world wide web.

# COVENANT THEOLOGICAL SEMINARY

*External Studies Office*
12330 Conway Road
St. Louis, MO 63141
**Contact:** Mr. Daniel S. Gilchrist, Director of Covenant Access
**Phone:** 800-264-8064
**Fax:** 314-434-4819
**Web:** http://www.covenantseminary.edu
**E-mail:** admissions@covenantseminary.edu

**ACCREDITATION:** North Central Association of Colleges and Schools

**INSTITUTIONALLY ADMINISTERED FINANCIAL AID:** Yes

## DEGREE OR CERTIFICATE PROGRAMS OFFERED
**Graduate**—*Graduate Certificate:* Theology. *MA:* Theology.

## NON-DEGREE-RELATED COURSE TOPICS OFFERED
**Graduate**—bible/biblical studies; ethnic and cultural studies; missions/missionary studies and missiology; philosophy and religion; religion/religious studies; theological and ministerial studies; theological studies and religious vocations, other.

# CRAVEN COMMUNITY COLLEGE

800 College Court
New Bern, NC 28562
**Contact:** Mrs. Janice Winfield, Admissions Secretary
**Phone:** 252-638-7227
**Fax:** 252-638-4649
**Web:** http://www.craven.cc.nc.us/
**E-mail:** winfielj@admin.craven.cc.nc.us

**ACCREDITATION:** Southern Association of Colleges and Schools

**INSTITUTIONALLY ADMINISTERED FINANCIAL AID:** Yes

## DEGREE OR CERTIFICATE PROGRAMS OFFERED
**Undergraduate**—*AAS:* Business Administration. *AGS:* Associate of General Education (AGE).

## NON-DEGREE-RELATED COURSE TOPICS OFFERED
**Undergraduate**—English composition; English creative writing; English language and literature, general; accounting; administrative and secretarial services; biology, general; business administration and management; communications, general; computer programming; computer systems networking and telecommunications; computer/information technology

administration and management; criminal justice and corrections; economics; history; psychology; quality control and safety technologies; sociology; visual and performing arts, other.

Non-credit—computer and information sciences, general.

# CROWN COLLEGE
## Crown Adult Programs

6425 County 30
St. Bonifacius, MN 55375
Contact: Dr. William J. Hyndman, Crown College Online
Phone: 952-446-4153
Fax: 952-446-4149
Web: http://www.crownonline.org
E-mail: cconline@crown.edu

ACCREDITATION: Accrediting Association of Bible Colleges

INSTITUTIONALLY ADMINISTERED FINANCIAL AID: Yes

eCollege.com  www.ecollege.com

### DEGREE OR CERTIFICATE PROGRAMS OFFERED
Undergraduate—AS: Christian Ministries. BS: Christian Ministry.
Graduate—MA: Church Leadership.

### NON-DEGREE-RELATED COURSE TOPICS OFFERED
Undergraduate—philosophy and religion.
Graduate—philosophy and religion.

# THE CULINARY INSTITUTE OF AMERICA
## CIA Self Study Programs

1946 Campus Drive
Hyde Park, NY 12538
Contact: Susan Cussen, Director of Marketing
Phone: 845-451-1471
Web: http://www.ciaprochef.com
E-mail: ciaprochef@culinary.edu

ACCREDITATION: Accrediting Commission of Career Schools and Colleges of Technology

INSTITUTIONALLY ADMINISTERED FINANCIAL AID: No

### DEGREE OR CERTIFICATE PROGRAMS OFFERED
Programs offered do not lead to a degree or other formal award.

### NON-DEGREE-RELATED COURSE TOPICS OFFERED
Non-credit—culinary arts and related services.

### Special Note
From the convenience of home or office, students can find invaluable professional development online from the Culinary Institute of America (CIA), a leader in culinary arts education.

The Techniques of Healthy Cooking course offering helps students take full advantage of consumers' ever-increasing preference for fresher, healthier cuisine. The program is based on the CIA's text *The Professional Chef's Techniques of Healthy Cooking*.

The Introduction to the Professional Kitchen course immerses students in the world of chefs, restaurants, and professional kitchens. Whether restaurant managers, distributor sales representatives, or food service professionals, the CIA's new program, based on its text *Cooking Essentials for the New Professional Chef*, helps enhance students' knowledge of the food service industry and broadens their understanding of the professional kitchen organization, ingredients, and tools.

Students are encouraged to take advantage of this e-learning opportunity to learn from the CIA. They can "hold the reins" to their future in this ever-changing field, right at their own computer.

Upon completion of CIA's distance learning courses, students obtain the following professional benefits: 5 ACF certification points, 3 Continuing Education Units (CEUs), and 1 CIA Certificate of Completion. Students can get all the benefits of a world-class culinary education in the comfort of their own workstation. Cost per person is $550.

To register or for more information, students should contact 800-888-7850 (toll-free) or visit CIA's Internet Learning Web site at http://www.ciaprochef.com.

# CULVER-STOCKTON COLLEGE

1 College Hill
Canton, MO 63435
Contact: Dr. David W. Wilson, Interim Dean of Academic Affairs
Phone: 217-231-6325
Fax: 217-231-6614
Web: http://www.culver.edu/
E-mail: dwilson@culver.edu

ACCREDITATION: North Central Association of Colleges and Schools

### DEGREE OR CERTIFICATE PROGRAMS OFFERED
Programs offered do not lead to a degree or other formal award.

# CUMBERLAND COUNTY COLLEGE
## Multimedia and Distance Learning Services

College Drive, PO Box 1500
Vineland, NJ 08362-0517
Contact: Amar Madineni, Assistant Dean of Instruction for Information Technology
Phone: 856-691-8600 Ext. 341
Fax: 856-691-9489
Web: http://www.cccnj.net
E-mail: amar@cccnj.net

ACCREDITATION: Middle States Association of Colleges and Schools

INSTITUTIONALLY ADMINISTERED FINANCIAL AID: Yes

## DEGREE OR CERTIFICATE PROGRAMS OFFERED

Programs offered do not lead to a degree or other formal award.

## NON-DEGREE-RELATED COURSE TOPICS OFFERED

**Undergraduate**—English composition; English creative writing; adult and continuing teacher education; anthropology; biology, general; business administration and management; foreign languages and literatures; journalism and mass communication, other; psychology; psychology, other; sociology.

# CUYAMACA COLLEGE

*Telecourse Program*

900 Rancho San Diego Parkway
El Cajon, CA 92019-4304
**Contact:** Mrs. Nancy Asbury, Administrative Secretary
**Phone:** 619-660-4401
**Fax:** 619-660-4493
**Web:** http://www.cuyamaca.net
**E-mail:** nancy.asubry@gcccd.net

**ACCREDITATION:** Western Association of Schools and Colleges
**INSTITUTIONALLY ADMINISTERED FINANCIAL AID:** Yes

## DEGREE OR CERTIFICATE PROGRAMS OFFERED

Programs offered do not lead to a degree or other formal award.

## NON-DEGREE-RELATED COURSE TOPICS OFFERED

**Undergraduate**—English language and literature, general; anthropology; astronomy; business; developmental and child psychology; economics; entrepreneurship; geological and related sciences; health and physical education/fitness; history; political science and government; psychology; sociology.

# CYPRESS COLLEGE

9200 Valley View Street
Cypress, CA 90630
**Contact:** David Wassenaar, Dean of Admission and Records
**Phone:** 714-484-7435
**Fax:** 714-484-7446
**E-mail:** dwassenaar@cypress.cc.ca.us

**ACCREDITATION:** Western Association of Schools and Colleges
**INSTITUTIONALLY ADMINISTERED FINANCIAL AID:** No

## DEGREE OR CERTIFICATE PROGRAMS OFFERED

Programs offered do not lead to a degree or other formal award.

## NON-DEGREE-RELATED COURSE TOPICS OFFERED

**Undergraduate**—business management and administrative services, other; economics; history; political science and government; psychology; sociology.

# DAKOTA COUNTY TECHNICAL COLLEGE

1300 145th Street, E, County Road 42
Rosemount, MN 55068
**Contact:** Patrick Lair, Admissions Coordinator
**Phone:** 651-423-8301
**Fax:** 651-423-8775
**Web:** http://www.dctc.mnscu.edu/
**E-mail:** patrick.lair@dctc.mnscu.edu

**ACCREDITATION:** North Central Association of Colleges and Schools

## DEGREE OR CERTIFICATE PROGRAMS OFFERED

Programs offered do not lead to a degree or other formal award.

## NON-DEGREE-RELATED COURSE TOPICS OFFERED

**Undergraduate**—English composition; English creative writing; English technical and business writing; mathematics; psychology; sociology.

# DAKOTA STATE UNIVERSITY

*Office of Distance Education*

201A Mundt Library
Madison, SD 57042-1799
**Contact:** Deb Gearhart, Director of Distance Education
**Phone:** 800-641-4309
**Fax:** 605-256-5208
**Web:** http://www.departments.dsu.edu/disted/
**E-mail:** dsuinfo@pluto.dsu.edu

**ACCREDITATION:** North Central Association of Colleges and Schools
**INSTITUTIONALLY ADMINISTERED FINANCIAL AID:** No

## DEGREE OR CERTIFICATE PROGRAMS OFFERED

**Undergraduate**—*BS:* Health Information Administration Degree Completion Program.
**Graduate**—*MEd:* Computer Education and Technology. *MSIS:* Information Systems.

## NON-DEGREE-RELATED COURSE TOPICS OFFERED

**Undergraduate**—English composition; English language and literature, general; computer and information sciences, general; computer and information sciences, other; computer programming; computer science; computer systems analysis; economics; education, other; educational psychology; health system/health services administration; human resources management; information sciences and systems; mathematics; music; psychology; sociology.
**Graduate**—computer and information sciences, other; education, other; educational/instructional media design; information sciences and systems.

**See full description on page 336.**

# DALLAS BAPTIST UNIVERSITY

*Dallas Baptist University Online (DBU Online)*

3000 Mountain Creek Parkway
Dallas, TX 75211-9209

**Contact:** Amy Walker, Online Student Coordinator
**Phone:** 800-460-8188
**Fax:** 214-333-5373
**Web:** http://dbuonline.org
**E-mail:** online@dbu.edu

**ACCREDITATION:** Southern Association of Colleges and Schools

**INSTITUTIONALLY ADMINISTERED FINANCIAL AID:** Yes

eCollege.com   *www.ecollege.com*

### DEGREE OR CERTIFICATE PROGRAMS OFFERED

Undergraduate—*BBA:* Business. *Certificate:* E-Commerce.
Graduate—*MAM:* Organizational Management. *MBA:* Business. *MEd:* Educational Organization and Administration.

See full description on page 338.

## DALLAS COUNTY COMMUNITY COLLEGE DISTRICT

*LeCroy Center for Educational Telecommunications*
9596 Walnut Street
Dallas, TX 75243-2112
**Contact:** Mrs. Karen McClendon, Administrative Assistant
**Phone:** 972-669-6550
**Fax:** 972-669-6668
**Web:** http://Dallas.dcccd.edu
**E-mail:** kmcclendon@dcccd.edu

**ACCREDITATION:** Southern Association of Colleges and Schools

**INSTITUTIONALLY ADMINISTERED FINANCIAL AID:** Yes

### DEGREE OR CERTIFICATE PROGRAMS OFFERED

Undergraduate—*AA:* Liberal Arts and General Studies. *AS:* General Studies.

### NON-DEGREE-RELATED COURSE TOPICS OFFERED

Undergraduate—English as a second language; English composition; English creative writing; accounting; biology, general; business marketing and marketing management; developmental and child psychology; mathematics, other; sociology.

See full description on page 340.

## DALLAS THEOLOGICAL SEMINARY

*External Studies Department*
3909 Swiss Avenue, Stearns-101
Dallas, TX 75204
**Contact:** Ben Scott, Director of External Studies
**Phone:** 214-841-3772
**Fax:** 214-841-3532
**Web:** http://www.dts.edu/ExternalStudies
**E-mail:** externalstudies@dts.edu

**ACCREDITATION:** Southern Association of Colleges and Schools

**INSTITUTIONALLY ADMINISTERED FINANCIAL AID:** No

### DEGREE OR CERTIFICATE PROGRAMS OFFERED

Programs offered do not lead to a degree or other formal award.

### NON-DEGREE-RELATED COURSE TOPICS OFFERED

Graduate—bible/biblical studies; biblical and other theological languages and literatures; education administration and supervision; education, other; missions/missionary studies and missiology; theological and ministerial studies.

## DANVILLE AREA COMMUNITY COLLEGE

*Distance Learning Department*
Instructional Media, 2000 East Main Street
Danville, IL 61832
**Contact:** Jon Spors, Director
**Phone:** 217-443-8577
**Fax:** 217-443-3178
**Web:** http://www.dacc.cc.il.us/
**E-mail:** jspors@dacc.cc.il.us

**ACCREDITATION:** North Central Association of Colleges and Schools

**INSTITUTIONALLY ADMINISTERED FINANCIAL AID:** Yes

### DEGREE OR CERTIFICATE PROGRAMS OFFERED

Undergraduate—*AAS:* Criminology.

### NON-DEGREE-RELATED COURSE TOPICS OFFERED

Undergraduate—English composition; accounting; agriculture/ agricultural sciences, other; anthropology; applied mathematics; astronomy; biological sciences/life sciences, other; business administration and management; business information and data processing services; communications, other; criminal justice and corrections; data processing technology; economics; electrical, electronics and communications engineering; environmental/environmental health engineering; geography; health professions and related sciences, other; history; internet and world wide web; mathematical statistics; mathematics; music; physics; psychology; sociology.

## DANVILLE COMMUNITY COLLEGE

*Learning Resource Center*
1008 South Main Street
Danville, VA 24541
**Contact:** Dr. Betty Jo Foster, Dean of Instruction
**Phone:** 434-797-8410
**Fax:** 434-797-8415
**Web:** http://www.dcc.vccs.edu
**E-mail:** bfoster@dcc.vccs.edu

**ACCREDITATION:** Southern Association of Colleges and Schools

**INSTITUTIONALLY ADMINISTERED FINANCIAL AID:** Yes

### DEGREE OR CERTIFICATE PROGRAMS OFFERED

Programs offered do not lead to a degree or other formal award.

## NON-DEGREE-RELATED COURSE TOPICS OFFERED

**Undergraduate**—English composition; accounting; business; business marketing and marketing management; child care and guidance workers and managers; communications, general; computer software and media applications; design and applied arts; drafting; foods and nutrition studies; graphic and printing equipment operators; health and physical education/fitness; mathematics; music.

# DAVENPORT UNIVERSITY ONLINE

415 East Fulton Street
Grand Raipds, MI 49503
**Contact:** Pam Jennings, Director of Marketing and Enrollment Management
**Phone:** 800-203-5323
**Fax:** 616-742-2076
**E-mail:** pam.jennings@davenport.edu

**ACCREDITATION:** North Central Association of Colleges and Schools
**INSTITUTIONALLY ADMINISTERED FINANCIAL AID:** Yes

## DEGREE OR CERTIFICATE PROGRAMS OFFERED

**Undergraduate**—*AAS:* Accounting; Automated Accounting Technology; Systems Analysis and Application Development. *ABA:* Computer Information Systems; Entrepreneurship. *AS:* Management; Marketing. *BBA:* Entrepreneurship; Industrial Management; Self-Directed Management. *BS:* Accountancy; E-Commerce (Bachelor of Applied Science—BAS); Human Resource Management; Management; Marketing. *Certificate:* Accounting Procedures; Microcomputer Applications. *Technical Certificate:* Human Resource Management; International Business; Leadership; Quality Leadership; Small Business Management.
**Graduate**—*MBA:* Accounting; Health Care Management; Management—Entrepreneurial Specialty; Management—Strategic Management Specialty.

## NON-DEGREE-RELATED COURSE TOPICS OFFERED

**Undergraduate**—accounting; business; business administration and management; business management and administrative services, other; business marketing and marketing management; computer and information sciences, general; computer/information technology administration and management; marketing management and research.
**Graduate**—accounting; business; business administration and management; business management and administrative services, other; health and medical administrative services.

**See full description on page 342.**

# DAWSON COMMUNITY COLLEGE
*Continuing and Extension Education Department*
300 College Drive
Glendive, MT 59330
**Contact:** Jolene Myers, Director of Admissions
**Phone:** 406-377-9410
**Fax:** 406-377-8132
**Web:** http://www.dawson.cc.mt.us/

**E-mail:** myers@dawson.cc.mt.us
**ACCREDITATION:** Northwest Association of Schools and Colleges
**INSTITUTIONALLY ADMINISTERED FINANCIAL AID:** Yes

## DEGREE OR CERTIFICATE PROGRAMS OFFERED
**Programs offered do not lead to a degree or other formal award.**

## NON-DEGREE-RELATED COURSE TOPICS OFFERED

**Undergraduate**—English composition; English creative writing; biology, general; business administration and management; communications, general; computer software and media applications; developmental and child psychology; psychology; sociology.

# DEFIANCE COLLEGE
*Design for Leadership*
701 North Clinton Street
Defiance, OH 43512
**Contact:** Dr. Richard Stroede, Vice President for Academic Affairs
**Phone:** 419-783-2402
**Fax:** 419-784-0426
**Web:** http://www.defiance.edu/pages/design_leadership.html
**E-mail:** dstroede@defiance.edu

**ACCREDITATION:** North Central Association of Colleges and Schools
**INSTITUTIONALLY ADMINISTERED FINANCIAL AID:** Yes

## DEGREE OR CERTIFICATE PROGRAMS OFFERED

**Undergraduate**—*AA:* Religious Education. *BA:* Religious Education. *Certificate:* African American Ministry Leadership; Church Education; Youth Ministry Leadership.

## NON-DEGREE-RELATED COURSE TOPICS OFFERED

**Undergraduate**—bible/biblical studies; religious education.

# DELAWARE TECHNICAL & COMMUNITY COLLEGE, JACK F. OWENS CAMPUS

PO Box 897
Dover, DE 19903
**Contact:** Michael A. Mills, Director of Distance Education
**Phone:** 302-857-1810
**Fax:** 302-857-1815
**Web:** http://www.dtcc.edu/
**E-mail:** mmills@outland.dtcc.edu

**ACCREDITATION:** Middle States Association of Colleges and Schools

## DEGREE OR CERTIFICATE PROGRAMS OFFERED

**Undergraduate**—*AAS:* Office Administration.

## NON-DEGREE-RELATED COURSE TOPICS OFFERED

**Undergraduate**—American (United States) history; Spanish language and literature; accounting; agriculture/agricultural sciences; biology, general; business marketing and marketing management; computer/

information technology administration and management; criminal justice and corrections; economics; journalism; mathematical statistics; mathematics; sociology.

# DELAWARE TECHNICAL & COMMUNITY COLLEGE, STANTON/WILMINGTON CAMPUS

*Distance Learning Programs and Outreach*

333 Shipley Street
Wilmington, DE 19801
**Contact:** Ms. Rebecca Bailey-Bell, Admissions Aide
**Phone:** 302-571-5366
**Web:** http://www.dtcc.edu/
**E-mail:** rbailey@hopi.dtcc.edu

**ACCREDITATION:** Middle States Association of Colleges and Schools
**INSTITUTIONALLY ADMINISTERED FINANCIAL AID:** Yes

### DEGREE OR CERTIFICATE PROGRAMS OFFERED
**Programs offered do not lead to a degree or other formal award.**

### NON-DEGREE-RELATED COURSE TOPICS OFFERED
**Undergraduate**—American (United States) history; American literature (United States); English composition; English technical and business writing; business; business administration and management; business marketing and marketing management; communications, other; developmental and child psychology; economics; educational/instructional media design; family and community studies; health professions and related sciences, other; history; human services; law and legal studies, other; mathematical statistics; mathematics, other; political science and government; psychology; social psychology; social sciences, general; sociology. **Non-credit**—computer software and media applications.

# DEL MAR COLLEGE

101 Baldwin
Corpus Christi, TX 78404
**Contact:** Donald Howard Tyler, Assistant Dean of Distance Learning
**Phone:** 361-698-1312
**Fax:** 361-698-1981
**Web:** http://www.delmar.edu/
**E-mail:** dtyler@delmar.edu

**ACCREDITATION:** Southern Association of Colleges and Schools
**INSTITUTIONALLY ADMINISTERED FINANCIAL AID:** Yes

### DEGREE OR CERTIFICATE PROGRAMS OFFERED
**Programs offered do not lead to a degree or other formal award.**

### NON-DEGREE-RELATED COURSE TOPICS OFFERED
**Undergraduate**—American (United States) history; American literature (United States); English composition; administrative and secretarial services; biology, general; computer and information sciences, general;

computer programming; data processing technology; internet and world wide web; music; psychology; real estate; sociology; tourism and travel services marketing operations.

# DELTA COLLEGE

*Distance Learning Office and Telelearning*

1960 Delta Road
University Center, MI 48710
**Contact:** Ms. Jane M. Adams, Senior Administrative Secretary
**Phone:** 989-686-9088
**Web:** http://www.delta.edu/
**E-mail:** jmadams@alpha.delta.edu

**ACCREDITATION:** North Central Association of Colleges and Schools
**INSTITUTIONALLY ADMINISTERED FINANCIAL AID:** Yes

### DEGREE OR CERTIFICATE PROGRAMS OFFERED
**Programs offered do not lead to a degree or other formal award.**

### NON-DEGREE-RELATED COURSE TOPICS OFFERED
**Undergraduate**—American (United States) history; English composition; Spanish language and literature; biology, general; business marketing and marketing management; developmental and child psychology; internet, general; law and legal studies, other; mathematical statistics; mathematics, other; microbiology/bacteriology; nursing; philosophy and religion; sociology.

# DELTA STATE UNIVERSITY

*Division of Continuing Education and Distance Learning*

Highway 8 West
Cleveland, MS 38733-0001
**Contact:** Division of Continuing Education and Distance Learning
**Phone:** 662-846-3000
**Fax:** 662-846-4016
**Web:** http://www.deltast.edu/

**ACCREDITATION:** Southern Association of Colleges and Schools

### DEGREE OR CERTIFICATE PROGRAMS OFFERED
**Programs offered do not lead to a degree or other formal award.**

# DENVER SEMINARY

PO Box 100000
Denver, CO 80250
**Contact:** Ms. Venita Doughty, Coordinator of Educational Technology
**Phone:** 303-762-6933
**Fax:** 303-761-8060
**Web:** http://www.densem.edu
**E-mail:** venita.doughty@densem.edu

**ACCREDITATION:** North Central Association of Colleges and Schools

## DEGREE OR CERTIFICATE PROGRAMS OFFERED

Programs offered do not lead to a degree or other formal award.

## NON-DEGREE-RELATED COURSE TOPICS OFFERED

**Graduate**—philosophy and religion.
**Non-credit**—philosophy and religion.

# DEPAUL UNIVERSITY

## School for New Learning

School for New Learning Distance Education, 25 East Jackson Boulevard, 2nd Floor
Chicago, IL 60604
**Contact:** Mr. Kenn Skorupa, Distance Education Advisor
**Phone:** 866-765-3678
**Fax:** 312-362-8809 Ext. 8809
**Web:** http://www.snlonline.net
**E-mail:** snl@depaul.edu

**ACCREDITATION:** North Central Association of Colleges and Schools

**INSTITUTIONALLY ADMINISTERED FINANCIAL AID:** Yes

## DEGREE OR CERTIFICATE PROGRAMS OFFERED

**Undergraduate**—*BA:* Individually Designed Focus Area; Various.

## NON-DEGREE-RELATED COURSE TOPICS OFFERED

**Undergraduate**—business; business administration and management; liberal arts and sciences, general studies and humanities; professional studies.

**See full description on page 344.**

# DEPAUW UNIVERSITY

101 East Seminary Street
Greencastle, IN 46135
**Contact:** Ms. Heather Kim, Associate Director of Admissions
**Phone:** 800-447-2495 Ext. 4106
**Fax:** 765-658-4007
**Web:** http://www.depauw.edu/
**E-mail:** hkim@depauw.edu

**ACCREDITATION:** North Central Association of Colleges and Schools

## DEGREE OR CERTIFICATE PROGRAMS OFFERED

Programs offered do not lead to a degree or other formal award.

# DES MOINES AREA COMMUNITY COLLEGE

## Distance Learning/Continuing Education

2006 South Ankeny Boulevard
Ankeny, IA 50021
**Contact:** Pat Thieben, Director of Distance Learning and Scheduling
**Phone:** 515-965-7086

**Fax:** 515-965-6002
**Web:** http://www.dmacc.org
**E-mail:** pathieben@dmacc.cc.ia.us

**ACCREDITATION:** North Central Association of Colleges and Schools

**INSTITUTIONALLY ADMINISTERED FINANCIAL AID:** Yes

eCollege.com www.ecollege.com

## DEGREE OR CERTIFICATE PROGRAMS OFFERED

Programs offered do not lead to a degree or other formal award.

## NON-DEGREE-RELATED COURSE TOPICS OFFERED

**Undergraduate**—English composition; accounting; business; business administration and management; computer science; data entry/microcomputer applications; developmental and child psychology; economics; health and medical administrative services; history; sociology.
**Non-credit**—computer software and media applications.

# DEVRY ONLINE

1 Tower Lane
Oakbrook Terrace, IL 60181
**Contact:** Ms. Donna Liljegren, Director of DeVry Online
**Phone:** 630-706-3257
**Fax:** 630-574-1969
**Web:** http://online.devry.edu/
**E-mail:** dliljegren@keller.edu

**ACCREDITATION:** North Central Association of Colleges and Schools

**INSTITUTIONALLY ADMINISTERED FINANCIAL AID:** Yes

eCollege.com www.ecollege.com

## DEGREE OR CERTIFICATE PROGRAMS OFFERED

**Undergraduate**—*BS:* Business Administration; Information Technology.

# DRAKE UNIVERSITY

## Distance Learning Program

Office of the Provost, 25th and University
Des Moines, IA 50311
**Contact:** Ms. Sandra K. Smeltzer, Assistant to the Provost
**Phone:** 515-271-4985
**Fax:** 515-271-3016
**Web:** http://www.multimedia.drake.edu/summer/
**E-mail:** sandra.smeltzer@drake.edu

**ACCREDITATION:** North Central Association of Colleges and Schools

**INSTITUTIONALLY ADMINISTERED FINANCIAL AID:** No

## DEGREE OR CERTIFICATE PROGRAMS OFFERED

Programs offered do not lead to a degree or other formal award.

## NON-DEGREE-RELATED COURSE TOPICS OFFERED

**Undergraduate**—American literature (United States); English composition; English literature (British and Commonwealth); Germanic languages and literatures; accounting; advertising; area, ethnic and cultural studies, other; biochemistry and biophysics; business; business administration and management; business information and data processing services; business quantitative methods and management science; business/managerial economics; communications, general; computer and information sciences, general; computer programming; economics; education, general; education, other; ethnic and cultural studies; fine arts and art studies; health professions and related sciences, other; history; human resources management; international relations and affairs; journalism and mass communications; liberal arts and sciences, general studies and humanities; mathematics; mathematics and computer science; peace and conflict studies; pharmacy; political science and government; psychology; social sciences and history, other; sociology; speech and rhetorical studies; student counseling and personnel services.

**Graduate**—English language and literature, general; advertising; business; business administration and management; economics; education, general; health professions and related sciences, other; history; human resources management; journalism and mass communications; law and legal studies; liberal arts and sciences, general studies and humanities; peace and conflict studies; pharmacy; political science and government; psychology; public administration; public administration and services, other; public health.

---

### Special Note

Distance education at Drake University includes an array of Web-based courses. These online courses are designed so that students can complete a course without having to attend class at a fixed time or place. During summer 2001, nearly 60 courses were offered for both undergraduate and graduate credit. All courses are transferable college credit.

Two new programs were developed for summer 2000: courses suitable for advanced high school students and/or students about to enter college and a cross-discipline program for students who want to become professional pharmacists. In addition, to provide useful information to new Web learners, the Web Learner Consultant Program was developed.

Students must register online for Web-based courses at http://www.multimedia.drake.edu/summer/. Additional information about Web-based courses is also available at http://www.drake.edu/summer/.

Experienced Drake faculty members teach every online course. Students rank Drake's distance education courses on the Web as highly satisfactory, particularly for the convenience, quality of instruction, variety of courses, and interactivity of the courses. Drake's Web-based program also provides access to on-campus library sources, advising, information about ordering books online, and discussion forums. This learner-centered course delivery system is best suited to those who know how to work independently, are self-starters and self-motivated, and are well-organized and know how to manage their time.

Since Drake began offering Web-based courses in 1997, the program has grown to serve registrants throughout the United States and several other countries. For more information on the Web-based program, students should contact Summer Programming at 800-44-DRAKE Ext. 2000 (toll-free) or e-mail at summer.sessions@drake.edu.

---

## DREXEL UNIVERSITY
### College of Business and Administration
3141 Chestnut Streets, 105 Matheson Hall
Philadelphia, PA 19104

**Contact:** Dr. Thomas J. Wieckowski, Director of Masters Programs
**Phone:** 215-895-1791
**Fax:** 215-895-1012
**E-mail:** wieck@drexel.edu

**ACCREDITATION:** Middle States Association of Colleges and Schools
**INSTITUTIONALLY ADMINISTERED FINANCIAL AID:** Yes

eCollege.com   www.ecollege.com

### DEGREE OR CERTIFICATE PROGRAMS OFFERED
**Graduate**—*MBA:* Business.

### NON-DEGREE-RELATED COURSE TOPICS OFFERED
**Graduate**—business administration and management.
**See full description on page 346.**

---

## DUKE UNIVERSITY
### Executive MBA Programs
Durham, NC 27708-0586
**Contact:** Kelli Kilpatrick
**Phone:** 919-660-7804
**Web:** http://www.fuqua.duke.edu/admin/gemba

**ACCREDITATION:** Southern Association of Colleges and Schools
**INSTITUTIONALLY ADMINISTERED FINANCIAL AID:** Yes

### DEGREE OR CERTIFICATE PROGRAMS OFFERED
**Graduate**—*MBA:* The Duke MBA—Global Executive.

### NON-DEGREE-RELATED COURSE TOPICS OFFERED
**Graduate**—accounting; business marketing and marketing management; finance, general; international business; mathematical statistics; organizational behavior studies.
**See full description on page 348.**

---

## DUQUESNE UNIVERSITY
### Center for Distance Learning
Rockwell Hall, 600 Forbes Avenue
Pittsburgh, PA 15206
**Contact:** Cynthia Golden, Executive Director
**Phone:** 412-396-6200
**Fax:** 412-396-5144
**Web:** http://www.distancelearning.duq.edu
**E-mail:** golden@duq.edu

**ACCREDITATION:** Middle States Association of Colleges and Schools
**INSTITUTIONALLY ADMINISTERED FINANCIAL AID:** Yes

### DEGREE OR CERTIFICATE PROGRAMS OFFERED
**Undergraduate**—*BS:* Degree Completion; Nursing. *Certificate:* Post-BSN; Post-BSN.
**Graduate**—*MBOL:* Liberal Arts. *MS:* Music Education. *MSN:* Nursing.
**Postgraduate and doctoral**—*PhD:* Nursing. *PharmD:* Nontraditional.

## NON-DEGREE-RELATED COURSE TOPICS OFFERED

**Undergraduate**—art history, criticism and conservation; educational psychology; environmental science/studies; philosophy and religion.
**Graduate**—computer software and media applications; curriculum and instruction; educational/instructional media design; environmental science/studies; philosophy and religion.

**See full description on page 350.**

# D'YOUVILLE COLLEGE

*Distance Learning*
HSB 102, 320 Porter Avenue
Buffalo, NY 14201
**Contact:** Dr. George Bishop, Dean of Arts, Sciences, and Professional Studies
**Phone:** 716-881-7606
**Fax:** 716-881-7760
**Web:** http://ddl.dyc.edu
**E-mail:** bishopgj@dyc.edu

**ACCREDITATION:** Middle States Association of Colleges and Schools
**INSTITUTIONALLY ADMINISTERED FINANCIAL AID:** Yes

## DEGREE OR CERTIFICATE PROGRAMS OFFERED
Programs offered do not lead to a degree or other formal award.

## NON-DEGREE-RELATED COURSE TOPICS OFFERED
**Undergraduate**—American literature (United States); English literature (British and Commonwealth); business administration and management; comparative literature; economics; education, general; health professions and related sciences, other; history; human resources management; international business; physics; political science and government; special education; teacher education, specific academic and vocational programs.
**Graduate**—business; education, general; health and medical administrative services; international business; nursing; special education.

# EAST CAROLINA UNIVERSITY

*Division of Continuing Studies*
Erwin Building, Room 215
Greenville, NC 27858
**Contact:** Carolyn Dunn, Marketing Coordinator
**Phone:** 800-398-9275
**Fax:** 252-328-2657
**Web:** http://www.options.ecu.edu
**E-mail:** dunnca@mail.ecu.edu

**ACCREDITATION:** Southern Association of Colleges and Schools
**INSTITUTIONALLY ADMINISTERED FINANCIAL AID:** Yes

> eCollege.com  *www.ecollege.com*

## DEGREE OR CERTIFICATE PROGRAMS OFFERED
**Undergraduate**—*BS:* Industrial Technology; Information Technologies.
**Graduate**—*Graduate Certificate:* Computer Network Professional; Professional Communication; Tele-Learning; Virtual Reality in Education and Training; Website Developer. *MLS:* Library Science. *MS:* Digital Communication Technology; Industrial Technology; Instructional Tech-

nology; Manufacturing; Nutrition and Dietetics; Occupational Safety; Speech Language and Auditory Pathology.

## NON-DEGREE-RELATED COURSE TOPICS OFFERED
**Undergraduate**—administrative and secretarial services; business communications; education, general; educational psychology; engineering/industrial management; hospitality services management; philosophy and religion.
**Graduate**—English technical and business writing; accounting; business administration and management; business management and administrative services, other; communication disorders sciences and services; computer science; computer systems networking and telecommunications; education, general; educational/instructional media design; fine arts and art studies; foods and nutrition studies; industrial production technologies; industrial/manufacturing engineering; internet and world wide web; library science/librarianship; psychology; quality control and safety technologies; special education.

**See full description on page 352.**

# EAST CENTRAL COLLEGE

PO Box 529, 1964 Prairie Dell Road
Union, MO 63084
**Contact:** Karen Klos, Instructional Design Coordinator
**Phone:** 636-583-5195 Ext. 2387
**Fax:** 636-583-6637
**Web:** http://www.ecc.cc.mo.us/
**E-mail:** klosk@ecmail.ecc.cc.mo.us

**ACCREDITATION:** North Central Association of Colleges and Schools
**INSTITUTIONALLY ADMINISTERED FINANCIAL AID:** Yes

## DEGREE OR CERTIFICATE PROGRAMS OFFERED
Programs offered do not lead to a degree or other formal award.

## NON-DEGREE-RELATED COURSE TOPICS OFFERED
**Undergraduate**—English composition; biology, general; business; computer and information sciences, general; computer software and media applications; drafting; economics; fine arts and art studies; health professions and related sciences, other; history; industrial/manufacturing engineering; internet and world wide web; marketing operations/marketing and distribution, other; psychology; speech and rhetorical studies.

# EASTERN CONNECTICUT STATE UNIVERSITY

*OnlineCSU*
83 Windham Street
Willimantic, CT 06226
**Contact:** Kathleen B. Fabian, Registrar
**Phone:** 860-465-5386
**Fax:** 860-465-4382
**Web:** http://onlinecsu.ctstateu.edu/
**E-mail:** fabiank@easternct.edu

**ACCREDITATION:** New England Association of Schools and Colleges
**INSTITUTIONALLY ADMINISTERED FINANCIAL AID:** Yes

## DEGREE OR CERTIFICATE PROGRAMS OFFERED

Programs offered do not lead to a degree or other formal award.

## NON-DEGREE-RELATED COURSE TOPICS OFFERED

**Undergraduate**—computer and information sciences, general; economics; education, general; mathematics; nursing; psychology; social work.
**Graduate**—computer and information sciences, general; criminal justice and corrections; education, general; information sciences and systems; nursing; social work.

# EASTERN ILLINOIS UNIVERSITY

*School of Adult and Continuing Education*

600 Lincoln Avenue
Charleston, IL 61920
**Contact:** Dr. L. Kaye Woodward, Director of Board of Trustees BA Program
**Phone:** 217-581-5618
**Fax:** 217-581-7076
**Web:** http://www.eiu.edu/
**E-mail:** bogba@eiu.edu

**ACCREDITATION:** North Central Association of Colleges and Schools

## DEGREE OR CERTIFICATE PROGRAMS OFFERED

**Undergraduate**—*BA:* Liberal Arts.

# EASTERN KENTUCKY UNIVERSITY

*Division of Extended Programs*

Box 27-A
Richmond, KY 40475
**Contact:** Kenneth R. Nelson, Director
**Phone:** 606-622-2001
**Fax:** 606-622-1177
**Web:** http://www.eku.edu/
**E-mail:** sosnelso@acs.eku.edu

**ACCREDITATION:** Southern Association of Colleges and Schools
**INSTITUTIONALLY ADMINISTERED FINANCIAL AID:** Yes

## DEGREE OR CERTIFICATE PROGRAMS OFFERED

Programs offered do not lead to a degree or other formal award.

## NON-DEGREE-RELATED COURSE TOPICS OFFERED

**Undergraduate**—American (United States) history; English composition; Spanish language and literature; anthropology; art history, criticism and conservation; biology, general; business marketing and marketing management; curriculum and instruction; educational psychology; family and marriage counseling; geography; journalism and mass communication, other; mathematics, other; philosophy and religion; radio and television broadcasting; sign language interpreter; sociology.
**Graduate**—curriculum and instruction; educational psychology.

# EASTERN MENNONITE UNIVERSITY

*Eastern Mennonite Seminary*

1200 Park Road
Harrisonburg, VA 22802-2462
**Contact:** Don Yoder, Director of Admissions, Seminary and Graduate Programs
**Phone:** 540-432-4257
**Fax:** 540-432-4444
**Web:** http://www.emu.edu/
**E-mail:** yoderda@emu.edu

**ACCREDITATION:** Southern Association of Colleges and Schools

## DEGREE OR CERTIFICATE PROGRAMS OFFERED

Programs offered do not lead to a degree or other formal award.

## NON-DEGREE-RELATED COURSE TOPICS OFFERED

**Graduate**—bible/biblical studies; theological and ministerial studies.

# EASTERN MICHIGAN UNIVERSITY

*Distance Education*

611 West Cross Street
Ypsilanti, MI 48197
**Contact:** Distance Education
**Phone:** 734-487-1081
**Fax:** 734-487-6695
**Web:** http://www.ce.emich.edu
**E-mail:** distance.education@emich.edu

**ACCREDITATION:** North Central Association of Colleges and Schools
**INSTITUTIONALLY ADMINISTERED FINANCIAL AID:** Yes

eCollege.com *www.ecollege.com*

## DEGREE OR CERTIFICATE PROGRAMS OFFERED

**Undergraduate**—*BS:* Dietetics.
**Graduate**—*Graduate Certificate:* Legal Administration. *MEngr:* Engineering.

## NON-DEGREE-RELATED COURSE TOPICS OFFERED

**Undergraduate**—Afro-American(Black) studies; American (United States) history; English composition; French language and literature; drama/theater arts, general; interior design; investments and securities; law and legal studies, other; medical genetics; military technologies; sociology; women's studies.
**Graduate**—Afro-American(Black) studies; law and legal studies, other.
See full description on page 354.

# EASTERN NEW MEXICO UNIVERSITY

*Extended Learning*

Station #9
Portales, NM 88130

**Contact:** Dr. Renee Neely, Extended Learning
**Web:** http://www.enmu.edu/distance/
**E-mail:** renee.neely@enmu.edu

**ACCREDITATION:** North Central Association of Colleges and Schools

### DEGREE OR CERTIFICATE PROGRAMS OFFERED

**Undergraduate—BBA:** Business Administration. **BEd:** Education. **BS:** University Studies. **BSN:** Nursing.
**Graduate—MA:** Education; English. **MBA:** Business Administration. **MS:** Communicative Disorders. **MSE:** Special Education.

### NON-DEGREE-RELATED COURSE TOPICS OFFERED

**Undergraduate**—accounting; sociology.
**Graduate**—accounting; sociology.

# EASTERN NEW MEXICO UNIVERSITY–ROSWELL

PO Box 6000
Roswell, NM 88202-6000
**Contact:** Dr. Diane June Klassen, Director of Learning Technology
**Phone:** 505-624-7284
**Fax:** 505-624-7284
**Web:** http://www.roswell.enmu.edu/
**E-mail:** diane.klassen@roswell.enmu.edu

**ACCREDITATION:** North Central Association of Colleges and Schools
**INSTITUTIONALLY ADMINISTERED FINANCIAL AID:** Yes

### DEGREE OR CERTIFICATE PROGRAMS OFFERED

Programs offered do not lead to a degree or other formal award.

### NON-DEGREE-RELATED COURSE TOPICS OFFERED

**Undergraduate**—English composition; administrative and secretarial services; biology, general; communications, general; health professions and related sciences, other; history; mathematics.

# EASTERN OREGON UNIVERSITY

## Division of Distance Education

Zabel Hall, 1 University Boulevard
La Grande, OR 97850-2899
**Contact:** Dr. Deirdre Jones, Inquiry Coordinator
**Phone:** 800-544-2195
**Fax:** 541-962-3627
**Web:** http://www.eou.edu/dde/
**E-mail:** dde@eou.edu

**ACCREDITATION:** Northwest Association of Schools and Colleges
**INSTITUTIONALLY ADMINISTERED FINANCIAL AID:** Yes

eCollege.com *www.ecollege.com*

### DEGREE OR CERTIFICATE PROGRAMS OFFERED

**Undergraduate—BA:** Business Administration; Philosophy, Politics and Economics. **BS:** Business and Economics; Fire Services Administration; Liberal Studies; Physical Education/Health.

### NON-DEGREE-RELATED COURSE TOPICS OFFERED

**Undergraduate**—English language and literature, general; accounting; agricultural business and management; anthropology; biology, general; botany; business; chemistry; dramatic/theater arts and stagecraft; economics; geography; health and physical education/fitness; music; philosophy; physics; political science and government; psychology.

### Special Note

Founded in 1929, Eastern Oregon University is a state-supported, comprehensive institution. Eastern is accredited by the Northwest Association of Schools and Colleges. The Division of Distance Education is the distance learning arm of the institution, with a long history of experience delivering both courses and degrees (the first courses were offered in 1978). In 2001–02, Eastern offers more than 400 courses at a distance and 6 different BA/BS distance degree programs: the multidisciplinary liberal studies degree; the philosophy, politics, and economics degree; the business/economics degree; the business administration degree; the physical education and health degree; and the fire services administration degree. Distance learning courses are offered in a variety of modalities (Web, computer conferencing, correspondence, weekend college) to accommodate the requirements of each degree program. All students are required to have e-mail access and Web-browsing capabilities.

More than 1,400 students are currently enrolled in the distance learning degree programs. The courses and degrees are available to students in the United States and Canada and to armed services personnel abroad. Eastern does not charge extra out-of-state tuition. Most of the courses are taught by the same faculty members who teach on-campus courses; the distance learning degrees are the same as those available on campus. Degree-seeking students receive close advising support and have access to full library services at a distance. The admission requirements for students entering the distance learning degree programs are the same as those for on-campus programs; Eastern is not an open admission university.

Students may take up to 8 quarter course units per term without being admitted. Specific information about enrollment is available at the online class registration site (http://webster.eou.edu/). For more information about courses or degree programs, students should e-mail to dde@eou.edu or visit the Division of Distance Education Web site (http://www.eou.edu/dde/) and fill out an online inquiry form.

# EASTERN WYOMING COLLEGE

## Outreach

3200 West C
Torrington, WY 82240
**Contact:** Dee Ludwig, Associate Dean of Instruction
**Phone:** 307-532-8221
**Web:** http://ewcweb.ewc.cc.wy.us

**E-mail:** dludwig@ewc.cc.wy.us

**ACCREDITATION:** North Central Association of Colleges and Schools

**INSTITUTIONALLY ADMINISTERED FINANCIAL AID:** No

### DEGREE OR CERTIFICATE PROGRAMS OFFERED

Programs offered do not lead to a degree or other formal award.

### NON-DEGREE-RELATED COURSE TOPICS OFFERED

**Undergraduate**—English composition; biology, general; business; computer and information sciences, general; economics; geological and related sciences; political science and government; sociology.

# EAST LOS ANGELES COLLEGE

1301 Avenida Cesar Chavez
Monterey Park, CA 91754
**Contact:** Ms. Kerrin McMahan, Coordinator of Online Education
**Phone:** 323-265-8774
**Web:** http://www.elac.cc.ca.us
**E-mail:** kerrin_m._mcmahan@laccd.cc.ca.us

**ACCREDITATION:** Western Association of Schools and Colleges

**INSTITUTIONALLY ADMINISTERED FINANCIAL AID:** Yes

### DEGREE OR CERTIFICATE PROGRAMS OFFERED

Programs offered do not lead to a degree or other formal award.

### NON-DEGREE-RELATED COURSE TOPICS OFFERED

**Undergraduate**—English composition; accounting; administrative and secretarial services; business information and data processing services; computer and information sciences, general; family/consumer resource management; fine arts and art studies; foods and nutrition studies; health and physical education/fitness; history; liberal arts and sciences, general studies and humanities; mathematics; philosophy; psychology; speech and rhetorical studies; visual and performing arts.

# EAST TENNESSEE STATE UNIVERSITY

*Office of Distance Education*

Box 70427
Johnson City, TN 37614-0427
**Contact:** Dr. Darcey M. Cuffman, Programming Coordinator
**Phone:** 423-439-6809
**Fax:** 423-439-8564
**Web:** http://online.etsu.edu
**E-mail:** cuffmand@etsu.edu

**ACCREDITATION:** Southern Association of Colleges and Schools

### DEGREE OR CERTIFICATE PROGRAMS OFFERED

**Undergraduate**—*BBA:* Business.
**Graduate**—*MA:* Professional Communication. *MBA:* Business Administration.

### NON-DEGREE-RELATED COURSE TOPICS OFFERED

**Undergraduate**—developmental and child psychology; education, general; education, other; educational psychology.
**Graduate**—education, general; education, other; educational psychology.

# EDISON STATE COMMUNITY COLLEGE

1973 Edison Drive
Piqua, OH 45356
**Contact:** Ann Marie Miller, Web Designer
**Phone:** 937-778-8600 Ext. 422
**Web:** http://www.edison.cc.oh.us/
**E-mail:** amiller@edison.cc.oh.us

**ACCREDITATION:** North Central Association of Colleges and Schools

### DEGREE OR CERTIFICATE PROGRAMS OFFERED

Programs offered do not lead to a degree or other formal award.

### NON-DEGREE-RELATED COURSE TOPICS OFFERED

**Undergraduate**—English composition; accounting; administrative and secretarial services; advertising; anthropology; art history, criticism and conservation; biology, general; business; business administration and management; business communications; business information and data processing services; business marketing and marketing management; cell biology; chemistry; child care and guidance workers and managers; computer and information sciences, general; computer engineering; computer programming; computer science; computer software and media applications; computer systems analysis; computer systems networking and telecommunications; computer/information technology administration and management; design and applied arts; drama/theater arts, general; ecology; economics; engineering design; engineering/industrial management; fine arts and art studies; human resources management; industrial production technologies; industrial/manufacturing engineering; internet and world wide web; mathematical statistics; mathematics; mathematics and computer science; nursing; philosophy; philosophy and religion; physics; sociology.
**Non-credit**—business; computer software and media applications; computer/information technology administration and management; human resources management; internet and world wide web.

# EDUKAN

245 Northeast 30th Road
Great Bend, KS 67530
**Contact:** Dr. Gillian Gabelmann, Executive Director
**Phone:** 620-792-9204
**Fax:** 620-792-5624
**Web:** http://www.edukan.org/
**E-mail:** gabelmanng@barton.cc.ks.us

**ACCREDITATION:** North Central Association of Colleges and Schools

**INSTITUTIONALLY ADMINISTERED FINANCIAL AID:** Yes

## DEGREE OR CERTIFICATE PROGRAMS OFFERED
Undergraduate—*AGS:* General Studies.

## NON-DEGREE-RELATED COURSE TOPICS OFFERED
Undergraduate—English composition; accounting; anthropology; astronomy; biological and physical sciences; biological sciences/life sciences, other; business; chemistry; communications, general; computer and information sciences, general; economics; ethnic and cultural studies; foreign languages and literatures; geography; mathematics; music; physical sciences, general; psychology; social sciences, general; sociology; speech and rhetorical studies; teacher education, specific academic and vocational programs.

See full description on page 356.

# ELAINE P. NUNEZ COMMUNITY COLLEGE

3710 Paris Road
Chalmette, LA 70043
**Contact:** Mr. Ernest Frazier, Coordinator of Continuing Education and Off-Campus Programs
**Phone:** 504-680-2461
**Web:** http://www.nunez.cc.la.us
**E-mail:** efrazier@nunez.cc.la.us

**ACCREDITATION:** Southern Association of Colleges and Schools
**INSTITUTIONALLY ADMINISTERED FINANCIAL AID:** Yes

## DEGREE OR CERTIFICATE PROGRAMS OFFERED
Programs offered do not lead to a degree or other formal award.

## NON-DEGREE-RELATED COURSE TOPICS OFFERED
Undergraduate—business; education, other; psychology; sociology.

# ELGIN COMMUNITY COLLEGE

1700 Spartan Drive
Elgin, IL 60123
**Contact:** Ms. Billie B. Barnett, Distance Learning Program Developer
**Phone:** 847-214-7945
**Fax:** 847-608-5479
**Web:** http://www.elgin.cc.il.us/
**E-mail:** bbarnett@mail.elgin.cc.il.us

**ACCREDITATION:** North Central Association of Colleges and Schools
**INSTITUTIONALLY ADMINISTERED FINANCIAL AID:** Yes

## DEGREE OR CERTIFICATE PROGRAMS OFFERED
Programs offered do not lead to a degree or other formal award.

## NON-DEGREE-RELATED COURSE TOPICS OFFERED
Undergraduate—American literature (United States); East European languages and literatures; East and Southeast Asian languages and literatures; English as a second language; English composition; English creative writing; English language and literature, general; English language and literature/letters, other; English technical and business writing; Germanic languages and literatures; Greek languages and literatures (modern); Middle Eastern languages and literatures; South Asian languages and literatures; accounting; administrative and secretarial services; anthropology; applied mathematics; archaeology; area, ethnic and cultural studies, other; astronomy; bilingual/bicultural education; biological and physical sciences; biology, general; botany; business; business administration and management; business communications; business information and data processing services; business management and administrative services, other; business/managerial economics; chemistry; child care and guidance workers and managers; clinical psychology; cognitive psychology and psycholinguistics; communications technologies; communications, general; communications, other; community health services; comparative literature; computer and information sciences, general; computer and information sciences, other; computer programming; computer science; computer software and media applications; computer systems analysis; computer systems networking and telecommunications; computer/information technology administration and management; counseling psychology; criminal justice and corrections; criminology; culinary arts and related services; data entry/microcomputer applications; data processing technology; dental services; design and applied arts; developmental and child psychology; drafting; dramatic/theater arts and stagecraft; economics; education, general; education, other; electrical and electronic engineering-related technology; engineering design; engineering mechanics; engineering, general; engineering-related technologies, other; engineering/industrial management; ethnic and cultural studies; family and community studies; film/video and photographic arts; financial management and services; fine arts and art studies; fire protection; food sciences and technology; foods and nutrition studies; foreign languages and literatures; foreign languages and literatures, other; general teacher education; geography; geological and related sciences; gerontology; health and medical administrative services; health and medical assistants; health and medical diagnostic and treatment services; health and medical laboratory technologies; health and medical preparatory programs; health professions and related sciences, other; heating, air conditioning and refrigeration mechanics and repairers; history; hospitality services management; human services; individual and family development studies; industrial and organizational psychology; industrial/manufacturing engineering; information sciences and systems; institutional food workers and administrators; internet and world wide web; journalism and mass communications; law and legal studies; liberal arts and sciences, general studies and humanities; marketing management and research; marketing operations/marketing and distribution, other; mathematical statistics; mathematics; mathematics and computer science; mathematics, other; mental health services; miscellaneous health aides; miscellaneous health professions; miscellaneous mechanics and repairers; miscellaneous physical sciences; music; nursing; philosophy; philosophy and religion; physical sciences, general; physical sciences, other; physics; plant sciences; political science and government; precision metal workers; psychology; psychology, other; public health; quality control and safety technologies; radio and television broadcasting; real estate; religion/religious studies; romance languages and literatures; science technologies, other; science, technology and society; social and philosophical foundations of education; social psychology; social sciences and history, other; social sciences, general; social work; sociology; special education; speech and rhetorical studies; teacher assistant/aide; teacher education, specific academic and vocational programs; teaching English as a second language/foreign language; telecommunications; tourism and travel services marketing operations; visual and performing arts; visual and performing arts, other; zoology.

# ELIZABETH CITY STATE UNIVERSITY

1704 Weeksville Road
Elizabeth City, NC 27909
**Contact:** Mrs. Kimberley N. Stevenson, Coordinator of the Virtual College
**Phone:** 252-335-3699
**Fax:** 252-335-3426
**Web:** http://www.ecsu.edu
**E-mail:** knstevenson@mail.ecsu.edu

**ACCREDITATION:** Southern Association of Colleges and Schools
**INSTITUTIONALLY ADMINISTERED FINANCIAL AID:** Yes

### DEGREE OR CERTIFICATE PROGRAMS OFFERED
Programs offered do not lead to a degree or other formal award.

### NON-DEGREE-RELATED COURSE TOPICS OFFERED
**Undergraduate**—accounting; business; business administration and management; business communications; business quantitative methods and management science; business/managerial economics; education, general; educational psychology; educational/instructional media design; history; human resources management; music; psychology; public administration; public policy analysis; special education; teacher education, specific academic and vocational programs.

# ELIZABETHTOWN COLLEGE

*Center for Continuing Education and Distance Learning*
1 Alpha Drive
Elizabethtown, PA 17022
**Contact:** Dr. John Joseph Kokolus, Dean of Continuing Education and Distance Learning
**Phone:** 717-361-1291
**Fax:** 717-361-1466
**Web:** http://www.etown.edu/cce
**E-mail:** kokolusj@etown.edu

**ACCREDITATION:** Middle States Association of Colleges and Schools
**INSTITUTIONALLY ADMINISTERED FINANCIAL AID:** Yes

### DEGREE OR CERTIFICATE PROGRAMS OFFERED
Programs offered do not lead to a degree or other formal award.

### NON-DEGREE-RELATED COURSE TOPICS OFFERED
**Undergraduate**—American literature (United States); English language and literature, general; accounting; anthropology; history.

# ELIZABETHTOWN COMMUNITY COLLEGE

*Distance Learning Program*
600 College Street Road
Elizabethtown, KY 42701

**Contact:** Dr. Jon Burke, Dean of Student Affairs
**Phone:** 270-769-2371 Ext. 305
**Fax:** 270-769-0736
**Web:** http://www.elizabethtowncc.com
**E-mail:** jon.burke@kctcs.net

**ACCREDITATION:** Southern Association of Colleges and Schools
**INSTITUTIONALLY ADMINISTERED FINANCIAL AID:** Yes

### DEGREE OR CERTIFICATE PROGRAMS OFFERED
Programs offered do not lead to a degree or other formal award.

### NON-DEGREE-RELATED COURSE TOPICS OFFERED
**Undergraduate**—American (United States) history; English composition; European history; business; foods and nutrition studies; nursing; social psychology.

# EMBRY-RIDDLE AERONAUTICAL UNIVERSITY

*Department of Distance Learning*
600 South Clyde Morris Boulevard
Daytona Beach, FL 32114-3900
**Contact:** Terry Whittum, Distance Learning Enrollment Manager
**Phone:** 386-226-4953
**Fax:** 386-226-7101
**Web:** http://www.ec.erau.edu/ddl
**E-mail:** whittumt@cts.db.erau.edu

**ACCREDITATION:** Southern Association of Colleges and Schools
**INSTITUTIONALLY ADMINISTERED FINANCIAL AID:** Yes

### DEGREE OR CERTIFICATE PROGRAMS OFFERED
**Undergraduate**—*AS:* Professional Aeronautics. *BS:* Management of Technical Operations; Professional Aeronautics.
**Graduate**—*MAS:* Aeronautical Science. *MBA:* Business Administration in Aviation.

### NON-DEGREE-RELATED COURSE TOPICS OFFERED
**Undergraduate**—English language and literature, general; English technical and business writing; applied mathematics; business; computer science; economics; social sciences, general.
**Graduate**—air transportation workers; business; psychology.

See full description on page 358.

# EMORY UNIVERSITY

*The Rollins School of Public Health*
1525 Clifton Road, Suite 107
Atlanta, GA 30322
**Contact:** Ms. Kara Brown, Assistant Director of Academic Programs
**Phone:** 404-727-3317
**Fax:** 404-727-8768
**Web:** http://www.sph.emory.edu/CMPH

**E-mail:** klbrow2@sph.emory.edu

**ACCREDITATION:** Southern Association of Colleges and Schools

**INSTITUTIONALLY ADMINISTERED FINANCIAL AID:** Yes

## DEGREE OR CERTIFICATE PROGRAMS OFFERED

Graduate—*MPH:* Career Master of Public Health Program.

## NON-DEGREE-RELATED COURSE TOPICS OFFERED

Graduate—public health.

### Special Note

The Career Master of Public Health (CMPH) program at the Rollins School of Public Health of Emory University is an innovative new way for public health professionals to prepare themselves as leaders in the 21st century. The CMPH is a 42-credit-hour Master of Public Health (MPH) degree program designed for those who have completed a bachelor's degree and who have a minimum of 5 years of professional experience.

The CMPH program runs for 7 semesters in a mixed format of on-campus face-to-face sessions and a Web-based community learning environment, providing working professionals the opportunity to earn an MPH without interrupting their career. Courses begin and end with on-campus face-to-face sessions; between the on-campus sessions, learners interact with classmates and instructors in a Web-based learning community. The mixed format ensures that students, regardless of location, receive the quality education Emory is known for, while gaining a familiarity with emerging technologies and developing close, rewarding relationships with faculty members and classmates.

The CMPH program combines curriculum relevant in today's public health environment with computer and Web-based skills critical for today's successful professionals. The CMPH curriculum is based on the goals and objectives of the "Ten Essential Public Health Services" as stated in the *Public Health Workforce: An Agenda for the 21st Century.*

The rich learning environment of the CMPH is due in part from the diversity of knowledge and experience learners bring to the program, as well as the knowledge and experience of Emory's quality faculty members, who are both practitioners as well as teachers.

# ERIE COMMUNITY COLLEGE, CITY CAMPUS

6205 Main Street
Williamsville, NY 14221
**Contact:** Ms. Marlene Arno, Director of Institutional Research
**Phone:** 716-851-1431
**Fax:** 716-851-1429
**Web:** http://www.ecc.edu/
**E-mail:** arno@ecc.edu

**ACCREDITATION:** Middle States Association of Colleges and Schools

**INSTITUTIONALLY ADMINISTERED FINANCIAL AID:** Yes

## DEGREE OR CERTIFICATE PROGRAMS OFFERED

Programs offered do not lead to a degree or other formal award.

## NON-DEGREE-RELATED COURSE TOPICS OFFERED

Undergraduate—geography; social sciences, general.

# ERIE COMMUNITY COLLEGE, NORTH CAMPUS

6205 Main Street
Williamsville, NY 14221
**Contact:** Ms. Marlene Arno, Director of Institutional Research
**Phone:** 716-851-1431
**Fax:** 716-851-1429
**Web:** http://www.ecc.edu/
**E-mail:** arno@ecc.edu

**ACCREDITATION:** Middle States Association of Colleges and Schools

**INSTITUTIONALLY ADMINISTERED FINANCIAL AID:** Yes

## DEGREE OR CERTIFICATE PROGRAMS OFFERED

Programs offered do not lead to a degree or other formal award.

## NON-DEGREE-RELATED COURSE TOPICS OFFERED

Undergraduate—English composition; accounting; biology, general; business administration and management; chemistry; computer and information sciences, general; dramatic/theater arts and stagecraft; economics; fine arts and art studies; geography; history; mathematics; miscellaneous health aides; music; physics; political science and government; psychology; social sciences, general; sociology.

# ERIE COMMUNITY COLLEGE, SOUTH CAMPUS

6205 Main Street
Williamsville, NY 14221
**Contact:** Ms. Marlene Arno, Director of Institutional Research
**Phone:** 716-851-1431
**Fax:** 716-851-1429
**Web:** http://www.ecc.edu/
**E-mail:** arno@ecc.edu

**ACCREDITATION:** Middle States Association of Colleges and Schools

**INSTITUTIONALLY ADMINISTERED FINANCIAL AID:** Yes

## DEGREE OR CERTIFICATE PROGRAMS OFFERED

Programs offered do not lead to a degree or other formal award.

## NON-DEGREE-RELATED COURSE TOPICS OFFERED

Undergraduate—English composition; English language and literature, general; accounting; business management and administrative services, other; economics; miscellaneous mechanics and repairers; philosophy; psychology; social sciences and history, other; sociology.

# EUGENE BIBLE COLLEGE

*External Studies Department*

2155 Bailey Hill Road
Eugene, OR 97405
**Contact:** Mr. David Earl Sinclair, Director of External Studies
**Phone:** 541-485-1780 Ext. 115
**Fax:** 541-343-5801
**Web:** http://www.ebc.edu
**E-mail:** distance-ed@ebc.edu

**ACCREDITATION:** Accrediting Association of Bible Colleges

**INSTITUTIONALLY ADMINISTERED FINANCIAL AID:** Yes

### DEGREE OR CERTIFICATE PROGRAMS OFFERED

Undergraduate—*Certificate:* One Year Bible Certificate.

### NON-DEGREE-RELATED COURSE TOPICS OFFERED

**Undergraduate**—English composition; English literature (British and Commonwealth); Greek languages and literatures (modern); applied mathematics; bible/biblical studies; biblical and other theological languages and literatures; biological and physical sciences; biology, general; computer and information sciences, general; education, general; educational psychology; history; mathematics; missions/missionary studies and missiology; music; religion/religious studies; religious education; religious/sacred music; school psychology; sociology; speech and rhetorical studies.

# EVERETT COMMUNITY COLLEGE

*Library/Media/Arts and Distance Learning*

2000 Tower Street
Everett, WA 98201
**Contact:** Jeanne Leader, Dean of Library, Media and Arts and Distance Learning
**Phone:** 425-388-9502
**Fax:** 425-388-9144
**Web:** http://www.evcc.ctc.edu
**E-mail:** jleader@evcc.ctc.edu

**ACCREDITATION:** Northwest Association of Schools and Colleges

**INSTITUTIONALLY ADMINISTERED FINANCIAL AID:** Yes

### DEGREE OR CERTIFICATE PROGRAMS OFFERED

Programs offered do not lead to a degree or other formal award.

### NON-DEGREE-RELATED COURSE TOPICS OFFERED

**Undergraduate**—English composition; anthropology; business; child care and guidance workers and managers; computer and information sciences, general; history; liberal arts and sciences, general studies and humanities; library science, other; mathematics; music; psychology; science technologies, other; social sciences, general; sociology.

# EVERGLADES COLLEGE

1500 Northwest 49th Street
Fort Lauderdale, FL 33309
**Contact:** Department of Admissions
**Phone:** 954-772-2655

**Fax:** 954-772-2695
**Web:** http://www.evergladescollege.edu/
**E-mail:** admissions@evergladescollege.edu

**ACCREDITATION:** Accrediting Commission of Career Schools and Colleges of Technology

**INSTITUTIONALLY ADMINISTERED FINANCIAL AID:** Yes

### DEGREE OR CERTIFICATE PROGRAMS OFFERED

Programs offered do not lead to a degree or other formal award.

# EVERGREEN VALLEY COLLEGE

*Telecourse Program*

3095 Yerba Buena Road
San Jose, CA 95121-2654
**Contact:** Janice Tomisaka, Program Specialist
**Phone:** 408-270-6422
**Fax:** 408-532-1858
**Web:** http://www.evc.edu
**E-mail:** jan.tomisaka@sjeccd.cc.ca.us

**ACCREDITATION:** Western Association of Schools and Colleges

**INSTITUTIONALLY ADMINISTERED FINANCIAL AID:** Yes

### DEGREE OR CERTIFICATE PROGRAMS OFFERED

Programs offered do not lead to a degree or other formal award.

### NON-DEGREE-RELATED COURSE TOPICS OFFERED

**Undergraduate**—Spanish language and literature; accounting; anthropology; astronomy; business; gerontology; history; music; psychology; sociology.

# EXCELSIOR COLLEGE

*Learning Services*

7 Columbia Circle
Albany, NY 12203
**Contact:** David Brigham, Director of Learning Services
**Phone:** 518-464-8500
**Fax:** 518-464-8777
**Web:** http://www.excelsior.edu
**E-mail:** david@excelsior.edu

**ACCREDITATION:** Middle States Association of Colleges and Schools

**INSTITUTIONALLY ADMINISTERED FINANCIAL AID:** Yes

### DEGREE OR CERTIFICATE PROGRAMS OFFERED

**Undergraduate**—*AA:* Liberal Arts. *AAS:* Administrative/Management Studies; Aviation Studies; Nursing; Technical Studies. *AS:* Business; Computer Software; Electronics Technology; Liberal Arts; Nuclear Technology; Nursing; Technology. *BA:* Liberal Arts; Liberal Studies. *BS:* Accounting; Computer Information Systems; Computer Software; Computer Technology; Electronics Technology; Finance; General Business; International Business; Liberal Arts; Liberal Studies; Management Information Systems; Management of Human Resources; Marketing; Nuclear Technology; Operations Management; Technology. *BSN:* Nursing. **Graduate**—*MA:* Liberal Studies. *MS:* Nursing.

## NON-DEGREE-RELATED COURSE TOPICS OFFERED

**Non-credit**—health professions and related sciences, other.

# FAIRMONT STATE COLLEGE

1201 Locust Avenue
Fairmont , WV 26554
**Contact:** Ms. Kit Conner, Program Specialist
**Phone:** 304-367-4208
**Fax:** 304-367-4881
**Web:** http://www.fscwv.edu/
**E-mail:** kconner@mail.fscwv.edu

**ACCREDITATION:** North Central Association of Colleges and Schools

## DEGREE OR CERTIFICATE PROGRAMS OFFERED

**Undergraduate**—**AAS:** Technical Studies in Information Systems.

## NON-DEGREE-RELATED COURSE TOPICS OFFERED

**Undergraduate**—English composition; business; business communications; economics; education, general; education, other; foods and nutrition studies; general teacher education; geography; history; information sciences and systems; internet and world wide web; liberal arts and sciences, general studies and humanities; multi/interdisciplinary studies, other; sociology.

# FASHION INSTITUTE OF TECHNOLOGY

7th Avenue at 27th Street
New York, NY 10001
**Contact:** Annette Piecora, Executive Assistant to the President
**Phone:** 212-217-8025
**Fax:** 212-217-7639
**Web:** http://www.fitnyc.suny.edu/
**E-mail:** fitonline@sfitva.cc.fitsuny.edu

**ACCREDITATION:** Middle States Association of Colleges and Schools

**INSTITUTIONALLY ADMINISTERED FINANCIAL AID:** Yes

## DEGREE OR CERTIFICATE PROGRAMS OFFERED

**Undergraduate**—**AAS:** Fashion Merchandising Management.

## NON-DEGREE-RELATED COURSE TOPICS OFFERED

**Undergraduate**—English as a second language; advertising; business marketing and marketing management; law and legal studies, other; management information systems and business data processing, general; photography.

**See full description on page 360.**

# FAYETTEVILLE TECHNICAL COMMUNITY COLLEGE

*Virtual Campus*
PO Box 35236
Fayetteville, NC 28303

**Contact:** Mr. Bobby J. Ervin, Associate Vice President for Learning Technologies
**Phone:** 910-678-8466
**Fax:** 910-678-8401
**Web:** http://www.faytech.cc.nc.us
**E-mail:** ervinb@ftccmail.faytech.cc.nc.us

**ACCREDITATION:** Southern Association of Colleges and Schools

**INSTITUTIONALLY ADMINISTERED FINANCIAL AID:** Yes

## DEGREE OR CERTIFICATE PROGRAMS OFFERED

**Undergraduate**—**AAS:** Accounting; Business; Criminal Justice Technology. **AGS:** General Education.

## NON-DEGREE-RELATED COURSE TOPICS OFFERED

**Undergraduate**—American literature (United States); accounting; administrative and secretarial services; biological and physical sciences; business; chemistry; child care and guidance workers and managers; computer and information sciences, general; computer/information technology administration and management; fine arts and art studies; history; marketing management and research.

# FEATHER RIVER COMMUNITY COLLEGE DISTRICT

570 Golden Eagle Avenue
Quincy, CA 95971
**Contact:** Dr. Jeanette Plankey, Interim Dean of Instruction
**Phone:** 530-283-0202
**Fax:** 530-283-3757
**Web:** http://www.frcc.cc.ca.us/
**E-mail:** jplankey@frcc.cc.ca.us

**ACCREDITATION:** Western Association of Schools and Colleges

## DEGREE OR CERTIFICATE PROGRAMS OFFERED

**Programs offered do not lead to a degree or other formal award.**

# FERRIS STATE UNIVERSITY

1010 Campus Drive, FLITE 460C
Big Rapids, MI 49307
**Contact:** Mr. Steve Cox, Producer and Director
**Phone:** 231-591-2721
**Fax:** 231-591-2785
**Web:** http://www.ferris.edu/
**E-mail:** coxs@ferris.edu

**ACCREDITATION:** North Central Association of Colleges and Schools

**INSTITUTIONALLY ADMINISTERED FINANCIAL AID:** Yes

## DEGREE OR CERTIFICATE PROGRAMS OFFERED

**Undergraduate**—**BSN:** Nursing.

## NON-DEGREE-RELATED COURSE TOPICS OFFERED

**Undergraduate**—American literature (United States); English language and literature, general; anthropology; biological sciences/life sciences, other; biology, general; chemistry; clinical psychology; community health

services; computer and information sciences, general; computer and information sciences, other; computer programming; education, general; mathematics; psychology; social work; sociology.
Graduate—computer and information sciences, general.

# FIELDING GRADUATE INSTITUTE

2112 Santa Barbara Street
Santa Barbara, CA 93105
**Contact:** Sylvia Williams, Communications Director
**Phone:** 805-898-2947
**Fax:** 805-898-4196
**Web:** http://www.fielding.edu/
**E-mail:** sawilliams@fielding.edu

**ACCREDITATION:** Western Association of Schools and Colleges
**INSTITUTIONALLY ADMINISTERED FINANCIAL AID:** Yes

## DEGREE OR CERTIFICATE PROGRAMS OFFERED
Undergraduate—*Certificate:* Neuropsychology.
Graduate—*MA:* Organizational Management; Organizational Development.
Postgraduate and doctoral—*EdD:* Educational Leadership and Change.
*PhD:* Clinical Psychology; Human and Organizational Development.

## NON-DEGREE-RELATED COURSE TOPICS OFFERED
Graduate—organizational behavior studies.

# FINGER LAKES COMMUNITY COLLEGE

4355 Lake Shore Drive
Canandaigua, NY 14424
**Contact:** Dr. James W. Ware, Vice President of Academic Affairs and Dean of the College
**Phone:** 716-394-3500 Ext. 7209
**Fax:** 716-394-5005
**Web:** http://www.flcc.edu
**E-mail:** warejw@flcc.edu

**ACCREDITATION:** Middle States Association of Colleges and Schools
**INSTITUTIONALLY ADMINISTERED FINANCIAL AID:** Yes

## DEGREE OR CERTIFICATE PROGRAMS OFFERED
Programs offered do not lead to a degree or other formal award.

## NON-DEGREE-RELATED COURSE TOPICS OFFERED
Undergraduate—biology, general; business; business communications; business marketing and marketing management; economics; law and legal studies; philosophy; psychology; sociology; tourism and travel services marketing operations.

# FLAGLER COLLEGE

St. Augustine, FL 32085
**Contact:** Ms. Mary Jane Dillon, Assistant to the President

**Web:** http://www.flagler.edu/
**E-mail:** dillonmj@flagler.edu
**ACCREDITATION:** Southern Association of Colleges and Schools

## DEGREE OR CERTIFICATE PROGRAMS OFFERED
Programs offered do not lead to a degree or other formal award.

# FLATHEAD VALLEY COMMUNITY COLLEGE

*Education Services*
777 Grandview Drive
Kalispell, MT 59901
**Contact:** Faith Hodges, Director of Institutional Research and Planning
**Phone:** 406-756-3812
**Fax:** 406-756-3815
**Web:** http://www.fvcc.cc.mt.us
**E-mail:** fhodges@mail.fvcc.cc.mt.us

**ACCREDITATION:** Northwest Association of Schools and Colleges
**INSTITUTIONALLY ADMINISTERED FINANCIAL AID:** Yes

## DEGREE OR CERTIFICATE PROGRAMS OFFERED
Programs offered do not lead to a degree or other formal award.

## NON-DEGREE-RELATED COURSE TOPICS OFFERED
Undergraduate—computer software and media applications; geography; sociology.

# FLORENCE-DARLINGTON TECHNICAL COLLEGE

*Learning Resources Division*
2715 West Lucas Street
Florence, SC 29501
**Contact:** Jane Lucas, Administration Specialist
**Phone:** 843-661-8133
**Fax:** 843-661-8217
**Web:** http://www.fdtc.org
**E-mail:** lucasj@flo.tec.sc.us

**ACCREDITATION:** Southern Association of Colleges and Schools
**INSTITUTIONALLY ADMINISTERED FINANCIAL AID:** Yes

## DEGREE OR CERTIFICATE PROGRAMS OFFERED
Undergraduate—*AA:* Liberal Arts. *AD:* Business; Criminal Justice.

## NON-DEGREE-RELATED COURSE TOPICS OFFERED
Undergraduate—English language and literature, general; English technical and business writing; Germanic languages and literatures; administrative and secretarial services; advertising; biology, general; botany; business and personal services marketing operations; carpenters; child care and guidance workers and managers; civil engineering/civil technology; computer/information technology administration and management; construction/building technology; cosmetic services; criminal justice and

corrections; data entry/microcomputer applications; developmental and child psychology; economics; electrical and electronic engineering-related technology; environmental control technologies; geography; health and medical assistants; health professions and related sciences, other; heating, air conditioning and refrigeration mechanics and repairers; history; international business; liberal arts and sciences, general studies and humanities; marketing management and research; mathematics; mathematics and computer science; mechanical engineering-related technologies; mechanics and repairers, other; miscellaneous engineering-related technologies; miscellaneous health professions; miscellaneous mechanics and repairers; philosophy; physical sciences, general; physics; precision metal workers; psychology; sociology.

**Non-credit**—English composition; English creative writing; Germanic languages and literatures; accounting; administrative and secretarial services; advertising; business administration and management; business and personal services marketing operations; carpenters; city/urban, community and regional planning; computer and information sciences, general; computer programming; computer systems networking and telecommunications; construction trades, other; construction/building technology; electrical and electronic engineering-related technology; electrical and electronics equipment installers and repairers; environmental control technologies; health and medical administrative services; health and medical assistants; heating, air conditioning and refrigeration mechanics and repairers; masons and tile setters; miscellaneous mechanics and repairers; real estate.

# FLORIDA COMMUNITY COLLEGE AT JACKSONVILLE

*Open Campus*
9911 Old Bay Meadows Road
Jacksonville, FL 32202
**Contact:** Maria J. Puzziferro, Instructional Program Manager
**Phone:** 904-997-2718
**Fax:** 904-997-2727
**Web:** http://www.distancelearning.org
**E-mail:** mpuzzife@fccj.org

**ACCREDITATION:** Southern Association of Colleges and Schools
**INSTITUTIONALLY ADMINISTERED FINANCIAL AID:** Yes

## DEGREE OR CERTIFICATE PROGRAMS OFFERED

Programs offered do not lead to a degree or other formal award.

## NON-DEGREE-RELATED COURSE TOPICS OFFERED

**Undergraduate**—American (United States) history; English composition; European history; French language and literature; Latin American studies; accounting; anatomy; anthropology; biology, general; business administration and management; business marketing and marketing management; computer science; criminology; developmental and child psychology; earth and planetary sciences; education, general; finance, general; foods and nutrition studies; geography; law and legal studies, other; liberal arts and sciences, general studies and humanities; mathematics, other; philosophy and religion; sociology.

# FLORIDA GULF COAST UNIVERSITY

*Enrollment Services*
10501 FGCU Boulevard, S
Fort Myers, FL 33965-6565
**Contact:** Department of Admissions
**Phone:** 941-590-7878
**Fax:** 941-590-7894
**Web:** http://www.fgcu.edu
**E-mail:** oar@fgcu.edu

**ACCREDITATION:** Southern Association of Colleges and Schools
**INSTITUTIONALLY ADMINISTERED FINANCIAL AID:** Yes

## DEGREE OR CERTIFICATE PROGRAMS OFFERED

**Undergraduate**—*BA:* Education. *BS:* Criminal Justice; Education; Health Services Administration. *Certificate:* Gerontology; Health Services Administration. *Endorsement:* English for Speakers of Other Languages.
**Graduate**—*MA:* Curriculum and Instruction. *MBA:* Business Administration. *MEd:* Curriculum and Instruction. *MPA:* Public Administration. *MS:* Health Professions Education; Health Services Administration.

## NON-DEGREE-RELATED COURSE TOPICS OFFERED

**Undergraduate**—English as a second language; accounting; business quantitative methods and management science; computer science; criminal justice and corrections; education administration and supervision; education, other; environmental/environmental health engineering; financial management and services; gerontology; health and medical administrative services; history; human services; marketing management and research; mathematics; nursing; psychology; public administration.
**Graduate**—English as a second language; education, other; public administration.

See full description on page 362.

# FLORIDA INSTITUTE OF TECHNOLOGY

*Extended Campus*
PO Box 260185
Tampa, FL 33615
**Contact:** Vicky W. Knerly, Senior Resident Administrator
**Phone:** 813-884-7365
**Fax:** 813-243-3548
**Web:** http://www.ec.fit.edu
**E-mail:** vgc@fit.edu

**ACCREDITATION:** Southern Association of Colleges and Schools
**INSTITUTIONALLY ADMINISTERED FINANCIAL AID:** Yes

## DEGREE OR CERTIFICATE PROGRAMS OFFERED

**Graduate**—*MBA:* Professional Master of Business Administration. *MPA:* Public Administration. *MS:* Acquisition and Contract Management; Health Management; Human Resources Management; Logistics Management; Materiel Acquisition Management; Operations Research; Project Management. *MSM:* Management.

## NON-DEGREE-RELATED COURSE TOPICS OFFERED

**Graduate**—accounting; business; business administration and management; business quantitative methods and management science; business/managerial economics; engineering/industrial management; health and medical administrative services; information sciences and systems; marketing management and research; public administration; systems engineering.

**Non-credit**—computer and information sciences, general; computer software and media applications; computer systems networking and telecommunications; financial management and services; information sciences and systems.

**See full description on page 364.**

# FLORIDA KEYS COMMUNITY COLLEGE

*Learning Resource Center*

5901 College Road
Key West, FL 33040
**Contact:** Bethany Klein, Admissions and Records
**Phone:** 305-296-9081 Ext. 293
**Web:** http://www.firn.edu/fkcc/library
**E-mail:** klein_b@firn.edu

**ACCREDITATION:** Southern Association of Colleges and Schools
**INSTITUTIONALLY ADMINISTERED FINANCIAL AID:** Yes

## DEGREE OR CERTIFICATE PROGRAMS OFFERED

Programs offered do not lead to a degree or other formal award.

## NON-DEGREE-RELATED COURSE TOPICS OFFERED

**Undergraduate**—anthropology; astronomy; business; education, general; geological and related sciences; library science, other; nursing; psychology; sociology.

# FLORIDA SCHOOL OF PROFESSIONAL PSYCHOLOGY

20 South Clark, 3rd Floor
Chicago, IL 60603
**Contact:** Ms. April Djakoniya, Coordinator of Online Services
**Phone:** 312-279-3839
**Fax:** 312-424-7282
**Web:** http://argosy.aspp.edu
**E-mail:** april@argosyeducation.com

**ACCREDITATION:** North Central Association of Colleges and Schools
**INSTITUTIONALLY ADMINISTERED FINANCIAL AID:** Yes

## DEGREE OR CERTIFICATE PROGRAMS OFFERED

Programs offered do not lead to a degree or other formal award.

## NON-DEGREE-RELATED COURSE TOPICS OFFERED

**Non-credit**—psychology.

# FLORIDA STATE UNIVERSITY

*Office for Distributed and Distance Learning*

3500-C University Center
Tallahassee, FL 32306-2550
**Contact:** Mr. Reinhart Lerch, Marketing Coordinator
**Phone:** 877-357-8283
**Fax:** 850-644-5803
**Web:** http://www.fsu.edu/~distance
**E-mail:** rlerch@oddl.fsu.edu

**ACCREDITATION:** Southern Association of Colleges and Schools
**INSTITUTIONALLY ADMINISTERED FINANCIAL AID:** Yes

## DEGREE OR CERTIFICATE PROGRAMS OFFERED

**Undergraduate**—*BS:* Computer and Information Sciences; Information Studies; Interdisciplinary Social Science. *BSN:* Nursing.
**Graduate**—*MS:* Criminology/Criminal Justice; Instructional Systems/Open and Distance Learning; Library and Information Studies; Mechanical Engineering; Risk Management/Insurance.

**See full description on page 366.**

# FLOYD COLLEGE

*Department of Extended Learning*

PO Box 1864
Rome, GA 30162
**Contact:** Carla Patterson, Director of Extended Learning
**Phone:** 706-802-5300
**Fax:** 706-802-5997
**Web:** http://www.fc.peachnet.edu/extendedlearning/
**E-mail:** carla_patterson@fc.peachnet.edu

**ACCREDITATION:** Southern Association of Colleges and Schools

## DEGREE OR CERTIFICATE PROGRAMS OFFERED

Programs offered do not lead to a degree or other formal award.

## NON-DEGREE-RELATED COURSE TOPICS OFFERED

**Undergraduate**—American (United States) history; English composition; European history; anatomy; developmental and child psychology; mathematics, other; physiology, human and animal; sign language interpreter; sociology.

# FOOTHILL COLLEGE

*Foothill Global Access*

12345 El Monte Road
Los Altos Hills, CA 94022
**Contact:** Art Turmelle, Coordinator, Distance Learning Program
**Phone:** 650-949-7614
**Fax:** 650-949-7123
**Web:** http://www.foothillcollege.org/
**E-mail:** turmelle@fhda.edu

**ACCREDITATION:** Western Association of Schools and Colleges
**INSTITUTIONALLY ADMINISTERED FINANCIAL AID:** Yes

## DEGREE OR CERTIFICATE PROGRAMS OFFERED

**Undergraduate—AA:** Economics; General Studies/Social Science; History; Psychology.

## NON-DEGREE-RELATED COURSE TOPICS OFFERED

**Undergraduate—**English as a second language; English composition; accounting; anthropology; archaeology; area, ethnic and cultural studies, other; art history, criticism and conservation; business administration and management; communications technologies; comparative literature; computer and information sciences, general; data entry/microcomputer applications; drama/theater arts, general; economics; film/cinema studies; financial management and services; foreign languages and literatures; history; library science/librarianship; music; psychology; radio and television broadcasting; social sciences, general; sociology.

# FORREST JUNIOR COLLEGE

601 East River Street
Anderson, SC 29624
**Contact:** Mrs. Brenda P. Cooley, Vice President of Administration and Programs
**Phone:** 864-225-7653 Ext. 204
**Fax:** 864-261-7471
**Web:** http://www.forrestcollege.com
**E-mail:** brenda@forrestcollege.com

**ACCREDITATION:** Accrediting Council for Independent Colleges and Schools

**INSTITUTIONALLY ADMINISTERED FINANCIAL AID:** No

## DEGREE OR CERTIFICATE PROGRAMS OFFERED
Programs offered do not lead to a degree or other formal award.

## NON-DEGREE-RELATED COURSE TOPICS OFFERED

**Undergraduate—**accounting; administrative and secretarial services; business; business administration and management; business and personal services marketing operations; business communications; business information and data processing services; business management and administrative services, other; business/managerial economics; computer and information sciences, general; computer and information sciences, other; computer software and media applications; computer systems networking and telecommunications; computer/information technology administration and management; health and medical administrative services; health and medical assistants; human resources management; law and legal studies; miscellaneous health aides; miscellaneous health professions.
**Non-credit—**computer and information sciences, general; computer and information sciences, other; computer systems networking and telecommunications; computer/information technology administration and management; health professions and related sciences, other.

# FORSYTH TECHNICAL COMMUNITY COLLEGE

*Distance Learning*
2100 Silas Creek Parkway
Winston-Salem, NC 27103
**Contact:** Dr. Bill Randall, Director of Distance Learning

**Phone:** 336-734-7311
**Fax:** 336-761-2598
**Web:** http://www.forsyth.tec.nc.us/
**E-mail:** brandall@forsyth.cc.ns.us

**ACCREDITATION:** Southern Association of Colleges and Schools

**INSTITUTIONALLY ADMINISTERED FINANCIAL AID:** Yes

## DEGREE OR CERTIFICATE PROGRAMS OFFERED

**Undergraduate—AA:** College Transfer. **AD:** Business Administration.

## NON-DEGREE-RELATED COURSE TOPICS OFFERED

**Undergraduate—**accounting; adult and continuing teacher education; anthropology; business marketing and marketing management; finance, general; law and legal studies, other; sociology.
**Non-credit—**American (United States) history; English composition; anatomy; management information systems and business data processing, general; mathematics, other; women's studies.

# FORT HAYS STATE UNIVERSITY

*Virtual College*
600 Park Street
Hays, KS 67601
**Contact:** Cynthia Elliott, Dean
**Phone:** 785-628-4291
**Fax:** 785-628-4037
**Web:** http://www.fhsu.edu/virtual_college
**E-mail:** v_college@tiger.fhsu.edu

**ACCREDITATION:** North Central Association of Colleges and Schools

**INSTITUTIONALLY ADMINISTERED FINANCIAL AID:** Yes

## DEGREE OR CERTIFICATE PROGRAMS OFFERED

**Undergraduate—BGS:** General Studies. **BS:** Elementary Education. **BSN:** Nursing.
**Graduate—MBA/MM:** Liberal Studies.
See full description on page 368.

# FRANCISCAN UNIVERSITY OF STEUBENVILLE

*Distance Learning*
1235 University Boulevard
Steubenville, OH 43952
**Contact:** Mrs. Lorrie Campana, Administrative Clerk
**Phone:** 740-283-6517 Ext. 4611
**Fax:** 740-284-7037
**Web:** http://www2.franuniv.edu/disted/
**E-mail:** distance@franuniv.edu

**ACCREDITATION:** North Central Association of Colleges and Schools

**INSTITUTIONALLY ADMINISTERED FINANCIAL AID:** No

## DEGREE OR CERTIFICATE PROGRAMS OFFERED
**Graduate—MA:** Theology.

## NON-DEGREE-RELATED COURSE TOPICS OFFERED

**Undergraduate**—philosophy; theological and ministerial studies.
**Graduate**—theological and ministerial studies.
**Non-credit**—philosophy; theological and ministerial studies.

# FRANKLIN PIERCE LAW CENTER
## *Education Law Institute*

2 White Street
Concord, NH 03301
**Contact:** Sarah E. Redfield, Professor
**Phone:** 603-228-1541
**Fax:** 603-228-1074
**Web:** http://www.edlaw.fplc.edu
**E-mail:** sredfield@fplc.edu

**ACCREDITATION:** American Bar Association

**INSTITUTIONALLY ADMINISTERED FINANCIAL AID:** Yes

eCollege.com *www.ecollege.com*

## DEGREE OR CERTIFICATE PROGRAMS OFFERED

**Graduate**—*CAGS:* Education Law. *MEd:* Education Law.

## NON-DEGREE-RELATED COURSE TOPICS OFFERED

**Graduate**—education, general; law and legal studies; special education.

# FRANKLIN UNIVERSITY
## *Technical and Non-Campus Based Programs*

201 South Grant Avenue
Columbus, OH 43215
**Contact:** Student Services, Admissions
**Phone:** 614-797-4700
**Fax:** 614-797-4799
**Web:** http://www.franklin.edu
**E-mail:** info@franklin.edu

**ACCREDITATION:** North Central Association of Colleges and Schools
**INSTITUTIONALLY ADMINISTERED FINANCIAL AID:** Yes

## DEGREE OR CERTIFICATE PROGRAMS OFFERED

**Undergraduate**—*BS:* Business Administration; Computer Science; Digital Communication; Health Care Management; Management Information Sciences; Public Safety Management; Technical Management.
**Graduate**—*MBA:* Online MBA.

## NON-DEGREE-RELATED COURSE TOPICS OFFERED

**Undergraduate**—accounting; business administration and management; computer science; financial management and services; health system/health services administration; marketing management and research.
**Graduate**—business administration and management.

See full description on page 370.

# FRANK PHILLIPS COLLEGE

1301 Roosevelt
Borger, TX 79007
**Contact:** Mr. Preston Haddan, Director of Extended Education
**Phone:** 800-687-2056 Ext. 775
**Fax:** 806-274-9834
**Web:** http://www.fpc.cc.tx.us/
**E-mail:** phaddan@fpc.cc.tx.us

**ACCREDITATION:** Southern Association of Colleges and Schools

**INSTITUTIONALLY ADMINISTERED FINANCIAL AID:** Yes

## DEGREE OR CERTIFICATE PROGRAMS OFFERED

**Programs offered do not lead to a degree or other formal award.**

## NON-DEGREE-RELATED COURSE TOPICS OFFERED

**Undergraduate**—American (United States) history; English composition; accounting; biology, general; business marketing and marketing management; developmental and child psychology; mathematics, other; social sciences, general.

# FREDERICK COMMUNITY COLLEGE

7932 Opossumtown Pike
Frederick, MD 21702
**Contact:** Ms. Deborah McClellan, Director of Student Advising
**Phone:** 301-846-2477
**Fax:** 301-846-2498
**Web:** http://www.fcc.cc.md.us/
**E-mail:** dmcclellan@fcc.cc.md.us

**ACCREDITATION:** Middle States Association of Colleges and Schools
**INSTITUTIONALLY ADMINISTERED FINANCIAL AID:** Yes

## DEGREE OR CERTIFICATE PROGRAMS OFFERED

**Undergraduate**—*AA:* General Studies Degree.

## NON-DEGREE-RELATED COURSE TOPICS OFFERED

**Non-credit**—English technical and business writing; accounting; business; business communications; business/managerial economics; communications, general; computer and information sciences, general; computer programming; computer software and media applications; computer systems networking and telecommunications; data entry/microcomputer applications; data processing technology; electrical and electronic engineering-related technology; health and physical education/fitness; home economics, general; internet and world wide web; marketing management and research; public relations and organizational communications; real estate; vehicle and equipment operators.

# FRESNO CITY COLLEGE

Fresno, CA 93741
**Contact:** John H. Cummings, Dean of Admission, Records, and Institutional Research
**Web:** http://www.fresnocitycollege.com

**E-mail:** john.cummings@scccd.com

**ACCREDITATION:** Western Association of Schools and Colleges

**INSTITUTIONALLY ADMINISTERED FINANCIAL AID:** Yes

### DEGREE OR CERTIFICATE PROGRAMS OFFERED

Programs offered do not lead to a degree or other formal award.

### NON-DEGREE-RELATED COURSE TOPICS OFFERED

**Undergraduate**—English composition; English creative writing; English language and literature, general; business administration and management; business information and data processing services; chemistry; computer and information sciences, general; computer systems networking and telecommunications; health and medical preparatory programs.

# FROSTBURG STATE UNIVERSITY

I.T.S. Center, Room 140, Pullen Hall
Frostburg, MD 21532
**Contact:** Ms. Ruth S. Richardson, Administrative Assistant
**Phone:** 301-687-4353
**Fax:** 301-687-3025
**Web:** http://www.frostburg.edu/
**E-mail:** rrichardson@frostburg.edu

**ACCREDITATION:** Middle States Association of Colleges and Schools

**INSTITUTIONALLY ADMINISTERED FINANCIAL AID:** No

### DEGREE OR CERTIFICATE PROGRAMS OFFERED

Programs offered do not lead to a degree or other formal award.

### NON-DEGREE-RELATED COURSE TOPICS OFFERED

**Undergraduate**—accounting; political science and government; sociology.
**Graduate**—business marketing and marketing management; curriculum and instruction; education administration and supervision; educational evaluation, research and statistics; psychology.

# FULLER THEOLOGICAL SEMINARY

*Individualized Distance Learning Program (IDL)*

135 North Oakland Avenue
Pasadena, CA 91182
**Contact:** Sonja Allen, Program Coordinator
**Phone:** 626-584-5266
**Web:** http://www.fuller.edu/
**E-mail:** idl@fuller.edu

**ACCREDITATION:** Western Association of Schools and Colleges

**INSTITUTIONALLY ADMINISTERED FINANCIAL AID:** No

eCollege.com  *www.ecollege.com*

### DEGREE OR CERTIFICATE PROGRAMS OFFERED

Programs offered do not lead to a degree or other formal award.

### NON-DEGREE-RELATED COURSE TOPICS OFFERED

**Graduate**—bible/biblical studies; theological and ministerial studies.
**Non-credit**—bible/biblical studies; theological and ministerial studies.

# FULLERTON COLLEGE

*Distance Education–Media Production Center*

321 East Fullerton
Fullerton, CA 92632
**Contact:** Jay Goldstein, Coordinator
**Phone:** 714-992-7487
**Fax:** 714-879-3972
**Web:** http://www.media.fullcoll.edu
**E-mail:** goldsteinj@hotmail.com

**ACCREDITATION:** Western Association of Schools and Colleges

### DEGREE OR CERTIFICATE PROGRAMS OFFERED

Programs offered do not lead to a degree or other formal award.

### NON-DEGREE-RELATED COURSE TOPICS OFFERED

**Undergraduate**—American (United States) history; English as a second language; English language and literature, general; accounting; biological and physical sciences; biology, general; business; business information and data processing services; computer software and media applications; developmental and child psychology; film/cinema studies; film/video and photographic arts; foreign languages and literatures; geography; health and physical education/fitness; history; journalism and mass communications; marketing management and research; oceanography; political science and government; psychology; sociology.

# GANNON UNIVERSITY

*Center for Adult Learning*

109 University Square
Erie, PA 16541
**Contact:** Gina Hagg, Adult Recruiter
**Phone:** 814-871-5563
**Fax:** 814-871-5827
**Web:** http://www.gannon.edu
**E-mail:** cfal@gannon.edu

**ACCREDITATION:** Middle States Association of Colleges and Schools

**INSTITUTIONALLY ADMINISTERED FINANCIAL AID:** Yes

### DEGREE OR CERTIFICATE PROGRAMS OFFERED

Programs offered do not lead to a degree or other formal award.

### NON-DEGREE-RELATED COURSE TOPICS OFFERED

**Undergraduate**—English composition; English creative writing; business communications; computer systems analysis; consumer and homemaking education; criminal justice and corrections; criminology; developmental and child psychology; economics; individual and family development studies; law and legal studies; marketing management and research; music; philosophy; psychology; religion/religious studies; theological studies and religious vocations, other.

# GARDNER-WEBB UNIVERSITY

Campus Box 7272
Boiling Springs, NC 28017

**Contact:** Dr. Anthony Negbenebor, Director of Graduate School of Business
**Phone:** 704-406-4489 Ext. 4489
**Fax:** 704-406-3895
**Web:** http://www.gardner-webb.edu/
**E-mail:** anegbenebor@gardner-webb.edu

**ACCREDITATION:** Southern Association of Colleges and Schools
**INSTITUTIONALLY ADMINISTERED FINANCIAL AID:** Yes

## DEGREE OR CERTIFICATE PROGRAMS OFFERED
Graduate—*MBA:* Business Administration. *MBA/M Acc:* Master of Accountancy.

## NON-DEGREE-RELATED COURSE TOPICS OFFERED
Graduate—accounting; business administration and management; business quantitative methods and management science; business/managerial economics; community health services; financial management and services; human resources management; information sciences and systems; international business; marketing management and research; taxation.

# GARLAND COUNTY COMMUNITY COLLEGE
## Distance Education
101 College Drive
Hot Springs, AR 71913
**Contact:** Dr. Luke Robins, Vice President for Instruction
**Phone:** 501-760-4202
**Fax:** 501-760-4100
**Web:** http://www.gccc.cc.ar.us
**E-mail:** lrobins@admin.gccc.cc.ar.us

**ACCREDITATION:** North Central Association of Colleges and Schools
**INSTITUTIONALLY ADMINISTERED FINANCIAL AID:** Yes

## DEGREE OR CERTIFICATE PROGRAMS OFFERED
Programs offered do not lead to a degree or other formal award.

## NON-DEGREE-RELATED COURSE TOPICS OFFERED
Undergraduate—English composition; English creative writing; applied mathematics; biology, general; business; business management and administrative services, other; consumer and homemaking education; history; microbiology/bacteriology; psychology; psychology, other; sociology.
Non-credit—business; business administration and management; computer and information sciences, general; computer software and media applications; computer systems networking and telecommunications; computer/information technology administration and management; nursing.

# GASTON COLLEGE
201 Highway 321 South
Dallas, NC 28034
**Contact:** Mrs. Kimberly C. Gelsinger, Director of Distance Education
**Phone:** 704-922-6515

**Fax:** 704-922-6443
**Web:** http://www.gaston.cc.nc.us
**E-mail:** gelsinger.kim@gaston.cc.nc.us

**ACCREDITATION:** Southern Association of Colleges and Schools
**INSTITUTIONALLY ADMINISTERED FINANCIAL AID:** Yes

## DEGREE OR CERTIFICATE PROGRAMS OFFERED
Programs offered do not lead to a degree or other formal award.

## NON-DEGREE-RELATED COURSE TOPICS OFFERED
Undergraduate—American literature (United States); English composition; English language and literature, general; accounting; biological sciences/life sciences, other; business; chemistry; communications, general; computer and information sciences, general; computer programming; computer software and media applications; criminal justice and corrections; criminology; geological and related sciences; information sciences and systems; internet and world wide web; law and legal studies; liberal arts and sciences, general studies and humanities; mathematics; psychology; teacher education, specific academic and vocational programs.

# GATEWAY COMMUNITY COLLEGE
60 Sargent Drive
New Haven, CT 06511
**Contact:** Ms. Catherine Surface, Director of Admission
**Phone:** 203-285-2013
**Fax:** 203-285-2018
**Web:** http://www.gwctc.commnet.edu/
**E-mail:** gw_surface@commnet.com

**ACCREDITATION:** New England Association of Schools and Colleges

## DEGREE OR CERTIFICATE PROGRAMS OFFERED
Programs offered do not lead to a degree or other formal award.

## NON-DEGREE-RELATED COURSE TOPICS OFFERED
Undergraduate—political science and government.

# GENESEE COMMUNITY COLLEGE
## Information Technology and Distance Learning
1 College Road
Batavia, NY 14020-9704
**Contact:** Robert G. Knipe, Dean
**Phone:** 716-343-0055 Ext. 6595
**Fax:** 716-343-0433
**Web:** http://www.genesee.suny.edu
**E-mail:** rgknipe@genesee.suny.edu

**ACCREDITATION:** Middle States Association of Colleges and Schools
**INSTITUTIONALLY ADMINISTERED FINANCIAL AID:** Yes

## DEGREE OR CERTIFICATE PROGRAMS OFFERED
Programs offered do not lead to a degree or other formal award.

## NON-DEGREE-RELATED COURSE TOPICS OFFERED

**Undergraduate**—English composition; English creative writing; European history; accounting; anthropology; art history, criticism and conservation; biology, general; business marketing and marketing management; developmental and child psychology; education, general; film/cinema studies; journalism and mass communication, other; mathematics, other; psychology; sociology; women's studies.

# GEORGE C. WALLACE COMMUNITY COLLEGE

Eufaula, AL 36072
**Contact:** Mr. Frank Barefield, Jr., Director of MIS, Distance Education, and Institutional Research
**Phone:** 334-687-3543 Ext. 4242
**Fax:** 334-687-0255
**Web:** http://www.wcc.cc.al.us
**E-mail:** fbarefield@wcc.cc.al.us

**ACCREDITATION:** Southern Association of Colleges and Schools

## DEGREE OR CERTIFICATE PROGRAMS OFFERED

**Programs offered do not lead to a degree or other formal award.**

## NON-DEGREE-RELATED COURSE TOPICS OFFERED

**Undergraduate**—English composition; biological and physical sciences; business; chemistry; computer and information sciences, general; economics.

# GEORGE MASON UNIVERSITY

4400 University Drive, MSN 5G1
Fairfax, VA 22030
**Contact:** Dr. Anne S. Agee, Executive Director of Division of Instructional Improvement and Instructional Technologies
**Phone:** 703-993-3178
**Fax:** 703-993-4343
**Web:** http://www.gmu.edu/
**E-mail:** aagee@gmu.edu

**ACCREDITATION:** Southern Association of Colleges and Schools
**INSTITUTIONALLY ADMINISTERED FINANCIAL AID:** Yes

## DEGREE OR CERTIFICATE PROGRAMS OFFERED

**Graduate**—*MA:* Recreation Resources Management.

## NON-DEGREE-RELATED COURSE TOPICS OFFERED

**Undergraduate**—English composition; English technical and business writing; business communications; computer and information sciences, other; computer science; criminal justice and corrections; geography; political science and government.
**Graduate**—computer systems networking and telecommunications; forestry and related sciences; information sciences and systems; parks, recreation and leisure facilities management; public administration and services, other.

# THE GEORGE WASHINGTON UNIVERSITY

801 22nd Street, NW, Suite 350
Washington, DC 20052
**Contact:** Dr. William Lynch, Director
**Phone:** 202-496-8369
**Fax:** 202-994-5048
**Web:** http://www.gwu.edu/
**E-mail:** blynch@gwu.edu

**ACCREDITATION:** Middle States Association of Colleges and Schools
**INSTITUTIONALLY ADMINISTERED FINANCIAL AID:** Yes

## DEGREE OR CERTIFICATE PROGRAMS OFFERED

**Undergraduate**—*Certificate:* Event Management; International Public Health-Community Oriented Primary Care Option; Records Management.
**Graduate**—*MA:* Educational Technology Leadership. *MBA/MHSA:* Clinical Health Sciences; Clinical Management and Leadership; Clinical Research Administration; Emergency Health Services. *MS:* Health Science; Project Management.

## NON-DEGREE-RELATED COURSE TOPICS OFFERED

**Undergraduate**—health professions and related sciences, other.
**Graduate**—business; education, general; health professions and related sciences, other.
**Non-credit**—business; education, general.
**See full description on page 372.**

# GEORGIA INSTITUTE OF TECHNOLOGY
*Center for Distance Learning*

613 Cherry Street
Atlanta, GA 30332-0385
**Contact:** Joe Boland, Director
**Phone:** 404-894-8572
**Fax:** 404-385-0322
**Web:** http://www.conted.gatech.edu/distance/
**E-mail:** joe.boland@conted.gatech.edu

**ACCREDITATION:** Southern Association of Colleges and Schools
**INSTITUTIONALLY ADMINISTERED FINANCIAL AID:** No

## DEGREE OR CERTIFICATE PROGRAMS OFFERED

**Graduate**—*MS:* Electrical Engineering; Environmental Engineering; Health Physics; Industrial and Systems Engineering; Mechanical Engineering.

## NON-DEGREE-RELATED COURSE TOPICS OFFERED

**Graduate**—aerospace, aeronautical and astronautical engineering; computer engineering; electrical, electronics and communication engineering; environmental/environmental health engineering; industrial/manufacturing engineering; mathematics; mechanical engineering.
**Non-credit**—aerospace, aeronautical and astronautical engineering; computer engineering; electrical, electronics and communication engineering;

environmental/environmental health engineering; industrial/manufacturing engineering; mathematics; mechanical engineering.

**See full description on page 374.**

# GEORGIA PERIMETER COLLEGE

*Center for Distance Learning*

555 North Indian Creek Drive
Clarkston, GA 30021-2396
**Contact:** Robert A. Harrell, Director of Distance Learning
**Phone:** 404-294-3490
**Fax:** 404-294-3492
**Web:** http://www.gpc.peachnet.edu/~dl
**E-mail:** rharrell@gpc.peachnet.edu

**ACCREDITATION:** Southern Association of Colleges and Schools

**INSTITUTIONALLY ADMINISTERED FINANCIAL AID:** Yes

## DEGREE OR CERTIFICATE PROGRAMS OFFERED

Undergraduate—*AS:* General Studies; Business Administration.

## NON-DEGREE-RELATED COURSE TOPICS OFFERED

Undergraduate—English language and literature, general; astronomy; biological and physical sciences; business administration and management; chemistry; communications, general; computer and information sciences, general; fire protection; foreign languages and literatures; general teacher education; geography; geological and related sciences; liberal arts and sciences, general studies and humanities; mathematics and computer science; nursing; physics; social sciences, general.

# GEORGIA SCHOOL OF PROFESSIONAL PSYCHOLOGY

20 South Clark, 3rd Floor
Chicago, IL 60603
**Contact:** Ms. April Djakoniya, Coordinator of Online Services
**Phone:** 312-279-3839
**Fax:** 312-424-7282
**Web:** http://argosy.aspp.edu
**E-mail:** april@argosyeducation.com

**ACCREDITATION:** North Central Association of Colleges and Schools

**INSTITUTIONALLY ADMINISTERED FINANCIAL AID:** Yes

## DEGREE OR CERTIFICATE PROGRAMS OFFERED

Programs offered do not lead to a degree or other formal award.

## NON-DEGREE-RELATED COURSE TOPICS OFFERED

Non-credit—psychology.

# GEORGIA SOUTHERN UNIVERSITY

*Distance Learning Center*

Post Office Box 8018
Statesboro, GA 30460
**Contact:** Alise Stokes, Administrative Secretary

**Phone:** 912-681-0882
**Fax:** 912-871-1424
**Web:** http://www2.gasou.edu/dlc
**E-mail:** astokes@gasou.edu

**ACCREDITATION:** Southern Association of Colleges and Schools

**INSTITUTIONALLY ADMINISTERED FINANCIAL AID:** Yes

## DEGREE OR CERTIFICATE PROGRAMS OFFERED

Programs offered do not lead to a degree or other formal award.

## NON-DEGREE-RELATED COURSE TOPICS OFFERED

Undergraduate—English composition; accounting; education administration and supervision; engineering mechanics; military studies; nursing; sociology.
Graduate—accounting; business management and administrative services, other; curriculum and instruction; public administration and services, other; sociology.

# GEORGIA STATE UNIVERSITY

*Division of Distance and Distributed Learning*

PO Box 4044
Atlanta, GA 30302-4044
**Contact:** Jacquelynn Sharpe, Instructional Services Coordinator
**Phone:** 404-651-3483
**Fax:** 404-651-3452
**Web:** http://www.gsu.edu/ddl
**E-mail:** dcejws@langate.gsu.edu

**ACCREDITATION:** Southern Association of Colleges and Schools

**INSTITUTIONALLY ADMINISTERED FINANCIAL AID:** Yes

## DEGREE OR CERTIFICATE PROGRAMS OFFERED

Programs offered do not lead to a degree or other formal award.

## NON-DEGREE-RELATED COURSE TOPICS OFFERED

Graduate—accounting; business; nursing.

# GLENDALE COMMUNITY COLLEGE

*Letters, Arts, and Sciences*

Instructional Services, 1500 North Verdugo Road
Glendale, CA 91208
**Contact:** Dr. Kristin Bruno, Dean
**Phone:** 818-240-1000 Ext. 5187
**Fax:** 818-551-5228
**Web:** http://www.glendale.cc.ca.us
**E-mail:** kbruno@glendale.cc.ca.us

**ACCREDITATION:** Western Association of Schools and Colleges

**INSTITUTIONALLY ADMINISTERED FINANCIAL AID:** Yes

## DEGREE OR CERTIFICATE PROGRAMS OFFERED

Programs offered do not lead to a degree or other formal award.

## NON-DEGREE-RELATED COURSE TOPICS OFFERED

**Undergraduate**—English as a second language; accounting; anthropology; business administration and management; computer science; developmental and child psychology; music; psychology; sociology.

# GLENVILLE STATE COLLEGE

Robert F. Kidd Library, 100 High Street
Glenville, WV 26351
**Contact:** Ed Messenger, Library Director
**Phone:** 304-462-4109 Ext. 311
**Fax:** 304-462-4049
**Web:** http://www.glenville.edu/
**E-mail:** messenger@glenville.edu

**ACCREDITATION:** North Central Association of Colleges and Schools

**INSTITUTIONALLY ADMINISTERED FINANCIAL AID:** Yes

## DEGREE OR CERTIFICATE PROGRAMS OFFERED

**Programs offered do not lead to a degree or other formal award.**

# GLOBAL UNIVERSITY OF THE ASSEMBLIES OF GOD

1211 South Glenstone Avenue
Springfield, MO 65804
**Contact:** Debbie A. Seevers, Director of Research and Evaluation
**Web:** http://www.globaluniversity.edu/
**E-mail:** dseevers@globaluniversity.edu

**ACCREDITATION:** Distance Education and Training Council

## DEGREE OR CERTIFICATE PROGRAMS OFFERED

**Undergraduate**—*AA:* Bible and Theology; Missions; Religious Education. *BA:* Bible and Theology; Missions; Religious Education.
**Graduate**—*MA:* Bible and Theology; Leadership-Christian; Missions; Religious Education.

### Special Note

Global University is the largest distance education institution in evangelical Christendom, providing adult continuing education, undergraduate, and graduate programs. Its headquarters are located in Springfield, Missouri.

Global University has more than 50 years in distance education experience through its Berean School of the Bible division and worldwide network for student support through its ICI international division. Present enrollment in the US is more than 16,000 adults of varying ages and denominations. It also serves students, schools, and churches outside the US through its network of 180 national offices in 160 countries. The mission of Global University is to integrate education and service through a worldwide network for student support; provide access to ministerial training, from adult continuing education to graduate level; produce curricular material in multiple languages; and serve the local church and Christian community through evangelism, discipleship, and leadership training via distributed learning methods. The University has experienced tremendous growth in educational technology. It offers a complete

BA degree in Bible and theology online. Students have 24-hour access to the voice-mail boxes of their personal student service representatives. The University has a presence on the Internet (http://www.globaluniversity.edu), where students and prospective students get detailed information about the services and programs that the institution offers. The site is updated regularly.

Global University provides access to its Christian education programs through its network of national offices and cooperative institutions, utilizing print, Internet, CD-ROM, videoconferencing, and audio and video delivery systems. The University is committed to providing high-quality distance education for students who must fit their studies between their families and their jobs or to those who desire to increase their biblical knowledge.

# GODDARD COLLEGE
*Distance Learning Programs*

123 Pitkin Road
Plainfield, VT 05667
**Contact:** Brenda Hawkins, Admissions
**Phone:** 800-468-4888
**Fax:** 802-454-1029
**Web:** http://www.goddard.edu
**E-mail:** admissions@goddard.edu

**ACCREDITATION:** New England Association of Schools and Colleges

**INSTITUTIONALLY ADMINISTERED FINANCIAL AID:** Yes

## DEGREE OR CERTIFICATE PROGRAMS OFFERED

**Undergraduate**—*BA:* Health Arts; Individualized Studies; Liberal Arts; Social Ecology.
**Graduate**—*MA:* Health Arts; Individualized Study in the Liberal Arts; Psychology and Counseling; Social Ecology; Teacher Education. *MFA:* Creative Writing; Interdisciplinary Arts.
**See full description on page 376.**

# GOGEBIC COMMUNITY COLLEGE

E4946 Jackson Road
Ironwood, MI 49938
**Contact:** Mr. James Lorenson, Dean of Instruction
**Phone:** 906-932-4231 Ext. 215
**Web:** http://www.gogebic.cc.mi.us/
**E-mail:** jiml@admin.gogebic.cc.mi.us

**ACCREDITATION:** North Central Association of Colleges and Schools

## DEGREE OR CERTIFICATE PROGRAMS OFFERED

**Programs offered do not lead to a degree or other formal award.**

## NON-DEGREE-RELATED COURSE TOPICS OFFERED

**Undergraduate**—English composition; accounting; ecology; history; journalism; sociology.

# GOLDEN GATE UNIVERSITY

## Cyber Campus

536 Mission Street
San Francisco, CA 94105
**Contact:** Alan Roper, Senior Program Administrator
**Phone:** 415-369-5263
**Fax:** 415-227-4502
**Web:** http://www.ggu.edu/
**E-mail:** cybercampus@ggu.edu

**ACCREDITATION:** Western Association of Schools and Colleges

### DEGREE OR CERTIFICATE PROGRAMS OFFERED

**Undergraduate—*Certificate:*** Finance(Undergraduate); Financial Planning(Undergraduate); Technology Management (Undergraduate).
**Graduate—*Graduate Certificate:*** Accounting; Finance; Financial Planning; Information Systems; Marketing; Taxation. ***MBA:*** Business Administration; E-Commerce(MBAeC). ***MBA/M Acc:*** Master of Accountancy. ***MBA/MSE:*** Public Administration. ***MS:*** E-Commerce; Finance; Financial Planning; Marketing; Taxation; Telecommunications Management. ***MSIS:*** Information Systems.

### NON-DEGREE-RELATED COURSE TOPICS OFFERED

**Undergraduate—**English composition; accounting; finance, general; management information systems and business data processing, general.
**Graduate—**English composition; accounting; business marketing and marketing management; finance, general; health system/health services administration; management information systems and business data processing, general.

# GONZAGA UNIVERSITY

## School of Professional Studies

502 East Boone, MSC 2616
Spokane, WA 99258
**Contact:** Shannon Zaranski, Assistant to the Dean of Professional Studies
**Phone:** 509-323-3569
**Fax:** 509-323-3566
**Web:** http://www.gonzaga.edu/
**E-mail:** zaranski@gu.gonzaga.edu

**ACCREDITATION:** Northwest Association of Schools and Colleges

### DEGREE OR CERTIFICATE PROGRAMS OFFERED

Programs offered do not lead to a degree or other formal award.

### NON-DEGREE-RELATED COURSE TOPICS OFFERED

**Graduate—**nursing.

# GORDON COLLEGE

255 Grapevine Road
Wenham, MA 01984
**Contact:** Mr. Chris Underation, Public Relations Specialist
**Phone:** 978-927.2306 Ext. 4037
**Fax:** 978-524.3771

**Web:** http://www.gordon.edu/
**E-mail:** cunderation@hope.gordon.edu

**ACCREDITATION:** New England Association of Schools and Colleges

eCollege.com  *www.ecollege.com*

### DEGREE OR CERTIFICATE PROGRAMS OFFERED

Programs offered do not lead to a degree or other formal award.

# GOUCHER COLLEGE

## Center for Graduate and Professional Studies

1021 Dulaney Valley Road
Baltimore, MD 21204
**Contact:** Noreen P. Mack, Director for Marketing and Program Development
**Phone:** 410-337-6200
**Fax:** 410-337-6085
**Web:** http://www.goucher.edu/
**E-mail:** nmack@goucher.edu

**ACCREDITATION:** Middle States Association of Colleges and Schools
**INSTITUTIONALLY ADMINISTERED FINANCIAL AID:** Yes

### DEGREE OR CERTIFICATE PROGRAMS OFFERED

**Graduate—*MA:*** Arts Administration; Historic Preservation. ***MFA:*** Creative Nonfiction.

### NON-DEGREE-RELATED COURSE TOPICS OFFERED

**Graduate—**education, general.

# GOVERNORS STATE UNIVERSITY

## Center for Extended Learning and Communications Services

1 University Parkway
University Park, IL 60466
**Contact:** Veronica Williams, Director
**Phone:** 708-534-3143
**Fax:** 708-534-8458
**Web:** http://www.govst.edu/
**E-mail:** v-williams@govst.edu

**ACCREDITATION:** North Central Association of Colleges and Schools

### DEGREE OR CERTIFICATE PROGRAMS OFFERED

**Undergraduate—*BA:*** Individualized Studies.

### NON-DEGREE-RELATED COURSE TOPICS OFFERED

**Undergraduate—**English composition; accounting; anthropology; art history, criticism and conservation; business marketing and marketing management; developmental and child psychology; geography; psychology; social work; sociology.
**Graduate—**anthropology; art history, criticism and conservation; developmental and child psychology; social work; sociology.

# GRACELAND UNIVERSITY

*Distance Learning*

College of Professional Studies, 1 University Place
Lamoni, IA 50140
**Contact:** Ms. Deb Jaeger, Executive Assistant
**Phone:** 641-784-5052
**Fax:** 641-784-5405
**Web:** http://www2.graceland.edu/
**E-mail:** djaeger@graceland.edu

**ACCREDITATION:** North Central Association of Colleges and Schools

## DEGREE OR CERTIFICATE PROGRAMS OFFERED

**Undergraduate—BA:** Accounting; Business Administration; Elementary Education; Information Technology; Liberal Studies; Sociology. **BSN:** Professional Nursing.
**Graduate—MEd:** Education. **MSN:** Clinical Nurse Specialist—Family Nursing; Family Nurse Practitioner; Health Care Administration.

## NON-DEGREE-RELATED COURSE TOPICS OFFERED

**Undergraduate—**American (United States) history; English composition; accounting; biology, general; business marketing and marketing management; curriculum and instruction; developmental and child psychology; drama/theater arts, general; educational psychology; finance, general; industrial and organizational psychology; microbiology/bacteriology; sociology.
**Graduate—**educational psychology.

# GRACE UNIVERSITY

*Grace University i-Studies*

1311 South 9th Street
Omaha, NE 68108
**Contact:** Terri Dingfield, Director of Admissions
**Phone:** 402-449-2831
**Fax:** 402-341-9587
**Web:** http://www.graceuniversity.edu
**E-mail:** admissions@graceu.edu

**ACCREDITATION:** Accrediting Association of Bible Colleges

## DEGREE OR CERTIFICATE PROGRAMS OFFERED

Programs offered do not lead to a degree or other formal award.

## NON-DEGREE-RELATED COURSE TOPICS OFFERED

**Undergraduate—**bible/biblical studies; history; psychology.

# GRAMBLING STATE UNIVERSITY

*Grambling State University Distance Learning*

100 Main Street
Grambling, LA 71245
**Contact:** Carolyn Wilson, Secretary
**Phone:** 318-274-6412
**Fax:** 318-274-3761
**Web:** http://www.gram.edu

**E-mail:** ctwilson@alphao.gram.edu

**ACCREDITATION:** Southern Association of Colleges and Schools
**INSTITUTIONALLY ADMINISTERED FINANCIAL AID:** No

## DEGREE OR CERTIFICATE PROGRAMS OFFERED

**Undergraduate—Certificate:** Paralegal Studies.

# GRAND CANYON UNIVERSITY

*College of Education*

3300 West Camelback Road
Phoenix, AZ 85017
**Contact:** Dr. Marilyn K. Wells, Director for Distance Learning
**Phone:** 800-600-5019 Ext. 2476
**Fax:** 602-589-2010
**Web:** http://www.grand-canyon.edu
**E-mail:** mwells@grand-canyon.edu

**ACCREDITATION:** North Central Association of Colleges and Schools
**INSTITUTIONALLY ADMINISTERED FINANCIAL AID:** Yes

## DEGREE OR CERTIFICATE PROGRAMS OFFERED

**Graduate—MAT:** Teaching.

## NON-DEGREE-RELATED COURSE TOPICS OFFERED

**Undergraduate—**special education.
**Graduate—**special education.

# GRAND RAPIDS BAPTIST SEMINARY

1001 East Beltline, NE
Grand Rapids, MI 49525
**Contact:** Peter G. Osborn, Director of Graduate Admissions
**Phone:** 616-222-1426
**Fax:** 616-222-1400
**Web:** http://www.grbs.edu
**E-mail:** grbs@cornerstone.edu

**ACCREDITATION:** North Central Association of Colleges and Schools
**INSTITUTIONALLY ADMINISTERED FINANCIAL AID:** Yes

## DEGREE OR CERTIFICATE PROGRAMS OFFERED

Programs offered do not lead to a degree or other formal award.

## NON-DEGREE-RELATED COURSE TOPICS OFFERED

**Graduate—**bible/biblical studies; biblical and other theological languages and literatures; religion/religious studies; theological studies and religious vocations, other.
**Non-credit—**bible/biblical studies; biblical and other theological languages and literatures; religion/religious studies; theological and ministerial studies.

# GRAND RAPIDS COMMUNITY COLLEGE

*Distance Learning Committee*

143 Bostwick, NE
Grand Rapids, MI 49503
**Contact:** Ms. Patti A. Trepkowski, Dean of Instructional Design and Information Technology
**Phone:** 616-234-4289
**Fax:** 616-234-3781
**Web:** http://www.grcc.cc.mi.us/
**E-mail:** ptrepkow@grcc.cc.mi.us

**ACCREDITATION:** North Central Association of Colleges and Schools
**INSTITUTIONALLY ADMINISTERED FINANCIAL AID:** Yes

## DEGREE OR CERTIFICATE PROGRAMS OFFERED
Programs offered do not lead to a degree or other formal award.

## NON-DEGREE-RELATED COURSE TOPICS OFFERED
**Undergraduate**—English composition; anthropology; applied mathematics; astronomy; business; business administration and management; business communications; computer systems networking and telecommunications; computer/information technology administration and management; criminal justice and corrections; developmental and child psychology; economics; film/video and photographic arts; geography; history; mathematical statistics; mathematics, other; philosophy; political science and government; psychology; social psychology; sociology; technology education/industrial arts.
**Non-credit**—communications, other; quality control and safety technologies.

# GRAND VALLEY STATE UNIVERSITY

*Division of Continuing Education*

301 West Fulton, Eberhard Center
Grand Rapids, MI 49504
**Contact:** Sandy Becker
**Phone:** 616-771-6616
**Web:** http://www.gvsu.edu/
**E-mail:** beckers@gvsu.edu

**ACCREDITATION:** North Central Association of Colleges and Schools

## DEGREE OR CERTIFICATE PROGRAMS OFFERED
Programs offered do not lead to a degree or other formal award.

## NON-DEGREE-RELATED COURSE TOPICS OFFERED
**Undergraduate**—accounting; business administration and management; criminal justice and corrections; educational psychology; liberal arts and sciences, general studies and humanities; nursing; social psychology; sociology.
**Graduate**—accounting; business administration and management; communications, general; education, general; educational psychology; nursing; public administration; social psychology; social work; sociology; special education.

# GRAND VIEW COLLEGE

*Camp Dodge Campus*

1200 Grandview Avenue
Des Moines, IA 50316
**Contact:** Ms. Sharon Timm, Director of Camp Dodge Campus
**Phone:** 515-245-4546
**Fax:** 515-263-2974
**Web:** http://www.gvc.edu/
**E-mail:** stimm@gvc.edu

**ACCREDITATION:** North Central Association of Colleges and Schools
**INSTITUTIONALLY ADMINISTERED FINANCIAL AID:** Yes

## DEGREE OR CERTIFICATE PROGRAMS OFFERED
Programs offered do not lead to a degree or other formal award.

## NON-DEGREE-RELATED COURSE TOPICS OFFERED
**Undergraduate**—economics; sociology.

# GRANTHAM COLLEGE OF ENGINEERING

PO Box 5700
Slidell, LA 70469-5700
**Contact:** Ms. Amy Hammer, Director of Admissions
**Phone:** 985-649-4191
**Fax:** 985-649-4183
**Web:** http://www.grantham.edu/
**E-mail:** admissions@grantham.edu

**ACCREDITATION:** Distance Education and Training Council

## DEGREE OR CERTIFICATE PROGRAMS OFFERED
**Undergraduate**—*AS:* Computer Science; Electronics Engineering Technology. *BS:* Computer Science; Electronics Engineering Technology.

## NON-DEGREE-RELATED COURSE TOPICS OFFERED
**Undergraduate**—English composition; electrical, electronics and communication engineering; mathematics, other.

# GREAT BASIN COLLEGE

1500 College Parkway
Elko, NV 89801
**Contact:** Dr. Garry Heberer, Executive Director for Extended Studies and Special Programs
**Phone:** 775-753-2213
**Fax:** 775-753-2186
**Web:** http://www.gbcnv.edu
**E-mail:** garry@gbcnv.edu

**ACCREDITATION:** Northwest Association of Schools and Colleges
**INSTITUTIONALLY ADMINISTERED FINANCIAL AID:** Yes

## DEGREE OR CERTIFICATE PROGRAMS OFFERED
Programs offered do not lead to a degree or other formal award.

## NON-DEGREE-RELATED COURSE TOPICS OFFERED

**Undergraduate**—English composition; business; computer and information sciences, general; engineering-related technologies, other; environmental health; geography; home economics, general; mathematics, other; nursing; political science and government; protective services, other; psychology; religion/religious studies; social sciences, general; sociology; teacher education, specific academic and vocational programs.

## GREEN RIVER COMMUNITY COLLEGE

*Distance Learning*
12401 Southeast 320th Street
Auburn, WA 98092
**Contact:** Paul Allen, Director of Distance Learning
**Phone:** 253-288-3354
**Web:** http://www.grcc.ctc.edu
**E-mail:** pallen@grcc.ctc.edu

**ACCREDITATION:** Northwest Association of Schools and Colleges
**INSTITUTIONALLY ADMINISTERED FINANCIAL AID:** Yes

## DEGREE OR CERTIFICATE PROGRAMS OFFERED

**Undergraduate**—*AA:* General Studies.

## NON-DEGREE-RELATED COURSE TOPICS OFFERED

**Undergraduate**—English composition; business; education, general; health and physical education/fitness; mathematics; social sciences, general.

## GRIGGS UNIVERSITY

*HSI/Griggs University*
PO Box 4437
Silver Spring, MD 20914-4437
**Contact:** Summer E. Porter, Director of Admissions and Registrar
**Phone:** 301-680-6579
**Fax:** 301-680-6526
**Web:** http://www.griggs.edu/
**E-mail:** sporter@griggs.edu

**ACCREDITATION:** Distance Education and Training Council

## DEGREE OR CERTIFICATE PROGRAMS OFFERED

**Undergraduate**—*AA:* Personal Ministries. *BA:* Religion; Theological Studies. *BS:* Church Business Management; Religious Education.

## NON-DEGREE-RELATED COURSE TOPICS OFFERED

**Undergraduate**—English language and literature, general; biology, general; business; communications, general; education, general; fine arts and art studies; foods and nutrition studies; geography; mathematics; political science and government; psychology; sociology; theological and ministerial studies.

## HAMILTON COLLEGE

*Center for Distance Education*
1924 D Street, SW
Cedar Rapids, IA 52404
**Contact:** Susan Spivey, Executive Director
**Phone:** 319-363-0481
**Fax:** 319-363-3812
**Web:** http://www.hamiltonia.edu
**E-mail:** spiveys@hamiltonia.edu

**ACCREDITATION:** Accrediting Council for Independent Colleges and Schools
**INSTITUTIONALLY ADMINISTERED FINANCIAL AID:** Yes

## DEGREE OR CERTIFICATE PROGRAMS OFFERED

**Programs offered do not lead to a degree or other formal award.**

## NON-DEGREE-RELATED COURSE TOPICS OFFERED

**Undergraduate**—English composition; English language and literature, general; accounting; administrative and secretarial services; business administration and management; business management and administrative services, other; communications, general; computer and information sciences, general; computer/information technology administration and management; economics; foods and nutrition studies; human resources management; law and legal studies; marketing management and research; mathematics; psychology; sociology.

## HAMLINE UNIVERSITY

1536 Hewitt Avenue
Saint Paul, MN 55104-1284
**Contact:** Dr. Andreas Schramm, Assistant Professor of Second Language and Teaching and Learning
**Phone:** 651-523-2009
**Fax:** 651-523-2489
**Web:** http://www.hamline.edu/
**E-mail:** aschramm@gw.hamline.edu

**ACCREDITATION:** North Central Association of Colleges and Schools
**INSTITUTIONALLY ADMINISTERED FINANCIAL AID:** Yes

## DEGREE OR CERTIFICATE PROGRAMS OFFERED

**Graduate**—*MAE:* Education; English as a Second Language.

## NON-DEGREE-RELATED COURSE TOPICS OFFERED

**Undergraduate**—anthropology.
**Graduate**—English as a second language; bilingual/bicultural education; education, general; education, other; educational/instructional media design; general teacher education; public administration and services, other; special education; teacher education, specific academic and vocational programs; teaching English as a second language/foreign language.
**Non-credit**—English as a second language; education administration and supervision; education, general; education, other; educational/instructional media design; public administration; public administration and services, other; teacher education, specific academic and vocational programs; teaching English as a second language/foreign language; urban affairs/studies.

# HARCOURT LEARNING DIRECT CENTER FOR DEGREE STUDIES

*Center for Degree Studies*

925 Oak Street
Scranton, PA 18515
**Contact:** Ms. Linda K. Smith, Manager of Data Processing
**Phone:** 570-342-7701
**Web:** http://www.harcourt-learning.com
**E-mail:** lsmith@harcourt.com

**ACCREDITATION:** Distance Education and Training Council
**INSTITUTIONALLY ADMINISTERED FINANCIAL AID:** No

## DEGREE OR CERTIFICATE PROGRAMS OFFERED
**Undergraduate—*AD:*** Accounting ASB; Applied Computer Science ASB; Business Management ASB; Engineering Technology AST; Hospitality Management ASB.

## NON-DEGREE-RELATED COURSE TOPICS OFFERED
**Non-credit**—accounting; administrative and secretarial services; child care and guidance workers and managers; computer programming; foods and nutrition studies; teacher assistant/aide.

# HARFORD COMMUNITY COLLEGE

401 Thomas Run Road
Bel Air, MD 21015
**Contact:** Ms. Cindi Barber, Distance Learning Technician
**Phone:** 410-836-4130
**Fax:** 410-836-4198
**Web:** http://www.harford.cc.md.us/
**E-mail:** cbarber@harford.cc.md.us

**ACCREDITATION:** Middle States Association of Colleges and Schools
**INSTITUTIONALLY ADMINISTERED FINANCIAL AID:** Yes

## DEGREE OR CERTIFICATE PROGRAMS OFFERED
**Undergraduate—*AA:*** General Studies.

## NON-DEGREE-RELATED COURSE TOPICS OFFERED
**Undergraduate**—computer and information sciences, general; computer programming; computer systems networking and telecommunications.
**Non-credit**—computer and information sciences, general; computer programming; computer systems networking and telecommunications.

# HARRISBURG AREA COMMUNITY COLLEGE

*Distance Education Office*

1 HACC Drive
Harrisburg, PA 17110
**Contact:** Elaine Stoneroad, Distance Education Manager
**Phone:** 717-780-2541
**Fax:** 717-780-1925
**Web:** http://www.hacc.edu/programs/disted/disted.cfm

**E-mail:** emstoner@hacc.edu
**ACCREDITATION:** Middle States Association of Colleges and Schools
**INSTITUTIONALLY ADMINISTERED FINANCIAL AID:** Yes

## DEGREE OR CERTIFICATE PROGRAMS OFFERED
Programs offered do not lead to a degree or other formal award.

## NON-DEGREE-RELATED COURSE TOPICS OFFERED
**Undergraduate**—American literature (United States); English composition; English language and literature, general; English literature (British and Commonwealth); English technical and business writing; accounting; anthropology; applied mathematics; biological and physical sciences; business; business administration and management; business management and administrative services, other; business/managerial economics; computer programming; computer science; computer software and media applications; criminal justice and corrections; developmental and child psychology; economics; engineering, general; foods and nutrition studies; geography; geological and related sciences; history; internet and world wide web; mathematical statistics; mathematics; mathematics and computer science; microbiology/bacteriology; philosophy; physical sciences, general; psychology; public health; sociology.

# HARTNELL COLLEGE

156 Homestaed Avenue
Salinas, CA 93901
**Contact:** Dr. Celia Barberena, Vice President of Student Services
**E-mail:** cberber@hartnell.cc.ca.us

**ACCREDITATION:** Western Association of Schools and Colleges
**INSTITUTIONALLY ADMINISTERED FINANCIAL AID:** Yes

## DEGREE OR CERTIFICATE PROGRAMS OFFERED
Programs offered do not lead to a degree or other formal award.

## NON-DEGREE-RELATED COURSE TOPICS OFFERED
**Undergraduate**—English as a second language; computer science; counseling psychology; health and medical assistants; health and medical preparatory programs.

# HARVARD UNIVERSITY

*Division of Continuing Education–Harvard Extension School*

51 Brattle Street
Cambridge, MA 02138
**Contact:** Academic Services
**Phone:** 617-495-4024
**Web:** http://www.extension.harvard.edu
**E-mail:** dce-distance-ed@harvard.edu

**ACCREDITATION:** New England Association of Schools and Colleges
**INSTITUTIONALLY ADMINISTERED FINANCIAL AID:** No

## DEGREE OR CERTIFICATE PROGRAMS OFFERED
Programs offered do not lead to a degree or other formal award.

## NON-DEGREE-RELATED COURSE TOPICS OFFERED

**Undergraduate**—Greek languages and literatures (modern); biology, general; environmental/environmental health engineering; museology/ museum studies; philosophy.

**Graduate**—Greek languages and literatures (modern); biology, general; computer science; environmental/environmental health engineering; museology/museum studies; philosophy.

**Non-credit**—Greek languages and literatures (modern); biology, general; computer science; environmental/environmental health engineering; museology/museum studies; philosophy.

# HAWKEYE COMMUNITY COLLEGE
## *Department of Academic Telecommunications*

1501 East Orange Road
Waterloo, IA 50704
**Contact:** Dr. Roger Rezabek, Director of Distance Learning
**Phone:** 319-296-4022
**Fax:** 319-296-9140
**Web:** http://www.hawkeye.cc.ia.us/academic/distance
**E-mail:** rrezabek@hawkeye.cc.ia.us

**ACCREDITATION:** North Central Association of Colleges and Schools
**INSTITUTIONALLY ADMINISTERED FINANCIAL AID:** Yes

## DEGREE OR CERTIFICATE PROGRAMS OFFERED

**Undergraduate**—*AA:* Arts and Sciences; Business Management; Liberal Arts. *AS:* Arts and Sciences.

## NON-DEGREE-RELATED COURSE TOPICS OFFERED

**Undergraduate**—computer systems networking and telecommunications.

# HAYWOOD COMMUNITY COLLEGE

185 Freedlander Drive
Clyde, NC 28716
**Contact:** Ms. Debbie Rowland, Coordinator of Admissions
**Phone:** 828-627-4505
**Fax:** 828-627-4513
**Web:** http://www.haywood.cc.nc.us/
**E-mail:** drowland@trieste.haywood.cc.nc.us

**ACCREDITATION:** Southern Association of Colleges and Schools
**INSTITUTIONALLY ADMINISTERED FINANCIAL AID:** Yes

## DEGREE OR CERTIFICATE PROGRAMS OFFERED

Programs offered do not lead to a degree or other formal award.

## NON-DEGREE-RELATED COURSE TOPICS OFFERED

**Undergraduate**—English composition; English language and literature, general; English technical and business writing; anthropology; business; business administration and management; business information and data processing services; computer and information sciences, general; economics; education, general; engineering-related technologies, other; fine arts and art studies; health and physical education/fitness; history; horticulture services operations and management; information sciences and systems;

liberal arts and sciences, general studies and humanities; mathematics and computer science; political science and government; psychology; religion/ religious studies; sociology.

**Non-credit**—computer software and media applications.

# HEARTLAND COMMUNITY COLLEGE

1500 West Raab Road
Normal, IL 61761
**Contact:** Mr. Padriac Sean Shinville, Division Chair of Alternative Learning and Developmental Education
**Phone:** 309-268-8414
**Fax:** 309-268-7986
**Web:** http://www.hcc.cc.il.us/
**E-mail:** padriac.shinville@hcc.cc.il.us

**ACCREDITATION:** North Central Association of Colleges and Schools
**INSTITUTIONALLY ADMINISTERED FINANCIAL AID:** Yes

## DEGREE OR CERTIFICATE PROGRAMS OFFERED

Programs offered do not lead to a degree or other formal award.

## NON-DEGREE-RELATED COURSE TOPICS OFFERED

**Undergraduate**—American literature (United States); English composition; accounting; business; child care and guidance workers and managers; communications, general; foods and nutrition studies; history; psychology.

# HEBREW COLLEGE

43 Hawes Street
Brookline, MA 02446
**Contact:** Nathan Ehrlich, Director, Center for Information Technology
**Phone:** 617-278-4929
**Fax:** 617-264-9264
**Web:** http://www.hebrewcollege.edu/online
**E-mail:** nathan@hebrewcollege.edu

**ACCREDITATION:** New England Association of Schools and Colleges
**INSTITUTIONALLY ADMINISTERED FINANCIAL AID:** Yes

## DEGREE OR CERTIFICATE PROGRAMS OFFERED

Programs offered do not lead to a degree or other formal award.

## NON-DEGREE-RELATED COURSE TOPICS OFFERED

**Undergraduate**—Jewish/Judaic studies; Middle Eastern languages and literatures; bible/biblical studies; biblical and other theological languages and literatures; education, other; foreign languages and literatures; philosophy and religion; religion/religious studies.

**Graduate**—Jewish/Judaic studies; Middle Eastern languages and literatures; bible/biblical studies; biblical and other theological languages and literatures; education, other; foreign languages and literatures; philosophy and religion; religion/religious studies.

**Non-credit**—Jewish/Judaic studies; Middle Eastern languages and literatures; bible/biblical studies; biblical and other theological languages and literatures; education, other; foreign languages and literatures; philosophy and religion; religion/religious studies.

# HIBBING COMMUNITY COLLEGE

1515 East 25th Street
Hibbing, MN 55746-3300
**Contact:** James Antilla, Director of Instructional Technology
**Phone:** 218-262-7250
**Fax:** 218-262-7222
**Web:** http://www.hcc.mnscu.edu/
**E-mail:** j.antilla@hcc.mnscu.edu

**ACCREDITATION:** North Central Association of Colleges and Schools

**INSTITUTIONALLY ADMINISTERED FINANCIAL AID:** Yes

## DEGREE OR CERTIFICATE PROGRAMS OFFERED
Programs offered do not lead to a degree or other formal award.

## NON-DEGREE-RELATED COURSE TOPICS OFFERED
**Undergraduate**—English composition; accounting; applied mathematics; area, ethnic and cultural studies, other; business administration and management; computer and information sciences, general; computer programming; computer science; computer software and media applications; data entry/microcomputer applications; drafting; economics; fine arts and art studies; foods and nutrition studies; health and medical preparatory programs; information sciences and systems; liberal arts and sciences, general studies and humanities; mathematics; multi/interdisciplinary studies, other; nursing; psychology.
**Non-credit**—accounting; computer and information sciences, general; computer software and media applications; internet and world wide web; real estate.

**See full description on page 378.**

# HILLSBOROUGH COMMUNITY COLLEGE

*Distance Learning Office*
PO Box 31127, BACA 207-E
Tampa, FL 33631-3127
**Contact:** Michael Comins, Director
**Phone:** 813-253-7017
**Fax:** 813-253-7196
**Web:** http://www.hcc.cc.fl.us/
**E-mail:** cominsm@mail.firn.edu

**ACCREDITATION:** Southern Association of Colleges and Schools

## DEGREE OR CERTIFICATE PROGRAMS OFFERED
Programs offered do not lead to a degree or other formal award.

## NON-DEGREE-RELATED COURSE TOPICS OFFERED
**Undergraduate**—English composition; biology, general; business marketing and marketing management; developmental and child psychology; finance, general; sociology.

# HILLSDALE FREE WILL BAPTIST COLLEGE

*Department of External Studies*
PO Box 7208
Moore, OK 73163-1208
**Contact:** Edwin L. Wade, Director of External Studies
**Phone:** 405-912-9000
**Fax:** 405-912-9050
**Web:** http://www.hc.edu
**E-mail:** xstudies@hc.edu

**ACCREDITATION:** Transnational Association of Christian Colleges and Schools

## DEGREE OR CERTIFICATE PROGRAMS OFFERED
Programs offered do not lead to a degree or other formal award.

# HOBE SOUND BIBLE COLLEGE

*Department of External Studies*
PO Box 1065
Hobe Sound, FL 33475
**Contact:** Mr. Dalbert N. Walker, Dean of External Studies
**Phone:** 561-546-5534 Ext. 1014
**Fax:** 561-545-1422
**E-mail:** hsbcexternal@aol.com

**ACCREDITATION:** Accrediting Association of Bible Colleges

**INSTITUTIONALLY ADMINISTERED FINANCIAL AID:** Yes

## DEGREE OR CERTIFICATE PROGRAMS OFFERED
**Undergraduate**—*BA:* General Christian Studies.

## NON-DEGREE-RELATED COURSE TOPICS OFFERED
**Undergraduate**—bible/biblical studies; missions/missionary studies and missiology; pastoral counseling and specialized ministries; philosophy and religion.
**Non-credit**—bible/biblical studies; education, general; missions/missionary studies and missiology; pastoral counseling and specialized ministries; philosophy and religion.

# HOCKING COLLEGE

*Instructional Development*
3301 Hocking Parkway
Nelsonville, OH 45764
**Contact:** Elaine V. Dabelko, Associate Vice President of Academic Affairs
**Phone:** 740-753-3591 Ext. 2272
**Fax:** 740-753-4097
**Web:** http://www.hocking.edu/
**E-mail:** dabelko_e@hocking.edu

**ACCREDITATION:** North Central Association of Colleges and Schools

## DEGREE OR CERTIFICATE PROGRAMS OFFERED
Programs offered do not lead to a degree or other formal award.

## NON-DEGREE-RELATED COURSE TOPICS OFFERED

**Undergraduate**—English composition; English language and literature, general; English technical and business writing; anatomy; communications, general; health and medical preparatory programs; hospitality services management; liberal arts and sciences, general studies and humanities; mathematics; psychology; social sciences, general.

# HOLMES COMMUNITY COLLEGE

## Distance Learning

PO Box 369
Goodman, MS 39079
**Contact:** Luther Boggan, Vice President for Academic Affairs
**Phone:** 662-472-9035
**Web:** http://www.holmes.cc.ms.us/distance_learning/online_courses/
**E-mail:** lboggan@holmes.cc.ms.us

**ACCREDITATION:** Southern Association of Colleges and Schools
**INSTITUTIONALLY ADMINISTERED FINANCIAL AID:** Yes

## DEGREE OR CERTIFICATE PROGRAMS OFFERED

**Programs offered do not lead to a degree or other formal award.**

## NON-DEGREE-RELATED COURSE TOPICS OFFERED

**Undergraduate**—accounting; business; business administration and management; business communications; computer science; economics; history; internet and world wide web; physical sciences, general; physics; psychology; sociology.

# HONOLULU COMMUNITY COLLEGE

## Outreach Office

874 Dillingham Boulevard
Honolulu, HI 96817
**Contact:** Sherrie Rupert, Coordinator of Distance Learning
**Phone:** 808-845-9151
**Fax:** 808-847-9829
**Web:** http://www.hcc.hawaii.edu
**E-mail:** srupert@hcc.hawaii.edu

**ACCREDITATION:** Western Association of Schools and Colleges
**INSTITUTIONALLY ADMINISTERED FINANCIAL AID:** Yes

## DEGREE OR CERTIFICATE PROGRAMS OFFERED

**Undergraduate**—*AA:* Arts.

## NON-DEGREE-RELATED COURSE TOPICS OFFERED

**Undergraduate**—English as a second language; English composition; English language and literature, general; anthropology; astronomy; business communications; computer and information sciences, general; construction trades, other; fire science/firefighting; foods and nutrition studies; geological and related sciences; history; polymer/plastics engineering; psychology; speech and rhetorical studies.

# HOPE INTERNATIONAL UNIVERSITY

## Distance Learning Department

2500 East Nutwood Avenue
Fullerton, CA 92831
**Contact:** Mr. Paul Alexander, Director of Distance Learning
**Phone:** 714-879-3901 Ext. 1251
**Web:** http://www.hiu.edu
**E-mail:** palexander@hiu.edu

**ACCREDITATION:** Western Association of Schools and Colleges
**INSTITUTIONALLY ADMINISTERED FINANCIAL AID:** Yes

| eCollege.com www.ecollege.com |
| --- |

## DEGREE OR CERTIFICATE PROGRAMS OFFERED

**Graduate**—*MBA:* International Development; Management; Non-Profit Management. *MSM:* International Development.

## NON-DEGREE-RELATED COURSE TOPICS OFFERED

**Undergraduate**—accounting; anthropology; bible/biblical studies; biblical and other theological languages and literatures; business; business administration and management; business and personal services marketing operations; business communications; business management and administrative services, other; business quantitative methods and management science; business/managerial economics; counseling psychology; developmental and child psychology; economics; enterprise management and operation; history; marketing management and research; psychology; psychology, other; religion/religious studies; religious education; theological studies and religious vocations, other.
**Graduate**—accounting; business; business administration and management; business and personal services marketing operations; business communications; business information and data processing services; business management and administrative services, other; business quantitative methods and management science; business/managerial economics; counseling psychology; history; marketing management and research; marketing operations/marketing and distribution, other; mathematics, other; religion/religious studies.

# HORRY-GEORGETOWN TECHNICAL COLLEGE

## Department of Distance Learning

2050 Highway 501 East, PO Box 261566
Conway, SC 29528
**Contact:** Ahmed Abdelsalam, Distance Learning Technician
**Phone:** 843-349-5311
**Fax:** 843-349-7533
**Web:** http://www.hor.tec.sc.us/distancelearning/distancelearning.htm
**E-mail:** abdelsalama@hor.tec.sc.us

**ACCREDITATION:** Southern Association of Colleges and Schools
**INSTITUTIONALLY ADMINISTERED FINANCIAL AID:** Yes

## DEGREE OR CERTIFICATE PROGRAMS OFFERED

**Programs offered do not lead to a degree or other formal award.**

## NON-DEGREE-RELATED COURSE TOPICS OFFERED

**Undergraduate**—American literature (United States); English composition; accounting; administrative and secretarial services; agriculture/agricultural sciences; astronomy; biological and physical sciences; business; business and personal services marketing operations; business communications; cognitive psychology and psycholinguistics; communications, other; computer science; criminal justice and corrections; developmental and child psychology; history; hospitality services management; individual and family development studies; internet and world wide web; mathematics, other; philosophy; religion/religious studies; romance languages and literatures; sociology.

# HOWARD COMMUNITY COLLEGE

*Office of Distance Learning*

10901 Little Patuxent Parkway
Columbia, MD 21044
**Contact:** Barbara Greenfeld, Director of Admissions
**Phone:** 410-772-4856
**Fax:** 410-715-2426
**Web:** http://www.howardcc.edu/distance
**E-mail:** bgreenfeld@howardcc.edu

**ACCREDITATION:** Middle States Association of Colleges and Schools
**INSTITUTIONALLY ADMINISTERED FINANCIAL AID:** Yes

## DEGREE OR CERTIFICATE PROGRAMS OFFERED

**Undergraduate**—*AA:* General Studies. *AAS:* General.

## NON-DEGREE-RELATED COURSE TOPICS OFFERED

**Undergraduate**—business administration and management; liberal arts and sciences, general studies and humanities.

# HUMBOLDT STATE UNIVERSITY

Office of Extended Education
Arcata, CA 95521
**Contact:** Carl Hansen, Director of Extended Education
**Phone:** 707-826-3731
**Fax:** 707-826-5885
**Web:** http://www.humboldt.edu/
**E-mail:** hansen@humboldt.edu

**ACCREDITATION:** Western Association of Schools and Colleges
**INSTITUTIONALLY ADMINISTERED FINANCIAL AID:** Yes

## DEGREE OR CERTIFICATE PROGRAMS OFFERED

Programs offered do not lead to a degree or other formal award.

## NON-DEGREE-RELATED COURSE TOPICS OFFERED

**Undergraduate**—economics; education, general; forestry and related sciences; mathematics; natural resources management and protective services; religion/religious studies; sociology.
**Non-credit**—natural resources management and protective services; sociology.

# HUNTER COLLEGE OF THE CITY UNIVERSITY OF NEW YORK

129 East 79th Street, 6th Floor
New York, NY 10021
**Contact:** Richard Hubbard, Technical Supervisor
**Phone:** 212-452-7484
**Fax:** 212-452-7485
**Web:** http://www.hunter.cuny.edu/
**E-mail:** richard.hubbard@hunter.cuny.edu

**ACCREDITATION:** Middle States Association of Colleges and Schools
**INSTITUTIONALLY ADMINISTERED FINANCIAL AID:** Yes

## DEGREE OR CERTIFICATE PROGRAMS OFFERED

Programs offered do not lead to a degree or other formal award.

## NON-DEGREE-RELATED COURSE TOPICS OFFERED

**Undergraduate**—Germanic languages and literatures; business administration and management; community health services; education, other; family and community studies; geography; health and medical assistants; home furnishings and equipment installers and consultants.
**Graduate**—family and community studies; geography.
**Non-credit**—home furnishings and equipment installers and consultants.

# HUSSON COLLEGE

*RN/BSN Online Program*

1 College Circle
Bangor, ME 04401
**Contact:** Ms. Mimi G. Padgett, RN, Director of RN Studies
**Phone:** 207-941-7079
**Fax:** 207-941-7883
**Web:** http://www.husson.edu/classroom
**E-mail:** padgettm@husson.edu

**ACCREDITATION:** New England Association of Schools and Colleges
**INSTITUTIONALLY ADMINISTERED FINANCIAL AID:** No

## DEGREE OR CERTIFICATE PROGRAMS OFFERED

**Undergraduate**—*BN:* Nursing.

## NON-DEGREE-RELATED COURSE TOPICS OFFERED

**Undergraduate**—English composition; English language and literature, general; foods and nutrition studies; gerontology; mathematical statistics; nursing; philosophy; psychology, other; speech and rhetorical studies.

# HUTCHINSON COMMUNITY COLLEGE AND AREA VOCATIONAL SCHOOL

*Instructional Technology*

1300 North Plum Street
Hutchinson, KS 67501
**Contact:** Ms. Janice Hilyard, Instructional Technology Director

**Phone:** 620-728-8145
**Fax:** 620-665-3310
**Web:** http://www.hutchcc.edu
**E-mail:** hilyardj@hutchcc.edu

**ACCREDITATION:** North Central Association of Colleges and Schools
**INSTITUTIONALLY ADMINISTERED FINANCIAL AID:** Yes

## DEGREE OR CERTIFICATE PROGRAMS OFFERED

Programs offered do not lead to a degree or other formal award.

## NON-DEGREE-RELATED COURSE TOPICS OFFERED

**Undergraduate**—English composition; business; communications, general; computer software and media applications; family and community studies; foreign languages and literatures; health and medical preparatory programs; history; mathematics; psychology; sociology; visual and performing arts, other.

# ILLINOIS EASTERN COMMUNITY COLLEGES, FRONTIER COMMUNITY COLLEGE

2 Frontier Drive
Fairfield, IL 62837
**Contact:** Mr. Jerry Hefley, Dean of the College
**Phone:** 618-842-3711 Ext. 4005
**Fax:** 618-842-6340
**Web:** http://www.iecc.cc.il.us./fcc
**E-mail:** hefleyj@iecc.cc.il.us

**ACCREDITATION:** North Central Association of Colleges and Schools
**INSTITUTIONALLY ADMINISTERED FINANCIAL AID:** Yes

## DEGREE OR CERTIFICATE PROGRAMS OFFERED

Programs offered do not lead to a degree or other formal award.

## NON-DEGREE-RELATED COURSE TOPICS OFFERED

**Undergraduate**—English composition; astronomy; business; business administration and management; computer programming; computer science; foods and nutrition studies; history; mathematical statistics; mathematics; music.

# ILLINOIS EASTERN COMMUNITY COLLEGES, LINCOLN TRAIL COLLEGE

11220 State Highway 1
Robinson, IL 62454
**Contact:** Dr. Gayle Saunders, Dean of the College
**Phone:** 618-544-8657 Ext. 1144
**Fax:** 618-544-7423
**Web:** http://www.iecc.cc.il.us/ltc
**E-mail:** saundersg@iecc.cc.il.us

**ACCREDITATION:** North Central Association of Colleges and Schools
**INSTITUTIONALLY ADMINISTERED FINANCIAL AID:** Yes

## DEGREE OR CERTIFICATE PROGRAMS OFFERED

Programs offered do not lead to a degree or other formal award.

## NON-DEGREE-RELATED COURSE TOPICS OFFERED

**Undergraduate**—English composition; astronomy; business; business administration and management; computer and information sciences, general; computer programming; computer science; computer software and media applications; foods and nutrition studies; history; mathematical statistics; mathematics; music.

# ILLINOIS EASTERN COMMUNITY COLLEGES, OLNEY CENTRAL COLLEGE

305 North West Street
Olney, IL 62450
**Contact:** Mr. Jackie L. Davis, Dean of Instruction
**Phone:** 618-395-7777 Ext. 2002
**Fax:** 618-395-5212
**Web:** http://www.iecc.cc.il.us/occ/
**E-mail:** davisj@iecc.cc.il.us

**ACCREDITATION:** North Central Association of Colleges and Schools
**INSTITUTIONALLY ADMINISTERED FINANCIAL AID:** Yes

## DEGREE OR CERTIFICATE PROGRAMS OFFERED

Programs offered do not lead to a degree or other formal award.

## NON-DEGREE-RELATED COURSE TOPICS OFFERED

**Undergraduate**—English composition; astronomy; business; business administration and management; computer and information sciences, general; computer programming; computer science; computer software and media applications; foods and nutrition studies; liberal arts and sciences, general studies and humanities; mathematical statistics; mathematics; music.

# ILLINOIS EASTERN COMMUNITY COLLEGES, WABASH VALLEY COLLEGE

2200 College Drive
Mt. Carmel, IL 62863
**Contact:** Mr. Wayne Henegar, Dean of Instruction
**Phone:** 618-262-8641 Ext. 3213
**Fax:** 618-262-5614
**Web:** http://www.iecc.cc.il.us/wvc
**E-mail:** henegarw@iecc.cc.il.us

**ACCREDITATION:** North Central Association of Colleges and Schools
**INSTITUTIONALLY ADMINISTERED FINANCIAL AID:** Yes

## DEGREE OR CERTIFICATE PROGRAMS OFFERED

Programs offered do not lead to a degree or other formal award.

## NON-DEGREE-RELATED COURSE TOPICS OFFERED

**Undergraduate**—English composition; adult and continuing teacher education; art history, criticism and conservation; astronomy; business; computer science; computer software and media applications; developmental and child psychology; foods and nutrition studies; history; journalism; mathematical statistics; mathematics; mathematics, other; music; radio and television broadcasting; sign language interpreter.

# ILLINOIS INSTITUTE OF TECHNOLOGY

### Distance Learning Technologies

Office of Academic Affairs, Graduate College, 3300 South Federal, Room 110A
Chicago, IL 60616-3793
**Contact:** Ms. Holli Pryor-Harris, Director of Client Services
**Phone:** 312-567-3167
**Fax:** 312-567-7140
**Web:** http://www.distance-education.iit.edu
**E-mail:** pryor@iit.edu

**ACCREDITATION:** North Central Association of Colleges and Schools
**INSTITUTIONALLY ADMINISTERED FINANCIAL AID:** No

## DEGREE OR CERTIFICATE PROGRAMS OFFERED

**Graduate**—*Graduate Certificate:* Advanced Electronics; Chemistry; Computer Engineering; Computer Networking and Telecommunications; Construction Management; Control Systems; Electricity Markets; Hazardous Waste Engineering; Indoor Air Quality; Intelligent Information Systems; Internet; Particle Processing; Pharmaceutical Processing; Polymer Operations Management; Power Engineering; Signal Processing; Software Engineering; Water and Wastewater Treatment; Wireless Communications. *MCE:* Chemical Engineering. *MChem:* Chemistry. *MMAE:* Mechanical and Aerospace Engineering. *MS:* Chemical Engineering; Chemistry; Computer Science; Electrical Engineering; Electrical and Computer Engineering; Electricity Markets; Environmental Engineering; Geotechnical Engineering; Health Physics; Manufacturing Engineering; Mechanical and Aerospace Engineering; Metallurgical and Materials Engineering; Public Works; Structural Engineering; Telecommunications and Software Engineering; Transportation Engineering.

## NON-DEGREE-RELATED COURSE TOPICS OFFERED

**Undergraduate**—biological sciences/life sciences, other; cell and molecular biology; computer science; electrical, electronics and communication engineering; engineering mechanics; mechanical engineering.
**Graduate**—aerospace, aeronautical and astronautical engineering; analytical chemistry; bioengineering and biomedical engineering; biological sciences/life sciences, other; chemical engineering; chemistry; civil engineering; computer engineering; computer science; construction and building finishers and managers; electrical, electronics and communication engineering; environmental/environmental health engineering; food sciences and technology; industrial/manufacturing engineering; inorganic chemistry; materials engineering; mechanical engineering; organic chemistry; telecommunications.

# ILLINOIS SCHOOL OF PROFESSIONAL PSYCHOLOGY, CHICAGO CAMPUS

20 South Clark, 3rd Floor
Chicago, IL 60603
**Contact:** Ms. April Djakoniya, Coordinator of Online Services
**Phone:** 312-279-3839
**Fax:** 312-424-7282
**Web:** http://argosy.aspp.edu
**E-mail:** april@argosyeducation.com

**ACCREDITATION:** North Central Association of Colleges and Schools
**INSTITUTIONALLY ADMINISTERED FINANCIAL AID:** Yes

## DEGREE OR CERTIFICATE PROGRAMS OFFERED
**Programs offered do not lead to a degree or other formal award.**

## NON-DEGREE-RELATED COURSE TOPICS OFFERED
**Non-credit**—psychology.

# ILLINOIS SCHOOL OF PROFESSIONAL PSYCHOLOGY, CHICAGO NORTHWEST CAMPUS

20 South Clark, 3rd Floor
Chicago, IL 60603
**Contact:** Ms. April Djakoniya, Coordinator of Online Services
**Phone:** 312-279-3839
**Fax:** 312-424-7282
**Web:** http://argosy.aspp.edu
**E-mail:** april@argosyeducation.com

**ACCREDITATION:** North Central Association of Colleges and Schools
**INSTITUTIONALLY ADMINISTERED FINANCIAL AID:** Yes

## DEGREE OR CERTIFICATE PROGRAMS OFFERED
**Programs offered do not lead to a degree or other formal award.**

## NON-DEGREE-RELATED COURSE TOPICS OFFERED
**Graduate**—counseling psychology.
**Non-credit**—psychology, other.

# ILLINOIS STATE UNIVERSITY

### Extended University

Campus Box 4090
Normal, IL 61790
**Contact:** Susan Van Klavern, Program Coordinator of Distance Learning
**Phone:** 309-438-5288
**Fax:** 309-438-5069
**Web:** http://www.exu.ilstu.edu

**E-mail:** sjvankl@ilstu.edu

**ACCREDITATION:** North Central Association of Colleges and Schools

**INSTITUTIONALLY ADMINISTERED FINANCIAL AID:** Yes

## DEGREE OR CERTIFICATE PROGRAMS OFFERED

**Undergraduate—*BSN:*** Nursing. ***Certification:*** Visual Impairment and Blindness.

## NON-DEGREE-RELATED COURSE TOPICS OFFERED

**Undergraduate—**English language and literature, general; business administration and management; communications, other; economics; education, other; foreign languages and literatures; health professions and related sciences, other; history; marketing management and research; music; visual and performing arts.
**Graduate—**curriculum and instruction; education administration and supervision; nursing; special education.

# ILLINOIS VALLEY COMMUNITY COLLEGE

*Learning Technologies*
815 North Orlando Smith Avenue
Oglesby, IL 61348
**Contact:** Emily Vescogni, Director
**Phone:** 815-224-0462
**Fax:** 815-224-0445
**Web:** http://www.ivcc.edu
**E-mail:** emily_vescogni@ivcc.edu

**ACCREDITATION:** North Central Association of Colleges and Schools

## DEGREE OR CERTIFICATE PROGRAMS OFFERED

**Programs offered do not lead to a degree or other formal award.**

## NON-DEGREE-RELATED COURSE TOPICS OFFERED

**Undergraduate—**English composition; English language and literature, general; accounting; advertising; agriculture/agricultural sciences; business; business communications; developmental and child psychology; geography; political science and government; psychology; psychology, other; social psychology; sociology.

# IMMACULATA COLLEGE

Box 300
Immaculata, PA 19345-0300
**Contact:** Dr. Elke Franke, Dean of College of LifeLong Learning
**Phone:** 610-647-4400 Ext. 3235
**Fax:** 610-647-0215
**Web:** http://www.immaculata.edu/
**E-mail:** efranke@immaculata.edu

**ACCREDITATION:** Middle States Association of Colleges and Schools

**INSTITUTIONALLY ADMINISTERED FINANCIAL AID:** Yes

## DEGREE OR CERTIFICATE PROGRAMS OFFERED

**Programs offered do not lead to a degree or other formal award.**

## NON-DEGREE-RELATED COURSE TOPICS OFFERED

**Undergraduate—**biological sciences/life sciences, other; computer software and media applications; environmental control technologies; foods and nutrition studies; history.
**Graduate—**education, general.

# INDIANA HIGHER EDUCATION TELECOMMUNICATION SYSTEM

714 North Senate Avenue
Indianapolis, IN 46202
**Contact:** Indiana College Network Student Services Center
**Phone:** 800-426-8899
**Fax:** 812-855-9380
**Web:** http://www.icn.org
**E-mail:** info@icn.org

**ACCREDITATION:** Accreditation varies across member institutions

**INSTITUTIONALLY ADMINISTERED FINANCIAL AID:** Yes

## DEGREE OR CERTIFICATE PROGRAMS OFFERED

**Undergraduate—*AA:*** Biblical Studies; General Arts; Justice Administration (Ministry Concentration). ***AAS:*** Accounting; Business Administration (Management and Marketing Specialties); Design Technology (Architecture Specialty); Law Enforcement. ***AS:*** Business Administration (Management Option); General Aviation Flight Technology; Histotechnology; Law Enforcement. ***BS:*** Completion Program in Vocational Trade-Industrial-Technical Area; Degree Completion in Mechanical Technology. ***BSN:*** Degree Completion Program in Nursing. ***Certificate:*** Corrections; Digital Signal Processing; Distance Education; General Studies; Information Technology; Justice and Ministry; Law Enforcement; Library/Media Services; Private Security. ***Endorsement:*** Graduate Endorsement in Driver Education; Undergraduate Endorsement in Driver Education. ***License:*** Graduate Licensure in School Administration.
**Graduate—*EMBA:*** Food and Agricultural Business. ***Graduate Certificate:*** Library/Media Services; Public Administration. ***MA:*** Criminology; Executive Development and Public Service. ***MAE:*** Educational Administration and Supervision; Elementary Education; Special Education. ***MBA:*** Business Administration. ***MS:*** Adult Education; Computer Science; Criminology; Electrical and Computer Engineering; Industrial Engineering; Interdisciplinary Engineering; Student Affairs Administration. ***MSE:*** Language Education.

## NON-DEGREE-RELATED COURSE TOPICS OFFERED

**Undergraduate—**English language and literature, general; anthropology; astronomy; biblical and other theological languages and literatures; business; computer science; criminal justice and corrections; economics; fine arts and art studies; foreign languages and literatures; geography; geological and related sciences; history; industrial/manufacturing engineering; journalism and mass communications; mathematics; nursing; philosophy; physics; psychology.

**See full description on page 380.**

# INDIANA INSTITUTE OF TECHNOLOGY

*Independent Study*
1600 East Washington Boulevard
Fort Wayne, IN 46803

Contact: Ms. Jill Wright, Admissions Counselor
Phone: 888-666-TECH Ext. 2258
Fax: 219-422-6309
Web: http://www.indtech.edu
E-mail: wright@indtech.edu

ACCREDITATION: North Central Association of Colleges and Schools
INSTITUTIONALLY ADMINISTERED FINANCIAL AID: Yes

## DEGREE OR CERTIFICATE PROGRAMS OFFERED

Undergraduate—*AS:* Business Administration. *BS:* Accounting. *BSBA:* Human Resources; Management; Marketing.

# INDIANA STATE UNIVERSITY
## *Division of Lifelong Learning*

Erickson Hall, Room 210-211
Terre Haute, IN 47809
Contact: Harry K. Barnes, Director of Office of Student Services
Phone: 888-237-8080
Fax: 812-237-8540
Web: http://indstate.edu/distance
E-mail: studentservices@indstate.edu

ACCREDITATION: North Central Association of Colleges and Schools
INSTITUTIONALLY ADMINISTERED FINANCIAL AID: Yes

## DEGREE OR CERTIFICATE PROGRAMS OFFERED

Undergraduate—*AS:* General Aviation Flight Technology. *BS:* Business Administration; Completion in Mechanical Technology; Completion in Vocational Trade-Industrial-Technical Area Major/ Career and Technology Education; Criminology; Electronics Technology; General Industrial Technology; Human Resource Development; Industrial Supervision; Insurance; Nursing. *Certificate:* Corrections; Law Enforcement; Library/ Media Services; Private Security; Public Administration. *Endorsement:* Driver Education; Emotional Disturbance. *License:* School Administration.
Graduate—*Graduate Certificate:* Library/Media Services. *MA:* Criminology; Nursing; Student Affairs Administration. *MS:* Criminology; Human Resource Development; Occupational Safety Management; Student Affairs Administration. *MSN:* Nursing.
Postgraduate and doctoral—*PhD:* Technology Management.

## NON-DEGREE-RELATED COURSE TOPICS OFFERED

Undergraduate—accounting; business; construction/building technology; criminology; curriculum and instruction; economics; education, general; education, other; electrical, electronics and communications engineering; fine arts and art studies; geography; history; insurance and risk management; international business; journalism; mathematical statistics; mathematics, other; psychology; sociology; special education.
Graduate—biological sciences/life sciences, other; criminology; curriculum and instruction; education administration and supervision; education, other; educational psychology; electrical and electronic engineering-related technology; health and physical education/fitness; human services; nursing; public administration; sociology; special education; student counseling and personnel services.

### Special Note

The DegreeLink Program offers eligible individuals an opportunity to transfer college credit to Indiana State University and complete selected Bachelor of Science degrees via distance education. Individuals who have completed designated degrees from Ivy Tech State College and Vincennes University may transfer credit as a 2-year block into one or more DegreeLink programs. In addition, individuals who have earned credits or an associate degree from any accredited collegiate institution are eligible for and encouraged to transfer credit on a course-by-course basis and complete a Bachelor of Science degree via distance technologies.

Baccalaureate degree-completion programs offered include business administration, community health, criminology, electronics technology, general industrial technology, human resource development, industrial supervision, insurance, mechanical technology, nursing, and vocational trade-industrial-technical.

A unique feature of the DegreeLink Program is a statewide network of area learning centers that offer free access to Internet-connected computers and student services coordinators who provide one-on-one assistance to in-state and out-of-state students and all individuals interested in DegreeLink.

Degree-completion courses are offered primarily via the Internet, print-based correspondence, videotape, and live televised courses that are accessible at more than 300 receiving sites in Indiana. Most DegreeLink programs can be completed via distance education within Indiana. Selected DegreeLink programs are accessible globally via the Internet.

For more information, students should call the Office of Student Services—Lifelong Learning at 888-237-8080 (toll-free) or visit the Web site at http://web.indstate.edu/degreelink.

See full description on page 382.

# INDIANA UNIVERSITY OF PENNSYLVANIA
## *School of Continuing Education*

100 Keith Hall, 390 Pratt Drive
Indiana, PA 15701
Contact: Dr. Kausalai Wijekumar, Director of Distance Education Development
Phone: 724-357-7695
Fax: 724-357-7597
Web: http://ces0100.soce.iup.edu/ceweb/index.htm
E-mail: kaywije@grove.iup.edu

ACCREDITATION: Middle States Association of Colleges and Schools
INSTITUTIONALLY ADMINISTERED FINANCIAL AID: Yes

## DEGREE OR CERTIFICATE PROGRAMS OFFERED

Graduate—*Graduate Certificate:* Safety Sciences.

## NON-DEGREE-RELATED COURSE TOPICS OFFERED

Undergraduate—chemistry; criminology; engineering-related technologies, other; foods and nutrition studies; geological and related sciences; mathematics; physics; political science and government.

Graduate—engineering-related technologies, other; physics.

**See full description on page 384.**

# INDIANA UNIVERSITY–PURDUE UNIVERSITY INDIANAPOLIS

425 University Boulevard
Indianapolis, IN 46202
**Contact:** Community Learning Network
**Phone:** 317-278-7600
**Web:** http://www.cln.iupui.edu/cp/distance-index.html

**ACCREDITATION:** North Central Association of Colleges and Schools

## DEGREE OR CERTIFICATE PROGRAMS OFFERED

**Programs offered do not lead to a degree or other formal award.**

# INDIANA UNIVERSITY SYSTEM

## School of Continuing Studies

PO Box 1345
Bloomington, IN 47402
**Contact:** Office of Distributed Education
**Phone:** 800-334-1011
**Web:** http://www.indiana.edu/~iude
**E-mail:** scs@iupui.edu

**ACCREDITATION:** North Central Association of Colleges and Schools

**INSTITUTIONALLY ADMINISTERED FINANCIAL AID:** No

## DEGREE OR CERTIFICATE PROGRAMS OFFERED

**Undergraduate—AA:** General Studies. **AGS:** General Studies. **AS:** Histotechnology; Histotechnology; Labor Studies; Labor Studies. **BGS:** General Studies. **BS:** Labor Studies; Labor Studies. **Certificate:** Distance Education; Information Technology; Labor Studies. **Diploma:** Diploma. **Graduate—MBA:** Business Administration; Business Administration. **MS:** Adult Education; Adult Education; Industrial Systems Technology; Instructional Systems Technology; Language Education; Music Technology; Music Technology; Therapeutic Recreation; Therapeutic Recreation. **MSE:** Language Education. **MSN:** Nursing.

## NON-DEGREE-RELATED COURSE TOPICS OFFERED

**Non-credit**—accounting; education, other; information sciences and systems.

# INDIANA WESLEYAN UNIVERSITY

## Distance Education Department

4301 South Washington Street
Marion, IN 46953
**Contact:** Adult Education Services
**Phone:** 800-895-0036
**Fax:** 765-677-2404
**Web:** http://IWUonline.com

**E-mail:** info@iwuonline.com

**ACCREDITATION:** North Central Association of Colleges and Schools

**INSTITUTIONALLY ADMINISTERED FINANCIAL AID:** Yes

## DEGREE OR CERTIFICATE PROGRAMS OFFERED

**Undergraduate—BS:** Business Information Systems; Management.
**Graduate—MBA:** Business Administration. **MEd:** Education.

## NON-DEGREE-RELATED COURSE TOPICS OFFERED

**Undergraduate**—English composition; computer and information sciences, general; earth and planetary sciences; history; internet and world wide web; mathematics; music; philosophy and religion.
**Graduate**—educational psychology.

**See full description on page 386.**

# INDIAN RIVER COMMUNITY COLLEGE

## Distance Learning

3209 Virginia Avenue
Ft. Pierce, FL 34981
**Contact:** Dr. Stephen Jack Maxwell, Vice President of Academic Affairs
**Phone:** 561-462-4704
**Fax:** 561-462-4796
**Web:** http://www.ircc.cc.fl.us/classrooms.htm
**E-mail:** smaxwell@ircc.cc.fl.us

**ACCREDITATION:** Southern Association of Colleges and Schools

**INSTITUTIONALLY ADMINISTERED FINANCIAL AID:** Yes

## DEGREE OR CERTIFICATE PROGRAMS OFFERED

**Undergraduate—AA:** General. **AS:** Instructional Services Technology—Library Technical Assistant.

## NON-DEGREE-RELATED COURSE TOPICS OFFERED

**Undergraduate**—English composition; English language and literature, general; anthropology; astronomy; biology, general; business administration and management; chemistry; criminal justice and corrections; economics; education, general; geography; history; library assistant; mathematics; psychology; sociology.

# IOWA LAKES COMMUNITY COLLEGE

1900 North Grand Avenue
Spencer, IA 51301
**Contact:** Ms. Kitty Conover, Spencer Center Director
**Phone:** 712-262-7141 Ext. 628
**Fax:** 712-262-4047
**Web:** http://www.ilcc.cc.ia.us
**E-mail:** kconover@ilcc.cc.ia.us

**ACCREDITATION:** North Central Association of Colleges and Schools

**INSTITUTIONALLY ADMINISTERED FINANCIAL AID:** Yes

## DEGREE OR CERTIFICATE PROGRAMS OFFERED

Undergraduate—*AA:* General Liberal Arts.

## NON-DEGREE-RELATED COURSE TOPICS OFFERED

**Undergraduate**—English composition; biological and physical sciences; business; computer software and media applications; liberal arts and sciences, general studies and humanities; social sciences, general; speech and rhetorical studies.
**Non-credit**—computer software and media applications.

# IOWA STATE UNIVERSITY OF SCIENCE AND TECHNOLOGY

## *Continuing Education and Communication Services*

3614 Administrative Services Building, Room 1717
Ames, IA 50011-3614
**Contact:** Lynette Spicer, Communication Specialist
**Phone:** 515-294-1327
**Fax:** 515-294-7767
**Web:** http://www.lifelearner.iastate.edu
**E-mail:** lspicer@iastate.edu

**ACCREDITATION:** North Central Association of Colleges and Schools
**INSTITUTIONALLY ADMINISTERED FINANCIAL AID:** Yes

## DEGREE OR CERTIFICATE PROGRAMS OFFERED

**Undergraduate**—*BS:* Professional Agriculture.
**Graduate**—*ME:* Systems Engineering. *MS:* Agriculture; Agronomy; Computer Engineering; Electrical Engineering; Mechanical Engineering; Statistics.

## NON-DEGREE-RELATED COURSE TOPICS OFFERED

**Undergraduate**—agriculture/agricultural sciences; atmospheric sciences and meteorology; biochemistry and biophysics; biology, general; economics; entomology; food sciences and technology; individual and family development studies; microbiology/bacteriology.
**Graduate**—agricultural economics; agriculture/agricultural sciences; atmospheric sciences and meteorology; biochemistry and biophysics; computer engineering; electrical, electronics and communication engineering; family/consumer resource management; food sciences and technology; mathematical statistics; mechanical engineering; microbiology/bacteriology.

# IOWA WESLEYAN COLLEGE

## *Office of Extended Learning*

601 North Main Street
Mount Pleasant, IA 52641-1398
**Contact:** Mr. David C. File, Associate Vice President and Dean of Extended Learning
**Phone:** 319-385-6247
**Fax:** 319-385-6296
**Web:** http://www.iwc.edu/
**E-mail:** exl@iwc.edu

**ACCREDITATION:** North Central Association of Colleges and Schools
**INSTITUTIONALLY ADMINISTERED FINANCIAL AID:** Yes

## DEGREE OR CERTIFICATE PROGRAMS OFFERED

Programs offered do not lead to a degree or other formal award.

## NON-DEGREE-RELATED COURSE TOPICS OFFERED

**Undergraduate**—English composition; accounting; anthropology; business administration and management; health and physical education/fitness; human resources management; mathematical statistics; psychology; sociology.

# IOWA WESTERN COMMUNITY COLLEGE

School of Arts and Sciences, Box 4-C
Council Bluffs, IA 51502
**Contact:** Dr. Bob Franzese, Dean
**Phone:** 712-325-3257
**Fax:** 712-325-3717
**Web:** http://iwcc.cc.ia.us
**E-mail:** bfranzes@iwcc.cc.ia.us

**ACCREDITATION:** North Central Association of Colleges and Schools
**INSTITUTIONALLY ADMINISTERED FINANCIAL AID:** Yes

## DEGREE OR CERTIFICATE PROGRAMS OFFERED

**Undergraduate**—*AA:* General Studies. *AAS:* Votech/Technology. *AS:* Criminal Justice.

## NON-DEGREE-RELATED COURSE TOPICS OFFERED

**Undergraduate**—English language and literature, general; accounting; biology, general; chemistry; fine arts and art studies; geological and related sciences; history; law and legal studies; liberal arts and sciences, general studies and humanities; mathematics; microbiology/bacteriology; nursing; philosophy and religion; political science and government; social work; sociology.
**Graduate**—English language and literature, general; biology, general; business; chemistry; economics; fine arts and art studies; history; mathematics; music; philosophy; psychology; sociology; speech and rhetorical studies.

# ISIM UNIVERSITY

501 South Cherry Street, #350
Denver, CO 80246
**Contact:** Ms. Kristine Kari Larson, Registrar
**Phone:** 303-333-4224 Ext. 172
**Fax:** 303-336-1144
**Web:** http://www.isim.edu/
**E-mail:** krislarson@isim.edu

**ACCREDITATION:** Distance Education and Training Council
**INSTITUTIONALLY ADMINISTERED FINANCIAL AID:** No

## DEGREE OR CERTIFICATE PROGRAMS OFFERED

**Graduate**—*MBA:* Business Administration. *MS:* Information Management.

**NON-DEGREE-RELATED COURSE TOPICS OFFERED**

**Graduate**—accounting.
**Non-credit**—professional studies.

# ISOTHERMAL COMMUNITY COLLEGE

Spindale, NC 28160
**Contact:** Mr. Eric Miller, Distance Learning Coordinator
**Phone:** 828-286-3636 Ext. 295
**Web:** http://www.isothermal.cc.nc.us/
**E-mail:** emiller@isothermal.cc.nc.us

**ACCREDITATION:** Southern Association of Colleges and Schools
**INSTITUTIONALLY ADMINISTERED FINANCIAL AID:** Yes

**DEGREE OR CERTIFICATE PROGRAMS OFFERED**
Programs offered do not lead to a degree or other formal award.

**NON-DEGREE-RELATED COURSE TOPICS OFFERED**

**Undergraduate**—English composition; English literature (British and Commonwealth); child care and guidance workers and managers; computer and information sciences, general; computer programming; criminal justice and corrections; economics; general teacher education; history; industrial and organizational psychology; political science and government; sociology.

# IVY TECH STATE COLLEGE–CENTRAL INDIANA

1 West 26th Street
Indianapolis, IN 46208-4777
**Contact:** Sonia Dickerson, Enrollment Manager
**Phone:** 317-921-4882
**Fax:** 317-921-4753
**Web:** http://www.ivy.tec.in.us/indianapolis/
**E-mail:** sdickers@ivy.tec.in.us

**ACCREDITATION:** North Central Association of Colleges and Schools
**INSTITUTIONALLY ADMINISTERED FINANCIAL AID:** Yes

**DEGREE OR CERTIFICATE PROGRAMS OFFERED**
**Undergraduate**—*AAS:* Early Childhood Education.

**NON-DEGREE-RELATED COURSE TOPICS OFFERED**

**Undergraduate**—English composition; accounting; business administration and management; communications, general; computer and information sciences, general; computer programming; computer software and media applications; computer systems analysis; computer systems networking and telecommunications; computer/information technology administration and management; economics; fire science/firefighting; hospitality services management; mathematics; physical sciences, general; physics; sociology.

# IVY TECH STATE COLLEGE–COLUMBUS

4475 Central Avenue
Columbus, IN 47203-1868
**Contact:** Lisa Morris, Manager of Admissions
**Phone:** 812-372-9925 Ext. 129
**Fax:** 812-372-0311
**Web:** http://www.ivy.tec.in.us/columbus/
**E-mail:** lmorris@ivy.tec.in.us

**ACCREDITATION:** North Central Association of Colleges and Schools
**INSTITUTIONALLY ADMINISTERED FINANCIAL AID:** Yes

**DEGREE OR CERTIFICATE PROGRAMS OFFERED**
**Undergraduate**—*AAS:* Early Childhood Education.

**NON-DEGREE-RELATED COURSE TOPICS OFFERED**

**Undergraduate**—English composition; accounting; business administration and management; communications, general; computer and information sciences, general; computer programming; computer software and media applications; computer systems analysis; computer systems networking and telecommunications; computer/information technology administration and management; economics; fire protection; history; mathematics; physical sciences, general; psychology; sociology.

# IVY TECH STATE COLLEGE–EASTCENTRAL

4301 South Cowan Road
Muncie, IN 47302-9448
**Contact:** Gail Chesterfield, Dean of Student Affairs
**Phone:** 765-289-2291
**Fax:** 765-289-2291
**Web:** http://www.ivy.tec.in.us/muncie/
**E-mail:** gchester@ivy.tec.in.us

**ACCREDITATION:** North Central Association of Colleges and Schools
**INSTITUTIONALLY ADMINISTERED FINANCIAL AID:** Yes

**DEGREE OR CERTIFICATE PROGRAMS OFFERED**
**Undergraduate**—*AAS:* Early Childhood Education.

**NON-DEGREE-RELATED COURSE TOPICS OFFERED**

**Undergraduate**—English composition; accounting; business administration and management; child care and guidance workers and managers; communications, general; computer and information sciences, general; computer programming; computer software and media applications; computer systems analysis; computer systems networking and telecommunications; computer/information technology administration and management; economics; history; mathematics; physical sciences, general; physics; psychology.

# IVY TECH STATE COLLEGE–KOKOMO

1815 East Morgan Street
Kokomo, IN 46903-1373

**Contact:** Alayne Cook, Admissions Coordinator
**Phone:** 765-459-0561
**Fax:** 765-454-5111
**Web:** http://www.ivy.tec.in.us/kokomo/
**E-mail:** acook@ivy.tec.in.us

**ACCREDITATION:** North Central Association of Colleges and Schools

**INSTITUTIONALLY ADMINISTERED FINANCIAL AID:** Yes

## DEGREE OR CERTIFICATE PROGRAMS OFFERED

**Undergraduate—*AAS:*** Early Childhood Education.

## NON-DEGREE-RELATED COURSE TOPICS OFFERED

**Undergraduate—**English composition; accounting; business administration and management; communications, general; computer and information sciences, general; computer programming; computer science; computer software and media applications; computer systems analysis; computer systems networking and telecommunications; computer/information technology administration and management; design and applied arts; economics; history; mathematics; physical sciences, general; physics; psychology; sociology.

# IVY TECH STATE COLLEGE-LAFAYETTE

3101 South Creasy Lane
Lafayette, IN 47903
**Contact:** Judy Doppelfeld, Director of Admissions
**Phone:** 765-772-9100
**Fax:** 765-772-9107
**Web:** http://www.laf.ivy.tec.in.us/
**E-mail:** jdoppelf@ivy.tec.in.us

**ACCREDITATION:** North Central Association of Colleges and Schools

**INSTITUTIONALLY ADMINISTERED FINANCIAL AID:** Yes

## DEGREE OR CERTIFICATE PROGRAMS OFFERED

**Undergraduate—*AAS:*** Early Childhood Education.

## NON-DEGREE-RELATED COURSE TOPICS OFFERED

**Undergraduate—**English composition; accounting; business administration and management; child care and guidance workers and managers; communications, general; computer and information sciences, general; computer programming; computer science; computer software and media applications; computer systems analysis; computer systems networking and telecommunications; computer/information technology administration and management; economics; hospitality services management; mathematics; physics; psychology.

# IVY TECH STATE COLLEGE-NORTH CENTRAL

## *Instructional Technology*

220 Dean Johnson Boulevard
South Bend, IN 46601
**Contact:** Leonard Thompson, Jr., Director of Admissions
**Phone:** 219-289-7001 Ext. 5423

**Fax:** 219-236-7177
**Web:** http://www.ivy.tec.in.us/southbend/
**E-mail:** lthompso@ivy.tec.in.us

**ACCREDITATION:** North Central Association of Colleges and Schools

**INSTITUTIONALLY ADMINISTERED FINANCIAL AID:** Yes

## DEGREE OR CERTIFICATE PROGRAMS OFFERED

**Undergraduate—*AAS:*** Early Childhood Education.

## NON-DEGREE-RELATED COURSE TOPICS OFFERED

**Undergraduate—**English composition; accounting; advertising; biology, general; business administration and management; communications, general; computer and information sciences, general; computer programming; computer software and media applications; computer systems analysis; computer systems networking and telecommunications; drafting; economics; history; hospitality services management; insurance and risk management; mathematics; physical sciences, general; physics; psychology; sociology.

# IVY TECH STATE COLLEGE-NORTHEAST

3800 North Anthony Boulevard
Fort Wayne, IN 46805-1489
**Contact:** Steve Scheer, Director of Admissions
**Phone:** 219-482-9171
**Fax:** 219-480-4252
**Web:** http://www.ivy.tec.in.us/fortwayne/
**E-mail:** sscheer@ivy.tec.in.us

**ACCREDITATION:** North Central Association of Colleges and Schools

**INSTITUTIONALLY ADMINISTERED FINANCIAL AID:** Yes

## DEGREE OR CERTIFICATE PROGRAMS OFFERED

**Undergraduate—*AAS:*** Early Childhood Education.

## NON-DEGREE-RELATED COURSE TOPICS OFFERED

**Undergraduate—**English composition; accounting; business administration and management; communications, general; computer and information sciences, general; computer programming; computer software and media applications; computer systems analysis; computer systems networking and telecommunications; computer/information technology administration and management; economics; history; marketing management and research; mathematics; nursing; physical sciences, general; psychology; sociology.

# IVY TECH STATE COLLEGE-NORTHWEST

1440 East 35th Avenue
Gary, IN 46409-1499
**Contact:** Twilla Lewis, Coordinator of Student Services
**Phone:** 219-981-1111
**Fax:** 219-981-4415
**Web:** http://www.gary.ivy.tec.in.us/

**E-mail:** tlewis@ivy.tec.in.us

**ACCREDITATION:** North Central Association of Colleges and Schools

**INSTITUTIONALLY ADMINISTERED FINANCIAL AID:** Yes

### DEGREE OR CERTIFICATE PROGRAMS OFFERED

**Undergraduate—*AAS:*** Early Childhood Education.

### NON-DEGREE-RELATED COURSE TOPICS OFFERED

**Undergraduate—**English composition; accounting; business administration and management; business marketing and marketing management; communications, general; computer programming; computer software and media applications; computer systems analysis; computer systems networking and telecommunications; economics; environmental science/studies; fire science/firefighting; hospitality services management; mathematics; nursing; physical sciences, general; psychology; sociology.

# IVY TECH STATE COLLEGE–SOUTHCENTRAL

8204 Highway 311
Sellersburg, IN 47172-1897
**Contact:** Randy Emily, Admissions Manager
**Phone:** 812-246-3301
**Fax:** 812-246-9905
**Web:** http://www.ivy.tec.in.us/sellersburg/
**E-mail:** remily@ivy.tec.in.us

**ACCREDITATION:** North Central Association of Colleges and Schools

**INSTITUTIONALLY ADMINISTERED FINANCIAL AID:** Yes

### DEGREE OR CERTIFICATE PROGRAMS OFFERED

**Undergraduate—*AAS:*** Early Childhood Education.

### NON-DEGREE-RELATED COURSE TOPICS OFFERED

**Undergraduate—**English composition; accounting; business administration and management; child care and guidance workers and managers; communications, general; computer and information sciences, general; computer programming; computer software and media applications; computer systems analysis; computer systems networking and telecommunications; computer/information technology administration and management; drafting; economics; industrial production technologies; mathematics; nursing; physical sciences, general; psychology; sociology.

# IVY TECH STATE COLLEGE–SOUTHEAST

590 Ivy Tech Drive
Madison, IN 47250-1881
**Contact:** Cindy Hutcherson, Coordinator of Admissions
**Phone:** 812-265-2580
**Fax:** 812-265-4028
**Web:** http://www.ivy.tec.in.us/madison/
**E-mail:** chutcher@ivy.tec.in.us

**ACCREDITATION:** North Central Association of Colleges and Schools

**INSTITUTIONALLY ADMINISTERED FINANCIAL AID:** Yes

### DEGREE OR CERTIFICATE PROGRAMS OFFERED

**Undergraduate—*AAS:*** Early Childhood Education.

### NON-DEGREE-RELATED COURSE TOPICS OFFERED

**Undergraduate—**English composition; accounting; business administration and management; communications, general; computer and information sciences, general; computer programming; computer software and media applications; computer systems analysis; computer systems networking and telecommunications; computer/information technology administration and management; drafting; economics; history; industrial equipment maintenance and repairers; mathematics; philosophy; physical sciences, general; political science and government; psychology; sociology.

# IVY TECH STATE COLLEGE–SOUTHWEST

3501 First Avenue
Evansville, IN 47710-3398
**Contact:** Helen Finke, Director of Admissions and Records
**Phone:** 812-426-2865
**Fax:** 812-429-9834
**Web:** http://www.ivy.tec.in.us/evansville/
**E-mail:** hfinke@ivy.tec.in.us

**ACCREDITATION:** North Central Association of Colleges and Schools

**INSTITUTIONALLY ADMINISTERED FINANCIAL AID:** Yes

### DEGREE OR CERTIFICATE PROGRAMS OFFERED

**Undergraduate—*AAS:*** Early Childhood Education.

### NON-DEGREE-RELATED COURSE TOPICS OFFERED

**Undergraduate—**English composition; accounting; business administration and management; communications, general; computer and information sciences, general; computer programming; computer software and media applications; computer systems analysis; computer systems networking and telecommunications; computer/information technology administration and management; drafting; economics; mathematics; nursing; physical sciences, general.

# IVY TECH STATE COLLEGE–WABASH VALLEY

7999 U.S. Highway 41
Terre Haute, IN 47802-4898
**Contact:** Michael Fisher, Admissions
**Phone:** 812-299-1121
**Fax:** 812-299-5723
**Web:** http://ivytech7.cc.in.us/
**E-mail:** mfisher@ivy.tec.in.us

**ACCREDITATION:** North Central Association of Colleges and Schools

**INSTITUTIONALLY ADMINISTERED FINANCIAL AID:** Yes

### DEGREE OR CERTIFICATE PROGRAMS OFFERED

**Undergraduate—*AAS:*** Accounting; Business Administration; Design; Early Childhood Education.

## NON-DEGREE-RELATED COURSE TOPICS OFFERED

**Undergraduate**—English composition; accounting; business administration and management; communications, general; computer and information sciences, general; computer programming; computer software and media applications; computer systems analysis; computer systems networking and telecommunications; computer/information technology administration and management; drafting; economics; health system/health services administration; history; mathematics; physical sciences, general; physics; political science and government; psychology; social psychology; sociology.

# IVY TECH STATE COLLEGE-WHITEWATER

2325 Chester Boulevard
Richmond, IN 47374-1298
**Contact:** Linda Przybysz, Admissions Coordinator
**Phone:** 765-966-2656
**Fax:** 765-962-8741
**Web:** http://www.ivy.tec.in.us/richmond/
**E-mail:** lprzybys@ivy.tec.in.us

**ACCREDITATION:** North Central Association of Colleges and Schools
**INSTITUTIONALLY ADMINISTERED FINANCIAL AID:** Yes

## DEGREE OR CERTIFICATE PROGRAMS OFFERED

**Undergraduate**—*AAS:* Early Childhood Education.

## NON-DEGREE-RELATED COURSE TOPICS OFFERED

**Undergraduate**—American (United States) history; English composition; accounting; business administration and management; child care and guidance workers and managers; communications, general; computer and information sciences, general; computer programming; computer software and media applications; computer systems analysis; computer systems networking and telecommunications; computer/information technology administration and management; economics; history; hospitality services management; mathematics; physical sciences, general; physics; psychology; sociology.

# JACKSONVILLE STATE UNIVERSITY

*Instructional Services Unit*

Ramona Wood Building, Room 101, 700 Pelham Road, North Jacksonville, AL 36265-1602
**Contact:** Dr. Franklin L. King, Director
**Phone:** 256-782-5616
**Fax:** 256-782-5959
**Web:** http://www.jsu.edu/
**E-mail:** fking@jsucc.jsu.edu

**ACCREDITATION:** Southern Association of Colleges and Schools
**INSTITUTIONALLY ADMINISTERED FINANCIAL AID:** Yes

## DEGREE OR CERTIFICATE PROGRAMS OFFERED

**Graduate**—*MPA:* Emergency Management.

## NON-DEGREE-RELATED COURSE TOPICS OFFERED

**Undergraduate**—American literature (United States); English composition; English language and literature, general; accounting; anthropology; applied mathematics; atmospheric sciences and meteorology; biological and physical sciences; business administration and management; business and personal services marketing operations; business information and data processing services; business management and administrative services, other; business quantitative methods and management science; business/managerial economics; child care and guidance workers and managers; computer and information sciences, general; computer and information sciences, other; computer programming; computer science; computer software and media applications; computer systems analysis; computer systems networking and telecommunications; computer/information technology administration and management; curriculum and instruction; data processing technology; developmental and child psychology; economics; education, general; education, other; educational evaluation, research and statistics; educational psychology; environmental control technologies; financial management and services; geography; geological and related sciences; health and physical education/fitness; health professions and related sciences, other; history; information sciences and systems; marketing management and research; marketing operations/marketing and distribution, other; mathematics; mathematics and computer science; medical basic sciences; medical residency programs; nursing; political science and government; psychology; public administration; quality control and safety technologies; school psychology; social sciences, general; social work; sociology; special education; student counseling and personnel services; teacher education, specific academic and vocational programs.

**Graduate**—accounting; business; business administration and management; business and personal services marketing operations; business communications; business information and data processing services; business management and administrative services, other; business quantitative methods and management science; business/managerial economics; computer and information sciences, general; computer and information sciences, other; computer engineering; computer programming; computer science; computer software and media applications; computer systems analysis; computer systems networking and telecommunications; computer/information technology administration and management; curriculum and instruction; developmental and child psychology; economics; education administration and supervision; education, general; education, other; educational evaluation, research and statistics; educational psychology; educational/instructional media design; family and community studies; financial management and services; financial services marketing operations; fire protection; health professions and related sciences, other; human resources management; individual and family development studies; information sciences and systems; marketing management and research; marketing operations/marketing and distribution, other; medical basic sciences; medical residency programs; miscellaneous health professions; public administration; public administration and services, other; quality control and safety technologies; social sciences, general; social work; sociology; special education; teacher education, specific academic and vocational programs.

# JAMES MADISON UNIVERSITY

*Distance Learning Center, Office of Continuing Education*

22 Carrier Library, MSC 1702
Harrisonburg, VA 22807

**Contact:** Dr. Jim Mazoue, Distance Learning Coordinator, Distributed and Distance Learning
**Phone:** 540-568-2591
**Fax:** 540-568-6734
**Web:** http://ddls.jmu.edu
**E-mail:** mazouejge@jmu.edu

**ACCREDITATION:** Southern Association of Colleges and Schools

### DEGREE OR CERTIFICATE PROGRAMS OFFERED

**Graduate—*MCC:*** Concentration in Information Security.

### NON-DEGREE-RELATED COURSE TOPICS OFFERED

**Undergraduate**—adult and continuing teacher education.

# JAMES SPRUNT COMMUNITY COLLEGE

*James Sprunt Community College Distance Learning*
221 James Sprunt Circle, PO Box 398
Kenansville, NC 28349
**Contact:** Mrs. Heather L. Lanier, Distance Learning Coordinator
**Phone:** 910-296-1334
**Fax:** 910-296-0731
**Web:** http://www.sprunt.com
**E-mail:** hlanier@jscc.cc.nc.us

**ACCREDITATION:** Southern Association of Colleges and Schools
**INSTITUTIONALLY ADMINISTERED FINANCIAL AID:** Yes

### DEGREE OR CERTIFICATE PROGRAMS OFFERED

**Programs offered do not lead to a degree or other formal award.**

### NON-DEGREE-RELATED COURSE TOPICS OFFERED

**Undergraduate**—English composition; English language and literature/letters, other; administrative and secretarial services; agricultural business and management; agriculture/agricultural sciences, other; animal sciences; business administration and management; business communications; communications, other; criminal justice and corrections; history; internet and world wide web; mathematics; psychology; religion/religious studies; sociology.
**Non-credit**—computer software and media applications.

# JAMESTOWN COMMUNITY COLLEGE

*Distance Education*
525 Falconer Street
Jamestown, NY 14702-0020
**Contact:** Admissions Office
**Phone:** 716-665-5220 Ext. 2239
**Fax:** 716-664-9592
**Web:** http://www.sunyjcc.edu

**E-mail:** admissions@mail.sunyjcc.edu
**ACCREDITATION:** Middle States Association of Colleges and Schools
**INSTITUTIONALLY ADMINISTERED FINANCIAL AID:** Yes

### DEGREE OR CERTIFICATE PROGRAMS OFFERED

**Undergraduate—*AS:*** Computer Science.

### NON-DEGREE-RELATED COURSE TOPICS OFFERED

**Undergraduate**—accounting; business administration and management; chemistry; computer science; fine arts and art studies; human resources management; philosophy; physics; sociology.

# JEFFERSON COLLEGE

*Learning Resources*
1000 Viking Drive
Hillsboro, MO 63050
**Contact:** Mr. Allan A. Wamsley, Director of Instructional Support Center
**Phone:** 636-797-3000 Ext. 342
**Fax:** 636-789-5801
**Web:** http://www.jeffco.edu/
**E-mail:** awamsley@jeffco.edu

**ACCREDITATION:** North Central Association of Colleges and Schools
**INSTITUTIONALLY ADMINISTERED FINANCIAL AID:** Yes

### DEGREE OR CERTIFICATE PROGRAMS OFFERED

**Programs offered do not lead to a degree or other formal award.**

### NON-DEGREE-RELATED COURSE TOPICS OFFERED

**Undergraduate**—American (United States) history; English composition; European history; French language and literature; Spanish language and literature; biology, general; mathematics, other; sociology.

# JEFFERSON COMMUNITY COLLEGE

*Division of Continuing Education*
1220 Coffeen Street
Watertown, NY 13601
**Contact:** Barry Jennison, Associate Dean for Continuing Education
**Phone:** 315-786-2233
**Fax:** 315-786-2391
**Web:** http://www.sunyjefferson.edu
**E-mail:** barry_jennison@ccmgate.sunyjefferson.edu

**ACCREDITATION:** Middle States Association of Colleges and Schools
**INSTITUTIONALLY ADMINISTERED FINANCIAL AID:** Yes

### DEGREE OR CERTIFICATE PROGRAMS OFFERED

**Programs offered do not lead to a degree or other formal award.**

### NON-DEGREE-RELATED COURSE TOPICS OFFERED

**Undergraduate**—English composition; English technical and business writing; business administration and management; business management and administrative services, other; computer programming; economics; history; mathematics, other; psychology; sociology.

# JEFFERSON DAVIS COMMUNITY COLLEGE

PO Box 958
Brewton, AL 36427
**Contact:** Dr. Anthony Molina, Dean of Instruction
**Phone:** 334-809-1500
**Fax:** 334-867-7399
**Web:** http://www.jdcc.net/

**ACCREDITATION:** Southern Association of Colleges and Schools
**INSTITUTIONALLY ADMINISTERED FINANCIAL AID:** No

## DEGREE OR CERTIFICATE PROGRAMS OFFERED
Programs offered do not lead to a degree or other formal award.

## NON-DEGREE-RELATED COURSE TOPICS OFFERED
**Undergraduate**—accounting; criminal justice and corrections; economics; health and physical education/fitness; mathematical statistics.

# JEWISH THEOLOGICAL SEMINARY OF AMERICA

3080 Broadway, Mailbox 90
New York, NY 10027
**Contact:** Department of Distance Learning
**Phone:** 212-678-8897
**Fax:** 212-749-9085
**Web:** http://courses.jtsa.edu/
**E-mail:** dlp@jtsa.edu

**ACCREDITATION:** Middle States Association of Colleges and Schools
**INSTITUTIONALLY ADMINISTERED FINANCIAL AID:** Yes

## DEGREE OR CERTIFICATE PROGRAMS OFFERED
**Graduate**—*MA:* Interdepartmental Studies—Judaic Studies; Jewish Education.

## NON-DEGREE-RELATED COURSE TOPICS OFFERED
**Undergraduate**—bible/biblical studies; biblical and other theological languages and literatures; religion/religious studies; religious education.
**Graduate**—bible/biblical studies; biblical and other theological languages and literatures; religion/religious studies; religious education.
**Non-credit**—bible/biblical studies; biblical and other theological languages and literatures; religion/religious studies; religious education.

# JOHN A. LOGAN COLLEGE

*Learning Resources*
700 Logan College Road
Carterville, IL 62918
**Contact:** Robert Fester, Advisor and Counselor

**Web:** http://www.jal.cc.il.us
**E-mail:** bob.fester@jal.cc.il.us

**ACCREDITATION:** North Central Association of Colleges and Schools
**INSTITUTIONALLY ADMINISTERED FINANCIAL AID:** Yes

## DEGREE OR CERTIFICATE PROGRAMS OFFERED
Programs offered do not lead to a degree or other formal award.

## NON-DEGREE-RELATED COURSE TOPICS OFFERED
**Undergraduate**—accounting; business.

# JOHN F. KENNEDY UNIVERSITY

12 Altarinda Road
Orinda, CA 94563-2603
**Contact:** Ellena Bloedorn, Director of Admissions and Records
**Phone:** 925-258-2212
**Fax:** 925-254-6964
**Web:** http://www.jfku.edu/
**E-mail:** ebloedor@jfku.edu

**ACCREDITATION:** Western Association of Schools and Colleges

## DEGREE OR CERTIFICATE PROGRAMS OFFERED
Programs offered do not lead to a degree or other formal award.

## NON-DEGREE-RELATED COURSE TOPICS OFFERED
**Undergraduate**—area, ethnic and cultural studies, other; business; business administration and management; education, general; ethnic and cultural studies; liberal arts and sciences, general studies and humanities; philosophy and religion; physical sciences, general; psychology.
**Graduate**—area, ethnic and cultural studies, other; biological sciences/life sciences, other; business administration and management; clinical psychology; counseling psychology; criminology; design and applied arts; developmental and child psychology; ethnic and cultural studies; fine arts and art studies; general teacher education; law and legal studies; museology/museum studies; peace and conflict studies; philosophy and religion; psychology; visual and performing arts.

# JOHNS HOPKINS UNIVERSITY

*School of Continuing Studies, Electronic and Distance Education*
Administration Office, Milton S. Eisenhower Library, 3400 North Charles Street
Baltimore, MD 21218
**Contact:** Dr. Candice V. Dalrymple, Associate Dean and Director, Center for Educational Resources
**Phone:** 410-516-8848
**Fax:** 410-516-5080
**Web:** http://webapps.jhu.edu/jhuniverse/academics/distance_education/
**E-mail:** cdalrymple@jhu.edu

**ACCREDITATION:** Middle States Association of Colleges and Schools
**INSTITUTIONALLY ADMINISTERED FINANCIAL AID:** Yes

eCollege.com  *www.ecollege.com*

## DEGREE OR CERTIFICATE PROGRAMS OFFERED

Programs offered do not lead to a degree or other formal award.

# JOHNSON BIBLE COLLEGE

*Distance Learning Office*

Box 777031
Knoxville, TN 37998
**Contact:** John C. Ketchen, Director of Distance Learning
**Phone:** 865-251-2254
**Fax:** 865-251-2285
**Web:** http://www.jbc.edu/
**E-mail:** jketchen@jbc.edu

**ACCREDITATION:** Accrediting Association of Bible Colleges

## DEGREE OR CERTIFICATE PROGRAMS OFFERED

**Graduate—***MA:* New Testament.

# JOHNSON COUNTY COMMUNITY COLLEGE

JCCC Billington Library, 12345 College Boulevard
Overland Park, KS 66210-1299
**Contact:** Dr. Mel Cunningham, Dean of Computer Instruction and Media Resources
**Phone:** 913-469-8500 Ext. 3882
**Fax:** 913-469-3816
**Web:** http://www.jccc.net
**E-mail:** mcunning@jccc.net

**ACCREDITATION:** North Central Association of Colleges and Schools
**INSTITUTIONALLY ADMINISTERED FINANCIAL AID:** Yes

## DEGREE OR CERTIFICATE PROGRAMS OFFERED

**Undergraduate—***AA:* Multidisciplinary Study. *AGS:* General Studies.

## NON-DEGREE-RELATED COURSE TOPICS OFFERED

**Undergraduate—**American (United States) history; English composition; English literature (British and Commonwealth); English technical and business writing; accounting; anthropology; biology, general; business marketing and marketing management; chemistry; computer software and media applications; computer systems networking and telecommunications; economics; environmental science/studies; mathematics; oceanography; paralegal/legal assistant; psychology; sociology; speech and rhetorical studies.
**Non-credit—**computer software and media applications; health and medical administrative services; health and medical preparatory programs; real estate.

# JOHN WOOD COMMUNITY COLLEGE

*Alternative and Distance Learning Center*

1301 South 48th Street
Quincy, IL 62305

**Contact:** Mark McNett, Director of Admissions
**Phone:** 217-224-6500
**Fax:** 217-224-4339
**Web:** http://www.jwcc.edu/instruct/olc/default.htm
**E-mail:** mcnett@jwcc.edu

**ACCREDITATION:** North Central Association of Colleges and Schools
**INSTITUTIONALLY ADMINISTERED FINANCIAL AID:** Yes

## DEGREE OR CERTIFICATE PROGRAMS OFFERED

**Undergraduate—***AA:* General Studies.

## NON-DEGREE-RELATED COURSE TOPICS OFFERED

**Undergraduate—**American (United States) history; Army R.O.T.C.; English composition; accounting; anatomy; anthropology; art history, criticism and conservation; astronomy; business; business administration and management; computer and information sciences, general; criminal justice and corrections; data entry/microcomputer applications; developmental and child psychology; economics; educational psychology; health and physical education/fitness; internet and world wide web; philosophy and religion; social psychology; sociology.
**Non-credit—**insurance and risk management.

# JONES COLLEGE

5353 Arlington Expressway
Jacksonville, FL 32211-5540
**Contact:** Mr. Thomas A. Clift, Director of Distance Learning
**Phone:** 904-743-1122 Ext. 134
**Fax:** 904-642-9231
**Web:** http://www.jones.edu/
**E-mail:** tclift@jones.edu

**ACCREDITATION:** Accrediting Council for Independent Colleges and Schools
**INSTITUTIONALLY ADMINISTERED FINANCIAL AID:** Yes

## DEGREE OR CERTIFICATE PROGRAMS OFFERED

Programs offered do not lead to a degree or other formal award.

## NON-DEGREE-RELATED COURSE TOPICS OFFERED

**Undergraduate—**English composition; English language and literature, general; accounting; business; business administration and management; business communications; business information and data processing services; community psychology; computer and information sciences, general; computer programming; computer systems analysis; health and medical assistants; law and legal studies; marketing operations/marketing and distribution, other; mathematics; social sciences, general; taxation.

# JONES INTERNATIONAL UNIVERSITY

9697 East Mineral Avenue
Englewood, CO 80112
**Contact:** Program in Business Communication
**Phone:** 800-811-5663
**Fax:** 303-784-8547

**Web:** http://www.jonesinternational.edu/
**E-mail:** info@international.edu

**ACCREDITATION:** North Central Association of Colleges and Schools

**INSTITUTIONALLY ADMINISTERED FINANCIAL AID:** Yes

### DEGREE OR CERTIFICATE PROGRAMS OFFERED

Undergraduate—*BA:* Business Communication.
Graduate—*MA:* Business Communication. *MBA:* Business Administration.

See full description on page 388.

# J. SARGEANT REYNOLDS COMMUNITY COLLEGE

### Division of Instructional Technologies and Distance Education

Center for Distance Education, PO Box 85622
Richmond, VA 23285-5622
**Contact:** Dr. S. Etkin, Assistant Coordinator, Center for Distance Education
**Web:** http://www.jsr.cc.va.us/itde/cde/default.htm
**E-mail:** setkin@jsr.cc.va.us

**ACCREDITATION:** Southern Association of Colleges and Schools

**INSTITUTIONALLY ADMINISTERED FINANCIAL AID:** Yes

### DEGREE OR CERTIFICATE PROGRAMS OFFERED

Undergraduate—*AAS:* Respiratory Therapy.

### NON-DEGREE-RELATED COURSE TOPICS OFFERED

Undergraduate—English composition; accounting; administrative and secretarial services; biology, general; business administration and management; chemistry; child care and guidance workers and managers; computer science; developmental and child psychology; economics; food sciences and technology; foreign languages and literatures; health and physical education/fitness; history; information sciences and systems; journalism and mass communications; marketing management and research; mathematics; miscellaneous health professions; nursing; political science and government; psychology; social sciences and history, other; sociology.

# JUDSON COLLEGE

### External Degree Program

PO Box 120
Marion, AL 36756
**Contact:** Angie M. Teague, Director of Adult Studies
**Phone:** 800-447-9472 Ext. 169
**Fax:** 334-683-5158
**Web:** http://home.judson.edu
**E-mail:** adultstudies@future.judson.edu

**ACCREDITATION:** Southern Association of Colleges and Schools

**INSTITUTIONALLY ADMINISTERED FINANCIAL AID:** No

### DEGREE OR CERTIFICATE PROGRAMS OFFERED

Undergraduate—*BA:* Business; Criminal Justice; English; History; Music; Psychology; Religious Studies. *BMin:* Ministry Studies. *BS:* Business; Criminal Justice; Psychology.

### NON-DEGREE-RELATED COURSE TOPICS OFFERED

Undergraduate—English composition; English language and literature, general; bible/biblical studies; business administration and management; criminal justice and corrections; education, general; history; music; political science and government; psychology; religion/religious studies; sociology.

# JUDSON COLLEGE

### Division of Continuing Education

1151 North State Street
Elgin, IL 60123
**Contact:** Ms. Sherri Deck, Customized Learning Center Operations Manager
**Phone:** 847-695-2500 Ext. 2227
**Fax:** 847-695-4880
**Web:** http://www.judsononline.org
**E-mail:** sdeck@judson-il.edu

**ACCREDITATION:** North Central Association of Colleges and Schools

**INSTITUTIONALLY ADMINISTERED FINANCIAL AID:** Yes

### DEGREE OR CERTIFICATE PROGRAMS OFFERED

Undergraduate—*BA:* Management and Leadership.

### NON-DEGREE-RELATED COURSE TOPICS OFFERED

Undergraduate—English composition; English creative writing; English language and literature, general; English technical and business writing; advertising; applied mathematics; astronomy; bible/biblical studies; business administration and management; business communications; communications, general; computer software and media applications; computer systems analysis; environmental control technologies; fine arts and art studies; foreign languages and literatures; history; human resources management; liberal arts and sciences, general studies and humanities; mathematics; political science and government; psychology; sociology.

# JUNIATA COLLEGE

Brumbaugh Science Center, 1700 Moore Street
Huntingdon, PA 16652
**Contact:** Dr. Loren K. Rhodes, Professor of Information Technology
**Phone:** 814-641-3620
**Fax:** 814-641-3685
**Web:** http://www.juniata.edu/
**E-mail:** rhodes@juniata.edu

**ACCREDITATION:** Middle States Association of Colleges and Schools

### DEGREE OR CERTIFICATE PROGRAMS OFFERED

Programs offered do not lead to a degree or other formal award.

# KANSAS CITY KANSAS COMMUNITY COLLEGE

*Distance Education*

7250 State Ave
Kansas City, KS 66112
**Contact:** Tamara Miller, Director of Distance Learning
**Phone:** 913-288-7136
**Fax:** 913-288-7663
**Web:** http://www.kckcc.cc.ks.us
**E-mail:** tmiller@toto.net

**ACCREDITATION:** North Central Association of Colleges and Schools
**INSTITUTIONALLY ADMINISTERED FINANCIAL AID:** Yes

## DEGREE OR CERTIFICATE PROGRAMS OFFERED
**Programs offered do not lead to a degree or other formal award.**

## NON-DEGREE-RELATED COURSE TOPICS OFFERED
**Undergraduate**—American literature (United States); English composition; English language and literature, general; accounting; administrative and secretarial services; anthropology; bilingual/bicultural education; biological and physical sciences; biology, general; business; business administration and management; business management and administrative services, other; computer and information sciences, general; computer and information sciences, other; computer science; computer software and media applications; computer systems networking and telecommunications; data entry/microcomputer applications; economics; foreign languages and literatures; history; liberal arts and sciences, general studies and humanities; marketing operations/marketing and distribution, other; philosophy; physical sciences, general; psychology; sociology.

# KANSAS STATE UNIVERSITY

*Division of Continuing Education, Continuing Learning*

13 College Court Building
Manhattan, KS 66506
**Contact:** Cyndy Trent, Bachelor Degree Completion Program Coordinator
**Phone:** 785-532-5575
**Fax:** 785-532-5637
**Web:** http://www.dce.ksu.edu
**E-mail:** degrees@dce.ksu.edu

**ACCREDITATION:** North Central Association of Colleges and Schools
**INSTITUTIONALLY ADMINISTERED FINANCIAL AID:** Yes

## DEGREE OR CERTIFICATE PROGRAMS OFFERED
**Undergraduate**—*BS:* Animal Science and Industry; Dietetics; Food Science and Industry; General Business; Interdisciplinary Social Sciences. *Certificate:* Food Science; Personal Financial Planning.
**Graduate**—*MS:* Agribusiness; Chemical Engineering; Civil Engineering; Electrical Engineering; Engineering Management; Family Financial Planning; Industrial/Organizational Psychology; Software Engineering.

## NON-DEGREE-RELATED COURSE TOPICS OFFERED
**Undergraduate**—American (United States) history; English language and literature, general; accounting; agricultural business and management; agricultural business and production, other; agriculture/agricultural sciences; agriculture/agricultural sciences, other; animal sciences; biochemistry; business; business administration and management; business management and administrative services, other; business marketing and marketing management; child care and guidance workers and managers; film/cinema studies; finance, general; financial management and services; food sciences and technology; foods and nutrition studies; horticulture science; labor/personnel relations and studies; management information systems and business data processing, general; mathematical statistics; organizational behavior studies; psychology; sociology; women's studies.
**Graduate**—agricultural business and management; chemical engineering; civil engineering; computer engineering; computer science; computer software and media applications; engineering mechanics; engineering science; engineering, general; engineering, other; engineering/industrial management; financial management and services; horticulture science; human resources management; industrial and organizational psychology; industrial/manufacturing engineering; labor/personnel relations and studies; mechanical engineering; psychology; public administration; quality control and safety technologies.
**Non-credit**—financial management and services; food sciences and technology.

**See full description on page 390.**

# KAPIOLANI COMMUNITY COLLEGE

*KCC Distance Learning*

Admissions Office, Ilima 102, 4303 Diamond Head Road
Honolulu, HI 96816
**Contact:** Cynthia L. Suzuki, Admissions Coordinator
**Phone:** 808-734-9448
**Fax:** 808-734-9456
**Web:** http://www.hawaii.edu/uhcc.e-learn
**E-mail:** cynthias@hawaii.edu

**ACCREDITATION:** Western Association of Schools and Colleges
**INSTITUTIONALLY ADMINISTERED FINANCIAL AID:** No

## DEGREE OR CERTIFICATE PROGRAMS OFFERED
**Programs offered do not lead to a degree or other formal award.**

## NON-DEGREE-RELATED COURSE TOPICS OFFERED
**Undergraduate**—English composition; English language and literature, general; anthropology; biology, general; education, other; foreign languages and literatures; geography; health and medical assistants; history; liberal arts and sciences, general studies and humanities; mathematics and computer science; psychology; zoology.

# KAPLAN COLLEGE

*Quest College Online*

1801 East Kimberly Road, Suite 1
Davenport, IA 52807-2095
**Contact:** Quest College Online
**Web:** http://www.kaplancollegeia.com/

**ACCREDITATION:** Accrediting Council for Independent Colleges and Schools

## DEGREE OR CERTIFICATE PROGRAMS OFFERED

**Programs offered do not lead to a degree or other formal award.**

# KEAN UNIVERSITY

1000 Morris Avenue
Union, NJ 07083
**Contact:** Dr. Jho-Ju Tu, Assistant Vice President for Academic and Instructional Technology
**Phone:** 908-527-2331
**Fax:** 908-352-6123
**Web:** http://www.kean.edu/

**ACCREDITATION:** Middle States Association of Colleges and Schools

**INSTITUTIONALLY ADMINISTERED FINANCIAL AID:** Yes

## DEGREE OR CERTIFICATE PROGRAMS OFFERED

**Graduate—***MAE:* Early Childhood Education.

## NON-DEGREE-RELATED COURSE TOPICS OFFERED

**Undergraduate**—accounting; apparel and accessories marketing operations; business; business and personal services marketing operations; business/managerial economics; criminal justice and corrections; curriculum and instruction; education administration and supervision; family and community studies; fine arts and art studies; health and medical administrative services; health and physical education/fitness; health professions and related sciences, other; marketing management and research; nursing; parks, recreation and leisure studies; sociology; special education.
**Graduate**—education administration and supervision; teacher education, specific academic and vocational programs.
**Non-credit**—business; computer and information sciences, general; computer software and media applications; education, general; personal and miscellaneous services, other; science technologies, other.

# KELLER GRADUATE SCHOOL OF MANAGEMENT

*Online Educational Center*
1 Tower Lane, 11th Floor
Oakbrook Terrace, IL 60181-4624
**Contact:** Michelle Alford, Director of Enrollment Management
**Phone:** 630-706-3275
**Fax:** 630-574-1973
**Web:** http://www.online.keller.edu
**E-mail:** malford@keller.edu

**ACCREDITATION:** North Central Association of Colleges and Schools

| eCollege .com *www.ecollege.com* |
| --- |

## DEGREE OR CERTIFICATE PROGRAMS OFFERED

**Undergraduate—***AIS:* Information Systems.
**Graduate—***MBA:* Various Concentrations. *MPM:* Project Management. *MS:* Accounting/Finance; Master of Human Resources Management (MHRM); Telecommunications. *MSIS:* Master of Information Systems Management (MISM).

## NON-DEGREE-RELATED COURSE TOPICS OFFERED

**Undergraduate**—accounting; financial management and services; marketing operations/marketing and distribution, other.
**Graduate**—accounting; business administration and management; finance, general; health system/health services administration; information sciences and systems; international business; marketing management and research; telecommunications.

**See full description on page 392.**

# KELLOGG COMMUNITY COLLEGE

*Distributed Learning*
450 North Avenue
Battle Creek, MI 49017
**Contact:** Charles F. Parker, Dean of Educational Services
**Phone:** 616-965-3931 Ext. 2390
**Web:** http://www.kellogg.cc.mi.us
**E-mail:** parkerc@kellogg.cc.mi.us

**ACCREDITATION:** North Central Association of Colleges and Schools

**INSTITUTIONALLY ADMINISTERED FINANCIAL AID:** Yes

## DEGREE OR CERTIFICATE PROGRAMS OFFERED

**Programs offered do not lead to a degree or other formal award.**

## NON-DEGREE-RELATED COURSE TOPICS OFFERED

**Undergraduate**—American (United States) history; English creative writing; Spanish language and literature; accounting; advertising; anthropology; biological and physical sciences; business marketing and marketing management; computer and information sciences, general; computer software and media applications; international business; journalism and mass communication, other; law and legal studies, other; mathematics, other; nursing; philosophy and religion; sociology.

# KENNESAW STATE UNIVERSITY

*Instructional Technology*
Kennesaw, GA 30188
**Contact:** Dr. Joe Head, Jr., Dean of Enrollment Services
**Web:** http://www.kennesaw.edu
**E-mail:** jhead@kennesaw.edu

**ACCREDITATION:** Southern Association of Colleges and Schools

**INSTITUTIONALLY ADMINISTERED FINANCIAL AID:** Yes

## DEGREE OR CERTIFICATE PROGRAMS OFFERED

**Graduate—***EMBA:* Business.

## NON-DEGREE-RELATED COURSE TOPICS OFFERED

**Undergraduate**—English composition; accounting; applied mathematics; business; chemistry; communications, general; computer science; education, general; health and physical education/fitness; nursing.
**Graduate**—business.

# KENTUCKY STATE UNIVERSITY

## KSU Distance Learning

400 East Main, HH 324
Frankfort, KY 40601
**Contact:** Diane Garrison, Director of Academic Computing
**Phone:** 502-597-6938
**Web:** http://www.kysu.edu/
**E-mail:** dgarrison@gwmail.kysu.edu

**ACCREDITATION:** Southern Association of Colleges and Schools

**INSTITUTIONALLY ADMINISTERED FINANCIAL AID:** Yes

### DEGREE OR CERTIFICATE PROGRAMS OFFERED
**Programs offered do not lead to a degree or other formal award.**

### NON-DEGREE-RELATED COURSE TOPICS OFFERED
**Undergraduate**—English composition; English language and literature, general; anthropology; computer and information sciences, general; computer programming; counseling psychology; drafting; engineering-related technologies, other; family and community studies; foreign languages and literatures; health and physical education/fitness; mathematics, other; miscellaneous health professions; psychology; psychology, other; rehabilitation/ therapeutic services; sociology.
**Non-credit**—crafts, folk art and artisanry; religion/religious studies.

# KETTERING UNIVERSITY

## Graduate School

1700 West 3rd Avenue
Flint, MI 48504
**Contact:** Betty Bedore, Coordinator of Graduate Publications
**Phone:** 810-762-7494
**Fax:** 810-762-9935
**Web:** http://www.kettering.edu
**E-mail:** bbedore@kettering.edu

**ACCREDITATION:** North Central Association of Colleges and Schools

**INSTITUTIONALLY ADMINISTERED FINANCIAL AID:** Yes

### DEGREE OR CERTIFICATE PROGRAMS OFFERED
**Graduate**—*MS:* Engineering; Manufacturing Management; Operations Management.

**See full description on page 394.**

# KING'S COLLEGE

## Distance Learning Program

133 North River Street
Wilkes-Barre, PA 18711
**Contact:** Bill Keating, Director of Distance Learning
**Phone:** 570-208-5960
**Fax:** 570-208-5961
**Web:** http://www.kings.edu/dstlrng
**E-mail:** wpkeatin@kings.edu

**ACCREDITATION:** Middle States Association of Colleges and Schools

**INSTITUTIONALLY ADMINISTERED FINANCIAL AID:** Yes

### DEGREE OR CERTIFICATE PROGRAMS OFFERED
**Programs offered do not lead to a degree or other formal award.**

### NON-DEGREE-RELATED COURSE TOPICS OFFERED
**Undergraduate**—American (United States) history; English creative writing; English language and literature, general; economics; psychology; sociology.

# KIRKSVILLE COLLEGE OF OSTEOPATHIC MEDICINE

## VTEL BK227

800 West Jefferson Street
Kirksville, MO 63501
**Contact:** Admissions
**Phone:** 800-626-KCOM Ext. 2237
**Fax:** 660-626-2969
**Web:** http://www.kcom.edu
**E-mail:** admissions@kcom.edu

**ACCREDITATION:** North Central Association of Colleges and Schools

eCollege.com   www.ecollege.com

### DEGREE OR CERTIFICATE PROGRAMS OFFERED
**Programs offered do not lead to a degree or other formal award.**

# KIRKWOOD COMMUNITY COLLEGE

6301 Kirkwood Boulevard, SW, 210 Linn Hall
Cedar Rapids, IA 52406
**Contact:** Wendell Maakestad, Director of Distance Learning
**Phone:** 319-398-5565
**Fax:** 319-398-5492
**Web:** http://www.kirkwood.cc.ia.us/
**E-mail:** wmaakes@kirkwood.cc.ia.us

**ACCREDITATION:** North Central Association of Colleges and Schools

**INSTITUTIONALLY ADMINISTERED FINANCIAL AID:** Yes

### DEGREE OR CERTIFICATE PROGRAMS OFFERED
**Undergraduate**—*AA:* Associate of Arts Programs; Liberal Arts.

### NON-DEGREE-RELATED COURSE TOPICS OFFERED
**Non-credit**—business; computer and information sciences, general; computer software and media applications; computer systems analysis; computer systems networking and telecommunications; data entry/ microcomputer applications; data processing technology.

# KNOWLEDGE SYSTEMS INSTITUTE

3420 Main Street
Skokie, IL 60076

**Contact:** Ms. Margaret M. Price, Office Manager
**Phone:** 847-679-3135
**Fax:** 847-679-3166
**Web:** http://distancelearning.ksi.edu/
**E-mail:** office@ksi.edu

**ACCREDITATION:** North Central Association of Colleges and Schools
**INSTITUTIONALLY ADMINISTERED FINANCIAL AID:** Yes

### DEGREE OR CERTIFICATE PROGRAMS OFFERED

Undergraduate—*Certificate:* Computer and Information Sciences.
Graduate—*MS:* Computer and Information Sciences.

### NON-DEGREE-RELATED COURSE TOPICS OFFERED

Undergraduate—computer programming; computer science.
Graduate—computer programming; computer science; information sciences and systems.

# KRANNERT GRADUATE SCHOOL OF MANAGEMENT

1310 Krannert Center, Suite 208
West Lafayette, IN 47907-1310
**Contact:** Erika C. Steuterman, Director of Executive Master's Programs
**Phone:** 765-494-7700
**Fax:** 765-494-0862
**Web:** http://www2.mgmt.purdue.edu/
**E-mail:** keepinfo@mgmt.purdue.edu

**ACCREDITATION:** North Central Association of Colleges and Schools
**INSTITUTIONALLY ADMINISTERED FINANCIAL AID:** No

### DEGREE OR CERTIFICATE PROGRAMS OFFERED

Graduate—*EMBA:* The Executive Master of Business Administration Program (EMB).

# LABETTE COMMUNITY COLLEGE

200 South 14th
Parsons, KS 67357
**Contact:** Dr. Brent E. Bates, Dean of Instruction
**Phone:** 620-820-1224
**Fax:** 620-421-4481
**Web:** http://www.labette.cc.ks.us/
**E-mail:** brentb@labette.cc.ks.us

**ACCREDITATION:** North Central Association of Colleges and Schools
**INSTITUTIONALLY ADMINISTERED FINANCIAL AID:** No

### DEGREE OR CERTIFICATE PROGRAMS OFFERED

Programs offered do not lead to a degree or other formal award.

### NON-DEGREE-RELATED COURSE TOPICS OFFERED

Undergraduate—English composition; computer programming; computer science; computer systems networking and telecommunications;

fine arts and art studies; geography; health and medical diagnostic and treatment services; health and physical education/fitness; history; mathematics; psychology; sociology.

# LAC COURTE OREILLES OJIBWA COMMUNITY COLLEGE

13466 West Trepania Road
Hayward, WI 54843
**Contact:** Dan Gretz, Academic Dean
**Phone:** 715-634-4790 Ext. 138
**Fax:** 715-634-5049
**Web:** http://www.geocities.com/athens/acropolis/4551/
**E-mail:** djgretz@lco-college.edu

**ACCREDITATION:** North Central Association of Colleges and Schools
**INSTITUTIONALLY ADMINISTERED FINANCIAL AID:** Yes

### DEGREE OR CERTIFICATE PROGRAMS OFFERED

Programs offered do not lead to a degree or other formal award.

### NON-DEGREE-RELATED COURSE TOPICS OFFERED

Undergraduate—earth and planetary sciences; environmental/environmental health engineering; ethnic and cultural studies; nursing.

# LACKAWANNA JUNIOR COLLEGE

*Distance Learning Center*
501 Vine Street
Scranton, PA 18509
**Contact:** Mr. Griffith R. Lewis, Senior Director of MIS
**Phone:** 570-961-7853
**Fax:** 570-961-7858
**Web:** http://www.ljc.edu
**E-mail:** lewisg@ljc.edu

**ACCREDITATION:** Middle States Association of Colleges and Schools
**INSTITUTIONALLY ADMINISTERED FINANCIAL AID:** Yes

### DEGREE OR CERTIFICATE PROGRAMS OFFERED

Programs offered do not lead to a degree or other formal award.

### NON-DEGREE-RELATED COURSE TOPICS OFFERED

Undergraduate—medical basic sciences; miscellaneous health professions.
Non-credit—medical basic sciences; miscellaneous health professions.

# LAFAYETTE COLLEGE

214 Skillman Library
Easton, PA 18042
**Contact:** Patricia A. Facciponti, Instructional Technologist
**Phone:** 610-330-5632
**Fax:** 610-252-0370
**Web:** http://www.lafayette.edu/~itech

**E-mail:** faccipop@lafayette.edu

**ACCREDITATION:** Middle States Association of Colleges and Schools

**INSTITUTIONALLY ADMINISTERED FINANCIAL AID:** Yes

## DEGREE OR CERTIFICATE PROGRAMS OFFERED

**Programs offered do not lead to a degree or other formal award.**

## NON-DEGREE-RELATED COURSE TOPICS OFFERED

**Undergraduate**—engineering mechanics; women's studies.

# LAKEHEAD UNIVERSITY

## Part-Time Studies

Regional Centre 0009, 955 Oliver Road
Thunder Bay, ON P7B 5E1, Canada
**Contact:** Part-time and Distance Education
**Phone:** 807-346-7730
**Fax:** 807-343-8008
**Web:** http://www.lakeheadu.ca
**E-mail:** parttime@lakeheadu.ca

**ACCREDITATION:** Provincially Chartered

## DEGREE OR CERTIFICATE PROGRAMS OFFERED

**Undergraduate**—*BA:* General Studies. *BSN:* Nursing. *BSW:* Social Work. *Certificate:* Certificate Program in Environmental Management; Certificate in Interdisciplinary Palliative Care; Environmental Assessment.

**See full description on page 396.**

# LAKELAND COLLEGE

## Lakeland Online

PO Box 358
Sheboygan, WI 53082-0359
**Contact:** Carol Butzen, Adult Education Counselor
**Phone:** 920-565-1293
**Fax:** 920-565-1341
**Web:** http://www.lakeland.edu
**E-mail:** butzencl@lakeland.edu

**ACCREDITATION:** North Central Association of Colleges and Schools
**INSTITUTIONALLY ADMINISTERED FINANCIAL AID:** Yes

## DEGREE OR CERTIFICATE PROGRAMS OFFERED

**Undergraduate**—*BA:* Accounting; Business Administration; Computer Science; Marketing.

## NON-DEGREE-RELATED COURSE TOPICS OFFERED

**Undergraduate**—accounting; business administration and management; business marketing and marketing management; computer science.
**Graduate**—business administration and management.

**See full description on page 398.**

# LAKELAND COMMUNITY COLLEGE

## Instructional Technology

7700 Clocktower Drive
Kirtland, OH 44094
**Contact:** Ms. Sherry Kocevar, Instructional Materials Coordinator
**Phone:** 440-953-7130
**Fax:** 440-953-9710
**Web:** http://www.lakeland.cc.oh.us/
**E-mail:** skocevar@lakeland.cc.oh.us

**ACCREDITATION:** North Central Association of Colleges and Schools
**INSTITUTIONALLY ADMINISTERED FINANCIAL AID:** Yes

## DEGREE OR CERTIFICATE PROGRAMS OFFERED

**Programs offered do not lead to a degree or other formal award.**

## NON-DEGREE-RELATED COURSE TOPICS OFFERED

**Undergraduate**—accounting; applied mathematics; art history, criticism and conservation; biology, general; business marketing and marketing management; computer and information sciences, general; economics; entrepreneurship; film/video and photographic arts; geography; health and physical education/fitness; history; mathematical statistics; sociology.
**Non-credit**—South Asian languages and literatures; accounting; administrative and secretarial services; advertising; business and personal services marketing operations; business communications; business information and data processing services; business management and administrative services, other; business quantitative methods and management science; business/managerial economics; communication disorders sciences and services; communications technologies; communications, general; communications, other; community health services; community organization, resources and services; computer and information sciences, general; computer and information sciences, other; computer engineering; computer programming; computer/information technology administration and management; data entry/microcomputer applications; data processing technology; engineering, other; enterprise management and operation; entrepreneurship; environmental control technologies; environmental/environmental health engineering; family and community studies; family/consumer resource management; film/video and photographic arts; financial management and services; financial services marketing operations; fine arts and art studies; floristry marketing operations; general retailing and wholesaling operations and skills; gerontology; health and physical education/fitness; health products and services marketing operations; health professions and related sciences, other; heating, air conditioning and refrigeration mechanics and repairers; historic preservation, conservation and architectural history; history; horticulture services operations and management; hospitality and recreation marketing operations; hospitality services management; quality control and safety technologies; real estate; soil sciences; special education; taxation; tourism and travel services marketing operations; veterinary clinical sciences (M.S., Ph.D.); wildlife and wildlands management.

# LAKE MICHIGAN COLLEGE

## Information Technologies

2755 East Napier Avenue
Benton Harbor, MI 49022

**Contact:** Todd Blake, Coordinator of Distance Learning
**Phone:** 616-927-3571
**Fax:** 616-927-8113
**Web:** http://www.lmc.cc.mi.us
**E-mail:** blake@lmc.cc.mi.us

**ACCREDITATION:** North Central Association of Colleges and Schools

**INSTITUTIONALLY ADMINISTERED FINANCIAL AID:** Yes

## DEGREE OR CERTIFICATE PROGRAMS OFFERED
Programs offered do not lead to a degree or other formal award.

## NON-DEGREE-RELATED COURSE TOPICS OFFERED
Undergraduate—accounting; biology, general; sociology.

# LAKE SUPERIOR COLLEGE

2101 Trinity Road
Duluth, MN 55811
**Contact:** Marie Carter Brooks, Online Student Counselor and Advisor
**Phone:** 218-725-7705
**Web:** http://www.lsc.mnscu.edu
**E-mail:** m.brooks@lsc.mnscu.edu

**ACCREDITATION:** North Central Association of Colleges and Schools

**INSTITUTIONALLY ADMINISTERED FINANCIAL AID:** Yes

## DEGREE OR CERTIFICATE PROGRAMS OFFERED
Programs offered do not lead to a degree or other formal award.

## NON-DEGREE-RELATED COURSE TOPICS OFFERED
Undergraduate—English composition; English technical and business writing; accounting; administrative and secretarial services; biological and physical sciences; business; business communications; civil engineering/ civil technology; communications, general; computer and information sciences, general; computer software and media applications; data entry/ microcomputer applications; financial management and services; fine arts and art studies; health and medical preparatory programs; mathematics; psychology; social psychology; sociology.

# LAKE SUPERIOR STATE UNIVERSITY
*Continuing Education*
Sault Sainte Marie, MI 49783
**Contact:** Susan K. Camp, Director of Continuing Education
**Phone:** 906-635-2802
**Fax:** 906-635-2762
**Web:** http://www.lssu.edu/conted
**E-mail:** scamp@lakers.lssu.edu

**ACCREDITATION:** North Central Association of Colleges and Schools

**INSTITUTIONALLY ADMINISTERED FINANCIAL AID:** Yes

## DEGREE OR CERTIFICATE PROGRAMS OFFERED
Programs offered do not lead to a degree or other formal award.

## NON-DEGREE-RELATED COURSE TOPICS OFFERED
Undergraduate—accounting; business administration and management; criminal justice and corrections; engineering/industrial management; nursing.

# LAKEVIEW COLLEGE OF NURSING

903 North Logan Avenue
Danville, IL 61832
**Contact:** Dr. JoAnn Marrs, President and Dean
**Phone:** 217-443-5238
**Fax:** 217-442-2279
**Web:** http://www.lakeviewcol.edu
**E-mail:** jmarrs@lakeviewcol.edu

**ACCREDITATION:** North Central Association of Colleges and Schools

**INSTITUTIONALLY ADMINISTERED FINANCIAL AID:** Yes

## DEGREE OR CERTIFICATE PROGRAMS OFFERED
Programs offered do not lead to a degree or other formal award.

## NON-DEGREE-RELATED COURSE TOPICS OFFERED
Undergraduate—nursing.

# LAMAR STATE COLLEGE–ORANGE

410 Front Street
Orange, TX 77630
**Contact:** Bobbie Burgess, Vice President of Student Services and Auxiliary Services
**Phone:** 409-883-7750
**Fax:** 409-882-3374
**Web:** http://www.orange.lamar.edu
**E-mail:** bobbie.burgess@lsco.lamar.edu

**ACCREDITATION:** Southern Association of Colleges and Schools

**INSTITUTIONALLY ADMINISTERED FINANCIAL AID:** No

## DEGREE OR CERTIFICATE PROGRAMS OFFERED
Programs offered do not lead to a degree or other formal award.

## NON-DEGREE-RELATED COURSE TOPICS OFFERED
Undergraduate—English composition; business administration and management; computer systems analysis; computer systems networking and telecommunications; health and medical preparatory programs.

# LAMAR UNIVERSITY
*Division of Continuing Education*
PO Box 10008
Beaumont, TX 77710
**Contact:** Ms. Orvelle Brown, Assistant Director
**Phone:** 409-880-8431
**Fax:** 409-880-8683
**Web:** http://hal.lamar.edu/%7Epsce

**E-mail:** brownok@hal.lamar.edu

**ACCREDITATION:** Southern Association of Colleges and Schools

**INSTITUTIONALLY ADMINISTERED FINANCIAL AID:** Yes

eCollege.com *www.ecollege.com*

### DEGREE OR CERTIFICATE PROGRAMS OFFERED

Programs offered do not lead to a degree or other formal award.

## LANSING COMMUNITY COLLEGE
*Virtual College*

9101 Academic Systems, PO Box 40010
Lansing, MI 48901-7210
**Contact:** Tim Brannan, Director of Distance Learning Educational Initiatives
**Phone:** 517-483-9940
**Fax:** 517-483-9676
**Web:** http://www.lcc.edu/distancelearning/
**E-mail:** tbrannan@lansing.cc.mi.us

**ACCREDITATION:** North Central Association of Colleges and Schools

**INSTITUTIONALLY ADMINISTERED FINANCIAL AID:** No

### DEGREE OR CERTIFICATE PROGRAMS OFFERED

Undergraduate—*AD:* Business.

### NON-DEGREE-RELATED COURSE TOPICS OFFERED

Undergraduate—English composition; English creative writing; accounting; drama/theater arts, general; earth and planetary sciences; law and legal studies, other; mathematics, other; social psychology; sociology.

## LAURENTIAN UNIVERSITY
*Centre for Continuing Education*

935 Ramsey Lake Road
Sudbury, ON P3E 2C6, Canada
**Contact:** Bettina Brockerhoff-Macdonald, Program Manager
**Phone:** 705-675-1151 Ext. 3942
**Fax:** 705-675-4897
**Web:** http://www.laurentian.ca/cce
**E-mail:** bbrockerhoff@nickel.laurentian.ca

**ACCREDITATION:** Provincially Chartered

**INSTITUTIONALLY ADMINISTERED FINANCIAL AID:** Yes

### DEGREE OR CERTIFICATE PROGRAMS OFFERED

Undergraduate—*BS:* Social Sciences. *BA:* Gerontology; History (in development); Langue et Linguistique (en developpement); Law and Justice (in development); Native Studies; Psychologie; Psychology; Religious Studies; Sciences Religieuses; Sociology; Sociology. *BS:* Liberal Science (in development). *BSN:* For registered nurses. *BSW:* Native Human Services; Service Social. *Certificate:* Family Life Studies and Human Sexuality; Family Life Studies and Human Sexuality; Gerontology; Law and Justice (in development).

## LEBANON VALLEY COLLEGE

101 North College Avenue
Annville, PA 17003
**Contact:** Dr. Barbara Jones Denison, Associate Dean for Graduate Studies and Continuing Education
**Phone:** 717-867-6214
**Web:** http://www.lvc.edu/
**E-mail:** denison@lvc.edu

**ACCREDITATION:** Middle States Association of Colleges and Schools

**INSTITUTIONALLY ADMINISTERED FINANCIAL AID:** No

### DEGREE OR CERTIFICATE PROGRAMS OFFERED

Programs offered do not lead to a degree or other formal award.

## LEHIGH CARBON COMMUNITY COLLEGE
*Office of Distance Learning*

4525 Education Park Drive
Schnecksville, PA 18078
**Contact:** Beverly Benfer, Director of Distance Learning and Instructional Technology
**Phone:** 610-799-1591
**Fax:** 610-799-1526
**Web:** http://www.lccc.edu/distancelearning.html
**E-mail:** bbenfer@lccc.edu

**ACCREDITATION:** Middle States Association of Colleges and Schools

**INSTITUTIONALLY ADMINISTERED FINANCIAL AID:** No

### DEGREE OR CERTIFICATE PROGRAMS OFFERED

Undergraduate—*AA:* Teacher Education. *AAS:* Business Administration and Management; E-Business Management; Health Information Technology.

### NON-DEGREE-RELATED COURSE TOPICS OFFERED

Undergraduate—American (United States) history; American literature (United States); English composition; English technical and business writing; French language and literature; Spanish language and literature; accounting; administrative and secretarial services; anthropology; art history, criticism and conservation; astronomy; biology, general; business; business administration and management; business and personal services marketing operations; business communications; business management and administrative services, other; business marketing and marketing management; child care and guidance workers and managers; computer and information sciences, general; computer and information sciences, other; computer software and media applications; data entry/microcomputer applications; economics; ethnic and cultural studies; finance, general; geography; health and medical administrative services; health and physical education/fitness; history; human resources management; journalism; law and legal studies, other; mathematical statistics; mathematics; philosophy; political science and government; psychology; sociology.

# LEHIGH UNIVERSITY
## Office of Distance Learning
205 Johnson Hall, 36 University Drive
Bethlehem, PA 18015
**Contact:** Peg Kercsmar, Manager
**Phone:** 610-758-5794
**Fax:** 610-758-6269
**Web:** http://www.distance.lehigh.edu
**E-mail:** mak5@lehigh.edu

**ACCREDITATION:** Middle States Association of Colleges and Schools

### DEGREE OR CERTIFICATE PROGRAMS OFFERED
Graduate—*MBA:* Business Administration. *ME:* Chemical Engineering; Polymer Science and Engineering. *MS:* Chemistry; Molecular Biology; Pharmaceutical Chemistry; Polymer Science and Engineering; Quality Engineering.

### Special Note
To enable working professionals to pursue graduate and continuing education at work, Lehigh University's Educational Satellite Network (LESN) carries live, on-campus classes that are broadcast by satellite to students at multiple corporate sites. Companies partner with Lehigh to offer their employees the opportunity to earn master's degrees in chemistry, chemical engineering, molecular biology, pharmaceutical chemistry, polymer science and engineering, quality engineering, and business administration (MBA).

Students express great satisfaction with Lehigh's distance education, particularly its convenience, quality instruction, and the University's responsiveness. This distance education enables students to receive the closest substitute to actual classroom participation possible—all on-campus courses are broadcast live to corporate sites so that students can interact on a real-time basis with instructors. Videotape back-up is available, and students have access to Lehigh's state-of-the-art computer and electronic library systems. Lehigh distance students completing a credit program receive the same degree as on-campus students. Noncredit courses are also available.

In addition, LESN-Online offers distance education courses using streaming video technology so students can simultaneously view the instructor and course graphics. Lehigh's online programs include a full M.S. in Pharmaceutical Chemistry, an executive education program offering a certificate in Supply Chain Management, and a selection of individual business courses. Most courses can be taken individually for credit or noncredit, or as part of a degree or certificate program.

Since Lehigh began offering distance education in 1992, LESN has grown to serve more than 800 students at more than 40 corporate sites including companies such as 3M, Air Products, Bristol Myers Squibb, GlaxoSmithKline, and Merck & Company.

# LESLEY UNIVERSITY
29 Everett Street
Cambridge, MA 02138
**Contact:** Jennifer Andrews, Program Advisor, Online Technology and Education Program
**Phone:** 617-349-8343

**Fax:** 617-349-8169
**Web:** http://www.lesley.edu/
**E-mail:** jandrews@mail.lesley.edu

**ACCREDITATION:** New England Association of Schools and Colleges

**INSTITUTIONALLY ADMINISTERED FINANCIAL AID:** Yes

### DEGREE OR CERTIFICATE PROGRAMS OFFERED
Graduate—*MEd:* Technology in Education.

### NON-DEGREE-RELATED COURSE TOPICS OFFERED
Graduate—curriculum and instruction; education, general; educational/instructional media design; technology education/industrial arts.
**See full description on page 400.**

# LETOURNEAU UNIVERSITY
## Graduate and Adult Continuing Studies
PO Box 7001
Longview, TX 75607-7001
**Contact:** Rodney Stanford, Director of Admissions
**Phone:** 903-233-3400
**Fax:** 903-233-3411
**Web:** http://www.letu.edu/academics/LU_Online/
**E-mail:** rodneystanford@letu.edu

**ACCREDITATION:** Southern Association of Colleges and Schools
**INSTITUTIONALLY ADMINISTERED FINANCIAL AID:** Yes

### DEGREE OR CERTIFICATE PROGRAMS OFFERED
Programs offered do not lead to a degree or other formal award.

### NON-DEGREE-RELATED COURSE TOPICS OFFERED
Undergraduate—English composition; English language and literature, general; bible/biblical studies; biology, general; communications, general; education, general; history; psychology.

# LEWIS AND CLARK COMMUNITY COLLEGE
5800 Godfrey Road
Godfrey, IL 62035
**Contact:** Mrs. Mary C. Hales, Dean of Applied Technology and Business
**Phone:** 618-468-4900
**Fax:** 618-468-7171
**Web:** http://www.lc.cc.il.us/
**E-mail:** mhales@lc.cc.il.us

**ACCREDITATION:** North Central Association of Colleges and Schools
**INSTITUTIONALLY ADMINISTERED FINANCIAL AID:** Yes

### DEGREE OR CERTIFICATE PROGRAMS OFFERED
Programs offered do not lead to a degree or other formal award.

### NON-DEGREE-RELATED COURSE TOPICS OFFERED
Undergraduate—American (United States) history; accounting; administrative and secretarial services; art history, criticism and conservation;

astronomy; biological sciences/life sciences, other; biology, general; business administration and management; business marketing and marketing management; business/managerial economics; communications, general; computer and information sciences, general; criminal justice and corrections; criminology; data entry/microcomputer applications; data processing technology; developmental and child psychology; economics; history; mathematics; music; psychology; speech and rhetorical studies; teacher assistant/aide.

**Non-credit**—computer software and media applications; curriculum and instruction.

# LEWIS-CLARK STATE COLLEGE
## Center for Individualized Programs
500 Eighth Avenue
Lewiston, ID 83501
**Contact:** Kathy L. Martin, Assistant Vice President of Extended Programs
**Phone:** 208-799-2358
**Fax:** 208-799-2444
**Web:** http://www.lcsc.edu/dlt
**E-mail:** kmartin@lcsc.edu

**ACCREDITATION:** Northwest Association of Schools and Colleges
**INSTITUTIONALLY ADMINISTERED FINANCIAL AID:** Yes

### DEGREE OR CERTIFICATE PROGRAMS OFFERED
**Programs offered do not lead to a degree or other formal award.**

### NON-DEGREE-RELATED COURSE TOPICS OFFERED
**Undergraduate**—English composition; administrative and secretarial services; business administration and management; business information and data processing services; child care and guidance workers and managers; communications, general; computer and information sciences, general; education, general; geological and related sciences; liberal arts and sciences, general studies and humanities; mathematics; psychology; social sciences, general; teaching English as a second language/foreign language. **Non-credit**—business management and administrative services, other; computer software and media applications; data entry/microcomputer applications; nursing; personal and miscellaneous services, other.

# LIBERTY UNIVERSITY
## External Degree Program
1971 University Boulevard
Lynchburg, VA 24502-2269
**Contact:** Mr. Lee Beaumont, Director of Enrollment Management
**Phone:** 800-424-9595
**Fax:** 800-628-7977
**Web:** http://www.liberty.edu/admissions/distance/index.cfm
**E-mail:** edpadmissions@liberty.edu

**ACCREDITATION:** Southern Association of Colleges and Schools
**INSTITUTIONALLY ADMINISTERED FINANCIAL AID:** Yes

### DEGREE OR CERTIFICATE PROGRAMS OFFERED
**Undergraduate**—*AA:* General Studies; Religion. *BS:* Business; Multidisciplinary Studies; Psychology; Religion.
**Graduate**—*MA:* Counseling; Professional Counseling. *MAR:* Religion. *MBA:* Business Administration. *MDiv:* Divinity. *MEd:* Education; School Counseling.
**Postgraduate and doctoral**—*EdD:* Education.

### NON-DEGREE-RELATED COURSE TOPICS OFFERED
**Undergraduate**—English composition; accounting; bible/biblical studies; biology, general; business; business marketing and marketing management; developmental and child psychology; economics; education, general; educational psychology; gerontology; philosophy; psychology; social psychology; taxation; theological studies and religious vocations, other.
**Graduate**—bible/biblical studies; business administration and management; business communications; curriculum and instruction; marketing management and research; pastoral counseling and specialized ministries; psychology; theological and ministerial studies.
**See full description on page 402.**

# LIFE BIBLE COLLEGE
## School of Distance Learning
1100 West Covina Boulevard
San Dimas, CA 91773
**Contact:** Brian Tomhave, Director
**Phone:** 909-599-5433 Ext. 359
**Fax:** 909-599-6690
**Web:** http://www.lifebible.edu
**E-mail:** sdl@lifebible.edu

**ACCREDITATION:** Accrediting Association of Bible Colleges

### DEGREE OR CERTIFICATE PROGRAMS OFFERED
**Undergraduate**—*AA:* Biblical Studies.

### NON-DEGREE-RELATED COURSE TOPICS OFFERED
**Undergraduate**—philosophy and religion.

# LIMESTONE COLLEGE
## The Block Program
1115 College Drive
Gaffney, SC 29340-3799
**Contact:** Mr. Frank Mitchell, Director of Institutional Research and Effectiveness
**Phone:** 864-489-7151 Ext. 390
**Fax:** 864-487-8706
**Web:** http://www.limestonevirtualcampus.net
**E-mail:** flmitchell@saint.limestone.edu

**ACCREDITATION:** Southern Association of Colleges and Schools
**INSTITUTIONALLY ADMINISTERED FINANCIAL AID:** Yes

### DEGREE OR CERTIFICATE PROGRAMS OFFERED
**Undergraduate**—*AA:* Business Administration; Computer Science Internet Management; Computer Science Management Information Systems; Computer Science Programming; Liberal Studies. *BA:* Human Resource

Development; Liberal Studies; Psychology. **BS:** Business Administration; Computer Science Internet Management; Computer Science Management Information Systems; Computer Science Programming; Liberal Studies.

# LINCOLN CHRISTIAN COLLEGE

*Distance Learning*
100 Campus View Drive
Lincoln, IL 62656
**Contact:** Admission
**Phone:** 217-732-3168 Ext. 2315
**Web:** http://www.lccs.edu
**E-mail:** coladmis@lccs.edu

**ACCREDITATION:** Accrediting Association of Bible Colleges
**INSTITUTIONALLY ADMINISTERED FINANCIAL AID:** Yes

## DEGREE OR CERTIFICATE PROGRAMS OFFERED
**Undergraduate—***Certificate:* Theological Studies.

## NON-DEGREE-RELATED COURSE TOPICS OFFERED
**Undergraduate—**Hebrew language and literature; adult and continuing teacher education; bible/biblical studies; biblical and other theological languages and literatures; business/managerial economics; counseling psychology; management information systems and business data processing, general; religion/religious studies; teaching English as a second language/foreign language; theological and ministerial studies; theological studies and religious vocations, other.
**Graduate—**Hebrew language and literature; bible/biblical studies; biblical and other theological languages and literatures; counseling psychology; religion/religious studies; teaching English as a second language/foreign language; theological and ministerial studies.
**Non-credit—**Hebrew language and literature; adult and continuing teacher education; bible/biblical studies; biblical and other theological languages and literatures; counseling psychology; management information systems and business data processing, general; religion/religious studies; theological and ministerial studies.

# LINCOLN LAND COMMUNITY COLLEGE

*Learning Resource Center*
5250 Shepherd Road, PO Box 19256
Springfield, IL 62794
**Contact:** Ms. Rebecca E. Parton, Coordinator of Distance Learning Services
**Phone:** 217-786-2351
**Web:** http://www.llcc.cc.il.us/ivc
**E-mail:** becky.parton@llcc.cc.il.us

**ACCREDITATION:** North Central Association of Colleges and Schools
**INSTITUTIONALLY ADMINISTERED FINANCIAL AID:** Yes

## DEGREE OR CERTIFICATE PROGRAMS OFFERED
Programs offered do not lead to a degree or other formal award.

## NON-DEGREE-RELATED COURSE TOPICS OFFERED
**Undergraduate—**English composition; English language and literature, general; administrative and secretarial services; business; business marketing and marketing management; computer and information sciences, general; computer systems networking and telecommunications; criminal justice and corrections; geological and related sciences; health and physical education/fitness; history; marketing management and research; mathematics; nursing; political science and government; psychology; sociology; women's studies.

# LONG BEACH CITY COLLEGE

4901 East Carson Street
Long Beach, CA 90808
**Contact:** Ms. Marcia Hedberg, Distance Learning
**Phone:** 562-938-4025
**Fax:** 562-938-4814
**Web:** http://de.lbcc.cc.ca.us
**E-mail:** mhedberg@lbcc.cc.ca.us

**ACCREDITATION:** Western Association of Schools and Colleges
**INSTITUTIONALLY ADMINISTERED FINANCIAL AID:** Yes

## DEGREE OR CERTIFICATE PROGRAMS OFFERED
Programs offered do not lead to a degree or other formal award.

## NON-DEGREE-RELATED COURSE TOPICS OFFERED
**Undergraduate—**English composition; English creative writing; anthropology; astronomy; biology, general; business administration and management; child care and guidance workers and managers; computer and information sciences, general; computer programming; computer science; computer software and media applications; computer systems networking and telecommunications; film/video and photographic arts; foods and nutrition studies; geography; history; international business; liberal arts and sciences, general studies and humanities; marketing management and research; mathematics; music; nursing; philosophy; political science and government; psychology; social psychology; sociology.

# LONG ISLAND UNIVERSITY, SOUTHAMPTON COLLEGE

239 Montauk Highway
Southampton, NY 11968
**Contact:** Victoria Colina-Brunne, Director of Enrollment Services
**Phone:** 631-287-8327
**Fax:** 631-287-8125
**E-mail:** vcolina@southampton.liu.edu

**ACCREDITATION:** Middle States Association of Colleges and Schools
**INSTITUTIONALLY ADMINISTERED FINANCIAL AID:** Yes

## DEGREE OR CERTIFICATE PROGRAMS OFFERED
Programs offered do not lead to a degree or other formal award.

## NON-DEGREE-RELATED COURSE TOPICS OFFERED

**Undergraduate**—English creative writing; business; communications, general; computer and information sciences, general; liberal arts and sciences, general studies and humanities; public administration; visual and performing arts.
**Graduate**—English creative writing; gerontology.

# LONGVIEW COMMUNITY COLLEGE

*Program for Adult College Education (PACE)*
500 Southwest Longview Road
Lee's Summit, MO 64063
**Contact:** Tamara Miller, PACE Outreach Coordinator
**Phone:** 816-672-2369
**Fax:** 816-672-2426
**Web:** http://www.kcmetro.cc.mo.us/LONGVIEW/LVHOME.HTML

**ACCREDITATION:** North Central Association of Colleges and Schools
**INSTITUTIONALLY ADMINISTERED FINANCIAL AID:** No

## DEGREE OR CERTIFICATE PROGRAMS OFFERED
**Programs offered do not lead to a degree or other formal award.**

## NON-DEGREE-RELATED COURSE TOPICS OFFERED
**Undergraduate**—English composition; accounting; biology, general; child care and guidance workers and managers; computer science; criminal justice and corrections; economics; education, general; engineering, general; environmental/environmental health engineering; fire protection; geography; heating, air conditioning and refrigeration mechanics and repairers; history; mathematics; philosophy; physical sciences, general; psychology; sociology.

# LORAIN COUNTY COMMUNITY COLLEGE

*Instructional Television*
1005 Abbe Road, N
Elyria, OH 44035
**Contact:** Ms. Mary Jane Palmer, Coordinator of Distance Learning
**Phone:** 440-366-7684
**Fax:** 440-366-4150
**Web:** http://www.lorainccc.edu/distlearn/
**E-mail:** mpalmer@lorainccc.edu

**ACCREDITATION:** North Central Association of Colleges and Schools
**INSTITUTIONALLY ADMINISTERED FINANCIAL AID:** Yes

## DEGREE OR CERTIFICATE PROGRAMS OFFERED
**Undergraduate**—*AA:* Universal Degree.

## NON-DEGREE-RELATED COURSE TOPICS OFFERED
**Undergraduate**—English as a second language; English composition; English creative writing; accounting; social psychology; sociology.
**Non-credit**—business; computer software and media applications; health professions and related sciences, other.

# LORD FAIRFAX COMMUNITY COLLEGE

173 Skirmisher Lane, PO Box 47
Middletown, VA 22845
**Contact:** Mrs. Nellie Manning, Distance Learning Office Support Specialist
**Phone:** 540-868-7190
**Fax:** 540-868-7100
**Web:** http://www.lf.vccs.edu
**E-mail:** lfmannn@lf.vccs.edu

**ACCREDITATION:** Southern Association of Colleges and Schools
**INSTITUTIONALLY ADMINISTERED FINANCIAL AID:** Yes

## DEGREE OR CERTIFICATE PROGRAMS OFFERED
**Programs offered do not lead to a degree or other formal award.**

## NON-DEGREE-RELATED COURSE TOPICS OFFERED
**Undergraduate**—English composition; accounting; applied mathematics; astronomy; biology, general; business; business marketing and marketing management; computer software and media applications; computer systems networking and telecommunications; economics; financial services marketing operations; fine arts and art studies; history; law and legal studies; liberal arts and sciences, general studies and humanities; materials engineering; mathematics; miscellaneous physical sciences; nursing; physical science technologies; physical sciences, general; physiological psychology/psychobiology; social psychology; sociology.
**Non-credit**—English as a second language; English technical and business writing; business; business administration and management; business and personal services marketing operations; business communications; business information and data processing services; business management and administrative services, other; business/managerial economics; communications, general; communications, other; computer and information sciences, general; computer and information sciences, other; computer software and media applications; computer systems analysis; computer systems networking and telecommunications; computer/information technology administration and management; culinary arts and related services; data processing technology; electrical and electronic engineering-related technology; electrical and electronics equipment installers and repairers; enterprise management and operation; industrial equipment maintenance and repairers; marketing operations/marketing and distribution, other; precision production trades, other; protective services, other; telecommunications.

# LOS ANGELES PIERCE COLLEGE

6201 Winnetka Avenue
Woodland Hills, CA 91371
**Contact:** Carlos Martinez, Dean of Academic Affairs
**Phone:** 818-710-4224
**Fax:** 818-710-9844
**Web:** http://www.lapc.cc.ca.us/
**E-mail:** martinc@laccd.cc.ca.us

**ACCREDITATION:** Western Association of Schools and Colleges
**INSTITUTIONALLY ADMINISTERED FINANCIAL AID:** No

## DEGREE OR CERTIFICATE PROGRAMS OFFERED

Programs offered do not lead to a degree or other formal award.

## NON-DEGREE-RELATED COURSE TOPICS OFFERED

**Undergraduate**—English composition; English language and literature, general; chemistry; computer science; computer software and media applications; mathematics; music; political science and government.

# LOUISIANA STATE UNIVERSITY AND AGRICULTURAL AND MECHANICAL COLLEGE

*Division of Instructional Support and Development*

118 Himes Hall
Baton Rouge, LA 70803
**Contact:** Tammy E. Adams, Director of Instructional Telecommunications
**Phone:** 225-388-1135
**Fax:** 225-388-5789
**Web:** http://www.lsu.edu/
**E-mail:** tadams3@lsu.edu

**ACCREDITATION:** Southern Association of Colleges and Schools

**INSTITUTIONALLY ADMINISTERED FINANCIAL AID:** Yes

## DEGREE OR CERTIFICATE PROGRAMS OFFERED

**Graduate**—*MS:* Library and Information Sciences.

## NON-DEGREE-RELATED COURSE TOPICS OFFERED

**Undergraduate**—English language and literature, general; business administration and management; communications, general; engineering, general; history; home economics, general; political science and government; psychology; sociology.
**Graduate**—agriculture/agricultural sciences; business administration and management; home economics, general; library science/librarianship; teacher education, specific academic and vocational programs.

# LOUISIANA STATE UNIVERSITY IN SHREVEPORT

*Division of Continuing Education and Public Service*

1 University Place
Shreveport, LA 71115
**Contact:** Meagan A. Killen, Telecommunications Specialist
**Phone:** 318-797-5120
**Fax:** 318-797-5395
**Web:** http://www.lsus.edu
**E-mail:** mkillen@pilot.lsus.edu

**ACCREDITATION:** Southern Association of Colleges and Schools
**INSTITUTIONALLY ADMINISTERED FINANCIAL AID:** No

## DEGREE OR CERTIFICATE PROGRAMS OFFERED

Programs offered do not lead to a degree or other formal award.

## NON-DEGREE-RELATED COURSE TOPICS OFFERED

**Undergraduate**—business administration and management; financial management and services; health and physical education/fitness; history; psychology; sociology.
**Graduate**—library science/librarianship.

# LOUISIANA TECH UNIVERSITY

*Center for Instructional Technology and Distance Learning*

PO Box 10408
Ruston, LA 71272
**Contact:** Mr. David R. Cargill, Director of Center for Instructional Technology and Distance Learning
**Phone:** 318-257-2912
**Fax:** 318-257-2731
**Web:** http://www.latech.edu/citdl
**E-mail:** david@latech.edu

**ACCREDITATION:** Southern Association of Colleges and Schools

**INSTITUTIONALLY ADMINISTERED FINANCIAL AID:** Yes

## DEGREE OR CERTIFICATE PROGRAMS OFFERED

Programs offered do not lead to a degree or other formal award.

## NON-DEGREE-RELATED COURSE TOPICS OFFERED

**Undergraduate**—English technical and business writing; architecture; biological sciences/life sciences, other; education administration and supervision; journalism and mass communications.
**Graduate**—English language and literature, general; bioengineering and biomedical engineering; education administration and supervision; foods and nutrition studies.

# LOWER COLUMBIA COLLEGE

1600 Maple Street
Longview, WA 98632
**Contact:** Scott W. Dennis, Distance Education Coordinator
**Phone:** 360-578-1428
**Web:** http://lcc.ctc.edu/
**E-mail:** sdennis@lcc.ctc.edu

**ACCREDITATION:** Northwest Association of Schools and Colleges

**INSTITUTIONALLY ADMINISTERED FINANCIAL AID:** Yes

## DEGREE OR CERTIFICATE PROGRAMS OFFERED

Programs offered do not lead to a degree or other formal award.

# LOYOLA UNIVERSITY CHICAGO

*Mundelein College*

6525 North Sheridan Road, Skyscraper 204
Chicago, IL 60626
**Contact:** Hilary Ward Schnadt, Associate Dean
**Phone:** 773-508-8000
**Fax:** 773-508-8008

**Web:** http://www.luc.edu/online
**E-mail:** hschnad@luc.edu

**ACCREDITATION:** North Central Association of Colleges and Schools

**INSTITUTIONALLY ADMINISTERED FINANCIAL AID:** Yes

eCollege.com   *www.ecollege.com*

## DEGREE OR CERTIFICATE PROGRAMS OFFERED

Undergraduate—*Certificate:* Database Applications; Networks and Telecommunications; Professional Certificate in Computer Science; Web Development.

## NON-DEGREE-RELATED COURSE TOPICS OFFERED

Undergraduate—biology, general; mathematical statistics; mathematics; philosophy; physics.
Graduate—nursing.
Non-credit—criminal justice and corrections.

See full description on page 404.

# LOYOLA UNIVERSITY NEW ORLEANS
## Off-Campus Learning Program

6363 St. Charles Avenue
New Orleans, LA 70118
**Contact:** Kristel Scheuermann, Off Campus Learning Program Coordinator
**Phone:** 504-865-3250
**Fax:** 504-865-3883
**Web:** http://www.loyno.edu/
**E-mail:** scheuer@loyno.edu

**ACCREDITATION:** Southern Association of Colleges and Schools

**INSTITUTIONALLY ADMINISTERED FINANCIAL AID:** Yes

## DEGREE OR CERTIFICATE PROGRAMS OFFERED

Undergraduate—*BSN:* Nursing.
Graduate—*MBA/MFS:* Criminal Justice. *MSN:* Nursing.

## NON-DEGREE-RELATED COURSE TOPICS OFFERED

Undergraduate—English composition; mathematical statistics; sociology.

# LYNN UNIVERSITY
## The Institute for Distance Learning

3601 North Military Trail
Boca Raton, FL 33431
**Contact:** Juliet Singh, Distance Learning Support
**Phone:** 561-237-7917
**Fax:** 561-237-7899
**Web:** http://www.lynn.edu/academics/distance
**E-mail:** jsingh@lynn.edu

**ACCREDITATION:** Southern Association of Colleges and Schools

**INSTITUTIONALLY ADMINISTERED FINANCIAL AID:** Yes

## DEGREE OR CERTIFICATE PROGRAMS OFFERED

Undergraduate—*BPS:* Behavioral Science; Business; Criminal Justice; Health Care Administration.

## NON-DEGREE-RELATED COURSE TOPICS OFFERED

Undergraduate—English composition; English language and literature, general; accounting; applied mathematics; biological and physical sciences; biological sciences/life sciences, other; biology, general; business; business administration and management; business communications; criminal justice and corrections; health and medical administrative services; hospitality services management; psychology; psychology, other; sociology.
Graduate—criminal justice and corrections; education, general.
Non-credit—aerospace, aeronautical and astronautical engineering.

See full description on page 406.

# MACON STATE COLLEGE
## Office of Distance Learning

Social Sciences Division, 100 College Station Drive
Macon, GA 31206-5144
**Contact:** Dr. Linda E. Grynkewich, Director of Distance Learning
**Phone:** 478-471-5755
**Fax:** 478-471-5756
**Web:** http://www.maconstate.edu
**E-mail:** lgrynkew@mail.maconstate.edu

**ACCREDITATION:** Southern Association of Colleges and Schools

**INSTITUTIONALLY ADMINISTERED FINANCIAL AID:** Yes

## DEGREE OR CERTIFICATE PROGRAMS OFFERED

Programs offered do not lead to a degree or other formal award.

## NON-DEGREE-RELATED COURSE TOPICS OFFERED

Undergraduate—English composition; English creative writing; accounting; business administration and management; computer and information sciences, general; computer software and media applications; computer systems analysis; computer systems networking and telecommunications; health and medical administrative services; nursing; psychology; sociology.
Non-credit—English creative writing; financial management and services; health and medical administrative services; human services; marketing operations/marketing and distribution, other.

# MAINE MARITIME ACADEMY

Castine, ME 04420
**Contact:** Dr. John Barlow, Interim Provost and Academic Dean
**Phone:** 207-326-2371
**Fax:** 207-326-2218
**Web:** http://www.mainemaritime.edu/
**E-mail:** jbarlow@mma.edu

**ACCREDITATION:** New England Association of Schools and Colleges

**INSTITUTIONALLY ADMINISTERED FINANCIAL AID:** No

## DEGREE OR CERTIFICATE PROGRAMS OFFERED

Undergraduate—*AD:* Ships Systems Design Technology.

# MALONE COLLEGE

*Malone College Online Learning*

515 25th Street, NW
Canton, OH 44709
**Contact:** Deborah Craven, Department Assistant
**Phone:** 330-471-8242
**Fax:** 330-471-8570
**Web:** http://www.malone-online.org
**E-mail:** onlineinquiry@malone.edu

**ACCREDITATION:** North Central Association of Colleges and Schools

**INSTITUTIONALLY ADMINISTERED FINANCIAL AID:** No

eCollege.com  *www.ecollege.com*

## DEGREE OR CERTIFICATE PROGRAMS OFFERED

Programs offered do not lead to a degree or other formal award.

## NON-DEGREE-RELATED COURSE TOPICS OFFERED

Undergraduate—English literature (British and Commonwealth); bible/biblical studies; biology, general; business; communications, general; developmental and child psychology; fine arts and art studies; health and physical education/fitness; history; philosophy; political science and government; psychology; social sciences and history, other; sociology.

# MANATEE COMMUNITY COLLEGE

*Distance Education*

PO Box 1849
Bradenton, FL 34206
**Contact:** Ms. Kathy Biggs, Director of Instructional Technology and Distance Learning
**Phone:** 941-752-5645
**Fax:** 941-727-6050
**Web:** http://www.mcc.cc.fl.us/
**E-mail:** biggsk@mcc.cc.fl.us

**ACCREDITATION:** Southern Association of Colleges and Schools

**INSTITUTIONALLY ADMINISTERED FINANCIAL AID:** Yes

## DEGREE OR CERTIFICATE PROGRAMS OFFERED

Programs offered do not lead to a degree or other formal award.

## NON-DEGREE-RELATED COURSE TOPICS OFFERED

Undergraduate—American (United States) history; English composition; accounting; art history, criticism and conservation; biology, general; business marketing and marketing management; developmental and child psychology; management information systems and business data processing, general; mathematical statistics; mathematics, other; microbiology/bacteriology; paralegal/legal assistant; philosophy and religion; sociology.

# MANCHESTER COMMUNITY COLLEGE

Great Path, MS 15, PO Box 1046
Manchester, CT 06045-1046
**Contact:** Cathy Miller, Director of Educational Technology and Distance Learning
**Phone:** 860-533-5253
**Fax:** 860-647-6238
**Web:** http://www.mcc.commnet.edu/
**E-mail:** maxcam@commnet.edu

**ACCREDITATION:** New England Association of Schools and Colleges

**INSTITUTIONALLY ADMINISTERED FINANCIAL AID:** Yes

## DEGREE OR CERTIFICATE PROGRAMS OFFERED

Programs offered do not lead to a degree or other formal award.

## NON-DEGREE-RELATED COURSE TOPICS OFFERED

Undergraduate—American (United States) history; English composition; English language and literature, general; Japanese language and literature; business communications; computer and information sciences, general; law and legal studies; occupational therapy; pharmacy; sociology.

# MANOR COLLEGE

700 Fox Chase Road
Jenkintown, PA 19046
**Contact:** Sally P. Mydlowec, Executive Vice President and Dean of Academic Affairs
**Phone:** 215-885-2360 Ext. 243
**Fax:** 215-576-6564
**Web:** http://www.manor.edu/
**E-mail:** smydlowec@manor.edu

**ACCREDITATION:** Middle States Association of Colleges and Schools

**INSTITUTIONALLY ADMINISTERED FINANCIAL AID:** Yes

## DEGREE OR CERTIFICATE PROGRAMS OFFERED

Programs offered do not lead to a degree or other formal award.

## NON-DEGREE-RELATED COURSE TOPICS OFFERED

Undergraduate—animal sciences; business; business administration and management; business marketing and marketing management; computer and information sciences, general; law and legal studies; psychology; religion/religious studies; sociology.

# MANSFIELD UNIVERSITY OF PENNSYLVANIA

*Center for Lifelong Learning*

211 Doane Center
Mansfield, PA 16933
**Contact:** Karen Norton, Director of Credit Programs
**Phone:** 717-662-4850
**Fax:** 717-662-4120
**Web:** http://cll.mnsfld.edu

**E-mail:** knorton@mnsfld.edu

**ACCREDITATION:** Middle States Association of Colleges and Schools

**INSTITUTIONALLY ADMINISTERED FINANCIAL AID:** Yes

### DEGREE OR CERTIFICATE PROGRAMS OFFERED

**Undergraduate—AS:** Criminal Justice.
**Graduate—MS:** School Library and Information Technologies.

# MAPLE WOODS COMMUNITY COLLEGE

### Distance Education Services

2601 Northeast Barry Road
Kansas City, MO 64156-1299
**Contact:** Mr. Leo J. Hirner
**Phone:** 816-759-4489
**Web:** http://www.kcmetro.cc.mo.us/maplewoods/mwhome.html

**ACCREDITATION:** North Central Association of Colleges and Schools

**INSTITUTIONALLY ADMINISTERED FINANCIAL AID:** Yes

### DEGREE OR CERTIFICATE PROGRAMS OFFERED

**Programs offered do not lead to a degree or other formal award.**

### NON-DEGREE-RELATED COURSE TOPICS OFFERED

**Undergraduate**—English composition; accounting; biology, general; child care and guidance workers and managers; computer science; criminal justice and corrections; economics; education, general; engineering design; engineering, general; fire protection; geography; history; mathematics; philosophy; physical sciences, general; psychology; sociology.

# MARANATHA BAPTIST BIBLE COLLEGE

745 West Main
Watertown, WI 53094
**Contact:** Miss Priscilla R. Spate, Secretary to the Registrar
**Phone:** 920-206-2342
**Fax:** 920-261-9109
**Web:** http://www.mbbc.edu/
**E-mail:** pspate@mbbc.edu

**ACCREDITATION:** North Central Association of Colleges and Schools

**INSTITUTIONALLY ADMINISTERED FINANCIAL AID:** Yes

### DEGREE OR CERTIFICATE PROGRAMS OFFERED

**Programs offered do not lead to a degree or other formal award.**

### NON-DEGREE-RELATED COURSE TOPICS OFFERED

**Undergraduate**—administrative and secretarial services; bible/biblical studies; business administration and management; child care and guidance workers and managers; education, general; general teacher education; music; nursing; pastoral counseling and specialized ministries; religion/religious studies; religious/sacred music; teacher education, specific academic and vocational programs.
**Graduate**—bible/biblical studies; pastoral counseling and specialized ministries.

# MARIAN COLLEGE OF FOND DU LAC

45 South National Avenue
Fond du Lac, WI 54935
**Contact:** Ms. Cheryl Shell, Registrar
**Phone:** 800-262-7426 Ext. 7618
**Fax:** 920-926-6708
**Web:** http://www.mariancollege.edu/
**E-mail:** cshell@mariancollege.edu

**ACCREDITATION:** North Central Association of Colleges and Schools

**INSTITUTIONALLY ADMINISTERED FINANCIAL AID:** No

### DEGREE OR CERTIFICATE PROGRAMS OFFERED

**Programs offered do not lead to a degree or other formal award.**

# MARION TECHNICAL COLLEGE

1467 Mt. Vernon Avenue
Marion, OH 43302
**Contact:** Tim E. Chambers, Dean of Business and Instructional Technologies
**Phone:** 740-389-4636 Ext. 237
**Fax:** 740-389-6136
**Web:** http://www.mtc.tec.oh.us/
**E-mail:** chamberst@mtc.tec.oh.us

**ACCREDITATION:** North Central Association of Colleges and Schools

**INSTITUTIONALLY ADMINISTERED FINANCIAL AID:** Yes

### DEGREE OR CERTIFICATE PROGRAMS OFFERED

**Programs offered do not lead to a degree or other formal award.**

### NON-DEGREE-RELATED COURSE TOPICS OFFERED

**Undergraduate**—business information and data processing services; computer and information sciences, general; computer software and media applications; computer systems analysis; mathematics.

# MARIST COLLEGE

### School of Management

Poughkeepsie, NY 12601
**Contact:** Dr. Gordon J. Badovick, Dean
**Phone:** 845-575-3225
**Fax:** 845-575-3640
**Web:** http://www.marist.edu/graduate
**E-mail:** gordon.badovick@marist.edu

**ACCREDITATION:** Middle States Association of Colleges and Schools

**INSTITUTIONALLY ADMINISTERED FINANCIAL AID:** Yes

### DEGREE OR CERTIFICATE PROGRAMS OFFERED

**Graduate—MBA:** Business Administration. **MPA:** Public Administration.

**See full description on page 408.**

# MARSHALL UNIVERSITY
## School of Extended Education
400 Hal Greer Boulevard, CB 216
Huntington, WV 25755-2140
**Contact:** Crystal Stewart, Program Coordinator
**Phone:** 304-696-2970
**Fax:** 304-696-2973
**Web:** http://www.marshall.edu
**E-mail:** stewar14@marshall.edu

**ACCREDITATION:** North Central Association of Colleges and Schools

### DEGREE OR CERTIFICATE PROGRAMS OFFERED
**Programs offered do not lead to a degree or other formal award.**

### NON-DEGREE-RELATED COURSE TOPICS OFFERED
**Undergraduate**—accounting; anthropology; business marketing and marketing management; communications, general; computer and information sciences, general; computer engineering; developmental and child psychology; educational psychology; geography; journalism; management information systems and business data processing, general; nursing; social work; sociology.
**Graduate**—accounting; computer and information sciences, general; educational psychology; marketing management and research; social work; sociology.

# MARTIN LUTHER COLLEGE
1995 Luther Court
New Ulm, MN 56073
**Contact:** Prof. John William Paulsen, Director of Special Services
**Phone:** 507-354-8221 Ext. 352
**Fax:** 507-354-8225
**Web:** http://www.mlc-wels.edu/
**E-mail:** paulsejw@mlc-wels.edu

**ACCREDITATION:** North Central Association of Colleges and Schools
**INSTITUTIONALLY ADMINISTERED FINANCIAL AID:** Yes

### DEGREE OR CERTIFICATE PROGRAMS OFFERED
**Programs offered do not lead to a degree or other formal award.**

### NON-DEGREE-RELATED COURSE TOPICS OFFERED
**Undergraduate**—bible/biblical studies.

# MARY BALDWIN COLLEGE
## Adult Degree Program
Staunton, VA 24401
**Contact:** Adult Degree Program
**Phone:** 800-822-2460
**Web:** http://www.mbc.edu
**E-mail:** adp@mbc.edu

**ACCREDITATION:** Southern Association of Colleges and Schools
**INSTITUTIONALLY ADMINISTERED FINANCIAL AID:** Yes

### DEGREE OR CERTIFICATE PROGRAMS OFFERED
**Programs offered do not lead to a degree or other formal award.**

### NON-DEGREE-RELATED COURSE TOPICS OFFERED
**Undergraduate**—East European languages and literatures; East and Southeast Asian languages and literatures; English language and literature, general; aerospace, aeronautical and astronautical engineering; anthropology; applied mathematics; biochemistry and biophysics; biology, general; business administration and management; chemistry; communications, general; computer and information sciences, general; computer science; economics; education, general; fine arts and art studies; health and medical administrative services; historic preservation, conservation and architectural history; history; human resources management; human services; marketing management and research; mathematics; medical basic sciences; military studies; multi/interdisciplinary studies, other; music; parks, recreation and leisure facilities management; philosophy; philosophy and religion; political science and government; psychology; religion/religious studies; religious education; social work; sociology; visual and performing arts.

# MARYCREST INTERNATIONAL UNIVERSITY
1607 West 12th Street
Davenport, IA 52804-4096
**Contact:** Dr. Marie E. Ven Horst, Institutional Researcher
**Phone:** 563-326-9259
**Fax:** 563-327-9606
**Web:** http://www.mcrest.edu/
**E-mail:** mvenhorst@mcrest.edu

**ACCREDITATION:** North Central Association of Colleges and Schools
**INSTITUTIONALLY ADMINISTERED FINANCIAL AID:** Yes

### DEGREE OR CERTIFICATE PROGRAMS OFFERED
**Graduate**—*MS:* Computer Science.

### NON-DEGREE-RELATED COURSE TOPICS OFFERED
**Undergraduate**—accounting; business; computer science; nursing.
**Graduate**—computer science.

# MARYLAND INSTITUTE, COLLEGE OF ART
## MICA On-Line
Baltimore, MD 21217
**Contact:** Continuing Studies
**Phone:** 410-225-2219
**Fax:** 410-225-2229
**Web:** http://www.mica.edu
**E-mail:** cs@mica.edu

**ACCREDITATION:** Middle States Association of Colleges and Schools
**INSTITUTIONALLY ADMINISTERED FINANCIAL AID:** No

### DEGREE OR CERTIFICATE PROGRAMS OFFERED
**Programs offered do not lead to a degree or other formal award.**

## NON-DEGREE-RELATED COURSE TOPICS OFFERED

**Undergraduate**—graphic design, commercial art and illustration.

# MARYLHURST UNIVERSITY
## Department of Distance Learning

17600 Pacific Highway, PO Box 261
Marylhurst, OR 97036
**Contact:** Web-Based Learning Office
**Phone:** 800-634-9982 Ext. 6319
**Web:** http://online.marylhurst.edu
**E-mail:** learning@marylhurst.edu

**ACCREDITATION:** Northwest Association of Schools and Colleges

**INSTITUTIONALLY ADMINISTERED FINANCIAL AID:** Yes

## DEGREE OR CERTIFICATE PROGRAMS OFFERED

**Undergraduate**—*BA:* Organizational Communications. *BS:* Management.
**Graduate**—*MBA:* Business Administration.

## NON-DEGREE-RELATED COURSE TOPICS OFFERED

**Undergraduate**—American (United States) history; American studies/civilization; English composition; English creative writing; Jewish/Judaic studies; anthropology; biology, general; business marketing and marketing management; educational psychology; film/cinema studies; finance, general; liberal arts and sciences, general studies and humanities; mathematical statistics; mathematics, other; philosophy and religion.
**Graduate**—business marketing and marketing management; finance, general; mathematical statistics; philosophy and religion.

# MARYWOOD UNIVERSITY
## Off Campus Degree Program

2300 Adams Avenue
Scranton, PA 18509-1598
**Contact:** General Program Information Staff
**Phone:** 800-836-6940
**Fax:** 570-961-4751
**Web:** http://www.marywood.edu/www2/conted_adm/conted.htm
**E-mail:** ocdp@ac.marywood.edu

**ACCREDITATION:** Middle States Association of Colleges and Schools

**INSTITUTIONALLY ADMINISTERED FINANCIAL AID:** Yes

## DEGREE OR CERTIFICATE PROGRAMS OFFERED

**Undergraduate**—*BS:* Accounting; Business Administration. *Certificate:* Comprehensive Business Skills; Office Administration; Professional Communications.

## NON-DEGREE-RELATED COURSE TOPICS OFFERED

**Undergraduate**—English composition; French language and literature; Spanish language and literature; accounting; administrative and secretarial services; advertising; art history, criticism and conservation; bible/biblical studies; business; business marketing and marketing management; communications, general; computer/information technology administration and management; data entry/microcomputer applications; earth and planetary sciences; economics; finance, general; history; human resources

management; international business; investments and securities; law and legal studies, other; management information systems and business data processing, general; marketing operations/marketing and distribution, other; mathematical statistics; mathematics, other; philosophy and religion; psychology; public relations and organizational communications; social sciences, general; sociology; taxation.

See full description on page 410.

# MASSACHUSETTS INSTITUTE OF TECHNOLOGY
## Center for Advanced Educational Services

77 Mass Avenue, Building 9-268B
Cambridge, MA 02139-4307
**Contact:** Janet Wasserstein, Development and Communications Officer
**Phone:** 617-253-1346
**Fax:** 617-252-1566
**Web:** http://www-caes.mit.edu
**E-mail:** janetw@mit.edu

**ACCREDITATION:** New England Association of Schools and Colleges

**INSTITUTIONALLY ADMINISTERED FINANCIAL AID:** No

## DEGREE OR CERTIFICATE PROGRAMS OFFERED

Programs offered do not lead to a degree or other formal award.

See full description on page 412.

# MASTER'S PENTECOSTAL BIBLE COLLEGE

780 Argyle Street
Peterborough, ON K9H 5T2, Canada
**Contact:** Rev. Tim M. Foster, Director of Distance Education and Technology
**Phone:** 705-748-9111 Ext. 155
**Fax:** 705-748-3931
**Web:** http://www.epbc.edu/
**E-mail:** tfoster@epbc.edu

**ACCREDITATION:** Provincially Chartered

**INSTITUTIONALLY ADMINISTERED FINANCIAL AID:** Yes

## DEGREE OR CERTIFICATE PROGRAMS OFFERED

**Undergraduate**—*AA:* Bachelor of Religious Education. *BA:* Bachelor of Theology.

## NON-DEGREE-RELATED COURSE TOPICS OFFERED

**Undergraduate**—bible/biblical studies; biblical and other theological languages and literatures; counseling psychology; missions/missionary studies and missiology; philosophy and religion; psychology, other; religion/religious studies; religious education; theological and ministerial studies; theological studies and religious vocations, other.

# MAUI COMMUNITY COLLEGE

*Distance Learning Program*

310 West Kaahumanu Avenue
Kahului, HI 96732
**Contact:** Debra Moreno, Secretary
**Phone:** 808-984-3525
**Fax:** 808-244-6595
**Web:** http://www.umaui.net/
**E-mail:** debra.moreno@mauicc.hawaii.edu

**ACCREDITATION:** Western Association of Schools and Colleges

## DEGREE OR CERTIFICATE PROGRAMS OFFERED

**Undergraduate—*AA:*** Liberal Arts. ***AAS:*** Administration of Justice. ***BA:*** Applied Social Sciences; Business Administration; English; Hawaiian Studies; Information and Computer Sciences; Liberal Studies; Marine Science. ***BEd:*** Elementary Education; Elementary Education/Special Education. ***BS:*** Computer Science. ***Certificate:*** Business; Substance Abuse. **Graduate—*Graduate Certificate:*** Telecommunication and Information Resource Management. ***MBA:*** Business Administration. ***MEd:*** Educational Administration; Educational Foundations. ***MLIS:*** Library and Information Science. ***MS:*** Information and Computer Sciences; Nursing. ***MSW:*** Social Work.

## NON-DEGREE-RELATED COURSE TOPICS OFFERED

**Undergraduate—**English composition; accounting; biology, general; developmental and child psychology; social psychology; social work; sociology.

# MAYLAND COMMUNITY COLLEGE

*Learning Resources Center*

Spruce Pine, NC 28777
**Contact:** Student Services
**Web:** http://www.mayland.cc.nc.us
**E-mail:** studentservices@mayland.cc.nc.us

**ACCREDITATION:** Southern Association of Colleges and Schools
**INSTITUTIONALLY ADMINISTERED FINANCIAL AID:** Yes

## DEGREE OR CERTIFICATE PROGRAMS OFFERED

**Programs offered do not lead to a degree or other formal award.**

## NON-DEGREE-RELATED COURSE TOPICS OFFERED

**Undergraduate—**English composition; art history, criticism and conservation; film/cinema studies; horticulture science.

# MAYSVILLE COMMUNITY COLLEGE

1755 US 68
Maysville, KY 41056
**Contact:** Mrs. Barbara J. Campbell, Assistant Dean of Extended Campus and Distance Learning
**Phone:** 606-759-7141 Ext. 116
**Fax:** 606-759-7176
**Web:** http://www.maycc.kctcs.net/

**E-mail:** barbara.campbell@kctcs.net

**ACCREDITATION:** Southern Association of Colleges and Schools
**INSTITUTIONALLY ADMINISTERED FINANCIAL AID:** Yes

## DEGREE OR CERTIFICATE PROGRAMS OFFERED

**Undergraduate—*AA:*** Business.

## NON-DEGREE-RELATED COURSE TOPICS OFFERED

**Undergraduate—**American (United States) history; English composition; English creative writing; English language and literature, general; European history; accounting; biology, general; business; chemistry; communications, general; computer and information sciences, general; developmental and child psychology; economics; education, general; electrical and electronic engineering-related technology; environmental science/studies; finance, general; fine arts and art studies; geography; history; industrial/manufacturing engineering; marketing management and research; mathematical statistics; mathematics; medical genetics; nursing; philosophy and religion; psychology; real estate; social sciences, general; sociology.

**Non-credit—**business administration and management; business and personal services marketing operations; computer software and media applications; foreign languages and literatures; law and legal studies.

# MAYVILLE STATE UNIVERSITY

*Enrollment Services Office*

330 Thirds Street, NE
Mayville, ND 58257
**Contact:** Dr. Gary Hagen, Vice President for Academic Affairs
**Phone:** 701-786-4787
**Fax:** 701-786-4748
**Web:** http://www.mayvillestate.edu
**E-mail:** gary_hagen@mail.masu.nodak.edu

**ACCREDITATION:** North Central Association of Colleges and Schools
**INSTITUTIONALLY ADMINISTERED FINANCIAL AID:** Yes

## DEGREE OR CERTIFICATE PROGRAMS OFFERED

**Programs offered do not lead to a degree or other formal award.**

## NON-DEGREE-RELATED COURSE TOPICS OFFERED

**Undergraduate—**business administration and management; child care and guidance workers and managers.

# MCDOWELL TECHNICAL COMMUNITY COLLEGE

*Educational Programs*

Route 1, Box 170
Marion, NC 28752-9724
**Contact:** Mr. Donald Glen Ford, Director of Distance Education
**Phone:** 828-652-0651
**Fax:** 828-652-1077
**Web:** http://www.mcdowelltech.cc.nc.us

E-mail: dongford@yahoo.com

ACCREDITATION: Southern Association of Colleges and Schools

INSTITUTIONALLY ADMINISTERED FINANCIAL AID: Yes

### DEGREE OR CERTIFICATE PROGRAMS OFFERED

Programs offered do not lead to a degree or other formal award.

### NON-DEGREE-RELATED COURSE TOPICS OFFERED

Undergraduate—accounting; business; education, general; information sciences and systems; liberal arts and sciences, general studies and humanities; psychology.

# MCLENNAN COMMUNITY COLLEGE

1400 College Drive
Waco, TX 76708

Contact: Randy Schormann, Associate Dean of Center for Instructional Innovation

Phone: 254-299-8711

Fax: 254-299-8785

Web: http://www.mclennan.cc

E-mail: rss@mcc.cc.tx.us

ACCREDITATION: Southern Association of Colleges and Schools

INSTITUTIONALLY ADMINISTERED FINANCIAL AID: No

### DEGREE OR CERTIFICATE PROGRAMS OFFERED

Programs offered do not lead to a degree or other formal award.

### NON-DEGREE-RELATED COURSE TOPICS OFFERED

Undergraduate—American literature (United States); English composition; business; communications, other; computer and information sciences, general; computer science; economics; history; mathematics; psychology.

# MEDICAL COLLEGE OF WISCONSIN

## Master of Public Health Degree Programs

Department of Preventive Medicine, 8701 Watertown Plank Road
Milwaukee, WI 53226

Contact: Mr. Kevin D. Brown, Associate Director of MPH Programs

Phone: 414-456-4510

Fax: 414-456-6160

Web: http://instruct.mcw.edu/prevmed

E-mail: mph@mcw.edu

ACCREDITATION: North Central Association of Colleges and Schools

INSTITUTIONALLY ADMINISTERED FINANCIAL AID: No

### DEGREE OR CERTIFICATE PROGRAMS OFFERED

Graduate—*MPH:* General Preventive Medicine; Health Services Administration; Occupational Medicine.

### NON-DEGREE-RELATED COURSE TOPICS OFFERED

Graduate—accounting; community health services; environmental health; finance, general; health system/health services administration; industrial and organizational psychology; organizational behavior studies; public health.

# MEMORIAL UNIVERSITY OF NEWFOUNDLAND

## School of Continuing Education

G. A. Hickman Building, E-3000
St. John's, NF A1B 3X8, Canada

Contact: Treena Parsons, Marketing

Phone: 709-737-7921

Fax: 709-737-7941

Web: http://www.ce.mun.ca

E-mail: cstudies@mun.ca

ACCREDITATION: Provincially Chartered

INSTITUTIONALLY ADMINISTERED FINANCIAL AID: Yes

### DEGREE OR CERTIFICATE PROGRAMS OFFERED

Undergraduate—*BBA:* Business Administration. *BComm:* Commerce (General). *BN:* Nursing (Post-Basic RN). *BSW:* Social Work (as a 2nd degree). *Certificate:* Business Administration; Career Development; Criminology; Library Studies; Municipal Administration; Newfoundland Studies; Public Administration; Records and Information Management. *Diploma:* Business Administration; Telelearning and Rural School Teaching.

### NON-DEGREE-RELATED COURSE TOPICS OFFERED

Undergraduate—Canadian studies; English composition; accounting; biology, general; developmental and child psychology; educational psychology; industrial and organizational psychology; social psychology; social work; sociology; women's studies.

Graduate—education, other; nursing; social work.

# MENDOCINO COLLEGE

## Distance Education

1000 Hensley Creek Road
Ukiah, CA 95482

Contact: Ms. Meridith Randall, Assistant Dean of Instruction

Phone: 707-468-3014

Fax: 707-463-6529

Web: http://www.mendocino.cc.ca.us/

E-mail: mrandall@mendocino.cc.ca.us

ACCREDITATION: Western Association of Schools and Colleges

INSTITUTIONALLY ADMINISTERED FINANCIAL AID: Yes

### DEGREE OR CERTIFICATE PROGRAMS OFFERED

Programs offered do not lead to a degree or other formal award.

### NON-DEGREE-RELATED COURSE TOPICS OFFERED

Undergraduate—American literature (United States); anthropology; business administration and management; computer and information sciences, general; computer software and media applications; data entry/microcomputer applications; developmental and child psychology; philosophy and religion; psychology; sociology.

## MERCER UNIVERSITY
### Office of Distance Learning
3001 Mercer University Drive
Atlanta, GA 30341
**Contact:** Ms. Elizabeth Simonetti Horner, Vice President of Educational Market Planning
**Phone:** 678-547-6187
**Fax:** 678-547-6102
**Web:** http://www.emercer.com
**E-mail:** horner_e@mercer.edu

**ACCREDITATION:** Southern Association of Colleges and Schools
**INSTITUTIONALLY ADMINISTERED FINANCIAL AID:** No

### DEGREE OR CERTIFICATE PROGRAMS OFFERED
Programs offered do not lead to a degree or other formal award.

### NON-DEGREE-RELATED COURSE TOPICS OFFERED
**Non-credit**—accounting; business administration and management; engineering, general; religious education.

## MERCY COLLEGE
### MerLIN
555 Broadway
Dobbs Ferry, NY 10522
**Contact:** Frank Bryce McCluskey, Jr., Dean of Online Education
**Phone:** 914-674-7521
**Fax:** 914-674-7518
**Web:** http://merlin.mercynet.edu
**E-mail:** fmccluskey@mercynet.edu

**ACCREDITATION:** Middle States Association of Colleges and Schools
**INSTITUTIONALLY ADMINISTERED FINANCIAL AID:** Yes

### DEGREE OR CERTIFICATE PROGRAMS OFFERED
**Undergraduate**—*AA:* Liberal Arts and Sciences. *AS:* Liberal Arts and Sciences. *BA:* Psychology. *BS:* Business Administration; Computer Science; Psychology.
**Graduate**—*MBA:* Business Administration. *MPA:* Health Sciences. *MS:* Banking; Direct Marketing; Internet Business Systems.

### NON-DEGREE-RELATED COURSE TOPICS OFFERED
**Undergraduate**—American (United States) history; English composition; European history; accounting; art history, criticism and conservation; biology, general; business marketing and marketing management; developmental and child psychology; environmental science/studies; finance, general; international business; law and legal studies, other; management information systems and business data processing, general; mathematical statistics; mathematics, other; social psychology; sociology.

**Graduate**—business marketing and marketing management; internet and world wide web; management information systems and business data processing, general.
**See full description on page 414.**

## MERIDIAN COMMUNITY COLLEGE
### Production Center
Drawer 536, 910 Highway 19 N
Meridian, MS 39307
**Contact:** Mr. Hubert E. Yates, Director of Distance Learning
**Phone:** 601-484-8819
**Fax:** 601-484-8824
**Web:** http://www.mcc.cc.ms.us/eplus
**E-mail:** hyates@mcc.cc.ms.us

**ACCREDITATION:** Southern Association of Colleges and Schools
**INSTITUTIONALLY ADMINISTERED FINANCIAL AID:** Yes

### DEGREE OR CERTIFICATE PROGRAMS OFFERED
Programs offered do not lead to a degree or other formal award.

### NON-DEGREE-RELATED COURSE TOPICS OFFERED
**Undergraduate**—American literature (United States); English composition; accounting; administrative and secretarial services; applied mathematics; biological and physical sciences; biological sciences/life sciences, other; business; business administration and management; business communications; business information and data processing services; communications, general; computer and information sciences, general; computer systems networking and telecommunications; computer/information technology administration and management; criminal justice and corrections; criminology; data entry/microcomputer applications; economics; fine arts and art studies; fire protection; foods and nutrition studies; geography; health and physical education/fitness; history; mathematics; music; psychology; sociology.

## METROPOLITAN COMMUNITY COLLEGE
### Student and Instructional Services
PO Box 3777
Omaha, NE 68103-0777
**Contact:** Arlene Jordan, Director of Enrollment Management
**Phone:** 402-457-2418
**Fax:** 402-457-2564
**Web:** http://www.mccneb.edu
**E-mail:** ajordan@metropo.mccneb.edu

**ACCREDITATION:** North Central Association of Colleges and Schools
**INSTITUTIONALLY ADMINISTERED FINANCIAL AID:** Yes

### DEGREE OR CERTIFICATE PROGRAMS OFFERED
**Undergraduate**—*AA:* Liberal Arts. *AAS:* Professional Studies.

### NON-DEGREE-RELATED COURSE TOPICS OFFERED
**Undergraduate**—English composition; French language and literature; Spanish language and literature; accounting; art history, criticism and

conservation; biology, general; business administration and management; film/cinema studies; finance, general; liberal arts and sciences, general studies and humanities; mathematics; music; philosophy and religion; physical sciences, general; political science and government; psychology; sociology.

# METROPOLITAN STATE UNIVERSITY

700 East 7th Street
Minneapolis, MN 55106
**Contact:** Dr. Janice Harring-Hendon, Director of Admissions
**Phone:** 651-772-7600
**Fax:** 651-772-7572
**Web:** http://www.metrostate.edu
**E-mail:** janice.harringhendon@metrostate.edu

**ACCREDITATION:** North Central Association of Colleges and Schools
**INSTITUTIONALLY ADMINISTERED FINANCIAL AID:** Yes

## DEGREE OR CERTIFICATE PROGRAMS OFFERED
Programs offered do not lead to a degree or other formal award.

## NON-DEGREE-RELATED COURSE TOPICS OFFERED
**Undergraduate**—English composition; anthropology; business administration and management; business marketing and marketing management; communications, other; management information systems and business data processing, general; nursing; philosophy.
**Graduate**—business marketing and marketing management; management information systems and business data processing, general.

# MIAMI-DADE COMMUNITY COLLEGE

## Virtual College
950 Northwest 20th Street
Miami, FL 33127-4693
**Contact:** Lloyd Hollingsworth, Student Services Coordinator and Webmaster
**Phone:** 305-237-4222
**Fax:** 305-237-4081
**Web:** http://www.mdcc.edu/vcollege/
**E-mail:** lholling@mdcc.edu

**ACCREDITATION:** Southern Association of Colleges and Schools
**INSTITUTIONALLY ADMINISTERED FINANCIAL AID:** Yes

## DEGREE OR CERTIFICATE PROGRAMS OFFERED
Programs offered do not lead to a degree or other formal award.

## NON-DEGREE-RELATED COURSE TOPICS OFFERED
**Undergraduate**—English as a second language; English composition; atmospheric sciences and meteorology; biology, general; curriculum and instruction; health and medical administrative services; individual and family development studies; international relations and affairs; liberal arts and sciences, general studies and humanities; mathematics; physical

sciences, other; political science and government; psychology; romance languages and literatures; social sciences, general.
**Non-credit**—health professions and related sciences, other.

# MICHIGAN STATE UNIVERSITY

## Outreach Instructional Programs
51 Kellogg Center
East Lansing, MI 48824
**Contact:** Jerry Rhead, Academic and Professional Programs Director, MSU Global
**Phone:** 517-432-1950
**Fax:** 517-432-1327
**Web:** http://www.vu.msu.edu
**E-mail:** rhead@msu.edu

**ACCREDITATION:** American Academy for Liberal Education

## DEGREE OR CERTIFICATE PROGRAMS OFFERED
**Undergraduate**—*Certificate:* Computer-Aided Design (CAD) Technologies; International Food Laws; Watershed Management.
**Graduate**—*Graduate Certificate:* Chemical Engineering; Criminal Justice; Facility Management; Global Management; Molecular Laboratory Diagnostics; Social Work. *MAE:* Education. *MS:* Beam Physics; Criminal Justice; Packaging.
**Postgraduate and doctoral**—*PhD:* Beam Physics.

## NON-DEGREE-RELATED COURSE TOPICS OFFERED
**Undergraduate**—chemical engineering; computer and information sciences, general; economics; food sciences and technology; geography; mathematics; social sciences, general; technology education/industrial arts; telecommunications.
**Graduate**—chemical engineering; community organization, resources and services; criminal justice and corrections; education administration and supervision; education, general; educational psychology; engineering, other; enterprise management and operation; health and medical laboratory technologies; nursing; social work; telecommunications.
**Non-credit**—chemical engineering; community organization, resources and services; computer and information sciences, general; social work.
**See full description on page 416.**

# MICHIGAN TECHNOLOGICAL UNIVERSITY

## Extended University Programs
1400 Townsend Drive
Houghton, MI 49931
**Contact:** Ms. Lynn A. Artman, Program Manager
**Phone:** 800-405-4678
**Fax:** 906-487-2463
**Web:** http://www.admin.mtu.edu/eup
**E-mail:** laartman@mtu.edu

**ACCREDITATION:** North Central Association of Colleges and Schools
**INSTITUTIONALLY ADMINISTERED FINANCIAL AID:** Yes

## DEGREE OR CERTIFICATE PROGRAMS OFFERED

**Undergraduate—*AAS:*** Engineering Technology. ***BS:*** Engineering; Surveying. ***Certificate:*** Engineering Design.
**Graduate—*MS:*** Electrical Engineering; Mechanical Engineering.
**Postgraduate and doctoral—*PhD:*** Electrical Engineering; Mechanical Engineering.

## NON-DEGREE-RELATED COURSE TOPICS OFFERED

**Undergraduate—**engineering mechanics; mechanical engineering; surveying.
**Graduate—**electrical, electronics and communication engineering; mechanical engineering.
**Non-credit—**engineering mechanics; mechanical engineering.

# MID-AMERICA BIBLE COLLEGE

## *DELTIC*

3500 SW 119th Street
Oklahoma City, OK 73170
**Contact:** Deanne Curtis-Mowry, Marketing Director for Distance Education
**Phone:** 405-692-3198
**Fax:** 405-692-3165
**Web:** http://www.mabc.edu
**E-mail:** dmowry@mabc.edu

**ACCREDITATION:** Accrediting Association of Bible Colleges
**INSTITUTIONALLY ADMINISTERED FINANCIAL AID:** Yes

## DEGREE OR CERTIFICATE PROGRAMS OFFERED

**Undergraduate—*BS:*** Pastoral Ministry.
**Graduate—*MA:*** Ministry.

## NON-DEGREE-RELATED COURSE TOPICS OFFERED

**Undergraduate—**bible/biblical studies; religion/religious studies.

# MIDDLESEX COMMUNITY COLLEGE

Academic Resources Building, Springs Road
Bedford, MA 01730
**Contact:** Mr. Sanford A. Arbogast, Instructional Technologist
**Phone:** 781-280-3739
**Fax:** 781-280-3771
**Web:** http://www.middlesex.cc.ma.us/
**E-mail:** arbogasts@middlesex.cc.ma.us

**ACCREDITATION:** New England Association of Schools and Colleges
**INSTITUTIONALLY ADMINISTERED FINANCIAL AID:** Yes

## DEGREE OR CERTIFICATE PROGRAMS OFFERED

**Undergraduate—*AAS:*** Liberal Studies. ***AS:*** Business Transfer. ***Certificate:*** Web Devolper.

## NON-DEGREE-RELATED COURSE TOPICS OFFERED

**Undergraduate—**English language and literature, general; business; computer software and media applications; liberal arts and sciences, general studies and humanities; mathematics; social sciences, general.

# MIDDLE TENNESSEE STATE UNIVERSITY

## *Division of Continuing Studies*

1301 East Main Street, Cope 113
Murfreesboro, TN 37132
**Contact:** Dianna Zeh, Director of Academic Outreach and Distance Learning
**Phone:** 615-898-5611
**Fax:** 615-904-8108
**Web:** http://www.mtsu.edu/learn
**E-mail:** dzeh@mtsu.edu

**ACCREDITATION:** Southern Association of Colleges and Schools
**INSTITUTIONALLY ADMINISTERED FINANCIAL AID:** Yes

## DEGREE OR CERTIFICATE PROGRAMS OFFERED

**Undergraduate—*BS:*** Liberal Studies; Professional Studies, Concentration in Information Technology; Professional Studies, Concentration in Organizational Leadership.
**Graduate—*MS:*** Mathematics.

## NON-DEGREE-RELATED COURSE TOPICS OFFERED

**Undergraduate—**American literature (United States); English composition; English language and literature, general; accounting; agricultural business and management; area, ethnic and cultural studies, other; astronomy; business administration and management; business communications; communications, general; criminal justice and corrections; economics; education, general; educational psychology; food sciences and technology; geological and related sciences; health and physical education/fitness; human resources management; journalism and mass communications; liberal arts and sciences, general studies and humanities; marketing operations/marketing and distribution, other; mathematics; nursing; political science and government; radio and television broadcasting; social sciences, general; social work; sociology.
**Graduate—**aerospace, aeronautical and astronautical engineering; economics; educational evaluation, research and statistics; marketing management and research; mathematics; nursing.

---

### Special Note

Middle Tennessee State University (MTSU) now offers accredited classes through a variety of technologies for students who may not be able to come to the campus.

Compressed video courses are instructed at one site and simultaneously sent to distant sites. Students and instructors can see one another on television monitors and talk to one another using microphones. Telecourses are offered via cable television or videotape. Students can view course segments on the MTSU cable channel or the local PBS affiliate or at the MTSU McWherter Learning Resources Center. Students consult with their instructors during telephone office hours or through e-mail. Students are required to attend an orientation, a midterm exam, and a final exam on campus.

Correspondence courses involve individual instruction of a student by an instructor. Typically, students study at home. Interaction between correspondence course faculty members and students consists of written assignments, testing, and assistance via such media as print/written word, telephone, fax, e-mail, and the World Wide Web. After registration, students receive a packet in the mail from the correspondence course coordinator, containing information about assignments and directions for completing and submitting them.

Online courses are taught primarily over the Internet through e-mail, newsgroups, distribution lists, and the World Wide Web. These various distance learning programs are closing the gap between students and the campus.

# MID-PLAINS COMMUNITY COLLEGE AREA

*Distance Learning*
1205 East 3rd
McCook, NE 69001
**Contact:** Ms. Judi Lynn Haney, Dean of Community Services
**Phone:** 308-345-6303 Ext. 225
**Fax:** 308-345-5744
**Web:** http://www.mpcca.cc.ne.us
**E-mail:** haneyj@mpcca.cc.ne.us

**ACCREDITATION:** North Central Association of Colleges and Schools
**INSTITUTIONALLY ADMINISTERED FINANCIAL AID:** Yes

## DEGREE OR CERTIFICATE PROGRAMS OFFERED
Programs offered do not lead to a degree or other formal award.

## NON-DEGREE-RELATED COURSE TOPICS OFFERED
**Undergraduate**—English composition; accounting; agricultural business and management; business; business administration and management; computer and information sciences, general; computer science; health and medical preparatory programs; psychology; sociology.
**Non-credit**—computer software and media applications.

# MIDWESTERN STATE UNIVERSITY

3410 Taft Boulevard
Wichita Falls, TX 76308-2099
**Contact:** Pamela Morgan, Director of Distance Education
**Phone:** 940-397-4785
**Fax:** 940-397-4861
**Web:** http://www.mwsu.edu/
**E-mail:** pamela.morgan@mwsu.edu

**ACCREDITATION:** Southern Association of Colleges and Schools
**INSTITUTIONALLY ADMINISTERED FINANCIAL AID:** Yes

## DEGREE OR CERTIFICATE PROGRAMS OFFERED
**Undergraduate**—*BAA:* Applied Arts and Sciences. *BSRS:* Radiologic Sciences.
**Graduate**—*MS:* Master of Science in Radiologic Sciences, Education or Administration Major.

## NON-DEGREE-RELATED COURSE TOPICS OFFERED
**Undergraduate**—business; business communications; communications, general; education, general; health professions and related sciences, other; psychology, other; public administration; sociology.
**Graduate**—business; education, other; health professions and related sciences, other; nursing.

# MILLERSVILLE UNIVERSITY OF PENNSYLVANIA

*MU Online*
PO Box 1002
Millersville, PA 17551
**Contact:** Bili Mattes, Director of Professional Training and Education
**Phone:** 717-872-3030
**Fax:** 717-871-2022
**Web:** http://muweb.millersville.edu/~conted/
**E-mail:** bili.mattes@millersville.edu

**ACCREDITATION:** Middle States Association of Colleges and Schools
**INSTITUTIONALLY ADMINISTERED FINANCIAL AID:** Yes

## DEGREE OR CERTIFICATE PROGRAMS OFFERED
Programs offered do not lead to a degree or other formal award.

## NON-DEGREE-RELATED COURSE TOPICS OFFERED
**Undergraduate**—atmospheric sciences and meteorology; economics; foreign languages and literatures; history; technology education/industrial arts.
**Graduate**—education, general; foreign languages and literatures; special education; technology education/industrial arts.

# MILWAUKEE SCHOOL OF ENGINEERING

*MSOE-TV*
1025 North Broadway
Milwaukee, WI 53202-3109
**Contact:** Mr. Kent Peterson, Manager of Internet Services
**Phone:** 414-277-7176
**Fax:** 414-277-7453
**Web:** http://www.msoe.edu/admiss
**E-mail:** peterson@msoe.edu

**ACCREDITATION:** North Central Association of Colleges and Schools
**INSTITUTIONALLY ADMINISTERED FINANCIAL AID:** No

## DEGREE OR CERTIFICATE PROGRAMS OFFERED
Programs offered do not lead to a degree or other formal award.

## NON-DEGREE-RELATED COURSE TOPICS OFFERED
**Graduate**—accounting; business marketing and marketing management; finance, general; international business; organizational behavior studies.

**Non-credit**—accounting; business marketing and marketing management; finance, general; international business; organizational behavior studies.

# MIMS GLOBAL LEADERSHIP EXECUTIVE PROGRAM

PO Box 830688
Richardson, TX 75083-0688
**Contact:** Dr. Anne M. Ferrante, Associate Director
**Phone:** 972-888-6467
**Fax:** 972-883-6164
**Web:** http://som.utdallas.edu/glemba
**E-mail:** ferrante@utdallas.edu

**ACCREDITATION:** Southern Association of Colleges and Schools
**INSTITUTIONALLY ADMINISTERED FINANCIAL AID:** Yes

### DEGREE OR CERTIFICATE PROGRAMS OFFERED
**Graduate**—*MBA:* Global Leadership Executive MBA.
**See full description on page 638.**

# MINERAL AREA COLLEGE

PO Box 1000
Park Hills, MO 63601
**Contact:** Mrs. Nancy G. Collier, Administrative Assistant to Arts and Sciences Dean
**Phone:** 573-518-2100
**Fax:** 573-518-2058
**Web:** http://www.mac.cc.mo.us/

**ACCREDITATION:** North Central Association of Colleges and Schools
**INSTITUTIONALLY ADMINISTERED FINANCIAL AID:** Yes

### DEGREE OR CERTIFICATE PROGRAMS OFFERED
Programs offered do not lead to a degree or other formal award.

### NON-DEGREE-RELATED COURSE TOPICS OFFERED
**Undergraduate**—English composition; Germanic languages and literatures; accounting; astronomy; biological sciences/life sciences, other; business administration and management; business quantitative methods and management science; health and medical preparatory programs; history; mathematics; psychology; social sciences and history, other.

# MINNESOTA SCHOOL OF PROFESSIONAL PSYCHOLOGY

20 South Clark, 3rd Floor
Chicago, IL 60603
**Contact:** Ms. April Djakoniya, Coordinator of Online Services
**Phone:** 312-279-3839
**Fax:** 312-424-7282
**Web:** http://argosy.aspp.edu

**E-mail:** april@argosyeducation.com
**ACCREDITATION:** North Central Association of Colleges and Schools
**INSTITUTIONALLY ADMINISTERED FINANCIAL AID:** Yes

### DEGREE OR CERTIFICATE PROGRAMS OFFERED
Programs offered do not lead to a degree or other formal award.

### NON-DEGREE-RELATED COURSE TOPICS OFFERED
**Non-credit**—psychology.

# MINNESOTA STATE UNIVERSITY MOORHEAD

PO Box 318
Moorhead, MN 56563
**Contact:** Ms. Jan A. Flack, Director of Continuing Studies
**Phone:** 218-236-2182
**Fax:** 218-287-5030
**Web:** http://www.mnstate.edu/continue?
**E-mail:** flackjan@mnstate.edu

**ACCREDITATION:** North Central Association of Colleges and Schools
**INSTITUTIONALLY ADMINISTERED FINANCIAL AID:** No

### DEGREE OR CERTIFICATE PROGRAMS OFFERED
Programs offered do not lead to a degree or other formal award.

### NON-DEGREE-RELATED COURSE TOPICS OFFERED
**Undergraduate**—English creative writing; business; community health services; ethnic and cultural studies; history; psychology; public health; sociology.
**Graduate**—educational evaluation, research and statistics; information sciences and systems.

# MINNESOTA WEST COMMUNITY AND TECHNICAL COLLEGE–WORTHINGTON CAMPUS

*Department of Distributed Education*
1450 Collegeway
Worthington, MN 56187
**Contact:** Ms. Crystal Strouth, Registrar
**Phone:** 507-372-3451
**Web:** http://www.mnwest.mnscu.edu
**E-mail:** cstrouth@wr.mnwest.mnscu.edu

**ACCREDITATION:** North Central Association of Colleges and Schools
**INSTITUTIONALLY ADMINISTERED FINANCIAL AID:** Yes

### DEGREE OR CERTIFICATE PROGRAMS OFFERED
**Undergraduate**—*AA:* Liberal Arts.

### NON-DEGREE-RELATED COURSE TOPICS OFFERED
**Undergraduate**—English composition; accounting; administrative and secretarial services; agricultural production workers and managers; animal sciences; biology, general; business management and administrative ser-

vices, other; computer programming; computer systems networking and telecommunications; computer/information technology administration and management; developmental and child psychology; heating, air conditioning and refrigeration mechanics and repairers; sociology.

# MINOT STATE UNIVERSITY
## Continuing Education
500 University Avenue West
Minot, ND 58707
**Contact:** Teresa Loftesnes, Director of Continuing Education
**Phone:** 701-858-3062
**Fax:** 701-858-4343
**Web:** http://online.minotstateu.edu
**E-mail:** loftesne@minotstateu.edu

**ACCREDITATION:** North Central Association of Colleges and Schools

**INSTITUTIONALLY ADMINISTERED FINANCIAL AID:** Yes

## DEGREE OR CERTIFICATE PROGRAMS OFFERED
Programs offered do not lead to a degree or other formal award.

## NON-DEGREE-RELATED COURSE TOPICS OFFERED
**Undergraduate**—American literature (United States); English composition; English language and literature, general; accounting; business administration and management; business information and data processing services; computer/information technology administration and management; criminal justice and corrections; education, general; general teacher education; history; nursing; philosophy; psychology; sociology; special education.
**Graduate**—business administration and management; business information and data processing services; special education.

## Special Note
Founded in 1913, Minot State University (MSU) has proven to be an integral part of the state and region it serves. Continuing education programs such as MSU Online and Correspondence have extended that influence globally. Online has assisted more than 1,500 students to achieve their academic and professional objectives through the delivery of university-level courses via the Internet. Online provides one-on-one interaction with a team of highly qualified faculty members, and courses are continually upgraded to meet the needs of an ever-changing workforce. The variety of courses allows students to work toward a degree program or to enhance their professional value while never stepping foot on campus. Online courses include accounting, business management, business information technology, driver's education, education, special education, psychology, and a wide variety of general education courses. Complementing the Online Program is the MSU Correspondence Program. Having served thousands of students across the US and Canada, Correspondence offers the working adult an affordable, flexible, and self-paced approach to learning. Students have the option of completing the courses within the traditional campus semester or utilizing the 9-month option. Correspondence courses include business management, criminal justice, English, history, mathematics, political science, and sociology. Many of these courses also fulfill general education requirements. For more information about the Online Program, contact Mark Timbrook, Online Advisor, 800-777-0750 Ext. 3218; e-mail: online@minotstateu.edu. For more information about the Correspondence Program, contact Trisha Roberts, Coordinator, 800-777-0750 Ext. 3359; e-mail: conted@minotstateu.edu. Web sites: http://online.minotstateu.edu or http://online.minotstateu.edu.

# MIRACOSTA COLLEGE
## MiraCosta CyberCollege
One Barnard Drive
Oceanside, CA 92056
**Contact:** Ms. Lori Schneider, Administrative Secretary
**Phone:** 760-795-6637
**Fax:** 760-795-6723
**Web:** http://www.miracosta.cc.ca.us
**E-mail:** lschneider@yar.miracosta.cc.ca.us

**ACCREDITATION:** Western Association of Schools and Colleges

**INSTITUTIONALLY ADMINISTERED FINANCIAL AID:** No

## DEGREE OR CERTIFICATE PROGRAMS OFFERED
Programs offered do not lead to a degree or other formal award.

## NON-DEGREE-RELATED COURSE TOPICS OFFERED
**Undergraduate**—English as a second language; English composition; biology, general; business; communications, general; computer software and media applications; economics; film/cinema studies; geological and related sciences; history; hospitality services management; music; philosophy; real estate.
**Non-credit**—English as a second language.

# MISSISSIPPI STATE UNIVERSITY
## Division of Continuing Education
PO Box 5247
Mississippi State, MS 39762
**Contact:** Mr. Michael K. Busby, Coordinator of Distance Education
**Phone:** 662-325-1559
**Fax:** 662-325-8666
**Web:** http://www.msstate.edu/dept/ced/
**E-mail:** mbusby@ce.msstate.edu

**ACCREDITATION:** Southern Association of Colleges and Schools

**INSTITUTIONALLY ADMINISTERED FINANCIAL AID:** Yes

## DEGREE OR CERTIFICATE PROGRAMS OFFERED
**Undergraduate**—**BS:** Elementary Education; Geoscience, Broadcast Meteorology; Interdisciplinary Studies in Vicksburg (3rd and 4th year program); Operational Meteorology. **Certificate:** Broadcast Meteorology; Computer Applications.
**Graduate**—**MBA:** Master of Business Administration at Columbus Air Force Base. **MBA/MALAS:** Vocational-Technical Licensure. **MPA:** Master of Public Policy and Administration. **MS:** Chemical Engineering; Civil Engineering; Counselor Education with a concentration in rehabilitation counseling; Counselor Education; Electrical and Computer Engineering; Geoscience; Industrial Engineering; Mechanical Engineering; Physical

Education—Emphasis in Health Education/Health Promotion; Physical Education; Systems Management. *MSE:* Master of Science in Elementary Education.

**Postgraduate and doctoral—*PhD:*** Chemical Engineering; Civil Engineering; Community College Leadership; Electrical and Computer Engineering; Industrial Engineering; Mechanical Engineering.

## NON-DEGREE-RELATED COURSE TOPICS OFFERED

**Undergraduate**—English as a second language; English composition; English creative writing; English language and literature, general; animal sciences; applied mathematics; astronomy; biology, general; botany; business; business administration and management; business quantitative methods and management science; chemistry; communications, general; communications, other; counseling psychology; curriculum and instruction; education, general; educational psychology; fine arts and art studies; foods and nutrition studies; foreign languages and literatures, other; forest production and processing; forestry and related sciences; general teacher education; health and physical education/fitness; health professions and related sciences, other; history; home economics, general; home economics, other; industrial production technologies; industrial/manufacturing engineering; liberal arts and sciences, general studies and humanities; mathematics; philosophy; physical sciences, general; physics; plant sciences; political science and government; real estate; technology education/industrial arts.

**Graduate**—chemical engineering; counseling psychology; curriculum and instruction; education administration and supervision; education, general; educational psychology; electrical, electronics and communication engineering; engineering mechanics; engineering/industrial management; environmental/environmental health engineering; health and physical education/fitness; health professions and related sciences, other; industrial/manufacturing engineering; mechanical engineering; public administration; public policy analysis; technology education/industrial arts; telecommunications.

**Non-credit**—English as a second language; accounting; administrative and secretarial services; applied mathematics; business; business administration and management; business and personal services marketing operations; business communications; business information and data processing services; business management and administrative services, other; business quantitative methods and management science; business/managerial economics; education administration and supervision; education, general; education, other; electrical and electronic engineering-related technology; electrical and electronics equipment installers and repairers; electrical and power transmission installers; electrical, electronics and communications engineering; environmental control technologies; environmental/environmental health engineering; financial management and services; food sciences and technology; forest production and processing; forestry and related sciences; health professions and related sciences, other; internet and world wide web; real estate; teacher education, specific academic and vocational programs; telecommunications; visual and performing arts; visual and performing arts, other; wildlife and wildlands management.

## Special Note

Mississippi State University was founded as a land-grant institution in 1878 to meet the needs of the people, institutions, and organizations of the state and nation through undergraduate and graduate education. Mississippi State University enrolls more than 15,000 students on the main campus, branch campus, and off-campus centers and through distance learning.

Mississippi State University is a Doctoral I university and is placed among the top 100 universities in the nation to receive federal research support. The University is fully accredited by the Southern Association of Colleges and Schools.

The Division of Continuing Education is an academic service arm of the University and is committed to meeting the academic needs of nontraditional students who are not able to attend classes on campus due to geographic location and/or career and personal commitments. With expertise in advanced telecommunication technology and its application in education, the Division of Continuing Education continues to be a leader in distance learning by utilizing the following delivery mediums: the Internet, videotapes, and the Mississippi Interactive Video Network (MIVN), which is a two-way, interactive audio/video network with 150 sites.

The division coordinates 7 programs that are offered though the MIVN—the Vocational Teacher Licensure Program; the Master of Science in counselor education, elementary education, early childhood development, and educational leadership of science in interdisciplinary studies; and courses leading to the Master of Instructional Technology. A Master of Science in physical education and health that is offered via videotape began in 1998. A certificate in computer applications is offered over the Internet and includes 12 semester hours of classes.

# MISSISSIPPI UNIVERSITY FOR WOMEN

## Continuing Education

Advanced Placement Services, 2170 East Eason Boulevard
Tupelo, MS 38801
**Contact:** Kathy McShane, Coordinator
**Phone:** 601-844-0284
**Fax:** 601-844-1927
**Web:** http://www.muw.edu/fibernet/
**E-mail:** kmshane@muw.edu.

**ACCREDITATION:** Southern Association of Colleges and Schools
**INSTITUTIONALLY ADMINISTERED FINANCIAL AID:** Yes

## DEGREE OR CERTIFICATE PROGRAMS OFFERED

Programs offered do not lead to a degree or other formal award.

## NON-DEGREE-RELATED COURSE TOPICS OFFERED

**Undergraduate**—biblical and other theological languages and literatures; medieval and renaissance studies.
**Graduate**—marketing management and research; marketing operations/marketing and distribution, other; nursing.

# MISSOURI BAPTIST COLLEGE

1 College Park Drive
St. Louis, MO 63126
**Contact:** Mrs. Amber Michelle Henry, Director of Distance Learning
**Phone:** 636-797-3000 Ext. 214
**Web:** http://www.mobap.edu/

**E-mail:** henrya@mobap.edu

**ACCREDITATION:** North Central Association of Colleges and Schools

**INSTITUTIONALLY ADMINISTERED FINANCIAL AID:** Yes

### DEGREE OR CERTIFICATE PROGRAMS OFFERED

Programs offered do not lead to a degree or other formal award.

### NON-DEGREE-RELATED COURSE TOPICS OFFERED

**Undergraduate**—religion/religious studies; teacher education, specific academic and vocational programs.

**Graduate**—teacher education, specific academic and vocational programs.

## MISSOURI SOUTHERN STATE COLLEGE

### Continuing Education

3950 East Newman Road
Joplin, MO 64801

**Contact:** Dr. Jerry Williams, Director of Continuing Education

**Phone:** 417-625-9384

**Fax:** 417-625-3024

**Web:** http://www.mssc.edu/

**E-mail:** williams-r@mail.mssc.edu

**ACCREDITATION:** North Central Association of Colleges and Schools

**INSTITUTIONALLY ADMINISTERED FINANCIAL AID:** Yes

### DEGREE OR CERTIFICATE PROGRAMS OFFERED

**Undergraduate**—*AA:* General Studies. *AS:* Law Enforcement. *BA:* Business; General Studies. *BS:* Criminal Justice.

### NON-DEGREE-RELATED COURSE TOPICS OFFERED

**Undergraduate**—accounting; biology, general; developmental and child psychology; journalism and mass communication, other; radio and television broadcasting; social psychology; sociology.

## MISSOURI WESTERN STATE COLLEGE

### Division of Continuing Education

4525 Downs Drive
St. Joseph, MO 64507

**Contact:** Continuing Education and Special Programs

**Phone:** 816-271-4100

**Fax:** 816-271-5922

**Web:** http://www.mwsc.edu/conted/fall/

**E-mail:** conteduc@mwsc.edu

**ACCREDITATION:** North Central Association of Colleges and Schools

### DEGREE OR CERTIFICATE PROGRAMS OFFERED

Programs offered do not lead to a degree or other formal award.

### NON-DEGREE-RELATED COURSE TOPICS OFFERED

**Undergraduate**—East European languages and literatures; English composition; English language and literature, general; accounting; biology,

general; business; chemistry; communications, general; computer science; construction/building technology; criminal justice and corrections; economics; education, general; engineering-related technologies, other; financial management and services; fine arts and art studies; health and physical education/fitness; law and legal studies; liberal arts and sciences, general studies and humanities; marketing management and research; mathematics; music; nursing; physics; social sciences, general.

**Graduate**—counseling psychology.

## MITCHELL COMMUNITY COLLEGE

### Distance Learning Technology

500 West Broad Street
Statesville, NC 28677

**Contact:** Dr. Gloria Rembert, Coordinator of Distance Learning

**Phone:** 704-878-3338

**Fax:** 704-878-3330

**Web:** http://www.mitchell.cc.nc.us

**E-mail:** grembert@mitchell.cc.nc.us

**ACCREDITATION:** Southern Association of Colleges and Schools

**INSTITUTIONALLY ADMINISTERED FINANCIAL AID:** No

### DEGREE OR CERTIFICATE PROGRAMS OFFERED

Programs offered do not lead to a degree or other formal award.

### NON-DEGREE-RELATED COURSE TOPICS OFFERED

**Undergraduate**—business administration and management; computer and information sciences, other; criminal justice and corrections.

## MOBERLY AREA COMMUNITY COLLEGE

101 College Avenue
Moberly, MO 63552

**Contact:** Dr. James Grant, Dean of Student Services

**Phone:** 660-263-4110 Ext. 239

**Web:** http://www.macc.cc.mo.us/

**E-mail:** jamesg@hp9000.macc.cc.mo.us

**ACCREDITATION:** North Central Association of Colleges and Schools

**INSTITUTIONALLY ADMINISTERED FINANCIAL AID:** Yes

### DEGREE OR CERTIFICATE PROGRAMS OFFERED

**Undergraduate**—*AAS:* Computer Information Systems.

### NON-DEGREE-RELATED COURSE TOPICS OFFERED

**Undergraduate**—accounting; business administration and management; child care and guidance workers and managers; computer science; electrical and electronic engineering-related technology; geography; history; industrial/manufacturing engineering; mathematics; psychology; sociology; speech and rhetorical studies.

# MOHAWK VALLEY COMMUNITY COLLEGE

*Educational Technology*

1101 Sherman Drive
Utica, NY 13501
**Contact:** Mr. Jeff Kimball, Coordinator for Distance Education
**Phone:** 315-792.5316
**Web:** http://www.mvcc.edu/
**E-mail:** jkimball@mvcc.edu

**ACCREDITATION:** Middle States Association of Colleges and Schools
**INSTITUTIONALLY ADMINISTERED FINANCIAL AID:** Yes

### DEGREE OR CERTIFICATE PROGRAMS OFFERED

Programs offered do not lead to a degree or other formal award.

### NON-DEGREE-RELATED COURSE TOPICS OFFERED

**Undergraduate**—American literature (United States); English composition; accounting; business/managerial economics; computer and information sciences, general; criminal justice and corrections; criminology; culinary arts and related services; developmental and child psychology; education, general; educational psychology; foods and nutrition studies; graphic design, commercial art and illustration; hospitality services management; internet and world wide web; mathematics; nursing; philosophy and religion; photography; psychology; social sciences, general; social work; sociology; special education.

# MONMOUTH UNIVERSITY

400 Cedar Avenue
West Long Branch, NJ 07764-1898
**Contact:** Miriam E. King, Vice President for Enrollment Management
**Phone:** 732-571-3413
**Fax:** 732-263-5101
**Web:** http://www.monmouth.edu/
**E-mail:** mking@monmouth.edu

**ACCREDITATION:** Middle States Association of Colleges and Schools
**INSTITUTIONALLY ADMINISTERED FINANCIAL AID:** Yes

### DEGREE OR CERTIFICATE PROGRAMS OFFERED

Programs offered do not lead to a degree or other formal award.

### NON-DEGREE-RELATED COURSE TOPICS OFFERED

**Undergraduate**—English composition; communications, general; education, general; liberal arts and sciences, general studies and humanities; philosophy.
**Graduate**—business; communications, general; computer science; criminal justice and corrections; education, general.

# MONTANA STATE UNIVERSITY–BILLINGS

116 Apsaruke Hall, 1500 North 30th Street
Billings, MT 59101

**Contact:** Mr. Kirk P. Lacy, Online University Coordinator
**Phone:** 406-657-2294
**Fax:** 406-657-2254
**Web:** http://www.msubonline.org
**E-mail:** klacy@msubillings.edu

**ACCREDITATION:** Northwest Association of Schools and Colleges
**INSTITUTIONALLY ADMINISTERED FINANCIAL AID:** Yes

eCollege.com    *www.ecollege.com*

### DEGREE OR CERTIFICATE PROGRAMS OFFERED

**Undergraduate**—*BA:* Communication/Organizational Communications/Mass Communication/Public Relations. *BS:* Liberal Studies with Concentration in Management and Communication.
**Graduate**—*MS:* Information Processing and Communications.

### NON-DEGREE-RELATED COURSE TOPICS OFFERED

**Undergraduate**—English composition; accounting; art history, criticism and conservation; biology, general; business; business administration and management; business communications; business marketing and marketing management; communications technologies; communications, general; curriculum and instruction; drama/theater arts, general; economics; education, general; geography; history; industrial and organizational psychology; liberal arts and sciences, general studies and humanities; mathematical statistics; mathematics; organizational behavior studies; physics; psychology; special education.
**Graduate**—communications, general; curriculum and instruction; education, general; health system/health services administration.

**See full description on page 418.**

# MONTANA STATE UNIVERSITY–BOZEMAN

*The Burns Telecommunications Center/Extended Studies*

EPS 128
Bozeman, MT 59717
**Contact:** Kelly Boyce, Program Manager
**Phone:** 406-994-6812
**Fax:** 406-994-7856
**Web:** http://btc.montana.edu/nten
**E-mail:** kboyce@montana.edu

**ACCREDITATION:** Northwest Association of Schools and Colleges

### DEGREE OR CERTIFICATE PROGRAMS OFFERED

**Graduate**—*MN:* Nursing. *MS:* Family and Financial Planning; Mathematics; Science Education. *MSE:* Education.

### NON-DEGREE-RELATED COURSE TOPICS OFFERED

**Undergraduate**—teacher education, specific academic and vocational programs.
**Graduate**—biological and physical sciences; biology, general; chemistry; earth and planetary sciences; health and physical education/fitness; mathematical statistics; mathematics; microbiology/bacteriology; physics; teacher education, specific academic and vocational programs.

# MONTANA TECH OF THE UNIVERSITY OF MONTANA

*Office of Extended Studies*

1300 West Park Street
Butte, MT 59701-8997
**Contact:** Ms. Kathy Williams, Administrative Assistant
**Phone:** 800-445-8324 Ext. 1
**Fax:** 406-496-4710
**Web:** http://www.mtech.edu
**E-mail:** admissions@mtech.edu

**ACCREDITATION:** Northwest Association of Schools and Colleges

**INSTITUTIONALLY ADMINISTERED FINANCIAL AID:** Yes

## DEGREE OR CERTIFICATE PROGRAMS OFFERED

**Undergraduate—*BS:*** Occupational Safety and Health.
**Graduate—*MPM:*** Project Engineering and Management.

## NON-DEGREE-RELATED COURSE TOPICS OFFERED

**Undergraduate—**English composition; English technical and business writing; computer software and media applications; health professions and related sciences, other; nursing.
**Graduate—**engineering/industrial management; health professions and related sciences, other.

# MONTCALM COMMUNITY COLLEGE

2800 College Drive
Sidney, MI 48885-9723
**Contact:** Kathie A. Lofts, Director of Admissions
**Phone:** 989-328-1250
**Fax:** 989-328-2950
**Web:** http://www.montcalm.cc.mi.us/
**E-mail:** admissions@montcalm.cc.mi.us

**ACCREDITATION:** North Central Association of Colleges and Schools

**INSTITUTIONALLY ADMINISTERED FINANCIAL AID:** Yes

## DEGREE OR CERTIFICATE PROGRAMS OFFERED

Programs offered do not lead to a degree or other formal award.

## NON-DEGREE-RELATED COURSE TOPICS OFFERED

**Undergraduate—**accounting; biology, general; business; business administration and management; computer programming; criminal justice and corrections; data entry/microcomputer applications; economics; international business; psychology.
**Non-credit—**accounting; business administration and management; computer and information sciences, general; health professions and related sciences, other.

# MONTGOMERY COUNTY COMMUNITY COLLEGE

*Learning Resources Unit*

340 DeKalb Pike, Box 400
Blue Bell, PA 19422

**Contact:** Mr. John Mastroni, Director of Distance Learning
**Phone:** 215-641-6589
**Fax:** 215-619-7182
**Web:** http://www.mc3.edu/crsprog/distlrn/distlrn.htm
**E-mail:** jmastron@mc3.edu

**ACCREDITATION:** Middle States Association of Colleges and Schools

**INSTITUTIONALLY ADMINISTERED FINANCIAL AID:** Yes

## DEGREE OR CERTIFICATE PROGRAMS OFFERED

**Undergraduate—*AGS:*** General Studies. ***AS:*** Liberal Studies. ***Certificate:*** International Studies.

## NON-DEGREE-RELATED COURSE TOPICS OFFERED

**Undergraduate—**English composition; Spanish language and literature; accounting; anthropology; biology, general; developmental and child psychology; mathematical statistics; social psychology; sociology.

# MOODY BIBLE INSTITUTE

*Moody Bible Institute External Studies Division*

820 North Lasalle Boulevard
Chicago, IL 60610
**Contact:** Independent Studies
**Phone:** 800-955-1123
**Fax:** 312-329-2081
**Web:** http://www.moody.edu/
**E-mail:** xstudies@moody.edu

**ACCREDITATION:** Accrediting Association of Bible Colleges

## DEGREE OR CERTIFICATE PROGRAMS OFFERED

**Undergraduate—*ABS:*** Biblical Studies. ***BS:*** Biblical Studies. ***Certificate:*** Biblical Studies.

## NON-DEGREE-RELATED COURSE TOPICS OFFERED

**Undergraduate—**English composition; bible/biblical studies; biblical and other theological languages and literatures; classical and ancient Near Eastern languages and literatures; counseling psychology; educational psychology; philosophy; philosophy and religion; physical sciences, general; psychology; religion/religious studies; religious education; theological and ministerial studies; theological studies and religious vocations, other.

# MORAINE VALLEY COMMUNITY COLLEGE

*Academic Services and Learning Technologies*

10900 South 88th Avenue
Palos Hills, IL 60465
**Contact:** Rod Seaney, Director of Alternative Learning
**Phone:** 708-974-5710
**Fax:** 708-974-1184
**Web:** http://www.moraine.cc.il.us/
**E-mail:** seaney@moraine.cc.il.us

**ACCREDITATION:** North Central Association of Colleges and Schools

**INSTITUTIONALLY ADMINISTERED FINANCIAL AID:** Yes

## DEGREE OR CERTIFICATE PROGRAMS OFFERED

Programs offered do not lead to a degree or other formal award.

## NON-DEGREE-RELATED COURSE TOPICS OFFERED

Undergraduate—English language and literature, general; astronomy; business; design and applied arts; developmental and child psychology; economics; engineering, other; film/cinema studies; geography; health professions and related sciences, other; history; philosophy and religion; physics; psychology; sociology.

# MOREHEAD STATE UNIVERSITY

## Office of Distance Learning

408 Ginger Hall
Morehead, KY 40351
**Contact:** Mr. Tim Young, Director
**Phone:** 606-783-2082
**Fax:** 606-783-5052
**Web:** http://www.morehead-st.edu/units/distance
**E-mail:** t.young@morehead-st.edu

**ACCREDITATION:** Southern Association of Colleges and Schools

**INSTITUTIONALLY ADMINISTERED FINANCIAL AID:** Yes

## DEGREE OR CERTIFICATE PROGRAMS OFFERED

Graduate—*MBA:* Business Administration.

## NON-DEGREE-RELATED COURSE TOPICS OFFERED

Undergraduate—accounting; business administration and management; business communications; business/managerial economics; computer and information sciences, general; education administration and supervision; education, other; foreign languages and literatures; health and medical assistants; health professions and related sciences, other; mathematics; nursing; physical sciences, other; social work; special education; technology education/industrial arts; veterinary medicine (D.V.M.).
Graduate—education administration and supervision; education, other; physical sciences, other; special education; teacher education, specific academic and vocational programs.

# MOTLOW STATE COMMUNITY COLLEGE

## Academic Affairs

PO Box 8500
Lynchburg, TN 37352
**Contact:** Ms. Wanda Fruehauf, Director of Admissions and Records
**Phone:** 931-393-1530
**Fax:** 931-393-1681
**Web:** HTTP://WWW.MSCC.CC.TN.US
**E-mail:** wfruehauf@mscc.cc.tn.us

**ACCREDITATION:** Southern Association of Colleges and Schools

**INSTITUTIONALLY ADMINISTERED FINANCIAL AID:** Yes

## DEGREE OR CERTIFICATE PROGRAMS OFFERED

Programs offered do not lead to a degree or other formal award.

## NON-DEGREE-RELATED COURSE TOPICS OFFERED

Undergraduate—business administration and management.
Non-credit—business administration and management.

# MOTT COMMUNITY COLLEGE

## Distance Learning Office

College in the Workplace, CM 2120, 1401 East Court Street
Flint, MI 48503
**Contact:** Lori France, Distance Learning Coordinator
**Phone:** 800-398-2715
**Fax:** 810-762-0282
**Web:** http://cwp.mcc.edu
**E-mail:** lfrance@edtech.mcc.edu

**ACCREDITATION:** North Central Association of Colleges and Schools

**INSTITUTIONALLY ADMINISTERED FINANCIAL AID:** Yes

## DEGREE OR CERTIFICATE PROGRAMS OFFERED

Undergraduate—*AA:* General Studies (for transferring). *AAS:* Computer Occupations Technology; General Business. *AGS:* General Studies (for transferring). *AS:* General Studies (for transferring).

## NON-DEGREE-RELATED COURSE TOPICS OFFERED

Undergraduate—English composition; advertising; anthropology; art history, criticism and conservation; biology, general; developmental and child psychology; sociology.

# MOUNTAIN EMPIRE COMMUNITY COLLEGE

## Office of Continuing and Distance Education

US Route 23, South, PO Drawer 700
Big Stone Gap, VA 24219
**Contact:** Susan Kennedy, Coordinator of Distance Education
**Phone:** 540-523-7488
**Fax:** 540-523-7486
**Web:** http://www.me.cc.va.us/Coned.htm
**E-mail:** skennedy@me.vccs.edu

**ACCREDITATION:** Southern Association of Colleges and Schools

**INSTITUTIONALLY ADMINISTERED FINANCIAL AID:** Yes

## DEGREE OR CERTIFICATE PROGRAMS OFFERED

Undergraduate—*AAS:* Business Administration; Education; General Studies; Liberal Arts; Water/Wastewater Specialization.

## NON-DEGREE-RELATED COURSE TOPICS OFFERED

Undergraduate—American (United States) history; English composition; Spanish language and literature; accounting; art history, criticism and conservation; biology, general; business marketing and marketing management; developmental and child psychology; environmental science/studies; law and legal studies, other; sociology.

# MOUNTAIN STATE UNIVERSITY
## The School of Extended and Distance Learning
PO Box 9003
Beckley, WV 25802-9003
**Contact:** Karen Carter-Harvey, Assistant Registrar
**Phone:** 304-253-7351 Ext. 1366
**Fax:** 304-253-9059
**Web:** http://www.cwv.edu/saell
**E-mail:** kcharvey@cwv.edu

**ACCREDITATION:** North Central Association of Colleges and Schools
**INSTITUTIONALLY ADMINISTERED FINANCIAL AID:** Yes

### DEGREE OR CERTIFICATE PROGRAMS OFFERED
**Undergraduate—AA:** Elementary Teacher Preparation; General Studies; Secondary Teacher Preparation. **AS:** Aviation Technology; Banking and Finance; Business Administration: Accounting; Business Administration: Business Law; Business Administration: General Business; Business Administration: Management; Business Administration: Office Management; Computer Information Technology; Computer Networking Technology; Criminal Justice; Environmental Studies; General Studies; Marketing; Medical Assisting; Secretarial Science: Administrative; Secretarial Science: Legal; Secretarial Science: Medical; Travel. **BA:** Interdisciplinary Studies: Psychology; Interdisciplinary Studies: Social and Behavioral Sciences. **BS:** Business Administration: Accounting; Business Administration: Business Law; Business Administration: General Business; Business Administration: Management; Business Administration: Office Management; Computer Networking; Criminal Justice; Health Care Management: Health Care Administration; Health Care Management: Health Care Informatics; Interdisciplinary Studies: Biology; Interdisciplinary Studies: Environmental Studies; Interdisciplinary Studies: Health Services Management; Interdisciplinary Studies: Natural Sciences; Interdisciplinary Studies: Pre-Medicine; Internet and E-Commerce; Marketing. **BSN:** RN to BSN. **Certificate:** Aviation Technology; General Business; Office Technology: Secretarial Skills; Office Technology: Word Processing; Travel and Tourism.

### NON-DEGREE-RELATED COURSE TOPICS OFFERED
**Undergraduate—**American (United States) history; English composition; English language and literature/letters, other; European history; accounting; advertising; anatomy; art history, criticism and conservation; astronomy; biochemistry; biology, general; botany; business; business administration and management; business management and administrative services, other; business marketing and marketing management; chemistry; criminal justice and corrections; criminology; developmental and child psychology; earth and planetary sciences; ecology; economics; environmental health; environmental science/studies; family and marriage counseling; finance, general; geography; gerontology; health system/health services administration; history; insurance and risk management; international business; labor/personnel relations and studies; law and legal studies, other; liberal arts and sciences, general studies and humanities; management information systems and business data processing, general; mathematical statistics; mathematics; mathematics, other; microbiology/bacteriology; music; nursing; organic chemistry; organizational behavior studies; philosophy; philosophy and religion; physical sciences, general; physics; physiology, human and animal; psychology; social psychology; social sciences and history, other; social sciences, general; social work; sociology.

**See full description on page 420.**

# MOUNT ALLISON UNIVERSITY
## Continuing and Distance Education
65 York Street
Sackville, NB E4L 1E4, Canada
**Contact:** Marilyn McCullough, Director
**Phone:** 506-364-2266
**Fax:** 506-364-2272
**Web:** http://www.mta.ca/continuingeducation
**E-mail:** mmccullough@mta.ca

**ACCREDITATION:** Provincially Chartered
**INSTITUTIONALLY ADMINISTERED FINANCIAL AID:** Yes

### DEGREE OR CERTIFICATE PROGRAMS OFFERED
**Undergraduate—BA:** English; History.

### NON-DEGREE-RELATED COURSE TOPICS OFFERED
**Undergraduate—**American (United States) history; Asian studies; European history; geography; mathematical statistics; mathematics, other.

# MT. HOOD COMMUNITY COLLEGE
26000 Southeast Stark Street
Gresham, OR 97030
**Contact:** Ms. Catherine Vogt, Administrative Assistant
**Phone:** 503-491-6953
**Fax:** 503-491-7389
**Web:** http://www.mhcc.cc.or.us/
**E-mail:** vogtc@mhcc.cc.or.us

**ACCREDITATION:** Northwest Association of Schools and Colleges
**INSTITUTIONALLY ADMINISTERED FINANCIAL AID:** Yes

### DEGREE OR CERTIFICATE PROGRAMS OFFERED
Programs offered do not lead to a degree or other formal award.

### NON-DEGREE-RELATED COURSE TOPICS OFFERED
**Undergraduate—**American literature (United States); English composition; English creative writing; English technical and business writing; accounting; administrative and secretarial services; astronomy; business administration and management; chemistry; child care and guidance workers and managers; computer and information sciences, general; computer software and media applications; economics; funeral services and mortuary science; health and medical administrative services; psychology.

# MOUNT SAINT VINCENT UNIVERSITY
## Distance Learning and Continuing Education
166 Bedford Highway
Halifax, NS B3M 2J6, Canada
**Contact:** Ms. Mary Hart-Baker, Program Assistant
**Phone:** 902-457-6437
**Fax:** 902-457-2618
**Web:** http://www.msvu.ca/distance

**E-mail:** mary.hart-baker@msvu.ca

**ACCREDITATION:** Provincially Chartered

**INSTITUTIONALLY ADMINISTERED FINANCIAL AID:** No

## DEGREE OR CERTIFICATE PROGRAMS OFFERED

**Undergraduate—BA:** Liberal Arts and General Studies. **BBA:** Business Administration. **BTHM:** Tourism and Hospitality Management. **Certificate:** Business Administration; French; Gerontology; Information Technology Management.
**Graduate—MEd:** Education.

## NON-DEGREE-RELATED COURSE TOPICS OFFERED

**Undergraduate—**French language and literature; accounting; advertising; sociology; women's studies.
**Graduate—**adult and continuing teacher education.

# MT. SAN ANTONIO COLLEGE

*Distance Learning*

Learning Resources, 1100 North Grand Avenue
Walnut, CA 91789
**Contact:** Kerry C. Stern, Dean
**Phone:** 909-594-5611 Ext. 5658
**Fax:** 909-468-3992
**Web:** http://vclass.mtsac.edu
**E-mail:** kstern@mtsac.edu

**ACCREDITATION:** Western Association of Schools and Colleges

**INSTITUTIONALLY ADMINISTERED FINANCIAL AID:** Yes

## DEGREE OR CERTIFICATE PROGRAMS OFFERED

**Programs offered do not lead to a degree or other formal award.**

## NON-DEGREE-RELATED COURSE TOPICS OFFERED

**Undergraduate—**English as a second language; English composition; English creative writing; accounting; anthropology; biology, general; business administration and management; business and personal services marketing operations; computer and information sciences, general; economics; journalism; law and legal studies, other; philosophy; psychology; real estate; religion/religious studies; sociology.
**Non-credit—**computer software and media applications.

# MOUNT WACHUSETT COMMUNITY COLLEGE

*Division of Continuing Education*

444 Green Street
Gardner, MA 01440
**Contact:** Ms. Melissa Howlett, Distance Learning Administrative Assistant
**Phone:** 978-632-6600 Ext. 273
**Fax:** 978-632-6155
**Web:** http://www.mwcc.mass.edu
**E-mail:** m_howlett@mwcc.mass.edu

**ACCREDITATION:** New England Association of Schools and Colleges

**INSTITUTIONALLY ADMINISTERED FINANCIAL AID:** Yes

## DEGREE OR CERTIFICATE PROGRAMS OFFERED

**Undergraduate—AS:** Business Administration; Criminal Justices; General Studies; Human Services.

## NON-DEGREE-RELATED COURSE TOPICS OFFERED

**Undergraduate—**American (United States) history; English composition; advertising; biology, general; business administration and management; business information and data processing services; business marketing and marketing management; computer programming; computer software and media applications; criminal justice and corrections; criminology; economics; family and marriage counseling; human services; mathematical statistics; mathematics, other; psychology; sociology.
**Non-credit—**computer software and media applications.

# MU DIRECT: CONTINUING AND DISTANCE EDUCATION

102 Whitten Hall
Columbia, MO 65211-6300
**Contact:** Juanita Smarr, Administrative Assistant
**Phone:** 800-545-2604
**Fax:** 573-882-5071
**Web:** http://MUdirect.missouri.edu
**E-mail:** mudirect@missouri.edu

**ACCREDITATION:** North Central Association of Colleges and Schools

**INSTITUTIONALLY ADMINISTERED FINANCIAL AID:** Yes

## DEGREE OR CERTIFICATE PROGRAMS OFFERED

**Undergraduate—Certificate:** Justice and Ministry; Justice and Ministry; Justice and Ministry.
**Graduate—MA:** Journalism—Media Management; Library and Information Science. **MEd:** Educational Administration Focus; Educational Technology Focus; Gifted Education Focus; Literacy Focus; Social Studies Focus. **MHSA:** Executive Program in Health Services Management. **MS:** Executive Program in Health Informatics; Nursing—Mental Health Nurse Practitioner; Nursing—Pediatric Nurse Practitioner; Nursing—Public Health or School Health.

## NON-DEGREE-RELATED COURSE TOPICS OFFERED

**Undergraduate—**agricultural business and management; health professions and related sciences, other; miscellaneous health professions; nursing.
**Graduate—**advertising; agricultural business and management; education administration and supervision; education, general; education, other; educational/instructional media design; health and medical administrative services; information sciences and systems; journalism and mass communications; library science, other; library science/librarianship; mental health services; nursing; radio and television broadcasting; real estate; teacher education, specific academic and vocational programs; technology education/industrial arts.
**Non-credit—**agricultural business and management; engineering/industrial management; real estate.

# MURRAY STATE UNIVERSITY

*Continuing Education*

PO Box 9
Murray, KY 42071-0009

**Contact:** Continuing Education
**Phone:** 800-669-7654
**Web:** http://www.murraystate.edu/

**ACCREDITATION:** Southern Association of Colleges and Schools

### DEGREE OR CERTIFICATE PROGRAMS OFFERED
Programs offered do not lead to a degree or other formal award.

### NON-DEGREE-RELATED COURSE TOPICS OFFERED
**Undergraduate**—American (United States) history; English composition; agricultural economics; anthropology; geography; journalism; law and legal studies, other; mathematics, other; philosophy and religion; radio and television broadcasting; sociology.

## NAROPA UNIVERSITY
*Outreach Office*
2130 Arapahoe Avenue
Boulder, CO 80302
**Contact:** Mr. Brian Van Way, Director of Distance Learning
**Phone:** 303-245-4703
**Fax:** 303-245-4749
**Web:** http://www.naropa.edu/distance
**E-mail:** brian@naropa.edu

**ACCREDITATION:** North Central Association of Colleges and Schools

**INSTITUTIONALLY ADMINISTERED FINANCIAL AID:** Yes

eCollege.com   *www.ecollege.com*

### DEGREE OR CERTIFICATE PROGRAMS OFFERED
**Graduate**—*Graduate Certificate:* Ecopsychology. *MA:* Transpersonal Psychology. *MAE:* Contemplative Education.

### NON-DEGREE-RELATED COURSE TOPICS OFFERED
**Undergraduate**—American literature (United States); English creative writing; anthropology; area, ethnic and cultural studies, other; clinical psychology; community psychology; comparative literature; counseling psychology; developmental and child psychology; ethnic and cultural studies; experimental psychology; gerontology; liberal arts and sciences, general studies and humanities; multi/interdisciplinary studies, other; peace and conflict studies; philosophy and religion; psychology; religion/religious studies.
**Graduate**—East and Southeast Asian languages and literatures; English language and literature, general; anthropology; area, ethnic and cultural studies, other; education, general; liberal arts and sciences, general studies and humanities; multi/interdisciplinary studies, other; psychology, other; religious education.

## NASH COMMUNITY COLLEGE
522 North Old Carriage Road, PO Box 7488
Rocky Mount, NC 27804-0488
**Contact:** Ms. Karen Hicks, Department Chair of Interdisciplinary Studies
**Phone:** 252-443-4011 Ext. 347
**Fax:** 252-451-4922

**Web:** http://www.nash.cc.nc.us/
**E-mail:** khicks@nash.cc.nc.us

**ACCREDITATION:** Southern Association of Colleges and Schools

**INSTITUTIONALLY ADMINISTERED FINANCIAL AID:** Yes

### DEGREE OR CERTIFICATE PROGRAMS OFFERED
Programs offered do not lead to a degree or other formal award.

### NON-DEGREE-RELATED COURSE TOPICS OFFERED
**Undergraduate**—English composition; business administration and management; computer and information sciences, general; criminal justice and corrections; history; mathematics, other; psychology.
**Non-credit**—computer and information sciences, general; enterprise management and operation; internet and world wide web.

## NASSAU COMMUNITY COLLEGE
*College of the Air*
1 Education Drive
Garden City, NY 11530-6793
**Contact:** Prof. Arthur l. Friedman, Coordinator of College of the Air
**Phone:** 516-572-7883
**Fax:** 516-572-0690
**Web:** http://www.sunynassau.edu
**E-mail:** friedma@sunynassau.edu

**ACCREDITATION:** Middle States Association of Colleges and Schools

**INSTITUTIONALLY ADMINISTERED FINANCIAL AID:** Yes

### DEGREE OR CERTIFICATE PROGRAMS OFFERED
Programs offered do not lead to a degree or other formal award.

### NON-DEGREE-RELATED COURSE TOPICS OFFERED
**Undergraduate**—English language and literature/letters, other; French language and literature; Italian language and literature; Spanish language and literature; accounting; anthropology; astronomy; atmospheric sciences and meteorology; business; business administration and management; business marketing and marketing management; communications, other; developmental and child psychology; economics; entrepreneurship; film/video and photographic arts; geological and related sciences; health and physical education/fitness; history; journalism and mass communication, other; law and legal studies, other; mathematical statistics; mathematics; mathematics, other; music; psychology; psychology, other; sociology.
**Non-credit**—mathematics.

## NATIONAL AMERICAN UNIVERSITY
*Department of Distance Learning*
321 Kansas City Street, PO Box 1780
Rapid City, SD 57709
**Contact:** Brian Pitts, Admissions Coordinator
**Phone:** 800-843-8892 Ext. 4895
**Fax:** 605-394-4871

**Web:** http://www.national.edu
**E-mail:** bpitts@national.edu

**ACCREDITATION:** North Central Association of Colleges and Schools

**INSTITUTIONALLY ADMINISTERED FINANCIAL AID:** Yes

## DEGREE OR CERTIFICATE PROGRAMS OFFERED

**Undergraduate—AAS:** Applied Management; Business Administration; General Education Studies; Information Technology. **BS:** Applied Management; Business Administration; Information Technology. **Diploma:** E-Commerce Professional; Web Developer.

## NON-DEGREE-RELATED COURSE TOPICS OFFERED

**Undergraduate—**accounting; astronomy; business management and administrative services, other; computer and information sciences, general; computer software and media applications; economics; hospitality services management; information sciences and systems; international business; marketing management and research; tourism and travel services marketing operations.

**See full description on page 422.**

# NATIONAL TECHNOLOGICAL UNIVERSITY

700 Centre Avenue
Fort Collins, CO 80526
**Contact:** Clintnette Willoughby, Registration Coordinator
**Phone:** 970-495-6405
**Fax:** 970-498-0601
**Web:** http://www.ntu.edu/
**E-mail:** cwilloughby@ntu.edu

**ACCREDITATION:** North Central Association of Colleges and Schools

## DEGREE OR CERTIFICATE PROGRAMS OFFERED

**Undergraduate—Certificate:** Chemical Engineering; Computer Engineering; Computer Science; Electrical Engineering; Engineering Management; Health Physics; Manufacturing Systems Engineering; Materials Science and Engineering; Software Engineering; Technical Japanese; Transportation Systems Engineering.
**Graduate—MBA:** Business Administration. **MBA/MPH:** Business Administration. **MS:** Chemical Engineering; Computer Engineering; Computer Science; Electrical Engineering; Engineering Management; Environmental Systems Management; Information Systems; Management of Technology; Manufacturing Systems Engineering; Materials Science and Engineering; Mechanical Engineering; Optical Science; Project Management; Software Engineering; Special Majors; Systems Engineering; Telecommunications.

## NON-DEGREE-RELATED COURSE TOPICS OFFERED

**Undergraduate—**engineering, other.
**Graduate—**engineering, other.

# NATIONAL UNIVERSITY

## NU Online

11255 North Torrey Pines Road
La Jolla, CA 92037

**Contact:** Dr. Jean M. Swenk, Director of Institutional Effectiveness and Planning
**Phone:** 858-642-8338
**Fax:** 858-642-8705
**Web:** http://www.online.nu.edu
**E-mail:** jswenk@nu.edu

**ACCREDITATION:** Western Association of Schools and Colleges

**INSTITUTIONALLY ADMINISTERED FINANCIAL AID:** Yes

eCollege.com   *www.ecollege.com*

## DEGREE OR CERTIFICATE PROGRAMS OFFERED

**Undergraduate—BA:** Global Studies. **BBA:** Business Administration. **BS:** Criminal Justice; Nursing. **Certificate of Completion:** CLAD Multiple or Single Subject Certificate; Preliminary Level 1 Education Specialist: Mild/Moderate Disabilities with Concurrent CLD/BCLAD; Preliminary and Professional Clear Multiple Subject Teaching with CLAD/BCLAD emphasis; Preliminary and Professional Clear Single Subject Teaching Credential with CLAD or BCLAD emphasis; Professional Certificate in Criminal Justice; Professional Tier I Administrative Services. **Certificate:** Electronic Commerce.
**Graduate—GMBA:** Business Administration. **MA:** Forensic Sciences. **MAT:** Teaching/Education with Credential Options. **MEd:** Cross Cultural Education with Credential Options. **MS:** Educational Administration; Educational Technology; Electronic Commerce; Instructional Technology; Nursing; Special Education with Credential Options.

## NON-DEGREE-RELATED COURSE TOPICS OFFERED

**Graduate—**educational psychology.

# NAZARENE THEOLOGICAL SEMINARY

1700 East Meyer Boulevard
Kansas City, MO 64131
**Contact:** Dr. Edwin H. Robinson, Dean of the Faculty
**Phone:** 816-333-6254
**Web:** http://www.nts.edu/
**E-mail:** rhrobinson@nts.edu

**ACCREDITATION:** Association of Theological Schools in the United States and Canada

**INSTITUTIONALLY ADMINISTERED FINANCIAL AID:** Yes

## DEGREE OR CERTIFICATE PROGRAMS OFFERED

**Programs offered do not lead to a degree or other formal award.**

## NON-DEGREE-RELATED COURSE TOPICS OFFERED

**Graduate—**religion/religious studies; religious education; theological and ministerial studies.

# NEUMANN COLLEGE

*neumannonline.org*

1 Neumann Drive
Aston, PA 19014-1298
**Contact:** Neumannonline
**Phone:** 610-558-5616

**Web:** http://neumannonline.org
**E-mail:** inquiry@neumannonline.org

**ACCREDITATION:** Middle States Association of Colleges and Schools

**INSTITUTIONALLY ADMINISTERED FINANCIAL AID:** Yes

eCollege.com *www.ecollege.com*

## DEGREE OR CERTIFICATE PROGRAMS OFFERED

Programs offered do not lead to a degree or other formal award.
See full description on page 424.

# NEW HAMPSHIRE COMMUNITY TECHNICAL COLLEGE, NASHUA/CLAREMONT

*Division of Continuing Education and Distance Learning*
1 College Drive
Claremont, NH 03743
**Contact:** Charles Kusselow, Director of Distance Learning
**Phone:** 800-837-0658 Ext. 2269
**Fax:** 603-543-1844
**Web:** http://www.claremont.tec.nh.us
**E-mail:** ckusselow@tec.nh.us

**ACCREDITATION:** New England Association of Schools and Colleges

**INSTITUTIONALLY ADMINISTERED FINANCIAL AID:** Yes

## DEGREE OR CERTIFICATE PROGRAMS OFFERED

Undergraduate—*AA:* Liberal Arts.

## NON-DEGREE-RELATED COURSE TOPICS OFFERED

Undergraduate—economics; foreign languages and literatures; history; mathematics; psychology; sociology.

# NEW HAMPSHIRE TECHNICAL INSTITUTE

5 Institute Drive
Concord, NH 03301
**Contact:** Mr. Paul Ambrose, Director of Distance Education
**Phone:** 603-271-2722
**Fax:** 603-271-2725
**Web:** http://www.nhti.net/
**E-mail:** pambrose@tech.nh.us

**ACCREDITATION:** New England Association of Schools and Colleges

**INSTITUTIONALLY ADMINISTERED FINANCIAL AID:** No

## DEGREE OR CERTIFICATE PROGRAMS OFFERED

Programs offered do not lead to a degree or other formal award.

# NEW JERSEY CITY UNIVERSITY

*Continuing Education*
2039 Kennedy Boulevard
Jersey City, NJ 07305-1597
**Contact:** Marie A. Fosello, Director of Special Programs
**Phone:** 201-200-3449
**Fax:** 201-200-2188
**Web:** http://newlearning.njcu.edu
**E-mail:** conted@njcu.edu

**ACCREDITATION:** Middle States Association of Colleges and Schools

**INSTITUTIONALLY ADMINISTERED FINANCIAL AID:** Yes

## DEGREE OR CERTIFICATE PROGRAMS OFFERED

Programs offered do not lead to a degree or other formal award.

## NON-DEGREE-RELATED COURSE TOPICS OFFERED

Undergraduate—business; criminal justice and corrections; economics; international relations and affairs; mathematics; physics; political science and government; public health.
Graduate—business administration and management; criminology; education administration and supervision; educational/instructional media design; public health; special education.

# NEW JERSEY INSTITUTE OF TECHNOLOGY

*Continuing Professional Education*
University Heights
Newark, NJ 07102
**Contact:** Gale Tenen Spak, Associate Vice President for Continuing and Distance Education
**Phone:** 973-596-8540
**Fax:** 973-596-3288
**Web:** http://www.njit.edu
**E-mail:** spak@njit.edu

**ACCREDITATION:** Middle States Association of Colleges and Schools

**INSTITUTIONALLY ADMINISTERED FINANCIAL AID:** Yes

## DEGREE OR CERTIFICATE PROGRAMS OFFERED

Undergraduate—*BA:* Information Systems. *BS:* Computer Science. *Certificate:* Computer Networking; E-Commerce; Information Systems, Design, and Development; Internet Applications Development; Internet Systems Engineering; Object-Oriented Design; Practice of Technology Communications; Programming Environmental Tools; Project Management; Telecommunications Networking.
Graduate—*MS:* Professional and Technical Communications. *MSE:* Engineering/Industrial Management. *MSIS:* Information Technology.

## NON-DEGREE-RELATED COURSE TOPICS OFFERED

Undergraduate—electrical, electronics and communication engineering; social psychology.
Graduate—chemical engineering; electrical, electronics and communication engineering; engineering/industrial management; environmental/environmental health engineering; industrial/manufacturing engineering; journalism.

See full description on page 426.

# NEWMAN UNIVERSITY
## Community Education

3100 McCormick Avenue
Wichita, KS 67213
**Contact:** Norman Correll, Director of Distance Learning
**Phone:** 316-942-4291 Ext. 222
**Fax:** 316-942-4483
**Web:** http://www.newmanu.edu
**E-mail:** cornelln@newmanu.edu

**ACCREDITATION:** North Central Association of Colleges and Schools
**INSTITUTIONALLY ADMINISTERED FINANCIAL AID:** Yes

eCollege *www.ecollege.com*

### DEGREE OR CERTIFICATE PROGRAMS OFFERED
**Undergraduate—BA:** Pastoral Ministry. **BS:** Business Management; Teacher Education. **BSN:** Nursing.
**Graduate—MS:** Adult Education; Building Leadership.

# NEW MEXICO INSTITUTE OF MINING AND TECHNOLOGY
## Distance Education Department

801 Leroy Place
Socorro, NM 87801
**Contact:** Mike Kloeppel, Director of Admissions
**Phone:** 505-835-5424
**Fax:** 505-835-5989
**Web:** http://www.nmt.edu
**E-mail:** mkloeppel@admin.nmt.edu

**ACCREDITATION:** North Central Association of Colleges and Schools
**INSTITUTIONALLY ADMINISTERED FINANCIAL AID:** Yes

### DEGREE OR CERTIFICATE PROGRAMS OFFERED
Programs offered do not lead to a degree or other formal award.

### NON-DEGREE-RELATED COURSE TOPICS OFFERED
**Undergraduate—**biology, general; chemical engineering; environmental/environmental health engineering; teacher education, specific academic and vocational programs.
**Graduate—**chemical engineering; environmental/environmental health engineering; teacher education, specific academic and vocational programs.

# NEW SCHOOL BACHELOR OF ARTS, NEW SCHOOL UNIVERSITY

66 West 12th Street, Room 401
New York, NY 10011
**Contact:** Ms. Gerianne Brusati, Associate Dean for Admissions
**Phone:** 212-229-5630
**Fax:** 212-989-3887
**Web:** http://www.nsu.newschool.edu/ba

**E-mail:** brusatig@newschool.edu
**ACCREDITATION:** Middle States Association of Colleges and Schools
**INSTITUTIONALLY ADMINISTERED FINANCIAL AID:** Yes

### DEGREE OR CERTIFICATE PROGRAMS OFFERED
Programs offered do not lead to a degree or other formal award.

### NON-DEGREE-RELATED COURSE TOPICS OFFERED
**Undergraduate—**liberal arts and sciences, general studies and humanities.

# NEW SCHOOL UNIVERSITY
## Distance Learning Program

68 Fifth Avenue, Suite 3
New York, NY 10011
**Contact:** Stephen J. Anspacher, Associate Provost for Distributed Learning Services
**Phone:** 212-229-5880
**Fax:** 212-989-2928
**Web:** http://www.dialnsa.edu
**E-mail:** sanspach@dialnsa.edu

**ACCREDITATION:** Middle States Association of Colleges and Schools
**INSTITUTIONALLY ADMINISTERED FINANCIAL AID:** Yes

### DEGREE OR CERTIFICATE PROGRAMS OFFERED
**Undergraduate—BA:** Liberal Arts.
**Graduate—MA:** Media Studies.

### NON-DEGREE-RELATED COURSE TOPICS OFFERED
**Undergraduate—**English as a second language; English composition; English creative writing; anthropology; business administration and management; city/urban, community and regional planning; communications, general; developmental and child psychology; economics; film/video and photographic arts; foreign languages and literatures; history; industrial and organizational psychology; internet and world wide web; journalism; journalism and mass communications; liberal arts and sciences, general studies and humanities; philosophy; psychology; social psychology; social sciences, general; sociology; teacher education, specific academic and vocational programs.
**Graduate—**English as a second language; English creative writing; teacher education, specific academic and vocational programs.
**Non-credit—**English as a second language; English composition; English creative writing; developmental and child psychology; industrial and organizational psychology; journalism; liberal arts and sciences, general studies and humanities; social psychology; sociology.

**See full description on page 428.**

# NEW YORK INSTITUTE OF TECHNOLOGY
## On-Line Campus

Carleton Avenue, PO Box 9029
Central Islip, NY 11729-9029
**Contact:** Mr. Stanley Silverman, Chair of Online Campus
**Phone:** 631-348-3317

**Fax:** 631-348-3399
**Web:** http://www.nyit.edu/olc
**E-mail:** stan@nyit.edu

**ACCREDITATION:** Middle States Association of Colleges and Schools

**INSTITUTIONALLY ADMINISTERED FINANCIAL AID:** Yes

### DEGREE OR CERTIFICATE PROGRAMS OFFERED

**Undergraduate—*BA:*** Interdisciplinary Studies. ***BPS:*** Hospitality Management; Interdisciplinary Studies. ***BS:*** Business Administration; Community Mental Health; Criminal Justice; Interdisciplinary Studies; Psychology; Sociology; Telecommunications Management.
**Graduate—*MBA:*** Business. ***MS:*** Energy Management.

### NON-DEGREE-RELATED COURSE TOPICS OFFERED

**Undergraduate**—English composition; accounting; anthropology; business marketing and marketing management; communications, general; finance, general; industrial/manufacturing engineering; interior design; mathematical statistics; mechanical engineering; philosophy and religion; social psychology; social work; sociology.
**Graduate**—accounting; business administration and management; business information and data processing services; business marketing and marketing management; educational/instructional media design.
**Non-credit**—computer and information sciences, general; computer and information sciences, other; computer software and media applications; computer/information technology administration and management; culinary arts and related services.

**See full description on page 430.**

# NEW YORK UNIVERSITY
## The Virtual College
48 Cooper Square
New York, NY 10003
**Contact:** Annie Stanton, Associate Director
**Phone:** 212-998-7193
**Fax:** 212-995-3550
**Web:** http://www.scps.nyu.edu/virtualms
**E-mail:** scps.virtualms@nyu.edu

**ACCREDITATION:** Middle States Association of Colleges and Schools

**INSTITUTIONALLY ADMINISTERED FINANCIAL AID:** Yes

### DEGREE OR CERTIFICATE PROGRAMS OFFERED

Programs offered do not lead to a degree or other formal award.

# NIPISSING UNIVERSITY
## Center for Continuing Business Education
100 College Drive, Box 5002
North Bay, ON P1B 8L7, Canada
**Contact:** Rhonda Pyper, Program Administrator
**Phone:** 705-474-3461 Ext. 4219
**Fax:** 705-475-0264
**Web:** http://www.unipissing.ca/ccbe/index.htm
**E-mail:** ccbe@unipissing.ca

**ACCREDITATION:** Provincially Chartered

**INSTITUTIONALLY ADMINISTERED FINANCIAL AID:** No

### DEGREE OR CERTIFICATE PROGRAMS OFFERED

**Undergraduate—*BComm:*** Financial Services.

### NON-DEGREE-RELATED COURSE TOPICS OFFERED

**Undergraduate**—financial management and services.

# NORTHAMPTON COUNTY AREA COMMUNITY COLLEGE
## College-at-Home Program
College Center 481, 3835 Green Pond Road
Bethlehem, PA 18020
**Contact:** Ms. Brenda J. Johnson, Director of Distance Learning
**Phone:** 610-861-4160
**Fax:** 610-861-5373
**Web:** http://www.northampton.edu
**E-mail:** bjohnson@northampton.edu

**ACCREDITATION:** Middle States Association of Colleges and Schools

**INSTITUTIONALLY ADMINISTERED FINANCIAL AID:** Yes

### DEGREE OR CERTIFICATE PROGRAMS OFFERED

**Undergraduate—*AA:*** Business Administration; General Studies; Individualized Transfer Studies. ***AAS:*** Accounting. ***AS:*** Business Management. ***Specialized diploma:*** Home-based Early Childhood Education; Library Technical Assistant.

### NON-DEGREE-RELATED COURSE TOPICS OFFERED

**Undergraduate**—English composition; English creative writing; English literature (British and Commonwealth); accounting; anthropology; astronomy; biological sciences/life sciences, other; biology, general; business; business administration and management; business communications; business management and administrative services, other; business/managerial economics; child care and guidance workers and managers; computer science; developmental and child psychology; economics; education, general; education, other; geography; geological and related sciences; health and physical education/fitness; journalism and mass communications; library assistant; mathematics; music; philosophy; psychology; social sciences, general; sociology.

# NORTH ARKANSAS COLLEGE
## Articulated Programs and Distance Learning
1515 Pioneer Drive
Harrison, AR 72601
**Contact:** Mr. John P. Walsh, Director of Distance Learning
**Phone:** 870-391-3308
**Fax:** 870-391-3250
**Web:** http://pioneer.northark.net/
**E-mail:** jwalsh@northark.cc.ar.us

**ACCREDITATION:** North Central Association of Colleges and Schools

**INSTITUTIONALLY ADMINISTERED FINANCIAL AID:** Yes

### DEGREE OR CERTIFICATE PROGRAMS OFFERED

Programs offered do not lead to a degree or other formal award.

## NON-DEGREE-RELATED COURSE TOPICS OFFERED

**Undergraduate**—English composition; English technical and business writing; accounting; anthropology; art history, criticism and conservation; business communications; business information and data processing services; economics; education, other; history.

# NORTH CAROLINA AGRICULTURAL AND TECHNICAL STATE UNIVERSITY

*Center for Distance Learning*

Fort IRC
Greensboro, NC 27411-1117
**Contact:** Mr. Rodney Harrigan, Vice Chancellor of Computing and Information Technology
**Phone:** 336-334-7856
**Web:** http://www.ncat.edu/
**E-mail:** harrigan@ncat.edu

**ACCREDITATION:** Southern Association of Colleges and Schools

**INSTITUTIONALLY ADMINISTERED FINANCIAL AID:** Yes

eCollege.com  www.ecollege.com

## DEGREE OR CERTIFICATE PROGRAMS OFFERED

**Undergraduate—*BS:*** Occupational Safety and Health.
**Graduate—*MS:*** Adult Education; Engineering; Instructional Technology; Physical Education; Technology Education.

## NON-DEGREE-RELATED COURSE TOPICS OFFERED

**Undergraduate**—construction and building finishers and managers; curriculum and instruction; education, other; electrical, electronics and communications engineering; teacher education, specific academic and vocational programs; technology education/industrial arts.
**Graduate**—computer science; curriculum and instruction; general teacher education; teacher education, specific academic and vocational programs; technology education/industrial arts.

**See full description on page 432.**

# NORTH CAROLINA CENTRAL UNIVERSITY

PO Box 19772
Durham, NC 27707
**Contact:** Tun K. Nyein, Assistant Director of Distance Learning
**Phone:** 919-530-7497
**Fax:** 919-530-7925
**Web:** http://www.nccu.edu/
**E-mail:** tnyein@wpo.nccu.edu

**ACCREDITATION:** Southern Association of Colleges and Schools

**INSTITUTIONALLY ADMINISTERED FINANCIAL AID:** Yes

## DEGREE OR CERTIFICATE PROGRAMS OFFERED

**Undergraduate—*BS:*** Criminal Justice; Nursing. ***Certificate:*** Recreation Management.

**Graduate—*MS:*** Hearing Disorders; Information Science; Library Science.

## NON-DEGREE-RELATED COURSE TOPICS OFFERED

**Undergraduate**—English as a second language; English composition; English language and literature, general; biological and physical sciences; business; business information and data processing services; clothing, apparel and textile workers and managers; clothing/apparel and textile studies; communications, general; communications, other; criminal justice and corrections; education administration and supervision; education, general; educational evaluation, research and statistics; home economics, general.
**Graduate**—communication disorders sciences and services; food products retailing and wholesaling operations; library science/librarianship; parks, recreation and leisure facilities management; special education.
**Non-credit**—English as a second language; foreign languages and literatures; health and medical diagnostic and treatment services; mathematics.

# NORTH CAROLINA COMMUNITY COLLEGE SYSTEM

200 West Jones Street
Raleigh, NC 27603
**Contact:** Distance Learning
**Phone:** 919-733-7051
**Fax:** 919-733-0680
**Web:** http://www.ncccs.cc.nc.us

**ACCREDITATION:** North Central Association of Colleges and Schools

**INSTITUTIONALLY ADMINISTERED FINANCIAL AID:** Yes

## DEGREE OR CERTIFICATE PROGRAMS OFFERED

**Programs offered do not lead to a degree or other formal award.**

## NON-DEGREE-RELATED COURSE TOPICS OFFERED

**Undergraduate**—English language and literature, general; accounting; business communications; business/managerial economics; communications, general; computer programming; criminal justice and corrections; data entry/microcomputer applications; economics; human resources management; law and legal studies; marketing management and research; mathematical statistics; mathematics; medical basic sciences; music.

# NORTH CAROLINA STATE UNIVERSITY

*Distance Education*

Campus Box 7401
Raleigh, NC 27695-7401
**Contact:** Michael Yoakam, Director of Distance Education
**Phone:** 919-515-9323
**Fax:** 919-515-6668
**Web:** http://distance.ncsu.edu
**E-mail:** michael_yoakam@ncsu.edu

**ACCREDITATION:** Southern Association of Colleges and Schools

**INSTITUTIONALLY ADMINISTERED FINANCIAL AID:** Yes

## DEGREE OR CERTIFICATE PROGRAMS OFFERED

**Undergraduate**—*Certificate:* Training and Development.
**Graduate**—*ME:* Video-Based Engineering Education. *MS:* Wood and Paper Science. *MT:* Textile Off-Campus Televised Education (TOTE).

## NON-DEGREE-RELATED COURSE TOPICS OFFERED

**Undergraduate**—American literature (United States); English composition; English language and literature, general; English technical and business writing; South Asian languages and literatures; accounting; agricultural and food products processing; anthropology; biological and physical sciences; business; chemistry; clothing/apparel and textile studies; communications, general; forestry and related sciences; health and physical education/fitness; history; mathematics; multi/interdisciplinary studies, other; music; parks, recreation and leisure facilities management; philosophy; political science and government; psychology; sociology; soil sciences; textile sciences and engineering; zoology.
**Graduate**—agricultural and food products processing; agricultural business and production, other; agriculture/agricultural sciences; chemical engineering; civil engineering; curriculum and instruction; education administration and supervision; engineering, general; textile sciences and engineering.

# NORTH CENTRAL MICHIGAN COLLEGE

1515 Howard Street
Petoskey, MI 49770
**Contact:** Mrs. Naomi DeWinter, Dean of Student Services
**Phone:** 231-439-6511
**Fax:** 231-348-6672
**Web:** http://www.ncmc.cc.mi.us/
**E-mail:** ndewi@ncmc.cc.mi.us

**ACCREDITATION:** North Central Association of Colleges and Schools
**INSTITUTIONALLY ADMINISTERED FINANCIAL AID:** Yes

## DEGREE OR CERTIFICATE PROGRAMS OFFERED

Programs offered do not lead to a degree or other formal award.

## NON-DEGREE-RELATED COURSE TOPICS OFFERED

**Undergraduate**—English language and literature, general; anthropology; history; philosophy; political science and government; psychology.

# NORTH CENTRAL MISSOURI COLLEGE

Trenton, MO 64683
**Contact:** Mrs. Linda L. Brown, Registrar
**Phone:** 660-359-3948 Ext. 205
**Web:** http://www.ncmc.cc.mo.us
**E-mail:** lbrown@mail.ncmc.cc.mo.us

**ACCREDITATION:** North Central Association of Colleges and Schools
**INSTITUTIONALLY ADMINISTERED FINANCIAL AID:** Yes

## DEGREE OR CERTIFICATE PROGRAMS OFFERED

Programs offered do not lead to a degree or other formal award.

## NON-DEGREE-RELATED COURSE TOPICS OFFERED

**Undergraduate**—English composition; mathematics.

# NORTH CENTRAL TEXAS COLLEGE

1525 West California
Gainesville, TX 76240
**Contact:** Dr. Eddie C. Hadlock, Vice President of Instruction
**Phone:** 940-668-4234
**Fax:** 940-668-4258
**Web:** http://www.nctc.cc.tx.us/
**E-mail:** ehadlock@nctc.cc.tx.us

**ACCREDITATION:** Southern Association of Colleges and Schools
**INSTITUTIONALLY ADMINISTERED FINANCIAL AID:** Yes

## DEGREE OR CERTIFICATE PROGRAMS OFFERED

Programs offered do not lead to a degree or other formal award.

## NON-DEGREE-RELATED COURSE TOPICS OFFERED

**Undergraduate**—English literature (British and Commonwealth); political science and government.

# NORTHCENTRAL UNIVERSITY

505 West Whipple Street
Prescott, AZ 86301
**Contact:** Shannon Cervantes, Admissions Assistant
**Phone:** 800-903-9381
**Fax:** 928-541-7817
**Web:** http://www.ncu.edu/
**E-mail:** enroll@ncu.edu

**ACCREDITATION:** North Central Association of Colleges and Schools
**INSTITUTIONALLY ADMINISTERED FINANCIAL AID:** Yes

## DEGREE OR CERTIFICATE PROGRAMS OFFERED

**Undergraduate**—*BA:* Psychology. *BBA:* Business Administration.
**Graduate**—*MA:* Psychology. *MBA:* Business Administration.
**Postgraduate and doctoral**—*PhD:* Business Administration; Psychology.

## NON-DEGREE-RELATED COURSE TOPICS OFFERED

**Undergraduate**—accounting; business administration and management; business information and data processing services; criminal justice and corrections; financial management and services; human resources management; industrial and organizational psychology.
**Graduate**—accounting; business administration and management; business information and data processing services; clinical psychology; criminal justice and corrections; engineering/industrial management; financial management and services; human resources management; international business.

See full description on page 434.

# NORTH CENTRAL UNIVERSITY
## Carlson Institute of Church Leadership

910 Elliot Avenue, S
Minneapolis, MN 55404
**Contact:** Carlson Institute of Church Leadership
**Phone:** 800-446-1176
**Fax:** 612-343-4435
**Web:** http://www.northcentral.edu/
**E-mail:** carlinst@northcentral.edu

**ACCREDITATION:** North Central Association of Colleges and Schools

### DEGREE OR CERTIFICATE PROGRAMS OFFERED

**Undergraduate—AA:** Christian Education; Theology. **BA:** Christian Education; Christian Studies; Church Ministries. **BS:** Christian Education; Christian Studies; Church Ministries. **Certificate:** Bible; Christian Education; Church Ministries.

### NON-DEGREE-RELATED COURSE TOPICS OFFERED

**Undergraduate**—English composition; Hebrew language and literature; educational psychology; journalism; philosophy and religion; sociology. **Non-credit**—English composition; Hebrew language and literature; educational psychology; journalism; philosophy and religion; sociology.

# NORTH COUNTRY COMMUNITY COLLEGE

20 Winona Avenue, PO Box 89
Saranac Lake, NY 12983-0089
**Contact:** Mr. Thomas J. Finch, Dean of Academic Affairs
**Phone:** 518-891-2915 Ext. 203
**Fax:** 518-891-5029
**Web:** http://www.nccc.edu/
**E-mail:** acdean@nccc.edu

**ACCREDITATION:** Middle States Association of Colleges and Schools
**INSTITUTIONALLY ADMINISTERED FINANCIAL AID:** Yes

### DEGREE OR CERTIFICATE PROGRAMS OFFERED

**Programs offered do not lead to a degree or other formal award.**

### NON-DEGREE-RELATED COURSE TOPICS OFFERED

**Undergraduate**—English composition; advertising; anthropology; art history, criticism and conservation; business communications; business marketing and marketing management; computer and information sciences, general; developmental and child psychology; earth and planetary sciences; economics; environmental science/studies; geography; human resources management; psychology; sociology.

# NORTH DAKOTA STATE UNIVERSITY
## Division of Continuing Education

PO Box 5819
Fargo, ND 58105
**Contact:** Continuing Education
**Phone:** 701-231-7015

**Fax:** 701-231-1016
**Web:** http://www.ndsu.edu/
**E-mail:** ndsu_continuing-ed@ndsu.nodak.edu

**ACCREDITATION:** North Central Association of Colleges and Schools
**INSTITUTIONALLY ADMINISTERED FINANCIAL AID:** No

eCollege.com  www.ecollege.com

### DEGREE OR CERTIFICATE PROGRAMS OFFERED

**Programs offered do not lead to a degree or other formal award.**

### NON-DEGREE-RELATED COURSE TOPICS OFFERED

**Undergraduate**—accounting; aerospace, aeronautical and astronautical engineering; developmental and child psychology; electrical and electronic engineering-related technology; mathematical statistics. **Graduate**—accounting; aerospace, aeronautical and astronautical engineering; electrical and electronic engineering-related technology.

**See full description on page 436.**

# NORTHEASTERN OKLAHOMA AGRICULTURAL AND MECHANICAL COLLEGE

200 I Street, NE
Miami, OK 74354
**Contact:** S. C. Brown, Distance Education Site Coordinator
**Phone:** 918-540-6296
**Fax:** 918-542-7065
**Web:** http://www.neoam.cc.ok.us
**E-mail:** distanceed@neoam.cc.ok.us

**ACCREDITATION:** North Central Association of Colleges and Schools
**INSTITUTIONALLY ADMINISTERED FINANCIAL AID:** Yes

### DEGREE OR CERTIFICATE PROGRAMS OFFERED

**Programs offered do not lead to a degree or other formal award.**

### NON-DEGREE-RELATED COURSE TOPICS OFFERED

**Undergraduate**—English composition; business; child care and guidance workers and managers; criminal justice and corrections; economics; education, general; film/video and photographic arts; geography; history; liberal arts and sciences, general studies and humanities; mathematics; music; psychology.

# NORTHEASTERN STATE UNIVERSITY
## Center for Academic Technology and Distance Learning

610 North Grand
Tahlequah, OK 74464
**Contact:** Dr. Donna G. Wood, Coordinator of Distance Learning
**Phone:** 918-456-5511 Ext. 5859
**Fax:** 918-458-2387 Ext. 5859
**Web:** http://arapaho.nsuok.edu/~wooddg/atc_files

**E-mail:** wooddg@nsuok.edu

**ACCREDITATION:** North Central Association of Colleges and Schools

**INSTITUTIONALLY ADMINISTERED FINANCIAL AID:** Yes

## DEGREE OR CERTIFICATE PROGRAMS OFFERED

**Undergraduate—*BSN:*** Bachelor of Science in Nursing for Registered Nurses.

## NON-DEGREE-RELATED COURSE TOPICS OFFERED

**Undergraduate—**American literature (United States); English composition; English creative writing; English language and literature, general; English technical and business writing; Germanic languages and literatures; accounting; anthropology; biology, general; business administration and management; criminal justice and corrections; education administration and supervision; education, general; educational evaluation, research and statistics; educational/instructional media design; financial management and services; foreign languages and literatures; hospitality services management; human resources management; law and legal studies; marketing management and research; nursing; sociology; special education; teacher education, specific academic and vocational programs; telecommunications.

**Graduate—**English language and literature, general; business administration and management; education administration and supervision.

# NORTHEASTERN UNIVERSITY

*Network Northeastern*

360 Huntington Avenue, 328 CP

Boston, MA 02115

**Contact:** Linda Alosso, Assistant Director

**Phone:** 617-373-5620

**Fax:** 617-373-5625

**Web:** http://www.neu.edu

**E-mail:** l.alosso@neu.edu

**ACCREDITATION:** New England Association of Schools and Colleges

## DEGREE OR CERTIFICATE PROGRAMS OFFERED

**Undergraduate—*Certificate:*** C++/Unix Programming.

**Graduate—*MSEE:*** Electrical and Computer Engineering. ***MSIS:*** Information Systems.

## NON-DEGREE-RELATED COURSE TOPICS OFFERED

**Undergraduate—**computer programming; computer/information technology administration and management; internet and world wide web; liberal arts and sciences, general studies and humanities; mathematics, other.

**Graduate—**electrical, electronics and communication engineering; engineering/industrial management; industrial/manufacturing engineering; information sciences and systems; mechanical engineering; nursing.

**Non-credit—**communications technologies; computer programming; computer systems networking and telecommunications; internet and world wide web; telecommunications.

**See full description on page 438.**

# NORTHEAST STATE TECHNICAL COMMUNITY COLLEGE

*Evening and Distance Education*

PO Box 246

Blountville , TN 37617

**Contact:** Ms. Tammy B. Street, Division Secretary

**Phone:** 423-323-0221

**Fax:** 423-323-0224

**Web:** http://nstcc.cc.tn.us

**E-mail:** tbstreet@nstcc.cc.tn.us

**ACCREDITATION:** Southern Association of Colleges and Schools

**INSTITUTIONALLY ADMINISTERED FINANCIAL AID:** Yes

## DEGREE OR CERTIFICATE PROGRAMS OFFERED

**Programs offered do not lead to a degree or other formal award.**

## NON-DEGREE-RELATED COURSE TOPICS OFFERED

**Undergraduate—**English composition; English language and literature, general; accounting; astronomy; biological and physical sciences; business administration and management; chemistry; computer and information sciences, general; economics; education, general; history; mathematics; music; psychology; social sciences, general; speech and rhetorical studies.

# NORTHERN ARIZONA UNIVERSITY

*NAU Net*

PO Box 4117

Flagstaff, AZ 86011

**Contact:** Distributed Learning Services Center

**Phone:** 800-426-8315

**Fax:** 520-523-1169

**Web:** http://www.nau.edu/statewide

**E-mail:** statewide.programs@nau.edu

**ACCREDITATION:** North Central Association of Colleges and Schools

**INSTITUTIONALLY ADMINISTERED FINANCIAL AID:** Yes

## DEGREE OR CERTIFICATE PROGRAMS OFFERED

**Undergraduate—*BA:*** Psychology; Spanish. ***BEd:*** Elementary Education; Secondary Education; Special and Elementary Education; Vocational Education. ***BLS:*** Biology; Criminal Justice; English; Enterprise in Society; Environmental Sciences; Learning and Pedagogy; Mathematics/Statistics; Parks and Recreation Management; Psychology; Sociology. ***BS:*** Construction Management; Criminal Justice; Dental Hygiene Completion Program; Environmental Sciences; Hotel and Restaurant Management; Interior Design; Nursing. ***BSAST:*** Computer Technology; Health Promotion; Justice Systems and Policy Planning. ***BSBA:*** Business Administration. ***BSW:*** Social Work. ***Certificate:*** Educational Technology; International Tourism Management; Parks and Recreation Management; Postdegree Elementary Education; Postdegree Secondary Education; Postdegree Special Education; Restaurant Management. ***Certification:*** Principalship; Superintendency; Supervisory. ***Endorsement:*** Bilingual Education; Early Childhood Education; English as a Second Language; Gifted Education; Math Education; Middle School Education; Reading Specialist; Special Education; Vocational Technological Education.

**Graduate—*MA:*** Counseling; English. ***MAT:*** English as a Second Language. ***MEd:*** Bilingual/Multicultural Education; Counseling/Human Relations; Counseling/School Counseling; Early Childhood Education; Educational Leadership; Educational Technology; Elementary Education; Secondary Education; Special Education; Vocational Education. ***MEngr:*** Engineering. ***MSM:*** Management.

**Postgraduate and doctoral—*EdD:*** Educational Leadership.

## NON-DEGREE-RELATED COURSE TOPICS OFFERED

**Undergraduate**—English language and literature, general; English language and literature/letters, other; English technical and business writing; art history, criticism and conservation; biology, general; business marketing and marketing management; chemistry; communication disorders sciences and services; communications, other; computer and information sciences, general; computer and information sciences, other; construction and building finishers and managers; criminal justice and corrections; curriculum and instruction; dental services; engineering, general; environmental science/studies; environmental/environmental health engineering; forestry and related sciences; geography; geological and related sciences; health and medical assistants; health and medical preparatory programs; health professions and related sciences, other; history; hospitality services management; liberal arts and sciences, general studies and humanities; marketing management and research; miscellaneous health professions; music; natural resources conservation; natural resources management and protective services; nursing; parks, recreation and leisure facilities management; philosophy; philosophy and religion; political science and government; social sciences, general; social work; sociology; special education.

**Graduate**—bilingual/bicultural education; business administration and management; community health services; curriculum and instruction; education administration and supervision; education, other; educational evaluation, research and statistics; educational psychology; educational/instructional media design; electrical and electronic engineering-related technology; health and medical administrative services; human resources management; mathematical statistics; physical therapy; public administration; public administration and services, other; public health; vocational home economics, other.

---

### Special Note

Northern Arizona University (NAU) is an accredited state university that has expanded its distance learning opportunities to include Web-based degree programs. A leader in distance education for more than 15 years, NAU has tried to meet the needs of place-bound students pursuing a degree. Serving more than 20,000 students, including over 5,000 off campus, NAU is home to award-winning degree programs in hotel and restaurant management and ecosystem science management, and it continues to be a leader in teacher education with more than a century of experience and dedication to the training and advancement of America's educators.

NAU provides a learner-centered approach to education with small class sizes and qualified instructors. NAU students benefit from the knowledge and experience of professors continually involved in their field of expertise. Whether attending classes on the 24 state-wide campuses or taking classes via distance learning, including interactive television, satellite broadcasting, or online through the Web, each student receives personal attention and class interaction. NAU continues to be a quality-assured and dynamically driven institution with a dedication to being a premier residential campus as well as a leader in technologically advanced distance education.

See full description on page 440.

# NORTHERN ESSEX COMMUNITY COLLEGE
## Business, International Programs and Non-Traditional Learning

100 Elliott Street
Haverhill, MA 01830-2399
**Contact:** Kenneth R. Robinson, Director, Center for Adult and Non-Traditional Learning
**Phone:** 978-556-3308
**Fax:** 978-556-3775
**Web:** http://www.necc.mass.edu
**E-mail:** krobinson@necc.mass.edu

**ACCREDITATION:** New England Association of Schools and Colleges
**INSTITUTIONALLY ADMINISTERED FINANCIAL AID:** Yes

### DEGREE OR CERTIFICATE PROGRAMS OFFERED
**Programs offered do not lead to a degree or other formal award.**

### NON-DEGREE-RELATED COURSE TOPICS OFFERED
**Undergraduate**—English composition; English technical and business writing; business administration and management; business communications; computer systems networking and telecommunications; health and medical administrative services; philosophy; psychology.
**Non-credit**—business administration and management; business information and data processing services; business quantitative methods and management science; computer science; computer systems networking and telecommunications; enterprise management and operation; entrepreneurship; fire protection; health and medical administrative services.

# NORTHERN ILLINOIS UNIVERSITY
## Division of Continuing Education

DeKalb, IL 60115-2860
**Contact:** Gail Crawford, Distance Education Coordinator
**Phone:** 815-753-6931
**Fax:** 815-753-6900
**Web:** http://www.niu.edu
**E-mail:** gcrawford@niu.edu

**ACCREDITATION:** North Central Association of Colleges and Schools
**INSTITUTIONALLY ADMINISTERED FINANCIAL AID:** No

### DEGREE OR CERTIFICATE PROGRAMS OFFERED
**Programs offered do not lead to a degree or other formal award.**

### NON-DEGREE-RELATED COURSE TOPICS OFFERED
**Graduate**—English composition; accounting; adult and continuing teacher education; business marketing and marketing management; curriculum and instruction; electrical, electronics and communication engineering; finance, general; management information systems and business data processing, general; mechanical engineering.

# NORTHERN KENTUCKY UNIVERSITY
## Office of Information Technology

501 Administrative Center
Highland Heights, KY 41099-5700

**Contact:** Karen Hamilton-LaRosa, Jr., Coordinator of Distance Learning Programs
**Phone:** 859-572-5701
**Fax:** 859-572-5566
**Web:** http://www.nku.edu/~it/
**E-mail:** larosa@nku.edu

**ACCREDITATION:** Southern Association of Colleges and Schools

**INSTITUTIONALLY ADMINISTERED FINANCIAL AID:** Yes

### DEGREE OR CERTIFICATE PROGRAMS OFFERED

Programs offered do not lead to a degree or other formal award.

### NON-DEGREE-RELATED COURSE TOPICS OFFERED

**Undergraduate**—English language and literature, general; Germanic languages and literatures; anthropology; biochemistry and biophysics; biological sciences/life sciences, other; business; business information and data processing services; business management and administrative services, other; communications, general; computer and information sciences, general; computer software and media applications; construction and building finishers and managers; entrepreneurship; geography; history; information sciences and systems; journalism; journalism and mass communications; liberal arts and sciences, general studies and humanities; marketing management and research; music; nursing; political science and government; psychology; public administration; social work; sociology.
**Graduate**—nursing; public administration; social sciences, general; social work; teacher education, specific academic and vocational programs.

# NORTHERN MICHIGAN UNIVERSITY

*Continuing Education*

1401 Presque Isle Avenue
Marquette, MI 49855
**Contact:** Joe Holman, Distance Education Specialist
**Phone:** 906-227-1683
**Fax:** 906-227-2108
**Web:** http://www.nmu.edu/ce
**E-mail:** jholman@nmu.edu

**ACCREDITATION:** North Central Association of Colleges and Schools

**INSTITUTIONALLY ADMINISTERED FINANCIAL AID:** Yes

### DEGREE OR CERTIFICATE PROGRAMS OFFERED

**Undergraduate**—*BBA:* Management. *BEd:* Elementary Education. *BS:* Social Science/Sociology. *BSW:* Social Work.
**Graduate**—*MBA/MPP:* Criminal Justice. *MN:* Nursing. *MPA:* Public Administration.

### NON-DEGREE-RELATED COURSE TOPICS OFFERED

**Undergraduate**—English composition; English creative writing; English language and literature, general; English technical and business writing; accounting; business; business marketing and marketing management; computer software and media applications; criminal justice and corrections; economics; geography; history; history and philosophy of science and technology; liberal arts and sciences, general studies and humanities; mathematical statistics; mathematics; psychology; social sciences, general; sociology; water transportation workers.

# NORTHERN NEW MEXICO COMMUNITY COLLEGE

921 Paseo de Onate
Espanola, NM 87532
**Contact:** Mr. Mike L. Costello, Enrollment Manager
**Phone:** 505-747-2193
**Fax:** 505-747-2191
**Web:** http://www.nnm.cc.nm.us/
**E-mail:** mikec@nnm.cc.nm.us

**ACCREDITATION:** North Central Association of Colleges and Schools

**INSTITUTIONALLY ADMINISTERED FINANCIAL AID:** Yes

### DEGREE OR CERTIFICATE PROGRAMS OFFERED

Programs offered do not lead to a degree or other formal award.

### NON-DEGREE-RELATED COURSE TOPICS OFFERED

**Undergraduate**—English composition; business administration and management; computer science; computer systems analysis; mathematics, other; psychology; sociology; speech and rhetorical studies.

# NORTHERN OKLAHOMA COLLEGE

PO Box 310
Tonkawa, OK 74653
**Contact:** Debra K. Herren, Instructional Technologist
**Phone:** 580-628-6330
**Fax:** 580-628-6256
**Web:** http://www.north-ok.edu
**E-mail:** dherren@nocaxp.north-ok.edu

**ACCREDITATION:** North Central Association of Colleges and Schools

**INSTITUTIONALLY ADMINISTERED FINANCIAL AID:** Yes

### DEGREE OR CERTIFICATE PROGRAMS OFFERED

Programs offered do not lead to a degree or other formal award.

### NON-DEGREE-RELATED COURSE TOPICS OFFERED

**Undergraduate**—English composition; English creative writing; accounting; geography; sociology.

# NORTHERN STATE UNIVERSITY

*Continuing Education*

1200 South Jay Street
Aberdeen, SD 57401-7198
**Contact:** Peggy Hallstrom, Registrar
**Phone:** 605-626-2012
**Fax:** 605-626-2587
**Web:** http://www.northern.edu
**E-mail:** hallstrp@northern.edu

**ACCREDITATION:** North Central Association of Colleges and Schools

**INSTITUTIONALLY ADMINISTERED FINANCIAL AID:** Yes

### DEGREE OR CERTIFICATE PROGRAMS OFFERED

Programs offered do not lead to a degree or other formal award.

## NON-DEGREE-RELATED COURSE TOPICS OFFERED

**Undergraduate**—English composition; English language and literature, general; Germanic languages and literatures; biological and physical sciences; business; chemistry; computer and information sciences, general; criminology; dramatic/theater arts and stagecraft; economics; educational psychology; foreign languages and literatures; health and physical education/fitness; library science/librarianship; mathematics; mathematics, other; music; sociology.

**Graduate**—education, general; educational psychology.

# NORTHERN VIRGINIA COMMUNITY COLLEGE

*Extended Learning Institute*

8333 Little River Turnpike
Annandale, VA 22003-3796
**Contact:** Jayne Townend, Admissions and Records
**Phone:** 703-323-3368
**Fax:** 703-323-3392
**Web:** http://www.nv.cc.va.us/
**E-mail:** nvtownj@nv.cc.va.us

**ACCREDITATION:** Southern Association of Colleges and Schools
**INSTITUTIONALLY ADMINISTERED FINANCIAL AID:** Yes

## DEGREE OR CERTIFICATE PROGRAMS OFFERED

**Undergraduate**—**AA:** Liberal Arts. **AAS:** Business Management; Business Management, Public Management Specialization; Information Systems Technology. **AS:** Business Administration; Engineering; General Studies. *Certificate:* Health Information Technology.

## NON-DEGREE-RELATED COURSE TOPICS OFFERED

**Undergraduate**—American (United States) history; English composition; English creative writing; French language and literature; Spanish language and literature; accounting; advertising; art history, criticism and conservation; biology, general; business marketing and marketing management; developmental and child psychology; drama/theater arts, general; film/cinema studies; finance, general; geography; journalism; law and legal studies, other; management information systems and business data processing, general; mathematical statistics; mathematics, other; mechanical engineering; organizational behavior studies; philosophy and religion; sociology.

# NORTH GEORGIA COLLEGE & STATE UNIVERSITY

*Distance Learning Services*

329 West Main Street
Dahlonega, GA 30597
**Contact:** Brian McCrary, Student Support Specialist
**Phone:** 706-864-1535
**Fax:** 706-864-1886
**Web:** http://www.ngcsu.edu
**E-mail:** bcmcrary@ngcsu.edu

**ACCREDITATION:** Southern Association of Colleges and Schools
**INSTITUTIONALLY ADMINISTERED FINANCIAL AID:** Yes

## DEGREE OR CERTIFICATE PROGRAMS OFFERED

Programs offered do not lead to a degree or other formal award.

## NON-DEGREE-RELATED COURSE TOPICS OFFERED

**Undergraduate**—Army R.O.T.C.; computer and information sciences, general; engineering, other; foreign languages and literatures; general teacher education; gerontology; international and comparative education; international relations and affairs; military studies; nursing; psychology; sociology; teacher education, specific academic and vocational programs.
**Graduate**—education administration and supervision; educational evaluation, research and statistics; general teacher education; gerontology; international and comparative education; nursing; psychology; public administration; public administration and services, other; sociology; teacher education, specific academic and vocational programs.
**Non-credit**—communications technologies; computer and information sciences, general; computer software and media applications; educational/instructional media design; food products retailing and wholesaling operations; food sciences and technology; foods and nutrition studies; general teacher education; health professions and related sciences, other; institutional food workers and administrators; internet and world wide web; mathematics; military studies; miscellaneous health professions; teacher education, specific academic and vocational programs.

# NORTH IDAHO COLLEGE

1000 West Garden Avenue
Coeur d'Alene, ID 83814
**Contact:** Dr. Candace Wheeler, Director of Distance Education
**Phone:** 208-769-3436
**Fax:** 208-769-7805
**Web:** http://www.nic.edu/
**E-mail:** candace_wheeler@nic.edu

**ACCREDITATION:** Northwest Association of Schools and Colleges
**INSTITUTIONALLY ADMINISTERED FINANCIAL AID:** Yes

## DEGREE OR CERTIFICATE PROGRAMS OFFERED

Programs offered do not lead to a degree or other formal award.

## NON-DEGREE-RELATED COURSE TOPICS OFFERED

**Undergraduate**—American literature (United States); English composition; accounting; anthropology; area, ethnic and cultural studies, other; biology, general; business; chemistry; child care and guidance workers and managers; communications, general; fine arts and art studies; gaming and sports officiating services; health and medical assistants; mathematics; philosophy; political science and government; psychology; sociology.

# NORTH IOWA AREA COMMUNITY COLLEGE

*Evening Credit Division*

500 College Drive
Mason City, IA 50401
**Contact:** Dr. Don Kamps, Evening Dean
**Phone:** 641-422-4326
**Fax:** 641-423-1711
**Web:** http://www.niacc.cc.ia.us/

**E-mail:** kampsdon@niacc.cc.ia.us

**ACCREDITATION:** North Central Association of Colleges and Schools

**INSTITUTIONALLY ADMINISTERED FINANCIAL AID:** Yes

### DEGREE OR CERTIFICATE PROGRAMS OFFERED

Undergraduate—*AA:* Associate of Arts—Pre-Baccalaureate.

### NON-DEGREE-RELATED COURSE TOPICS OFFERED

Undergraduate—English composition; biology, general; business; chemistry; economics; geography; history; mathematics; philosophy; psychology; speech and rhetorical studies; visual and performing arts.
Non-credit—child care and guidance workers and managers; computer software and media applications; nursing; public health.

# NORTH PARK UNIVERSITY

3225 West Foster Avenue
Chicago, IL 60625
**Contact:** Ms. Christy Thomas, Assistant Dean
**Phone:** 773-244-6287
**Web:** http://www.northpark.edu/
**E-mail:** cthomas@northpark.edu

**ACCREDITATION:** North Central Association of Colleges and Schools

**INSTITUTIONALLY ADMINISTERED FINANCIAL AID:** No

### DEGREE OR CERTIFICATE PROGRAMS OFFERED

Programs offered do not lead to a degree or other formal award.

### NON-DEGREE-RELATED COURSE TOPICS OFFERED

Graduate—theological and ministerial studies.
Non-credit—theological and ministerial studies.

# NORTH SEATTLE COMMUNITY COLLEGE

*Distance Learning Office*
9600 College Way, N, 3NC2329A
Seattle, WA 98103
**Contact:** Dr. Tom Braziunas, Distance Learning Manager
**Phone:** 206-527-3619
**Fax:** 206-527-3748
**Web:** http://www.virtualcollege.org
**E-mail:** tbraziun@sccd.ctc.edu

**ACCREDITATION:** Northwest Association of Schools and Colleges

**INSTITUTIONALLY ADMINISTERED FINANCIAL AID:** Yes

### DEGREE OR CERTIFICATE PROGRAMS OFFERED

Undergraduate—*AA:* General Studies.

### NON-DEGREE-RELATED COURSE TOPICS OFFERED

Undergraduate—American literature (United States); English as a second language; English composition; English creative writing; English language and literature, general; accounting; anthropology; area, ethnic and cultural studies, other; astronomy; biological and physical sciences; business; chemistry; child care and guidance workers and managers; computer and information sciences, general; computer programming; computer science; computer systems networking and telecommunications; economics; education, general; environmental health; ethnic and cultural studies; family and community studies; film/video and photographic arts; geological and related sciences; information sciences and systems; international business; internet and world wide web; journalism and mass communication, other; journalism and mass communications; liberal arts and sciences, general studies and humanities; library science, other; marketing management and research; mathematics; mathematics and computer science; mathematics, other; music; philosophy; philosophy and religion; physics; political science and government; psychology; social sciences and history, other; sociology; speech and rhetorical studies; visual and performing arts.
Non-credit—international business; international relations and affairs; marketing management and research; marketing operations/marketing and distribution, other.

# NORTHWEST ARKANSAS COMMUNITY COLLEGE

*Northwest Arkansas Distance Education*
CEF 1225, One College Drive
Bentonville, AR 72712
**Contact:** Mr. Clint Brooks, Distance Learning Coordinator
**Phone:** 501-619-4382
**Fax:** 501-519-4383
**Web:** http://www.nwacc.net/disted
**E-mail:** cbrooks@nwacc.cc.ar.us

**ACCREDITATION:** North Central Association of Colleges and Schools

**INSTITUTIONALLY ADMINISTERED FINANCIAL AID:** Yes

### DEGREE OR CERTIFICATE PROGRAMS OFFERED

Programs offered do not lead to a degree or other formal award.

### NON-DEGREE-RELATED COURSE TOPICS OFFERED

Undergraduate—English composition; English language and literature, general; accounting; agriculture/agricultural sciences; business communications; chemistry; computer and information sciences, other; fine arts and art studies; history; internet and world wide web; mathematics; psychology; sociology.
Non-credit—mathematics, other.

# NORTHWESTERN COLLEGE

*Center for Distance Education*
3003 Snelling Avenue, N
St. Paul, MN 55113
**Contact:** Betty Piper, Student Relations Coordinator
**Phone:** 651-631-5494
**Fax:** 651-631-5133
**Web:** http://www.distance.nwc.edu
**E-mail:** bap@nwc.edu

**ACCREDITATION:** North Central Association of Colleges and Schools

**INSTITUTIONALLY ADMINISTERED FINANCIAL AID:** Yes

## DEGREE OR CERTIFICATE PROGRAMS OFFERED

**Undergraduate—*BA:*** Intercultural Ministries. ***Certificate:*** Certificate in Bible.

## NON-DEGREE-RELATED COURSE TOPICS OFFERED

**Undergraduate—**Greek languages and literatures (modern); archaeology; astronomy; bible/biblical studies; chemistry; ethnic and cultural studies; history; liberal arts and sciences, general studies and humanities; mathematics; missions/missionary studies and missiology; psychology; religion/religious studies.

**See full description on page 442.**

# NORTHWESTERN MICHIGAN COLLEGE

## Distance Education Services

Educational Media Technologies, 1701 East Front Street
Traverse City, MI 49686
**Contact:** Janet Oliver, Director
**Phone:** 231-955-1075
**Fax:** 231-955-1080
**Web:** http://www.nmc.edu/flo/
**E-mail:** joliver@nmc.edu

**ACCREDITATION:** North Central Association of Colleges and Schools
**INSTITUTIONALLY ADMINISTERED FINANCIAL AID:** Yes

## DEGREE OR CERTIFICATE PROGRAMS OFFERED

**Undergraduate—*AAS:*** General Education Transfer Degree. ***AD:*** Nursing. ***Certificate:*** Network Administration; Web Development.

## NON-DEGREE-RELATED COURSE TOPICS OFFERED

**Undergraduate—**American (United States) history; English composition; English creative writing; English technical and business writing; European history; anthropology; biology, general; business administration and management; business communications; business information and data processing services; computer and information sciences, general; computer and information sciences, other; computer programming; computer software and media applications; computer systems networking and telecommunications; criminal justice and corrections; history; internet and world wide web; law and legal studies; mathematics, other; music; nursing; philosophy; psychology, other; sociology.

# NORTHWESTERN STATE UNIVERSITY OF LOUISIANA

Electronic Learning, 203 Roy Hall
Natchitoches, LA 71497
**Contact:** Mrs. Darlene Williams, Electronic Learning Systems Coordinator
**Phone:** 318-357-6355
**Fax:** 318-357-5573
**Web:** http://www.nsula.edu/ensu
**E-mail:** darlene@alpha.nsula.edu

**ACCREDITATION:** Southern Association of Colleges and Schools
**INSTITUTIONALLY ADMINISTERED FINANCIAL AID:** Yes

## DEGREE OR CERTIFICATE PROGRAMS OFFERED

**Undergraduate—*AA:*** Criminal Justice. ***AGS:*** General Studies. ***BSN:*** Nursing. ***BSRS:*** Radiologic Technology.
**Graduate—*MA:*** Adult Education. ***MAE:*** Educational Technology.

## NON-DEGREE-RELATED COURSE TOPICS OFFERED

**Undergraduate—**English composition; English creative writing; English language and literature, general; English technical and business writing; accounting; business administration and management; chemistry; computer and information sciences, general; computer software and media applications; criminal justice and corrections; education, other; educational/instructional media design; fine arts and art studies; general teacher education; history; journalism and mass communications; library science, other; marketing management and research; mathematics; nursing; physical sciences, general; psychology; social work.
**Graduate—**education administration and supervision; education, other; educational evaluation, research and statistics; educational psychology; educational/instructional media design; psychology; special education.

# NORTHWESTERN TECHNICAL COLLEGE

265 Bicentennial Trail
Rock Springs, GA 30739
**Contact:** Darryl Harrison, Dean of Distance Education
**Phone:** 706-764-3593
**Fax:** 706-764-3566
**Web:** http://www.nwtcollege.org
**E-mail:** dharriso@nwtcollege.org

**ACCREDITATION:** Southern Association of Colleges and Schools
**INSTITUTIONALLY ADMINISTERED FINANCIAL AID:** No

## DEGREE OR CERTIFICATE PROGRAMS OFFERED

**Undergraduate—*Certificate:*** Medical Coding; Microsoft Officer User Specialist.

# NORTHWEST IOWA COMMUNITY COLLEGE

## ICN Office

603 West Park Street
Sheldon, IA 51250
**Contact:** Colette W. Scott, ICN Coordinator
**Phone:** 712-324-5061
**Fax:** 712-324-4136
**Web:** http://www.nwicc.cc.ia.us
**E-mail:** cscott@nwicc.cc.ia.us

**ACCREDITATION:** North Central Association of Colleges and Schools
**INSTITUTIONALLY ADMINISTERED FINANCIAL AID:** Yes

## DEGREE OR CERTIFICATE PROGRAMS OFFERED

Programs offered do not lead to a degree or other formal award.

## NON-DEGREE-RELATED COURSE TOPICS OFFERED

**Undergraduate—**American literature (United States); English composition; English creative writing; English language and literature, general;

business/managerial economics; educational psychology; foreign languages and literatures; history; mathematical statistics; psychology; psychology, other; social psychology; social sciences and history, other; social sciences, general; sociology; speech and rhetorical studies.

# NORTHWEST MISSOURI STATE UNIVERSITY

*Center for Information Technology in Education*
OL 246
Maryville, MO 64468
**Contact:** Dr. Roger Lee Von Holzen, Director of Center for Information Technology in Education
**Phone:** 660-562-1532
**Fax:** 660-562-2153
**Web:** http://www.NorthwestOnline.org
**E-mail:** rvh@mail.nwmissouri.edu

**ACCREDITATION:** North Central Association of Colleges and Schools
**INSTITUTIONALLY ADMINISTERED FINANCIAL AID:** Yes

eCollege.com  *www.ecollege.com*

**DEGREE OR CERTIFICATE PROGRAMS OFFERED**
**Undergraduate—BS:** Accounting; Business Management.

**NON-DEGREE-RELATED COURSE TOPICS OFFERED**
**Undergraduate—**American (United States) history; drama/theater arts, general; earth and planetary sciences; geography.

# NORTHWEST TECHNICAL COLLEGE

*Distance Education*
150 2nd Street, SW, Suite B, Box 309
Perham, MN 56573
**Contact:** Ms. Linda Cordell, Administrative Assistant
**Phone:** 218-347-6225
**Fax:** 218-347-6210
**Web:** http://www.ntc-online.com/distance
**E-mail:** linda.cordell@mail.ntc.mnscu.edu

**ACCREDITATION:** North Central Association of Colleges and Schools
**INSTITUTIONALLY ADMINISTERED FINANCIAL AID:** Yes

**DEGREE OR CERTIFICATE PROGRAMS OFFERED**
**Undergraduate—AAS:** Microcomputer and Network Technology.

# NORWICH UNIVERSITY

*New College / Vermont College Graduate Program Online*
36 College Street
Montpelier, VT 05602
**Contact:** Ms. Margaret L. Harmon, Co-Director of Admissions
**Phone:** 802-828-8804

**Fax:** 802-828-8855
**Web:** http://www.norwich.edu/vermontcollege
**E-mail:** harmonm@norwich.edu

**ACCREDITATION:** New England Association of Schools and Colleges
**INSTITUTIONALLY ADMINISTERED FINANCIAL AID:** Yes

**DEGREE OR CERTIFICATE PROGRAMS OFFERED**
**Undergraduate—BA:** Liberal Arts.
**Graduate—CAGS:** Graduate Study. **MA:** Art Therapy; Liberal Arts. **MEd:** Education. **MFA:** Visual Art; Writing.
**See full description on page 444.**

# NOVA SOUTHEASTERN UNIVERSITY

*Masters in Clinical Vision Research*
3200 South University Drive
Ft. Lauderdale, FL 33328
**Contact:** Dr. Josephine Shallo-Hoffman, Chair, Research and Graduate Programs
**Phone:** 954-262-1464
**Fax:** 954-262-3875
**Web:** http://www.nova.edu/optometry
**E-mail:** shoffman@nova.edu

**ACCREDITATION:** Southern Association of Colleges and Schools
**INSTITUTIONALLY ADMINISTERED FINANCIAL AID:** Yes

**DEGREE OR CERTIFICATE PROGRAMS OFFERED**
**Graduate—MS:** Clinical Vision Research.

**NON-DEGREE-RELATED COURSE TOPICS OFFERED**
**Graduate—**data processing technology; educational evaluation, research and statistics; health professions and related sciences, other; medical clinical sciences (M.S., Ph.D.).

# NOVA SOUTHEASTERN UNIVERSITY

*Wayne Huizenga Graduate School of Business and Entrepreneurship*
3100 Southwest 9th Avenue
Fort Lauderdale, FL 33315
**Contact:** Mr. Steven Harvey, Director of Marketing
**Phone:** 800-672-7223 Ext. 5047
**Web:** http://www.huizenga.nova.edu
**E-mail:** harvey@huizenga.nova.edu

**ACCREDITATION:** Southern Association of Colleges and Schools
**INSTITUTIONALLY ADMINISTERED FINANCIAL AID:** Yes

**DEGREE OR CERTIFICATE PROGRAMS OFFERED**
**Graduate—MBA:** Business Administration. **MBA/M Acc:** Accounting. **MPA:** Public Administration.

## NON-DEGREE-RELATED COURSE TOPICS OFFERED

**Graduate**—accounting; business management and administrative services, other; financial management and services; marketing management and research.

**See full description on page 446.**

# NYACK COLLEGE

1 South Boulevard
Nyack, NY 10960
**Contact:** Office of the Registrar
**Phone:** 845-358-1710 Ext. 121
**Fax:** 845-353-6429
**Web:** http://www.nyackcollege.edu/
**E-mail:** enroll@nyack.edu

**ACCREDITATION:** Middle States Association of Colleges and Schools

eCollege.com *www.ecollege.com*

## DEGREE OR CERTIFICATE PROGRAMS OFFERED

Programs offered do not lead to a degree or other formal award.

# OHIO NORTHERN UNIVERSITY

*Raabe College of Pharmacy*

525 South Main Street
Ada, OH 45810
**Contact:** Dr. Karen Kier, Director of Non-Traditional Pharm.D Program
**Phone:** 419-772-2307
**Fax:** 419-772-1917
**Web:** http://www.onu.edu/pharmacy/ntpd/default.asp
**E-mail:** k-kier@onu.edu

**ACCREDITATION:** North Central Association of Colleges and Schools
**INSTITUTIONALLY ADMINISTERED FINANCIAL AID:** No

## DEGREE OR CERTIFICATE PROGRAMS OFFERED

**Postgraduate and doctoral**—*PharmD:* Pharmacy.

## NON-DEGREE-RELATED COURSE TOPICS OFFERED

**Graduate**—pharmacy.

# OHIO UNIVERSITY

*Independent Study*

302 Tupper Hall
Athens, OH 45701
**Contact:** Independent and Distance Learning Programs
**Phone:** 800-444-2910
**Fax:** 740-593-2901
**Web:** http://www.ohiou.edu/independent/
**E-mail:** independent.study@ohio.edu

**ACCREDITATION:** North Central Association of Colleges and Schools
**INSTITUTIONALLY ADMINISTERED FINANCIAL AID:** Yes

## DEGREE OR CERTIFICATE PROGRAMS OFFERED

**Undergraduate**—*AA:* Arts and Humanities; Social Sciences. *AIS:* Individualized Studies. *AS:* Mathematics; Natural Science.
**Graduate**—*MBA/MPA:* Specialized Studies.

## NON-DEGREE-RELATED COURSE TOPICS OFFERED

**Undergraduate**—American literature (United States); English composition; English creative writing; English language and literature, general; English technical and business writing; accounting; administrative and secretarial services; anthropology; biological and physical sciences; biology, general; business; chemistry; communications, general; criminology; developmental and child psychology; economics; educational psychology; foreign languages and literatures; geography; history; human resources management; journalism; journalism and mass communications; marketing management and research; mathematics; philosophy and religion; psychology; sociology; tourism and travel services marketing operations; women's studies.

**See full description on page 448.**

# OHLONE COLLEGE

*Learning Resources and Instructional Technology Division*

43600 Mission Boulevard
Fremont, CA 94539-5884
**Contact:** Dr. Shirley S. Peck, Dean
**Phone:** 510-659-6166
**Fax:** 510-659-6265
**Web:** http://online.ohlone.cc.ca.us/
**E-mail:** speck@ohlone.cc.ca.us

**ACCREDITATION:** Western Association of Schools and Colleges
**INSTITUTIONALLY ADMINISTERED FINANCIAL AID:** Yes

## DEGREE OR CERTIFICATE PROGRAMS OFFERED

Programs offered do not lead to a degree or other formal award.

## NON-DEGREE-RELATED COURSE TOPICS OFFERED

**Undergraduate**—English as a second language; English composition; anthropology; business administration and management; computer science; fine arts and art studies; foods and nutrition studies; foreign languages and literatures; geography; journalism and mass communication, other; library science, other; photography; physical therapy; sociology; speech and rhetorical studies.

# OKALOOSA-WALTON COMMUNITY COLLEGE

*Distance Learning*

1170 Martin Luther King Jr. Boulevard
Fort Walton Beach, FL 32547
**Contact:** Mrs. Wanda C. Edwards, Coordinator of Distance Learning
**Phone:** 850-863-0701
**Fax:** 850-863-6560
**Web:** http://www.owcc.cc.fl.us

**E-mail:** edwardsw@owcc.net

**ACCREDITATION:** Southern Association of Colleges and Schools

**INSTITUTIONALLY ADMINISTERED FINANCIAL AID:** Yes

## DEGREE OR CERTIFICATE PROGRAMS OFFERED
Programs offered do not lead to a degree or other formal award.

## NON-DEGREE-RELATED COURSE TOPICS OFFERED
**Undergraduate**—English composition; accounting; biology, general; business communications; chemistry; computer and information sciences, general; criminal justice and corrections; economics; educational psychology; general retailing and wholesaling operations and skills; internet and world wide web; philosophy; physical sciences, general; political science and government; psychology; quality control and safety technologies; sociology.

# OKLAHOMA CITY COMMUNITY COLLEGE
*Distance Education*
7777 South May Avenue
Oklahoma City, OK 73159
**Contact:** Ms. Glenda Kay Prince, Coordinator of Distance Education
**Phone:** 405-682-1611 Ext. 7424
**Fax:** 405-685-8399
**Web:** http://www.okc.cc.ok.us/distanced
**E-mail:** gprince@okc.cc.ok.us

**ACCREDITATION:** North Central Association of Colleges and Schools

**INSTITUTIONALLY ADMINISTERED FINANCIAL AID:** Yes

## DEGREE OR CERTIFICATE PROGRAMS OFFERED
Programs offered do not lead to a degree or other formal award.

## NON-DEGREE-RELATED COURSE TOPICS OFFERED
**Undergraduate**—American literature (United States); English composition; English language and literature, general; accounting; astronomy; biological and physical sciences; biology, general; business; business administration and management; business communications; business/managerial economics; child care and guidance workers and managers; computer science; developmental and child psychology; economics; geography; geological and related sciences; history; law and legal studies, other; liberal arts and sciences, general studies and humanities; marketing operations/marketing and distribution, other; mathematical statistics; mathematics; music; philosophy; philosophy and religion; physical sciences, general; political science and government; psychology; sociology.

# OKLAHOMA CITY UNIVERSITY
*Program in Prior Learning and University Studies*
2501 North Blackwelder
Oklahoma City, OK 73106
**Contact:** Bill Jacquemain, Admissions Counselor and Recruiter
**Phone:** 405-521-5292
**Web:** http://www.okcu.edu/plus

**E-mail:** plus@okcu.edu

**ACCREDITATION:** North Central Association of Colleges and Schools

**INSTITUTIONALLY ADMINISTERED FINANCIAL AID:** Yes

## DEGREE OR CERTIFICATE PROGRAMS OFFERED
Programs offered do not lead to a degree or other formal award.

## NON-DEGREE-RELATED COURSE TOPICS OFFERED
**Undergraduate**—business; communications, general; fine arts and art studies; liberal arts and sciences, general studies and humanities; social sciences, general.

# OKLAHOMA STATE UNIVERSITY
*Distance Learning*
Independent and Correspondence Study, 470 Student Union
Stillwater, OK 74078
**Contact:** Cecilia Boardman, Senior Office Assistant
**Phone:** 405-744-6390
**Fax:** 405-744-7793
**Web:** http://www.okstate.edu/outreach/distance
**E-mail:** ics-inf@okstate.edu

**ACCREDITATION:** North Central Association of Colleges and Schools

**INSTITUTIONALLY ADMINISTERED FINANCIAL AID:** Yes

## DEGREE OR CERTIFICATE PROGRAMS OFFERED
**Graduate**—*MAg:* Agricultural Education. *MBA:* Business Administration. *MS:* Agricultural Education; Computer Science; Control Systems Engineering; Electrical Engineering; Engineering Technology Management; Environmental Science/Management; Fire and Emergency Management Administration; Telecommunications Management.

## NON-DEGREE-RELATED COURSE TOPICS OFFERED
**Undergraduate**—American (United States) history; English composition; English creative writing; English technical and business writing; French language and literature; Spanish language and literature; accounting; agricultural economics; agriculture/agricultural sciences, other; animal sciences; anthropology; business administration and management; business communications; business marketing and marketing management; chemical engineering; communication disorders sciences and services; counseling psychology; developmental and child psychology; economics; education, other; educational psychology; electrical and electronic engineering-related technology; engineering science; family and community studies; finance, general; fire science/firefighting; foods and nutrition studies; foreign languages and literatures; geography; geological and related sciences; health and physical education/fitness; history; horticulture services operations and management; individual and family development studies; journalism; law and legal studies, other; management information systems and business data processing, general; mathematical statistics; mathematics, other; music; organizational behavior studies; philosophy; political science and government; psychology; sociology.
**Graduate**—chemical engineering; educational evaluation, research and statistics; electrical, electronics and communication engineering; environmental/environmental health engineering; fire science/firefighting; industrial/manufacturing engineering; mechanical engineering.
**Non-credit**—English technical and business writing; communications, other; community health services; computer programming; fire protection; real estate; special education.

# OLD DOMINION UNIVERSITY

*Office of Distance Learning and Extended Education*

Gornto TELETECHNET Center
Norfolk, VA 23529
**Contact:** Dr. Jeanie Kline, Director of Distance Learning Operations
**Phone:** 757-683-3163
**Fax:** 757-683-5492
**Web:** http://www.odu.edu/
**E-mail:** jkline@odu.edu

**ACCREDITATION:** Southern Association of Colleges and Schools

**INSTITUTIONALLY ADMINISTERED FINANCIAL AID:** Yes

## DEGREE OR CERTIFICATE PROGRAMS OFFERED

**Undergraduate—*BA:*** Criminal Justice. ***BS:*** Computer Science; Criminal Justice; Education -Teacher Preparation; Human Services Counseling; Occupational and Technical Studies. ***BSBA:*** Business Administration. ***BSET:*** Civil Engineering Technology; Electrical Engineering Technology; Mechanical Engineering Technology. ***BSN:*** Nursing.
**Graduate—*MBA/M Acc:*** Taxation. ***MEM:*** Engineering Management. ***MS:*** Education—Pre K Through 6; Occupational and Technical Studies; Special Education. ***MSN:*** Leadership in Nursing and Health Care Systems.

## NON-DEGREE-RELATED COURSE TOPICS OFFERED

**Undergraduate**—accounting; business communications; business information and data processing services; business marketing and marketing management; business quantitative methods and management science; business/managerial economics; communications, general; community health services; computer and information sciences, general; computer science; computer systems networking and telecommunications; criminal justice and corrections; education, other; engineering-related technologies, other; finance, general; industrial and organizational psychology; journalism; management information systems and business data processing, general; nursing; philosophy; social psychology; sociology.
**Graduate**—accounting; aerospace, aeronautical and astronautical engineering; business marketing and marketing management; education, other; electrical, electronics and communication engineering; engineering/industrial management; environmental/environmental health engineering; finance, general; management information systems and business data processing, general; mechanical engineering; nursing.

**See full description on page 450.**

# OLIVET NAZARENE UNIVERSITY

*School of Graduate and Adult Studies*

PO Box 592
Kankakee, IL 60901
**Contact:** Kim Johnston, Programs Specialist
**Phone:** 815-939-5184
**Fax:** 815-939-5390
**Web:** http://www.olivet.edu
**E-mail:** kjohnsto@olivet.edu

**ACCREDITATION:** North Central Association of Colleges and Schools

**INSTITUTIONALLY ADMINISTERED FINANCIAL AID:** Yes

## DEGREE OR CERTIFICATE PROGRAMS OFFERED

**Graduate—*MEd:*** Education.

## NON-DEGREE-RELATED COURSE TOPICS OFFERED

**Graduate**—curriculum and instruction.

# OLYMPIC COLLEGE

Media Services and Distance Learning, 1600 Chester Avenue
Bremerton, WA 98337-1699
**Contact:** Ms. Cara J. Corkill, Media Assistant
**Phone:** 360-475-7773
**Fax:** 360-475-7775
**Web:** http://www.oc.ctc.edu
**E-mail:** ccorkill@oc.ctc.edu

**ACCREDITATION:** Northwest Association of Schools and Colleges

**INSTITUTIONALLY ADMINISTERED FINANCIAL AID:** Yes

## DEGREE OR CERTIFICATE PROGRAMS OFFERED

Programs offered do not lead to a degree or other formal award.

## NON-DEGREE-RELATED COURSE TOPICS OFFERED

**Undergraduate**—English creative writing; English language and literature/letters, other; accounting; anthropology; business communications; business/managerial economics; child care and guidance workers and managers; computer and information sciences, general; economics; fine arts and art studies; history; liberal arts and sciences, general studies and humanities; mathematics; political science and government; psychology, other; radio and television broadcasting; sociology.

# OPEN LEARNING AGENCY

*Career and College Prep./College Courses and Programs/B.C. Open University Courses and Programs*

Box 82080
Burnaby, BC V5C 6J8, Canada
**Contact:** Ms. Kristine Smalcel Pederson, Supervisor, Admissions and Education Information
**Phone:** 604-431-3300
**Fax:** 604-431-3444
**Web:** http://www.ola.ca
**E-mail:** student@ola.bc.ca

**ACCREDITATION:** Provincially Chartered

**INSTITUTIONALLY ADMINISTERED FINANCIAL AID:** Yes

## DEGREE OR CERTIFICATE PROGRAMS OFFERED

**Undergraduate—*AA:*** General Studies. ***AS:*** General Studies. ***BA:*** Fine Arts; General Program; General Studies; Major Program; Music Therapy; Music, Jazz Studies; Music, Performance. ***BBA:*** Business Administration; Business Administration, Public Sector Management Option. ***BGS:*** General Studies. ***BHS:*** Physiotherapy; Psychiatric Nursing; Respiratory Therapy. ***BS:*** Business in Real Estate; Design; General Program; Major Program; Tourism Management. ***BST:*** Computing; Technology Management.

# ORAL ROBERTS UNIVERSITY

Adult Learning Service Center, 7777 South Lewis Avenue
Tulsa, OK 74171
**Contact:** Mrs. Kathryn Neal, Assistant Director of Adult Learning Service Center
**Phone:** 800-643-7976
**Fax:** 918-495-7965
**Web:** http://www.oru.edu/
**E-mail:** kneal@oru.edu

**ACCREDITATION:** North Central Association of Colleges and Schools
**INSTITUTIONALLY ADMINISTERED FINANCIAL AID:** No

eCollege.com   www.ecollege.com

## DEGREE OR CERTIFICATE PROGRAMS OFFERED

**Undergraduate—BS:** Business Administration; Christian Care and Counseling; Church Ministries; Elementary Education with Certification; Liberal Studies. **Certificate:** Non-Profit Management; Theology.

**Graduate—MA:** Practical Theology. **MAE:** Christian School Administration; Christian School Curriculum; Christian School Post-secondary Administration; Christian School Teaching; Early Childhood Education; Teaching English as a Second Language (TESL). **MAM:** Non-Profit Management. **MDiv:** Divinity.

**Postgraduate and doctoral—DMin:** Ministry. **EdD:** Christian School Administration (Post-secondary); Christian School Administration (PK-12); Public School Administration.

## NON-DEGREE-RELATED COURSE TOPICS OFFERED

**Non-credit—**bible/biblical studies; theological and ministerial studies.

### Special Note

At Oral Roberts University (ORU), "Into Every Person's World" means enabling students to reach their educational goals wherever they live. ORU's External Academic Degree Program offers Bachelor of Science degrees via correspondence in business administration, church ministries, Christian care and counseling, and liberal studies.

For those interested in teaching, ORU's School of Education offers a Bachelor of Science in elementary education. Students complete two thirds of the degree through independent study and the remaining third by attending short sessions on campus 3 times per year.

With Prior Learning Assessment, students in any of the above programs can earn college credit for learning on the job or in other situations. Transferring credits from another accredited institution and credit by examination are additional ways to earn credit.

Graduate degrees increase professional marketability. ORU offers the following through combinations of modular, correspondence, and Internet study: Master of Management (concentration in non-profit management), Master of Divinity, Master of Arts in practical theology, Master of Arts in Education (concentrations in Christian school teaching, Christian school curriculum, Christian school postsecondary administration, Christian school administration, teaching English as a second language (TESL), and early childhood education), Doctor of Ministry, and Doctor of Education in educational leadership (concentrations in Christian school administration (PK–12), Christian school administration (postsecondary), and public school administration).

For information on distance education degrees, residential study, or campus visits, students should contact ORU at 800-643-7976 (toll-free) or http://www.oru.edu.

# ORANGEBURG-CALHOUN TECHNICAL COLLEGE

3250 St. Matthews Road
Orangeburg, SC 29115
**Contact:** Mike Hammond, Dean
**Phone:** 803-535-1267
**Fax:** 803-535-1388
**Web:** http://www.octech.org/
**E-mail:** hammondm@org.tec.sc.us

**ACCREDITATION:** Southern Association of Colleges and Schools
**INSTITUTIONALLY ADMINISTERED FINANCIAL AID:** Yes

## DEGREE OR CERTIFICATE PROGRAMS OFFERED
Programs offered do not lead to a degree or other formal award.

## NON-DEGREE-RELATED COURSE TOPICS OFFERED

**Undergraduate—**English composition; English literature (British and Commonwealth); English technical and business writing; business; computer systems networking and telecommunications; computer/information technology administration and management; criminal justice and corrections; economics; history; mathematics; psychology; sociology.

# ORANGE COAST COLLEGE

2701 Fairview Road
Costa Mesa, CA 92626
**Contact:** Dr. Nancy Kidder, Administrative Dean, Admissions and Records and International Programs
**Phone:** 714-432-0202
**Web:** http://www.orangecoastcollege.com
**E-mail:** nkidder@mail.occ.cccd.edu

**ACCREDITATION:** Western Association of Schools and Colleges
**INSTITUTIONALLY ADMINISTERED FINANCIAL AID:** Yes

## DEGREE OR CERTIFICATE PROGRAMS OFFERED
Programs offered do not lead to a degree or other formal award.

## NON-DEGREE-RELATED COURSE TOPICS OFFERED

**Undergraduate—**English composition; business management and administrative services, other; computer programming; computer software and media applications; computer/information technology administration and management; electrical and electronics equipment installers and repairers; foods and nutrition studies; music.

# OREGON HEALTH & SCIENCE UNIVERSITY
*School of Nursing*
OHSU SON 4N, 3181 Southwest Sam Jackson Park Road
Portland, OR 97201

**Contact:** Gabrielle M. Petersen, Academic Program Counselor
**Phone:** 503-494-3805
**Fax:** 503-494-3691
**Web:** http://www.ohsu.edu/son
**E-mail:** petersen@ohsu.edu

**ACCREDITATION:** Northwest Association of Schools and Colleges

**INSTITUTIONALLY ADMINISTERED FINANCIAL AID:** Yes

eCollege.com  www.ecollege.com

### DEGREE OR CERTIFICATE PROGRAMS OFFERED

**Undergraduate—*BSN:*** Nursing.

# OREGON STATE UNIVERSITY

## Distance and Continuing Education

4943 The Valley Library
Corvallis, OR 97331-4504
**Contact:** Student Services
**Phone:** 800-235-6559
**Fax:** 541-737-2734
**Web:** http://statewide.orst.edu
**E-mail:** ostateu@orst.edu

**ACCREDITATION:** Northwest Association of Schools and Colleges

**INSTITUTIONALLY ADMINISTERED FINANCIAL AID:** Yes

### DEGREE OR CERTIFICATE PROGRAMS OFFERED

**Undergraduate—*BA:*** Liberal Studies. ***BS:*** Environmental Sciences; General Agriculture; Liberal Studies; Natural Resources.
**Graduate—*MS:*** Nutrition and Food Management.

### NON-DEGREE-RELATED COURSE TOPICS OFFERED

**Undergraduate—**American (United States) history; American literature (United States); English composition; English creative writing; English language and literature, general; English technical and business writing; European history; Spanish language and literature; agricultural business and management; agricultural economics; agriculture/agricultural sciences; agriculture/agricultural sciences, other; anthropology; area, ethnic and cultural studies, other; atmospheric sciences and meteorology; biology, general; botany; cell and molecular biology; chemistry; communications, general; conservation and renewable natural resources, other; developmental and child psychology; ecology; economics; education, general; environmental science/studies; fishing and fisheries sciences and management; forestry and related sciences; forestry, general; geological and related sciences; health system/health services administration; history; history and philosophy of science and technology; liberal arts and sciences, general studies and humanities; mathematical statistics; mathematics, other; natural resources conservation; natural resources management and protective services; oceanography; philosophy; philosophy and religion; plant sciences; political science and government; psychology; public health; social sciences and history, other; sociology; soil sciences; wildlife and wildlands management; women's studies.
**Graduate—**adult and continuing teacher education; agriculture/agricultural sciences; education administration and supervision; education, general; environmental/environmental health engineering; fishing and fisheries sciences and management; foods and nutrition studies; health and medical administrative services; health system/health services administration; natural resources conservation; wildlife and wildlands management.

**See full description on page 452.**

# OTERO JUNIOR COLLEGE

1802 Colorado
La Junta, CO 81050
**Contact:** Dr. Thomas J. Armstrong, Vice President for Instruction
**Phone:** 719-384-6884
**Fax:** 719-384-6935
**E-mail:** tom.armstrong@ojc.cccoes.edu

**ACCREDITATION:** North Central Association of Colleges and Schools

**INSTITUTIONALLY ADMINISTERED FINANCIAL AID:** Yes

eCollege.com  www.ecollege.com

### DEGREE OR CERTIFICATE PROGRAMS OFFERED

**Programs offered do not lead to a degree or other formal award.**

### NON-DEGREE-RELATED COURSE TOPICS OFFERED

**Undergraduate—**English composition; accounting; business marketing and marketing management; law and legal studies, other; management information systems and business data processing, general; mathematics, other; social psychology; sociology; women's studies.

# OTTAWA UNIVERSITY

## Kansas City Campus

20 Corporate Woods, 10865 Grandview Drive
Overland Park, KS 66210
**Contact:** Karen Adams, Enrollment Manager
**Phone:** 888-404-6852
**Fax:** 913-451-0806
**Web:** http://www.ottawa.edu
**E-mail:** adamsk@ottawa.edu

**ACCREDITATION:** North Central Association of Colleges and Schools

**INSTITUTIONALLY ADMINISTERED FINANCIAL AID:** Yes

### DEGREE OR CERTIFICATE PROGRAMS OFFERED

**Undergraduate—*BA:*** Management of Health Services.
**Graduate—*MA:*** Human Resources. ***MBA:*** Business Administration.

### NON-DEGREE-RELATED COURSE TOPICS OFFERED

**Undergraduate—**health system/health services administration.

**See full description on page 454.**

# OUACHITA TECHNICAL COLLEGE

PO Box 816, 1 College Circle
Malvern, AR 72104
**Contact:** Ms. Linda Johnson, Dean for Enrollment Management and Registrar
**Phone:** 501-332-3658 Ext. 1118

**Fax:** 501-337-9382
**Web:** http://www.otcweb.org
**E-mail:** lindaj@otcweb.org

**ACCREDITATION:** North Central Association of Colleges and Schools
**INSTITUTIONALLY ADMINISTERED FINANCIAL AID:** Yes

### DEGREE OR CERTIFICATE PROGRAMS OFFERED
Programs offered do not lead to a degree or other formal award.

### NON-DEGREE-RELATED COURSE TOPICS OFFERED
**Undergraduate**—English composition; computer and information sciences, general; computer systems networking and telecommunications; earth and planetary sciences; environmental science/studies; internet and world wide web; labor/personnel relations and studies; mathematics; philosophy; psychology; sociology.

## OWENS COMMUNITY COLLEGE
*Center for Development and Training*
PO Box 10000, AVCC 152
Toledo, OH 43699-1947
**Contact:** Dr. Ron Skulas, Alternative Learning Coordinator
**Phone:** 419-661-7061
**Fax:** 419-661-7801
**Web:** http://www.owens.cc.oh.us/
**E-mail:** rskulas@owens.cc.oh.us

**ACCREDITATION:** North Central Association of Colleges and Schools
**INSTITUTIONALLY ADMINISTERED FINANCIAL AID:** Yes

### DEGREE OR CERTIFICATE PROGRAMS OFFERED
**Undergraduate**—*AAB:* E-Business Technology. *Certificate:* Supervision.

### NON-DEGREE-RELATED COURSE TOPICS OFFERED
**Undergraduate**—English composition; accounting; business; business information and data processing services; child care and guidance workers and managers; communications, general; computer and information sciences, general; economics; entrepreneurship; environmental/environmental health engineering; foreign languages and literatures; history; human resources management; internet and world wide web; journalism and mass communications; liberal arts and sciences, general studies and humanities; mathematics; philosophy; psychology; sociology.

## OZARKS TECHNICAL COMMUNITY COLLEGE
PO Box 5958
Springfield, MO 65801
**Contact:** Shirley Lawler, Dean of Academic Services
**Web:** http://www.otc.cc.mo.us/
**E-mail:** slawler@otc.cc.mo.us

**ACCREDITATION:** North Central Association of Colleges and Schools
**INSTITUTIONALLY ADMINISTERED FINANCIAL AID:** Yes

### DEGREE OR CERTIFICATE PROGRAMS OFFERED
Programs offered do not lead to a degree or other formal award.

### NON-DEGREE-RELATED COURSE TOPICS OFFERED
**Undergraduate**—English composition; biochemistry and biophysics; biological and physical sciences; communications, general; history; liberal arts and sciences, general studies and humanities; mathematics; political science and government.

## PACIFIC GRADUATE SCHOOL OF PSYCHOLOGY
*Master's Degree (M.S.) in Psychology*
940 East Meadow Drive
Palo Alto, CA 94303
**Contact:** Ms. Tonaka Kendrick, Admissions Coordinator
**Phone:** 800-818-6136
**Fax:** 650-493-6147
**Web:** http://www.pgsp.edu/njdistance.htm
**E-mail:** t.kendrick@pgsp.edu

**ACCREDITATION:** Western Association of Schools and Colleges
**INSTITUTIONALLY ADMINISTERED FINANCIAL AID:** Yes

### DEGREE OR CERTIFICATE PROGRAMS OFFERED
**Graduate**—*MS:* Psychology.

### NON-DEGREE-RELATED COURSE TOPICS OFFERED
**Graduate**—psychology.

## PACIFIC OAKS COLLEGE
*Distance Learning*
5 Westmoreland Place
Pasadena, CA 91103
**Contact:** Betty Jones, Director of Distance Learning
**Phone:** 626-397-1320
**Fax:** 626-397-1380
**Web:** http://www.pacificoaks.edu
**E-mail:** bjones@pacificoaks.edu

**ACCREDITATION:** Western Association of Schools and Colleges
**INSTITUTIONALLY ADMINISTERED FINANCIAL AID:** Yes

### DEGREE OR CERTIFICATE PROGRAMS OFFERED
**Undergraduate**—*BA:* Human Development.
**Graduate**—*MA:* Human Development. *MCM:* Early Childhood Education; Human Development.

## PALO ALTO COLLEGE
*Extended Services*
1400 West Villaret
San Antonio, TX 78224
**Contact:** Mr. Robert L. Garza, Director of Distance Learning
**Phone:** 210-921-5494
**Fax:** 210-921-5328
**Web:** http://www.accd.edu/pac

**E-mail:** robogarz@accd.edu

**ACCREDITATION:** Southern Association of Colleges and Schools

**INSTITUTIONALLY ADMINISTERED FINANCIAL AID:** Yes

### DEGREE OR CERTIFICATE PROGRAMS OFFERED

Programs offered do not lead to a degree or other formal award.

### NON-DEGREE-RELATED COURSE TOPICS OFFERED

**Undergraduate**—American (United States) history; American literature (United States); English composition; accounting; agricultural economics; biology, general; business administration and management; chemistry; communications, general; computer and information sciences, general; computer science; criminal justice and corrections; economics; health and physical education/fitness; mathematics; political science and government; psychology; sociology.

# THE PARALEGAL INSTITUTE, INC.

2933 West Indian School Road, Drawer 11408
Phoenix, AZ 85061-1408
**Contact:** Christine Jasinski, Director of Operations
**Phone:** 602-212-0501
**Fax:** 602-212-0502
**Web:** http://www.theparalegalinstitute.com/
**E-mail:** paralegalinst@mindspring.com

**ACCREDITATION:** Distance Education and Training Council

**INSTITUTIONALLY ADMINISTERED FINANCIAL AID:** No

### DEGREE OR CERTIFICATE PROGRAMS OFFERED

**Undergraduate**—*AA:* Paralegal.

### NON-DEGREE-RELATED COURSE TOPICS OFFERED

**Undergraduate**—English composition; English creative writing; business administration and management; business management and administrative services, other; mathematics; psychology.

# PARKLAND COLLEGE

*Distance Education*
2400 West Bradley Avenue
Champaign, IL 61821
**Contact:** Haiti Eastin, Program Coordinator
**Phone:** 217-353-2342
**Fax:** 217-353-2241
**Web:** http://online.parkland.cc.il.us
**E-mail:** heastin@parkland.cc.il.us

**ACCREDITATION:** North Central Association of Colleges and Schools

**INSTITUTIONALLY ADMINISTERED FINANCIAL AID:** Yes

### DEGREE OR CERTIFICATE PROGRAMS OFFERED

**Undergraduate**—*AA:* Mass Communication: Advertising/Public Relations; Mass Communications (Journalism); Psychology. *AAS:* Business Management. *AGS:* General Studies. *AS:* Business Administration; Business Education.

### NON-DEGREE-RELATED COURSE TOPICS OFFERED

**Undergraduate**—American (United States) history; English composition; accounting; adult and continuing teacher education; anatomy; anthropology; art history, criticism and conservation; biology, general; business marketing and marketing management; developmental and child psychology; drama/theater arts, general; earth and planetary sciences; journalism; journalism and mass communication, other; law and legal studies, other; mathematical statistics; mathematics, other; social psychology; sociology.

# PARK UNIVERSITY

*School for Extended Learning*
Distance Learning, 778 Radian Drive
Heath, OH 43056
**Contact:** Ms. Cathy Beatty, Administrator
**Phone:** 800-492-2538
**Fax:** 740-522-6051
**Web:** http://www.park.edu/dist/index.htm
**E-mail:** cbeatty@cgate.net

**ACCREDITATION:** North Central Association of Colleges and Schools

**INSTITUTIONALLY ADMINISTERED FINANCIAL AID:** No

### DEGREE OR CERTIFICATE PROGRAMS OFFERED

Programs offered do not lead to a degree or other formal award.

### NON-DEGREE-RELATED COURSE TOPICS OFFERED

**Undergraduate**—American (United States) history; American literature (United States); English composition; English creative writing; English language and literature, general; accounting; biology, general; business administration and management; business marketing and marketing management; communications, general; computer and information sciences, general; computer programming; computer science; computer systems analysis; criminal justice and corrections; criminology; economics; finance, general; geography; health system/health services administration; human resources management; journalism; labor/personnel relations and studies; law and legal studies, other; mathematical statistics; organizational behavior studies; philosophy and religion; psychology; social psychology.

See full description on page 456.

# PASCO-HERNANDO COMMUNITY COLLEGE

10230 Ridge Road
New Port Richey, FL 34654-5199
**Contact:** Mr. Michael Malizia, Director of Admissions and Student Records
**Phone:** 727-816-3261
**Fax:** 727-816-3389
**Web:** http://www.pasco-hernandocc.com
**E-mail:** michael_malizia@pasco-hernandocc.com

**ACCREDITATION:** Southern Association of Colleges and Schools

**INSTITUTIONALLY ADMINISTERED FINANCIAL AID:** Yes

## DEGREE OR CERTIFICATE PROGRAMS OFFERED

Programs offered do not lead to a degree or other formal award.

## NON-DEGREE-RELATED COURSE TOPICS OFFERED

**Undergraduate**—English composition; English literature (British and Commonwealth); anthropology; biology, general; business; business administration and management; computer systems networking and telecommunications; general teacher education; history; internet and world wide web; physical sciences, other; psychology; social sciences and history, other; sociology.

**Non-credit**—English technical and business writing; business and personal services marketing operations; business communications; computer and information sciences, general; computer software and media applications; family/consumer resource management; health products and services marketing operations.

# PASSAIC COUNTY COMMUNITY COLLEGE

1 College Boulevard
Paterson, NJ 07505-1179
**Contact:** Rick Perdew, Coordinator of Instructional Technology
**Phone:** 973-684-5790
**Fax:** 973-684-4079
**Web:** http://www.pccc.cc.nj.us/
**E-mail:** rperdew@pccc.cc.nj.us

**ACCREDITATION:** Middle States Association of Colleges and Schools
**INSTITUTIONALLY ADMINISTERED FINANCIAL AID:** Yes

## DEGREE OR CERTIFICATE PROGRAMS OFFERED

Programs offered do not lead to a degree or other formal award.

## NON-DEGREE-RELATED COURSE TOPICS OFFERED

**Undergraduate**—English language and literature, general; business; communications, general; computer and information sciences, general; health professions and related sciences, other; mathematical statistics; mathematics, other; physical sciences, general.

# PATRICK HENRY COMMUNITY COLLEGE

*Learning Resource Center*
PO Box 5311
Martinsville, VA 24115
**Contact:** Carolyn R. Byrd, Director of Instructional Support Services
**Phone:** 540-656-0211
**Fax:** 540-656-0327
**Web:** http://www.ph.vccs.edu
**E-mail:** phbyrdc@ph.cc.va.us

**ACCREDITATION:** Southern Association of Colleges and Schools
**INSTITUTIONALLY ADMINISTERED FINANCIAL AID:** Yes

## DEGREE OR CERTIFICATE PROGRAMS OFFERED

Programs offered do not lead to a degree or other formal award.

## NON-DEGREE-RELATED COURSE TOPICS OFFERED

**Undergraduate**—American (United States) history; English composition; English literature (British and Commonwealth); accounting; art history, criticism and conservation; business information and data processing services; computer systems networking and telecommunications; computer/information technology administration and management; developmental and child psychology; economics; sociology.

# PEIRCE COLLEGE

*Peirce College Non-Traditional Education*
1420 Pine Street
Philadelphia, PA 19102
**Contact:** OnLine Program Advisors
**Phone:** 877-670-9190
**Fax:** 215-545-3685
**Web:** http://www.peirce.edu
**E-mail:** online@peirce.edu

**ACCREDITATION:** Middle States Association of Colleges and Schools
**INSTITUTIONALLY ADMINISTERED FINANCIAL AID:** Yes

eCollege.com   *www.ecollege.com*

## DEGREE OR CERTIFICATE PROGRAMS OFFERED

**Undergraduate**—*AS:* Business Administration; Information Technology. *BS:* Business Administration; Information Technology.

## NON-DEGREE-RELATED COURSE TOPICS OFFERED

**Undergraduate**—business administration and management; computer/information technology administration and management.

### Special Note

Online courses are structured to provide students with the maximum amount of personalized attention from professors and to keep real-time discussion groups manageable. Students are required to actively participate by completing homework assignments, papers, and online exams. Each course is 7 weeks in length, with new classes starting every 3½ weeks. Students can register and begin their studies before all transcripts and other supporting documentation is completed. Credits from previous college work are accepted, although no prior college experience is required, and there are no age limits on enrollment. Peirce College brings the campus directly to the learner. Peirce Online offers one of the lowest private college tuition costs in the country.

See full description on page 458.

# PENNSYLVANIA COLLEGE OF TECHNOLOGY

1 College Avenue
Williamsport, PA 17701
**Contact:** Vicki Paulina, Director of Instructional Technology and Distance Learning
**Phone:** 570-326-3761 Ext. 7628
**Fax:** 570-321-5559

**Web:** http://www.pct.edu/
**E-mail:** vpaulina@pct.edu

**ACCREDITATION:** Middle States Association of Colleges and Schools

**INSTITUTIONALLY ADMINISTERED FINANCIAL AID:** Yes

## DEGREE OR CERTIFICATE PROGRAMS OFFERED

**Undergraduate—BS:** Applied Health Studies; Automotive Technology; Dental Hygiene; Technology Management.

## NON-DEGREE-RELATED COURSE TOPICS OFFERED

**Undergraduate**—accounting; art history, criticism and conservation; biology, general; business marketing and marketing management; dental services; finance, general; history and philosophy of science and technology; international business; mathematical statistics; organizational behavior studies; philosophy and religion.

---

### Special Note

Pennsylvania College of Technology offers online baccalaureate degree completion programs in 4 areas of study.

Applied health studies is a completion program for individuals who are certified, licensed, or registered in health-care professions. Credentialed (certified, licensed, registered, or degreed) health-care practitioners who meet admissions requirements are eligible for this program. This degree provides the opportunity to increase knowledge base in management and administrative issues and expand knowledge and skills to establish a more marketable multiskilled background. Graduates become credentialed health-care practitioners.

Automotive technology management provides automotive technicians the opportunity to pursue a baccalaureate degree. This program prepares students for advanced positions in the field of transportation technology and in related fields such as technical education, manufacturer representative, insurance review specialist, shop manager, technical specialist, and fleet operations.

Dental hygiene is a completion program that prepares students for advanced positions in the traditional field of dental hygiene, as well as opportunities in related fields such as dental hygiene educator, legislative aide, health/patient advocate, insurance review specialist, public health hygienist, health-care manager, geriatric oral health specialist, and special population care provider.

Technology management is a 2+2 degree program, providing an opportunity for students who have earned an associate degree in a technical/professional area of study to continue study toward a baccalaureate degree. The program provides a final 2 years of study concentrating on the development of business/management skills, preparing students for advanced positions in technical/professional areas related to a specific associate degree field.

---

# THE PENNSYLVANIA STATE UNIVERSITY UNIVERSITY PARK CAMPUS

*Department of Distance Education/World Campus*
207 Mitchell Building
University Park, PA 16802
**Contact:** Distance Education Advising Office

**Phone:** 800-252-3592
**Fax:** 814-865-3290
**Web:** http://www.worldcampus.psu.edu
**E-mail:** psude@outreach.psu.edu

**ACCREDITATION:** Middle States Association of Colleges and Schools

**INSTITUTIONALLY ADMINISTERED FINANCIAL AID:** No

## DEGREE OR CERTIFICATE PROGRAMS OFFERED

**Undergraduate—AA:** Letters, Arts, and Sciences. **AS:** Business Administration; Dietetic Food Systems Management; Hotel, Restaurant, and Institutional Management; Human Development and Family Studies. **BA:** Letters, Arts, and Sciences. ***Certificate:*** Adult Development and Aging Services; Advanced Business Management; Basic Supervisory Leadership; Business Management; Children, Youth and Family Services; Counselor Education-Chemical Dependency; Customer Relationship Management; Dietary Manager; Dietetics and Aging; Educational Technology Integration; General Business; Geographic Information Systems; Human Resources; Legal Issues for Business Professionals; Legal Issues for Those Dealing with the Elderly; Logistics and Supply Chain Management; Marketing Management; Noise Control Engineering; Paralegal Program; Retail Management; Small Business Management; Turfgrass Management; Webmaster; Writing Social Commentary.
**Graduate—MBA-EP:** iMBA. **MEd:** Adult Education.

## NON-DEGREE-RELATED COURSE TOPICS OFFERED

**Undergraduate**—American (United States) history; English composition; English creative writing; English technical and business writing; French language and literature; Spanish language and literature; accounting; animal sciences; anthropology; art history, criticism and conservation; biological and physical sciences; biology, general; business; business administration and management; business communications; business marketing and marketing management; chemistry; communications, general; comparative literature; criminal justice and corrections; earth and planetary sciences; economics; educational evaluation, research and statistics; enterprise management and operation; environmental science/studies; ethnic and cultural studies; finance, general; fine arts and art studies; foods and nutrition studies; foreign languages and literatures; geography; geological and related sciences; gerontology; health and physical education/fitness; health system/health services administration; history; hospitality services management; human resources management; individual and family development studies; industrial and organizational psychology; information sciences and systems; institutional food workers and administrators; investments and securities; journalism; journalism and mass communications; labor/personnel relations and studies; law and legal studies, other; management information systems and business data processing, general; marketing operations/marketing and distribution, other; mathematical statistics; mathematics; mathematics, other; music; organic chemistry; organizational behavior studies; philosophy; physics; physiology, human and animal; political science and government; psychology; religion/religious studies; romance languages and literatures; science, technology and society; sociology; speech and rhetorical studies; visual and performing arts; wildlife and wildlands management.
**Graduate**—adult and continuing teacher education; alcohol/drug abuse counseling; architectural environmental design; business administration and management; business quantitative methods and management science; business/managerial economics; curriculum and instruction; education administration and supervision; educational/instructional media design; electrical, electronics and communication engineering; electromechanical instrumentation and maintenance technology; environmental

control technologies; marketing operations/marketing and distribution, other; mathematical statistics; transportation and materials moving workers, other.

**Non-credit**—agricultural and food products processing; agricultural business and management; architectural environmental design; business administration and management; business communications; geography; human resources management; internet and world wide web; paralegal/legal assistant; wildlife and wildlands management.

**See full description on page 460.**

# PENN VALLEY COMMUNITY COLLEGE

*Distance Education and Media*

3201 Southwest Traffic Way
Kansas City, MO 64111-2764
**Contact:** Charles Gosselin, Associate Dean of Instructional Technology
**Phone:** 816-759-4489
**Fax:** 816-759-4367
**Web:** http://www.kcmetro.cc.mo.us/pennvalley/pvhome.html
**E-mail:** gosselin@pennvalley.cc.mo.us

**ACCREDITATION:** North Central Association of Colleges and Schools
**INSTITUTIONALLY ADMINISTERED FINANCIAL AID:** Yes

## DEGREE OR CERTIFICATE PROGRAMS OFFERED
**Programs offered do not lead to a degree or other formal award.**

## NON-DEGREE-RELATED COURSE TOPICS OFFERED
**Undergraduate**—English composition; accounting; biology, general; child care and guidance workers and managers; computer science; criminal justice and corrections; economics; education, general; engineering science; engineering, general; fire science/firefighting; geography; history; mathematics; philosophy; physical sciences, general; psychology; sociology.

# PENSACOLA JUNIOR COLLEGE

*Distance Learning Department*

1000 College Boulevard
Pensacola, FL 32504
**Contact:** Dr. Bill Waters, Director
**Phone:** 850-484-1238
**Fax:** 850-484-1237
**Web:** http://www.distance.pjc.cc.fl.us
**E-mail:** bwaters@pjc.cc.fl.us

**ACCREDITATION:** Southern Association of Colleges and Schools

## DEGREE OR CERTIFICATE PROGRAMS OFFERED
**Undergraduate**—*AA:* General.

## NON-DEGREE-RELATED COURSE TOPICS OFFERED
**Undergraduate**—developmental and child psychology; social psychology; sociology.

# PEPPERDINE UNIVERSITY

*Program in Educational Technology*

Graduate School of Education and Psychology, 400 Corporate Pointe
Culver City, CA 90230
**Contact:** Ms. Gabriella Miramontes, Enrollment Specialist
**Phone:** 800-347-4849
**Web:** http://gsep.pepperdine.edu/gsep
**E-mail:** gsep@pepperdine.edu

**ACCREDITATION:** Western Association of Schools and Colleges
**INSTITUTIONALLY ADMINISTERED FINANCIAL AID:** Yes

## DEGREE OR CERTIFICATE PROGRAMS OFFERED
**Graduate**—*MA:* Educational Technology.
**Postgraduate and doctoral**—*EdD:* Educational Technology.

# PHILADELPHIA UNIVERSITY

School House Lane and Henry Avenue
Philadelphia, PA 19144
**Contact:** Dr. Judith McKee, Dean of Graduate and Continuing Studies
**Phone:** 215-951-2900
**Web:** http://www.philau.edu/
**E-mail:** mckeej@philau.edu

**ACCREDITATION:** Middle States Association of Colleges and Schools
**INSTITUTIONALLY ADMINISTERED FINANCIAL AID:** No

eCollege.com *www.ecollege.com*

## DEGREE OR CERTIFICATE PROGRAMS OFFERED
**Graduate**—*MBA:* Textile & Apparel Marketing. *MS:* Midwifery.

# PIEDMONT COLLEGE

*Georgia State Academic and Medical System (GSAMS)*

PO Box 10
Demorest, GA 30535
**Contact:** Dr. James Mellichamp, Vice President of Academic Affairs
**Phone:** 706-776-0110
**Fax:** 706-776-2811
**Web:** http://www.piedmont.edu
**E-mail:** jmellichamp@piedmont.edu

**ACCREDITATION:** Southern Association of Colleges and Schools
**INSTITUTIONALLY ADMINISTERED FINANCIAL AID:** Yes

## DEGREE OR CERTIFICATE PROGRAMS OFFERED
**Programs offered do not lead to a degree or other formal award.**

## NON-DEGREE-RELATED COURSE TOPICS OFFERED
**Undergraduate**—English composition; South Asian languages and literatures; communications, general; history; mathematics; sociology.

# PIERCE COLLEGE

## Developmental Education

9401 Farwest Drive, SW
Lakewood, WA 98498
**Contact:** Martha Makaneole, Programs Assistant
**Phone:** 253-964-6244
**Fax:** 253-964-6299
**Web:** http://www.pierce.ctc.edu/distance
**E-mail:** mmakaneo@pierce.etc.edu

**ACCREDITATION:** Northwest Association of Schools and Colleges

**INSTITUTIONALLY ADMINISTERED FINANCIAL AID:** Yes

### DEGREE OR CERTIFICATE PROGRAMS OFFERED
**Programs offered do not lead to a degree or other formal award.**

### NON-DEGREE-RELATED COURSE TOPICS OFFERED
**Undergraduate**—English composition; English creative writing; English language and literature, general; French language and literature; anthropology; applied mathematics; astronomy; biology, general; business communications; computer and information sciences, general; computer and information sciences, other; developmental and child psychology; earth and planetary sciences; geological and related sciences; history; music; philosophy and religion; physical sciences, general; physics.

# PIKES PEAK COMMUNITY COLLEGE

## Learning Technologies

5675 South Academy Boulevard
Colorado Springs, CO 80906-5498
**Contact:** Julie Witherow, Director of Distance Education
**Phone:** 719-540-7539
**Fax:** 719-540-7532
**Web:** http://www.ppcc.cccoes.edu
**E-mail:** witherow@ppcc.cccoes.edu

**ACCREDITATION:** North Central Association of Colleges and Schools

**INSTITUTIONALLY ADMINISTERED FINANCIAL AID:** Yes

eCollege.com   *www.ecollege.com*

### DEGREE OR CERTIFICATE PROGRAMS OFFERED
**Undergraduate**—*AAS:* Fire Science Technology.

### NON-DEGREE-RELATED COURSE TOPICS OFFERED
**Undergraduate**—English composition; English language and literature, general; English technical and business writing; accounting; anthropology; business; business administration and management; business communications; computer science; computer software and media applications; criminal justice and corrections; design and applied arts; fire protection; history; journalism and mass communications; natural resources conservation; political science and government; radio and television broadcasting; social psychology; sociology.
**Non-credit**—accounting; radio and television broadcasting; social psychology; sociology.

# PIMA COMMUNITY COLLEGE

## Telecommunications and Production Service

Student Services, 401 North Bonita Avenue
Tucson, AZ 85709-5030
**Contact:** Mr. Jim Johnson, Dean of Student Services
**Phone:** 520-206-6482
**Fax:** 520-206-6482
**Web:** http://www.pimacc.pima.edu
**E-mail:** jejohnson@pimacc.pima.edu

**ACCREDITATION:** North Central Association of Colleges and Schools

**INSTITUTIONALLY ADMINISTERED FINANCIAL AID:** Yes

### DEGREE OR CERTIFICATE PROGRAMS OFFERED
**Undergraduate**—*AA:* General Studies.

### NON-DEGREE-RELATED COURSE TOPICS OFFERED
**Undergraduate**—English composition; sociology.

# PINE TECHNICAL COLLEGE

## Distance Education Center

900 Fourth Street
Pine City, MN 55063
**Contact:** Phil Schroeder, Dean of Student Services
**Phone:** 320-629-6764
**Web:** http://www.ptc.tec.mn.us
**E-mail:** phil.schroeder@ptc.tec.mn.us

**ACCREDITATION:** North Central Association of Colleges and Schools

**INSTITUTIONALLY ADMINISTERED FINANCIAL AID:** Yes

### DEGREE OR CERTIFICATE PROGRAMS OFFERED
**Programs offered do not lead to a degree or other formal award.**

### NON-DEGREE-RELATED COURSE TOPICS OFFERED
**Undergraduate**—English composition; accounting; business management and administrative services, other; health professions and related sciences, other.

# PITT COMMUNITY COLLEGE

## Distance Education Department

Highway 11 South, PO Drawer 7007
Greenville, NC 27835-7007
**Contact:** Elaine Seeman, Director of Distance Learning
**Phone:** 252-321-4608
**Fax:** 252-321-4401
**Web:** http://www.pitt.cc.nc.us
**E-mail:** eseeman@pcc.pitt.cc.nc.us

**ACCREDITATION:** Southern Association of Colleges and Schools

**INSTITUTIONALLY ADMINISTERED FINANCIAL AID:** Yes

### DEGREE OR CERTIFICATE PROGRAMS OFFERED
**Undergraduate**—*AAS:* Business Administration; Computer Programming; Health Information Technology; Information Systems Generalist. *Certificate:* Administrative Manager Certificate; Basic Accounting Cer-

tification; Computer Software Applications Certificate; Data Entry Applications Certificate; Emerging Technologies for Educators; Healthcare Leadership and Management; Home Office Computing; Information Systems Technology Certificate; Leadership Certificate; Management Application and Principles Certificate; Marketing Certificate; Medical Office Administration Certificate; Object Oriented Programming Certificate; Starting Your Own Business; WordProcessing/Transcription Certificate.

### NON-DEGREE-RELATED COURSE TOPICS OFFERED

**Undergraduate**—English composition; accounting; advertising; alcohol/drug abuse counseling; biochemistry; biology, general; business marketing and marketing management; international business; law and legal studies, other; philosophy and religion; sociology.
**Non-credit**—English creative writing; adult and continuing teacher education; finance, general.

## PITTSBURG STATE UNIVERSITY

Division of Continuing Studies, 1701 South Broadway
Pittsburg, KS 66762
**Contact:** Mrs. Suzie K. Long, Director
**Phone:** 620-235-4181
**Fax:** 620-235-4174
**Web:** http://www.pittstate.edu/
**E-mail:** slong@pittstate.edu

**ACCREDITATION:** North Central Association of Colleges and Schools
**INSTITUTIONALLY ADMINISTERED FINANCIAL AID:** Yes

### DEGREE OR CERTIFICATE PROGRAMS OFFERED
**Programs offered do not lead to a degree or other formal award.**

### NON-DEGREE-RELATED COURSE TOPICS OFFERED
**Undergraduate**—technology education/industrial arts.
**Graduate**—education administration and supervision; human resources management.

## PLATTSBURGH STATE UNIVERSITY OF NEW YORK

*Distance Learning Office*
101 Broad Street, Sibley Hall, 418 A
Plattsburgh, NY 12901
**Contact:** Ms. Cheryl Marshall, Coordinator of Distance Learning Office
**Phone:** 518-564-4234
**Fax:** 518-564-4236
**Web:** http://www.plattsburgh.edu/cll
**E-mail:** cheryl.marshall@plattsburgh.edu

**ACCREDITATION:** Middle States Association of Colleges and Schools
**INSTITUTIONALLY ADMINISTERED FINANCIAL AID:** Yes

### DEGREE OR CERTIFICATE PROGRAMS OFFERED
**Undergraduate**—*BS:* Nursing.

### NON-DEGREE-RELATED COURSE TOPICS OFFERED
**Undergraduate**—English as a second language; anthropology; area, ethnic and cultural studies, other; economics; ethnic and cultural studies; fine arts and art studies; health and physical education/fitness; library science, other; marketing management and research; mathematical statistics; nursing; political science and government.
**Graduate**—business administration and management; education, other; entrepreneurship.

## PORTLAND COMMUNITY COLLEGE

*Distance Learning Department*
PO Box 19000
Portland, OR 97219
**Contact:** Barbara Baker, Distance Learning Support
**Phone:** 503-977-4730
**Fax:** 503-977-4858
**Web:** http://www.distance.pcc.edu
**E-mail:** bbaker@pcc.edu

**ACCREDITATION:** Northwest Association of Schools and Colleges

### DEGREE OR CERTIFICATE PROGRAMS OFFERED
**Undergraduate**—*AGS:* General Studies. *Certificate:* Medical Assisting.
**Graduate**—*MBA/M Ed:* General Studies.

### NON-DEGREE-RELATED COURSE TOPICS OFFERED
**Undergraduate**—American (United States) history; English composition; English creative writing; accounting; anthropology; biology, general; business marketing and marketing management; computer and information sciences, general; computer and information sciences, other; computer software and media applications; dental services; developmental and child psychology; earth and planetary sciences; fire science/firefighting; geography; health professions and related sciences, other; law and legal studies, other; mathematical statistics; mathematics, other; oceanography; social sciences, general; sociology.
**Non-credit**—English composition; English creative writing; English technical and business writing; computer programming; computer software and media applications; computer systems networking and telecommunications; health professions and related sciences, other; internet and world wide web; miscellaneous health professions.

## PORTLAND STATE UNIVERSITY

*Independent Study*
PO Box 751
Portland, OR 97207-0751
**Contact:** Thomas Luba, Director of Distance Learning
**Phone:** 800-547-8887
**Fax:** 503-725-4840
**Web:** http://www.pdx.edu/
**E-mail:** lubat@pdx.edu

**ACCREDITATION:** Northwest Association of Schools and Colleges
**INSTITUTIONALLY ADMINISTERED FINANCIAL AID:** Yes

## DEGREE OR CERTIFICATE PROGRAMS OFFERED

Programs offered do not lead to a degree or other formal award.

## NON-DEGREE-RELATED COURSE TOPICS OFFERED

**Undergraduate**—English composition; English language and literature, general; business administration and management; chemistry; criminal justice and corrections; economics; geography; geological and related sciences; history; mathematical statistics; mathematics, other; psychology; religion/religious studies; sociology.

# PRAIRIE BIBLE COLLEGE

*Prairie Distance Education*

Box 4000
Three Hills, AB T0M 2N0, Canada
**Contact:** Dr. Arnold L. Stauffer, Associate Dean
**Phone:** 403-443-3036
**Fax:** 403-443-3099
**Web:** http://www.pbi.ab.ca/distanceed
**E-mail:** distance.ed@pbi.ab.ca

**ACCREDITATION:** Provincially Chartered

**INSTITUTIONALLY ADMINISTERED FINANCIAL AID:** No

## DEGREE OR CERTIFICATE PROGRAMS OFFERED

**Undergraduate**—*AA:* Religious Studies. *BMin:* Ministry. *Certificate:* Bible.
**Graduate**—*Graduate Certificate:* Theological Studies.

## NON-DEGREE-RELATED COURSE TOPICS OFFERED

**Undergraduate**—English composition; European history; anthropology; philosophy and religion.
**Graduate**—American (United States) history; anthropology.

# PRAIRIE STATE COLLEGE

*Learning Resources Center*

202 South Halsted Street
Chicago Heights, IL 60411
**Contact:** Mary Welsh, Director of Admissions
**Phone:** 708-709-3513
**Fax:** 708-755-2587
**Web:** http://www.prairie.cc.il.us/
**E-mail:** mwelsh@prairie.cc.il.us

**ACCREDITATION:** North Central Association of Colleges and Schools

## DEGREE OR CERTIFICATE PROGRAMS OFFERED

Programs offered do not lead to a degree or other formal award.

## NON-DEGREE-RELATED COURSE TOPICS OFFERED

**Undergraduate**—English composition; accounting; business communications; computer and information sciences, general.

# PRATT COMMUNITY COLLEGE AND AREA VOCATIONAL SCHOOL

348 Northeast SR 61
Pratt, KS 67124
**Contact:** Adm. Pam M. Dietz, Assistant to the Vice President
**Phone:** 620-672-9800 Ext. 238
**Fax:** 620-672-5641 Ext. 238
**Web:** http://www.pcc.cc.ks.us/
**E-mail:** pamd@pcc.cc.ks.us

**ACCREDITATION:** North Central Association of Colleges and Schools

**INSTITUTIONALLY ADMINISTERED FINANCIAL AID:** Yes

eCollege.com  *www.ecollege.com*

## DEGREE OR CERTIFICATE PROGRAMS OFFERED

**Undergraduate**—*AS:* General Studies.

## NON-DEGREE-RELATED COURSE TOPICS OFFERED

**Undergraduate**—accounting; business administration and management.

# PRESCOTT COLLEGE

220 Grove Avenue
Prescott, AZ 86301
**Contact:** Admissions
**Phone:** 800-628-6364
**Web:** http://www.prescott.edu/
**E-mail:** admissions@prescott.edu

**ACCREDITATION:** North Central Association of Colleges and Schools

## DEGREE OR CERTIFICATE PROGRAMS OFFERED

**Undergraduate**—*BA:* Adult Degree Completion Program.
**Graduate**—*MA:* Adventure Education; Counseling and Psychology; Education; Environmental Studies; Humanities.

See full description on page 462.

# PRESENTATION COLLEGE

1500 North Main Street
Aberdeen, SD 57401
**Contact:** Mickie L. Metzinger, Registrar
**Phone:** 605-229-8424
**Fax:** 605-229-8332
**Web:** http://www.presentation.edu/
**E-mail:** metzingerm@presentation.edu

**ACCREDITATION:** North Central Association of Colleges and Schools

**INSTITUTIONALLY ADMINISTERED FINANCIAL AID:** Yes

## DEGREE OR CERTIFICATE PROGRAMS OFFERED

Programs offered do not lead to a degree or other formal award.

## NON-DEGREE-RELATED COURSE TOPICS OFFERED

**Undergraduate**—English composition; mathematical statistics; mathematics, other; nursing; sign language interpreter; social work; sociology.

# PRESTONSBURG COMMUNITY COLLEGE

1 Bert T. Combs Drive
Prestonsburg, KY 41653
**Contact:** Ms. Della F. Pack, Staff Support Associate for Distance Learning
**Phone:** 606-886-3863 Ext. 284
**Fax:** 606-886-6200
**Web:** http://www.prestonsburgcc.com/
**E-mail:** della.pack@kctcs.net

**ACCREDITATION:** Southern Association of Colleges and Schools
**INSTITUTIONALLY ADMINISTERED FINANCIAL AID:** Yes

## DEGREE OR CERTIFICATE PROGRAMS OFFERED

**Undergraduate—AA:** Associate in Arts Degree (Business Transfer Framework).

## NON-DEGREE-RELATED COURSE TOPICS OFFERED

**Undergraduate—**English language and literature, general; administrative and secretarial services; business; business management and administrative services, other; computer and information sciences, general; computer/information technology administration and management; history; mathematical statistics; mathematics; political science and government.

# PRINCETON THEOLOGICAL SEMINARY

*Center of Continuing Education*
20 Library Place
Princeton, NJ 08540-6824
**Contact:** Mr. David H. Wall, Program Coordinator
**Phone:** 609-497-7990
**Fax:** 609-497-0709
**E-mail:** david.wall@ptsem.edu

**ACCREDITATION:** Middle States Association of Colleges and Schools
**INSTITUTIONALLY ADMINISTERED FINANCIAL AID:** No

## DEGREE OR CERTIFICATE PROGRAMS OFFERED

Programs offered do not lead to a degree or other formal award.

## NON-DEGREE-RELATED COURSE TOPICS OFFERED

**Non-credit—**bible/biblical studies; religious education; theological and ministerial studies.

# PROVIDENCE COLLEGE AND THEOLOGICAL SEMINARY

*Department of Continuing Education*
Otterburne, MB R0A 1G0, Canada
**Contact:** Mr. Richard J. Smith, Associate Director of Enrollment
**Phone:** 204-433-7488 Ext. 293
**Fax:** 204-433-7158
**Web:** http://www.seminary.ca

**E-mail:** rsmith@providence.mb.ca
**ACCREDITATION:** Provincially Chartered
**INSTITUTIONALLY ADMINISTERED FINANCIAL AID:** Yes

## DEGREE OR CERTIFICATE PROGRAMS OFFERED

Programs offered do not lead to a degree or other formal award.

## NON-DEGREE-RELATED COURSE TOPICS OFFERED

**Graduate—**area, ethnic and cultural studies, other; bible/biblical studies; biblical and other theological languages and literatures; counseling psychology; education, other; missions/missionary studies and missiology; pastoral counseling and specialized ministries; religion/religious studies; theological and ministerial studies; theological studies and religious vocations, other.

# PUEBLO COMMUNITY COLLEGE

*Educational Technology and Telecommunications*
Distance Learning Office, 900 West Orman Avenue
Pueblo, CO 81004-1499
**Contact:** Jo-Ann Kipple, Coordinator for Distance Learning
**Phone:** 719-549-3380
**Fax:** 719-549-3419
**Web:** http://www.pcc.cccoes.edu
**E-mail:** jo-ann.kipple@pcc.cccoes.edu

**ACCREDITATION:** North Central Association of Colleges and Schools
**INSTITUTIONALLY ADMINISTERED FINANCIAL AID:** Yes

eCollege.com www.ecollege.com

## DEGREE OR CERTIFICATE PROGRAMS OFFERED

**Undergraduate—AA:** General Education; Public Administration. **AAS:** Business; Library Technician. **Certificate:** Agricultural Business; Early Childhood Professions Program; Library Technician.

## NON-DEGREE-RELATED COURSE TOPICS OFFERED

**Undergraduate—**English composition; English language and literature, general; accounting; agricultural business and management; astronomy; biology, general; business; chemistry; computer programming; economics; film/video and photographic arts; foreign languages and literatures; geography; health professions and related sciences, other; library assistant; mathematics; philosophy; physics; psychology; sociology.

# PULASKI TECHNICAL COLLEGE

3000 West Scenic Drive
North Little Rock, AR 72118
**Contact:** Ms. Laura Richardson South, Enrollment Coordinator
**Phone:** 501-812-2231
**Fax:** 501-812-2316
**Web:** http://www.ptc.tec.ar.us
**E-mail:** lsouth@mail.ptc.tec.ar.us

**ACCREDITATION:** North Central Association of Colleges and Schools
**INSTITUTIONALLY ADMINISTERED FINANCIAL AID:** Yes

## DEGREE OR CERTIFICATE PROGRAMS OFFERED

Programs offered do not lead to a degree or other formal award.

## NON-DEGREE-RELATED COURSE TOPICS OFFERED

**Undergraduate**—American literature (United States); English composition; English creative writing; English literature (British and Commonwealth); biology, general; business; computer and information sciences, general; computer systems analysis; computer systems networking and telecommunications; journalism and mass communications; psychology.

# PURDUE UNIVERSITY
*Distance Education Services*

1586 Stewart Center, Room 116
West Lafayette, IN 47907-1586
**Contact:** Joetta S. Burrous, Director
**Phone:** 765-496-3338
**Fax:** 765-496-6384
**Web:** http://www.vet.purdue.edu
**E-mail:** jburrous@purdue.edu

**ACCREDITATION:** North Central Association of Colleges and Schools

## DEGREE OR CERTIFICATE PROGRAMS OFFERED

**Graduate**—*EMBA:* Agribusiness Management. *EMS:* Business. *MS:* Industrial Engineering. *MSCE:* Civil Engineering. *MSE:* Engineering. *MSEE:* Electrical and Computer Engineering. *MSME:* Mechanical Engineering.

## NON-DEGREE-RELATED COURSE TOPICS OFFERED

**Undergraduate**—health professions and related sciences, other; hospitality services management; veterinary clinical sciences (M.S., Ph.D.).
**Graduate**—business administration and management; engineering, general; fine arts and art studies.
**Non-credit**—agriculture/agricultural sciences; engineering, general.

# PURDUE UNIVERSITY
*Krannert Executive Education Programs*

1310 Krannert Center
West Lafayette, IN 47907-1310
**Contact:** Krannert Executive Education
**Phone:** 765-494-7700
**Fax:** 765-494-0862
**Web:** http://www2.mgmt.purdue.edu/
**E-mail:** keepinfo@mgmt.purdue.edu

**ACCREDITATION:** North Central Association of Colleges and Schools

## DEGREE OR CERTIFICATE PROGRAMS OFFERED

Programs offered do not lead to a degree or other formal award.
See full description on page 464.

# PURDUE UNIVERSITY NORTH CENTRAL
*Mathematics and Physics Section*

1401 South US 421
Westville, IN 46391
**Contact:** Barbara J. Birchfield, Director of Learning Center

**Phone:** 219-785-5438
**Fax:** 219-785-5470
**Web:** http://www.purduenc.edu
**E-mail:** barbarab@purduenc.edu

**ACCREDITATION:** North Central Association of Colleges and Schools

**INSTITUTIONALLY ADMINISTERED FINANCIAL AID:** Yes

## DEGREE OR CERTIFICATE PROGRAMS OFFERED

Programs offered do not lead to a degree or other formal award.

## NON-DEGREE-RELATED COURSE TOPICS OFFERED

**Undergraduate**—computer and information sciences, general; mathematical statistics.

# QUINEBAUG VALLEY COMMUNITY COLLEGE

742 Upper Maple Street
Danielson, CT 06239
**Contact:** Dr. Toni Thomas Moumouris, Enrollment and Transition Counselor
**Phone:** 860-774-1130 Ext. 318
**Fax:** 860-779-2998
**Web:** http://www.qvcc.commnet.edu/
**E-mail:** qv_moumouris@commnet.edu

**ACCREDITATION:** New England Association of Schools and Colleges

**INSTITUTIONALLY ADMINISTERED FINANCIAL AID:** No

## DEGREE OR CERTIFICATE PROGRAMS OFFERED

**Undergraduate**—*AS:* General Studies. *Certificate:* Health Information Management Technology.

## NON-DEGREE-RELATED COURSE TOPICS OFFERED

**Undergraduate**—astronomy; history; liberal arts and sciences, general studies and humanities; sociology.

# RADFORD UNIVERSITY

Graduate College, Division of Extended Education
Radford, VA 24142
**Contact:** Dr. Garry Ellerman, Associate Dean and Director of Extended Education
**Phone:** 540-831-5429
**Fax:** 540-831-6119
**Web:** http://www.radford.edu/
**E-mail:** gellerma@radford.edu

**ACCREDITATION:** Southern Association of Colleges and Schools

**INSTITUTIONALLY ADMINISTERED FINANCIAL AID:** Yes

## DEGREE OR CERTIFICATE PROGRAMS OFFERED

Programs offered do not lead to a degree or other formal award.

## NON-DEGREE-RELATED COURSE TOPICS OFFERED

**Graduate**—business; business administration and management; business communications; business/managerial economics; communications, general; community health services; criminology; curriculum and instruction;

education administration and supervision; financial management and services; general teacher education; health and medical administrative services; health and medical diagnostic and treatment services; health and medical preparatory programs; health professions and related sciences, other; miscellaneous health professions; nursing; romance languages and literatures.

**Non-credit**—accounting; business administration and management; business and personal services marketing operations; business management and administrative services, other; computer and information sciences, general; computer and information sciences, other; computer software and media applications; nursing; public health.

# RANDOLPH COMMUNITY COLLEGE

*Virtual Campus*

629 Industrial Park Avenue, PO Box 1009
Asheboro, NC 27203
**Contact:** Celia Hurley, Director of Teaching Excellence and Distance Education
**Phone:** 336-633-0299
**Fax:** 336-629-4695
**Web:** http://www.virtualrandolph.org
**E-mail:** cthurley@randolph.cc.nc.us

**ACCREDITATION:** Southern Association of Colleges and Schools

**INSTITUTIONALLY ADMINISTERED FINANCIAL AID:** Yes

## DEGREE OR CERTIFICATE PROGRAMS OFFERED
**Programs offered do not lead to a degree or other formal award.**

## NON-DEGREE-RELATED COURSE TOPICS OFFERED
**Undergraduate**—English composition; European history; accounting; anthropology; business marketing and marketing management; computer and information sciences, general; economics; finance, general; historic preservation, conservation and architectural history; history; law and legal studies, other; music; philosophy and religion; psychology; sociology.

# RAPPAHANNOCK COMMUNITY COLLEGE

*Flexible Learning Opportunities (FLO)*

52 Campus Drive
Warsaw, VA 22572
**Contact:** Kristy Walker, Assistant for Distance Learning
**Phone:** 804-333-6786
**Fax:** 804-333-0106
**Web:** http://www.rcc.vccs.edu
**E-mail:** kwalker@rcc.vccs.edu

**ACCREDITATION:** Southern Association of Colleges and Schools

**INSTITUTIONALLY ADMINISTERED FINANCIAL AID:** Yes

## DEGREE OR CERTIFICATE PROGRAMS OFFERED
**Undergraduate**—*AS:* General Studies.

## NON-DEGREE-RELATED COURSE TOPICS OFFERED
**Undergraduate**—American literature (United States); English composition; accounting; business administration and management; business communications; community health services; criminal justice and corrections; fine arts and art studies; health and physical education/fitness; history; mathematics; psychology; religion/religious studies; sociology.

# RARITAN VALLEY COMMUNITY COLLEGE

*Distance Learning*

PO Box 3300
Somerville, NJ 08876
**Contact:** Chuck Chulvick, Vice President of Learning Services
**Phone:** 908-526-1200 Ext. 8409
**Fax:** 908-526-0255
**Web:** http://www.raritanval.edu/newhometest/frameset/virtualcampus.html
**E-mail:** cchulvic@raritanval.edu

**ACCREDITATION:** Middle States Association of Colleges and Schools

**INSTITUTIONALLY ADMINISTERED FINANCIAL AID:** Yes

## DEGREE OR CERTIFICATE PROGRAMS OFFERED
**Programs offered do not lead to a degree or other formal award.**

## NON-DEGREE-RELATED COURSE TOPICS OFFERED
**Undergraduate**—American literature (United States); English composition; English creative writing; English language and literature, general; anthropology; applied mathematics; area, ethnic and cultural studies, other; computer and information sciences, general; computer and information sciences, other; computer programming; computer software and media applications; computer systems networking and telecommunications; computer/information technology administration and management; criminology; economics; family and community studies; history; law and legal studies; marketing management and research; mathematics; nursing; psychology; social work; sociology.

# RED ROCKS COMMUNITY COLLEGE

*Learning and Resource Center*

5420 Miller Street
Arvada, CO 80002
**Contact:** Diane Hegeman, Associate Vice President
**Phone:** 303-914-6017
**Fax:** 303-420-9572
**Web:** http://www.rrcc.cccoes.edu
**E-mail:** diane.hegeman@rrcc.cccoes.edu

**ACCREDITATION:** North Central Association of Colleges and Schools

**INSTITUTIONALLY ADMINISTERED FINANCIAL AID:** Yes

eCollege.com    www.ecollege.com

## DEGREE OR CERTIFICATE PROGRAMS OFFERED

**Undergraduate—AAS:** Building Code Enforcement; Business; Construction Technology—Emphasis in Construction Electrician; Construction Technology—Emphasis in Power Technology; Emergency Management and Planning.

## NON-DEGREE-RELATED COURSE TOPICS OFFERED

**Undergraduate**—English as a second language; English composition; accounting; applied mathematics; art history, criticism and conservation; computer and information sciences, general; computer programming; computer science; computer software and media applications; computer systems analysis; computer systems networking and telecommunications; data processing technology; developmental and child psychology; geography; history; mathematics; social psychology; sociology.

# REGENT UNIVERSITY

## Distance Education

1000 Regent University Drive
Virginia Beach, VA 23464
**Contact:** Distance Education
**Phone:** 757-226-4127
**Fax:** 757-226-4381
**Web:** http://www.regent.edu
**E-mail:** admissions@regent.edu

**ACCREDITATION:** Southern Association of Colleges and Schools

## DEGREE OR CERTIFICATE PROGRAMS OFFERED

**Programs offered do not lead to a degree or other formal award.**

### Special Note

Regent University is a pioneer in online/distance learning and currently offers more than 20 graduate programs online via its Worldwide Campus. Regent ranks in the upper third of all colleges and universities in its use of technology in learning. In addition to this distinction, Regent embraces the Judeo-Christian tradition and enjoys a highly ecumenical environment. With faith as the foundation of its mission, Regent prepares leaders to make a positive impact upon American society and the world. Unique among universities, Regent offers graduate-level study in 8 professional fields—business, communication and the arts, divinity, education, government, law, psychology and counseling (currently not available online), and organizational leadership. In addition to the main campus in Virginia Beach, Regent offers programs at its Graduate Center in the northern Virginia/Washington, DC, area. In addition to sharing similar commitments toward faith and values, Regent University online students also share an interest in technology-based learning, the motivation and ability to pursue studies independently, and strong written and oral communication skills.

See full description on page 466.

# REND LAKE COLLEGE

## Learning Resource Center

Ina, IL 62846

**Contact:** Andrea Witthoft, Director of Learning Resources and Instructional Technology
**Phone:** 618-437-5321 Ext. 277
**Fax:** 618-437-5598
**Web:** http://www.rlc.cc.il.us
**E-mail:** witthoft@rlc.cc.il.us

**ACCREDITATION:** North Central Association of Colleges and Schools
**INSTITUTIONALLY ADMINISTERED FINANCIAL AID:** Yes

## DEGREE OR CERTIFICATE PROGRAMS OFFERED

**Programs offered do not lead to a degree or other formal award.**

## NON-DEGREE-RELATED COURSE TOPICS OFFERED

**Undergraduate**—Latin American studies; anthropology; horticulture science; mathematics; microbiology/bacteriology; nursing.

# RENSSELAER POLYTECHNIC INSTITUTE

## Office of Professional and Distance Education

Center for Industrial Innovation, Suite 4011, 110 8th Street
Troy, NY 12180
**Contact:** Heliena T. Fox, Recruitment Representative for Alumni and Individual Programs
**Phone:** 518-276-8351
**Fax:** 518-276-8026
**Web:** http://www.rsvp.rpi.edu
**E-mail:** rsvp@rpi.edu

**ACCREDITATION:** Middle States Association of Colleges and Schools
**INSTITUTIONALLY ADMINISTERED FINANCIAL AID:** No

## DEGREE OR CERTIFICATE PROGRAMS OFFERED

**Undergraduate—Certificate:** Bioinformatics; Computer Graphics and Data Visualization; Computer Networks; Computer Science; Database Systems Design; E-Business; Electric Power Engineering; Graphical User Interfaces; Human-Computer Interaction; Information Technology; Management and Technology; Manufacturing Systems Engineering; Microelectronics Manufacturing Engineering; Microelectronics Technology and Design; Quality and Reliability; Service Systems; Software Engineering. **Graduate—MBA:** Management and Technology. **ME:** Computer and Systems Engineering; Electric Power Engineering; Electrical Engineering; Mechanical Engineering. **MS:** Computer Science; Electric Power Engineering; Electrical Engineering; Engineering Science; Industrial and Management Engineering; Information Technology; Management; Mechanical Engineering; Technical Communications.

See full description on page 468.

# RENTON TECHNICAL COLLEGE

3000 Northeast 4th Street
Renton, WA 98056-4195
**Contact:** Mr. Mike Dahl, Special Programs Coordinator and Counselor
**Phone:** 425-235-2352 Ext. 5544
**Fax:** 425-235-7832
**Web:** http://www.renton-tc.ctc.edu/

**E-mail:** mdahl@rtc.ctc.edu

**ACCREDITATION:** Northwest Association of Schools and Colleges

**INSTITUTIONALLY ADMINISTERED FINANCIAL AID:** No

**DEGREE OR CERTIFICATE PROGRAMS OFFERED**

Programs offered do not lead to a degree or other formal award.

# THE RICHARD STOCKTON COLLEGE OF NEW JERSEY

*Office of Distance Education*

PO Box 195
Pomona, NJ 08240-0195
**Contact:** Mr. Mark Jackson, Director of Media Services and Distance Education
**Phone:** 609-652-4811
**Fax:** 609-748-5562
**Web:** http://www.stockton.edu
**E-mail:** mark.jackson@stockton.edu

**ACCREDITATION:** Middle States Association of Colleges and Schools

**INSTITUTIONALLY ADMINISTERED FINANCIAL AID:** Yes

**DEGREE OR CERTIFICATE PROGRAMS OFFERED**

Programs offered do not lead to a degree or other formal award.

**NON-DEGREE-RELATED COURSE TOPICS OFFERED**

**Undergraduate**—English composition; anthropology; applied mathematics; business administration and management; business marketing and marketing management; film/video and photographic arts; gerontology; health professions and related sciences, other; journalism and mass communication, other; liberal arts and sciences, general studies and humanities; nursing; photography; psychology; sociology; women's studies.

# RICHLAND COMMUNITY COLLEGE

*Lifelong Learning Division*

1 College Park
Decatur, IL 62521
**Contact:** Ms. Catherine L. Sebok, Extension Coordinator
**Phone:** 217-875-7200 Ext. 558
**Fax:** 217-875-6965
**E-mail:** csebok@richland.cc.il.us

**ACCREDITATION:** North Central Association of Colleges and Schools

**INSTITUTIONALLY ADMINISTERED FINANCIAL AID:** Yes

**DEGREE OR CERTIFICATE PROGRAMS OFFERED**

Programs offered do not lead to a degree or other formal award.

**NON-DEGREE-RELATED COURSE TOPICS OFFERED**

**Undergraduate**—English composition; English creative writing; European history; accounting; art history, criticism and conservation; business communications; developmental and child psychology; internet and world wide web; psychology; social psychology; sociology.

# RIO HONDO COLLEGE

3600 Workman Mill Road
Whittier, CA 90601
**Contact:** Joe Ramirez, Dean, Counseling and Matriculation
**Phone:** 562-692-0921 Ext. 3146
**Web:** http://www.rh.cc.ca.us/
**E-mail:** jramirez@rh.cc.ca.us

**ACCREDITATION:** Western Association of Schools and Colleges

**INSTITUTIONALLY ADMINISTERED FINANCIAL AID:** Yes

**DEGREE OR CERTIFICATE PROGRAMS OFFERED**

Programs offered do not lead to a degree or other formal award.

**NON-DEGREE-RELATED COURSE TOPICS OFFERED**

**Undergraduate**—English composition; English language and literature, general; accounting; anthropology; business management and administrative services, other; computer and information sciences, general; computer programming; economics; education, other; fine arts and art studies; fire protection; geological and related sciences; history; international business; library science, other; mathematics; political science and government; psychology; romance languages and literatures; sociology.

# RIO SALADO COLLEGE

*Distance Learning*

2323 West 14th Street
Tempe, AZ 85281
**Contact:** Student Services
**Phone:** 480-517-8540
**Web:** http://www.rio.maricopa.edu
**E-mail:** student.services@email.rio.maricopa.edu

**ACCREDITATION:** North Central Association of Colleges and Schools

**INSTITUTIONALLY ADMINISTERED FINANCIAL AID:** Yes

**DEGREE OR CERTIFICATE PROGRAMS OFFERED**

**Undergraduate**—*AA:* General Studies. *AGS:* General Studies.

See full description on page 470.

# ROBERT MORRIS COLLEGE

*Department of Enrollment Management*

600 Fifth Avenue
Pittsburgh, PA 15219
**Contact:** Darcy B. Tannehill, Dean of Pittsburgh Center
**Phone:** 412-227-6472
**Fax:** 412-281-5539
**Web:** http://www.robert-morris.edu
**E-mail:** tannehil@robert-morris.edu

**ACCREDITATION:** Middle States Association of Colleges and Schools

**INSTITUTIONALLY ADMINISTERED FINANCIAL AID:** Yes

eCollege.com *www.ecollege.com*

**DEGREE OR CERTIFICATE PROGRAMS OFFERED**

**Undergraduate**—*BS:* Information Systems. *BSBA:* Accounting; Management.

## NON-DEGREE-RELATED COURSE TOPICS OFFERED

**Undergraduate**—English composition; English language and literature, general; accounting; business marketing and marketing management; communications, other; computer systems analysis; finance, general; history; hospitality and recreation marketing operations; industrial and organizational psychology; law and legal studies, other; management information systems and business data processing, general; physical sciences, general; psychology; sociology.

**See full description on page 472.**

# ROCHESTER COMMUNITY AND TECHNICAL COLLEGE

851 30th Avenue, SE
Rochester, MN 55904-4999
**Contact:** Nancy Shumaker, Registrar
**Phone:** 507-285-7461
**Web:** http://www.roch.edu/

**ACCREDITATION:** North Central Association of Colleges and Schools

## DEGREE OR CERTIFICATE PROGRAMS OFFERED

**Undergraduate**—*Certificate:* Digital Arts: Computer Graphics.

## NON-DEGREE-RELATED COURSE TOPICS OFFERED

**Undergraduate**—English composition; administrative and secretarial services; biology, general; child care and guidance workers and managers; computer software and media applications; economics; individual and family development studies.

# ROCHESTER INSTITUTE OF TECHNOLOGY

*Graduate Enrollment Services*
Bausch & Lomb Center, 58 Lomb Memorial Drive
Rochester, NY 14623
**Contact:** Mr. Joseph T. Nairn, Director of Office of Part-time Enrollment Services
**Phone:** 716-475-2229
**Fax:** 716-475-7164
**Web:** http://online.rit.edu
**E-mail:** opes@rit.edu

**ACCREDITATION:** Middle States Association of Colleges and Schools

**INSTITUTIONALLY ADMINISTERED FINANCIAL AID:** Yes

## DEGREE OR CERTIFICATE PROGRAMS OFFERED

**Undergraduate**—*BS:* Applied Arts and Science; Electrical and Mechanical Engineering Technology; Environmental Management; Safety Technology; Telecommunications. *Certificate:* Basic Quality Management; Digital Imaging and Publishing; Disaster and Emergency Management; Environmental Management Science; Health Systems Administration; Industrial Environmental Management; Safety and Health Technology; Structural Design; Technical Communications; Telecommunications Network Management; Voice Communications.
**Graduate**—*Graduate Certificate:* Integrated Health Systems, Health Systems Finance; Statistical Quality. *MS:* Applied Statistical Quality; Cross Disciplinary Professional Studies; Environmental Health and Safety

Management; Graphic Arts Publishing; Health Systems Administration; Imaging Science; Information Technology; Software Development and Management.

## NON-DEGREE-RELATED COURSE TOPICS OFFERED

**Undergraduate**—English composition; electrical, electronics and communication engineering; engineering mechanics; engineering/industrial management; environmental science/studies; mechanical engineering; sociology.
**Graduate**—electrical, electronics and communication engineering.

**See full description on page 474.**

# ROCKHURST UNIVERSITY

1100 Rockhurst Road
Kansas City, MO 64110
**Contact:** Ms. Margaret M. Millard, Institutional Research Coordinator
**Phone:** 816-501-4617
**Fax:** 816-501-4136
**Web:** http://www.rockhurst.edu/
**E-mail:** peg.millard@rockhurst.edu

**ACCREDITATION:** North Central Association of Colleges and Schools

**INSTITUTIONALLY ADMINISTERED FINANCIAL AID:** Yes

## DEGREE OR CERTIFICATE PROGRAMS OFFERED

**Programs offered do not lead to a degree or other formal award.**

## NON-DEGREE-RELATED COURSE TOPICS OFFERED

**Undergraduate**—computer programming; computer science; computer/information technology administration and management; history; philosophy and religion; psychology; social sciences, general.
**Graduate**—business; business administration and management; financial management and services; financial services marketing operations; marketing management and research.

# ROCKINGHAM COMMUNITY COLLEGE

PO Box 38
Wentworth, NC 27375
**Contact:** Dr. William E. Knight, Executive Vice President
**Phone:** 336-342-4261 Ext. 2137
**Fax:** 336-349-9986
**Web:** http://www.rcc.cc.nc.us/
**E-mail:** knightw@rcc.cc.nc.us

**ACCREDITATION:** Southern Association of Colleges and Schools

**INSTITUTIONALLY ADMINISTERED FINANCIAL AID:** No

## DEGREE OR CERTIFICATE PROGRAMS OFFERED

**Programs offered do not lead to a degree or other formal award.**

## NON-DEGREE-RELATED COURSE TOPICS OFFERED

**Undergraduate**—business; computer software and media applications; data entry/microcomputer applications; economics.
**Non-credit**—administrative and secretarial services; bilingual/bicultural education; business; business administration and management; business

and personal services marketing operations; business communications; business information and data processing services; business management and administrative services, other; business quantitative methods and management science; business/managerial economics; communications technologies; communications, general; communications, other; community health services; computer and information sciences, general; computer programming; computer science; computer software and media applications; computer systems analysis; computer systems networking and telecommunications; data entry/microcomputer applications; data processing technology; design and applied arts; entrepreneurship; financial management and services; fire protection; health and medical diagnostic and treatment services; human services; industrial production technologies; international business; internet and world wide web; law and legal studies; marketing management and research; marketing operations/marketing and distribution, other; materials science; public health.

# ROCKLAND COMMUNITY COLLEGE

## Telecourse and Distance Learning Department
145 College Road, Room 4124
Suffern, NY 10901
**Contact:** Lynne Koplik, Distance Education Supervisor
**Phone:** 845-574-4780
**Fax:** 845-356-5811
**Web:** http://www.sunyrockland.edu
**E-mail:** lkoplik@sunyrockland.edu

**ACCREDITATION:** Middle States Association of Colleges and Schools
**INSTITUTIONALLY ADMINISTERED FINANCIAL AID:** Yes

### DEGREE OR CERTIFICATE PROGRAMS OFFERED
Undergraduate—*AA:* Liberal Arts and Sciences.

### NON-DEGREE-RELATED COURSE TOPICS OFFERED
Undergraduate—health professions and related sciences, other; liberal arts and sciences, general studies and humanities; nursing.

# ROGERS STATE UNIVERSITY

## Distance Learning
1701 West Will Rogers Boulevard
Claremore, OK 74017
**Contact:** Lane Wood, Online Coordinator
**Phone:** 918-343-7751
**Fax:** 918-343-7595
**Web:** http://www.rsuonline.edu
**E-mail:** lwood@rsu.edu

**ACCREDITATION:** North Central Association of Colleges and Schools
**INSTITUTIONALLY ADMINISTERED FINANCIAL AID:** Yes

eCollege.com *www.ecollege.com*

### DEGREE OR CERTIFICATE PROGRAMS OFFERED
Undergraduate—*AA:* Business Administration; Liberal Arts. *AAS:* Applied Technology. *AS:* Computer Science. *BA:* Liberal Arts. *BAA:* Applied Technology. *BS:* Information Technology.

# ROGER WILLIAMS UNIVERSITY

## Open Program
150 Washington Street
Providence, RI 02903
**Contact:** Mary Dionisopoulos, Administrative Assistant
**Phone:** 401-254-3530
**Fax:** 401-254-3560
**Web:** http://www.rwu.edu
**E-mail:** jws@alpha.rwu.edu

**ACCREDITATION:** New England Association of Schools and Colleges
**INSTITUTIONALLY ADMINISTERED FINANCIAL AID:** Yes

eCollege.com *www.ecollege.com*

### DEGREE OR CERTIFICATE PROGRAMS OFFERED
Undergraduate—*BS:* Business Management; Criminal Justice; Industrial Technology; Public Administration.

### NON-DEGREE-RELATED COURSE TOPICS OFFERED
Undergraduate—accounting; anthropology; biology, general; business administration and management; business marketing and marketing management; criminal justice and corrections; engineering/industrial management; history and philosophy of science and technology; industrial/manufacturing engineering; insurance and risk management; investments and securities; law and legal studies, other; philosophy and religion; public administration; sociology.

**See full description on page 476.**

# ROOSEVELT UNIVERSITY

## External Studies Program
430 South Michigan, Room 124
Chicago, IL 60605
**Contact:** Karen S. Gersten, Associate Dean
**Phone:** 312-281-3129
**Fax:** 312-281-3132
**Web:** http://www.roosevelt.edu/
**E-mail:** kgersten@roosevelt.edu

**ACCREDITATION:** North Central Association of Colleges and Schools
**INSTITUTIONALLY ADMINISTERED FINANCIAL AID:** Yes

### DEGREE OR CERTIFICATE PROGRAMS OFFERED
**Programs offered do not lead to a degree or other formal award.**

### NON-DEGREE-RELATED COURSE TOPICS OFFERED
Undergraduate—American (United States) history; English composition; accounting; business; business administration and management; business communications; business information and data processing services; computer and information sciences, general; computer programming; economics; education, general; finance, general; financial management and services; geography; history; hospitality services management; law and legal studies; law and legal studies, other; physical sciences, general; psychology; social psychology; social sciences, general.
Graduate—business administration and management; education, general.

# ROWAN-CABARRUS COMMUNITY COLLEGE

Salisbury, NC 28145
**Contact:** Debra Humphrey NeeSmith, Director of Distance Education
**Phone:** 704-637-0760 Ext. 799
**E-mail:** neesmithd@rccc.cc.nc.us

**ACCREDITATION:** Southern Association of Colleges and Schools

**INSTITUTIONALLY ADMINISTERED FINANCIAL AID:** Yes

### DEGREE OR CERTIFICATE PROGRAMS OFFERED

**Undergraduate—*AA:*** Arts and Sciences. ***AAS:*** Business Administration.

### NON-DEGREE-RELATED COURSE TOPICS OFFERED

**Undergraduate—**American literature (United States); English composition; English language and literature, general; astronomy; business administration and management; business/managerial economics; child care and guidance workers and managers; computer and information sciences, general; computer software and media applications; computer/information technology administration and management; criminal justice and corrections; criminology; economics; history; internet and world wide web; marketing operations/marketing and distribution, other; music; philosophy and religion; psychology; sociology.
**Non-credit—**English composition; business; computer and information sciences, general; computer software and media applications; computer systems networking and telecommunications; tourism and travel services marketing operations.

# ROYAL ROADS UNIVERSITY

2005 Sooke Road
Victoria, BC V9B 5Y2, Canada
**Contact:** Ann Nightingale, Director, Learner Services and Registrar
**Phone:** 250-391-2505
**Fax:** 250-391-2522
**Web:** http://www.royalroads.ca/
**E-mail:** ann.nightingale@royalroads.ca

**ACCREDITATION:** Provincially Chartered

**INSTITUTIONALLY ADMINISTERED FINANCIAL AID:** Yes

### DEGREE OR CERTIFICATE PROGRAMS OFFERED

**Undergraduate—*BComm:*** Entrepreneurial Management. ***BS:*** Environmental Science.
**Graduate—*MA:*** Conflict Analysis and Management; Distributed Learning; Environment and Management; Leadership and Training. ***MBA:*** Digital Technologies Management; Executive Management; Human Resources Management; Public Relations and Communication Management. ***MS:*** Environment and Management.

### NON-DEGREE-RELATED COURSE TOPICS OFFERED

**Graduate—**business administration and management; business communications; business information and data processing services; business management and administrative services, other; communications, other; education administration and supervision; human resources management; public administration and services, other; public relations and organizational communications.

# RUTGERS, THE STATE UNIVERSITY OF NEW JERSEY, NEW BRUNSWICK

*Office of Vice President for Continuous Education and Outreach*
83 Somerset Street
New Brunswick, NJ 08903
**Contact:** Dr. Raphael J. Caprio, Vice President of Continuous Education and Outreach
**Phone:** 732-932-5935
**Fax:** 732-932-9225
**Web:** http://ce1766.rutgers.edu/distance-learning.html
**E-mail:** caprio@andromeda.rutgers.edu

**ACCREDITATION:** Middle States Association of Colleges and Schools

### DEGREE OR CERTIFICATE PROGRAMS OFFERED

Programs offered do not lead to a degree or other formal award.
See full description on page 478.

# RYERSON POLYTECHNIC UNIVERSITY

*Distance Education*
Continuing Education, 350 Victoria Street
Toronto, ON M5B 2K3, Canada
**Contact:** Dr. Richard Malinski, Director
**Phone:** 416-979-5132
**Fax:** 416-595-9602
**Web:** http://ce-online.ryerson.ca/de
**E-mail:** malinski@ryerson.ca

**ACCREDITATION:** Provincially Chartered

**INSTITUTIONALLY ADMINISTERED FINANCIAL AID:** Yes

### DEGREE OR CERTIFICATE PROGRAMS OFFERED

Programs offered do not lead to a degree or other formal award.

# SACRED HEART UNIVERSITY

*University College/ Continuing Education*
5151 Park Avenue
Fairfield, CT 06432
**Contact:** Edward Donato, Associate Dean of University College
**Phone:** 203-371-7836
**Fax:** 203-365-7500
**Web:** http://uc.sacredheart.edu
**E-mail:** donatoe@sacredheart.edu

**ACCREDITATION:** New England Association of Schools and Colleges

**INSTITUTIONALLY ADMINISTERED FINANCIAL AID:** No

### DEGREE OR CERTIFICATE PROGRAMS OFFERED

**Undergraduate—*BA:*** Leadership Studies. ***BSN:*** Nursing.

## NON-DEGREE-RELATED COURSE TOPICS OFFERED

**Undergraduate**—English composition; English language and literature, general; business marketing and marketing management; chemistry; communications, other; computer science; finance, general; health and physical education/fitness; history; international business; law and legal studies, other; nursing; organizational behavior studies.
**Graduate**—accounting; computer science; economics; education, general; financial management and services.

---

### Special Note

Sacred Heart University's dynamic link to adult and corporate communities, University College, brings Sacred Heart's resources and programs to the adult learner through regional campus locations in Derby, Fairfield, Shelton, and Stamford, Connecticut; on-site at local corporations; or through distance learning.

Founded in 1963, Sacred Heart was created to embody a new direction within American Catholic higher education, led and staffed by laity and independent and locally oriented. As the University grew, the vision and mission expanded, producing a high-quality institution that now serves a regional, national, and international purpose. University College has maintained the founding premise of the University by continuing to serve the needs of adults in their quest for knowledge; personal, professional, and spiritual growth; and continuous learning.

The University offers its distance learning courses on a semester-based calendar. Most courses are delivered asynchronously, so students can schedule their own "work time." Small class size ensures personal attention in the Web-based courses. Sacred Heart employs Jones Knowledge.Com as its partner in delivering online courses. This partnership provides students with redundant hardware systems, 24-hour support, and state-of-the-art software.

Sacred Heart offers undergraduate distance learning courses in disciplines such as business administration and management, business law, chemistry, comparative literature, computer science, English composition, history, international business, mathematics, media studies, nursing, philosophy, and sports marketing. It also offers a complete degree program for registered nurses who wish to complete a Bachelor of Science in Nursing. The RN-to-BSN program is accredited by the National League for Nursing Accrediting Commission and requires 57 credits in nursing; 30 credits may be awarded for previous nursing work. A graduate certificate in educational technology for certified teachers, consisting of 4 Web-based courses, and a baccalaureate degree in leadership studies are also available. All MBA prerequisites are available online, as is the Sports Business University, a partnership to provide relevant business education to the sports industry. A graduate-level program in geriatric rehabilitation will be available next academic year.

For further information, students should contact Edward Donato, Associate Dean, University College at 203-371-7836 or at donatoe@sacredheart.edu.

---

# SADDLEBACK COLLEGE
*Office of Instruction*
AGB 126, 28000 Marguerite Parkway
Mission Viejo, CA 92692
**Contact:** Ms. Sheri L. Nelson, Senior Administrative Assistant
**Phone:** 949-582-4515

**Fax:** 949-347-0438
**Web:** http://saddlebackcollege.net
**E-mail:** snelson@saddleback.cc.ca.us

**ACCREDITATION:** Western Association of Schools and Colleges
**INSTITUTIONALLY ADMINISTERED FINANCIAL AID:** Yes

## DEGREE OR CERTIFICATE PROGRAMS OFFERED
Programs offered do not lead to a degree or other formal award.

## NON-DEGREE-RELATED COURSE TOPICS OFFERED
**Undergraduate**—American (United States) history; English composition; English creative writing; accounting; anthropology; business information and data processing services; business management and administrative services, other; business marketing and marketing management; computer science; developmental and child psychology; history; individual and family development studies; law and legal studies, other; library science, other; marketing operations/marketing and distribution, other; music; oceanography; political science and government; social sciences and history, other; sociology.

---

# ST. AMBROSE UNIVERSITY
518 West Locust Street
Davenport, IA 52803-2898
**Contact:** Dr. Donald Moeller, Provost
**Phone:** 563-333-6211
**Fax:** 563-333-6243
**Web:** http://www.sau.edu/
**E-mail:** dmoeller@sau.edu

**ACCREDITATION:** North Central Association of Colleges and Schools
**INSTITUTIONALLY ADMINISTERED FINANCIAL AID:** Yes

## DEGREE OR CERTIFICATE PROGRAMS OFFERED
Programs offered do not lead to a degree or other formal award.

## NON-DEGREE-RELATED COURSE TOPICS OFFERED
**Undergraduate**—business administration and management; journalism and mass communication, other; philosophy.
**Graduate**—business administration and management; mathematical statistics; occupational therapy; physical therapy; special education.

---

# SAINT CHARLES COMMUNITY COLLEGE
*Distance Learning*
Learning Resource Center, 4601 Mid Rivers Mall Drive
St. Peters, MO 63376
**Contact:** Ms. Gwen Bell, Distance Learning Secretary
**Phone:** 636-922-8470
**Fax:** 636-922-8434
**Web:** http://www.stchas.edu/distance/dlmain.shtml
**E-mail:** gbell@chuck.stchas.edu

**ACCREDITATION:** North Central Association of Colleges and Schools
**INSTITUTIONALLY ADMINISTERED FINANCIAL AID:** Yes

## DEGREE OR CERTIFICATE PROGRAMS OFFERED

Programs offered do not lead to a degree or other formal award.

## NON-DEGREE-RELATED COURSE TOPICS OFFERED

**Undergraduate**—anthropology; biology, general; business; criminal justice and corrections; health and physical education/fitness; history; music; political science and government; psychology; sociology.

# ST. CLAIR COUNTY COMMUNITY COLLEGE

323 Erie Street, PO Box 5015
Port Huron, MI 48061-5015
**Contact:** Linda Davis, Instructional Designer
**Phone:** 810-989-5765
**Web:** http://www.stclair.cc.mi.us/
**E-mail:** ldavis@stclair.cc.mi.us

**ACCREDITATION:** North Central Association of Colleges and Schools
**INSTITUTIONALLY ADMINISTERED FINANCIAL AID:** Yes

## DEGREE OR CERTIFICATE PROGRAMS OFFERED

Programs offered do not lead to a degree or other formal award.

## NON-DEGREE-RELATED COURSE TOPICS OFFERED

**Undergraduate**—English composition; astronomy; business administration and management; business communications; chemistry; communications, other; computer and information sciences, general; electrical and electronic engineering-related technology; general teacher education; mathematics; nursing; social sciences, general; sociology.

# ST. CLOUD STATE UNIVERSITY

*Center for Continuing Studies*

Center for Continuing Studies, 720 4th Avenue, S
St. Cloud, MN 56301
**Contact:** Ms. Patricia A. Kallevig, Director of Distributed Learning
**Phone:** 320-255-3081
**Fax:** 320-654-5041
**Web:** http://www.stcloudstate.edu/
**E-mail:** pakallevig@stcloudstate.edu

**ACCREDITATION:** North Central Association of Colleges and Schools
**INSTITUTIONALLY ADMINISTERED FINANCIAL AID:** Yes

## DEGREE OR CERTIFICATE PROGRAMS OFFERED

**Undergraduate**—*AA:* Liberal Arts.
**Graduate**—*MCM:* Applied Psychology; Marketing; Self Designed Studies; Self Designed; Speech Communication. *MEd:* Educational Administration.

## NON-DEGREE-RELATED COURSE TOPICS OFFERED

**Undergraduate**—anthropology; biology, general; education of the speech impaired; environmental science/studies; sociology.
**Graduate**—English as a second language; journalism and mass communication, other.

# ST. CLOUD TECHNICAL COLLEGE

*Central Minnesota Distance Learning Network*

1540 Northway Drive
St. Cloud, MN 56303
**Contact:** Ms. Jodi Elness, Director of Enrollment Management
**Phone:** 320-654-5087
**Fax:** 320-654-5981
**Web:** http://www.sctconline.com
**E-mail:** jme@cloud.tec.mn.us

**ACCREDITATION:** North Central Association of Colleges and Schools
**INSTITUTIONALLY ADMINISTERED FINANCIAL AID:** No

## DEGREE OR CERTIFICATE PROGRAMS OFFERED

Programs offered do not lead to a degree or other formal award.

## NON-DEGREE-RELATED COURSE TOPICS OFFERED

**Non-credit**—business; child care and guidance workers and managers; computer and information sciences, general; computer science; medical basic sciences.

# ST. EDWARD'S UNIVERSITY

*New College*

Center for Academic Progress, 3001 South Congress Avenue
Austin, TX 78704-6489
**Contact:** Ms. Amy Bush, New College Recruitment Coordinator
**Phone:** 512-448-8745
**Fax:** 512-428-1032
**Web:** http://www.stedwards.edu
**E-mail:** amyb@admin.stedwards.edu

**ACCREDITATION:** Southern Association of Colleges and Schools
**INSTITUTIONALLY ADMINISTERED FINANCIAL AID:** Yes

## DEGREE OR CERTIFICATE PROGRAMS OFFERED

Programs offered do not lead to a degree or other formal award.

## NON-DEGREE-RELATED COURSE TOPICS OFFERED

**Undergraduate**—English language and literature, general; accounting; anthropology; business administration and management; business communications; business/managerial economics; communications, general; criminal justice and corrections; economics; geography; history; human resources management; human services; marketing operations/marketing and distribution, other; philosophy; philosophy and religion; social sciences and history, other.
**Graduate**—accounting; business administration and management; business communications; business/managerial economics; financial services marketing operations; human resources management; human services; marketing management and research; marketing operations/marketing and distribution, other; peace and conflict studies; public relations and organizational communications.

# SAINT FRANCIS UNIVERSITY

*Academic Affairs*

Loretto, PA 15940

**Contact:** Dr. Peter Skoner, Assistant Vice President for Academic Affairs

**Web:** http:// www.francis.edu

**E-mail:** pskoner@francis.edu

**ACCREDITATION:** Middle States Association of Colleges and Schools

**INSTITUTIONALLY ADMINISTERED FINANCIAL AID:** Yes

## DEGREE OR CERTIFICATE PROGRAMS OFFERED

**Graduate—*MMS:*** Medicine.

# ST. JOHN'S UNIVERSITY

8000 Utopia Parkway
Jamaica, NY 11439

**Contact:** Mr. Jeffery E. Olson, Associate Vice President and Associate Provost

**Phone:** 718-990-5705

**Fax:** 718-990-2456

**Web:** http://www.stjohns.edu/

**E-mail:** olsonj@stjohns.edu

**ACCREDITATION:** Middle States Association of Colleges and Schools

**INSTITUTIONALLY ADMINISTERED FINANCIAL AID:** Yes

## DEGREE OR CERTIFICATE PROGRAMS OFFERED

**Programs offered do not lead to a degree or other formal award.**

## NON-DEGREE-RELATED COURSE TOPICS OFFERED

**Undergraduate—**English composition; English language and literature, general; biological and physical sciences; business; business administration and management; communications, general; economics; history; law and legal studies; paralegal/legal assistant; pharmacy.

**Graduate—**business management and administrative services, other; business/managerial economics; education, general; finance, general.

# SAINT JOSEPH'S COLLEGE

*Graduate & Professional Studies*

278 Whites Bridge Road
Standish, ME 04084-5263

**Contact:** Lynne Robinson, Director of Admissions

**Phone:** 800-752-4723

**Fax:** 207-892-7480

**Web:** http://www.sjcme.edu/gps

**E-mail:** admiss@sjcme.edu

**ACCREDITATION:** New England Association of Schools and Colleges

**INSTITUTIONALLY ADMINISTERED FINANCIAL AID:** Yes

## DEGREE OR CERTIFICATE PROGRAMS OFFERED

**Undergraduate—*AS:*** Criminal Justice. ***ASM:*** Business Administration. ***BLS:*** American Studies; Christian Tradition. ***BS:*** Criminal Justice; General Studies; Health Care Administration; Long-Term Care Administration. ***BSBA:*** Business Administration. ***BSN:*** Nursing. ***BSPA:*** Professional Arts. ***BSRC:*** Respiratory Care. ***BSRS:*** Radiological Sciences. ***Certificate:*** American Studies; Business Administration; Christian Tradition; Criminal Justice; Health Care Finance; Health Care Management; Long-Term

Care Administration; Medical and Dental Practice Administration; Parish Nursing; Pastoral Studies; Professional Studies.

**Graduate—*MA:*** Pastoral Studies. ***MHSA:*** Health Services Administration. ***MSE:*** Education. ***MSN:*** Nursing.

## NON-DEGREE-RELATED COURSE TOPICS OFFERED

**Undergraduate—**English composition; accounting; business administration and management; criminology; developmental and child psychology; educational evaluation, research and statistics; educational psychology; health and medical administrative services; human services; industrial and organizational psychology; marketing management and research; multi/interdisciplinary studies, other; pastoral counseling and specialized ministries; philosophy and religion; social psychology; sociology.

**Graduate—**accounting; business administration and management; business/managerial economics; curriculum and instruction; education administration and supervision; educational evaluation, research and statistics; health and medical administrative services; philosophy and religion; public administration; religion/religious studies; theological and ministerial studies.

**Non-credit—**pastoral counseling and specialized ministries; religion/religious studies.

**See full description on page 480.**

# SAINT LEO UNIVERSITY

*Center for Distance Learning*

PO Box 6665, MC2008
Saint Leo, FL 33574

**Contact:** Office of Admission

**Phone:** 800-334-5532

**Fax:** 352-588-8257

**Web:** http://www.saintleo.edu/degrees/degrees.html

**E-mail:** admission@saintleo.edu

**ACCREDITATION:** Southern Association of Colleges and Schools

## DEGREE OR CERTIFICATE PROGRAMS OFFERED

**Undergraduate—*BA:*** Accounting; Business Administration. ***BS:*** Computer Information Systems.

---

**Special Note**

Saint Leo University, a leader in adult education since 1974, offers several options in obtaining an accredited degree on line. Saint Leo University's complete online programs include bachelor's degrees in accounting, business administration (management), and computer information systems. The programs are available through the Center for Online Learning (http://www.saintleo.com). Alternative delivery classes are delivered on line through the School of Continuing Education's Distance Learning System to supplement site-based programs that are offered at the regional campuses. A wide array of courses is available in such subjects as computer information systems, management, philosophy, and psychology. New course content is added every semester, and students should call or visit the Web site (http://saintleodl.eduprise.com) for complete information.

The distance learning courses are delivered by a variety of methods, including Web-based synchronous and asynchronous techniques, e-mail, and audio/video. The majority of the courses permit the learner to complete the courses at home, provided that they have access to a properly equipped computer and telephone connections.

The online programs are designed to permit adult learners to complete their degrees without on-campus residential requirements. The online course system provides the ability to register for courses, receive student services, and complete instruction on line. This flexible program is ideal for working professionals who desire to complete a bachelor's degree but cannot afford to do so by placing their careers on hold.

# ST. LOUIS COMMUNITY COLLEGE SYSTEM
*Telelearning Services*
300 South Broadway
St. Louis, MO 63102
**Contact:** Mr. Dan Bain, Director of Telelearning Services
**Phone:** 314-539-5056
**Fax:** 314-539-5005
**Web:** http://stlcc.cc.mo.us/distance
**E-mail:** dbain@stlcc.cc.mo.us

**ACCREDITATION:** North Central Association of Colleges and Schools
**INSTITUTIONALLY ADMINISTERED FINANCIAL AID:** Yes

## DEGREE OR CERTIFICATE PROGRAMS OFFERED
Undergraduate—*AA:* General.

# SAINT LOUIS UNIVERSITY
*School of Nursing*
3525 Caroline Street
St. Louis, MO 63104-1099
**Contact:** Director, Marketing and Recruitment
**Phone:** 314-577-8993
**Fax:** 314-577-8949
**E-mail:** slunurse@slu.edu

**ACCREDITATION:** North Central Association of Colleges and Schools
**INSTITUTIONALLY ADMINISTERED FINANCIAL AID:** Yes

## DEGREE OR CERTIFICATE PROGRAMS OFFERED
Undergraduate—*BSN:* Nursing-RN-BSN Completion.
Graduate—*MBA/Pharm D:* Nursing. *MSN:* Nursing. *PMC:* Nursing.

**Special Note**
Saint Louis University School of Nursing is a leader in nursing distance education. It was the first nursing school in the US to offer complete master's degree programs in nursing online through the World Wide Web.

Currently, MSN, MSN (research), and post-master's certificate programs are available online for the adult, family, gerontological, and pediatric nurse practitioner tracks and for the adult and gerontological clinical nurse specialist tracks. Students complete all course work for the degree program through distance education. The online nurse practitioner tracks are designed to follow the same curriculum and program objectives required of on-campus students. Faculty members work with students to help select clinical sites and

preceptors that are compatible with the students' and the program's objectives. To participate, students must be comfortable using PC hardware and software and should have an e-mail account and be proficient in accessing the World Wide Web. Students enrolled in the online programs have access to the University's main and health sciences libraries and resources via the Internet.

On campus, the School offers several BSN programs; master's programs in adult nursing (CNS, NP), family and community health nursing (PHNS, NP), gerontological nursing (CNS, NP), perinatal nursing (CNS), and psychiatric–mental health nursing (CNS); and a doctoral program in nursing.

Saint Louis University is accredited by the North Central Association of Colleges and Schools. The School of Nursing is fully accredited by the National League for Nursing Accrediting Commission and the Missouri State Board of Nursing and has preliminary approval by the Committee on Collegiate Education of the American Association of Colleges of Nursing. The master's programs are accredited by the National League for Nursing Council for Baccalaureate and Higher Degree Programs.

# SAINT MARY-OF-THE-WOODS COLLEGE
*Women's External Degree Program*
Guerin Hall
Saint Mary-of-the-Woods, IN 47876
**Contact:** Ms. Gwen J. Hagemeyer, Director of WED Admission
**Phone:** 812-535-5186
**Fax:** 812-535-4900
**Web:** http://www.smwc.edu/
**E-mail:** wedadms@smwc.edu

**ACCREDITATION:** North Central Association of Colleges and Schools
**INSTITUTIONALLY ADMINISTERED FINANCIAL AID:** Yes

## DEGREE OR CERTIFICATE PROGRAMS OFFERED
Undergraduate—*AA:* Humanities; Paralegal Studies. *AS:* Accounting; Early Childhood Education; General Business; Gerontology. *BA:* English; History and Political Studies; Humanities; Journalism; Mathematics; Paralegal Studies; Professional Writing; Social Science/History; Theology. *BS:* Accounting Information Systems; Accounting; Business Administration; Computer Information Systems; Digital Media Communication; Early Childhood Education; Elementary Education; Equine Business Management; Gerontology; Human Resource Management; Human Services; Marketing; Not for Profit: Child Care Administration; Not for Profit: Financial Administration; Not for Profit: Human Services; Not for Profit: Public Relations; Occupational Therapy Applications; Psychology; Secondary Education—English; Secondary Education—Mathematics; Secondary Education—Social Studies; Special Education. *Certificate:* Gerontology; Legal Nurse; Paralegal Studies; Theology.
Graduate—*MA:* Art Therapy; Earth Literacy; Music Therapy; Pastoral Theology.

**See full description on page 482.**

# ST. NORBERT COLLEGE
*Program in Education*
100 Grant Street
De Pere, WI 54115

Contact: Mr. Daniel Meyer, Dean of Admissions
Phone: 920-403-3005
Fax: 920-403-4072
Web: http://www.snc.edu/mse
E-mail: daniel.meyer@snc.edu

ACCREDITATION: North Central Association of Colleges and Schools

INSTITUTIONALLY ADMINISTERED FINANCIAL AID: Yes

## DEGREE OR CERTIFICATE PROGRAMS OFFERED

Graduate—*MSE:* Inquiry and Applied Research for Educational Change.

## NON-DEGREE-RELATED COURSE TOPICS OFFERED

Undergraduate—liberal arts and sciences, general studies and humanities.
Graduate—business; education, general; foreign languages and literatures; liberal arts and sciences, general studies and humanities.
Non-credit—English as a second language; business administration and management; education, general; financial management and services; foreign languages and literatures; religion/religious studies.

# SAINT PAUL SCHOOL OF THEOLOGY

5123 Truman Road
Kansas City, MO 64127
Contact: Admissions
Phone: 800-825-0378
Fax: 816-483-9605
Web: http://www.spst.edu/
E-mail: admiss@spst.edu

ACCREDITATION: North Central Association of Colleges and Schools

## DEGREE OR CERTIFICATE PROGRAMS OFFERED

Programs offered do not lead to a degree or other formal award.

# ST. PETERSBURG COLLEGE

*Electronic Campus*
PO Box 13489
St. Petersburg, FL 33733
Contact: Lynda Womer, Program Director
Phone: 727-394-6116
Fax: 727-394-6124
Web: http://e.spjc.edu
E-mail: womerl@spjc.edu

ACCREDITATION: Southern Association of Colleges and Schools

INSTITUTIONALLY ADMINISTERED FINANCIAL AID: Yes

## DEGREE OR CERTIFICATE PROGRAMS OFFERED

Undergraduate—*AA:* General. *AS:* Veterinary Technology.

## NON-DEGREE-RELATED COURSE TOPICS OFFERED

Undergraduate—American (United States) history; English composition; English creative writing; European history; French language and literature; Spanish language and literature; accounting; anatomy; anthropology; art history, criticism and conservation; biology, general; business marketing and marketing management; developmental and child psychology; earth and planetary sciences; family and marriage counseling; finance, general; fire science/firefighting; fire services administration; journalism; mathematical statistics; mathematics, other; microbiology/bacteriology; oceanography; philosophy and religion; social psychology; sociology.

# SAINT PETER'S COLLEGE

*Institute for the Advancement of Urban Education*
2641 Kennedy Boulevard
Jersey City, NJ 07306-5997
Contact: Dr. Richard J. Hamilton, Dean of Evening and Summer Programs
Phone: 201-915-9010
Web: http://www.spc.edu
E-mail: hamilton_r@spc.edu

ACCREDITATION: Middle States Association of Colleges and Schools

INSTITUTIONALLY ADMINISTERED FINANCIAL AID: No

## DEGREE OR CERTIFICATE PROGRAMS OFFERED

Programs offered do not lead to a degree or other formal award.

## NON-DEGREE-RELATED COURSE TOPICS OFFERED

Undergraduate—American (United States) history; anthropology; criminal justice and corrections; psychology; sociology.
Graduate—curriculum and instruction.

---

**Special Note**

Saint Peter's College currently offers distance learning graduate education courses through videotape as well as selected graduate and undergraduate courses via ITV (interactive television). During the 2000–01 academic year, the College offered designated graduate and undergraduate Web-based courses.

Graduate education students can work at their own pace on any of the nine 3-credit courses that were developed with the direct participation of and within the context of the expressed needs of K–12 teachers, school administrators, college faculty members, and students. These courses can be applied toward a Saint Peter's Master of Arts in Education with a concentration in urban education as well as toward other degrees and certificates at Saint Peter's or most other graduate education programs. The concentration in urban education, with a careful choice of electives, leads to eligibility for Supervisor of Instruction. The courses are offered at a significant discount. The College also offers selected graduate education courses at a discount via its ATV facilities. The courses can be used as electives in other concentrations at the College.

Advanced high school seniors and juniors can take advantage of the ITV rooms in their schools to join introductory 3-credit college classes. The classes are acceptable to virtually any college in the nation.

For more information, students should contact the Institute for the Advancement of Urban Education at 201-915-9329 or via e-mail at iauedept@spcvxa.spc.edu or visit the Web site at http://www.spc.edu/iaue.

---

# SALVE REGINA UNIVERSITY

*Extension Study*

100 Ochre Point Avenue
Newport, RI 02840-4192
**Contact:** Charles H. Reed, Director of Extension Studies
**Phone:** 401-341-2212
**Fax:** 401-341-2931
**Web:** http://www.salve.edu/
**E-mail:** reedc@salve.edu

**ACCREDITATION:** New England Association of Schools and Colleges
**INSTITUTIONALLY ADMINISTERED FINANCIAL AID:** Yes

## DEGREE OR CERTIFICATE PROGRAMS OFFERED

**Undergraduate—*BA:*** Liberal Studies. ***BS:*** Business. ***Certificate:*** Management and Correctional Administration; Management.
**Graduate—*MA:*** Human Development; International Relations. ***MBA:*** Business Administration. ***MS:*** Management.

## NON-DEGREE-RELATED COURSE TOPICS OFFERED

**Undergraduate—**English language and literature, general; English technical and business writing; business administration and management; nursing; philosophy and religion.
**Graduate—**human resources management.
**See full description on page 484.**

# SAM HOUSTON STATE UNIVERSITY

*Correspondence Course Division*

PO Box 2536
Huntsville, TX 77341-2536
**Contact:** Gail M. Wright, Correspondence Course Coordinator
**Phone:** 936-294-1003
**Fax:** 936-294-3703
**Web:** http://www.shsu.edu/~cor_www
**E-mail:** cor_gmw@shsu.edu

**ACCREDITATION:** Southern Association of Colleges and Schools
**INSTITUTIONALLY ADMINISTERED FINANCIAL AID:** No

## DEGREE OR CERTIFICATE PROGRAMS OFFERED

**Programs offered do not lead to a degree or other formal award.**

## NON-DEGREE-RELATED COURSE TOPICS OFFERED

**Undergraduate—**American (United States) history; English creative writing; accounting; anthropology; business marketing and marketing management; economics; family/consumer resource management; finance, general; geography; inorganic chemistry; insurance and risk management; law and legal studies, other; mathematics, other; organic chemistry; photography; sociology.
**See full description on page 486.**

# SAMPSON COMMUNITY COLLEGE

PO Box 318
Clinton, NC 28329

**Contact:** Amy Noel, Distance Learning Coordinator
**Phone:** 910-592-8081 Ext. 5044
**Web:** http://www.sampson.cc.nc.us/
**E-mail:** anoel@sampson.cc.nc.us

**ACCREDITATION:** Southern Association of Colleges and Schools
**INSTITUTIONALLY ADMINISTERED FINANCIAL AID:** Yes

## DEGREE OR CERTIFICATE PROGRAMS OFFERED

**Programs offered do not lead to a degree or other formal award.**

## NON-DEGREE-RELATED COURSE TOPICS OFFERED

**Undergraduate—**animal sciences; business administration and management; computer and information sciences, general; sociology.

# SAMUEL MERRITT COLLEGE

*Academic Affairs*

370 Hawthorne Avenue
Oakland, CA 94609
**Contact:** Mr. John Garten-Shuman, Director of Admission
**Phone:** 800-607-6377
**Fax:** 510-869-6525
**Web:** http://www.samuelmerritt.edu
**E-mail:** jgartens@samuelmerritt.edu

**ACCREDITATION:** Western Association of Schools and Colleges
**INSTITUTIONALLY ADMINISTERED FINANCIAL AID:** Yes

## DEGREE OR CERTIFICATE PROGRAMS OFFERED

**Graduate—*MSN:*** Nursing.

# SANDHILLS COMMUNITY COLLEGE

*Division of Curriculum Education*

3395 Airport Road
Pinehurst, NC 28374
**Contact:** Prof. Richard N. Lewis, Jr., Chair, Department of Languages
**Phone:** 910-695-3856
**Fax:** 910-692-6918
**Web:** http://www.sandhills.cc.nc.us
**E-mail:** lewisr@email.sandhills.cc.nc.us

**ACCREDITATION:** Southern Association of Colleges and Schools
**INSTITUTIONALLY ADMINISTERED FINANCIAL AID:** Yes

## DEGREE OR CERTIFICATE PROGRAMS OFFERED

**Programs offered do not lead to a degree or other formal award.**

## NON-DEGREE-RELATED COURSE TOPICS OFFERED

**Undergraduate—**English composition; English language and literature, general; English technical and business writing; biological and physical sciences; business management and administrative services, other; economics; education, other; film/cinema studies; geography; health professions and related sciences, other; history; political science and government; psychology; sociology.

# SAN DIEGO STATE UNIVERSITY

## Academic Affairs

5500 Campanile Drive
San Diego, CA 92182-8010
**Contact:** Ms. Treacy Lau, Principal Coordinator for Distributed Learning
**Phone:** 619-594-0919
**Fax:** 619-594-7443
**Web:** http://www.sdsu.edu/dl
**E-mail:** dl@mail.sdsu.edu

**ACCREDITATION:** Western Association of Schools and Colleges
**INSTITUTIONALLY ADMINISTERED FINANCIAL AID:** Yes

### DEGREE OR CERTIFICATE PROGRAMS OFFERED

**Undergraduate—*BA:*** CSU Consortial Jewish Studies Major. ***Certificate:*** Education Technology.
**Graduate—*MA:*** Rehabilitation Science Counseling. ***MAE:*** Education Leadership.

### NON-DEGREE-RELATED COURSE TOPICS OFFERED

**Undergraduate**—American (United States) history; Jewish/Judaic studies; adult and continuing teacher education; business; educational/instructional media design; geological and related sciences; physiology, human and animal; teacher education, specific academic and vocational programs.
**Graduate**—adult and continuing teacher education; business; educational/instructional media design.
**Non-credit**—English creative writing; business; computer software and media applications; education, general.

# SAN JACINTO COLLEGE NORTH CAMPUS

8060 Spencer Highway
Pasadena, TX 77501
**Contact:** Dr. Del Long, Director of Admission
**Phone:** 281-476-1819
**Fax:** 281-478-2720
**Web:** http://www.sjcd.cc.tx.us/distlearn
**E-mail:** dlong@sjcd.cc.tx.us

**ACCREDITATION:** Southern Association of Colleges and Schools
**INSTITUTIONALLY ADMINISTERED FINANCIAL AID:** Yes

### DEGREE OR CERTIFICATE PROGRAMS OFFERED

Programs offered do not lead to a degree or other formal award.

### NON-DEGREE-RELATED COURSE TOPICS OFFERED

**Undergraduate**—American literature (United States); English composition; English creative writing; English language and literature, general; English literature (British and Commonwealth); English technical and business writing; accounting; applied mathematics; business; business administration and management; business communications; business information and data processing services; business management and administrative services, other; computer and information sciences, general; computer and information sciences, other; computer software and media applications; computer systems networking and telecommunications; criminal justice and corrections; criminology; developmental and

child psychology; fine arts and art studies; foods and nutrition studies; health and medical administrative services; health and medical preparatory programs; health professions and related sciences, other; industrial production technologies; information sciences and systems; journalism and mass communications; marketing management and research; mathematics; mathematics and computer science; mathematics, other; pharmacy; psychology; psychology, other; public administration; public administration and services, other; real estate; social psychology; social work; sociology.

# SAN JOAQUIN DELTA COLLEGE

## Instructional Development

5151 Pacific Avenue
Stockton, CA 95207
**Contact:** Kathryn Campbell, Dean of Instruction for Instructional Development and Regional Education
**Phone:** 209-954-5039
**Fax:** 209-954-5600
**Web:** http://www.deltacollege.org
**E-mail:** kcampbell@sjdccd.cc.ca.us

**ACCREDITATION:** Western Association of Schools and Colleges
**INSTITUTIONALLY ADMINISTERED FINANCIAL AID:** Yes

eCollege.com    www.ecollege.com

### DEGREE OR CERTIFICATE PROGRAMS OFFERED

**Undergraduate—*AA:*** Liberal Arts and Science. ***Certificate:*** Early Childhood Education Assistant; Merchandising; Supervision and Management.

### NON-DEGREE-RELATED COURSE TOPICS OFFERED

**Undergraduate**—American literature (United States); English composition; accounting; advertising; business marketing and marketing management; child care and guidance workers and managers; computer science; history; interior design; law and legal studies, other; mathematics, other; nursing; philosophy and religion; psychology; sociology.
**See full description on page 488.**

# SANTA BARBARA CITY COLLEGE

## SBCC Online

721 Cliff Drive
Santa Barbara, CA 93109
**Contact:** Michael Gallegos, Dean, Educational Technologies
**Phone:** 805-965-0581 Ext. 2914
**Fax:** 805-963-7222
**Web:** http://sbcc.net
**E-mail:** gallegos@sbcc.net

**ACCREDITATION:** Western Association of Schools and Colleges
**INSTITUTIONALLY ADMINISTERED FINANCIAL AID:** Yes

### DEGREE OR CERTIFICATE PROGRAMS OFFERED

Programs offered do not lead to a degree or other formal award.

### NON-DEGREE-RELATED COURSE TOPICS OFFERED

**Undergraduate**—American literature (United States); English language and literature, general; accounting; applied mathematics; biological and physical sciences; business; chemistry; communications, general; community health services; computer science; ethnic and cultural studies; foreign languages and literatures; health and medical assistants; history; internet and world wide web; music; philosophy and religion; psychology; sociology.

# SANTA MONICA COLLEGE

## SMC Online

1900 Pico Boulevard
Santa Monica, CA 90405
**Contact:** Winniphred Stone, Associate Dean of Distance Education
**Phone:** 310-434-3761
**Fax:** 310-434-3769
**Web:** http://smconline.org
**E-mail:** stone_winniphred@smc.edu

**ACCREDITATION:** Western Association of Schools and Colleges
**INSTITUTIONALLY ADMINISTERED FINANCIAL AID:** Yes

eCollege.com *www.ecollege.com*

### DEGREE OR CERTIFICATE PROGRAMS OFFERED
**Programs offered do not lead to a degree or other formal award.**
See full description on page 490.

# SANTA ROSA JUNIOR COLLEGE

1501 Mendocino Avenue
Santa Rosa, CA 95401
**Contact:** Dr. Richard Sapanaro, Director of Open Learning
**Phone:** 707-524-1757
**Fax:** 707-527-4545
**Web:** http://www.santarosa.edu/
**E-mail:** rsapanaro@santarosa.edu

**ACCREDITATION:** Western Association of Schools and Colleges
**INSTITUTIONALLY ADMINISTERED FINANCIAL AID:** Yes

### DEGREE OR CERTIFICATE PROGRAMS OFFERED
**Programs offered do not lead to a degree or other formal award.**

### NON-DEGREE-RELATED COURSE TOPICS OFFERED
**Undergraduate**—accounting; administrative and secretarial services; anthropology; atmospheric sciences and meteorology; business communications; business marketing and marketing management; communications technologies; communications, general; computer and information sciences, general; computer software and media applications; criminal justice and corrections; family and community studies; foreign languages and literatures, other; liberal arts and sciences, general studies and humanities; library science/librarianship; philosophy; psychology; real estate; sociology; visual and performing arts.
**Non-credit**—English creative writing.

# SAUK VALLEY COMMUNITY COLLEGE

173 Illinois Route 2
Dixon, IL 61021

**Contact:** Alan Pfeifer, Director of Academic Computing
**Phone:** 815-288-5511 Ext. 218
**Fax:** 815-288-5958
**Web:** http://www.svcc.edu/
**E-mail:** pfeifer@svcc.edu

**ACCREDITATION:** North Central Association of Colleges and Schools
**INSTITUTIONALLY ADMINISTERED FINANCIAL AID:** Yes

### DEGREE OR CERTIFICATE PROGRAMS OFFERED
**Programs offered do not lead to a degree or other formal award.**

### NON-DEGREE-RELATED COURSE TOPICS OFFERED
**Undergraduate**—American (United States) history; English composition; accounting; biology, general; criminal justice and corrections; economics; international business; mathematics, other; psychology; sociology.

# SAYBROOK GRADUATE SCHOOL AND RESEARCH CENTER

450 Pacific, Third Floor
San Francisco, CA 94133
**Contact:** Mindy Myers, Vice President for Admissions and Recruitment
**Phone:** 800-825-4480 Ext. 6196
**Fax:** 415-433-9271 Ext. 6196
**Web:** http://www.saybrook.edu/
**E-mail:** mmyers@saybrook.edu

**ACCREDITATION:** Western Association of Schools and Colleges
**INSTITUTIONALLY ADMINISTERED FINANCIAL AID:** Yes

### DEGREE OR CERTIFICATE PROGRAMS OFFERED
**Graduate**—*MA:* Human Science; Organizational Systems; Psychology Licensure; Psychology.
**Postgraduate and doctoral**—*PhD:* Human Science; Individualized PhD, Advanced Standing Doctoral Students; Individualized PhD, Post Masters; Organizational Studies; Psychology.

### NON-DEGREE-RELATED COURSE TOPICS OFFERED
**Graduate**—cognitive psychology and psycholinguistics; community health services; counseling psychology; developmental and child psychology; peace and conflict studies; psychology; public policy analysis; social psychology.
See full description on page 492.

# SCHENECTADY COUNTY COMMUNITY COLLEGE

78 Washington Avenue
Schenectady, NY 12305
**Contact:** Steve McIntosh, Director of Instructional Technology Center
**Phone:** 518-381-1253
**Web:** http://www.sunysccc.edu

**E-mail:** mcintosb@gw.sunysccc.edu

**ACCREDITATION:** Middle States Association of Colleges and Schools

**INSTITUTIONALLY ADMINISTERED FINANCIAL AID:** Yes

## DEGREE OR CERTIFICATE PROGRAMS OFFERED

Programs offered do not lead to a degree or other formal award.

## NON-DEGREE-RELATED COURSE TOPICS OFFERED

**Undergraduate**—English composition; English technical and business writing; accounting; astronomy; business administration and management; culinary arts and related services; enterprise management and operation; fire protection; history; hospitality services management; law and legal studies; mathematics; music.
**Non-credit**—English as a second language; English creative writing.

# SCHILLER INTERNATIONAL UNIVERSITY

453 Edgewater Drive
Dunedin, FL 34698
**Contact:** Ms. Susan Russeff, Associate Director of Admissions
**Phone:** 727-736-5082 Ext. 239
**Fax:** 727-734-0359
**Web:** http://www.schiller.edu/
**E-mail:** susan_russeff@schiller.edu

**ACCREDITATION:** Accrediting Council for Independent Colleges and Schools

**INSTITUTIONALLY ADMINISTERED FINANCIAL AID:** Yes

## DEGREE OR CERTIFICATE PROGRAMS OFFERED

**Graduate**—*MBA:* International Business.

## NON-DEGREE-RELATED COURSE TOPICS OFFERED

**Undergraduate**—English composition; accounting; business administration and management; business communications; business/managerial economics; history; human resources management; international business; marketing management and research; mathematics; physical sciences, general.
**Graduate**—accounting; business/managerial economics; computer/information technology administration and management; hospitality services management; human resources management; international business; marketing management and research; mathematical statistics; tourism and travel services marketing operations.

### Special Note

Schiller International University (SIU), with 8 campuses in 6 countries and a leader in global education, was founded in 1964. SIU is an independent, licensed, and accredited institution offering a curriculum of more than 300 courses in 16 areas of study that lead to associate, bachelor's, and master's degrees. Currently SIU offers its MBA program with a concentration in international business in a distance learning format. Concentrations in international hotel and tourism management and management of information technology are being developed.

Students can combine online courses with a residential program to complete degree requirements or elect to take the complete program online. Selected graduate- and undergraduate-level courses are also offered in a distance learning format. Courses are taught by highly qualified faculty members trained in methods of distance learning instruction. Each course includes a textbook, a study guide, and Web-based course materials. The study guides have been developed by SIU's teaching faculty.

The University has developed a number of methods to assist students in distance learning programs. Each student receives a copy of SIU's publication *A Guide to Distance Learning.* Specially trained faculty mentors are always available by e-mail for consultation, and technical assistance is available 24 hours per day. Distance learning students have access to the full range of support services that are presently used by all SIU students.

Eligibility for financial aid for distance learning is currently available to those who qualify in the form of private scholarships or alternative student loans (private loans).

# SCHOOLCRAFT COLLEGE
*Distance Learning Office*
18600 Haggerty Road
Livonia, MI 48152
**Contact:** Elgene W. Doinidis, Coordinator
**Phone:** 734-462-4532
**Fax:** 734-462-4589
**Web:** http://www.schoolcraft.cc.mi.us
**E-mail:** edoinidi@schoolcraft.cc.mi.us

**ACCREDITATION:** North Central Association of Colleges and Schools

## DEGREE OR CERTIFICATE PROGRAMS OFFERED

**Undergraduate**—*AA:* Liberal Arts. *AGS:* Liberal Arts.
**Graduate**—*MSBA:* Omnibus.

## NON-DEGREE-RELATED COURSE TOPICS OFFERED

**Undergraduate**—English composition; business; developmental and child psychology; sociology.

# SCHOOL FOR INTERNATIONAL TRAINING
*Instructional Technology*
SIT Extension, Kipling Road, PO Box 0676
Brattleboro, VT 05302-0676
**Contact:** Ms. Meredith McDill, Director of Extension Programs
**Phone:** 802-258-3324
**Fax:** 802-258-3248
**Web:** http://www.sit.edu/extension/index.html
**E-mail:** meredith.mcdill@sit.edu

**ACCREDITATION:** New England Association of Schools and Colleges

**INSTITUTIONALLY ADMINISTERED FINANCIAL AID:** No

## DEGREE OR CERTIFICATE PROGRAMS OFFERED

Programs offered do not lead to a degree or other formal award.

## NON-DEGREE-RELATED COURSE TOPICS OFFERED

**Non-credit**—English language and literature, general; human resources management; international business; teacher education, specific academic and vocational programs; teaching English as a second language/foreign language.

# SEABURY-WESTERN THEOLOGICAL SEMINARY

2122 Sheridan Road
Evanston, IL 60201
**Contact:** Ms. Susan A. Shroff, Registrar and Manager of Academic Affairs
**Phone:** 847-328-9300 Ext. 26
**Fax:** 847-328-9624
**Web:** http://www.seabury.edu/
**E-mail:** susan-shroff@seabury.edu

**ACCREDITATION:** North Central Association of Colleges and Schools

## DEGREE OR CERTIFICATE PROGRAMS OFFERED

Programs offered do not lead to a degree or other formal award.

## NON-DEGREE-RELATED COURSE TOPICS OFFERED

**Graduate**—theological and ministerial studies.
**Non-credit**—theological and ministerial studies.

# SEATTLE CENTRAL COMMUNITY COLLEGE

## Distance Learning Program

1701 Broadway, BE1148
Seattle, WA 98122-2400
**Contact:** Queenie L. Baker, Director
**Phone:** 800-510-1724
**Fax:** 206-287-5562
**Web:** http://distantlearning.net
**E-mail:** qbaker@sccd.ctc.edu

**ACCREDITATION:** Northwest Association of Schools and Colleges
**INSTITUTIONALLY ADMINISTERED FINANCIAL AID:** Yes

## DEGREE OR CERTIFICATE PROGRAMS OFFERED

**Undergraduate**—*AA:* Liberal Arts. *Certificate:* Teaching English as a Second Language.

## NON-DEGREE-RELATED COURSE TOPICS OFFERED

**Undergraduate**—American studies/civilization; Asian studies; English composition; Spanish language and literature; accounting; anthropology; developmental and child psychology; environmental science/studies; film/cinema studies; geography; journalism; journalism and mass communication, other; mathematical statistics; mathematics, other; medieval and renaissance studies; oceanography; philosophy and religion; sociology.

## Special Note

Since its founding in 1967, Seattle Central Community College has developed into a school with a national reputation for innovative educational programs. Located in Seattle, Washington, Seattle Central is one of the largest colleges in the state, with an enrollment of 10,000 students. The College is unique among the state's community colleges for its ethnic and cultural diversity. Each year, more students from Seattle Central go on to 4-year institutions than from any other community college in the state.

If the ultimate goal is a 4-year degree, the Associate of Arts (AA) degree via distance learning provides freshman- and sophomore-level classes recognized by most universities. For those not sure about college, distance learning may help them decide. Students can enroll via distance learning in an individual course that interests them or helps improve their knowledge and skills and earn credit toward an AA degree, or they can earn a certificate in a specific technical area. There are several reasons why distance learning may work for students, including those with a work or home schedule conflict, disability or homebound situation, lifestyle preferences, traffic gridlock, or a residence too far from a college. It can also be a good match with the student's learning style or simply more convenient.

Seattle Central's distance learning program offers courses in a variety of formats, including correspondence courses, telecourses, videocassette courses, and online courses.

For more information, students should contact the Distance Learning Program at 800-510-1724 (toll-free) or by e-mail (dislrn@sccd.ctc.edu) or visit the home page (http://www.distantlearning.net).

# SEMINOLE COMMUNITY COLLEGE

## Distance Learning Department

100 Weldon Boulevard
Sanford, FL 32773
**Contact:** Mrs. Wilma Lopez Hodges, Instructional Technology Specialist
**Phone:** 407-328-4722 Ext. 3232
**Fax:** 407-328-2233
**Web:** http://scc-fl.com/dl
**E-mail:** hodgesw@scc-fl.com

**ACCREDITATION:** Southern Association of Colleges and Schools
**INSTITUTIONALLY ADMINISTERED FINANCIAL AID:** Yes

## DEGREE OR CERTIFICATE PROGRAMS OFFERED

Programs offered do not lead to a degree or other formal award.

## NON-DEGREE-RELATED COURSE TOPICS OFFERED

**Undergraduate**—English composition; English technical and business writing; administrative and secretarial services; anthropology; area, ethnic and cultural studies, other; astronomy; atmospheric sciences and meteorology; business information and data processing services; computer and information sciences, general; computer programming; computer science; computer software and media applications; computer systems analysis; computer systems networking and telecommunications; criminal justice and corrections; criminology; data entry/microcomputer applications; data processing technology; economics; education, general; electrical and electronic engineering-related technology; electrical and electronics equipment installers and repairers; family and community studies; geography; geological and related sciences; history; liberal arts and sciences, general studies and humanities; library science, other; psychology; social psychology; social sciences, general; teacher education, specific academic and vocational programs.

**Non-credit**—health and medical administrative services; protective services, other.

# SEQUOIA INSTITUTE

200 Whitney Place
Freemont, CA 94539-7663
**Contact:** Mr. Hank Gallegus, Coordinator of AAS Degree Program
**Web:** http://www.sequoiainstitute.com/
**E-mail:** hgallegus@sequoiainstitute.com

**ACCREDITATION:** Accrediting Commission of Career Schools and Colleges of Technology

**INSTITUTIONALLY ADMINISTERED FINANCIAL AID:** Yes

eCollege.com   *www.ecollege.com*

## DEGREE OR CERTIFICATE PROGRAMS OFFERED

**Undergraduate**—*AAS:* Automotive Technology and HVAC Technology.

# SETON HALL UNIVERSITY

## *SetonWorldWide*

Kozsloski Hall, 400 South Orange Avenue
South Orange, NJ 07079
**Contact:** Dr. Philip DiSalvio, Director
**Phone:** 973-761-9086
**Fax:** 973-761-9234
**Web:** http://www.setonworldwide.net
**E-mail:** disalvph@shu.edu

**ACCREDITATION:** Middle States Association of Colleges and Schools
**INSTITUTIONALLY ADMINISTERED FINANCIAL AID:** Yes

eCollege.com   *www.ecollege.com*

## DEGREE OR CERTIFICATE PROGRAMS OFFERED

**Undergraduate**—*BSN:* RN to BSN.
**Graduate**—*MA:* Counseling; Educational Administration and Supervision; Healthcare Administration; Strategic Communication and Leadership. *MSN:* Nurse Practitioner.

## NON-DEGREE-RELATED COURSE TOPICS OFFERED

**Graduate**—accounting; health system/health services administration.
**See full description on page 494.**

# SETON HILL COLLEGE

## *Academic Affairs*

Seton Hill Drive
Greensburg, PA 15601

**Contact:** Dr. Rich Cerullo, Director of Information and Communication Technology
**Phone:** 724-830-1589
**Fax:** 724-830-1294
**Web:** http://www.setonhill.edu
**E-mail:** cerullo@setonhill.edu

**ACCREDITATION:** Middle States Association of Colleges and Schools
**INSTITUTIONALLY ADMINISTERED FINANCIAL AID:** Yes

## DEGREE OR CERTIFICATE PROGRAMS OFFERED

**Programs offered do not lead to a degree or other formal award.**

## NON-DEGREE-RELATED COURSE TOPICS OFFERED

**Undergraduate**—communications, other; history; political science and government.
**Graduate**—English creative writing.

# SEWARD COUNTY COMMUNITY COLLEGE

PO Box 1137
Liberal, KS 67905
**Contact:** Mr. Dale L. Reed, Associate Dean of Educational Services
**Phone:** 620-626-3137
**Fax:** 620-629-2715
**Web:** http://www.sccc.net
**E-mail:** dreed@sccc.net

**ACCREDITATION:** North Central Association of Colleges and Schools
**INSTITUTIONALLY ADMINISTERED FINANCIAL AID:** Yes

eCollege.com   *www.ecollege.com*

## DEGREE OR CERTIFICATE PROGRAMS OFFERED

**Programs offered do not lead to a degree or other formal award.**

## NON-DEGREE-RELATED COURSE TOPICS OFFERED

**Undergraduate**—American literature (United States); English composition; accounting; advertising; agriculture/agricultural sciences; biology, general; business information and data processing services; chemistry; communications, general; computer software and media applications; computer/information technology administration and management; economics; geography; history; mathematical statistics; mathematics; psychology.

# SHASTA BIBLE COLLEGE

## *Individualized Distance Learning*

2980 Hartnell Avenue
Redding, CA 96002
**Contact:** Pastor George Gunn, Dean of Admissions and Records
**Phone:** 530-221-4275
**Fax:** 530-221-6929
**Web:** http://www.shasta.edu

**E-mail:** ggunn@shasta.edu

**ACCREDITATION:** Transnational Association of Christian Colleges and Schools

**INSTITUTIONALLY ADMINISTERED FINANCIAL AID:** Yes

### DEGREE OR CERTIFICATE PROGRAMS OFFERED
Programs offered do not lead to a degree or other formal award.

### NON-DEGREE-RELATED COURSE TOPICS OFFERED
Undergraduate—education, other.

# SHASTA COLLEGE

PO Box 496006, 11555 Old Oregon Trail
Redding, CA 96049
**Contact:** Dr. James E. Poulsen, Dean of Extended Education and Evening Programs
**Phone:** 530-225-4814
**Fax:** 530-225-4983
**Web:** http://www.shastacollege.edu/
**E-mail:** jpoulsen@shastacollege.edu

**ACCREDITATION:** Western Association of Schools and Colleges

**INSTITUTIONALLY ADMINISTERED FINANCIAL AID:** No

### DEGREE OR CERTIFICATE PROGRAMS OFFERED
Programs offered do not lead to a degree or other formal award.

### NON-DEGREE-RELATED COURSE TOPICS OFFERED
Undergraduate—English composition; biological and physical sciences; business administration and management; history; liberal arts and sciences, general studies and humanities; social sciences, general.

# SHAWNEE STATE UNIVERSITY
*Nursing Department*

940 Second Street, Health Sciences Building, Room 122
Portsmouth, OH 45662
**Contact:** Dr. Cheryl Boyd, Chair of Nursing Department
**Phone:** 740-355-2378
**E-mail:** cboyd@shawnee.edu

**ACCREDITATION:** North Central Association of Colleges and Schools

**INSTITUTIONALLY ADMINISTERED FINANCIAL AID:** Yes

### DEGREE OR CERTIFICATE PROGRAMS OFFERED
Programs offered do not lead to a degree or other formal award.

### NON-DEGREE-RELATED COURSE TOPICS OFFERED
Undergraduate—English as a second language; English language and literature, general; accounting; anthropology; biology, general; business administration and management; business information and data processing services; chemistry; computer and information sciences, general; computer engineering; computer programming; education, general; electromechanical instrumentation and maintenance technology; environmental control technologies; fine arts and art studies; foreign languages and literatures, other; geography; health and medical assistants; health and medical laboratory technologies; health and physical education/fitness; history; journalism and mass communications; law and legal studies;

mathematical statistics; mathematics; music; nursing; philosophy; physical sciences, general; political science and government; psychology; sociology.

# SHERIDAN COLLEGE

PO Box 1500
Sheridan, WY 82801
**Contact:** Mark Englert, Dean of Arts and Sciences
**Phone:** 307-674-6446 Ext. 6135
**Fax:** 307-674-4293
**E-mail:** menglert@sc.cc.wy.us

**ACCREDITATION:** North Central Association of Colleges and Schools

**INSTITUTIONALLY ADMINISTERED FINANCIAL AID:** Yes

### DEGREE OR CERTIFICATE PROGRAMS OFFERED
Programs offered do not lead to a degree or other formal award.

### NON-DEGREE-RELATED COURSE TOPICS OFFERED
Undergraduate—English composition; English creative writing; Spanish language and literature; accounting; agricultural business and production, other; business; business marketing and marketing management; business/managerial economics; data entry/microcomputer applications; economics; food products retailing and wholesaling operations.

# SHIPPENSBURG UNIVERSITY OF PENNSYLVANIA
*Extended Studies*

1871 Old Main Drive
Shippensburg, PA 17257-2299
**Contact:** Dr. Kathleen Howley, Dean of Extended Studies
**Phone:** 717-477-1348
**Fax:** 717-477-4050
**Web:** http://www.ship.edu/~virtual
**E-mail:** kmhowl@wharf.ship.edu

**ACCREDITATION:** Middle States Association of Colleges and Schools

**INSTITUTIONALLY ADMINISTERED FINANCIAL AID:** Yes

### DEGREE OR CERTIFICATE PROGRAMS OFFERED
Programs offered do not lead to a degree or other formal award.

### NON-DEGREE-RELATED COURSE TOPICS OFFERED
Undergraduate—English language and literature, general; biology, general; communications, general; criminal justice and corrections; economics; education, other; geography; mathematics; philosophy; physics; psychology; teacher education, specific academic and vocational programs.
Graduate—English language and literature, general; mathematics; mathematics and computer science.

# SIMPSON COLLEGE
*Division of Adult Learning*

701 North C Street
Indianola, IA 50125

**Contact:** Walter Pearson, Director
**Phone:** 515-961-1615
**Fax:** 515-961-1498
**Web:** http://www.simpson.edu/dal
**E-mail:** adultlrn@simpson.edu

**ACCREDITATION:** North Central Association of Colleges and Schools
**INSTITUTIONALLY ADMINISTERED FINANCIAL AID:** Yes

eCollege.com  www.ecollege.com

## DEGREE OR CERTIFICATE PROGRAMS OFFERED
Programs offered do not lead to a degree or other formal award.

## NON-DEGREE-RELATED COURSE TOPICS OFFERED
**Undergraduate**—communications, general; criminal justice and corrections; sociology.

# SINCLAIR COMMUNITY COLLEGE
*Distance Learning Division*
444 West Third Street
Dayton, OH 45402
**Contact:** Linda M. PaHud, Coordinator of Distance Learning Services
**Phone:** 937-512-2694
**Fax:** 937-512-2891
**Web:** http://www.sinclair.edu/distance
**E-mail:** linda.pahud@sinclair.edu

**ACCREDITATION:** North Central Association of Colleges and Schools
**INSTITUTIONALLY ADMINISTERED FINANCIAL AID:** Yes

## DEGREE OR CERTIFICATE PROGRAMS OFFERED
**Undergraduate—AA:** Liberal Arts. **AS:** Business Administration. **Certificate:** Software Applications for the Professional. **Certification:** Radiologic Technology Continuing Education.

## NON-DEGREE-RELATED COURSE TOPICS OFFERED
**Undergraduate**—English as a second language; English composition; English technical and business writing; accounting; administrative and secretarial services; art history, criticism and conservation; business administration and management; business marketing and marketing management; computer software and media applications; computer systems networking and telecommunications; developmental and child psychology; economics; electrical, electronics and communication engineering; history; law and legal studies, other; mathematics; miscellaneous health professions; photography; psychology; sociology.
**Non-credit**—health professions and related sciences, other.
See full description on page 496.

# SKIDMORE COLLEGE
*Graduate Programs*
850 Broadway
Saratoga Springs, NY 12866
**Contact:** Dr. David P. Glaser, Director of Master of Arts in Liberal Studies
**Phone:** 518-580-5480 Ext. 5489

**Fax:** 518-580-5486
**Web:** http://www.skidmore.edu/administration/mals/
**E-mail:** dglaser@skidmore.edu

**ACCREDITATION:** Middle States Association of Colleges and Schools
**INSTITUTIONALLY ADMINISTERED FINANCIAL AID:** Yes

## DEGREE OR CERTIFICATE PROGRAMS OFFERED
**Graduate—MA:** Liberal Studies.

## NON-DEGREE-RELATED COURSE TOPICS OFFERED
**Graduate**—liberal arts and sciences, general studies and humanities.
See full description on page 498.

# SKIDMORE COLLEGE
*University Without Walls*
Saratoga Springs, NY 12866
**Contact:** Cornel Reinhart, Director
**Phone:** 518-580-5450
**Fax:** 518-580-5449
**Web:** http://www.skidmore.edu/uww
**E-mail:** uww@skidmore.edu

**ACCREDITATION:** Middle States Association of Colleges and Schools
**INSTITUTIONALLY ADMINISTERED FINANCIAL AID:** Yes

## DEGREE OR CERTIFICATE PROGRAMS OFFERED
**Undergraduate—BA:** Individualized Studies.

## NON-DEGREE-RELATED COURSE TOPICS OFFERED
**Undergraduate**—English composition; English creative writing; French language and literature; accounting; biology, general; developmental and child psychology; environmental health; geography; journalism; microbiology/bacteriology; social work; sociology.
See full description on page 500.

# SLIPPERY ROCK UNIVERSITY OF PENNSYLVANIA
200 Maltby Center
Slippery Rock, PA 16057
**Contact:** Dr. James Kushner, Dean of Lifelong Learning
**Phone:** 724-738-4484
**Fax:** 724-738-4483
**Web:** http://www.sru.edu/
**E-mail:** james.kushner@sru.edu

**ACCREDITATION:** Middle States Association of Colleges and Schools
**INSTITUTIONALLY ADMINISTERED FINANCIAL AID:** Yes

## DEGREE OR CERTIFICATE PROGRAMS OFFERED
**Graduate—MS:** Park and Resource Management. **MSN:** Family Nurse Practitioner Graduate Program.

## NON-DEGREE-RELATED COURSE TOPICS OFFERED
**Undergraduate**—accounting; computer science; education, general; education, other; geological and related sciences; nursing; philosophy; psychology.

Graduate—counseling psychology; education, general; education, other; educational psychology; special education.

Non-credit—computer software and media applications.

# SONOMA STATE UNIVERSITY
## Liberal Studies Special Sessions Degree Programs

1801 East Cotati Avenue
Rohnert Park, CA 94928-3609
Contact: Beth Warner, Administrative Coordinator
Phone: 707-664-3977
Fax: 707-664-2613
Web: http://www.sonoma.edu/exed/Degrees/dindex.html
E-mail: beth.warner@sonoma.edu

ACCREDITATION: Western Association of Schools and Colleges
INSTITUTIONALLY ADMINISTERED FINANCIAL AID: Yes

### DEGREE OR CERTIFICATE PROGRAMS OFFERED
Undergraduate—*BA:* Liberal Studies.
Graduate—*MA:* Action for a Viable Future.

# SOUTHEAST ARKANSAS COLLEGE

1900 South Hazel Street
Pine Bluff, AR 71603
Contact: Kim Brown-King, Coordinator of Distance Learning
Phone: 870-543-5988
Web: http://www.seark.org/

ACCREDITATION: North Central Association of Colleges and Schools
INSTITUTIONALLY ADMINISTERED FINANCIAL AID: Yes

### DEGREE OR CERTIFICATE PROGRAMS OFFERED
Programs offered do not lead to a degree or other formal award.

### NON-DEGREE-RELATED COURSE TOPICS OFFERED
Undergraduate—English composition; anthropology; business; business administration and management; business communications; business management and administrative services, other; business/managerial economics; economics; geography; health and physical education/fitness; history; marketing management and research; mathematics; psychology; sociology.

# SOUTHEAST COMMUNITY COLLEGE, BEATRICE CAMPUS

4771 West Scott Road
Beatrice, NE 68310
Contact: Bob Morgan, Distance Learning Coordinator
Phone: 402-228-3468 Ext. 326
Fax: 402-228-2218
E-mail: bmorgan@scc.cc.ne.us

ACCREDITATION: North Central Association of Colleges and Schools
INSTITUTIONALLY ADMINISTERED FINANCIAL AID: Yes

### DEGREE OR CERTIFICATE PROGRAMS OFFERED
Undergraduate—*AAS:* Business Administration; Radiologic Technology Program; Surgical Technology. *Certification:* Food Service Training Program. *License:* Nursing Home Administration.

### NON-DEGREE-RELATED COURSE TOPICS OFFERED
Undergraduate—English composition; English language and literature, general; English technical and business writing; accounting; biological sciences/life sciences, other; business; economics; health and medical administrative services; health professions and related sciences, other; history; institutional food workers and administrators; liberal arts and sciences, general studies and humanities; mathematics; miscellaneous health professions; philosophy; psychology; social psychology; speech and rhetorical studies.
Non-credit—business quantitative methods and management science; mathematics.

# SOUTHEAST COMMUNITY COLLEGE, LINCOLN CAMPUS
## Academic Education

8800 O Street
Lincoln, NE 68520
Contact: Randy Hiatt, Director of Distance and Extended Education
Phone: 402-437-2705
Fax: 402-437-2541
Web: http://www.college.secc.cc.ne.us/
E-mail: rhiatt@scc.cc.ne.us

ACCREDITATION: North Central Association of Colleges and Schools
INSTITUTIONALLY ADMINISTERED FINANCIAL AID: Yes

### DEGREE OR CERTIFICATE PROGRAMS OFFERED
Undergraduate—*AAS:* Business Administration; Surgical Technology. *AS:* Radiological Technology.

### NON-DEGREE-RELATED COURSE TOPICS OFFERED
Undergraduate—American (United States) history; English composition; European history; Spanish language and literature; accounting; adult and continuing teacher education; anthropology; applied mathematics; business administration and management; earth and planetary sciences; geography; law and legal studies, other; philosophy and religion; sociology.
Non-credit—agricultural business and management; child care and guidance workers and managers; family and community studies; health professions and related sciences, other.

# SOUTHEASTERN ILLINOIS COLLEGE
## Distance Learning

3575 College Road
Harrisburg, IL 62946
Contact: Mr. Gary Jones, Media Specialist
Phone: 618-252-6376 Ext. 2265
Fax: 618-252-2713

**Web:** http://sic.cc.il.us/virtual.htm
**E-mail:** gjones@sic.cc.il.us

**ACCREDITATION:** North Central Association of Colleges and Schools
**INSTITUTIONALLY ADMINISTERED FINANCIAL AID:** Yes

### DEGREE OR CERTIFICATE PROGRAMS OFFERED
Programs offered do not lead to a degree or other formal award.

### NON-DEGREE-RELATED COURSE TOPICS OFFERED
**Undergraduate**—English language and literature, general; business; educational psychology; health professions and related sciences, other; history; home economics, other; mathematics; philosophy; political science and government; psychology; religion/religious studies.

## SOUTHEASTERN OKLAHOMA STATE UNIVERSITY

*Telecommunications*
1405 North 4th, PO Box 4238
Durant , OK 74701
**Contact:** Wayne Williamson, Director of Telecommunications
**Phone:** 580-745-2100
**Fax:** 580-745-2101
**Web:** http://www.sosu.edu
**E-mail:** wwilliamson@sosu.edu

**ACCREDITATION:** North Central Association of Colleges and Schools
**INSTITUTIONALLY ADMINISTERED FINANCIAL AID:** Yes

### DEGREE OR CERTIFICATE PROGRAMS OFFERED
Programs offered do not lead to a degree or other formal award.

### NON-DEGREE-RELATED COURSE TOPICS OFFERED
**Undergraduate**—accounting; business; computer science; criminology; economics; education, other; history; mathematics; nursing; physiological psychology/psychobiology.

## SOUTHEASTERN UNIVERSITY

*Southeastern University Distance learning Degree Program*
501 I Street, SW
Washington , DC 20024
**Contact:** Mr. Jack Flinter, Director of Admissions
**Phone:** 202-488-8162 Ext. 211
**Web:** http://www.seu.edu
**E-mail:** jflinter@admin.seu.edu

**ACCREDITATION:** Middle States Association of Colleges and Schools
**INSTITUTIONALLY ADMINISTERED FINANCIAL AID:** No

### DEGREE OR CERTIFICATE PROGRAMS OFFERED
Programs offered do not lead to a degree or other formal award.

### NON-DEGREE-RELATED COURSE TOPICS OFFERED
**Undergraduate**—public administration.
**Graduate**—public administration.

## SOUTHEAST MISSOURI STATE UNIVERSITY

*Extended Learning*
Cape Girardeau, MO 63701
**Contact:** Dennis Charles Holt, Vice Provost
**Phone:** 573-651-2262
**Fax:** 573-651-2829
**Web:** http://cstl.semo.edu/extlearning/
**E-mail:** dholt@semo.edu

**ACCREDITATION:** North Central Association of Colleges and Schools
**INSTITUTIONALLY ADMINISTERED FINANCIAL AID:** Yes

### DEGREE OR CERTIFICATE PROGRAMS OFFERED
Programs offered do not lead to a degree or other formal award.

### NON-DEGREE-RELATED COURSE TOPICS OFFERED
**Undergraduate**—English as a second language; English composition; English language and literature, general; biology, general; business administration and management; business communications; community psychology; criminal justice and corrections; curriculum and instruction; developmental and child psychology; economics; education, other; educational/instructional media design; foreign languages and literatures; general teacher education; history; mathematics; nursing; philosophy; philosophy and religion; psychology; social psychology; speech and rhetorical studies.

## SOUTHERN ARKANSAS UNIVERSITY TECH

*Business and Industry Productivity Center*
PO Box 3499
East Camden, AR 71711
**Contact:** Robert D. Gunnels, Chair, Arts and Sciences and Business Administration
**Phone:** 870-574-4541
**Fax:** 870-574-4477
**Web:** http://www.sautech.edu
**E-mail:** rgunnels@sautech.edu

**ACCREDITATION:** North Central Association of Colleges and Schools
**INSTITUTIONALLY ADMINISTERED FINANCIAL AID:** Yes

### DEGREE OR CERTIFICATE PROGRAMS OFFERED
Programs offered do not lead to a degree or other formal award.

### NON-DEGREE-RELATED COURSE TOPICS OFFERED
**Undergraduate**—English composition; biological and physical sciences; business administration and management; computer science; history; mathematics, other; philosophy.

## SOUTHERN CHRISTIAN UNIVERSITY

*Extended Learning Program*
1200 Taylor Road
Montgomery, AL 36117-3553

**Contact:** Rick Johnson, Admissions Officer
**Phone:** 800-351-4040 Ext. 213
**Fax:** 334-387-3878
**Web:** http://www.southernchristian.edu
**E-mail:** rickjohnson@southernchristian.edu

**ACCREDITATION:** Southern Association of Colleges and Schools
**INSTITUTIONALLY ADMINISTERED FINANCIAL AID:** Yes

### DEGREE OR CERTIFICATE PROGRAMS OFFERED

**Undergraduate—BA:** Biblical Studies. **BS:** Human Development; Liberal Studies; Management Communication; Ministry/Bible.
**Graduate—MA:** Biblical Studies. **MDiv:** Christian Ministry; Family Therapy. **MS:** Christian Ministry; Counseling/Family Therapy; Organizational Leadership.
**Postgraduate and doctoral—DMin:** Christian Ministry; Family Therapy.

### NON-DEGREE-RELATED COURSE TOPICS OFFERED

**Undergraduate—**human services; liberal arts and sciences, general studies and humanities; missions/missionary studies and missiology; organizational behavior studies; pastoral counseling and specialized ministries; philosophy and religion; religion/religious studies; theological and ministerial studies.
**Graduate—**human services; missions/missionary studies and missiology; organizational behavior studies; pastoral counseling and specialized ministries; philosophy and religion; religion/religious studies; theological and ministerial studies.
**Non-credit—**human services; liberal arts and sciences, general studies and humanities; missions/missionary studies and missiology; organizational behavior studies; pastoral counseling and specialized ministries; philosophy and religion; religion/religious studies; theological and ministerial studies.

See full description on page 502.

# SOUTHERN CONNECTICUT STATE UNIVERSITY

## School of Extended Learning

501 Crescent Street
New Haven, CT 06515
**Contact:** Christine Barrett, Interim Assistant Dean for Special Programs
**Phone:** 203-392-6195
**Fax:** 203-392-5252
**Web:** http://www.southernct.edu
**E-mail:** barrettc@southernct.edu

**ACCREDITATION:** New England Association of Schools and Colleges
**INSTITUTIONALLY ADMINISTERED FINANCIAL AID:** Yes

### DEGREE OR CERTIFICATE PROGRAMS OFFERED

**Graduate—MS:** Library Science.

# SOUTHERN ILLINOIS UNIVERSITY CARBONDALE

## Office of Distance Education

Washington Square C, Mailcode 6705
Carbondale, IL 62901-6705

**Contact:** Dr. Susan Edgren, Assistant Director
**Phone:** 618-453-5659
**Fax:** 618-453-5668
**Web:** http://www.siu.edu/siuc/
**E-mail:** sedgren@siu.edu

**ACCREDITATION:** North Central Association of Colleges and Schools
**INSTITUTIONALLY ADMINISTERED FINANCIAL AID:** Yes

### DEGREE OR CERTIFICATE PROGRAMS OFFERED

Programs offered do not lead to a degree or other formal award.

### NON-DEGREE-RELATED COURSE TOPICS OFFERED

**Undergraduate—**East and Southeast Asian languages and literatures; advertising; agricultural business and management; agricultural mechanization; anatomy; biology, general; business; communications technologies; criminal justice and corrections; education administration and supervision; education, other; engineering-related technologies, other; geography; health and medical preparatory programs; history; marketing management and research; mathematics; music; parks, recreation and leisure studies; philosophy; political science and government; real estate; rehabilitation/therapeutic services; religion/religious studies; sociology.
**Graduate—**educational/instructional media design; journalism and mass communications; rehabilitation/therapeutic services; telecommunications.
**Non-credit—**marketing management and research.

# SOUTHERN ILLINOIS UNIVERSITY EDWARDSVILLE

## Office of Continuing Education

Box 1084
Edwardsville, IL 62026
**Contact:** Lynn Heidinger-Brown, Director of Continuing Education
**Phone:** 618-650-3210
**Fax:** 618-650-2629
**Web:** http://www.siue.edu/CE/
**E-mail:** ldieter@siue.edu

**ACCREDITATION:** North Central Association of Colleges and Schools
**INSTITUTIONALLY ADMINISTERED FINANCIAL AID:** Yes

### DEGREE OR CERTIFICATE PROGRAMS OFFERED

Programs offered do not lead to a degree or other formal award.

### NON-DEGREE-RELATED COURSE TOPICS OFFERED

**Graduate—**geography; nursing.

# SOUTHERN METHODIST UNIVERSITY

## School of Engineering–Distance Learning

PO Box 750335
Dallas, TX 75275-0335
**Contact:** Stephanie Dye, Associate Director of Distance Education

Phone: 214-768-3232
Fax: 214-768-3778
Web: http://www.engr.smu.edu
E-mail: sdye@engr.smu.edu

ACCREDITATION: Southern Association of Colleges and Schools
INSTITUTIONALLY ADMINISTERED FINANCIAL AID: Yes

### DEGREE OR CERTIFICATE PROGRAMS OFFERED

Graduate—*MS:* Civil Engineering; Computer Science; Electrical Engineering; Engineering Management; Environmental Engineering; Environmental Systems Management; Facilities Management; Manufacturing Systems Management; Mechanical Engineering; Operations Research; Software Engineering; Systems Engineering; Telecommunications.

### NON-DEGREE-RELATED COURSE TOPICS OFFERED

Graduate—civil engineering; computer science; electrical, electronics and communication engineering; engineering/industrial management; environmental/environmental health engineering; mechanical engineering; systems engineering; telecommunications.

See full description on page 504.

# SOUTHERN NEW HAMPSHIRE UNIVERSITY

*Distance Education Program*

2500 North River Road
Manchester, NH 03106
Contact: Janet Byrne, Supervisor of Academic Advising
Phone: 603-645-9766
Fax: 603-645-9706
Web: http://de.snhu.edu/
E-mail: j.byrne@minerva.snhu.edu

ACCREDITATION: New England Association of Schools and Colleges
INSTITUTIONALLY ADMINISTERED FINANCIAL AID: Yes

### DEGREE OR CERTIFICATE PROGRAMS OFFERED

Undergraduate—*AA:* Liberal Arts. *AS:* Business. *BA:* Liberal Arts. *BBA:* Business Administration. *BS:* Business Studies; Communication; Marketing. *Certificate:* Accounting; Business Administration; Computer Information Systems; Health Administration; Human Resources Management; International Business.
Graduate—*MBA:* Business Administration. *MS:* Business Education; International Business.

### NON-DEGREE-RELATED COURSE TOPICS OFFERED

Undergraduate—English composition; English creative writing; accounting; advertising; business marketing and marketing management; developmental and child psychology; finance, general; international business; law and legal studies, other; mathematical statistics; organizational behavior studies; sociology.
Graduate—accounting; advertising; business marketing and marketing management; finance, general; international business; mathematical statistics; organizational behavior studies.

### Special Note

Established in 1932, Southern New Hampshire University (SNHU) is a private, nonprofit coeducational institution. The campus rests on nearly 300 acres situated along the banks of the Merrimack River in Manchester, New Hampshire. SNHU offers certificate and degree programs in business, liberal arts, and hospitality, with degrees beginning at the associate level and continuing to the Ph.D. The SNHU Distance Education program offers certificate and degree programs up to the master's level and is one of the largest and fastest-growing programs in New England. It is both regionally and nationally accredited by the New England Association of Schools and Colleges, the Association of Collegiate Business Schools and Programs, and the New England Postsecondary Education Commission. SNHU is a recognized leader in asynchronous learning and 100% Internet-based instruction. Total enrollments will exceed 7,000 for the 2001–02 academic year. The 6 undergraduate terms are 8 weeks in length, and the 4 graduate terms are 12 weeks in length. Distance Education has an open-enrollment policy. The undergraduate residency requirement is 30 semester hours through SNHU, including 12 hours from the major for the bachelor's and 9 hours from the major for the associate degree. Each student's final 24 semester hours must be through SNHU. The graduate program typically limits transfer credit to 6 semester hours. Classes are normally limited to 18 enrollments, providing a significant measure of faculty-student interaction and at a level not found in more traditional class environments. Blackboard CourseInfo™ software is the standard delivery product for all SNHU online courses.

See full description on page 506.

# SOUTHERN UNIVERSITY AND AGRICULTURAL AND MECHANICAL COLLEGE

*Continuing Distance Education*

PO Box 9772
Baton Rouge, LA 70821
Contact: Mr. Hilton Joseph LaSalle, III, Distance Education Coordinator
Phone: 225-771-2613 Ext. 2613
Fax: 225-771-2654 Ext. 2654
Web: http://www.subr.edu
E-mail: hiltonl307@sus.edu

ACCREDITATION: Southern Association of Colleges and Schools
INSTITUTIONALLY ADMINISTERED FINANCIAL AID: No

### DEGREE OR CERTIFICATE PROGRAMS OFFERED

Programs offered do not lead to a degree or other formal award.

### NON-DEGREE-RELATED COURSE TOPICS OFFERED

Undergraduate—biology, general; computer science; education administration and supervision; special education.
Graduate—nursing; public administration; special education.
Non-credit—special education.

# SOUTH FLORIDA COMMUNITY COLLEGE

Arts and Sciences, 600 West College Drive
Avon Park, FL 33825-9356
**Contact:** Dr. David Sconyers, Dean of School of Arts and Sciences
**Phone:** 863-784-7329
**Fax:** 863-453-2365
**Web:** http://www.sfcc.cc.fl.us/
**E-mail:** sconda3951@sfcc.cc.fl.us

**ACCREDITATION:** Southern Association of Colleges and Schools

## DEGREE OR CERTIFICATE PROGRAMS OFFERED
**Programs offered do not lead to a degree or other formal award.**

# SOUTH PIEDMONT COMMUNITY COLLEGE

680 Highway 74 West, PO Box 126
Polkton, NC 28170
**Contact:** Ms. Julia Grace May, Director of Distance Learning
**Phone:** 704-272-7635 Ext. 260
**Fax:** 704-272-7542
**Web:** http://www.southpiedmont.org
**E-mail:** jmay@spcc.cc.nc.us

**ACCREDITATION:** Southern Association of Colleges and Schools
**INSTITUTIONALLY ADMINISTERED FINANCIAL AID:** Yes

## DEGREE OR CERTIFICATE PROGRAMS OFFERED
**Programs offered do not lead to a degree or other formal award.**

## NON-DEGREE-RELATED COURSE TOPICS OFFERED
**Undergraduate**—English composition; accounting; biology, general; computer and information sciences, general; computer/information technology administration and management; economics; education administration and supervision; family and community studies; financial management and services; health professions and related sciences, other; marketing operations/marketing and distribution, other; teacher education, specific academic and vocational programs.

# SOUTH PLAINS COLLEGE

1401 South College
Levelland, TX 79336
**Contact:** Ms. Andrea Grimaldo Rangel, Dean of Admissions and Records
**Phone:** 806-894-9611 Ext. 2370
**Fax:** 806-897-2371
**Web:** http://www.spc.cc.tx.us/
**E-mail:** arangel@spc.cc.tx.us

**ACCREDITATION:** Southern Association of Colleges and Schools
**INSTITUTIONALLY ADMINISTERED FINANCIAL AID:** Yes

## DEGREE OR CERTIFICATE PROGRAMS OFFERED
**Programs offered do not lead to a degree or other formal award.**

## NON-DEGREE-RELATED COURSE TOPICS OFFERED
**Undergraduate**—psychology.

# SOUTH PUGET SOUND COMMUNITY COLLEGE

Library and Media Center, 2011 Mottman Road, SW
Olympia, WA 98512
**Contact:** Russell Rose, Director
**Phone:** 360-754-7711 Ext. 258
**Fax:** 360-664-0780
**Web:** http://www.spscc.ctc.edu/
**E-mail:** rrose@spscc.ctc.edu

**ACCREDITATION:** Northwest Association of Schools and Colleges

## DEGREE OR CERTIFICATE PROGRAMS OFFERED
**Programs offered do not lead to a degree or other formal award.**

## NON-DEGREE-RELATED COURSE TOPICS OFFERED
**Undergraduate**—anthropology; education, other; history.

# SOUTHWEST BAPTIST UNIVERSITY

1600 University Avenue
Bolivar, MO 65613-2597
**Contact:** College Credit Through Correspondence
**Phone:** 417-328-1599
**Fax:** 417-328-1514
**Web:** http://falcon.sbuniv.edu/cctc/CCTCHP.html
**E-mail:** cctc@sbuniv.edu

**ACCREDITATION:** North Central Association of Colleges and Schools

## DEGREE OR CERTIFICATE PROGRAMS OFFERED
**Programs offered do not lead to a degree or other formal award.**

## NON-DEGREE-RELATED COURSE TOPICS OFFERED
**Undergraduate**—English language and literature, general; biological and physical sciences; foods and nutrition studies; marketing management and research.

# SOUTHWESTERN ASSEMBLIES OF GOD UNIVERSITY
*School of Distance Education*

Waxahachie, TX 75165
**Contact:** Rev. Jason Scott Edwards, Assistant Director for Enrollment
**Phone:** 972-937-4010
**Fax:** 972-923-2980
**Web:** http://www.sagu.edu

**E-mail:** info@sagu.edu

**ACCREDITATION:** Accrediting Association of Bible Colleges

**INSTITUTIONALLY ADMINISTERED FINANCIAL AID:** Yes

### DEGREE OR CERTIFICATE PROGRAMS OFFERED

**Undergraduate—BA:** Business; Church Ministries; Education; Professional Studies. **BS:** Business; Church Ministries; Education; Professional Studies.

### NON-DEGREE-RELATED COURSE TOPICS OFFERED

**Undergraduate—**English composition; English creative writing; accounting; biology, general; developmental and child psychology; educational psychology; social psychology; sociology.

## SOUTHWESTERN BAPTIST THEOLOGICAL SEMINARY

### Department of Continuing Education

PO Box 22487
Fort Worth, TX 76122
**Contact:** Gary Waller, Director of Distance Learning
**Phone:** 817-923-1921 Ext. 3510
**Fax:** 817-921-8763
**Web:** http://www.swbts.edu/
**E-mail:** gww@swbts.edu

**ACCREDITATION:** Southern Association of Colleges and Schools

**INSTITUTIONALLY ADMINISTERED FINANCIAL AID:** Yes

### DEGREE OR CERTIFICATE PROGRAMS OFFERED

Programs offered do not lead to a degree or other formal award.

### NON-DEGREE-RELATED COURSE TOPICS OFFERED

**Undergraduate—**bible/biblical studies; religion/religious studies; religious education; theological and ministerial studies.
**Graduate—**bible/biblical studies; biblical and other theological languages and literatures; education administration and supervision; education, other; educational evaluation, research and statistics; educational psychology; educational/instructional media design; family and community studies; foreign languages and literatures; pastoral counseling and specialized ministries; philosophy and religion; psychology; psychology, other; religion/religious studies; religious education; religious/sacred music; theological and ministerial studies; theological studies and religious vocations, other.

## SOUTHWESTERN COLLEGE

900 Otay Lakes Road
Chula Vista, CA 91910
**Contact:** Greg R. Sandoval, Interim Dean of Academic Information Services
**Phone:** 619-482-6347
**Fax:** 619-482-6417
**Web:** http://www.swc.cc.ca.us/
**E-mail:** gsandoval@swc.cc.ca.us

**ACCREDITATION:** Western Association of Schools and Colleges

**INSTITUTIONALLY ADMINISTERED FINANCIAL AID:** Yes

### DEGREE OR CERTIFICATE PROGRAMS OFFERED

Programs offered do not lead to a degree or other formal award.

### NON-DEGREE-RELATED COURSE TOPICS OFFERED

**Undergraduate—**English as a second language; anthropology; astronomy; child care and guidance workers and managers; economics; history; political science and government; psychology; sociology.
**Non-credit—**English as a second language.

## SOUTHWESTERN COMMUNITY COLLEGE

1501 West Townline Street
Creston, IA 50801
**Contact:** Stacy Gibbs, Director of Distance Learning
**Phone:** 641-782-7081 Ext. 324
**Fax:** 641-782-3312
**Web:** http://www.swcc.cc.ia.us/
**E-mail:** gibbs@swcc.cc.ia.us

**ACCREDITATION:** North Central Association of Colleges and Schools

**INSTITUTIONALLY ADMINISTERED FINANCIAL AID:** Yes

### DEGREE OR CERTIFICATE PROGRAMS OFFERED

**Undergraduate—AA:** Liberal Arts.

### NON-DEGREE-RELATED COURSE TOPICS OFFERED

**Undergraduate—**American studies/civilization; English composition; accounting; anatomy; art history, criticism and conservation; biology, general; environmental science/studies; geography; journalism; mathematics, other; philosophy and religion; sociology.

## SOUTHWESTERN COMMUNITY COLLEGE

447 College Drive
Sylva, NC 28779
**Contact:** Ms. Myrna Campbell, Director of Enrollment Management
**Phone:** 828-586-4091 Ext. 253
**Fax:** 828-586-3129
**Web:** http://www.southwest.cc.nc.us/
**E-mail:** myrna@southwest.cc.nc.us

**ACCREDITATION:** Southern Association of Colleges and Schools

**INSTITUTIONALLY ADMINISTERED FINANCIAL AID:** No

### DEGREE OR CERTIFICATE PROGRAMS OFFERED

Programs offered do not lead to a degree or other formal award.

### NON-DEGREE-RELATED COURSE TOPICS OFFERED

**Undergraduate—**English creative writing; English language and literature, general; accounting; business; business information and data processing services; child care and guidance workers and managers; communications, general; computer and information sciences, general; computer science; criminal justice and corrections; data processing technology; economics; foreign languages and literatures; health and medical laboratory technologies; history; marketing management and research; mathematics; political science and government; psychology; religion/religious studies; visual and performing arts.

# SOUTHWEST MISSOURI STATE UNIVERSITY

## College of Continuing Education and the Extended University

901 South National
Springfield, MO 65804
**Contact:** Ms. Diana Garland, Associate Director of Academic Outreach
**Web:** http://ce.smsu.edu
**E-mail:** dianagarland@smsu.edu

**ACCREDITATION:** North Central Association of Colleges and Schools
**INSTITUTIONALLY ADMINISTERED FINANCIAL AID:** Yes

### DEGREE OR CERTIFICATE PROGRAMS OFFERED

**Undergraduate—BS:** Elementary Education. **BSN:** Nursing.
**Graduate—MBA:** Business Administration. **MS:** Administrative Studies; Computer Information Systems; Elementary Education. **MSW:** Social Work.

### NON-DEGREE-RELATED COURSE TOPICS OFFERED

**Undergraduate—**American (United States) history; Spanish language and literature; accounting; alcohol/drug abuse counseling; anthropology; biology, general; business marketing and marketing management; film/cinema studies; finance, general; mathematics, other; nursing; social work; sociology.
**Graduate—**accounting; business marketing and marketing management; curriculum and instruction; education administration and supervision; education, general; finance, general; social work.
**Non-credit—**alcohol/drug abuse counseling.

# SOUTHWEST STATE UNIVERSITY

## Office of Distance Learning

1501 State Street
Marshall, MN 56258
**Contact:** Office of Distance Learning
**Phone:** 507-537-6251
**Fax:** 507-537-6252
**Web:** http://www.southwest.msus.edu/program/index.cfm?programid=37&program=Distance%20Learning,%20Dept.%20of

**ACCREDITATION:** North Central Association of Colleges and Schools

### DEGREE OR CERTIFICATE PROGRAMS OFFERED

Programs offered do not lead to a degree or other formal award.

# SOUTHWEST TEXAS STATE UNIVERSITY

## Correspondence and Extension Studies

302 ASB North, 601 University Drive
San Marcos, TX 78666

**Contact:** Carolyn Bettelheim, Administrative Assistant
**Phone:** 512-245-2322
**Fax:** 512-245-8934
**Web:** http://www.ideal.swt.edu/correspondence
**E-mail:** corrstudy@swt.edu
**ACCREDITATION:** Southern Association of Colleges and Schools
**INSTITUTIONALLY ADMINISTERED FINANCIAL AID:** No

### DEGREE OR CERTIFICATE PROGRAMS OFFERED

Programs offered do not lead to a degree or other formal award.

### NON-DEGREE-RELATED COURSE TOPICS OFFERED

**Undergraduate—**English composition; English creative writing; English language and literature, general; English language and literature/letters, other; English literature (British and Commonwealth); Spanish language and literature; art history, criticism and conservation; biological sciences/life sciences, other; biology, general; criminal justice and corrections; dance; geography; health and medical administrative services; health system/health services administration; history; mathematics; mathematics and computer science; music; philosophy; political science and government; psychology; sociology; teacher education, specific academic and vocational programs.
**Graduate—**geography; mathematics.
**Non-credit—**education, other; health and medical administrative services.

### Special Note

The century-old Southwest Texas State University (SWT) is a state-supported university that *Money* magazine named as one of the top 10 educational values in the United States in 1998. With nearly 50 years of experience in distributed learning, the distance education program at SWT was developed to provide up-to-date service to all students. Most courses are available in a print-based format, while some courses contain audio and video components.

As it enters the millennium, SWT provides more Internet-delivered courses, including new graduate-level geography courses, which are also available in a print-based format. The program seeks to include students who do not have access to new technologies, which has made the program popular worldwide.

Courses typically cost $189 per 3-credit-hour course ($63 per credit hour) for undergraduate credit and $285 per 3-credit-hour course ($95 per credit hour) for graduate credit. In addition, undergraduate and graduate correspondence students are assessed a $25 administrative fee for each course in which they enroll. Students outside the U.S. should add $50 per course for overseas postage. Courses are written and taught by departmentally approved instructors. Students have 12 months to complete a course and may apply for a 6-month extension. All applications from Texas residents are reviewed for compliance with TASP regulations. Students may apply directly to the Office of Correspondence and Extension Studies. For current course listings, students should visit the Web site (http://www.ideal.swt.edu/correspondence) or call 512-245-2322 for a catalog.

# SPERTUS INSTITUTE OF JEWISH STUDIES

618 South Michigan Avenue
Chicago, IL 60605

**Contact:** Admissions
**Phone:** 888-322-1769
**Fax:** 312-922-6406
**Web:** http://www.spertus.edu/
**E-mail:** college@spertus.edu

**ACCREDITATION:** North Central Association of Colleges and Schools

## DEGREE OR CERTIFICATE PROGRAMS OFFERED

Programs offered do not lead to a degree or other formal award.

### Special Note

Accredited by the North Central Association of Colleges and Schools, Spertus currently offers 4 degree programs on a distance learning basis: the Master of Science in Jewish Studies (MSJS), the Master of Science in Jewish Education (MSJE), the Doctor of Jewish Studies (DJS), and the Doctor of Science in Jewish Studies (DSJS).

The MSJS and the MSJE are designed for students with an accredited undergraduate degree and a desire to enrich their Jewish education or acquire a professional credential in Jewish education or Jewish communal service. The MSJS and MSJE programs are identical, except that students in the MSJE must choose a concentration area in Jewish education. Courses are delivered in a variety of ways, including distance learning packages, intensive seminars, and independent study. The programs progress at the learner's individual rate. Distance learners are encouraged to spend a minimum of 6 days per year at Spertus's Chicago campus for intensive course work. Fifty quarter hours are required for the degrees. Tuition is currently $200 per quarter hour. Scholarships, in the form of partial tuition remission, are available.

The DJS is designed for in-service Jewish clergy, educators, and communal service workers who are interested in and committed to building upon and enhancing previously acquired Judaica knowledge and professional skills and who desire to make a cutting-edge contribution to their respective fields. Admission to the DJS program is highly selective. Eighteen courses are required for the degree: 7 reading courses, 7 intensive seminars, and 4 courses toward the completion of a Project Demonstrating Excellence.

The DSJS program has been designed primarily for students who already hold a master's degree in Jewish studies and who want to explore how the wisdom of the Jewish past—as embodied in its sacred and significant texts and in the diverse historical experiences of the Jewish people—can be utilized to address the perplexities and problems of Jewish life in the present—both communal and individual. The DSJS program requires 18 courses, including 7 core courses; 3 text courses; 5 courses on issues, problems, methodologies, and major intellectual or historical figures in Jewish history; and 3 research and writing courses related to a final project. (In some cases, additional prerequisite courses may also be required.) Tuition for both the DJS and DSJS programs is currently $250 per quarter hour.

For more information, students should contact the Office of the Registrar at 888–322–1769 (toll-free), fax: 312–922–6406, or e-mail: college@spertus.edu or visit the Web site at http://www.spertus.edu.

# SPOKANE FALLS COMMUNITY COLLEGE

3410 West Ft. George Wright Drive, MS 3020
Spokane, WA 99224
**Contact:** Kyla Bates, Program Coordinator
**Phone:** 509-533-3216
**Web:** http://www.sfcc.spokane.cc.wa.us/
**E-mail:** distancelearning@sfcc.spokane.cc.wa.us

**ACCREDITATION:** Northwest Association of Schools and Colleges
**INSTITUTIONALLY ADMINISTERED FINANCIAL AID:** Yes

## DEGREE OR CERTIFICATE PROGRAMS OFFERED
**Undergraduate—AA:** General.

## NON-DEGREE-RELATED COURSE TOPICS OFFERED
**Undergraduate—**English composition; English language and literature, general; astronomy; biological and physical sciences; business; computer software and media applications; economics; entrepreneurship; foreign languages and literatures; geography; geological and related sciences; gerontology; health and physical education/fitness; history; journalism and mass communications; liberal arts and sciences, general studies and humanities; mathematics; music; philosophy; social sciences, general.
**Non-credit—**computer software and media applications.

# SPOON RIVER COLLEGE

23235 North County 22
Canton, IL 61520
**Contact:** Sharon Wrenn, Dean of Student Services
**Phone:** 309-647-4645
**Fax:** 309-649-6235
**Web:** http://www.spoonrivercollege.net/
**E-mail:** info@src.cc.il.us

**ACCREDITATION:** North Central Association of Colleges and Schools
**INSTITUTIONALLY ADMINISTERED FINANCIAL AID:** Yes

## DEGREE OR CERTIFICATE PROGRAMS OFFERED
**Undergraduate—AA:** General.

## NON-DEGREE-RELATED COURSE TOPICS OFFERED
**Undergraduate—**English composition; English language and literature, general; biology, general; child care and guidance workers and managers; education, general; fine arts and art studies; health professions and related sciences, other; philosophy and religion.
**Non-credit—**computer software and media applications.

# SPRING ARBOR UNIVERSITY

106 East Main Street
Spring Arbor, MI 49283
**Contact:** Dr. John Nemecek, Assistant Dean of School of Adult Studies
**Phone:** 517-750-6351
**Fax:** 517-750-6602
**Web:** http://www.arbor.edu/

**E-mail:** jnemecek@arbor.edu

**ACCREDITATION:** North Central Association of Colleges and Schools

**INSTITUTIONALLY ADMINISTERED FINANCIAL AID:** Yes

eCollege.com   *www.ecollege.com*

### DEGREE OR CERTIFICATE PROGRAMS OFFERED

Graduate—*MIM:* Organizational Management.

### NON-DEGREE-RELATED COURSE TOPICS OFFERED

Undergraduate—English composition; English creative writing; business administration and management; business marketing and marketing management; computer software and media applications; history; music; philosophy; psychology; sociology.

Graduate—business administration and management; business communications; business marketing and marketing management; business/managerial economics; international business.

See full description on page 508.

# STANFORD UNIVERSITY

### Stanford Center for Professional Development

496 Lomita Hall, Room 401
Stanford, CA 94305-4036
**Contact:** Frank Schroeder, SITN Customer Relations
**Phone:** 650-725-6950
**Fax:** 650-725-2868
**Web:** http://scpd.stanford.edu
**E-mail:** frankschroeder@stanford.edu

**ACCREDITATION:** Western Association of Schools and Colleges

**INSTITUTIONALLY ADMINISTERED FINANCIAL AID:** No

### DEGREE OR CERTIFICATE PROGRAMS OFFERED

Graduate—*MBA/MAIS:* Aerospace Engineering; Computer Science; Electrical Engineering; Materials Science and Engineering; Mechanical Engineering. *MS:* Management Science and Engineering.

### NON-DEGREE-RELATED COURSE TOPICS OFFERED

Graduate—aerospace, aeronautical and astronautical engineering; bioengineering and biomedical engineering; electrical, electronics and communication engineering; engineering/industrial management; industrial/manufacturing engineering; mechanical engineering.

Non-credit—aerospace, aeronautical and astronautical engineering; electrical, electronics and communication engineering; engineering/industrial management; industrial/manufacturing engineering; mechanical engineering.

See full description on page 510.

# STANLY COMMUNITY COLLEGE

141 College Drive
Albemarle, NC 28001
**Contact:** Barbara Wiggins, Director of Evening and Weekend College
**Phone:** 704-991-0266
**Fax:** 704-982-0819
**Web:** http://www.stanly.cc.nc.us/

**E-mail:** wigginbo@stanly.cc.nc.us

**ACCREDITATION:** Southern Association of Colleges and Schools

**INSTITUTIONALLY ADMINISTERED FINANCIAL AID:** Yes

### DEGREE OR CERTIFICATE PROGRAMS OFFERED

Programs offered do not lead to a degree or other formal award.

### NON-DEGREE-RELATED COURSE TOPICS OFFERED

Undergraduate—English composition; accounting; applied mathematics; biology, general; business administration and management; business information and data processing services; business marketing and marketing management; child care and guidance workers and managers; computer and information sciences, general; computer and information sciences, other; criminal justice and corrections; developmental and child psychology; human services; nursing; psychology; sociology.

# STATE UNIVERSITY OF NEW YORK AT OSWEGO

### Office of Distance Learning

Oswego, NY 13126
**Contact:** Division of Continuing Education
**Phone:** 315-312-2270
**Fax:** 315-312-3078
**Web:** http://www.oswego.edu
**E-mail:** ced@oswego.edu

**ACCREDITATION:** Middle States Association of Colleges and Schools

### DEGREE OR CERTIFICATE PROGRAMS OFFERED

Undergraduate—*BA:* Communications.

### NON-DEGREE-RELATED COURSE TOPICS OFFERED

Undergraduate—European history; Russian language and literature; business administration and management; business/managerial economics; journalism and mass communication, other; marketing management and research; mathematical statistics; radio and television broadcasting.

See full description on page 512.

# STATE UNIVERSITY OF NEW YORK COLLEGE AT BROCKPORT

350 New Campus Drive
Brockport, NY 14589
**Contact:** Dr. Diane Elliott, Assistant Vice President of Graduate Studies
**Phone:** 716-395-2525
**Fax:** 716-395-2515
**Web:** http://www.brockport.edu/
**E-mail:** delliott@brockport.edu

**ACCREDITATION:** Middle States Association of Colleges and Schools

**INSTITUTIONALLY ADMINISTERED FINANCIAL AID:** Yes

### DEGREE OR CERTIFICATE PROGRAMS OFFERED

Programs offered do not lead to a degree or other formal award.

## NON-DEGREE-RELATED COURSE TOPICS OFFERED

**Undergraduate**—business administration and management; computer science; health professions and related sciences, other; internet and world wide web.

**Graduate**—parks, recreation, leisure and fitness studies, other; public administration.

# STATE UNIVERSITY OF NEW YORK COLLEGE AT CORTLAND

PO Box 2000
Cortland, NY 13045
**Contact:** Gradin Avery, Director of Admissions
**Phone:** 607-753-4741
**Fax:** 607-753-5998
**Web:** http://www.cortland.edu/
**E-mail:** admissions@cortland.edu

**ACCREDITATION:** Middle States Association of Colleges and Schools

**INSTITUTIONALLY ADMINISTERED FINANCIAL AID:** Yes

## DEGREE OR CERTIFICATE PROGRAMS OFFERED

Programs offered do not lead to a degree or other formal award.

## NON-DEGREE-RELATED COURSE TOPICS OFFERED

**Undergraduate**—English creative writing; area, ethnic and cultural studies, other; parks, recreation, leisure and fitness studies, other; philosophy; social sciences and history, other; sociology.

**Graduate**—education administration and supervision; parks, recreation, leisure and fitness studies, other.

# STATE UNIVERSITY OF NEW YORK COLLEGE AT FREDONIA

*Office of Lifelong Learning/SUNY Learning Network*

LoGrasso Hall
Fredonia, NY 14048
**Contact:** Mr. Grant Umberger, Associate Director of Lifelong Learning
**Phone:** 716-673-3177
**Fax:** 716-673-3175
**Web:** http://sln.suny.edu
**E-mail:** grant.umberger@fredonia.edu

**ACCREDITATION:** Middle States Association of Colleges and Schools

**INSTITUTIONALLY ADMINISTERED FINANCIAL AID:** Yes

## DEGREE OR CERTIFICATE PROGRAMS OFFERED

Programs offered do not lead to a degree or other formal award.

## NON-DEGREE-RELATED COURSE TOPICS OFFERED

**Undergraduate**—English language and literature, general; Germanic languages and literatures; accounting; anthropology; area, ethnic and cultural studies, other; biochemistry and biophysics; biology, general; business administration and management; chemistry; communication disorders sciences and services; communications, general; computer and information sciences, general; criminal justice and corrections; dance;

dramatic/theater arts and stagecraft; economics; education, general; general teacher education; history; mathematics; music; philosophy; physics; social work; sociology; visual and performing arts.

**Graduate**—English language and literature, general; biology, general; chemistry; communication disorders sciences and services; education administration and supervision; education, general; music.

**See full description on page 518.**

# STATE UNIVERSITY OF NEW YORK COLLEGE AT ONEONTA

*Academic Support Services*

135 Netzer Administration Building
Oneonta, NY 13820
**Contact:** Dr. Marguerite Culver, Interim Dean
**Phone:** 607-436-2548
**Fax:** 607-436-2548
**Web:** http://www.oneonta.edu
**E-mail:** culvermm@oneonta.edu

**ACCREDITATION:** Middle States Association of Colleges and Schools

**INSTITUTIONALLY ADMINISTERED FINANCIAL AID:** Yes

## DEGREE OR CERTIFICATE PROGRAMS OFFERED

Programs offered do not lead to a degree or other formal award.

## NON-DEGREE-RELATED COURSE TOPICS OFFERED

**Undergraduate**—business administration and management.

# STATE UNIVERSITY OF NEW YORK COLLEGE OF AGRICULTURE AND TECHNOLOGY AT MORRISVILLE

134 Glabreath Hall
Morrisville, NY 13408
**Contact:** Ms. Christine Cring, Coordinator of Distance Learning
**Phone:** 315-684-6430
**Fax:** 315-684-6024
**Web:** http://www.morrisville.edu/
**E-mail:** cringca@morrisville.edu

**ACCREDITATION:** Middle States Association of Colleges and Schools

**INSTITUTIONALLY ADMINISTERED FINANCIAL AID:** Yes

## DEGREE OR CERTIFICATE PROGRAMS OFFERED

Programs offered do not lead to a degree or other formal award.

## NON-DEGREE-RELATED COURSE TOPICS OFFERED

**Undergraduate**—English composition; English creative writing; English technical and business writing; accounting; business; business quantitative methods and management science; computer/information technology administration and management; hospitality services management; internet and world wide web; mathematics.

# STATE UNIVERSITY OF NEW YORK COLLEGE OF TECHNOLOGY AT ALFRED

10 Upper College Drive
Alfred, NY 14802
**Contact:** Wendy Dresser-Rectenwald, Director of CCET
**Phone:** 607-587-4544
**Fax:** 607-587-3295
**Web:** http://www.alfredstate.edu
**E-mail:** dressews@alfredtech.edu

**ACCREDITATION:** Middle States Association of Colleges and Schools

**INSTITUTIONALLY ADMINISTERED FINANCIAL AID:** Yes

## DEGREE OR CERTIFICATE PROGRAMS OFFERED

**Undergraduate—AAS:** Court and Real-Time Reporting; Health Information Technology/Medical Records. **Certificate:** Coding and Reimbursement Specialist; Medical Transcription.

## NON-DEGREE-RELATED COURSE TOPICS OFFERED

**Undergraduate—**biological and physical sciences; biological sciences/life sciences, other; biology, general; business; business administration and management; business management and administrative services, other; chemistry; health and medical administrative services; health and medical assistants; health and medical preparatory programs; health professions and related sciences, other; law and legal studies; liberal arts and sciences, general studies and humanities; medical basic sciences; miscellaneous health professions.

# STATE UNIVERSITY OF NEW YORK COLLEGE OF TECHNOLOGY AT CANTON

*Academic Affairs*
Canton, NY 13617
**Contact:** Barbara Porter, Registrar
**Phone:** 315-386-7647
**Fax:** 315-379-3819
**Web:** http://www.canton.edu
**E-mail:** porter@canton.edu

**ACCREDITATION:** Middle States Association of Colleges and Schools

**INSTITUTIONALLY ADMINISTERED FINANCIAL AID:** Yes

## DEGREE OR CERTIFICATE PROGRAMS OFFERED

**Programs offered do not lead to a degree or other formal award.**

## NON-DEGREE-RELATED COURSE TOPICS OFFERED

**Undergraduate—**animal sciences; business administration and management; computer and information sciences, general; criminal justice and corrections; insurance marketing operations; physical sciences, other.

# STATE UNIVERSITY OF NEW YORK EMPIRE STATE COLLEGE

*Center for Distance Learning*
Three Union Avenue
Saratoga Springs, NY 12866

**Contact:** Ms. Lorena Gonzalez, Secretary of Communications
**Phone:** 518-587-2100 Ext. 300
**Fax:** 518-587-2660
**Web:** http://www.esc.edu/cdl
**E-mail:** lorena.gonzalez@ esc.edu

**ACCREDITATION:** Middle States Association of Colleges and Schools

**INSTITUTIONALLY ADMINISTERED FINANCIAL AID:** Yes

## DEGREE OR CERTIFICATE PROGRAMS OFFERED

**Undergraduate—AA:** Business, Management and Economics; Community and Human Services; Cultural Studies; Educational Studies; Historical Studies; Human Development; Interdisciplinary Studies; Labor Studies; Science, Math and Technology; Social Theory, Social Structure and Change; The Arts. **AS:** Business, Management and Economics; Community and Human Services; Cultural Studies; Educational Studies; Historical Studies; Human Development; Interdisciplinary Studies; Labor Studies; Science, Math and Technology; Social Theory, Social Structure and Change; The Arts. **BA:** Business, Management and Economics; Community and Human Services; Cultural Studies; Educational Studies; Historical Studies; Human Development; Interdisciplinary Studies; Labor Studies; Science, Math and Technology; Social Theory, Social Structure and Change; The Arts. **BPS:** Business, Management and Economics; Community and Human Services. **BS:** Business, Management and Economics; Community and Human Services; Cultural Studies; Educational Studies; Historical Studies; Human Development; Interdisciplinary Studies; Labor Studies; Science, Math and Technology; Social Theory, Social Structure and Change; The Arts.

## NON-DEGREE-RELATED COURSE TOPICS OFFERED

**Undergraduate—**American (United States) history; English composition; accounting; biology, general; finance, general; fire services administration; international business; labor/personnel relations and studies; law and legal studies, other; management information systems and business data processing, general; mathematical statistics; mathematics, other; organizational behavior studies; social psychology; sociology.

**See full description on page 514.**

# STATE UNIVERSITY OF NEW YORK INSTITUTE OF TECHNOLOGY AT UTICA/ROME

*SUNY Learning Network*
PO Box 3050
Utica, NY 13504-3050
**Contact:** Dr. Thomas Tribunella, Associate Professor
**Phone:** 315-792-7126
**Fax:** 315-792-7138
**Web:** http://sln.suny.edu
**E-mail:** ftjt@sunyit.edu

**ACCREDITATION:** Middle States Association of Colleges and Schools

**INSTITUTIONALLY ADMINISTERED FINANCIAL AID:** Yes

## DEGREE OR CERTIFICATE PROGRAMS OFFERED

**Graduate—MS:** Accountancy; Health Services Administration.

## NON-DEGREE-RELATED COURSE TOPICS OFFERED

**Undergraduate**—accounting; business; business administration and management; communications, general; health and medical administrative services; health professions and related sciences, other; human resources management; nursing.

**Graduate**—accounting; business; business administration and management; communications, general; health and medical administrative services; health professions and related sciences, other; human resources management; nursing; taxation.

**See full description on page 516.**

# STATE UNIVERSITY OF WEST GEORGIA

*Special Programs*

Honors House
Carrollton, GA 30118
**Contact:** Melanie Clay, Distance Education Administrator
**Phone:** 770-836-4647
**Fax:** 770-836-4666
**Web:** http://www.westga.edu
**E-mail:** melaniec@westga.edu

**ACCREDITATION:** Southern Association of Colleges and Schools

## DEGREE OR CERTIFICATE PROGRAMS OFFERED

**Graduate**—*MEd:* Educational Leadership; Media and Technology.

## NON-DEGREE-RELATED COURSE TOPICS OFFERED

**Undergraduate**—American (United States) history; English as a second language; English composition; English creative writing; European history; accounting; art history, criticism and conservation; business marketing and marketing management; drama/theater arts, general; educational psychology; history; journalism and mass communication, other; law and legal studies, other; management information systems and business data processing, general; mathematics, other; political science and government; social sciences, general; sociology.

**Graduate**—American (United States) history; European history; accounting; educational psychology.

**Non-credit**—public administration; special education; teacher education, specific academic and vocational programs.

# STEPHEN F. AUSTIN STATE UNIVERSITY

SFA Box 13038
Nacogdoches, TX 75962-3038
**Contact:** Ms. Andra Floyd, Distance Education Support Specialist
**Phone:** 936-468-1919
**Fax:** 936-468-1308
**Web:** http://www.sfasu.edu/
**E-mail:** de@sfasu.edu

**ACCREDITATION:** Southern Association of Colleges and Schools
**INSTITUTIONALLY ADMINISTERED FINANCIAL AID:** Yes

## DEGREE OR CERTIFICATE PROGRAMS OFFERED

**Undergraduate**—*Certificate:* Elementary Education.

## NON-DEGREE-RELATED COURSE TOPICS OFFERED

**Undergraduate**—English technical and business writing; agriculture/agricultural sciences; apparel and accessories marketing operations; business administration and management; criminal justice and corrections; curriculum and instruction; educational psychology; social work.

**Graduate**—educational psychology; general teacher education.

# STEPHENS COLLEGE

*School of Graduate and Continuing Education*

1200 East Broadway
Columbia, MO 65215
**Contact:** School of Graduate and Continuing Education
**Phone:** 800-388-7579
**Fax:** 573-876-7237
**Web:** http://www.stephens.edu/gce
**E-mail:** sce@stephens.edu

**ACCREDITATION:** North Central Association of Colleges and Schools
**INSTITUTIONALLY ADMINISTERED FINANCIAL AID:** No

## DEGREE OR CERTIFICATE PROGRAMS OFFERED

**Undergraduate**—*BA:* Business Administration; English; Law, Philosophy and Rhetoric; Psychology. *BS:* Education; Health Care and Second Area; Health Information Administration; Health Science and Second Area. *Certificate:* Education; Health Information Administration.

**Graduate**—*MBA:* Clinical Information Systems Management; Entrepreneurial Studies; Management.

## NON-DEGREE-RELATED COURSE TOPICS OFFERED

**Undergraduate**—English creative writing; English language and literature, general; accounting; biology, general; business; computer and information sciences, general; developmental and child psychology; economics; education, general; health and medical administrative services; history; law and legal studies; mathematics; philosophy; psychology; religion/religious studies; social sciences, general.

**Graduate**—accounting; business marketing and marketing management; entrepreneurship; finance, general; marketing management and research; mathematical statistics.

**See full description on page 520.**

# STEVENS INSTITUTE OF TECHNOLOGY

*Graduate School*

Castle Point on Hudson
Hoboken, NJ 07030
**Contact:** Robert Ubell, Dean of Online Learning
**Phone:** 800-496-4935
**Fax:** 201-216-8044
**Web:** http://www.webcampus.stevens.edu
**E-mail:** webcampus@stevens-tech.edu

**ACCREDITATION:** Middle States Association of Colleges and Schools
**INSTITUTIONALLY ADMINISTERED FINANCIAL AID:** Yes

## DEGREE OR CERTIFICATE PROGRAMS OFFERED

**Graduate—*Graduate Certificate:*** Atmospheric and Environmental Science and Engineering; Concurrent Engineering; Elements of Computer Science; Project Management; Technology Applications in Science; Technology Management; Telecommunications Management; Wireless Communications. ***MEE:*** Computer Science; Wireless Communications. ***MS:*** Telecommunications Management.

## NON-DEGREE-RELATED COURSE TOPICS OFFERED

**Graduate—**management information systems and business data processing, general; management science.

See full description on page 522.

# STONY BROOK UNIVERSITY, STATE UNIVERSITY OF NEW YORK

*Electronic Extension Program*

School of Professional Development, N 215 SBS Building
Stony Brook, NY 11794-4310
**Contact:** Kim Garvin, Assistant Director
**Phone:** 631-632-9484
**Fax:** 631-632-7872
**Web:** http://www.stonybrook.edu/spd/CDL.htm
**E-mail:** kgarvin@notes.cc.sunysb.edu

**ACCREDITATION:** Middle States Association of Colleges and Schools

**INSTITUTIONALLY ADMINISTERED FINANCIAL AID:** No

## DEGREE OR CERTIFICATE PROGRAMS OFFERED

**Graduate—*MA:*** Liberal Studies.

## NON-DEGREE-RELATED COURSE TOPICS OFFERED

**Graduate—**education, general; liberal arts and sciences, general studies and humanities.

# STRAYER UNIVERSITY

*Strayer Online*

PO Box 487
Newington, VA 22122
**Contact:** Mr. James A. Anderson, Campus Dean of Strayer Online
**Phone:** 888-360-1588
**Fax:** 703-339-1783
**Web:** http://www.online.strayer.edu
**E-mail:** ja@strayer.edu

**ACCREDITATION:** Middle States Association of Colleges and Schools

**INSTITUTIONALLY ADMINISTERED FINANCIAL AID:** Yes

## DEGREE OR CERTIFICATE PROGRAMS OFFERED

**Undergraduate—*AA:*** Accounting; Acquisition and Contract Management; Business Administration; Computer Information Systems; Computer Networking; Economics; General Studies; Marketing. ***BS:*** Accounting; Business Administration; Computer Information Systems; Computer Networking; Economics; International Business. ***Diploma:*** Accounting; Computer Information Systems.

**Graduate—*MS:*** Business Administration; Communications Technology; Information Systems; Professional Accounting.

## NON-DEGREE-RELATED COURSE TOPICS OFFERED

**Undergraduate—**English composition; English language and literature, general; accounting; anthropology; area, ethnic and cultural studies, other; business; economics; financial management and services; foreign languages and literatures; history; information sciences and systems; international business; law and legal studies; marketing operations/marketing and distribution, other; mathematics; political science and government; psychology; sociology.

**Graduate—**accounting; business; economics; information sciences and systems; law and legal studies; mathematics.

See full description on page 524.

# SUFFOLK COUNTY COMMUNITY COLLEGE

*Office of Academic Affairs*

533 College Road
Selden, NY 11784
**Contact:** Dr. Sandra Susman Palmer, Coordinator of Distance Education and Academic Chair of Department of Fine Arts
**Phone:** 631-451-4352
**Fax:** 631-451-4631
**Web:** http://www.sunysuffolk.edu
**E-mail:** susmans@sunysuffolk.edu

**ACCREDITATION:** Middle States Association of Colleges and Schools

**INSTITUTIONALLY ADMINISTERED FINANCIAL AID:** Yes

## DEGREE OR CERTIFICATE PROGRAMS OFFERED

Programs offered do not lead to a degree or other formal award.

## NON-DEGREE-RELATED COURSE TOPICS OFFERED

**Undergraduate—**American (United States) history; Asian studies; English composition; English creative writing; European history; accounting; art history, criticism and conservation; business marketing and marketing management; developmental and child psychology; earth and planetary sciences; law and legal studies, other; mathematics, other; philosophy and religion; radio and television broadcasting; sociology; women's studies.

# SUFFOLK UNIVERSITY

*Suffolk eMBA*

8 Ashburton Place, S-1142
Boston, MA 02108-2770
**Contact:** Ms. Christine Maher, Assistant Director
**Phone:** 617-973-5383
**Fax:** 617-723-0139
**Web:** http://www.suffolkemba.org
**E-mail:** cmaher@suffolk.edu

**ACCREDITATION:** New England Association of Schools and Colleges

**INSTITUTIONALLY ADMINISTERED FINANCIAL AID:** Yes

## DEGREE OR CERTIFICATE PROGRAMS OFFERED

**Undergraduate—*Certificate:*** Advanced Professional Certificate.
**Graduate—*MBA:*** Business Administration.

## NON-DEGREE-RELATED COURSE TOPICS OFFERED

**Undergraduate—**accounting.
**Graduate—**accounting; business; business marketing and marketing management; finance, general; international business; investments and securities; management information systems and business data processing, general; organizational behavior studies.

**See full description on page 526.**

# SUSSEX COUNTY COMMUNITY COLLEGE

## Academic Affairs

1 College Hill
Newton, NJ 07860
**Contact:** Dr. Thomas Isekenegbe, Associate Dean
**Phone:** 973-300-2136
**Fax:** 973-300-2277
**Web:** http://www.sussex.cc.nj.us
**E-mail:** thomasi@sussex.cc.nj.us

**ACCREDITATION:** Middle States Association of Colleges and Schools
**INSTITUTIONALLY ADMINISTERED FINANCIAL AID:** Yes

## DEGREE OR CERTIFICATE PROGRAMS OFFERED

**Undergraduate—*Certificate:*** Legal Studies.

## NON-DEGREE-RELATED COURSE TOPICS OFFERED

**Undergraduate—**English language and literature, general; computer science; criminal justice and corrections; mathematics; psychology.

# SYRACUSE UNIVERSITY

## Division of Continuing Education

700 University Avenue
Syracuse, NY 13244-2530
**Contact:** Mr. Robert Colley, Director of Marketing Communications and Distance Education
**Phone:** 315-443-3225
**Fax:** 315-443-4174
**Web:** http://www.suce.syr.edu
**E-mail:** mcolley@syr.edu

**ACCREDITATION:** Middle States Association of Colleges and Schools
**INSTITUTIONALLY ADMINISTERED FINANCIAL AID:** Yes

## DEGREE OR CERTIFICATE PROGRAMS OFFERED

**Undergraduate—*AA:*** Liberal Arts. ***BA:*** Liberal Studies. ***CBS:*** Library Science.
**Graduate—*MA:*** Advertising Design; Illustration. ***MBA:*** Business Administration. ***MS:*** Communications Management; Engineering Management; Information Resource Management; Nursing; Telecommunications Network Management. ***MSS:*** Social Sciences.

## NON-DEGREE-RELATED COURSE TOPICS OFFERED

**Undergraduate—**English composition; English creative writing; English language and literature, general; accounting; anthropology; computer programming; entrepreneurship; geography; philosophy and religion; psychology; sociology; textile sciences and engineering.
**Graduate—**nursing; psychology; sociology.
**Non-credit—**financial management and services; textile sciences and engineering.

**See full description on page 528.**

# SYRACUSE UNIVERSITY

## School of Management

900 South Crouse Avenue
Syracuse, NY 13244-2130
**Contact:** Paula C. O'Callaghan, Director of Mid-Career and Executive Education
**Phone:** 315-443-9216
**E-mail:** paula@som.syr.edu

**ACCREDITATION:** Middle States Association of Colleges and Schools
**INSTITUTIONALLY ADMINISTERED FINANCIAL AID:** No

## DEGREE OR CERTIFICATE PROGRAMS OFFERED

**Programs offered do not lead to a degree or other formal award.**

## NON-DEGREE-RELATED COURSE TOPICS OFFERED

**Graduate—**accounting; business; business administration and management; financial management and services; marketing management and research.

---

**Special Note**

Founded in 1977, the Independent Study MBA Program at Syracuse University is the nation's longest-running AACSB International–accredited distance learning MBA program. The 1-week residency at the beginning of each trimester is the hallmark of this program. During the week on campus, or at one of the international sites, students are taught by the same faculty members who have taught in the full-time and part-time evening MBA program at Syracuse. The week is composed of intensive classes and informal time with faculty members and other students. The beginning of each course is the class time during the residency week. For new students the first day consists of an orientation program and the registration process, followed by a reception with faculty members and returning students. For continuing students the first day consists of exams for the classes taken in the last trimester, followed by the reception. Then all students take intensive classes in the School of Management building over the next 5 days. Classes are small, typically 15–30 students per course. At the conclusion of the residency week, students leave Syracuse with an understanding of the requirements for completion of their courses. They communicate extensively between residencies with their professors and classmates via e-mail. The course ends with the exam, if required, at the following residency. Following the model, students typically take 2 courses each trimester per year, completing 18 credits toward the MBA each year. The MBA can be completed in approximately 3 years for most students. Admission is conducted on a rolling basis year-round. New students who are accepted may begin at any of the residencies, which occur annually in January, May, and August. Basic requirements for admission consideration are a bachelor's degree from a regionally accredited institution, GMAT score, TOEFL score for international applicants, and the completed application, including 1 recommendation letter. Admission is competitive. An online application is available at http://Embark.com. The Admissions Office can be reached at 315-443-9214; e-mail: MBAinfo@som.syr.edu; Web site: http://www.som.syr.edu/isp.

See full description on page 530.

# TACOMA COMMUNITY COLLEGE
## Distance Learning Program
6501 South 19th Street
Tacoma, WA 98466
**Contact:** Teresita Hartwell, Associate Dean for Distance Learning
**Phone:** 253-566-6005
**Fax:** 253-566-5398
**Web:** http://www.tacoma.ctc.edu/inst_dept/distancelearning/
**E-mail:** thartwel@tcc.tacoma.ctc.edu

**ACCREDITATION:** Northwest Association of Schools and Colleges

**INSTITUTIONALLY ADMINISTERED FINANCIAL AID:** Yes

### DEGREE OR CERTIFICATE PROGRAMS OFFERED
**Programs offered do not lead to a degree or other formal award.**

### NON-DEGREE-RELATED COURSE TOPICS OFFERED
**Undergraduate**—English composition; anthropology; applied mathematics; biology, general; computer and information sciences, general; design and applied arts; geography; health professions and related sciences, other; human services; library science, other; music; political science and government; psychology; sociology.
**Non-credit**—business administration and management; business information and data processing services; computer and information sciences, general.

# TAFT COLLEGE
29 Emmons Park Drive
Taft, CA 93268
**Contact:** Mr. Raymond L. Hatch, Distance Learning Instructional Coordinator
**Phone:** 661-763-7759
**Fax:** 661-763-7705
**Web:** http://www.taft.cc.ca.us/
**E-mail:** rhatch@taft.org

**ACCREDITATION:** Western Association of Schools and Colleges

**INSTITUTIONALLY ADMINISTERED FINANCIAL AID:** Yes

### DEGREE OR CERTIFICATE PROGRAMS OFFERED
**Undergraduate**—*AA:* CJA.

### NON-DEGREE-RELATED COURSE TOPICS OFFERED
**Undergraduate**—English composition; English creative writing; English language and literature, general; English language and literature/letters, other; accounting; applied mathematics; biological and physical sciences;

business; business administration and management; child care and guidance workers and managers; computer science; criminal justice and corrections; geological and related sciences; history; mathematical statistics; mathematics; mathematics, other; psychology; sociology.

# TARLETON STATE UNIVERSITY
## Center for Instructional Technology and Distance Learning
Box T-0810
Stephenville, TX 76402
**Contact:** Ms. Joann K. Wheeler, Director
**Phone:** 254-968-9050
**Fax:** 254-968-9540
**Web:** http://online2.tarleton.edu
**E-mail:** jkwheeler@tarleton.edu

**ACCREDITATION:** Southern Association of Colleges and Schools

**INSTITUTIONALLY ADMINISTERED FINANCIAL AID:** Yes

### DEGREE OR CERTIFICATE PROGRAMS OFFERED
**Programs offered do not lead to a degree or other formal award.**

### NON-DEGREE-RELATED COURSE TOPICS OFFERED
**Undergraduate**—English composition; English creative writing; English language and literature, general; English technical and business writing; applied mathematics; business administration and management; business/managerial economics; cognitive psychology and psycholinguistics; community health services; counseling psychology; curriculum and instruction; economics; education administration and supervision; financial management and services; health and physical education/fitness; history; home economics, other; human resources management; mathematics, other; nursing; political science and government; psychology, other.
**Graduate**—business marketing and marketing management; curriculum and instruction; educational psychology; history; social sciences, general.

# TARRANT COUNTY COLLEGE DISTRICT
## Center for Distance Learning
53-1 Campus Drive
Fort Worth, TX 76119
**Contact:** Dr. Kevin R. Eason, Assistant Director of Distance Learning
**Phone:** 817-515-4430
**Fax:** 817-515-4400
**Web:** http://www.tcjc.cc.tx.us/
**E-mail:** kevin.eason@tccd.net

**ACCREDITATION:** Southern Association of Colleges and Schools

**INSTITUTIONALLY ADMINISTERED FINANCIAL AID:** Yes

### DEGREE OR CERTIFICATE PROGRAMS OFFERED
**Undergraduate**—*AA:* General Studies.

### NON-DEGREE-RELATED COURSE TOPICS OFFERED
**Undergraduate**—English composition; English creative writing; accounting; biology, general; developmental and child psychology; engineering

mechanics; liberal arts and sciences, general studies and humanities; mechanical engineering; social psychology; sociology.

# TAYLOR UNIVERSITY, WORLD WIDE CAMPUS

## College of Lifelong Learning

1025 West Rudisill Boulevard
Fort Wayne, IN 46807-2197
**Contact:** Mr. Kevin J. Mahaffy, Director of Enrollment Services
**Phone:** 219-744-8750
**Fax:** 219-744-8796
**Web:** http://wwcampus.tayloru.edu
**E-mail:** wwcampus@tayloru.edu

**ACCREDITATION:** North Central Association of Colleges and Schools
**INSTITUTIONALLY ADMINISTERED FINANCIAL AID:** Yes

### DEGREE OR CERTIFICATE PROGRAMS OFFERED

**Undergraduate—AA:** Biblical Studies; Justice Administration—Ministry Concentration; Justice Administration—Public Policy Concentration; Liberal Arts (General Studies). **Certificate:** Christian Worker; Justice and Ministry.

### NON-DEGREE-RELATED COURSE TOPICS OFFERED

**Undergraduate—**American literature (United States); English composition; English language and literature, general; English literature (British and Commonwealth); area studies; bible/biblical studies; biblical and other theological languages and literatures; biological and physical sciences; biology, general; business; business administration and management; business information and data processing services; business/managerial economics; computer and information sciences, general; computer/information technology administration and management; counseling psychology; criminal justice and corrections; developmental and child psychology; economics; education, general; educational psychology; educational/instructional media design; fine arts and art studies; geography; history; information sciences and systems; journalism and mass communications; liberal arts and sciences, general studies and humanities; mathematics; medieval and renaissance studies; missions/missionary studies and missiology; multi/interdisciplinary studies, other; music; pastoral counseling and specialized ministries; peace and conflict studies; philosophy; philosophy and religion; physical sciences, general; professional studies; psychology; religion/religious studies; religious education; religious/sacred music; social psychology; social sciences and history, other; social sciences, general; sociology; speech and rhetorical studies; theological and ministerial studies; theological studies and religious vocations, other; urban affairs/studies.

See full description on page 532.

# TEACHERS COLLEGE, COLUMBIA UNIVERSITY

## Distance Learning Project

525 West 120th Street, Box 132
New York, NY 10027
**Contact:** Distance Learning Project
**Phone:** 888-633-6933

**Fax:** 212-678-3291
**Web:** http://dlp.tc.columbia.edu
**E-mail:** dlp@columbia.edu

**ACCREDITATION:** Middle States Association of Colleges and Schools
**INSTITUTIONALLY ADMINISTERED FINANCIAL AID:** Yes

### DEGREE OR CERTIFICATE PROGRAMS OFFERED

**Undergraduate—Certificate:** Designing Interactive Multimedia Instruction; Teaching and Learning with Technology.

### NON-DEGREE-RELATED COURSE TOPICS OFFERED

**Undergraduate—**cognitive psychology and psycholinguistics; education, other; educational/instructional media design; mathematical statistics.

See full description on page 534.

# TEMPLE UNIVERSITY

## Online Learning Program

1801 North Broad Street, TUZIP 040-14
Philadelphia, PA 19122-6096
**Contact:** Tim Walsh, Students Information System Director
**Phone:** 215-204-5050
**Fax:** 215-204-3756
**Web:** http://oll.temple.edu
**E-mail:** walsh@temple.edu

**ACCREDITATION:** Middle States Association of Colleges and Schools
**INSTITUTIONALLY ADMINISTERED FINANCIAL AID:** Yes

### DEGREE OR CERTIFICATE PROGRAMS OFFERED

Programs offered do not lead to a degree or other formal award.

### NON-DEGREE-RELATED COURSE TOPICS OFFERED

**Undergraduate—**English language and literature, general; anthropology; architecture; area, ethnic and cultural studies, other; business; communications technologies; communications, general; economics; education, general; educational/instructional media design; film/video and photographic arts; geological and related sciences; industrial and organizational psychology; internet and world wide web; journalism and mass communications; mathematics; multi/interdisciplinary studies, other; music; nursing; physics; psychology.

**Graduate—**English language and literature, general; accounting; business; business administration and management; communications technologies; communications, general; community health services; dentistry (D.D.S., D.M.D.); economics; education administration and supervision; engineering, general; geological and related sciences; health professions and related sciences, other; journalism and mass communications; materials engineering; music; podiatry (D.P.M., D.P., Pod.D.); social work; telecommunications.

# TENNESSEE TEMPLE UNIVERSITY

## School of External Studies

1815 Union Avenue
Chattanooga, TN 37404
**Contact:** School of External Studies
**Phone:** 800-553-4050 Ext. 4288
**Web:** http://www.tntemple.edu/external_studies/general.htm

**E-mail:** ttuinfo@tntemple.edu

**ACCREDITATION:** Accrediting Association of Bible Colleges

## DEGREE OR CERTIFICATE PROGRAMS OFFERED

**Undergraduate—AS:** Biblical Studies. **BS:** Biblical Studies.

## NON-DEGREE-RELATED COURSE TOPICS OFFERED

**Undergraduate—**East European languages and literatures; English composition; Greek languages and literatures (modern); bible/biblical studies; biblical and other theological languages and literatures; biology, general; liberal arts and sciences, general studies and humanities; mathematics; pastoral counseling and specialized ministries; philosophy; political science and government; psychology; religion/religious studies; religious education; religious/sacred music.

### Special Note

Tennessee Temple University (TTU) was founded with the intent to provide a strong academic education integrated within the framework of the Bible, which TTU believes is the only source of ultimate truth. In line with this founding purpose, the TTU School of External Studies offers an Associate of Science and a Bachelor of Science degree in biblical studies. The course requirements provide an outstanding theological basis for every student's education, which becomes the cement that holds all of the other building blocks of education together into a unified body of knowledge and wisdom.

The courses are offered to anyone from the United States or around the world. TTU works with missionaries on varied schedules. Students also find that TTU's prices fit well into most budgets.

Students who have scheduling conflicts at home or work, are disabled or homebound, or are geographically too far away from a college campus and want an outstanding, biblically based, and integrated academic education should contact TTU.

# TEXAS A&M UNIVERSITY

## Office of Distance Education

510 Blocker, 1478 TAMU
College Station, TX 77843
**Contact:** Dr. Elizabeth D. Tebeaux, Director of Distance Education
**Phone:** 979-845-4415
**Fax:** 979-845-4415
**Web:** http://www.tamu.edu/ode/disted
**E-mail:** e-tebeaux@tamu.edu

**ACCREDITATION:** Southern Association of Colleges and Schools

**INSTITUTIONALLY ADMINISTERED FINANCIAL AID:** Yes

## DEGREE OR CERTIFICATE PROGRAMS OFFERED

**Graduate—MAg:** Agricultural Development, Plant Science, or Natural Resource Development. **MEd:** Educational Technology. **MEngr:** Petroleum Engineering. **MS:** Educational Human Resource Development; Engineering Systems Management.

## NON-DEGREE-RELATED COURSE TOPICS OFFERED

**Graduate—**agriculture/agricultural sciences; education administration and supervision; educational/instructional media design; engineering-related technologies, other; engineering/industrial management; human resources management; petroleum engineering; plant sciences; wildlife and wildlands management.

**See full description on page 536.**

# TEXAS A&M UNIVERSITY–CORPUS CHRISTI

6300 Ocean Drive
Corpus Christi, TX 78412-5503
**Contact:** Ms. Margaret Dechant, Director of Admissions and Records
**Phone:** 361-825-2624
**Fax:** 361-825-5887
**E-mail:** margaret.dechant@mail.tamucc.edu

**ACCREDITATION:** Southern Association of Colleges and Schools

**INSTITUTIONALLY ADMINISTERED FINANCIAL AID:** Yes

## DEGREE OR CERTIFICATE PROGRAMS OFFERED

**Graduate—MBA/MHSA:** Health Science. **MSN:** Nursing Administration.

## NON-DEGREE-RELATED COURSE TOPICS OFFERED

**Undergraduate—**mathematical statistics.
**Graduate—**education, other.

# TEXAS A&M UNIVERSITY–KINGSVILLE

## Center for Distance Learning and Continuing Education

700 University Boulevard, MSC 147
Kingsville, TX 78363-8202
**Contact:** Dr. Tadeo Reyna, Jr., Director
**Phone:** 361-593-2861 Ext. 2854
**Fax:** 361-593-2859
**Web:** http://www.tamuk.edu/distancelearning
**E-mail:** t-reyna@tamuk.edu

**ACCREDITATION:** Southern Association of Colleges and Schools

**INSTITUTIONALLY ADMINISTERED FINANCIAL AID:** Yes

## DEGREE OR CERTIFICATE PROGRAMS OFFERED

Programs offered do not lead to a degree or other formal award.

## NON-DEGREE-RELATED COURSE TOPICS OFFERED

**Undergraduate—**geography.
**Graduate—**English as a second language; bilingual/bicultural education; education administration and supervision; environmental/environmental health engineering.

# TEXAS A&M UNIVERSITY–TEXARKANA

PO Box 5518
Texarkana, TX 75503-6518

**Contact:** Mrs. Patricia Black, Director of Admissions and Registrar
**Phone:** 903-223-3069
**Fax:** 903-223-3140
**Web:** http://www.tamut.edu/
**E-mail:** pat.black@tamut.edu

**ACCREDITATION:** Southern Association of Colleges and Schools

**INSTITUTIONALLY ADMINISTERED FINANCIAL AID:** Yes

### DEGREE OR CERTIFICATE PROGRAMS OFFERED

**Graduate—*MEd:*** Educational Administration.

### NON-DEGREE-RELATED COURSE TOPICS OFFERED

**Undergraduate—**accounting; business marketing and marketing management.
**Graduate—**business information and data processing services; economics; education administration and supervision.

# TEXAS CHRISTIAN UNIVERSITY
## *Cyberlearning*

TCU Box 297024
Fort Worth, TX 76129
**Contact:** Dr. Leo W. Munson, Associate Vice Chancellor for Academic Support
**Phone:** 817-257-7104
**Fax:** 817-257-7484
**Web:** http://www.tcu.edu/
**E-mail:** l.munson@tcu.edu

**ACCREDITATION:** Southern Association of Colleges and Schools

**INSTITUTIONALLY ADMINISTERED FINANCIAL AID:** Yes

> eCollege.com  *www.ecollege.com*

### DEGREE OR CERTIFICATE PROGRAMS OFFERED

**Graduate—*MS:*** Nursing.

### NON-DEGREE-RELATED COURSE TOPICS OFFERED

**Undergraduate—**American (United States) history; art history, criticism and conservation; biology, general; drama/theater arts, general.

**See full description on page 538.**

# TEXAS TECH UNIVERSITY
## *Extended Studies*

Box 42191
Lubbock, TX 79409-2191
**Contact:** Mrs. Michele L. Moskos, Marketing Director of Extended Studies
**Phone:** 806-742-7200 Ext. 276
**Fax:** 806-742-7277
**Web:** http://www.dce.ttu.edu
**E-mail:** dldegrees.oes@ttu.edu

**ACCREDITATION:** Southern Association of Colleges and Schools
**INSTITUTIONALLY ADMINISTERED FINANCIAL AID:** Yes

### DEGREE OR CERTIFICATE PROGRAMS OFFERED

**Undergraduate—*BGS:*** General Studies.
**Graduate—*MA:*** Technical Communication. ***ME:*** Engineering. ***MS:*** Petroleum Engineering; Restaurant, Hotel and Institutional Management; Software Engineering; Systems and Engineering Management.
**Postgraduate and doctoral—*EdD:*** Agricultural Education.

### NON-DEGREE-RELATED COURSE TOPICS OFFERED

**Undergraduate—**American (United States) history; American literature (United States); English composition; English literature (British and Commonwealth); English technical and business writing; European history; Spanish language and literature; accounting; agricultural economics; agriculture/agricultural sciences; anthropology; business administration and management; business marketing and marketing management; developmental and child psychology; economics; educational psychology; food sciences and technology; foods and nutrition studies; history; horticulture services operations and management; journalism and mass communications; law and legal studies; liberal arts and sciences, general studies and humanities; mathematics, other; music; psychology; social psychology; sociology; tourism and travel services marketing operations.
**Graduate—**English technical and business writing; agriculture/agricultural sciences; animal sciences; architecture; chemical engineering; civil engineering; computer and information sciences, other; computer science; curriculum and instruction; education administration and supervision; education, general; education, other; educational/instructional media design; electrical and electronic engineering-related technology; engineering, general; engineering, other; environmental/environmental health engineering; family/consumer resource management; industrial/manufacturing engineering; mathematical statistics; mathematics; mechanical engineering; music; petroleum engineering; plant sciences; textile sciences and engineering; visual and performing arts.
**Non-credit—**Spanish language and literature; agricultural economics; architecture; business administration and management.

**See full description on page 540.**

# TEXAS WOMAN'S UNIVERSITY

PO Box 425649
Denton, TX 76204
**Contact:** Dr. Lynda Murphy, Coordinator of Distance Education
**Phone:** 940-898-3405
**Fax:** 940-898-3412
**Web:** http://www.twu.edu/
**E-mail:** lmurphy@twu.edu

**ACCREDITATION:** Southern Association of Colleges and Schools

### DEGREE OR CERTIFICATE PROGRAMS OFFERED

**Undergraduate—*AA:*** CJA.
**Graduate—*MLS:*** Library Science. ***MS:*** Speech-Language Pathology.
**Postgraduate and doctoral—*PhD:*** Nursing.

### NON-DEGREE-RELATED COURSE TOPICS OFFERED

**Undergraduate—**English language and literature, general; bilingual/bicultural education; family/consumer resource management; home economics, general; nursing; occupational therapy; sociology.
**Graduate—**bilingual/bicultural education; business; computer and information sciences, general; education, general; family/consumer resource

management; health and physical education/fitness; library science/librarianship; mathematical statistics; nursing; occupational therapy; physical therapy.

# THOMAS EDISON STATE COLLEGE
## DIAL–Distance and Independent Adult Learning

101 West State Street
Trenton, NJ 08608-1176
**Contact:** Mr. Gordon Holly, Director of Admissions
**Phone:** 609-984-1150
**Fax:** 609-984-8447
**Web:** http://www.tesc.edu
**E-mail:** admissions@tesc.edu

**ACCREDITATION:** Middle States Association of Colleges and Schools
**INSTITUTIONALLY ADMINISTERED FINANCIAL AID:** Yes

eCollege.com  *www.ecollege.com*

## DEGREE OR CERTIFICATE PROGRAMS OFFERED

**Undergraduate—AA:** Arts. **ASAST:** Air Traffic Control; Aviation Flight Technology; Aviation Maintenance Technology; Computer Science Technology; Electrical Technology; Mechanical Engineering Technology; Medical Imaging; Nuclear Engineering Technology; Nuclear Medicine; Radiation Protection; Radiation Therapy; Respiratory Care. **ASM:** Accounting; Administrative Office Management; Banking; Finance; General Management; Hotel/Motel/Restaurant Management; Human Resource Management; Insurance; International Business; Marketing; Real Estate; Retailing Management; Small Business Management/Entrepreneurship; Transportation/Distribution Management. **ASNSM:** Computer Science; Mathematics. **ASPSS:** Administration of Justice; Child Development Services; Community Services; Emergency Disaster Management; Gerontology; Legal Services; Mental Health and Rehabilitation Services; Recreation Services. **BA:** Chemistry; Communications; Economics; English; History; Humanities; Labor Studies; Liberal Studies; Natural Sciences/Mathematics; Philosophy; Political Science; Psychology; Religion; Social Sciences/History; Sociology. **BS:** Mental Health and Rehabilitative Services. **BSAST:** Air Traffic Control; Aviation Flight Technology; Aviation Maintenance Technology; Computer Science Technology; Electronics Engineering Technology; Environmental Sciences; Insurance; Medical Engineering Technology; Medical Imaging; Nuclear Engineering Technology; Nuclear Medicine; Radiation Protection; Radiation Therapy; Respiratory Care. **BSBA:** Accounting; Administrative Office Management; Advertising Management; Banking; General Management; Hospital Health Care Administration; Hotel/Motel/Restaurant Management; Human Resources Management; International Business; Marketing; Operations Management; Organizational Management; Retailing Management; Small Business Management/Entrepreneurship; Transportation/Distribution Management. **BSN:** Nursing.
**Graduate—MA:** Professional Studies. **MSM:** Management.

## NON-DEGREE-RELATED COURSE TOPICS OFFERED

**Undergraduate—**Afro-American(Black) studies; American (United States) history; Asian studies; English composition; Spanish language and literature; accounting; anthropology; art history, criticism and conservation; biology, general; developmental and child psychology; earth and planetary sciences; environmental science/studies; family and marriage counseling;

finance, general; organizational behavior studies; philosophy and religion; social psychology; sociology; women's studies.
**See full description on page 542.**

# TIDEWATER COMMUNITY COLLEGE

121 College Place
Norfolk, VA 23510
**Contact:** Dr. George C. Lassetter, III, Assistant to the Dean for Distributed Teaching, Learning, and Services
**Phone:** 757-822-1069
**Fax:** 757-822-1086
**Web:** http://www.tc.cc.va.us/
**E-mail:** tclassc@tc.cc.va.us

**ACCREDITATION:** Southern Association of Colleges and Schools
**INSTITUTIONALLY ADMINISTERED FINANCIAL AID:** Yes

## DEGREE OR CERTIFICATE PROGRAMS OFFERED
**Programs offered do not lead to a degree or other formal award.**

## NON-DEGREE-RELATED COURSE TOPICS OFFERED

**Undergraduate—**English composition; accounting; administrative and secretarial services; astronomy; data entry/microcomputer applications; economics; mathematics; psychology; sociology.
**Non-credit—**information sciences and systems.

# TIFFIN UNIVERSITY
## School of Off-Campus Learning

155 Miami Street
Tiffin, OH 44883
**Contact:** Dr. Charles R. Christensen, Director of Tiffin Online
**Phone:** 866-TU-WIRED
**Fax:** 419-443-5011
**Web:** http://www.tiffin-global.org
**E-mail:** onlineed@tiffin.edu

**ACCREDITATION:** North Central Association of Colleges and Schools
**INSTITUTIONALLY ADMINISTERED FINANCIAL AID:** Yes

eCollege.com  *www.ecollege.com*

## DEGREE OR CERTIFICATE PROGRAMS OFFERED
**Graduate—MBA:** Business Administration. **MCJ:** Criminal Justice.

# TOMPKINS CORTLAND COMMUNITY COLLEGE
## Instructional and Learning Resources

170 N Street
Dryden, NY 13053
**Contact:** Student Service Representative
**Phone:** 607-844-6582
**Web:** http://www.sunytccc.edu/e-tc3/e-tc3.htm

E-mail: ssr@sunytccc.edu

ACCREDITATION: Middle States Association of Colleges and Schools

### DEGREE OR CERTIFICATE PROGRAMS OFFERED

Undergraduate—*AAS:* Chemical Dependency Studies Counseling; Hotel and Restaurant Management; Paralegal Studies.

### NON-DEGREE-RELATED COURSE TOPICS OFFERED

Undergraduate—English as a second language; English composition; English language and literature, general; accounting; alcohol/drug abuse counseling; business; business communications; business marketing and marketing management; business quantitative methods and management science; communications, general; computer and information sciences, general; computer programming; computer software and media applications; developmental and child psychology; fine arts and art studies; hospitality services management; international business; internet and world wide web; law and legal studies; law and legal studies, other; mathematics; psychology; psychology, other; social psychology; sociology; visual and performing arts.

**See full description on page 544.**

# TOURO UNIVERSITY INTERNATIONAL

10542 Calle Lee, #102
Los Alamitos, CA 90720
**Contact:** Wei Ren, Registrar
**Phone:** 714-816-0366
**Fax:** 714-816-0367
**Web:** http://www.tourou.edu/
**E-mail:** registration@tourou.edu

ACCREDITATION: Middle States Association of Colleges and Schools

INSTITUTIONALLY ADMINISTERED FINANCIAL AID: Yes

### DEGREE OR CERTIFICATE PROGRAMS OFFERED

Undergraduate—*BS:* Bachelor of Science.
Graduate—*MBA:* Business Administration. *MS:* Health Sciences.
Postgraduate and doctoral—*PhD:* Business Administration; Health Sciences.

**See full description on page 546.**

# TREASURE VALLEY COMMUNITY COLLEGE

*Division of Extended Learning*
650 College Boulevard
Ontario, OR 97914
**Contact:** Mike Woodhead, Director of Continuing and Distance Education
**Phone:** 541-881-8822 Ext. 283
**Fax:** 541-881-2743
**Web:** http://www.tvcc.cc
**E-mail:** woodhead@tvcc.cc

ACCREDITATION: Northwest Association of Schools and Colleges

INSTITUTIONALLY ADMINISTERED FINANCIAL AID: No

### DEGREE OR CERTIFICATE PROGRAMS OFFERED

Programs offered do not lead to a degree or other formal award.

### NON-DEGREE-RELATED COURSE TOPICS OFFERED

Undergraduate—biology, general; business; chemistry; computer and information sciences, other; computer programming; mathematics, other; music; physical sciences, general; psychology; sociology.

# TRIDENT TECHNICAL COLLEGE

7000 Rivers Avenue, PO Box 118067
Charleston, SC 29423-8067
**Contact:** Ms. Edna Boroski, Instructional Support Coordinator for Distance Learning
**Phone:** 843-574-6931
**Fax:** 843-574-6595
**Web:** http://www.tridenttech.org
**E-mail:** boroskie@telli.trident.tec.sc.us

ACCREDITATION: Southern Association of Colleges and Schools

INSTITUTIONALLY ADMINISTERED FINANCIAL AID: Yes

### DEGREE OR CERTIFICATE PROGRAMS OFFERED

Programs offered do not lead to a degree or other formal award.

### NON-DEGREE-RELATED COURSE TOPICS OFFERED

Undergraduate—English composition; English technical and business writing; accounting; administrative and secretarial services; business; business administration and management; business information and data processing services; business/managerial economics; computer and information sciences, general; computer programming; computer software and media applications; computer/information technology administration and management; criminal justice and corrections; data entry/microcomputer applications; economics; history; mathematics; psychology; quality control and safety technologies; sociology; speech and rhetorical studies; telecommunications; visual and performing arts.

# TRINITY INTERNATIONAL UNIVERSITY

*Division of Open Studies*
2065 Half Day Road
Deerfield, IL 60015
**Contact:** Mr. Jason M. Miller, Distance Education Coordinator
**Phone:** 847-317-6554
**Fax:** 847-317-6509
**Web:** http://www.tiu.edu/etrinity
**E-mail:** distance@tiu.edu

ACCREDITATION: North Central Association of Colleges and Schools

INSTITUTIONALLY ADMINISTERED FINANCIAL AID: No

### DEGREE OR CERTIFICATE PROGRAMS OFFERED

Programs offered do not lead to a degree or other formal award.

### NON-DEGREE-RELATED COURSE TOPICS OFFERED

Graduate—bible/biblical studies; religion/religious studies; religious education; theological and ministerial studies.

# TRI-STATE UNIVERSITY

1 University Avenue
Angola, IN 46703
**Contact:** Ms. Sara Yarian, Director of Admission
**Phone:** 219-665-4132
**Fax:** 219-665-4578
**Web:** http://www.tristate.edu/
**E-mail:** admit@tristate.edu

**ACCREDITATION:** North Central Association of Colleges and Schools
**INSTITUTIONALLY ADMINISTERED FINANCIAL AID:** No

## DEGREE OR CERTIFICATE PROGRAMS OFFERED
Programs offered do not lead to a degree or other formal award.

## NON-DEGREE-RELATED COURSE TOPICS OFFERED
**Undergraduate**—accounting; business; business administration and management; economics; fine arts and art studies; geological and related sciences; history; law and legal studies; liberal arts and sciences, general studies and humanities; marketing management and research; social sciences, general.

# TRITON COLLEGE
## Alternative Learning at Triton

2000 5th Avenue
River Grove, IL 60171
**Contact:** Bruce Scism, Associate Vice President of Instructional Technology
**Phone:** 708-456-0300 Ext. 3868
**Fax:** 708-583-3121
**Web:** http://www.triton.cc.il.us
**E-mail:** bscism@triton.cc.il.us

**ACCREDITATION:** North Central Association of Colleges and Schools
**INSTITUTIONALLY ADMINISTERED FINANCIAL AID:** Yes

## DEGREE OR CERTIFICATE PROGRAMS OFFERED
Programs offered do not lead to a degree or other formal award.

## NON-DEGREE-RELATED COURSE TOPICS OFFERED
**Undergraduate**—American (United States) history; English composition; Latin American studies; Spanish language and literature; accounting; anthropology; art history, criticism and conservation; biology, general; business marketing and marketing management; developmental and child psychology; drama/theater arts, general; educational psychology; law and legal studies, other; mathematical statistics; philosophy and religion; social psychology; sociology.

# TROY STATE UNIVERSITY
## Distance Learning Center

Distance Learning Center, 304 Wallace Hall
Troy, AL 36082
**Contact:** Mr. Doc Kunkle, Student Support Director
**Phone:** 334-670-5875
**Fax:** 334-670-5679
**Web:** http://www.tsulearn.net

**E-mail:** dkunkle2@trojan.troyst.edu
**ACCREDITATION:** Southern Association of Colleges and Schools
**INSTITUTIONALLY ADMINISTERED FINANCIAL AID:** Yes

## DEGREE OR CERTIFICATE PROGRAMS OFFERED
**Undergraduate**—**AA:** Business; General Education.
**Graduate**—**EMBA:** Business Administration. **MBA/PhD:** Criminal Justice. **MCE:** Resource Management. **MS:** Human Resource Management; International Relations; Public Administration.

## NON-DEGREE-RELATED COURSE TOPICS OFFERED
**Undergraduate**—accounting.
**Graduate**—educational psychology.
**Non-credit**—adult and continuing teacher education.
**See full description on page 548.**

# TROY STATE UNIVERSITY DOTHAN
## Information Services

500 University Drive
Dotham, AL 36304
**Contact:** Ronnie Creole, Director for Information Services
**Phone:** 334-983-6556 Ext. 314
**Fax:** 334-983-6322
**Web:** http://www.tsud.edu
**E-mail:** admissions@tsud.edu

**ACCREDITATION:** Southern Association of Colleges and Schools
**INSTITUTIONALLY ADMINISTERED FINANCIAL AID:** Yes

## DEGREE OR CERTIFICATE PROGRAMS OFFERED
Programs offered do not lead to a degree or other formal award.

## NON-DEGREE-RELATED COURSE TOPICS OFFERED
**Undergraduate**—English composition; philosophy and religion; sociology.

# TROY STATE UNIVERSITY–FLORIDA REGION
## Distance Learning

81 Beal Parkway, SE
Fort Walton Beach, FL 32548
**Contact:** Ms. Jan Barnes, TSUFL Distance and Partnership Programs Student Services Specialist
**Phone:** 850-301-2150
**Fax:** 850-796-2969
**Web:** http://www.tsufl.edu/distancelearning
**E-mail:** distlearn@tsufl.edu

**ACCREDITATION:** Southern Association of Colleges and Schools
**INSTITUTIONALLY ADMINISTERED FINANCIAL AID:** Yes

## DEGREE OR CERTIFICATE PROGRAMS OFFERED
**Undergraduate**—**AS:** Business Administration; General Education. **BS:** (BAS) Resources Management; Computer Science; Management.

**NON-DEGREE-RELATED COURSE TOPICS OFFERED**

**Undergraduate**—English language and literature, general; business; business information and data processing services; computer programming; computer/information technology administration and management; economics; education, general; family and community studies; mathematics; organizational behavior studies; social sciences and history, other; social sciences, general.

# TROY STATE UNIVERSITY MONTGOMERY

## External Degree Program–Professional Studies

PO Drawer 4419, Rosa Parks Library and Museum, Room 310
Montgomery, AL 36103
**Contact:** Mr. David W. Barham, MSC, Director of External
Degree Program
**Phone:** 334-241-9553
**Fax:** 800-355-TSUM Ext. 553
**Web:** http://www.tsum.edu/DL/
**E-mail:** dbarham@tsum.edu

**ACCREDITATION:** Southern Association of Colleges and Schools
**INSTITUTIONALLY ADMINISTERED FINANCIAL AID:** Yes

**DEGREE OR CERTIFICATE PROGRAMS OFFERED**

**Undergraduate—AS:** Business Administration; Business, History, Political Science, Psychology, Social Science, Child Care; General Education; History; Political Science; Psychology; Social Sciences. **BA:** Business Administration; English; History; Political Science; Psychology; Resources Management (Business), English, History, Political Science, Psychology, Social Science; Social Sciences. **BS:** Business Administration; English; History; Political Science; Psychology; Resources Management (Business), English, History, Political Science, Psychology, Social Science; Social Sciences.

**NON-DEGREE-RELATED COURSE TOPICS OFFERED**

**Undergraduate**—English composition; Spanish language and literature; accounting; business marketing and marketing management; developmental and child psychology; economics; finance, general; geography; history; law and legal studies, other; organizational behavior studies; philosophy; physical sciences, general; political science and government; sociology.

# TULANE UNIVERSITY

## University College

New Orleans, LA 70118
**Contact:** Dr. Julia Grace Houston, Director of Media Arts and
Distance Education
**Phone:** 504-862-8000 Ext. 1672
**Fax:** 504-865-5562
**Web:** http://www.tulane.edu/~uc
**E-mail:** jhousto@tulane.edu

**ACCREDITATION:** Southern Association of Colleges and Schools
**INSTITUTIONALLY ADMINISTERED FINANCIAL AID:** Yes

**DEGREE OR CERTIFICATE PROGRAMS OFFERED**

**Programs offered do not lead to a degree or other formal award.**

**NON-DEGREE-RELATED COURSE TOPICS OFFERED**

**Undergraduate**—English composition; business and personal services marketing operations; computer and information sciences, general; internet and world wide web.

# TULSA COMMUNITY COLLEGE

## Distance Learning Office

909 South Boston Avenue
Tulsa, OK 74119-2095
**Contact:** Randy Dominguez, Dean of Distance Learning
**Phone:** 918-595-7143
**Fax:** 918-595-7306
**Web:** http://www.tulsa.cc.ok.us/dl
**E-mail:** rdomingu@tulsa.cc.ok.us

**ACCREDITATION:** North Central Association of Colleges and Schools
**INSTITUTIONALLY ADMINISTERED FINANCIAL AID:** Yes

**DEGREE OR CERTIFICATE PROGRAMS OFFERED**

**Programs offered do not lead to a degree or other formal award.**

**NON-DEGREE-RELATED COURSE TOPICS OFFERED**

**Undergraduate**—American literature (United States); English composition; English literature (British and Commonwealth); English technical and business writing; accounting; business; business administration and management; computer programming; computer science; computer software and media applications; computer systems networking and telecommunications; computer/information technology administration and management; developmental and child psychology; economics; financial management and services; fine arts and art studies; foreign languages and literatures; geography; geological and related sciences; history; law and legal studies; liberal arts and sciences, general studies and humanities; mathematics; philosophy; psychology; sociology; telecommunications.

# TUNXIS COMMUNITY COLLEGE

271 Scott Swamp Road
Farmington, CT 06032
**Contact:** Lucretia Holley, Director of Admissions
**Phone:** 860-679-9152
**Fax:** 860-676-8906
**Web:** http://www.tunxis.commnet.edu/tole
**E-mail:** tx_admissions@commnet.edu

**ACCREDITATION:** New England Association of Schools and Colleges
**INSTITUTIONALLY ADMINISTERED FINANCIAL AID:** Yes

**DEGREE OR CERTIFICATE PROGRAMS OFFERED**

**Undergraduate—AA:** Criminal Justice; General Studies/Liberal Arts.
**Certificate:** Corrections Pre-certification.

**NON-DEGREE-RELATED COURSE TOPICS OFFERED**

**Non-credit**—information sciences and systems.

# TUSKEGEE UNIVERSITY

Center for Continuing Education, Kellogg Conference Center
Tuskegee, AL 36088
**Contact:** Dr. Henry J. Findlay, Professor and Director of Program Development
**Phone:** 334-724-4316
**Fax:** 334-724-4199
**Web:** http://www.tusk.edu/
**E-mail:** findlleyh@tusk.edu

**ACCREDITATION:** Southern Association of Colleges and Schools

## DEGREE OR CERTIFICATE PROGRAMS OFFERED
**Programs offered do not lead to a degree or other formal award.**

## NON-DEGREE-RELATED COURSE TOPICS OFFERED
**Non-credit**—English creative writing; English technical and business writing; communications technologies; computer and information sciences, general; education, other; ethnic and cultural studies; mathematics and computer science; real estate; religious education; teacher assistant/aide.

# TYLER JUNIOR COLLEGE

*Learning Resources*
PO Box 9020
Tyler, TX 75711
**Contact:** Gay Howard, Secretary of Learning Resources
**Phone:** 903-510-2529
**Fax:** 903-510-2643
**Web:** http://www.tyler.cc.tx.us/academics/distance-learning.htm
**E-mail:** ghow@tjc.tyler.cc.tx.us

**ACCREDITATION:** Southern Association of Colleges and Schools
**INSTITUTIONALLY ADMINISTERED FINANCIAL AID:** Yes

## DEGREE OR CERTIFICATE PROGRAMS OFFERED
**Undergraduate**—*AA:* Business Administration; General Studies. *AAS:* Business Management; Emergency Medical Service Professions [Paramedic Option]; Information Systems Networking Technologies [Novell].

## NON-DEGREE-RELATED COURSE TOPICS OFFERED
**Undergraduate**—American (United States) history; American literature (United States); English composition; English creative writing; Spanish language and literature; accounting; administrative and secretarial services; anatomy; art history, criticism and conservation; astronomy; biology, general; business; business administration and management; business communications; computer and information sciences, general; computer and information sciences, other; computer programming; computer science; computer software and media applications; computer systems analysis; computer systems networking and telecommunications; computer/information technology administration and management; criminal justice and corrections; economics; education, general; environmental science/studies; fire protection; internet and world wide web; law and legal studies, other; liberal arts and sciences, general studies and humanities; mathematics, other; music; paralegal/legal assistant; political science and government; psychology; sign language interpreter; sociology.
**Non-credit**—accounting; business; business administration and management; business information and data processing services; computer and

information sciences, general; computer programming; educational/instructional media design; information sciences and systems; internet and world wide web.

# ULSTER COUNTY COMMUNITY COLLEGE

*SUNY at Ulster Online Degree Program*
Stone Ridge, NY 12484
**Contact:** Susan Weatherly, Admissions Recruiter
**Phone:** 800-724-0833 Ext. 5018
**Fax:** 914-687-5090
**Web:** http://www.ulster.cc.ny.us/
**E-mail:** weathers@sunyulster.edu

**ACCREDITATION:** Middle States Association of Colleges and Schools

## DEGREE OR CERTIFICATE PROGRAMS OFFERED
**Undergraduate**—*AS:* Liberal Arts.

## NON-DEGREE-RELATED COURSE TOPICS OFFERED
**Undergraduate**—liberal arts and sciences, general studies and humanities.

# THE UNION INSTITUTE

*Center for Distance Learning*
440 East McMillan Street
Cincinnati, OH 45206-1925
**Contact:** Dr. Timothy Mott, Dean
**Phone:** 800-486-3116
**Fax:** 513-861-9026
**Web:** http://www.tui.edu
**E-mail:** tmott@tui.edu

**ACCREDITATION:** North Central Association of Colleges and Schools
**INSTITUTIONALLY ADMINISTERED FINANCIAL AID:** Yes

## DEGREE OR CERTIFICATE PROGRAMS OFFERED
**Undergraduate**—*BA:* Liberal Arts and Sciences. *BS:* Liberal Arts and Sciences.
**Postgraduate and doctoral**—*PhD:* Interdisciplinary Studies.

## NON-DEGREE-RELATED COURSE TOPICS OFFERED
**Graduate**—organizational behavior studies.
**See full description on page 550.**

# UNITED STATES OPEN UNIVERSITY

6 Denny Road, Suite 301
Wilmington, DE 19809
**Contact:** Ms. Kathleen Hebbel, Manager of Business Development and Outreach
**Phone:** 800-232-7705
**Fax:** 302-765-9503
**Web:** http://www.open.edu/

**E-mail:** k.v.hebbel@open.edu

**ACCREDITATION:** Middle States Association of Colleges and Schools

**INSTITUTIONALLY ADMINISTERED FINANCIAL AID:** No

## DEGREE OR CERTIFICATE PROGRAMS OFFERED

**Undergraduate—BA:** Business Administration; Computing; English; European Studies; Humanities; Information Technology; International Studies; Liberal Arts; Social Sciences.
**Graduate—MBA:** Business Administration. **MS:** Computing. **MSIS:** Information Systems Management.

# UNITED STATES SPORTS ACADEMY

*Continuing Education and Distance Learning*

One Academy Drive
Daphne, AL 36526-7055
**Contact:** Dr. Cynthia Ryder, Vice President of Academic Affairs
**Phone:** 334-626-3303 Ext. 136
**Web:** http://www.ussa.edu
**E-mail:** ceryder@ussa.edu

**ACCREDITATION:** Southern Association of Colleges and Schools

**INSTITUTIONALLY ADMINISTERED FINANCIAL AID:** Yes

eCollege.com *www.ecollege.com*

## DEGREE OR CERTIFICATE PROGRAMS OFFERED

**Undergraduate—Certificate:** Continuing Education Certificate in Body Building; Continuing Education Certificate in Coaching Figure Skating; Continuing Education Certificate in Conditioning and Nutrition; Continuing Education Certificate in Fitness and Exercise Physiology; Continuing Education Certificate in Mental Skills in Sports; Continuing Education Certificate in Personal Training; Continuing Education Certificate in Sport Recreation Management; Continuing Education Certificate in Sports Agency; Continuing Education Certificate in Sports Coaching; Continuing Education Certificate in Sports Medicine.
**Graduate—MSS:** Health and Fitness Management; Recreational Management; Sport Art; Sports Coaching; Sports Management; Sports Medicine.

## NON-DEGREE-RELATED COURSE TOPICS OFFERED

**Undergraduate—**parks, recreation and leisure facilities management.
**See full description on page 552.**

# UNIVERSITÈ DE MONTRÈAL

*Faculté de L'éducation Permanente, Formation á Distance*

C.P. 6128, succursale Centre-Ville
Montréal , QC H3C 3J7, Canada
**Contact:** M. Bernard Morin, Coordonnateur
**Phone:** 514-343-6111 Ext. 2852
**Fax:** 514-343-6943
**Web:** http://www.fep.umontreal.ca/distance/

**E-mail:** bernard.morin@umontreal.ca

**ACCREDITATION:** Provincially Chartered

**INSTITUTIONALLY ADMINISTERED FINANCIAL AID:** Yes

## DEGREE OR CERTIFICATE PROGRAMS OFFERED

**Undergraduate—Certificate:** Certificat en Gérontologie.

## NON-DEGREE-RELATED COURSE TOPICS OFFERED

**Undergraduate—**architecture; astronomy; health professions and related sciences, other; nursing; public relations and organizational communications.
**Non-credit—**communications, other.

# UNIVERSITÈ DU QUÈBEC Á RIMOUSKI

Cours médiatisés, 300, Allée des Ursulines
Rimouski, QC G5L 3A1, Canada
**Contact:** Director of Distance Education
**Phone:** 418-723-1986 Ext. 1665
**Fax:** 418-723-1986 Ext. 1865
**Web:** http://www.uquebec.ca/
**E-mail:** marie-france_ouellet@uqar.uquebec.ca

**ACCREDITATION:** Provincially Chartered

**INSTITUTIONALLY ADMINISTERED FINANCIAL AID:** Yes

## DEGREE OR CERTIFICATE PROGRAMS OFFERED

**Undergraduate—Certificate:** Education contemporaine.

## NON-DEGREE-RELATED COURSE TOPICS OFFERED

**Undergraduate—**developmental and child psychology; education, other; educational psychology; psychology.

# UNIVERSITÈ SAINTE-ANNE

Pointe-de-L'Église
Digby County, NS B0W 1M0, Canada
**Contact:** Dr. Betty A. Dugas, Director
**Phone:** 902-769-2114 Ext. 134
**Fax:** 902-769-2930
**Web:** http://ustanne-59.ustanne.ednet.ns.ca/
**E-mail:** bdugas@ustanne.ednet.ns.com

**ACCREDITATION:** Provincially Chartered

**INSTITUTIONALLY ADMINISTERED FINANCIAL AID:** Yes

## DEGREE OR CERTIFICATE PROGRAMS OFFERED

Programs offered do not lead to a degree or other formal award.

# THE UNIVERSITY ALLIANCE

9417 Princess Palm Avenue
Tampa, FL 33619
**Contact:** Admissions
**Phone:** 800-404-7355
**Web:** http://www.universityalliance.com/

**E-mail:** info@universityalliance.com

**ACCREDITATION:** Accreditation varies across member institutions

**INSTITUTIONALLY ADMINISTERED FINANCIAL AID:** Yes

## DEGREE OR CERTIFICATE PROGRAMS OFFERED

**Undergraduate—AA:** Liberal Arts. **AS:** Business. **BA:** Accounting; Business Administration and Accounting; Business Administration and Management; Business Administration; Criminology. **BS:** Computer Information Systems; Nursing.

## NON-DEGREE-RELATED COURSE TOPICS OFFERED

**Undergraduate—**English language and literature, general; accounting; computer science; criminology; economics; fine arts and art studies; marketing management and research; mathematics; philosophy; political science and government; psychology; religion/religious studies; social sciences, general.

# UNIVERSITY AT BUFFALO, THE STATE UNIVERSITY OF NEW YORK

*Millard Fillmore College Distance Learning Office*

128 Parker Hall
Buffalo, NY 14214-3007
**Contact:** Dr. George Lopos, Dean
**Phone:** 716-829-3131
**Fax:** 716-829-2475
**Web:** http://www.mfc.buffalo.edu
**E-mail:** mfc-inquire@buffalo.edu

**ACCREDITATION:** Middle States Association of Colleges and Schools

**INSTITUTIONALLY ADMINISTERED FINANCIAL AID:** No

## DEGREE OR CERTIFICATE PROGRAMS OFFERED

**Programs offered do not lead to a degree or other formal award.**

## NON-DEGREE-RELATED COURSE TOPICS OFFERED

**Undergraduate—**English composition; advertising; communications, general; computer systems networking and telecommunications; computer/information technology administration and management; film/cinema studies; law and legal studies; psychology; public relations and organizational communications.

# UNIVERSITY COLLEGE OF THE FRASER VALLEY

*UCFV Online*

45635 Yale Road
Chilliwack, BC V2P 6T4, Canada
**Contact:** Dr. Wendy E. Burton, University College Professor
**Phone:** 604-792-0025 Ext. 2413
**Fax:** 604-792-2388
**Web:** http://www.ucfv.bc.ca/online

**E-mail:** burton@ucfv.bc.ca

**ACCREDITATION:** Provincially Chartered

**INSTITUTIONALLY ADMINISTERED FINANCIAL AID:** Yes

eCollege.com *www.ecollege.com*

## DEGREE OR CERTIFICATE PROGRAMS OFFERED

**Programs offered do not lead to a degree or other formal award.**

## NON-DEGREE-RELATED COURSE TOPICS OFFERED

**Undergraduate—**English composition; accounting; agriculture/agricultural sciences; anthropology; biological sciences/life sciences, other; business administration and management; business communications; child care and guidance workers and managers; communications technologies; communications, general; comparative literature; computer and information sciences, general; criminology; curriculum and instruction; education administration and supervision; educational evaluation, research and statistics; fine arts and art studies; geography; history; human services; library assistant; philosophy; philosophy and religion; psychology; sociology; teaching English as a second language/foreign language.
**Non-credit—**computer software and media applications; data entry/microcomputer applications; data processing technology.

# THE UNIVERSITY OF AKRON

*Information Services*

Bierce Library
Akron, OH 44325-3501
**Contact:** Dr. John J. Hirschbuhl, Director Instructional Learning and Scholar and Learner Services
**Phone:** 330-972-6507
**Fax:** 330-972-5238
**Web:** http://gozips.uakron.edu/is/clientserv
**E-mail:** jhirsch@uakron.edu

**ACCREDITATION:** North Central Association of Colleges and Schools

**INSTITUTIONALLY ADMINISTERED FINANCIAL AID:** Yes

## DEGREE OR CERTIFICATE PROGRAMS OFFERED

**Programs offered do not lead to a degree or other formal award.**

## NON-DEGREE-RELATED COURSE TOPICS OFFERED

**Undergraduate—**English composition; English technical and business writing; Japanese language and literature; accounting; biology, general; business; communications, general; education, general; educational/instructional media design; general teacher education; geography; mathematics; nursing; psychology; public administration; social work; sociology.
**Graduate—**education, general; educational evaluation, research and statistics; educational/instructional media design; nursing; social work.
**Non-credit—**communications technologies; computer and information sciences, general; computer and information sciences, other; computer programming; computer software and media applications; computer systems analysis; computer systems networking and telecommunications; computer/information technology administration and management; data entry/microcomputer applications; data processing technology; information sciences and systems.

# THE UNIVERSITY OF ALABAMA

## College of Continuing Studies

Box 870388
Tuscaloosa, AL 35487-0388
**Contact:** Student Inquiries, Division of Distance Education
**Phone:** 205-348-9278
**Fax:** 205-348-0249
**Web:** http://bama.disted.ua.edu
**E-mail:** disted@ccs.ua.edu

**ACCREDITATION:** Southern Association of Colleges and Schools

### DEGREE OR CERTIFICATE PROGRAMS OFFERED

**Graduate—MS:** Engineering; Environmental Engineering; Nursing Case Management. **MSAE:** Aerospace Engineering. **MSCE:** Civil Engineering. **MSE:** Engineering Management. **MSEE:** Electrical Engineering. **MSME:** Mechanical Engineering.

### NON-DEGREE-RELATED COURSE TOPICS OFFERED

**Undergraduate—**American literature (United States); English language and literature, general; accounting; astronomy; biological and physical sciences; biology, general; business; communications, general; computer science; criminal justice and corrections; economics; foreign languages and literatures; geography; history; home economics, general; hospitality services management; journalism and mass communications; mathematics; philosophy; philosophy and religion; real estate; telecommunications. **Graduate—**accounting; advertising; aerospace, aeronautical and astronautical engineering; chemical engineering; electrical, electronics and communication engineering; engineering mechanics; environmental/environmental health engineering; industrial/manufacturing engineering; nursing.

**See full description on page 554.**

# UNIVERSITY OF ALASKA ANCHORAGE

## Center for Distributed Learning

3211 Providence Drive, K-134
Anchorage, AK 99508-8269
**Contact:** Mr. R. David Stephens, Manager
**Phone:** 907-786-4488
**Fax:** 907-786-4485
**Web:** http://uaaonline.alaska.edu
**E-mail:** dave@uaa.alaska.edu

**ACCREDITATION:** Northwest Association of Schools and Colleges
**INSTITUTIONALLY ADMINISTERED FINANCIAL AID:** Yes

### DEGREE OR CERTIFICATE PROGRAMS OFFERED

Programs offered do not lead to a degree or other formal award.

### NON-DEGREE-RELATED COURSE TOPICS OFFERED

**Undergraduate—**English composition; accounting; biology, general; business administration and management; developmental and child psychology; economics; fine arts and art studies; foreign languages and literatures; geography; history; journalism and mass communication, other; nursing; philosophy; social sciences and history, other; sociology. **Graduate—**education, general; education, other; engineering, other; history; social work.

# UNIVERSITY OF ALASKA FAIRBANKS

## Center for Distance Education and Independent Learning

PO Box 756700
Fairbanks, AK 99775
**Contact:** Bob Anderl, Acting Director
**Phone:** 907-474-5353
**Fax:** 907-474-5402
**Web:** http://www.uaf.edu/
**E-mail:** distance@uaf.edu

**ACCREDITATION:** Northwest Association of Schools and Colleges
**INSTITUTIONALLY ADMINISTERED FINANCIAL AID:** Yes

### DEGREE OR CERTIFICATE PROGRAMS OFFERED

**Undergraduate—AA:** General Studies. **AAS:** Community Health; Early Childhood Development; Human Services Technology; Microcomputer Support Specialist. **BA:** Rural Development; Social Work. **Certificate:** Community Health; Early Childhood Development; Microcomputer Support Specialist.

### NON-DEGREE-RELATED COURSE TOPICS OFFERED

**Undergraduate—**American literature (United States); English composition; English creative writing; English language and literature, general; English language and literature/letters, other; English literature (British and Commonwealth); English technical and business writing; Latin language and literature (ancient and medieval); advertising; anthropology; art history, criticism and conservation; biology, general; business; business administration and management; computer and information sciences, general; computer science; computer software and media applications; drafting; dramatic/theater arts and stagecraft; economics; educational psychology; ethnic and cultural studies; family and community studies; film/cinema studies; foreign languages and literatures; geography; history; journalism; journalism and mass communications; leatherworkers and upholsterers; library science/librarianship; mathematical statistics; mathematics; mathematics, other; philosophy; philosophy and religion; psychology; radio and television broadcasting; real estate; social sciences and history, other; social sciences, general; social work; sociology; women's studies. **Graduate—**education administration and supervision; education, other; educational psychology; political science and government.

**See full description on page 556.**

# UNIVERSITY OF ALASKA SOUTHEAST, KETCHIKAN CAMPUS

2600 Seventh Avenue
Ketchikan, AK 99901
**Contact:** Barbara Oleson, Coordinator of Distance Learning
**Phone:** 907-443-2201 Ext. 230
**Fax:** 907-443-5602
**E-mail:** nnbao@uaf.edu

**ACCREDITATION:** Northwest Association of Schools and Colleges
**INSTITUTIONALLY ADMINISTERED FINANCIAL AID:** Yes

## DEGREE OR CERTIFICATE PROGRAMS OFFERED

**Undergraduate—AAS:** Business; Health Practitioner; Office Management Technology. **BA:** Rural Development; Social Work. **BEd:** Education. **Certificate:** Business; Health Practitioner.
**Graduate—MA:** Education; Rural Development; Social Work.

## NON-DEGREE-RELATED COURSE TOPICS OFFERED

**Undergraduate—**American (United States) history; European history; accounting; anthropology; art history, criticism and conservation.

# UNIVERSITY OF ALASKA SOUTHEAST, SITKA CAMPUS

1332 Seward Avenue
Sitka, AK 99835
**Contact:** Denise Blankenship, Distance Education Coordinator
**Phone:** 907-747-6653 Ext. 714
**Fax:** 907-747-7768
**Web:** http://www.alaska.edu/
**E-mail:** denise.blankenship@uas.alaska.edu

**ACCREDITATION:** Northwest Association of Schools and Colleges
**INSTITUTIONALLY ADMINISTERED FINANCIAL AID:** Yes

## DEGREE OR CERTIFICATE PROGRAMS OFFERED

**Undergraduate—AA:** General Studies. **AAS:** Computer Information Office Systems; Early Childhood Education; Environmental Technology; Health Information Management. **BA:** Liberal Arts. **Certificate:** CDA in Early Childhood Education; Computer Information and Office Systems; Environmental Technology.

## NON-DEGREE-RELATED COURSE TOPICS OFFERED

**Undergraduate—**English composition; English creative writing; accounting; biology, general; developmental and child psychology; environmental science/studies; journalism; social psychology; sociology.

# THE UNIVERSITY OF ARIZONA
*Extended University, Distance Learning Program*
PO Box 210158, University Services Building, Room 302
Tucson, AZ 85721-0158
**Contact:** Pam Shack, Program Coordinator, Distance Learning
**Phone:** 520-626-4573
**Fax:** 520-621-2099
**Web:** http://www.eu.arizona.edu/dist/
**E-mail:** pshack@u.arizona.edu

**ACCREDITATION:** North Central Association of Colleges and Schools
**INSTITUTIONALLY ADMINISTERED FINANCIAL AID:** No

## DEGREE OR CERTIFICATE PROGRAMS OFFERED

**Undergraduate—Certificate:** Professional Graduate Certificate in Systems Engineering.
**Graduate—Graduate Certificate:** Reliability and Quality Engineering. **MEngr:** Engineering. **MS:** Optical Sciences.

## NON-DEGREE-RELATED COURSE TOPICS OFFERED

**Graduate—**aerospace, aeronautical and astronautical engineering; chemical engineering; electrical, electronics and communication engineering; engineering mechanics; engineering/industrial management; industrial/manufacturing engineering; library science/librarianship; mechanical engineering.
**Non-credit—**aerospace, aeronautical and astronautical engineering; computer engineering; engineering, general; mechanical engineering; systems engineering.

## Special Note

Students can update their technical skills and gain new perspectives on their fields through distance learning classes at the University of Arizona. Courses are taught by top faculty members and incorporate the latest research and technological developments. Students can choose the distance learning courses and formats that best meet their needs. The University offers classes via videotape, the NTU network, CD-ROM, and the Internet.

The University offers a wide range of technical courses in areas such as aerospace and mechanical engineering, electrical and computer engineering, optical sciences, reliability and quality engineering, and systems and industrial engineering. The Tri-University Master of Engineering degree, administered jointly by the University of Arizona, Arizona State University, and Northern Arizona University, is designed by faculty members from all 3 universities with input from industry professionals to meet the individual educational needs of practicing engineers.

The Professional Graduate Certificate in Systems Engineering, a program of the University of Arizona College of Engineering and Mines, is available totally at a distance. Students learn how to ensure that a system satisfies its requirements throughout the entire system life cycle, from cradle to grave, to increase a system's probability of success, reduce the risk of failure, and reduce total life-cycle cost.

The University's online master's degree program in information resources and library science offers Internet-based courses. Other Web-based courses will join the lineup in the months ahead.

For further details, students should contact 520-626-2079 or 800-478-9508 (toll-free), e-mail at distance@u.arizona.edu, or visit the University's Web site at http://www.eu.arizona.edu/~dist/.

# UNIVERSITY OF ARKANSAS
*Division for Continuing Education*
Office of Credit Studies, 2 East Center Street
Fayetteville, AR 72701
**Contact:** Gary McHenry, Director
**Phone:** 501-575-3648
**Fax:** 501-575-7232
**Web:** http://www.uacted.uark.edu
**E-mail:** gmchenry@uark.edu

**ACCREDITATION:** North Central Association of Colleges and Schools
**INSTITUTIONALLY ADMINISTERED FINANCIAL AID:** No

## DEGREE OR CERTIFICATE PROGRAMS OFFERED

**Undergraduate—BS:** Human Resource Development.

## NON-DEGREE-RELATED COURSE TOPICS OFFERED

**Undergraduate—**American (United States) history; English composition; French language and literature; Latin language and literature (ancient and medieval); Spanish language and literature; curriculum and instruction; developmental and child psychology; drama/theater arts, general; educational psychology; environmental science/studies; geography; industrial and organizational psychology; journalism; law and legal studies, other; mathematics, other; microbiology/bacteriology; philosophy and religion; social work; sociology.

# UNIVERSITY OF ARKANSAS AT LITTLE ROCK

## Off-Campus Programs

2801 South University Avenue
Little Rock, AR 72204-1099
**Contact:** Donna Rae Eldridge, Research, Assessment, and Media Coordinator
**Phone:** 501-569-8632
**Fax:** 501-569-8538
**Web:** http://www.ualr.edu/~occp/
**E-mail:** dreldridge@ualr.edu

**ACCREDITATION:** North Central Association of Colleges and Schools
**INSTITUTIONALLY ADMINISTERED FINANCIAL AID:** Yes

### DEGREE OR CERTIFICATE PROGRAMS OFFERED

Graduate—*MA:* Rehabilitation Counseling.

### NON-DEGREE-RELATED COURSE TOPICS OFFERED

Undergraduate—English creative writing; anthropology; criminal justice and corrections; geography; health professions and related sciences, other; history; journalism and mass communications; liberal arts and sciences, general studies and humanities; mathematics; music; philosophy; political science and government; psychology; radio and television broadcasting; sociology.
Graduate—gerontology.

# UNIVERSITY OF BALTIMORE

## UBOnline

1420 North Charles Street
Baltimore, MD 21201
**Contact:** Julia Pitman, Associate Director of Admissions
**Phone:** 877-APPLYUB
**Fax:** 410-837-4793
**Web:** http://www.ubalt.edu
**E-mail:** admissions@ubmail.ubalt.edu

**ACCREDITATION:** Middle States Association of Colleges and Schools
**INSTITUTIONALLY ADMINISTERED FINANCIAL AID:** Yes

### DEGREE OR CERTIFICATE PROGRAMS OFFERED

Undergraduate—*BS:* Business Administration; Criminal Justice; Psychology.
Graduate—*MBA:* Business Administration.

### NON-DEGREE-RELATED COURSE TOPICS OFFERED

Undergraduate—English creative writing.
Graduate—accounting; business marketing and marketing management.
**See full description on page 558.**

# UNIVERSITY OF BRIDGEPORT

## Office of Distance Learning

303 University Avenue
Bridgeport, CT 06601
**Contact:** Mr. Michael J. Giampaoli, Director of Distance Education
**Phone:** 203-576-4851
**Fax:** 203-576-4852
**Web:** http://www.bridgeport.edu/disted/index.html
**E-mail:** ubonline@bridgeport.edu

**ACCREDITATION:** New England Association of Schools and Colleges
**INSTITUTIONALLY ADMINISTERED FINANCIAL AID:** Yes

### DEGREE OR CERTIFICATE PROGRAMS OFFERED

Graduate—*MS:* Human Nutrition.

### NON-DEGREE-RELATED COURSE TOPICS OFFERED

Undergraduate—business administration and management; business quantitative methods and management science; computer systems networking and telecommunications; computer/information technology administration and management; economics; educational/instructional media design.
Graduate—computer software and media applications; computer systems networking and telecommunications; educational/instructional media design.
Non-credit—computer systems networking and telecommunications.
**See full description on page 560.**

# THE UNIVERSITY OF BRITISH COLUMBIA

## Distance Education and Technology

2329 West Mall, University Services Building, Room 1170
Vancouver, BC V6T 1Z4, Canada
**Contact:** Heather Francis, Manager of New Business Development
**Phone:** 604-822-6565
**Fax:** 604-822-8636
**Web:** http://det.ubc.ca
**E-mail:** heather.francis@ubc.ca

**ACCREDITATION:** Provincially Chartered
**INSTITUTIONALLY ADMINISTERED FINANCIAL AID:** Yes

### DEGREE OR CERTIFICATE PROGRAMS OFFERED

Undergraduate—*Certificate:* Rehabilitation Services.
Graduate—*MBA/MA:* Education.

### NON-DEGREE-RELATED COURSE TOPICS OFFERED

Undergraduate—Canadian studies; English language and literature, general; French language and literature; Germanic languages and literatures; agricultural economics; agriculture/agricultural sciences; animal sciences; civil engineering; computer and information sciences, general; dental services; education, general; environmental control technologies; film/cinema studies; forestry, general; history; landscape architecture; library science, other; medieval and renaissance studies; oceanography; rehabilitation/therapeutic services; social work; urban affairs/studies; women's studies.

**Graduate**—education, general; forestry and related sciences; natural resources management and protective services; rehabilitation/therapeutic services.

**Non-credit**—natural resources management and protective services; rehabilitation/therapeutic services.

## Special Note

The Distance Education & Technology (DE&T) division of Continuing Studies develops and delivers programs, courses, and learning materials for individual and institutional clients who require cost-effective, quality education delivered in flexible formats. Established as the Department of University Extensions at UBC in 1949, the division continues to collaborate with twelve UBC faculties plus Continuing Studies program areas to produce distance education services and courses to serve local, national, and international clients.

UBC currently offers more than 120 courses via distance technology, including print-based materials, audio, video, CD-ROM, and World Wide Web and other Internet services. In addition, DE&T at UBC is now developing more than 25 new courses annually, many with an online component. DE&T's inventory consists of degree-credit, noncredit, certificate, and diploma courses. For a complete list of courses and projects, students should visit the Web site at http://det.cstudies.ubc.ca or call 604-822-6500 or 800-754-1811 (toll-free in British Columbia and Yukon) for a printed catalog and registration requirements.

Those who are interested in DE&T's consultation and collaboration services, course development, training, research, or technological expertise should visit the DE&T Web site at http://det.cstudies.ubc.ca or the Director's Web site at http://bates.cstudies.ubc.ca. Dr. Tony Bates, Director of DE&T, is a founding member of the British Open University, has authored 7 books on distance education, and has consulted for UNESCO, the World Bank, and other institutions in more than 30 countries. Along with a staff of 25 people, Dr. Bates has initiated several partnership franchises with organizations offering distance education around the world.

# UNIVERSITY OF CALIFORNIA, BERKELEY

## Center for Media and Independent Learning

2000 Center Street, Suite 400
Berkeley, CA 94704
**Contact:** UC Extension Online
**Phone:** 510-642-4124
**Web:** http://www.unex.berkeley.edu/
**E-mail:** askcmil@uclink.berkeley.edu

**ACCREDITATION:** Western Association of Schools and Colleges
**INSTITUTIONALLY ADMINISTERED FINANCIAL AID:** No

## DEGREE OR CERTIFICATE PROGRAMS OFFERED

Programs offered do not lead to a degree or other formal award.

## NON-DEGREE-RELATED COURSE TOPICS OFFERED

**Undergraduate**—English language and literature, general; accounting; advertising; agriculture/agricultural sciences; anthropology; architecture;

astronomy; biology, general; botany; business; communications technologies; communications, general; communications, other; comparative literature; computer and information sciences, other; computer programming; computer software and media applications; counseling psychology; dance; data entry/microcomputer applications; data processing technology; developmental and child psychology; economics; education, general; education, other; ethnic and cultural studies; film/cinema studies; financial management and services; fine arts and art studies; international business; internet and world wide web; music; peace and conflict studies; philosophy; plant sciences; psychology; women's studies.

# UNIVERSITY OF CALIFORNIA, DAVIS

## UC Davis Extension

1333 Research Park Drive
Davis, CA 95616
**Contact:** Kathy Gleed, Director of Student Services
**Phone:** 530-757-8777
**Fax:** 530-757-8558
**Web:** http://www.universityextension.ucdavis.edu/distancelearning
**E-mail:** kgleed@unexmail.ucdavis.edu

**ACCREDITATION:** Western Association of Schools and Colleges
**INSTITUTIONALLY ADMINISTERED FINANCIAL AID:** No

## DEGREE OR CERTIFICATE PROGRAMS OFFERED

Programs offered do not lead to a degree or other formal award.

## NON-DEGREE-RELATED COURSE TOPICS OFFERED

**Undergraduate**—business quantitative methods and management science; computer programming; computer science; computer software and media applications; computer systems analysis; computer systems networking and telecommunications; computer/information technology administration and management; food sciences and technology; internet and world wide web.

**Non-credit**—English composition; foreign languages and literatures.

See full description on page 562.

# UNIVERSITY OF CALIFORNIA, LOS ANGELES

## University Extension

10995 LeConte Avenue, Room 714
Los Angeles, CA 90024
**Contact:** Ms. Sande Shima, Project Representative
**Phone:** 310-825-2648
**Fax:** 310-267-4783
**Web:** http://www.unex.ucla.edu
**E-mail:** sshimabu@unex.ucla.edu

**ACCREDITATION:** Western Association of Schools and Colleges
**INSTITUTIONALLY ADMINISTERED FINANCIAL AID:** Yes

eCollege.com  www.ecollege.com

## DEGREE OR CERTIFICATE PROGRAMS OFFERED

Programs offered do not lead to a degree or other formal award.

## NON-DEGREE-RELATED COURSE TOPICS OFFERED

**Graduate**—English technical and business writing; archaeology; design and applied arts; economics; film/video and photographic arts; foreign languages and literatures, other; health and physical education/fitness; liberal arts and sciences, general studies and humanities; mathematics; philosophy and religion; psychology; social sciences, general; visual and performing arts.

# UNIVERSITY OF CALIFORNIA, RIVERSIDE

## University Extension

Riverside, CA 92507
**Contact:** Eric Blum, Director
**Phone:** 909-787-4111 Ext. 1637
**Web:** http://www.ucr.edu/
**E-mail:** eblum@ucx.ucr.edu

**ACCREDITATION:** Western Association of Schools and Colleges
**INSTITUTIONALLY ADMINISTERED FINANCIAL AID:** No

## DEGREE OR CERTIFICATE PROGRAMS OFFERED

**Programs offered do not lead to a degree or other formal award.**

## NON-DEGREE-RELATED COURSE TOPICS OFFERED

**Non-credit**—agriculture/agricultural sciences, other; education, other.

# UNIVERSITY OF CALIFORNIA, SANTA BARBARA

## Off-Campus Studies

Santa Barbara, CA 93106
**Contact:** Howard Adamson, Manager of Off-Campus Studies
**Phone:** 805-893-8841
**Fax:** 805-893-8719
**Web:** http://www.xlrn.ucsb.edu
**E-mail:** hadamson@xlrn.ucsb.edu

**ACCREDITATION:** Western Association of Schools and Colleges
**INSTITUTIONALLY ADMINISTERED FINANCIAL AID:** No

## DEGREE OR CERTIFICATE PROGRAMS OFFERED

**Graduate**—*MS:* Computer Science; Electrical and Computer Engineering.

## NON-DEGREE-RELATED COURSE TOPICS OFFERED

**Undergraduate**—English composition; English creative writing; developmental and child psychology; educational psychology; sociology.
**Graduate**—electrical, electronics and communication engineering.
**Non-credit**—English as a second language; English composition; English creative writing; accounting; computer systems networking and telecommunications; developmental and child psychology; electrical, electronics and communication engineering; industrial and organizational psychology; social psychology; sociology.

# UNIVERSITY OF CENTRAL ARKANSAS

## Division of Continuing Education

201 Donaghey Avenue
Conway, AR 72035
**Contact:** Sondra Pugh, Secretary to Guided Study
**Phone:** 501-450-3118
**Fax:** 501-450-5277
**Web:** http://www.uca.edu
**E-mail:** sondrap@ecom.ucs.edu

**ACCREDITATION:** North Central Association of Colleges and Schools
**INSTITUTIONALLY ADMINISTERED FINANCIAL AID:** Yes

## DEGREE OR CERTIFICATE PROGRAMS OFFERED

**Programs offered do not lead to a degree or other formal award.**

## NON-DEGREE-RELATED COURSE TOPICS OFFERED

**Undergraduate**—English creative writing; business marketing and marketing management; finance, general; geography.
**Graduate**—curriculum and instruction; geography; occupational therapy; physical therapy.
See full description on page 564.

# UNIVERSITY OF CENTRAL FLORIDA

## Center for Distributed Learning

12424 Research Parkway, Suite 264
Orlando, FL 32826-3269
**Contact:** Dr. Steven E. Sorg, Assistant Vice President and Director of Center for Distributed Learning
**Phone:** 407-207-4910
**Fax:** 407-207-4911
**Web:** http://distrib.ucf.edu
**E-mail:** distrib@mail.ucf.edu

**ACCREDITATION:** Southern Association of Colleges and Schools
**INSTITUTIONALLY ADMINISTERED FINANCIAL AID:** Yes

## DEGREE OR CERTIFICATE PROGRAMS OFFERED

**Undergraduate**—*BA:* Liberal Studies. *BS:* Education; Liberal Studies. *BSET:* Engineering Technology. *BSN:* Nursing.
**Graduate**—*MChem:* Forensic Chemistry. *MEd:* Educational Media.

## NON-DEGREE-RELATED COURSE TOPICS OFFERED

**Undergraduate**—electrical, electronics and communication engineering; health system/health services administration; industrial/manufacturing engineering; mathematical statistics; sociology.
**Graduate**—electrical, electronics and communication engineering; health system/health services administration; industrial/manufacturing engineering; mathematical statistics; mechanical engineering.
See full description on page 566.

# UNIVERSITY OF CENTRAL OKLAHOMA

*Distance Learning Technologies*

Information Technology Distance Learning, 100 North University Drive, Box 98
Edmond, OK 73034-5209
**Contact:** Stacy Meiser, Distance Learning Supervisor
**Phone:** 405-974-5395
**Fax:** 405-974-3845
**Web:** http://www.ucok.edu/cyber
**E-mail:** smeiser@ucok.edu

**ACCREDITATION:** North Central Association of Colleges and Schools

**INSTITUTIONALLY ADMINISTERED FINANCIAL AID:** Yes

### DEGREE OR CERTIFICATE PROGRAMS OFFERED

Programs offered do not lead to a degree or other formal award.

### NON-DEGREE-RELATED COURSE TOPICS OFFERED

**Undergraduate**—English as a second language; English language and literature, general; art history, criticism and conservation; education administration and supervision; education, other; funeral services and mortuary science; library science/librarianship; sociology.
**Graduate**—English as a second language; English language and literature, general; art history, criticism and conservation; education administration and supervision; education, other; funeral services and mortuary science; library science/librarianship; sociology.

# UNIVERSITY OF CHARLESTON

*Off-Campus Programs*

2300 MacCorkle Avenue, SE
Charleston, WV 25304
**Contact:** Ms. Claudia Cox, Admissions Counselor
**Phone:** 304-357-4750
**Web:** http://www.uchaswv.edu/academic/it/
**E-mail:** ccox@uchaswv.edu

**ACCREDITATION:** North Central Association of Colleges and Schools

**INSTITUTIONALLY ADMINISTERED FINANCIAL AID:** Yes

### DEGREE OR CERTIFICATE PROGRAMS OFFERED

**Undergraduate**—*AS:* Information Technology.

### NON-DEGREE-RELATED COURSE TOPICS OFFERED

**Undergraduate**—information sciences and systems.

# UNIVERSITY OF CHICAGO

5835 South Kimbark Avenue, Judd Hall 207
Chicago, IL 60637
**Contact:** Graham School of General Studies
**Phone:** 773-702-1726
**Web:** http://www.uchicago.edu/
**E-mail:** gsal-rs@uchicago.edu

**ACCREDITATION:** North Central Association of Colleges and Schools

### DEGREE OR CERTIFICATE PROGRAMS OFFERED

Programs offered do not lead to a degree or other formal award.

# UNIVERSITY OF CINCINNATI

*College of Evening and Continuing Education (CECE)*

PO Box 210019
Cincinnati, OH 45221-0019
**Contact:** Ms. Melody Clark, Academic Director of Office of Distance Education
**Phone:** 513-556-9154
**Fax:** 513-556-6380
**Web:** http://www.uc.edu/
**E-mail:** melody.clark@uc.edu

**ACCREDITATION:** North Central Association of Colleges and Schools

### DEGREE OR CERTIFICATE PROGRAMS OFFERED

**Undergraduate**—*BS:* Addiction Studies; Fire Science Administration.

### NON-DEGREE-RELATED COURSE TOPICS OFFERED

**Undergraduate**—alcohol/drug abuse counseling; business; computer software and media applications; criminal justice and corrections; fire science/firefighting; geography; geological and related sciences; history; philosophy; philosophy and religion; women's studies.
**Non-credit**—business; computer and information sciences, general.

# UNIVERSITY OF CINCINNATI RAYMOND WALTERS COLLEGE

*Outreach and Continuing Education*

9555 Plainfield Road
Cincinnati, OH 45236-1096
**Contact:** Dr. Susan Kemper, Assistant Dean
**Phone:** 513-745-5776
**Fax:** 513-745-8315
**Web:** http://www.rwc.uc.edu
**E-mail:** susan.kemper@uc.edu

**ACCREDITATION:** North Central Association of Colleges and Schools

**INSTITUTIONALLY ADMINISTERED FINANCIAL AID:** Yes

### DEGREE OR CERTIFICATE PROGRAMS OFFERED

Programs offered do not lead to a degree or other formal award.

### NON-DEGREE-RELATED COURSE TOPICS OFFERED

**Undergraduate**—English composition; sociology.

# UNIVERSITY OF COLORADO AT BOULDER

*Center for Advanced Training in Engineering and Computer Science (CATECS)*

435 UCB
Boulder, CO 80309

**Contact:** Robin M.W. McClanahan, Publications and Marketing Manager
**Phone:** 303-492-0212
**Fax:** 303-492-5987
**Web:** http://www.colorado.edu/CATECS
**E-mail:** catecs-info@colorado.edu

**ACCREDITATION:** North Central Association of Colleges and Schools
**INSTITUTIONALLY ADMINISTERED FINANCIAL AID:** Yes

eCollege.com *www.ecollege.com*

## DEGREE OR CERTIFICATE PROGRAMS OFFERED

**Undergraduate—*Certification:*** Engineering Management; Power Electronics.
**Graduate—*ME:*** Aerospace Engineering; Computer Science; Electrical and Computer Engineering; Engineering Management; Telecommunications. ***MS:*** Aerospace Engineering; Electrical and Computer Engineering; Telecommunications.

## NON-DEGREE-RELATED COURSE TOPICS OFFERED

**Undergraduate**—aerospace, aeronautical and astronautical engineering; civil engineering; computer engineering; computer science; electrical and electronic engineering-related technology; engineering/industrial management; mechanical engineering; telecommunications.
**Graduate**—aerospace, aeronautical and astronautical engineering; civil engineering; computer engineering; electrical and electronic engineering-related technology; engineering/industrial management; mechanical engineering; telecommunications.
**Non-credit**—aerospace, aeronautical and astronautical engineering; biology, general; civil engineering; computer engineering; electrical and electronic engineering-related technology; engineering/industrial management; mechanical engineering; telecommunications.

# UNIVERSITY OF COLORADO AT COLORADO SPRINGS

## CU-NET

PO Box 7150
Colorado Springs, CO 80933-7150
**Contact:** Linda Aaker, Program Coordinator, CU-Net
**Phone:** 719-262-3597
**Fax:** 719-262-3592
**Web:** http://www.uccs.edu/~it
**E-mail:** laaker@mail.uccs.edu

**ACCREDITATION:** North Central Association of Colleges and Schools
**INSTITUTIONALLY ADMINISTERED FINANCIAL AID:** No

## DEGREE OR CERTIFICATE PROGRAMS OFFERED

Programs offered do not lead to a degree or other formal award.

## NON-DEGREE-RELATED COURSE TOPICS OFFERED

**Undergraduate**—history.
**Graduate**—education, general; education, other; educational evaluation, research and statistics; engineering, other; engineering-related technologies, other.

# UNIVERSITY OF COLORADO AT DENVER

## CU Online

Campus Box 198, PO Box 173364
Denver, CO 80217-3364
**Contact:** Patty Godbey, Assistant Director
**Phone:** 303-556-6505
**Fax:** 303-556-6530
**Web:** http://www.cudenver.edu/cuonline
**E-mail:** inquiry@cuonline.edu

**ACCREDITATION:** North Central Association of Colleges and Schools
**INSTITUTIONALLY ADMINISTERED FINANCIAL AID:** Yes

## DEGREE OR CERTIFICATE PROGRAMS OFFERED

**Undergraduate—*BA:*** Sociology.
**Graduate—*MBA:*** Business Administration. ***MBA/M Div:*** Geographic Information Systems (GIS). ***MEM:*** Engineering Management. ***MPA:*** Public Administration.
**Postgraduate and doctoral—*PharmD:*** Pharmacy.

## NON-DEGREE-RELATED COURSE TOPICS OFFERED

**Undergraduate**—American (United States) history; American literature (United States); English composition; English creative writing; English language and literature, general; English technical and business writing; Latin language and literature (ancient and medieval); accounting; anthropology; biochemistry and biophysics; biology, general; cell biology; civil engineering; communications, general; computer programming; drama/theater arts, general; economics; engineering mechanics; engineering science; engineering, general; ethnic and cultural studies; fine arts and art studies; foreign languages and literatures; geography; geological and related sciences; history; industrial and organizational psychology; liberal arts and sciences, general studies and humanities; mathematical statistics; mathematics, other; mechanical engineering; medical genetics; music; philosophy and religion; physics; political science and government; psychology; social psychology; sociology.
**Graduate**—accounting; business; business administration and management; business and personal services marketing operations; business communications; business information and data processing services; business management and administrative services, other; business quantitative methods and management science; business/managerial economics; education, general; education, other; educational psychology; engineering design; engineering mechanics; engineering physics; engineering science; engineering, general; engineering, other; engineering-related technologies, other; engineering/industrial management; management information systems and business data processing, general; marketing management and research; marketing operations/marketing and distribution, other; nursing; political science and government; public administration; public administration and services, other; public policy analysis; sociology.
**Non-credit**—American literature (United States); English composition; English creative writing; English language and literature, general; English technical and business writing; accounting; anthropology; architecture; area, ethnic and cultural studies, other; biochemistry and biophysics; biology, general; business; business administration and management; business and personal services marketing operations; business communications; business information and data processing services; business management and administrative services, other; business quantitative methods and management science; business/managerial economics; civil engineering; civil engineering/civil technology; computer programming;

economics; engineering design; engineering mechanics; engineering physics; engineering science; engineering, general; engineering, other; engineering-related technologies, other; engineering/industrial management; ethnic and cultural studies; fine arts and art studies; foreign languages and literatures; geography; geological and related sciences; history; liberal arts and sciences, general studies and humanities; marketing management and research; marketing operations/marketing and distribution, other; mathematics; mathematics, other; music; physics; psychology; public administration; public administration and services, other; public policy analysis.

**See full description on page 568.**

# UNIVERSITY OF CONNECTICUT
## University Center for Instructional Media and Technology
249 Glenbrook Road, Box U-2001
Storrs, CT 06269-2001
**Contact:** Mr. Richard L. Gorham, Director of University Center for Instructional Media & Technology
**Phone:** 860-486-2161
**Fax:** 860-486-1766
**Web:** http://www.ucimt.uconn.edu
**E-mail:** richard.gorham@uconn.edu

**ACCREDITATION:** New England Association of Schools and Colleges
**INSTITUTIONALLY ADMINISTERED FINANCIAL AID:** Yes

## DEGREE OR CERTIFICATE PROGRAMS OFFERED
Programs offered do not lead to a degree or other formal award.

## NON-DEGREE-RELATED COURSE TOPICS OFFERED
**Undergraduate**—American literature (United States); English language and literature, general; English language and literature/letters, other; accounting; aerospace, aeronautical and astronautical engineering; agricultural and food products processing; agricultural business and management; agricultural business and production, other; animal sciences; anthropology; apparel and accessories marketing operations; applied mathematics; biochemistry and biophysics; bioengineering and biomedical engineering; biological and physical sciences; biological sciences/life sciences, other; biology, general; business administration and management; business communications; business information and data processing services; business management and administrative services, other; business quantitative methods and management science; business/managerial economics; cell and molecular biology; chemical engineering; chemistry; civil engineering; cognitive psychology and psycholinguistics; communication disorders sciences and services; communications, general; comparative literature; computer and information sciences, general; computer and information sciences, other; computer engineering; computer programming; computer science; computer systems analysis; computer systems networking and telecommunications; computer/information technology administration and management; counseling psychology; curriculum and instruction; economics; education administration and supervision; education, general; engineering mechanics; engineering, general; engineering-related technologies, other; ethnic and cultural studies; foreign languages and literatures; geography; mathematics; nursing; pharmacy; philosophy; physical sciences, general; plant sciences; political science and government; professional studies; sociology; taxation; urban affairs/studies; visual and performing arts; zoology.
**Graduate**—accounting; anthropology; bioengineering and biomedical engineering; biological and physical sciences; biology, general; business

# UNIVERSITY OF CONNECTICUT
## College of Continuing Studies
1 Bishop Circle, Unit 4056
Storrs, CT 06269-4056
**Contact:** Ms. Holly B. Gingras, Program Coordinator
**Phone:** 860-486-1080
**Fax:** 860-486-0756
**Web:** http://continuingstudies.uconn.edu/onlinecourses/index.html
**E-mail:** ccsonline@access.ced.uconn.edu

**ACCREDITATION:** New England Association of Schools and Colleges
**INSTITUTIONALLY ADMINISTERED FINANCIAL AID:** Yes

## DEGREE OR CERTIFICATE PROGRAMS OFFERED
**Undergraduate**—*Certificate:* Himalayan Studies; Information Technology; Occupational Safety and Health Program.
**Graduate**—*Graduate Certificate:* Humanitarian Studies—MA pending approval.

## NON-DEGREE-RELATED COURSE TOPICS OFFERED
**Undergraduate**—area, ethnic and cultural studies, other; business administration and management; business information and data processing services; computer and information sciences, other; ethnic and cultural studies; health professions and related sciences, other; human services; information sciences and systems; liberal arts and sciences, general studies and humanities; miscellaneous health professions; multi/interdisciplinary studies, other.
**Graduate**—business administration and management; health professions and related sciences, other; human services; liberal arts and sciences, general studies and humanities; miscellaneous health professions; multi/interdisciplinary studies, other.
**Non-credit**—computer software and media applications; health professions and related sciences, other; insurance marketing operations; miscellaneous health professions; real estate.

# UNIVERSITY OF DALLAS
## Center for Distance Education
1845 East Northgate Drive
Irving, TX 75062-4736
**Contact:** Kate McCoy, Distance Learning Coordinator
**Phone:** 800-832-5622
**Fax:** 972-721-4009
**Web:** http://imba.udallas.edu

The administration and management; chemical engineering; computer and information sciences, general; curriculum and instruction; dental residency programs; education administration and supervision; educational evaluation, research and statistics; educational psychology; educational/instructional media design; engineering, general; family and community studies; geography; landscape architecture; marketing management and research; mathematics and computer science; ocean engineering; pharmacy; plant sciences; polymer/plastics engineering; psychology; sociology; taxation; urban affairs/studies.

**E-mail:** kmccoy@gsm.udallas.edu

**ACCREDITATION:** American Academy for Liberal Education

**INSTITUTIONALLY ADMINISTERED FINANCIAL AID:** Yes

eCollege.com *www.ecollege.com*

## DEGREE OR CERTIFICATE PROGRAMS OFFERED

**Graduate—***Graduate Certificate:* E-Commerce Management; Health Services Management; Information Technology; Telecommunications Management. *MBA:* E-Commerce Management; Health Services Management; Information Technology; Telecommunications Management. *MCIS:* Health Services Management; Information Technology; Sports Management; Telecommunications Management.

## NON-DEGREE-RELATED COURSE TOPICS OFFERED

**Graduate—**accounting; business marketing and marketing management; engineering/industrial management; finance, general; health system/health services administration; insurance and risk management; international business; investments and securities; management information systems and business data processing, general; organizational behavior studies.

See full description on page 570.

# UNIVERSITY OF DELAWARE
*Division of Continuing and Distance Education*
211 Clayton Hall
Newark, DE 19716
**Contact:** Mary Pritchard, Director
**Phone:** 302-831-6442
**Fax:** 302-831-3292
**Web:** http://www.udel.edu/ce/udonline/
**E-mail:** maryvp@udel.edu

**ACCREDITATION:** Middle States Association of Colleges and Schools

**INSTITUTIONALLY ADMINISTERED FINANCIAL AID:** Yes

## DEGREE OR CERTIFICATE PROGRAMS OFFERED

**Undergraduate—***BS:* Hotel, Restaurant, and Institutional Management; Nursing.
**Graduate—***MME:* Mechanical Engineering. *MSN:* Health Services Administration.

## NON-DEGREE-RELATED COURSE TOPICS OFFERED

**Undergraduate—**American (United States) history; animal sciences; biology, general; business marketing and marketing management; chemical engineering; chemistry; civil engineering; communications, general; criminal justice and corrections; economics; education, general; electrical, electronics and communication engineering; engineering science; hospitality services management; individual and family development studies; mathematics, other; mechanical engineering; music; nursing; organizational behavior studies; philosophy and religion; political science and government; sociology; urban affairs/studies.
**Graduate—**chemical engineering; civil engineering; education, general; electrical, electronics and communication engineering; engineering mechanics; health professions and related sciences, other; mechanical engineering; nursing; public administration; urban affairs/studies.

**Non-credit—**business management and administrative services, other; electrical, electronics and communication engineering; mechanical engineering.

See full description on page 572.

# UNIVERSITY OF DENVER
*University College*
2199 South University Park
Denver, CO 80208
**Contact:** Mr. Jason Wyrick, Director of Information Management
**Phone:** 303-871-2085
**Fax:** 303-871-4047
**Web:** http://www.learning.du.edu
**E-mail:** jwyrick@du.edu

**ACCREDITATION:** North Central Association of Colleges and Schools

**INSTITUTIONALLY ADMINISTERED FINANCIAL AID:** Yes

## DEGREE OR CERTIFICATE PROGRAMS OFFERED

**Graduate—***CAGS:* American Indian Studies; Business Environmental Management; Ecotourism Management; Environmental Health and Safety Management; Environmental Management; Environmental Regulatory Compliance; Geographic Information Systems; Management of Hazardous Materials; Natural Resource Management; Network Analysis and Design; Telecommunications. *MBA/MES:* Environmental Policy and Management. *MBATM:* Telecommunications. *MCIS:* Computer Information Systems.

## NON-DEGREE-RELATED COURSE TOPICS OFFERED

**Undergraduate—**American studies/civilization.
**Graduate—**American studies/civilization; English creative writing.

# THE UNIVERSITY OF FINDLAY
*Global Campus*
1000 North Main Street
Findlay, OH 45840
**Contact:** Dr. Doris L. Salis, Dean of Adult and Continuing Education
**Phone:** 419-424-4600
**Fax:** 419-424-4822
**Web:** http://gcampus.findlay.edu
**E-mail:** salis@mail.findlay.edu

**ACCREDITATION:** North Central Association of Colleges and Schools

**INSTITUTIONALLY ADMINISTERED FINANCIAL AID:** Yes

## DEGREE OR CERTIFICATE PROGRAMS OFFERED

**Undergraduate—***BS:* Business Management; Criminal Justice Administration; Environmental Management; Technical Communications.
**Graduate—***MBA:* Business Administration. *MS:* Environmental Management.

## NON-DEGREE-RELATED COURSE TOPICS OFFERED

**Undergraduate—**accounting; business; business administration and management; business/managerial economics; chemistry; communications, other; economics; ethnic and cultural studies; fine arts and art studies;

human resources management; international business; marketing management and research; mathematical statistics; mathematics; philosophy and religion; religion/religious studies; social sciences, general; sociology; visual and performing arts.

**Graduate**—accounting; business; business administration and management; business communications; business/managerial economics; educational/instructional media design; environmental control technologies; human resources management; marketing management and research; marketing operations/marketing and distribution, other; public administration.

**Non-credit**—accounting; business; business administration and management; business and personal services marketing operations; computer and information sciences, general; computer programming; computer software and media applications; computer systems networking and telecommunications; computer/information technology administration and management; data entry/microcomputer applications; data processing technology; entrepreneurship; environmental control technologies; financial management and services; financial services marketing operations; human resources management; marketing management and research; natural resources management and protective services.

See full description on page 574.

# UNIVERSITY OF FLORIDA
## Florida Campus Direct
2209 Northwest 13th Street
Gainesville, FL 32611-3172
**Contact:** Christopher D. Sessums, Director of Distance Learning
**Phone:** 352-392-1711
**Fax:** 352-392-6950
**Web:** http://www.fcd.ufl.edu
**E-mail:** csessum@doce.ufl.edu

**ACCREDITATION:** Southern Association of Colleges and Schools
**INSTITUTIONALLY ADMINISTERED FINANCIAL AID:** Yes

### DEGREE OR CERTIFICATE PROGRAMS OFFERED
**Graduate**—*Graduate Certificate:* Forensic Toxicology. *MAg:* Agricultural Education; Communications; Food and Resource Economics. *MBA:* Business Administration. *MBS:* Audiology; Health Services Administration. *MS:* International Construction Management. *MSHA:* Occupational Therapy.
**Postgraduate and doctoral**—*PharmD:* Pharmacy.

### NON-DEGREE-RELATED COURSE TOPICS OFFERED
**Undergraduate**—English as a second language; English composition; biology, general; chemistry; horticulture science.

# UNIVERSITY OF FLORIDA
## Department of Occupational Therapy
2710 Rew Circle, Suite 100
Ocoee, FL 34761
**Contact:** Intelicus
**Phone:** 800-431-6687
**Web:** http://www.intelicus.com/ot/default.htm

**ACCREDITATION:** Southern Association of Colleges and Schools

### DEGREE OR CERTIFICATE PROGRAMS OFFERED
Programs offered do not lead to a degree or other formal award.
See full description on page 576.

# UNIVERSITY OF FLORIDA
## Professional Program in Pharmacy
1600 Southwest Archer Road, P-100, PO Box 100483
Gainesville, FL 32610-0483
**Contact:** Mr. Gregory Michael Zuest, Coordinator of Academic Support Services
**Phone:** 352-846-2307
**Fax:** 352-392-3479
**Web:** http://www.cop.ufl.edu/wppd
**E-mail:** greg@cop.ufl.edu

**ACCREDITATION:** Southern Association of Colleges and Schools
**INSTITUTIONALLY ADMINISTERED FINANCIAL AID:** Yes

### DEGREE OR CERTIFICATE PROGRAMS OFFERED
**Postgraduate and doctoral**—*PharmD:* Working Professional Doctor of Pharmacy Program.
See full description on page 578.

# UNIVERSITY OF GEORGIA
## Georgia Center for Continuing Education
Athens, GA 30602-3603
**Contact:** Melissa Pettigrew
**Phone:** 800-877-3243
**Fax:** 706-542-6635
**Web:** http://www.gactr.uga.edu/usgis
**E-mail:** ugis@arches.uga.edu

**ACCREDITATION:** Southern Association of Colleges and Schools

### DEGREE OR CERTIFICATE PROGRAMS OFFERED
Programs offered do not lead to a degree or other formal award.
See full description on page 652.

# UNIVERSITY OF GREAT FALLS
## Center for Distance Learning
1301 20th Street, S
Great Falls, MT 59405
**Contact:** Jim Gretch, Production Manager
**Phone:** 406-791-5320
**Fax:** 406-791-5394
**Web:** http://www.ugf.edu/dl/dl.htm
**E-mail:** jgretch@ugf.edu

**ACCREDITATION:** Northwest Association of Schools and Colleges
**INSTITUTIONALLY ADMINISTERED FINANCIAL AID:** Yes

### DEGREE OR CERTIFICATE PROGRAMS OFFERED
**Undergraduate**—*BA:* Criminal Justice; Paralegal Studies; Psychology; Sociology. *BBA:* Business Administration.

Graduate—*MSIS:* Information Systems.

### NON-DEGREE-RELATED COURSE TOPICS OFFERED

**Undergraduate**—English language and literature, general; English technical and business writing; accounting; advertising; astronomy; business administration and management; business/managerial economics; counseling psychology; criminal justice and corrections; developmental and child psychology; history; human services; internet and world wide web; law and legal studies; liberal arts and sciences, general studies and humanities; marketing management and research; mathematics; philosophy and religion; psychology; sociology.
**Graduate**—computer and information sciences, general.

# UNIVERSITY OF GUELPH
## Office of Open Learning and Distance Education
Guelph, ON N1G 2W1, Canada
**Contact:** Office of Open Learning
**Phone:** 519-824-4120
**Web:** http://www.open.uoguelph.ca/index.html

**ACCREDITATION:** Provincially Chartered

### DEGREE OR CERTIFICATE PROGRAMS OFFERED
**Undergraduate**—*Certificate of Achievement:* Food Science.

### NON-DEGREE-RELATED COURSE TOPICS OFFERED
**Undergraduate**—English composition; French language and literature; anthropology; biology, general; cell biology; developmental and child psychology; ecology; environmental science/studies; finance, general; geography; industrial and organizational psychology; mathematical statistics; microbiology/bacteriology; social psychology; sociology.

# UNIVERSITY OF HAWAII AT MANOA
## Outreach College
2440 Campus Road, Box 447
Honolulu, HI 96822
**Contact:** Jaishree Odin, Interim Assistant Dean of Outreach College
**Phone:** 800-956-8547
**Fax:** 808-956-5666
**Web:** http://www.aln.hawaii.edu
**E-mail:** jodin@outreach.hawaii.edu

**ACCREDITATION:** Western Association of Schools and Colleges
**INSTITUTIONALLY ADMINISTERED FINANCIAL AID:** Yes

### DEGREE OR CERTIFICATE PROGRAMS OFFERED
**Undergraduate**—*BA:* Information and Computer Science; Liberal Studies—Human Resource Management; Liberal Studies—Information Resource Management. *Certificate:* Database Management.
**Graduate**—*MS:* Information and Computer Science.

# UNIVERSITY OF HOUSTON
## Division of Distance and Continuing Education
4242 South Mason Road
Katy, TX 77450
**Contact:** Mrs. Lorraine Cirlos-Martinez, Distance Education Advisor
**Phone:** 281-395-2800
**Fax:** 281-395-2629
**Web:** http://www.uh.edu/uhdistance
**E-mail:** deadvisor@uh.edu

**ACCREDITATION:** Southern Association of Colleges and Schools

### DEGREE OR CERTIFICATE PROGRAMS OFFERED
**Undergraduate**—*BA:* English; History; Psychology. *BS:* Hotel and Restaurant Management; Psychology. *BST:* Computer Drafting Design; Technology Leadership and Supervision.
**Graduate**—*MEE:* Electrical Engineering. *MHM:* Hospitality Management. *MIE:* Engineering Management. *MS:* Computer Science. *MSOT:* Training and Development.

### NON-DEGREE-RELATED COURSE TOPICS OFFERED
**Undergraduate**—English creative writing; Spanish language and literature; anthropology; developmental and child psychology; educational psychology; film/cinema studies; social psychology; sociology.
**Graduate**—Spanish language and literature; curriculum and instruction; educational psychology; electrical, electronics and communication engineering; industrial/manufacturing engineering; social work.

**See full description on page 580.**

# UNIVERSITY OF HOUSTON–DOWNTOWN
One Main Street
Houston, TX 77002
**Contact:** Chris Brown, Enrollment Services
**Phone:** 713-221-8423
**Fax:** 713-221-8157
**Web:** http://www.uhd.edu/
**E-mail:** brownc@dt.uh.edu

**ACCREDITATION:** Southern Association of Colleges and Schools
**INSTITUTIONALLY ADMINISTERED FINANCIAL AID:** Yes

### DEGREE OR CERTIFICATE PROGRAMS OFFERED
**Programs offered do not lead to a degree or other formal award.**

### NON-DEGREE-RELATED COURSE TOPICS OFFERED
**Undergraduate**—English language and literature/letters, other; accounting; business administration and management; business marketing and marketing management; criminal justice and corrections; developmental and child psychology; finance, general; history; industrial and organizational psychology; international business; law and legal studies, other; liberal arts and sciences, general studies and humanities; management information systems and business data processing, general; marketing operations/marketing and distribution, other; mathematical statistics; political science and government; sociology.

# UNIVERSITY OF HOUSTON-VICTORIA

3005 North Ben Wilson Street
Victoria, TX 77901-4450
**Contact:** Ms. Jane Mims, Coordinator of MBA Program
**Phone:** 361-570-4234
**Web:** http://www.vic.uh.edu/
**E-mail:** mimsj@vic.uh.edu

**ACCREDITATION:** Southern Association of Colleges and Schools
**INSTITUTIONALLY ADMINISTERED FINANCIAL AID:** Yes

## DEGREE OR CERTIFICATE PROGRAMS OFFERED

**Undergraduate—*BS:*** Computer Science; Mathematics.
**Graduate—*MBA:*** Business. ***MEd:*** Education.

# UNIVERSITY OF IDAHO

*Engineering Outreach*
PO Box 441014
Moscow, ID 83844-1014
**Contact:** Ms. Diane Bancke, Administrative Manager
**Phone:** 800-824-2889
**Fax:** 208-885-9249
**Web:** http://www.uidaho.edu/eo/
**E-mail:** outreach@uidaho.edu

**ACCREDITATION:** Northwest Association of Schools and Colleges
**INSTITUTIONALLY ADMINISTERED FINANCIAL AID:** Yes

## DEGREE OR CERTIFICATE PROGRAMS OFFERED

**Undergraduate—*Certificate:*** Advanced Material Design; Applied Geotechnics; Character Education; Communication Systems; Heating, Ventilation, and Air Conditioning (HVAC) Systems; Power System Protection and Relaying; Secure and Dependable Computing Systems; Structural Engineering; Water Resources Engineering.
**Graduate—*MAT:*** Teaching Mathematics. ***MEngr:*** Biological and Agricultural Engineering; Civil Engineering; Computer Engineering; Electrical Engineering; Engineering Management; Mechanical Engineering. ***MS:*** Biological and Agricultural Engineering; Computer Engineering; Computer Science; Electrical Engineering; Environmental Science; Geological Engineering; Psychology.
**Postgraduate and doctoral—*PhD:*** Computer Science; Electrical Engineering.

## NON-DEGREE-RELATED COURSE TOPICS OFFERED

**Undergraduate**—agricultural engineering; biology, general; chemical engineering; civil engineering; computer engineering; computer programming; computer science; electrical, electronics and communication engineering; engineering/industrial management; geography; mathematical statistics; mathematics, other; mechanical engineering; psychology.
**Graduate**—agricultural engineering; business management and administrative services, other; chemical engineering; computer engineering; computer science; electrical, electronics and communication engineering; engineering/industrial management; environmental/environmental health engineering; mathematical statistics; mathematics, other; mechanical engineering; philosophy and religion; psychology.

**Non-credit**—computer programming; electrical, electronics and communications engineering.
See full description on page 582.

# UNIVERSITY OF IDAHO

*Independent Study in Idaho*
PO Box 443225
Moscow, ID 83844-3225
**Contact:** Jeanne Workman, Registration Coordinator
**Phone:** 208-885-6641
**Fax:** 208-885-5738
**Web:** http://www.academic.uidaho.edu/indep-study
**E-mail:** jeannew@uidaho.edu

**ACCREDITATION:** Northwest Association of Schools and Colleges
**INSTITUTIONALLY ADMINISTERED FINANCIAL AID:** No

## DEGREE OR CERTIFICATE PROGRAMS OFFERED

Programs offered do not lead to a degree or other formal award.

## NON-DEGREE-RELATED COURSE TOPICS OFFERED

**Undergraduate**—English composition; English language and literature, general; accounting; advertising; anthropology; business; computer software and media applications; economics; education, other; history; library science, other; mathematics; microbiology/bacteriology; philosophy; physics; political science and government; psychology; sociology.
**Graduate**—library science, other.

# UNIVERSITY OF ILLINOIS

*University of Illinois Online*
176 Henry Administration Building, 506 South Wright Street, MC 353
Urbana, IL 61801
**Contact:** University of Illinois Online
**Phone:** 800-633-UIOL
**Web:** http://www.online.uillinois.edu
**E-mail:** uiol-info@uillinois.edu

**ACCREDITATION:** North Central Association of Colleges and Schools
**INSTITUTIONALLY ADMINISTERED FINANCIAL AID:** Yes

## DEGREE OR CERTIFICATE PROGRAMS OFFERED

Programs offered do not lead to a degree or other formal award.
See full description on page 584.

# UNIVERSITY OF ILLINOIS AT CHICAGO

*Office of Continuing Education and Public Service/ Office of External Education*
601 South Morgan Street, M/C 140
Chicago , IL 60607
**Contact:** Mr. Roy Mathew, Assistant Director of Academic Programs

**Phone:** 312-355-1767
**Web:** http://www.uic.edu/depts/uionline/
**E-mail:** rmathew@uic.edu

**ACCREDITATION:** North Central Association of Colleges and Schools
**INSTITUTIONALLY ADMINISTERED FINANCIAL AID:** Yes

### DEGREE OR CERTIFICATE PROGRAMS OFFERED

**Graduate**—*MEngr:* Engineering. *MS:* Health Professions Education.
**Postgraduate and doctoral**—*PharmD:* Continuing Curriculum Option (CCO) Pathway to PharmD Degree.

### NON-DEGREE-RELATED COURSE TOPICS OFFERED

**Graduate**—business; education, other; engineering, general; health professions and related sciences, other; internet and world wide web; marketing management and research; medical clinical sciences (M.S., Ph.D.); nursing; pharmacy; public health.
**Non-credit**—health and medical administrative services; health and medical diagnostic and treatment services; internet and world wide web; marketing management and research; nursing.

# UNIVERSITY OF ILLINOIS AT SPRINGFIELD

*Office of Technology-Enhanced Learning*
HRB 79, PO Box 19243
Springfield, IL 62794-9243
**Contact:** Ray Schroeder, Director
**Phone:** 217-206-7317
**Fax:** 217-206-7539
**Web:** http://online.uis.edu
**E-mail:** schroeder.ray@uis.edu

**ACCREDITATION:** North Central Association of Colleges and Schools
**INSTITUTIONALLY ADMINISTERED FINANCIAL AID:** No

### DEGREE OR CERTIFICATE PROGRAMS OFFERED

**Undergraduate**—*BLS:* Liberal Studies.
**Graduate**—*MEd:* Master in Teaching Leadership Degree Concentration. *MS:* Management Information Systems.

### NON-DEGREE-RELATED COURSE TOPICS OFFERED

**Undergraduate**—accounting; biology, general; business administration and management; chemistry; communications, general; computer science; human resources management; mathematical statistics; mathematics; philosophy; psychology; public administration; women's studies.
**Graduate**—education, other; management information systems and business data processing, general.

See full description on page 586.

# UNIVERSITY OF ILLINOIS AT URBANA–CHAMPAIGN

*Academic Outreach*
601 East John Street
Champaign, IL 61820
**Contact:** Faye Lesht, Head of Academic Outreach
**Phone:** 217-333-3061

**Fax:** 217-244-8481
**Web:** http://www.outreach.uiuc.edu
**E-mail:** f-lesht@uiuc.edu

**ACCREDITATION:** North Central Association of Colleges and Schools
**INSTITUTIONALLY ADMINISTERED FINANCIAL AID:** No

### DEGREE OR CERTIFICATE PROGRAMS OFFERED

**Programs offered do not lead to a degree or other formal award.**

### NON-DEGREE-RELATED COURSE TOPICS OFFERED

**Undergraduate**—American literature (United States); Asian studies; English language and literature, general; French language and literature; Latin language and literature (ancient and medieval); Russian language and literature; anthropology; business administration and management; counseling psychology; film/cinema studies; geography; gerontology; health professions and related sciences, other; history; industrial and organizational psychology; mathematics; political science and government; social psychology; sociology.
**Graduate**—curriculum and instruction; electrical, electronics and communication engineering; engineering mechanics; mechanical engineering.

---

### Special Note

University of Illinois at Urbana-Champaign offers a variety of distance learning courses at the undergraduate and graduate levels as well as master's degree programs. More than 130 undergraduate courses are available in a correspondence format. Enrollments are accepted at any time. Some courses use e-mail for submission of work. The NetMath program provides a number of tutored undergraduate math courses via the Internet.

Several graduate degree programs are delivered using the Internet, with a few also offered via videotape. These include master's degree programs in library and information sciences, curriculum and instruction, human resource education, electrical engineering, general engineering, mechanical engineering, theoretical and applied mechanics, and computer science. Admission to degree programs is competitive. Combined on-campus and online programs are being developed in the fields of veterinary medicine and agricultural education. Internet-based graduate course sequences include a series of courses in French translation. Distance learning degree programs are identical to the campus program and are taught primarily by regular campus faculty members. Library and other support services are provided. Internet courses are generally available nationally and, in some cases, internationally. Videoconferencing courses are offered at various locations, primarily in Illinois. Information about offerings can be obtained from Academic Outreach.

To be eligible for student loans, distance learners must be officially admitted to a degree program at the University and enrolled at least part-time.

Organizations interested in contractual courses or programs for their constituencies should contact Academic Outreach. For more information, students should also contact Academic Outreach at 800-252-1360 Ext. 3-3061 (toll-free) or visit the Web site at http://www.outreach.uiuc.edu.

---

See full description on page 588.

# THE UNIVERSITY OF IOWA
## Center for Credit Programs

116 International Center
Iowa City, IA 52242
**Contact:** Ms. Angela Ward, Pre-Admission Coordinator
**Phone:** 319-335-2575
**Fax:** 319-335-2740
**Web:** http://www.uiowa.edu/~ccp
**E-mail:** angela-ward@uiowa.edu

**ACCREDITATION:** North Central Association of Colleges and Schools

**INSTITUTIONALLY ADMINISTERED FINANCIAL AID:** Yes

### DEGREE OR CERTIFICATE PROGRAMS OFFERED
**Undergraduate—BLS:** Liberal Studies.

### NON-DEGREE-RELATED COURSE TOPICS OFFERED
**Undergraduate—**Afro-American(Black) studies; American (United States) history; American studies/civilization; Asian studies; European history; French language and literature; Latin language and literature (ancient and medieval); Spanish language and literature; anthropology; earth and planetary sciences; environmental health; geography; journalism; mathematical statistics; mathematics, other; nursing; social work; sociology; women's studies.
**Graduate—**Afro-American(Black) studies; American (United States) history; Asian studies; European history; anthropology; earth and planetary sciences; environmental health; geography; journalism; mathematical statistics; mathematics, other; social work; sociology; women's studies.

**See full description on page 590.**

# UNIVERSITY OF KANSAS
## Academic Outreach Programs

1515 St. Andrews Drive
Lawrence, KS 66047-1625
**Contact:** Continuing Education
**Phone:** 785-864-KUCE
**Fax:** 785-864-7895
**Web:** http://www.kumc.edu/kuce/aop/
**E-mail:** enroll@ukans.edu

**ACCREDITATION:** North Central Association of Colleges and Schools

### DEGREE OR CERTIFICATE PROGRAMS OFFERED
**Programs offered do not lead to a degree or other formal award.**

### NON-DEGREE-RELATED COURSE TOPICS OFFERED
**Undergraduate—**East and Southeast Asian languages and literatures; English language and literature, general; French language and literature; Spanish language and literature; anthropology; biology, general; communication disorders sciences and services; communications, general; economics; environmental control technologies; film/cinema studies; geography; geological and related sciences; history; mathematics; music; philosophy and religion; political science and government; psychology; religion/religious studies; social psychology; social sciences, general; sociology.
**Graduate—**curriculum and instruction; developmental and child psychology; education, general; ethnic and cultural studies; history; music; psychology.

**Non-credit—**gerontology; medical basic sciences; nursing; social work.

# UNIVERSITY OF LA VERNE
## Distance Learning Center

1950 3rd Street
La Verne, CA 91750
**Contact:** Mrs. Alene Harrison, Distance Learning Center Registrar
**Phone:** 909-985-0944 Ext. 5301
**Fax:** 909-981-8695
**Web:** http://www.ulv.edu/dlc/dlc.html
**E-mail:** harrisoa@ulv.edu

**ACCREDITATION:** Western Association of Schools and Colleges

**INSTITUTIONALLY ADMINISTERED FINANCIAL AID:** Yes

### DEGREE OR CERTIFICATE PROGRAMS OFFERED
**Undergraduate—BS:** Public Administration.

### NON-DEGREE-RELATED COURSE TOPICS OFFERED
**Undergraduate—**English composition; English creative writing; anthropology; biology, general; chemistry; developmental and child psychology; history; philosophy; speech and rhetorical studies.

# THE UNIVERSITY OF LETHBRIDGE

Web: http://www.uleth.ca/

**ACCREDITATION:** Provincially Chartered

### DEGREE OR CERTIFICATE PROGRAMS OFFERED
**Programs offered do not lead to a degree or other formal award.**

# UNIVERSITY OF LOUISVILLE
## Department of Special Education

School of Education, EDU 158
Louisville, KY 40292
**Contact:** Denzil Edge, Director of Distance Education
**Phone:** 502-852-0559
**Fax:** 502-852-3976
**Web:** http://www.louisville.edu/edu/edsp/distance
**E-mail:** denzil.edge@louisville.edu

**ACCREDITATION:** Southern Association of Colleges and Schools

**INSTITUTIONALLY ADMINISTERED FINANCIAL AID:** Yes

### DEGREE OR CERTIFICATE PROGRAMS OFFERED
**Graduate—MEd:** Autism/Assistive Technology; Moderate/Severe Disabilities; Orientation and Mobility; Special Education; Visual Impairment.

### NON-DEGREE-RELATED COURSE TOPICS OFFERED
**Graduate—**special education.

**Graduate**—animal sciences; anthropology; business; civil engineering; education, general; electrical, electronics and communication engineering; liberal arts and sciences, general studies and humanities; mechanical engineering; social work.

**Non-credit**—electrical, electronics and communication engineering.

## Special Note

University of Louisville, Department of Special Education, located in Louisville, Kentucky, is an accredited college (National Council for Accreditation of Teacher Education) that offers teacher certification and master's degrees in special education with an emphasis on visual impairment, autism, assistive technology, orientation and mobility, and moderate/severe disabilities. The Distance Education Program of the Department of Special Education is entering its 8th year of operations and now provides 45 courses through advanced technologies, including interactive television, compressed video, videostreaming, and the World Wide Web. As the University is committed to offering distance education students the same high-quality services and support as on-campus students enjoy, students have continuous access to library services, professors, and colleagues via listserv connections and e-mail.

Based on the need for teacher preparation in the area of visual impairment, the Department of Special Education has created a new delivery system that combines summer institutes, conducted in collaboration with the Kentucky School for the Blind, and distance education courses during the fall and spring. Students participating in programs with a concentration in autism or assistive technology can complete their course of study through distance education courses.

All programs are available to students nationally and internationally. For the academic year 2001–02, the tuition rate for non-Kentucky residents is $592.00 per credit hour. Many states offer financial aid for students in the field of special education. Additional information may be obtained by visiting the Department of Special Education's Web site (http://www.louisville.edu/edu/edsp) or by contacting Dr. Denzil Edge/Pam Drake at 502-852-0560 or toll-free at 800-334-8635 Ext. 0560 or via e-mail (info@de.education.louisville.edu).

## UNIVERSITY OF MAINE

*Continuing Education Division*
5713 Chadbourne Hall
Orono, ME 04469-5713
**Contact:** James F. Toner, Associate Director
**Phone:** 207-581-3142
**Fax:** 207-581-3141
**Web:** http://dll.umaine.edu/ced
**E-mail:** jim.toner@umit.maine.edu

**ACCREDITATION:** New England Association of Schools and Colleges
**INSTITUTIONALLY ADMINISTERED FINANCIAL AID:** Yes

### DEGREE OR CERTIFICATE PROGRAMS OFFERED
Programs offered do not lead to a degree or other formal award.

### NON-DEGREE-RELATED COURSE TOPICS OFFERED
**Undergraduate**—Asian studies; English as a second language; English composition; English creative writing; accounting; biology, general; developmental and child psychology; educational psychology; electrical, electronics and communication engineering; environmental health; horticulture science; mechanical engineering; social psychology; sociology; surveying; women's studies.

## UNIVERSITY OF MAINE AT FARMINGTON

Merrill Hall, 224 Main Street
Farmington, ME 04938
**Contact:** Doug Rawlings, Director of Institutional Research
**Phone:** 207-778-7292
**Fax:** 207-778-7510
**Web:** http://www.umf.maine.edu/
**E-mail:** rawlings@maine.maine.edu

**ACCREDITATION:** New England Association of Schools and Colleges
**INSTITUTIONALLY ADMINISTERED FINANCIAL AID:** Yes

### DEGREE OR CERTIFICATE PROGRAMS OFFERED
Programs offered do not lead to a degree or other formal award.

## UNIVERSITY OF MAINE AT MACHIAS

*Behavioral Science External Degree Program*
9 O'Brien Avenue
Machias, ME 04654
**Contact:** Stacy Peabody, Distance Education Assistant
**Phone:** 207-255-1374
**Fax:** 207-255-4864
**Web:** http://www.umm.maine.edu/
**E-mail:** speabody@maine.edu

**ACCREDITATION:** New England Association of Schools and Colleges
**INSTITUTIONALLY ADMINISTERED FINANCIAL AID:** Yes

### DEGREE OR CERTIFICATE PROGRAMS OFFERED
**Undergraduate**—*BA:* Behavioral Science (External Degree Program).

### NON-DEGREE-RELATED COURSE TOPICS OFFERED
**Undergraduate**—American literature (United States); English creative writing; English language and literature, general; business; mathematical statistics; political science and government; psychology; social sciences, general.

## UNIVERSITY OF MAINE AT PRESQUE ISLE

181 Maine Street
Presque Isle, ME 04769
**Contact:** Mr. Ed A. Dery, ITV Coordinator
**Phone:** 207-768-9648
**Fax:** 207-764-5833
**Web:** http://www.umpi.maine.edu/

**E-mail:** dery@polaris.umpi.maine.edu

**ACCREDITATION:** New England Association of Schools and Colleges

### DEGREE OR CERTIFICATE PROGRAMS OFFERED
Programs offered do not lead to a degree or other formal award.

### NON-DEGREE-RELATED COURSE TOPICS OFFERED
Undergraduate—English composition.

# UNIVERSITY OF MANITOBA
*Distance Education Program*
188 Continuing Education Complex
Winnipeg, MB R3T 2N2, Canada
**Contact:** Distance Education Student Support
**Phone:** 204-474-8028
**Fax:** 204-474-7660
**Web:** http://www.umanitoba.ca/distance
**E-mail:** de_advisor@umanitoba.ca

**ACCREDITATION:** Provincially Chartered

**INSTITUTIONALLY ADMINISTERED FINANCIAL AID:** Yes

### DEGREE OR CERTIFICATE PROGRAMS OFFERED
Undergraduate—*BA:* 3 Year General. *BN:* Nursing. *BSW:* Social Work.
Graduate—*Graduate Certificate:* Education.

### NON-DEGREE-RELATED COURSE TOPICS OFFERED
Undergraduate—East European languages and literatures; English language and literature, general; anthropology; computer science; economics; education administration and supervision; geography; geological and related sciences; history; mathematics; microbiology/bacteriology; nursing; philosophy; political science and government; psychology; religion/religious studies; social work; sociology.
Graduate—education administration and supervision; education, other; romance languages and literatures; social work.
Non-credit—education, general; horticulture science; quality control and safety technologies.

# UNIVERSITY OF MARYLAND, BALTIMORE COUNTY
*UMBC Continuing Education*
1000 Hilltop Circle
Baltimore, MD 21250
**Contact:** Donna Taylor, Associate Vice Provost
**Phone:** 410-455-2797
**Fax:** 410-455-1115
**Web:** http://www.umbc.edu/
**E-mail:** connect@umbc.edu

**ACCREDITATION:** Middle States Association of Colleges and Schools
**INSTITUTIONALLY ADMINISTERED FINANCIAL AID:** No

### DEGREE OR CERTIFICATE PROGRAMS OFFERED
Graduate—*Graduate Certificate:* Distance Learning. *MS:* Emergency Health Services. *MSIS:* Information Systems.

### NON-DEGREE-RELATED COURSE TOPICS OFFERED
Undergraduate—mechanical engineering.
Graduate—education, other; educational/instructional media design.

# UNIVERSITY OF MARYLAND, COLLEGE PARK
*Instructional Television System*
Mitchell Building, First Floor
College Park, MD 20742-5231
**Contact:** Single Point of Contact
**Phone:** 301-341-3572
**Fax:** 301-314-1282
**Web:** http://www.e-learning.umd.edu
**E-mail:** e-learning@umail.umd.edu

**ACCREDITATION:** Middle States Association of Colleges and Schools

### DEGREE OR CERTIFICATE PROGRAMS OFFERED
Programs offered do not lead to a degree or other formal award.
See full description on page 592.

# UNIVERSITY OF MARYLAND, COLLEGE PARK
*A. James Clark School of Engineering*
Reliability Engineering Program, 2100 Marie Mount Hall
College Park, MD 20742-7531
**Contact:** Dr. Marvin L. Roush, Professor of Reliability Engineering
**Phone:** 301-405-7299
**Fax:** 301-314-9601
**Web:** http://www.enre.umd.edu/enreumd.htm
**E-mail:** roush@eng.umd.edu

**ACCREDITATION:** Middle States Association of Colleges and Schools
**INSTITUTIONALLY ADMINISTERED FINANCIAL AID:** No

### DEGREE OR CERTIFICATE PROGRAMS OFFERED
Undergraduate—*Certificate:* Reliability Engineering.
Graduate—*ME:* Reliability Engineering. *MS:* Reliability Engineering.
Postgraduate and doctoral—*PhD:* Reliability Engineering.

### NON-DEGREE-RELATED COURSE TOPICS OFFERED
Undergraduate—engineering physics; engineering science; engineering, general; engineering, other; engineering-related technologies, other; fire protection; materials engineering; nuclear engineering.
Graduate—engineering physics; engineering science; engineering, general; engineering, other; engineering-related technologies, other; fire protection; materials engineering; nuclear engineering.
See full description on page 594.

# UNIVERSITY OF MARYLAND UNIVERSITY COLLEGE
*Office of Distance Education and Lifelong Learning*
3501 University Boulevard East
Adelphi, MD 20783

**Contact:** Undergraduate Enrollment Team
**Phone:** 800-581-UMUC
**Web:** http://www.umuc.edu
**E-mail:** umucinfo@nova.umuc.edu

**ACCREDITATION:** Middle States Association of Colleges and Schools
**INSTITUTIONALLY ADMINISTERED FINANCIAL AID:** Yes

## DEGREE OR CERTIFICATE PROGRAMS OFFERED

**Undergraduate—*BA:*** Behavioral and Social Sciences; Communication Studies; Computer and Information Sciences; Fire Science; Humanities; Management; Paralegal Studies. ***BS:*** Liberal Studies.
**Graduate—*MS:*** Computer Systems Management; Environmental Management; Management.

See full description on page 596.

# UNIVERSITY OF MASSACHUSETTS AMHERST

*Division of Continuing Education and Video Instructional Program*

Continuing Education Building, 358 North Pleasant Street
Amherst, MA 01003-9296
**Contact:** Kevin Aiken, Director, Division of Continuing Education
**Phone:** 413-545-2111
**Fax:** 413-545-3351
**Web:** http://www.umass.edu/contined
**E-mail:** kaiken@admin.umass.edu

**ACCREDITATION:** New England Association of Schools and Colleges
**INSTITUTIONALLY ADMINISTERED FINANCIAL AID:** Yes

eCollege.com   *www.ecollege.com*

## DEGREE OR CERTIFICATE PROGRAMS OFFERED

**Undergraduate—*BS:*** HRTA; Nursing (RN to BS). ***Certificate:*** Arts Management.
**Graduate—*MBA:*** Business Administration. ***MCSE:*** Computer Science. ***MPH:*** Public Health Practice. ***MS:*** Electrical and Computer Engineering; Engineering Management; Nursing.

## NON-DEGREE-RELATED COURSE TOPICS OFFERED

**Undergraduate—**English language and literature, general; accounting; business marketing and marketing management; community health services; conservation and renewable natural resources, other; criminal justice and corrections; education, other; electrical, electronics and communication engineering; foods and nutrition studies; journalism and mass communications; marketing management and research; natural resources conservation; psychology; sociology; wildlife and wildlands management.
**Graduate—**accounting; chemical engineering; education administration and supervision; electrical, electronics and communication engineering; engineering/industrial management; environmental health; industrial/manufacturing engineering; mechanical engineering.
**Non-credit—**chemical engineering; electrical, electronics and communication engineering; engineering/industrial management; financial management and services; industrial/manufacturing engineering; marketing

operations/marketing and distribution, other; mechanical engineering; public relations and organizational communications.
See full description on page 600.

# UNIVERSITY OF MASSACHUSETTS BOSTON

*Corporate, Continuing and Distance Education*

100 Morrissey Boulevard
Boston, MA 02125-3393
**Contact:** Ms. Katharine Grant Galaitsis, Assistant to the Dean
**Phone:** 617-287-7925
**Fax:** 617-287-7297
**Web:** http://www.conted.umb.edu
**E-mail:** kitty.galaitsis@umb.edu

**ACCREDITATION:** New England Association of Schools and Colleges
**INSTITUTIONALLY ADMINISTERED FINANCIAL AID:** Yes

eCollege.com   *www.ecollege.com*

## DEGREE OR CERTIFICATE PROGRAMS OFFERED
Programs offered do not lead to a degree or other formal award.

## NON-DEGREE-RELATED COURSE TOPICS OFFERED

**Undergraduate—**English technical and business writing; area, ethnic and cultural studies, other; business administration and management; cell and molecular biology; communications technologies; computer and information sciences, general; computer science; curriculum and instruction; education, other; international relations and affairs; music; nursing; sociology; student counseling and personnel services; teaching English as a second language/foreign language.
See full description on page 602.

# UNIVERSITY OF MASSACHUSETTS DARTMOUTH

*Division of Continuing Education, University of Massachusetts at Dartmouth*

Old Westport Road
North Dartmouth, MA 02747
**Contact:** Mr. Greg Stone, CyberEd Coordinator
**Phone:** 508-999-8077
**E-mail:** gstone@umassd.edu

**ACCREDITATION:** New England Association of Schools and Colleges
**INSTITUTIONALLY ADMINISTERED FINANCIAL AID:** Yes

## DEGREE OR CERTIFICATE PROGRAMS OFFERED
Programs offered do not lead to a degree or other formal award.

## NON-DEGREE-RELATED COURSE TOPICS OFFERED

**Undergraduate—**English technical and business writing; Jewish/Judaic studies; astronomy; biology, general; chemistry; communications, general; fine arts and art studies; nursing; women's studies.
**Graduate—**English technical and business writing.

Non-credit—communications technologies; computer programming; computer software and media applications.

See full description on page 604.

# UNIVERSITY OF MASSACHUSETTS LOWELL

*Continuing Studies and Corporate Education*

1 University Avenue
Lowell, MA 01854-2881
**Contact:** Steven Tello, Assistant Director of Distance Learning
**Phone:** 978-934-2467
**Fax:** 978-934-4064
**Web:** http://cybered.uml.edu
**E-mail:** cybered@uml.edu

**ACCREDITATION:** New England Association of Schools and Colleges
**INSTITUTIONALLY ADMINISTERED FINANCIAL AID:** Yes

## DEGREE OR CERTIFICATE PROGRAMS OFFERED

**Undergraduate—AS:** Information Technology. **BLS:** Bachelor of Liberal Arts Degree (BLA). **BS:** Information Technology with Business Minor; Information Technology. **Certificate:** Contemporary Communications; Data/Telecommunications; Fundamentals of Information Technology; Graduate Certificate in Clinical Pathology; Graduate Certificate in Photonics and Optoelectronics; Intranet Development; Multimedia Applications; Plastics Engineering Technology; UNIX.
**Graduate—Certificate:** UNIX.

## NON-DEGREE-RELATED COURSE TOPICS OFFERED

**Undergraduate—**English composition; adult and continuing teacher education; business; business communications; communications, general; computer and information sciences, general; computer programming; ethnic and cultural studies; information sciences and systems; journalism; liberal arts and sciences, general studies and humanities; mathematics and computer science; philosophy; social sciences and history, other; sociology; telecommunications.
**Graduate—**education administration and supervision; education, general; electrical and electronic engineering-related technology; health and medical laboratory technologies; health professions and related sciences, other; teacher education, specific academic and vocational programs.
**Non-credit—**teacher education, specific academic and vocational programs.

See full description on page 606.

# UNIVERSITY OF MASSACHUSETTS SYSTEM

*UMassOnline*

Boston, MA 02108
**Contact:** Dr. Jack M. Wilson, CEO of UMassOnline
**Phone:** 617-287-7160
**Web:** http://www.umassonline.net/
**E-mail:** info@umassonline.net

**ACCREDITATION:** New England Association of Schools and Colleges
**INSTITUTIONALLY ADMINISTERED FINANCIAL AID:** Yes

## DEGREE OR CERTIFICATE PROGRAMS OFFERED

**Undergraduate—AS:** Information Technology. **BA:** Liberal Arts. **BS:** HRTA; Information Technology; Nursing (RN to BS). **Certificate:** Arts Management; Contemporary Communications; Data/Telecommunications; Fundamentals of Information Technology; Intranet Development; Multimedia Applications; Online Communications Skills; UNIX.
**Graduate—Graduate Certificate:** Clinical Pathology; Photonics and Optoelectronics. **MBA:** Business Administration. **MEd:** Educational Administration. **MPH:** Public Health Practice. **MS:** Nursing.

## NON-DEGREE-RELATED COURSE TOPICS OFFERED

**Undergraduate—**American literature (United States); English language and literature, general; accounting; astronomy; biology, general; botany; business; business administration and management; business communications; business information and data processing services; chemistry; communications, general; comparative literature; computer and information sciences, other; computer programming; computer systems analysis; computer/information technology administration and management; conservation and renewable natural resources, other; counseling psychology; economics; education, general; fine arts and art studies; foods and nutrition studies; journalism and mass communications; marketing management and research; mathematics; miscellaneous physical sciences; natural resources conservation; philosophy; physical sciences, general; psychology; sociology; telecommunications; wildlife and wildlands management.
**Graduate—**accounting; biological and physical sciences; business administration and management; counseling psychology; education administration and supervision; educational/instructional media design; nursing.
**Non-credit—**computer software and media applications; internet and world wide web; marketing operations/marketing and distribution, other; public administration; public relations and organizational communications; visual and performing arts, other.

See full description on page 598.

# UNIVERSITY OF MEDICINE AND DENTISTRY OF NEW JERSEY

65 Bergen Avenue
Newark, NJ 07107
**Contact:** Mr. Brian Lewis, Manager of Enrollment Services
**Web:** http://www.umdnj.edu/
**E-mail:** lewisbj@umdnj.edu

**ACCREDITATION:** Middle States Association of Colleges and Schools
**INSTITUTIONALLY ADMINISTERED FINANCIAL AID:** Yes

## DEGREE OR CERTIFICATE PROGRAMS OFFERED

**Undergraduate—BS:** Health Sciences.

# THE UNIVERSITY OF MEMPHIS

*Extended Programs*

376 Administration Building
Memphis, TN 38152-3370
**Contact:** Sheila D. Owens, Manager
**Phone:** 901-678-3807
**Fax:** 901-678-5112
**Web:** http://www.extended.memphis.edu/

**E-mail:** sowens@memphis.edu

**ACCREDITATION:** Southern Association of Colleges and Schools

## DEGREE OR CERTIFICATE PROGRAMS OFFERED
**Programs offered do not lead to a degree or other formal award.**

## NON-DEGREE-RELATED COURSE TOPICS OFFERED
**Undergraduate**—English composition; English language and literature, general; biology, general; computer and information sciences, general; criminal justice and corrections; curriculum and instruction; fire services administration; health and physical education/fitness; history; journalism and mass communications; multi/interdisciplinary studies, other; music; nursing; psychology; public administration; speech and rhetorical studies. **Graduate**—English language and literature, general; journalism.

### Special Note
Practicing professionals in print and electronic journalism, advertising, and public relations find the University of Memphis's online master's degree program in journalism highly attractive. This fully accredited program is delivered via the Internet to students around the world.

The degree requires 30 to 36 semester hours—30 hours, including a 6-hour thesis; 33 hours, including a 3-hour professional project; or 36 hours of course work. Three-semester-hour courses are offered and begin each September, January, and June. Students who take a full course load each semester can complete the degree program in 18 months, although most students choose to take fewer courses per semester.

Students complete a 12-hour core curriculum (law, theory, research, and administration) and then select from a broad range of electives. Students may review these courses at http://umvirtual.memphis.edu/masscomm. More information concerning the University and the Department of Journalism can be found at http://www.memphis.edu. Students can apply for admission to the program at http://www.people.memphis.edu/~gradsch/adminfo.html.

Candidates for admission to the program are expected to have completed undergraduate degrees with a grade point average of 3.0 on a 4.0 scale and attained scores of 480 or better on the verbal portion and 420 or better on the quantitative portion of the Graduate Record Examinations or a score of 40 on the Miller Analogies Test. Students may take up to 9 hours if they have not yet taken either test.

For more information, students should contact Rick Fischer, Coordinator of the Online Program (rfischer@memphis.edu) or Dr. David Arant, Journalism Graduate Studies Coordinator (darant@memphis.edu).

## UNIVERSITY OF MICHIGAN
*Media Union*
Center for Professional Development, College of Engineering,
2121 Bonisteel Boulevard
Ann Arbor, MI 48109-2092
**Contact:** Kathy Friedrichs
**Phone:** 734-647-7200
**Fax:** 734-647-7182
**Web:** http://cpd.engin.umich.edu
**E-mail:** kamf@umich.edu

**ACCREDITATION:** North Central Association of Colleges and Schools

## DEGREE OR CERTIFICATE PROGRAMS OFFERED
**Graduate**—*ME:* Manufacturing Engineering. *MEngr:* Automotive Engineering.

## NON-DEGREE-RELATED COURSE TOPICS OFFERED
**Non-credit**—engineering/industrial management.

## UNIVERSITY OF MICHIGAN–FLINT
*Distance Learning Program*
Room 266, University Pavilion
Flint, MI 48502-1950
**Contact:** Office of the Registrar
**Web:** http://www.umflintonline.org/
**E-mail:** admin@umflintonline.org

**ACCREDITATION:** North Central Association of Colleges and Schools

| eCollege.com | *www.ecollege.com* |

## DEGREE OR CERTIFICATE PROGRAMS OFFERED
**Programs offered do not lead to a degree or other formal award.**

## NON-DEGREE-RELATED COURSE TOPICS OFFERED
**Undergraduate**—accounting; computer science; health and medical diagnostic and treatment services; marketing management and research; nursing; social work.

**Graduate**—accounting; human resources management; marketing management and research.

### Special Note
The University of Michigan–Flint is committed to the highest standards of teaching, learning, scholarship, and creative endeavors in online education. The new virtual campus continues the historic tradition of excellence that distinguishes all 3 University of Michigan campuses.

The UM-Flint Online program offers a variety of courses traditionally offered on campus through UM-Flint's 4 Schools and Colleges. Online courses have been developed by distinguished faculty members and enjoy the same credits and recognition as their on-campus counterparts. They provide the convenience of bringing the University of Michigan–Flint's quality education into the student's home or office.

The UM-Flint Online program offers 2 comprehensive online degrees. Students can earn a Master of Business Administration through the new NetPlus MBA, which is offered through Blackboard™ at http://online.umflint.edu. Students may also enroll in the registered nurse to Bachelor of Science in Nursing degree (RN to BSN) program, which is offered through eCollege™ at http://umflintonline.org.

The University of Michigan–Flint is dedicated to developing online educational opportunities that meet the educational needs of diverse student populations. To inquire about upcoming courses or for more information about online classes, students should call 810-762-3123 or visit the above Web sites.

# UNIVERSITY OF MINNESOTA, MORRIS

## College of Continuing Education-GenEdWeb Program

225 Community Services Building, 600 East 4th Street
Morris, MN 56267
**Contact:** Ms. Karen M. Johnson, Program Associate
**Phone:** 800-842-0030
**Fax:** 320-589-1661
**Web:** http://genedweb.mrs.umn.edu
**E-mail:** johnsokm@mrs.umn.edu

**ACCREDITATION:** North Central Association of Colleges and Schools
**INSTITUTIONALLY ADMINISTERED FINANCIAL AID:** Yes

### DEGREE OR CERTIFICATE PROGRAMS OFFERED
**Programs offered do not lead to a degree or other formal award.**

### NON-DEGREE-RELATED COURSE TOPICS OFFERED
**Undergraduate**—English composition; education, general; mathematical statistics; mathematics; political science and government; psychology; teacher education, specific academic and vocational programs.

# UNIVERSITY OF MINNESOTA, TWIN CITIES CAMPUS

## Independent and Distance Learning

CCE Student Support Services, 150 Wesbrook Hall, 77 Pleasant Street, SE
Minneapolis, MN 55455
**Contact:** Receptionist
**Phone:** 800-234-6564
**Fax:** 612-625-1511
**Web:** http://www.idl.umn.edu
**E-mail:** adv@cce.umn.edu

**ACCREDITATION:** North Central Association of Colleges and Schools
**INSTITUTIONALLY ADMINISTERED FINANCIAL AID:** Yes

### DEGREE OR CERTIFICATE PROGRAMS OFFERED
**Programs offered do not lead to a degree or other formal award.**

### NON-DEGREE-RELATED COURSE TOPICS OFFERED
**Undergraduate**—American (United States) history; American studies/civilization; English composition; English creative writing; English language and literature, general; European history; French language and literature; Germanic languages and literatures; Latin language and literature (ancient and medieval); Russian language and literature; Spanish language and literature; accounting; agriculture/agricultural sciences; agriculture/agricultural sciences, other; anthropology; art history, criticism and conservation; astronomy; biochemistry and biophysics; biology, general; business administration and management; business marketing and marketing management; classical and ancient Near Eastern languages and literatures; developmental and child psychology; ecology; economics; finance, general; foods and nutrition studies; foreign languages and literatures; geography; geological and related sciences; history; journalism; management information systems and business data processing, general; mathematics; mechanical engineering; music; nursing; occupational

therapy; philosophy; psychology; public health; romance languages and literatures; social work; speech and rhetorical studies; women's studies.
**Graduate**—bioengineering and biomedical engineering; geological and related sciences; public health; speech and rhetorical studies.
**See full description on page 608.**

# UNIVERSITY OF MISSOURI-COLUMBIA

## Center for Distance and Independent Study

136 Clark Hall
Columbia, MO 65211-4200
**Contact:** Ms. Terrie Nagel, Student Services Adviser
**Phone:** 800-609-3727
**Fax:** 573-882-6808
**Web:** http://cdis.missouri.edu
**E-mail:** nagelt@missouri.edu

**ACCREDITATION:** North Central Association of Colleges and Schools
**INSTITUTIONALLY ADMINISTERED FINANCIAL AID:** No

### DEGREE OR CERTIFICATE PROGRAMS OFFERED
**Programs offered do not lead to a degree or other formal award.**

### NON-DEGREE-RELATED COURSE TOPICS OFFERED
**Undergraduate**—Afro-American(Black) studies; American literature (United States); English composition; English creative writing; English language and literature, general; English language and literature/letters, other; English literature (British and Commonwealth); English technical and business writing; French language and literature; Germanic languages and literatures; Russian language and literature; Spanish language and literature; accounting; agricultural engineering; animal sciences; anthropology; area, ethnic and cultural studies, other; astronomy; atmospheric sciences and meteorology; bible/biblical studies; business administration and management; business marketing and marketing management; business/managerial economics; communications, other; computer science; computer software and media applications; criminal justice and corrections; criminology; curriculum and instruction; developmental and child psychology; economics; education, general; educational evaluation, research and statistics; educational psychology; engineering mechanics; entomology; family and community studies; family/consumer resource management; finance, general; foreign languages and literatures, other; geography; geological and related sciences; health and medical administrative services; health and physical education/fitness; health system/health services administration; horticulture science; law and legal studies, other; mathematical statistics; mathematics, other; peace and conflict studies; philosophy; psychology; psychology, other; romance languages and literatures; social psychology; sociology; women's studies.
**Graduate**—English literature (British and Commonwealth); animal sciences; business marketing and marketing management; communications, other; counseling psychology; criminal justice and corrections; criminology; curriculum and instruction; education administration and supervision; education, general; education, other; educational evaluation, research and statistics; educational psychology; family and community studies; history; organizational behavior studies; political science and government; special education.
**Non-credit**—city/urban, community and regional planning; fire protection.

## Special Note

Building on its long history of bringing individual distance education courses to students around the world, the University of Missouri–Columbia offers distance degrees and interactive online courses through MU Direct: Continuing and Distance Education. The courses, usually conducted within the time frame of one semester, allow students to interact with faculty members and classmates while "attending" class virtually at their convenience—anytime, day or night.

Cited in several publications as one of the nation's best values in higher education, the University of Missouri–Columbia is one of only 31 public universities selected for membership in the Association of American Universities. Graduate degrees are available in several health-care fields, including 3 nursing specialty areas, health administration, and informatics. Bachelor's completion programs are offered online for registered nurses, radiographers, and respiratory therapists. Some programs require on-campus class work. Teachers may conveniently pursue a master's degree in educational technology, social studies, gifted education, literacy, or administration. The first four of these options can be completed entirely at a distance, or any course may be taken individually as well. Certificate programs are offered in several education areas and in computerized tomography and magnetic resonance imaging. Two unique courses leading to national certification in rural real estate appraisal may be taken on either a credit or noncredit basis.

Students should check MU Direct's Web site (http://MUdirect.missouri.edu) for the most current offerings as well as online advising and access to registration, library services, textbook purchasing, and other academic resources. Questions also are welcome at 800-545-2604 (toll-free) or via e-mail at MUdirect@missouri.edu.

See full description on page 610.

# UNIVERSITY OF MISSOURI–ROLLA

## Department of Engineering Management

Enginering Management Building, Room 223
Rolla, MO 65409
**Contact:** Ms. Krista Chambers, Teleconference Program Specialist
**Phone:** 573-341-4990
**Fax:** 573-341-6990
**Web:** http://www.umr.edu/~emgt
**E-mail:** krista@umr.edu

**ACCREDITATION:** North Central Association of Colleges and Schools
**INSTITUTIONALLY ADMINISTERED FINANCIAL AID:** No

### DEGREE OR CERTIFICATE PROGRAMS OFFERED

**Graduate**—*MS:* Engineering Management; Systems Engineering.

### NON-DEGREE-RELATED COURSE TOPICS OFFERED

**Graduate**—accounting; computer and information sciences, general; engineering science; engineering, general; engineering/industrial management; industrial/manufacturing engineering.

# UNIVERSITY OF MISSOURI–ST. LOUIS

## Video Instructional Program

Information Technology Services, 412 CCB, 8001 Natural Bridge Road
St. Louis, MO 63121
**Contact:** Marcel G. Bechtoldt, Assistant Director
**Phone:** 314-516-6173
**Fax:** 314-516-6007
**Web:** http://www.umsl.edu/technology/videosupport/distancelearning/distancelearning.html
**E-mail:** bechtoldt@umsl.edu

**ACCREDITATION:** North Central Association of Colleges and Schools

### DEGREE OR CERTIFICATE PROGRAMS OFFERED

**Undergraduate**—*BN:* Nursing.
**Graduate**—*MBA:* Business Administration; Nursing.

### NON-DEGREE-RELATED COURSE TOPICS OFFERED

**Undergraduate**—developmental and child psychology; radio and television broadcasting.

# THE UNIVERSITY OF MONTANA–MISSOULA

## Continuing Education

Missoula, MT 59812
**Contact:** Dr. Sharon E. Alexander, Dean
**Phone:** 406-243-2900
**Web:** http://www.umt.edu
**E-mail:** alexands@selway.umt.edu

**ACCREDITATION:** Northwest Association of Schools and Colleges
**INSTITUTIONALLY ADMINISTERED FINANCIAL AID:** Yes

eCollege.com www.ecollege.com

### DEGREE OR CERTIFICATE PROGRAMS OFFERED

**Undergraduate**—*BA:* Liberal Studies. *Endorsement:* Library Media.
**Graduate**—*MBA:* Business Administration. *MEd:* Counselor Education; Curriculum Studies; Educational Leadership.
**Postgraduate and doctoral**—*EdD:* Educational Leadership. *PharmD:* Pharmacy.

### NON-DEGREE-RELATED COURSE TOPICS OFFERED

**Undergraduate**—English creative writing; curriculum and instruction; forestry, general.
**Graduate**—business administration and management; library science, other.

# UNIVERSITY OF NEBRASKA AT OMAHA

Arts and Sciences Hall #202, 6001 Dodge Street
Omaha, NE 68123

**Contact:** Shelley Schafer, Manager of Off-Campus and Distance Education
**Phone:** 402-554-4831
**Fax:** 402-554-2231
**Web:** http://www.unomaha.edu/
**E-mail:** srschafer@unomaha.edu

**ACCREDITATION:** North Central Association of Colleges and Schools
**INSTITUTIONALLY ADMINISTERED FINANCIAL AID:** Yes

## DEGREE OR CERTIFICATE PROGRAMS OFFERED

**Undergraduate**—*BGS:* Aviation Studies.
**Graduate**—*MPA:* Public Administration.

## NON-DEGREE-RELATED COURSE TOPICS OFFERED

**Undergraduate**—astronomy; computer and information sciences, general; history; information sciences and systems; psychology; sociology; telecommunications; urban affairs/studies.

# UNIVERSITY OF NEBRASKA MEDICAL CENTER

### CON Rural Nursing Education/CON Graduate Program

985330 Nebraska Medical Center
Omaha, NE 68198-5330
**Contact:** Robin Moreau, Staff Assistant
**Phone:** 402-559-4110
**Fax:** 402-559-6379
**Web:** http://www.unmc.edu/nursing
**E-mail:** rmoreau@unmc.edu

**ACCREDITATION:** North Central Association of Colleges and Schools
**INSTITUTIONALLY ADMINISTERED FINANCIAL AID:** Yes

## DEGREE OR CERTIFICATE PROGRAMS OFFERED

**Undergraduate**—*BSN:* Nursing.

# UNIVERSITY OF NEVADA, LAS VEGAS

### Distance Education

4505 Maryland Parkway, Box 451038
Las Vegas, NV 89154
**Contact:** Pauline Saunders, Program Manager of Distance Education
**Phone:** 702-895-0745
**Fax:** 702-895-3850
**Web:** http://www.unlv.edu/infotech/Distance_Education
**E-mail:** psaunders@ccmail.nevada.edu

**ACCREDITATION:** Northwest Association of Schools and Colleges

## DEGREE OR CERTIFICATE PROGRAMS OFFERED

**Undergraduate**—*BA:* Social Science Studies.
**Graduate**—*EMA:* Hotel Administration. *Graduate Certificate:* Instructional Technology.

## NON-DEGREE-RELATED COURSE TOPICS OFFERED

**Undergraduate**—English as a second language; developmental and child psychology.

## Special Note

Beginning in the fall semester 2001, the University of Nevada, Las Vegas, offers a baccalaureate degree in social science. This degree completion program is intended primarily for students who have completed, or nearly completed, the equivalent of the first 2 years of college. Students completing this undergraduate program obtain a broad, interdisciplinary understanding of many issues addressed by research in the social sciences. In addition, UNLV offers a series of courses in 2 areas of interest to the hospitality industry: casino management and hotel administration. These classes, using mostly videotape augmented by Internet and/or telephone, may be taken by any adult anywhere. While all of the courses count in the undergraduate program at UNLV, they may also be useful for individuals in the industry who want to acquire competency in particular areas without enrolling in a degree program. If there is enough interest, UNLV may aggregate these courses into a certificate program in the future. Courses developed so far include Introduction to the Casino, Gaming Device Management, Gaming Regulations and Control, Introduction to the Hospitality Industry, and Lodging Operations. UNLV also offers an executive master's degree in hotel administration. For more information, students should contact Distance Education, University of Nevada, Las Vegas, 702-895-0334; e-mail: distanceed@ccmail.nevada.edu.

# UNIVERSITY OF NEVADA, RENO

### Independent Study and Division of Continuing Education

Independent Study 050
Reno, NV 89557
**Contact:** Kerri Garcia, Director
**Phone:** 775-784-4652
**Fax:** 775-784-1280
**Web:** http://www.dce.unr.edu/istudy
**E-mail:** istudy@scs.unr.edu

**ACCREDITATION:** Northwest Association of Schools and Colleges
**INSTITUTIONALLY ADMINISTERED FINANCIAL AID:** Yes

## DEGREE OR CERTIFICATE PROGRAMS OFFERED

Programs offered do not lead to a degree or other formal award.

## NON-DEGREE-RELATED COURSE TOPICS OFFERED

**Undergraduate**—American (United States) history; American studies/civilization; European history; French language and literature; Italian language and literature; Spanish language and literature; accounting; advertising; anthropology; business marketing and marketing management; criminal justice and corrections; developmental and child psychology; earth and planetary sciences; geography; journalism; sociology.
**Graduate**—education, general.
**Non-credit**—business communications.

See full description on page 612.

# UNIVERSITY OF NEW BRUNSWICK

## Department of Extension and Summer Session

Distance Education and Off-Campus Service, PO Box 4400
Fredericton, NB E3b 5A3, Canada
**Contact:** Barry Hughes, Open Access Learning Program
**Phone:** 506-453-4802
**Fax:** 506-453-3572
**Web:** http://www.unb.ca/coned
**E-mail:** bhughes@unb.ca

**ACCREDITATION:** Provincially Chartered

### DEGREE OR CERTIFICATE PROGRAMS OFFERED

**Undergraduate**—*BEd:* Adult Education. *BN:* Nursing. *Certificate:* Adult Education.
**Graduate**—*MEd:* Adult Education. *MN:* Nursing.

### NON-DEGREE-RELATED COURSE TOPICS OFFERED

**Undergraduate**—accounting; adult and continuing teacher education; biology, general; business administration and management; educational psychology; electrical, electronics and communication engineering; mathematical statistics; microbiology/bacteriology; organizational behavior studies; sociology.
**Graduate**—adult and continuing teacher education; educational psychology.
**Non-credit**—English creative writing.

# UNIVERSITY OF NEW ENGLAND

## Master of Science in Education Program

716 Stevens Avenue
Portland, ME 04103
**Contact:** Certificate of Advanced Graduate Study in Educational Leadership Program
**Phone:** 207-797-7261 Ext. 4360
**Fax:** 207-878-2434
**Web:** http://www.uneonline.org
**E-mail:** cags@mailbox.une.edu

**ACCREDITATION:** New England Association of Schools and Colleges
**INSTITUTIONALLY ADMINISTERED FINANCIAL AID:** Yes

eCollege.com   *www.ecollege.com*

### DEGREE OR CERTIFICATE PROGRAMS OFFERED

Programs offered do not lead to a degree or other formal award.
See full description on page 614.

# UNIVERSITY OF NEW HAMPSHIRE

## Interactive Instructional Television Center

Division of Continuing Education, 6 Garrison Avenue
Durham, NH 03824
**Contact:** William F. Murphy, Dean
**Phone:** 603-862-1938

**Fax:** 603-862-1113
**Web:** http://www.learn.unh.edu
**E-mail:** wfm@christa.unh.edu

**ACCREDITATION:** New England Association of Schools and Colleges
**INSTITUTIONALLY ADMINISTERED FINANCIAL AID:** Yes

### DEGREE OR CERTIFICATE PROGRAMS OFFERED

Programs offered do not lead to a degree or other formal award.

### NON-DEGREE-RELATED COURSE TOPICS OFFERED

**Graduate**—business administration and management; computer science; foods and nutrition studies; health professions and related sciences, other; mathematical statistics; mechanical engineering.
**Non-credit**—business; civil engineering/civil technology.

# UNIVERSITY OF NEW MEXICO

## Distance Education Center

Extended University, 1634 University Boulevard, NE
Albuquerque, NM 87131
**Contact:** Melissa Hilleary, Senior Program Manager
**Phone:** 505-277-0014
**Fax:** 505-277-8975
**Web:** http://e-unm.unm.edu
**E-mail:** hilleary@unm.edu

**ACCREDITATION:** North Central Association of Colleges and Schools
**INSTITUTIONALLY ADMINISTERED FINANCIAL AID:** Yes

### DEGREE OR CERTIFICATE PROGRAMS OFFERED

**Undergraduate**—*BN:* Nursing.
**Graduate**—*MSN:* Nursing Administration.

### NON-DEGREE-RELATED COURSE TOPICS OFFERED

**Undergraduate**—English composition; English creative writing; anthropology; astronomy; chemical engineering; civil engineering; computer engineering; computer science; economics; education administration and supervision; education, general; electrical, electronics and communication engineering; family and community studies; history; mathematics; mechanical engineering; nuclear engineering; nursing; pharmacy; philosophy; political science and government; psychology; sociology.
**Graduate**—English creative writing; chemical engineering; civil engineering; computer engineering; computer science; electrical, electronics and communication engineering; family and community studies; mechanical engineering; nuclear engineering; nursing; public administration.

# UNIVERSITY OF NEW ORLEANS

## UNO Metropolitan College

New Orleans, LA 70148
**Contact:** Dr. Carl E. Drichta, Associate Dean
**Phone:** 504-280-7100
**Fax:** 504-280-7317
**Web:** http://www.uno.edu/~meco/SREC/distance_learning_at_uno.htm
**E-mail:** cdrichta@uno.edu

**ACCREDITATION:** Southern Association of Colleges and Schools

### DEGREE OR CERTIFICATE PROGRAMS OFFERED

**Programs offered do not lead to a degree or other formal award.**

# UNIVERSITY OF NORTH ALABAMA

*Educational Technology Services/Distance Learning*

Box 5005
Florence, AL 35632-0001
**Contact:** Brenda J. Wilson, Coordinator of Distance Learning
**Phone:** 256-765-4651
**Fax:** 256-765-4863
**Web:** http://www.una.edu/
**E-mail:** bhill@unanov.una.edu

**ACCREDITATION:** Southern Association of Colleges and Schools

**INSTITUTIONALLY ADMINISTERED FINANCIAL AID:** Yes

> eCollege.com   *www.ecollege.com*

### DEGREE OR CERTIFICATE PROGRAMS OFFERED

**Graduate—***EMBA:* Executive Business Administration.

### NON-DEGREE-RELATED COURSE TOPICS OFFERED

**Undergraduate—**American (United States) history; American studies/civilization; English composition; business marketing and marketing management; geography; sociology.
**Graduate—**American studies/civilization.

# THE UNIVERSITY OF NORTH CAROLINA AT CHAPEL HILL

*The William and Ida Friday Center for Continuing Education*

CB 1020
Chapel Hill, NC 27599-1020
**Contact:** Carol McDonnell, Student Services Manager
**Phone:** 800-862-5669
**Fax:** 919-962-5549
**Web:** http://www.fridaycenter.unc.edu
**E-mail:** cbmcdonn@email.unc.edu

**ACCREDITATION:** Southern Association of Colleges and Schools

### DEGREE OR CERTIFICATE PROGRAMS OFFERED

**Programs offered do not lead to a degree or other formal award.**

### NON-DEGREE-RELATED COURSE TOPICS OFFERED

**Undergraduate—**Afro-American(Black) studies; American (United States) history; American studies/civilization; English as a second language; English composition; English creative writing; European history; French language and literature; Italian language and literature; Latin language and literature (ancient and medieval); Russian language and literature; Spanish language and literature; accounting; anthropology; art history, criticism and conservation; biology, general; business communications; chemistry; computer and information sciences, general; drama/theater arts, general; economics; environmental science/studies; geography; health system/health services administration; history; journalism; journalism and mass communications; mathematical statistics; mathematics, other; music; oceanography; parks, recreation and leisure studies; philosophy; philosophy and religion; physics; sociology.
**Non-credit—**foreign languages and literatures; nursing.

### Special Note

The Friday Center for Continuing Education at the University of North Carolina at Chapel Hill has offered distance education opportunities since 1913. Currently, 3 distance education programs that offer college-level courses for academic credit are available. Independent Studies is a print-based correspondence program offering more than 120 courses. Students may enroll at any time of year, work independently with their instructors, and have up to 9 months to complete their courses. Carolina Courses Online offers nearly 40 courses over the Internet. Courses offered through this program are based on the traditional semester schedule, and many of the courses can be taken during the summer months. Students work in classes of approximately 25 and communicate with each other and their instructor via e-mail and discussion forums. Self-paced Study Online also delivers courses over the Internet but with flexible scheduling, similar to Independent Studies. Students can enroll at any time of year and work independently with their instructor. In each of these programs, students work with course materials prepared under the direction of academic departments at UNC-CH; content, instruction, and quality are comparable to classroom courses. At the present time, an entire online degree program is not available, but the courses offered through these programs can be used toward degrees earned at UNC-CH and at other institutions. Founded in 1793, the University of North Carolina at Chapel Hill is the oldest public university in the United States, and its commitment to outreach and public service dates back to its earliest days.

# THE UNIVERSITY OF NORTH CAROLINA AT CHARLOTTE

*Continuing Education, Extension and Summer Programs*

9201 University City Boulevard
Charlotte, NC 28223
**Contact:** Ms. Diane M. Locklin, Senior Program Manager
**Phone:** 704-687-4457
**Fax:** 704-687-3158
**Web:** http://www.uncc.edu/disted
**E-mail:** dmlockli@email.uncc.edu

**ACCREDITATION:** Southern Association of Colleges and Schools

**INSTITUTIONALLY ADMINISTERED FINANCIAL AID:** Yes

### DEGREE OR CERTIFICATE PROGRAMS OFFERED

**Undergraduate—***BSET:* Engineering Technology; Fire Science. *BSN:* RN/BSN Completion Program.

# THE UNIVERSITY OF NORTH CAROLINA AT GREENSBORO

*Division of Continual Learning and Summer Session*

1100 West Market Street, 3rd Floor, PO Box 26170
Greensboro, NC 27402-6170

**Contact:** William H. Taylor, Director of Distance Learning and Professional Development
**Phone:** 336-334-5414
**Fax:** 336-334-5628
**Web:** http://www.uncg.edu/dcl
**E-mail:** whtaylor@uncg.edu

**ACCREDITATION:** Southern Association of Colleges and Schools
**INSTITUTIONALLY ADMINISTERED FINANCIAL AID:** Yes

eCollege.com *www.ecollege.com*

## DEGREE OR CERTIFICATE PROGRAMS OFFERED

**Undergraduate—BS:** Birth-Kindergarten Teacher Licensure; Community Health Education. **BSN:** Nursing. **License:** Add-on Teacher Licensure in Special Education.
**Graduate—MA:** Liberal Studies. **MEd:** Curriculum and Instruction; School Administration; Special Education (Cross-Categorical Emphasis). **MLIS:** Library and Information Studies. **MSN:** Nursing.

## NON-DEGREE-RELATED COURSE TOPICS OFFERED

**Undergraduate—**American (United States) history; English language and literature/letters, other; astronomy; chemistry; family and community studies; fine arts and art studies; geological and related sciences; philosophy; religion/religious studies; sociology.
**Graduate—**English as a second language; French language and literature; Latin language and literature (ancient and medieval); Spanish language and literature; business administration and management; curriculum and instruction; fine arts and art studies; historic preservation, conservation and architectural history; information sciences and systems; liberal arts and sciences, general studies and humanities; library science, other; special education; teaching English as a second language/foreign language.
**Non-credit—**English creative writing; ethnic and cultural studies; liberal arts and sciences, general studies and humanities; library science, other; multi/interdisciplinary studies, other; romance languages and literatures.

# THE UNIVERSITY OF NORTH CAROLINA AT PEMBROKE

## The Interactive Video Facility

1 University Drive
Pembroke, NC 28372
**Contact:** Miss Emily Autumn Love, Interactive Video Facility Manager
**Phone:** 910-521-6563
**Fax:** 910-521-6564
**Web:** http://www.uncp.edu/ivf
**E-mail:** emily.love@uncp.edu

**ACCREDITATION:** Southern Association of Colleges and Schools
**INSTITUTIONALLY ADMINISTERED FINANCIAL AID:** Yes

## DEGREE OR CERTIFICATE PROGRAMS OFFERED

Programs offered do not lead to a degree or other formal award.

## NON-DEGREE-RELATED COURSE TOPICS OFFERED

**Undergraduate—**agricultural and food products processing; agricultural business and management; agriculture/agricultural sciences; business; business and personal services marketing operations; economics; forestry and related sciences.

**Graduate—**business.

# UNIVERSITY OF NORTH DAKOTA

## Division of Continuing Education

Extended Degree Programs, Box 9021
Grand Forks, ND 58202-9021
**Contact:** Lynette Krenelka, Program Director
**Phone:** 877-450-1842
**Fax:** 701-777-4282
**Web:** http://www.conted.und.edu
**E-mail:** lynette_krenelka@mail.und.nodak.edu

**ACCREDITATION:** North Central Association of Colleges and Schools
**INSTITUTIONALLY ADMINISTERED FINANCIAL AID:** Yes

## DEGREE OR CERTIFICATE PROGRAMS OFFERED

**Undergraduate—BS:** Chemical Engineering; Electrical Engineering; Mechanical Engineering.
**Graduate—MBA:** Business Administration. **MEd:** Education Leadership; Special Education. **MPA:** Public Administration. **MS:** Elementary Education; General Studies (Secondary Education); Rural Health Nursing; Space Studies. **MSW:** Social Work.
**Postgraduate and doctoral—PhD:** Higher Education.

## NON-DEGREE-RELATED COURSE TOPICS OFFERED

**Undergraduate—**accounting; biology, general; business administration and management; chemical engineering; chemistry; electrical, electronics and communication engineering; engineering mechanics; geography; industrial and organizational psychology; library science, other; mechanical engineering; physics; social work.
**Graduate—**education, other; social work.

# UNIVERSITY OF NORTHERN COLORADO

## Center for Professional Development

Campus Box 21, Candelaria 1281
Greeley, CO 80639
**Contact:** Receptionist
**Phone:** 800-232-1749
**Fax:** 970-351-2519
**Web:** http://www.unco.edu/center
**E-mail:** front.deskcpdo@exchange.unco.edu

**ACCREDITATION:** North Central Association of Colleges and Schools
**INSTITUTIONALLY ADMINISTERED FINANCIAL AID:** Yes

eCollege.com *www.ecollege.com*

## DEGREE OR CERTIFICATE PROGRAMS OFFERED

**Undergraduate—BS:** Nursing (RN to BSN). **Internship Certificate:** Dietetics.
**Graduate—Graduate Certificate:** Gerontology. **MA:** Communication Disorders, Speech-Language Pathology; Special Education, Moderate Needs Emphasis; Special Education, Severe Needs Vision Emphasis.

## NON-DEGREE-RELATED COURSE TOPICS OFFERED

**Undergraduate**—biology, general; communication disorders sciences and services; community health services; economics; geography; geological and related sciences; gerontology; health and medical administrative services; health professions and related sciences, other; human services; mathematics; nursing; political science and government; rehabilitation/therapeutic services; special education.

**Graduate**—education, other.

# UNIVERSITY OF NORTHERN IOWA

## Division of Continuing Education

Credit Programs, 124 SHC
Cedar Falls, IA 50614-0223
**Contact:** Kent Johnson, Associate Director
**Phone:** 319-273-5970
**Fax:** 319-273-2872
**Web:** http://www.uni.edu/contined/gcs
**E-mail:** kent.johnson@uni.edu

**ACCREDITATION:** North Central Association of Colleges and Schools
**INSTITUTIONALLY ADMINISTERED FINANCIAL AID:** No

## DEGREE OR CERTIFICATE PROGRAMS OFFERED

**Undergraduate**—*BLS:* Liberal Studies.

## NON-DEGREE-RELATED COURSE TOPICS OFFERED

**Undergraduate**—accounting; business marketing and marketing management; developmental and child psychology; educational psychology; social psychology; social work; sociology.

**Graduate**—developmental and child psychology; educational psychology; social work; sociology.

# UNIVERSITY OF NORTH FLORIDA

4567 St. Johns Bluff Road, South
Jacksonville, FL 32224-2465
**Contact:** Dr. Dennis Gayle, Associate Vice President for Academic Affairs
**Phone:** 904-620-2700
**Fax:** 904-620-2787
**Web:** http://www.unf.edu/
**E-mail:** dgayle@unf.edu

**ACCREDITATION:** Southern Association of Colleges and Schools
**INSTITUTIONALLY ADMINISTERED FINANCIAL AID:** Yes

## DEGREE OR CERTIFICATE PROGRAMS OFFERED

**Programs offered do not lead to a degree or other formal award.**

## NON-DEGREE-RELATED COURSE TOPICS OFFERED

**Undergraduate**—computer and information sciences, general; curriculum and instruction; health professions and related sciences, other; nursing; sociology.

**Graduate**—curriculum and instruction; health professions and related sciences, other; human services; special education.

# UNIVERSITY OF NORTH TEXAS

## Center for Distributed Learning

PO Box 311277
Denton, TX 76203-1277
**Contact:** Marcilla Collinsworth, Director of Admissions
**Phone:** 800-UNT-8211
**Fax:** 940-565-2408
**Web:** http://courses.unt.edu
**E-mail:** marcilla@acad.admin.unt.edu

**ACCREDITATION:** Southern Association of Colleges and Schools
**INSTITUTIONALLY ADMINISTERED FINANCIAL AID:** Yes

## DEGREE OR CERTIFICATE PROGRAMS OFFERED

**Undergraduate**—*Certificate:* Library and Information Sciences. *Endorsement:* Gifted and Talented Education.

**Graduate**—*Graduate Certificate:* Applied Gerontology; Behavior Analysis. *MLS:* Library Science. *MS:* Applied Gerontology; Computer Education and Cognitive Systems; Criminal Justice; Hospitality Management; Information Sciences; Merchandising.

## NON-DEGREE-RELATED COURSE TOPICS OFFERED

**Undergraduate**—English technical and business writing; anthropology; apparel and accessories marketing operations; art history, criticism and conservation; business administration and management; business marketing and marketing management; clothing/apparel and textile studies; computer and information sciences, general; computer software and media applications; computer/information technology administration and management; criminal justice and corrections; curriculum and instruction; data entry/microcomputer applications; developmental and child psychology; economics; educational/instructional media design; electrical and electronic engineering-related technology; engineering-related technologies, other; family and community studies; family/consumer resource management; food products retailing and wholesaling operations; food sciences and technology; health and physical education/fitness; history; history and philosophy of science and technology; hospitality and recreation marketing operations; hospitality services management; journalism and mass communications; library science, other; library science/librarianship; marketing management and research; mathematics; miscellaneous engineering-related technologies; music; psychology, other; public administration; social sciences, general; social work; special education.

**Graduate**—apparel and accessories marketing operations; business administration and management; business marketing and marketing management; chemistry; clothing/apparel and textile studies; communications technologies; community organization, resources and services; computer and information sciences, general; computer software and media applications; criminal justice and corrections; curriculum and instruction; education administration and supervision; education, general; education, other; educational evaluation, research and statistics; educational psychology; educational/instructional media design; electrical and electronic engineering-related technology; family and community studies; family/consumer resource management; food sciences and technology; gerontology; health and medical administrative services; hospitality and recreation marketing operations; hospitality services management; human resources management; industrial and organizational psychology; information sciences and systems; library science, other; library science/librarianship; rehabilitation/therapeutic services; social and philosophical foundations of education; social sciences, general; special education.

# UNIVERSITY OF NORTHWESTERN OHIO

## Division of Distance Learning

1441 North Cable Road
Lima, OH 45805
**Contact:** Mr. Rick Morrison, Director of Admissions
**Phone:** 419-227-3141
**Fax:** 419-226-6926
**Web:** http://www.unoh.edu
**E-mail:** morris_r@unoh.edu

**ACCREDITATION:** North Central Association of Colleges and Schools

### DEGREE OR CERTIFICATE PROGRAMS OFFERED

**Undergraduate—*AAB:*** Accounting; Agribusiness; Automotive Management; Business Administration; Information Systems Technology; Legal Assisting; Marketing; Marketing, Management and Technology; Medical Assistant Technology; Secretarial (Administrative, Legal, Medical); Travel Management; Word Processing-Administrative Support. ***BS:*** Accounting; Business Administration; Health Care Administration.

### NON-DEGREE-RELATED COURSE TOPICS OFFERED

**Undergraduate—**American (United States) history; English composition; accounting; advertising; agricultural economics; business marketing and marketing management; geography; international business; law and legal studies, other; mathematical statistics; mathematics, other; philosophy and religion; sociology.

# UNIVERSITY OF NOTRE DAME

## Executive Programs

126 Mendoza College of Business
Notre Dame, IN 46556
**Contact:** Leo Burke, Associate Dean and Director of Executive Education
**Phone:** 800-631-3622
**Fax:** 219-631-6783
**Web:** http://executive.nd.edu
**E-mail:** burke.77@nd.edu

**ACCREDITATION:** North Central Association of Colleges and Schools
**INSTITUTIONALLY ADMINISTERED FINANCIAL AID:** Yes

### DEGREE OR CERTIFICATE PROGRAMS OFFERED

**Graduate—*MBA:*** EMBA (Chicago-based); EMBA (South Bend-based).

### NON-DEGREE-RELATED COURSE TOPICS OFFERED

**Graduate—**accounting; business; business administration and management; business communications; business management and administrative services, other; business quantitative methods and management science; business/managerial economics; economics; financial management and services; marketing operations/marketing and distribution, other; mathematical statistics; taxation.
**Non-credit—**accounting; business; business administration and management; business communications; business management and administrative services, other; business quantitative methods and management science; business/managerial economics; economics; financial manage-

ment and services; marketing management and research; marketing operations/marketing and distribution, other; mathematical statistics; taxation.

See full description on page 616.

# UNIVERSITY OF OKLAHOMA

## College of Continuing Education

1700 Asp Avenue
Norman, OK 73072
**Contact:** Larry D. Hayes, Information Assistant for Office of the Vice President for University Outreach and College of Continuing Education
**Phone:** 800-522-0772 Ext. 4414
**Fax:** 405-325-7196
**Web:** http://www.occe.ou.edu
**E-mail:** lhayes@ou.edu

**ACCREDITATION:** North Central Association of Colleges and Schools

### DEGREE OR CERTIFICATE PROGRAMS OFFERED

**Graduate—*MA:*** Advanced Programs.

### NON-DEGREE-RELATED COURSE TOPICS OFFERED

**Undergraduate—**English composition; anthropology; astronomy; business administration and management; business communications; chemistry; communications, general; dramatic/theater arts and stagecraft; economics; education, general; engineering, general; financial management and services; geography; geological and related sciences; health and physical education/fitness; history; journalism and mass communications; library science, other; marketing management and research; mathematics; philosophy; political science and government; sociology.
**Graduate—**communications, general; economics; education administration and supervision; education, other; educational psychology; human resources management; public administration; social work.

See full description on page 618.

# UNIVERSITY OF OREGON

## Distance Education

1277 University of Oregon
Eugene, OR 97403-1277
**Contact:** Sandra Gladney, Program Coordinator
**Phone:** 541-346-4231
**Fax:** 541-346-3545
**Web:** http://de.uoregon.edu
**E-mail:** dasst@continue.uoregon.edu

**ACCREDITATION:** Northwest Association of Schools and Colleges

eCollege.com www.ecollege.com

### DEGREE OR CERTIFICATE PROGRAMS OFFERED

**Graduate—*MS:*** Applied Information Management.

### NON-DEGREE-RELATED COURSE TOPICS OFFERED

**Undergraduate—**English language and literature, general; astronomy; economics; geological and related sciences; oceanography; physics; political science and government; visual and performing arts, other.

**Graduate**—information sciences and systems; management information systems and business data processing, general.

**See full description on page 620.**

# UNIVERSITY OF PENNSYLVANIA
## Distance Education

PennAdvance Program, College of General Studies, 3440 Market Street, Suite 100
Philadelphia, PA 19104-3335
**Contact:** Ms. Colleen Gasiorowski, Admissions Coordinator
**Phone:** 215-898-1684
**Fax:** 215-573-2053
**Web:** http://www.upenn.edu/schools_prog/distance.html
**E-mail:** gasiorow@sas.upenn.edu

**ACCREDITATION:** Middle States Association of Colleges and Schools
**INSTITUTIONALLY ADMINISTERED FINANCIAL AID:** Yes

eCollege.com  *www.ecollege.com*

### DEGREE OR CERTIFICATE PROGRAMS OFFERED
**Graduate**—*MN:* Masters in Nursing. *MSE:* Telecommunications.

### NON-DEGREE-RELATED COURSE TOPICS OFFERED
**Undergraduate**—English composition; English creative writing; English literature (British and Commonwealth); anthropology; biological and physical sciences; cell and molecular biology; dramatic/theater arts and stagecraft; economics; fine arts and art studies; geological and related sciences; liberal arts and sciences, general studies and humanities; mathematical statistics; mathematics; physics; psychology.
**Graduate**—educational/instructional media design; electrical, electronics and communications engineering; environmental/environmental health engineering; fine arts and art studies; nursing; systems engineering; telecommunications.
**Non-credit**—English composition; English creative writing; business; dentistry (D.D.S., D.M.D.); electrical, electronics and communications engineering; systems engineering; telecommunications.

**See full description on page 622.**

# UNIVERSITY OF PHOENIX
## University of Phoenix Online

3157 East Elwood Street
Phoenix, AZ 85034
**Contact:** Mr. Larry Etherington, Director of Marketing
**Phone:** 800-366-9699
**Fax:** 602-735-9632
**Web:** http://www.uoponline.com
**E-mail:** larry.etherington@phoenix.edu

**ACCREDITATION:** North Central Association of Colleges and Schools
**INSTITUTIONALLY ADMINISTERED FINANCIAL AID:** Yes

### DEGREE OR CERTIFICATE PROGRAMS OFFERED
**Undergraduate**—*BS:* Business Accounting; Business Administration; Business Management; Business Marketing; E-Business; Information Technology; Management; Nursing.

**Graduate**—*MA:* Education/Curriculum and Instruction; Education/Curriculum and Technology; Education/E-Education; Organizational Management. *MBA:* Accounting; Business Administration; E-Business; Global Management; Health Care Management; Technology Management. *MS:* Computer Information Systems; Nursing.

### NON-DEGREE-RELATED COURSE TOPICS OFFERED
**Undergraduate**—accounting; business marketing and marketing management.
**Graduate**—accounting; business marketing and marketing management; international business; management information systems and business data processing, general; organizational behavior studies.
**Non-credit**—business; business administration and management; business communications; business management and administrative services, other; financial management and services; human resources management; international business; marketing management and research; miscellaneous health professions.

**See full description on page 624.**

# UNIVERSITY OF PITTSBURGH
## Office of Extended Education

College of General Studies, 451 Cathedral of Learning, Fifth Avenue
Pittsburgh, PA 15260
**Contact:** Ms. Mary Hanlon, Student Support Services
**Phone:** 412-624-7206
**Fax:** 412-624-3836
**Web:** http://www.pitt.edu/
**E-mail:** reg5@cgs.pitt.edu

**ACCREDITATION:** Middle States Association of Colleges and Schools
**INSTITUTIONALLY ADMINISTERED FINANCIAL AID:** Yes

### DEGREE OR CERTIFICATE PROGRAMS OFFERED
**Undergraduate**—*BA:* Humanities; Social Sciences.
**Graduate**—*MBA:* Business Administration. *MEd:* Elementary Education.

### NON-DEGREE-RELATED COURSE TOPICS OFFERED
**Undergraduate**—English composition; anthropology; educational psychology; mathematical statistics; philosophy and religion.
**Graduate**—curriculum and instruction.

### Special Note

University of Pittsburgh, accredited by the Middle States Association of Colleges and Schools, is a state-related university founded in 1787, with distance learning since 1972. Through more than 150 distance learning courses with minimal on-campus requirements, students can earn a Bachelor of Arts in administration of justice, humanities, or social sciences. In fall 2000, 1,200 students were enrolled in courses offered at a distance from the University. Distance learners earn degree credit equivalent to on-campus courses using course materials designed specifically for the program by University faculty members. These distance learning courses are delivered via the World Wide Web, videotapes, interactive television, computer software, and print materials from the main campus in Pittsburgh and from the 4 branch campuses located in Bradford, Greensburg, Johnstown, and Titusville. Students and faculty members may meet in person or contact each other via mail, telephone, fax, e-mail, interactive television, or the World Wide Web. For more information, students should call 412-624-7210 or visit the Web site at http://www.pitt.edu/~~~cgs/.

---

# UNIVERSITY OF PITTSBURGH AT JOHNSTOWN

114 Blackington Hall
Johnstown, PA 15904
**Contact:** Mrs. Judith Freedman, Coordinator of Distance Education and Professional Development
**Phone:** 814-269-2099
**Fax:** 814-269-7075
**Web:** http://www.upj.pitt.edu
**E-mail:** jfreedma@pitt.edu

**ACCREDITATION:** Middle States Association of Colleges and Schools
**INSTITUTIONALLY ADMINISTERED FINANCIAL AID:** Yes

### DEGREE OR CERTIFICATE PROGRAMS OFFERED
Programs offered do not lead to a degree or other formal award.

### NON-DEGREE-RELATED COURSE TOPICS OFFERED
**Graduate**—nursing.

# UNIVERSITY OF RICHMOND
### School of Continuing Studies
Emergency Management Degree Program
Richmond, VA 23173
**Contact:** Dr. Walter G. Green, III, Assistant Professor of Emergency Management
**Phone:** 804-287-1246
**Fax:** 804-289-8138
**Web:** http://www.richmond.edu/~contstud/
**E-mail:** wgreen@richmond.edu

**ACCREDITATION:** Southern Association of Colleges and Schools
**INSTITUTIONALLY ADMINISTERED FINANCIAL AID:** Yes

### DEGREE OR CERTIFICATE PROGRAMS OFFERED
Programs offered do not lead to a degree or other formal award.

# UNIVERSITY OF ST. AUGUSTINE FOR HEALTH SCIENCES
### Division of Distance Education
1 University Boulevard
St. Augustine, FL 32086
**Contact:** Dr. Richard Jensen, Dean of Division of Advanced Studies
**Phone:** 904-826-0084 Ext. 262
**Fax:** 904-826-0085
**Web:** http://www.usa.edu

**E-mail:** info@usa.edu
**ACCREDITATION:** Distance Education and Training Council
**INSTITUTIONALLY ADMINISTERED FINANCIAL AID:** Yes

### DEGREE OR CERTIFICATE PROGRAMS OFFERED
**Graduate—MS:** Health Science (MHSc).
**Postgraduate and doctoral—DPT:** Transitional Doctor of Physical Therapy. **PhD:** Health Science (DHSc).

### NON-DEGREE-RELATED COURSE TOPICS OFFERED
**Graduate**—occupational therapy; physical therapy.
**Non-credit**—health professions and related sciences, other.

# UNIVERSITY OF ST. FRANCIS
500 North Wilcox Street
Joliet, IL 60435
**Contact:** Charles M. Beutel, Registrar
**Phone:** 815-740-3391
**Fax:** 815-740-5084
**Web:** http://www.stfrancis.edu/
**E-mail:** cbeutel@stfrancis.edu

**ACCREDITATION:** North Central Association of Colleges and Schools
**INSTITUTIONALLY ADMINISTERED FINANCIAL AID:** Yes

### DEGREE OR CERTIFICATE PROGRAMS OFFERED
**Undergraduate—BS:** Health Arts; Professional Arts.
**Graduate—MBA:** Business. **MHSA:** Health Services. **MSM:** Business Management.

### NON-DEGREE-RELATED COURSE TOPICS OFFERED
**Undergraduate**—business; health professions and related sciences, other.
**Graduate**—business administration and management; health system/health services administration.

See full description on page 626.

# UNIVERSITY OF SAINT FRANCIS
2701 Spring Street
Fort Wayne, IN 46763
**Contact:** Dr. Carla L. Mueller, Director of Distance Education and Online Curriculum Development
**Phone:** 219-434-3257
**Fax:** 219-434-7601
**Web:** http://www.sf.edu/
**E-mail:** cmueller@sf.edu

**ACCREDITATION:** North Central Association of Colleges and Schools
**INSTITUTIONALLY ADMINISTERED FINANCIAL AID:** Yes

### DEGREE OR CERTIFICATE PROGRAMS OFFERED
**Graduate—MSN:** Nursing.

### NON-DEGREE-RELATED COURSE TOPICS OFFERED
**Undergraduate**—nursing.
**Graduate**—nursing.

# UNIVERSITY OF ST. THOMAS

School of Continuing Studies, Mail #5002, 2115 Summit Avenue
St. Paul, MN 55105
**Contact:** Dr. Gene Scapanksi, Dean
**Phone:** 651-962-5959
**Fax:** 651-962-5965
**Web:** http://www.stthomas.edu/scs
**E-mail:** gascapanski@stthomas.edu

**ACCREDITATION:** North Central Association of Colleges and Schools

**INSTITUTIONALLY ADMINISTERED FINANCIAL AID:** Yes

## DEGREE OR CERTIFICATE PROGRAMS OFFERED
Programs offered do not lead to a degree or other formal award.

## NON-DEGREE-RELATED COURSE TOPICS OFFERED
**Undergraduate**—Germanic languages and literatures; music; philosophy; sociology.

# UNIVERSITY OF SARASOTA

*Enrollment Management*

5250 17th Street
Sarasota, FL 34235
**Contact:** Ms. Linda Volz, Director of Admissions
**Phone:** 941-379-0404 Ext. 222
**Fax:** 941-379-5964
**Web:** http://www.sarasota.edu/
**E-mail:** linda_volz@embanet.com

**ACCREDITATION:** Southern Association of Colleges and Schools

## DEGREE OR CERTIFICATE PROGRAMS OFFERED
**Undergraduate**—*BSBA:* Business Administration. *Certificate:* Business Areas.
**Graduate**—*MBA:* Business Administration. *MBA-EP:* Accounting; Information Systems; International Business; Management; Marketing. *MCRP/MPA:* Education.
**Postgraduate and doctoral**—*EdD:* Counseling Psychology; Higher Education Administration; Pastoral Community Counseling.

## NON-DEGREE-RELATED COURSE TOPICS OFFERED
**Graduate**—business marketing and marketing management; curriculum and instruction; finance, general; health system/health services administration; international business; management information systems and business data processing, general.

# UNIVERSITY OF SASKATCHEWAN

*Extension Credit Studies*

117 Science Place, Kirk Hall, Room 330
Saskatoon, SK S7N 5C8, Canada
**Contact:** Ms. Grace Milashenko, Independent Studies Coordinator
**Phone:** 306-966-5562
**Fax:** 306-966-5590
**Web:** http://www.extension.usask.ca

**E-mail:** grace.milashenko@usask.ca

**ACCREDITATION:** Provincially Chartered

**INSTITUTIONALLY ADMINISTERED FINANCIAL AID:** No

## DEGREE OR CERTIFICATE PROGRAMS OFFERED
Programs offered do not lead to a degree or other formal award.

## NON-DEGREE-RELATED COURSE TOPICS OFFERED
**Undergraduate**—English language and literature, general; English literature (British and Commonwealth); adult and continuing teacher education; agriculture/agricultural sciences; anthropology; archaeology; computer science; curriculum and instruction; economics; geography; geological and related sciences; history; philosophy; political science and government; psychology; religion/religious studies; sociology.
**Non-credit**—English as a second language; agricultural business and management; agricultural business and production, other; botany; education, other; educational/instructional media design; horticulture services operations and management; landscape architecture; soil sciences; teaching English as a second language/foreign language.

# UNIVERSITY OF SCIENCE AND ARTS OF OKLAHOMA

PO Box 82345
Chickasha, OK 73018
**Contact:** Dr. Alan D. Todd, Director of Instructional Technology
**Phone:** 405-574-1277
**Fax:** 405-574-1396
**Web:** http://www.usao.edu/
**E-mail:** factoddad@usao.edu

**ACCREDITATION:** North Central Association of Colleges and Schools

**INSTITUTIONALLY ADMINISTERED FINANCIAL AID:** Yes

## DEGREE OR CERTIFICATE PROGRAMS OFFERED
Programs offered do not lead to a degree or other formal award.

## NON-DEGREE-RELATED COURSE TOPICS OFFERED
**Undergraduate**—mathematics, other.

# UNIVERSITY OF SIOUX FALLS

1101 West 22nd Street, Jorden Hall
Sioux Falls, SD 57105
**Contact:** Dr. Kirby D. Wilcoxson, Senior Vice President of Academic Affairs
**Phone:** 605-331-6675
**Fax:** 605-331-6615
**Web:** http://www.usiouxfalls.edu/
**E-mail:** kirby.wilcoxson@usiouxfalls.edu

**ACCREDITATION:** North Central Association of Colleges and Schools

**INSTITUTIONALLY ADMINISTERED FINANCIAL AID:** Yes

eCollege.com  *www.ecollege.com*

## DEGREE OR CERTIFICATE PROGRAMS OFFERED

Programs offered do not lead to a degree or other formal award.

## NON-DEGREE-RELATED COURSE TOPICS OFFERED

**Undergraduate**—fine arts and art studies; geography; health and physical education/fitness; history; sociology.
**Graduate**—education administration and supervision; educational evaluation, research and statistics.

# UNIVERSITY OF SOUTH ALABAMA

## USA Online

75 North University Boulevard, UCOM 3600
Mobile, AL 36688-0002
**Contact:** Dr. Thomas L. Chilton, Associate Dean of Education
**Phone:** 334-380-2738
**Fax:** 334-380-2748
**Web:** http://usaonline.southalabama.edu
**E-mail:** tchilton@usamail.usouthal.edu

**ACCREDITATION:** Southern Association of Colleges and Schools

**INSTITUTIONALLY ADMINISTERED FINANCIAL AID:** Yes

eCollege.com www.ecollege.com

## DEGREE OR CERTIFICATE PROGRAMS OFFERED

**Undergraduate**—*BSN:* Nursing. *Certification:* Educational Administration.
**Graduate**—*MBA:* General. *MEd:* Educational Leadership; Educational Media (Library Media); Special Education (Gifted). *MS:* Instructional Design and Development.

## NON-DEGREE-RELATED COURSE TOPICS OFFERED

**Graduate**—accounting; business administration and management; education administration and supervision; educational psychology; educational/instructional media design; finance, general; special education.

See full description on page 628.

# UNIVERSITY OF SOUTH CAROLINA

## Department of Distance Education and Instructional Support

Independent Learning Program, 915 Gregg Street
Columbia, SC 29208
**Contact:** Ms. Robin Dandridge, Independent Learning Coordinator
**Phone:** 803-777-6285
**Fax:** 803-777-6264
**Web:** http://www.sc.edu/deis/student.services
**E-mail:** rdandrid@gwm.sc.edu

**ACCREDITATION:** Southern Association of Colleges and Schools

**INSTITUTIONALLY ADMINISTERED FINANCIAL AID:** Yes

## DEGREE OR CERTIFICATE PROGRAMS OFFERED

**Graduate**—*MBA:* Business Administration. *ME:* Chemical Engineering; Civil and Environmental Engineering; Computer Engineering; Electrical Engineering; Mechanical Engineering. *MLIS:* Library and Information Sciences. *MS:* Chemical Engineering; Civil and Environmental Engineering; Computer Engineering; Electrical Engineering; Mechanical Engineering.
**Postgraduate and doctoral**—*PhD:* Chemical Engineering; Computer Engineering; Electrical Engineering; Mechanical Engineering.

## NON-DEGREE-RELATED COURSE TOPICS OFFERED

**Undergraduate**—English language and literature, general; English technical and business writing; accounting; astronomy; business administration and management; economics; financial management and services; foreign languages and literatures; geography; health professions and related sciences, other; history; international relations and affairs; marketing operations/marketing and distribution, other; mathematics; music; philosophy; psychology; social work; sociology.

# UNIVERSITY OF SOUTH CAROLINA SPARTANBURG

800 University Way
Spartanburg, SC 29303-4999
**Contact:** Andrew Tate Crosland, Associate Vice Chancellor
**Phone:** 864-503-5285
**Fax:** 864-503-5262
**Web:** http://www.uscs.edu/
**E-mail:** acrosland@gw.uscs.edu

**ACCREDITATION:** Southern Association of Colleges and Schools

**INSTITUTIONALLY ADMINISTERED FINANCIAL AID:** Yes

## DEGREE OR CERTIFICATE PROGRAMS OFFERED

**Undergraduate**—*BSN:* Baccalaureate Nursing.
**Graduate**—*MCL:* Nursing.

## NON-DEGREE-RELATED COURSE TOPICS OFFERED

**Undergraduate**—English language and literature, general; business; education, general; geography; nursing; political science and government.
**Graduate**—education, general.

# UNIVERSITY OF SOUTH CAROLINA SUMTER

200 Miller Road
Sumter, SC 29150
**Contact:** Dr. Robert Ferrell, Director of Admissions
**Phone:** 803-938-3762
**Fax:** 803-775-2180
**Web:** http://www.uscsumter.edu/
**E-mail:** bobf@uscsumter.edu

**ACCREDITATION:** Southern Association of Colleges and Schools

**INSTITUTIONALLY ADMINISTERED FINANCIAL AID:** No

## DEGREE OR CERTIFICATE PROGRAMS OFFERED

Programs offered do not lead to a degree or other formal award.

## NON-DEGREE-RELATED COURSE TOPICS OFFERED

**Undergraduate**—American literature (United States); community health services; education administration and supervision; education, general;

educational evaluation, research and statistics; engineering, general; history; hospitality and recreation marketing operations; hospitality services management; public administration; public health.

# UNIVERSITY OF SOUTH DAKOTA

## State-Wide Educational Services

414 East Clark Street
Vermillion, SD 57069
**Contact:** State-Wide Educational Services
**Phone:** 800-233-7937
**Fax:** 605-677-6118
**Web:** http://www.usd.edu/
**E-mail:** swes@usd.edu

**ACCREDITATION:** North Central Association of Colleges and Schools
**INSTITUTIONALLY ADMINISTERED FINANCIAL AID:** Yes

### DEGREE OR CERTIFICATE PROGRAMS OFFERED
Undergraduate—*AA:* General Studies.

### NON-DEGREE-RELATED COURSE TOPICS OFFERED
Undergraduate—English composition; accounting; art history, criticism and conservation; biology, general; communications, general; comparative literature; criminal justice and corrections; drama/theater arts, general; educational/instructional media design; film/cinema studies; geography; history; journalism and mass communication, other; mathematical statistics; mathematics, other; nursing; political science and government; sociology.
Graduate—criminal justice and corrections; education administration and supervision; education, other; technology education/industrial arts.
Non-credit—real estate.

# UNIVERSITY OF SOUTHERN COLORADO

## Division of Continuing Education

2200 Bonforte Boulevard
Pueblo, CO 81001-4901
**Contact:** Joanna Ponce, Assistant Program Manager
**Phone:** 877-872-9653
**Fax:** 719-549-2438
**Web:** http://www.uscolo.edu/

**ACCREDITATION:** North Central Association of Colleges and Schools
**INSTITUTIONALLY ADMINISTERED FINANCIAL AID:** Yes

### DEGREE OR CERTIFICATE PROGRAMS OFFERED
Undergraduate—*BS:* Social Sciences. *Certificate:* Paralegal Studies.
**See full description on page 630.**

# UNIVERSITY OF SOUTHERN INDIANA

## Distance Education Programming

8600 University Boulevard
Evansville, IN 47712

**Contact:** Dr. Saxon Reasons, Programming Manager, Instructional Technology Services
**Phone:** 800-813-4238
**Fax:** 812-465-7131
**Web:** http://www.usi.edu/distance
**E-mail:** saxrea@usi.edu

**ACCREDITATION:** North Central Association of Colleges and Schools
**INSTITUTIONALLY ADMINISTERED FINANCIAL AID:** Yes

### DEGREE OR CERTIFICATE PROGRAMS OFFERED
Undergraduate—*AS:* Communications. *BS:* Health Professions and Related Sciences. *BSN:* Nursing.
Graduate—*MSN:* Nursing.

### NON-DEGREE-RELATED COURSE TOPICS OFFERED
Undergraduate—English composition; English language and literature, general; English literature (British and Commonwealth); advertising; biology, general; communications, general; computer/information technology administration and management; dental services; economics; educational psychology; environmental science/studies; foreign languages and literatures; general teacher education; gerontology; health and medical administrative services; journalism; journalism and mass communication, other; journalism and mass communications; nursing; political science and government; psychology; public relations and organizational communications; radio and television broadcasting; speech and rhetorical studies; visual and performing arts.
Graduate—economics; health professions and related sciences, other; marketing management and research; nursing; social work.
Non-credit—entrepreneurship; human resources management.

# UNIVERSITY OF SOUTHERN MISSISSIPPI

## Department of Continuing Education

Box 5055
Hattiesburg, MS 39406-5055
**Contact:** Ms. Sue Pace, Director
**Phone:** 601-266-4210
**Fax:** 601-266-5839
**Web:** http://www.cice.usm.edu/ce/
**E-mail:** sue.pace@usm.edu

**ACCREDITATION:** Southern Association of Colleges and Schools
**INSTITUTIONALLY ADMINISTERED FINANCIAL AID:** No

### DEGREE OR CERTIFICATE PROGRAMS OFFERED
Programs offered do not lead to a degree or other formal award.

### NON-DEGREE-RELATED COURSE TOPICS OFFERED
Undergraduate—English creative writing; accounting; anthropology; biology, general; business marketing and marketing management; community health services; criminology; electrical, electronics and communication engineering; geography; management information systems and business data processing, general; mathematics, other; medical genetics; philosophy and religion; sociology.
Graduate—biochemistry and biophysics; cognitive psychology and psycholinguistics; community health services; construction/building technology; consumer and homemaking education; criminal justice and corrections; curriculum and instruction; demography/population studies;

economics; educational evaluation, research and statistics; family and community studies; geography; health and physical education/fitness; individual and family development studies; mathematical statistics; nursing; parks, recreation, leisure and fitness studies, other; public health; social and philosophical foundations of education; social work; special education.

**Non-credit**—communications, general; health and medical administrative services; health and medical assistants; health and medical preparatory programs; tourism and travel services marketing operations.

# THE UNIVERSITY OF TENNESSEE

## Department of Distance Education and Independent Study

1534 White Avenue
Knoxville, TN 37996
**Contact:** Mr. Brad Fox, Assistant Director for Learner Services
**Phone:** 865-974-5087
**Fax:** 865-974-4684
**Web:** http://anywhere.tennessee.edu
**E-mail:** fox@outreach.utk.edu

**ACCREDITATION:** Southern Association of Colleges and Schools
**INSTITUTIONALLY ADMINISTERED FINANCIAL AID:** Yes

### DEGREE OR CERTIFICATE PROGRAMS OFFERED

**Undergraduate**—*Technical Certificate:* Internet Database Mastery.
**Graduate**—*EMBA:* Physician Executive MBA. *Graduate Certificate:* Applied Statistics; Nuclear Criticality Safety. *MS:* Industrial Engineering; Information Sciences; Nuclear Engineering.

### NON-DEGREE-RELATED COURSE TOPICS OFFERED

**Undergraduate**—American (United States) history; English composition; European history; French language and literature; Spanish language and literature; accounting; agricultural economics; anthropology; business management and administrative services, other; curriculum and instruction; developmental and child psychology; economics; forestry, general; geography; mathematical statistics; mathematics, other; philosophy and religion; physics; social psychology; sociology.
**Non-credit**—English creative writing; business marketing and marketing management; information sciences and systems; internet and world wide web; internet, general.

**See full description on page 632.**

# THE UNIVERSITY OF TENNESSEE AT MARTIN

## Office of Extended Campus and Continuing Education

110 Gooch Hall
Martin, TN 38238-5050
**Contact:** Katy Crapo, Coordinator
**Phone:** 901-587-7089
**Fax:** 901-587-7984
**Web:** http://www.utm.edu

**E-mail:** kcrapo@utm.edu

**ACCREDITATION:** Southern Association of Colleges and Schools
**INSTITUTIONALLY ADMINISTERED FINANCIAL AID:** Yes

### DEGREE OR CERTIFICATE PROGRAMS OFFERED

**Graduate**—*MBA:* Business Administration. *MSE:* Education.

### NON-DEGREE-RELATED COURSE TOPICS OFFERED

**Undergraduate**—accounting; business; business administration and management; education administration and supervision; fine arts and art studies; special education; teacher education, specific academic and vocational programs.
**Graduate**—accounting; business; business administration and management; education administration and supervision; special education; teacher education, specific academic and vocational programs.

# THE UNIVERSITY OF TEXAS AT ARLINGTON

## Center for Distance Education

Box 19077
Arlington, TX 76015
**Contact:** Mr. David W. Davis, Director of Distance Education and Engineering
**Phone:** 817-272-2352
**Fax:** 817-272-5630
**Web:** http://distance.uta.edu
**E-mail:** ddavis@uta.edu

**ACCREDITATION:** Southern Association of Colleges and Schools
**INSTITUTIONALLY ADMINISTERED FINANCIAL AID:** Yes

### DEGREE OR CERTIFICATE PROGRAMS OFFERED

**Graduate**—*ME:* Aerospace Engineering; Computer Science and Engineering; Mechanical Engineering. *MS:* Industrial Engineering. *MSCE:* Civil Engineering. *MSEE:* Electrical Engineering.

### NON-DEGREE-RELATED COURSE TOPICS OFFERED

**Undergraduate**—English composition; biology, general; criminology; political science and government; sociology.
**Graduate**—aerospace, aeronautical and astronautical engineering; curriculum and instruction; electrical, electronics and communication engineering; engineering mechanics; environmental/environmental health engineering; finance, general; industrial/manufacturing engineering; mechanical engineering; urban affairs/studies.

---

**Special Note**

The University of Texas at Arlington (UTA) is a Carnegie Doctoral I institution with a nationwide reputation for the design and delivery of Internet-based classes. High-quality courses and programs and first-rate student support services cause more than 90 percent of UTA distance learners to express high levels of satisfaction.

UTA provides both Internet-based certificate and degree programs through the University of Texas System TeleCampus. Programs include the MBA Online and master's degrees in electrical engineering and computer science.

For educators, UTA offers the unique opportunity to complete graduate course work in reading, which leads to the English as a Second Language (ESL) Endorsement, granted through the state of Texas. This endorsement prepares them to teach children from all cultural and language backgrounds and is required for those teachers in the state of Texas who are working with students in grades K–12 whose first language is not English. UTA also offers an online Master of Education in curriculum and instruction in which the course work has the added distinction of preparatory work for certificates granted through the state of Texas: the Reading Specialist Certificate, the Master Reading Teacher Certificate, and the ESL Endorsement.

For further information, students should visit UTA's Web site at http://distance.uta.edu or call the Center for Distance Education at 888-UTA-DIST (toll-free).

---

# THE UNIVERSITY OF TEXAS AT AUSTIN

## Continuing and Extended Education

PO Box 7700
Austin, TX 78713-7700
**Contact:** Olga Garza, Manager of Student Services
**Phone:** 888-232-4723
**Fax:** 512-475-7933
**Web:** http://www.utexas.edu/
**E-mail:** dec@utexas.edu

**ACCREDITATION:** Southern Association of Colleges and Schools
**INSTITUTIONALLY ADMINISTERED FINANCIAL AID:** Yes

### DEGREE OR CERTIFICATE PROGRAMS OFFERED
Programs offered do not lead to a degree or other formal award.
See full description on page 634.

# THE UNIVERSITY OF TEXAS AT DALLAS

## School of Management

Richardson, TX 75080
**Contact:** Mr. George E. Barnes, Director of Global MBA Online
**Phone:** 972-883-2783
**Fax:** 972-883-2799
**Web:** http://som.utdallas.edu/globalmba
**E-mail:** gbarnes@utdallas.edu

**ACCREDITATION:** Southern Association of Colleges and Schools
**INSTITUTIONALLY ADMINISTERED FINANCIAL AID:** Yes

### DEGREE OR CERTIFICATE PROGRAMS OFFERED
Graduate—*MBA:* Business.
See full description on page 638.

# THE UNIVERSITY OF TEXAS AT TYLER

## Interactive Television

Enrollment Management, 3900 University Boulevard
Tyler, TX 75799

**Contact:** Pam Morrow, Information Specialist
**Phone:** 903-566-7205
**Fax:** 903-566-7068
**Web:** http://www.uttyler.edu
**E-mail:** pmorrow@mail.uttyl.edu

**ACCREDITATION:** Southern Association of Colleges and Schools
**INSTITUTIONALLY ADMINISTERED FINANCIAL AID:** Yes

### DEGREE OR CERTIFICATE PROGRAMS OFFERED
Undergraduate—*BSN:* Nursing.

### NON-DEGREE-RELATED COURSE TOPICS OFFERED
Undergraduate—accounting; anthropology; biology, general; business; computer science; criminal justice and corrections; geography; history; marketing management and research; mathematics; sociology.
Graduate—business administration and management; computer science; health professions and related sciences, other; nursing; public administration.

# THE UNIVERSITY OF TEXAS MEDICAL BRANCH AT GALVESTON

Office of Institutional Analysis, 150 Gail Borden Building, Route 0677
Galveston, TX 77555-0677
**Contact:** Dr. Christine Anne Stroup-Benham, Interim Director
**Phone:** 409-747-1653
**Fax:** 409-747-1654
**Web:** http://www.utmb.edu/
**E-mail:** cbenham@utmb.edu

**ACCREDITATION:** Southern Association of Colleges and Schools
**INSTITUTIONALLY ADMINISTERED FINANCIAL AID:** Yes

### DEGREE OR CERTIFICATE PROGRAMS OFFERED
Programs offered do not lead to a degree or other formal award.

### NON-DEGREE-RELATED COURSE TOPICS OFFERED
Undergraduate—health and medical laboratory technologies; health professions and related sciences, other; nursing.
Graduate—medical clinical sciences (M.S., Ph.D.); nursing.

# THE UNIVERSITY OF TEXAS OF THE PERMIAN BASIN

## REACH Program Center

4901 East University
Odessa, TX 79762-0001
**Contact:** Carrie Vasquez, Administrative Secretary
**Phone:** 915-552-2870
**Fax:** 915-522-2871
**Web:** http://www.utpb.edu/reach/

**E-mail:** vasquez_c@utpb.edu

**ACCREDITATION:** Southern Association of Colleges and Schools

**INSTITUTIONALLY ADMINISTERED FINANCIAL AID:** Yes

## DEGREE OR CERTIFICATE PROGRAMS OFFERED

**Undergraduate—*BA:*** Criminal Justice.
**Graduate—*MBA:*** Business Administration. *MS:* Kinesiology.

## NON-DEGREE-RELATED COURSE TOPICS OFFERED

**Undergraduate—**English as a second language; English composition; art history, criticism and conservation; curriculum and instruction; drama/theater arts, general; education, other; geography; health and physical education/fitness; history; industrial and organizational psychology; journalism and mass communications; mathematics; philosophy and religion; psychology; sociology.

**Graduate—**English as a second language; criminal justice and corrections; criminology; curriculum and instruction; education administration and supervision; educational psychology; general teacher education; health and physical education/fitness; mathematical statistics; teacher education, specific academic and vocational programs.

# THE UNIVERSITY OF TEXAS SYSTEM

## UT TeleCampus

210 West Sixth Street, Suite 2.100
Austin, TX 78701
**Contact:** Ms. Susan Smith, Student Services Coordinator
**Phone:** 888-TEXAS 16
**Fax:** 512-499-4715
**Web:** http://www.telecampus.utsystem.edu
**E-mail:** telecampus@utsystem.edu

**ACCREDITATION:** Southern Association of Colleges and Schools

**INSTITUTIONALLY ADMINISTERED FINANCIAL AID:** Yes

## DEGREE OR CERTIFICATE PROGRAMS OFFERED

**Undergraduate—*BS:*** Criminal Justice—Completion Degree. *Certificate:* Chess and Education Online; Graduate Telecommunications Engineering; Reading Specialist. *Certification:* Master Reading Teacher. *Endorsement:* English as a Second Language (ESL).
**Graduate—*MBA:*** Business Administration and Management. *MEd:* Curriculum and Instruction; Educational Technology; Kinesiology. *MS:* Computer Science and Engineering; Computer Science; Electrical Engineering; Kinesiology.

## NON-DEGREE-RELATED COURSE TOPICS OFFERED

**Undergraduate—**English composition; English creative writing; English language and literature, general; English language and literature/letters, other; accounting; biology, general; chemistry; comparative literature; curriculum and instruction; developmental and child psychology; economics; education, general; education, other; educational/instructional media design; fine arts and art studies; foreign languages and literatures; geography; geological and related sciences; health and medical laboratory technologies; history; liberal arts and sciences, general studies and humanities; mathematical statistics; mathematics; mathematics, other; music; physical sciences, general; physical sciences, other; physics; political science and government; psychology; social and philosophical foundations of education; social sciences and history, other; social sciences,

general; sociology; teacher education, specific academic and vocational programs; visual and performing arts.
**Graduate—**developmental and child psychology; education, general; education, other; educational psychology; educational/instructional media design; health and medical assistants; health professions and related sciences, other; nursing; social and philosophical foundations of education; teacher assistant/aide; teacher education, specific academic and vocational programs; teaching English as a second language/foreign language.

**See full description on page 640.**

# UNIVERSITY OF THE INCARNATE WORD

## Universe Online

4301 Broadway, CPO 324
San Antonio, TX 78209
**Contact:** Universe Online
**Phone:** 877-827-2702
**Fax:** 210-829-2756
**Web:** http://www.uiw.edu/online
**E-mail:** virtual@universe.uiwtx.edu

**ACCREDITATION:** Southern Association of Colleges and Schools

**INSTITUTIONALLY ADMINISTERED FINANCIAL AID:** Yes

## DEGREE OR CERTIFICATE PROGRAMS OFFERED

**Programs offered do not lead to a degree or other formal award.**
**See full description on page 642.**

# UNIVERSITY OF THE SCIENCES IN PHILADELPHIA

600 South 43rd Street
Philadelphia, PA 19104-4418
**Contact:** Ms. Joyce D'Angelo, Assistant for College of Graduate Studies
**Phone:** 215-596-8937
**Fax:** 215-895-1185
**Web:** http://www.usip.edu/
**E-mail:** j.dangel@usip.edu

**ACCREDITATION:** Middle States Association of Colleges and Schools

**INSTITUTIONALLY ADMINISTERED FINANCIAL AID:** No

## DEGREE OR CERTIFICATE PROGRAMS OFFERED

**Programs offered do not lead to a degree or other formal award.**

## NON-DEGREE-RELATED COURSE TOPICS OFFERED

**Graduate—**English technical and business writing; health professions and related sciences, other.

# UNIVERSITY OF TOLEDO

## Division of Distance Learning

Toledo, OH 43604-1005

**Contact:** Janet Green, Interim Assistant Director for Enrollment Management
**Phone:** 419-321-5130
**Fax:** 419-321-5147
**Web:** http://www.dl.utoledo.edu
**E-mail:** jgreen@utnet.utoledo.edu

**ACCREDITATION:** North Central Association of Colleges and Schools
**INSTITUTIONALLY ADMINISTERED FINANCIAL AID:** Yes

## DEGREE OR CERTIFICATE PROGRAMS OFFERED

**Undergraduate—AA:** Business Management Technology. **BA:** Adult Liberal Studies. **Certificate:** Business Management Technology. **Graduate—MA:** Liberal Studies.

## NON-DEGREE-RELATED COURSE TOPICS OFFERED

**Undergraduate**—developmental and child psychology; journalism and mass communication, other; mathematical statistics; philosophy and religion; sociology; women's studies.
**Non-credit**—adult and continuing teacher education.

## Special Note

The University of Toledo (UT) established the Division of Distance Learning (DL) in June 1995 to meet its distance learning mission. The Division of Distance Learning connects UT and educational opportunities wherever they may exist. This is accomplished by responding to market needs and synergistically joining the instructional design of learner-centered course work with innovative uses of technology and teacher preparation for global instruction. Distance learning courses are taught via videotapes, compressed video using ISDN lines, UT's Virtual Campus, coax cable technology, and CD-ROM. Student-faculty interaction is accomplished through face-to-face or compressed video meetings, telephone, or e-mail or via chat room discussions on the Internet.

The University of Toledo is a nationally recognized, comprehensive public university with a broad range of undergraduate and graduate programs that serve more than 18,000 students from all 50 states and 98 countries. Seven colleges award undergraduate degrees: Arts and Sciences, Business Administration, Education, Engineering, Health and Human Services, Pharmacy, and University College. Advanced degrees are offered through the Graduate School and the College of Law. Courses may be offered via distance learning from any of the colleges. Academic success in a flexible anytime, anywhere environment is the DL goal. Each year, distance learning works with colleges throughout the University to provide comprehensive degree and certificate programs taught by leading UT faculty members. Current online degree programs include business management technologies, computer science and engineering technology third- and fourth-year degree completion, adult liberal studies, Master of Liberal Studies, and Master of Science in engineering.

The Division of Distance Learning is administered by Karen Rhoda, PhD, Interim Director of the Division of Distance Learning. Students should contact the division (telephone: 419–321–5130; fax: 419–321–5147; e-mail: jgreen@utnet.utoledo.edu) for an inventory of current offerings, or students can have their company, school, or agency representative call to discuss how distance learning can meet the educational needs of their organization. Students should visit the World Wide Web at http://www.dl.utoledo.edu.

# UNIVERSITY OF TULSA
## College of Business Administration
600 South College, BAH 215
Tulsa, OK 74104-3189
**Contact:** Mrs. Nanette C. Alix, iMBA(TM) Enrollment Coordinator
**Phone:** 918-631-3211
**Fax:** 918-631-3672
**Web:** http://www.imba.utulsa.edu
**E-mail:** nanette-alix@utulsa.edu

**ACCREDITATION:** North Central Association of Colleges and Schools
**INSTITUTIONALLY ADMINISTERED FINANCIAL AID:** Yes

## DEGREE OR CERTIFICATE PROGRAMS OFFERED

**Graduate—MBA:** Business Administration.

## NON-DEGREE-RELATED COURSE TOPICS OFFERED

**Graduate**—accounting; business; business administration and management; business information and data processing services; business management and administrative services, other; business quantitative methods and management science; business/managerial economics; computer and information sciences, general; computer systems networking and telecommunications; computer/information technology administration and management; economics; enterprise management and operation; entrepreneurship; financial management and services; human resources management; information sciences and systems; international business; internet and world wide web; law and legal studies; marketing management and research; marketing operations/marketing and distribution, other; telecommunications.

See full description on page 644.

# UNIVERSITY OF UTAH
## Distance Education
ULEARN, 1901 East South Campus Drive, Room 1215
Salt Lake City, UT 84112-9359
**Contact:** Roberta Lopez, Program Coordinator
**Phone:** 801-585-1906
**Fax:** 801-581-6267
**Web:** http://ulearn.utah.edu
**E-mail:** rlopez@aoce.utah.edu

**ACCREDITATION:** Northwest Association of Schools and Colleges
**INSTITUTIONALLY ADMINISTERED FINANCIAL AID:** No

## DEGREE OR CERTIFICATE PROGRAMS OFFERED

Programs offered do not lead to a degree or other formal award.

## NON-DEGREE-RELATED COURSE TOPICS OFFERED

**Undergraduate**—English creative writing; English literature (British and Commonwealth); anthropology; area, ethnic and cultural studies, other; art history, criticism and conservation; atmospheric sciences and meteorology; biology, general; chemistry; communications, general; developmental and child psychology; economics; educational psychology; financial management and services; foods and nutrition studies; geography; gerontology; history; mathematical statistics; mathematics; mathematics, other;

music; organic chemistry; physics; physiology, human and animal; political science and government; psychology; sign language interpreter; social psychology.

**Non-credit**—geological and related sciences.

**See full description on page 646.**

# UNIVERSITY OF VERMONT
## Distance Learning Network
460 South Prospect Street
Burlington, VT 05401
**Contact:** Mr. Mark A. Fitzsimmons, Director of Distance Learning Network
**Phone:** 802-656-8019
**Fax:** 802-656-1347
**Web:** http://learn.uvm.edu
**E-mail:** mark.fitzsimmons@uvm.edu

**ACCREDITATION:** New England Association of Schools and Colleges
**INSTITUTIONALLY ADMINISTERED FINANCIAL AID:** Yes

### DEGREE OR CERTIFICATE PROGRAMS OFFERED
**Graduate**—*MS:* Education Leadership. *MSN:* Nursing. *MSW:* Social Work.

### NON-DEGREE-RELATED COURSE TOPICS OFFERED
**Undergraduate**—English creative writing; animal sciences; chemistry; communication disorders sciences and services; dental services; electrical, electronics and communication engineering; history; mathematics, other; nursing; sociology.
**Graduate**—communication disorders sciences and services; library science/librarianship; nursing; psychology; public administration.
**Non-credit**—English composition; English language and literature, general; biological and physical sciences.

**See full description on page 648.**

# UNIVERSITY OF VIRGINIA
## Educational Technologies
PO Box 400160
Charlottesville, VA 22904
**Contact:** Office of Admissions
**Phone:** 434-982-3200
**Fax:** 434-924-3587
**Web:** http://www.virginia.edu/
**E-mail:** undergrad-admission@virginia.edu

**ACCREDITATION:** Southern Association of Colleges and Schools

eCollege.com  *www.ecollege.com*

### DEGREE OR CERTIFICATE PROGRAMS OFFERED
Programs offered do not lead to a degree or other formal award.

# UNIVERSITY OF WASHINGTON
## Extension
5001 25th Avenue, NE
Seattle, WA 98105

**Contact:** UW Educational Outreach
**Phone:** 800-543-2320
**Web:** http://www.washington.edu/students/distance/
**E-mail:** distance@u.washington.edu

**ACCREDITATION:** Northwest Association of Schools and Colleges

### DEGREE OR CERTIFICATE PROGRAMS OFFERED
Programs offered do not lead to a degree or other formal award.

### NON-DEGREE-RELATED COURSE TOPICS OFFERED
**Undergraduate**—American literature (United States); East European languages and literatures; English composition; English creative writing; English language and literature, general; English technical and business writing; Greek languages and literatures (modern); accounting; business communications; chemistry; cognitive psychology and psycholinguistics; communications, general; criminology; curriculum and instruction; developmental and child psychology; economics; education, general; educational psychology; ethnic and cultural studies; geography; geological and related sciences; gerontology; history; international business; journalism and mass communications; library science/librarianship; marketing management and research; mathematical statistics; mathematics; mathematics, other; music; pharmacy; philosophy; political science and government; psychology; religion/religious studies; social psychology; sociology; speech and rhetorical studies; urban affairs/studies.
**Non-credit**—English as a second language; English creative writing; English language and literature, general; business administration and management; computer programming; internet and world wide web.

# UNIVERSITY OF WATERLOO
## Distance and Continuing Education
Waterloo, ON N2L 3G1, Canada
**Contact:** Information and Student Services
**Phone:** 519-888-4050
**Fax:** 519-746-6393
**Web:** http://dce.uwaterloo.ca
**E-mail:** distance@uwaterloo.ca

**ACCREDITATION:** Provincially Chartered
**INSTITUTIONALLY ADMINISTERED FINANCIAL AID:** Yes

### DEGREE OR CERTIFICATE PROGRAMS OFFERED
**Undergraduate**—*BA:* Canadian Studies; Classical Studies; Economics; English; French; Geography; History; Humanities; Philosophy; Psychology; Religious Studies; Social Development Studies; Social Sciences; Sociology. *BES:* Geography. *BGS:* General Studies, Non-Major. *BS:* General Science, Non-Major.
**Graduate**—*MS:* Master of Applied Science Management Science, Technology Management.

### NON-DEGREE-RELATED COURSE TOPICS OFFERED
**Undergraduate**—American (United States) history; American literature (United States); Canadian studies; English composition; English literature (British and Commonwealth); European history; French language and literature; Germanic languages and literatures; Greek languages and literatures (modern); Hebrew language and literature; Jewish/Judaic studies; Latin language and literature (ancient and medieval); Russian language and literature; Spanish language and literature; accounting; anthropology; applied mathematics; area, ethnic and cultural studies, other; astronomy; bible/biblical studies; biblical and other theological

languages and literatures; biochemistry; biological and physical sciences; biological sciences/life sciences, other; biology, general; cell and molecular biology; chemistry; computer and information sciences, general; computer science; dance; developmental and child psychology; earth and planetary sciences; ecology; economics; educational psychology; environmental science/studies; ethnic and cultural studies; family and community studies; foreign languages and literatures; geography; geological and related sciences; gerontology; history; insurance and risk management; investments and securities; liberal arts and sciences, general studies and humanities; mathematical statistics; mathematics; mathematics, other; medical genetics; medieval and renaissance studies; microbiology/bacteriology; miscellaneous physical sciences; multi/interdisciplinary studies, other; organic chemistry; organizational behavior studies; peace and conflict studies; philosophy; philosophy and religion; physical and theoretical chemistry; physical sciences, general; physics; physiology, human and animal; psychology; religion/religious studies; social psychology; social sciences and history, other; social sciences, general; social work; sociology; women's studies.

**Graduate**—engineering/industrial management; industrial/manufacturing engineering; management information systems and business data processing, general.

**Non-credit**—English composition; chemistry; mathematics, other; physics.

# UNIVERSITY OF WISCONSIN COLLEGES

## UWC On-line

780 Regent Street, PO Box 8680
Madison, WI 53708-8680
**Contact:** Ms. Leanne Johnson, Academic Advisor
**Phone:** 877-449-1877
**Web:** http://www.uwcolleges.com
**E-mail:** academicadvisor@uwc.edu

**ACCREDITATION:** North Central Association of Colleges and Schools
**INSTITUTIONALLY ADMINISTERED FINANCIAL AID:** Yes

### DEGREE OR CERTIFICATE PROGRAMS OFFERED
**Undergraduate**—*AAS:* Liberal Arts.

### NON-DEGREE-RELATED COURSE TOPICS OFFERED
**Undergraduate**—English composition; English language and literature, general; biological and physical sciences; biology, general; communications, other; engineering, other; fine arts and art studies; geography; history; journalism and mass communications; mathematical statistics; mathematics; music; philosophy; political science and government; psychology; sociology.

# UNIVERSITY OF WISCONSIN–EAU CLAIRE

130 Schofield
Eau Claire, WI 54702
**Contact:** Sue E. Shelton, Registrar
**Phone:** 715-836-3887
**Fax:** 715-836-3846
**Web:** http://www.uwec.edu/

**E-mail:** sheltose@uwec.edu
**ACCREDITATION:** North Central Association of Colleges and Schools
**INSTITUTIONALLY ADMINISTERED FINANCIAL AID:** Yes

### DEGREE OR CERTIFICATE PROGRAMS OFFERED
**Undergraduate**—*BSN:* Nursing Degree Completion Program. *License:* School Library Media.

### NON-DEGREE-RELATED COURSE TOPICS OFFERED
**Undergraduate**—business administration and management; library science, other; nursing.
**Non-credit**—accounting; economics; financial management and services; information sciences and systems; marketing management and research; nursing.

# UNIVERSITY OF WISCONSIN–EXTENSION

## Learning Innovations

505 South Rosa Road
Madison, WI 53719-1257
**Contact:** Learner Services
**Phone:** 800-442-6460
**Fax:** 608-262-4096
**Web:** http://learn.wisconsin.edu/
**E-mail:** info@learn.uwsa.edu

**ACCREDITATION:** North Central Association of Colleges and Schools

### DEGREE OR CERTIFICATE PROGRAMS OFFERED
Programs offered do not lead to a degree or other formal award.

### NON-DEGREE-RELATED COURSE TOPICS OFFERED
**Undergraduate**—East European languages and literatures; English language and literature, general; French language and literature; Hebrew language and literature; Italian language and literature; Spanish language and literature; biology, general; business; business communications; chemistry; criminal justice and corrections; criminology; engineering, general; ethnic and cultural studies; family and community studies; financial management and services; financial services marketing operations; history; human resources management; law and legal studies; marketing management and research; mathematical statistics; mathematics; music; natural resources management and protective services; peace and conflict studies; philosophy and religion; physics; psychology; quality control and safety technologies; religion/religious studies; teacher education, specific academic and vocational programs.

# UNIVERSITY OF WISCONSIN–MADISON

500 Lincoln Drive
Madison, WI 53706
**Web:** http://www.wisc.edu/

**ACCREDITATION:** North Central Association of Colleges and Schools

### DEGREE OR CERTIFICATE PROGRAMS OFFERED
**Undergraduate**—*BS:* Nursing. *Certificate:* Distance Education.

**Graduate**—*MBA/MS:* Engineering. *MEngr:* Professional Practice; Technical Japanese. *MS:* Computer Engineering; Electrical Engineering; Mechanical Engineering.
**Postgraduate and doctoral**—*PharmD:* Pharmacy.

## NON-DEGREE-RELATED COURSE TOPICS OFFERED

**Undergraduate**—civil engineering; electrical and electronic engineering-related technology; family and community studies; food sciences and technology; foreign languages and literatures; geological and related sciences; mechanical engineering; nursing; organizational behavior studies.
**Graduate**—business; civil engineering; electrical, electronics and communication engineering; engineering, general; family and community studies; marketing management and research; mechanical engineering; nursing; organizational behavior studies; pharmacy; political science and government; social work.

# UNIVERSITY OF WISCONSIN-MILWAUKEE

## Distance Learning and Instructional Support

161 West Wisconsin Avenue, #6000
Milwaukee, WI 53203
**Contact:** Nancy Morris, Distance Learning Manager
**Phone:** 414-227-3223
**Fax:** 414-227-3396
**Web:** http://www.uwm.edu/UniversityOutreach/deuwm
**E-mail:** nanm@uwm.edu

**ACCREDITATION:** North Central Association of Colleges and Schools
**INSTITUTIONALLY ADMINISTERED FINANCIAL AID:** Yes

eCollege.com www.ecollege.com

## DEGREE OR CERTIFICATE PROGRAMS OFFERED

**Undergraduate**—*Certificate:* Internet Technologies; State and Local Taxation; Wisconsin Credential Program for Child Care Administrators.
**Graduate**—*MLIS:* Library and Information Science.
**Postgraduate and doctoral**—*PhD:* Nursing.

## NON-DEGREE-RELATED COURSE TOPICS OFFERED

**Undergraduate**—accounting; computer and information sciences, general; finance, general; information sciences and systems; organizational behavior studies.
**Graduate**—accounting; child care and guidance workers and managers; computer and information sciences, general; computer and information sciences, other; education administration and supervision; education, general; education, other; library science, other; library science/librarianship; taxation.
**Non-credit**—computer and information sciences, other; computer software and media applications; computer systems networking and telecommunications; liberal arts and sciences, general studies and humanities; transportation and materials moving workers, other.

# UNIVERSITY OF WISCONSIN-PARKSIDE

900 Wood Road, PO Box 2000
Kenosha, WI 53141-2000

**Contact:** Dr. William Blanchard, Director of Institutional Research and Assessment Services
**Phone:** 262-595-2235
**Fax:** 262-595-2630
**Web:** http://www.uwp.edu/
**E-mail:** william.blanchard@uwp.edu

**ACCREDITATION:** North Central Association of Colleges and Schools
**INSTITUTIONALLY ADMINISTERED FINANCIAL AID:** Yes

## DEGREE OR CERTIFICATE PROGRAMS OFFERED

Programs offered do not lead to a degree or other formal award.

## NON-DEGREE-RELATED COURSE TOPICS OFFERED

**Undergraduate**—Germanic languages and literatures; biological sciences/life sciences, other; biology, general; cell and molecular biology; communications, general; criminal justice and corrections; foreign languages and literatures; mathematics; nursing.
**Graduate**—accounting; business; business administration and management; business information and data processing services; business quantitative methods and management science; business/managerial economics; economics; financial management and services; marketing operations/marketing and distribution, other; mathematical statistics.
**Non-credit**—engineering science; gerontology; law and legal studies.

# UNIVERSITY OF WISCONSIN-PLATTEVILLE

## Distance Learning Center

B12 Karrmann Library, 1 University Plaza
Platteville, WI 53818
**Contact:** Distance Learning Center
**Phone:** 800-362-5460
**Fax:** 608-342-1071
**Web:** http://www.uwplatt.edu/~disted
**E-mail:** disted@uwplatt.edu

**ACCREDITATION:** North Central Association of Colleges and Schools
**INSTITUTIONALLY ADMINISTERED FINANCIAL AID:** Yes

## DEGREE OR CERTIFICATE PROGRAMS OFFERED

**Undergraduate**—*BS:* Business Administration. *Certificate:* Leadership and Human Performance Certificate and Human Resource Management Certificate; Project Management.
**Graduate**—*Advanced Graduate Diploma:* Criminal Justice. *MEngr:* Engineering. *MS:* Criminal Justice; Project Management.

## NON-DEGREE-RELATED COURSE TOPICS OFFERED

**Undergraduate**—accounting; business administration and management; business marketing and marketing management; communications, general; economics; finance, general; geography; human resources management; mathematics; music; speech and rhetorical studies.
**Graduate**—adult and continuing teacher education; business; civil engineering; communications, general; criminal justice and corrections; industrial/manufacturing engineering; management science; mathematics; mechanical engineering; psychology.

# UNIVERSITY OF WISCONSIN–RIVER FALLS

*Outreach Office*
410 South 3rd Street
River Falls, WI 54022-5001
**Contact:** Katrina Larsen, Outreach Program Manager
**Phone:** 715-425-3276
**Fax:** 715-425-3785
**Web:** http://www.uwrf.edu/outreach/
**E-mail:** katrina.larsen@uwrf.edu

**ACCREDITATION:** North Central Association of Colleges and Schools
**INSTITUTIONALLY ADMINISTERED FINANCIAL AID:** Yes

## DEGREE OR CERTIFICATE PROGRAMS OFFERED
**Programs offered do not lead to a degree or other formal award.**

## NON-DEGREE-RELATED COURSE TOPICS OFFERED
**Undergraduate**—accounting; agriculture/agricultural sciences; astronomy; business; business administration and management; communications, general; drama/theater arts, general; liberal arts and sciences, general studies and humanities; political science and government; teacher education, specific academic and vocational programs.
**Graduate**—teacher education, specific academic and vocational programs.
**Non-credit**—agriculture/agricultural sciences; business; business administration and management; education, general; teacher education, specific academic and vocational programs.

# UNIVERSITY OF WISCONSIN–STEVENS POINT

*University Telecommunications and Distance Learning Resources*
2100 Main Street
Stevens Point, WI 54481
**Contact:** Mr. Jerry L. Rous, Outreach Program Manager
**Phone:** 715-346-3301
**Fax:** 715-346-4641
**Web:** http://www.uwsp.edu/extension
**E-mail:** jrous@uwsp.edu

**ACCREDITATION:** North Central Association of Colleges and Schools
**INSTITUTIONALLY ADMINISTERED FINANCIAL AID:** No

## DEGREE OR CERTIFICATE PROGRAMS OFFERED
**Programs offered do not lead to a degree or other formal award.**

## NON-DEGREE-RELATED COURSE TOPICS OFFERED
**Undergraduate**—American (United States) history; English technical and business writing; Japanese language and literature; Russian language and literature; anthropology; business administration and management; communications technologies; communications, general; computer and information sciences, general; computer science; education, general; environmental/environmental health engineering; foreign languages and literatures; mathematical statistics; mathematics.
**Graduate**—American (United States) history; English technical and business writing; business communications; business management and

administrative services, other; communications, general; computer and information sciences, general; computer programming; computer software and media applications; economics; education, general; education, other; history; mathematical statistics; mathematics, other; social and philosophical foundations of education; technology education/industrial arts.
**Non-credit**—English creative writing; business administration and management; business communications; environmental/environmental health engineering; forestry and related sciences.

# UNIVERSITY OF WYOMING

*The Outreach School*
PO Box 3274
Laramie, WY 82071-3274
**Contact:** Ms. Judith E. Atencio, Program Associate for Outreach Credit Programs, The Outreach School
**Phone:** 800-448-7801
**Fax:** 307-766-3445
**Web:** http://outreach.uwyo.edu
**E-mail:** occ@uwyo.edu

**ACCREDITATION:** North Central Association of Colleges and Schools
**INSTITUTIONALLY ADMINISTERED FINANCIAL AID:** Yes

eCollege.com www.ecollege.com

## DEGREE OR CERTIFICATE PROGRAMS OFFERED
**Undergraduate**—*BA:* Criminal Justice; Social Sciences. *BS:* Business Administration; Family and Consumer Sciences (Professional Child Development Option); Psychology; Social Sciences. *BSN:* Nursing, RN to BSN; Nursing, RN to BSN. *Certificate:* Land Surveying. *Certification:* Real Estate.
**Graduate**—*MA:* Education—Adult and Post-Secondary Education; Education—Special Education; Education—Teaching and Learning. *MBA:* Business Administration. *MPA:* Public Administration. *MS:* Education—Instructional Technology; Kinesiology and Health; Nursing (Community Health Clinical Specialist); Nursing (Nurse Educator Option); Speech-Language Pathology. *MSW:* Social Work.

## NON-DEGREE-RELATED COURSE TOPICS OFFERED
**Undergraduate**—Afro-American(Black) studies; Army R.O.T.C.; English composition; astronomy; communications, general; education, general; ethnic and cultural studies; geography; history; labor/personnel relations and studies; liberal arts and sciences, general studies and humanities; mathematical statistics; social psychology; women's studies.
**Graduate**—educational psychology; history; labor/personnel relations and studies.

**See full description on page 650.**

# UNIVERSITY SYSTEM COLLEGE FOR LIFELONG LEARNING

College for Lifelong Learning, 125 North State Street
Concord, NH 03301
**Contact:** Ms. Karen R. King, Registrar
**Phone:** 603-228-3000 Ext. 312
**Fax:** 603-229-0964

**Web:** http://www.cll.edu
**E-mail:** k_king@unhf.unh.edu

**ACCREDITATION:** New England Association of Schools and Colleges
**INSTITUTIONALLY ADMINISTERED FINANCIAL AID:** Yes

### DEGREE OR CERTIFICATE PROGRAMS OFFERED
**Programs offered do not lead to a degree or other formal award.**

### NON-DEGREE-RELATED COURSE TOPICS OFFERED

**Undergraduate**—adult and continuing teacher education; communications, general; computer and information sciences, general; criminal justice and corrections; health system/health services administration; investments and securities; liberal arts and sciences, general studies and humanities; management information systems and business data processing, general; social sciences, general.

# UPPER IOWA UNIVERSITY
## External Degree
PO Box 1861
Fayette, IA 52142
**Contact:** Barbara J. Schultz, Director of External Degree
**Phone:** 888-877-3742
**Fax:** 563-425-5353
**Web:** http://www.uiu.edu
**E-mail:** extdegree@uiu.edu

**ACCREDITATION:** North Central Association of Colleges and Schools
**INSTITUTIONALLY ADMINISTERED FINANCIAL AID:** Yes

### DEGREE OR CERTIFICATE PROGRAMS OFFERED

**Undergraduate—AA:** Business; Liberal Arts. **BS:** Accounting; Business; Human Resources Management; Human Services; Management; Marketing; Public Administration (General); Public Administration (Law Enforcement/Fire Science); Social Sciences; Technology and Information Management.

### NON-DEGREE-RELATED COURSE TOPICS OFFERED

**Undergraduate**—American (United States) history; English composition; accounting; art history, criticism and conservation; biology, general; business marketing and marketing management; communications, general; earth and planetary sciences; industrial and organizational psychology; international business; labor/personnel relations and studies; law and legal studies, other; management information systems and business data processing, general; mathematical statistics; political science and government; psychology; public administration; sociology.

**Non-credit**—American (United States) history; English composition; accounting; art history, criticism and conservation; biology, general; business marketing and marketing management; communications, general; industrial and organizational psychology; international business; labor/personnel relations and studies; law and legal studies, other; management information systems and business data processing, general; mathematical statistics; political science and government; psychology; public administration; sociology.

**See full description on page 654.**

# UTAH STATE UNIVERSITY
## Independent and Distance Education
3080 Old Main Hill, Merrill Library, Room 208
Logan, UT 84322-3080
**Contact:** Vincent J. Lasserty, Director of Independent and Time Enhanced Learning
**Phone:** 800-233-2137
**Fax:** 435-797-2709
**Web:** http://extension.usu.edu
**E-mail:** enroll@ext.usu.edu

**ACCREDITATION:** Northwest Association of Schools and Colleges
**INSTITUTIONALLY ADMINISTERED FINANCIAL AID:** Yes

### DEGREE OR CERTIFICATE PROGRAMS OFFERED

**Undergraduate—BBA:** Business Administration.
**Graduate—MPA:** Public Administration.
**See full description on page 656.**

# VALDOSTA STATE UNIVERSITY
## Division of Public Services
Room 124, Regional Center for Continuing Education
Valdosta, GA 31698
**Contact:** Philip D. Allen, Interim Director of Public Services
**Phone:** 912-245-6484
**Fax:** 912-333-5397
**Web:** http://www.valdosta.edu/distance
**E-mail:** pdallen@valdosta.edu

**ACCREDITATION:** Southern Association of Colleges and Schools
**INSTITUTIONALLY ADMINISTERED FINANCIAL AID:** Yes

eCollege.com  *www.ecollege.com*

### DEGREE OR CERTIFICATE PROGRAMS OFFERED

**Undergraduate—AA:** General Studies. **BA:** Criminal Justice; General Studies; Management; Political Science. **BBA:** Business Administration and Management. **BS:** Adult and Vocational Education; Education—Middle Grades; Education. **BSN:** Nursing.

**Graduate—MBA:** Business Administration. **MCP:** Education. **MEd:** Adult and Vocational Education; Early Childhood Education. **MPA:** Public Administration. **MSN:** Nursing. **MSW:** Social Work.

**Postgraduate and doctoral—EdD:** Curriculum and Instructional Technology.

### NON-DEGREE-RELATED COURSE TOPICS OFFERED

**Undergraduate**—English composition; English language and literature, general; business; computer science; design and applied arts; financial management and services; health and physical education/fitness; history; marketing management and research; mathematics; philosophy; political science and government; psychology.

**Graduate**—business administration and management; design and applied arts; education, other; political science and government; psychology; public administration; social work.

# VANGUARD UNIVERSITY OF SOUTHERN CALIFORNIA

55 Fair Drive
Costa Mesa, CA 92626
**Contact:** Dr. Phil Robinette, Dean
**Phone:** 714-556-3610 Ext. 247
**Fax:** 714-957-9317
**Web:** http://www.vanguard.edu/
**E-mail:** probinette@vanguard.edu

**ACCREDITATION:** Western Association of Schools and Colleges

**INSTITUTIONALLY ADMINISTERED FINANCIAL AID:** Yes

eCollege.com  www.ecollege.com

**DEGREE OR CERTIFICATE PROGRAMS OFFERED**

Programs offered do not lead to a degree or other formal award.

**NON-DEGREE-RELATED COURSE TOPICS OFFERED**

Undergraduate—business; psychology; religion/religious studies.

# VERMONT TECHNICAL COLLEGE

PO Box 500
Randolph Center, VT 05061
**Contact:** Michael Dempsey, Registrar
**Phone:** 802-728-1630
**Fax:** 802-728-1390
**Web:** http://www.vtc.vsc.edu/
**E-mail:** mdempsey@vtc.edu

**ACCREDITATION:** New England Association of Schools and Colleges

**INSTITUTIONALLY ADMINISTERED FINANCIAL AID:** Yes

**DEGREE OR CERTIFICATE PROGRAMS OFFERED**

Programs offered do not lead to a degree or other formal award.

**NON-DEGREE-RELATED COURSE TOPICS OFFERED**

Undergraduate—business communications; computer and information sciences, general; history; social sciences and history, other.

# VICTORIA COLLEGE

Victoria, TX 77901
**Contact:** Becky Payne, Counselor
**Web:** http://www.vc.cc.tx.us/
**E-mail:** payne@vc.cc.tx.us

**ACCREDITATION:** Southern Association of Colleges and Schools

**INSTITUTIONALLY ADMINISTERED FINANCIAL AID:** Yes

**DEGREE OR CERTIFICATE PROGRAMS OFFERED**

Programs offered do not lead to a degree or other formal award.

**NON-DEGREE-RELATED COURSE TOPICS OFFERED**

Undergraduate—English composition; English language and literature, general; accounting; chemistry; child care and guidance workers and managers; computer and information sciences, general; computer software and media applications; computer systems networking and telecom-munications; data processing technology; economics; fine arts and art studies; history; law and legal studies; mathematics; nursing; psychology. **Non-credit**—computer software and media applications.

# VILLANOVA UNIVERSITY

*Division of Par-time Studies/Summer Sessions*
Villanova, PA 19008
**Contact:** Mr. James R. Johnson, Director of Part-Time Studies
**Web:** http://www.parttime.villanova.edu
**E-mail:** james.johnson@villanova.edu

**ACCREDITATION:** Middle States Association of Colleges and Schools

**INSTITUTIONALLY ADMINISTERED FINANCIAL AID:** Yes

**DEGREE OR CERTIFICATE PROGRAMS OFFERED**

Programs offered do not lead to a degree or other formal award.

**NON-DEGREE-RELATED COURSE TOPICS OFFERED**

Undergraduate—American literature (United States); accounting; biological sciences/life sciences, other; business administration and management; business information and data processing services; business/managerial economics; communications, general; economics; electrical, electronics and communications engineering; engineering design; industrial and organizational psychology; marketing management and research; mathematical statistics; mechanical engineering; nursing; philosophy; political science and government; sociology.
Graduate—accounting; business administration and management; business information and data processing services; business quantitative methods and management science; business/managerial economics; civil engineering; electrical and electronic engineering-related technology; financial management and services; marketing management and research; nursing.

# VINCENNES UNIVERSITY

*Distance Education/Degree Completion*
1002 North First Street
Vincennes, IN 47591
**Contact:** Prof. Vernon E. Houchins, Dean of Continuing Studies
**Phone:** 812-888-5900
**Fax:** 812-888-2054
**Web:** http://www.vinu.edu or http://vublackboard.vinu.edu
**E-mail:** disted@indian.vinu.edu

**ACCREDITATION:** North Central Association of Colleges and Schools

**INSTITUTIONALLY ADMINISTERED FINANCIAL AID:** Yes

**DEGREE OR CERTIFICATE PROGRAMS OFFERED**

Undergraduate—*AAS:* Business Studies; General Studies; Law Enforcement Studies; Technology Apprenticeship. *AS:* Behavioral Sciences; Business Administration; General Studies Surgical Technology Degree Completion; General Studies; Health Information Management; Law Enforcement Studies; Recreation Management—Therapeutic Option; Technology Apprenticeship. *Certificate of Completion:* Administrative Office Technology—Office Software Specialist; Community Rehabilitation. *Certificate:* General Studies.
Graduate—*Graduate Certificate:* Surgical Technology Accelerated Option, Certificate of Graduation.

## NON-DEGREE-RELATED COURSE TOPICS OFFERED

**Undergraduate**—English composition; English creative writing; accounting; area, ethnic and cultural studies, other; business administration and management; business marketing and marketing management; chemistry; computer and information sciences, general; developmental and child psychology; earth and planetary sciences; education, general; fire science/firefighting; mathematics; psychology; rehabilitation/therapeutic services; social work; sociology; speech and rhetorical studies.

# VIRGINIA COMMONWEALTH UNIVERSITY

## *Office of Academic Technology*

901 Park Avenue, Suite B-30
Richmond, VA 23284-3008
**Contact:** Sonja Moore, Director of Distance Education
**Phone:** 804-828-8470
**Fax:** 804-828-9001
**Web:** http://www.vcu.edu/
**E-mail:** somoore@vcu.edu

**ACCREDITATION:** Southern Association of Colleges and Schools
**INSTITUTIONALLY ADMINISTERED FINANCIAL AID:** Yes

## DEGREE OR CERTIFICATE PROGRAMS OFFERED

**Graduate**—*MSHA:* Health Administration.
**Postgraduate and doctoral**—*PhD:* Health-Related Sciences.

## NON-DEGREE-RELATED COURSE TOPICS OFFERED

**Undergraduate**—English creative writing; English language and literature, general; communications, general; computer and information sciences, general; education, general; foreign languages and literatures; physics; psychology.
**Graduate**—health professions and related sciences, other; health system/health services administration.

### Special Note

The Executive Program is an innovative 22-month course of study that leads to the degree of Master of Science Health Administration (MSHA). The course of study can be completed by persons residing anywhere and working full-time in health care. It is a distance learning program accomplished mainly over the World Wide Web, with 6 one-week on-campus sessions over a 22-month period of study. The program is designed for self-motivated, experienced professionals seeking graduate education in management for continued career advancement. The program is offered by the Department of Health Administration in the School of Allied Health Professions at Virginia Commonwealth University (VCU), on the Medical College of Virginia (MCV) campus in Richmond.

To be considered for admission, an applicant must hold a baccalaureate degree from an institution of higher learning recognized by VCU and have at least a 2.75 grade point average (GPA) for all undergraduate work completed. Applicants with less than a 2.75 undergraduate GPA who have exceptional work experience will be considered for admission with provisional status. The applicant must also submit scores on a standardized aptitude test for graduate studies. Applicants holding professional degrees (e.g., MD, DDS, JD, and PharmD) may have testing requirements waived upon petition to

the graduate dean. Applicants should have at least 5 years of increasingly responsible work experience. The specific experience profile depends upon an individual's particular profession or occupation. A resume should accurately and completely describe an applicant's accomplishments. No specific prerequisite course work is required for application to the program. Upon acceptance, associates complete independent study modules in 3 areas: microeconomics, accounting, and quantitative analysis.

For more information, prospective students can visit the Web site (http://www.had.vcu.edu) or can call 804-828-0719.

# VIRGINIA POLYTECHNIC INSTITUTE AND STATE UNIVERSITY

## *Institute for Distance and Distributed Learning*

3044 Torgersen Hall
Blacksburg, VA 24061
**Contact:** Mrs. Cate K. Mowrey, Marketing and Media Specialist
**Phone:** 540-231-9584
**Fax:** 540-231-2079
**Web:** http://iddl.vt.edu and http://vto.vt.edu
**E-mail:** catem@vt.edu

**ACCREDITATION:** Southern Association of Colleges and Schools
**INSTITUTIONALLY ADMINISTERED FINANCIAL AID:** Yes

## DEGREE OR CERTIFICATE PROGRAMS OFFERED

**Graduate**—*MA:* Curriculum and Instruction-Instructional Technology Emphasis. *MBA:* Business Administration. *MS:* Career and Technical Education; Civil Infrastructure Engineering; Civil and Environmental Engineering; Computer Engineering; Curriculum and Instruction-Health Promotion Emphasis; Curriculum and Instruction-Physical Education Emphasis; Electrical and Computer Engineering; Engineering Administration; Master of Information Technology; Materials Science and Engineering; Ocean Engineering; Political Science; Systems Engineering.

## NON-DEGREE-RELATED COURSE TOPICS OFFERED

**Undergraduate**—Afro-American(Black) studies; American (United States) history; English creative writing; Spanish language and literature; art history, criticism and conservation; biology, general; business marketing and marketing management; chemical engineering; electrical, electronics and communication engineering; engineering/industrial management; environmental/environmental health engineering; finance, general; geography; industrial/manufacturing engineering; mathematics, other; mechanical engineering; medieval and renaissance studies; microbiology/bacteriology; sociology; women's studies.
**Graduate**—Spanish language and literature; accounting; aerospace, aeronautical and astronautical engineering; curriculum and instruction; electrical, electronics and communication engineering; engineering/industrial management; environmental/environmental health engineering; industrial/manufacturing engineering; management information systems and business data processing, general; mathematical statistics; mechanical engineering; organizational behavior studies; women's studies.
**Non-credit**—administrative and secretarial services; adult and continuing teacher education; architecture; business administration and management; computer and information sciences, general; computer software

and media applications; computer/information technology administration and management; education, other; financial management and services; special education.

See full description on page 658.

# VIRGINIA WESTERN COMMUNITY COLLEGE

*Distance Learning*

PO Box 14007
Roanoke, VA 24038
**Contact:** Dr. Inez Farrell, Instructional Technologist
**Phone:** 540-857-6202
**Web:** http://www.vw.vccs.edu
**E-mail:** ifarrell@vw.vccs.edu

**ACCREDITATION:** Southern Association of Colleges and Schools
**INSTITUTIONALLY ADMINISTERED FINANCIAL AID:** Yes

## DEGREE OR CERTIFICATE PROGRAMS OFFERED

Undergraduate—*AAS:* Dental Hygiene. *AS:* Business Administration; General Studies; Social Science.

## NON-DEGREE-RELATED COURSE TOPICS OFFERED

Undergraduate—American literature (United States); English composition; accounting; business administration and management; business information and data processing services; economics; fine arts and art studies; health and medical administrative services; history; journalism and mass communications; mathematics; music; philosophy; political science and government; psychology; sociology.

# VOLUNTEER STATE COMMUNITY COLLEGE

*Distance Learning/College at Home*

1480 Nashville Pike
Gallatin, TN 37066
**Contact:** Mr. Seth H. Sparkman, Director of Distance Learning
**Phone:** 615-230-5145
**Fax:** 615-451-5843
**Web:** http://www.vscc.cc.tn.us
**E-mail:** ssparkman@vscc.cc.tn.us

**ACCREDITATION:** Southern Association of Colleges and Schools
**INSTITUTIONALLY ADMINISTERED FINANCIAL AID:** Yes

## DEGREE OR CERTIFICATE PROGRAMS OFFERED

Programs offered do not lead to a degree or other formal award.

## NON-DEGREE-RELATED COURSE TOPICS OFFERED

Undergraduate—English composition; English creative writing; accounting; applied mathematics; astronomy; biological and physical sciences; biology, general; business; business information and data processing services; business marketing and marketing management; chemistry; communications, general; computer and information sciences, general; culinary arts and related services; developmental and child psychology; economics; educational psychology; geography; history; industrial and

organizational psychology; mathematics; medical basic sciences; philosophy; psychology; social psychology; social work; sociology.

# WAKE TECHNICAL COMMUNITY COLLEGE

9101 Fayetteville Road
Raleigh, NC 27603-5696
**Contact:** Diana Osborne, Assistant Coordinator of Distance Education
**Phone:** 919-662-3432
**Fax:** 919-779-3360
**Web:** http://www.wake.tec.nc.us
**E-mail:** dgosborn@gwmail.wake.tec.nc.us

**ACCREDITATION:** Southern Association of Colleges and Schools

## DEGREE OR CERTIFICATE PROGRAMS OFFERED

Programs offered do not lead to a degree or other formal award.

## NON-DEGREE-RELATED COURSE TOPICS OFFERED

Undergraduate—English composition; business; computer and information sciences, general; geological and related sciences; psychology; sociology.

# WALDEN UNIVERSITY

155 South 5th, Suite 200
Minneapolis, MN 55401
**Contact:** Mick Schommer
**Phone:** 612-338-7224 Ext. 1281
**Web:** http://www.waldenu.edu/
**E-mail:** mschommer@waldenu.edu

**ACCREDITATION:** North Central Association of Colleges and Schools
**INSTITUTIONALLY ADMINISTERED FINANCIAL AID:** Yes

## DEGREE OR CERTIFICATE PROGRAMS OFFERED

Graduate—*MS:* Education; Psychology; Public Health.
Postgraduate and doctoral—*PhD:* Applied Management and Decision Sciences; Education; Health Services; Human Services; Professional Psychology.

## NON-DEGREE-RELATED COURSE TOPICS OFFERED

Graduate—adult and continuing teacher education; developmental and child psychology; educational psychology; finance, general; health system/health services administration; industrial and organizational psychology; management information systems and business data processing, general; social psychology; social work.

See full description on page 660.

# WALLA WALLA COMMUNITY COLLEGE

*Distance Learning Department*

500 Tausick Way
Walla Walla, WA 99362

**Contact:** Ms. Hildy J. Helgeson, Distance Learning Program Assistant
**Phone:** 509-527-4331
**Fax:** 509-527-4325
**Web:** http://www.wallawalla.cc/
**E-mail:** hildy.helgeson@wwcc.ctc.edu

**ACCREDITATION:** Northwest Association of Schools and Colleges
**INSTITUTIONALLY ADMINISTERED FINANCIAL AID:** Yes

### DEGREE OR CERTIFICATE PROGRAMS OFFERED
Programs offered do not lead to a degree or other formal award.

### NON-DEGREE-RELATED COURSE TOPICS OFFERED
**Undergraduate**—accounting; agricultural business and management; agriculture/agricultural sciences; anthropology; biology, general; business; child care and guidance workers and managers; comparative literature; computer software and media applications; criminal justice and corrections; mathematics; mathematics and computer science; philosophy; plant sciences; sociology; soil sciences.
**Non-credit**—English creative writing; administrative and secretarial services; business administration and management; business and personal services marketing operations; business management and administrative services, other; computer software and media applications; computer systems networking and telecommunications; criminal justice and corrections; data entry/microcomputer applications; enterprise management and operation; entrepreneurship; film/video and photographic arts; general retailing and wholesaling operations and skills; human resources management; industrial production technologies; law and legal studies; marketing operations/marketing and distribution, other; personal and miscellaneous services, other; quality control and safety technologies.

# WALSH COLLEGE OF ACCOUNTANCY AND BUSINESS ADMINISTRATION

PO Box 7007
Troy, MI 48007-7006
**Contact:** Karen Mahaffy, Interim Director of Admissions and Advising
**Phone:** 248-823-1500
**Fax:** 248-689-0938
**Web:** http://www.walshcollege.edu/
**E-mail:** kmahaffy@walshcollege.edu

**ACCREDITATION:** North Central Association of Colleges and Schools
**INSTITUTIONALLY ADMINISTERED FINANCIAL AID:** Yes

### DEGREE OR CERTIFICATE PROGRAMS OFFERED
**Undergraduate**—*Certificate:* Interactive Marketing.
**Graduate**—*MBA:* Business.

### NON-DEGREE-RELATED COURSE TOPICS OFFERED
**Undergraduate**—business marketing and marketing management.
**Graduate**—accounting; business administration and management; business marketing and marketing management; business quantitative methods and management science; marketing operations/marketing and distribution, other.

**Non-credit**—business administration and management; business marketing and marketing management.

# WALTERS STATE COMMUNITY COLLEGE
*Evening and Distance Education Office*
500 South Davy Crockett Parkway
Morristown, TN 37813-6899
**Contact:** Dave Roberts, Dean
**Phone:** 423-585-6899
**Fax:** 423-585-6853
**Web:** http://vc.wscc.cc.tn.us/
**E-mail:** dave.roberts@wscc.cc.tn.us

**ACCREDITATION:** Southern Association of Colleges and Schools
**INSTITUTIONALLY ADMINISTERED FINANCIAL AID:** Yes

### DEGREE OR CERTIFICATE PROGRAMS OFFERED
Programs offered do not lead to a degree or other formal award.

### NON-DEGREE-RELATED COURSE TOPICS OFFERED
**Undergraduate**—American literature (United States); English composition; English creative writing; Spanish language and literature; anthropology; business; business marketing and marketing management; computer science; criminal justice and corrections; culinary arts and related services; gerontology; health and physical education/fitness; history; human resources management; mathematics; music; nursing; physical therapy; psychology; real estate; sociology.

# WARNER SOUTHERN COLLEGE
5301 U.S. Highway 27 South
Lake Wales, FL 33853
**Contact:** Deborah Jayne Oesch-Minor, Associate Director of Distance Ministry Programs
**Phone:** 800-309-9563 Ext. 7599
**Fax:** 863-638-3702
**Web:** http://www.warner.edu/
**E-mail:** oeschd@warner.edu

**ACCREDITATION:** Southern Association of Colleges and Schools
**INSTITUTIONALLY ADMINISTERED FINANCIAL AID:** Yes

eCollege.com   *www.ecollege.com*

### DEGREE OR CERTIFICATE PROGRAMS OFFERED
**Undergraduate**—*AA:* Church Ministry. *BA:* Church Ministry. *Certificate:* Church Ministry.

### NON-DEGREE-RELATED COURSE TOPICS OFFERED
**Undergraduate**—theological and ministerial studies.

# WASHINGTON STATE UNIVERSITY
*Distance Degree Programs*
104 Van Doren Hall, PO Box 645220
Pullman, WA 99164-5220

**Contact:** Ms. Jaqueline M. Almdale, Program Assistant for Recruitment and Retention, and Distance Degree Programs
**Phone:** 800-222-4978
**Fax:** 509-335-7529
**Web:** http://www.distance.wsu.edu
**E-mail:** jalmdale@wsu.edu

**ACCREDITATION:** Northwest Association of Schools and Colleges

**INSTITUTIONALLY ADMINISTERED FINANCIAL AID:** Yes

### DEGREE OR CERTIFICATE PROGRAMS OFFERED

Undergraduate—*BA:* Business Administration; Criminal Justice; Human Development; Social Sciences. *BS:* General Agriculture.
Graduate—*MAg:* Agriculture.

### NON-DEGREE-RELATED COURSE TOPICS OFFERED

Undergraduate—American (United States) history; American studies/civilization; Asian studies; English composition; English creative writing; European history; French language and literature; Spanish language and literature; accounting; anthropology; biology, general; business marketing and marketing management; developmental and child psychology; finance, general; insurance and risk management; international business; investments and securities; law and legal studies, other; mathematical statistics; social psychology; sociology; women's studies.
Graduate—agricultural and food products processing; agricultural business and management; agricultural business and production, other; agricultural engineering; agricultural supplies and related services; agriculture/agricultural sciences.

See full description on page 662.

# WASHTENAW COMMUNITY COLLEGE

*Office of Distance Learning*
4800 East Huron River Drive
Ann Arbor, MI 48106
**Contact:** Ms. Michele S. Meissner
**Phone:** 734-477-8556
**Fax:** 734-677-2220
**Web:** http://www.wccnet.org
**E-mail:** meissner@wccnet.org

**ACCREDITATION:** North Central Association of Colleges and Schools

**INSTITUTIONALLY ADMINISTERED FINANCIAL AID:** Yes

### DEGREE OR CERTIFICATE PROGRAMS OFFERED

Programs offered do not lead to a degree or other formal award.

### NON-DEGREE-RELATED COURSE TOPICS OFFERED

Undergraduate—English composition; administrative and secretarial services; business administration and management; communications, general; construction and building finishers and managers; dental services; internet and world wide web; law and legal studies, other.

# WAYLAND BAPTIST UNIVERSITY

1900 West 7th Street, CMB 735
Plainview, TX 79072

**Contact:** Mr. Stan DeMerritt, Registrar
**Phone:** 806-296-4706
**Fax:** 806-296-4580
**Web:** http://www.wbu.edu/
**E-mail:** demerritt@mail.wbu.edu

**ACCREDITATION:** Southern Association of Colleges and Schools

**INSTITUTIONALLY ADMINISTERED FINANCIAL AID:** Yes

### DEGREE OR CERTIFICATE PROGRAMS OFFERED

Programs offered do not lead to a degree or other formal award.

### NON-DEGREE-RELATED COURSE TOPICS OFFERED

Undergraduate—business administration and management; education, other; management information systems and business data processing, general.
Graduate—accounting; business administration and management; financial management and services; management information systems and business data processing, general; marketing operations/marketing and distribution, other.

# WAYNE COMMUNITY COLLEGE

3000 Wayne Memorial Drive
Goldsboro, NC 27533
**Contact:** Michele Turnage, Web Base Instruction Coordinator
**Phone:** 919-735-5152 Ext. 765
**Fax:** 919-736-9425
**Web:** http://www.wayne.cc.nc.us/
**E-mail:** shell@wcc.wayne.cc.nc.us

**ACCREDITATION:** Southern Association of Colleges and Schools

**INSTITUTIONALLY ADMINISTERED FINANCIAL AID:** Yes

### DEGREE OR CERTIFICATE PROGRAMS OFFERED

Programs offered do not lead to a degree or other formal award.

### NON-DEGREE-RELATED COURSE TOPICS OFFERED

Undergraduate—English language and literature, general; agricultural business and management; business; business administration and management; computer systems networking and telecommunications; computer/information technology administration and management; criminal justice and corrections; data processing technology; economics; history; internet and world wide web; visual and performing arts.

# WAYNE STATE COLLEGE

*Regional Education and Distance Learning*
1111 Main Street
Wayne, NE 68787
**Contact:** Dr. Robert O. McCue, Associate Vice President for Academic Affairs
**Phone:** 402-375-7232
**Fax:** 402-375-7204
**Web:** http://www.wsc.edu
**E-mail:** bomccue1@wsc.edu

**ACCREDITATION:** North Central Association of Colleges and Schools

**INSTITUTIONALLY ADMINISTERED FINANCIAL AID:** Yes

## DEGREE OR CERTIFICATE PROGRAMS OFFERED

Programs offered do not lead to a degree or other formal award.

## NON-DEGREE-RELATED COURSE TOPICS OFFERED

**Undergraduate**—business administration and management; foreign languages and literatures; home economics, general; industrial/manufacturing engineering; mathematics; special education.

**Graduate**—business administration and management; counseling psychology; education administration and supervision; educational/instructional media design; internet and world wide web.

# WAYNE STATE UNIVERSITY

## College of Lifelong Learning

2608 Academic/Administrative Building.
Detroit, MI 48202
**Contact:** Ms. Arthurine Turner, Administrative Manager
**Phone:** 313-577-6960
**Fax:** 313-577-5466
**Web:** http://fls.cll.wayne.edu/
**E-mail:** aturner@wayne.edu

**ACCREDITATION:** North Central Association of Colleges and Schools

## DEGREE OR CERTIFICATE PROGRAMS OFFERED

**Graduate**—*MA:* Electronics and Computer Control Systems.

## NON-DEGREE-RELATED COURSE TOPICS OFFERED

**Undergraduate**—social psychology; sociology.
**Graduate**—electrical, electronics and communication engineering.

# WEBER STATE UNIVERSITY

## Distance Learning and Independent Study

4005 University Circle
Ogden, UT 84408-4005
**Contact:** Distance Learning Customer Services
**Phone:** 801-626-6785
**Fax:** 801-626-8035
**Web:** http://weber.edu/ce/dl
**E-mail:** dist-learn@weber.edu

**ACCREDITATION:** Northwest Association of Schools and Colleges

**INSTITUTIONALLY ADMINISTERED FINANCIAL AID:** Yes

## DEGREE OR CERTIFICATE PROGRAMS OFFERED

**Undergraduate**—*AAS:* Clinical Laboratory Technician; Health Information Technology; Respiratory Therapy. *AS:* Criminal Justice; General Studies; Respiratory Therapy. *BS:* Advanced Respiratory Therapy; Clinical Laboratory Sciences; Health Administrative Services; Health Promotion; Radiological Sciences. *Certificate:* Health Care Coding and Classification; Nuclear Medicine; Production and Inventory Management—APICS; Radiation Therapy; Radiological Sciences.

## NON-DEGREE-RELATED COURSE TOPICS OFFERED

**Undergraduate**—American (United States) history; English composition; English creative writing; English language and literature, general; European history; French language and literature; accounting; anthropology; art history, criticism and conservation; botany; business; business

administration and management; business marketing and marketing management; business quantitative methods and management science; communications, general; computer and information sciences, other; counseling psychology; criminal justice and corrections; drama/theater arts, general; electrical, electronics and communication engineering; finance, general; foods and nutrition studies; geography; gerontology; health and physical education/fitness; health professions and related sciences, other; health system/health services administration; history; interior design; journalism and mass communication, other; management information systems and business data processing, general; mathematical statistics; mathematics; mathematics, other; music; nursing; organizational behavior studies; philosophy; political science and government; psychology; social psychology; social work; sociology.

See full description on page 664.

# WEBSTER UNIVERSITY

## Collaborative Learning–Academic Affairs

470 East Lockwood
St. Louis, MO 63119
**Contact:** Bruce Humphrey, Interim Director of Distance Learning Center
**Web:** http://online.webster.edu
**E-mail:** humphery@webster.edu

**ACCREDITATION:** North Central Association of Colleges and Schools

**INSTITUTIONALLY ADMINISTERED FINANCIAL AID:** Yes

## DEGREE OR CERTIFICATE PROGRAMS OFFERED

Programs offered do not lead to a degree or other formal award.

## NON-DEGREE-RELATED COURSE TOPICS OFFERED

**Undergraduate**—computer programming; computer software and media applications.

# WENATCHEE VALLEY COLLEGE

John A. Brown Library, 1300 5th Street
Wenatchee, WA 98801
**Contact:** Erica Swanson, Coordinator of Distance Learning Support Center
**Phone:** 509-664-2539
**Fax:** 509-664-2542
**Web:** http://wvc.ctc.edu/
**E-mail:** eswanson@wvcmail.ctc.edu

**ACCREDITATION:** Northwest Association of Schools and Colleges

**INSTITUTIONALLY ADMINISTERED FINANCIAL AID:** Yes

## DEGREE OR CERTIFICATE PROGRAMS OFFERED

**Undergraduate**—*AAS:* Liberal Arts and Sciences.

# WESTERN BAPTIST COLLEGE

## Management and Communication Online Program/ Family Studies Online Program

Adult Studies, 5000 Deer Park Drive, SE
Salem, OR 97301

**Contact:** Ms. Nancy L. Martyn, Director of Adult Studies
**Phone:** 503-375-7585
**Fax:** 503-375-7583
**Web:** http://www.wbc.edu
**E-mail:** nmartyn@wbc.edu

**ACCREDITATION:** Northwest Association of Schools and Colleges
**INSTITUTIONALLY ADMINISTERED FINANCIAL AID:** Yes

## DEGREE OR CERTIFICATE PROGRAMS OFFERED

Undergraduate—*BS:* Psychology/Sociology.

## NON-DEGREE-RELATED COURSE TOPICS OFFERED

Undergraduate—bible/biblical studies.

See full description on page 666.

# WESTERN CAROLINA UNIVERSITY
## Continuing Education and Summer School

138 Outreach Center
Cullowhee, NC 28723
**Contact:** Oakley Winters, Dean of Continuing Education
**Phone:** 828-227-7397
**Fax:** 828-227-7115
**Web:** http://cess.wcu.edu
**E-mail:** winters@wcu.edu

**ACCREDITATION:** Southern Association of Colleges and Schools
**INSTITUTIONALLY ADMINISTERED FINANCIAL AID:** Yes

## DEGREE OR CERTIFICATE PROGRAMS OFFERED

Graduate—*MPM:* Project Management.

# WESTERN CONNECTICUT STATE UNIVERSITY
## Online CSU

181 White Street
Ridgefield, CT 06877
**Contact:** Mr. Peter Serniak, Director of Continuing Education
**Phone:** 203-837-8229
**Fax:** 203-837-8338
**Web:** http://www.wcsu.edu/
**E-mail:** serniakp@wcsu.edu

**ACCREDITATION:** New England Association of Schools and Colleges
**INSTITUTIONALLY ADMINISTERED FINANCIAL AID:** No

## DEGREE OR CERTIFICATE PROGRAMS OFFERED

Programs offered do not lead to a degree or other formal award.

## NON-DEGREE-RELATED COURSE TOPICS OFFERED

Undergraduate—anthropology; area, ethnic and cultural studies, other; computer science; criminology; health professions and related sciences, other; history; mathematics, other; political science and government; psychology; sociology.
Graduate—education, other.

# WESTERN GOVERNORS UNIVERSITY

2040 East Murray Holladay Road, Suite 106
Salt Lake City, UT 84117
**Contact:** Wendy Gregory, Enrollment Manager
**Phone:** 801-274-3280
**Fax:** 801-274-3305
**Web:** http://www.wgu.edu/
**E-mail:** wgregory@wgu.edu

**ACCREDITATION:** Northwest Association of Schools and Colleges
**INSTITUTIONALLY ADMINISTERED FINANCIAL AID:** Yes

## DEGREE OR CERTIFICATE PROGRAMS OFFERED

Undergraduate—*AA:* General Education. *AAS:* Information Technology, CNE Emphasis; Information Technology, Network Administration. *AS:* Business; Information Technology. *BS:* Business, IT Management; Computer Information Systems. *Certificate:* Information Technology, Network Administration.
Graduate—*Graduate Certificate:* Instructional Design; Technology Proficiency. *MA:* Learning and Technology.

## NON-DEGREE-RELATED COURSE TOPICS OFFERED

Undergraduate—English composition; English language and literature, general; accounting; applied mathematics; area, ethnic and cultural studies, other; biology, general; business; business communications; chemistry; communications, general; computer science; computer systems analysis; computer systems networking and telecommunications; developmental and child psychology; economics; education, general; foreign languages and literatures; geography; history; information sciences and systems; internet and world wide web; marketing management and research; mathematics; philosophy; philosophy and religion; physical sciences, general; physics; political science and government; psychology; sociology.
Graduate—English as a second language; education administration and supervision; education, general; educational evaluation, research and statistics; educational/instructional media design; teacher education, specific academic and vocational programs; teaching English as a second language/foreign language.
Non-credit—business; business administration and management; business communications; computer and information sciences, general; computer and information sciences, other; computer programming; computer science; computer software and media applications; computer systems analysis; computer systems networking and telecommunications.

See full description on page 668.

# WESTERN ILLINOIS UNIVERSITY
## School of Extended and Continuing Education

5 Horrabin Hall, 1 University Circle
Macomb, IL 61455
**Contact:** Extended Education
**Phone:** 309-298-2496
**Fax:** 309-298-2226
**Web:** http://wie.edu/users/miebis
**E-mail:** robbie_morelli@ccmail.wiu.edu

**ACCREDITATION:** North Central Association of Colleges and Schools

## DEGREE OR CERTIFICATE PROGRAMS OFFERED

Programs offered do not lead to a degree or other formal award.

## NON-DEGREE-RELATED COURSE TOPICS OFFERED

**Undergraduate**—accounting; business; counseling psychology; economics; education administration and supervision; finance, general; human resources management; zoology.
**Graduate**—biology, general; economics.

# WESTERN IOWA TECH COMMUNITY COLLEGE

4647 Stone Avenue, PO Box 5199
Sioux City, IA 51102-5199
**Contact:** Lora Vander Zwaag, Director of Admissions
**Phone:** 712-274-8733 Ext. 1353
**Fax:** 712-274-6412
**Web:** http://www.witcc.com
**E-mail:** vanderl@witcc.com

**ACCREDITATION:** North Central Association of Colleges and Schools

**INSTITUTIONALLY ADMINISTERED FINANCIAL AID:** Yes

## DEGREE OR CERTIFICATE PROGRAMS OFFERED

**Undergraduate**—*AA:* Liberal Arts Transfer.

## NON-DEGREE-RELATED COURSE TOPICS OFFERED

**Undergraduate**—business; computer and information sciences, general; health and medical administrative services; history; international business. **Non-credit**—business; computer software and media applications; personal and miscellaneous services, other; quality control and safety technologies.

# WESTERN MICHIGAN UNIVERSITY

*Department of Distance Education*
Ellsworth A-103
Kalamazoo, MI 49008-5161
**Contact:** Rosemary Nichols, Office Manager
**Phone:** 616-387-4129
**Fax:** 616-387-4226
**Web:** http://www.wmich.edu
**E-mail:** rosemary.nicholas@wmich.edu

**ACCREDITATION:** North Central Association of Colleges and Schools

**INSTITUTIONALLY ADMINISTERED FINANCIAL AID:** Yes

## DEGREE OR CERTIFICATE PROGRAMS OFFERED

Programs offered do not lead to a degree or other formal award.

## NON-DEGREE-RELATED COURSE TOPICS OFFERED

**Undergraduate**—Afro-American(Black) studies; anthropology; engineering/industrial management; geography; occupational therapy; social work; sociology.

# WESTERN NEBRASKA COMMUNITY COLLEGE

*Information Technology*
1601 East 27th Street
Scottsbluff, NE 69361
**Contact:** Mr. Mark A. Sinner, Distance Learning Coordinator
**Phone:** 308-635-6142
**Fax:** 308-635-6100
**Web:** http://wncc.net/
**E-mail:** sinnerm@wncc.net

**ACCREDITATION:** North Central Association of Colleges and Schools

**INSTITUTIONALLY ADMINISTERED FINANCIAL AID:** Yes

## DEGREE OR CERTIFICATE PROGRAMS OFFERED

Programs offered do not lead to a degree or other formal award.

## NON-DEGREE-RELATED COURSE TOPICS OFFERED

**Undergraduate**—English composition; developmental and child psychology; sociology.

# WESTERN NEVADA COMMUNITY COLLEGE

160 Campus Way
Fallon, NV 89406
**Contact:** Walter Lewis, Distance Education Technician
**Phone:** 775-423-7565
**Fax:** 775-423-8029
**Web:** http://www.wncc.nevada.edu/
**E-mail:** wlewis@wncc.nevada.edu

**ACCREDITATION:** Northwest Association of Schools and Colleges

## DEGREE OR CERTIFICATE PROGRAMS OFFERED

Programs offered do not lead to a degree or other formal award.

## NON-DEGREE-RELATED COURSE TOPICS OFFERED

**Undergraduate**—Spanish language and literature; accounting; biology, general; culinary arts and related services; education, other; electrical, electronics and communication engineering; geography; management science; mechanical engineering; nursing; sociology.

# WESTERN OREGON UNIVERSITY

*Division of Extended and Summer Studies*
345 North Monmouth Avenue
Monmouth, OR 97361
**Contact:** LaRon Tolley, Distance Education Manager
**Phone:** 503-838-8697
**Fax:** 503-838-8473
**Web:** http://www.wou.edu

**E-mail:** tolleyl@wou.edu

**ACCREDITATION:** Northwest Association of Schools and Colleges

**INSTITUTIONALLY ADMINISTERED FINANCIAL AID:** Yes

eCollege.com www.ecollege.com

### DEGREE OR CERTIFICATE PROGRAMS OFFERED

**Undergraduate—*BS:*** Fire Services Administration.

### NON-DEGREE-RELATED COURSE TOPICS OFFERED

**Undergraduate**—social psychology.

# WESTERN PIEDMONT COMMUNITY COLLEGE

1001 Burkemont Avenue
Morganton, NC 28655
**Contact:** Jim Reed, Director of Admissions
**Phone:** 828-438-6051
**Fax:** 828-438-6015
**Web:** http://www.wp.cc.nc.us/
**E-mail:** jreed@wp.cc.nc.us

**ACCREDITATION:** Southern Association of Colleges and Schools

**INSTITUTIONALLY ADMINISTERED FINANCIAL AID:** Yes

### DEGREE OR CERTIFICATE PROGRAMS OFFERED

**Undergraduate—*AAS:*** Business Administration; Paralegal Studies.

### NON-DEGREE-RELATED COURSE TOPICS OFFERED

**Undergraduate**—English composition; accounting; administrative and secretarial services; business; business administration and management; business information and data processing services; business/managerial economics; computer and information sciences, general; computer programming; computer software and media applications; computer systems networking and telecommunications; criminal justice and corrections; economics; fine arts and art studies; geography; human resources management; internet and world wide web; psychology; sociology; taxation.

# WESTERN SEMINARY

*Center for Lifelong Learning*
5511 Southeast Hawthorne Boulevard
Portland, OR 97215
**Contact:** Jon Raibley, Assistant Director of Center for Lifelong Learning
**Phone:** 800-547-4546
**Fax:** 503-517-1801
**Web:** http://www.westernseminary.edu
**E-mail:** jlraible@westernseminary.edu

**ACCREDITATION:** Northwest Association of Schools and Colleges

**INSTITUTIONALLY ADMINISTERED FINANCIAL AID:** Yes

### DEGREE OR CERTIFICATE PROGRAMS OFFERED

**Programs offered do not lead to a degree or other formal award.**

### NON-DEGREE-RELATED COURSE TOPICS OFFERED

**Graduate**—bible/biblical studies; biblical and other theological languages and literatures; religion/religious studies; religious education; theological and ministerial studies; theological studies and religious vocations, other. **Non-credit**—bible/biblical studies; biblical and other theological languages and literatures; religion/religious studies; religious education; theological and ministerial studies; theological studies and religious vocations, other.

# WESTERN UNIVERSITY OF HEALTH SCIENCES

College of Graduate Nursing, 309 East Second Street, College Plaza
Pomona, CA 91766
**Contact:** Ms. Sarah Douville, Assistant Program Director
**Phone:** 909-469-5523
**Fax:** 909-469-5521
**Web:** http://www.westernu.edu
**E-mail:** sdouville@westernu.edu

**ACCREDITATION:** Western Association of Schools and Colleges

**INSTITUTIONALLY ADMINISTERED FINANCIAL AID:** Yes

### DEGREE OR CERTIFICATE PROGRAMS OFFERED

**Undergraduate—*Certificate:*** Family Nurse Practitioner.
**Graduate—*MSN:*** Nursing.

### NON-DEGREE-RELATED COURSE TOPICS OFFERED

**Graduate**—nursing.
**Non-credit**—nursing.

# WESTERN WASHINGTON UNIVERSITY

*Extended Education and Summer Programs*
516 High Street
Bellingham, WA 98225-5293
**Contact:** Bunny Starbuck, Program Assistant
**Phone:** 360-650-3650
**Fax:** 360-650-6858
**Web:** http://www.wwu.edu/~extended
**E-mail:** extendedprograms@wwu.edu

**ACCREDITATION:** Northwest Association of Schools and Colleges

**INSTITUTIONALLY ADMINISTERED FINANCIAL AID:** No

### DEGREE OR CERTIFICATE PROGRAMS OFFERED

**Undergraduate—*BA:*** Human Services. ***Certificate:*** Microsoft Certified System Engineers.

### NON-DEGREE-RELATED COURSE TOPICS OFFERED

**Undergraduate**—American (United States) history; American literature (United States); Asian studies; Canadian studies; East and Southeast Asian languages and literatures; English creative writing; English language and literature, general; European history; French language and literature; Greek languages and literatures (modern); anthropology; biblical and other theological languages and literatures; biology, general; business quantitative methods and management science; curriculum and instruction; developmental and child psychology; economics; education administration and supervision; education, general; educational psychology; environmental science/studies; general teacher education; history; human services; mathematical statistics; mathematics; mathematics, other; medieval and renaissance studies; psychology; romance languages and literatures; sociology; teacher education, specific academic and vocational programs; teaching English as a second language/foreign language; women's studies.

**Non-credit**—computer software and media applications; computer systems networking and telecommunications.

**See full description on page 670.**

# WESTERN WISCONSIN TECHNICAL COLLEGE

PO Box 308
Independence, WI 54747
**Contact:** Jennifer Ann Brave, Distance Learning Coordinator
**Phone:** 715-985-3392
**Fax:** 715-985-2580
**Web:** http://www.western.tec.wi.us
**E-mail:** bravej@western.tec.wi.us

**ACCREDITATION:** North Central Association of Colleges and Schools

**INSTITUTIONALLY ADMINISTERED FINANCIAL AID:** Yes

## DEGREE OR CERTIFICATE PROGRAMS OFFERED

**Undergraduate**—*AD:* Supervisory Management.

## NON-DEGREE-RELATED COURSE TOPICS OFFERED

**Non-credit**—accounting; computer and information sciences, general; family and community studies; fire protection; miscellaneous health aides; real estate.

# WESTERN WYOMING COMMUNITY COLLEGE

*Extended Education*
2500 College Drive, PO Box 428
Rock Springs, WY 82902
**Contact:** Mr. Billy Smith, Director of Extended Education
**Phone:** 307-382-1757 Ext. 1757
**Fax:** 307-382-1812 Ext. 1812
**Web:** http://www.wwcc.cc.wy.us/dist_ed/distance.htm
**E-mail:** wsmith@wwcc.cc.wy.us

**ACCREDITATION:** North Central Association of Colleges and Schools

**INSTITUTIONALLY ADMINISTERED FINANCIAL AID:** Yes

## DEGREE OR CERTIFICATE PROGRAMS OFFERED

**Undergraduate**—*AA:* General.

## NON-DEGREE-RELATED COURSE TOPICS OFFERED

**Undergraduate**—English composition; accounting; administrative and secretarial services; anthropology; applied mathematics; biological and physical sciences; business; business administration and management; chemistry; computer software and media applications; dramatic/theater arts and stagecraft; economics; ethnic and cultural studies; foods and nutrition studies; general teacher education; health and medical assistants; philosophy.

**Special Note**

Western Wyoming Community College is located on the high desert plains of southwestern Wyoming and has a service area of 25,000 square miles. Because of the distance and small populations in some of the local communities, it was essential for the College to enter the distance learning field.

Western's goal is to provide high-quality instruction to students who might not otherwise be able to continue their education. The College offers videotaped courses, compressed video instruction, and Internet courses that are part of an associate degree program. Standards are the same as they are for traditional instruction, and students are able to complete degree requirements from their home. Western is interested in drawing students from around the country and the world to their classes because they believe it enriches the learning experience for all concerned. Some Wyoming people rarely venture outside the state, and they welcome the chance to interact with students from other cultures and backgrounds.

Because Western is a state-supported institution, tuition and fees are very low, so students on a tight budget find the College to be very attractive. On average, 77% of students receive some type of financial assistance to attend the College. Western offers both need- and academic-based aid.

Western is accredited by the North Central Association of Colleges and Schools, so transfer of courses taken is not a problem. Students who plan carefully are able to complete the first 2 years of their bachelor's degree and transfer with junior status. Occupational students find that they are well prepared for jobs in their field.

Students should visit the Web site at http://www.wwcc.cc.wy.us.

# WEST LOS ANGELES COLLEGE

*Distance Learning Center*
9000 Overland Drive
Culver City, CA 90230
**Contact:** Mr. Eric Jean Ichon, Distance Learning Coordinator
**Phone:** 310-287-4305
**Web:** http://www.wlac.cc.ca.us/dised
**E-mail:** ichone@wmail.wlac.cc.ca.us

**ACCREDITATION:** Western Association of Schools and Colleges

**INSTITUTIONALLY ADMINISTERED FINANCIAL AID:** Yes

eCollege.com  *www.ecollege.com*

## DEGREE OR CERTIFICATE PROGRAMS OFFERED

**Programs offered do not lead to a degree or other formal award.**

## NON-DEGREE-RELATED COURSE TOPICS OFFERED

**Undergraduate**—English composition; English creative writing; English language and literature, general; English technical and business writing; accounting; business; business management and administrative services, other; computer science; computer/information technology administration and management; criminal justice and corrections; dental clinical sciences/graduate dentistry (M.S., Ph.D.); design and applied arts; health and medical preparatory programs; history; individual and family development studies; international relations and affairs; law and legal studies; marketing management and research; music; tourism and travel services marketing operations.

# WEST SHORE COMMUNITY COLLEGE

3000 North Stiles Road
Scottville, MI 49454-0277
**Contact:** Patti Davidson, Director of Distance Learning and Information Technology
**Phone:** 231-845-6211 Ext. 3106
**Fax:** 231-845-0207
**Web:** http://www.westshore.cc.mi.us/
**E-mail:** pldavidson@westshore.cc.mi.us

**ACCREDITATION:** North Central Association of Colleges and Schools
**INSTITUTIONALLY ADMINISTERED FINANCIAL AID:** Yes

## DEGREE OR CERTIFICATE PROGRAMS OFFERED

**Programs offered do not lead to a degree or other formal award.**

## NON-DEGREE-RELATED COURSE TOPICS OFFERED

**Undergraduate**—English composition; advertising; biology, general; business administration and management; business marketing and marketing management; geological and related sciences; mathematics, other; sociology.

# WEST VIRGINIA NORTHERN COMMUNITY COLLEGE

Admissions Office
Wheeling, WV 26003
**Contact:** Ms. Bonny Ellis, Director of Student Admissions and Counseling
**Phone:** 304-233-5900 Ext. 4218
**Fax:** 304-232-0965
**Web:** http://www.northern.wvnet.edu/
**E-mail:** bellis@northern.wvnet.edu

**ACCREDITATION:** North Central Association of Colleges and Schools
**INSTITUTIONALLY ADMINISTERED FINANCIAL AID:** No

## DEGREE OR CERTIFICATE PROGRAMS OFFERED

**Programs offered do not lead to a degree or other formal award.**

## NON-DEGREE-RELATED COURSE TOPICS OFFERED

**Undergraduate**—American (United States) history; English composition; accounting; biology, general; management information systems and business data processing, general; mathematics, other; microbiology/bacteriology; sociology.

# WEST VIRGINIA UNIVERSITY

## Extended Learning

306 CERC Building, PO Box 6808
Morgantown, WV 26506-6808

**Contact:** Ms. Cindy K. Hart, Coordinator of Distance Learning
**Phone:** 304-293-3852
**Fax:** 304-293-3853
**Web:** http://www.wvu.edu/~exlearn/
**E-mail:** lkhart@mail.wvu.edu

**ACCREDITATION:** North Central Association of Colleges and Schools
**INSTITUTIONALLY ADMINISTERED FINANCIAL AID:** Yes

## DEGREE OR CERTIFICATE PROGRAMS OFFERED

**Undergraduate**—*Certificate:* Integrated Marketing Communications Program.
**Graduate**—*EMBA:* Business Administration; Health. *MA:* Special Education. *MS:* Software Engineering. *MSN:* Nursing.

## NON-DEGREE-RELATED COURSE TOPICS OFFERED

**Undergraduate**—English composition; English creative writing; English literature (British and Commonwealth); English technical and business writing; history; journalism and mass communications; mathematics.
**Graduate**—biology, general; chemistry; community health services; public health; technology education/industrial arts.

# WEST VIRGINIA UNIVERSITY INSTITUTE OF TECHNOLOGY

## Extension and Community Service

Vining Library
Montgomery, WV 25136
**Contact:** Rodney Stewart, Director
**Phone:** 304-442-3200
**Fax:** 304-442-3090
**Web:** http://www2.wvutech.edu/academics/extended/index.html
**E-mail:** rstewart@wvutech.edu

**ACCREDITATION:** North Central Association of Colleges and Schools
**INSTITUTIONALLY ADMINISTERED FINANCIAL AID:** No

## DEGREE OR CERTIFICATE PROGRAMS OFFERED

**Programs offered do not lead to a degree or other formal award.**

## NON-DEGREE-RELATED COURSE TOPICS OFFERED

**Undergraduate**—accounting; administrative and secretarial services; computer software and media applications; economics; history; internet and world wide web; management information systems and business data processing, general; mathematics; nursing; sociology.
**Graduate**—electrical, electronics and communication engineering.

# WEST VIRGINIA WESLEYAN COLLEGE

## Outreach Education

59 College Avenue
Buckhannon, WV 26201
**Contact:** Jennifer Bunner, Coordinator of Distance Education
**Phone:** 888-340-7574
**Fax:** 304-473-8429
**Web:** http://www.wvwc.edu/aca/distanceed/

**E-mail:** distanceed@wvwc.edu

**ACCREDITATION:** North Central Association of Colleges and Schools

**INSTITUTIONALLY ADMINISTERED FINANCIAL AID:** Yes

### DEGREE OR CERTIFICATE PROGRAMS OFFERED

**Undergraduate—*BSN:*** Nursing.

### NON-DEGREE-RELATED COURSE TOPICS OFFERED

**Undergraduate—**Afro-American(Black) studies; American (United States) history; English language and literature, general; European history; accounting; anatomy; biological sciences/life sciences, other; business communications; business marketing and marketing management; computer and information sciences, general; criminology; developmental and child psychology; fine arts and art studies; foods and nutrition studies; geological and related sciences; health and physical education/fitness; liberal arts and sciences, general studies and humanities; mathematics, other; music; nursing; physiology, human and animal; political science and government; sociology; women's studies.

## WHEATON COLLEGE

*Distance Learning*

Wheaton, IL 60187

**Contact:** Douglas Milford, Director

**Phone:** 630-752-5944

**Fax:** 630-752-5935

**Web:** http://www.wheaton.edu/distancelearning

**E-mail:** distance.learning@wheaton.edu

**ACCREDITATION:** North Central Association of Colleges and Schools

**INSTITUTIONALLY ADMINISTERED FINANCIAL AID:** No

eCollege.com   *www.ecollege.com*

### DEGREE OR CERTIFICATE PROGRAMS OFFERED

**Programs offered do not lead to a degree or other formal award.**

### NON-DEGREE-RELATED COURSE TOPICS OFFERED

**Graduate—**bible/biblical studies; theological and ministerial studies; theological studies and religious vocations, other.

**Non-credit—**bible/biblical studies; theological and ministerial studies.

**See full description on page 672.**

## WHITTIER COLLEGE

13406 Philadelphia Street

Whittier, CA 90608

**Contact:** Jamie J. Shepherd, Director of Learning Support Services

**Phone:** 562-907-4233

**Fax:** 562-907-4980

**Web:** http://www.whittier.edu/

**E-mail:** jshepherd@whittier.edu

**ACCREDITATION:** Western Association of Schools and Colleges

**INSTITUTIONALLY ADMINISTERED FINANCIAL AID:** No

### DEGREE OR CERTIFICATE PROGRAMS OFFERED

**Programs offered do not lead to a degree or other formal award.**

## WICHITA STATE UNIVERSITY

*Media Resources Center*

1845 Fairmount

Wichita, KS 67260-0057

**Contact:** Mary Morriss, Telecourse Coordinator

**Phone:** 316-978-7766

**Fax:** 316-978-3575

**Web:** http://www.mrc.twsu.edu/mrc/telecourse

**E-mail:** morriss@mrc.twsu.edu

**ACCREDITATION:** North Central Association of Colleges and Schools

### DEGREE OR CERTIFICATE PROGRAMS OFFERED

**Programs offered do not lead to a degree or other formal award.**

### NON-DEGREE-RELATED COURSE TOPICS OFFERED

**Undergraduate—**accounting; anthropology; astronomy; biology, general; business administration and management; communications, general; comparative literature; family/consumer resource management; geography; gerontology; history; music; psychology; sociology; speech and rhetorical studies.

**Graduate—**economics.

## WILFRID LAURIER UNIVERSITY

*Office of Part-Time Studies and Continuing Education*

75 University Avenue, W

Waterloo, ON N2G 2H3, Canada

**Contact:** Linda Neumeister, Distance Education Coordinator

**Phone:** 519-884-0710 Ext. 3211

**Fax:** 519-884-0181

**Web:** http://www.wlu.ca/pts

**E-mail:** lneumeis@wlu.ca

**ACCREDITATION:** Provincially Chartered

### DEGREE OR CERTIFICATE PROGRAMS OFFERED

**Undergraduate—*BA:*** Geography; Sociology.

### NON-DEGREE-RELATED COURSE TOPICS OFFERED

**Undergraduate—**English language and literature, general; French language and literature; accounting; anthropology; biology, general; developmental and child psychology; economics; environmental science/studies; fine arts and art studies; geography; investments and securities; law and legal studies, other; medical genetics; religion/religious studies; social work; sociology.

## WILLIAM JEWELL COLLEGE

500 College Hill

Liberty, MO 64068

**Contact:** Dr. Steve Schwegler, Associate Dean

**Phone:** 816-781-7700 Ext. 5399

**Fax:** 816-415-5015

**Web:** http://www.jewell.edu/

**E-mail:** schweglers@william.jewell.edu

**ACCREDITATION:** North Central Association of Colleges and Schools

## DEGREE OR CERTIFICATE PROGRAMS OFFERED

Programs offered do not lead to a degree or other formal award.

## NON-DEGREE-RELATED COURSE TOPICS OFFERED

**Undergraduate**—English composition; accounting; business information and data processing services; business management and administrative services, other; history.

# WILLIAM PATERSON UNIVERSITY OF NEW JERSEY

*The Center for Continuing Education and Distance Learning (CEDL)*

College Hall 120, PO Box 913
Wayne, NJ 07474-0913
**Contact:** Ms. Kathy Garbowski
**Phone:** 973-720-2354
**Fax:** 973-720-2298
**Web:** http://www.wpunj.edu/cedl/dl.htm
**E-mail:** garbowskik@wpunj.edu

**ACCREDITATION:** Middle States Association of Colleges and Schools
**INSTITUTIONALLY ADMINISTERED FINANCIAL AID:** No

## DEGREE OR CERTIFICATE PROGRAMS OFFERED

Programs offered do not lead to a degree or other formal award.

## NON-DEGREE-RELATED COURSE TOPICS OFFERED

**Undergraduate**—American literature (United States); English composition; English creative writing; accounting; anthropology; applied mathematics; botany; business administration and management; communications, other; conservation and renewable natural resources, other; criminal justice and corrections; curriculum and instruction; environmental/ environmental health engineering; foods and nutrition studies; history; marketing management and research; marketing operations/marketing and distribution, other; music; ocean engineering; philosophy; public health.
**Graduate**—English technical and business writing; educational/ instructional media design; mathematical statistics; nursing.
**Non-credit**—business communications; business management and administrative services, other; enterprise management and operation; entrepreneurship.

# WILLIAM RAINEY HARPER COLLEGE

*Learning Resource Center*

1200 West Algonquin Road
Palatine, IL 60067-7398
**Contact:** Fran Hendrickson, Program Assistant
**Phone:** 847-925-6586
**Fax:** 847-925-6037
**Web:** http://www.harper.cc.il.us/doit
**E-mail:** fhendric@harper.cc.il.us

**ACCREDITATION:** North Central Association of Colleges and Schools
**INSTITUTIONALLY ADMINISTERED FINANCIAL AID:** Yes

## DEGREE OR CERTIFICATE PROGRAMS OFFERED

Programs offered do not lead to a degree or other formal award.

## NON-DEGREE-RELATED COURSE TOPICS OFFERED

**Undergraduate**—English composition; English language and literature, general; accounting; astronomy; business communications; business management and administrative services, other; developmental and child psychology; geography; marketing operations/marketing and distribution, other; physical and theoretical chemistry; psychology; sociology.

# WILLIAMSBURG TECHNICAL COLLEGE

601 Martin Luther King, Jr Avenue
Kingstree, SC 29556
**Contact:** Rusty Elliott, Dean of Instruction
**Phone:** 843-355-4138
**Web:** http://www.williamsburgtech.com/
**E-mail:** elliott@wil.tec.sc.us

**ACCREDITATION:** Southern Association of Colleges and Schools

## DEGREE OR CERTIFICATE PROGRAMS OFFERED

Programs offered do not lead to a degree or other formal award.

# WILMINGTON COLLEGE

320 DuPont Highway
New Castle, DE 19720
**Contact:** Dr. JoAnn Ciuffetelli, Assistant Director of Admissions
**Phone:** 302-328-9407 Ext. 104
**Fax:** 302-328-5902
**Web:** http://www.wilmcoll.edu/
**E-mail:** jciuf@wilmcoll.edu

**ACCREDITATION:** Middle States Association of Colleges and Schools
**INSTITUTIONALLY ADMINISTERED FINANCIAL AID:** Yes

## DEGREE OR CERTIFICATE PROGRAMS OFFERED

Programs offered do not lead to a degree or other formal award.

# WISCONSIN INDIANHEAD TECHNICAL COLLEGE, NEW RICHMOND CAMPUS

1019 South Knowles
New Richmond, WI 54017
**Contact:** Susan Yohnk, Admissions Advisor
**Phone:** 715-246-6561 Ext. 4339
**Fax:** 715-246-2777
**Web:** http://www.witc.tec.wi.us/
**E-mail:** syohnk@witc.tec.wi.us

**ACCREDITATION:** North Central Association of Colleges and Schools
**INSTITUTIONALLY ADMINISTERED FINANCIAL AID:** Yes

## DEGREE OR CERTIFICATE PROGRAMS OFFERED
**Undergraduate—*AAS:*** Programmer/Analyst.

## NON-DEGREE-RELATED COURSE TOPICS OFFERED
**Undergraduate—**English technical and business writing; accounting; business administration and management; computer programming; education, general; psychology, other.

# WORCESTER POLYTECHNIC INSTITUTE
### Advanced Distance Learning Network
100 Institute Road
Worcester, MA 01609-2280
**Contact:** Pamela S. Shelley, Assistant Director of Advanced Distance Learning Network
**Phone:** 508-831-5220
**Fax:** 508-831-5881
**Web:** http://www.wpi.edu/+ADLN
**E-mail:** adln@wpi.edu

**ACCREDITATION:** New England Association of Schools and Colleges
**INSTITUTIONALLY ADMINISTERED FINANCIAL AID:** Yes

## DEGREE OR CERTIFICATE PROGRAMS OFFERED
**Graduate—*CAGS:*** Fire Protection Engineering; Wireless Communications. ***CGMS:*** Management. ***Graduate Certificate:*** Environmental Engineering. ***MBA:*** Business Administration. ***MS:*** Civil Engineering; Environmental Engineering; Fire Protection Engineering.

## NON-DEGREE-RELATED COURSE TOPICS OFFERED
**Graduate—**accounting; business administration and management; business marketing and marketing management; communications technologies; engineering/industrial management; environmental/environmental health engineering; finance, general; fire science/firefighting; industrial/manufacturing engineering; international business; management information systems and business data processing, general; marketing operations/marketing and distribution, other; organizational behavior studies.

See full description on page 674.

# WORCESTER STATE COLLEGE
Office of Graduate and Continuing Education, 486 Chandler Street, Sullivan 120
Worcester, MA 01602-2597
**Contact:** Ms. Rayanne LaPierre, Graduate Admissions Counselor
**Phone:** 508-929-8120
**Fax:** 508-929-8100
**Web:** http://www.worcester.edu/
**E-mail:** rlapierre@worcester.edu

**ACCREDITATION:** New England Association of Schools and Colleges
**INSTITUTIONALLY ADMINISTERED FINANCIAL AID:** No

## DEGREE OR CERTIFICATE PROGRAMS OFFERED
Programs offered do not lead to a degree or other formal award.

## NON-DEGREE-RELATED COURSE TOPICS OFFERED
**Undergraduate—**English language and literature, general; communications, general; mathematics.
**Graduate—**education, general.
**Non-credit—**business; computer and information sciences, general.

# WYTHEVILLE COMMUNITY COLLEGE
1000 East Main Street
Wytheville, VA 24382
**Contact:** Mr. David Carter-Tod, Instructional Technologist and Distance Learning Contact
**Phone:** 540-223-4784
**Fax:** 540-223-4778
**Web:** http://www.wcc.vccs.edu/
**E-mail:** wccartd@wcc.vccs.edu

**ACCREDITATION:** Southern Association of Colleges and Schools
**INSTITUTIONALLY ADMINISTERED FINANCIAL AID:** Yes

## DEGREE OR CERTIFICATE PROGRAMS OFFERED
**Undergraduate—*Certificate:*** Web Page Design.

## NON-DEGREE-RELATED COURSE TOPICS OFFERED
**Undergraduate—**American (United States) history; English composition; accounting; administrative and secretarial services; biology, general; business marketing and marketing management; computer and information sciences, general; computer programming; computer software and media applications; computer systems analysis; computer systems networking and telecommunications; cosmetic services; developmental and child psychology; drafting; economics; health and physical education/fitness; health professions and related sciences, other; history; ophthalmic/optometric services; optometry (O.D.); physics; religion/religious studies.

# YORK COLLEGE OF PENNSYLVANIA
### Special Programs
1 Country Club Road
York, PA 17405
**Contact:** Leroy M. Keeney, Director of Special Programs
**Phone:** 717-846-7788
**Fax:** 717-849-1607
**Web:** http://www.ycp.edu
**E-mail:** lkeeney@ycp.edu

**ACCREDITATION:** Middle States Association of Colleges and Schools
**INSTITUTIONALLY ADMINISTERED FINANCIAL AID:** Yes

## DEGREE OR CERTIFICATE PROGRAMS OFFERED
Programs offered do not lead to a degree or other formal award.

## NON-DEGREE-RELATED COURSE TOPICS OFFERED
**Undergraduate—**accounting; finance, general; investments and securities.
**Non-credit—**accounting; agricultural business and management; agricultural production workers and managers; applied mathematics; business

administration and management; communications, general; human resources management; mathematics.

# YORK TECHNICAL COLLEGE
## Distance Learning Department
452 South Anderson Road
Rock Hill, SC 29730
**Contact:** Anita McBride, Department Manager
**Phone:** 803-981-7044
**Fax:** 803-981-7193
**Web:** http://www.yorktech.com
**E-mail:** mcbride@york.tec.sc.us

**ACCREDITATION:** Southern Association of Colleges and Schools

**INSTITUTIONALLY ADMINISTERED FINANCIAL AID:** Yes

### DEGREE OR CERTIFICATE PROGRAMS OFFERED
Programs offered do not lead to a degree or other formal award.

### NON-DEGREE-RELATED COURSE TOPICS OFFERED
**Undergraduate**—English composition; English language and literature, general; accounting; business; business administration and management; computer science; developmental and child psychology; economics; electrical, electronics and communication engineering; environmental/environmental health engineering; history; industrial/manufacturing engineering; mathematics; nursing; philosophy; psychology; sociology.

# YORK UNIVERSITY
Centre for Distance Education, 4700 Keele Street, Room 215 Atkinson
Toronto, ON M3J 1P3, Canada
**Contact:** Ms. Amalia Syligardakis, Supervisor of Centre for Distance Education
**Phone:** 416-736-2100 Ext. 30705
**Fax:** 416-736-5439
**Web:** http://www.yorku.ca/
**E-mail:** amalias@yorku.ca

**ACCREDITATION:** Provincially Chartered

**INSTITUTIONALLY ADMINISTERED FINANCIAL AID:** Yes

### DEGREE OR CERTIFICATE PROGRAMS OFFERED
**Undergraduate**—*BA:* Public Service Studies. *BBA:* Administrative Studies.

### NON-DEGREE-RELATED COURSE TOPICS OFFERED
**Undergraduate**—accounting; business administration and management; business communications; business quantitative methods and management science; business/managerial economics; communications, general; economics; fine arts and art studies; history; human resources management; liberal arts and sciences, general studies and humanities; marketing management and research; mathematics; nursing; philosophy; political science and government; psychology, other; public administration and services, other; religion/religious studies; social sciences, general; social work; sociology.
**Non-credit**—accounting; air transportation workers; business administration and management; computer software and media applications; mathematics, other; social work.

# YUBA COLLEGE
## Learning Resource Center
2088 North Beale Road
Marysville, CA 95901
**Contact:** Miss Jeanette O'Bryan, Distance Learning and Media Specialist
**Phone:** 530-741-6754
**Fax:** 530-741-6824
**Web:** http://www.yuba.cc.ca.us
**E-mail:** jobryan@yuba.cc.ca.us

**ACCREDITATION:** Western Association of Schools and Colleges

**INSTITUTIONALLY ADMINISTERED FINANCIAL AID:** Yes

### DEGREE OR CERTIFICATE PROGRAMS OFFERED
**Undergraduate**—*AAS:* General Studies.

### NON-DEGREE-RELATED COURSE TOPICS OFFERED
**Undergraduate**—American literature (United States); English composition; Spanish language and literature; anthropology; design and applied arts; education, other; family and community studies; foreign languages and literatures, other; history; human resources management; journalism and mass communications; mathematical statistics; mathematics; nursing; psychology, other; veterinary medicine (D.V.M.).

# IN-DEPTH DESCRIPTIONS

The following two-page descriptions were prepared for this book by the institutions. An institution's absence from this section does not constitute an editorial decision on the part of Peterson's. Rather, it was offered as an open forum for institutions to expand upon the information provided in the previous section of this book. The descriptions are arranged alphabetically by institution name.

# AIU Online—American InterContinental University

## *Information Technology and Business Degree Programs*

Atlanta, Georgia

*American InterContinental University (AIU), founded in 1970 in Lucerne, Switzerland, is a private, coeducational, nondenominational institution. Evolving from that single campus, the institution today consists of AIU Online and residential campuses in Atlanta and Dunwoody, Georgia; Los Angeles, California; London, England; and Dubai, United Arab Emirates. AIU has a total enrollment of more than 4,500 students who represent 110 countries and participate in a variety of programs: information technology, business, and visual communications and design.*

*AIU is accredited by the Commission on Colleges of the Southern Association of Colleges and Schools (SACS) and is approved by the Nonpublic Postsecondary Education Commission (Georgia), the Bureau of Private Post Secondary and Vocational Education (California), the State Board of Independent Colleges and Universities (Florida), and the Educational Licensure Commission (District of Columbia). The London campus is also approved as an accredited institution in the United Kingdom by the Open University.*

## DISTANCE LEARNING PROGRAM

AIU Online's virtual campus offers a master's degree in information technology, a bachelor's degree in information technology, and an associate degree completion program in business. In addition, AIU Online's Web-based virtual campus offers students complete support throughout their degree program of study from Admissions Services, Academic Services, Financial Services, Career Services, and Technical Support Services.

## DELIVERY MEDIA

The Web-based degree programs delivered from AIU Online are specifically designed for the student who will access the course from a standard home or work personal computer. Recommended PC specifications are provided to students at the time of enrollment to ensure the best accessibility to distance learning resources and an optimal learning experience.

## PROGRAMS OF STUDY

Information Technology (IT) is the one of the fastest-growing industries in the world, offering excellent long-term career opportunities. According to the Information Technology Association of America, 10 percent, a staggering 850,000 IT positions, will stand open in the United States through 2001. This unfulfilled demand for IT professionals and the prospect of a lucrative career are only a couple of many reasons students are choosing AIU Online's master's or bachelor's of information technology degree programs. In addition to the master's and bachelor's of information technology degree programs, AIU Online offers an associate degree completion program in business.

## STUDENT SERVICES

To ensure an overall high-quality educational experience and academic success, several student support services are provided to AIU Online students. Admissions Services, Academic Services, Financial Services, Career Services, and Technical Sup-port Services are all accessible through a secured Web site to AIU Online students. Online students can check the status of their account, degree plan, and personal information 24 hours a day through this secured Web site. In addition to the services listed above, Technical Support is also available through regular e-mail and by a toll-free telephone number. Career Services offers placement assistance to AIU Online graduates.

## CREDIT OPTIONS

In addition to college credit earned at accredited postsecondary institutions, the following can also be evaluated for academic credit equivalency: CLEP Examination, Advanced Placement (AP) tests, Computer Competency Examination, Extrainstitutional Credit/Experiential Learning, and DANTES/Military Credit.

## FACULTY

AIU Online places special emphasis on the educational, professional, and personal growth of each student. To help students succeed in these areas, AIU Online provides experienced faculty members who bring their real-world experience and expertise, along with their academic credentials, to their students. Faculty members are expected to lead a rich, collaborative online learning experience to facilitate the educational process for each and every student. All faculty members teaching online receive training and guidance in online delivery methods and pedagogy. Through this, AIU Online students are ensured that the University places training of the online faculty as a first concern in offering online courses and degree programs.

## ADMISSION

To be considered for admission to AIU Online, applicants must submit an application, a $50 application fee, and fulfill all admission requirements for the program, as described below. Selection of students for admission into degree programs of study is based on an individual assessment of each applicant. Each applicant must submit to the Admissions Office proof of high school graduation or the equivalent and participate in an admissions interview, arranged by the admissions personnel. If the applicant's first language is not English or the applicant graduated from a non-English-speaking university, a TOEFL score of 500 (undergraduate) or 550 (graduate) or other acceptable proof of English proficiency must be submitted.

## TUITION AND FEES

Tuition and fee schedules for programs of study are reviewed with students at the time of entrance. Fees are charged for applications for admission and graduation. A fee is also charged for rescheduling registration. The registration fee can be made by cash, check, money order, or MasterCard or Visa credit card. Some students may qualify for tuition assistance, financial aid, or veterans benefits.

## FINANCIAL AID

AIU Online's Financial Aid Department is committed to providing every student with the assistance necessary to ensure that each student receives the maximum financial aid available to those who qualify.

AIU Online participates in various federal and state student financial assistance programs. These financial aid programs are designed to provide assistance to students who are currently enrolled or accepted for enrollment but whose financial resources are unable to meet the full cost of their education. In addition, alternative financing options are available to those who qualify, making their attendance through AIU Online a reality.

## APPLYING

To apply for admission, a prospective student must submit an application along with a $50 application fee. An online application can be found at the Web address listed below.

---

### CONTACT

Jay Skiba
National Director of Admissions and Marketing
AIU Online
2895 Greenspoint Parkway, Suite 400
Hoffman Estates, Illinois 60195
Telephone: 877-701-3800, Ext. 3656 (toll-free)
E-mail: info@aiu-online.com
Web site: http://www.aiu-online.com

# Alliant International University

## *School of Education*
San Diego, California

eCollege.com   *www.ecollege.com*

United States International University (USIU) and Alliant University/CSPP, one of the country's largest graduate schools of psychology, have joined forces to create a new multinational university with eight campuses in California, Kenya, and Mexico.

The new Alliant International University (AIU) serves more than 6,000 students. California campuses include Fresno, Irvine, Los Angeles, Sacramento, San Diego, and the San Francisco–Bay Area, with international campuses in Nairobi and Mexico City.

Alliant International University programs focus on interdisciplinary approaches to social issues, problems, and challenges. The University prepares individuals to address social and human behavior issues in all domains of life. It focuses on building and enhancing human capital in a multicultural, technologically complex, and globally interdependent society.

Alliant International University is accredited by the Western Association of Schools and Colleges. This accreditation applies to both traditional and online programs.

## DISTANCE LEARNING PROGRAM

The online Master of Arts in Technology and Learning program provides the same high level of personal attention, support, and service that on-campus students receive at AIU. The online program is primarily tailored to teachers and professionals, so they can progress in their field while maintaining busy schedules.

## DELIVERY MEDIA

Faculty members provide feedback and support to students on a continual basis. Instructors utilize threaded discussions, audio and video clips, group projects, and an integration of Web-based resources. AIU Online students need the following minimum equipment: Windows 95 or later on a 90-MHz Pentium PC or MacOS 8.1 or later on a 604 PowerPC processor (Macintosh); 32 MB RAM; 28.8 modem; sound card; and speakers. Technical support is provided by eCollege.com through their 24-hour, seven-day-a-week HelpDesk.

## PROGRAM OF STUDY

The Master of Arts in Technology and Learning program is composed of eleven courses (45 units) and may be completed in as little as fifteen months. Students may complete the courses conveniently from their homes, schools, or office computers. The frequency and duration of classes are the same as those of equivalent on-campus courses; the teaching methods and learning environment have been modified to make them effective for delivering the program at a distance. The method of delivery in many ways models appropriate usage of technology in education. Thus, the main objective of the program, "to provide students with the skills and understanding necessary to utilize technology to facilitate learning," is enhanced by the online delivery mode.

## STUDENT SERVICES

Alliant International University provides AIU Online students with the following services via the Internet: admissions, registration, financial aid application and processing, academic advisement, and bookstore and library services.

## CREDIT OPTIONS

For the master's program, Alliant International University may accept up to 8 units of transfer credit from other accredited higher education institutions. Course work being considered for transfer must be equivalent to AIU course work for which it is being applied. Students are required to submit transcripts, course descriptions, and other documents for faculty review.

## FACULTY

The entire program's faculty participates in the planning and development of online courses. In addition, there are two online-dedicated AIU Technology and Learning professors and a number of adjunct instructors. AIU Online's student-faculty ratio is 15:1.

## ADMISSION

Applicants must meet the general requirements for admission to the University, which include a bachelor's degree, a minimum GPA of 2.5, two letters of recommendation, official transcripts, and a personal essay.

## TUITION AND FEES

Tuition and fees for the 2001–02 academic year are $295 per unit and a $250 per course distance education fee. The cost of textbooks and materials is additional and varies.

## FINANCIAL AID

AIU Online students may apply for scholarships and all federal, state, and institutional programs (such as grants and loans), as appropriate. In addition, new applicants to the online master's program may qualify for a $500 tuition credit.

## APPLYING

Prospective AIU Online students should go to the Web site below to begin the admissions process. At this Web site, students may complete the application process, apply for financial aid, pay their tuition and fees, consult their academic advisers, register for classes, and attend classes 100 percent online.

---

**CONTACT**
Students should visit the Web site for more information.
Web site: http://www.usiuonline.net

---

American College
of Computer
& Information Sciences

# The American College of Computer and Information Sciences

## Distance Learning Programs

Birmingham, Alabama

---

*The American College of Computer and Information Sciences (ACCIS) is a privately owned independent college, originally founded in 1988 as the American Institute for Computer Sciences. The board of directors adopted the College's new name in January 2001 in order to better represent the credentials the College awards: undergraduate and graduate degree programs in computer science and information systems. ACCIS students typically are adult professionals who wish to study via a self-paced format. ACCIS is accredited by the Accrediting Commission of the Distance Education and Training Council (DETC).*

## DISTANCE LEARNING PROGRAM

The College currently offers Bachelor of Science (B.S.) degree programs in information systems (IS) and computer science, and an Master of Science (M.S.) degree program in computer science. All courses follow a self-paced format, with online chat sessions and full-time faculty assistance offered during weekdays. There is no on-campus residency or scheduled class attendance; students may enroll anywhere at anytime. ACCIS currently services approximately 3,000 active students located in more than 120 countries.

## DELIVERY MEDIA

ACCIS course delivery uses a mixture of texts and technology in all degree programs. Multimedia tutorials offer interactive examples of online learning and self-tests on course concepts. All tutorials are also available via CD-ROM format. Online labs present additional reference material and tutorials written by faculty members.

Faculty-student interaction is achieved by small groups meeting weekly for online chats and lectures covering specific course topics. In addition, one-on-one assistance with full-time faculty members are available via phone, fax and e-mail.

Course assignments, progress tests, and final examinations are required in courses; many courses also require programming assignments. All graded work may be mailed to the school; however, ACCIS uses online testing and feedback software with many courses. Students may also submit work electronically.

Students must have a computer with Windows 95/98 or NT, a CD-ROM drive, and Internet access. Some IS courses require a sound card.

## PROGRAMS OF STUDY

All ACCIS curricula follow guidelines established by leading technology organizations, including the Association for Computing Machinery (ACM) and the Institute for Electronic and Electrical Engineers (IEEE). Both B.S. programs require 120 credit hours, with 60 hours in the core curriculum and 60 hours in the major. The core curriculum offers courses in written communications, humanities, behavioral and social sciences, and business.

The B.S. in information systems is designed for students who desire a broad-based knowledge of computer information systems as they are used in modern organizational settings. Required courses include foundation subjects, such as programming basics, database administration, networking, and IS management. Students may choose suggested elective tracts in C++/Java programming, Web design, Web programming, and database programming. Electives include e-commerce, ASP, telecommunications, Visual Basic, and JavaScript.

The B.S. in computer science uses C++ as core language. It prepares students for real-world object-oriented programming. Fundamental programming concepts include data structures, software engineering, computer architecture and operating systems. Electives include Java, Visual Basic, artificial intelligence, algorithm design and analysis, and data communications and networking.

The M.S. in computer science is designed for students who have an undergraduate computer science or a closely-related degree. The program requires 36 credit hours and offers an in-depth treatment of theoretical foundations and methodologies in computer science. Topics include algorithm design, communication networks, database systems, software engineering, compiler design, and parallel processing.

## STUDENT SERVICES

ACCIS offers an array of services to assist students in becoming involved participants in the online learning process and in preparing for careers in technology.

Students can access a number of services through the College's Web site (listed below). Course labs link students directly to online tutorials, interactive exercises, and resources that apply to concepts covered in each course. Bulletin board discussions thread a variety of conversations. A career center leads students to assessment worksheets, resume builders, interviewing tips, employment tests and negotiating skills. The library links to leading online libraries, features a "Software Station" for downloadable freeware and shareware, offers access to IT publications, and provides an online reference section. ListServs for each course provide another medium for moderated student communication. Students receive weekly e-mails from the College that notify them of upcoming events or changes.

ACCIS also sponsors a number of organizations and events of interest to students. The Mentor Program matches strong ACCIS students and graduates with individuals who need additional help to improve their academic performance. ACCIS's student chapter of the ACM is the only purely distance learning chapter of this well-known professional organization. Monthly meetings offer networking and chats with industry professionals. Delta Epsilon Tau annually honors and inducts outstanding ACCIS students during its Alumni/Student Council conference. Online graduation ceremonies celebrate the achievement of ACCIS alumni.

## CREDIT OPTIONS

ACCIS admissions staff members want to help new students begin at the most advanced point possible in their programs. Since most new students have completed prior college work and have many years of work experience, it is not unusual for students to meet the 60 credit hours required in the core curriculum through transfer and life and work experience credit. Students may receive up to a total of 80 hours of credit through a combination of credits transferred from other accredited, degree-granting programs or awarded for life and work experience. Of the 80 hours, up to 20 may be applied to the student's major. Students may receive up to 30 hours for life and work experience.

## FACULTY

ACCIS has 26 full- and part-time faculty members. Seventy percent of all ACCIS faculty members have earned their terminal or M.B.A. degrees. All full-time faculty members have traditional classroom teaching experience as well as distance learning experience.

## ADMISSION

Graduation from high school or satisfactory completion of the GED to enter an undergraduate program is required for admission into the B.S. programs. A bachelor's degree in computer science or a related discipline is required for admission into the M.S. program.

## TUITION AND FEES

Tuition includes all instruction and faculty-produced course materials. Students purchase textbooks separately. Tuition for the B.S. programs is $105 per credit hour. Tuition for the M.S. program is $135 per credit hour. Individual courses may be taken for $445 (undergraduate) and $565 (graduate). There is no application fee. All books can be purchased online through Specialty Books, ACCIS' textbook partner.

## FINANCIAL AID

More than half of all ACCIS students receive financing assistance. ACCIS offers both interest-free and low-cost finance plans. Students may also gain financing through Sallie Mae Corporation. In addition, more than 350 employers have reimbursed their employees for tuition through the ACCIS Business Benefits Program.

## APPLYING

ACCIS offers open enrollment; students may begin their programs at any time. Both printed and online applications are available. An admissions adviser is assigned to each applicant. Advisers work with prospective students by phone and e-mail to design a program most appropriate for the individual. The ACCIS Admissions Committee evaluates documents and transcripts provided by the student and awards life and work experience credit and transfer credit. Enrollment process can be as short as one week. Following enrollment, each student completes the online orientation course that covers all ACCIS policies and procedures and introduces services and course materials.

**CONTACT**
American College of Computer and Information Sciences
2101 Magnolia Avenue
Suite 200
Birmingham, Alabama 35205
Telephone: 205-323-6191
          800-729-2427 (toll-free in the U.S.)
E-mail: admiss@accis.edu
Web site: http://www.accis.edu

# American Military University

## *Distance Learning Programs*

Manassas Park, Virginia

*American Military University (AMU) is a private higher-education institution that is accredited by the Distance Education and Training Council, whose accrediting commission is recognized by the U.S. Department of Education. The University is licensed by the State Council on Higher Education for Virginia to offer both graduate and undergraduate degrees and certificates. From its inception, AMU has been exclusively a distance learning institution and, in 1995, became one of the first to achieve recognized accreditation. AMU was founded in 1991 to provide distance learning military studies degrees to military personnel. Over the years, the mission broadened to include government, corporate, and civilian communities, with curricula expanding into management, national security, criminal justice, intelligence, and international relations disciplines. The University's administrative offices are in Manassas Park, Virginia, about 45 miles east of Washington, D.C.*

## DISTANCE LEARNING PROGRAM

AMU is exclusively a distance learning institution. All 600 courses are Web based and accessible around the clock through the Electronic Campus from wherever students have Internet access. Students are led through the four-week, eight-week, or fifteen-week courses with a Student Course Guide that lists weekly study requirements and assignments.

## DELIVERY MEDIA

AMU delivers and supports more than 600 courses through its Electronic Campus, with classrooms served by Educator® courseware by Ucompass. Through these electronic classrooms, students communicate with professors and each other using LISTSERV, discussion groups, bulletin boards, chat rooms, and e-mail and submit assignments, receive feedback, and take examinations. Electronic communications are supplemented by phone consultations during professors' office hours, with most classes restricted to 25 students to ensure adequate student-professor interaction.

## PROGRAMS OF STUDY

AMU offers graduate and undergraduate degree programs and certificate programs.

Graduate nonthesis programs, consisting of 36 semester hours/twelve courses and a comprehensive final examination, are offered in national security studies, military studies, air warfare, land warfare, naval warfare, unconventional warfare, intelligence, Civil War studies, American Revolution studies, defense management, criminal justice, and management. There are cooperative graduate degree programs in transportation management and marine engineering with the Global Maritime and Transportation School of the U.S. Merchant Marine Academy and in peacekeeping operations with the United Nations Institute for Training and Research (UNITAR).

Certificate programs, consisting of 15 semester hours/five courses, are offered in twenty-five specialties within the curriculum and in area studies, period studies, and both historical and contemporary study areas.

Undergraduate programs include the Associate of Arts in general studies, a 63-semester-hour program with 30 semester hours of specified general education courses and electives, and the Bachelor of Arts, a 120-semester-hour program that mirrors the associate degree's lower-division requirements and includes upper-division major requirements of 39 semester hours, with 18 hours of electives. The bachelor's degree is offered in international relations; interdisciplinary studies; military management; intelligence studies; criminal justice, with an internship for law enforcement practitioners; management, with a career-counseling concentration; military history, with American or world concentrations; and marketing, with an internship program for military recruiters. Certificate programs are offered in five specialties.

## SPECIAL PROGRAMS

Special programs include undergraduate internships in marketing, for military recruiters; in criminal justice, for practicing law enforcement professionals; and in civic responsibility, open to all students; Graduate Challenge Examinations for U.S. Army Officer Basic and Captain Career Courses; graduate credit programs for the U.S. Marine Corps Basic Course (TBS) and Amphibious Warfare School (AWS); articulation agreements with Blue Ridge Community College in criminal justice, with Army Management Staff College in defense management, and with Potomac College; an undergraduate career counseling concentration within the management degree for military retention officials; and an undergraduate certificate program in information technology.

## STUDENT SERVICES

The Student Service and Technology Center provides an orientation that prepares students for online distance learning, including navigating the Electronic Campus, using the Online Research Center, utilizing the functions of the Educator® classrooms and software, transfer credit evaluations, academic program development, financial aid, and other services. Most student service functions are available online for students to submit changes and check their status.

## CREDIT OPTIONS

Credits may be earned through AMU by traditional courses, challenge examinations, internships, and independent study. Courses may be audited without credit. AMU accepts transfer credit from accredited institutions, training and experience credit recommended by the American Council on Education, and credit by examinations (CLEP, DANTES, etc.).

Credit acceptance by programs is associate degree, up to 45 semester hours; bachelor's degree, up to 90 semester hours; and graduate degree, up to 15 semester hours.

## FACULTY

The 180 faculty members are primarily adjunct professors active in the disciplines they instruct. All faculty members meet traditional accreditation standards with regard to degrees and professional preparation.

## ADMISSION

Graduate students must possess an accredited baccalaureate degree and a minimum 2.7 GPA in their final 60 undergraduate semester hours. Undergraduate students must have a high school diploma or GED certificate. No examinations are required for admission.

## TUITION AND FEES

Tuition is $250 per semester hour for both graduate and undergraduate programs. There is no admission fee. Transfer credit evaluations are $75, and the graduation fee is $100, which includes a framed and matted diploma.

## FINANCIAL AID

Undergraduate students receive merit scholarships covering up to 25 percent of tuition, and book grants provide all required textbooks. More than $400,000 in financial aid was distributed to undergraduate students in 2000, covering 100 percent of eligible students. All students are eligible for Sallie Mae education loans. At this time, AMU does not participate in Title IV funding programs, although the U.S. Department of Education is evaluating distance learning programs for possible inclusion in the program.

## APPLYING

All students apply online at no cost through the Web site Visitor Center. Notifications are made by e-mail, and admission is confirmed after all transcripts and other documents are received. All students go through an online interactive orientation.

---

### CONTACT

Office of University Relations
American Military University
9104-P Manassas Drive
Manassas Park, Virginia 20111
Telephone: 877-468-6268 (toll-free)
Fax: 703-330-5109
E-mail: info@amunet.edu
Web site: http://www.amunet.edu

---

# Athabasca University

## Distance Learning

Athabasca, Alberta, Canada

*Athabasca University (AU) was created as a publicly funded and fully accredited university under the statutes of the Province of Alberta, Canada. Athabasca University specializes in the delivery of distance education courses and programs.*

*The main office is located in the town of Athabasca, 145 kilometres north of Edmonton, with satellite learning centres in Calgary and Edmonton.*

*Athabasca University's mission statement reflects a commitment to innovation, flexibility, excellence in teaching, research and scholarship, and service in the community. Emphasis has also been placed on international development and building a base for public trust and private support.*

*Athabasca University is a full member of the Association of Universities and Colleges of Canada, the Association of Commonwealth Universities, the International Council for Open and Distance Education, the Canadian Association for Distance Education, and the Canadian Association for Graduate Studies.*

## DISTANCE LEARNING PROGRAM

Athabasca University's primary focus is the delivery of courses and programs by distance and online methods at both the undergraduate and graduate levels. Students can pursue studies at their own pace in their own home or workplace, completing a program or individual courses. AU courses are accessed by 25,000 individuals annually.

## DELIVERY MEDIA

Athabasca University uses a variety of learning methods, including multimedia online activities, print materials, e-mail, the Internet, CD-ROMs, computer software, audioconferencing, videoconferencing, audiotapes, videotapes, TV, and radio. Any particular course might use a combination of these methods. Some courses are also available in the classroom, taught in association with one of AU's partners. Students have support from professors, tutors, advisers, and service departments through contact by e-mail and telephone (toll-free in Canada and the U.S.).

## PROGRAM OF STUDY

Graduate degree and diploma programs offered are the Master of Arts–integrated studies, Master of Business Administration, Master of Distance Education, Master of Health Studies, Master of Science–information systems, advanced graduate diploma: advanced nursing practice, advanced graduate diploma in distance education (technology), and the advanced graduate diploma in management. Undergraduate degrees offered are the Bachelor of Administration, Bachelor of Administration (postdiploma), three-year Bachelor of Arts degree, three-year Bachelor of Arts general degree, four-year Bachelor of Arts (joint program with Mount Royal College), four-year Bachelor of Arts, Bachelor of Commerce, Bachelor of General Studies, Bachelor of Nursing (post-RN), Bachelor of Professional Arts, Bachelor of Science with a major in human science, Bachelor of Science (postdiploma), Bachelor of Science in human science (postdiploma), Bachelor of Science in computing and information systems, and Bachelor of Science in computing and information systems (postdiploma).

University certificate programs are offered in accounting, advanced accounting, administration, career development, computers and management information systems, counseling women, English language studies, French language proficiency, health development administration, home health nursing, computing and information systems, industrial relations and human resources, labour studies, and public administration.

In addition, there are University diploma programs in arts and inclusive education.

## SPECIAL PROGRAMS

A new Canadian Virtual University is centered at AU. The CVU-UVC is an innovative partnership of seven Canadian universities. The partnership offers 1,500 courses, including 160 online that can be combined to complete 100 recognized university credentials. For details, students should visit http://www.cvu-uvc.ca.

AU is a founding partner and the only Canadian member of Global Alliance, a consortium of ten leading universities in North America, Europe, and Australia. The alliance is a new concept in "e-education" that allows students to link to the Internet, take courses, and complete degrees. For information, students should visit http://www.gua.com.

Athabasca University has more than 125 partnerships with colleges, universities, and the private sector to provide learning options for students. Approximately twenty of these alliances are international (Japan, China, England, Jamaica, Mexico, Malaysia, Trinidad, South Africa, and Taiwan).

Athabasca University is providing management courses through e-classes® to about 50 Canadian Aboriginal students over the next two years. Students will be provided assistance with the cost of tuition and computers. Aboriginal advisers provide program planning and registration advice.

## STUDENT SERVICES

Athabasca University provides high-quality service to all students. There are a number of departments that offer information and advice, including the Information Centre, Academic Centres, Learning Centres, Learning Services–Tutorial, Office of the Registrar, Course Materials, Computing Services Help Desk, and Library Services. The first point of contact for questions or to reach any of these services is the Information Centre at 800-788-9041 (toll-free in Canada and the U.S.) or 780-675-6100 (international).

## CREDIT OPTIONS

Athabasca University grants credit for approved courses completed at other recognized postsecondary institu-

tions, and its credits are eligible for transfer to programs at other universities worldwide. Some students can apply for a Prior Learning Assessment, which evaluates nonformal university-level learning for credit toward a credential.

Athabasca University courses are generally either 3 credits or 6 credits. Typically, a three-year degree program requires 90 credits and four-year degree programs require 120 credits.

## FACULTY

Athabasca University employs 124 faculty members and 220 part-time tutors, with 96 percent having a doctorate or an advanced degree. Academic staff members and tutors contribute to Athabasca University's high student satisfaction rating.

## ADMISSION

Admission is year-round, and anyone 18 years of age or older is eligible for admission, regardless of previous educational experience, with or without a high school diploma. (A few programs and courses may have academic or geographic restrictions).

## TUITION AND FEES

Textbooks, course materials, and fees are included in each registration. Undergraduate 3-credit registration costs

Can$444 for in-province students and Can$694 for international students. For 6-credit registration, students pay Can$776 (provincial) and Can$1026 (international). Graduate program fees vary by program.

## FINANCIAL AID

Financial assistance is available to full- and part-time students from Alberta Students Finance or the financial aid agency where a student resides. The amount varies according to need.

In-province students obtain a financial aid package from Athabasca University. Out-of-province students should contact the financial aid agency in their locale.

All students are automatically considered for academic awards and scholarships without application unless specified otherwise. Award recipients are announced twice per year at Convocation.

## APPLYING

Admission to undergraduate programs is year-round. Applicants should consider postal and processing times when a particular starting time is desired. They should complete a General Application Form and Course Registration Form and submit them with applicable fees. Forms are available in the Calendar, by fax, or on the Web.

---

### CONTACT

Athabasca University Information Centre
1 University Drive
Athabasca, Alberta T9S 3A3
Canada
Telephone: 780-675-6100
         800-788-9041 (toll-free in Canada and the U.S.)
Fax: 780-675-6437
E-mail: auinfo@athabascau.ca
Web site: http://www.athabascau.ca

---

# Auburn University

## Graduate Outreach Program

Auburn, Alabama

---

> Auburn University was chartered in 1856 as the East Alabama Male College. In 1872, Auburn became a state institution—the first land-grant university in the South to be separate from a state university. Auburn University, selected as one of the nation's top 100 college buys by The Student Guide to America's 100 Best College Buys 1999, is dedicated to serving the state and the nation through instruction, research, and extension. Auburn University is accredited by the Commission on Colleges of the Southern Association of Colleges and Schools.
>
> The campus consists of more than 1,800 acres, with a student body of approximately 21,500. Auburn University, the largest school in the state of Alabama, is located in east-central Alabama. The city of Auburn has a population of about 35,000. Auburn is known for its small-town, friendly atmosphere and is often referred to as "the loveliest village on the Plain."

## DISTANCE LEARNING PROGRAM

In response to industry's request, Auburn's College of Engineering began offering courses to off-campus students through the Graduate Outreach Program in 1984. The College of Business made Master of Business Administration (M.B.A.) courses available in 1990. The Graduate Outreach Program allows professionals the opportunity to continue their education while maintaining full-time employment. The program serves more than 400 students in forty states. The M.B.A. program is accredited by AACSB–The International Association for Management Education.

*Note for international inquirers: Due to material distribution methods, the current distance learning program service area is limited to the U.S. and Canada and to U.S. military personnel with APO or FPO mailing addresses.*

## DELIVERY MEDIA

The Graduate Outreach Program makes every effort to ensure that the off-campus students receive the same high-quality education as on-campus students. Live classes are videotaped daily and distributed in standard VHS format. Professors establish telephone office hours and/or e-mail communication so that off-campus students may receive answers to any questions they may have. E-mail accounts are established for the Graduate Outreach Program students. Most faculty members also utilize the Internet to post handouts and class materials.

## PROGRAMS OF STUDY

The Graduate Outreach Program offers master's degrees in eight different disciplines in engineering, the Master of Management Information Systems, the Master of Accounting, and the Master of Business Administration degree. The Master of Aerospace Engineering, Chemical Engineering, Civil Engineering, Computer Science and Engineering, Electrical and Computer Engineering, Industrial and Systems Engineering, Materials Engineering, and Mechanical Engineering are all nonthesis programs without residency requirements. Each candidate must pass an on-campus, comprehensive, oral examination covering the program of study to graduate. The examination covers the major and minor subjects, including any research or special projects involved. The Master of Science degree, offered in eight disciplines, requires a formal written thesis and at least one quarter of full-time residence.

In the Master of Business Administration program, students may earn a concentration in either finance, health care administration, human resource management, marketing, operations management, management information systems, or management of technology. The program consists of 36 to 42 semester hours of course work, including a minimum of 15 elective hours. Applicants are required to complete a course in calculus and statistics prior to entering the program. Students with nonbusiness undergraduate degrees may be required to pass foundations exams in economics, finance, marketing, management, and accounting. Incoming students are also advised to have a working knowledge of word processing and spreadsheet software and an elementary understanding of database applications. M.B.A. students must visit the campus for three to five days during their last quarter prior to graduating for on-campus presentations.

Nondegree professional development courses are available for those who need to meet job requirements or professional certification.

## SPECIAL PROGRAMS

Career and job placement assistance is available through Auburn University's Career and Student Development Services. Accessibility to the R. B. Draughon Library is also available. A valid Auburn University student identification card is required to check out resources. The Division of University Computing provides University-wide computing and networking services to students. Computer accounts are free of charge to currently enrolled students.

## CREDIT OPTIONS

Graduate credit taken in residence at another approved graduate school may be transferred to Auburn University, but is not accepted until the student has completed at least 9 hours of work in the Graduate School at Auburn University. No prior commitment is made concerning whether transfer credit will be accepted. A student must earn at least 21 semester hours or half of the total hours required for a master's degree (whichever is greater) at Auburn University. No transfer credit is approved without two official transcripts. No course in which a grade lower than B was earned may be transferred.

## FACULTY

The Auburn University faculty consists of more than 1,200 members. Eighty percent of the faculty members hold a doctoral degree, and 88 percent hold a terminal degree in their field.

## ADMISSION

An applicant to the Graduate School must hold a bachelor's degree or its equivalent from an accredited college or university. The Graduate Record Examinations (GRE) is required for admission to the College of Engineering, and the Graduate Management Admission Test (GMAT) is required for admission to the M.B.A. program. Admission is based on the grade point average of university-level courses, GRE or GMAT scores, and recommendation letters from instructors and supervisors. Students can be informed by the Graduate Outreach Program on how they can enroll as off-campus students once they are accepted by the Graduate School.

## TUITION AND FEES

The Graduate Outreach Program fees are $397 per credit hour for engineering and the M.B.A. program. There is no longer a part-time registration fee. Registration schedules and fee bills are mailed to the student prior to the beginning of each quarter.

## FINANCIAL AID

Military personnel who have been accepted into the Graduate School may apply for tuition aid through DANTES at their local education office. Many of the Graduate Outreach Program students receive tuition assistance through their employer's tuition reimbursement plan. The Auburn University Office of Student Financial Aid assists in the awarding of grants, loans, and scholarships for qualified full-time students.

## APPLYING

To apply for admission, a prospective student must return a Graduate School application, an M.B.A. application (if applicable), a $25 nonrefundable application fee, three letters of recommendation, GRE or GMAT scores, and two official transcripts of all undergraduate and subsequent course work from the respective institutions. An online application is now available for Graduate School applicants (http://gradweb.duc.auburn.edu/webapp/appfrm_web.mv). This ensures a quicker response in most cases.

---

### CONTACT

James C. Brandt
Student Services
Graduate Outreach Program
202 Ramsay Hall
Auburn University
Auburn, Alabama 36849-5336
Telephone: 888-844-5300 (toll-free)
Fax: 334-844-2519
E-mail: jcbrandt@eng.auburn.edu
Web site: http://www.auburn.edu/gop/

# Baker College

## Baker On-line

Flint, Michigan

Baker College, founded in the true American tradition as a small business college in 1888, is a private, nonprofit, accredited, coeducational institution. The College has more than a dozen campuses and branch locations in the Midwest and has a total enrollment of more than 17,000 students. The College is uniquely designed for one purpose: to provide high-quality higher education that enables graduates to be successful throughout their challenging and rewarding careers. The College offers diploma; certificate; and associate, bachelor's, and master's degree programs in the fields of business, technical, and health service fields. Total commitment to the students' employment success in uniquely evident in all aspects of the College's operations.

Baker College is accredited by the Commission on Institutions of Higher Education of the North Central Association of Colleges and Schools. Baker College is an equal opportunity/affirmative action institution.

## DISTANCE LEARNING PROGRAM

Baker On-Line offers the convenience of classroom accessibility 24 hours a day, seven days a week, from virtually anywhere in the world. Because students do all classroom work off-line, schedules are flexible. A student goes on line to send and receive completed work and other materials. It is not a self-paced program. Courses begin and end on specific dates, and class work is assigned deadlines.

## DELIVERY MEDIA

Students are required to have a computer with the following minimum requirements: a 486 computer system or higher, a 3.5 high-density floppy drive, a 28.8 bps modem (minimum), and a hard drive capacity exceeding the student's current demands by at least 100 megabytes. A CD-ROM and an Internet service provider are required. The virtual classroom is the common meeting area for all students taking classes on line. Communication is accomplished by sending messages back and forth from the student's computer to the classroom computer. Each classroom has a unique name, and only students taking that class have access to the virtual classroom. This ensures privacy for all students.

## PROGRAMS OF STUDY

Baker On-Line offers the delivery of high-quality, respected courses and programs that enable a student to earn an associate, bachelor's, or master's degree at home, on the road, or anywhere in the world.

The Associate of Business Administration degree has been designed specifically for the on-line college environment, where students have a variety of choices in filling out the degree plan. The curriculum gives students a good background of business facts and knowledge upon which to build or enhance a career in business.

The Bachelor of Business Administration degree is a program designed for the working professional that combines core course work with independent research and experiential credit to provide a contemporary business degree for today's business environment. Each core course contains focused study in the content area accompanied by independent research.

The Master of Business Administration degree program seeks to combine the best of conventional academic training with the best of field-based learning. Most typical business disciplines are represented in the curriculum because the College believes that a successful manager must be conversant with different aspects of running any of today's organizations or companies. Students may also elect to focus their studies in one of the following areas: computer information systems, health-care management, human resource management, industrial management, integrated health care, international business, leadership studies, or marketing.

## SPECIAL PROGRAMS

Baker On-Line offers undergraduate courses at all levels to support all of the campuses and their program offerings as a convenience for students who may have trouble commuting to a campus. Baker On-Line publishes a listing each quarter showing which classes will be offered.

## STUDENT SERVICES

Every Baker College student is assigned an e-mail account on the BakerNet system. Through this system, students can communicate with each other and their instructors and with members of the graduate school staff. Students may also use their accounts to access the World Wide Web. They also have access to the Baker College Library System and FALCON, a consortium of libraries that supports an online catalog database of more than 500,000 holdings. Students also have access to InfoTrac periodical indexing databases, the UMI/ProQuest General Periodicals On-Disc full-article imaging station, Books-in-Print with Reviews, and all available Internet and World Wide Web resources.

Baker College offers a renowned Lifetime Employment Service, with access to thousands of career opportunities and employment databases, to all students. This service can be used for the rest of one's life.

## CREDIT OPTIONS

Baker College recognizes the expediency of understandable and universally accepted standards related to transfer of academic credit. The College follows the Michigan Association of Collegiate Registrars and Admissions Officers Official Policies and recognizes the College-Level Examination Program (CLEP) or other standardized tests.

## FACULTY

The focus of Baker's faculty is somewhat different from that of traditional universities. Instead of placing an emphasis on empirical research, Baker values practitioner-oriented education. Faculty members remain con-

tinually active in their professions by consulting, conducting seminars, running their own businesses, writing, volunteering in their communities, and working with other organizations. The faculty-student ratio in distance education is 1:10.

## ADMISSION

Graduate program candidates must have a bachelor's degree from an accredited institution and a 2.5 or better GPA in their undergraduate work, be able to display appropriate communication skills, submit three letters of reference, submit a current resume, and have completed no less than three years of full-time work. Undergraduates must have graduated from high school, completed a GED, or passed an Ability to Benefit assessment before entering.

## TUITION AND FEES

Undergraduate tuition for the 2001–02 school year is $155 per credit hour. Graduate tuition is $235 per credit hour. The cost of books ranges from $200 to $300 per quarter.

## FINANCIAL AID

Students who are accepted into Baker College may be considered for several forms of state, federal, and insti-

tutional financial aid. Students are requested to complete the Free Application for Federal Student Aid (FAFSA) and return it directly to the College.

## APPLYING

Baker College uses a rolling admission process, so there are no deadlines for applications. Students are allowed to begin in any quarter. Once the Admissions Committee receives an application, applicants usually receive a decision in approximately four weeks. Once accepted, students participate in a three-week online orientation. They are not required to visit a campus at any time.

### CONTACT

Chuck J. Gurden
Director of On-Line Admissions
Center for Graduate Studies
Baker College
1116 West Bristol Road
Flint, Michigan 48507-9843
Telephone: 810-766-4390
         800-469-3165 (toll-free)
Fax: 810-766-4399
E-mail: gurden_c@corpfl.baker.edu
Web site: http://online.baker.edu

# Bellevue University

## Online Programs

Bellevue, Nebraska

---

Bellevue University is one of Nebraska's largest fully accredited independent colleges. It is accredited by the Higher Learning Commission and the North Central Association of Colleges and Schools' Commission on Institutions of Higher Education (NCA-CIHE). Programs serve the needs of more than 3,400 students annually (600 online) and cater to working adult students as well as traditional undergraduate students. Benefits include accelerated degree completion programs, online programs, an online library, and cooperative credit transfer agreements. Associate degrees are accepted in full, and credit is given for corporate and military training.

## DISTANCE LEARNING PROGRAM

Bellevue University is an information-age institution of higher learning with progressive options for online graduate and undergraduate degrees. Graduate and undergraduate programs are offered online, on campus, and in centers throughout the region, preparing students for an ever-changing environment.

## DELIVERY MEDIA

Online education is about taking classes and earning a degree entirely through the Internet. With Internet access, students go online to take classes, participate in discussions with professors and fellow students, conduct research at the online library, and interact with their online adviser. Online classes are small to give the cyberactive learning advantage that characterizes Bellevue University.

## PROGRAMS OF STUDY

Undergraduate programs are offered in an accelerated, cohort-based format. The program in business administration of technical studies emphasizes techniques, procedures, and methods for managing the technical functions of business. The business information systems program prepares students who do not have computer technology degrees or course work for management within IT and positions with technical applications. The program in criminal justice administration focuses on management and opportunities in the criminal justice system. The program is designed for individuals working in, or who are closely associated with, the criminal justice system. The e-business program covers the interchange and processing of information using electronic techniques for conducting business within a framework of generally accepted standards and practices. The program in global business management provides the knowledge, skills, and abilities to evaluate and manage international businesses. The health-care administration program provides a systems perspective for those interested in pursuing management opportunities in health care. The program in leadership provides students the theoretical and practical preparation they need to assume positions of leadership in the professional ranks of organizations. The management program gives students a comprehensive background in the skills, methods, and theories that undergird effective management. The management of human resources program covers methods and practices of the human resource management professional. The management information systems program emphasizes business knowledge and management skills for individuals working in the management information systems field.

Bellevue University Online offers five graduate programs. The Master of Business Administration (M.B.A.) program covers the tools and methods required to run a business. Thirty-six credit hours of course work are required. The schedule of course offerings permits an individual working full-time to complete all the requirements for the M.B.A. degree in eighteen months (two classes per term). Students who do not have an undergraduate degree in business generally take the Foundation (12 credits) and the Core (24 credits) to complete the degree. M.B.A. concentrations are offered in accounting, cyber law, finance, international management, and management information systems.

The Master of Science in Computer Information Systems program has strong elements of both business and computer/telecommunication subjects. Students with business or computer undergraduate preparation typically finish the program with 36 credits of graduate work. For students without a computer background, there are an additional 6 credits of prerequisite courses.

The Master of Science in health-care administration program provides clinical health-care providers with an opportunity to pursue in depth the various areas of planning, organizing, leading, and controlling as they provide administrative guidance to others within their health-related organization.

Students in the Master of Arts in Management program develop a working knowledge of the application of quantitative techniques, marketing analysis, human resource management, financial analysis, influencing behavior in organizations, and sensitivity to the legal environment in which operations occur.

The Master of Arts in leadership program encourages individual thought, synthesis of group contribution, and assimilation of practical and theoretical teachings. Its mission is to combine leadership philosophy, derived from great leaders and their writings, with concepts and theoretical models of organizational leadership.

## CREDIT OPTIONS

Bellevue University grants credit for college-level learning that a student has obtained through sources other than college classes. Students may be granted credit for college-level learning acquired outside of a regionally accredited college setting. Procedures are in place to assess student learning from non–regionally accredited institutions, American Council on Education recommendations, corporate training or programs, CLEP/DANTES tests, and the Experiential Learning Assessment.

## FACULTY

The Bellevue University full-time and adjunct faculty consists of 95 men and 53 women teaching students from freshman to graduate level. The student-faculty ratio is 20:1.

## ADMISSION

Online degree completion programs are offered in an accelerated format. To qualify for undergraduate programs, students must have at least 60 credit hours from an accredited institution or an associate degree. To qualify for graduate programs, students must have a baccalaureate degree from an accredited institution, a minimal 2.5 GPA over the course of the last two years of undergraduate work, two letters of recommendation, and a completed essay.

## TUITION AND FEES

Tuition and fees vary by program. For more information, students should contact the University at the phone number listed below.

## FINANCIAL AID

Financial assistance is available from the federal and state governments, the institution, and private sources. Financial aid includes grants, scholarships, work-study programs, and student loans. Grants and scholarships do not have to be repaid.

## APPLYING

Individuals interested in applying should transmit the application online or by mail, pay fees, and submit transcripts for evaluation. Admissions counselors work with students to complete the official admissions process. An educational degree plan is completed for each student, defining requirements needed to achieve each student's degree goal.

---

### CONTACT

Bellevue University
1000 Galvin Road South
Bellevue, Nebraska 68005
Telephone: 800-756-7920 (toll-free)
Web site: http://www.bellevue.edu

# Berkeley College

## Berkeley College Online

Waldwick, New Jersey

*Since its inception in 1931, Berkeley College has evolved and expanded, and is recognized as a premier educator in the New York metropolitan area. The College prepares people of all generations for successful careers in business. All of our five urban and suburban campuses are accredited by the Commission on Higher Education of the Middle States Association of Colleges and Schools. The New York and New Jersey campuses are authorized to confer bachelor's degrees and associate degrees.*

## DISTANCE LEARNING PROGRAM

Berkeley College brings its classrooms to students with the same high standards of its on-site courses. Both online and on-site, Berkeley College's strengths are in giving students connections through a balanced program of academic preparation, professional training, and hands-on experience through internships.

## DELIVERY MEDIA

Berkeley supports each one of its online students with an instructor, classmates, and an academic adviser, all of whom are just an e-mail away.

Berkeley has always taught courses to all generations. With the understanding that many students may need to balance work, family, and social responsibilities with their course work, a Berkeley student may log on, though the power of the Internet, to a Berkeley course from anywhere in the world, anytime they want.

## PROGRAMS OF STUDY

Small classes, one-on-one coaching, and emphasis on the development of creative and analytical skills are the hallmarks of Berkeley's teaching. With 25 people or less in each course,

many Berkeley students feel they have more contact with the faculty members.

The following distance learning courses are offered in fall, via the Internet: College Writing Skills; College Reading Skills; Fundamentals of Math I; Fundamentals of Math II; English Composition I; English Composition III; Business Organization and Management; Business in a Digital World; Managing for Change; Principles of Marketing; International Business; World Civilization (2 sections); Health/Heredity; Sociology; Macroeconomics; Gender, Race, and Class; and Psychology.

## SPECIAL PROGRAMS

Students can take approximately the first half of their course work toward an associate or bachelor's business degree at home, online. The remainder of the program must be completed on-site at Berkeley College. It's a great way to save the money and time otherwise spent on travel/commuting, meals, residence facilities, etc.

Bachelor's degree programs are offered in business administration–office systems management, business administration–management, business administration–marketing, general business, international business, and e-business.

Associate degree programs include business administration–manage-

ment, business administration–marketing, business administration–office systems management, international business (A.S. degree), international business (A.A.S. degree), and e-business.

## STUDENT SERVICES

Online learners may use all of Berkeley's services, from libraries to academic advisers. More than 20 Berkeley placement professionals are on the staff to help with students' resumes and interviewing skills. With many connections to professionals in the business world, placement professionals also arrange interviews for students with many of the finest corporations in the New York area.

The Berkeley balance of conceptual and practical education results in 95 percent of their graduates gaining employment in positions related to their course work.

## CREDIT OPTIONS

Transfer counselors help students transfer their previously earned credits to Berkeley. Prior learning experiences (including alternatives to classroom instruction) may help students earn credits and complete their program ahead of schedule.

## FACULTY

Berkeley's practitioner faculty members are leaders in their fields. They share real-world insights and help students in many practical and theoretical ways.

## ADMISSION

Basic requirements for admission to Berkeley College include graduation from an accredited high school or equivalent and entrance exam or SAT/ACT scores. A personal interview is strongly recommended. The following credentials must be submitted as part of the application process: a completed application form, a nonrefundable $35 application fee, and an unofficial transcript (for currently enrolled high school students) or a high school diploma or its equivalent (for high school graduates). Students who graduated from an accredited high school or its equivalent and attended a college or university are considered transfer students. To be considered for admission, transfer students must submit an application for admission and the nonrefundable $35 application fee, a transcript from each college or university attended, and a high school transcript or GED. For all students, applications are accepted after credentials are received.

To be admitted directly to the upper-division, students must have completed either a relevant associate degree or at least 60 semester/90 quarter credits in appropriate course work (with a grade of C or better) at Berkeley or another regionally accredited institution.

## TUITION AND FEES

In 2001–02, day students pay $13,185 for tuition. At the Westchester campus, boarding students pay an additional residence fee of $4800. Students at Berkeley's New York City campus are housed at Sussex House, a newly renovated eight-story building located on the edge of Times Square. It is only five blocks from the College's Academic Center. A wide variety of residence options are available at Sussex House.

## FINANCIAL AID

Scholarships and grants totaling approximately $7 million are available at Berkeley. Many full and partial scholarships are available. Grants are also made on the basis of financial need.

Berkeley protects students against tuition increases. In most colleges, tuition continually increases. To help students complete the program of their choice within a budget, Berkeley College makes the distinctive promise of protecting them from any tuition increase as long as they maintain continuous, full-time enrollment.

## APPLYING

Applications are accepted on an ongoing basis. Current students who wish to apply for online learning must obtain approval from an Academic Dean. Prospective students who wish to apply as online learning students should submit an online application on the Web site (listed below). An orientation session shows prospective students how to log on and navigate through various screens.

---

### CONTACT

Berkeley College
Central Admissions Office
100 West Prospect Street
Waldwick, New Jersey 07463
Telephone: 201-652-1346 Ext. 143
        800-446-5400 (toll-free)
E-mail: info@berkeleycollege.edu
Web site: http://www.berkeleycollege.edu

# Boston University

## *College of Engineering*
## *Department of Manufacturing Engineering*

Boston, Massachusetts

*Boston University, incorporated in 1869, is an independent, coeducational, nonsectarian university, open to members of all minority groups. Its 22,515 full-time students and 2,559 faculty members make it one of the largest independent universities in the world. The Department of Manufacturing Engineering offers B.S., M.S., and Ph.D. degrees and was the first department in the country with an ABET-accredited B.S. program in manufacturing engineering. Interaction with local industry through research and part-time-study corporate programs has created a focus on state-of-the-art educational and research issues.*

## DISTANCE LEARNING PROGRAM

The Interactive-Compressed Video (ICV) graduate program in manufacturing engineering, comprised of courses identical to those for the on-campus degree, is designed to satisfy the needs of part-time students in industry. The department is a pioneer in distance learning, graduating its first student with an M.S. degree entirely attained by ICV in 1992.

## DELIVERY MEDIA

The department maintains three state-of-the-art PictureTel video-conferencing systems. These systems transmit at speeds ranging from switched 56 to the full-motion video capability of 384 K. PictureTel equipment is compatible with other PictureTel equipment, as well as equipment from other vendors, if those systems meet H.320 standards for video and audio.

## PROGRAMS OF STUDY

Courses focus on the technical aspects of design and production. Three concentrations are offered for the master's degree via ICV: manufacturing systems, manufacturing operations management, and process design. While not all of the courses available on campus are offered via ICV, sufficient courses are offered to enable a student to complete all requirements for the M.S. degree in manufacturing engineering, which may be completed in approximately three years.

A limited number of special/nondegree students are admitted each semester. Persons not wishing to pursue a graduate degree may enroll in courses for which they meet prerequisite requirements. Special/nondegree students may apply at any time prior to completing a third course for admission to the degree program. Only three courses taken as a special/nondegree student may be applied to the master's degree.

## SPECIAL PROGRAMS

The department encourages all part-time students in industry to visit the campus and become familiar with the resources it can offer. The faculty particularly welcomes the opportunity provided in these visits to develop more significant and lasting relationships with the part-time video students. Matriculated students who wish to visit the campus have access to all facilities, including University libraries and athletic facilities.

Another feature of the program is that each instructor is expected to visit the company at least once during each course offering so that students get to know their instructors firsthand.

Boston University has developed a substantial collaborative relationship with the Fraunhofer Resource Center Massachusetts. A state-of-the-art laboratory supporting this endeavor houses exceptional equipment for work in high-performance machining and rapid prototyping. The Boston University/Fraunhofer collaboration engages manufacturing engineering students and faculty members in programs of contract industrial research directed toward finding practical solutions to actual problems from manufacturing industry customers. Although participation by Fraunhofer personnel in ICV education is limited at present, this interaction is expected to increase.

## CREDIT OPTIONS

The master's program in manufacturing engineering consists of 36 credit hours (ordinarily nine courses), of which no fewer than 28 credits must be earned at

Boston University and at least 20 credits from technically oriented courses. A cumulative grade point average of at least 3.0 (B) is required for all courses taken at Boston University and for all courses offered for the degree.

## FACULTY

The Department of Manufacturing Engineering has about 20 full-time faculty members. All are actively engaged in industrial problems through writing, consulting, and research.

## ADMISSION

Students accepted into the master's program in manufacturing engineering are expected to have earned a bachelor's degree in engineering. Students with strong mathematics backgrounds and aptitudes, but nonengineering degrees, may also apply.

## TUITION AND FEES

Tuition for 2001–02 is $809 per credit hour. There is an additional registration fee of $40 per semester. Students may pay as individuals and seek reimbursement from their company, or the University can bill the company.

## FINANCIAL AID

No departmental financial aid is offered. Students are typically sponsored by their companies.

## APPLYING

Students seeking special student status should contact the department. Students seeking admission to the M.S. program should request and complete an application packet.

### CONTACT

Elizabeth Spencer-Dawes
Distance Learning Administrator
Department of Manufacturing Engineering
Boston University
15 St. Mary's Street
Boston, Massachusetts 02215
Telephone: 617-353-2943
Fax: 617-353-5548
E-mail: icv@bu.edu
Web site: http://www.bu.edu/mfg/icv

# Brenau University

## Online Education

Gainesville, Georgia

---

Brenau University, founded in 1878, is a historic, private, comprehensive university in Gainesville, Georgia. The University's two colleges, the coeducational Evening and Weekend College (EWC) and the Women's College, have complementary missions.

The online programs serve a population of students who are unable or unwilling to attend campus-based classes. Degree and certificate programs are offered entirely online, with a focus on collaborative learning. The EWC serves a growing population of working adult men and women returning to school by offering degree and certificate programs and other classes in five additional locations across the state (Atlanta, Athens, Augusta, Kings Bay, and Waleska). The Women's College, located on the picturesque main campus in Gainesville, has provided a single-gender liberal arts education since its founding in 1878.

Brenau University is accredited by the Southern Association of Colleges and Schools.

## DISTANCE LEARNING PROGRAM

Brenau's goal is to be a leader in the development and provision of quality online programs using the latest distance learning technology. Its online programs, first offered in 1998, were developed to serve working adult students and provide maximum flexibility without compromising learning outcomes or academic rigor.

## DELIVERY MEDIA

Online classes are delivered via the Internet using the popular Blackboard program. Other common support programs are also used to enhance the delivery of course materials. Dialogue among students, using an asynchronous bulletin board system, is central to the collaborative learning goal. Online students bring with them varied life and work experiences that, when shared with classmates and combined with theory, improve the discussion of the subject at hand.

## PROGRAMS OF STUDY

Brenau University currently offers fully online degree programs in business, education, and nursing.

Brenau's first online degree program, an RN to B.S.N. bridge program, provides registered nurses the opportunity for career advancement by earning a bachelor's degree. This 120-hour program offers students an experienced and educated faculty of registered nurses with master's degrees and/or doctoral degrees. The clinical portion of this program may be completed in the student's local community, supervised by an approved preceptor.

M.B.A.'s in leadership development and accounting are available from the School of Business at Brenau University, where the faculty has twenty-four years of experience in M.B.A. programs and there is flexible scheduling for weekend, evening, and online classes. Students can reach their professional goals easily with Brenau's accelerated ten-course, 30-hour M.B.A. in leadership development program or the twelve-course, 36-hour M.B.A. in accounting program. Many states are now adopting the 150-hour educational requirement to sit for the CPA exam. Brenau students earn the required credits by earning an M.B.A.

The Master of Education in early childhood education has been a degree program at Brenau for years. Now it is available online in an eleven-course cohort program, which requires 33–36 credit hours, depending on the student's choice of a capstone activity (comprehensive exam or research project).

## SPECIAL PROGRAMS

Brenau University's Department of Business Administration offers an accelerated M.B.A. program in leadership development. Online students require a minimum of four semesters to complete the degree requirements. Classes are small and offer students asynchronous discussion, work-related collaborative projects, and computer-based business simulations. These activities are designed to guarantee participation in online classes.

Nonbusiness majors interested in earning an M.B.A. in leadership development or accounting are interested in Brenau University's BA500, an intensive business foundations course that covers all undergraduate business basics in the fields of economics, management, marketing, quantitative methods, accounting, and computer applications. Esteemed faculty members from each of these fields collaborate to teach this unique 6-semester-hour course.

## STUDENT SERVICES

In addition to online application, advising, and registration, other student services are available online. These include career services, which support students in job searches and career selection, and crisis counseling provided by a licensed counselor via e-mail and telephone. The Brenau Trustee Library catalog is available online, and document delivery and interlibrary loan are offered for supplemental materials.

## CREDIT OPTIONS

Brenau University courses offer 3 semester credits, except for 1-credit labs. Up to 6 semester hours of transfer credits from other regionally accredited institutions may be appropriately transferred as part of a planned program of study.

Alternative credit options toward a Brenau University degree (credit earned from advanced placement exams, international baccalaureate programs, CLEP, military credit, experiential credit, or challenge exams) are limited to a total of 27 semester hours.

## FACULTY

All online instructors have successfully completed an in-house training program offered online. Professors teaching in graduate programs have doctorates in their fields and years of corporate and/or practical experience.

## ADMISSION

Prospective students must submit a Brenau University application, and transcripts from every institution previously attended as well as standardized test scores (GMAT, GRE, MAT, TOEFL) must be sent directly to the University's admissions office for consideration.

## TUITION AND FEES

All online classes are currently $350 per semester hour. Limited fees apply to course labs only. Tuition rates are addressed prior to each academic year. Tuition is payable by check, money order, or credit card (Visa or MasterCard).

## FINANCIAL AID

The FAFSA financial aid application is available online. Online students who qualify are eligible for all need-based financial aid programs, including Pell Grants, other federal grants and loan programs, state-direct loans for students in nursing, and institutional grants.

Program-specific funds are also available. A total of 1,633 (56 percent) of Brenau University students received some type of financial aid this past academic year. Student loan applications are handled by the Office of Scholarships and Financial Assistance (770-534-6152).

## APPLYING

Prospective students must send a completed application and a $30 application fee. Faculty advising is conducted via e-mail, fax, and/or telephone. Students need only consult their advisers upon entering a program of study. Returning students may register online in a secure environment.

---

### CONTACT

Heather S. Gibbons, Ph.D.
Director of Online Education
Brenau University
One Centennial Circle
Gainesville, Georgia 30501
Telephone: 770-718-5328
Fax: 770-718-5329
E-mail: online@lib.brenau.edu
Web site: http://online.brenau.edu

---

# Caldwell College

## External Degree Program

### Caldwell, New Jersey

*Caldwell College is a Catholic, coeducational, four-year liberal arts institution committed to intellectual rigor, individual attention, and the ethical values of the Judeo-Christian academic tradition. Founded in 1939 by the Sisters of St. Dominic, the College is accredited by the Middle States Association of Colleges and Universities, chartered by the State of New Jersey, and registered with the Regents of the University of the State of New York. Located on a 100-acre wooded campus in a quiet suburban community 20 miles from New York City, Caldwell provides a serene and secure environment conducive to study and learning.*

*Caldwell College offers a 13:1 student-faculty ratio, small classes, and individual attention. Professors know their students by name, challenge them to strive for excellence, and provide the support needed to achieve it. This close relationship between faculty members and students also leads to a spirit of friendship throughout the campus community. Approximately half of the 2,039 men and women enrolled at the College are adults pursuing degrees both full-time and part-time or obtaining new skills to compete in the changing marketplace. Through the College's Center for Continuing Education, these adults seek personal growth, professional enrichment, and career advancement. All students find the staff ready to provide the personalized academic planning that will help them succeed in their studies and careers.*

## DISTANCE LEARNING PROGRAM

Caldwell College pioneered the external degree concept in 1979, becoming the first higher education institution in the state of New Jersey to offer students the option of completing their degrees without attending on-campus classes. Caldwell designed the program especially for busy adults whose work or family commitments make it difficult to follow a weekly on-campus academic schedule. Traditional course work is presented in a flexible and convenient format. External Degree students are required to be on campus only for External Degree Saturday at the beginning of each semester. Students pursuing their bachelor's degrees through the External Degree Program use the same textbooks and complete the same course work as their on-campus counterparts.

## DELIVERY MEDIA

Students learn with the guidance of an academic mentor and through interaction with the faculty via phone, personal conferences, e-mail, mailing or faxing of assignments, audiocassette, videocassette, and computer technologies.

## PROGRAM OF STUDY

The External Degree Program offers seventeen majors. Bachelor of Science degrees are offered in accounting, business administration, computer information systems, international business, marketing, and management. Bachelor of Arts degrees are offered in art (some on-campus work is required for art majors), communication arts, criminal justice, English, history, political science, psychology, religious studies, sociology, and social studies.

Eligibility for a degree requires completion of 122 credits and a GPA of at least 2.0 (C). This includes completing 57 liberal arts and science core curriculum credits, requirements specific to the student's major, and open electives. Students must also complete major courses with a minimum grade of C and satisfy all other departmental requirements. Overall, a minimum of 45 credits must be taken at Caldwell

College, with the last 30 credits of the 122-credit requirement completed at the College before a degree is awarded. Transfer students must complete at least half the total number of credits for a given major at Caldwell College.

Students enrolled in undergraduate or graduate distance education programs at other institutions are permitted to enroll as visiting (nonmatriculated) students in the Caldwell College External Degree Program. Visiting External Degree students may register for courses offered in accounting, business administration, international business, management, and marketing only and must be age 23 or older. Course registration opens three weeks prior to the beginning of each semester. Permission to enroll as a visiting student is granted by the Director of the External Degree Program through the Center for Continuing Education. Visiting students are required to attend new-student orientation and mandatory meetings with instructors on External Degree Saturday to receive course materials. In order to participate in this program, students must submit a completed External Degree Visiting Student Application form with a $10 processing fee to the Center for Continuing Education. Visiting students may register for two courses per semester (four courses per year) and have access to the Caldwell College Library. Tuition costs are the same as those for all other External Degree Program students and are payable at the time of registration.

## SPECIAL PROGRAMS

Students majoring in business administration, English, or psychology who have earned at least 60 prior college credits in courses applicable to their major may apply for Accelerated Degree Completion through the External Degree Program. Students admitted to the Accelerated Degree Completion Program can complete their degrees within two years by taking approximately 27 credits per year (9 credits per term) or an equivalent combination of course credits and College Level Examination Program, Prior Learning Assessment, internships, and/or cooperative education credits. Each student is expected to work closely with an academic adviser in developing and following a specific course of study.

## STUDENT SERVICES

All of the following services are available to External Degree students. The Jennings Library and the Academic Computing Center are open on evenings and weekends. Students have the ability to access the library's vast database from their home computers. The library's home page also provides links to the Internet and other databases and informational resources. The Career Development Center, Campus Minister, Counseling Office, and Learning Center are also available during the evening by appointment. The college bookstore is open evenings and during External Degree Saturday. The Learning Center assists students in academic skill development for all majors through tutoring.

## CREDIT OPTIONS

Credit is given for courses completed at an accredited college or university with a grade of C or above, provided it is appropriate to the curriculum chosen at Caldwell College. Students may transfer no more than 75 credits from a baccalaureate institution or 60 credits from a junior college. Students may earn credits by examination through standardized testing (CLEP, DANTES, OHIO, and TECEP). Credit is also awarded for noncollegiate military or corporate training courses accredited by the American Council on Education. Credits may be earned through the Prior Learning Assessment portfolio development process.

## ADMISSION

Students who are 23 years of age or older and who possess a high school diploma or the GED and have com-

pleted at least 12 college credits may matriculate as an External Degree student upon acceptance to the College. Those students with fewer than 12 college credits must complete the following courses to be eligible for the External Degree Program: EN/101 Basic Composition, EN/111 Literary Types and Themes, PS/111 Re-entry Seminar for Adults, and one liberal arts core course. These courses are not available via the distance learning format, but they can be completed at any college.

## TUITION AND FEES

Tuition for all students is $357 per credit. The additional cost for books is the responsibility of the student.

## FINANCIAL AID

External Degree students are eligible for several of the federal financial aid programs available to full-time students, including Pell Grants and various loans. Approximately 10 percent of External Degree students receive Pell Grants, 70 percent Stafford Loans, 10 percent Caldwell College Grants, and 2 percent Federal Supplemental Educational Opportunity Grants. Tuition Aid Grants are available for full-time External Degree students. Academic advisers of the Center for Continuing Education and the staff of the Financial Aid Office also inform students of special privately funded scholarship opportunities for which they may qualify.

## APPLYING

Students wishing to pursue a degree through the External Degree Program must submit the following to the Office of Corporate Education and Adult Undergraduate Admissions: a completed application for adult undergraduate admission; a nonrefundable application fee of $40 made payable to Caldwell College (the student's Social Security number should be included on the memo line); official transcripts from high schools, career schools, or colleges previously attended (GED certification may be submitted in place of a high school tran-

script); and a photocopy of the student's Social Security card. There is no testing for adults. All application material must be received by the Office of Adult Undergraduate Admissions by the deadline date of each semester, approximately one month prior to the beginning of classes.

Students in the External Degree Program may enroll for a minimum of one and a maximum of five courses per semester, depending on their personal schedules and abilities. The program offers three semesters: fall, spring, and summer. Students are required to be on campus only for the External Degree Saturday at the beginning of each semester. New students attend an orientation program and participate in workshops designed to enhance their college experience. On External Degree Saturday, students meet with their faculty mentor and receive an overview of the course material, faculty evaluation criteria, and dates that assignments are due. Students also attend department meetings and learn about recent developments and career options in their chosen fields of study. Prior to each semester, students consult with their academic advisers for guidance in selecting courses. Academic counseling is available through the semester as a supportive, ongoing service.

### CONTACT

Jack Albalah, Director
Corporate and Adult Undergraduate Admissions
Caldwell College
9 Ryerson Avenue
Caldwell, New Jersey 07006
Telephone: 973-618-3285
888-864-9518 (toll-free)
Fax: 973-618-3660
E-mail: jalbalah@caldwell.edu
Web site:
http://www.caldwell.edu/adult-admissions.

# California State University, Dominguez Hills

## Division of Extended Education

Carson, California

---

*California State University, Dominguez Hills, is a national leader in distance learning, named by* Forbes *magazine as one of the top twenty Cyber universities. Founded in 1960, the University is one of twenty-three California State University (CSU) campuses, and has the largest distance learning program in the CSU system. The University offered its first distance learning degree in 1974, and in 1995 offered the first online master's degree program ever accredited by the Western Association of Schools and Colleges.*

*CSU Dominguez Hills continues to be in the forefront of distance learning technology and academic excellence, garnering numerous awards, including the Best Distance Learning Teacher from the U.S. Distance Learning Association, a 1999 Omni Intermedia Award, a 1999 Aegis Award, two Telly Awards, and a Top 100 Producer award from* AV Video Multimedia Producer *magazine..*

*The CSU Dominguez Hills campus is located in the South Bay Area of Los Angeles and is accredited by the Western Association of Schools and Colleges.*

## DISTANCE LEARNING PROGRAM

The distance learning unit is part of the Division of Extended Education, whose mission is to extend the resources of the University to better serve the communities of which it is a part. The University has more than 2,000 students enrolled in distance learning programs in all fifty states and more than sixty countries.

## DELIVERY MEDIA

All distance learning courses have a Web site, and participants can interact with faculty and staff members via e-mail, telephone, and correspondence. Courses are conducted via live Internet, where students participate in a live, interactive educational environment, including video transmission of the lecture; via asynchronous Internet, where participants log in at their convenience to complete class assignments and engage in discussion groups with their peers; via television, where CSUDH broadcasts 24 hours a day on cable systems throughout Southern California; and via correspondence.

## PROGRAMS OF STUDY

Dominguez Hills currently offers five degree and four certificate programs via distance learning. There are no on-campus requirements for any CSUDH distance learning program.

The Master of Arts in Humanities offers a broad interdisciplinary exposure to all of the areas of the humanities—history, literature, philosophy, music, and art, with emphasis on their interrelating effects and influences. The student may specialize in a particular discipline of the humanities or in specific cultural thematic areas that can be traced across all of the humanistic disciplines. The program is conducted via correspondence, and 30 semester units are required for graduation.

Participants in the Master of Science in Quality Assurance (MSQA) receive education in both the technical and administrative foundations of quality assurance, an interdisciplinary profession utilized in management in manufacturing, service, government, and health-care organizations. The MSQA has been developed by experienced and dedicated professionals to ensure course offerings meet the constantly changing requirements for improved organizational competitiveness. All course work for the MSQA is conducted via asynchronous Internet, and it requires 33 units of approved graduate course work.

The Behavioral Science Master's Degree program in Negotiation and Conflict Management teaches participants valuable skills and knowledge that may be applied directly to police work, counseling, human resources management, labor relations, supervision, administration, alternative dispute resolution, arbitration, public policy, social work, teaching, intercultural and community conflicts, corporate contracts, and purchasing. This is a 33-semester-unit graduate program that can be completed in two years. In addition to course work, all students must complete a 3-unit internship during the second year and pass a comprehensive examination at the conclusion of the program. The program is conducted via live, interactive Internet and television broadcast.

The Master of Science in Nursing program prepares professional nurses for advanced and specialized practice. The curriculum is organized around the role of the nurse in societal institutions, with emphasis on the application of theory through excellence in professional practice, and the advancement of the profession through research, leadership, and scholarship for the ultimate benefit of the health-care needs of society. Role emphasis options include clinical nurse specialist in gerontological nursing and nursing education.

The Bachelor of Science completion program in nursing offers an individualized approach to nursing education designed for the self-directed, employed professional. It is one of the largest post-licensure programs in the United States. Graduates are equipped to function as leaders, managers, and resource persons in a variety of health-care settings. Course work for the B.S. in nursing degree is conducted via Web sites, discussion groups, e-mail, and videotape. It requires 124 semester units for graduation.

The Assistive Technology Certificate program prepares individuals to comply with state and federal laws that require that school personnel be prepared to offer a full range of assistive technology services to disabled persons. The online program is useful to educational administrators, teachers, special education teachers, occupational and physical therapists, speech and language specialists, rehabilitation specialists, program specialists, resource specialists, and psychologists.

The Certificate in Production and Inventory Control is conducted entirely online and is designed for those who wish to gain a broad education in the principles of production and inventory control. The program is taught by professionals certified in production and inventory management who are currently employed in the field.

The Certificate Award in Purchasing is designed for those who wish to gain a broad education in the principles of procurement management. Conducted online, the program is also designed to help students prepare for the National Association of Purchasing Managers Certified Purchasing Manager certification exam.

The certificate-completion program in quality assurance allows professionals to gain certification in specialized areas of quality as well as prepare for American Society for Quality Exams. Conducted online, students who successfully complete three master's degree-level courses and the associated capstone course can earn a certificate of completion in quality management, quality engineering, quality auditing, reliability engineering, or software quality engineering.

## SPECIAL PROGRAMS

The Center for Training and Development at CSUDH works closely with the business community to develop custom-designed training programs to help meet the demands of the fast-paced workplace of the new millennium. Programs are delivered via distance learning, on-site, and on the CSUDH campus.

## STUDENT SERVICES

Faculty members are available to students via e-mail, telephone, and mail. Student services available at a distance include academic advising, technical support, and online tutoring and access to the library and bookstore.

## CREDIT OPTIONS

Depending on the specific program, students may transfer credit earned at other accredited colleges and universities. For more information, students should consult the Web site, listed below.

## FACULTY

CSU Dominguez Hills has more than 100 faculty members teaching distance learning courses. Most of these faculty members have doctoral degrees in their chosen fields.

## ADMISSION

Admission requirements vary for each program. Students should consult the CSUDH distance learning Web site, listed below, for specific program requirements.

## TUITION AND FEES

Tuition and fees vary for each program. Students should consult the CSUDH distance learning Web site, listed below, for specific cost information.

## FINANCIAL AID

More than $33 million in financial aid is disbursed to CSUDH students each year. Approximately 68 percent of CSUDH students receive some form of financial assistance, and most financial aid programs are available to qualified distance learning students. For further information, students should visit the financial aid Web site at http://www.csudh.edu/fin_aid.

## APPLYING

Application processes vary for each program, and campus visits are not required for any program. Students should consult the CSUDH distance learning Web site for specific application information.

---

**CONTACT**

Extended Education Registration Office
California State University, Dominguez Hills
1000 East Victoria Street
Carson, California 90747
Telephone: 310-243-3741
877-GO-HILLS (toll-free)
Fax: 310-516-3971
E-mail: eereg@csudh.edu
Web site: http://www.csudh.edu/dominguezonline

---

# Carnegie Mellon University

## *Distance Learning Programs*

Pittsburgh, Pennsylvania

---

*Founded by industrialist Andrew Carnegie as the Carnegie Technical Schools in 1900, Carnegie Mellon University has emerged as one of the nation's top private research institutions. Today, it includes seven colleges—Carnegie Institute of Technology, College of Fine Arts, College of Humanities and Social Sciences, Graduate School of Industrial Administration, H. John Heinz III School of Public Policy and Management, Mellon College of Science, and School of Computer Science—and more than sixty research centers and institutes. Its internationally recognized programs encompass the areas of computer science, engineering, fine arts, liberal arts, public and private management, science, and technology. This Pittsburgh-based university is accredited by the Middle States Association of Colleges and Schools (MSA). The colleges within the University are accredited by various accrediting bodies that are specific to their disciplines.*

## DISTANCE LEARNING PROGRAM

Students worldwide can benefit from Carnegie Mellon's educational and research resources through a variety of graduate-level certificate and degree programs in management and information technology. Programs include the Certificate in Software Engineering (CSE); Master of Science in Technology–Software Engineering (M.S.I.T.-S. E.) and Master of Software Engineering (M.S.E., corporate-sponsored); Master of Science in Information Technology–Management (M.S.I.T.-I. T.M., corporate-sponsored); the Master of Medical Management (M.M.M.); Flex-Mode (company-sponsored); and Computational Finance.

## DELIVERY MEDIA

The latest Web, CD, and teleconferencing technologies are the primary delivery media for Carnegie Mellon's distance learning programs. Faculty members and students interact regularly via e-mail, interactive chat, threaded bulletin boards, and teleconferencing. In the Software Engineering and IT Management programs, videotaped lectures and just-in-time CDs are used to deliver lectures and libraries of supporting materials. The

CDs also contain transcripts and outlines of the lectures, as well as links to support materials such as slide presentations, readings, and Web pages. Further, the technology provides keyword search capabilities.

## PROGRAMS OF STUDY

The software engineering certificate and degree programs include the five core courses of the School of Computer Science's Master of Software Engineering program and prepare students to excel as software engineers and project leaders. The Certificate in Software Engineering (CSE) program provides software professionals with continuing education credit in the five core courses. The Master of Science in Information Technology–Software Engineering (M.S.I.T.-S.E.) program provides software professionals with credit for the five course courses as well as four elective courses drawn from the School of Computer Science and an applied practicum project designed to facilitate the integration of the course work. Finally, the Master of Software Engineering (M.S.E.) program is a corporate-sponsored program similar to the M.S.I.T.-S.E. with a software studio component in the place of the practicum. Whereas the practicum involves individual work,

the studio component of the M.S.E. program is a collaborative practical experience in software engineering and requires that the students participating are colocated (hence the need for corporate sponsorship).

The Master of Science in Information Technology–Management (M.S.I.T.-I. T.M.) program offered through the H. J. Heinz III School of Public Policy and Management provides business and information technology professionals with credit for five core information technology courses as well as seven electives in the management and strategic use of information technology. This program is available on campus or at a distance via a corporate partnership.

The Master of Medical Management (M.M.M.) program, also offered through the Heinz School, is open to physicians who have completed a prerequisite program through the American College of Physicians Executives. Through distance learning and on-campus sessions, the M.M.M. program prepares physicians to lead health-care organizations.

Carnegie Mellon's Graduate School of Industrial Administration (GSIA) offers two long-distance programs via interactive video technologies: the company-sponsored Flex-Mode Program (at company locations; see Special Programs) and the Computational Finance Program (Pittsburgh and New York City). Combining the resources of four Carnegie Mellon colleges, the Computational Finance Program lets participants move seamlessly among the fields of computer science, finance, mathematics, and statistics. This lets them gain an understanding of current practices in the financial industry, as well as high-level skills and conceptual framework for career growth.

## SPECIAL PROGRAMS

All students in Flex-Mode Program (Master of Industrial Administration courses) offered through Carnegie Mellon's Graduate School of Industrial Administration are company sponsored. This program uses teleconferencing to deliver courses to company locations. The three-year program is just as comprehensive as the school's full-time master's degree track, covering areas such as quantitative managerial decision making, business communication, and the political environment for business leaders.

## STUDENT SERVICES

Small class sizes in the various programs enhance the delivery of many student services, such as technical orientations in the use of distance learning technologies, evening and weekend phone access to teaching and technical assistants, and online enrollment. Individualized Web pages for each course offered in the Software Engineering and IT Management programs facilitate access to student services and contact with instructors, courseware specialists, and administrators. Student services information for the GSIA distance learning programs is available through the program-specific Web sites.

## CREDIT OPTIONS

In the Software Engineering programs, courses can be taken not-for-credit, for continuing education units (CEU), for-credit, or for credit toward a master's degree. Students taking courses not-for-credit or for continuing education units must retake the course in order to get credit for it. Students taking courses for credit toward a master's degree must be accepted into the master's degree program. Additional information about the various credit options for the Software Engineering programs is available through the Software Engineering Distance Education Web site. Credit information for the GSIA programs is available through the GSIA program Web site.

## FACULTY

Faculty members for the Software Engineering programs are drawn from the School of Computer Science, the Software Engineering Institute, the Master of Software Engineering program, and industry. Information about individual faculty members can be found on the Software Engineering Distance Education Web site. Faculty members for the M.S.I.T.-I.T.M. program are drawn from the Heinz School, the Software Engineering Institute, the School of Computer Science, and the information technology industry. Faculty member information for the GSIA programs is available through their Web sites.

## ADMISSION

Students interested in Carnegie Mellon distance learning programs must apply to the appropriate school just as campus-based students do. decisAdmission standards are essentially the same for both types of programs. Program-specific requirements are available through the specific program Web sites.

## TUITION AND FEES

While tuition rates vary among programs, the rates for a specific distance learning program and a similar campus-based program are generally the same. Program-specific tuition details are available through the specific program Web site or contact person listed below.

## FINANCIAL AID

The amount and type of financial aid varies from program to program. Program-specific financial aid information is available through the specific program Web site or contact person listed below.

## APPLYING

Procedures for application, acceptance, and orientation differ for each Carnegie Mellon distance learning program. Students interested in applying for a specific program should request an application through that program's Web site or from the contact person listed below.

### CONTACT

Michael Carriger, Associate Director of M.S.E. for Distance Education
Telephone: 412-268-6191
Fax: 412-268-5576
E-mail: dist-ed@cs.cmu.edu
Web site: http://www.distance.cmu.edu/

Karyn Moore, Program Director, M.S.I.T.-I.T.M.
Telephone: 412-268-8465
Fax: 412-268-7036
E-mail: karyn@cmu.edu
Web site: http://www.mism.cmu.edu/

Megan O'Donnell, Assistant Director, Master of Medical Management Program
Telephone: 412-268-4481
Fax: 412-268-7036
E-mail: mo@andrew.cmu.edu

Flex-Mode Program
Web site: http://www.flexmode.gsia.cmu.edu

Computational Finance
Web site: http://www.fastweb.gsia.cmu.edu/MSCF

# Central Michigan University

## College of Extended Learning
## Distance/Distributed Learning

Mount Pleasant, Michigan

*Since its founding in 1892, Central Michigan University (CMU) has grown from a small teachers' college into a world class Midwestern university offering more than 150 programs at the bachelor's level and nearly 60 programs at the master's, specialist's, and doctoral level. CMU is accredited by the North Central Association of Colleges and Schools. This accreditation includes all on- and off-campus programs. The College of Extended Learning is an institutional member of the Council for Adult and Experiential Learning; the Adult Education Association; the Alliance: An Association of Alternative Degree Programs for Adults; and the National Association of Institutions in Military Education.*

## DISTANCE LEARNING PROGRAM

Distance/Distributed Learning is a division of CMU's College of Extended Learning, which serves off-campus students. Distance learning at CMU has its roots in the University's correspondence study program, which was created more than 70 years ago. As CMU's commitment to distance learning grew, the University developed a number of options for students to complete courses outside of the traditional classroom setting.

## DELIVERY MEDIA

Students have a choice of delivery systems, including print-based learning packages, World Wide Web courses, and video/televised courses. Courses are offered in a twelve-week format with specific start and end dates.

Learning packages are print-based courses that use textbooks and study guides but can also include audio and videocassettes and the use of e-mail and/or Internet chat rooms to enrich the content.

World Wide Web courses use Web technology to involve the student in interactive learning. Students can interact with instructors and others through e-mail chat sessions and mes-

sage forums. Student lecture materials and assignments are all online. Textbooks are still required.

Televised or video courses are available on the Central Michigan University Public Television Network and also on videotape. These courses include a study guide, text, and supplementary materials.

## PROGRAMS OF STUDY

Distance/Distributed Learning offers undergraduate degree programs and graduate programs with additional classes being added each term.

Bachelor's degrees are available through the Bachelor of Science with an option in community development and the Bachelor of Science with a major in administration.

The 36-semester-hour Master of Science in Administration degree approaches administration and management from a broader perspective than other graduate-level programs. The M.S.A. features eight concentrations, including general, human resources, health services, hospitality and tourism, international, public, and software engineering administration; and information resource management. Currently, general administration is the only concentration available via distance learning.

## SPECIAL PROGRAMS

The Master of Science in Nutrition and Dietetics is designed to provide advanced training in human nutritional sciences for new and experienced professionals. The M.S. in Nutrition and Dietetics is available through distance learning courses, although practical internships are still required.

Also available entirely through distance learning is the Au.D. program, created by CMU exclusively for professional audiologists. It is based on a minimum 36 to 40 credit-hour sequence and a comprehensive exam. There is a 12-hour capstone experience in lieu of a formal thesis. The courses are self-paced, and it is possible to complete the program within two years.

## STUDENT SERVICES

Central Michigan University's Distance/Distributed Learning offers students many timesaving services. In addition to touch-tone (phone-in) registrations and online admissions, textbook purchases, academic advising, and library resources are available via a toll-free phone call, fax, or the World Wide Web.

Central Michigan University offers library support services tailored to meet the needs of the adult learner. Students can contact CMU's Off Campus Library Services and request reference assistance, book loans, and copies of journal articles. An online catalog of book and periodical holdings as well as subject databases are available.

## FACULTY

Faculty members who teach off-campus courses are drawn from the regular CMU faculty, other colleges and universities, government, and business and industry. Faculty members are approved for teaching assignments by the department chairperson on the basis of their academic and professional qualifications. Selection criteria vary from department to department. Additionally, all graduate course approvals are subject to the approval of the Graduate Dean.

## ADMISSION

Distance/Distributed Learning courses are part of the regular offerings of Central Michigan University. Students must be admitted to CMU in order to take distance learning courses. The minimum requirement for admission to CMU undergraduate programs is a high school diploma or GED certificate. Students can be awarded up to 60 hours of credit toward the bachelor's degree and up to 10 hours of credit toward the master's degree for relevant work, training, and other life experiences through CMU's Prior Learning Assessment Program.

Graduate applicants must have a baccalaureate or equivalent degree from an institution that has received regional accreditation or recognized standing at the time the student attended.

Audiology applicants must have a graduate degree in audiology with a minimum grade point average of 3.0 in graduate work, and either the ASHA Certificate of Clinical Competence in Audiology or a valid state license to practice audiology. Five years of professional audiological experience beyond the master's degree is also required.

## TUITION AND FEES

Tuition for the distance learning program is $183 per credit hour for undergraduate students and $245 per credit hour for graduate students. Tuition for the Audiology Ph.D. program is $250 per credit hour at the government rate or $351 at the nongovernment rate.

Additional fees (per credit hour) include a $50 admission fee, $50 graduation fee, $65 prior learning application fee, and a $40 prior learning assessment fee.

## FINANCIAL AID

Financial aid is available to those students who qualify. Students interested in financial aid are encouraged to contact CMU for more information.

## APPLYING

Students interested in taking classes through Distance/Distributed Learning are encouraged to apply for regular admission to Central Michigan University. Admission applications can be downloaded from the Web site listed below.

---

### CONTACT

Central Michigan University
Distance/Distributed Learning
College of Extended Learning
Mount Pleasant, Michigan 48859
Telephone: 800-688-4268 (toll-free)
Fax: 989-774-1822
Web site: http:// www.ddl.cmich.edu

---

# Central Missouri State University

*Office of Extended Campus–Distance Learning*

Warrensburg, Missouri

---

Founded in 1871, Central Missouri State University is a state university offering approximately 150 areas of study to 11,500 undergraduate and graduate students. In 1996, Central Missouri State University was designated Missouri's lead institution for professional technology, an area long recognized as one of the University's greatest strengths. The new mission has expanded this commitment and means that Central will continue to integrate the latest technologies into every level of its comprehensive liberal arts curriculum. Central is committed to acquiring, disseminating, and utilizing technology to enhance the University's comprehensive educational mission. Central is accredited by the North Central Association of Colleges and Schools.

## DISTANCE LEARNING PROGRAM

Central's main Distance Learning Program provides undergraduate- and graduate-level courses through two-way interactive television and Web-based courses. The program currently includes one doctoral degree, three master's degrees, and numerous graduate and undergraduate courses. From fall 1994 through spring 2001, Central provided instruction to more than 3,800 graduate, undergraduate, and high school students in a distance learning environment.

Central Missouri State University is a member of Missouri Learners Network, a voluntary, collaborative project among Missouri postsecondary institutions. The Missouri Learners Network was developed to share information, promote educational opportunities, and act as a referral service for students searching for distance educational opportunities.

## DELIVERY MEDIA

Central uses a variety of technologies to deliver its distance learning courses. These include two-way, interactive television; broadcast television; and Internet technologies, including video and audio streaming. Central links to the Missouri Research and Educational Network (MOREnet) statewide backbone, which connects all of Missouri's

public higher education institutions and several K–12 schools, to provide Internet-based and interactive television programming. Finally, Central's complement of six 2-way videoconferencing facilities, which are capable of dedicated T-1, ISDN, H.323, T.120, and audioconferencing, allow Central to provide distance learning content to anywhere in the world.

## PROGRAMS OF STUDY

The Master of Science in Criminal Justice is designed for those students who wish to enter or progress in the criminal justice fields of law enforcement, corrections, and juvenile justice or for those who plan to seek positions in leadership, professional specialization, research, or instruction in criminal justice. Completion of the program requires a minimum of 36 credit hours in required and elective courses. The master's degree program is delivered by interactive television and will also be available online beginning in fall 2001.

The Master of Science in Library Information Technology is a 32-credit-hour degree program that produces skilled information specialists who can retrieve relevant information to increase competitive advantage and productivity. This degree, with its emphasis on Internet resources, is of interest to educators, information specialists, Webmasters, and school librarians. It can

also serve as the core for an education specialist degree in learning resources for those who have earned a master's degree. Online courses in the degree program are available beginning fall 2001. The online degree program, beginning summer 2002, will plan for cohort groups to spend two weeks on campus for two consecutive summers—all other course work will be Web-based.

The Master of Science in Industrial Management is designed for students who are preparing for upward mobility in supervisory or management positions in business and industry, manufacturing, quality control or quality systems management, or related positions. This is a 33-credit-hour degree program, with selected courses delivered online in fall 2001. The complete program is expected to be delivered online by the end of fall 2002. Students may enter the course cycle at the beginning of any semester. The program presents a balanced management curriculum with course work and skill development in such areas as leadership, quality control, plant layout, operations research, and production planning.

Central is one of a consortium of seven higher education institutions that collectively offer the Ph.D. in Technology Management. This degree requires a minimum of 90 hours above an undergraduate degree and includes a dissertation. There is a short residency requirement; the majority of the course work is Internet-based. The Doctor of Philosophy in Technology Management program is designed to prepare students for positions of leadership in the public and private sectors of society. Students develop skills in research procedures, acquire expertise in instructional processes, and are able to provide service to the industrial and educational community.

In addition, the following degree programs offer courses via distance learning: the Bachelor of Science in Crisis and Disaster Management, the Master of Science in Education, the Master of Science in Library Science and Information Services, and the Master of Science in Rural Family Nursing.

## SPECIAL PROGRAMS

Central's Distance Learning Program builds upon the existing curriculum offerings at Central as well as offerings that address special distance learning needs.

Central's distance learning students are eligible to participate in the same opportunities as on-campus students. These include study tours and internships in many disciplines.

The Office of Career Services reports a 95 percent placement rate for Central graduates within six months of graduation.

## STUDENT SERVICES

A toll-free University number, 800-SAY-CMSU, allows access to offices involved with student services: extended campus–distance learning, admissions, academic advising, registrar, financial aid, revenue, accounts receivable, University housing, and the Graduate School. All students enrolled at Central are issued a mainframe Internet account. The HELP Desk is available to Central students needing technical computer assistance. Distance learning students receive individualized course information prior to the start of each semester as well as information regarding University resources available to them. Online library resources are available for distance learning and off-campus students. Access is also available to LUIS, the online card catalog for the James C. Kirkpatrick Library, a new state-of-the-art facility dedicated in March 1999. An online writing lab (OWL) provides writing assistance to distance learning students. A toll-free number provides ordering and delivery service for textbooks from the University Bookstore.

## CREDIT OPTIONS

The University accepts undergraduate transfer students from other accredited colleges and universities and evaluates their credit on the same bases used for other Central students. Thus, admission requires students to be in good standing and to have a grade point average of C (2.0) or better, computed by Central's methods. Students may be considered on an individual basis if their GPA is less than 2.0. For entering graduate students, Central will accept up to 8 hours of transfer credits in graduate work.

## FACULTY

Faculty members at Central exemplify the goals of the institution as they balance personal attention with expertise in their respective fields. Approximately 70 percent of the 443 full-time faculty members hold doctoral degrees. The undergraduate student-faculty ratio is 17:1; the graduate student-faculty ratio is 3:1.

## ADMISSION

A rolling admission policy is employed at Central. First-time undergraduate students, students returning after an absence of one or more semesters, and students who desire to enroll as visiting students should contact the Office of Admissions at 660-543-4290 or 800-SAY-CMSU (toll-free).

First-time graduate students taking Extended Campus courses may be admitted either by completing the Graduate School application in person or when calling to enroll in a class. Students must submit official copies of their transcripts to the Graduate School. Graduate students may enroll in up to 6 credit hours before finalizing their admission.

Students currently attending another university may enroll as visiting students. Graduate students who are not seeking a degree may enroll as non-degree-seeking students.

A nonrefundable application fee of $25 is due upon submission of the application. This applies to first-time applications only.

## TUITION AND FEES

For 2001–02, graduate tuition is $210 and undergraduate tuition is $147 per credit hour for interactive television courses. For Internet-based courses, graduate tuition is $179 per credit hour, and undergraduate tuition is $137 per credit hour. Doctoral courses are $192 per credit hour.

## FINANCIAL AID

Central recognizes a student's continuing need for financial assistance. Federal grant and loan funds are available for eligible students who have been accepted for regular degree programs at Central. Application eligibility information may be obtained by contacting the Office of Financial Aid and Veteran Services at 660-543-4040 or the toll-free number below. Students who are veterans may also be considered for VA educational benefits to help with tuition costs.

The University participates in all federal student financial aid grant, loan, and employment programs. Visiting and non-degree-seeking students are not eligible to receive federal financial aid.

## APPLYING

Undergraduate students should contact the Admissions Office at 660-543-4290 or the toll-free number listed below. Graduate students should contact the Graduate School at 660-543-4621 or at the toll-free number.

### CONTACT

Debbie Bassore
Assistant Director for Distance
  Learning
Office of Extended Campus
Humphreys 403
Central Missouri State University
Warrensburg, Missouri 64093
Telephone: 660-543-8480
            800-SAY-CMSU (toll-
            free)
Fax: 660-543-8333
E-mail: bassore@cmsu1.cmsu.edu
Web site:
  http://www.cmsu.edu/extcamp

# Champlain College

*Online Distance Learning Program*
*Continuing Education Division*

Burlington, Vermont

---

*Since 1878, Champlain College has been dedicated to providing education that reflects the realities and needs of the contemporary workplace. It offers professional certificates and two-year and four-year degree programs that are designed to provide sound professional training or updating for careers in today's complex world, as well as to provide broadening education in the humanities and general education. Champlain College is recognized as one of the leading career-building colleges in northern New England, and it has earned the respect of business, technical, and human services professions for its outstanding career-oriented education.*

## DISTANCE LEARNING PROGRAM

Champlain College is a pioneer in the use of computer technologies in distance learning applications. Champlain College Online serves hundreds of students in the United States and internationally. Champlain offers complete degree and professional certificate programs that may be accessed online at any time of day.

Champlain College is an independent, nonprofit four- and two-year college. It is accredited by the New England Association of Schools and Colleges. It first offered distance learning courses in 1993, with more than eighty courses offered in 2000–01.

## DELIVERY MEDIA

Those who have access to a computer and the World Wide Web can access Champlain College Online. Once connected, students find messages posted from the instructor and classmates either in the course forum or in private e-mail. All communication occurs online and includes discussion comments from classmates, lectures, instructional material, and assignments. The material covered in Champlain College's online classes is the same as in traditional courses.

## PROGRAMS OF STUDY

Champlain College offers an extensive array of traditionally delivered, career-oriented four- and two-year degrees. Through its distance learning program, the College offers both Professional Certificates and Associate in Science (A.S.) degrees in accounting, business, e-commerce, international business management, management, software development, telecommunications, and Web site development and management. The College also offers Bachelor in Science (B.S.) degrees in professional studies and in computer information systems, both of which are designed to complement associate degrees in career areas. Professional certificates require successful completion of 16 to 24 credits. Associate degrees require completion of 60 credits, half of which must be taken through Champlain College. The bachelor's degree requires completion of 120 credits, at least 45 of which must be taken through Champlain. Students can also take individual courses on a nonmatriculated basis.

## SPECIAL PROGRAMS

The College has several expanding international programs that offer degree programs to students in Israel, Malaysia, and the United Arab Emirates. All of these programs incorporate distance learning into the curriculum.

Corporate partnerships are also available for businesses that are interested in training employees. Since classes are available at anytime, from anywhere the Internet can be accessed, distance learning allows businesses to offer high-quality training programs to employees—even when different shifts, different locations, and even different time zones are involved.

## STUDENT SERVICES

Champlain College provides a number of services to adult learners. Distance learners receive academic advising from the Advising and Registration Center and the Career Planning Office, a full range of online library services, and access to the Computer Help Desk and an online bookstore.

## CREDIT OPTIONS

Students may transfer credits earned through other accredited postsecondary institutions. Depending on the program selected, students may also transfer credit for life/work experience or credits from approved testing programs. Champlain accepts credit through approved portfolio assessment programs, CLEP, DANTES, and PONSI.

## FACULTY

Champlain's strength lies in its faculty. More than 120 full-time and part-time faculty members focus their primary energies on teaching. Faculty members have completed programs of advanced study, and many have doctoral or terminal degrees.

## ADMISSION

Admission requirements for degree programs include graduation from a recognized secondary school or possession of a high school equivalency certificate and submission of SAT I or ACT scores. Students who have been out of high school for several years and who may not have taken all of the course work that is required for acceptance to a particular major or who have not taken SAT or ACT tests should speak with an admission counselor or academic adviser about how to apply. Admission to the cer-tificate program requires submission of a high school transcript (or GED) and a current resume. Given the method of instructional delivery, online students should be self-moti-vated and possess effective reading and writing skills as well as basic com-puter skills.

## TUITION AND FEES

In 2001–02, tuition is $350 per credit; most courses are 3 credits. The ap-plication fee is $35. Textbooks may be purchased on line through the bookstore. There are no additional fees.

## FINANCIAL AID

Payment and financial aid options de-pend on personal circumstances and whether students attend full- or part-time. The College participates in sev-eral federal financial aid programs, including Federal Pell Grant and Fed-eral Stafford Student Loan, and state loan and grant programs.

## APPLYING

Students may enroll for online courses as nonmatriculating students by regis-tering online or by mail, fax, or tele-phone. The College reviews applica-tions for degree programs when they are received. A short, online orienta-tion is required for all online students prior to gaining access to their courses.

---

**CONTACT**

Cheryl Letourneau, Program Coordinator
Champlain College Online
Champlain College
163 South Willard Street
Burlington, Vermont 05402
Telephone: 802-865-6449
       888-545-3459 (toll-free)
Fax: 802-865-6447
E-mail: online@champlain.edu
Web site: http://www.champlain.edu

---

# Charter Oak State College

New Britain, Connecticut

Charter Oak State College was established in 1973 by the Connecticut Legislature to provide an alternate way for adults to earn a college degree. The College offers associate and bachelor's degrees and is regionally accredited by the New England Association of Schools and Colleges. Charter Oak is a Servicemembers Opportunity College.

Charter Oak's degree program was designed to be especially appealing to people who work full-time and have family and financial responsibilities as well. The program is designed for independent adult learners who have the capacity and motivation to pursue a degree program that provides flexibility in how, where, and when they can earn credits. The Charter Oak program assumes that its students possess a basic understanding of the elements of a degree program and that they will seek guidance as often as necessary to progress satisfactorily with their studies.

Charter Oak teaches no classes. Students earn credits based on faculty evaluation of courses transferred from regionally accredited colleges and universities, noncollegiate sponsored instruction, standardized tests, special assessment, contract learning, and portfolio assessment.

One of the hallmarks of Charter Oak State College is its individualized professional advisement services. Each student is assigned to an academic adviser, who is a specialist in the student's chosen field of study. That adviser is accessible via telephone, fax, or e-mail and works closely with the student to develop a plan of study for completion of the degree program.

## DISTANCE LEARNING PROGRAM

Charter Oak State College offers an external degree program and so, by definition, is a distance learning institution. Students earn their credits "externally" and transfer them into the College; there is no residence requirement. Charter Oak offers more than a dozen distance learning courses each semester. Courses run for a period of sixteen weeks but may be completed in less time with the permission of faculty members.

## DELIVERY MEDIA

The College offers a selection of distance learning courses. Some of the courses use videotapes and texts and some are online courses. The courses are facilitated by faculty mentors who are accessible by e-mail, telephone, and U.S. mail. Students purchase texts at a distance from a designated bookstore and rent videotapes from a mail-order service. A catalog of offerings is available each semester.

## PROGRAMS OF STUDY

Charter Oak State College offers four degrees in general studies: Associate of Arts, Associate of Science, Bachelor of Arts, and Bachelor of Science. To earn an associate degree, a student must complete at least 60 credits; a bachelor's degree requires at least 120 credits.

A Charter Oak degree is more than an accumulation of the required number of credits. At least one half of the credits toward a degree must be earned in subjects traditionally included among the liberal arts and sciences: humanities, mathematics, natural sciences, and social sciences. Achievement in these areas demonstrates breadth of learning. In addition, students pursuing a baccalaureate degree must complete a concentration, consisting of at least 36 credits, that demonstrates depth of learning.

A concentration plan, in conjunction with an essay, must be submitted to the faculty for approval. Concentrations may be constructed in many areas, including applied arts, art history, the behavioral sciences, business, child study, communication, computer science, engineering studies, fire science technology, human services, individualized studies, languages, liberal studies, literature, music history, the natural sciences, religious studies, the social sciences, and technology studies.

## SPECIAL PROGRAMS

The College has evaluated a number of noncollegiate courses and programs that can be used in Charter Oak degree programs. Many health-care specialties from hospital-based programs are included, such as medical laboratory technician, nurse practitioner, physician assistant, radiologic technologist, registered nurse, and respiratory therapist or technician. Other evaluations include the Child Development Associate (CDA) credential; the FAA Airman Certificate; Famous Artists School in Westport, Connecticut; Institute of Children's Literature in West Redding, Connecticut; the National Opticianry Competency Examination; the Contact Lens Registry Examination; and several fire certifications, including Fire Marshal, Deputy Fire Marshal, Fire Inspector, Fire Fighter III, Fire Officer I or II, and Fire Service Instructor I or II.

## CREDIT OPTIONS

Students can transfer credits from other regionally accredited colleges and universities; age of credits is not a factor in their transferability. There is no limit to the number of credits that can be earned using standardized examinations, prior learning, including ACE-evaluated military credits, ACE and PONSI-evaluated noncollegiate learning, and portfolio assessment.

## FACULTY

Full-time faculty members from public and independent institutions of higher education in Connecticut are appointed to serve as consulting examiners at Charter Oak.

## ADMISSION

Admission is open to any person 16 years or older, regardless of level of formal education, who is able to demonstrate college-level achievement. To be admitted, a student must have earned 9 college-level credits from acceptable sources of credit.

## TUITION AND FEES

All students pay a $45 application fee; Connecticut residents pay a first-year enrollment fee of $475 and nonresidents pay $686. Active-duty service-members and their spouses pay a special active-duty military fee for all Charter Oak fees and services that is equivalent to the in-state resident fee. All baccalaureate degree candidates pay a Concentration Proposal Review fee of $255. All students pay a graduation fee of $145. Tuition for video-based courses is $74 per credit for Connecticut residents and $110 per credit for nonresidents; tuition for all online courses is $107 per credit for Connecticut residents and $146 per credit for nonresidents. All students pay a $15 registration fee.

## FINANCIAL AID

Financial aid is available in the form of fee waivers and foundation grants, as well as federal financial aid (Title IV) funds. Fee-waiver awards are made available through the College's financial resources and may be applied to the cost for the Enrollment And Records Conversion fee, Concentration Proposal Review fee, Annual Advisement and Records Maintenance fee, Reinstatement fee, and the Graduation fee. The foundation grants are made available through generous contributions from both private and corporate donations. These grants are for enrolled students. Federal aid is also available to those who qualify.

The following fees are eligible for Title IV funds: Enrollment And Records Conversion fee, Concentration Proposal Review fee, Annual Advisement and Records Maintenance fee, and the Reinstatement fee. Federal aid may be applied to the cost associated with tuition for COSC video-based courses, COSC contract learning courses, online and/or onsite courses at any CTDLC consortium member institution. For information, or to receive the appropriate application for aid, please contact the financial aid office. Veterans Administration benefits are also available for eligible students.

## APPLYING

Charter Oak reviews applications on a rolling basis; students may enroll anytime during the year.

### CONTACT

Admissions Office
Charter Oak State College
55 Paul Manafort Drive
New Britain, Connecticut 06053-2142
Telephone: 860-832-3800
Fax: 860-832-3999
Web site: http://www.cosc.edu

# City University

## Distance Learning Option

Renton, Washington

City University was founded in 1973 on the philosophy that everyone should have access to quality higher education. The University upholds this philosophy by offering programs that are well designed, cost effective, and convenient. The University's progressive approach to education has fueled its growth from a single classroom in downtown Seattle to the largest private university in the state of Washington. It is a private, nonprofit institution and is accredited by the Northwest Association of Schools and Colleges.

City University's programs cover a variety of academic fields ranging from business management and technology to humanities, social sciences, counseling, and teacher preparation. The majority of faculty members actively work in the fields they teach. The combination of innovative program design and outstanding instruction make City University an exceptional higher learning institution.

## DISTANCE LEARNING PROGRAM

In keeping with its mission of providing convenient, accessible education, City University offers most of its degree programs through distance learning (DL). The DL option makes degree programs available through traditional correspondence and electronically, through the World Wide Web. City University serves approximately 4,600 students annually through DL.

## DELIVERY MEDIA

City University offers DL and electronic DL programs. Electronic DL students complete course work through the University's online instructional center, using computers and the World Wide Web. DL students communicate with instructors by e-mail or by phone, mail, or fax. Electronic DL students need an e-mail address, a computer with a modem, Internet access, and CD-ROM capacity.

## PROGRAMS OF STUDY

City University's undergraduate programs prepare students to compete in today's marketplace. Students may complete an Associate of Science (A.S.), a Bachelor of Science (B.S.), or a Bachelor of Arts (B.A.) degree. Within these degrees, students may pursue one of several areas of study, including business administration, accounting, sociology, management specialty, computer systems, international studies, marketing, philosophy, political science, mass communications, journalism, and e-commerce. Undergraduate courses are 5 credits each; 180 credits are required for completion of a B.S. or B.A. degree.

City University's graduate business and public administration programs prepare management professionals for leadership roles at local, national, and international levels. Students may pursue a graduate certificate or a Master of Business Administration (M.B.A.), with an array of specialties; a Master of Public Administration (M.P.A.); a combined M.B.A./M.P.A.; a Master of Science in either project management or computer systems; or an M.A. in management degree. Most graduate courses are worth 3 credits; total required credits range from 45 to 60. City University also offers programs in education and human services. Students may pursue a Master of Education (M.Ed.) in curriculum and instruction or educational technology, or they may pursue an M.A. degree in counseling psychology. Total required credits for these programs range from 45 to 73.

## SPECIAL PROGRAMS

City University has an "open door" admissions policy. Students may begin a distance learning course at the beginning of any month, and there is no application deadline. City University has partnerships with several institutions and organizations worldwide. Through these affiliations, the University offers in-house programs and evaluates prior training for college-level credit.

All of City University's programs are geared for adult students. From its student body to its faculty and staff, City University is a community of professionals. All who are associated with the University understand the needs of adult learners who are seeking quality education that applies to their individual lifestyle.

## STUDENT SERVICES

Students may register by touch-tone phone. Academic advising and assistance is available from a distance learning adviser by phone, fax, or e-mail. Students have full access to the library, including an online search service; a reference librarian, via a toll-free phone number; and a mailing service for circulation books and articles.

## CREDIT OPTIONS

Undergraduate students may transfer up to 90 approved lower-division and 45 approved upper-division credits from approved institutions for baccalaureate programs. The Prior Learning Assessment Program lets students earn credits through documented experiential learning. Students may receive credit for the CLEP or other standardized tests. Graduate students may transfer up to 12 credits from approved programs.

## FACULTY

There are more than 250 faculty members included in the distance learning program, 36 of whom are full-time. More than 25 percent of the full-time faculty members have terminal degrees.

## ADMISSION

Undergraduate programs are generally open to applicants over 18 years of age who hold a high school diploma or GED. Admission to graduate programs requires that students hold a baccalaureate degree from an accredited or otherwise recognized institution. Additional requirements apply to education and human services programs. International students whose first language is not English are required to submit a TOEFL score of at least 540 for admission to undergraduate programs and 565 for graduate programs.

## TUITION AND FEES

Undergraduate tuition is $173 per credit, and graduate tuition is $309 per credit. The application fee is $75.

## FINANCIAL AID

For more information, students should contact the Student Financial Services Department (telephone: 800-426-5596, toll-free).

## APPLYING

DL students may enroll on a rolling admissions basis. Students must speak with an academic adviser to complete the initial enrollment. Students should then submit the application form, nonrefundable application fee, and admission documents to the Office of Admissions and Student Affairs. Official transcripts should be sent to the Office of the Registrar.

---

### CONTACT

DL/Online Advisor
Office of Admissions and Student Affairs
City University
919 Southwest Grady Way
Renton, Washington 98055
Fax: 425-277-2437

Office of the Registrar
335 116th Avenue, SE
Bellevue, Washington 98004
Fax: 425-637-9689

Telephone: 425-637-1010
　　　　　800-422-4898 (toll-free)
　　　　　425-450-4660 (TTY)
Web site: http://www.cityu.edu

---

# Clarkson College

Omaha, Nebraska

*Clarkson College is a regionally accredited private institution, with exceptional programs in health-care business, nursing, occupational therapy assistant studies, physical therapist assistant studies, and radiologic technology and medical imaging. The College offers the personal qualities of a small institution and the technological advantages found within a larger educational environment. Founded in 1888, it was the first school of nursing in Nebraska and was approved to grant academic degrees in 1984. Clarkson College is accredited by the Commission on Institutions of Higher Education and the North Central Association of Colleges and Schools.*

*The mission of Clarkson College is to improve the quality of patient care by offering undergraduate and graduate health science degrees. The College provides high-quality education to prepare competent, thoughtful, ethical, and compassionate health-care professionals for service to individuals, families, and communities.*

*Clarkson College recognizes that all students do not have the opportunity to give up employment and/or move to a college campus to continue their education. Clarkson offers the opportunity for working adults to complete degree programs through a variety of delivery methods.*

## DISTANCE LEARNING PROGRAM

The Clarkson College Distance Education Program currently serves about 150 students in thirty states. Since distance education is an outreach of the College's current programs, it is governed by the academic and administrative policies in effect. Distance students follow the same semester schedule, pay the same tuition, and receive the same support services as on-campus students. Distance Education Programs have the same accreditation as on-campus programs.

## DELIVERY MEDIA

Clarkson delivers theory course work to students via the Internet, mail, videotape and audiotape, fax transmission, computer e-mail, and telephone conferencing. Clarkson advisers help students to access and use the computer system. Syllabi, textbooks, and study questions are available on line; follow-up calls are made by faculty members. Tests are mailed to proctors in the students' area who monitor test-taking.

Students must have access to a computer with a modem, a fax machine, a VCR, and an audiocassette player. All students are required to have either a telephone answering machine or voice mail and access to the Internet and e-mail.

## PROGRAMS OF STUDY

Registered nurses who hold a diploma or associate degree can complete the Bachelor of Science in Nursing (B.S.N.). All courses can be taken by distance education. The B.S.N. requires 130 credit hours. Clarkson's Master of Science in Nursing (M.S.N.), which requires 18 credit hours of core courses plus appropriate credit hours in a selected option, allows nurses to enhance their career mobility. Options include nursing administration (additional 18 credit hours), nursing education (additional 18 credit hours), and family nurse practitioner (addi-

tional 27 credit hours). M.S.N. students are required to come to campus for thesis defense or comprehensive exams. M.S.N.–F.N.P. students must come to campus five times for testing and assessment. Clinicals are completed using qualified preceptors in the student's community. M.S.N.–F.N.P. students who wish to study via distance learning must reside in Nebraska, Iowa, Wyoming, South Dakota, Missouri, Kansas, or Colorado.

The Bachelor of Science in medical imaging is open to ARRT Registered Technologists and/or board-eligible graduates of an associate degree or diploma program in radiography. Students can earn their bachelor's degree (128 credit hours) in medical imaging completely through distance education.

The B.S. in health-care business (128 credit hours) prepares students to assume leadership roles in the health-care industry. The program is available entirely through distance education.

## SPECIAL PROGRAMS

There are no special programs offered in distance learning education at Clarkson College.

## STUDENT SERVICES

Distance education students have access to many of the same resources as on-campus students. Distance students have regular contact with the Coordinator of Distance Education, who serves as a liaison between students and faculty members. The coordinator assists the students in the areas of advisement, registration, and textbook orders, which are accomplished through phone calls, faxes, and e-mail. Distance students' research and informational needs are supported by the College Library Services. Library resources are available via phone, computer, or fax, allowing students the ability to search for articles and books. Distance students have access to the College library loan services. Students also receive a listing of other students enrolled in the same courses for the semester, which facilitates communication with fellow students to discuss course work and share information. Distance students have access to career planning, counseling, and academic skill development services through the Student Success Center.

## CREDIT OPTIONS

Students can transfer credits taken at other regionally accredited institutions if the course work is comparable and there is evidence of satisfactory scholarship (at least a C in undergraduate courses and a B for graduate courses). In major course work, up to one third of the total number of credit hours in the major may be transferred. Registered nurses can receive 47 credit hours for their previous nursing education. An ARRT Registered Technologist can receive 44 credit hours for previous radiography education. Students beginning graduate programs may transfer no more than 9 semester credit hours from other institutions. Advanced placement students may take the College-Level Examination Program (CLEP).

## FACULTY

Clarkson College has 28 full-time and 9 part-time faculty members instructing distance education courses, 10 percent of whom hold doctoral degrees.

## ADMISSION

Distance education students are subject to the same admissions requirements as on-campus students. Undergraduate students must have a C+ GPA or higher and an ACT score of 20 or better. Graduate students must have a 3.0 GPA on a 4.0 scale and have completed an appropriate undergraduate degree from an accredited college or university. There are certain program-specific admission requirements.

## TUITION AND FEES

Distance students pay the same tuition as on-campus students. For the 2000–01 academic year, undergraduate tuition is $289 per credit hour and graduate tuition is $334 per credit hour. There is an additional $18 per credit hour in fees. Distance students pay a $75 per semester distance fee.

## FINANCIAL AID

Distance students are eligible for many of the financial aid opportunities as on-campus students. Scholarships, grants, and loans are available to meet the individual financial needs of students who qualify.

Scholarships are awarded to outstanding applicants. Students are required to submit the completed Free Application for Federal Student Aid (FAFSA) and the Clarkson College Financial Aid Information Form for eligibility for all forms of aid.

## APPLYING

The enrollment policy at Clarkson College allows potential students to apply at any time during the year. A completed application form, accompanied by the $15 application fee, and all official transcripts (high school and previous colleges) should be submitted when seeking admission. Students who have graduated from high school in the past two years must also submit ACT or SAT scores.

### CONTACT
Tony Damewood
Dean of Enrollment Management
Clarkson College
101 South 42nd Street
Omaha, Nebraska 68131-2739
Telephone: 402-552-3100
          800-647-5500 (toll-free)
E-mail: admiss@clarksoncollege.edu
Web site: http://www.clarksoncollege.edu

# The College of Mount St. Joseph

## Distance Learning Programs

Cincinnati, Ohio

*As a private, Catholic, liberal arts college founded in 1920, the College of Mount St. Joseph has a rich history of preparing students for the future. Today, the Mount has more than 2,200 students and offers an outstanding liberal arts curriculum that emphasizes values, integrity, and social responsibility, as well as practical career preparation. Required courses in humanities, science, and the arts are complemented by opportunities for cooperative work experience, specialized professionally oriented courses, development of computer skills through a universal computing requirement, and extracurricular opportunities to give students the broad-based background that is in high demand among employers.*

*The College is accredited by the North Central Association of Colleges and Schools.*

## DISTANCE LEARNING PROGRAM

A leader in the field of technology, the College of Mount St. Joseph is committed to providing convenient, accessible, and high-quality education. The Mount's online programs provide a flexible alternative for those wanting to further their education, but for whom attending regularly scheduled classes would be difficult or impossible.

## DELIVERY MEDIA

While all courses are taken via distance delivery, distance learning programs require a two weekend sessions at the Mount's campus in Cincinnati, Ohio. During this time, program participants learn the technical skills necessary to succeed in the program, meet their classmates, and become familiar with the College services available to them.

The distance program uses Web-based interactive learning materials, videotapes, and textbooks for "classroom" instruction and provides for student/teacher and student/student interaction through a variety of communication vehicles, includ-ing telephone, voice mail, e-mail, and teleconferences.

## PROGRAMS OF STUDY

The Mount offers two certificate programs via distance learning. The Paralegal Studies Certificate Online is a postdegree certificate available to anyone holding either an associate or a bachelor's degree. The Paralegal Studies for Nurses Certificate Online is a postdegree certificate available to RNs holding a Bachelor of Science in Nursing degree. Both programs are approved by the American Bar Association. Both certificates require 33 credit hours. Courses are offered in sequence and can be completed in twenty months. Courses may also be elected individually and taken as part of a bachelor's or associate's degree. Classes begin in August and January and are limited to 20 students.

## STUDENT SERVICES

The College of Mount St. Joseph is known for outstanding student support and extends the same services to students learning at a distance. Technical service is available via a toll-free support line from 8 a.m. to 11 p.m. Eastern time. The College library offers many resources in electronic form, including its catalog, journal indexes, journal articles, and reference materials. An electronic reserves system provides distance learners with Web access to articles placed on reserve by their professors. Because access to library resources, including LEXIS, has been built using Web technologies, integration with a predominant Web-based distance program is ensured.

Students also have access to the bookstore, which provides delivery and online ordering. Other student services include advising, financial aid, career counseling and placement, a Wellness Center, and an Academic Performance Center.

## FACULTY

The Mount's two distance programs make use of the same faculty as their on-campus counterparts. This includes 1 full-time and 12 part-time faculty members, 8 of whom have doctoral degrees.

## ADMISSION

To be admitted to the Paralegal Studies Certificate Online program, a student must have either an associate or a bachelor's degree from an accredited institution.

To be admitted to the Paralegal Studies for Nurses Certificate Online program, a student must be an RN with a Bachelor of Science in Nursing degree from an accredited institution and have had at least 2,000 hours of clinical experience.

## CREDIT OPTIONS

There are no credit options for the distance learning programs at the College of Mount St. Joseph.

## TUITION AND FEES

Tuition is $363 per credit hour. The application fee is $25.

## FINANCIAL AID

There are several financing options, including Stafford loans or interest-free monthly payments. Students should call Student Financial Services at 800-654-9314 Ext. 4418 (toll-free), or 513-244-4418 for more information.

## APPLYING

Classes begin in August and January. Students should submit the application form, nonrefundable application fee, transcripts, and admission documents to the Office of Admission.

---

**CONTACT**

Georgana Taggart, Program Director
College of Mount St. Joseph
5701 Delhi Road
Cincinnati, Ohio 45233
Telephone: 513-244-4952 (Paralegal Studies)
           513-244-4531 (Admission Office)
           800-654-9314 (toll-free)
Fax: 513-244-4601
E-mail: georgana_taggart@mail.msj.edu
Web site: http://www.msj.edu/paralegal

# Colorado Community Colleges Online

COMMUNITY COLLEGES OF
**COLORADO** ONLINE
Denver, Colorado

eCollege .com  *www.ecollege.com*

*CCCOnline was founded in 1995 as a significant innovation of the Colorado Community Colleges, a fourteen-college state system. CCCOnline develops and delivers the excellent degree and certificate programs of the system colleges via Internet technologies. CCCOnline students register through, and are awarded their degrees/certificates from, one of the Colorado Community Colleges, which are accredited by the North Central Association of Colleges and Schools.*

*CCCOnline was one of the first of its kind to offer a postsecondary degree completely asynchronously. CCCOnline partners with Colorado Community Colleges to provide unlimited access to its programs. It has articulated its degree program with the public four-year colleges in Colorado and several out-of-state colleges.*

## DISTANCE LEARNING PROGRAM

CCCOnline has served 9,000 students in all fifty states as well as Canada, the Caribbean, South America, Europe, and Asia. Students can receive the Associate of Arts (A.A.) degree and various occupational degrees/certificates from their home or office without ever visiting a campus. Student support services are available at a distance as well.

## DELIVERY MEDIA

Course work includes Internet, CD-ROM materials, and videotape, depending on the course of study. Students need only a computer and Internet access to complete an A.A. degree. Presentations, discussions, and study groups with classmates and faculty members occur online and through electronic mail.

## PROGRAMS OF STUDY

CCCOnline offers fully-accredited degrees/certificates at a dis-
tance. By accessing the CCCOnline Web site (listed with contact information), students can obtain degrees/certificates that are awarded by one of the fourteen Colorado Community Colleges. These programs include freshman- and sophomore-level general education courses that transfer toward the completion of a baccalaureate degree. The A.A. degree of the Colorado Community Colleges is a low-cost, high-quality, accredited degree that offers variety, flexibility, and a learner-centered curriculum. The A.A. degree requires 60 hours (38 hours of core curriculum and 22 hours of general education electives). Fifteen hours must be completed through a Colorado Community College. Students completing the core curriculum are guaranteed transferability to Colorado four-year colleges. Colorado Community College currently manages the following degree programs: A.A.S. in business, offered by all Colorado Community College consortial partners; A.A.S. in construction technology (with an emphasis in construction electrician), offered by Red Rocks Community College; A.A.S. in convergent technology, offered by Arapahoe Community College; A.A.S. in emergency management and planning, offered by Red Rocks Community College; A.A.S. in library technician studies, offered by Pueblo Community College; A.A.S. in occupational safety and health technology, offered by Trinidad State Junior College; A.A.S. in construction technology (with an emphasis in power technology), offered by Red Rocks Community College; A.A. (with an emphasis in public administration), offered by all Colorado Community College consortial partners.

Certificate programs offered include agricultural business, computer networking, and early childhood professional studies (through several community colleges); convergent technologies (through Arapahoe Community College); emergency management and planning (through Red Rocks Community College); library technician studies (through Pueblo Community College); Microsoft Certified System Engineer (MCSE) certification (through Northeastern Junior College); and occupational safety and health technology (through Trinidad State Junior College).

## STUDENT SERVICES

CCCOnline is dedicated to the satisfaction and success of its students. Colorado Community Colleges provide easy access to the complete array of student enrollment, academic, financial aid, special support, and career counseling services. An Online Writing Lab (OWL) and an Online Math Lab (OML) are available to all students. Library access is provided through various Internet library resources, interlibrary loan, and by the Colorado Association for Research Libraries.

## FACULTY

CCCOnline uses full-time and part-time faculty members from Colorado Community Colleges. These faculty members have won regional and national awards for teaching skills and have long experience with a student-centered philosophy.

## ADMISSION

Colorado Community Colleges are open-door institutions, admitting anyone 16 years of age or older. A high school diploma or GED is not required for admission.

## TUITION AND FEES

In-state and out-of-state tuition is $122.70 per credit hour.

## FINANCIAL AID

General financial aid programs are available through all Colorado Community Colleges and include the Federal Pell Grant, Federal Supplemental Educational Opportunity Grant, Federal Perkins Loan, Federal Stafford Student Loan, and Federal Work-Study Programs.

## APPLYING

Distance learners can enroll at the Web site (listed below) or in person at any Colorado Community College campus.

---

### CONTACT

John Schmahl
Director of Student Support Services
CCCOnline
9075 East Lowry Boulevard
Denver, Colorado 80220
Telephone: 303-365-8807
          800-801-5040 (toll-free)
Fax: 303-365-8822
E-mail: john.schmahl@heat.cccoes.edu
Web site: http://www.ccconline.org

# Colorado State University

## *Division of Educational Outreach*

Fort Collins, Colorado

---

*Colorado State University has served the people of Colorado as the state's land-grant university since 1870. Today, the campus in Fort Collins is home to 22,000 students pursuing degrees at all levels in a wide range of subjects in the liberal arts, engineering, business, natural resources, agriculture, and the sciences. The University's instructional outreach activities go far beyond the campus and the state of Colorado.*

## DISTANCE LEARNING PROGRAM

Colorado State University's distance education courses are designed to begin or to finish a degree, to explore new topics, to enrich life, and to give students an opportunity to develop a level of proficiency in professional development. Approximately 2,500 individuals from all over the country and overseas enrolled in distance education courses from Colorado State University during the 1999–2000 academic year.

## DELIVERY MEDIA

Colorado State offers courses in online, print, and video formats. All courses are supported by Colorado State University faculty members. Students may contact course faculty members via telephone, fax, e-mail, or regular mail. Students should call Educational Outreach for contact information for an instructor.

## PROGRAMS OF STUDY

Colorado State University's Network for Learning (CSUN) links learners to all of Colorado State's distance options—correspondence courses, telecourses, distance degree programs, online courses, face-to-face programs at satellite locations, and those offering a mix of media.

As an institution, Colorado State has been involved in distance education since 1967 and was one of the first schools to utilize technology in distance education.

*Independent Study: Correspondence Study, Telecourses, and Online Courses* removes the traditional boundaries of time and location for the distance learner. Through the use of a study guide, textbooks, videotapes, the Internet, and applicable reference materials, students have the opportunity to participate in an individualized mode of instruction offering a high degree of flexibility. Students interested in correspondence courses and telecourses may enroll at any time, set their own pace, and choose the most convenient time and place to study. Online courses are taught according to the regular University semester schedule.

*Distance degrees* offer working professionals the opportunity to earn credit from Colorado State without coming to campus. These are semester-based, primarily videotaped programs, with some online courses and programs. Whether students are working on their degree or taking courses to stay current in their field, distance degrees offer the flexibility to pursue educational objectives as work schedules permit.

Courses are available in several disciplines, including agriculture, business, computer science, engineering, fire service, human resource development, and statistics. Distance degree students are located throughout the United States and Canada and at U.S. military APO and FPO addresses. At this time, only correspondence courses and online courses and degrees are available to overseas students. More than 1,000 motivated people have earned their degrees, and countless others have taken individual courses to enhance their skill base or keep current with the latest technology.

## SPECIAL PROGRAMS

Colorado State also provides other distance education opportunities. These courses are open-entry/open-exit, meaning students may register at any time and take from six to twelve months to complete, depending on the course. Many of the courses can be used for specific programs, such as Child Care Administration Certification, the Gerontology Interdisciplinary Studies Program, the Educator's Portfolio Builder, or Seed Analyst Training.

The state of Colorado requires certification of all child-care center directors and substitute directors by the State Department of Human Services. Certification requires both experience working with young children and specific education. Colorado State University is proud to offer courses through distance education that satisfy the educational requirements. Other states may have individual specific educational requirements. Students should contact the appropriate agency in their area for further information.

The Gerontology Interdisciplinary Studies Certificate Program helps individuals increase their knowledge, skills, and effectiveness in working with older adults. The objectives of the program are congruent with standards and guidelines for gerontology programs advocated by the Association of Gerontology in Higher Education (AGHE), of which Colorado State is an institutional member.

The Educator's Portfolio Builder distance education courses are designed for independent, self-paced learning. Students choose an area of interest and focus; they can mix and match and build the portfolio that meets their individual professional development needs. Courses are designed for practicing teachers, with assignments and activities relevant to teachers and students, and they are all college-credit courses. Instructors are Colorado State University faculty members. They are available to answer questions and give feedback via telephone, fax, e-mail, or regular mail.

An innovative Seed Analyst Training Program consisting of four distance learning (correspondence) courses has been developed by the National Seed Storage Laboratory and Colorado State University. The courses were prepared over a two-year period by University professors and other experts with the support of the Colorado seed industry. The four courses cover the basics of seed analyst training: 1) Seed Anatomy and Identification, 2) Seed Development and Metabolism, 3) Seed Purity Analysis, and 4) Seed Germination and Viability.

Advising through the University HELP/Success Center is offered to all those interested in continuing their learning. There is no fee for academic advising services. Students may schedule an appointment with an academic adviser by calling 970-491-7095. The Extended University Programs librarian is available to assist students with identifying and accessing library materials. Students should call 970-491-6952 to speak with the librarian.

## CREDIT OPTIONS

All credits earned through distance education are recorded on a Colorado State University transcript. Distance education courses are the same as on-campus courses and are accredited by each department. A student currently enrolled in a degree program elsewhere is responsible for checking with the appropriate official at the degree-granting institution to make certain the course will apply.

## FACULTY

Distance education faculty members must meet the same high standards any Colorado State University faculty member must meet. Most of the distance faculty members are faculty members within the department granting the course credit. Faculty members are available to answer questions and give feedback via telephone, fax, e-mail, or regular mail.

## ADMISSION

Anyone who has the interest, desire, background, and ability may register for distance learning courses. However, if prerequisites are listed for a course, they must be met. Registration in distance learning courses does not constitute admission to Colorado State University.

## TUITION AND FEES

Tuition for distance degrees for the 2001–02 academic year is $448 per semester credit hour (business courses), $436 per semester credit hour (nonbusiness courses), or $360 per credit hour (online courses). Tuition for other distance education courses for the 2001–02 academic year is $160 per semester credit hour.

## FINANCIAL AID

Colorado State University courses are approved for the DANTES program. Eligible military personnel should process DANTES applications through their education office. For information regarding veterans' benefits, students should contact the VA office at Colorado State University. With the exception of distance degrees, distance learning is not a degree-granting program and is therefore not eligible for federal grants. Students are encouraged to seek scholarship aid from organizations and local civic groups that may sponsor such study.

## APPLYING

There is no application for distance education. Students should simply register for the course(s) of interest by mail, fax, telephone, or in person and pay the tuition. To complete a degree via distance degrees, admittance to the University is required.

---

### CONTACT

For more information about these and other distance courses from Colorado State University or for registration information:

Telephone: 970-491-5288
877-491-4336 (toll-free)
Fax: 970-491-7885
E-mail: info@learn.colostate.edu
Web site: http://www.learn.colostate.edu

---

# Connecticut State University

## OnlineCSU

Hartford, Connecticut

*The Connecticut State University System (CSU) is fully accredited and the largest public university in Connecticut, with more than 35,000 students, 2,800 employees, and 150,000 alumni. OnlineCSU is the virtual classroom of the four Connecticut State Universities—Central Connecticut State University, Eastern Connecticut State University, Southern Connecticut State University, and Western Connecticut State University. Created in 1998 as a board initiative, OnlineCSU supports CSU's mission to provide affordable and high-quality active learning opportunities that are geographically and technologically accessible. The collaborative efforts of the four Universities provide a stronger educational resource for students in Connecticut and around the world.*

## DISTANCE LEARNING PROGRAM

As the virtual classroom of the four Connecticut State Universities, OnlineCSU offers a wide variety of undergraduate and graduate-level courses. OnlineCSU itself is not a university; students matriculate in and/or take classes from one of the four institutions and go to class via the OnlineCSU virtual classroom. Courses are approved for credit and are generally transferable within the CSU system and beyond. Launched in 1998 with 70 students, OnlineCSU successfully educated nearly 1,000 students in the spring 2001 semester.

## DELIVERY MEDIA

OnlineCSU is an asynchronous learning environment; students and teachers do not need to log on at the same time. Faculty members and students share documents and interact regularly through chat rooms, threaded discussions, and e-mail. The equipment requirements for taking an OnlineCSU course are: Windows 95/MacOs 7.5.5 or greater; a Pentium 75 or Power PC or faster processor, with 16 MB or more of RAM and a 28.8-kbps or faster modem; and an Internet service provider.

## PROGRAMS OF STUDY

OnlineCSU offers a Master of Library Science (M.L.S.) degree. This program is offered by Southern Connecticut State University's Department of Library Science and Instructional Technology. Southern's M.L.S. program integrates library science, information science, and instructional technology and offers preparation for carers in various types of libraries, including academic, public, special, and school libraries, and a range of alternative information science occupations. The Master of Library Science degree program is accredited by the American Library Association. The school media specialist concentration is also approved by the Connecticut State Board of Education and offers Connecticut-certified teachers the opportunity to obtain cross-endorsement as a school media specialist through the online program. A minimum of 36 credits, taken as part of a planned program, is required for the Master of Library Science degree. Some specialization alternatives may require additional credits.

Other online master's degree programs under consideration include accounting, educational technology, and data mining; a certificate in data mining is also being considered. In-formation about these programs will be posted to the Web site as it becomes available.

## SPECIAL PROGRAMS

Online learners are invited to participate in the same programs that are available to on-campus students. The four Connecticut State Universities offer a full range of special programs for students, including internships, work-study programs, study-abroad programs, and more. More information can be obtained by linking to the four University Web sites from the OnlineCSU site (listed below).

## STUDENT SERVICES

All OnlineCSU students have full access to CSU's online library services, including full-text resources; online bookstores; and a round-the-clock, toll-free help desk. In addition, all of the on-campus student services, such as academic advising, financial aid, and career counseling, are available to OnlineCSU students.

## CREDIT OPTIONS

CSU is a fully accredited university system, and the courses that are offered through OnlineCSU are part of the regular curriculum of the four Connecticut State Universities. Therefore, these credits should be transferable to other higher-education institutions.

## FACULTY

Regular CSU faculty members teach all of the courses offered through

OnlineCSU. At CSU, the faculty members who develop the course teach the course, whether the course is delivered on campus or online.

## ADMISSION

Students wishing to enroll in the online Master of Library Science (M.L.S.) degree program can do so completely online. Other than the M.L.S. degree, students wishing to matriculate at one of the four CSUs must apply to the University of choice using the on-campus application process. For information about the M.L.S. degree, students should contact Mary Brown at brown@scsud.ctstateu.edu or by calling 860-392-5781.

## TUITION AND FEES

In summer 2001, part-time graduate students, both in-state and out-of-state, paid $260 per credit hour. Part-time undergraduate students, both in-state and out-of-state, paid $220 per credit hour. All students who took a class via OnlineCSU paid a $32 online fee per class.

## FINANCIAL AID

Students who receive financial aid may be able to apply all or part of this aid to the OnlineCSU courses.

## APPLYING

OnlineCSU courses are open to full- and part-time students, whether or not they matriculated at one of the four CSU universities. Students register for OnlineCSU courses online through the Web site (listed below). Registration data is forwarded to the appropriate University for approval. No orientation is required. Students complete a self-rated questionnaire, Is Online Learning For Me, and are asked to consult regularly with their advisers regarding online learning choices.

---

### CONTACT

Robin Worley
Telephone: 860-493-0023
Fax: 860-493-0080
E-mail: worleyr@sysoff.ctstateu.edu
Web site: http://www.OnlineCSU.ctstateu.edu

---

# Dakota State University

## *Office of Distance Learning*

Madison, South Dakota

---

Dakota State University (DSU), established in 1881, has offered Web courses since 1990 and recently expanded its distance education program to provide technology-based education to students nationally and internationally. The University's Center of Excellence is in information systems. The faculty members pride themselves on the integration of technology into the curricula. DSU is accredited by Commission on Institutions of Higher Education of the North Central Association of Colleges and Schools.

## DISTANCE LEARNING PROGRAM

DSU Online is an integral part of the University and in its five years has served more than 2,560 students with online and now ITV courses. The program offers a variety of undergraduate and graduate courses in IT and other areas. Through innovation in technology the Office of Distance Education delivers DSU programs to diverse populations throughout the state, the nation, and the world, applying technology with a personal touch.

## DELIVERY MEDIA

At Dakota State, the primary delivery method for distance courses is the Internet. DSU's online courses are set up for student-to-instructor and student-to-student interaction through e-mail, phone, and Web discussion boards. The courses range from self-paced to highly interactive and are conducted on a semester basis. This past year, DSU has started delivering courses over the state's Digital Dakota Network (DDN), which can be made accessible to sites out of the state.

## PROGRAMS OF STUDY

Distance-delivered degree programs at Dakota State University include a Bachelor of Science (B.S.) in health information administration (HIA), a degree completion program; a Master of Science in Information Systems (M.S.I.S.); and a Master of Science (M.S.) in computer education and technology. Baccalaureate degree programs are being developed in information systems and e-commerce.

The health information administration program offers preparation for a professional area of service in hospitals, clinics, and related health facilities and agencies. Graduates are prepared to serve as entry-level health information administrators. The HIA program is for those students who already have their ARTS/RHITS and want to complete the bachelor's degree.

The Master of Science in Information Systems is an advanced degree program designed to prepare graduates for leadership positions in the information technology field. The M.S.I.S. program provides the technical foundations of computer science

combined with key business concepts and applications. The program focuses on the integration of information technology with business problems and opportunities, enabling information systems professionals to understand technological issues as well as business concepts and fundamentals.

The M.S. in computer education and technology program is designed to equip educators to function in a new paradigm, the information age school. It equips information age educators to be leaders in educational technology; current in teaching, learning processes and practices, research technologies, and designs; and knowledgeable of technologies, programming skills, and technology-based current educational tools and products.

## SPECIAL PROGRAMS

Dakota State University also offers the high school fast track program, where high school students can take the DSU online courses for dual credit while in high school and get a "jump start" on college.

## STUDENT SERVICES

The Office of Distance Education strives to provide all campus services to DSU distance students. Distance students have online registration, as well as online access to the bookstore and library—all done through the Office of Distance Education

Web site, listed below. There is a student guide with the policies and procedures for distance students.

## CREDIT OPTIONS

Degree-seeking students can transfer in credit or earn credit by AP and CLEP exams, department credit by exam, or earn credit for prior learning or work experience up to 32 credit hours for a baccalaureate degree. The details can be found in the online catalog on the DSU Web site, listed below.

## FACULTY

The majority of the distance courses are taught by full-time faculty members of Dakota State, in addition to 1 part-time faculty member. Twenty-three of the distance faculty members have earned doctoral degrees, including the 1 part-time faculty member. The remaining 7 instructors are at the master's degree level.

## ADMISSION

Distance students, until they become degree seeking, need not formally apply to the University to take the distance courses. Students can register online on the Distance Education Web site (listed below), as well as by phone, fax, and at the office.

## TUITION AND FEES

Tuition is set yearly by the South Dakota Board of Regents and currently distance courses are categorized under the self-support rate. The current rate is $142.25 per credit hour for undergraduate courses and $181.60 per credit hour for graduate courses. This rate is for both in-state and out-of-state students.

## FINANCIAL AID

Financial aid is available for degree-seeking students only and is processed by the DSU Financial Aid Office.

## APPLYING

For distance students want to applying for degree status, there is an online application form on the DSU Web site, listed below.

---

### CONTACT

Deb Gearhart, Director of Distance Education or
Susan Eykamp, Secretary
Office of Distance Education
201A Karl Mundt Library
Dakota State University
Madison, South Dakota 57042
Telephone: 605-256-5049
　　　　　800-641-4209
Fax: 605-256-5208
E-mail: dsuinfo@pluto.dsu.edu
Web site: http://www.dsu.edu (DSU)
　　　　　http://www.departments.dsu.edu/disted/
　　　　　(Distance Education)

---

# Dallas Baptist University

## Distance Education Program

Dallas, Texas

*The purpose of Dallas Baptist University (DBU) is to provide Christ-centered, high-quality higher education in the arts, sciences, and professional studies at both the undergraduate and graduate levels to traditional age and adult students in order to produce servant leaders who have the ability to integrate faith and learning through their respective callings.*

*Dallas Baptist University celebrated its 100th anniversary in 1998 and in fall 1999 reached a record enrollment of 3,921 students on campus and across a nine-state region.*

*The adult degree-completion program received national recognition in 1992, and the Master of Business Administration is one of the few M.B.A. programs available on line that has both regional and national accreditation.*

*All degree programs are accredited by the Southern Association of Colleges and Schools, 1866 Southern Lane, Decatur, Georgia 30033-4097 (telephone: 404-670-4501). The Graduate School of Business M.B.A. program is also accredited by ACBSP.*

## DISTANCE LEARNING PROGRAM

The Distance Education Program provides students with the same high-quality degree programs, student services support, library access, and technology access as local students receive on the main campus. Multiple technologies served more than 800 distance education students by March 2001. Students may take courses from anywhere in the world.

## DELIVERY MEDIA

Internet courses are instructor led from password-protected Web sites with a wide variety of interactions, such as chat rooms and threaded discussion. Students must have appropriate computer equipment, technical skills, and Internet access via a Web browser. The online courses are offered via the eCollege.com system.

Two-way audio/video courses are provided for corporate clients over their videoconferencing networks.

Both undergraduate and graduate business degree programs are available.

Video courses are instructor led using a VHS format.

Audio courses are standard 60-minute cassettes.

## PROGRAMS OF STUDY

Dallas Baptist University offers a Bachelor of Business Studies degree in business administration and management through the College of Adult Education via distance education. Students may earn up to 30 semester credit hours through the successful completion of an academic portfolio. A total of 66 semester hours can be transferred from a regionally accredited two-year college, and an unlimited number of semester hours can be transferred from a regionally accredited four-year institution for students who earned a GPA of 2.0 or above. A minimum of 126 semester hours is required for graduation, with 32 semester hours taken from DBU.

Courses required for the M.B.A. degree are available through distance education. The M.B.A. program consists of a 24-semester-hour core plus a student-selected concentration of 12 semester hours. Some applicants may need to add 3–18 semester hours of foundational courses if their undergraduate degree is not in business. An M.B.A. in management and a new concentration in e-commerce are now available completely online.

The management curriculum is designed to serve the educational needs of business managers and professionals who desire to enhance their management skills or acquire new skills. A variety of courses are provided in strategy, research, quantitative analysis, financial management, marketing, and international business. The e-commerce concentration provides both the business and technical knowledge needed to succeed in the exciting new world of electronic commerce.

DBU welcomes corporations that are interested in providing these degree programs to employees via the Internet or videoconferencing networks. For more information, companies should contact the University.

## SPECIAL PROGRAMS

College credit for knowledge gained through life and work experiences is available to adults who have at least four years of full-time work experience. This is accomplished through the College of Adult Education.

Dallas Baptist University's internship program provides students with opportunities to participate in an experimental work environment supervised by a professor and a business professional. The internship offers research, observation, study, and work in an approved organization. An international study program offers students international business knowledge through periodic overseas travel. Up to 6 semester hours of credit may be earned.

Special programs available to distance learners include on-site classes held at corporations in the Dallas/Fort Worth metroplex area and corporate sites in Texas, Oklahoma, Arkansas, Kansas, Georgia, Florida, and Missouri. Currently, Dallas Baptist University teaches undergraduate and/or graduate classes at twenty-five corporate sites.

## STUDENT SERVICES

Distance education students receive the same high-quality degree programs, administrative support, library access, technology access, bookstore services, academic advising, and access to the University Writing Center as local students receive on the main campus. Student computer equipment and computer skills are tested via the Internet prior to admission to the Internet courses. Any technical problems are identified for the student.

## CREDIT OPTIONS

For the Bachelor of Business Studies degree, students can transfer earned academic credits from accredited two-year colleges, accredited four-year institutions, CLEP examinations, and ACE/PONSI.

For the M.B.A. program, students may transfer up to 6 semester hours of graduate-level courses.

Students can supplement distance education courses with DBU's weekend and miniterm courses.

## FACULTY

Courses are taught by the same faculty members who teach on-campus classes to assure high-quality learning. Graduate students do not teach at DBU.

## ADMISSION

In addition to the University's standard admission requirements, a brief computer skills assessment is required for Internet courses. For degree-specific requirements, students should contact the University.

## TUITION AND FEES

Tuition for 2001–02 undergraduate online courses is $365 per credit hour. Graduate online courses are $375 per credit hour. There is a $40 fee for video courses and a $20 fee for audio courses.

## FINANCIAL AID

A variety of federal, state, and private funds may be available for students who meet specific requirements.

For institutional scholarships, students must be in good standing and satisfactorily progressing toward their educational goals. Other eligibility requirements may exist for specific awards.

For federal or state financial assistance, a student must meet the guidelines established by the U.S. Department of Education and the state of Texas.

Students interested in such assistance should contact the Financial Aid Office for more information (telephone: 214-333-5363).

## APPLYING

Applicants may apply online at http://www.dbu.edu or by requesting an application packet. Undergraduates must submit an application, official transcripts, and/or GED scores and an essay on why they wish to attend DBU. Applicants to the Graduate School of Business M.B.A. program must submit an application, transcripts, GMAT scores, two references, a resume, and an essay. Students for whom English is a second language must submit a minimum TOEFL score of 550.

---

### CONTACT
Distance Education Program
Dallas Baptist University
3000 Mountain Creek Parkway
Dallas, Texas 75211-9299
Telephone: 214-333-5337 (undergraduate program)
214-333-5242 (graduate program)
800-460-8188 (toll-free online program)
E-mail: caed@dbu.edu (undergraduate program)
graduate@dbu.edu (graduate program)
online@dbu.edu (online program)
Web site: http://www.dbu.edu
http://www.dbuonline.org

# Dallas Community Colleges

## Distance Learning Program

Dallas, Texas

More than 250,000 students have enrolled in the Distance Learning Program of the Dallas Community College (DCC) District since it began in 1972. Currently, approximately 10,000 students enroll in the program each academic year. The Dallas Community Colleges program is a product of the collaboration of seven colleges, all accredited by the Commission on Colleges of the Southern Association of Colleges and Schools to award the associate degree. The program draws its strength from the full-time faculty members of these colleges and from more than twenty-five years of experience in the development and implementation of distance learning courses, which are used by many colleges worldwide.

## DISTANCE LEARNING PROGRAM

The Dallas Distance Learning Program provides greater access to educational opportunities for learners in Dallas County and worldwide through the delivery of flexible, cost-effective courses. These courses are offered through a variety of technologies and lead to the Associate of Arts (A.A.) or the Associate of Sciences (A.S.) degree. The Distance Learning Program also provides opportunities for skill development or enhancement in career fields such as business. Dallas also provides a variety of noncredit courses.

## DELIVERY MEDIA

Video-based telecourses include a preproduced video series with print materials. Students may lease videos or view them on television (Dallas area only). Class interaction is offered through the telephone, fax, and mail. Students are required to have a TV, VCR, and telephone.

Video-based telecourse PLUS includes the same materials as above with online activities. Minimum requirements to access the sites are Netscape 4.0 or Internet Explorer 4.0.

Online courses are conducted entirely on the Internet. These courses require a computer, an Internet connection, an e-mail account, and Netscape Navigator 4.0 or Internet Explorer 4.0 or higher.

Some courses require additional hardware, software, or telephone resources. Print-based courses include print materials and participation in specialized activities. Courses may require a VCR or telephone.

## PROGRAMS OF STUDY

The Associate of Arts and the Associate of Sciences degrees require the completion of 61 credit hours, which includes a 48-credit-hour core plus an additional 13 credit hours of electives. The A.A. and A.S. degrees may be earned in their entirety through the Distance Learning Program of the Dallas Community Colleges.

More than 100 courses are available in a variety of subjects, including business, communications, computer programming, electronics, health, humanities and arts, literature, mathematics, office technology and software, sciences, and social sciences.

Students who plan to transfer to a four-year institution should consult the catalog of that institution to ensure that selected courses will both transfer and apply toward the intended major.

## SPECIAL PROGRAMS

Dallas participates in the special open-enrollment Navy College PACE program that reaches ships, submarines, and remote sites of the U.S. Navy. More than 10,000 military personnel have enrolled in courses through Dallas since 1992. Dallas is also a participant in Western Governor's University and Southern Regional Electronic Campus, which offers courses to students in the U.S. and abroad. Dallas Community Colleges also deliver credit and noncredit courses to employees of major corporations based in the north Texas area and beyond.

## STUDENT SERVICES

Distance learners have access to admission and enrollment processes as well as library services, including an online search, study skills assistance, and academic advising. There are services that are available through the Web site or by fax, telephone, or mail.

## CREDIT OPTIONS

The DCC transfers many passing grade credits from other colleges accredited through one of the U.S. regional associations. The DCC registrar completes course evaluations as needed for degree planning.

Credits earned through credit-by-examination, military experience, and the U.S. Armed Forces Institute are reviewed by the registrar. Credit may be granted if applicable. The DCC requires that at least 25 percent of the credit hours required for graduation be taken by instruction rather than these methods.

## FACULTY

Most of the courses in the Distance Learning Program are taught by full-time faculty members who also teach on-campus classes. Each of the more than 100 faculty members holds credentials approved by the Colleges' accrediting agency. To ensure high-quality instruction, the number of students assigned to a faculty member in a distance learning course is limited.

## ADMISSION

Students must have a high school diploma or its equivalent, be at least 18 years of age, or receive special approval for admission as outlined in the DCC catalog. Texas students must also fulfill testing requirements as mandated by state law. International students must take the TOEFL.

## TUITION AND FEES

Tuition and fees vary with the learner's residence and the number of credit hours. This may range from approximately $84 per 3-credit course for a local Dallas resident to $389 per 3-credit course for an out-of-state student. Other expenses may include tape leasing and the cost of study guides, textbooks, and course-related software.

## FINANCIAL AID

Students accepted for enrollment may be considered for several forms of institutional and federal financial aid. Veterans and financial aid recipients should consult an adviser before enrolling in distance learning courses.

## APPLYING

Applicants should submit an official application along with appropriate documentation, such as an official high school transcript, GED scores, or official transcripts from previous colleges, and should complete any required assessment procedures. The DCC application is available on line or through the mail.

### CONTACT
Distance Learning Program
Dallas Community Colleges
9596 Walnut Street
Dallas, Texas 75243
Telephone: 972-669-6400
   888-468-4268 (toll-free)
   972-669-6410 (for recorded information)
Fax: 972-669-6409
Web site: http://dallas.dcccd.edu

# Davenport University

## Davenport University Online

Grand Rapids, Michigan

---

*Davenport University has offered specialized, career-focused business education for more than 135 years. In addition, since early 1999, Davenport University has been accredited to offer master's, bachelor's, and associate degrees completely online—with no on-campus residency requirement. However, if students wish to use on-campus services or take a combination of online and on-campus courses, Davenport has twenty-seven locations throughout Michigan and northern Indiana. Accredited by the Higher Learning Commission and a member of the North Central Association of Colleges and Schools (NCA), Davenport's online courses are developed by its own faculty members, all of whom are certified to instruct in the online environment. This ensures that the online degree programs and courses are of consistently high quality and that Davenport University can accomplish its mission of preparing individuals and organizations to excel in the knowledge-driven environment of the twenty-first century.*

## DISTANCE LEARNING PROGRAM

Davenport Online offers the convenience of classroom accessibility 24 hours a day, seven days a week from virtually anywhere in the world. Online courses are truly interactive. Through group assignments, online research projects, and case study analyses, students collaborate with peers and immediately apply textbook theory to real business situations. The computer is simply a tool through which to communicate. Courses begin and end on specific dates, and class work is assigned deadlines.

## DELIVERY MEDIA

All online courses are delivered through the Internet using the Blackboard learning platform. It is recommended that the student's computer meet the following minimum specifications: Pentium 100 MHz Processor or Macintosh - Power PC 601 100 MHz; 16 megs of RAM; 28.8 modem; Internet access through an ISP (Internet Service Provider), including e-mail; Web browser: Netscape 4.0 or higher, Internet Explorer 4.0 or higher (AOL users should use the Netscape browser); monitor resolution: 640 x 480; and word processing software. A CD-ROM is strongly recommended.

## PROGRAMS OF STUDY

Complete online degree programs include an M.B.A. in strategic or entrepreneurial management; bachelor's degrees in accounting, e-commerce, marketing, and management (including human resource, industrial, entrepreneurship, and general management); and associate degrees in accounting, computer information systems, marketing, and management. Davenport Online also offers technical specialties and preparation for certification in the areas of management, marketing, international business, leadership, small business management, and more.

## FACULTY

All faculty members who teach with Davenport Online have at least a master's degree in the area of study and practical work experience. Their combined knowledge of theory and practice enhances the learning environment. All faculty members must complete an instructional design training program to become certified as an online instructor.

## ADMISSION

Online course work relies heavily on written communication and problem-solving skills. Students are eligible to enroll in Davenport online courses where assessment indicates their readiness for the first college-level writing courses (non-developmental) and the first college-level math course (non-developmental) required for their degree. In addition, students who do not have credit for College Writing I/Composition I must enroll in that course during their first online session. This may be done concurrently with another course.

## TUITION AND FEES

Davenport University Online undergraduate tuition is $830 per course; master's-level tuition is $930 per course. A $35 technology fee is assessed each term.

## FINANCIAL AID

Financial aid, such as grants, loans, and scholarships, is available to all qualified students. Students must first fill out a Free Application for Federal Student Aid (FAFSA) to begin the process. Many students receive tuition assistance through their employer's tuition reimbursement plan.

## APPLYING

Student must apply and be admitted to Davenport University. Students can complete an online application at the Web site listed below. There is a $25 application fee for admission into the undergraduate school and a $50 application fee for admission into the M.B.A. program. Once students have been admitted, they receive detailed information about how to schedule and activate their courses and how to purchase their books online through MBS Direct.

---

**CONTACT**

Pam Jennings
Director of Marketing & Enrollment Management
Davenport University Online
415 East Fulton Street
Grand Rapids, Michigan 49503
Telephone: 800-203-5323 (toll-free)
Fax: 800-811-2658 (toll-free)
E-mail: DUOnline@davenport.edu
Web site: http://www.online.davenport.edu

---

# DePaul University

## School for New Learning
## Center for Distance Education

Chicago, Illinois

> *Founded more than a century ago, DePaul University is one of the largest universities in the United States and the fastest growing of its size and type, serving more than 20,000 students. DePaul attracts students from all fifty U.S. states and sixty-five other countries, ensuring multiple perspectives.*
>
> *The School for New Learning (SNL) was established thirty years ago as one of the eight schools and colleges of DePaul. SNL is a national leader in the design and delivery of competency-based learning for adults. In 1999, SNL was ranked by CAEL (the Council for Adult and Experiential Learning) as one of the six best institutions for serving adult learners in higher education. Choosing from among colleges and universities all across North America, CAEL called SNL a "cutting edge pioneer" and "truly innovative in the understanding of the need to improve education." DePaul University and the School for New Learning are fully accredited, which means that the degree earned is honored throughout the world.*

## DISTANCE LEARNING PROGRAM

SNL's Distance Education Program allows adult students, 24 years or older, to earn a Bachelor of Arts degree from DePaul University without ever visiting a campus. SNL provides excellent learning opportunities and individualized service to adult students.

The Bachelor of Arts degree consists of fifty requirements allocated across three areas: focus area, lifelong learning skills, and liberal arts. Students meet the requirements through DePaul courses, transfer courses, proficiency examinations, demonstration of prior learning, and independent study. Unique to SNL is its emphasis on experience. The fifty degree requirements are competency-based, and all offerings honor adult experience and provide opportunities to extend learning through additional experience.

## DELIVERY MEDIA

The Distance Education Program uses various platforms, such as the World Wide Web, CD-ROMs, and e-mail, for course work and for connecting students, faculty members, advisers, professional experts, and classmates.

## PROGRAMS OF STUDY

Students receive a Bachelor of Arts degree from DePaul University. Unique to this program is that students individualize their study by designing a focus area relevant to their life and work goals. Approximately 60 percent of current SNL students graduate with a focus related to business, and other students study any area they choose.

In order to ensure both academic quality and focus area expertise, students work in a personalized committee format during their academic program. A committee consists of the student, faculty mentor, and a professional adviser. The faculty mentor is a DePaul faculty member who works directly with the student throughout his or her program. The professional adviser is an expert in the field in which the student would like to focus. The student selects the professional adviser, with the help of the faculty mentor, to act as a guide to the student, particularly in the focus area.

## STUDENT SERVICES

DePaul University offers students the following resources and services: admission, registration, identification cards, access to the library, career counseling, writing and math assistance, financial aid, academic advising, the bookstore, and more.

Students have continuing academic and administrative support throughout their academic programs. Advisers and counselors are available to serve students efficiently and effectively.

## CREDIT OPTIONS

There is no maximum to the number of transfer credits accepted in the Distance Education Program, although certain courses will not transfer. Courses with a grade of C- or better from accredited institutions are accepted for credit. Students may also transfer college-level learning from life and work experience into the program.

## FACULTY

The faculty members within the SNL community are dedicated to individualized, student-centered education in a collaborative environment. All have graduate degrees and experience in the fields in which they teach. The faculty members teach about what they know best.

## ADMISSION

Students must be 24 years or older, be proficient in use of the English language, and have completed secondary education.

Students' computers must meet the following technical requirements in order for them to participate: Windows 98 or higher, at least 32 MB or RAM, 56K baud modem, sound card, speakers, CD-ROM drive, monitor 800 x 600, and Internet access. Macintosh systems should meet equivalent requirements.

## TUITION AND FEES

Tuition and fees for the 2001–02 academic year are $319 per credit hour. The cost of textbooks varies from class to class.

## FINANCIAL AID

Financial aid opportunities are available to DePaul's SNL students. For more information, students should visit DePaul's financial aid Web site at http://www.depaul.edu/~saccount/.

## APPLYING

Applications for admission are accepted year-round. Students should visit SNL's Web site, listed below, to request that an interactive CD containing information about the program and an application for admission be sent to them (this request can also be made by e-mail or telephone).

## CONTACT

School for New Learning
Center for Distance Education
DePaul University
25 East Jackson Boulevard
Chicago, Illinois 60604
Telephone: 312-362-8821
        866-SNL-FORU (toll-free)
Fax: 312-362-8809
E-mail: snl@depaul.edu
Web site: http://snlonline.net

# Drexel University

## *MBA Online*

Philadelphia, Pennsylvania

*In 1891, near the end of a long and prosperous life, Philadelphia financier Anthony J. Drexel founded the Drexel Institute of Art, Science, and Industry. As society's need for technically proficient leaders grew, so did Mr. Drexel's Institution, first becoming Drexel Institute of Technology in 1936 and then Drexel University in 1970. Today, more than 6,800 undergraduate and 2,800 graduate students attend Drexel's six colleges and three schools. The Bennett S. LeBow College of Business founded its M.B.A. degree program in 1947 and currently has 900 students in the M.B.A., five M.S. programs, and the APC program. Located on 49 acres in Philadelphia's University City neighborhood, Drexel's programs are enhanced by the industrial, commercial, professional, and cultural activities of the nation's fourth-largest metropolitan area.*

## DISTANCE LEARNING PROGRAM

MBA Online is a Web-based version of the renowned Drexel M.B.A. program. It is fully a part of the graduate program in the College of Business, with the same admissions standards, same faculty, and same degree program. The mission of MBA Online is to serve the needs of graduate students whose schedule or location prevent them from otherwise participating in a high-quality M.B.A. program.

The first year, or foundation level, is an open enrollment program of ten courses. The second year, or advanced year, is a cohort track open by special admission. There are 25 students per cohort. The curriculum of the advanced year is delivered as a "techno-MBA," designed to meet the needs of professionals in technology-related positions. The technology-management focus is derived from a selection of courses from the Management Information Systems (MIS) area, as well as those developed by

the Center for e-Commerce Management. The curriculum uses enterprise-wide business simulations at the beginning and end of the program, as well as a unique case study in the application of Enterprise Resource Planning. It is designed to meet the needs of professionals and managers who wish to enhance their skills in the rapidly emerging technology-oriented marketplace.

Unique features of the program include focus on ERP as a unifying theme; focus on e-commerce as an important framework for the future; technology-management orientation; cutting-edge technology for program delivery, utilizing the strength of simulation experiences; the Business Mentors program, which features a highly placed executive in a mentorship role; and an active advisory board of executives that provides continuous improvement of the program.

## DELIVERY MEDIA

The MBA Online program is delivered over the World Wide

Web in the asynchronous mode via the eCollege.com system. Students need a computer, an Internet service provider, and Web navigation software. No other special equipment or software is needed. Since the program is Web based, students have access to their classes from anywhere they can plug into the Web. The MBA Online site carries not only all of the educational materials that the student needs to participate but communications features as well in order to communicate with the instructor, fellow students, advisers, and support services.

## PROGRAM OF STUDY

MBA Online comprises two parts: ten required foundation-level M.B.A. classes in an open enrollment program (i.e., any accepted student can register for these courses to meet requirements in the regular "real-time" program or the online program) and sixteen advanced-level M.B.A. classes. Students who qualify and wish to complete the M.B.A. entirely online are admitted to a select group of 25 students, called a cohort, at the advanced level. Cohorts start in September and April of each year. Students complete a sixteen-course sequence with their cohorts over a twenty-one-month period. Students in the advanced-level MBA Online are required to attend three residencies at the beginning, middle, and end of the program. These residencies are structured as concentrated weekend workshops and include a real-time course component that continues online throughout the academic quarter. The first two residencies are conducted at the headquarters hotel in Philadelphia. The final residency is a unique experience in international business at Drexel's London, England, campus. Other than these three residencies, students are not required to come onto campus. At the foundation level, there is no residency requirement.

## STUDENT SERVICES

All services available to on-campus students are also available to distance learning students. They are accessible through hot links on the MBA Online Web site. These links include academic advisers, cashier, and bookstore and access to the resources of Drexel's Hagerty Library.

## CREDIT OPTIONS

Course credits earned at the undergraduate and graduate levels may be transferred into the program to meet foundation-level requirements. Credit is granted based on academic course work only; no credit is granted on the basis of professional experience. At the foundation level, credit for all eight courses may be transferred from undergraduate programs or other previous study.

## FACULTY

There are 85 full-time and 21 part-time faculty members on staff at the LeBow Business College. Ninety-two percent of the full-time faculty members hold a Ph.D. in their fields. Instructors are regular members of the faculty of the LeBow College of Business at Drexel University and meet all of the requirements as faculty members of one of the nation's premier institutions for professional education. Students interact with each of their instructors regularly, and, in most cases, instructors are experienced in teaching the same courses in "real time" on campus. All instructors are committed to their students' success in the course.

## ADMISSION

All applicants must have received a bachelor's degree from an accredited college or university. Students must submit a fee, college transcripts, GMAT scores, TOEFL scores for international students, an essay, and letters of recommendation for admission to the advanced level.

## TUITION AND FEES

Tuition for the twenty-one-month advanced-level program for the cohort beginning in the academic year 2000 was $31,500. Students should see the Web site for tuition for individual courses in the open enrollment program.

## FINANCIAL AID

There is no financial aid specifically for the MBA Online program at this time. Students may contact the graduate financial aid officer, Mr. Robert Forest (rdf22@drexel.edu), for information on applicable federal and state loan and grant programs.

## APPLYING

Applications may be made through the MBA Online Web site.

---

**CONTACT**

Dr. Thomas Wieckowski
Director of Master's Programs in Business
Bennett S. LeBow College of Business
Drexel University
3141 Chestnut Street
Philadelphia, Pennsylvania 19104
Telephone: 215-895-1791
E-mail: mba@drexel.edu
Web site: http://mbaonline.lebow.drexel.edu

---

# Duke University

## *The Fuqua School of Business*

Durham, North Carolina

*Chartered in 1924 and accredited by AACSB–The International Association for Management Education in 1979, Duke University is one of the world's preeminent research and teaching universities. Duke consistently ranks among the top schools in the annual survey of "America's Best Colleges" by* U.S. News & World Report. *In addition to 6,000 undergraduates from ninety-six countries, Duke is home to 5,000 graduate students studying arts and sciences, business, divinity, engineering, the environment, and law and medicine.*

*Founded in 1969, Duke University's Fuqua School of Business is an established world leader among M.B.A. and executive education programs. Fuqua ranked fifth in the most recent biennial rankings of the best business schools by* Business Week. U.S. News & World Report *ranked Fuqua second in Executive M.B.A. programs among all schools in 2001. In the summer of 1999, Duke University established the Fuqua School of Business Europe in Frankfurt, Germany.*

## DISTANCE LEARNING PROGRAM

*Cross Continent:* The Duke M.B.A. Cross Continent program allows high-potential young managers to earn an internationally focused M.B.A. degree in less than two years, utilizing a format that minimizes the disruption of career and personal life. Three class sections, each comprised of 50 to 55 students, are enrolled concurrently. One is based on Duke's Durham, North Carolina, campus, and the other in Frankfurt, Germany, at the Fuqua School of Business Europe. Each term includes one week of intensive residential learning, coupled with significant team-oriented Internet-enabled learning.

*Global Executive:* The Duke M.B.A. Global Executive program enrolls approximately 90 mid- to senior-level executives from all over the world who wish to earn an internationally focused M.B.A. degree while minimizing the disruption of their careers and personal life. With five separate residencies in North America, Europe, Asia, and South America, the program is designed specifically to capitalize on its unique combination of "place and space." By combining face-to-face residential sessions (place) with Internet-mediated learning (space), the

program helps students develop skills in the core functional areas of business, as well as learn how to think and manage globally. Moreover, through frequent interaction with international classmates, Global Executive students are exposed to a wealth of ideas and approaches to each topic studied.

## DELIVERY MEDIA

*Cross Continent:* In the course of the twenty-month program, Cross Continent students attend nine weeks of residential sessions (8 one-week learning sessions plus a week of orientation), mostly on their primary campus, with one to three residential sessions on the other campus. The remainder of the program is delivered via an innovative Internet-enabled learning platform. Students complete sixteen courses over 8 ten-week terms.

*Global Executive:* Global Executive students attend eleven weeks of classroom sessions on four different continents. The program is broken into five academic terms, each of which is preceded by a two-week residency (the first term includes an extra week of orientation). The first and last residencies are held at Fuqua's Durham campus. The other three residential learning

sessions take place in Europe, Asia, and South America. The remainder of the Global Executive program is delivered via interactive distance education.

## PROGRAMS OF STUDY

*Cross Continent:* In the Duke M.B.A. Cross Continent program, all students take the same courses together in the same sequence, with a heavy emphasis on teamwork. Four of the sixteen courses offered are electives. The courses are designed to build from fundamental business knowledge to functional and strategy courses.

*Global Executive:* The Duke M.B.A. Global Executive curriculum, delivered by Duke's world-class faculty, offers a rigorous general management education with a focus on global management. Global Executive is also a lock-step program, and courses are designed to build from fundamental business courses to functional and strategy courses.

## STUDENT SERVICES

Both the Cross Continent and Global Executive programs offer library services online 24 hours a day, seven days a week. The programs offer extensive technical and operational support.

## CREDIT OPTIONS

All credits must be earned in both the Cross Continent (48 credit hours) and Global Executive (45 credit hours) programs. No transferred credits are accepted.

## FACULTY

Duke's Fuqua School of Business has one faculty body that teaches across all of its M.B.A. degree programs and executive education programs. The School employs 75 full-time, tenure-track and 48 part-time/adjunct faculty members. All of the 123 faculty members hold the Ph.D.

## ADMISSION

*Cross Continent:* Applicants to the Duke M.B.A. Cross Continent should have three to nine years of professional work experience, a bachelor's degree or equivalent, company sponsorship, GMAT scores, and TOEFL scores (if applicable). Interviews are strongly recommended.

*Global Executive:* Applicants to the Duke M.B.A. Global Executive program should have a minimum of ten years of professional experience, an undergraduate degree from an accredited four-year college or university or equivalent, strong quantitative skills, proficient written and verbal English skills, company sponsorship, and TOEFL scores (if applicable). Interviews are required.

## TUITION AND FEES

*Cross Continent:* The Duke M.B.A. Cross Continent program tuition for 2002 is $75,000. This includes all room and board during residential learning sessions and all books and materials. It does not include travel to and from residencies, laptop computers, and Internet service providers.

*Global Executive:* The Duke M.B.A. Global Executive program tuition for 2002 is $95,000. This includes all room and board during residential learning sessions and all books and materials. It does not include travel to and from residencies, laptop computers, and Internet service providers.

## FINANCIAL AID

Financial assistance is available to eligible students in the form of International Student Loans, Federal Stafford Loans, or private loans.

## APPLYING

Applicants should request application materials from the addresses below or access an application on each program's respective Web site located at http://www.fuqua.duke.edu.

---

### CONTACT

Karen Courtney, Director of Recruiting and Admissions, Cross Continent
The Fuqua School of Business
1 Towerview Drive
Durham, North Carolina 27708
Telephone: 919-660-7804
Fax: 919-660-8044
E-mail: fuqua-cross-continent@mail.duke.edu
Web site: http://www.fuqua.duke.edu

Lisa Lee, Associate Director of Recruiting and Admissions, Global Executive
The Fuqua School of Business
1 Towerview Drive
Durham, North Carolina 27708
Telephone: 919-660-7804
Fax: 919-660-8044
E-mail: globalexec@fuqua.duke.edu
Web site: http://www.fuqua.duke.edu

Fuqua School of Business Europe
Taunusanlage 21
D-60325 Frankfurt am Main
Germany
Telephone: 49-69-972699-0
Fax: 49-69-972699-99
E-mail: europe@fuqua.duke.edu
Web site: http://www.fuqua.duke.edu

# Duquesne University
## *Distance Learning Programs*
### Pittsburgh, Pennsylvania

*Duquesne University first opened its doors as the Pittsburgh Catholic College of the Holy Ghost in October 1878 with an enrollment of 40 students. Today Duquesne has more than 10,000 students in nine schools, who come from 110 nations and enjoy the University's global environment steeped in Duquesne's unique tradition of education for the mind, the heart, and the soul.*

*Known for its innovative educational programs for traditional and nontraditional students, Duquesne has been consistently ranked among America's top ten Catholic universities by* U.S. News & World Report. *It is rated as very competitive by* Barron's Profiles of American Colleges *and as one of* Barron's 300 Best Buys in College Education. *Duquesne has been listed among the 100 Most Wired Colleges by* Yahoo! Internet Life *magazine for three consecutive years. Duquesne is accredited by the Middle States Association of Colleges and Schools.*

## DISTANCE LEARNING PROGRAM

Distance learning opportunities are available in the areas of education, leadership, music, nursing, and pharmacy. Students are offered the best in online education and benefit from the same resources as students on campus, with access to Duquesne's library and technology resources. An outstanding faculty and a substantial student support system provide students with the opportunity to take courses from anywhere in the world.

## DELIVERY MEDIA

Distance learning courses are led by Duquesne faculty using Blackboard's CourseInfo, WebCT, or FirstClass. Students are able to interact with professors during online office hours or with other classmates using chatrooms or message boards.

Students are expected to use equipment that meets the University system requirements, have access to the Internet through a Web browser, and possess relevant technology skills.

## PROGRAMS OF STUDY

Duquesne University offers online graduate programs in a variety of academic areas. New programs are anticipated to be added to the current offerings. A complete list of courses offered each semester can be found at http://www.duq.edu/distancelearning/. In addition to complete degree programs, the University also offers a number of individual undergraduate and graduate online courses.

The School of Leadership and Professional Advancement offers a Master of Arts in leadership and liberal studies program that focuses on self-assessment and development of skills that are crucial to the leader's role, as well as an examination of the world in which today's leaders function. The School also offers an online bachelor's degree completion program. Students entering with an associate degree or its equivalent can obtain a degree in two years.

The School of Education, also new in fall 2000, offers instructional technology certificate programs that give K–12 educators, technology coordinators, higher education faculty members, and corporate business trainers the opportunity to enhance their approach to effectively linking teaching and learning.

The School of Music offers a Master of Music Education that emphasizes national standards, leadership, and advocacy.

The School of Nursing is the only school to offer both undergraduate and graduate online programs for RN to B.S.N., M.S.N., and Ph.D. degrees; post-B.S.N. certificates in RN First Assistant (RNFA) and nursing informatics; and post-master's degree programs in nursing administration, nursing education, family nurse practitioner (FNP), transcultural nursing, and psychiatric–mental health.

The School of Pharmacy offers a non-traditional Doctor of Pharmacy (Pharm.D.) program that is targeted for adult learners and is designed as an accessible and flexible way for working pharmacy practitioners to obtain a Doctor of Pharmacy degree.

## SPECIAL PROGRAMS

Designed for adult students, the online Master of Arts in Leadership and Liberal Studies (M.L.L.S.) is designed to enhance leadership capabilities and an understanding of the world in which tomorrow's leaders must function. Online M.L.L.S. students come from a variety of disciplines in the for-profit, nonprofit, and government sectors worldwide. The Master of Arts in Leadership and Liberal Studies is the recipient of the national Distinguished Credit Program Award by the Association of Continuing Higher Education and the national Outstanding Leadership Program for 1999 award from the Association for Leadership Educators. While the focus of the program is to cultivate the ability to lead at any level, individuals also develop and refine skills in critical thinking, problem solving, motivating and empowering others, communicating effectively and persuasively, and sharing knowledge with a community of like-minded professionals. For more information on this program, students should visit http://www.leadership.duq.edu.

## STUDENT SERVICES

Textbooks and other materials are available through mail order from the Duquesne bookstore or online via the Duquesne distance learning Web site (listed below).

Students have continuous support for the duration of their studies. A Help Desk is available through online chats, e-mail, or telephone to assist students in troubleshooting connectivity problems or other technically related questions.

## CREDIT OPTIONS

Credit transfer and degree completion requirements vary with each individual school and program. Information on program specifications can be found from the list of available programs at the Web site for individual schools and programs (listed below).

## FACULTY

While they are leaders in the community and in their professions, Duquesne's dynamic faculty members make students their highest priority. Online classes cover identical curricula and are taught by the same distinguished faculty members as on-campus courses.

## ADMISSION

Admissions for the distance education programs are handled separately through each school offering online programs and courses. Admission procedures and requirements can be found at the Web site for individual schools and programs (listed below).

## TUITION AND FEES

Tuition and fee schedules vary from school to school. Information can be found by clicking on the appropriate school at the Web site for individual schools and programs (listed below).

## FINANCIAL AID

Financial aid opportunities vary according to the program. For more information, students should consult http://www.duq.edu/StudentLife/services/financial/financial.html or the school administering the program.

## APPLYING

Application procedures and requirements vary by program. Students should see the admissions section within each program by visiting the Web site for individual schools and programs.

---

**CONTACT**

Center for Distance Learning
Duquesne University
600 Forbes Avenue
Pittsburgh, Pennsylvania 15282
Telephone: 800-283-3853 (toll-free)
E-mail: virtualcampus@duq.edu
Web site: http://www.duq.edu/distancelearning

---

# East Carolina University

## Division of Continuing Studies

Greenville, North Carolina

*Founded in 1907, East Carolina University (ECU) is the third-largest of the sixteen institutions comprising the University of North Carolina and offers baccalaureate, master's, specialist, and doctoral degrees in the liberal arts and sciences and professional fields, including medicine. Fully accredited by the Southern Association of Colleges and Schools, the University's goal is to provide students with a rich and distinctive educational experience. ECU's commitment to providing outstanding off-campus education opportunities spans more than fifty years. The Division of Continuing Studies provides a portal (http://www.options.ecu.edu) to the resources of the University as well as assistance that allows adult learners to choose programs that fit both their schedules and their academic goals. East Carolina University is constantly evaluating its distance learning programs to utilize the latest technology and is committed to meeting the evolving needs of the lifelong learner.*

## DISTANCE LEARNING PROGRAM

East Carolina University's academic community has developed a diverse offering of distance learning programs in direct response to the needs of students. A number of fully online programs are currently available, with additional programs under development. ECU is committed to providing programs designed to meet the professional needs and demanding schedules of busy, working adults. The latest offerings can be found on the Division of Continuing Studies Web site (listed below).

## DELIVERY MEDIA

East Carolina University's Web-based courses are offered via either Web sites created by the instructor, which contain course materials and interactive tools, or courses contained in the Blackboard course management system. Faculty members may employ a variety of communication tools within their courses, including threaded discussion groups, small group work, asynchronous Web-based chats, and instant messaging. In addition, faculty members may elect to deliver es-sential components of their courses via audio and video streaming or distributions of CDs, or by utilizing desktop video conferencing technologies.

## PROGRAMS OF STUDY

The M.S. in instructional technology program prepares students to be designers and developers of computer-based instructional materials for education, government, and business.

The M.S. in nutrition and dietetics program provides advanced academic training for individuals employed or planning to seek employment as registered dietitians.

The M.S. in speech, language, and auditory pathology program provides services that include the identification, description, evaluation, and remediation of all forms of speech, hearing, and language problems in children and adults.

The M.L.S. in library science program prepares students for careers in librarianship. The program is approved by NCATE/AASL, NC DPI, and the NC Public Library Certification Commission.

The M.S.I.T. in digital communications technology program emphasizes the use of information processing systems to effectively communicate, process information, access data, and solve problems in industry.

The M.S.I.T. in manufacturing program emphasizes the design, management, and control of human and technological systems in manufacturing.

The M.S.O.S. in occupational safety program emphasizes the management of safety programs, as well as the technical aspects of industrial safety and health.

There are several Graduate Certificate Programs.

The Computer Network Professional (CNP): Successful completion of the CNP also prepares an individual to sit for the Microsoft Certified Systems Engineer (MCSE) certification exam.

Professional Communication: Teachers who must design professional communication curricula and corporate trainers who must provide on-site communication training can benefit from this program.

Virtual Reality in Education and Training: Provides interested persons with an opportunity to learn to use basic virtual reality software and to apply that knowledge in educational and training settings.

Tele-Learning: Provides interested persons an opportunity to learn the basic principles of distance delivery of classes, to manage distance-delivered classes, and to evaluate their effectiveness.

Website Developer: Successful completion of the Website Developer certificate program prepares an individual to sit for an industry-standard professional certificate examination—the Microsoft Site Builder exam.

In addition to the programs detailed above, East Carolina University offers undergraduate degree completion programs that utilize associate degrees and course work from other institutions to complete the following degrees: BSBE in information technologies and the BSIT in industrial technology.

## STUDENT SERVICES

Distance learners at East Carolina University have access to library services, the campus network, e-mail accounts, the bookstore, registration, and academic advising at a distance. Academic advisers are available by phone, e-mail, fax, and in person to assist students with course selection.

## CREDIT OPTIONS

Transfer credit is granted on academic course work within degree-specific limits, and no credit is granted on the basis of professional experience. CLEP course credit may also be available.

## FACULTY

ECU's approximately 1,300 full-time faculty members, the majority of whom hold terminal degrees, teach both the on-campus and distance learning courses.

## ADMISSION

Before registering for a course, students must first apply and be admitted to ECU. Students may be admitted as degree seeking or as nondegree or visiting students. Admission for students seeking a degree is based on their previous academic record and standardized test scores. A performance-based admission policy is available for adult students. In addition, graduate students are required to submit letters of recommendation.

## TUITION AND FEES

Undergraduate tuition and technology fees are $54 per semester hour for in-state residents, $203 per semester hour for out-of-state students, and $319 per semester hour for in-state nonresidents. Graduate tuition and technology fees are $80 per semester hour for in-state residents, $203 per semester hour for out-of-state students, and $465 per semester hour for in-state nonresidents. Graduate students taking undergraduate courses are charged graduate tuition. The rates are projected and subject to change without prior written notice.

## FINANCIAL AID

Distance learning students are eligible to apply for financial aid and are encouraged to contact the Office of Financial Aid at 252-328-6610, faques@mail.ecu.edu, or via the Web at http://www.ecu.edu/financial/ for more information.

## APPLYING

Prospective students must submit an application, accompanied by a fee of $45, for admission. Applications can also be obtained online from the Division of Continuing Studies at http://www.options.ecu.edu. While most programs accept students year-round, students are urged to apply early. No on-campus orientation is required for distance learning students.

### CONTACT

Carolyn Dunn
Division of Continuing Studies
215 Erwin Building
East Carolina University
Greenville, North Carolina 27858-4353
Telephone: 252-328-2657
          800-398-9275 (toll-free)
Fax: 252-328-1600
E-mail: dcs@mail.ecu.edu
Web site:
    http://www.options.ecu.edu

# Eastern Michigan University

## Distance Education

Ypsilanti, Michigan

eCollege.com *www.ecollege.com*

*Eastern Michigan University (EMU) is a public, comprehensive, metropolitan university that offers programs in the arts, sciences, and professions. Founded in 1849, the University comprises more than 24,000 students who are served by 680 full-time faculty members as well as 1,200 staff members—on campus, off campus, and electronically. EMU offers undergraduate, graduate, specialist, doctoral, and certificate programs in its Colleges of Arts and Sciences, Business, Education, Health and Human Services, and Technology.*

*Eastern Michigan University continues to be the largest producer of educational personnel in the United States, including the largest producer of special education personnel, mathematics teachers, and science teachers, and is among the top ten producers of educational administrators. The University is fully accredited by the North Central Association of Colleges and Schools.*

*Eastern Michigan University's Continuing Education Office offers programs and courses online, at off-campus locations throughout the state, on weekends, in the evenings during the week, and in accelerated formats.*

## DISTANCE LEARNING PROGRAM

EMU's Distance Education program offers students the following three convenient distance learning options. Online courses allow students to attend class when it's convenient for their busy schedule—early in the morning, during the weekend, or even at 2 a.m. Whether students live just 5 or 500 miles from EMU's campus, they are able to learn conveniently, using a computer from their home, office, hotel room, military base, or "virtually" any other location in the world. Independent Learning courses are the second distance learning option. These allow students to enroll anytime, learn at their own pace, avoid commuting and parking inconveniences, satisfy general education requirements, and submit course work via Internet, fax, or U.S. mail. The third option is Interactive Television courses, which allow students to enroll in a single course that may be offered at multiple locations.

## DELIVERY MEDIA

Courses are delivered via World Wide Web, videotapes, print, and ITV. Students may meet in person or interact via e-mail, World Wide Web, mail, telephone, fax, or interactive television.

## PROGRAMS OF STUDY

The Master of Science in Engineering Management degree program is appropriate for a wide range of industrial and technically focused professionals who may have previously pursued a four-year degree in technology, business, engineering, or science. The Master of Liberal Studies in Technology degree program enhances students' career options by helping them gain the technology perspective required of contemporary managers and administrators. A graduate certificate in business administration is also offered. It is designed for the busy professional who would like to learn more about business, but, at this time, may not be interested in the M.B.A. or similar graduate business degrees. The graduate certificate in legal administration is the first of its kind offered in the Midwest and can stand alone as a means of updating knowledge, exploring a new discipline, or redirecting a career. It can also constitute an area of concentration within EMU's Master of Liberal Studies program. The Bachelor of Science in applied technology degree program is designed for those who wish to continue their education and earn a Bachelor of Science degree. This program is ideally suited for the individual who has received an associate degree in a technical area at a community college. The Bachelor of Science in dietetics degree program prepares students to work as registered dietitians in the high-tech science of applying knowledge of food and nutrition to health.

## SPECIAL PROGRAMS

The Independent Learning course, Prior Learning and Portfolio Development (DIS/AADV 279), which is required for students seeking credit for prior learning through portfolio assessment, helps students identify competencies and document experience to create a portfolio to present for assessment by faculty members in appropriate departments.

## STUDENT SERVICES

Distance learners can complete their online education entirely via the Internet. Registration, book buying, discussions, homework assignments, and exams are all available at the click of a computer mouse.

## CREDIT OPTIONS

Students may transfer credits from another institution or may earn credits through examinations, portfolio assessment, military training, or business training.

## FACULTY

More than 100 faculty members from EMU's academic departments currently teach online, independent learning, and interactive television courses at EMU.

## ADMISSION

Students may register by mail, fax, e-mail, and World Wide Web and in person.

## TUITION AND FEES

In 2000–01, per credit hour rates for Michigan and Ohio residents were $104.50 for lower-level (000-200) undergraduate courses, $111.75 for upper-level (300-400) undergraduate courses, $180 for lower-level (500-600) graduate courses, and $225 for upper-level (700 and above) graduate courses.

Rates per credit hour for nonresidents in 2000–01 were $308 for lower-level undergraduate courses, $345 for upper-level undergraduate courses, $400 for lower-level graduate courses, and $450 for upper-level graduate courses.

A registration fee of $40 per semester and a general fee of $20 per credit hour are also assessed. In addition to tuition and other applicable fees, online students are assessed an additional per-credit-hour program fee.

All tuition and fees are subject to change by action of the EMU Board of Regents without prior notice and at any time.

## FINANCIAL AID

For financial aid information, students should visit http://www.emich.edu/public/fin_aid/finhome.html or call 734-487-0455.

## APPLYING

Undergraduate admission requirements include a completed application; a $25 application fee; transcripts from all high schools, colleges, or universities previously attended; and ACT or SAT I scores for persons with fewer than 12 college credits who are under 21 (no ACT or SAT I test scores are required for individuals over the age of 21). Individuals with 12 or more transferable credits apply as transfer students and usually do not need to send high school transcripts.

Graduate admission requirements include a completed application, a $30 application fee, and all transcripts from any colleges or universities the student has attended. In addition, each graduate program has its own requirements, which may include any or all of the following: proof of a GRE or GMAT score, a personal statement, one or more letters of recommendation, and a teaching certificate, for students planning to study education. (Students should contact the graduate coordinator in their department of interest to determine which of these are required).

---

## CONTACT

Distance Education
Continuing Education
Eastern Michigan University
101 Boone Hall
Ypsilanti, Michigan 48197
Telephone: 800-777-3521 (toll-free)
E-mail: distance.education@emich.edu
Web site: http://www.emuonline.edu
http://www.emich.edu/ce

# EduKan Consortium

Great Bend, Kansas

*The Western Kansas Community College Virtual Education Consortium (EduKan) brings students a new way of receiving their college courses. In 1999 EduKan launched a series of college courses via the Internet. EduKan consists of the following colleges: Barton County Community College, Colby Community College, Dodge City Community College, Garden City Community College, Pratt Community College, and Seward County Community College.*

## DISTANCE LEARNING PROGRAM

The Western Kansas Community College Virtual Education Consortium (EduKan) began offering classes via the Internet in 1999. Enrollments have increased every semester since that time. Students who enroll in the online program can take course work that leads to an associate degree from one of six participating institutions. The institutions involved include Barton County Community College, in Great Bend; Colby Community College, in Colby; Dodge City Community College, in Dodge City; Garden City Community College, in Garden City; Pratt Community College, in Pratt; and Seward County Community College, in Liberal.

## DELIVERY MEDIA

Students must have access to a computer with Windows 95 or 98 or Mac OS. In addition, a computer with multimedia capability, a modem, a full-service Web browser, audio and video capability, an Internet provider, and an e-mail account is required. Some classes may also require the student to view videos via a TV and VCR. EduKan has partnered with eCollege.com to provide their virtual campus and their Internet course system.

## PROGRAMS OF STUDY

More than forty courses will be offered through EduKan in multisemester formats. These courses include: Fundamentals of Writing, English Composition I and II, Speech I, Intermediate Algebra, College Algebra, Principles of Biology, Physical Science, Introduction to Astronomy, General Psychology, Human Growth and Development, Principles of Macroeconomics, World and Regional Geography, American Government, Native American Culture, Introduction to Sociology, Personal Finance, Human Relations, History and Criticism of Art I and II, American History Since 1865, World Literature, Introduction to Music, Introduction to Ethics, Accounting I and II, Horse Production, Cultural Anthropology, Anatomy & Physiology I and II, Introduction to Business, General Chemistry, Introduction to Computers, Microcomputer Applications, Web Page Design, Principles of Microeconomics, Foundations of Modern Education, Children's Literature, Spanish I and II, Basic Applied Math, Beginning Algebra, and Personal and Community Health. Each course provides a solid foundation that leads to an Associate of General Studies degree, with transferability to four-year colleges and universities.

## SPECIAL PROGRAMS

These courses are recommended for adult learners who may not be able to take traditional classes due to conflicting schedules, multiple responsibilities, and/or long driving distances. High school and college students who would like to get a head start on their college education are good candidates as well.

## STUDENT SERVICES

EduKan provides a wide array of services to students online. They include academic advising, career placement assistance, library services, transcript request, business office services, bookstore access, and more. The goal is to provide any essential campus service via the Internet.

## CREDIT OPTIONS

All courses are offered for college credit and, with the exception of the developmental courses, count toward graduation requirements at any of the institutions. Courses are offered on a semester basis, and most are offered for 3–5 credit hours per course.

## FACULTY

All faculty members have teaching experience and online training and are respected members of their institutions. Their complete biographies are listed online. More than 85 percent of the faculty members also teach full-time at the member institutions.

## ADMISSION

Kansas community colleges operate under an open admissions policy. Admission and enrollment forms are standardized for all six EduKan schools and are outlined on the EduKan Web site (listed below). Current high school students may get a start in their college education through this process, but most students who are admitted are high school or GED graduates or transfer students. Each college is also a member of the Servicemen's Opportunity College.

## TUITION AND FEES

Tuition is $115 per credit hour, excluding textbooks. The cost is the same for all students, regardless of Kansas residency status.

## FINANCIAL AID

Financial aid is available through the participating colleges. Some part-time scholarships are available. Federal financial aid can also be completed online.

## APPLYING

Students may apply to and learn more about EduKan via the Web site.

---

### CONTACT

Gillian Gabelmann, Executive Director
245 Northeast 30th Road
Great Bend, Kansas 67530
Telephone: 877-4EDUKAN (toll-free)
E-mail: gabelmannm@barton.cc.ks.us
Web site: http://www.edukan.org

---

# Embry-Riddle Aeronautical University

## *Extended Campus*
Daytona Beach, Florida

Embry-Riddle Aeronautical University is an independent, nonsectarian, nonprofit coeducational university with a history dating back to the early days of aviation. The University is accredited by the Commission on Colleges of the Southern Association of Colleges and Schools. Residential campuses in Daytona Beach, Florida, and Prescott, Arizona, provide education in a traditional setting. The Extended Campus network of education centers throughout the United States and Europe and the Distance Learning Program serve civilian and military working adults around the world. Embry-Riddle Aeronautical University has served the public and private sectors of aviation through education for more than seventy years and is the only accredited not-for-profit university in the world totally oriented to aviation/aerospace. Alumni are employed in all facets of civilian and military aviation.

## DISTANCE LEARNING PROGRAM

Since 1970, Embry-Riddle has provided educational opportunities for professionals working in civilian and military aviation and aerospace careers. To meet the varied needs of the adult working student, Embry-Riddle established the Extended Campus, which includes the College of Career Education's classroom and distance learning operations.

The Extended Campus maintains a comprehensive system of academic quality control, sustaining the requirements and elements of courses as delivered on the residential campuses. The curricula, academic standards, and academic policies are the same throughout the University and are modified only to accommodate certain requirements resulting from different delivery methods.

The College of Career Education provides working adults with the opportunity to earn undergraduate and graduate degrees through a network of teaching centers spread across the United States and Europe and through distance learning. The College operates more than 130 resident centers and teaching sites in thirty-six states

and five European nations. Resident centers and teaching sites are found at or near major aviation industry installations, both civilian and military. When students are not located near a center or a teaching site, they can enroll in many of the same programs through distance learning. All teaching centers and the distance learning programs are approved for veterans educational benefits. Students receive personalized academic advisement whether they take their classes in the classroom or by distance learning. Classroom instruction is conducted during hours convenient for working students, and distance learning students can work on their studies at any time and at any place that is convenient for them. Degree requirements are completed through a combination of course work, transfer credit, prior learning assessment, or by achieving the University's required scores in standardized national testing programs, such as CLEP or DANTES.

## DELIVERY MEDIA

The Distance Learning bachelor's and master's degree courses are delivered via the Internet. Each class is hosted on a private Embry-Riddle Web site,

where students and professors interact by way of a bulletin board–type discussion forum. As a result, students are not required to log on to the Web site at specific times, but they may access their course work at a time most convenient to them. To participate in a Distance Learning class, students need access to a personal computer and the World Wide Web.

## PROGRAMS OF STUDY

At the graduate level, Embry-Riddle offers the Master of Business Administration in Aviation (M.B.A./A.) and the Master of Aeronautical Science (M.A.S.) degrees. The M.B.A./A. degree program is designed to emphasize the application of modern management concepts, methods, and tools to the challenges of aviation and general business. The special intricacies of aviation are woven into a strong, traditional business foundation and examined in greater detail through a wide variety of specified electives.

The M.B.A./A. requires completion of 36 credits, including a core of aviation business courses (27 credits), aviation business specified electives (6 credits), and the Graduate Research Project (3 credits).

The M.A.S. degree with specializations in operations, management, human factors, or safety requires 36 semester hours of course work. The M.A.S. program was designed to enable the aviation/aerospace professional to master the application of modern management concepts, methods, and tools to the challenges of aviation and general business. The special intricacies of aviation are woven into a strong, traditional management foundation and examined in greater detail through the wide variety of electives. M.A.S. core topics (12 credit hours) include air transportation, aircraft and space craft development, human factors in aviation/aerospace, and research methods and statistics. Specialization courses (12 credit hours) provide a strong knowledge base of subject material required. Each of the four courses provides the student with skills needed in the professional arena. Electives and a graduate research project (GRP) (12 credit hours) provide students with the ability to tailor their degrees, adding greater breadth and depth in aviation/aerospace–related intellectual pursuits.

Undergraduate degree offerings include Associate of Science and Bachelor of Science degrees in professional aeronautics and a Bachelor of Science degree in management of technical operations (BSMTO).

The professional aeronautics degree program was conceived and developed especially for individuals who have already established and progressed in an aviation career. The curriculum is designed to build upon the knowledge and skills acquired through training and experience in one of the many aviation occupations. The combination of aviation experience and required and elective courses in aeronautical science, management, computer science, economics, communications, humanities, social science, mathematics, and physical science prepares graduates for career growth and increased responsibility. The Bachelor of Science in professional aeronautics requires 120 credit hours, and the Associate of Science in professional aeronautics requires 60 credit hours.

The Bachelor of Science in management of technical operations degree requires successful completion of 120

credit hours. Designed for the student who possesses some technical expertise either through previous course work, licensing, or experience, this degree provides the student a flexible yet solid business program.

The Associate of Science in aviation business administration degree requires successful completion of 60 credit hours. This degree provides courses in general education and an introduction to business coupled with some business applications.

## CREDIT OPTIONS

Master's degree applicants may transfer up to 12 semester hours of credit into the University. Credit must be from a regionally accredited institution with a grade of B or better and awarded within seven years of application to Embry-Riddle. Courses must be applicable to the M.A.S. degree program.

Undergraduate applicants may transfer credit from regionally accredited institutions with the letter grade of D or better. Advanced standing credit may be awarded for prior learning achieved through postsecondary education, testing, and work or training experience.

## FACULTY

The faculty is a blend of traditionally prepared academicians and leaders with significant industry track records. Nearly all faculty members have doctorate or terminal degrees.

## ADMISSION

Admission to the master's degree program requires a bachelor's degree from a regionally accredited institution. Admission to the undergraduate programs is unique to each degree.

## TUITION AND FEES

Tuition for master's degree courses is $331 per credit hour. Textbook and shipping fees vary from $50 to $125 per course based on textbook prices.

Undergraduate tuition is $152 per credit hour. Other fees vary by course. Each course is 3 semester credit hours.

## FINANCIAL AID

Students accepted for enrollment may be considered for several forms of federal financial aid. There are three different federal programs available. Additional information is provided at time of application.

All Embry-Riddle degree programs have been approved by the Department of Veterans' Affairs for enrollment of persons eligible to receive benefits from U.S. Department of Veterans' Affairs (DVA).

## APPLYING

Applications must be submitted with appropriate documentation, such as official high school transcripts, GED scores, or official transcripts from previous colleges or universities.

### CONTACT

Terry E. Whittum, Director
Linda Dammer, Assistant Director
Distance Learning Enrollment Office
Embry-Riddle Aeronautical University
600 South Clyde Morris Boulevard
Daytona Beach, Florida 32114-3900
Telephone: 800-359-3728 (toll-free)
Fax: 904-226-7627
E-mail: dlinfo@db.erau.edu
Web site: http://www.embryriddle.edu

# Fashion Institute of Technology

## On-Line Program
### New York, New York

*The Fashion Institute of Technology, a State University of New York (SUNY) college of art and design, business and technology, has been educating professionals for careers in the fashion and related fields since 1944. FIT now offers its students thirty-one degree programs in areas of study where industry has made New York City its focal point. Many of them are innovative and one of a kind, such as the country's only two-year program in accessories design and the only bachelor's degree program in home products development and marketing.*

*FIT is an accredited institutional member of the Middle States Association of Colleges and Schools, the National Association of Schools of Art and Design, and the Foundation for Interior Design Education Research. FIT serves more than 5,700 full-time students and 5,400 part-time students who come from all fifty states and sixty-five countries.*

## DISTANCE LEARNING PROGRAM

The college's online program serves students by offering a variety of courses as well as a curriculum that can lead to the fashion merchandising management (FMM) one-year A.A.S. degree. Students who already possess a degree from another college or who have earned 30 transferable credits may apply to the one-year FMM program, which is offered entirely online.

The FMM program provides a sound grasp of the practical aspects of the fashion industry, which is essential to building a successful merchandising career. Students take courses in buying, merchandising, retail operations, product development, team management, and wholesale strategies of selling. They learn about the fashion industry at every level and how each segment is affected by both domestic and global influences. Graduates find careers with retail stores, wholesale showrooms, or buying offices.

## DELIVERY MEDIA

FIT delivers its courses through the SUNY Learning Network (SLN), an electronic forum where students and professors learn collaboratively via the Internet. Courses may require the use of specific software programs and computer hardware products to complete course requirements. Prior to registering for an online course, students should test their access to the SLN Web site at http://www.sln.suny.edu.

## PROGRAMS OF STUDY

FIT's online program currently offers courses leading to the fashion merchandising management one-year A.A.S. degree. These courses include introduction to the fashion industry, merchandise planning and control, fashion merchandising (principles and techniques), advertising and promotion, apparel design and production analysis, textile fundamentals, fashion business practices, consumer motivation in fashion, product development, introduction to direct marketing, workshop in fashion merchandising management, import buying, and product development.

Other online offerings include starting a small business, English as a second language, professional procedures in commercial photography, photography portfolio development for the World Wide Web, introduction to business law, information systems in business management, and multimedia computing for advertising and marketing communications.

For detailed descriptions of each course, students should visit the FIT Web site at http://www.fitnyc.suny.edu/academic.

## SPECIAL PROGRAMS

FIT is developing additional online courses and degree programs. The college plans to add required liberal arts courses providing students with the opportunity to complete the FMM two-year A.A.S. program entirely online. Students should periodically check the FIT Web site for online course updates.

## CREDIT OPTIONS

Students may apply up to 30 credits earned through subject examinations (CLEP and Advanced Placement) and transfer credit toward fulfillment of degree requirements at FIT. Students who have completed courses at accredited institutions receive credit for course work similar to courses at FIT and in which a grade of C or better has been achieved. Complete information about obtaining academic credit by evaluation is available from the Registrar's Office at 212-217-7676.

## FACULTY

Currently, there are more than 200 full-time faculty members and approximately 690 part-time faculty members. In addition to their academic backgrounds, all of FIT's faculty members have extensive experience in the diverse industries from which they come. This enables them to bring the immediacy of their continuing professional activity to their teaching.

## ADMISSION

All applicants must have a high school diploma or the equivalent and must supply their high school transcript showing average and rank in class. Transfer students must provide official college transcripts. FIT operates on a rolling admission basis.

For additional information on how to apply or obtain specific admissions requirements or to obtain a SUNY application form, applicants should call the FIT Admissions Office at 212-217-7675, send e-mail to fitinfo@fitsuny.edu, or visit the World Wide Web at the address listed below.

## TUITION AND FEES

Undergraduate tuition is currently $109 per credit for New York State residents and $265 per credit for all others. In addition, course instructors may require the purchase of textbooks, reference materials, and supplies. Additional fees may apply. For the most updated tuition and fee information, applicants should visit the Web at http://www.sln.suny.edu/sln or at FIT's Web site, listed below.

## FINANCIAL AID

Financial aid is available to eligible students and includes PELL, TAP, and Stafford Loans. Applications are available through FIT's Financial Aid Office (telephone: 212-217-7177), local high schools, libraries, and post offices. Additional information regarding financial aid is available at the FIT Web site.

## APPLYING

Anyone can register for an online course on a nonmatriculating basis. To matriculate toward the FMM degree program, students must apply through the usual application process. Applicants can apply in one of the following ways: online at the FIT Web site; submission by mail of a downloaded application form; or by filling out the State University of New York application.

For more information, applicants should call the FIT Admissions Office at 212-217-7675, or send e-mail to fitinfo@fitsuny.edu.

---

### CONTACT

Director of Distance Learning
Fashion Institute of Technology
Seventh Avenue at 27th Street
New York, New York 10001
Telephone: 212-217-7911 (online program information)
          212-217-7910 (general information)
Fax: 212-217-7481
E-mail: fitonline@fitsuny.edu
Web site: http://www.fitnyc.suny.edu

---

# Florida Gulf Coast University

## Distance Learning Programs

Fort Myers, Florida

*Florida Gulf Coast University (FGCU) opened its doors to students in August 1997 and is housed on a state-of-the art campus located on the southwest coast of Florida between Fort Myers and Naples. Its primary mission is undergraduate education, providing a broad range of programs in arts and sciences, business, technology, environmental science, education, allied health, and social services. Graduate programs at the master's level are also provided. FGCU was founded as a dual-mode institution to provide a full range of on-campus degree programs and selected degree programs for distance learners. FGCU is fully accredited by the Southern Association of Colleges and Schools (SACS). The University now serves a regional, state, and national audience with these programs. Additional information about the University and its programs may be found on the World Wide Web at http://www.fgcu.edu.*

## DISTANCE LEARNING PROGRAM

Distance learning at FGCU is an instructional strategy that is central to the University's mission. FGCU is committed to the development of innovative distance learning course designs that utilize a technology-rich learning environment. FGCU's distance-learning students receive personalized attention from faculty members strategically selected to accomplish high-quality instruction and exceptional service.

## DELIVERY MEDIA

FGCU supports five methods of distance learning delivery: the Internet, videotape, two-way interactive video, broadcast video, and e-mail. Each course uses one or more of these methods, depending on the intended learning outcomes. All distance-learning courses currently being offered include extensive Web site and e-mail communication. The use of video is incorporated into many, but not all, courses.

## PROGRAMS OF STUDY

There are currently four master's and two bachelor's degree programs of-fered by FGCU via distance learning. Brief descriptions of these programs appear below. For full details, students should visit the Web site (http://itech.fgcu.edu/distance) and select Programs and Courses to see course offerings in the current semester.

The Master of Business Administration (M.B.A.) provides a challenging curriculum designed to prepare students for leadership positions in organizations. Leadership, teamwork, information technology, entrepreneurial vision, and global awareness are integrated throughout the program. All courses for this program are available at a distance. For more information, students should visit the Web site at http://www.fgcu.edu/cob/mba.

The Curriculum and Instruction–Educational Technology (M.A./M.Ed.) graduate program at FGCU is designed to provide a theoretical foundation and practical skills. The emphasis is on enabling students to provide leadership in distance learning, provide technical support and education in schools or colleges, and design and implement courses in computer programming, applica-tions, and literacy. This program is offered largely through Internet courses, with two special, on-campus summer institutes. For more information, students should visit the Web site at http://soe.fgcu.edu/soe/programs/CIM.html.

The interdisciplinary Master of Science in Health Science program offers a choice of four concentrations: health professions education, practice, health services administration, and gerontology. The education and practice concentrations are limited to those qualified in a health profession. All courses for this program are available at a distance. For more information, students should visit the Web site at http://www.fgcu.edu/chp/discipline.

The Master of Public Administration (M.P.A.) is an applied degree program that prepares students for successful administrative careers in the public sector. It is designed for students who have significant in-service experience and for students who have little prior work experience in public agencies. All courses for this program are available at a distance. For more information, students should visit the Web site at http://spss.fgcu.edu.

The Bachelor of Science in criminal justice degree program prepares students for careers in criminal justice professions and/or graduate education. The curriculum provides students the opportunity to acquire knowledge of the roles and challenges faced by police, courts, and corrections and their interrelationship within the justice system. All upper-division undergraduate courses for this program are available at a distance to those students who have completed at least 60 hours of undergraduate course work. For more information, students should visit the Web site at http://spss.fgcu.edu.

The interdisciplinary Bachelor of Science in Health Science program is designed to provide career advancement opportunities for entry-level health profession practitioners and individuals who seek careers in health care, such as physical therapy. All of the upper-division undergraduate courses for this program are available at a distance to those students who have completed at least 60 hours of undergraduate course work. For more information, students should visit the Web site at http://www.fgcu.edu/chp/discipline.

## SPECIAL PROGRAMS

The English for Speakers of Other Languages (ESOL) endorsement program at FGCU strives to prepare graduate students, teachers, and school personnel to teach and work with limited English proficient students (LEP) and/or English language learners (ELL) in K–12 school environments. This includes teaching ELL/LEP students in mainstream settings and in pullout programs and serving as advocates by sharing the information and knowledge gained with other professionals working with culturally and linguistically diverse student populations. Learning experiences are varied, including on-campus courses at the graduate level and distance delivery. These professional learning experiences are supported by regular interaction among students and professors.

Florida Gulf Coast University is part of a consortium of forty-six universities that participate in the National Technological University (NTU) Satellite Network, serving the needs of engineers, technical professionals, and managers using advanced telecommunications technology. Degrees and certificates are awarded at the master's level to candidates sponsored by corporations or organizations affiliated with NTU. Students who wish to participate need to confirm NTU sponsorship with employers.

## STUDENT SERVICES

Many of the services for students on campus also are available to students at a distance. A spirit of cooperation within Student Services fosters a learning environment that promotes the academic success and personal and career development of students, with an emphasis on leadership skills, community services, and an appreciation for diversity. For more information, students should visit the Web site at http://condor.fgcu.edu.

## CREDIT OPTIONS

Credits earned through distance education are recorded on a Florida Gulf Coast University transcript in the same manner as credits earned in on-campus courses. Individuals may enroll as non–degree-seeking or degree seeking students, but there are limits on the amount of credit awarded to non–degree-seeking students that may be transferred to a degree seeking program. Students should contact the Office of the Admissions at OAR@fgcu.edu or 888-889-1095 (toll-free) for additional details and assistance.

## FACULTY

Distance education faculty members meet all of the standards set forth by the Southern Association of Colleges and Schools and the State of Florida. All are full-time or adjunct members within the department granting the course credit. They are available to answer questions and provide feedback via telephone, fax, e-mail, or regular mail.

## ADMISSION

Admission decisions are based on standards set by the Board of Regents for the State University System of Florida. Criteria for admissions depend on student status: degree seeking or non–degree-seeking, graduate or undergraduate, transferring to FGCU or just beginning college education. More information, students should visit the Web site at http://condor.fgcu.edu/ES/ARR/lg_category.htm.

## TUITION AND FEES

Current tuition and fees are published on the Web site at http://condor.fgcu.edu/ES. For the 2000–01 academic year, these were $69.68 per credit hour for undergraduate Florida residents, $146.13 for graduate residents, $314.29 for undergraduate nonresidents, and $524.91 for graduate nonresidents.

## FINANCIAL AID

The University offers a comprehensive program of financial assistance for traditional and nontraditional students pursuing undergraduate or graduate degrees. The Financial Aid and Scholarships Office is responsible for helping students secure the necessary funds to pursue education. The office is proactive in offering information to enrolled and prospective students about the availability of financial assistance. Students should contact the Financial Aid and Scholarships Office at FASO@fgcu.edu or 941-590-7920.

## APPLYING

Students may apply for admission as a degree seeking or non–degree-seeking student via the Web site by completing the University's Application for Admission at http://www.fgcu.edu/online.html. To complete the application, students must include a $20 application fee with their completed and signed residency statement.

---

**CONTACT**

Florida Gulf Coast University
10501 FGCU Boulevard South
Fort Myers, Florida 33965-6565
Telephone: 914-590-7878
          888-889-1095 (toll-free)
941-590-7886 (TTY)
E-mail: oar@fgcu.edu
Web site: http://www.fgcu.edu

# Florida Institute of Technology

## The Extended Campus
Melbourne, Florida

Florida Institute of Technology is an accredited, coeducational, independently controlled and supported university that is committed to the pursuit of excellence in teaching and research. Undergraduate programs are offered in science and engineering, aviation, business, humanities, psychology, and communications. Doctoral degrees are offered in science, engineering, and psychology while master's degrees are offered in aeronautics, business, communication, and more.

Founded in 1958, Florida Tech is rich in history, with links to the nation's space program. Originally founded to offer continuing education opportunities to scientists, engineers, and technicians at what is now NASA's Kennedy Space Center, the University's growth has paralleled the area's rapid development.

Florida Tech is located in Melbourne on Florida's Space Coast, home to space shuttle launches and landings, marine science research projects, and alternative energy development projects.

## DISTANCE LEARNING PROGRAM

The Extended Campus has reached out to career professionals since 1972 and has awarded more than 9,000 master's degrees in management, engineering, and science. Since 1995, it has also offered online distance learning programs. Graduates include corporate and government leaders, top-rank military officers, and five astronauts.

Nine graduate programs and eleven graduate certificate programs are available completely online. Online enrollments exceed 400 per semester.

## DELIVERY MEDIA

Using Blackboard as the learning management system, courses are offered via the Internet. Text information is supported by audio and video clips. Interaction between instructors and students and among students is provided through e-mail, synchronous chats, and asynchronous threaded discussions.

## PROGRAMS OF STUDY

Programs currently being offered include a 36-hour professional Master of Business Administration (M.B.A.) with concentrations available in contract and acquisition management, information systems, human resource management, and e-business; a 36-hour Master of Public Administration (M.P.A.); a 33-hour M.S. in health management; a 33-hour M.S. in acquisition and contract management; a 33-hour M.S. in human resources management; a 33-hour M.S. in logistics management; a 33-hour M.S. in management, with concentrations available in acquisition and contract management, health services management, human resources management, information systems, logistics management, transportation management, and e-business; a 33-hour M.S. in materiel acquisition management; and a 33-hour M.S. in systems management, with concentrations available in information systems and operations research. All programs require a set of core requirements and a set of electives. Some programs require the completion of specific prerequisites prior to enrollment. Some courses in the programs require prerequisites. All courses are 3 semester hours. Details on each program of study may be found at http://www.segs.fit.edu. Course prerequisites may be found at http://www.fit.edu/catalog/.

Graduate certificate programs may be obtained in the following management areas: business, health services, human resources, information systems, program, systems, quality, transportation, and materiel acquisition. Each certificate program requires the completion of five 3-semester-hour courses. The curriculum consists of one required course and four electives chosen from a specified list.

## STUDENT SERVICES

Library service is provided via remote access to all internal holdings and to several electronic databases through http://www.lib.fit.edu. Access is provided to currently registered students via a personal identification number and password for certain restricted databases.

Recommendations for the purchase of computers and related equipment are available at http://www.segs.fit.edu.

Academic advising is provided through e-mail, fax, and telephone contact on a request basis.

Distance learning students are eligible to use the University's career placement services.

## CREDIT OPTIONS

Graduate students may transfer a maximum of 12 graduate credit hours to a Florida Tech master's degree program. To be eligible for transfer, the courses must have been taken for graduate credit at a regionally accredited university within the past six years and have been completed with a grade of A or B. A limited number of military schools have been evaluated by the American Council on Education and the school's faculty and are recommended for some transfer credit award.

## FACULTY

There are 14 full-time and 20 to 30 part-time faculty members in the distance learning program. More than 95 percent possess a doctorate in their teaching discipline or in a field closely related to it.

## ADMISSION

Applicants must have a minimum cumulative GPA of 3.0 for regular admission to graduate studies. Students with a cumulative GPA lower than 3.0 may be granted provisional admission with additional supporting materials. Applicants not initially qualifying may enroll as continuing education students and take up to four graduate courses for academic credit. Special rules apply to students admitted as continuing education students.

## TUITION AND FEES

As of 2001–02, the per-credit-hour tuition rate is $330. The application fee is $50.

## FINANCIAL AID

As a general rule, a graduate student must be enrolled half-time (at least 5 credit hours per term) as a regular student in a degree program and must be a U.S. citizen or an eligible non-U.S. citizen to qualify for federal and/or state financial aid. Specific information is available through the University's Office of Student Financial Assistance. Graduate students should file prior to March 20 to ensure timely processing and must re-apply for financial aid each year. Students must maintain satisfactory academic progress as defined by the Office of Student Financial Assistance to continue receiving financial assistance.

## APPLYING

Application is available online through http://www.segs.fit.edu. Applicants must sign and mail an affidavit attesting to the accuracy of the application to the University's Graduate Admission Office. Official transcripts are required from all colleges/universities attended. Students may be provisionally authorized to attend one academic term while their admission documents are being collected and submitted for evaluation.

---

**CONTACT**

Extended Campus for Distance Learning
School of Extended Graduate Studies
Florida Institute of Technology
150 West University Boulevard
Melbourne, Florida 32901
Telephone: 813-884-7365
Fax: 813-243-3548
E-mail: vgc@fit.edu
Web site: http://www.segs.fit.edu

# Florida State University

## Office of Distributed and Distance Learning

Tallahassee, Florida

> Since its founding 150 years ago, Florida State University has been guided by its mission to meet the higher education needs of the people of Florida and the U.S. The University remains rooted in its tradition of encouraging critical inquiry, promoting lifelong learning, and responding to radical transformations within professions and society—most recently, the technological revolution.
>
> FSU's distance programs integrate student/teacher collaboration, comprehensive student support, and current technology to deliver a university learning experience. Students develop a core of intellectual tools that enable them to learn efficiently and adapt quickly to new settings and challenges, long after earning their degree.

## DISTANCE LEARNING PROGRAM

Students learning from a distance receive the same high-quality education and degrees as those students who complete on-campus programs. (No distinction is made on transcripts.) Using computers and online classrooms, students and instructors exchange ideas and course work via the Internet. Students ask questions via e-mail, collaborate on group projects using a range of communication tools, and post to online class discussions at any time, day or night. Florida State University integrates course design and technology to support students in building and sustaining learning communities.

## DELIVERY MEDIA

To provide distance students a complete and easy-to-use online learning environment, FSU partnered with a leading educational software corporation to create the leading product of its kind. Students "attend" class through course Web sites that deliver communication tools (including discussion boards, live chat, and e-mail) and course materials. FSU's online environment includes nearly every component of a face-to-face class and some that are only possible via technology. Distance learning at FSU is accessible from anywhere an Internet connection is available.

## PROGRAMS OF STUDY

Bachelor's degree programs are open to students who have earned an Associate in Arts degree and meet the University's admission and specific departmental requirements for transfer students. The junior- and senior-level courses (60 semester hours) in these baccalaureate programs lead to a bachelor's degree in computer and information science (with a major in computer science or software engineering); information studies; interdisciplinary social science (with a concentration in economics, geography, or sociology); or nursing (limited geographical access).

Master's degree programs are open to students who have earned a bachelor's degree and meet University graduate entrance and specific departmental requirements. Master of Science degrees via distance learning are available in criminology (with a major in criminal justice studies); library and information studies; instructional systems (with a major in open and distance learning); mechanical engineering; and risk management/insurance.

## SPECIAL PROGRAMS

Florida State University has been selected as one of only sixteen institutions to offer distance learning degree-track programs to U.S. Navy personnel and their families through the Navy College Program. FSU has the further distinction of being the only university approved for all Navy ratings. The University is also a participating institution in Army University Access Online, a project whose goal is to deliver distance learning courses to U.S. soldiers throughout the world.

## STUDENT SERVICES

Florida State University has developed a team exclusively focused on supporting students in its distance learning programs. Team members include a lead faculty member (who is responsible for assuring course quality), mentors and/or graduate assistants, and distance learning support staff. Mentors/graduate assistants are selected by FSU faculty members for their background and knowledge of the particular discipline, as well as for their ability to guide and encourage a cohort of students. Cohorts are limited to approximately 20 students to enable mentors/graduate assistants to provide each student with tutorial guidance and attention.

## CREDIT OPTIONS

Florida State University generally awards credit for classes (offered at a comparable level) taken at regionally accredited community colleges, colleges, and universities in the U.S.

and from fully recognized international institutions. After a student is admitted to the University, the Office of Admissions Transfer Credit Evaluations examines the student's transcripts to determine what credit will transfer toward a bachelor's degree from FSU.

## FACULTY

Approximately 90 percent of the teaching faculty members hold doctorates or other terminal degrees. FSU has had 5 Nobel laureates on its faculty. The faculty currently includes 10 National Academy of Sciences elected members and 12 American Academy of Arts and Sciences fellows.

## ADMISSION

All applicants must submit official transcripts from each institution previously attended. Applicants for bachelor's degree programs with 60 or more transferable semester hours must have a 2.5 (out of 4.0) minimum GPA, unless they have earned an Associate in Arts degree from a Florida public institution. Individual departments may have additional requirements.

Master's degree program admission involves gaining acceptance by the department or school in which the applicant expects to study. While there are minimum University admission requirements, the departments can, and frequently do, set admission standards significantly higher than these minimums. Applicants should first determine departmental requirements.

## TUITION AND FEES

Tuition rates differ depending on whether a student is a Florida resident or an out-of-state resident, and an undergraduate or graduate student. Fee rates for on-campus programs differ slightly from those for distance learning programs.

## FINANCIAL AID

Distance students may have access to many of the same types of financial aid as residential students. To quality, students need to be enrolled for at least 6 hours per semester. Qualifying for financial aid is sometimes a lengthy process, and it should be started at least two semesters in advance of the term for which financial aid is expected. FSU's Office of Financial Aid provides assistance in determining eligibility for financial aid. The academic coordinator for each distance degree program can also answer questions about obtaining financial aid.

## APPLYING

Applications may be submitted online and are accepted one year in advance of the start semester. Notification typically takes four to six weeks from the time all necessary credentials are received. An initial orientation is required and is available online. Registering for courses may also be done online or by phone.

---

**CONTACT**

Florida State University
Office for Distributed and Distance Learning
3500-C University Center
Tallahassee, Florida 32306-2550
Telephone: 877-357-8283 (toll-free)
Fax: 850-644-5803
E-mail: inquiries@oddl.fsu.edu
Web site: http://www.fsu.edu/~distance

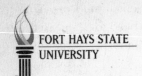

# Fort Hays State University

## *Virtual College*

Hays, Kansas

*Celebrating a Century of Excellence in Education. The year 2002 marks the 100th anniversary of Fort Hays State University, founded in 1902. Through the years, Fort Hays State University (FHSU) has developed a reputation for excellent teaching, academic research, and community partnerships with the people of Kansas and beyond. Today, FHSU serves 5,000 on-campus students and nearly 2,500 distance education students throughout the world. FHSU looks forward to a second century of service and excellence in a knowledge-driven, global society. FHSU is regionally accredited by the North Central Association of Colleges and Schools.*

## DISTANCE LEARNING PROGRAM

The Virtual College is the division of Fort Hays State University that delivers the bachelor's and master's courses and degree programs offered through the University's four academic units: Arts and Sciences, Business and Leadership, Education, and Health and Life Sciences. The Virtual College has been a leader in distance learning for more than twenty years and currently offers more than 500 distance learning courses each semester. The College's programs have the same academic rigor as on-campus courses and are designed and taught by the same on-campus, full-time faculty.

## DELIVERY MEDIA

The Virtual College delivers distance learning course work through asynchronous and synchronous modes. Asynchronous delivery (anytime/any place) includes: the Internet, videotapes, audiotapes, and CD-ROMs. Synchronous delivery (same time/ different locations) includes: interactive television (ITV), Telenet2 in Kansas, in person, independent study, and specially arranged delivery. Virtual College courses provide students with a great deal of interaction with the faculty through e-mail, chat rooms, telephone, fax, and regular mail. Courses include readings in leading textbooks and study manuals, exercises, simulations, online discussions, live chats, videos and other appropriate learning activities.

## PROGRAMS OF STUDY

Fort Hays State University offers several degrees entirely through the convenience of the Virtual College. The Bachelor of General Studies (B.G.S.) is a 124-credit-hour degree that is granted by the College of Arts and Sciences. The B.G.S. allows students to customize a 21-credit-hour concentration in an area of the student's choice. Some include business, organizational leadership, justice studies, information networking and telecommunications, human services, and gerontology, among others. The University diploma states the student's area of concentration.

Up to 94 credits may be transferred from any accredited institution with a maximum of 64 credits of lower division courses. Up to 64 credits of ACE-approved credits for military experience and credit-by-exam is permitted. An individual adviser is assigned to work with each student in order to fulfill career and personal goals. Required courses include 6 credits of English composition; 3 credits of computer literacy; 12 credits each from humanities, natural sciences, and mathematics; and social and behavioral sciences. There are no college algebra or foreign language requirements, but they may be taken as electives.

The Master of Liberal Studies is a 31-credit-hour degree that is granted by the College of Arts and Sciences. This interdisciplinary graduate program consists of a 10-hour core requirement and 18 hours of a customized study and a 3-hour culminating experience. There is no thesis required and students have up to six years to complete their degree.

There is no residency requirement and an FHSU adviser oversees the program of study. Up to 15 graduate hours can be transferred into the program from an accredited institution, if it has been completed within the last six years.

Other degrees offered through the Virtual College include the Bachelor of Science in justice studies (B.S.), the Bachelor of Science in Nursing (B.S.N./RN to B.S.N.), and the Master of Science in Nursing (nursing administration track or nursing education track). For more information, students can access the Web site at http://www.fhsu.edu/virtual_college.

## SPECIAL PROGRAMS

FHSU offers certifications in specialized areas. The Cisco Certified Network Associate (CCNA) prep courses prepare students to take the highly sought after CCNA exam. The program consists of two, 3-hour courses: internetworking certification I and II. These courses are delivered through the Internet with audio and video streaming.

More than twenty-five CD-ROM and Internet courses are offered in partnership with NETg. Topics include financial management, written communications, time management, self-development skills, and many more. These 1-credit offerings are self-paced training CD-ROMs that begin each month.

In partnership with the National Association of State Directors in Special Education (NASDSE), FHSU offers CD-ROM and Internet-learning kits to prepare teachers for special certification in assistive technology and special education. One-credit offerings are available at the graduate and undergraduate level.

## STUDENT SERVICES

FHSU provides numerous services in order to accommodate distance learning students. Class registration and enrollment is available online each semester. Online library resources include 12,500 journals that are available as full-text or annotations. For information or technical assistance, a toll-free help desk is available 24 hours, seven days a week.

Books, media, and other instructional materials are delivered directly to students through the convenience of online and toll-free telephone orders. Students also receive discounts on laptops, Internet service, and hardware and software support. For soon-to-be or recent graduates, resume writing, job counseling, placement services, and free online resume posting is available.

The B.G.S. adviser is Joleen Briggs, Coordinator for Interdisciplinary Studies; the M.L.S. adviser is Dr. Lou Caplan, Assistant Dean for Interdisciplinary Studies. For other advisement, contact Dr. Patricia Griffin, Director of Academic Advising. Cindy Elliott is Dean of the Virtual College, Michael Michaelis is Assistant to the Dean.

## CREDIT OPTIONS

Students may receive a complimentary degree analysis by sending transcripts of previous college course work taken at accredited institutions. Military transcripts are also accepted. Credit may be earned through credit-by-exam (CLEP, DANTES, Advanced Placement, EXCELSIOR) and ACE-approved military experience. Credits received through the Virtual College at FHSU may be transferred to other colleges and universities and are not distinguished from other credits on a student's transcript.

## FACULTY

Faculty members who teach the courses offered through the Virtual College are the same highly credentialed, full-time faculty members as those teaching courses on campus. Faculty members hold doctorates or terminal degrees in their respective fields. Some undergraduate courses may be taught by graduate teaching assistants, or qualified adjunct faculty members, under the supervision of doctorate-holding faculty. All Virtual College courses are designed and developed by full-time faculty members.

## ADMISSION

As of fall 2001, applicants who have not yet reached the age of 21 must meet qualified admissions requirements, including a minimum of 21 composite ACT score, rank in the upper third of their graduating class, or have a 2.0 high school GPA. There are no admissions requirements for students over the age of 21. Students who desire to earn graduate credit must be admitted to FHSU Graduate School.

## TUITION AND FEES

Virtual College tuition is the same for students living in state or out of state. Tuition for fall 2001 through summer 2002 is $83 per credit hour for undergraduates and $112 per credit hour for graduate students. Fees vary depending upon the course-delivery mode. Media fees for Internet, CD-ROM, and video courses, for instance, are $30 for a 1 credit hour course, $35 for a 2-credit-hour course, $40 for a 3-credit-hour course, and $45 for a 4-credit-hour course. Payment for tuition and fees may be made by check, credit card, fee installment agreement, or with financial aid.

## FINANCIAL AID

FHSU administers all Federal Title IV financial aid programs according to U.S. Department of Education guidelines, based on family and student needs. Helpful financial aid representatives assist students with the required forms and are available through the FHSU toll free number. Major loan programs include subsidized and unsubsidized Stafford loans and parent loans. In addition, the office administers institutional work programs, scholarships, and Veterans Administration benefits. Students must file the Free Application for Federal Student Aid (FAFSA).

## APPLYING

Students can apply online at the Internet address http://www.fhsu.edu/virtual_college, or through regular mail with the application available in the Virtual College schedule book. Once admitted, students register for courses online or with their assigned academic adviser. A $25 nonrefundable admission fee is required ($35 for international students).

---

### CONTACT

Fort Hays State University
Virtual College
600 Park Street
Hays, Kansas 67601
Telephone: 800-628-FHSU (toll-free)
Fax: 785-628-4037
E-mail: v_college@fhsu.edu
Web site: http://www.fhsu.edu/virtual_college

---

# Franklin University
## *Community College Alliance and Online Degree Programs*
Columbus, Ohio

*Franklin University is an independent, nonprofit institution of higher education and is best characterized by its student-centered philosophy. Annually, 7,000 students—the majority of whom work full-time and are more than 32 years of age—pursue programs leading to a bachelor's degree in fifteen undergraduate majors and four master's degree programs. Franklin University has been offering online courses since 1996 and has made the decision to increase its course offerings through distance learning methods. In 1998, the University began the Community College Alliance (CCA) program that provides a bachelor's degree completion program to community college graduates via the Internet. The University also offers six-week Balanced Learning Format courses that allow students to complete eight courses per year, either on line, on-site, or through a combined online/on-site format.*

## DISTANCE LEARNING PROGRAM

Through educational alliances with more than 100 community colleges in the U.S. and Canada, the Community College Alliance Program (CCA) enables community college graduates to earn a bachelor's degree from Franklin without leaving their community. Students complete their degrees through a combination of on-site courses at the community college and online courses with Franklin. Franklin's Balanced Learning Format includes accelerated courses, which allow students to complete a course in just six weeks.

## DELIVERY MEDIA

Students in Franklin's online programs can get all the help they need via the Internet. Chat rooms are set up so students can interact with each other and with faculty members. Students enrolled directly through Franklin need access to a multimedia computer, a modem, and the Internet (and the ability to create, send, and receive e-mail). In addition, some instructors may require access to other equipment, such as a fax machine, a VCR, and an audio cassette player.

Students enrolled through the CCA program also must have access to a computer and the World Wide Web.

## PROGRAMS OF STUDY

Students enrolled in the CCA can complete a Bachelor of Science degree in one of six majors. Business administration combines a knowledge of general business practices with analytical ability that is suited to today's problem-solving tasks. Computer science is for students who are interested in applying, designing, and implementing computer systems. Graduates are prepared to seek a wide variety of jobs, including software engineer, systems analyst, and database administrator or to pursue graduate school. Health-care management recognizes the fact that health-care reform is inevitable and that the industry needs leaders with a vision for the future. This major program develops leaders of change in the health-care profession. Management information systems (MIS) graduates are prepared for careers in a variety of areas, including systems analysis, application development, and computer support. Technical management is designed to comple-

ment the existing skills that are acquired through a two-year technical degree. This major program is for people who want to move into management and leadership roles in their technical organization. The public safety management major prepares public safety professionals to be upwardly mobile in their agencies. Franklin also offers a variety of online courses that can be applied to any of the University's fifteen undergraduate majors through its campus-based programs.

## SPECIAL PROGRAMS

In today's evolving business organizations, employees are being asked to take on many responsibilities that cross functional lines. Often, those employees have no formal training for completing their increased responsibilities. In response to these additional educational demands, Franklin University has developed eighteen professional certificates for those with or without undergraduate degrees. Each certificate program consists of three or four courses that are designed to enhance the knowledge of the business professional who is interested in personal growth or career or business development.

## STUDENT SERVICES

Through Franklin University's student-centered approach, each student is matched with a Student Services Associate (SSA) who, along with the course instructor, becomes an important contact at the University. SSAs serve as an initial, as well as long-term, resource for helping the student with admission and course scheduling until the academic goals are achieved.

## CREDIT OPTIONS

Franklin University has a transfer credit policy that is more liberal than most other institutions. More than 70 percent of Franklin students have transferred credit from other colleges and universities. Students also can earn credit outside the classroom through College-Level Examination Program (CLEP), ACT Proficiency Program (ACT-PEP), Franklin University Proficiency Exams (FUPE), or Prior Learning Portfolios.

## FACULTY

Franklin faculty members enrich the classroom, both virtual and physical, with special talents and abilities drawn from successful careers in business, industry, government, and social service. Franklin University faculty members are working professionals who bring real-world experience to the classroom.

## ADMISSION

Students applying to the CCA program must have an associate's degree or have completed 60 semester credit hours or 90 quarter credit hours to be admitted to the program.

## TUITION AND FEES

For the 2001–02 academic year, tuition for online courses from Franklin University is $212 per credit hour for standard courses and $258 per credit hour for computer science and MIS courses.

## FINANCIAL AID

Franklin offers a variety of financial aid options, including a deferred payment plan for students whose employers offer a tuition reimbursement program. Approximately 75 percent of Franklin students receive some type of financial assistance through grants, scholarships, loans, employer tuition reimbursement, and student employment. Franklin University awards nearly 225 scholarships every year to new and current students.

## APPLYING

Anyone who is a graduate of an accredited high school or has passed the GED is eligible for admission as a degree-seeking student. Those seeking a bachelor's degree must complete an admission application and forward an official high school transcript or an official GED test score report. To apply transfer credits from another institution, all official transcripts should be forwarded to Franklin University directly from the previous institution(s). However, a student can begin a distance learning course before the transcripts have been received. Students who would like to take courses as non-degree-seeking students do not need to be high school graduates.

---

**CONTACT**

Community College Alliance
Franklin University
201 South Grant Avenue
Columbus, Ohio 43215
Telephone: 614-797-4700
          888-341-6237 (toll-free)
Fax: 888-625-8678 (toll-free)
E-mail: alliace@franklin.edu
Web site: http://www.alliance.franklin.edu

---

# The George Washington University

## School of Public Health and Health Services
Washington, D.C.

The George Washington University School of Public Health and Health Services (SPHHS) is the newest and most rapidly growing school among the eight schools that constitute the George Washington University. The SPHHS is the only school of public health in the nation's capital and is fully accredited by the Council on Education for Public Health (CEPH). The School was chartered in 1997 and, along with the School of Medicine and Health Sciences, constitutes the George Washington University Medical Center. Distance education programs have been part of the SPHHS since 1998.

## DISTANCE LEARNING PROGRAM

The Graduate Certificate Program (GCP) may be taken exclusively by distance education. These 18–credit-hour programs may be transferred to the 36–credit-hour Master of Public Health (M.P.H.) program, which may be completed on an intensive basis on campus and may include a limited number of additional distance education courses. Nearly 100 students have enrolled in SPHHS distance education programs. The public health generalist (PHG) program is fully established and graduated its first students in 2000.

## DELIVERY MEDIA

SPHHS distance education courses are delivered via the World Wide Web utilizing the Prometheus system. Students communicate via e-mail with their faculty course director, the Director of the Office of Distance Education, and the Office of Student Services. The George Washington University has developed the Prometheus system to provide coordinated curriculum and administrative systems for distance education students.

## PROGRAMS OF STUDY

The 18–credit-hour GCP offered by the SPHHS is designed as a self-contained curriculum providing knowledge and skills needed for health professions, including management and health information systems positions. The GCP is also designed to link with and transfer credits to the Master of Public Health program.

The PHG program includes courses covering all core curriculum required for master's degrees by the CEPH. All PHG courses may be transferred to any track of the M.P.H. program (administrative medicine, community oriented primary care, environmental and occupational health, epidemiology/biostatistics, health promotion/disease prevention, international health, and maternal and child health).

## SPECIAL PROGRAMS

The SPHHS Wertlieb Educational Institute for Long Term Care Management offers two online courses on aging and disabilities and management of long-term care programs and facilities. These courses are available in the summer 2001 semester, which takes place in late May and ends in mid-August. These courses are open to undergraduate and graduate students, as well as interested professionals. Taken together with other undergraduate and graduate courses, such as ethics, human resources, and finance, these courses can fulfill the education requirements in a majority of states for students to take the examination to become licensed long-term care administrators. The two courses may be taken by students enrolled in other universities.

SPHHS programs are generally designed for adult learners. Students may enroll as part of collaborative programs with international institutions. These may include Monash University's campus in Malaysia, the National School of Public Health of Southern Africa, Cairo University, and Hebrew University–Hadassah School of Public Health.

The University's College of Professional Studies offers group rates for programs arranged through an employer.

## STUDENT SERVICES

Student services are provided through the Offices of Distance Education and Student Services. Access to online services of the Himmelfarb Health Sciences Library and other online services of the George Washington University are provided.

## CREDIT OPTIONS

Graduate Certificate programs are 18 credit hours and may be transferred, upon acceptance, to the 36–credit-hour M.P.H. program. The two long-term care courses are 3 credits each.

## FACULTY

More than 20 full-time faculty members serve as course directors for distance education courses. Full-time faculty members at the assistant professor level and above have doctoral or other terminal degrees.

## ADMISSION

Admission to the GCP requires a bachelor's degree with a minimum GPA of 3.0 (4.0 scale), or submission of an average score of 500 on the verbal and the quantitative portions of the GRE or the 50th percentile of the GMAT or MCAT. Language testing may be required for international applicants. No letters of recommendation are required, and the GRE is waived for applicants with a 3.0 or greater undergraduate GPA or master's degree or higher. Provisional admissions are also considered. The application deadline for fall semester is August 1.

Admission to the PHG may occur in the fall or spring semester. The program may be completed in one or two years or, with permission, over a longer period of time.

## TUITION AND FEES

Tuition, beginning in the summer semester 2001–02, is $742.50 per credit hour. Fees are $35 per semester.

## FINANCIAL AID

Distance Education students are eligible for the Alternative Loan Program and may be eligible for Federal Financial Aid. Partial scholarships are offered that may cover up to 6 credits of course work. Special employer-based rates may also be available. Applicants should contact the Office of Student Financial Assistance at 202-994-6620 or visit their Web site at http://gwired.gwu.edu/finaid.

## APPLYING

To receive an admissions application and further information, students should contact the SPHHS Office of Admissions.

---

### CONTACT

SPHHS Office of Admissions
The George Washington University
Ross Hall 106
2300 Eye Street, Northwest
Washington, D.C. 20037-2336

Telephone: 202-994-2160
E-mail sphhsinfo@gwumc.edu
Web site: http://www.gwumc.edu/sphhs

---

# Georgia Institute of Technology
## *Center for Distance Learning*
Atlanta, Georgia

Founded in 1885, the Georgia Institute of Technology is the Southeast's largest technological institution. Georgia Tech is located on a 330-acre campus near downtown Atlanta—the financial, communications, and cultural hub of the Southeast. The Institute's mission is to be a leader among those few technological universities whose alumni, faculty, students, and staff define, expand, and communicate the frontiers of knowledge and innovation.

U.S. News & World Report consistently lists Georgia Tech among the fifty best universities in the nation. Georgia Tech also makes their list of the top graduate engineering programs in the country. Seven of the engineering options were ranked in the top ten, with several in the top five.

In addition to its high-quality undergraduate and graduate instructional programs, Tech has a world-class research program, with $232 million in new grants and contracts awarded during the 2000 fiscal year. This ranks Tech as the South's number one public institution in engineering research.

## DISTANCE LEARNING PROGRAM

Georgia Tech's Center for Distance Learning serves more than 450 distance learning students and is housed within a unit that reports directly to the provost. Georgia Tech is accredited by the Southern Association of Colleges and Schools. Engineering disciplines are accredited by the Accrediting Board for Engineering and Technology, Inc.

## DELIVERY MEDIA

Video cameras record instructor presentations and student-instructor interaction during regular Georgia Tech graduate classes. The videotapes and supporting materials are sent to off-campus students, who take courses without having to come to the campus. Selected courses are available at some locations via video-conferencing, satellite, and the Internet. Students enrolled in the program communicate with their Georgia Tech professor by telephone, fax, and/or electronic mail. Students have access to the Georgia Tech Electronic Library and the computer system via a business or home computer and a modem. Access is also provided over the Internet.

## PROGRAMS OF STUDY

The Georgia Tech video-based distance delivery program provides high-quality graduate-level courses that can be applied to several master's degree programs. The Master of Science in Electrical and Computer Engineering is offered with options in computer engineering, digital signal processing, power, and telecommunications; all options require 30 hours of course work. The Master of Science (M.S.) and the Master of Science in Environmental Engineering (M.S.Env. E.) degrees are offered with concentrations in water quality, surface and subsurface systems, hazardous and solid waste, and air quality; all programs require 30 hours of course work or the equivalent. The Master of Science in Health Physics/Radiological Engineering degree requires 30 hours of course work. The Master of Science in Industrial Engineering is offered with specializations in au-

tomation, production and logistics systems, and statistical process control and quality assurance; it requires 30 hours of course work, students must hold an undergraduate degree from an ABET-accredited engineering curriculum. The Master of Science in Mechanical Engineering is offered with specializations in thermal science and mechanical systems; it requires 30 hours of course work.

Specific information on admission and degree requirements can be obtained by calling the academic coordinators for each area. Students should call the contact name for additional information.

## SPECIAL PROGRAMS

Georgia Tech offers a series of graduate-level credit courses in mechanical engineering (ME) that enable qualified students around the world to earn a Georgia Tech master's degree in ME completely on line. Once all the required courses are developed and offered, Georgia Tech will become the first and only university in the nation to offer a master's degree in ME in an asynchronous mode via the desktop. Also, in the fall semester of 2000, Georgia Tech began offering online graduate courses in electrical engineering that can be applied toward master's degrees in this discipline.

All Georgia Tech online graduate courses use state-of-the-art streaming audio and video technologies synchronized with slides, simulations, and other multimedia and make maximum use of the pedagogical advantages offered by Web-based courseware and instruction. Further information about these new online degree programs is available at the

Georgia Tech Center for Distance Learning Web site (http://www.conted.gatech.edu/distance/gatech-online.html).

A Certificate in Manufacturing provides students with the fundamentals in support of education and research in manufacturing. Each student pursuing the certificate develops knowledge and skills in a particular discipline coupled with a general knowledge of the entire manufacturing enterprise and an ability to work well as a member of a team. The certificate emphasizes the philosophy that it is not possible to educate engineers, managers, or scientists in all aspects of manufacturing. Accordingly, the program is structured to broaden and enhance the education of students who are enrolled in traditional academic disciplines. The program encourages students to develop knowledge in multiple disciplines from class work and experiences in multidisciplinary team activities. Thus, the program balances technical depth with a broad exposure and comprehension of the problems (and potential solutions) facing industry in the manufacturing arena. The Certificate in Manufacturing is obtained as part of a graduate degree program (M.S. or Ph.D.) from the Georgia Institute of Technology. Students must complete a graduate degree to obtain the certificate. The certificate program consists of a set of key courses that are fundamental to manufacturing, from the which the students select 12 semester hours or 18 quarter hours. Students are also required to attend seminars.

## CREDIT OPTIONS

Students earn credit toward their degree by registering for and completing courses delivered by videotape. Requirements for each course are the same as for on-campus students enrolled in the course. A student may receive transfer credit of up to 6 hours for graduate-level courses (approved by the academic adviser) taken at an accredited institution in the United States or Canada and not used for credit toward another degree.

## FACULTY

There are 672 full-time faculty members at Georgia Tech, 93 percent with doctoral degrees. One hundred ten, or 16 percent, teach in the distance learning program.

## ADMISSION

Admission requirements vary among the academic disciplines. To apply, individuals should contact the academic adviser or admissions office in the School to which he or she is applying.

## TUITION AND FEES

Video enrollment fees for in-state and out-of-state students for the 2000–01 academic year were $530 per credit hour. Fees are subject to change each year. There are no supplemental fees; however, students must purchase their own textbooks.

## FINANCIAL AID

There are no financial aid programs available through Georgia Tech for distance learning students. Most employers have programs that will help students pay the course fees. The Department of Veterans Affairs has approved the Georgia Tech Video Program as independent study. Georgia Tech has a memorandum of understanding with DANTES and with the Air Force.

## APPLYING

Application materials can be obtained from the School to which the student is applying. Applicants must submit an Application for Admission, three letters of recommendation, a biographical sketch, two official transcripts of all previous college work, and scores from the Graduate Record Examinations (GRE). Decisions are made by the individuals Schools.

---

**CONTACT**

Program Coordinator
Center for Distance Learning
Georgia Institute of Technology
Atlanta, Georgia 30332-0240
Telephone: 404-894-3378
Fax: 404-894-8924
Web site: http://www.conted.gatech.edu/distance/

# Goddard College
## *Distance Learning Programs*
Plainfield, Vermont

*Goddard College pioneered distance learning and became the first college to offer accredited distance learning programs. Goddard continues to experiment and innovate by employing various styles of learning and learning modes. In addition to the individually designed low-residency B.A., M.A., and M.F.A. programs, the College also has an undergraduate resident program. Goddard was chartered in 1938 and is accredited by NEASC.*

*Goddard's campus is situated on 250 acres of rolling forest and meadows in rural Vermont. The main campus buildings include the former farm buildings of the historic Martin Estate and two other clusters of buildings, added in the 1960s, that consist of the library, the dormitories, and an arts complex. Plainfield is located in central Vermont, about 10 miles northeast of Montpelier, the state's capital.*

## DISTANCE LEARNING PROGRAM

The low-residency, student-designed programs enable students to study across the liberal arts at the undergraduate and graduate levels and to pursue several professional graduate programs. The College also offers an M.F.A. in creative writing and an M.F.A. in the interdisciplinary arts in a low-residency mode.

## DELIVERY MEDIA

Twice a year, at the outset of each semester, students come to the Vermont campus for an intensive weeklong collaboration with fellow students as well as a faculty mentor to plan their semester's work through detailed study plans that enable them to reach their individual long-term learning goals. Throughout the rest of the semester, students work independently in their own communities, communicating with their mentor every three weeks.

## PROGRAMS OF STUDY

Goddard offers the B.A. and the M.A. in individualized study, for which students craft diverse programs across the liberal arts. The areas of interest that studies cover include but are not limited to literature and writing, the performing arts, community organization and development, cultural theory, environmental studies, gay and lesbian studies, history, health arts, holistic health systems, women's studies, and philosophy.

Also offered are M.A. degrees in environmental studies, psychology/counseling, teacher education, and health arts. M.F.A. degrees are offered in creative writing and in interdisciplinary arts.

For the B.A. degree, students must earn a minimum of 120 semester hours of credit. For the M.A. in individualized study, the M.A. in teacher education, the M.A. in environmental studies, and the M.A. in health arts, students must earn a minimum of

36 semester hours of credit. For the M.A. in psychology and counseling, students must earn a minimum of 48 semester hours of credit. The M.F.A. degree in creative writing requires a minimum of 48 semester hours of credit, and the M.F.A. in interdisciplinary arts requires a minimum of 60 semester hours of credit.

## SPECIAL PROGRAMS

Students in the low-residency programs can make use of study leaves, internships, apprenticeships, and travel-abroad opportunities as well as summer programs with the Institute for Social Ecology in Plainfield. Up to 45 B.A. credits may also be granted for life experience through an assessment of prior learning.

## CREDIT OPTIONS

A maximum of 90 semester hours of credit may be transferred at the undergraduate level. Up to 12 transfer credits may be considered at the graduate level. In lieu of tests and grades, Goddard uses a written evaluative system, whereby each semester's work is viewed as successful or not. Each successful undergraduate semester is worth 15 credit hours, while each successful graduate semester is worth 12 credit hours.

## FACULTY

Each of Goddard's programs is served by a body of core faculty members plus associate faculty members who are chosen for their general training as well as their individual areas of expertise. The faculty-student ratio is 1:10. Ninety percent of faculty members have terminal degrees in their fields.

## ADMISSION

Goddard's admissions policy is inclusive rather than exclusive. Instead of grade point averages and test scores, applicants are judged on their interest, readiness, and willingness to begin study with the College and their apparent potential to complete college-level work. Previous credit must have been gained at accredited schools.

## TUITION AND FEES

Tuition for the undergraduate program is $4115 per semester. M.A. tuition is $4825 per semester, and M.F.A. tuition is $4912 per semester. All fees include the costs of the residencies. The College reserves the right to change the tuition and fees.

## FINANCIAL AID

Financial aid is based on financial need. Eligible undergraduate students may qualify for the Federal Pell Grant as well as various state grants. Guaranteed student loans, based on eligibility, are also available to both graduate and undergraduate students. Last year, more than $1.5 million was awarded in financial aid to Goddard students. Of Goddard's newly enrolled students, 100 percent received financial aid.

## APPLYING

Goddard College accepts applications on a rolling basis, and prospective students must supply required documents. Students applying to the M.F.A. programs must also provide an appropriate portfolio. Application materials can be acquired by contacting Admissions or via the College's Web site (address below).

### CONTACT

Brenda Hawkins
Admissions
Goddard College
123 Pitkin Road
Plainfield, Vermont 05667
Telephone: 800-468-4888 (toll-free)
Fax: 802-454-1029
E-mail: admissions@goddard.edu
Web site:
   http://www.goddard.edu

# Hibbing Community College

## Distance Learning

Hibbing, Minnesota

> *Hibbing Community College, a technical and community college, provides excellence in lifelong educational and career opportunities in a responsive learning environment.*
>
> *Hibbing Community College (HCC) offers associate degrees that transfer and can be applied as the first two years of a baccalaureate degree, career programs, continuing education classes, and workshops and certificates for updating job skills.*
>
> *HCC is accredited by the North Central Association of Colleges and is part of the Minnesota State Colleges and Universities System (MnSCU).*
>
> *Hibbing was one of the first towns in the nation to expand educational opportunities by opening a two-year college in 1916. Thus, Hibbing Community College is one of the oldest two-year colleges in Minnesota and the nation.*
>
> *Today, HCC serves more than 1,800 students each semester, including more than 300 online students.*

## DISTANCE LEARNING PROGRAM

Hibbing Community College offers courses online that fulfill the requirements of the Minnesota Transfer Curriculum for the first two years of a baccalaureate degree program. Other courses in development include some that are hybrids. HCC is working hard to meet the needs of students who need to learn anywhere, any time.

## DELIVERY MEDIA

HCC's online courses use Anlon software. Students have access through HCC's Web pages and interact with the instructor and other students via e-mail and the Message Center (bulletin board discussion). Some courses require online or other testing at proxy sites. Student support is exceptional, with staff members on hand for technical help, advisement, or other student services.

## PROGRAMS OF STUDY

Students may complete the Minnesota Transfer curriculum require-ments entirely online. A selection of courses within these ten categories allows students to continue the pursuit of a baccalaureate degree with any of the four-year institutions within the Minnesota State Colleges and Universities system. Some of the courses include Drawing 1, Computer Applications, C++ Programming, AutoCAD 2D, Freshman Composition, U.S. History to 1877, Native American History, Medical Terminology, Psychology of Adjustment, General Psychology, Fitness Walking, and Industrial Safety.

## SPECIAL PROGRAMS

Hibbing Community College offers customized training to business and corporate clients in many areas. Computer, safety and health, and business courses are the most popular.

## STUDENT SERVICES

HCC offers a full range of student services for its online students. All students have access to a free online orientation and are able to use the library services (WebPALS). Interlibrary loan service allows students to obtain any materials available throughout the Minnesota State Colleges and Universities' libraries. Students simply request these materials online by entering their account number.

Registration is entirely online. Application forms are downloadable from the college Web site. Transcripts are required from other institutions and need to be requested for forwarding to HCC.

Computer services provides support for online students. One e-mail and phone number is used for one-stop assistance with any technical matters.

Financial aid application and support is available online. HCC has a toll-free number for students who may need help with anything that develops. Online students receive the same attention as the residential students.

## CREDIT OPTIONS

Credits earned at accredited colleges, technical schools, or universities may be transferred to Hibbing Community College depending upon the applicability of the credit earned to the student's program. Articulation agreements within Minnesota facilitate smooth transition to HCC programs. HCC is one member of a statewide consortium of thirty-five community, technical, and four-year colleges and universities.

## FACULTY

Hibbing Community College has 65 full-time and 35 part-time faculty members. HCC has state-of-the-art technology and faculty members who are well trained in its use. All online faculty members have received extensive training in online course development and delivery. In addition, HCC has an instructional technology department that provides a high degree of support for faculty members at all times, including during online course delivery. If faculty members cannot answer students' questions about online issues, instructional support is available to solve any problems that arise.

## ADMISSION

Hibbing Community College is committed to open admissions. The basic requirement of an applicant is a high school diploma or GED certificate. A person who has neither a high school diploma nor a GED certificate may be admitted if, at the discretion of the college, that person demonstrates potential for being a successful college student. Admission to HCC does not guarantee admission to college-level courses.

Students may contact the direct number for admissions. All online students may contact Counselor Kathy Nucech directly, by telephone at 218-262-6752, or by e-mail at k.nucech@hcc.mnscu.edu.

For technical support or other information, students may contact Jim Antilla, Director of Instructional Technology (e-mail: j.antilla@hcc.mnscu. edu) or Shelly McCauley, Instructional Technology Assistant (e-mail: s.mccauley@hccgwy.mnscu.edu). They may be reached by telephone at 218-263-2970 or 800-224-4422 (toll-free).

## TUITION AND FEES

Tuition is projected to be $76.50 per credit (resident rate) for 2001–02. Rates are the same for residents and nonresidents for all online courses. A technology fee of $8 per credit also applies.

## FINANCIAL AID

Most of the students attending Hibbing Community College, a technical and community college, are eligible for some form of financial aid. While a part of the responsibility for financing a college education will be assumed by the students and/or their parents, HCC helps students explore options to receive aid. Complete information is available on the HCC Web site at http://www.hcc.mnscu. edu.

## APPLYING

Applications are available online at the HCC Web site. Transcripts are required from previous schools attended. Fees are also due before courses begin. More information is available at the Web site and e-mail listed below.

### CONTACT

Admissions (admissions@hcc. mnscu.edu)
Hibbing Community College
1515 East 25th Street
Hibbing, Minnesota 55746
Telephone: 800-224-4422
Fax: 218-262-6717
E-mail: admissions@hcc.mnscu. edu
Web site:
    http://www.hcc.mnscu.edu

# Indiana Higher Education Telecommunication System

## *Indiana College Network*

Indianapolis, Indiana

*Since 1967, Indiana's colleges and universities have cooperatively managed telecommunications networks through IHETS to share resources and disseminate a wide variety of educational opportunities. In 1992, the institutions established the Indiana Partnership for Statewide Education (now known as the Indiana College Network) as the vehicle for collaboration in program planning, delivery of student services, needs assessment and promotion, faculty development, and evaluation. The Network's goal is to ensure that lifelong learning is available via distance education to Indiana citizens wherever they may live and work. Technology developments mean that many of the same programs are available on campus and around the world. Consortium members are Ball State University, Independent Colleges of Indiana, Indiana State University, Indiana University, Ivy Tech State College, Purdue University, University of Southern Indiana, and Vincennes University.*

## DISTANCE LEARNING PROGRAM

Each consortium member is fully accredited and responsible for its own programs. Collectively, enrollments on a statewide basis approach 20,500 in college credit courses and 8 million in elementary/high school classes and electronic field trips; hundreds of others are served locally, regionally, or globally by correspondence programs. IHETS has adopted the umbrella label "Indiana College Network" to refer to the comprehensive array of degree programs and learning opportunities provided by Indiana's higher education institutions.

## DELIVERY MEDIA

Partnership institutions use a variety of delivery methods, including the Internet, satellite television (one-way video with two-way audio), two-way interactive videoconferencing, computer disks and CD-ROMs, videotape, public or cable television, and independent study by correspondence. Some degrees are available entirely via satellite to specially equipped Receive Sites, but most degrees permit students to take course work in a com-

bination of delivery methods. Most programs with "live" interaction are still available only within Indiana, though more are becoming available at locations throughout the United States.

## PROGRAMS OF STUDY

Certificate and degree programs are listed with the name of the originating institution: Certificate in Distance Education (Indiana University); Certificate in General Studies (Vincennes University); Certificate in Labor Studies (Indiana University); Certificate in Public Library, Librarian IV and V (Indiana University); Certificate in School Library/Media and Information Technology (Indiana University); Christian Worker Certificate (Taylor University); Technical Certificate in Child Development (Ivy Tech State College); Technical Certificate in Histotechnology (Indiana University); Associate of Applied Science (A.A.S.) in accounting (Ivy Tech State College); A.A.S. in business administration (Ivy Tech State College); A.A.S. in child development (Ivy Tech State College); A.A.S. in design technology (Ivy Tech State College); Associate of Arts (A.A.) in general arts (Ball State University);

Associate of General Studies (Indiana University); Associate of Science (A.S.) or A.A. in behavioral sciences (Vincennes University); A.S. in business administration (Ball State University); A.S. in business administration (Vincennes University); A.S. in communications (University of Southern Indiana); A.S. in computer technology (Purdue University Calumet); A.S. in general aviation flight technology (Indiana State University); A.S. or A.A.S. in general studies (Vincennes University); A.S. in histotechnology (Indiana University); A.S. in labor studies (Indiana University); A.S. or A.A.S. in law enforcement (Vincennes University); A.S. in social science (Vincennes University); A.S. in veterinary technology (Purdue University); Bachelor of General Studies (Indiana University); Bachelor of Science (B.S.) in electronics technology (Indiana State University); B.S. in business administration (Indiana State University); B.S. in community health (Indiana State University); B.S. in criminology (Indiana State University); B.S. in general industrial supervision (Indian State University); B.S. in health services (University of Southern Indiana); B.S. in human resource development (Indiana State University); B.S. in insurance (Indiana State University); B.S. in labor studies (Indiana University); B.S. in mechanical technology (Indiana State University); B.S. in nursing (Ball State University); B.S. in nursing (Indiana State University); B.S. in nursing (University of Southern Indiana); B.S. in vocational-trade-industrial-technical education (Indiana State University); Master of Arts (M.A.) in executive development and public service (Ball State University); M.A. or Master of Science (M.S.) in student affairs administration (Indiana State University); M.A. or M.S. in criminology (Indiana

State University); Master of Arts in Education (M.A.Ed.) in educational administration and supervision (Ball State University); M.A.Ed. in elementary education (Ball State University); M.A. Ed. in special education (Ball State University); Master of Business Administration (M.B.A.) (Ball State University); Master of Business Administration (Indiana University); M.B.A. in agribusiness (Purdue University); Master of Science (M.S.). in adult education (Indiana University); M.S in computer science (Ball State University); M.S. or M.A. in criminology (Indiana State University); Master of Science in Education (M.S.Ed.) in language education (Indiana University); M.S. in electrical engineering (Purdue University); M.S. or M.A. in health and safety (Indiana State University); M.S. in human resource development (Indiana State University); M.S. in industrial engineering (Purdue University); M.S. in music technology (Indiana University); M.S. or Master of Science in Engineering (M.S.E) in interdisciplinary engineering (Purdue University); M.S. in mechanical engineering (Purdue University); M.S. in nursing (Ball State University); M.S. in nursing (Indiana State University); M.S. in nursing (Indiana University); M.S. in nursing (Purdue University Calumet); M.S. in recreation (Indiana University), and M.S. in technology (Purdue University).

Several other programs were nearing authorization at the time of this publication. Information is available in the separate listings for the institutions or via the World Wide Web.

## STUDENT SERVICES

All of the partner institutions participate in a library automation network, which makes library catalogs accessible via the Internet. Most professors expect students at a distance to use the Internet for library research and class-related communications. Students are generally expected to obtain Internet access from a local provider, but Learning Centers in Indiana house computers with dial-up access for students unable to obtain affordable service.

## CREDIT OPTIONS

The undergraduate degree programs listed here allow some credit to be transferred from other institutions; the amount varies for each program. The Indiana University (IU) general studies degree programs are tailored for adults to permit credit transfer and learning portfolios along with courses to be taken to complete the degree. All other degrees are the same programs as those offered to students on campus; many courses are taken simultaneously by students on and off campus. Graduate degree programs typically allow limited credit transfer.

## FACULTY

Faculty members' credentials vary among the institutions, but professors in the university programs are almost exclusively full-time institutional faculty members with terminal degrees.

## ADMISSION

Admission requirements are the same as those for on-campus programs, with special flexibility in the IU general studies programs. Older or reentering students are not usually required to take or retake SAT or other standardized tests.

## TUITION AND FEES

Fees are highly variable, with a range of $67 to $139 per credit hour for in-state undergraduate students; some institutions charge an additional $25 per credit hour to help cover support-service costs for students at a distance.

## FINANCIAL AID

Since most distance education students are independent, employed adults attending college part-time, few receive federal or state financial aid, although it is the personal circumstances rather than the delivery methods that reduce or eliminate benefits. Many students are receiving support from Veterans Administration benefits or from employer tuition reimbursement programs.

## APPLYING

Application and acceptance processes are approximately the same for on- and off-campus students, although distant students usually apply through special distance education or program coordinators at the offering institutions rather than through the main college or university admissions office.

---

**CONTACT**

Indiana College Network (ICN) Student Services Center
2805 East Tenth Street
Bloomington, Indiana 47408
Telephone: 800-426-8899 (toll-free)
Fax: 812-855-9380

Additional information, including a searchable database of courses and degree programs, is available at the Partnership's Web site: http://www.icn.org.

# Indiana State University

## *Distance Education Program*

Terre Haute, Indiana

---

Indiana State University is a medium-sized, comprehensive university accredited by the North Central Association of Colleges and Schools. Founded in 1865, the University has grown to serve a student population that includes 11,000 students from all fifty states and eighty-two countries. International students comprise 13 percent of the student population.

Attention to and concern for the individual is reflected in the institution's offerings. Flexible and responsive programs are designed to facilitate student attainment of academic, vocational, and personal goals. Classes are designed to meet the needs of full-time and part-time students. Nondegree study is also available for those seeking personal growth, transferable credit, and enrichment through lifelong learning.

In addition to offering distance programs and courses, the University offers undergraduate and graduate programs in more than 120 areas of study on the Indiana State University campus in Terre Haute, Indiana.

## DISTANCE LEARNING PROGRAM

Indiana State University (ISU) has offered distance programs since 1969. Many programs can be completed entirely via distance education; others require minimal campus visits. Selected distance programs and numerous courses can be completed by out-of-state and international students. More than 1,000 students enroll in ISU distance learning courses each semester.

## DELIVERY MEDIA

Courses are offered via the Internet, videotapes, correspondence, and live television accessible at 300 sites in Indiana. Television courses offer live, two-way interaction among students and the instructor. Students enrolled in correspondence courses work independently, interacting with their instructor via written communications. Students in Internet courses and some videotape courses interact via e-mail and Internet chat rooms. Equipment requirements depend on course format and may include an Internet-connected computer, VCR, and audio cassette player.

## PROGRAMS OF STUDY

Students may complete individual undergraduate or graduate courses; each semester, more than 100 ISU courses are offered via distance education. In addition, eligible students may complete numerous undergraduate and graduate degrees and professional development programs.

Undergraduate degree programs include an Associate of Science in general aviation flight technology and bachelor degree completion programs in business administration, community health, criminology, electronics technology, general industrial technology, human resource development, industrial supervision, insurance, mechanical technology, nursing, and vocational trade-industrial-technical. Undergraduate nondegree programs include basic and advanced certificate programs in corrections, law enforcement, and private security; an endorsement in driver education; and a certification program in library/media services.

Graduate degree programs include a doctoral program in technology management and master's programs in criminology, health and safety, human resource development, nursing, and student affairs administration. Graduate nondegree programs include endorsement programs in driver education and emotional disturbance, a licensure program in educational administration, and certification programs in public administration and library/media services.

## SPECIAL PROGRAMS

DegreeLink is a bachelor's degree completion program that enables individuals to transfer previously earned credit to ISU and complete selected bachelor's degrees via distance education. Students may transfer credit earned from Ivy Tech State College, Vincennes University, or another accredited institution.

The Library/Media Services Certification Program consists of 27 hours of library and media courses leading to an undergraduate minor and certification or graduate certification in library/media services.

The Ph.D. in technology management is offered through the School of Technology in cooperation with a consortium of eight other universities. Course work includes a general technology core, a technical specialization, cognate studies, an internship, and a research core and dissertation.

## STUDENT SERVICES

Indiana State University offers distance learners a comprehensive package of services, including academic advisement, a virtual bookstore, library services, technical support, and career counseling. The Office of Student Services–Lifelong Learning offers one-stop assistance to individuals interested in pursuing undergraduate and graduate courses and programs via distance learning.

## CREDIT OPTIONS

Students earn credit by registering for and completing semester-based courses offered on campus or via distance learning. In addition, undergraduate students may opt to earn credit via year-based study. Undergraduate students are eligible to transfer up to 64 credit hours from two-year accredited institutions or 94 hours from four-year accredited institutions. Selected programs enable undergraduates to earn credit for prior work experience, by examination, and through portfolios. Graduate students are eligible to transfer selected credit; each department determines the number of hours transferable.

## FACULTY

Distance courses are developed and taught by ISU's 536 full-time faculty members. Working with instructional designers and media specialists, faculty members transform on-campus courses to distance formats.

## ADMISSION

Admission requirements vary by program of study. For information, prospective students should contact the Office of Student Services–Lifelong Learning.

## TUITION AND FEES

All distance learners pay Indiana residence fees. Undergraduate tuition is $128 per credit hour; graduate tuition is $154 per credit hour. Tuition is subject to change.

## APPLYING

Individuals may obtain undergraduate and graduate applications, information, and assistance by contacting the Office of Student Services–Lifelong Learning.

---

### CONTACT

Harry K. Barnes, Director
Office of Student Services–Lifelong Learning
Indiana State University
Erickson Hall, Room 210–211
Terre Haute, Indiana 47809
Telephone: 888-237-8080 (toll-free)
Fax: 812-237-8540
E-mail: studentservices@indstate.edu
Web site: http://indstate.edu/distance

---

# Indiana University of Pennsylvania

## School of Continuing Education—Distance Education

Indiana, Pennsylvania

With its original 1875 building still standing at the heart of its campus, Indiana University of Pennsylvania (IUP) has a long tradition of academic excellence. The University is recognized as a "Public Ivy" in company with other public colleges and universities that offer academic environments comparable to those at Ivy League schools but at affordable prices. IUP provides an intellectually challenging experience to more than 13,000 students at the University's three campuses, all easily accessible from Pittsburgh and the Middle Atlantic region. IUP is the largest member of Pennsylvania's State System of Higher Education and the only one authorized to confer doctoral degrees.

Academic offerings include more than 100 undergraduate majors with a variety of internship and study-abroad programs, more than forty master's degree programs, and eight doctoral degree programs. Unusual opportunities for research at all levels and the Robert E. Cook Honors College provide special challenges for academic growth. The variety and quality of instruction are characteristic of a big university, yet at IUP, close, one-to-one relationships develop within the teaching framework, and a strong sense of community prevails.

## DISTANCE LEARNING PROGRAM

Indiana University of Pennsylvania continues its outstanding tradition in learning with the addition of new programs and courses in distance learning. These programs and courses are designed with emphasis on active learning and use of the most current Web-based technologies.

## DELIVERY MEDIA

The courses use Web-based delivery enhanced with streaming video, audio, and other tools. The University uses CD-ROM, WebCT, printed materials, and an orientation guide for use by distance learning students.

## PROGRAMS OF STUDY

The Department of Safety Sciences at Indiana University of Pennsylvania offers a graduate program of studies leading to a Certificate of Recognition (COR) in Safety Sciences. The 12-credit COR introduces the student to the fundamentals of occupational safety and health, stressing the recognition, evaluation, and control of common workplace hazards. The COR is designed for those individuals who already have a bachelor's degree and have safety and health program activities as peripheral responsibilities within an organization. Professionals who benefit from this certificate are human resource managers, occupational health and environmental health professionals, and others who have safety responsibilities.

All students are required to successfully complete a minimum of 12 graduate credits, of which 6 hours are core courses. The student must choose the remaining 6 hours of elective courses. Three credits may be applied toward the M.S. in safety sciences.

There are two required core courses (6 hours):

Principles of Occupational Safety (SAFE 645) provides a fundamental knowledge of the technical and managerial aspects of the safety and health function within an organization. The effects of loss incidents, accident causation, safety and health legislation, and safety program development are some of the managerial aspects covered in this course. The technical aspects of the course focus on recognition, evaluation, and control of common safety, fire, and repetitive motion hazards in the workplace.

Principles of Occupational Health (SAFE 667) provides comprehensive coverage of the industrial hygienist's responsibility for recognition, evaluation, and control of environmental stressors arising in or from the workplace. Students learn how to recognize and evaluate exposures to chemical, physical, and biological hazards. Emphasis is placed on the identification of appropriate control strategies, including program development and evaluation of health hazards.

Two elective courses totaling 6 hours must be selected from the following:

Radiological Health (SAFE 562) involves the study of problems associated with ionizing radiation in the human environment. Emphasis is given to biological effects, radiation measurement, dose computational techniques, exposure control, and local and federal regulations. The study and use of various radiological instruments is included.

Advanced Safety Administration (SAFE 623) analyzes the management structure for its procedures, organizations, policies, and departmental competencies as they relate to safety. Ways to audit and improve management's safety effectiveness are covered.

Pollution Control (SAFE 630) introduces the student to both management and engineering strategies in the prevention and control of pollution of the environment from industrial activities. The course includes a brief history of pollution, legal aspects of prevention and control, management of major types of industrial wastes, and the control of releases into both water and air.

Construction Safety (SAFE 643) provides an in-depth treatment of hazard recognition, evaluation, and control principles used in the construction industry. Extensive coverage of federal standards is given, together with the means by which a construction safety program can be developed and administered.

Disaster Preparedness (SAFE 673) outlines requirements necessary to develop workable plans for natural and industrial types of disasters and emergencies. Principles and techniques for preparing for various types of disasters, loss prevention measures, and preservation of organization resources are discussed.

## SPECIAL PROGRAMS

IUP offers both undergraduate and graduate-level courses online for continued professional development.

IUP has developed courses for continuing professional development of educators. In Pennsylvania, these courses may fulfill Act 48 In-Service requirements for maintaining teacher certification.

The IUP Web-based Instruction for Physics Certification (WIN PC) is a unique series of graduate courses (23 credits) in physics for science and mathematics teachers seeking professional development and to satisfy state physics certification requirements.

Those interested in IUP's special programs should visit the Web site listed below and select Distance Education for the most current course offerings and registration information.

## STUDENT SERVICES

IUP offers numerous services to distance learners, including online library services with electronic reserves, bookstore, advising via e-mail, Web-based registration, and access to e-mail. The University also has a complete career placement center.

## FACULTY

More than 200 IUP faculty members, with experience in using WebCT, are eligible to teach online.

## ADMISSION

General admission information for Indiana University of Pennsylvania is available on the Web at http://www.iup.edu/ (select Admissions from the menu listed on the screen).

The admission procedures for enrollment into the Certificate of Recognition in Safety Sciences program are the same as the Graduate School and Research for a graduate degree program. The requirements for this program include a baccalaureate degree with a minimum 2.6 GPA. As with the M.S. in safety sciences, there is no requirement for the GRE. Applicants apply for Certificate of Recognition Status as a student in the IUP Graduate School and Research.

Enrollment into the Act 48 In-Service Development for Educators graduate-level courses requires an application to the Graduate School and Research and a copy of Level I (or higher) teaching certification. Information is available online at the Web site listed below.

Enrollment into the WIN PC graduate-level program of courses requires an application to the Graduate School and Research and a copy of Level I (or higher) teaching certification. Information is available online at the Web site listed below.

## TUITION AND FEES

For undergraduate students, tuition is $158 per credit for in-state residents and $395 per credit for out-of-state residents. For graduate students, tuition is $230 per credit for in-state residents and $389 per credit for out-of-state residents.

The off-campus instructional fee for part-time students is $95, and it is $190 for full-time students. The registration fee for the fall or spring semesters is $20 per academic semester.

The summer registration fee is $10 per session. The application fee is $30.

## FINANCIAL AID

IUP's Financial Aid Office offers financial information and counseling to all students attending the University. More information on financial aid is available on the Web at http://www.iup.edu/.

## APPLYING

For an application and registration information, applicants should contact the IUP School of Continuing Education at the e-mail address or the telephone numbers listed below.

### CONTACT

School of Continuing Education
100 Keith Hall, 390 Pratt Drive
Indiana University of
    Pennsylvania
Indiana, Pennsylvania 15705
Telephone: 724-357-2228
        800-845-0131 (toll-
        free)
Fax: 724-357-7695
E-mail: ce-ocp@grove.iup.edu
Web site: http://www.iup.edu/
    contin/

# IWUonline Indiana Wesleyan University

## Online Degree Programs

Marion, Indiana

Indiana Wesleyan University (IWU) is a Christian comprehensive university founded in 1920 that is committed to liberal arts and professional education. Through innovative degree programs for adult and residential students, IWU has become one of the fastest-growing private universities in America. More than 7,000 students are enrolled in programs leading to undergraduate and graduate degrees both online and at seventy locations.

Affiliated with The Wesleyan Church, IWU is a "Christ-centered academic community committed to changing the world by developing students in character, scholarship, and leadership." IWU is accredited by the North Central Association of Colleges and Schools.

## DISTANCE LEARNING PROGRAM

IWUonline offers four degree programs to working adult professionals who must overcome time and geographic barriers in order to obtain a degree. The curriculum for the online degree programs is built upon IWU's successful site-based programs, which are held in traditional classroom settings.

## DELIVERY MEDIA

IWUonline students learn in a "virtual classroom" forum and interact with faculty members and fellow students concerning a broad range of issues. Each student interacts online with fellow classmates and professors, allowing for group learning. Web page discussion forums, live chats, and collaborative software allow for both synchronous and asynchronous interaction between faculty members and students. Students need an IBM-compatible computer, a modem, and Internet connection to participate in the program.

## PROGRAMS OF STUDY

IWUonline offers four online degree programs. Two online bachelor's degree completion programs in business are offered: Bachelor of Science in Management (B.S.M.) and Bachelor of Science in Business Information Systems (B.S.B.I.S.). The two online graduate degree programs are Master of Business Administration (M.B.A.) and Master of Education (M.Ed.)

Each online degree program is taught in a lock-step sequence to cohort groups of approximately 15 to 18 students. Students complete one course at a time in an accelerated format. No campus visit or residencies are required with any of the online degree programs.

The Online B.S.M. core program (40 credit hours) is completed in approximately 20 months. The Online B.S.B.I.S. core program (52 credit hours) is completed in approximately 30 months.

The Online M.B.A. core program (41 credit hours) is completed in approximately 24 months, and the Online M.Ed. core program for teachers (30 credit hours) is completed in approximately 20 months.

## STUDENT SERVICES

Since the online degree programs are designed for working adult professionals, IWU strives to make the IWUonline experience as conve-

nient as possible. All textbooks and other study materials are mailed to students prior to each class. IWUonline also offers off-campus library services to all students completing online degree programs. Students may request copies of articles and other items by e-mail or a toll-free telephone number. Academic advising is provided, as well. Students receive technical assistance before starting their first course, with similar help continuing throughout the duration of the program.

## CREDIT OPTIONS

Students applying for the bachelor's degree completion programs may transfer at least 60 credits earned from a regionally accredited institution. IWU also awards credit for prior learning and accepts credit earned through CLEP and DANTES tests.

## FACULTY

Experienced, well-trained faculty members provide guidance for students as they master the knowledge base and seek to apply what they are learning in their vocational settings. Because of the "practitioner focus" of the online degree programs, many of the faculty members are full-time professionals who facilitate learning on a part-time basis. All faculty members hold advanced degrees.

## ADMISSION

Students who wish to be admitted to the bachelor's degree completion programs must have completed 60 credit hours of transferable credit obtained at an accredited college or university with a minimum overall grade point average of 2.0. In addition, a minimum of two years' significant full-time work experience beyond high school is required.

Students who wish to be admitted to the Online M.B.A. program must have completed a baccalaureate degree from a regionally accredited college or university with an overall grade point average of at least 2.5, a minimum of three years' significant full-time work experience, and prior course work in math, economics, finance, and accounting.

Students who wish to be admitted to the Online M.Ed. program must have a baccalaureate degree in education from a regionally accredited college or university with a minimum overall grade point average of 2.75, at least one year of full-time teaching experience, and a valid (not necessarily current) teaching license.

## TUITION AND FEES

The total cost of the online degree programs includes tuition for the core program, books, and fees. The cost of the Online B.S.M. program is $11,656 for U.S. students and $12,346 for international students. The cost of the Online B.S.B.I.S. program is $17,365 for U.S. students and $18,176 for international students. The cost of the Online M.B.A. program is $17,581 for U.S. students and $18,519 for international students. The cost of the Online M.Ed. program is $9812 for U.S. students and $10,434 for international students.

## FINANCIAL AID

Indiana Wesleyan University offers a variety of assistance to those students who require financial aid.

Through IWU's Financial Aid Office, students receive help in exploring alternatives to financing their education, including installment tuition payment plans, employer reimbursement programs, and student loan programs. Generally, government-sponsored financial aid is not available for international students.

## APPLYING

Prospective students are asked to complete an application data form and a brief narrative statement. Two recommendation forms and official transcripts from all colleges or universities at which the student completed undergraduate course work are also required. Applicants are advised to start the application process at least one month prior to the scheduled cohort group start date.

---

### CONTACT

College of Adult and Professional Studies
Indiana Wesleyan University
4301 South Washington Street
Marion, Indiana 46953-5279
Telephone: 800-895-0036 (toll-free)
Fax: 765-677-2404
E-mail: info@IWUonline.com
Web site: http://www.IWUonline.com
 http://www.indwes.edu

# Jones International University

## *Program in Business Communication*

### Englewood, Colorado

*Jones International University™, Ltd. (JIU), offers courses, professional and executive education, and degree programs entirely online. According to e-learning magazine, "The university laid the foundation for online education and continues to pave the way in this space."*

*JIU's degree programs represent a true best practice for online education: students take what they learn in the classroom and put it to use at work immediately. JIU courses are developed specifically for online delivery by highly respected faculty members from leading universities around the world.*

*JIU's programs are an exciting option for students around the world who are committed to investing in their future, enabling their professional success, and tackling the challenges of working in today's rapidly changing business environment. JIU interactive courses facilitate new ideas and impart the knowledge, confidence, and credentials students need to succeed.*

## DISTANCE LEARNING PROGRAM

Harnessing the power of the Internet, JIU was the first entirely online university to gain United States regional accreditation. JIU's 3,000 students in fifty-seven countries use the Internet and a Web browser to log into their courses, access their course materials, and participate in discussions any time and anywhere it is convenient.

## DELIVERY MEDIA

JIU's courses are conducted entirely online. They take full advantage of the Internet, streaming audio, video, and other emerging technologies to foster communication and skill acquisition. Students work collaboratively with instructors and classmates using e-mail and asynchronous forums. This international "community of learners" offers a highly interactive exchange of ideas and experiences for a truly innovative learning experience. Using the Internet, students learn at home, at work, or even while traveling.

## PROGRAMS OF STUDY

JIU's M.B.A. students work both independently and collaboratively with classmates to analyze and resolve real business problems. Students translate business theory into action steps for professional success. JIU offers seven high-demand M.B.A.'s: global enterprise management, e-commerce, health-care management, entrepreneurship, information technology management, negotiation and conflict management, and project management.

Keeping up to speed with emerging e-learning techniques and technologies has never been more challenging. JIU offers six skill-packed M.Ed. programs: research and assessment, corporate training and knowledge management, global leadership and administration, library and resource management, e-learning: technology and design, and general studies.

Students in the Master of Arts in business communications program master the valuable skills of human communication, emerging communication technologies, and oral and written communication skills. Through this course of study, students learn the tools and expert knowledge that lead to improved workplace performance, creativity, and leadership.

JIU's B.A. in business communication degree completion program blends theory and practice for the effective management of communication. This program teaches students the skills that are necessary for creative thinking, innovation, entrepreneurship, and leadership.

## SPECIAL PROGRAMS

JIU offers more than forty Professional and Executive Education Programs, ranging from project management to team effectiveness. These focused programs are ideal for students who want to explore a new area of interest or sharply hone their skills for increased success in a targeted area of business. Students receive an outstanding education while taking advantage of the convenience, quality, and cost efficiency of online learning.

Credits earned in these programs can be transferred toward the completion of a JIU degree program.

Students can get the education they need to maintain their edge in today's rapidly changing marketplace in programs such as Mastering e-Commerce, Successful Entrepreneurship, Information Technology Management, Project Management, Using the Internet in Business, Financial Management in the Digital Age, Team Strategies for the Effective Executive, Managing the Global Enterprise, Marketing Electronically, Oral and Written Business Communication, and Advanced Public Relations for the Wired World.

## STUDENT SERVICES

Students purchase textbooks through JIU's online bookstore and use the e-global library™, a Web-based library, to access reference resources and other support materials online. Student Advisors provide academic guidance to students, including establishing academic and career goals. JIU offers technical assistance for issues relating to the JIU Web site and courses 24 hours a day, seven days a week.

## CREDIT OPTIONS

Students in the B.A. program may transfer at least 60 and no more than 90 credits that they have earned through other regionally accredited institutions toward their JIU B.A. Students in JIU's master's programs may transfer up to 9 credits earned through regionally accredited institutions toward their degree. JIU also awards credit for prior learning and accepts credit earned through CLEP and DANTES tests.

## FACULTY

JIU has 7 full-time faculty members and approximately 200 part-time faculty members. Seventy-five percent of the faculty members hold doctorates, and 25 percent have master's degrees.

## ADMISSION

Students seeking admission to JIU's degree programs must submit a completed application package, including a nonrefundable $75 application fee, a resume, official transcripts from all colleges previously attended, a writing sample, and references.

## TUITION AND FEES

Tuition for 3-credit courses at the bachelor's level is $690. Tuition for 3-credit courses at the master's level is $825. An application fee, a one-time registration fee, and a per-course technology fee also apply.

## FINANCIAL AID

JIU students can apply for student loans from Sallie Mae or PLATO. Both loan options are available to U.S. citizens, U.S. nationals, or permanent U.S. residents.

Students may be qualified for financial assistance under the Montgomery GI Bill, the Dependents' Education Assistance Program, and the Veteran's Educational Assistance Program.

JIU also offers scholarships to limited groups of potential students. For a current list of available scholarships, students should visit JIU's Web site (address listed below).

## APPLYING

Student applications are accepted on a continual basis throughout the year. Courses start every month, and students may begin courses before their applications are complete. Course orientation is available at all times, entirely online.

---

### CONTACT

Jones International University
9697 East Mineral Avenue
Englewood, Colorado 80112
Telephone: 303-784-8904
        800-811-5663 (toll-free, U.S. only)
Fax: 303-784-8547
E-mail: info@international.edu
Web site: http://www.jonesinternational.edu

---

# Kansas State University

## *Division of Continuing Education*
## *Distance Education*

Manhattan, Kansas

*Kansas State University (KSU or K-State) was founded on February 16, 1863, as a land-grant institution under the Morrill Act. Originally located on the grounds of the old Bluemont Central College, which was chartered in 1858, the University was moved to its present site in 1875.*

*The 664-acre campus is in Manhattan, 125 miles west of Kansas City, via Interstate 70, in the rolling Flint Hills of northeast Kansas. The Salina campus, 70 miles west of Manhattan, was established through a merger of the former Kansas College of Technology with the University. This was made possible by an enactment of the 1991 Kansas Legislature.*

*KSU is accredited by the North Central Association of Colleges and Schools (NCA). One of the six universities governed by the Kansas Board of Regents, Kansas State University continues to fulfill its historic educational mission in teaching, research, and public service.*

## DISTANCE LEARNING PROGRAM

Kansas State University innovatively offers high-quality courses and degree programs to students who are not geographically located near the Manhattan campus. KSU utilizes cutting-edge technologies that enhance the learning environment and extend it far beyond the University's physical boundaries.

Adults across the country want to complete their education, advance their careers, or change their professions. Success requires dedication, self-direction, and perseverance on the part of the student. Distance education offered by K-State provides people with an opportunity to pursue these goals without leaving a current job or family. KSU offers bachelor's degrees and master's degrees at a distance.

## DELIVERY MEDIA

K-State offers courses through a variety of delivery methods. Most courses follow regular K-State semester dates. Some courses require minimum computer system requirements.

Kansas State University offers more than 250 courses per year through distance education. Courses are offered in a variety of subject areas and students can take many of these without enrolling in a degree program.

Delivery methods include use of videotapes and audiotapes, the World Wide Web, listservs, e-mail, discussion rooms, guided study, desktop video, community-based outreach courses, independent study, correspondence course work with other institutions, military training credit evaluations (based on American Council for Education Guidelines), portfolio/experiential credit assessments, standardized test taking, credit by examination and competency assessments, and petitions for special exams.

## PROGRAMS OF STUDY

K-State has been offering degree completion programs through distance education for more than twenty-five years. The goal of the Distance Education Degree Completion Programs is to help students complete the last two years of a Bachelor of Science degree. K-State staff is avail-

able to help students get started, stay directed, and earn a Bachelor of Science degree.

A student's requirements include a minimum of 30 KSU hours, with 20 of the last 30 hours earned from K-State. Students may transfer a maximum of 60 credit hours to KSU from a community college. The average student completes a bachelor's degree in two to six years; the pace is up to the student.

Bachelor's degree completion programs are offered in animal science and industry, general business, food science and industry, interdisciplinary social science, early childhood education (limited to Kansas), and course work leading to a degree in dietetics.

Master's degree programs offered include agribusiness, industrial/organizational psychology, family financial planning, electrical engineering, civil engineering, chemical engineering, software engineering, and engineering management.

## SPECIAL PROGRAMS

Certificate/endorsement programs are also offered. These programs include a food science certificate program, English as a second language (ESL) endorsement (limited to Kansas), and early childhood education (limited to Kansas).

K-State is a member of Service Members Opportunity College for the SOCAD-2 flexible-degree network. This network guarantees worldwide transfer of credit for military personnel who take courses from participating colleges and universities.

## STUDENT SERVICES

Each person in the Bachelor's Degree Completion Program receives individual advising. A program of study is developed to meet the specific needs of each student.

Library services are available to students enrolled in degree completion programs. A K-State library services facilitator helps students access materials in the K-State library. For more information, students should visit the library Web site at http://www.ksu.edu/dce/as/library/.

Financial aid is available for students seeking degrees. More information may be found at http://www.dce.ksu.edu/dce/division/finaid.html.

The Division of Continuing Education student handbook is available on the Web at http://www.dce.ksu/edu/dce/division/studenthandbook.html.

The technical support help desk can provide a variety of technical support services once a student is enrolled in a distance education course and has paid the media fee. For information about the help desk, students should visit the Web site at http://online.ksu.edu/support/.

## FACULTY

Kansas State University is an accredited institution offering credit courses through distance education. Distance education courses are taught by faculty members who teach K-State on-campus courses.

## ADMISSION

Each distance education degree program has specific admission requirements and procedures. Bachelor's degree completion programs require an application fee of $30. Admission information is available for each program at the Web address listed below.

## TUITION AND FEES

Course fees are set by the Kansas Board of Regents and vary from year to year. In 2001–02, undergraduate tuition is $102 per credit hour. Graduate tuition is $146 per credit hour. Students pay an additional media fee and other fees.

## FINANCIAL AID

Students may be eligible for financial aid for distance education courses if federal requirements are met, they are admitted and enrolled in a degree program in Kansas State University, and they are enrolled in a minimum of 6 credit hours of Kansas State University course work. Each student is assigned a financial aid adviser.

The Maurine Allison O'Bannon Scholarship, perpetuating the memory of Maurine Allison O'Bannon at Kansas State University, provides $375 to undergraduate students and $450 to graduate students who are in degree

programs at KSU and enrolled in Division of Continuing Education courses.

The Dorothy Thompson Scholarship is a memorial scholarship of approximately $400 per semester. The recipient must be a new or continuing nontraditional student who desires to complete a degree program at K-State, demonstrate financial need, and be a U.S. citizen. Preference is given to undergraduate students, enrolled in at least 12 hours, who have an interested in law or public service and a goal of developing or influencing public policy.

The Robert F. Sykes Scholarship honors Robert F. Sykes and funds a scholarship for a graduate of an accredited college of engineering who is pursuing a graduate degree in civil engineering or engineering management at Kansas State University via distance education.

## APPLYING

The application process for each program varies. For complete information on a specific program, students can access the Web site at the address listed below or contact the Division of Continuing Education at 785-532-5687 or 800-622-2KSU (toll-free) or e-mail academic-services@dce.ksu.edu.

---

**CONTACT**

Division of Continuing Education
Kansas State University
13 College Court Building
Manhattan, Kansas 66506-6002
Telephone: 785-532-5566
   800-432-8222 (toll-free)
Fax: 785-532-5637
E-mail: info@dce.ksu.edu
Web site: http://www.dce.ksu.edu

---

# Keller Graduate School of Management

## Online Education Center

Oakbrook Terrace, Illinois

*The mission of Keller Graduate School of Management is to provide working adults with high-quality, practitioner-oriented graduate management degree programs with an emphasis on excellence in teaching and service. To accomplish this mission, the School operates ethically, professionally, and respectfully toward the individual and seeks to consistently achieve the ideals on which it was founded. Keller was founded in Chicago in 1973 on the idea that the most important components of management education are effective teaching and student mastery of practical management skills. The first class had 7 full-time students. By the late seventies, some 900 Keller students were pursuing their M.B.A.s in an evening program introduced in 1974. Today, more than 9,000 participants across the country annually benefit from the School's educational offerings.*

*Keller Graduate School of Management is accredited by the Higher Learning Commission and a member of the North Central Association of Colleges and Schools, 30 North LaSalle Street, Chicago, Illinois 60602 (312-263-0456).*

## DISTANCE LEARNING PROGRAM

Keller's distance learning, delivered through the School's Online Education Center, integrates today's high-tech capabilities with Keller's proven educational methodologies. The result is solid education enhanced by the latest in interactive information technology—computer-mediated e-mail and threaded conversations, videotapes, and the Internet—that enables students to send and receive feedback from instructors as well as to participate in various group and team activities with fellow online students. Keller's Online Education Center serves approximately 1,000 participants per term.

## DELIVERY MEDIA

Computer-mediated e-mail, threaded conversations, videotapes, and the Internet enable students to send and receive feedback from instructors as well as participate in various group and team activities with fellow online students. Typical distance learning technologies at Keller include the School's online site (http://online.keller.edu), which is accessible twenty-four hours a day and offers course syllabi and assignments, Keller's virtual library, and other Web-based resources; text and course materials, available through Keller's online bookstore; CD-ROM companion disks; and study notes on "instructor lectures," which are on the Web site for student review

## PROGRAMS OF STUDY

Keller currently offers master's degree programs online in business administration (M.B.A.), accounting and financial management (M.A.F.M.), human resource management (M.H.R.M.), information systems management (M.I.S.M.), public administration (M.P.A.), project management (M.P.M.), and telecommunications management (M.T.M.). Graduate certificates are also available for students who wish to develop their expertise in accounting, business administration, educational management, electronic commerce, entrepreneurship, financial analysis, human resources, project management, health services, information systems, and telecommunications management without completing a degree.

The M.B.A. curriculum emphasizes the practical skills and concepts businesses demand from management professionals and blends management theory with real-world applications. Students in this sixteen-course program must complete five management core and five program-specific courses that provide a broad business background. For the remaining six courses, students can custom design a course of study that best suits their needs and interests. The M.A. F.M. program equips students with the knowledge, skills, and abilities necessary to function as accounting and financial managers in public accounting, industry, education, or government. Students must select an emphasis on CPA, CMA/CFM, or CFA professional certification exam preparation and must complete five advanced courses in accounting and finance, including an integrative capstone course focusing on solving real-world problems; three, four, or five professional exam-preparation courses; and one elective. In addition, six accounting foundation courses are required. The M.H.R.M. program prepares students to be more productive in their organizations by teaching concepts and skills needed to plan, control, and direct organizational requirements for effective and efficient use of human resources. Students must complete fifteen courses, including five management core and seven program-specific courses. Three elective courses must also be completed. The M.I.S.M. program equips students with the skills necessary to effectively function as systems analysts, IS project leaders, and MIS managers. Students in the fifteen-course program must complete five courses in management foundations, four in IS applications, two in IS tools, and three in project management as well as an integrative capstone course focused on solving a real-world problem. In addition, an IS technical foundation course is required of those without an IS background. The M.P.A. program focuses on developing concepts and skills necessary to become effective managers in organizations lying outside the boundaries of the traditional business environment. Course work blends theory and practice to build knowledge in key areas, such as leadership and human resources, budgeting and accounting, project management, information systems, public policy formulation and implementation, and public relations and marketing. Students pursue either a government management, nonprofit management, or public health management emphasis. Students electing the government or nonprofit management emphasis must complete fifteen courses: seven management core, six emphasis-specific, and two elective courses. One emphasis-specific course is a capstone project integrating material learned across key public administration areas. Students following the health management emphasis must complete seven management core courses, seven 3-credit-hour courses in the School of Health Management at Kirksville College of Osteopathic Medicine, the M.P.A. capstone course, and at least 7 credit hours of electives chosen from Keller and Kirksville offerings. The M.P.M. program is designed to help students develop the ability to solve real-world management problems and to exercise sound management judgment through practical application of project management concepts and skills. Students must successfully complete five-management core and six program-specific courses. Three elective courses must also be completed. The M.T.M. program is designed to equip students with managerial skills and technical knowledge of telecommunications to enable them to develop and manage telecommunications applications for the strategic benefit of their organizations. The fifteen required courses include four management core, seven program-specific, two technology applications, and two project management courses. In addition, a technical foundation course, which provides the fundamentals necessary for success in the program, is required of students without a telecommunications background.

In addition to fulfilling the graduation requirements for their specific programs, all students must also achieve a cumulative grade point average of 2.70 or higher (on a 4.0 scale) and fulfill all financial obligations to the School.

## STUDENT SERVICES

In addition to offering high-quality education via distance learning, Keller is committed to providing distance learning students with electronic access to the same full range of Keller support services available to students attending courses at Keller centers. Through the School's online site, students can access admission and registration information, career services information, academic advising, and financial aid information. Keller also maintains an online library, which provides access to resources such as full-text periodical databases and online short courses for self-instruction. These resources are available twenty-four hours a day, seven days a week, to Keller students and faculty and staff members.

## FACULTY

To ensure uniformity of content and rigor in course work delivered via Keller's Online Education Center, the School taps the expertise of seasoned faculty members who have undergone specialized training designed to prepare and present courses through distance learning and then supplement course delivery with a variety of online instructional activities, all of which focus squarely on course objectives.

## ADMISSION

For regular admission, applicants must hold a baccalaureate degree from a U.S. institution accredited by, or in candidacy status with, a regional accrediting agency recognized by the U.S. Department of Education (international applicants must hold a degree equivalent to a U.S. baccalaureate degree); ensure that the registrar receives an official transcript; pass the Graduate Management Admission Test, the Graduate Record Examinations, or Keller's alternative admission test; complete a personal interview with an admissions representative; and complete a written application. Applicants with postbaccalaureate degrees from accredited graduate schools must complete an application and an interview as well as document their degree. However, they do not need to take an admissions test.

Keller's admission process is streamlined, so students learn quickly whether they have been accepted.

## TUITION AND FEES

Online tuition per course is $1620. After acceptance into Keller, new students pay a $100 deposit, which is credited toward the first term's tuition. Tuition is payable in full at registration or in installments of two or three payments (with small handling fees for the latter two choices). Books and materials average $100 per course.

## FINANCIAL AID

Federal Stafford Loan Student Loan money is available to Keller students through the Federal Family Education Loan Program (FFELP).

### CONTACT

Keller Graduate School of
    Management
One Tower Lane, Suite 1140
Oakbrook Terrace, Illinois 60181
Telephone: 800-839-9009
Web site: http://online.keller.edu

# Kettering University

## Graduate Studies Department

Flint, Michigan

---

*In 1919, the Industrial Fellowship League of Flint sponsored a night school for employees of Flint-area industries. General Motors Corporation agreed to underwrite the school in 1926, and General Motors Institute was born. In 1982, GMI became independent of General Motors when the private corporation "GMI Engineering and Management Institute" was established. In January 1998, GMI changed its name to Kettering University. Kettering continues to maintain a close affiliation with industry, as it has throughout its history.*

*In the fall of 1982, Kettering began a video-based distance learning graduate program leading to a Master of Science in Manufacturing Management degree. In 1990, the Master of Science in Engineering degree was initiated.*

*Kettering's mission is to serve society by preparing leaders to meet the technical and managerial needs of business and industry in both the public and private sectors. World renowned as America's Co-op College, Kettering focuses on practice rather than theory. Continuing the University's long and continuous association with industry and the working student, the Master of Science degrees have a strong orientation toward manufacturing. Kettering is accredited by the Commission on Institutions of Higher Education of the North Central Association of Colleges and Schools.*

## DISTANCE LEARNING PROGRAM

Offering flexibility and convenience, these programs were developed to fit the needs of working professionals. The educational process consists of the on-campus presentation, off-campus communication of the courses via videotape, telephone contact, and evaluation.

The video-based program is offered at host companies where the number of prospective students is sufficient. The video-based distance learning program serves approximately 800 students at host companies throughout the United States, Canada, and Mexico. The program, however, is not a correspondence course. It is a rigorous, bona fide graduate program.

## DELIVERY MEDIA

Kettering's distance learning program is video-based, and tapes are delivered to established industrial learning centers throughout the United States. Industrial partners at the centers provide video equipment for classes. Students at the centers have telephone, facsimile, and e-mail access to the professors. A regular schedule of telephone communication is established in the first session of each course. For some courses, students may need access to a personal computer for homework.

## PROGRAMS OF STUDY

Kettering offers a Master of Science in Manufacturing Management (M.S.M.M.) degree requiring 54 credit hours, a Master of Science in Operations Manage-ment (M.S.O.M.) degree requiring 48 credit hours, and a Master of Science in Engineering (M.S.Eng.) degree that requires 45 credit hours. Students in the engineering program can specialize in mechanical design or manufacturing engineering.

The University designed the Master of Science programs to be terminal professional degrees for engineers and managers. The programs are particularly attractive to working professionals who want to extend and broaden their related skills. Although designed as terminal degrees, they also provide preparation for study at the doctoral level.

The M.S.M.M. degree is a part-time program designed to be completed in three years. Areas of study include finance and economics, quantitative skills and computer applications, management and administration, and manufacturing engineering.

The M.S.O.M. is a new degree program, designed to be completed in two years on a part-time basis. Offered as an interdisciplinary degree program, the M.S.O.M. combines the core areas of business administration with systems and process engineering skills from the engineering disciplines. The M.S.O.M. takes tools and methodologies most often associated with manufacturing and applies them to service industries and nonmanufacturing areas of manufacturing businesses. The M.S.Eng.

degree can be completed in one year full-time or two years on a part-time basis. There is no thesis required for any of the M.S. programs.

## CREDIT OPTIONS

Credits are earned by completing courses; however, students may transfer up to 9 credit hours. Credit may be transferred for grades of B or better upon the recommendation of the candidate's adviser and is granted only for completed graduate study. Credit is not given for experience.

Anyone interested in transfer credit should obtain an application for transfer credit from the Graduate Office.

## FACULTY

There are 41 full- and part-time professors teaching in the Graduate Studies program. Ninety-seven percent of the faculty members have doctoral or other terminal academic degrees.

## ADMISSION

No one is accepted into the program without a bachelor's degree. A bachelor's degree in engineering is required for the Master of Science in Engineering degree program. Requirements include a minimum 3.0 grade point average in undergraduate work, scores on the GRE, and two supervisor recommendations. The same requirements apply to on-campus and distance learning students.

## TUITION AND FEES

In 2000–01, graduate tuition was $1281 per 3-credit course. There is no application fee, but there is a $45 registration fee per course. The same fees apply to out-of-state students.

## APPLYING

Kettering accepts applications for fall and winter terms only. The deadline for fall application is July 15 and for winter, November 1.

---

### CONTACT

Betty Bedore
Coordinator, Graduate Publications
Office of Graduate Studies
Kettering University
1700 West Third Avenue
Flint, Michigan 48504-4898
Telephone: 810-762-7494
        888-464-4723 (toll-free)
Fax: 810-762-9935
E-mail: bbedore@kettering.edu
Web site: http://www.kettering.edu/official/acad/grad/

# Lakehead University

## Part-Time and Distance Education

Thunder Bay, Ontario, Canada

> *Lakehead University is committed to excellence and innovation in undergraduate and graduate teaching, service, research, and other scholarly activity. As part of this commitment, Lakehead is dedicated to a student-centered learning environment by offering a wide range of programs and courses that are designed to meet the needs of its students.*

## DISTANCE LEARNING PROGRAM

Through extensive offerings by the Office of Part-Time and Distance Education, the University extends its programming to students regionally, nationally, and internationally. Lakehead offers credit courses for University degrees and certificates with interactive, accessible, and convenient approaches. Ongoing development supports new course offerings annually.

## DELIVERY MEDIA

A variety of modes are used in distance education courses, including online delivery instruction, print materials, audioconferencing, videoconferencing, computer conferencing, and simulcast lectures. Lakehead's new Advanced Technology and Academic Centre, a state-of-the-art facility to be completed in 2002, will further enhance advanced technological applications to support "at-a-distance" course delivery.

## PROGRAMS OF STUDY

Students may choose from a wide range of programs and courses on- and off-campus. Four programs—the Bachelor of Arts (general program), Bachelor of Science in Nursing for registered nurses, Interdisciplinary Palliative Care Certificate Program, and Certificate in En-vironmental Management—may be completed entirely at a distance.

The Bachelor of Arts general program provides latitude in choice of courses within a general framework; courses are designed to acquaint students with a broad range of thought in the liberal arts. Fifteen full courses are required.

The Bachelor of Science in Nursing degree program is for registered nurses and uses multimode delivery methods, including print-packages, audioconferencing, and computer conferencing. Students are encouraged to contact the Office of Admissions and Recruitment for details regarding admission criteria and program requirements.

The objectives of the Certificate Program in Environmental Management are to develop an understanding of the basic premises, theories, and practices associated with environmental management and provide an insight into the ways in which management can be employed to mitigate a wide range of environmental problems.

Courses pertaining to the following programs are also offered annually: Bachelor of Education (professional development), Master of Education, and Joint Doctor of Philosophy in Educational Studies.

## SPECIAL PROGRAMS

Ongoing development of print, online, and online-enhanced courses (i.e., print materials and online tools such as bulletin boards and chat programs) provides for continuing variety in the selection of courses offered. For online courses, a PC with Windows 95/98 or a PowerMac, a connection to the Internet, and either Netscape 4.51 to 4.76 or Internet Explorer 4.0 to 5.5 are required. Online course selection varies. Current courses include Biomedical Ethics, Educational Administrative Theory, Environmental Assessment and Management, Foundations of Curriculum, Introduction to Interdisciplinary Palliative Care, Introductory Statistics, Introduction to Bio Mechanics, Policy Making in Education, Research and the Internet I and II, Sensation and Perception, Social Philosophy, and Social Psychology.

## STUDENT SERVICES

To assist students in their studies, Lakehead provides a wide range of student support services, including academic advising, library services, learning assistance, individual/peer tutoring, career planning, and personal counseling.

## CREDIT OPTIONS

When applying for admission with advanced standing, students must provide school records and official transcripts from the institutions attended. For information regarding the transfer of credits, students should contact the Office of Admissions and Recruitment at 807-343-8500 (fax: 807-343-8156; e-mail: liaison@lakeheadu.ca).

## FACULTY

Lakehead University has 260 faculty members as well as sessional lecturers appointed by academic units. Approximately 30 faculty members and sessional lecturers are appointed annually as instructors of distance education courses.

## ADMISSION

Admission to Lakehead University is necessary for registration in distance education courses. Applicants are encouraged to visit Lakehead's Web site or contact the Office of Admissions and Recruitment regarding specific program requirements.

## TUITION AND FEES

The 2001–02 tuition fees for undergraduate degree programs are $797.60 (excluding education) per full-course and $398.80 (excluding education) per half-course for Canadian residents and landed immigrants and $1734 per full-course and $867 per half-course for nonresidents on a student visa. For graduate degree programs, the fees are $1948.80 per full-course and $974.40 per half-course for Canadian residents and landed immigrants and $3600 per full-course and per $1800 half-course for nonresidents on a student visa.

## FINANCIAL AID

Students are encouraged to contact the Financial Aid Office regarding scholarships, bursaries, and financial assistance programs (telephone: 807-343-8206; fax: 807-346-7760; e-mail: financial.aid@lakeheadu.ca).

## APPLYING

Full descriptions of programs and courses are available on the University's Web site. Application forms for distance education courses may be obtained by contacting the Office of Part-Time and Distance Education.

---

### CONTACT

Lakehead University
Office of Part-Time
    and Distance Education
Regional Centre 0009
955 Oliver Road
Thunder Bay, Ontario P7B 5E1
Canada
Telephone: 807-346-7730
Fax: 807-343-8008
E-mail: parttime@lakeheadu.ca
Web site: http://www.lakeheadu.ca

# Lakeland College

## Lakeland College Online

Sheboygan, Wisconsin

*Lakeland College, an independent four-year liberal arts institution in Sheboygan, Wisconsin, was founded in 1862 to provide higher education opportunities for Wisconsin's new frontiersmen. Lakeland became an early adopter of the distance learning concept when, in 1978, it established its first lifelong learning satellite campus. This program has since grown to include ten locations throughout Wisconsin. In 1997, continuing its innovation in education, Lakeland became a world leader in online education and one of the few fully accredited colleges and universities nationwide that offer full bachelor's degrees totally online.*

*Located about 50 miles north of Milwaukee, Lakeland has an enrollment of more than 4,000 students in its on-campus undergraduate and graduate, lifelong learning, international, and electronically delivered online programs. All Lakeland courses and programs are fully accredited by the North Central Association of Colleges and Schools.*

## DISTANCE LEARNING PROGRAM

Lakeland offers complete bachelor's degrees in five majors. Courses are conducted online from start to finish, including all prerequisites, and are delivered entirely at each student's convenience. The same fully accredited courses and degrees as those offered on-site are available. More than 2,500 students from across the country and overseas register annually.

## DELIVERY MEDIA

Through national online educational services provider and leader Convene, Lakeland College Online uses a Web-based platform, IZIO, that allows students to participate in an online system orientation and to communicate at their convenience with the College, faculty members, and fellow students. Minimum hardware requirements are an IBM or 100 percent–compatible computer with a Pentium processor and 32 mb RAM, a 150-meg hard drive, and a 56k modem. Recommended specifications are a Pentium II–class computer (200 Mhz or higher) with 128 mb RAM;

Windows 95, 98, or NT; and a 10-gig hard drive. As the course delivery software is Web-based and requires students to spend significant amounts of time online, a dedicated modem or high-speed (DSL or cable modem) Internet access are recommended.

## PROGRAM OF STUDY

Each online course is 4 credits, and each program of study requires students to complete a minimum of 128 credits. Lakeland accepts many transfer credits from other schools. The business administration major encompasses the coordination, implementation, promotion, supervision, and direction of activities of organizations and individuals. Students who wish to be generalists in business find that this program meets their needs. The accounting program prepares students for positions in business and industry. Graduates who have completed the accounting major and a few additional courses are qualified to sit for the CPA and CMA examinations. The computer science program offers a sound basis for careers in information technology, business applications programming, and sys-

tems analysis. The marketing major explores consumers' needs and desires for products and services and their willingness to pay for them. Students are prepared for a wide variety of tasks in diverse areas. The specialized administration major is available to students who wish to complete a bachelor's degree after having completed an associate degree in certain technical fields.

## SPECIAL PROGRAMS

Lakeland is accredited to offer an online bachelor's degree in specialized administration that is available only to students with associate degrees in a technical field.

## STUDENT SERVICES

Lakeland College Online students can do all of the following online: apply for admission, register for classes, participate in chat groups, work with a personal admission counselor for academic advising, and access the Lakeland bookstore and library. Ordering textbooks online is encouraged. Students also have access to career planning and placement services.

## CREDIT OPTIONS

Online courses are 4 credits each. Online students may enroll in three courses without being accepted for admission. Students seeking a degree must be accepted for admission. Degree programs have a minimum requirement of 128 credits.

Lakeland accepts credits transferred from most other regionally accredited schools. Credits earned in the online program can be combined with credits earned on campus to complete a degree.

## FACULTY

Lakeland College Online courses are taught by both on-campus instructors and adjunct faculty members. Of the current online faculty members, 85 percent hold advanced academic degrees in their chosen discipline.

## ADMISSION

Students must have a high school diploma or its equivalent. They can take three courses before applying for admission. International students must apply for admission before taking classes. Nonnative speakers of English must have a minimum TOEFL score of 500.

## TUITION AND FEES

All students pay a $25 application fee. Tuition for all online courses is $725 per 4-credit undergraduate course. Books and other materials (computer course software or other required resources) are additional.

## FINANCIAL AID

Financial aid and/or military benefits are available to any qualifying student who is enrolled part-time (taking at least two courses) or full-time if they have already been accepted to Lakeland.

## APPLYING

Applications are available by e-mailing online@lakeland.edu, visiting the College's Web site at http://www.lakeland.edu, or calling toll-free at 888-LAKENET (525-3638). Students are asked to submit their application, nonrefundable application fee, and high school and postsecondary school transcripts. Students are notified of acceptance by e-mail. System orientation is offered completely online.

---

**CONTACT**

Katherine Van Sluys
Lakeland College Online
P.O. Box 359
Sheboygan, Wisconsin 53082-0359
Telephone: 888-LAKENET (525-3638, toll-free)
Fax: 920-565-1341
E-mail: vansluysks@lakeland.edu
Web site: http://www.lakeland.edu/online

 **Lesley University**

## *Distance Learning Programs*

### Cambridge, Massachusetts

*Lesley prepares women and men for professional careers in education, human services, management, and the arts. Since 1909, Lesley has been a leader and innovator in educating for professions that put people first. Lesley is accredited by the New England Association of Schools and Colleges.*

*Lesley offers interdisciplinary and self-designed graduate and undergraduate degree programs in a low- or no-residency format. Central to Lesley is the conviction that people matter, and that adult students bring knowledge and experience with them that can inform their own study and enrich the Lesley learning community.*

*The goal of a Lesley education is to empower students with the knowledge, skills, and practical experience they need to succeed as catalysts and leaders in their professions, their own lives, and the world in which they live.*

## DISTANCE LEARNING PROGRAM

Lesley offers self-designed study options at the graduate and undergraduate level. Students range in age from 24 to 70 and older, and come from all over the world. A pioneer in independent and interdisciplinary study, Lesley has been helping students develop their unique interests into practical, academic degree programs for nearly thirty years. These programs feature brief, intensive residencies in between faculty-guided self-study.

## DELIVERY MEDIA

Lesley's nontraditional degree programs combine the best of distance and face-to-face education by providing participation in a learning community, both virtual and actual, and intensive faculty guidance enhanced by technology. During the residency period, students attend workshops, presentations, and small study groups to plan their customized learning contracts. Students then study and work at home, submitting work-in-progress to faculty advisers. Advisers are always available via phone, e-mail, and through personal meeting. There is

no residency requirement for the independent study degree program.

## PROGRAMS OF STUDY

Students seeking an undergraduate degree from the Adult Baccalaureate College may combine a wide range of disciplines to shape their own specialization. Sample majors include, but are not limited to, psychology, counseling, human development, writing, women's and gender studies, environmental studies, history, art entrepreneurship, management, holistic health, and expressive therapy. Projects must include research, writing, a substantive biography, and expressive components. The Bachelor of Arts in behavioral science (B.A.B.S.), Bachelor of Arts in liberal studies (B.A.L.S.), and Bachelor of Science (B.S.) may be awarded. Students must complete a total of 128 credits in order to receive a bachelor's degree.

At the Graduate School of Arts and Social Sciences, Lesley's interdisciplinary and individualized programs are designed for those graduate students who want to put their personal stamp on their education. Flexibility of academic specialization is the hallmark

of these programs, and graduate students with unique interests that cross or reach past traditional academic disciplines can craft a personalized study program in consultation with Lesley's renowned faculty. An emphasis on integrating life and professional experiences with academic study informs all of Lesley's graduate programs. Students may earn the Master of Arts (M.A.) in independent study, the M.A. in interdisciplinary studies, the Master of Education (M.Ed.) in independent study, or the Certificate of Advanced Graduate Study (C.A.G.S.) in independent study.

## STUDENT SERVICES

Students in off-campus and independent study programs are given full and complete access to all administrative Student Services functions (Registrar, Bursar, Financial Aid, etc.) In addition, Lesley offers all students access to a variety of library resources including subject databases and other resources via the Internet, instructional materials, and telephone reference services. Lesley negotiates agreements with college and university libraries near national sites for library services to Lesley students. The Career Resource Center provides a wide range of career planning and job services. Students in both graduate and undergraduate programs may communicate with their faculty adviser by phone, mail, and e-mail and in person.

## CREDIT OPTIONS

At the undergraduate level, students may transfer up to 96 credits of approved course work. Credits must be from an accredited institution and a letter grade of C (2.0) or better must have been awarded. Undergraduate students may receive a total of 16 credits through the College Level Exam Program (CLEP). The combined total of test credits and transfer credits may not exceed 96 credits. Lesley also recognized the extensive work experience and life skills of its adult students. Accepted degree candidates who document and evaluate past experiences relevant to their course of study may petition to receive a maximum of 48 prior learning assessment credits.

## FACULTY

There are 11 full-time faculty members within the interdisciplinary and independent study programs at Lesley University, at both the undergraduate and graduate levels. All possess earned doctorates, and many specialize in adult learning. In addition to full-time faculty, Lesley employs adjunct faculty practitioners who offer real-world experience and specialization in a variety of disciplines. The student-faculty ratio for these programs is less than 7:1, and all students receive personalized attention from a dedicated faculty adviser.

## ADMISSION

Admission requirements and procedures vary by program and students are encouraged to identify a potential area of study in advance. Students should visit the Lesley admissions Web site (http://www.lesley. edu/grad_admiss.html) for a detailed description of admissions policies and procedures.

## TUITION AND FEES

Undergraduate tuition is $280 per credit for the 2001–02 academic year.

Graduate tuition is $475 per credit for the 2001–02 academic year.

## FINANCIAL AID

Financial aid is available to qualified students. To be considered for financial aid, students must complete a Free Application for Federal Student Aid and a Lesley University Financial Aid Request Form. Students should call 800-999-1959, Ext. 8710 for more details, or visit the Lesley financial aid Web site (http://www.lesley.edu/financial.html).

## APPLYING

Prospective students may request a bachelor's or master's application from the Office of Graduate and Adult Baccalaureate Admissions by calling 800-999-1959, Ext. 8300, or by downloading an application from the admissions Web site (http://www.lesley.edu/grad_admiss.html).

## CONTACT

Adult Baccalaureate College
Olive Silva, Program Advisor
29 Everett Street, Cambridge, MA 02138
Telephone: 800-999-1959, Ext. 8478 (toll-free)
Fax: 617-349-8420
E-mail: iro@mail.lesley.edu
Web site: http://www.lesley.edu/abc.html

Graduate School of Arts and Social Sciences
Lisa Lombardi, Program Advisor
29 Everett Street, Cambridge, MA 02138
Telephone: 800-999-1959 Ext. 8454 (toll-free)
Fax: 617-349-8124
E-mail: lombardi@mail.lesley.edu
Web site: http://www.lesley.edu/gsass.html

# Liberty University

## Distance Learning Program

Lynchburg, Virginia

> Liberty University (LU) was founded in 1971 as a private, independent, Christian, comprehensive institution. Since then, Liberty has grown to an enrollment of more than 17,000 students through its various undergraduate and graduate divisions, the Liberty Baptist Theological Seminary, the Distance Learning Program, and the Liberty Bible Institute. Liberty University is accredited by the Commission on Colleges of the Southern Association of Colleges and Schools to award associate, bachelor's, master's, and doctoral degrees.

## DISTANCE LEARNING PROGRAM

Liberty University offers adult students the opportunity to pursue an accredited college degree at a distance on the associate, bachelor's, master's, and doctoral levels. The University assists students who are pursuing a degree with such services as transcript evaluation, academic advising, and degree planning. Flexible semesters allow course work to begin at the most convenient times for students.

## DELIVERY MEDIA

Course lectures are presented both online and through prerecorded VHS videocassettes that students purchase along with the required print materials, such as books, workbooks, and study notes (all class materials are required to complete each class). Testing is monitored by a University-approved proctor. Students in need of class assistance may contact the assigned academic adviser, faculty member, and library services via phone, fax, e-mail, or regular mail.

## PROGRAMS OF STUDY

Liberty University's Distance Learning Program offers associate degrees in general studies and religion. Baccalaureate degrees are offered in business (accounting, finance, marketing, and management), multidisciplinary studies, psychology, and religion. Students may pursue a master's degree in professional counseling. A 36-credit-hour traditional program and a 48-credit-hour licensure program are available. Other master's degrees include the Master of Arts in religion, the Master of Divinity, the Master of Business Administration, and the Master of Education (M.Ed.). The M.Ed. programs are approved by the Virginia Department of Education for the licensure of school personnel. The LU School of Education also offers the Doctor of Education (Ed.D.), with an emphasis in educational leadership, through distance learning.

## SPECIAL PROGRAMS

Distance learners have access to library services, the campus computer network, e-mail services, academic advising, tutoring, and career placement assistance.

## CREDIT OPTIONS

Credit is given for courses completed at an accredited institution, provided the credit is appropriate to the curriculum chosen at Liberty University. Undergraduate students may also earn credit through standardized testing (CLEP, PEP, DANTES, and ICE), advanced placement, portfolio assessment, military training (ACE), and business training.

## FACULTY

There are 171 full-time and 104 part-time faculty members at Liberty University. Of the 171 full-time faculty members, 49 work specifically for the Distance Learning Program in either a full-time or part-time capacity. Faculty members who work with the Distance Learning Program hold a master's, doctorate, or other terminal degree in their field of specialty and are specially trained in order to ensure the best-quality education possible for students.

## ADMISSION

An application with a $35 nonrefundable fee must be submitted prior to admittance. All official transcripts must be sent to the Office of Admissions to determine acceptance to a degree program and the evaluation of credit.

## TUITION AND FEES

For the 2001–02 academic year, tuition for the undergraduate and seminary programs is $130 per semester hour. Military accelerated personnel in the program pay $180 per semester hour. Graduate tuition is $215 per semester hour. Course materials are a separate charge and must be purchased by the student through the University's supplier, MBS Direct (telephone: 800-325-3252, toll-free).

## FINANCIAL AID

Liberty offers a full range of state (Virginia Tuition Assistance Grant), federal (Pell Grant), and school-sponsored financial assistance programs for those enrolled as matriculated students. Forms for state and federal aid can be obtained through the University's Web site (address below) or by calling the Office of Admissions. All students who apply for a Federal Stafford Student Loan must submit a Free Application for Federal Student Aid (FAFSA).

## APPLYING

Distance learning students can apply for admission at any time of the year. Correspondence between the student and the University is conducted through the Office of Admissions. The student has 120 days from the enrollment date to complete each class.

### CONTACT

Dr. Patricia Thompson, Executive Director for
  Administrative and Academic Affairs
Distance Learning Program
Liberty University
1971 University Boulevard
Lynchburg, Virginia 24502
Telephone: 800-424-9595 (toll-free)
Fax: 800-628-7977 (toll-free)
E-mail: edpadmissions@liberty.edu
Web site: http://www.liberty.edu

# Loyola University Chicago

## *Mundelein College*
Chicago, Illinois

*Loyola University Chicago is one of the largest of the twenty-eight American Jesuit colleges and universities. Fully accredited by the North Central Association of Colleges and Schools and other relevant accrediting agencies, the University includes the Loyola University Medical Center and four other campuses, three in the Chicago metropolitan area and one in Rome, Italy. Loyola's nine colleges and schools have an enrollment of nearly 14,000 students. Loyola University Chicago emphasizes the Jesuit tradition of developing the intellectual, social, moral, and spiritual aspects of the individual.*

## DISTANCE LEARNING PROGRAM

Mundelein College is partnering with eCollege.com to provide online, Web-based courses. All courses offered in the Web-based format are the same as courses that are offered on campus and are taught by the regular full-time faculty members. All courses are as interactive and virtual as possible, including threaded discussions, collaborative learning opportunities, video streaming, and faculty member office hours. Students have a complete range of online services, including a bookstore, academic advising, and learning support.

## DELIVERY MEDIA

All courses offered are Web based. Communication with faculty members, fellow students, and other academic services is conducted primarily by e-mail. Admissions and registration are Web based. All assignments are "handed in" via e-mail.

To participate in the program, students must have a minimum of a Pentium I (or equivalent Macintosh) with modem and access to the Internet. Students should have a basic understanding of how to use e-mail and the Internet.

## PROGRAMS OF STUDY

The College offers complete certificate programs in computer science—Web development, networks and telecommunications, and database applications—at beginning and advanced levels. Students can begin these programs with a minimal understanding of computers and finish with the skills necessary to master the rapid development of computer technologies. Students with prior computer knowledge may earn a certificate in a particular area (Web development, networks and telecommunications, or database applications) more quickly or may widen the breadth of their knowledge through the professional certificate in computer science program. Students gain an understanding of Oracle and Microsoft software, Visual Basic, Java, C++, PERL, and Object-Oriented Programming. Students learn Internet programming, client/server applications, data mining, protocols and applications for data and voice communication, and the skills to build interactive Web services as distributed client/server systems.

The College also offers individual online courses in fields such as biology, math, philosophy, and physics.

For more information, students should visit the Web site at http://online.luc.edu or send e-mail to online@luc.edu.

## CREDIT OPTIONS

All courses are fully accredited and taken for credit. The courses can be transferred to other colleges and universities, or they can be used to complete either the bachelor's degree in computer science or the Bachelor of General and Integrative Studies at Loyola University Chicago. These courses can also be used to provide the prerequisite background to apply for either the master's degrees in computer science or the information systems management at Loyola.

## ADMISSION

Applicants for the certificate program must have graduated from high school or have passed the GED. There are no prerequisites or computer competency tests required. Initial course placement is determined from each student's computer background. Students should e-mail their questions about initial course placement to online@luc.edu.

## TUITION AND FEES

Tuition for the online courses is currently $371 per semester hour. Tuition is subject to change. Other general expenses include costs for books and software and vary depending on the course.

## APPLYING

Students can apply online at http://www.luc.edu/schools/mundelein/onlineapp.html. To apply, students need only to complete an application and include a one-time application fee of $25. No transcripts are required to apply for the certificate programs.

## CONTACT

Hilary Ward Schnadt
Mundelein College
Loyola University Chicago
6525 North Sheridan Road
Chicago, Illinois 60626
Telephone: 773-508-8004
E-mail: hschnad@luc.edu
Web site: http://online.luc.edu

# Lynn University

## Institute for Distance Learning (IDL)

Boca Raton, Florida

---

*Founded in 1962 and located in Boca Raton, Florida, Lynn University is a private coeducational institution whose primary purposes are education; the preservation, discovery, dissemination, and creative application of knowledge; and the preparation of its graduates with the academic foundation for lifelong learning. Service, scholarly activity that includes research, and ongoing professional development allow the faculty, in conjunction with the entire University community, to fulfill its purposes: facilitating student-centered learning and fostering the intellectual life of the University.*

## DISTANCE LEARNING PROGRAM

Lynn University delivers its academic programs at both the undergraduate and graduate levels to students who cannot participate in a traditional classroom-based environment at the main campus. The aim of the University is to be a global institution for the twenty-first century, where learners have access to higher learning opportunities independent of time schedules and geographical limitations.

The Institute for Distance Learning (IDL) is designed to facilitate educational opportunities for independent self-directed learners using technology and flexible delivery methods. The design and implementation of the programs recognizes and values prior skills and knowledge that mature global learners bring to the educational experience. In fulfilling its mission, the Institute delivers both credit and noncredit course work at the undergraduate and graduate levels to meet the needs of learners seeking academic work and lifelong learning experiences.

## DELIVERY MEDIA

IDL delivers interactive distance learning courses using Internet technology that allows interactions between faculty members and students, students and other students, and students and resources (e.g., books, journals, electronic library services, Internet resources). In addition, videoconferencing facilities are in place, which are used to deliver interactive courses from the main campus to remote sites.

## PROGRAMS OF STUDY

The Southern Association of Colleges and Schools (SACS) has approved Lynn University to offer complete distance learning degree programs via the Web. The Bachelor of Professional Studies (B.P.S.) degree, designed for adult learners seeking college credit for prior learning, is available entirely via course work over the Internet. Majors available are business, behavioral science, healthcare administration, and hospitality administration. In addition, numerous undergraduate, graduate, and doctoral courses, as well as noncredit courses and certificate courses in hospitality and aviation are available via the Web. The course listing is available at http://www.lynn.edu/academics/distance.

## SPECIAL PROGRAMS

IDL also facilitates a variety of noncredit accelerated courses that can be tailored to address corporate needs. Customized courses on selected topics in business and technology can be delivered via video conferencing or over the Web.

## CREDIT OPTIONS

Most online courses are 3 credits each. Courses with labs are 4 credits. Courses offered with less than 3 credits are identified in the catalog. Lynn University accepts transfer credits from most other regionally accredited schools. Credits earned in the online program can be combined with credits earned on campus to complete a degree.

## FACULTY

The faculty and staff members of IDL are highly qualified and committed to providing quality instruction and learning opportunities for self-directed learners. Along with excellent academic credentials, the faculty members are primarily practitioners in their fields of expertise, thus providing the theoretical context for the practical applications of the subject matter.

## ADMISSION

Admission to the Bachelor of Professional Studies degree program requires five years of post–high school professional work experience. This program is intended for adult learners who have significant skills and knowledge that can be translated into college-level credits. The process involves the participation in a 1-credit portfolio seminar where the development of a portfolio documenting the prior learning is explained and initiated. Students may earn a minimum of 3 credits, and up to 30 credits, through this process.

Individuals participating in any course work via distance learning (for college credit or certificate programs) must demonstrate proficiency in the use of Office 97 (minimum), e-mail composition and file attachments, and downloading and uploading files.

## TUITION AND FEES

The application fee for all new students is a one-time nonrefundable $50 fee. The tuition fees and registration fees follow the pricing established for the respective colleges and noncredit programs. For the 2001–02 academic year, the fees are as follows: undergraduate, $230 per credit hour (adult evening division); graduate, $440 per credit hour; doctoral, $555 per credit hour; noncredit, tuition varies with the individual courses. Students should check the Web site for further details. There is a registration fee of $30 at the beginning of each term enrolled; lab fees of $30 to $60, depending on the specific course; and a portfolio administration fee of $75 per credit placed on transcript. More information and specific details regarding fees are available in the catalog.

## FINANCIAL AID

Financial aid is available to any qualified Lynn student. For specific information, students should contact the financial aid office at 561-237-7941.

## APPLYING

Students wishing to enroll in undergraduate courses, noncredit courses, or in the Bachelor of Professional Studies degree program apply through the Center for Professional and Continuing Education (CPCE). The College of Graduate Studies administers graduate and doctoral courses.

Applications may be obtained on the University Web page at http://www.lynn.edu/academics/distance or by phone, fax, or e-mail.

### CONTACT

Mary L. Tebes, M.Ed.
Executive Director
Lynn University
The Institute for Distance Learning
3601 North Military Trail
Boca Raton, Florida 33431
Telephone: 561-237-7850
Fax: 561-237-7899
Web site: http://www.lynn.edu

# Marist College

## *School of Management*

Poughkeepsie, New York

---

*Marist College is an independent, coeducational liberal arts and sciences institution located in Poughkeepsie, New York. Marist began offering graduate programs in 1972 and currently serves some 750 graduate students from all over the world. Marist has been listed among the finest colleges and universities in America by both the* Barron's Guide *and* U.S. News & World Report.

*Marist is registered by the New York State Education Department, Office of Higher Education and the Professions, and is accredited by the Middle States Association of Colleges and Schools.*

## DISTANCE LEARNING PROGRAM

Marist College was among the nation's frontrunners in distance learning, offering working adults the unique opportunity to complete challenging graduate programs in business administration or public administration entirely on the Web. Professionals from as far away as Europe, India, and China currently count themselves as members of the Marist College family.

Marist's M.B.A. and M.P.A. programs provide an unsurpassed mix of quality, convenience, and flexibility. Students for whom regularly scheduled on-site classes are difficult may pursue equally challenging graduate course work at their convenience from anywhere in the world.

## DELIVERY MEDIA

Cutting-edge instructional technology enables students to interact extensively with their instructors and classmates. Communication is ongoing via e-mail, bulletin boards, group conference rooms, or private chat rooms.

A personal computer with a Pentium 166 processor, 32 megabytes of RAM, a 28.8 modem (56K recommended), and access to the World Wide Web

via MS Explorer, Netscape 4.0, or America Online browser version 4.0 are required for the program. In addition, to insure compatibility in reading attached files and sharing work with other classmates, Microsoft Office 97 is essential throughout the program.

## PROGRAMS OF STUDY

Marist's online graduate programs in business administration and public administration are available to students worldwide. Candidates for either program must meet the admissions criteria required by that program and must have completed a baccalaureate degree from an accredited institution. International applicants must submit official TOEFL and TWE scores for admission.

Marist's M.B.A. is designed to cultivate managers who are capable of effective decision-making in today's complex business environment. Emphasis is placed on the management process and the behavioral influences that significantly affect the success of modern organizations. Graduates of the program possess the strategic perspective necessary to identify opportunities and risks in a rapidly changing economic environment. Course requirements consist of a combination of foundation, core, and elective courses designed to de-

velop the professional analytical, communication, and leadership skills needed to keep pace with the competitive demands of a global economy.

Marist's M.P.A. is designed to provide students with the knowledge and skills necessary for effective public-sector and not-for-profit program management. The M.P.A. program consists of ten core courses and three subfield courses in which students do reading, research, and writing. Subfields include criminal justice administration, health services administration, human services administration, and nonprofit agency administration.

The curriculum stresses the ethical, legal, and social context of administration. Graduates are proficient in understanding and developing positive organizational behavior and effectively utilizing a full range of management and administrative techniques to solve problems, address issues, and lead important programs.

## CREDIT OPTIONS

The M.B.A. program requires a minimum of 30 credit hours, with a maximum of 51 credit hours, for the degree. Up to 21 credits of foundation courses may be waived, based on prior graduate or undergraduate study. Transfer credits are not applicable to foundation course work. Instead, particular foundation requirements are waived on the basis of prior study.

Transfer of credits into the M.B.A. or M.P.A. program requires the prior approval of the program director. Up to 6 graduate credits may be transferred from a regionally accredited graduate program to satisfy graduate core and/or elective requirements. Criteria considered in awarding transfer credit include the grade received (must be B or higher), the level of the course in the program at which it was taken, and the course content. Transfer credit is awarded for core courses only if the course is substantially equivalent to the Marist course requirement.

## FACULTY

The Marist College faculty comprises highly experienced credentialed educators, many of whom are skilled professionals with practical hands-on experience in corporate, government, not-for-profit, and community settings. Faculty members regularly take part in research, publishing, and consulting and are frequently called upon by various organizations and institutions for their expertise in their given academic areas.

## ADMISSION

The M.B.A. and M.P.A. programs are concerned with the interest, apti- tude, and capacity of a prospective student as indicated in the applicant's previous academic record, achievement on the Graduate Management Admission Test (GMAT) or Graduate Record Examinations (GRE), and past professional achievement and growth. Each applicant's credentials are evaluated on an individual basis. Specific requirements for admission and completion vary by program. At a minimum, all applicants must submit the graduate application, application fee, official transcripts, and current resume. A personal statement is required of M.P.A. candidates. The GMAT/GRE is waived for applicants who already hold a master's degree.

## TUITION AND FEES

Tuition for the 2001–02 academic year is $462 per credit, plus a $30 registration fee per semester and a one-time matriculation fee of $30. A $30 nonrefundable application fee is required at application.

## FINANCIAL AID

Marist College offers merit-based and need-based financial programs to assist students in meeting the cost of their graduate education. To be eligible, a student must be matriculated in a graduate program and maintain satisfactory academic progress each semester. Awards are made without reference to racial or ethnic origin, sex, age, religion, marital status, or disability. The process of applying for aid should begin in early summer for fall admittance and mid-fall for spring admittance.

## APPLYING

Student wishing to pursue their M.B.A. or M.P.A. on line should follow the same procedures as campus-based graduate students. All admissions documents should be sent directly to the Office of Graduate Admissions.

---

### CONTACT

Graduate Admissions
School of Graduate and Continuing Education
Marist College
North Road
Poughkeepsie, New York 12601
Telephone: 845-575-3800
      888-877-7900 (toll-free)
Fax: 845-575-3166
E-mail: graduate@marist.edu
Web site: http://www.Marist.edu/graduate

# Marywood University

## Off Campus Degree Program
Scranton, Pennsylvania

*Marywood University is an independent, comprehensive Catholic institution owned and sponsored by the Sisters, Servants of the Immaculate Heart of Mary, Scranton, Pennsylvania, and collaboratively staffed by lay and religious personnel. Its mission is the education of men and women of all ages in undergraduate, graduate, and continuing education programs. The University serves a wide range of students, both nationally and internationally, while maintaining a concern for the education of women, culturally diverse persons, and first-generation students. Committed to spiritual, ethical, and religious values and a tradition of service, Marywood University provides a framework that enables students to develop fully as persons and master the professional and leadership skills necessary for meeting human needs on regional and global levels.*

## DISTANCE LEARNING PROGRAM

Marywood University's Off Campus Degree Program, founded in 1975, is a challenging system of education designed to meet the needs of industrious adults. The flexible format of directed independent study allows for learning at a pace consistent with professional and personal responsibilities and goals. In 2000–01, eighty-two courses were offered through distance learning, with an enrollment of more than 150 students.

## DELIVERY MEDIA

Courses are delivered via print or online. Student and faculty communication links are by e-mail, a toll-free phone number, and fax.

## PROGRAMS OF STUDY

A candidate for a baccalaureate degree must present a minimum of 126 credits of college work that fulfill all general and departmental requirements; 60 of these credits must be earned at Marywood. Ordinarily, at least one half of the credits required for a major must be earned at Marywood University.

To fulfill graduation requirements, each degree-seeking student in the Off Campus Degree Program must complete a total of 12 credits in residency, including two courses in liberal arts and two courses in business.

Marywood University's Off Campus Degree Program offers the following baccalaureate degrees: Bachelor of Science in accounting (126 credits) and Bachelor of Science in business administration (126 credits), with concentrations in financial planning, management, and marketing.

## SPECIAL PROGRAMS

A certificate is a formally organized sequence of courses that culminates in a certificate of achievement in a particular area of study. Credits earned toward the certificate may be applied to an undergraduate degree program. Marywood University's School of Continuing Education offers the following certificate programs: certificate in comprehensive business skills (48 credits), certificate in office administration (24 credits), and a certificate in professional communications (24 credits).

Many students enroll in Marywood's Off Campus Degree Program with the goal of becoming a Certified Public Accountant. Students interested in sitting for the CPA examination should contact their respective state's Board of Accountancy for eligibility requirements. Many students also enroll in business and liberal arts courses for personal and/or professional enrichment.

## STUDENT SERVICES

Distance learners have access to library services, the campus computer network, e-mail services, academic advising, career placement assistance, and bookstore at a distance.

## CREDIT OPTIONS

Academic credits may be accepted in direct transfer from colleges and universities that have been approved by regional accrediting commissions. Academic credit or waivers for other college-level learning can be awarded through standardized testing such as CLEP, DANTES, and Advanced Placement. Some departments allow challenge exams and place-out exams. Students may be able to present a portfolio to show they have acquired college-level learning for particular courses.

Marywood subscribes to the standards for quality assurance set forth by the Council for Adult and Experiential Learning.

## FACULTY

All courses are developed and mentored by Marywood University faculty. All faculty members have advanced degrees; 57 percent are full-time and 43 percent are part-time.

## ADMISSION

The Undergraduate Admissions Committee establishes guidelines for admission to the undergraduate programs at Marywood University. All completed applications are reviewed under these guidelines, in compliance with the Marywood requirements of satisfactory academic preparation for college-level work.

## TUITION AND FEES

Tuition is $312 per credit. Additional costs include a text and materials fee ($95), a deferred payment fee ($30), a registration fee ($50 for 3 credits, $100 for 4 to 11 credits, $300 for 12 or more credits), and an application fee ($40).

## FINANCIAL AID

Marywood administers financial aid for degree-seeking students through grant and loan programs. Eligibility is based on demonstrated financial need. Federal Pell Grants and Stafford Loans may apply. Endowed scholarships are used to provide support, on the basis of academic excellence, to qualified students enrolled in the Off Campus Degree Program. Ninety-six percent of Marywood students receive some type of financial aid. More than $9 million in financial aid was awarded in the 2000–01 academic year.

## APPLYING

Individuals who wish to apply for admission must submit a completed application form, the required application fee, high school transcripts, college transcripts, and a personal/professional essay. Students who completed a GED must forward a copy of their GED certificate, which should include the GED score. International students must submit results for the Test of English as a Foreign Language (TOEFL).

---

### CONTACT

For further information, students should contact:

Off Campus Degree Program
Marywood University
2300 Adams Avenue
Scranton, Pennsylvania 18509
800-836-6940 (toll-free)
Fax: 570-961-4751
E-mail: OCDP@ac.marywood.edu
Web site: http://www.marywood.edu/disted/

---

# Massachusetts Institute of Technology

## Center for Advanced Educational Services (CAES)

Cambridge, Massachusetts

*The Massachusetts Institute of Technology (MIT) is one of the world's outstanding universities. MIT is independent, coeducational, and privately endowed. It is organized into five schools that contain twenty-one academic departments, as well as many interdepartmental programs, laboratories, and centers whose work extends beyond traditional departmental boundaries.*

*The Institute was founded in 1865 by William Barton Rogers. Rogers's philosophy envisioned a new kind of institution relevant to the times and the nation's needs, where students would be educated in the application as well as the acquisition of knowledge. A distinguished natural scientist, Rogers stressed the importance of basic research and believed that professional competence was best fostered by the coupling of teaching and research and attention to real-world problems.*

*MIT's programs in engineering, the sciences, economics, management, linguistics, architecture, and other areas are internationally recognized, and leaders in industry and government routinely draw on the expertise of MIT faculty members.*

## DISTANCE LEARNING PROGRAM

The Center for Advanced Educational Services (CAES) offers various undergraduate, graduate, and professional development educational programs via multimodal distance learning. These programs follow the Independent Learning model of distance learning delivery. Students are provided with a variety of materials, including a course guide and detailed syllabus, and access to a faculty member who provides guidance, answers questions, and evaluates their work. These programs are most often delivered in an asynchronous manner. Several of the Independent Learning programs may also be redistributed through CAES partnerships with leading universities and organizations around the world.

## DELIVERY MEDIA

Off-campus learners use a combination of communication technologies for course delivery, including videostreaming, satellite broadcast, the Internet, videotapes, CD-ROM, e-mail, and voicemail. The design of MIT's distance learning programs recognizes the benefits of student-professor and student-student interaction. Depending upon the specific programs, students may need access to one or more of the following: an e-mail account, the Internet, a videotape player, a satellite downlink, and/or a voicemail account. At a minimum, the Web-based portion of the programs requires a Pentium or Power Macintosh computer with a Web browser.

## PROGRAMS OF STUDY

Programs that exist through the Center for Advanced Educational Services range from entirely asynchronous independent learning to entirely synchronous group-based learning. At present, there is no degree-granting program offered through CAES. However, some of the courses can be taken for MIT credit that may later be applied toward a degree-granting program. There is a four course program in System Dynamics that is offered asynchronously over the Web via videostreaming and CD-ROM. A certificate is awarded upon successful completion of this off-campus program. Many of the courses offered are taken for professional development, and Continuing Education Units (CEUs) are available upon request. In addition, participants can take professional development courses at their home organizations synchronously through satellite broadcast, asynchronously through videostreaming, CD-ROM, videotapes, or lecture by an onsite visiting professor.

The Advanced Study Program provides lifelong learning opportunities for working professionals to be a part of the MIT experience. ASP courses delivered via distance learning technologies allow learners to participate remotely instead of coming to the MIT campus. Participants in the off-campus courses benefit through interaction with other learners in different locations by sharing concepts and ideas through online study groups and direct e-mail contact with faculty members. Presentation of program content is through videostreaming over the World Wide Web and is supplemented by print, CD-ROM, and Internet activity. More information on these programs can be found at http://caes.mit.edu/asp/off_campus/index.html.

Professional development (noncredit) courses that are offered through a joint venture with NTUC/PBS The Business and Technology Network provide continuous improvement opportunities for managers, consultants, engineers, and other knowledge workers. More information on these programs can be found at http://www-caes/programs/index.html.

The Professional Institute (PI) can bring its intensive, one-week, professional development courses to groups in organizations from industry, government, and academia. Taught by MIT faculty, topics over a span of engineering, science, management, and technology. For a full course listing, students may visit the Web at http://web.mit.edu/professional/summer/.

## CREDIT OPTIONS

Both credit and noncredit courses are offered through CAES. Distance learners participating in the Advanced Study Program are eligible to receive MIT credit, in addition to certificates of completion, for course work that is successfully completed. Students enrolled in professional development (noncredit) courses are eligible for certificates of participation after course requirements are met, and they may also receive Continuing Education Units (CEUs) upon request.

## FACULTY

The Center for Advanced Educational Services draws from all faculty members across the Institute. The MIT faculty numbers approximately 1,100, with a total teaching staff of more than 2,000.

## ADMISSION

Applicants seeking for-credit and professional development courses are accepted based upon their academic training and professional experience. In order to maintain the highest standards, CAES reserves the right to select those applicants whose qualifications and experiences suggest that they will receive the most benefit from a given program.

## TUITION AND FEES

Tuition is based on the type of academic credit provided. For-credit courses, delivered live through the Advanced Study Program, carry full MIT tuition for qualified candidates. Tuition for professional development courses, delivered through Strategic Partner Relationships and the Professional Institute, is based on arrangements established by those institutions.

## FINANCIAL AID

There is no financial aid provided for any of the distance learning programs offered through the Center for Advanced Educational Services.

## APPLYING

Individuals interested in applying to any of the CAES distance learning programs need to submit an application, along with the required supporting documents.

---

### CONTACT

Center for Advanced Educational Services
Massachusetts Institute of Technology
77 Massachusetts Avenue
Room 9-434
Cambridge, Massachusetts 02139-4307
Web site: http://www-caes.mit.edu
Advanced Study Program telephone: 617-253-6128
Advanced Study Program fax: 617-258-8831
E-mail: caes-courses@mit.edu
NTUC/PBS The Business and Technology Network
    telephone: 617-253-0247
NTUC/PBS The Business and Technology Network fax:
    617-253-8301
E-mail: caes-courses@mit.edu
Professional Institute telephone: 617-253-2101
Professional Institute fax: 617-253-8042
E-mail: professional-institute@mit.edu

# Mercy College

## MerLIN Online Learning Program

Dobbs Ferry, New York

*Mercy College is a comprehensive college that offers both undergraduate and graduate degrees. Founded in 1950 by the Sisters of Mercy, the College became independent in 1969. The guiding principles of the College are service to the community through the education of both traditional and nontraditional students, reliance on the liberal arts and sciences as the foundation of education, and dedication to teaching and the advancement of knowledge.*

*The College provides programs in the liberal arts and sciences as well as career-oriented, preprofessional, and professional degree programs; offers activities and services that enrich students' intellectual, social, personal, and work lives; and serves students with varied backgrounds through innovative learning methodologies and flexible scheduling at multiple locations.*

*Mercy College is accredited by the Middle States Association of Colleges and Schools and the New York State Board of Regents of the University of the State of New York. Programs in accounting, nursing, paralegal studies, physical and occupational therapy, social work, and veterinary technology have additional accreditations.*

## DISTANCE LEARNING PROGRAM

MerLIN, the Mercy Long-distance Instructional Network, offers courses without time restrictions, wherever students have access to the Internet. The same high-quality educational experience is available online as in Mercy's traditional courses. There are currently more than 3,000 students matriculated for degrees or taking individual courses in the program. Each semester more than 200 courses are offered through MerLIN. Courses are convenient but not self-paced. Faculty members have incorporated weekly online discussions and Web-based activities and assignments in their MerLIN courses. Students must be prepared to log in to their courses a minimum of three times per week.

## DELIVERY MEDIA

Learning and communication in a MerLIN course takes place in a group environment with other students and the professor. Courses incorporate streaming media for audio and video, hyperlinks, and synchronous chat. Students enrolling in a MerLIN course must have basic computer and Internet skills, including word processing, e-mail, and Web searching. Access to a computer with a modem (at least 56 kbs) as well as an Internet service provider is necessary. A sound card and speakers are recommended.

## PROGRAMS OF STUDY

The Online Learning Program offers the Master of Business Administration, Master of Science in banking, Master of Science in direct marketing, Master of Science in Internet business systems, Bachelor of Arts in business administration, Bachelor of Science in computer science, Bachelor of Science in psychology, and Associate of Arts or Associate of Science in liberal studies degrees.

## SPECIAL PROGRAMS

College services available to the traditional student are provided to distance learning students, including access to the College's library, computer support, and student advising. Individual and group tutoring is available to students studying via MerLIN. An online bookstore allows students to purchase all textbooks via the Internet.

## CREDIT OPTIONS

Mercy College accepts transfer credit from accredited institutions of higher education. In order to have credits accepted in transfer, a student must be matriculated in a degree program, and the credits must be applicable to degree requirements. A maximum of 75 credits may be accepted in transfer from an accredited two-year institution and a maximum of 90 credits from a four-year institution. Up to 18 credits can be earned through CLEP's general examinations. All evaluation of transcripts for the purpose of determining transferable credits is done on an individual basis.

## FACULTY

All Online Learning Program courses are taught by experienced Mercy College faculty members. More than 80 percent of the 75 faculty members teaching in the program have a doctorate or other terminal degree.

## ADMISSION

All students are required to have an admission interview. Individual arrangements can be made for telephone interviews. Some applicants may be required to take a placement examination. Individual graduate and undergraduate programs may have additional requirements.

## TUITION AND FEES

Undergraduate tuition in 2000–01 was $4250 per semester for 12 to 18 credits and $355 per credit for less than 12 credits. Graduate tuition was $435 per credit for M.B.A., M.S. in direct marketing, and M.S. in Internet business systems programs and $525 per credit for the M.S. in banking program. There is a $35 application fee for both undergraduate and graduate students.

## FINANCIAL AID

Financial assistance is available in the form of scholarships, grants, loans, and employment for eligible matriculated students. All students requesting financial assistance are requested to file the Free Application for Federal Student Aid (FAFSA). Mercy College awarded $310,000 in scholarships and $1.5 million in grants to students last year.

## APPLYING

Students may complete an application on line or on paper via mail. First-time distance learning students are required to take an online orientation course that covers the basics of how to log in, participate in courses, send and receive messages, and access the online resources.

---

### CONTACT

Joy Colelli, Vice President of Enrollment Management
Dr. Frank McCluskey, Director of Online Learning
Mercy College
555 Broadway
Dobbs Ferry, New York 10533
Telephone: 914-674-7527
Fax: 914-674-7382
E-mail: admission@mercynet.edu
Web site: http://merlin.mercynet.edu

# Michigan State University

East Lansing, Michigan

*Michigan State University (MSU), founded in 1855, is a research-intensive, land-grant university, offering more than 200 programs at the bachelor's through doctoral levels. It is one of only fifty-eight members of the prestigious American Association of Universities and is a member of the Big Ten Conference.*

*The core of MSU's land-grant tradition is the belief that educational opportunities should be available to the widest possible audience. Six guiding principles reflect the land-grant tradition at MSU: access to quality education, active learning, the generation of new knowledge, problem solving, diversity, and making people matter. A recently announced Technology Guarantee ensures students an intensive, quality-based technological experience (with increased interactive instruction) and lifelong access to MSU technology.*

*The University's outreach mission, involving all fourteen of its colleges, emphasizes the extension of knowledge to serve the needs of individuals, groups, and communities.*

## DISTANCE LEARNING PROGRAM

MSU serves more than 7,000 off-campus students per year in Michigan and around the world. Offerings expand each year. The University is fully accredited by the North Central Association of Colleges and Schools, and individual programs are accredited, where appropriate, by professional associations. MSU's distance education programs are offered by the individual academic departments, not by a centralized continuing education unit.

## DELIVERY MEDIA

MSU uses interactive and satellite television (usually viewed at local sites), the Internet, computer conferencing, and e-mail. Access to a computer with a modem is important. Students are in frequent contact with faculty members by e-mail and/or telephone.

## PROGRAMS OF STUDY

At sites throughout the state, MSU offers master's-level programs in adver-

tising, business, child development, community services, educational administration, family studies, nursing, public relations, social work, and teacher education.

The distance learning programs currently available worldwide include courses and programs offered via the MSU Virtual University in chemical engineering, computing, computer-aided design, criminal justice, education, facility management, hospitality management, international food law, Jewish studies, medical lab diagnostics, nursing, packaging, physics, social work, telecommunications, and watershed management.

Master's degree programs require a minimum of 30 semester credits (some require more), and bachelor's programs require 120 credits. Students who wish to take courses without or before applying to a degree program may enroll as Lifelong Education students.

## SPECIAL PROGRAMS

MSU's off-campus programs are fully equivalent to on-campus programs,

follow the same curriculum, have the same entrance and graduation requirements, and charge the same tuition and fees. Courses are almost always taught by the University's regular faculty, not by local adjuncts.

## STUDENT SERVICES

All students receive University e-mail accounts, access to the Internet, and library services. Off-campus students may seek research assistance or request books and articles by telephone, fax, or mail from the MSU libraries.

## CREDIT OPTIONS

MSU accepts transfer credit from accredited institutions but does not offer or accept credit through assessment of prior learning. Some College-Level Examination Program (CLEP) and Advanced Placement credits are accepted. For a bachelor's degree, at least 30 semester credits must be earned at MSU; for a master's degree, at least 21 credits of a 30-credit program must be earned at MSU.

## FACULTY

MSU has 2,614 faculty members, with 1,993 in the tenure system; about 2,392 are appointed on a full-time basis. Almost all MSU faculty members hold doctoral or other terminal degrees. The regular on-campus faculty members provide 90 percent of the instruction in off-campus programs.

## ADMISSION

Distance learners meet the same admission requirements as on-campus students. Admission to undergraduate programs is based on high school grade point average, recent trend of grades, other activities and accomplishments, SAT or ACT scores, and recommendations.

Master's program admission is based on grade point average for the third and fourth years of undergraduate study, other relevant accomplishments, GRE scores, recommendations, and the availability of space in the program.

## TUITION AND FEES

Upper division undergraduate tuition for 2000–01 was $169.75 for Michigan residents and $422.50 for out-of-state students; graduate tuition was $237 for Michigan residents and $479.50 for out-of-state students. Matriculation and technology fees were $301 for full-time students (5 or more credits) and $246 for part-time students. Lifelong Education students (those not in a degree program) paid $237 per credit hour (graduate or undergraduate, resident or nonresident), with no additional fees. There was an additional Engineering Program fee of $249 for full-time status and $138 for part-time status.

## FINANCIAL AID

Distance learners are eligible for the same federal and state and University financial aid programs as on-campus students, based on part-time or full-time status. However, graduate assistantships are usually not available to students at a distance because they involve on-campus assigned work hours. One fellowship program is targeted specifically for reentry adult students, the Mildred B. Erickson Fellowship.

## APPLYING

Applications are accepted all year. However, some programs only accept new students in the fall semester. In some programs, students must attend an orientation program either on campus or at a local site.

---

### CONTACT

For more information regarding Michigan State University Online Programs, students should visit the Web site at http://www.vu.msu.edu or call 800-500-1554.

---

# Montana State University–Billings

## *MSU–B Online Program*

Billings, Montana

*Established in 1927, Montana State University–Billings provides excellent instructional and learning opportunities in the arts and sciences as well as in its professional programs in business, technology, human services, rehabilitation, and education. MSU–Billings is accredited by the Northwest Association of Schools and Colleges, and its various degree programs, including teacher education, are accredited by other individual organizations. The University offers a wide variety of preprofessional and certification programs and awards degrees at the associate's, bachelor's, and master's levels to over 4000 students annually. For more information on Montana State University–Billings, please visit the University Web site.*

## DISTANCE LEARNING PROGRAM

Through the Montana State University–Billings (MSU–B) Online Program established in the fall of 1998, MSU–Billings is pleased to offer students an opportunity to take college courses via the Internet as a way of overcoming barriers of time and place. The program ensures that students can achieve their personal, professional, and academic goals while not having to sacrifice the other things that are important in their lives. The program currently offers more than ninety online courses annually to approximately 2,000 students.

## DELIVERY MEDIA

All MSU–B online classes are delivered entirely via the Internet using the sophisticated eCollege.com online course delivery system. This system provides for complete course content hosting whereby all readings, assignments, multimedia tutorials, audio and video streaming media, and instructional documents, are provided online. In addition to hosting course content, the delivery system provides access to a variety of cutting-edge online interaction tools including centralized e-mail, internet and course search tools, chat rooms, and threaded discussions, as well as an online journal, calendar, webliography, document sharing, exam manager, and gradebook features. Minimal hardware, software, and Internet connectivity requirements exist for all online classes.

## PROGRAMS OF STUDY

Students can select from three online degree programs through MSU–B Online, including the Bachelor of Science in Liberal Studies (B.S.L.S.) with a concentration in management and communication; a Bachelor of Arts (B.A.) degree with an organizational communication Major, and the B.S.L.S. degree completion program.

The B.S.L.S. degree completion program uses the same curriculum as the full four-year B.S.L.S. degree, but allows students to transfer or substitute prior academic coursework into the program while completing the thematic concentration in management and communication. To complete the B.S.L.S. degree or the B.S.L.S. degree completion program, individuals must earn a minimum of 120 credits with a cumulative grade point average of 2.0 or better. In addition, all students must satisfy the General Education requirements at MSU–Billings. MSU–Billings will accept transfer students with completed A.A. or A.S. degrees from other institutions as having fulfilled their MSU–Billings General Education requirements. Sudents must complete a minimum of 30 credits through MSU–Billings, 36 upper division credits, and 30 credits of the management and communications thematic concentration.

The organizational communication degree program shares the same requirements as the B.S.L.S. degree program described above, with the exception of a major core of online organizational communications classes instead of the 30-credit Management and Communication concentration. The degree is designed to educate students entering the fields of business and social service as managers, public relations personnel, trainers, human resource officers, and corporate communication staff. This option is excellent preparation for graduate study in communication or law.

## SPECIAL PROGRAMS

Through the MSU–B Online Program, students can complete the B.S.L.S. degree completion program described above, which offers a thematic concentration in management and communication. Additionally, students can complete a variety of courses in General Education Requirements typically required of undergraduate students.

## STUDENT SERVICES

MSU–B Online provides online students with access to all student services offered to MSU–Billings on-site students, including admissions, degree planning and advising, financial aid, ordering books and supplies, fee payment, library, twenty-four-hour online course HelpDesk support, and a number of other student support services. In addition, all students enrolling in an online class receive access to an online orientation course that is designed to help students learn how to use the course delivery system and to maximize their success and satisfaction in online learning.

## FACULTY

All 30 faculty members who teach classes online for the MSU–B Online Program are full-time faculty of Montana State University–Billings. In addition to teaching their online classes, these faculty members teach equivalent courses in traditional on-site classes. Eighty-six percent of the University's faculty members hold the highest degrees in their fields.

## ADMISSION

The requirements for admission to MSU–B are the same as those for individuals taking classes on-site.

## TUITION AND FEES

Tuition and fees for online classes are the same as for taking classes on-site with an additional $36 per credit nonrefundable fee that is assessed for all Internet courses. The exact rate of tuition and fees depends upon the number of credits taken and whether the student is a resident or nonresident of Montana.

## FINANCIAL AID

Financial aid is awarded to more than 60 percent of the University population—including students taking courses online—in the form of grants, scholarships, tuition waivers, employment, and loans.

## APPLYING

All students wishing to enroll in MSU–B Online courses or degree programs should do so by submitting an online application and registration form.

### CONTACT

Kirk Lacy
MSU–B Online Coordinator
College of Professional Studies
   and Lifelong Learning
Apsaruke Hall 116
Montana State University–Billings
1500 North 30th Street
Billings, Montana 59101
Telephone: 406-657-2294
            800-708-0068
            (toll-free)
Fax: 406-657-2254
E-mail: inquiry@msubonline.org
Web site: http://www.
   msubonline.org
or http://www.msubillings.edu

# Mountain State University/CJ-Direct

## Administration of Criminal Justice
## Bachelor of Science Degree Program

Beckley, West Virginia

---

*Mountain State University is a private, not-for-profit college located in southern West Virginia. As a graduate and baccalaureate degree-granting institution, Mountain State University continues to provide programs designed to lead to gainful employment for its graduates. Mountain State University remains committed to its founding philosophy that every individual should have the opportunity to obtain an education and maximize his or her human potential.*

## DISTANCE LEARNING PROGRAM

Mountain State University is partnered with CJ-Direct, a division of Compass Knowledge Group, to deliver an accredited, affordable, and convenient program designed specifically for the working adult. CJ-Direct uses the unique Compass Learning System™, along with the latest distance learning delivery technologies.

## DELIVERY MEDIA

The fulfillment of the program's learning objectives occurs through a combination of multimedia presentations and readings, Internet discussion sessions, and peer and professional support systems. The program uses the Internet to provide the highest quality and amount of peer/faculty interaction possible. All relevant course information is posted on the course Web site, a centralized interaction portal for students, instructors, facilitators, and program administrators.

## PROGRAM OF STUDY

To complete the degree, students must earn a total of 129 credit hours of course work consisting of a 48-credit administration of criminal justice component, a 33-credit career component, a 36-credit general education component, and a 12-credit elective component. Students are awarded credit for learning that took place during their work experiences, training programs, and previously completed college courses. The University also offers a variety of options for earning these credits.

## SPECIAL PROGRAMS

Mountain State University recognizes that adult learners are busy and have demanding work and family responsibilities. The Bachelor of Science program allows working professionals to complete the majority of their studies at their convenience, in the comfort of their own homes.

## STUDENT SERVICES

Each learner participates in a small group that is led by a qualified facilitator. This facilitator provides one-to-one mentoring and assists students in achieving the program's objectives. Students also participate in a virtual community, which includes chat sessions, message board postings, and e-mail correspondence with mentors and peers. In addition, students can receive personal research assistance via Mountain State University's online Academic Resources Library.

## CREDIT OPTIONS

The University offers a variety of options for earning credits, and students may gain credit by participating in any or all of them. Some of these options include (but are not limited to) transfer credit, independent study courses, prior learning assessment (PLA), and standardized examinations, such as CLEP and the advanced placement (AP) program.

## FACULTY

Faculty members possess graduate degrees and work experience in either the criminal justice or management fields. Facilitators (one-on-one student mentors) are criminal justice professionals with years of real-world experience.

## ADMISSION

To be admitted to the program, students must be at least 25 years old. Other admission requirements include a minimum of 40 transferable semester-credit hours earned through various credit options (or previous college credit), at least 2 years of work experience, and a transferable grade point average of 2.0 or better.

## TUITION AND FEES

Tuition for course work is $175 per credit ($170 per credit for independent study). Additional fees include a $25 application fee and $200 to $500 per semester for books. Other options for earning credit are available for nominal fees.

## FINANCIAL AID

A complete range of financial assistance programs from federal, state, institutional, and private agency sources are available to help students afford their educational goals. Mountain State University participates in funding such as Pell grants, Federal Supplemental Educational Opportunity Grants, and Stafford guaranteed loans. To download the appropriate forms, students should visit the Web site http://www.fafsa. ed.gov. Mountain State University's Federal Code number is 003807. In addition, Mountain State University courses are approved for U.S. Department of Veterans Affairs benefits.

## APPLYING

Students should submit a completed Mountain State University application for admission, a $25 application fee, and a resume and cover letter. A completed application also includes official transcripts/educational records for all previous institutions attended (including military transcript DD214) and standardized test scores (CLEP, DANTES, etc.).

---

**CONTACT**

Michael Adams
Admissions Advisor
2704 Rew Circle, Suite 105
Ocoee, Florida 34761
800-645-5078 (toll-free)
Fax: 407-573-2015
E-mail: Cwheatley@compassknowledge.com
Web site: http://www.cj-direct.com
http://www.compassknowledge.com.

---

# National American University

## *Distance Learning Program*

Rapid City, South Dakota

*Since 1941, National American University (NAU) has been serving the needs of adult students. In keeping with that mission, the University began to offer courses online in 1996. Since then, National American University has been approved to offer full-degree programs via the online format. National American University's innovative approach to student services emphasizes personal contact and 24-hour service to ensure the success of its students. Highly personalized attention and a full range of student services are available to every online student. Online courses at National American University provide students with a unique learning experience. Through highly interactive classes, students communicate frequently with instructors and classmates from around the world.*

## DISTANCE LEARNING PROGRAM

Asynchronous courses, bachelor's degree programs, and professional diplomas are available on line through National American University's Distance Learning Program. Online degree programs include applied management, business administration, and information technology. Professional diploma programs include e-commerce, Webmaster studies, and Microsoft network management. National American University is accredited by the Commission on Institutions of Higher Education of the North Central Association of Colleges and Schools.

## DELIVERY MEDIA

Utilizing evolving technology, professional instructors provide students with an interactive learning environment that surpasses the boundaries of the traditional classroom. Students accessing courses through the Internet explore sites on the virtual campus, such as the study carrel, the lecture hall, and the student union. Students receive information concerning learning objectives, course content, and assignments to be completed on line. Through asynchronous discussion, students engage in educational dialogue with instructors and peers at times convenient to their own schedules.

To make the students' online learning experience as successful as possible, National American University recommends the following hardware and software configurations: Pentium processor or equivalent; a RAM of 16 Mb or better; Windows 95, 98, or NT; and an Internet browser. In addition, students need a word processor and access to e-mail.

## PROGRAMS OF STUDY

Students may complete individual courses or pursue a bachelor's degree in one of three academic disciplines: applied management, business administration, and information technology. Students can also pursue three professional diplomas: Microsoft network management, e-commerce, and Webmaster studies. Four terms are offered each year, with classes from eight to eleven weeks in length.

## SPECIAL PROGRAMS

National American University offers business and corporate clients customized programs in the areas of business and computers.

## STUDENT SERVICES

National American University offers a full range of student services for its online students. All online students are enrolled in a free online orientation, which introduces students to National American University's virtual campus. Students may utilize the online library 24 hours a day and may access resources such as ProQuest Direct, FirstSearch, Net Advantage, and Encyclopedia Americana Online.

For the convenience of online students, applications and registrations may also be completed on line. Academic advisers are available to assist applicants with quarterly academic advising and placement. The NAU bookstore offers students the opportunity to purchase textbooks and supplementary materials through the mail. Students who need additional help in their online courses can receive free online tutoring. Financial assistance services are provided through National American University's Financial Aid Office. Technical support is available to distance learning students 24 hours a day. For more information, students are encouraged to visit the catalog on the University's Web site (listed below).

## CREDIT OPTIONS

Credits earned at accredited business or technical schools, colleges, or universities may be transferred to National American University depending on comparability of subject matter and the applicability of the credit earned to the student's program. The student must have received a grade of C or better for each of the courses transferred. In addition, a student may obtain up to 50 percent of the required credit hours toward graduation from nontraditional methods, including experiential learning/portfolio credit awarded by National American University, evaluated corporate training certificates, work experience credit, and nontranscripted military training.

National American University also accepts credit earned through national standardized examinations, including the College-Level Examination Program (CLEP), the Defense Activity for Non-Traditional Education Support (DANTES), and the American College Testing Proficiency Examination Program (ACT PEP).

## FACULTY

National American University online faculty members are experienced professionals with both appropriate academic credentials and professional experience. All online faculty members receive extensive training in online course facilitation and are required to respond to student inquiries and assignments within 24 hours. The combination of cutting-edge technology and caring, concerned faculty members allows students to achieve more both academically and professionally.

## ADMISSION

Graduation from an accredited high school is a requirement for admis-sion. Those who have satisfied graduation requirements through the General Educational Development test (GED) are also eligible for admission. In addition, students enrolled in online courses must sign and return a self-directed learner/accountability statement to help ensure that the student understands the nature and requirements of online course work.

## TUITION AND FEES

Tuition and fees are due on the first day of each quarter unless advance arrangements are made. A commitment for tuition and fees is made for three academic quarters, subject to the current refund policy. Students may qualify for short-term financial assistance to complete their registration. Tuition for online courses is $200 per credit hour. Select information technology courses have a separate fee schedule.

## FINANCIAL AID

Financial aid is available to those who qualify. Financial aid advisers are available to assist students through the process of applying for financial aid. It is suggested that students check with their companies to determine the availability of financial assistance.

## APPLYING

On-campus students enrolling in online courses must follow the same procedures (listed in the University catalog) as do other students taking courses on campus. Students enrolling in National American University's online courses must complete an application for admission (available on line), submit an original high school transcript or a certificate of GED and all college transcripts, complete a self-directed learner statement, and submit an application fee of $25.

Students whose native language is not English are required to provide a TOEFL score of at least 500. TOEFL scores should be forwarded directly from ETS and must be less than two years old. For more information on TOEFL, students should contact ETS at 609-921-9000 or at http://www.toefl.org.

International applicants must also complete an admissions application and return it with the $45 application fee and a $100 refundable tuition deposit; obtain official transcripts and diplomas from all high schools, colleges, and universities attended (non-English documents must be accompanied by certified English translations); and pay quarterly tuition and fees (in U.S. dollars) in advance.

**CONTACT**
Jeffrey Bailie, Director of Distance Learning Operations
Jon Outland, Associate Academic Dean for Distance
    Learning
Jim Leonard, Director of Technology
Distance Learning Program
National American University
321 Kansas City Street
Rapid City, South Dakota 57701
Telephone: 800-843-8892 Ext. 4933 (toll-free)
Fax: 605-394-4871
E-mail: dladmissions@national.edu
Web site: http://www.national.edu

# Neumann College

## *neumannonline.org*

Aston, Pennsylvania

*Founded and sponsored by the Sisters of St. Francis of Philadelphia, Neumann College is a Catholic, coeducational institution of higher learning in the Franciscan tradition. The educational philosophy is based on the concepts that knowledge, while valuable in itself, is best used in the service of others and that learning is a lifelong process. The College offers undergraduate degrees in a broad variety of subjects, five graduate programs, and accelerated associate and bachelor's degree programs for adults. Faculty members bring to online courses the same commitment to personal attention that they exhibit in the classroom. A recent expansion of programs and services, coupled with the College's commitment to first-rate academic instruction and real-world career preparation, has caused Neumann's popularity to boom in recent years. The College's total enrollment stands at more that 1,660 students.*

## DISTANCE LEARNING PROGRAM

An implicit part of Neumann College's mission is that it recognizes its responsibility to offer educational programs that anticipate and respond to the changing needs of society. Neumannonline.org is particularly attractive to those students who are motivated self-starters and who enjoy a learning environment with no time constraints or distance barriers. A variety of courses are available each semester at http://www.neumannonline.org.

## DELIVERY MEDIA

Neumannonline.org is an integrated system that uses an interactive syllabus. Lectures are a combination of virtual lecture, real audio, and real video. Discussion groups, online chats, and threaded discussions provide collaboration between faculty members and students. E-mail and the message center are vehicles for communication and information. Students need access to a suitable multimedia computer with an Internet connection and an e-mail account, Internet Explorer or Netscape Navigator (version 4.0 or later), and

RealPlayer Basic. More details and a system checkup are available at http://www.neumannonline.org.

The online courses are offered via the eCollege.com system.

## PROGRAMS OF STUDY

Neumann College offers an Associate of Arts degree and majors leading to Bachelor of Arts and Bachelor of Science degrees.

Bachelor of Arts degree candidates may choose a major from the following: communication arts, early childhood/elementary education, English, international studies (dual degree with international business), liberal arts, political science, or psychology.

Bachelor of Science degree candidates may choose a major from the following: accounting, biological science, business administration, computer and information management, environmental studies and education, international business (dual degree with international studies), marketing, nursing, psychology, or sport management.

Neumann College also offers academic programs leading to Master of

Science degrees in education, nursing, pastoral care and counseling, sport management, and physical therapy.

## SPECIAL PROGRAMS

Neumann offers an Associate of Arts degree that can be completed entirely online. The program's special 6-credit courses (twice the standard 3-credit value) ensure that students make accelerated progress toward their degree, and online faculty members give students the personal attention they need to succeed. After meeting the Associate of Arts degree requirements, students can earn an accelerated bachelor's degree with just ten additional courses.

## STUDENT SERVICES

The mission of the Career Development Office is to promote a values-based approach to career and life planning, with opportunities for career exploration through community service activities, service learning, and internship and cooperative education experiences.

The Computer Center consists of four state-of-the art classrooms/labs and a central administrative office area. Neumann College has a local area network (LAN), which connects academic and Internet computer resources. This network consolidates a number of functions, such as printing, e-mail, and support for the instructional use of computers. Access to the Internet, Web browsing, and Neumann's Web site are also available.

The Learning Assistance Center enables students to meet Neumann's academic standards and successfully attain their personal educational goals. The center assists students with specific direction in the organization and writing of papers and research documentation, provides tutorial assistance, and aids in developing students' study and test-taking skills.

The Neumann College Library plays a crucial role in the learning experience of the student and in the teaching and researching needs of the faculty. The heart of the collection is available on Francis, Neumann College Library's online catalog, which lists the College's more than 76,000 books and more than 52,000 audiovisual materials. Neumann subscribes to approximately 1,700 periodicals, many of which are available online in full-text databases.

## CREDIT OPTIONS

The curriculum for the College's academic major is divided into four sections: core requirements, major requirements, allied requirements, and general electives. Traditional students are required to have 43 core credits, with a minimum of 30 credits in the academic major. Allied requirements vary from one major to another, and the general electives are designated courses of study that students may pursue to meet their needs or interests. The number of required general electives is based on the student's academic program.

Neumann College offers various supplemental ways of earning credits. Advanced Placement tests; challenge examinations; ACT, CLEP, and DANTES examinations; directed study; an independent study program; portfolio assessment; study abroad; and summer session courses are the various methods through which a student can earn credits.

## FACULTY

The Neumann College faculty consists of 53 full-time faculty members and 130 per-course faculty members, all of whom are dedicated to the intellectual and affective development of the students as well as to portraying the spirit and values of St. Francis of Assisi by developing a sense of responsibility, which fosters and respects diversity.

## ADMISSION

Admission to Neumann College is open to all students, regardless of race, religion, creed, or national origin. Distance learners must meet the same requirements as traditional college students. An application for admission to Neumann College can be accessed online at the Web address listed below.

## TUITION AND FEES

In 2001–02, part-time undergraduate tuition is $350 per credit. Graduate tuition is $440 per credit for all programs except physical therapy, which is $590 per credit. Various fees include a graduation fee of $80, a portfolio assessment application fee of $80, a liberal studies certificate fee of $25, and a transcript fee of $3. There is a late payment fine of $45 and a returned check penalty of $35.

## FINANCIAL AID

Neumann College accepts all financial aid forms. The College, however, recommends the Free Application for Federal Student Aid (FAFSA) because there is no fee required to process this form. More information about financial aid can be obtained by writing to or calling the Office of Admissions and Financial Aid (610-558-5521). The Neumann College Title IV code is 003988.

## APPLYING

Students who wish to apply to Neumann College may do so by following instructions found at the Web address listed below, or they may call the admissions office.

### CONTACT

Telephone: 610-558-5616
E-mail: inquiry@neumannonline.org
Web site: http://neumannonline.org

# New Jersey Institute of Technology

## Division of Continuing Professional Education
## Distance Learning—Extension Programs

Newark, New Jersey

*Founded in 1881, New Jersey Institute of Technology (NJIT) is New Jersey's technological research university. An international leader in scientific and technological education, NJIT educates students to become frontrunners in the global marketplace. The university seeks students who are seriously committed to education and can bring energy, creativity, and a practical outlook to solving today's pressing problems. The degree programs are demanding, rewarding, and highly regarded by employers.*

*Since publication in 1978 of* The Networked Nation: Human Communication via Computers, *by NJIT's Professors Murray Turrof and S. Roxanne Hiltz, the university has served as a leader in distance education. With four degree programs and six graduate certificate programs offered completely through distance learning, NJIT course work is made available to students regardless of their geographic location. For the adult professional, in particular, NJIT courses provide the flexibility and convenience needed to fit in with work, family, and community responsibilities. NJIT's customer-service orientation allows each student to receive the personal attention that is required for successful completion of a degree program or certificate.*

## DISTANCE LEARNING PROGRAM

Via distance learning, NJIT conducts full undergraduate and graduate degree programs, graduate certificates, and individual college courses using today's home electronics to provide the college experience. By virtue of the academic quality, focus, and advanced delivery format, NJIT helps adult men and women cross one bridge to knowledge acquisition leading to gainful employment.

## DELIVERY MEDIA

Today's home electronics can be used in a new way to pursue education. Through integration of the personal computer, streaming audio, streaming video, on-line chat, threaded discussion, videocassette recorder (VCR), television, and telephone, the classroom can be a student's home, office, or any place other than the college campus. Each NJIT course consists of two components: a telelecture conducted by NJIT faculty members and an electronic dis-

cussion through which students conduct dialogue with a mentor and other classmates at any time of the day or night. The medium of the telelecture is streaming video, streaming audio, or video (furnished as a set of stand-alone, leased videotapes that are shipped to the student's home or office for replaying in sequence).

## PROGRAMS OF STUDY

The university offers seven complete degree programs via distance learning with two new programs, the Master of Science in Internet Engineering and the Master of Science in Computer Engineering, coming soon. The 129-credit Bachelor of Arts in information systems program provides students with a solid foundation in applying the principles of computing and information systems to business and industrial problems and managerial decision making. The 127-credit Bachelor of Science in information systems program prepares students to integrate, design, deploy, and manage computing and telecom-

munication resources and services. Graduates are ready to contribute to the development and evolution of technology infrastructures in organizations.

The 134-credit Bachelor of Science in computer science program provides students with the most comprehensive treatment of computers, with considerable breadth and depth in computer science topics, the sciences, mathematics, and supporting interdisciplinary studies. Coming soon is the new 127-credit applied computing degree of Bachelor of Science in information technology. IT is the convergence of telecommunications and computing. The discipline addresses the integration, design, deployment, and management of computing and telecommunication resources and services, as well as the development of technology infrastructures in organizations.

The 36-credit Master of Science in Information Systems program has been designed to train individuals who can assume responsibility for analyzing and organizing the information needs and resources of an organization and develop systems to respond to those needs.

The 30-credit Master of Science in Engineering Management program has been designed to develop engineers and other technically trained individuals for leadership roles in technology-based, project-oriented enterprises. It provides individuals with the broad-based knowledge and skills to succeed as managers of organizations and of projects from conceptualization through implementation. The 30-credit Master of Science in professional and technical communication program prepares students for careers in the rapidly growing field of technical communication. This degree enables students to acquire an understanding of information technologies and to approach communication issues with new problem-solving skills.

In addition, students who wish to complete individual undergraduate or graduate courses in one or more of a dozen academic disciplines may enroll on a nonmatriculated basis.

## SPECIAL PROGRAMS

Through the Division of Continuing Professional Education, the administrative unit in which distance learning program is housed, NJIT offers several graduate-level certificates that are available in their entirety or in part via distance learning techniques, including e-commerce, computer networks, object-oriented design (C++), client/server architecture, project management, practice of technical communications, telecommunications networking, Internet applications development, and information systems design and development. Each certificate, worth 12 graduate credits, can be used as a springboard to advanced degree study at NJIT or elsewhere. Consisting of four courses, each certificate is in a topic area considered by today's corporations to be employable "hot tracks" through the year 2005.

## CREDIT OPTIONS

Students may be awarded transfer credit at the time of admission for courses that were completed at other institutions and are equivalent to courses offered by NJIT. A minimum grade of C must be earned in a course in order to receive transfer credit.

## FACULTY

Ninety-eight percent of NJIT's full-time faculty members hold the terminal degree in their field.

## ADMISSION

Admission policies for the NJIT distance learning programs follow the same admission criteria as do traditionally delivered NJIT academic programs. In general, admission on a nonmatriculated basis to an undergraduate course requires possession of a high school diploma or General Equivalency Degree. Admission as a nonmatriculated student to a graduate course requires possession, at minimum, of an undergraduate degree from an accredited college or university with a grade point average that meets NJIT academic department standards for regular admission as a Master of Science degree candidate. In general, an acceptable grade point average is no lower than a 2.8 on a 4.0 scale.

## TUITION AND FEES

In 2000–01, undergraduate tuition was $216 per credit for New Jersey residents and $434 per credit for nonresidents. Graduate tuition was $406 per credit for New Jersey residents and $558 per credit for nonresidents. Graduate certificate students pay in-state tuition regardless of location. Required supplemental fees, not including rental of video telelectures, totaled $247 for a 3-credit course taken during the 2000–01 academic year. Updated tuition and fees can be found online (http://www.njit.edu/cpe).

## FINANCIAL AID

NJIT's Office of Financial Aid provides counseling and administers loans, scholarships, and grants to qualified students. Federal and state programs and private, industrial, and university resources are utilized to support the university's financial aid programs.

## APPLYING

Students may apply on a nonmatriculated basis by mail, fax, or online (http://www.njit.edu/cpe). To apply for admission on a matriculated basis, students should contact the Office of Admissions at 973-596-3300 or 800-925-6548 (toll-free) to request a degree application or use the online matriculated application form (http://www.njit.edu).

---

### CONTACT
Division of Continuing Professional Education
New Jersey Institute of Technology
University Heights, New Jersey 07102-1982
Telephone: 973-596-3060
Fax: 973-596-3203
Web site: http://www.njit.edu/DL

---

# The New School

## New School Online University

New York, New York

*The New School was founded in 1919 as America's first university for adults. Over the years, it has grown into an accredited, degree-granting institution comprising seven divisions (The New School, the Graduate Faculty of Political and Social Science, the Robert J. Milano Graduate School of Management and Urban Policy, Parsons School of Design, Mannes College of Music, Eugene Lang College, and the School of Dramatic Arts). About 40,000 students attend the University annually, bringing a wide variety of cultures, perspectives, aspirations, priorities, interests, and talents. But the New School has never neglected its original mission: it continues to serve the intellectual, cultural, artistic, and professional needs and interests of adult students.*

## DISTANCE LEARNING PROGRAM

The New School Online University (NSOU) distance learning program first went online with seven non-credit courses in 1994. Since then, NSOU has grown into a full cyberspace campus, offering 300 courses each year for credit and non-credit, as well as master's-level courses and bachelor's degrees on line. NSOU courses are often sections of the same courses that are taught on the Greenwich Village campus and are created and led by the same distinguished faculty. The New School and its programs, including NSOU, are accredited by the Commission on Higher Education of the Middle States Association of Colleges and Schools and chartered as a university by the Regents of the University of the State of New York.

## DELIVERY MEDIA

NSOU courses are offered through interactive computer conferencing via the Internet's World Wide Web facility. Programs are asynchronous and fully interactive, meaning that students receive instruction, ask questions of the instructor and each other, discuss issues, and actively participate in the class, all from home or office. It is recommended that students acquire the highest-speed connection that they can afford (28.8 bps modem minimum) from their Internet Service Providers (ISPs), and guidelines are available for those students who need help in identifying and arranging for service from a local ISP. Students and faculty also need computers (PC or Mac) capable of running one of today's graphical Web browsers (Internet Explorer recommended).

## PROGRAMS OF STUDY

Credit, noncredit, and degree courses are offered in many curriculum areas, including the social sciences, humanities, writing, and communication. The New School's Bachelor of Arts degree in liberal arts is offered through NSOU. Students work closely with an academic adviser (on line) to clarify their educational objectives, assess intellectual strengths and weaknesses, evaluate past academic accomplishments, and then draw on the curriculum available through NSOU to design a program of study reflecting their individual needs and goals. The process of organizing and synthesizing his or her own education is the essential and ongoing responsibility of every New School student. Applicants to the online B.A. program must have completed 60 semester credits of course work at an accredited college prior to matriculation. In general, students are required to complete an additional 60 credits to graduate; more information may be obtained by sending e-mail to nsadmissions@newschool.edu. In addition to courses offered in fulfillment of B.A. requirements, students may study through NSOU for credits that may be applied to the New School's M.A. in Media Studies and several other graduate degrees.

## SPECIAL PROGRAMS

Almost all New School courses, including those offered through NSOU, are available for credit or noncredit registration. About half of the students study each semester not for credit but for personal enrichment or intellectual stimulation. A significant proportion of the remaining half study for general credit, which means that the credit earned is transferable to a degree program elsewhere. The balance of the students in NSOU study for credit to be applied to one of the University's degree programs (predominantly the New School B.A. and M.A. in Media Studies). Through its Institute for Professional Development (IPD), the New School's Distance Learning Program seeks to make courses, certificates, and degree programs available to employees through special arrangements with organizations and other employers; for more information, students may send e-mail to dialexec@dialnsa. edu. All New School distance learning students have access to the full range of facilities on the cyberspace campus, including faculty office hours, library support, an orientation center, and 24-hour technical support (on line and by telephone). There is also a full program of public events, performances, social gatherings—even the New School's unique art collection.

## CREDIT OPTIONS

For matriculated students, the academic credits earned upon successful completion of an NSOU course are applied toward degree requirements. Matriculants may earn credit for prior academic and other developmental work; specific information may be obtained by e-mail from advisors@dialnsa.edu. Students who are degree candidates at another college or university or have not yet entered an undergraduate degree program may register for general credit. Students receive academic credit for each course successfully completed. Students at other institutions should make arrangements for transfer of credit at their home institutions prior to registering for NSOU courses. Students may also elect to take online courses on a noncredit basis. The University does not maintain a permanent record of noncredit enrollment, although students may request a "Record of Attendance" should verification of enrollment be necessary. Students may send e-mail to advisors@dialnsa.edu for more information or clarification.

## FACULTY

Close to 700 of the New School's 1,800 instructors have completed the preparation required to teach on line.

In the core curriculum areas (humanities, social sciences, writing, and communication), about 68 percent of New School faculty members have earned the doctorate or other terminal degree in their fields of specialty.

## ADMISSION

General requirements for B.A. matriculants are that they have completed 60 semester credits at an accredited college and that they be at least 24 years of age. Specific information can be obtained by sending e-mail to nsadmissions@newschool. edu or calling 212-229-5630. Noncredit and general credit students may simply review course offerings and complete registration online at http:// www.dialnsa.edu at any time.

## TUITION AND FEES

For the 2001–02 academic year, matriculated students enrolled in the B.A. program pay $588 per credit; for those enrolled in the M.A. in Media Studies, the cost is $730 per credit. All degree students pay a $100 registration fee per term. General credit students pay $660 per credit for New School courses and $730 per credit for Parsons courses. General credit students pay a $60 registration fee per term. Noncredit tuition varies by course and is listed with each description. Some courses carry additional lab, materials, or other fees; these are also listed with each description. The noncredit registration fee is $10 per term.

## FINANCIAL AID

The New School offers a full range of state, federal, and New School–sponsored programs for students enrolled in degree programs, depending on the jurisdiction in which the NSOU student resides. Students at other institutions may be eligible for financial support from those institutions. Applicants must file the FAFSA form; this form may be obtained from the Financial Aid Office. No student should decide against applying to New School University for financial reasons. For specific information and assistance, students may send e-mail to finance@dialnsa. edu or call 212-229-8930.

## APPLYING

Students may send e-mail to nsadmissions@newschool.edu or call 212-229-5630 or 800-862-5039 (toll-free) to find out about online information sessions. All new students are required to participate in a weeklong, online orientation program.

---

**CONTACT**

Office of Admissions
    and Advising
The New School
66 West 12th Street, Room 401
New York, New York 10011
Telephone: 212-229-5630
800-862-5039 (toll-free)
Fax: 212-989-2928
E-mail: nsadmissions@newschool.
    edu
Web site: http://www.dialnsa.edu

# NYIT New York Institute of Technology

## Online Campus

Old Westbury, New York

New York Institute of Technology (NYIT) is a fully accredited, private, independent, nonsectarian, coeducational college that educates more than 10,000 undergraduate, graduate and professional students on three physical campuses—in Old Westbury and Central Islip, Long Island, and New York City, near Lincoln Center—and a virtual campus via the Internet. Founded in 1955, NYIT is committed to providing career-focused, technology-based education to all qualified students, and to providing educational opportunity to students who might otherwise be excluded from higher education due to their socioeconomic situations or status as nontraditional learners. More than 100 programs of study are available to NYIT students in traditional academic settings and through groundbreaking distance learning options. NYIT is also home to the New York College of Osteopathic Medicine (NYCOM), the only osteopathic medical school in New York State.

## DISTANCE LEARNING PROGRAM

New York Institute of Technology's Online Campus offers students the opportunity to earn an undergraduate or graduate degree via the Internet from NYIT, consistently ranked among the nation's finest colleges and universities by major publications. Only a computer, modem, and Internet service provider are required.

## DELIVERY MEDIA

NYIT's Online Campus uses a fully integrated Web application that allows text, graphics, audio, and multimedia activities. To access the Online Campus, students need a computer with a 486 or higher processor, a minimum 14.4bps modem, and a current Web browser. It is recommended that students use either Netscape Navigator or Microsoft Internet Explorer and download the most recent version of that software before beginning online courses.

## PROGRAMS OF STUDY

NYIT offers four undergraduate degrees and one graduate degree entirely online. Undergraduate programs include the college's core curriculum and concentrated preprofessional and professional courses in the area of study. Graduate programs offer advanced course work in the area of study that emphasizes solutions-based outcomes. All programs incorporate technology into all aspects of the curricula.

The Bachelor of Science in behavioral sciences prepares students for careers or graduate study in psychology, sociology, criminal justice, or community mental health.

The Bachelor of Science in business administration prepares students for careers or graduate study in business, including management, finance, marketing, e-commerce, and international business.

The Bachelor of Professional Studies in hospitality management prepares students for careers as leaders in the hospitality industries, including travel and tourism, business conferencing, and food and beverage services.

The Bachelor of Arts, Sciences, or Professional Studies in interdisciplinary studies allows students to design their own degree programs by combining a core curriculum with three concentration areas from a choice of sixteen in professional services, liberal arts, business, and physical, natural, and social sciences.

The Master of Science in energy management prepares students for careers as leaders in all aspects of energy management and usage, including environmental management, conservation, energy technology, and hazardous materials management.

## SPECIAL PROGRAMS

All NYIT students with a 2.5 GPA or above are eligible to take individual courses online through the Online Campus. Undergraduate courses are available in business, communication arts, computer science, economics, English, life sciences, mathematics, physics, social sciences, and speech; graduate courses are available in business administration and instructional technology.

## STUDENT SERVICES

All Online Campus students have access to on-campus facilities and are assigned student e-mail accounts. The NYIT libraries offer online access to a number of academic research and professional databases in such fields as education, engineering, architecture, and medicine, as well as general educational databases, including ProQuest Direct and SIRS Knowledge Source.

## CREDIT OPTIONS

NYIT offers a generous transfer credit policy to all students who have previous educational experience at accredited colleges and universities. Undergraduate students must complete a minimum of 30 credits at NYIT, with some individual programs requiring additional credits. Students transferring from a two-year school are eligible for a maximum of 70 transfer credits. Graduate students may be eligible to transfer up to 6 graduate credits if they are equivalent to courses in the NYIT program. NYIT also accepts CLEP, DANTES, and RCE.

## FACULTY

NYIT faculty members are both academic and professional experts in their fields. The majority possess the terminal degree for their disciplines, participate in research and professional development, and serve as professional mentors to their students.

## ADMISSION

Candidates for admission must possess a high-school diploma or equivalent, take the SAT or ACT, fill out an application form (available online) and pay a nonrefundable application fee of $50. Transfer students must forward copies of previous college transcripts. Online Campus students must choose a qualified proctor while taking online classes, and first-time online students must take a special course during their first semester.

## TUITION AND FEES

For the 2001–02 academic year, the undergraduate tuition is $470 per credit; graduate tuition is $545 per credit. Tuition cost is subject to change. For updates and additional fees, prospective students should visit the NYIT Web site, listed below.

## FINANCIAL AID

NYIT offers generous financial aid to all qualified students. Most financial aid options are available to Online Campus students. NYIT participates in federal and New York State programs including direct loans, TAP, and Pell, and offers a number of NYIT-exclusive scholarships for academic excellence, community service, and financial need. Prospective students should visit the NYIT Web site, listed below, for a complete list of finanacial aid options.

## APPLYING

Online Campus students must fill out an NYIT undergraduate or graduate application, which is available either via mail or on the NYIT Web site. A nonrefundable fee of $50 must accompany the application, which should be mailed back to the NYIT Office of Admissions.

---

### CONTACT

For information about the Online Campus, prospective students should contact:

Ms. Katie Lyons
Assistant Director of Admissions
New York Institute of Technology
P.O. Box 9029
Central Islip, New York 11722-9029
Telephone: 631-348-3050
E-mail: klyons@nyit.edu
Web site: http://www.nyit.edu

# North Carolina Agricultural and Technical State University

## Center for Distance Learning

Greensboro, North Carolina

eCollege.com  www.ecollege.com

*North Carolina Agricultural and Technical State University (NC A&T), a public, comprehensive, land-grant university, is accredited by the Commission on Colleges of the Southern Association of Colleges and Schools to award bachelor's, master's, and doctoral degrees. The University offers degree programs in technology, education, agriculture, and arts and sciences at the bachelor's and master's levels; in nursing and business at the bachelor's level only; and in electrical and mechanical engineering at the doctoral level. The University was established by an act of the General Assembly of North Carolina in 1891 as an agricultural and mechanical college and became a constituent institution of the University of North Carolina system in 1972. The mission statement of the University reads in part, "to . . . develop innovative instructional programs that will meet the needs of a diverse student body and the expectation of the various professions . . . to develop and maintain undergraduate and graduate programs of high academic quality and excellence."*

## DISTANCE LEARNING PROGRAM

Distance learning at NC A&T, administered in close cooperation with the academic departments, enables students to access courses and degree programs of the University at convenient sites and times. More than 600 people are currently taking classes on-site, via interactive video, and via Web-based instruction.

## DELIVERY MEDIA

As of fall 1999, courses are delivered on- and off-campus using two methods of delivery. Asynchronous instruction allows students to determine their own times for instruction. This form of instruction includes such learning tools as e-mail, listserves, and online discussion boards. Synchronous instruction requires the participation of all students at a set time. Some examples of synchronous instruction include computer conferencing and interactive video, which includes streaming video, audio, and graphics. Students and instructors also interact via group chatroom sessions and individual sessions.

## PROGRAMS OF STUDY

The Center for Distance Learning provides the opportunity for students taking courses online to work towards degrees in six programs. These programs include five Master of Science degrees in adult education, architectural engineering, instructional technology, health and physical education, and vocational/industrial education. The Center for Distance Learning also offers one Bachelor of Science degree in occupational safety and health. This program, which deals with occupational safety and health hazards, has proven popular with military organizations and business and factory employees.

In physical education, the M.S. degree/G license-teaching/administration option, a 33 semester-hour program, is offered via on-site, interactive video, and Web-based instruction. Students must take the 12 semester-hour physical education required core, 9 semester hours in the area of interest, 6 semester hours in education, and 6 semester hours of electives.

Adult education courses are offered via interactive video, on-site instruction, and Web-based instruction. The program of study consists of a professional core curriculum of 21 semester hours, with a minimum of 15 semester hours in a research or practice concentration. The concentration entails graduate research and cognate studies in an adult education specialty (thesis option) or an adult education practice concentration (nonthesis option). Practice concentrations are currently designed in community education, counseling, higher education, human resource development, and instructional technology.

Technological education courses are offered via Web-based and on-site instruction. The program requires at least 30 semester hours of graduate-level courses, which include a 12 semester-hour concentration in technology or vocational/industrial education courses, leading to the G license in technology education or trade and industrial education or to vocational education director.

Instructional technology courses are offered via Web-based instruction. The program requires at least 39 semester hours of graduate level courses. Distance learners can follow four tracks: business and industry, media coordinator, instructional technologist-computers, and instructional technologist-telecommunications.

## SPECIAL PROGRAMS

The Center for Distance Learning provides the opportunity for students taking courses online to work towards degrees in six programs. These programs include master's degrees in computer science, adult education, instructional technology, health and physical education, and reading education. Although these programs are still in the planning stages, students may take the available online courses and apply them towards their current degree program. Another program in the planning stages is a bachelor's degree in occupational safety and health.

## STUDENT SERVICES

Library services are available to distance learners through the online library Web site and on-site visits. Library orientation and bibliographic resources are posted on the Web site to help students locate materials for research. Students may also access various library holdings through this site. Students are issued student identification cards for obtaining access to library services at other institutions.

Academic advising information located on the online course Web site offers distance learning students the same resources found on campus. Advisement for distance learners is conducted via the Internet, e-mail, regular mail, telephone, interactive video, and on-site visits.

## CREDIT OPTIONS

The University allows 6 transfer credits (semester hours) from another accredited graduate program toward graduate degrees and up to 80 semester hours in transfer toward undergraduate degrees. Credit may be earned by examination for any undergraduate course for which a suitable examination has been adopted or prepared by the academic department. Credit may also be granted for the successful completion of standardized tests under the College Level Examination Program (CLEP) for specific approved courses.

## FACULTY

Twenty-eight full-time and 8 part-time faculty members teach in the distance learning programs. All of the full-time faculty members hold terminal degrees.

## ADMISSION

All distance learners must be formally admitted to the University. Distance learners must also meet the on-campus admissions requirements of the programs to which they are applying. Non-degree-seeking students may enroll in off-campus credit courses after special admissions to the University. Degree-seeking students may earn 9 semester hours off campus prior to admission. After completing the admissions process, all distance learners must complete the Distance Learning Agreement Form.

## TUITION AND FEES

In-state undergraduate students pay $33 per semester hour for tuition, an education technology fee of $8 per semester hour, and a student identification card fee of $5 per semester hour, for a total of $46 per semester hour. Out-of-state undergraduate students pay $125 per semester hour for tuition, an education technology fee of $8 per semester hour, and a student identification card fee of $5 per semester hour, for a total of $138 per semester hour.

In-state graduate students pay $50 per semester hour for tuition, an education technology fee of $10 per semester hour, and a student identification card fee of $5 per semester hour, for a total of $65 per semester hour. Out-of-state graduate students pay $125 per semester hour for tuition, an education technology fee of $10 per semester hour, and a student identification card fee of $5 per semester hour, for a total of $140 per semester hour.

## FINANCIAL AID

Distance learning students who qualify for financial aid may expect assistance through a variety of sources, which may include loans or grants. Typical sources of financial aid include Federal Pell Grants, state need-based grants, Federal Perkins Loans, and Federal Direct Student Loans. Distance learning tuition and fees do not apply to students who obtain financial aid. Detailed information pertaining to federal and state programs may be found in the *Student Financial Aid Handbook.* For financial aid information, students may contact the Student Financial Aid Office (336-334-7973).

## APPLYING

Distance learners may apply to the Office of Undergraduate Admissions for all undergraduate programs and to the School of Graduate Studies for all graduate programs. Undergraduate applicants must complete the undergraduate application, remit a $35 application fee, and have previous college and high school transcripts mailed to the undergraduate admissions office. SAT I scores (for those under age 24) also need to be submitted.

Applicants to programs within the School of Graduate Studies must complete the graduate application and remit a $35 application fee and three letters of recommendation. Required test scores from admissions examinations vary by department.

To enroll in a distance learning course, students need to contact the Center for Distance Learning for specific on-site, telephone, and online registration dates and times. No formal application process is necessary.

### CONTACT

Inquiries should be directed to:
Mrs. Patricia White, Student
    Services Coordinator
Center for Distance Learning
North Carolina Agricultural and
    Technical State University
1020 E. Wendover Avenue
Suite 202
Greensboro, North Carolina
    27411
Telephone: 336-256-0355 (office)
                888-498-6752 (toll-
                free)
Fax: 336-256-0357
E-mail: distance@ncat.edu
Web site: http://www.ncat.edu

# Northcentral University
## *Distance Learning*
### Prescott, Arizona

*Northcentral University (NCU) is dedicated to its motto, "We Put People First in Distance Learning." NCU is a private distance learning institution offering bachelor's, master's, and doctoral degrees in psychology and business. Arizona state law, rule R4-39-107(B), states that "to be provisionally licensed to operate degree programs or to grant degrees, an existing private, nonaccredited, degree-granting institution shall demonstrate reasonable and timely progress toward obtaining accreditation with an accrediting agency recognized by the United States Department of Education or the Council for Higher Education Accreditation. 'Reasonable and timely' means the continuous, diligent and successful pursuit of the various stages of accreditation within the time periods established by the accrediting agency and as determined by the board." NCU's Board of Directors is committed to obtaining regional accreditation. An NCA site evaluation team has recommended initial candidacy. More information is available on the school's Web site at http://www.ncu.edu.*

## DISTANCE LEARNING PROGRAM

Northcentral University provides a self-paced learning program in which faculty mentors serve as guides rather than lecturers. Enrollment is continuous so that students can arrange start dates for their convenience. Students are free to complete courses at any time within a four-month semester and are encouraged to advance to the next semester's courses ahead of schedule. Academic advisers and faculty mentors communicate one-on-one with students through voice or electronic contact. Students have access to NCU's Electronic Library Resource Center; the research librarian is available for assistance.

## DELIVERY MEDIA

Learners are advised and guided through the courses through direct, individual contact with faculty mentors via phone, fax, e-mail, and other electronic media. Each program is an organized process designed to meet educational objectives in the shortest time frame possible.

Upon enrolling in a course, the learner receives a syllabus and a course outline. Learners purchase books from local bookstores or online suppliers.

The purpose of active self-learning is to encourage the learner to apply knowledge acquired in the courses to practical situations and to use faculty mentors as resources and facilitators in the process of learning. The learner demonstrates mastery of the course material and its relevance by completing required assignments.

## PROGRAMS OF STUDY

NCU offers degree programs through distance learning in two recognized professional areas: business and technology and psychology. Many specializations are available so that students can tailor course work to their specific career or personal interests.

A bachelor's degree requires 120 semester units, with 48 units in general education. At least 40 units must be completed through NCU.

A master's degree requires 40 semester units beyond the bachelor's degree. NCU accepts up to 8 units for relevant graduate courses completed at an accredited college.

A doctoral degree requires 96 semester units beyond the bachelor's degree. NCU accepts up to 48 units for relevant graduate courses completed at an accredited college.

The Doctor of Philosophy (Ph.D.) program prepares learners for scholarship, systematic inquiry, and research. The degree requirements include 24 graduate units in dissertation preparation courses and the submission and defense of an acceptable dissertation. A dissertation handbook, clearly outlined procedures, and a helpful, interested faculty committee assist the learner. The dissertation process is demanding, but high academic recognition is the reward for rigorous effort and scholarship.

## SPECIAL PROGRAMS

Specializations available for graduate programs in business administration include applied computer science, criminal justice administration, financial management, health-care administration, human resources management, international business, management, management information systems, management of engineering and technology, and public administration.

Specializations in psychology include general psychology, industrial organizational psychology, and behavioral psychology/health medicine.

## STUDENT SERVICES

NCU recognizes that the life experiences, learning needs, and learning patterns of adults differ significantly from those of the traditional college student. NCU was designed as a new kind of university, where "we put people first in distance learning." NCU provides adult learners with an education comparable to the best that can be found at traditional campus-based institutions, at a more affordable cost and without being required to reside on campus. Students have the opportunity to learn at their own pace, at times and in places compatible with commitments of family, work, and leisure. In a supportive, collaborative learning environment, students acquire knowledge that is relevant to their lives and careers. Faculty members offer individual treatment, professional assessment, and timely feedback on performance. Modern technology enables students to access information and to confer with colleagues around the world. A learner advocate is available to help students understand the system.

## CREDIT OPTIONS

Payment options allow payment for the program either in full, by semester, or monthly. Service charges apply to multiple payment plans. All charges are enumerated on the enrollment agreement that is electronically accepted by both the learner and University.

## FACULTY

All faculty mentors have accredited graduate degrees; 75 percent have doctorate degrees. Many are active in professional practice as well as academic work.

## ADMISSION

Each learner at NCU must have an e-mail address with the capability to send and receive attachments and a Java-enabled browser to access the NCU Web site. Doctorate learners must have a PC camera.

For admission to a bachelor's program, students are required to have a high school diploma, GED, or their equivalent. A 450 TOEFL score is required for applicants for whom English is not the primary language.

For admission to a master's program, students must have a bachelor's degree from NCU or an accredited institution.

For admission to a doctorate program, students are required to have earned a master's degree or its equivalent from NCU or an accredited institution. A 500 TOEFL score is required for applicants to graduate programs whose primary language is not English.

## TUITION AND FEES

Tuition for the degree program is based on the number of units required at the rate of $165 per unit. Additional fees are assessed for ap-

plication evaluation, dissertation, adding or dropping courses, library or identification card replacement, and other specific items.

## FINANCIAL AID

NCU students qualify for SLM loans.

## APPLYING

To apply on line, students should go to the Web site listed below and fill out the application. Admissions screening counselors contact applicants to coordinate the fee, statement of intent, transcripts, and other documentation. Students who are merely seeking information should click on the "information only" icon to receive a bulletin and other information through the mail or call the toll-free telephone number listed below.

### CONTACT

Northcentral University
505 West Whipple Street
Prescott, Arizona 86301
Telephone: 928-541-7777
            800-903-9381
            (toll-free)
Fax: 928-541-7817
Web site: http://www.ncu.edu

# North Dakota State University

## *Division of Continuing Education*

Fargo, North Dakota

*Founded in 1890, North Dakota State University (NDSU) affirms its heritage as the land-grant institution of North Dakota. Located on the state's eastern border in Fargo, North Dakota's largest city, the University strives to be a leader in information systems, technology transfer, economic development, and lifelong learning. It encompasses a broad spectrum of curriculum offerings, scholarly activity, and service. NDSU is one of two major research universities in an 11-institution state university system, and is accredited by the North Central Association of Colleges and Secondary Schools (NCA).*

## DISTANCE LEARNING PROGRAM

Most distance learning opportunities are administered through the Division of Continuing Education. NDSU provides courses for undergraduate students, graduate students, and those seeking professional development. Courses are delivered through an array of distance delivery systems, including online, video- and print-based individual study, video conferencing, and any combination of these technologies. NDSU provides a high quality, convenient, and user-friendly environment for all of its distance education opportunities. A number of specialty courses and programs are in development. The most current information is at http://www.ndsu.edu/conted.

## DELIVERY MEDIA

NDSU supports a variety of distance delivery systems, including online, video- and print-based individual study, video conferencing, and any combination of these technologies. Technological support is available to individuals participating in courses. Students may interact with instructors via mail, telephone, e-mail, or fax. Students should have reasonably current computers, software, and browsers.

## PROGRAM OF STUDY

In 1974, NDSU offered its first distance learning course. Today, NDSU offers more than 100 distance learning courses. Many distance education courses at NDSU help individuals to become more specialized in their field of choice. Some examples of specialized courses offered through NDSU are forensic accounting, cardiovascular engineering, signal integrity, aircraft manufacturing, character education, and teacher development. Many courses are available for undergraduate credit, graduate credit, or may be taken for professional development. NDSU also offers courses for dual-credit. Dual-credit means high school juniors and seniors in good academic standing may take courses for high school credits and also earn simultaneous undergraduate college credit to jump-start their college education.

## SPECIAL PROGRAMS

In conjunction with several regional universities, NDSU offers a master's degree in family financial planning online. This unique collaborative degree allows students to take at least one class from each university and choose from which university they would like to receive their degree. Students have a wonderful opportunity to experience many universities through each university's online environment. Two additional master's programs, one in gerontology and the other in youth development, are in development. Also available through NDSU is a minor in aeromanufacturing (pending). This innovative minor option is a combination of manufacturing and aircraft content. The aeromanufacturing minor prepares individuals to work in the aviation industry, either in aircraft structural design and manufacturing or in support of aircraft operations.

## STUDENT SERVICES

Students taking courses from a distance have access to a wide array of electronic library materials.

## CREDIT OPTIONS

The Office of the Registrar determines all credits transferred into NDSU. Students may transfer credits from another institution or may earn credits through examinations, portfolio assessment, military training, or business training. NCA accreditation makes transfer of credits to other institutions easier.

## FACULTY

NDSU faculty members are very experienced in their fields and are dedicated to teaching distance education. Approximately 75 percent of Continuing Education faculty members who teach distance education hold a doctoral degree; the remaining hold an advanced degree.

## ADMISSION

All students enrolling in a Continuing Education course must be admitted to the University, either as degree-seeking or non-degree-seeking students. Requirements may differ. More information is available from the University.

## TUITION AND FEES

Tuition and fees vary. Generally, distance-based courses carry one fee. Current prices are on the website. There is also an application fee of $25 for undergraduate students and $30 for graduate students. All fees are subject to change without notice.

## FINANCIAL AID

Students may apply for financial aid by completing and submitting the Free Application for Federal Student Assistance (FAFSA). Other forms of financial aid may come from scholarships, loans, grants, or the student's employer.

## APPLYING

Students are encouraged to contact NDSU Continuing Education to obtain the application materials and/or to seek assistance with the application procedure.

### CONTACT

NDSU - Continuing Education
University Station
P.O. Box 5819
Fargo, North Dakota 58105
Telephone: 701-231-7015
800-726-1724
Fax: 701-231-7016
E-mail: ndsu_continuing-ed@ndsu.nodak.edu
Web site: http://www.ndsu.edu/conted

# Northeastern University

## OnLine and TV Distance Education Programs

Boston, Massachusetts

*Founded in 1898, Northeastern University's (NU) mission as a national, private, research university that is student-oriented, practice-oriented, and urban, is to provide individuals with the opportunity for upward mobility through excellence in education. For close to a century, cooperative education has been the keystone of Northeastern's uniqueness. Students are offered the opportunity to apply lessons of the classroom directly to the workplace through the co-op program.*

*Northeastern University's main campus is situated on 60 acres in Boston's Back Bay. The University offers seven undergraduate colleges, nine graduate and professional schools, two part-time undergraduate divisions, and a number of continuing and special education programs and institutes. Northeastern has a long history of serving the educational needs of nontraditional students.*

*Northeastern University is accredited by the New England Association of Schools and Colleges, Inc.*

## DISTANCE LEARNING PROGRAM

Network Northeastern, the distance learning unit, provides credit and noncredit programs to corporate, business and university sites, and individuals in the Commonwealth of Massachusetts and the United States through live, interactive television, videotape, and online programs. Since 1983, Network Northeastern has served thousands of students regionally and nationally as part of adult and continuing education unit at the University.

## DELIVERY MEDIA

For students located outside the Boston area, Northeastern University Online (NUOL) makes continuing education convenient and accessible. NUOL offers undergraduate and noncredit certificate programs entirely on line. Courses are asynchronous and accessible twenty-four hours a day. Students have e-mail and phone contact with their instructors and chat/conference sections of each online course. Students complete all of their work on line and are never required to attend class on campus.

## PROGRAMS OF STUDY

NUOL offers eight different complete certificate programs and one degree completion program. The technical communications Bachelor of Science degree with the track in technical writing for computer science prepares students for careers as technical writers in the computer industry. Certificates offered include advanced Web design, computer programming, database design and administration, Internet technologies (both Webmaster and Internet commerce tracks), and technical writing (undergraduate course credit). Data communications, Java developer studies, and Webmaster technology (noncredit) are also offered. Students can take selected courses, earn an entire certificate, and also use courses toward a degree program. Undergraduate courses can be used toward a given certificate or toward an undergraduate degree at Northeastern or transferred to another institution. The noncredit certificates carry CEU (continuing education unit) credit, but cannot be used toward a degree. For most programs, students can earn a certificate in a year or less.

Once registered in the online program, students have access to their courses twenty-four hours a day, seven days a week. Students work within the term they register but can often work at their own pace within the confines of the course syllabus. Regular contact with the instructor is encouraged and posted conferences for student discussion within the class are an integral part of the course program. Courses are offered four times a year—summer, fall, winter, and spring quarters. The program operates on an open-enrollment basis. For information about programs, schedule, and registration, students should visit the Web site at the address listed below.

## STUDENT SERVICES

Twenty-four hour a day access to courses is provided as well as a toll-free number for assistance with advising, registration, tuition payment, or other help. All registration for online courses is completed on line. Students may also contact instructors and order books in this manner.

## CREDIT OPTIONS

Students may take courses for credit or noncredit. Most certificate programs that offer undergraduate credit are designed to also be transferred into a related degree program. The number of transfer credits which can be allowed into an NU certificate varies by certificate. Students should check with Northeastern University regarding specific transfer restrictions.

## FACULTY

All online instructors are industry professionals who teach for the University part-time. Ninety-five percent of the online faculty members have master's degrees or higher.

## ADMISSION

Admission to the online program is on an open admissions basis. Students simply register and begin taking their courses.

## TUITION AND FEES

For academic year 2001–02, undergraduate courses are $740 per three-hour course or $995, $1030, and $1200 for noncredit courses.

## FINANCIAL AID

Students must be admitted to a degree program to qualify for financial aid. A student must be a U.S. citizen or eligible noncitizen. All students applying for aid must submit a Free Application for Federal Student Aid (FAFSA) to the Federal Student Aid program. Northeastern University also requires that a student complete an institutional application. A student should begin the process twelve weeks before the beginning of the quarter. To obtain an application, students should call the Office of Student Financial Services at 617-373-3190.

## APPLYING

Students should register online for courses at the Web site listed below. There is no application fee.

---

### CONTACT

Demet Yener
Assistant Director
Network Northeastern
Northeastern University
360 Huntington Avenue
328 CP
Boston, Massachusetts 02115
Telephone: 877-375-6865 (toll-free)
Fax: 617-373-5625
E-mail: d.yener@neu.edu
Web site: http://www.NUOL.edu

---

# Northern Arizona University

## Distributed Learning: Worldwide Campus

Flagstaff, Arizona

---

*Established in 1899, Northern Arizona University (NAU) has maintained a tradition of excellence over the past century, taking pride in its focus on academic excellence and combining highly respected career-oriented programs, a wide choice of majors, and an emphasis on liberal arts and close faculty-student interaction. With twenty-three campus locations throughout Arizona and a growing number of distance programs, NAU serves more than 20,000 students from all fifty states and sixty-three countries. The NAU mission is to provide educational opportunities in both residential and nonresidential environments as well as to offer instruction that employs a variety of strategies to support distance learning. NAU continues to lead in the preparation of Arizona teachers, the enrollment of Native American students, and nationally and internationally recognized programs within the health and hospitality professions as well as natural resources conservation and management.*

## DISTANCE LEARNING PROGRAM

With ten years of experience, NAU's distance learning program offers eight online degree and certificate programs, with more in the planning stages. The degree students earn online is the same accredited degree awarded to a campus-based student. Although every degree cannot be offered via distance technology, NAU works to meet the needs of its Web-based learners.

## DELIVERY MEDIA

NAU offers distance classes via the Web and Interactive Instructional Television (within Arizona). In conjunction with the DISH network, students can participate in satellite broadcast classes. All delivery methods allow the instructors and students to interact via e-mail or online chat rooms. Textbooks and materials are available through the NAU bookstore.

## PROGRAMS OF STUDY

Dedicated to providing all NAU students with a high-quality education, a degree received via distance technology is the same accredited degree awarded on the NAU campus, holding students and faculty members to the same standards of excellence. NAU currently offers eight degrees and certification programs through distance learning technology: Bachelor of Arts in liberal studies, parks and recreation management emphasis; Certification in Parks and Recreation Management; Bachelor of Applied Science, heath promotion; Bachelor of Science, hotel and restaurant management; Bachelor of Science in Dental Hygiene; Bachelor of Science in Nursing; Master of Education, educational technology; and Master of Engineering. Each of these programs of study was developed based on the needs of distance students.

## SPECIAL PROGRAMS

A member of the Arizona Regents University, NAU works in conjunction with Arizona State University and the University of Arizona to offer students access to courses and degrees not offered by NAU. Students select a home campus by which all services, including registration, are provided for the student. Students may earn credit from all three institutions, which transfer to degree programs at any one of the three universities.

Western Governor's University is an online university offering Web-based classes from a variety of educational institutions in sixteen states, Guam, and Canada. NAU is a provider of classes for WGU. Students enrolled in these classes are considered non-degree seeking for NAU purposes, though they may be earning a degree from WGU. Students pay 1½ times in-state tuition.

## STUDENT SERVICES

NAU distance students are eligible for a free e-mail account that provides electronic access to academic records, online registration, and other online student services. Academic advising is available to distance students either online or through NAU's toll-free number. Students who do not have a computer and live in Arizona can complete their class at one of the twenty-three NAU statewide computer labs.

## CREDIT OPTIONS

To be eligible for financial aid, students must be admitted to a degree or certification program. Classes may be taken for audit or professional development credit; however, space may be limited due to for-credit student demand. Most classes are evaluated with a letter-grade. However, some classes are offered on a pass/fail only basis. These classes are outlined in the current NAU undergraduate and graduate catalogs.

## FACULTY

Distance learning courses are developed and taught by NAU faculty members as well as highly qualified part-time instructors, more than 70 percent of whom hold a doctorate or other terminal degree in their field.

## ADMISSION

NAU has a rolling admissions policy. Program admission is required for some degrees and is indicated on the NAU Web site. There is a $45 graduate application fee and a $50 nonresident undergraduate application fee.

## TUITION AND FEES

Nonresident students taking only Web or satellite courses are eligible for a special reduced tuition rate of 1½ times in-state tuition. Some classes may have additional fees attached (students should see the online course catalog for those fees).

## FINANCIAL AID

The amount of financial aid awarded to students is based upon their need as computed from the Free Application for Federal Student Aid (FAFSA). Scholarships are awarded based on academic excellence as well as need. In the 2000–01 academic year, more than $70 million was available for financial aid programs. About 60 percent of NAU students receive some form of aid. Students requiring financial aid or other benefits must comply with deadlines.

## APPLYING

Undergraduate applicants must provide transcripts from high school and all higher education institutions attended. Graduate applicants must hold a baccalaureate degree from an accredited institution and provide transcripts of college course work. Students should refer to the NAU catalog for specific program requirements.

---

### CONTACT

Distributed Learning: Worldwide Campus
Northern Arizona University
P.O. Box 4117
Flagstaff, Arizona 86001
Telephone: 800-426-8315 (toll-free)
Fax: 520-523-1169
E-mail: worldwide.campus@nau.edu
Web site: http://www.nau.edu/statewide

# Northwestern College

## Center for Distance Education
St. Paul, Minnesota

*Northwestern College, founded in 1902, is an independent, Christian four-year college. It is accredited by the North Central Association of Colleges and Schools. It first offered distance learning courses in 1994. In 2000–01, the College offered twenty-six courses at a distance and had approximately 1000 new distance enrollments.*

## DISTANCE LEARNING PROGRAM

The Center for Distance Education (CDE) is at the forefront of delivering high quality, Christ-centered education in a flexible and convenient format. Distance Education's courses are developed by Northwestern College faculty members who are experts in their fields. Students come from all around the United States, as well as from many countries around the world. The CDE offers a certificate of Bible, a Bachelor of Arts in intercultural ministries, postsecondary enrollment options, and twenty-six courses in Bible, history, science, and general education that can be applied to the previously mentioned programs. CDE courses are accessible via the Internet from anywhere around the world and are ideally suited for missionaries or military personnel working overseas.

## DELIVERY MEDIA

The Center for Distance Education delivers all course materials to the student's home via regular mail. Course materials consist of the following media: videotapes, audiotapes, CD-ROMs, the World Wide Web, and print. Materials are sent out at the beginning of each semester. The following equipment may be required: a television, videocassette player, computer, and Internet access. Assignments and tests may be submitted via e-mail or through regular mail.

Most courses are print and video based. All CDE courses have a CourseSite on the Internet that is used for interaction between students and instructors through discussion forums; although varying degrees of participation are required in an online format. Students and teachers may meet in person or interact via regular mail, telephone, fax, e-mail, or the World-Wide Web; however, the primary mode of interaction is through written comments on tests and assignments.

## PROGRAMS OF STUDY

Through the Center for Distance Education, a student may complete undergraduate-level course work to obtain a certificate in Bible or a Bachelor of Arts degree in intercultural ministries. The certificate in Bible, also known as the 30/30 Plan, prepares students for Christian ministry through the completion of 30 credits in thirty months. The program provides in-depth training in Bible study and develops credentials for Christian ministry. All credits earned in the certificate program may be applied to a degree program at Northwestern. The degree in intercultural ministries is designed for students who have previously completed two years of postsecondary course work and are serious about full time ministry. While the major is targeted at those preparing for, or currently involved in missions endeavors, the Christian, whether abroad or at home, who de-

sires to understand more fully God's evangelistic purposes, will benefit from the intercultural ministries program. Degrees currently under development are an Associate of Arts and a Bachelor of Arts in biblical studies.

## SPECIAL PROGRAMS

The Post Secondary Enrollment Option (PSEO) is a program open to high-school juniors and seniors who are public-, private-, and home-schooled and who are residents of the State of Minnesota. This program allows high school students to take courses through Northwestern College's Center for Distance Education. Through PSEO, students may earn credit that applies to both high school and college. Credits earned under this program are applicable to degree programs at Northwestern or other institutions. The State of Minnesota pays tuition, book, and application fees.

## STUDENT SERVICES

Distance learners have access to library services, academic advising, tutoring, career placement assistance, and the bookstore at a distance. Northwestern College's Bernsten Resource Center aids distance students with research and resource acquisition for projects and papers. The CDE Web site contains helpful links to other sites related to biblical studies, church history, mission agencies, and reference resources.

## CREDIT OPTIONS

Students may transfer credits from another institution or may earn credits through examinations, portfolio assessment, life experience, or military training.

## FACULTY

There are approximately 10 full-time and 7 part-time faculty members involved in these programs. Of this faculty group, 100 percent hold advanced degrees. Ninety percent of the full-time faculty and 60 percent of the part-time faculty hold doctoral degrees.

## ADMISSION

In order to qualify for a certificate or degree program, students must meet the admission requirements of Northwestern College. Students should contact the Center for Distance Education for specific requirements. Students not seeking to earn credits toward a degree or a certificate are allowed to take up to 16 credits without formal admission to the college. PSEO applicants must have a composite ACT of 18 or higher, a letter of recommendation from a high school official, suitable scores on the state benchmark examination, as well as an ability to demonstrate competence in college-level work.

## TUITION AND FEES

There is a one-time, non-refundable $25 registration fee at the time of registration ($50 for ICM). Course fees are $200 per semester credit, plus a mandatory materials fee of $60 per course. Students enrolled in the Bible certificate and intercultural ministries programs receive a tuition discount that brings the cost to $180 per semester credit. Noncredit courses are $100 per course.

## FINANCIAL AID

Financial aid is available to distance learners.

## APPLYING

Information can be obtained either online or by contacting the Center of Distance Education at the address and telephone number listed below. Students may register by mail, fax, telephone, e-mail, World Wide Web, or in person. The process is simple: applicants must complete registration either online or on the form mailed to them, mail in the nonrefundable application fee to CDE, pay a tuition deposit, and arrange a payment plan.

---

### CONTACT

The Center for Distance Education
Northwestern College
3003 Snelling Avenue North
St. Paul, Minnesota 55113
Telephone: 651-631-5495
　　　　　　800-308-5495 (toll-free)
Fax: 651-631-5133
E-mail: distance@nwc.edu
Web site: http://www.distance.nwc.edu

---

# Norwich University

## *Vermont College*
Montpelier, Vermont

*A leader in innovative education tailored to the needs of its diverse student body, Norwich University is a comprehensive university that combines a wide range of brief-residency undergraduate and graduate degree programs on its Vermont College campus in Montpelier, Vermont, with a Corps of Cadets and traditional undergraduates on its Northfield, Vermont, campus. Now offering both undergraduate and graduate online options, Vermont College is also the first campus in the United States dedicated exclusively to brief-residency distance learning programs. The College enrolls more than 1,000 students from around the world. Students may spend from two days to two weeks on campus, studying in a community of learners who share similar interests, or they participate in vibrant online learning communities. Norwich University is accredited by the New England Association of Schools and Colleges.*

## DISTANCE LEARNING PROGRAM

Vermont College programs offer brief on-campus residencies; independent, self-designed study; one-to-one mentoring; flexible schedules; and academic excellence. Vermont College is located in Montpelier, Vermont, 35 miles south of Burlington International Airport. Boston, Massachusetts, and Montreal, Canada, are both an easy 3-hour drive via interstate highways. New York City, 300 miles south, is accessible by car, plane, train, or bus.

## DELIVERY MEDIA

Most programs require limited residency on the Montpelier or Brattleboro campuses. New College uses Internet technology to provide its distance learning programs, as does the graduate program's online option.

## PROGRAMS OF STUDY

Every degree program is carefully designed by the student and faculty members to meet the particular needs and goals of the student. The emphasis is on interdisciplinary, multicultural studies in the humanities and social sciences through a powerful integration of theory and practical application.

The undergraduate division offers two program options. The Adult Degree Program (ADP) offers a bachelor's degree in liberal studies that working students can earn in eighteen months to four years. Like all Vermont College programs, the ADP features flexible, individualized study and mentored instruction. New College, founded in 1997, is the newest undergraduate option at Norwich University. It offers a bachelor's degree in liberal studies for traditional-aged students that utilizes Internet technology.

Vermont College offers a variety of graduate programs as well. Since 1969, the Graduate Program has offered a Master of Arts (M.A.) with concentrations in humanities and social sciences that can be completed in a minimum of eighteen months through individually tailored study plans.

The Master of Arts in Art Therapy program offers the M.A.A.T. degree and features clinical training in the student's geographic area of choice throughout the United States and parts of Canada.

The newest graduate offering is the Master of Education (M.Ed.) degree. It is a part-time program that features areas of study in curriculum and instruction (including a teaching licensure option), educational leadership (including an administrative licensure option), guidance (including a guidance licensure option), and issues in education.

Established in 1981, the Master of Fine Arts in writing offers a two-year terminal degree for adult students and working writers, with concentrations in poetry, prose, and creative nonfiction.

The Master of Fine Arts in writing for children program offers a two-year terminal degree for adult students and working writers, with concentrations in picture book, middle grade, and young adult.

The Master of Fine Arts in visual art is a two-year terminal degree program for working artists, with areas of study that include painting, drawing, printmaking, sculpture, photography, craft as fine art, video/film, and nontraditional media.

The graduate division also offers a Certificate of Advanced Graduate Study, a postgraduate program that offers concentrations in school psychology, guidance counseling, community psychology, educational administration, leadership studies, and integrated studies.

## STUDENT SERVICES

Two comprehensive libraries, Kreitzberg Library on the Northfield campus and Gary Library on the Montpelier campus, support research and study. Because students study where they live, Vermont College has interlibrary loan arrangements with many schools and local libraries. The library collections are linked with automated catalogs that are accessible on campus and via personal computers from anywhere in the world.

## CREDIT OPTIONS

Credit and requirements for graduation vary by program. Students can contact Vermont College for specific credit option information.

## FACULTY

More than 150 scholars, artists, and writers form the faculty at Vermont College. The faculty members possess both outstanding academic and professional qualifications. Students study with faculty members during on-campus residencies, developing close working relationships and gaining insights that help them better shape their studies. Following the residency, students work one-to-one with faculty mentors throughout the ensuing term of study.

## ADMISSION

Admission requirements vary by program but rely on a variety of measures. Students are asked to send transcripts from previous education, professional references, and an essay detailing life experience and education goals. Students should contact the appropriate admissions counselor for detailed information.

## TUITION AND FEES

Tuition varies by program but ranges from $4525 to $6000 per semester.

Comprehensive fees include room and board for on-campus residencies. Students are responsible for travel to and from the campus as well as for books and materials necessary for their study.

## FINANCIAL AID

To be considered for financial aid, Vermont College requires students to complete a Free Application for Federal Student Aid (FAFSA). To request this form or to ask questions, students can contact the financial planning office (telephone: 800-336-6794 Ext. 8709). The financial aid process can take up to three months to complete.

## APPLYING

Applicants should contact the University for specific application information.

---

**CONTACT**

Office of Admissions
Vermont College
Montpelier, Vermont 05602
Telephone: 800-336-6794 (toll-free)
Fax: 802-828-8855
E-mail: vcadmis@norwich.edu
Web site: http://www.norwich.edu/vermontcollege

# Nova Southeastern University

## The School of Computer and Information Sciences

Fort Lauderdale, Florida

*A major force in educational innovation, the School of Computer and Information Sciences (SCIS) provides educational programs of distinction to prepare students for leadership roles in computer science, information systems, information science, and computing technology in education. It is distinguished by its ability to offer on-campus, online, and combined on-campus/online formats that enable professionals to pursue M.S., Ph.D., and Ed.D. degrees without career interruption. Ranked by* Forbes *magazine as one of the nation's top twenty cyber-universities, and listed in the* Princeton Review's *"The Best Distance Learning Graduate Schools," the School pioneered online graduate education with its creation of the first electronic classroom. It has been offering online graduate programs and programs with an online component since 1983. All four online M.S. programs are now part of the Southern Regional Electronic Campus (SREC). SCIS has more than 1,100 students. It conducts about 250 online graduate classes per year. It has online students in forty-six states and thirty-five other countries. Through its research, the School advances knowledge, improves professional practice, and contributes to understanding in the computer and information sciences. As part of its programs in computing technology in education, the School's faculty members and Ph.D. students conduct a considerable amount of research and experimentation in online learning environments, with emphasis on online pedagogy. Located on a beautiful 232-acre campus in Fort Lauderdale, Nova Southeastern University (NSU) serves approximately 23,000 students and is the largest independent institution of higher education in Florida. It ranks twenty-fifth in the size of its graduate programs among the 1,560 universities in the U.S. with graduate programs and tenth among independent universities. In addition to SCIS, NSU has an undergraduate college and graduate schools of medicine, dentistry, pharmacy, allied health, optometry, law, psychology, education, business, oceanography, and social and systemic studies. To date, the institution has produced approximately 63,000 alumni. Since 1971, NSU has enjoyed full accreditation by the Commission on Colleges of the Southern Association of Colleges and Schools.*

## DISTANCE LEARNING PROGRAM

All of SCIS's programs of study (four master's degree programs and five doctoral degree programs) are offered in distance learning formats. Online master's programs require no on-campus classroom attendance. Part-time students may complete the M.S. degree in eighteen months. Doctoral programs use one of two formats: cluster or institute. Cluster students attend four cluster meetings per year, held quarterly over an extended weekend (Friday, Saturday, and half-day Sunday) at the University. Cluster

terms start in March and September. Cluster weekends take place in March, June, September, and December. Institute students attend a weeklong institute twice a year at the University. Institutes are held in mid-January and mid-July at the start of each five-month term. Doctoral programs also have an online component. Clusters and institutes bring together students and faculty members for participation in courses, workshops, and dissertation counseling. Between meetings, students complete assignments, research papers, and projects and participate in online activities.

## DELIVERY MEDIA

Online activities involve the use of Web pages to access course materials, announcements, e-mail, the electronic library, and other information, plus a range of activities that facilitate frequent student-professor and student-student interaction. These may include online forums using threaded bulletin boards and chat rooms. In addition, the School provides a system that enables students to submit assignments online in multimedia formats and to receive their professors' online reviews of assignments in the same multimedia formats. Some online courses may include electronic classroom sessions. Students are provided computer accounts but must obtain their own Internet service providers and use their own computers. New students are provided an orientation on computer and software requirements, online access, online tools and methods, and library resources.

## PROGRAMS OF STUDY

The School offers programs leading to the M.S. degree in computer information systems, computer science, computing technology in education, and management information systems; the Ph.D. in computer information systems, computer science, computing technology in education, information systems, and information science; and the Ed.D. in computing technology in education. The M.S. requires 36 credit hours (thesis optional) and may be completed in eighteen months. An option for early admission into the doctoral program from the master's program is available. To earn the M.S. in eighteen months, the student must enroll in two courses each term. Terms are twelve weeks long, and there are four terms each year. Master's terms start in September, January, April, and July. Doctoral programs require 64 credits, including eight 3-credit courses, four 4-credit projects, and the dissertation. They may be completed in three years. The Ph.D. in computer science and computer information systems are offered in cluster format. Doctoral programs in information systems, information science, and computing technology in education are offered in cluster and institute formats. Students attend clusters or institutes during the first two years of the program while completing course work. Cluster terms start in March and September. Institute terms start in January and July.

## SPECIAL PROGRAMS

SCIS has four special programs: (1) a graduate certificate program in information resources management for federal employees, (2) a graduate certificate program in information systems for corporations, (3) short course and workshop programs for several companies, and (4) a comprehensive series of technology-oriented courses that have been approved for teacher certification in computer science (grades K–12) by Florida's Bureau of Teacher Certification.

## CREDIT OPTIONS

Master's applicants may request transfer of up to 6 graduate credits. Courses proposed for transfer must have grades of at least B. Credit is not awarded for life or work experience.

## FACULTY

SCIS has 20 full-time and 10 part-time faculty members. All faculty members teaching at the graduate level have doctoral degrees.

## ADMISSION

The master's applicant must have an undergraduate degree with a GPA of at least 2.5 and a GPA of at least 3.0 in an appropriate major. The doctoral applicant must have a master's degree with an appropriate graduate major and a graduate GPA of at least 3.25. Degrees must be from regionally accredited institutions. All applicants must submit a summary of professional experience or a score report from the GRE. English proficiency is a requirement for admission.

## TUITION AND FEES

Tuition is $395 per credit for master's students; for doctoral students, tuition is $4450 per five-month term, or $445 per credit. The registration fee is $30.

## FINANCIAL AID

To qualify for financial assistance, a student must be admitted, must be a U.S. citizen or an eligible permanent resident, and must plan on registering for a minimum of 6 credit hours per term. A prospective student who requires financial assistance should apply for it while still a candidate for admission. For financial assistance information or application forms, students should call 800-522-3243 (toll-free).

## APPLYING

Admission decisions are made on a rolling basis. To ensure evaluation for the desired starting term, reviewable applications must be received at least one month prior to the start of that term. The application fee is $50. Late applications that cannot be processed in time for the desired starting term are considered for the next term. Applicants may be granted provisional admission status pending completion of the application process. Admission forms, brochures, and the graduate catalog may be downloaded from the School's Web site, listed below. Master's terms start in September, January, April, and July. Doctoral cluster terms start in September and March. Doctoral institute terms start in January and July.

---

**CONTACT**

The School of Computer and Information Sciences
Nova Southeastern University
6100 Griffin Road
Fort Lauderdale, Florida 33314-4416
Telephone: 954-262-2000
        800-986-2247 (toll-free)
E-mail: scisinfo@nova.edu
Web site: http://www.scis.nova.edu

# Ohio University

## Lifelong Learning Programs

Athens, Ohio

Ohio University, founded in 1804, was the first institution of higher learning in the Northwest Territory. Today it offers all the resources of a major university—diverse intellectual stimulation and an abundance of social and cultural activities—in a quiet, small-city setting. In addition to the main campus in Athens, the University has six regional centers in the southeast quadrant of Ohio.

Ohio University offers degrees in more than 325 subject areas through its colleges: Arts and Sciences, Business, Communication, Education, Engineering and Technology, Fine Arts, Health and Human Services, Honors Tutorial, Osteopathic Medicine, and University College. The University is accredited by the North Central Association of Colleges and Schools and holds membership in a number of professional organizations; in addition, many academic programs are accredited by their respective associations.

Ohio University has also been a leader in providing learning opportunities for nontraditional students, including more than seventy-five years of correspondence education, credit for college-level learning from life experience, and the external-student degree program.

## DISTANCE LEARNING PROGRAM

Independent and Distance Learning (IDL) serves students at a distance through correspondence and online courses, course credit by examination, and individual learning contracts. Credit earned through one of these options is considered residential credit and may be applied without limit to a degree program at Ohio University or transferred to another institution (subject to any conditions set by the accepting institution). Approximately 300 courses are currently available through Independent and Distance Learning; the program has about 4,000 course enrollments each year.

The External Student Program (ESP) assists students at a distance who are working toward Ohio University degrees with such services as transcript evaluation, advising, degree planning, and liaison with other University offices and departments. The College Program for the Incarcerated (CPI) offers the same services to in- carcerated individuals, along with comprehensive fees unique to this program and staff experienced in meeting the special needs of this population.

## DELIVERY MEDIA

Correspondence between students and instructors, using the postal system or fax, is the primary delivery system for IDL courses. E-mail lesson service and videotape supplements are being incorporated into an increasing number of courses. The number of courses using the Internet and World Wide Web for instructional delivery and communications between students and instructors is growing. Online courses are available as self-paced (IDL) and as term-based (Ohio University Online).

## PROGRAMS OF STUDY

To earn a degree, students must enroll with the External Student Program. Students are assigned an ad- viser to assist them in fulfilling degree requirements, including assistance in choosing courses and creating the degree proposals.

Three associate degrees are available: Associate in Arts (A.A.), Associate in Science (A.S.), and Associate in Individualized Studies (A.I.S.). All require the completion of 96 quarter hours of credit; at least 30 quarter hours of credit from Ohio University.

The A.I.S. is a self-designed degree; students are required to submit a proposal outlining their course of study and area of concentration (which must consist of a minimum of 30 quarter hours of study). At least 30 of the 96 quarter hours of credit must be completed after admission to the A.I.S. program.

Through the Bachelor of Specialized Studies (B.S.S.), students design individualized baccalaureate-degree programs, creating unique majors that combine courses from two or more departments. Students must have sophomore rank and a minimum cumulative grade point average of 2.0 in order to submit a proposal. The proposal specifies the course of study and an area of concentration of at least 45 quarter hours (which cannot duplicate an existing major). At least 45 hours must be earned after admission to the B.S.S. progra; at least 80 hours of the 192 hours total for the degree must be at the junior/senior level. An adviser assists students through the entire B.S.S. proposal process.

## SPECIAL PROGRAMS

The M.B.A. Without Boundaries is a structured two-year graduate-degree program offered by the College of Business. Designed for working professionals, it combines several intensive on-site seminar sessions with group and individual projects completed at the student's own location using the OUMBA Intranet to access learning modules, collaborate with other students, and communicate with faculty members. Enrollment is limited.

The Institutes for Adult Learners are held twice a year on the Ohio University campus. Institute students earn credit, usually four quarters per course, become acquainted with the campus and faculty, and participate in a residential experience with other nontraditional students. Courses are taught in intensive, one-week classroom formats supplemented by individual work before and after the Institute.

## CREDIT OPTIONS

Students at a distance who are interested in completing an Ohio University degree through the External Student Program can use a combination of credit earned through the Institutes, credit for experiential learning documented through a portfolio process, transfer credit (including military and professional training equivalencies established by the American Council on Education), and Independent and Distance Learning options. Students may apply 24 quarter hours of experiential learning credit to-

ward an associate degree; 48 quarter hours may be applied toward a bachelor's degree.

Regularly enrolled students on any Ohio University campus may use IDL or experiential learning credit toward their degrees with their college's approval.

## FACULTY

All Independent Study courses are taught by permanent Ohio University faculty members; more than 90 percent of the 125 faculty members teaching in the program have a doctorate or other terminal degree.

## ADMISSION

Enrollment in IDL courses is open to anyone who can profit from the learning. Enrollment in a course does not constitute formal admission to the University. Students must have a high school diploma to be admitted to the External Student program; transfer students must have a minimum 2.0 cumulative grade point average. Admission to the External Student Program does not guarantee on-campus admission to a specific degree program at Ohio University.

## TUITION AND FEES

Fees for IDL courses in 2001–02 are correspondence and online courses,

$85 per quarter hour; course credit by examination, $44 per quarter hour; and Independent Learning projects, $95 per quarter hour. Fees for the External Student Program are a $125 application fee and, in subsequent years, a $75 annual matriculation fee. In 2001–02, students seeking credit for experiential learning pay $380 for the required portfolio development course plus $160 per course assessment (paid after completion of the portfolio development course).

## FINANCIAL AID

Students may use veterans' benefits and employer reimbursement to pay course and program fees. Federal and state financial aid cannot be applied to courses and fees through Independent Study or the External Student Program. Standard tuition and fees paid by on-campus students cannot be applied to Independent Study courses.

## APPLYING

Students may enroll in Independent and Distance Learning courses at any time; enrollment forms are provided in the IDL catalog and at the program's World Wide Web site. A separate application process is required for the External Student Program; forms are provided in the External Student bulletin or may be requested from the ESP office.

---

### CONTACT

Director, Independent and
Distance Learning Programs
302 Tupper Hall
Ohio University
Athens, Ohio 45701
Telephone: 740-593-2910
Fax: 740-593-2901
E-mail: independent.study@ohio.
edu
Web site: http://www.ohiou.edu/
independent/

Counselor, External Student
Program/College Program for the
Incarcerated
301 Tupper Hall
Ohio University
Athens, Ohio 45701
Telephone: 740-593-2150
Fax: 740-593-0452
E-mail: external.student@ohio.
edu
or cpi@ohio.edu
Web site: http://www.ohiou.edu/
adultlearning/overview.htm

M.B.A. Without Boundaries
Dr. Richard Milter
Bromley Hall
Ohio University
Athens, Ohio 45701
Telephone: 740-593-2072
E-mail: milter@ohiou.edu
Web site: http://mbawb.cob.
ohiou.edu/

# Old Dominion University

## Distance Learning/TELETECHNET

Norfolk, Virginia

Old Dominion University, a state-assisted institution in Norfolk, Virginia, is part of a metropolitan and historic area with a population of approximately 1.4 million. Established in 1930, the University enrolls more than 18,000 students, including 4,000 graduate students, and operates centers in Hampton, Portsmouth, and Virginia Beach as well as TELETECHNET locations throughout the commonwealth of Virginia and several additional states.

Old Dominion University is accredited by the Commission on Colleges of the Southern Association of Colleges and Schools (1866 Southern Lane, Decatur, Georgia 30033-4097; telephone: 404-679-4501) to award baccalaureate, master's, and doctoral degrees and certificates of advanced study. The undergraduate and graduate business programs are fully accredited by AACSB–The International Association for Management Education. The graduate and undergraduate education programs are accredited by the National Council for Accreditation of Teacher Learning Education. The engineering technology programs are fully accredited by the Technology Accreditation Commission of the Accreditation Board for Engineering and Technology, Inc. (TAC/ABET). The nursing program is accredited by the National League for Nursing Accrediting Commission.

## DISTANCE LEARNING PROGRAM

Old Dominion is recognized as an international leader in telecommunications with the creation of TELETECHNET, a distance learning network in partnership with community colleges, military installations, and corporations. Within TELETECHNET, Old Dominion University offers degrees through courses televised to off-campus sites across the country and has an enrollment of more than 5,000 students. Students earn baccalaureate degrees from Old Dominion by completing the first two years of course work at their local community college or other accredited institutions. Old Dominion provides the remaining course work at the site primarily through telecourses using audio and video technologies. In addition to eighteen baccalaureate degrees, TELETECHNET also offers seven master's degrees.

## DELIVERY MEDIA

Old Dominion University courses are delivered by Ku-band digital satellite with one-way video and two-way audio for interaction between faculty members and students. Classes originate in Norfolk and are transmitted to receiving sites in five states, the District of Columbia, and the Bahamas. Several classes are also offered in a Web-based format, providing students greater flexibility in completion of course work. In addition, a number of classes are streamed over the Internet, where students have access to them at home or at work.

## PROGRAMS OF STUDY

Old Dominion's TELETECHNET program offers baccalaureate degrees in business administration, computer science, criminal justice, engineering technology, health sciences, human services counseling, interdisciplinary studies (elementary school education, leading to a master's degree, and professional communication), medical technology, nursing (RN to B.S.N.), and occupational and technical studies.

The following master's degrees are offered: Master of Engineering Management, Master of Science in Education (elementary school education, which is tied to the bachelor's program, and special education, which meets certification and endorsement requirements in learning disabilities, mental retardation, and emotional/behavioral disorders), Master of Science in Nursing (family nurse practitioner studies), Master of Science in Occupational and Technical Studies, and Master of Taxation.

In addition to the bachelor's and master's programs, certificate programs in public management and survey science are offered. Other programs are in the development stage for TELETECHNET.

## STUDENT SERVICES

TELETECHNET students have the advantage of checking out videotapes of class presentations if they miss a session due to family responsibilities or job conflicts. Computer labs, which are connected to the main campus and have Internet access, are available at each site for the students' use.

The Old Dominion library supports the TELETECHNET students by providing library resources, services, and reference assistance that are required for successful completion of course work, research papers and projects, and independent reading and research. Services are available primarily through the library's Web site (http://www.lib.odu.edu), with telephone, e-mail, and fax requests also provided.

## CREDIT OPTIONS

Students can transfer credits earned at other accredited postsecondary institutions to Old Dominion University and can receive credit through the College-Level Examination Program (CLEP) for certain courses. Returning adult students may also have the option of applying for academic credit through the Experiential Learning Program. This program evaluates college-level learning gained outside the college classroom. Examples are military and workplace training, independent study, professional certification, portfolios, and examination.

## FACULTY

More than 50 percent of Old Dominion University's full-time faculty members have taught on television, and this percentage continues to grow as TELETECHNET expands its degree offerings. Specialized training for this unique teaching environment is provided to ensure high-quality instruction for students.

## ADMISSION

Prospective students must submit an application accompanied by a $30 fee for degree-seeking admission and request that official transcripts from all previous colleges be sent to the Office of Distance Learning for evaluation of credits earned (transfer admission generally requires a minimum 2.2 grade point average).

## TUITION AND FEES

Old Dominion's TELETECHNET program offers affordable tuition for students. Undergraduate TELETECHNET tuition for the 2001–02 school year is $123 per credit for Virginia residents (outside the Hampton Roads area of Virginia) and $408 per credit for nonresidents. Graduate tuition is $202 per credit for in-state students and $534 per credit for out-of-state students. Tuition for TELETECHNET USA sites (those outside of Virginia) is $129 per credit for undergraduates and $202 per credit for graduate students. There is a required general services fee of $8 for each semester.

## FINANCIAL AID

Old Dominion University is a direct lending institution and awards financial aid from federally funded and state-funded programs as well as from privately funded sources. The University requires all students applying for need-based assistance to complete the Free Application for Federal Student Aid (FAFSA). Those applying for merit-based awards must complete the Old Dominion University Scholarship Application.

## APPLYING

The deadline for admission for the fall semester for transfer students and graduate students is June 1. The deadline for nursing students is February 1. The deadline for applying for the spring semester is November 1. The summer semester deadline is April 1. Decisions are made on a rolling basis, and applicants are notified of their admission status within four weeks after receipt of all application materials.

### CONTACT

Dr. Jeanie P. Kline
Director of Distance Learning
  Operations
424 Gornto TELETECHNET
  Center
Old Dominion University
Norfolk, Virginia 23529
Telephone: 800-YOU-2ODU
  (800-968-2638, toll-free)
Fax: 757-683-5492
E-mail: ttnet@odu.edu
Web site: http://www.odu.
  edu/home/distance

# Oregon State University

## *Distance and Continuing Education*

Corvallis, Oregon

*Founded in 1868 and accredited by the Commission on Colleges of the Northwest Association of Schools and Colleges, Oregon State University (OSU) is one of a select number of schools nationwide to receive the Carnegie Foundation's highest rating for education and research. A land-grant, sea-grant, and space-grant university, Oregon State serves the state of Oregon, the nation, and the world through its teaching, research, and outreach efforts. Today, OSU is home to more than 16,500 students who are pursuing their degrees in one of 220 undergraduate and graduate academic degree programs. The American Productivity and Quality Center recently named Oregon State a top university for providing electronic services to students.*

## DISTANCE LEARNING PROGRAM

During fall term 2000, more than 1,000 individuals throughout Oregon and the world were enrolled in OSU courses off campus. Each term, students have access to more than 140 distance courses in more than thirty-five subjects in areas as diverse as education, fisheries and wildlife, history, math, and psychology. Courses are designed as part of bachelor's completion programs, undergraduate minors, certificate programs, and some graduate-level course work.

## DELIVERY MEDIA

Oregon State offers the majority of its distance courses via the Web, videotapes, and through independent study with an assigned instructor. Courses often entail a combination of delivery methods, such as a video course with class interaction through an electronic listserv or Web site. Students communicate with instructors and administrative staff via e-mail, phone, fax, or regular mail. Certain courses and programs are also delivered through face-to-face instruction or interactive television broadcasting (ITV) at statewide locations.

## PROGRAMS OF STUDY

Oregon State is one of a handful of universities nationwide pioneering the field of online education. Most of the 140 distance courses offered each term include some online component such as e-mail communication with faculty members, and more than seventy courses are currently offered partially or entirely on the Web.

Bachelor's degrees can be acquired in a "2+2" or dual-enrollment program, in which students typically complete their first two years of lower-division requirements through a community college or other institution. They can complete their degree from anywhere in the world by taking upper-division course work through OSU Distance and Continuing Education. Students may select from a Bachelor of Arts/Bachelor of Science (B.A./B.S.) in liberal studies (a preprofessional elementary education option is available statewide), a B.S. in environmental sciences, a B.S. in general agriculture, and a B.S. in natural resources. Students in bachelor's programs must accumulate a minimum of 180 quarter credit hours to graduate.

A minor in natural resources is available worldwide; a communication minor is available statewide in Oregon.

Minors usually include at least 27 quarter credit hours of study and can be pursued as part of a bachelor's program or added to a transcript after graduation.

A Master of Science (M.S.) degree in nutrition and food science with an area of concentration in dietetics management is delivered primarily through Web-based courses. The program is geared for registered dietitians and prepares them for management responsibilities. The degree may be completed in three years by taking two to three courses per term.

Graduate-level course work delivered over the Web is also available to students interested in education, public health, and some liberal arts disciplines. These courses are part of campus-based graduate programs at Oregon State but may also be available to students off campus who meet specific course prerequisites.

## SPECIAL PROGRAMS

During 2001–02, a new online certificate program in Web design fundamentals is scheduled to be available for individuals who are interested in becoming a Webmaster or for those who are eager to build and update their Internet skill set. During 2001–02, this fundamentals Web design program, as well as an advanced Web design program, are scheduled to be delivered on-site throughout Oregon.

A preservice professional technical licensure program for Oregon educators provides preparation for professional technical teachers in arts and communication, business and management, and industrial and engineering systems. The curriculum includes 46 credits, with course work organized into two blocks (Web courses and related school-based practicums and student teaching).

For more information on the Oregon Professional Technical Licensure Program, students can contact Dr. Sylvia Twomey, Program Coordinator, by e-mail (pte@orst.edu).

### STUDENT SERVICES

Oregon State makes it a priority to provide excellent student services to distance learners. The Advising Center provides advising services and program information to students everywhere, via e-mail, fax, and a toll-free number. Students also have access to comprehensive online library services, a toll-free hotline for computer consulting, online writing assistance, and a myriad of resources accessible from the Distance and Continuing Education Web site, listed below. *OSU E-News,* a free electronic newsletter, provides timely tips to help distance students succeed.

### CREDIT OPTIONS

All credits earned through distance education are recorded on an Oregon State University transcript and do not appear any differently than on-campus courses. Each course falls under the same accreditation ratings of the individual department from which it originates. Transfer students

enrolled in academic programs must have previous credits evaluated by an OSU adviser to ensure that program requirements are met. Forty-five of the last 75 credit hours for bachelor's completion programs must be Oregon State University courses.

### FACULTY

Oregon State has more than 2,700 faculty members, with 1,119 in the tenure system. Eighty-seven percent of faculty members in professorial ranks have doctoral degrees. OSU distance education faculty members must adhere to the same quality standards as any faculty member teaching on campus.

### ADMISSION

Students taking distance learning courses to meet OSU degree requirements must be admitted to the University through the regular admission process and must meet the requirements for admission. Nondegree enrollment requires no formal admission and no admission fees or requirements and can be obtained by contacting the registrar at 541-737-4331 and requesting a "Quick Admit."

### TUITION AND FEES

Effective fall 2001, tuition for undergraduate distance degree courses is

$130 per quarter credit hour for most courses. Graduate-level courses are generally $250–$290 per quarter credit, depending upon the program. Additional fees may be assessed for tape rental or other course materials.

### FINANCIAL AID

Distance learners are eligible for financial aid programs according to the same rules as on-campus students. Generally, to be considered, a student must be fully admitted to the University and taking at least 6 quarter hours. Some scholarships are open to part-time distance learning students. Students can consult specific information on the Web (http://osu.orst.edu/admin/finaid).

### APPLYING

Distance learners seeking an OSU degree should apply through the regular application process. Some of the distance programs at the graduate level are cohort based and require admission prior to fall quarter. The undergraduate distance degree programs accept students year-round. It is recommended that students seek initial advising prior to the application process. Registration for individual courses generally requires no application other than to contact the registrar for admission as a nondegree or part-time student.

---

### CONTACT

Distance and Continuing Education
Attention: Advising Center
4943 The Valley Library
Oregon State University
Corvallis, Oregon 97331-4504
Telephone: 541-737-2676
          800-235-6559 (toll-free)
Fax: 541-737-2734
E-mail: ostateu@orst.edu
Web site: http://statewide.orst.edu

# Ottawa University

## *Distance Learning Programs*

Overland Park, Kansas

> *Ottawa University, founded in 1865, is a private liberal arts college affiliated with the American Baptist Churches. Its mission is to provide distinctive higher education programs within a Christian context. Ottawa University aspires to provide programs that serve people of all ages, across national boundaries, and through a variety of delivery systems. It is accredited by the Commission on Institutions of Higher Education of the North Central Association of Colleges and Schools.*

## DISTANCE LEARNING PROGRAM

The goal of Ottawa University's distance learning programs is to provide a unique delivery system that maintains personal involvement yet offers the convenience students need to complete a degree while juggling the demands of work and family responsibility.

## DELIVERY MEDIA

Through a combination of face-to-face and online interaction, students can complete an undergraduate degree in management of health services or their choice of two graduate degrees, a Master of Arts degree in human resources and a Master of Business Administration (M.B.A.). With a personal computer, modem, an Internet provider, and word processing capability, students access the University's Web-based courseware to complete assignments and continue interactive discussions with their instructors and classmates. No face-to-face meetings are required in the police science or law enforcement programs, as these programs are offered entirely online.

## PROGRAMS OF STUDY

Ottawa University has been offering distance learning programs since 1974. The management of health ser-

vices degree is an undergraduate degree specifically designed for the health-care professional. The degree is for those who manage and work closely with others in health-care organizations or who want to move into administrative positions. The program is designed to be completed within one year. Students meet four times per year and then complete their course work online.

In response to today's demand for technologically savvy employees, Ottawa University began its undergraduate degree in information technology in the spring of 2000. The University plans to launch this degree online in the fall of 2002.

The Bachelor of Arts (B.A.) degree in police science is for police officers who have completed a Rio Salado–affiliated police academy within the U.S. and have received the Associate of Applied Science degree in law enforcement technology from Rio. The Bachelor of Arts degree in law enforcement administration is available for those police officers who have successfully completed another state-sanctioned police academy in the U.S., hold an associate degree or equivalent credits from another institution, or hold a bachelor's degree in another discipline. This program is also available to non–police officers who are committed to the pursuit of a police career.

The Master of Arts (M.A.) degree in human resources has been offered online since 1989. This program is designed to be completed within two years. Classes meet three times per year for an intensive weekend, and the remainder of the course work and interaction with the instructor and classmates are completed online.

Ottawa's Master of Business Administration is designed to offer students a unique perspective in graduate business education in a convenient and flexible format. Students in the M.B.A. program meet for four intensive weekends per year and complete required course work online. These weekend sessions can be completed at Ottawa University's Kansas City, Milwaukee, and Arizona (Phoenix, Mesa, Scottsdale, and Tempe) locations in January 2002. Sessions will be offered in the Pacific Rim in fall 2002.

## STUDENT SERVICES

Distance learners have access to academic advising throughout the length of their program. Computer support is also available if students encounter courseware difficulties.

## CREDIT OPTIONS

The B.A. in management of health services degree is a 32-hour program. Students can transfer in credit from regionally accredited institutions, and various health-care professions have been evaluated for direct transfer of credit. CLEP, DANTES, and credit for experiential learning are other means of earning credit. A minimum of 128 hours are required for graduation. The B.A. in information technology degree requires 58 hours in the major. Students can transfer in credit from regionally accredited institutions, and hours can also be earned for industry-recognized certifications. The B.A. in police science and the B.A. in law enforcement administration degree programs require 44 hours of upper-division credits, with a total of 124 hours required for the degree. The M.A. in human resources and the M.B.A. are both 36-hour programs. Students can transfer in up to 9 hours of relevant graduate course work.

## FACULTY

Ottawa University faculty members who participate in the distance education programs are full-time faculty members or degreed adjuncts in their various areas of expertise.

## ADMISSION

Students who desire admission to the undergraduate programs must possess a high school diploma or its equivalent. Transcripts from any other institutions previously attended must also be submitted. Graduate-level programs require a baccalaureate degree from a regionally accredited college or university, three letters of recommendation, an essay, a current resume, and a minimum GPA of 3.0 on a 4.0 scale.

## TUITION AND FEES

Costs vary and depend upon the program. Students should contact either of the people indicated below for tuition information.

## FINANCIAL AID

Financial aid is available and depends upon the program. Students can direct questions regarding financial aid to the contacts listed below.

## APPLYING

An application fee is required for all programs. Students may contact either of the people indicated below for further application information.

---

### CONTACT

Program Information:

Karen Adams
Enrollment Manager
Building 20
10865 Grandview Drive
Overland Park, Kansas 66210-1503
Telephone: 888-404-6852 (toll-free)
Fax: 913-451-0806
E-mail: adamsk@ottawa.edu
Web site: http://www.ottawa.edu

Marketing Information:

Mary Steigerwald
Director of New Program Development
300 North Corporate Drive, Suite 110
Brookfield, Wisconsin 53045-5865
Telephone: 262-879-0200
Fax: 262-879-0096
E-mail: steigerwald@ottawa.edu
Web site: http://www.ottawa.edu

# Park University

## School for Extended Learning

Parkville, Missouri

---

*Park University was founded in 1875 and is accredited by the Commission on Institutions of Higher Education of the North Central Association of Colleges and Schools. Programs in liberal arts are offered through the School of Arts and Sciences, and the School for Extended Learning offers Bachelor of Science degrees. Many undergraduate courses are offered through the Internet. Graduate programs in public affairs, education, and business administration are also offered.*

*Park University endeavors to educate students who will be characterized by literacy, open-mindedness, and professionalism. To foster the accomplishment of this goal, Park University is committed to providing a distinctive learning environment that is characterized by accessibility, sensitivity, and excellence.*

## DISTANCE LEARNING PROGRAM

Park University has been involved in distance learning courses since 1996 and currently offers more than seventy-five distance learning courses each term, which provide the student with the option of studying where and when it is convenient.

## DELIVERY MEDIA

Students in distance learning courses should have basic computer literacy skills. The necessary equipment includes a Windows-compatible computer with a 28.8 kbps or higher modem and Netscape Navigator or an equivalent. The AOL browser is not supported by Park's online courses. Courses are designed for accelerated sessions of eight weeks. Students interact with instructors and other students through classroom threads and assignments.

## PROGRAM OF STUDY

Park University currently offers degree completion courses online in criminal justice administration, management/computer information systems, management/marketing, man-

agement/human resources, and social psychology. Online courses are offered in psychology; adult development and aging; agency administration; the American Civil War; American foreign policy in the twentieth century; business; business communications writing; business ethics; business law; business policy; chemistry and society; compensation management; complex organizations; computers in society; computer systems and design analysis; criminal investigation; criminal justice administration; criminal justice and the community; criminal law; criminology; early American literature; expository and research writing; financial management; financial institutions and markets; human ecology; human resources development; information systems; introduction to computers; juvenile delinquency; labor relations; macroeconomics; management; modern literature; organizational behavior; organizational development and change; network/data communications; personal financial management; principles of marketing; probation and parole; productions and operations management; professional writing; programming; public administration; Russia in the twentieth century; science, technol-

ogy, and society; scientific and technical writing; small business management; social psychology; supervision; tests and measurements; world physical geography; and World War II.

Special seminars are given in journalism on the Web and management. New courses are being developed on a continuous basis.

## SPECIAL PROGRAMS

Programs are offered in an accelerated eight-week format. Online student services include bookstore, library, registration, financial aid, and advising.

## CREDIT OPTIONS

Park University online courses are transferable to programs at other regionally accredited institutions. Park accepts credit from regionally accredited institutions. It accepts up to 84 hours of C or better work from two-year schools. Official transcripts from previous colleges or universities, official test reports or transcripts from CLEP, USAFI, DANTES, and ACT/PEP documentation are needed to accompany an application. Credit may also be awarded for military service and Validated Learning Equivalency up to 24 hours.

## FACULTY

Park University has 117 Internet faculty instructors, all of whom have advanced degrees. All of the instructors have taught their online classes for Park in a face-to-face academic environment.

## ADMISSION

Park online programs are open to anyone who has completed an associate degree or has 60 transferable college credits, is 25 years old who has 30 transferable college credits, or is in the military on active duty.

## TUITION AND FEES

The tuition for the 2001–02 academic year is $172 per credit hour. The application and evaluation fee is $25. There is a discounted rate of $128 per credit hour for active duty military students and where special contracts exist. All online courses require a $10 per credit hour Internet fee.

## FINANCIAL AID

Financial assistance may be awarded to full- and part-time students who qualify.

## APPLYING

Degree-seeking students must meet all admission standards for Park University. Students seeking Internet course work for transfer credit to another college or university must pay a one-time $25 application fee.

For more information, students should contact Park University at the telephone number below or visit the Web site.

---

**CONTACT**
School for Extended Learning
Park University
8700 Northwest River Park Drive
Parkville, Missouri 64152-3795
Telephone: 816-741-2000 Ext. 6777
          877-505-1059 (toll-free)
E-mail: internet@mail.park.edu
Web site: http://www.park.edu

---

# Peirce College

## Distance Learning Program

Philadelphia, Pennsylvania

*The institutional mission of Peirce, since 1865, has been to provide a quality business, legal, and information technology education to a diverse student population in an academic environment that supports the professional excellence of faculty and staff members, alumni, and employers.*

## DISTANCE LEARNING PROGRAM

Online courses are structured to provide students with the maximum amount of personalized attention from professors and to keep real-time discussion groups manageable. Students are required to actively participate by completing homework assignments, papers, and online exams. Each course is seven weeks in length, with new classes starting every 3½ weeks. Students can register and begin their studies before all transcripts and other supporting documentation are completed. Credits from previous college work are accepted, although no prior college is required, and there are no age limits on enrollment. Peirce College brings the campus directly to the learner. Peirce Online offers one of the lowest private college tuitions in the country.

Peirce Online was launched in fall 2000. This delivery system ushered the College into the asynchronous learning environment. Students can now work toward a degree from the comfort of their home and/or workplace while staying in close contact with their professors by telephone, e-mail, and Internet. Students can earn an associate degree in eighteen months and a bachelor's degree in thirty-six months with the Peirce College Online Program.

## PROGRAMS OF STUDY

Students may receive their bachelor's or associate degrees online in either business administration with a concentration in management, or information technology with a concentration in technology management.

Peirce Online focuses on business and information technology. Students may also earn a bachelor's or associate degree in one or more of several on-site degree programs, such as business administration with a concentration in accounting, marketing, or management; information technology with a concentration in technology management, business systems administration, or networking; or paralegal studies. Peirce maintains strong business community relationships and continually upgrades courses to reflect hiring trends. In all degree programs, students must take general education core courses in English; communications; humanities; and social science, math, or science. Supervised cooperative education is available in all programs. Most of the bachelor's degree programs include a capstone course in the last term of the program.

A minimum of 60 credits is required for an associate degree and 120 credits for a bachelor's degree. Certificates of Proficiency require 27 to 30 credits. Student may enroll in programs in the Online format in which classes begin every 3½ weeks; traditional day and evening format over the fall, spring, and summer term of each academic year; in an accelerated evening or weekend format; or in Friday-only format, through Peirce Corporate College Program.

The College Peirce College is a four-year, nonprofit, independent, coeducational college that was founded in 1865. Peirce is committed to the philosophy that education should be practical and useful and that each student's ambitions are important.

Peirce College is accredited by the Commission on Higher Education of the Middle States Association of Colleges and Schools and the Pennsylvania Department of Education to award associate and bachelor degrees. Peirce is also accredited by the Association of Collegiate Business Schools and Programs (ACBSP).

## STUDENT SERVICES

Classrooms and laboratories are designed and equipped for up-to-date teaching and learning techniques. Peirce College and its facilities are handicapped accessible. Peirce College has many networked classrooms with state-of-the-art equipment that reflects what is currently used in the workplace. A comprehensive package of instructional and tutorial software can be accessed through the network. In addition, a dedicated technology lab serves the career-related needs of Peirce students.

The Peirce College library provides services to students and faculty members.

## FACULTY

Peirce College has 30 full-time and 284 adjunct faculty members with diverse professional backgrounds. Most of the faculty members have advanced degrees and many are practitioners in their field. Attorneys, certified public accountants, psychologists, market analysts, computer experts, health-care professionals, business managers, and other professionals are among the teaching staff members at Peirce. Small classes ensure that faculty members are readily available to offer professional advice to individual students. Faculty members also serve as career and academic advisers.

## ADMISSION

It is the policy of Peirce College to offer admissions to applicants without regard to sex, sexual orientation, ancestry, age, race, creed, color, national origin, or an individual handicap. Admission is based on the student's academic record, work experience, personal qualifications, and aptitude for the program selected. Requirements include a high school diploma or general equivalency diploma and a high school transcript and significant work experience. SAT sources are not required, but are recommended.

## TUITION AND FEES

In 2001–02, tuition and fees are $325 per credit hour for day, evening, and online students. Books and supplies average about $80 per course. Costs are subject to change.

## FINANCIAL AID

About 90 percent of the College's students received approximately $7 million in financial aid. Financial assistance includes scholarships, grants, loans, and on-campus employment. Peirce College participates in most federal and state aid programs. Scholarships and grants from College sources are available for both new and returning students. Applicants for aid must submit the Free Application for Federal Student Aid (FAFSA).

## APPLYING

The application/registration process can be completed online at the online learning Web site listed below. The entire process should take approximately 15 minutes. Students may begin classes and pursue their educational goals as the Peirce College staff members gather required documentation and transcripts.

---

### CONTACT
Center for Enrollment Services
Peirce College
1420 Pine Street
Philadelphia, Pennsylvania 19102-4699
Telephone: 215-670-9217
Fax: 215-546-5996
E-mail: info@peirce.edu
Web site: http://www.peirce.edu
Online learning Web site: www.peirceonline.net

# The Pennsylvania State University

## *Distance Education*

University Park, Pennsylvania

*From agricultural college to world-class learning community, the story of the Pennsylvania State University (Penn State) is one of an expanding mission of teaching, research, and public service. Conceived in 1855, when the commonwealth of Pennsylvania chartered the school at the request of the Pennsylvania State Agricultural Society, today Penn State is one of America's ten largest universities, enrolling more than 80,000 students at twenty-four locations throughout the state.*

*Penn State has been a pioneer in distance education since 1892, when it founded one of the nation's first correspondence study programs. Now, with the addition of an online World Campus, the University has reaffirmed its commitment to providing educational access to learners everywhere.*

## DISTANCE LEARNING PROGRAM

Penn State Distance Education offers both World Campus and Independent Learning programs. The World Campus makes some of Penn State's most highly regarded undergraduate, graduate, and continuing professional education programs available anytime, anywhere through the World Wide Web, computer interfacing, CD-ROM, and other media. Penn State's Independent Learning offers more than 150 undergraduate credit courses and a variety of noncredit courses that contribute to bachelor's and associate's degree and several certificate programs.

## DELIVERY MEDIA

The World Campus uses multiple technologies to present information, facilitate interaction among students and faculty members, give access to learning resources, and provide learner support. World Campus courses are technology based and delivered via the World Wide Web, and most are offered on a semester basis, with students and faculty members interacting together in a group.

Penn State's Independent Learning program assigns each student to a Penn State instructor to communicate with by mail, telephone, fax, and/or e-mail. Students can register for courses at any time throughout the year.

## PROGRAMS OF STUDY

The World Campus provides signature Penn State programs to adult learners that can help them advance professionally and remain competitive in today's ever-changing marketplace. A master's degree in adult education is offered, in addition to associate degrees. Associate degrees are offered in dietetic food systems management and hotel, restaurant, and institutional management. Postbaccalaureate credit certificate programs are available in community and economic development, counselor education–chemical dependency, educational technology integration, logistics and supply-chain management, and noise control engineering. Undergraduate certificates are offered in customer relationship management, dietary manager studies, hospitality management, turfgrass management, and logistics and supply-chain management. The noncredit certificate programs available are basic supervisory leadership, geographic information systems, and Webmaster studies. Courses are also available in advanced antenna engineering, architectural lighting design, reliability engineering, semiconductor device reliability, and fundamentals of engineering (EIT Review). For the most up-to-date information on available programs and courses, students should visit the Web site listed below.

Through Independent Learning, courses can be taken for general interest or applied toward degree programs. A bachelor's degree completion program is offered in letters, arts, and sciences. Associate degrees are offered in business administration, human development and family studies, and letters, arts, and sciences. Credit certificate programs include advanced business management; business management; children, youth, and family services; dietetics and aging; general business; human resources; marketing management; retail management; small business management; and writing social commentary. The noncredit certificate programs offered are legal issues for business professionals, legal issues for those dealing with the elderly, and paralegal studies. For more information, students should visit the Web site listed below.

## SPECIAL PROGRAMS

Independent Learning provides a bachelor's degree program in partnership with the University of Iowa, called LionHawk, in which students who complete the letters, arts, and sciences associate degree are automatically accepted into the Bachelor of Liberal Arts Studies program at Iowa. No on-campus study is required for either degree.

Penn State Distance Education uses interactive videoconferencing to link faculty members with students at other Penn State locations and at work sites globally. This distributed classroom approach to distance education extends access to Penn State graduate programs. It allows spontaneous student-to-faculty member interaction as well as student-to-student interaction through real-time, two-way audio and two-way video connections. Additionally, these programs rely on Internet communications to further enhance interaction and increase students' access to resources. For more information about Distributed Learning, students should call the toll-free telephone number listed below.

## CREDIT OPTIONS

Credits earned through World Campus or Independent Learning courses are equivalent to credits earned on campus at Penn State. Advanced standing credits may be awarded for college-level work taken at regionally accredited institutions, provided that the course grade earned is equivalent to a grade of A, B, or C at Penn State and that the credits are useful to the student's program of study.

## FACULTY

Penn State has a distinguished faculty of 4,100 teachers and researchers. Penn State has consistently ranked among the top ten universities in the nation in the number of faculty members who win Fulbright Scholarships for study abroad, and numerous faculty members hold memberships in the National Academies of Sciences, Engineering, or Medicine.

## ADMISSION

For admission into the Independent Learning degree programs, graduation from a regionally accredited high school or a passing grade on the GED test is required, as are SAT or ACT scores. For requirements for Independent Learning certificate programs, students should contact the Distance Education office. Students should visit the Web site listed below for specific World Campus admission requirements.

## TUITION AND FEES

For 2001-02, the tuition for lower-level credit courses numbered 000 to 299 is $143 per semester-hour credit, while tuition for upper-level credit courses numbered 300 to 499 is $275 per semester-hour credit. Courses in post-baccalaureate certificates and graduate level courses are $317 per credit (some programs may have a higher rate). Noncredit tuition varies by course. A $30 processing fee is charged for every course enrollment. Students should contact the Department of Distance Education/World Campus or visit the Web site below for the most up-to-date details on tuition and fees.

## FINANCIAL AID

Independent Learning courses are not eligible for financial aid because enrollment is accepted at any time of the year and a student can take up to eight months to complete a course. This flexibility takes Independent Learning courses out of the traditional semester timeframe on which the awarding of financial aid is based. World Campus credit courses with a set start and end date may qualify for financial aid depending on a student's degree status and credit load. Students are encouraged to contact the Penn State Office of Student Aid at 814-863-0465 or studentaid@psu.edu. Additional information is also available on line: www.psu.edu/studentaid

## APPLYING

To apply or register for Penn State Distance Education programs and courses, visit the Web site below for downloadable forms, or contact the department via phone, fax, or e-mail.

---

### CONTACT

Penn State Distance Education
The Pennsylvania State University
207 Mitchell Building
University Park, Pennsylvania 16802-3602
Telephone: 814-865-5403 (local and international)
          800-252-3592 (toll-free within the United States)
Fax: 814-865-3290
E-mail: psuwd@outreach.edu (World Campus)
      psude@cde.psu.edu (Independent Learning)
Web site: http://www.worldcampus.psu.edu

---

# Prescott College

## Distance Learning Program

Prescott, Arizona

> *Prescott College was founded in 1966 based upon the idea that learning occurs in the world of experience as well as in the mind. Prescott College seeks to develop the whole person through a unified educational experience in which the acquisition of knowledge and skills is combined with the individual's search for identity and meaning. The College is accredited by the North Central Association of Colleges and Schools and grants bachelor's and master's degrees in several fields. It is the mission of Prescott College to educate students of diverse ages and backgrounds to understand, thrive in, and enhance the world community and environment.*
>
> *Prescott is located in central Arizona, surrounded by national forests and high plains, at an elevation of higher than 5,200 feet. With four mild seasons and beautiful surroundings, Prescott offers a diversity of outside activities, including rock climbing, hiking, mountain biking, and nearby canoeing, rafting, and snow skiing. The city has a population of more than 35,000, including the 125-member Yavapai Apache Indian Tribe, and the county has a population of more than 150,000. Prescott is an interesting combination of old and new. There are more than 500 buildings in Prescott that are recorded on the National Register of Historic Places. Prescott is about 2 hours from Phoenix.*

## DISTANCE LEARNING PROGRAM

Approximately 300 students are enrolled in the program. Degree-seeking students must attend a three-day New Student Orientation and a subsequent three-day Liberal Arts Seminar in Prescott, Arizona. During their programs students continue to work full-time in their home communities while completing course work and meeting regularly with local mentors. Prescott College also has a resident undergraduate program and a limited residency Master of Arts program.

## DELIVERY MEDIA

Students meet core faculty members during their New Student Orientation in Prescott and subsequently maintain contact through e-mail, telephone, fax, and mail. Students typically have twelve to eighteen hours of in-person meetings with a mentor per course.

## PROGRAM OF STUDY

Prescott College's Adult Degree Program (ADP) provides a community-based, independent study model for completion of the Bachelor of Arts degree and post-baccalaureate programs for students pursuing teacher certification. The majority of Adult Degree students are enrolled in the Teacher Education/Certification Program or are pursuing competencies (majors) in counseling psychology/human services, environmental studies, sustainable community development, or management. In addition, many students design individualized programs in areas such as anthropology, art, communications, creative writing, criminal justice, holistic health, humanities, political science, public administration, and women's studies. Enrolled students may develop and submit a life/work experience portfolio for evaluation of credits based on demonstration of prior college-level learning.

All students work with core faculty members and their curriculum committee to design their individualized programs. Programs provide a framework for meaningful, self-directed learning. Competencies (majors) may be broad and interdisciplinary in content or more narrowly focused to reflect particular student career goals. Students are encouraged to include liberal arts as one of their breadth (minor) areas. Teacher certification course work follows Arizona guidelines but programs have been successfully adapted for certification in other states.

To facilitate community-based education, students find mentors in their home communities who agree to work with them for one, two, or three courses. Mentors are approved by core faculty members. They must complete a credential file and meet Adult Degree Program criteria, including a minimum of a master's degree and, preferably, teaching experience at the college level. Interested mentors are often found at universities and community colleges, at local elementary and high schools, and in business and other professional fields. Students are expected to direct their own learning using mentors as resources and guides. Finding mentors also provides students with a valuable network of professionals in their field of study. Often, these connections lead to internships, recommendations, and jobs. Mentors are paid a stipend for working with ADP students.

## SPECIAL PROGRAMS

Prescott College Adult Degree Program students have been involved in many community-based programs, such as Teach for America. Students are encouraged to include internships and practica as part of their demonstration of competence, a graduation requirement.

## STUDENT SERVICES

The Student Services Office serves all students during their time with Prescott College. Career development information is updated regularly. Guided by the philosophy of Prescott College's Adult Degree Program and the Association of Colleges and Research Libraries' (ACRL) "Guidelines for Extended Campus Library Services," Prescott College provides a high level of library service equal to that available to students enrolled elsewhere in traditional programs.

## CREDIT OPTIONS

Courses completed above remedial level at other regionally accredited colleges, with a grade of C or better, are transferable. Relevant courses are applied to the competence and breadth areas during initial advising. In some cases, courses from unaccredited colleges may be documented through a conversion portfolio for which Prescott College credit may be awarded. This option is available after admission into the undergraduate program. CLEP (College Level Examination Program) scores may be submitted for evaluation.

## ADMISSION

The focus of the admissions process is to help ensure that students who are admitted enter a program suited to their individual goals. Prescott College Admissions Counselors are available to assist students during the admissions process. More information is available from the Admissions Office at the address and telephone number listed below.

## TUITION AND FEES

In 2001–02, full-time tuition per six-month enrollment period (18 to 24 quarter credits) is $3825. Part-time tuition (including less than 18 or more than 24 quarter credits) is $210 per credit-hour. There is a $25 nonrefundable application fee.

## FINANCIAL AID

Prescott College's Financial Aid Office makes every attempt to ensure that all qualified students can attend and assists them in finding financial aid, given individual eligibility. The types of financial aid available are Federal Pell Grants, Prescott College grants, Federal Perkins Loans, Arizona State Student Incentive Grants, Federal Supplemental Educational Opportunity Grants, work-study programs, Federal Stafford Student Loans, the Arizona Voucher Program, campus employment, and scholarships.

More than 65 percent of the students at Prescott College receive financial aid. Prescott College uses the Free Application for Federal Student Aid (FAFSA) to determine a student's financial need. Aid is awarded on a first-come, first-served basis until all available funds are used. FAFSA forms take four to six weeks to process, so students should submit them early, even if their plans are indefinite.

## APPLYING

Students are encouraged to submit completed applications by the priority due date for the term in which they plan to enroll. After the priority due date has passed, applications are accepted and reviewed on a rolling, or first-come, first-served, basis. Additional clarification is available from the Admissions Office at 800-628-6364 (Prescott) or 888-797-4680 (Tucson).

### CONTACT

Admissions Office, ADP
Prescott College
220 Grove Avenue
Prescott, Arizona 86301
Telephone: 800-628-6364 (toll-free)
Fax: 520-776-5242
E-mail: admissions@prescott.edu
Web site:
 http://www.prescott.edu

# Purdue University

## *Krannert Executive Education Programs*

West Lafayette, Indiana

---

*Purdue University, a state-supported land-grant university, was founded in 1869. It was named after its chief benefactor, John Purdue, and is known for its academic excellence and affordable education. The West Lafayette campus offers nearly 6,700 courses in the Schools of Agriculture, Management, Consumer and Family Sciences, Pharmacy, Nursing and Health Sciences, Education, Science, Engineering, Technology, Liberal Arts, and Veterinary Medicine. The goals of the University are symbolized in its emblem, the griffin, whose three-part shield represents education, research, and service. Purdue is accredited by the North Central Association of Colleges and Schools.*

## DISTANCE LEARNING PROGRAM

The Krannert Executive Education Programs (KEEP) began its distance learning programs in 1983. The programs were developed specifically for mid-level managers or managers-to-be who are unable to attend classes on a full-time basis. The programs have unique scheduling that makes it possible for participants to be drawn from a wide geographical area. Six 2-week residencies spread across twenty-two months, from orientation to graduation, allow its participants to meet their educational goals while simultaneously fulfilling their job responsibilities. During the nineteen months the students are off campus, they utilize the Internet and World Wide Web, online discussion forums and chatrooms, and other electronic media to stay in touch with each other, the faculty, and Executive Education support staff. These nationally ranked programs are part of the Krannert Graduate School of Management and admit 55 students in each cohort.

## DELIVERY MEDIA

KEEP supports its programs via the World Wide Web. Students need a Windows-compatible laptop computer, an Internet service provider, and Web browser software to access the KEEP Web site and communication support tools. Since the program is Internet-based, students have access to their course Web sites, faculty members, and program support staff anywhere they can connect to the Web. Students are expected to have the current version of Microsoft Office installed on their systems for the purpose of completing their group and individual assignments.

## PROGRAMS OF STUDY

An M.B.A. is offered through two unique programs: the Executive Master of Science in Management (EMS) Program and the International Master in Management (IMM) Program.

The EMS Program begins each July with an orientation session where the participants are introduced to the course work, the instructors, and the KEEP information technology system. The courses have an applied policymaking orientation and make extensive use of case studies and other experiential material. The third module has an emphasis on international business, and the last residency in the third module is spent at an international location. Upon completion of the program, the Master of Science in Management (M.S.M.) degree is awarded by Purdue University.

The IMM Program is taught in conjunction with Tilburg University in the Netherlands and the Budapest University of Economic Sciences (BUES) in Hungary. It is structured like the EMS Program, but the residencies alternate among the campuses of the three collaborating institutions. Orientation initiates the program each January. Graduation yields two master's degrees: a Master of Science in Management (M.S.M.) degree from Purdue and an M.B.A. from either Tilburg or BUES.

The EMS and IMM Programs are intensive and demanding, which is consistent with a graduate professional program in management. Serious preparation is expected, and academic standards are carefully maintained to ensure integrity of the earned degrees. As a result, however, the educational benefits are substantial, and the degrees earned are significant professional credentials.

## SPECIAL PROGRAMS

Both the EMS and IMM Programs are open to executive students worldwide and are accredited by AACSB–The International Association for Management Education. Both national and international students are attracted to the program.

## STUDENT SERVICES

Students may maintain contact with faculty members, support staff, and KEEP administration on a daily basis, if necessary. Other resources include online library services, tutoring, campus computer networks, e-mail services, academic advising, and online discussion forums and chatrooms.

## CREDIT OPTIONS

The programs are cohort in nature; that is, all students in each class enter together, take a common set of courses, and graduate together. There are 48 total credits, 16 per module, that participants must complete within two years.

## FACULTY

Classes are taught by the senior faculty members of the Krannert Graduate School of Management at Purdue, the Tias Business School at Tilburg University, the Budapest University of Economic Sciences, and by experienced teachers from other U.S. and international programs. All faculty members have taught extensively in executive programs containing distance learning aspects, have substantial research and publication records, and have experience as consultants to corporations and government agencies.

## ADMISSION

Successful applicants are expected to have a GMAT score of 520 or higher, a completed baccalaureate degree with a grade point average of B or better, a minimum of five years of work experience in positions of increasing professional responsibility, a current position of significant responsibility, and three supporting letters of recommendation. Any applicant whose first language is not English must have a minimum TOEFL score of 213 on the computer-based test or 550 on the paper-based test.

## TUITION AND FEES

The total cost for each program is $45,000 ($15,000 per each of the three modules). The tuition covers books and course material, instructional costs, lodging, and most meals during the residencies. Tuition is due before the first residency of each program module. The EMB Program features an international trip in its last module, for which there is an additional charge.

## FINANCIAL AID

EMBA loans offered through Purdue's financial aid office are available. Applications may be completed at a distance.

## APPLYING

Candidates may apply online at any time. As admission to the program is on a rolling basis throughout the year until class capacity is reached, early application is recommended. Upon receipt of all necessary documents, the application will be reviewed by the Program Admissions Committee and, upon approval, submitted to Purdue's Graduate School for the final decision. Typically, a candidate can expect word of his or her application status within two weeks of receipt of all application documentation.

---

### CONTACT

Erika C. Steuterman
Director, Executive Master's Programs
Purdue University
1310 Krannert Center, Suite 206
West Lafayette, Indiana 47907-1310
Telephone: 765-494-7700
Fax: 765-494-0862
E-mail: keepinfo@mgmt.purdue.edu
Web site: http://www2.mgmt.purdue.edu

# Regent University

## Online Distance Learning Programs

Virginia Beach, Virginia

---

*Regent University is a graduate institution offering twenty-eight master's and doctoral degree programs from a Judeo-Christian worldview. Regent's eight colleges and schools include the Graduate School of Business, College of Communication and the Arts, School of Divinity, School of Education, Robertson School of Government, School of Law, Center for Leadership Studies, and School of Psychology and Counseling (currently not offering programs online).*

*Since its founding in 1977, Regent University has grown to an enrollment of more than 2,400 students. In addition to the main campus in Virginia Beach, Regent also offers programs at its Graduate Center, Northern Virginia/D.C. More than twenty-two degree programs are offered online via the Regent Worldwide Campus. Regent University is accredited by the Commission on Colleges of the Southern Association of Colleges and Schools (1866 Southern Lane, Decatur, Georgia 30033-4097; telephone: 404-679-4501) to award the master's and doctoral degrees and is a candidate for accreditation to award the bachelor's degree. The School of Law is fully accredited by the American Bar Association. The School of Divinity is accredited by the Association of Theological Schools (ATS). The Council for Accreditation of Counseling and Related Educational Programs (CACREP), a specialized accrediting body recognized by the Council for Higher Education Accreditation (CHEA), has conferred accreditation to the following program areas offered by the School of Psychology and Counseling of Regent University: community counseling (M.A.) and school counseling (M.A.).*

## DISTANCE LEARNING PROGRAM

Regent University serves more than 810 students via its online Worldwide Campus through programs in communication (M.A., Ph.D.), journalism (M.A.), organizational leadership (M.A., Ph.D., Doctor of Strategic Leadership (D.S.L.)), business (M.B.A., M.A.), law (LL.M., Master of International Taxation (M.I.T.)), education (M.Ed., Ed.D.), and divinity (M.A., M.Div.). Each fully accredited program is taught from a Judeo-Christian perspective, allowing students to apply relevant ethical values to their professional pursuits within a scholarly framework.

## DELIVERY MEDIA

Degrees are offered online via the Regent Worldwide Campus. Students receive study materials via e-mail. Some materials, such as videotapes, may be sent to the student via postal services. Students submit papers and quizzes to instructors via e-mail. Chat rooms are used for class interaction. Detailed requirements are outlined in each admissions packet and are available at http://www.regent.edu/distance.

## PROGRAMS OF STUDY

Online distance learning programs in the College of Communication and the Arts include the M.A. and Ph.D. in communication and the M.A. in journalism. The Center for Leadership Studies offers the M.A. and Ph.D. in organizational leadership and the D.S.L. The Graduate School of Business offers the M.B.A. and the M.A. in management. The School of Law offers the LL.M. in international taxa-

tion and the M.I.T. The School of Education offers the M.Ed. and the Ed.D. The School of Divinity offers the M.A. in biblical studies and practical theology and the M.Div.

## SPECIAL PROGRAMS

Regent University offers the Accelerated Scholars and Professionals Program (ASAP), which allows some students to enter their master's program without having received a bachelor's degree. Successful applicants to this program have accrued a minimum of 90 credits toward their undergraduate degree and have acquired significant life experience (determined by an admissions committee) in a professional area relevant to their chosen master's program.

## CREDIT OPTIONS

For all online distance programs, students may transfer up to 25 percent of the total credits required for their chosen degree. Credits must be taken from an approved institution (determined by each Regent school) and must reflect grades of B or better.

## FACULTY

Regent online distance learning courses are taught by the same full- and part-time faculty members who teach on campus. Regent has a distinguished faculty of 109 men and women of varying religious denominations and ethnic origins.

## ADMISSION

With the exception of ASAP students, admission to Regent University requires a completed four-year bachelor's degree for master's programs and a completed master's degree for doctoral programs from an institution that is state and regionally accredited. Applicants possessing earned degrees from nonaccredited institutions are considered on an individual basis.

While each Regent school maintains specific admissions criteria, the following are considered common: a minimum cumulative undergraduate GPA of 3.0 in the desired area, submission of test scores (MAT, GMAT, or GRE), maturity in spiritual and/or character qualities, and personal goals that are consistent with the mission and goals of Regent University.

International admissions requirements also vary among Regent schools. Students should contact the school of their choice for specific information.

## TUITION AND FEES

Tuition for online/distance learning programs is as follows: Professional M.B.A., $24,912 (total); Executive M.B.A., $25,884 (total); M.A. in management, $350 per credit; M.A. in communication and M.A. in journalism, $450 per credit; M.A. in organizational leadership, $375 per credit; Ph.D. in organizational leadership and D.S.L., $500 per credit; M.Ed., $357 per credit; Ed.D., $465 per credit; M.A. in biblical studies, M.A. in practical theology, and M.Div., $295 per credit; and LL.M. in international taxation and M.I.T., $624 per credit. Fees vary by program.

## FINANCIAL AID

Students accepted for enrollment may apply for Federal Stafford Student Loans and a variety of school-specific scholarships and grants. Veterans' benefits also apply.

## APPLYING

Application deadlines and processes vary among schools. Students should contact the individual school for specific information.

---

### CONTACT

Regent University
1000 Regent University Drive
Virginia Beach, Virginia 23464-9800
Telephone: 800-373-5504 (Central Enrollment Management, toll-free)
E-mail: admissions@regent.edu
Web site: http://www.regent.edu

To contact distance learning programs directly:
Graduate School of Business (telephone: 800-477-3642 (toll-free); e-mail: bizschool@regent.edu)
College of Communication and the Arts (telephone: 757-226-4116; e-mail: commcollege@regent.edu)
Center for Leadership Studies (telephone: 757-226-3063; e-mail: leadercenter@regent.edu)
School of Divinity (telephone: 800-723-6162 (toll-free); e-mail: divschool@regent.edu)
School of Education (telephone: 888-713-1595 (toll-free); e-mail: eduschool@regent.edu)
Robertson School of Government (telephone: 888-800-7735 (toll-free); e-mail: govschool@regent.edu)
School of Law (telephone: 877-850-8435 (toll-free); e-mail: lawschool@regent.edu)

# Rensselaer Polytechnic Institute

## Professional and Distance Education

Troy, New York

*Founded in 1824, Rensselaer Polytechnic Institute in Troy, New York, is America's oldest private technological university. Internationally regarded as a prominent research institute with strong ties to industry, Rensselaer offers graduate and undergraduate degrees in engineering, science, management, architecture, and humanities and social science. Since 1995, Rensselaer's highly successful curriculum-renewal efforts have been recognized with three of the most prestigious awards in higher education: the Hesburgh Award for Faculty Development to Enhance Undergraduate Teaching, the Boeing Outstanding Educator Award, and the Pew Leadership Award for the Renewal of Undergraduate Education. National rankings in U.S. News & World Report and Success have provided acclaim for Rensselaer's graduate programs in engineering, management, and entrepreneurship. For the fourth year in a row, Yahoo! Internet Life magazine ranked Rensselaer among the top five "most-wired" campuses in the nation.*

## DISTANCE LEARNING PROGRAM

Rensselaer's distance learning program, RSVP, provides fifteen master's degree programs and sixteen certificate programs, as well as graduate courses and noncredit seminars, to working professionals at their work sites, homes, or other convenient locations. More than 1,300 working professionals from many of this nation's leading corporations participate each semester without having to travel to the campus.

In operation since 1987, RSVP is a highly respected program in the field of distance learning. In 1993, it was named "Best Distance Learning Program—Higher Education" by the United States Distance Learning Association. In 1996, the same organization recognized it as having an "Outstanding Partnership with a Corporation" for the development and delivery of its M.S. program in the management of technology to General Motors. RSVP is known for an emphasis on high quality, customer service, excellent production values, and innovation.

## DELIVERY MEDIA

RSVP delivers courses using a range of technologies that include satellite broadcasts, videoconferencing, videotapes, and the Internet. These technologies are integrated so that the same event can be transmitted to multiple locations in different delivery formats. Most programs can be received in a live, interactive mode. A growing number of classes are now being videostreamed on the Internet, making it possible for individual students, as well as those at corporate sites, to pursue Rensselaer graduate studies at a distance and at any time of the day or night. The World Wide Web also provides for e-mail or chat interaction with the instructor and staff members and provides electronic access to course materials.

## PROGRAMS OF STUDY

Working professionals may complete individual courses, four-course certificate programs, or full master's degrees through RSVP. The credits and degrees received are identical to those received by campus-based students. Most content is at the graduate level. In addition, noncredit seminars and workshops are offered in a range of technical areas.

Master's degrees are available in the following areas: business administration (M.B.A.), computer science, computer and systems engineering, electrical engineering (microelectronics), electric power engineering, engineering science (manufacturing systems engineering and microelectronics manufacturing engineering), industrial and management engineering (quality engineering and service systems), information technology, management (with optional concentrations in management information systems or human-computer interaction), mechanical engineering, and technical communications.

Certificates are available in the following areas: bioinformatics, computer graphics and data visualization, computer networks, computer science, database systems design, graphical user interfaces, human-computer interaction, management and technology, manufacturing systems engineering, mechanical engineering, microelectronics manufacturing engineering, microelectronics technology and design, quality and reliability, service systems, and software engineering.

In 1999, RSVP launched a series of new information technology degree and certificate programs called IT at a Distance. Qualified students may pursue courses leading to IT-related degrees or certificates at home or office using videostreaming on the World Wide Web and through Rensselaer's new 80/20 model for interactive Web-based delivery. In addition, Rensselaer alumni may now pursue these or any RSVP programs as individual students. Students should contact the Office of Professional and Distance Education for Web delivery schedules.

RSVP delivers approximately seventy-five courses annually via distance learning technology to both individual students and employees at more than sixty sites of many of the nation's leading corporations and other organizations. Participants include AT&T, Consolidated Edison, DuPont, U.S. Department of Defense, Federal Highway Administration, Ford, General Electric, General Motors, Hyperion Solutions, IBM, J. P. Morgan, Lockheed Martin, Lotus Development Corporation, Lucent Technology, Perkin-Elmer, Pitney Bowes, Quantum Corp., United Technologies, and Xerox, among others.

In nondegree programming, Rensselaer also provides several programs per year of one to five days in length, depending on content and audience need. In recent years, programs have been offered in bioinformatics, colloid chemistry, computer and information technology, polymer chemistry, multiphase flow and heat transfer, chemical mechanical planarization, and highway capacity, among other areas. Employees from many Fortune 500 companies and other leading organizations have attended these programs.

## SPECIAL PROGRAMS

RSVP frequently works with corporate, government, and military sponsors who arrange to bring Rensselaer's programs on-site for their employees. Similar arrangements can be made with regional partners (i.e., community colleges, professional organizations, and education centers). Partner sites agree to receive courses and provide all local administrative support, which often includes a library of instructional materials. Because many programs are offered in response to the needs of sponsors, it is possible to add new courses or programs based on interest and sufficient enrollments.

## STUDENT SERVICES

Professional and Distance Education staff members serve as the interface to the rest of the Rensselaer campus for RSVP student services, including admission, registration, academic advising, instructional materials, transfer credits, and degree clearance. Students also have direct access to Rensselaer's Student Information System and the library via the World Wide Web.

## CREDIT OPTIONS

Except for the M.B.A., all master's programs are 30-credit minimum, ten-course degrees. Students in the master's programs can transfer up to two graduate-level courses (6 credits) that have been completed at other institutions, assuming that the courses are approved as acceptable in the plan of study by an academic adviser and were completed with a grade of B or better. The M.B.A. is a 60-credit program with the possibility of waiving 3 to 12 credits based on prior knowledge and/or work experience. Certificate programs require the successful completion of a four-course sequence of graduate-level courses. No course work can be transferred into the certificate program.

## FACULTY

The RSVP faculty is drawn from approximately 400 full-time Rensselaer scholars, teachers, and researchers. Their doctorates or other degrees are from the world's leading universities. The faculty members who teach in the distance learning program also teach on campus, and more than 80 full-time faculty members have taught in the program to date.

## ADMISSION

Students interested in credit courses and degree programs must apply to Rensselaer in the same manner as campus-based students, and admission standards are essentially the same. Transcripts of all college-level work and three letters of recommendation must be supplied for degree admission. Transcripts are also required for certificates. There are no admission requirements for short courses and seminars.

## TUITION AND FEES

Tuition for all credit courses is invoiced at the same rate as for campus-based students. For the 2000–01 academic year, that was $700 per credit hour, or $2100 per 3-credit course. The only other costs are for the application fee ($45), a transcript fee ($35), and the cost of instructional materials. Costs for noncredit seminars and workshops vary.

## FINANCIAL AID

Most students currently enrolled in the program have their tuition costs paid through their employers. If desired, students enrolled in the credit courses and programs can, like their colleagues on campus, apply for state and federal bank loans.

## APPLYING

Application deadlines are typically set at six weeks prior to the first day of class, and admission decisions are made as soon as the completed application is received. Application materials for credit courses and programs are provided to participating locations and are also available upon request. Registration forms for noncredit seminars and workshops are included in the program announcements.

### CONTACT

Heliena Fox, Recruitment
    Representative
Individual and Alumni Programs
Office of Professional and
    Distance Education
Rensselaer Polytechnic Institute
Center for Industrial Innovation,
    Suite 4011
Troy, New York 12180
Telephone: 518-276-8351
Fax: 518-276-8026
E-mail: rsvp@rpi.edu
Web site:
    http://www.rsvp.rpi.edu

# Rio Salado College

## Distance Learning Program

Tempe, Arizona

> Rio Salado College was established in 1978 to provide active, working adults with flexible educational opportunities designed for convenience. Known as "the college without walls," Rio Salado does not maintain a traditional campus. Instead, courses are delivered for diverse populations using customized programs and partnerships, accelerated formats, and 300 distance learning courses, which allow students to take courses anytime and anyplace. Rio Salado is one of the ten Maricopa Community Colleges, the largest community college district in the U.S.
>
> Rio Salado is accredited by The Higher Learning Commission, a member of the North Central Association, 30 North LaSalle Street, Suite 2400, Chicago, Illinois 60602.
>
> Rio Salado's reputation for excellence and innovation has often attracted regional and national attention. The College has earned many awards, including Outstanding Web Site in Higher Education (North American Web Association); the Paragon Award for Most Creative Use of Technology (National Council for Marketing and Public Relations) and the Award of Excellence for Distance Learning (Council for the Advancement and Support of Education). Rio Salado has also been profiled in the New York Times, the Chronicle of Higher Education, the Business Journal, the Arizona Republic, on National Public Radio, and in many specialty publications such as Converge magazine and University Business.

## DISTANCE LEARNING PROGRAM

"Let the College come to you" is the prevailing philosophy at Rio Salado. Rio Salado College makes it possible to earn an associate degree through distance learning. Rio offers 300 distance learning courses, with 200 of those on the Internet. More than 25,000 distance learning enrollments will occur this academic year. All distance courses encourage maximum interaction between student and instructor. Students choose their own study times and submit assignments by mail, fax, or computer. Instructors are available by phone, fax, and e-mail.

## DELIVERY MEDIA

Rio Salado offers three delivery formats: the Internet (including CD-ROM), audio and videocassettes, and print-based materials. Courses delivered on the Internet require a service provider, Macintosh/Windows capability, and a minimum of 8 MB of RAM. Programs are available worldwide.

## PROGRAMS OF STUDY

Distance learning classes are primarily academic in nature and include accounting, anthropology, art humanities, biology, business, chemistry, child/family studies, communication, computers, counseling and personal development, economics, education, English, geology, health science, history, humanities, integrated studies, management and supervision, mathematics, office automated systems, philosophy, political science, psychology, Spanish, and theater.

Degrees offered are the Associate of Applied Science (A.A.S), the Associate of General Studies (A.G.S.), the Associate of Transfer Partnership (A.T.P.), the Associate of Arts (A.A.), the Associate of Business (A.Bus.), and the Associate of Science (A.S.). An option is available in general requirements or special requirements for the A.A., A.Bus., and A.S. degree programs.

## SPECIAL PROGRAMS

Rio Salado College provides a variety of Level I and Level II computer courses leading to an A.A.S. degree and/or certificates of completion in computer technology, plus nine areas of specialization, including desktop publishing, networking, Web master, business office technology, office user specialist preparation skills, programming, technology helpdesk support, and technology troubleshooting. Sample individual courses include Windows 98, Internet Explorer, and Microsoft Office 97 and 2000.

The Law Enforcement Technology Program is available to police officers across the U.S. This associate degree program transfers seamlessly into the Bachelor of Police Science degree program offered by Ottawa University in partnership with Rio Salado.

The Professional Development Program for K–12 Teachers was developed for teachers, by teachers, and is available entirely online. Credits are accepted by the Arizona Department of Education and can lead to approved endorsements.

The Rio Salado Teacher Preparation Program is available to Arizona residents who hold a baccalaureate degree but lack Arizona teaching credentials. The eight courses in the Teacher Preparation Program can be taken anytime and anyplace through the Internet.

The Arizona Dental Assocation Clinical Dental Assisting Program is offered over the Internet. Unique distance lab kits allow students to complete most of the lab work at home. A short lab practicum is taught on-site at a state-of-the-art dental clinic in the Phoenix area. Information on all these programs is available through Rio Salado academic advisers.

## STUDENT SERVICES

All major student services are online, including registration, career and academic counseling, tutoring, book orders, and scholarship applications. Two easy-to-follow tutorials assist first-time Internet users. In addition, a technology help desk is available seven days a week, 360 days a year.

## CREDIT OPTIONS

Because Rio Salado College is accredited by the Higher Learing Commission, its credits are recognized nationwide. Students who plan to transfer credits outside Arizona are encouraged to confer with an adviser to obtain specific information as to how the credits will fit into their curriculum or program of study.

## FACULTY

In addition to full-time residential faculty members, Rio Salado College capitalizes on the professional career experience and expertise that more than 600 adjunct faculty members bring to the learning environment. As well as being content specialists, Rio Salado faculty members are specially trained in effective teaching techniques for distance learning.

## ADMISSION

With only a few exceptions, students may begin their distance classes any one of twenty-six times throughout the year—new classes start every two weeks. This open-entry format allows students to enroll anytime and have up to thirteen weeks to complete their courses.

For regular and distance classes, students may be admitted under any of the following classifications: college transfer, high school/GED graduate, or 18 years of age or older. Special admission requirements and forms are available for international students or students who do not qualify for any of these classifications.

## TUITION AND FEES

Students pay tuition according to their residency status. Tuition for Arizona residents is $43 per credit hour, plus a $5-per-semester registration fee. Tuition for nonresidents is $125 per credit hour, plus a $5-per-semester registration fee. Tuition and fees are subject to change.

## FINANCIAL AID

Whether taking regular or distance learning courses, eligible students can apply for grants, work-study, and scholarships. To be eligible for federal financial aid, students must meet application criteria and select a program of study. The application process is approximately eight weeks long, so students should plan ahead.

## APPLYING

Registration can be completed by Touch-Tone phone (480-731-8255 or toll-free at 800-729-1197) or via the World Wide Web (listed below). Along with a completed application, students need to provide an official high school transcript, GED scores, or official transcripts from previously attended colleges.

## CONTACT

Rio Salado College
Student Services
2323 West 14th Street
Tempe, Arizona 85281
Telephone: 480-517-8540
Web site: http://www.rio.maricopa.edu

# Robert Morris College

Pittsburgh, Pennsylvania

*Robert Morris College, an independent coeducational institution of higher education, it is accredited by the Middle States Association of Colleges and Secondary Schools. It is authorized by the Department of Education of the Commonwealth of Pennsylvania to award the Doctor of Science degree, the Master of Science degree, the Master of Business Administration degree, the Bachelor of Science in Business Administration degree, the Bachelor of Arts degree, and the Bachelor of Science degree. With a student population of approximately 4,800, the College offers high-quality undergraduate and graduate degree programs that integrate the liberal arts with professional programs.*

*Robert Morris College was admitted to candidacy status for the AACSB–The International Association for Management Education in March of 1995. This accreditation process encourages the pursuit of diverse paths to high quality in business education, and the College is active in this process.*

*The College has two convenient campuses. The main campus is located in Moon Township, a suburb of Pittsburgh, 17 miles from downtown and 5 miles from the Pittsburgh International Airport. The Pittsburgh Campus is located in the heart of the financial and banking area of downtown Pittsburgh and is the center for the Robert Morris College Online programs.*

## DISTANCE LEARNING PROGRAM

The mission of the College's online programs is to offer a high-quality and affordable education to adult students in a manner that is convenient. Adults bring a variety of experiences to the educational setting, and instructional methods should enhance and use these experiences. The faculty is trained to facilitate the adult learner.

## DELIVERY MEDIA

Robert Morris College's cutting-edge distance learning programs use the Internet for online instruction. The online method allows for e-mail, interactive chat, audio and video streaming, threaded discussions, instructional connections to additional Web sites, and access to the electronic library, journals, and document sharing, among other things. Online courses require students to have access to a computer and an Internet provider as well as an e-mail account.

## PROGRAMS OF STUDY

By utilizing the Internet, students are able to participate in courses online at their convenience. This provides them with greater freedom to complete their course requirements and the flexibility to do so when their schedules permit. A Bachelor of Science in Business Administration degree (B.S.B.A) majoring in accounting, management, or information systems may be completed in as little as four years. Students with transfer credits may finish in even less time.

The program currently requires that students also attend class at the Pittsburgh Campus. The class time is minimal, only 1 hour per week per class. Therefore, students in this program can attend college "full-time," qualify for the maximum amount of financial aid, and have their day completed at 1:40 p.m. each Saturday. The remainder of their class work is completed online, via the Internet. This program allows maximum convenience while still providing students with the opportunity to interact with their professor and classmates in person each week. They only attend classes forty weeks out of each calendar year, leaving them with twelve weeks of vacation.

## STUDENT SERVICES

Robert Morris College's distance students still have access to all of the student services available to the on-campus students. Such services include enrollment counseling, the Freedom Card functions, the RMC library, student financial services options, and financial aid counseling.

## FACULTY

The faculty of Robert Morris College offers students the best of both worlds. Instructors include full-time faculty members as well as adjunct professors. The faculty members bring real-world experience and knowledge to the classroom as well as the theoretical background that is necessary for a well-rounded educational experience.

## TUITION AND FEES

Undergraduate tuition for 2000–01 was $282 per credit hour. A college fee of $16 per credit and a technology fee of $20 per credit were also charged.

## APPLYING

To be considered for admission into any program for any term at Robert Morris College, students must complete an admissions application. Please be sure to complete the application in its entirety. An online application may be completed on the Web site at: http://www.robert-morris.edu. The application fee is waived for all applicants who complete and submit the application online.

Robert Morris College is on rolling admissions. This means that there is no official date by which a student must apply for admission. However, students are advised to send in their application as soon as they have decided to include Robert Morris College in their college search, in order to ensure prompt processing time. A $30 nonrefundable application fee is required of all hard-copy applicants.

### CONTACT

For further details and information, students should contact the Office of Enrollment Services at 800-762-0097 (toll-free) or http://www.robert-morris.edu or see the online campus at http://www.rmconline.org.

# R·I·T Rochester Institute of Technology

## Online Learning

Rochester, New York

---

Online Learning at RIT offers a broad selection of courses and full degree programs, all regionally accredited by the Middle States Association of Colleges and Schools. With more than twenty years of experience in distance education, RIT offers one of the largest and most established online learning programs in the U.S.

## DISTANCE LEARNING PROGRAM

Rochester Institute of Technology is one of the nation's leaders in online learning education programs. The online learning program empowers the student by providing anytime, anywhere access to courses, while maintaining essential interaction between faculty members and students. RIT online learning students have access to more than thirty full degree and certificate programs, including eight graduate degrees, four undergraduate degrees, nineteen certificate programs, and more than 300 courses. The commitment to quality education is an inherent part of RIT online learning programs. The faculty members are world renowned and leaders in the subject matter they teach.

## DELIVERY MEDIA

All course interaction takes place online. RIT provides students with online courseware to access their courses. RIT distance learning emphasizes student-instructor interaction over the Internet. Professors deliver course materials through the Internet. Many courses also use a combination of textbooks, videotapes, audiotapes, audio conferences, chats, electronic library resources, and other components that enhance that particular course experience. Students submit most assignments online, but professors may also choose to fax or mail assignments. Students may register online, by fax, and through touch-tone telephone. Students may order course materials online and have complete access to a full range of library services and academic advising online.

In order to participate, students must have full access to the Internet and a personal computer. Students must have basic computer skills and some Internet experience to be successful. In addition, a VCR that is capable of playing NTSC (American standard video) and a telephone are required. For specific computer requirements, students should visit the Web page listed in the Contact section.

## PROGRAMS OF STUDY

All programs offered through RIT are available to students worldwide. Applications for all programs are available online. Most students have some college experience before coming to RIT, but admission into the certificates and the bachelor's-level programs can be accommodated without previous college experience. Master's degree candidates must meet the admissions standards required by that program and must have completed a baccalaureate degree from an accredited institution. International applicants must demonstrate English proficiency, usually through the Test of English as a Foreign Language (TOEFL). TOEFL scores vary by program, but most programs require a score of 550 or better. For graduate students, undergraduate transcripts and two professional recommendations must be submitted.

The B.S. in applied arts and science presents a flexible opportunity for a student, with the help of an academic adviser, to create a program tailored to meet his or her educational needs. It requires the completion of 180 credit hours. Sixteen concentrations are available.

The B.S. in electrical/mechanical engineering technology has broadened its scope to an anytime, anywhere program, with the exception of some lab experiences that must be completed over several weekends at RIT or by taking an alternative course from an approved institution. The undergraduate degree requires 193 credit hours. This program is accredited by ABET-TAC.

The B.S. in telecommunications engineering technology (the technical option) is currently available to both working professionals and full-time students. The academic emphasis is placed on backbone technologies that transmit, switch, and manage networks and the information they carry. Individuals who have no background or have not completed basic lab work in this field may need to come to RIT for intensified weekend labs. This program is accredited by ABET-TAC.

The B.S. in safety technology is structured to be at the leading edge of this field, providing high-quality academic preparation and relevant work experience. All students completing RIT's safety technology bachelor's degree program are eligible to take the associate safety professional examination upon graduation. Individuals may enter the upper-division program from an associate degree program or with two years of college, including appropriate courses in math, science, and liberal arts.

The M.S. in applied statistics is designed for full-time professionals who want to learn state-of-the art statistical techniques to enhance their careers and their value to their companies. Students must complete 45 credits. Admission to the degree program is granted to qualified holders of a baccalaureate degree from an accredited college or university who have acceptable mathematics credits, including one academic year of calculus.

The M.S. in software development and management consists of 48 credit hours, comprising the software engineering core foundation, the software engineering project, and electives. A minimal background is required in mathematics (discrete structures, statistics) and computing (programming in a high-level language, data structures, elementary computer architecture, and digital logic).

The M.S. in information technology consists of 48 credit hours of graduate study in core courses, with a choice of electives and concentrations in telecommunications technology, telecommunications management, and software development and management. Entering students are expected to have programming skills at an intermediate level in an appropriate language and understand the fundamentals of computer hardware.

The M.S. in health systems administration is designed to meet the needs of health professionals who desire a non-clinical degree in management and administration. Students typically enter in cohort groups, which improves the learning environment, and take two courses per quarter until completion of the 57 credit hours.

The M.S. in cross-disciplinary professional studies consists of 48 credit hours, which comprise two or three concentrations from various areas. These areas are designed to give the student a comprehensive and customized plan of graduate study tailored to meet either career or educational objectives. Students must take a course in interdisciplinary research techniques and finish a capstone project to complete this degree.

The M.S. in environmental health and safety management requires 48 credit hours drawn from core courses like environmental health and safety management system design and performance measurement, 12 credits from professional electives, and 12 credits from the graduate thesis and graduate project.

The M.S. in imaging science is being offered to working professionals and students around the world. The worldwide demand for specialists in imaging science is well documented. The program emphasizes a systems approach to the study of imaging science, and, with a background in science or engineering, this degree prepares the student for positions in research, product development, and management in the imaging industry. The program requires completion of 45 credits.

The M.S. in microelectronics manufacturing engineering is designed for students with a B.S. degree in microelectronic engineering or other related engineering areas. The degree requires the completion of nine 4-credit courses and a 9-credit thesis for a total of 45 credits.

RIT also offers nineteen certificates for those wanting to improve or obtain skills in specialized areas. Courses in the certificate programs may be applied toward a degree.

## CREDIT OPTIONS

Students have a number of options available for credit, including transfer credit, credit by exam, College-Level Examination Program (CLEP), Regents College exam, credit for educational experiences in the armed forces, credit for educational experiences in noncollegiate organizations, and credit for nontraditional learning. Advisers work with students to evaluate the number of credits that can be transferred, since the number of non-RIT credits accepted varies by program.

## FACULTY

RIT's faculty members are world-renowned and teach both on-campus and distance education courses. More than 200 full-time and part-time faculty members teach distance learning courses.

## ADMISSION

Requirements for admission and completion of degree or certificate programs vary by academic department. Students should refer to Program of Study descriptions.

## TUITION AND FEES

Graduate tuition is $587 per credit hour. Undergraduate tuition, based on program code, is $268 per credit hour for lower-division courses and $294 per credit hour for upper-division courses.

## FINANCIAL AID

RIT offers a full range of traditional financial aid programs as well as a number of innovative financing plans. Scholarships and assistantships are available to matriculated students in most graduate departments. The process of applying for aid should begin during the month of January in the year the student wishes to enroll.

## APPLYING

Online learning students follow the same procedures as all other students attending RIT. Decisions for selection rest within each college. Correspondence between the student and the Institute is conducted through the Offices of Part-Time and Graduate Enrollment Services, which reviews applications as they are received.

### CONTACT

Offices of Part-Time and Graduate Enrollment Services
Rochester Institute of Technology
58 Lomb Memorial Drive
Rochester, New York 14623-5604
Telephone: 716-475-2229
800-CALL-RIT (toll-free)
Fax: 716-475-7164
E-mail: online@rit.edu
Web site: http://online.rit.edu

# Roger Williams University
## *Open College*
Bristol and Providence, Rhode Island

*Accredited by the New England Association of Schools and Colleges, Roger Williams University (RWU) is an independent institution that was founded in 1956. Roger Williams University offers students a strong foundation in the liberal arts and sciences, combined with a variety of professional programs. The University's Core Curriculum introduces all students to a wide range of subjects—in the humanities, natural and social sciences, history, and fine arts—to broaden their horizons and help them develop the building blocks for lifelong learning and professional success. For the third consecutive year,* U.S. News & World Report *named Roger Williams University a "Top-Tier" Northern Liberal Arts College.*

*The University's Open College is a comprehensive external degree program designed for people interested in nontraditional education. Most of the students are working adults who are able to pursue their educational programs with little or no interference with their personal or professional commitments.*

## DISTANCE LEARNING PROGRAM

Since its inception in 1974, more than 3,600 students have graduated from the Open College at Roger Williams University. In the 2000–01 academic year, 125 courses were offered via distance learning. The average distance learning enrollment is 600 students per semester.

Academic programs are divided into regular semesters of study, including fall, spring, and summer. Campus residency is not required.

## DELIVERY MEDIA

The Open College emphasizes an external approach to education, and the instructional methods available to off-campus students include nonclassroom courses, such as external courses, internships, online courses, and independent study courses. Some of the external courses may include guided instruction via videotapes, audiotapes, computer software, computer conferencing, World Wide Web, e-mail, and print. Students and teachers may meet in person or interact via audioconferencing, mail, telephone, fax, e-mail, and World Wide Web. The following equipment may be required: fax machine, computer, Internet access, and e-mail.

## PROGRAMS OF STUDY

Distance education through the Open College at Roger Williams University offers baccalaureate degrees in business management, criminal justice, industrial technology, public administration, and social science.

The business management major provides students with "marketplace" skills such as problem solving, information gathering and processing, and project managing. The degree also prepares students to appreciate the overall challenges of a business operation and to function effectively within an integrated business environment.

The criminal justice major is designed for students who are employed, or who are seeking employment, in direct law enforcement professions or public or private criminal justice–related agencies.

The industrial technology major is designed for students with technical and/or managerial backgrounds and interests and who are employed or seeking employment in manufacturing or service industries.

The public administration major prepares students for government service on the federal, state, or local level and for employment in non-profit organizations and international administration.

The social science major is designed for students with interests in more than one social science area and whose interests cannot be accommodated by a single discipline. Typically, students select a combination of courses that reflect personal or professional interests and represent a coherent program with one or more specific focuses or themes.

To earn a baccalaureate degree, a minimum of 120 credits are required through any combination of learning experiences, including credit for previous college work, military training and experience, CLEP exams, and credit documentation. Students are required to complete a minimum of 30 credits through the Open College at Roger Williams University. Also, a minimum 2.0 grade point average is required in all courses carrying a letter grade and in all required major courses.

Each student is assigned to a faculty adviser who works with the student to develop an education and degree plan. The adviser also assists in registration, credit documentation, and enrollment procedures; identifies appropriate courses and learning experiences; and supervises student work.

## SPECIAL PROGRAMS

The Open College at Roger Williams University offers internships, co-ops, and practica for employment-related learning experiences in all academic degree programs.

## STUDENT SERVICES

All college services available to the traditional student are also available to distance learning students, including access to the University's library, computer support, tutoring, advising, and career placement.

## CREDIT OPTIONS

Many students are able to enter the Open College with considerable advanced standing. Students may reduce the total time required for completion of studies and degree requirements with up to three years of credit from military service and training, transfer of credits obtained from other colleges, credit documentation that awards credit for life and job-related learning experiences, and College-Level Examination Program (CLEP) or other advanced credit exams.

## FACULTY

The Open College at Roger Williams University has a total of 47 faculty members to provide instruction. Eighteen are full-time faculty members at RWU (38 percent), and 29 are part-time (adjunct) faculty members (62 percent). Twenty-six faculty members (55 percent) have doctoral or other terminal degrees. All faculty members have at least one graduate degree.

## ADMISSION

Admissions preference is given to students who are able to enter with advanced standing, based on credits already acquired from previous college attendance, military training, employment experiences, and/or CLEP exams. Also, preference is given to students who have access to various educational and learning resources in the event such resources need to be incorporated into their academic programs. Resources may include, but are not limited to, libraries, classroom courses at local colleges, local proctors, potential sites for internship placement, and computers.

## TUITION AND FEES

Open College tuition varies by program and ranged from $705 to $1200 per 3-credit course for the 2000–01 academic year. The application fee is $35; no registration fee is required.

## FINANCIAL AID

Aside from various forms of military tuition assistance that might be available to service members, Open College students are eligible for all of the traditional forms of financial aid that are normally associated with adult and continuing education students. Approximately 50 percent of distance learning students receive financial assistance (excluding employer reimbursement programs).

## APPLYING

Applications must be submitted with appropriate documentation, such as a resume, official high school transcripts, GED scores, or official transcripts from previous colleges or universities. Service members must submit a copy of credit recommendations for all military training and experience from Form DD295, prepared by military education officers, or SMART/AARTS transcripts.

### CONTACT

John Stout, Dean
Open College
Roger Williams University
150 Washington Street
Providence, Rhode Island 02903
Telephone: 401-254-3530
            800-458-7144 Ext. 3530 (toll-free)
Fax: 401-254-3560
E-mail: jws@alpha.rwu.edu
Web site: http://www.rwu.edu

# Rutgers, The State University of New Jersey

## *RutgersOnline*

New Brunswick, New Jersey

*Rutgers University, which comprises twenty-nine undergraduate colleges and graduate and professional schools, is the flagship institution of New Jersey's public higher education system. It is a vibrant and diverse community of more than 48,000 students enrolled in over 280 degree programs, 35,000 students enrolled in continuing professional development courses, 10,000 faculty and staff members, and more than 300,000 living alumni.*

*Founded more than 230 years ago in 1766, Rutgers is distinguished as one of the oldest institutions of higher learning in the country. At the same time, modern-day Rutgers qualifies as the youngest of America's major public research universities. In the span of the last forty years, Rutgers has risen from a disparate collection of schools, geographically dispersed and operating largely independently, into the ranks of the nation's most prestigious educational institutions. That advancement was recognized in 1989 when Rutgers was asked to join the Association of American Universities, comprising the top research universities in North America. Driving all of Rutgers' activities, whether teaching, research, or service, is the defining characteristic of a great research university: the continuous and vigorous creation of intellectual capital and the new discoveries and insights that drive the advancement of human knowledge contributing to the improvement of the human condition.*

*RutgersOnline extends the services and reach of the University, providing students with the opportunity to telecommute to campus from virtually anywhere. RutgersOnline students benefit from some of Rutgers most distinguished faculty members through online courses that are equivalent to traditional courses offered on campus. Graduate courses in nursing and communication and library studies were among the first offered during 1999–2000. Additional courses in budgeting, management, accountancy, and education are being developed and will be available within the next year.*

## DISTANCE LEARNING PROGRAM

Rutgers University seeks to use distance learning to promote the three-fold mission of teaching, research, and service, providing the same high-quality academic program that is found on campus. RutgersOnline extends access to the resources of the University through the Internet-based distance learning program, especially for nontraditional, working adult students who are off campus. The hallmarks of the distance learning program are high quality in the academic program, a high level of interactivity for active learning, and access to a wide range of resources found only at a top research university.

## DELIVERY MEDIA

Internet-based courses delivered through RutgersOnline provide asynchronous access to selected courses from anywhere in the world. Students need computer and Internet access. Full hardware and software requirements are detailed at http://www.rutgersonline.net.

RutgersOnline courses are highly interactive and use various software-based tools to enhance student-faculty and student-student interaction, including threaded discussion, e-mail, and chat room.

## PROGRAMS OF STUDY

In fall 1999, RutgersOnline began offering courses in nursing and library studies, primarily at the graduate level. Various certificate programs will be offered in the near future. Several online master's degrees are anticipated in the future, as well, beginning with a master's degree in nursing. In addition, courses are being developed in the budgeting and management areas, accounting, economics, adult education with a focus on adult literacy, and selected liberal arts areas. Most courses offered by RutgersOnline will be at the graduate level. In addition, several non-credit, professional development courses have been offered, and others are being developed.

## STUDENT SERVICES

Students of the RutgersOnline distance learning program have access to a wide range of student services online. Admissions, financial aid, and library and other services are available online. In addition, online students have a 24-hour-a-day, seven-day-a-week Help Desk to support the technical aspects of their online learning. The Help Desk is available by e-mail and toll-free phone number.

## TUITION AND FEES

Tuition and fees are variable, depending upon the school offering the course. The average is approximately $800 for a New Jersey resident for an undergraduate 3-credit course to approximately $1600 for a nonresident for an undergraduate 3-credit course. Graduate course tuition and fees for residents are approximately $1400 for a 3-credit course and approximately $2000 for nonresidents.

## FINANCIAL AID

All forms of student financial aid are available to assist matriculated students enrolling in Rutgers undergraduate or graduate degree programs and utilizing Rutgers University distance learning courses. The application process, particular undergraduate and graduate program specifications, and other key eligibility information can be accessed through the Office of Financial Aid's Web page at http://studentaid.rutgers.edu.

## APPLYING

Distance learning students apply and register through the respective school offering the online course. For matriculating students, online registration is available through the main Rutgers University Web site at http://www.rutgers.edu.

---

### CONTACT

For more information about RutgersOnline, prospective students should first review all of the information at the Web site listed below. Program and course questions should be directed to the appropriate individulas as listed on the Web site. General questions can be directed to:

Dr. Richard J. Novak
Executive Director for Continuous Education and
Distance Learning
Telephone: 732-932-3491
Fax: 732-932-2588
E-mail: ce1766@rci.rutgers.edu
Web site: http://www.ce1766.rutgers.edu/online

---

# Saint Joseph's College of Maine

## *Division of Graduate and Professional Studies*

Standish, Maine

*Saint Joseph's College was founded in 1912 by the Sisters of Mercy and chartered by the Maine legislature in 1915. The College grants degrees in keeping with the mission of the College and the ministries of the Sisters of Mercy. Saint Joseph's is a liberal arts college that nurtures intellectual, spiritual, and social growth in students of all ages and all faiths within a value-centered environment.*

*In 1970, Saint Joseph's became a coeducational institution, and in 1976, the Distance Education Program was introduced to serve the needs of the nontraditional adult learner nationwide.*

*Saint Joseph's is located on the shores of Sebago Lake, 18 miles from Portland. More than 1,000 students attend classes on the 331-acre campus. The beautiful lakefront of the campus faces the White Mountains. The region's natural beauty and the proximity of the College to Maine's popular ski resorts appeal to the outdoor enthusiast in winter. The nearby rocky Atlantic coastline and picturesque New England countryside offer an ideal setting for the summer experience.*

## DISTANCE LEARNING PROGRAM

Saint Joseph's College offers the adult learner an opportunity to integrate formal education in the liberal arts tradition with professional experience. Saint Joseph's College is accredited by the New England Association of Schools and Colleges. The Graduate and Professional Studies program provides academic options in a variety of disciplines leading to undergraduate and graduate certificates and to associate, baccalaureate, and graduate degrees. Each option is designed to reflect the special nature of Saint Joseph's commitment to its students. The Graduate and Professional Studies program currently enrolls about 4,000 active students, and approximately 7,000 Saint Joseph's alumni earned their degrees through the distance program.

## DELIVERY MEDIA

Faculty-directed independent study is a highly flexible, accessible mode of education that allows students to

study where they are. Upon enrollment, students receive the texts, materials, and study guides for their courses. Some courses require access to a computer or a VCR. Approximately half of the 200 courses offered through the Division of Graduate and Professional Studies are available online via the Internet. Faculty members assist each student with their studies through a combination of written feedback on assignments, telephone consultations, and e-mail. An academic adviser is assigned to work with each student from the first enrollment through to graduation. Undergraduate and graduate degree programs require one 2-week summer residency at the campus in Maine. Nondegree classes are also offered.

## PROGRAMS OF STUDY

The Graduate and Professional Studies program offers the following degree and certificate programs: a Master of Science in education with an emphasis in teaching and learning (33 credits), which serves two major pro-

fessional arenas—K–12 school systems and adult education programs; a master's degree in health services administration (42 credits) for senior management roles in complex organizations; a Master of Arts in pastoral studies (33 credits) for those who seek to minister to the evolving needs of church and society; the Bachelor of Science (128 credits), with majors in health-care administration and long-term-care administration; the Bachelor of Science in professional arts (128 credits), a degree-completion program for licensed health-care professionals with concentrations in health-care administration, human services, and psychology; the Bachelor of Science in general studies (128 credits), a degree-completion program for adult students transferring a minimum of 30 credits, with concentrations in business administration, human services, psychology, and adult education and training; the Bachelor of Science in radiologic science (128 credits), a postcertification baccalaureate degree for radiologic science professionals; the Bachelor of Science in respiratory care (128 credits), a postcertification baccalaureate degree for respiratory care professionals; the Bachelor of Science in criminal justice (128 credits) to provide individuals currently working in law enforcement a well-rounded curriculum; the Bachelor of Arts in liberal studies (128 credits), an interdisciplinary degree program with concentrations in American studies, and the Christian tradition; the Bachelor of Science in business administration (128 credits), with concentrations in management and banking (a joint venture with the American Institute of Banking); the Associate of Science in criminal justice (66 credits), a foundation for the Bachelor of

Science in criminal justice; the Associate of Science in management (66 credits), a foundation for the Bachelor of Science in business administration; graduate certificates (18 credits) in health-care finance, designed to provide nonfinancial health-care managers with an in-depth background in health-care financial management; medical/dental administration for physicians and dentists; pastoral studies for those seeking to secure or enhance positions in a wide spectrum of ministries; and undergraduate certificate programs (18 credits) in business administration, health-care management, long-term-care administration, criminal justice, Christian tradition, American studies, and professional studies (self-designed). Students who would like to take individual courses may enroll as continuing education students.

## SPECIAL PROGRAMS

The Department of Nursing offers a Master of Science in Nursing with specializations in nursing administration, nursing education, and parish nursing (48 credits); a graduate certificate in parish nursing (18 credits); and a Bachelor of Science in Nursing with an RN to B.S.N. track (129 credits) for students at a distance. The Division of Graduate and Professional Studies is a member of the Army University Access Online program, and assists other active and nonactive military personnel in their educational pursuits as a member of Servicemembers Opportunity Colleges (SOC).

## CREDIT OPTIONS

The Graduate and Professional Studies program acknowledges the value of certain formal learning and career-based experience. For most programs, the College follows the American Council on Education guidelines in granting transfer credit for courses of study from accredited colleges or universities with a grade of C or better; ACE/PONSI-approved credit; ACE-approved military training and experience credits; CEUs earned through professional seminars, workshops, internships, and in-service education classes as elective credit; and CLEP, ACT/PEP, and DANTES exams. A maximum of 30 credits can be accepted by exam.

## FACULTY

More than 100 full-time and part-time faculty members serve students in the Graduate and Professional Studies program. Many teach in the traditional program as well as in distance education. All excel in their fields and have experience with nontraditional students.

## ADMISSION

Admission requirements vary by program of study. Prospective students should contact the Admissions Office for the Graduate and Professional Studies program at 800-752-4723 (toll-free) with specific questions about admission requirements. Information can also be obtained from the Web site listed below.

## TUITION AND FEES

In the 2001–02 academic year, tuition is $200 per credit hour ($600 per 3-credit course) at the undergraduate level and $240 per credit hour ($720 per 3-credit course) at the graduate level. Application fees are $50 for degree programs and $25 for certificate programs and continuing education. A complete fee schedule is available in the program catalogs.

## FINANCIAL AID

Students may be eligible for the Federal Pell Grant and/or Federal Stafford Student Loan. Applying for financial aid is an individualized process requiring consultation and evaluation. For more information and assistance, students should call the Financial Aid Office at 800-752-1266 (toll-free).

## APPLYING

Students are accepted on a rolling admissions basis and, therefore, can apply and begin their studies at any time during the year. Students can apply online at http://www.sjcme.edu/gps or by contacting the Admissions Office at the number listed below.

---

**CONTACT**

Admissions Office
Division of Graduate and Professional Studies
Saint Joseph's College of Maine
278 Whites Bridge Road
Standish, Maine 04084-5263
Telephone: 800-752-4723 (toll-free)
Fax: 207-892-7480
E-mail: admiss@sjcme.edu
Web site: http://www.sjcme.edu/gps

---

# Saint Mary-of-the-Woods College

## *Women's External Degree Program*

Saint Mary-of-the-Woods, Indiana

*Founded in 1840, Saint Mary-of-the-Woods College (SMWC) is the nation's oldest Catholic liberal arts college for women and is accredited by the North Central Association of Colleges and Schools. The College offers the rich traditions of academic excellence and dedication to educating women personally and professionally for responsible roles in society. The diverse student community of 1,400 includes traditional resident students, commuters, student mothers and children, and distance learners at both the undergraduate and graduate levels. A hallmark of the College is an emphasis on personalized service.*

*The general studies curriculum required of all undergraduates is designed to develop the communication and analytical skills needed for success in college and in the professional world.*

## DISTANCE LEARNING PROGRAM

Since 1973, the Women's External Degree (WED) program has provided the College curriculum to contemporary adult women who juggle multiple responsibilities yet need or want a college degree. Now serving 1,000 women, this structured but flexible independent study program is based on five-month semesters that begin with in-person appointments with instructors and faculty advisers and leads to a degree in one of more than twenty majors.

## DELIVERY MEDIA

Faculty members and students communicate by telephone, voice mail, e-mail, and postal service. All full-time faculty members, some adjuncts, and many students have access to e-mail. Computers with modems are not required, except for accounting, CIS, and digital media communication majors, but access to a computer or word processor is strongly recommended. Some courses use videotapes, audiotapes, or optional computer programs.

## PROGRAMS OF STUDY

The College is chartered to grant the degrees Associate in Arts, Associate in Science, Bachelor of Arts, and Bachelor of Science to women and the Master of Arts degree to both women and men.

Undergraduates complete the general studies curriculum, courses required for their chosen major, and additional electives to total 125 semester hours for a baccalaureate degree and 65 semester hours for an associate degree; a minimum of 30 hours must be earned at the College.

Associate majors available through WED are accounting, early childhood education, general business, gerontology, humanities, and paralegal studies. Baccalaureate majors are accounting, accounting information systems, business administration, computer information systems, digital media communications, education (early childhood, elementary, and secondary), English, equine business management, gerontology, history/political science, human resource management, human services, humanities, journalism, marketing, mathematics, not-for-profit administration, occupational therapy applications, paralegal studies, professional writing, psychology, social sciences (history concentration), and theology.

There are no geographical restrictions, except that education majors must reside within 200 miles of campus for faculty supervision of field experience and student teaching.

The Master of Arts in pastoral theology program is designed for persons who are or plan to be engaged in ministry and for those seeking personal enrichment in theological study.

The Master of Arts in earth literacy program is designed for persons who care for and advocate a sustainable and just earth community.

The Master of Arts in art therapy program is designed for persons who use or plan to use art in therapy or art as therapy. This program emphasizes understanding and applying theories to art therapy, counseling, and psychopathology.

The Master of Arts in music therapy program is designed for professional music therapists who seek an advanced understanding of the therapeutic uses of music, especially as applied to psychotherapy and medicine. Master of Arts degrees require 36 to 40 credit hours.

## SPECIAL PROGRAMS

SMWC offers several learning formats: traditional campus-based study, distance learning, and a third format that combines independent study with intensive weekend seminars on campus. WED students may combine these formats in any semester of study; about 400 choose to enroll in weekend alternative format courses each year. However, all degrees offered through WED may be completed entirely through distance learning at home, with the exception of several paralegal, digital media communication, and equine courses, which must be taken via alternative format on campus on weekends.

## STUDENT SERVICES

Full-time faculty members serve as academic advisers to the WED students in their departments, meeting each semester to monitor progress and plan subsequent semesters. A WED staff of 8 provides additional support, advocacy, registrarial assistance, and information, including a quarterly newsletter for distance learners. One WED staff person provides referral to other campus services, such as career development (available by phone and in person) and library materials by mail.

## CREDIT OPTIONS

Students may transfer credit earned at other accredited colleges and universities, although some credits may be too dated to meet the requirements. WED encourages students to earn credit for previous college-level learning through CLEP and DANTES, ACE/CCRS awards, and portfolio ap-

plications documenting other prior learning. At least 30 semester hours of course work must be earned under the direct supervision of SMWC faculty members.

## FACULTY

Fifty-seven full-time and 55 adjunct faculty members serve as instructors and academic advisers to WED students. Sixty percent of full-time faculty members have doctoral or other terminal degrees.

## ADMISSION

Applicants must have earned a high school diploma or GED certificate and demonstrate potential for success in a distance learning program. SAT I scores are required for applicants who have been out of high school for less than five years. Academic history, employment and other life experience, writing skills, and stated goals are considered. Applicants for whom English is a second language must submit TOEFL scores.

## TUITION AND FEES

For 2001–02, undergraduate tuition for the WED program is $294 per semester hour. Fees include a $30 ap-

plication fee, a one-time fee of $80 for the initial on-campus residency (not including housing), an annual $50 general fee, and modest materials fees for laboratory courses.

## FINANCIAL AID

Available financial aid includes Federal Pell grants, student loans, and, for residents only, Indiana Higher Education grants. In 2000–01, the College processed about $2.7 million from these sources on behalf of WED students. The College awards small WED grants to eligible seniors and offers 10 percent tuition discounts through cooperating employers; this institutional aid totaled $63,000 in 2000–01. Finally, the WED staff maintains a directory of private grants and scholarships and encourages WED students to apply for them. More than half of WED students receive some form of aid.

## APPLYING

Applications are reviewed when all materials are received; the evaluation process is usually completed within a month. Two-day orientation residencies are held on campus five times each year and conclude with enrollment in the initial semester.

## CONTACT

**Admission:**
Gwen Hagemeyer
WED Admission Director
Saint Mary-of-the-Woods College
Saint Mary-of-the-Woods, Indiana
   47876
Telephone: 812-535-5186
      800-926-SMWC
      (toll-free)
Fax: 812-535-4900
E-mail: wedadms@smwc.edu
Web site: http://www.smwc.edu

**Graduate Programs:**
Mary Lou Dolan, C.S.J.
Earth Literacy Director
Telephone: 812-535-5160
Fax: 812-535-5228
E-mail: mldolan@smwc.edu
     elm@smwc.edu
Kathy Gotshall
Art Therapy Program
Telephone: 812-535-5151
E-mail: kgotshal@smwc.edu

Virginia Unverzagt
Pastoral Theology Director
Telephone: 812-535-5170
Fax: 812-535-4613
E-mail: vunver@smwc.edu

Tracy Richardson
Music Therapy Program
Telephone: 812-535-5154
E-mail: trichardson@smwc.edu

# Salve Regina University

## Extension Study

Newport, Rhode Island

---

*Salve Regina is an independent, coeducational institution of higher learning that confers degrees in the arts and sciences. It teaches in the tradition of the Catholic Church and according to the Mission of the Sisters of Mercy who continue as its sponsors. Salve Regina's Charter was amended in June 1991 to change its name to Salve Regina University.*

*The University serves approximately 2,200 men and women from many states and foreign countries. Alumni number more than 12,000. Its 65-acre oceanfront campus in Newport's Ochre Point historic district includes twenty-two new and adapted buildings.*

*The University, through teaching and research, prepares men and women for responsible lives by imparting and expanding knowledge, developing skills, and cultivating enduring values. Through liberal arts and professional programs, students develop their abilities for thinking clearly and creatively, enhance their capacity for sound judgment, and prepare for the challenge of learning throughout their lives.*

*The graduate programs of Salve Regina University have two broad goals: to help the individual who enrolls to realize his or her own full potential and to prepare this individual for helping others do the same. Specific objectives of each graduate program are three-fold: to create an opportunity for critical analysis and problem solving from a Judeo-Christian perspective, to stimulate growth in wisdom by integrating the knowledge and experience gained by the student both inside and outside the classroom, and to emphasize the importance of ethics in each program's curriculum.*

## DISTANCE LEARNING PROGRAM

The Graduate Extension Study alternative is designed to meet the needs of students whose personal and professional circumstances make regular on-campus study impossible. Courses at the graduate level as well as systematic programs leading to the completion of requirements for the master's degree are available for eligible students. Extension Study is a highly personalized alternative to the traditional classroom approach to learning. It involves a one-on-one relationship with instructors who guide students' learning and monitor their progress through the course. Detailed syllabi prepared by faculty members provide a structured, step-by-step approach to learning while allowing students the utmost flexibility in organizing their study time.

## DELIVERY MEDIA

Students can register online, by mail, or in person for Extension Study courses. Once registered, students receive a detailed syllabus and their textbooks by mail, as well as contact information for their professor. Salve Regina Extension Study also has a course Web site where students can find their syllabus online, communicate and interact with their classmates and professor, and find links to other helpful and related sites. In addition, an online information center gives students important information on everything from applying for admission to filing for degree.

## PROGRAMS OF STUDY

Four distance learning master's degree programs are offered in business administration, human development, international relations, and management.

The Master of Business Administration program is designed to prepare graduates for professional careers in organizations that operate in a rapidly changing environment. It is directed towards developing managers and focuses on finance, economics, accounting, organizational behavior, strategic management, and ethics.

The Master of Arts program in human development focuses on psychological, spiritual, emotional, and intellectual development. Students discover new ways to think, to learn, and to promote self-development both for themselves and others.

The Master of Arts in international relations focuses on new ways to achieve global harmony and justice. The program, planned for those who seek a broader and deeper understanding of the contemporary world, helps to prepare students for an increasingly interdependent twenty-first century. Courses address individual needs and prepare students for enhanced careers in government, international organizations, business, finance, teaching, and research.

The Master of Science program in management offers a solid theoretical and practical management foundation and integrates information systems into the management role.

Salve Regina University is a fully accredited member of the New England Association of Schools and Colleges (NEASC). Having met the criteria of NEASC's Commission on Institutions of Higher Education for quality and integrity through periodic peer reviews, the University is considered to have the resources to pursue its stated purposes and has shown great promise that its educational programs will continue into the future. NEASC accreditation is impartial and applies to the entire institution; it does not guarantee specific courses, programs, or individual graduate competency. Accreditation provides reasonable assurances regarding quality of student opportunities. Inquiries about NEASC accreditation may be directed to the Vice President for Academic Affairs at Salve Regina or to the Commission on Institutions of Higher Education, NEASC, 209 Burlington Road, Bedford, MA 01730-1433. (Telephone: 617-271-0022, E-mail: cihe@neasc.org)

## SPECIAL PROGRAMS

The certificate program in management is for students who already have a bachelor's degree, and includes 15 hours of graduate credit. It offers opportunities for those who desire a graduate education without formal pursuit of a master's degree. The certificate program in management/correctional administration does not require a bachelor's degree. Twelve credits hours are required.

Salve Regina University also participates with the Global Risk Management Institute in providing courses for the Fellow in Risk Management (FRM). The FRM is an advanced designation specifically for risk managers and others who want to further their education and improve their risk management skills. To take courses, the student must first apply and be accepted by the Global Risk Management Institute.

All students taking seven or more courses through the Extension Study program need to complete a residency requirement. The Graduate Extension Study Institute or Summer Institute is a four-day on-campus experience which is usually held the first weekend in June. The Institute enables students to interact with faculty members and other students, fulfill residency requirements, identify with the University, and experience the beauty of Salve Regina's campus. Alternatively, those students who are close enough to campus to commute, may take a course on campus at any time to meet their residency requirement.

## CREDIT OPTIONS

The master's degree programs are all twelve courses (36 credits). Students have six months to complete each course. Students normally register for up to two courses at a time. Students have up to five years to complete all of the requirements for the degree; however, at a rate of four courses per year, students are generally able to complete the degree in three years if they are able to complete two courses every six months. The transfer policy may allow up to 40 percent of the program credit requirements. Students who have completed courses approved by the American Council of Education (ACE) at nondegree granting military or professional schools may request additional transfer credits.

## FACULTY

The faculty members are a valued resource; many teach full time on campus and others are adjunct faculty members who are successful professionals within their field. They come from leading doctoral, M.B.A., and law programs and represent a wide variety of backgrounds. Their superior teaching skills, academic training and research, and knowledge of practical application bring a wealth of experience to the curriculum.

## ADMISSION

Men and women with bachelor's degrees from accredited institutions of higher learning who are considered to have the ability to pursue graduate study and show a desire for personal development are admitted following a careful evaluation of their credentials, without regard to age, race, sex, creed, national or ethnic origin, or handicap.

## TUITION AND FEES

Tuition is $450 per credit hour for all Extension Study courses. All courses are 3 credit hours. Fees include application ($50), incomplete/delay of grade ($100), master's degree graduation ($150), transcript ($5), and prerequisite courses ($500).

## FINANCIAL AID

Salve Regina University assists students in applying for loans through the Federal Family Educational Loan Programs, particularly the Federal Stafford Loans. These loans are available to all students and may be used to fund education at the University provided the student maintains continuous quantitative and qualitative progress. Benefit plans for veterans and active duty service persons and employers' tuition reimbursement plans are welcome.

## APPLYING

A Graduate Extension Study catalog with application may be requested from the Graduate Admissions Office. The address and phone number are listed below. The following must be submitted to the Graduate Admissions office: application form, nonrefundable application fee, official transcripts from all accredited degree granting institutions attended, two letters of recommendation, standardized test score no more than five years old (GRE, MAT, GMAT, or LSAT), a personal statement of intent of study, and a nonrefundable commitment deposit upon acceptance. The TOEFL and official transcript evaluations are required of international students.

### CONTACT

Associate Director
Graduate Extension Study
Salve Regina University
100 Ochre Point Avenue
Newport, Rhode Island 02840
Telephone: 800-GO-SALVE (toll-free)
Fax: 401-341-2931
E-mail: graduate-studies@salve.edu
Web site: http://www.salve.edu

# Sam Houston State University

## *Distance Learning*

Huntsville, Texas

---

Sam Houston State University (SHSU), located in Huntsville, Texas, serves one of the most diverse populations of any educational institution in the state. The University is committed to the development of its creative resources so that it can adapt to the changing educational needs of its constituency while maintaining high quality in the traditional curricula.

Sam Houston State University, a member institution in the Texas State University System and the Southern Association of Colleges and Schools (SACS) as an accredited institution of higher learning, is organized academically into four colleges: Arts and Sciences, Education and Applied Science, Business Administration, and Criminal Justice. More than 12,500 students are offered an extensive range of bachelor's and master's degrees, as well as the Doctor of Philosophy in criminal justice, the Doctor of Philosophy in forensic clinical psychology, and the Doctor of Education in educational leadership.

## DISTANCE LEARNING PROGRAM

SHSU offers three graduate programs and three undergraduate majors entirely online. The online courses offer students anytime, anywhere access to course material while allowing multiple means of interactivity and communication with faculty members.

## DELIVERY MEDIA

Sam Houston State University's distance learning options are available interactively via the World Wide Web, e-mail, video, and telecourses. Students and faculty members correspond by telephone, mail, fax, e-mail, and online chat.

## PROGRAMS OF STUDY

The Master of Science (M.S.) degree in criminal justice is designed for individuals in middle management positions in a criminal justice agency, or for those who have a reasonable expectation of being promoted to such a position. This degree requires the completion of 36 credit hours. For more information, prospective students should visit the Web site http://www.shsu.edu/cjcenter/College.

The Master of Education (M.Ed.) in reading degree plan is designed for those holding an elementary or secondary teaching certificate and can lead to certification as a reading specialist. The degree requires the completion of a minimum of 36 hours of graduate credit. For more information, prospective students should visit the Web at http://www.shsu.edu/~edu_lls.

The Master of Arts (M.A.) in military history program is designed for active duty military, military retirees, and others interested in military history. This degree requires the completion of 36 credit hours (nonthesis option) or 30 credit hours (thesis option). For more information, prospective students should visit the Web at http://www.shsu.edu/~his_www.

The undergraduate history, criminal justice, and criminal justice, victim studies majors are designed for students who may want to combine online courses with course work on campus, or for those who may want to complete all the required classes for a major at home. These majors require 36 credit hours. For more information, prospective students should visit the Web at http://www.shsu.edu/~his_www for history and http://www.shsu.edu/cjcenter/College for criminal justice, and criminal justice, victim studies.

## SPECIAL PROGRAMS

Students in the Houston, Texas area have access to SHSU's distance learning courses at the University Center in The Woodlands, Texas. Degrees include business administration, M.B.A.; criminal justice, M.S.; elementary education, M.Ed.; secondary education, M.Ed.; educational leadership: administrator supervisors certificate, M.Ed.; English, M.A.; history, M.A.; postbaccalaureate teacher certification; accounting, B.B.A.; applied arts and sciences, B.A.A.S.; biology, B.A. or B.S.; criminal justice, B.A. or B.S.; geography, B.A. or B.S.; management, B.B.A.; political science, B.A. or B.S.; and psychology, B.S. Prospective students should visit the Web at http://www.tuc.edu.

## STUDENT SERVICES

Online library services, computer services, and academic advising are available to all students. Telephone numbers, fax numbers, and e-mail addresses are readily available from SHSU's Web site (http://www.shsu.edu). SHSU also offers access to student services by phone through the campus operator (telephone: 936-294-1111).

## CREDIT OPTIONS

Distance learners have the same options for credit as on-campus students, including transfer credit.

## FACULTY

The 505 full-time faculty members are recognized regionally, nationally, and internationally with many teaching both on-campus and distance learning courses.

## ADMISSION

Requirements for admission and completion of degree vary by academic department. Students should refer to Programs of Study and Applying sections.

## TUITION AND FEES

Graduate tuition is $247 and undergraduate tuition is $265 per 3-credit course. A distance learning fee of $303 per 3-credit course applies to all online courses.

Tuition for distance learning courses at the University Center is $383 for 3-credit graduate and undergraduate courses. There is also a University Center fee of $25 per credit.

## FINANCIAL AID

SHSU offers several financial aid programs including grants, scholarships, and loans. The process of applying for financial aid should be completed by March 31 of the year the student wishes to enroll.

## APPLYING

Students seeking admission to bachelor degree programs must submit an application to the Undergraduate Admissions office via the corresponding Web site or contact the Undergraduate Admissions office by phone (both listed below). Students seeking admission to master's degree programs must submit an application to Graduate Studies via the corresponding Web site or contact Graduate Studies by phone (both listed below).

---

**CONTACT**

Academic Instructional Technology and Distance Learning
Sam Houston State University
P.O. Box 2179
Huntsville, Texas 77340
Telephone: 936-294-1828 (Undergraduate Admissions)
           936-294-1971 (Graduate Studies)
Web site: http://www.shsu.edu/~vaf_jlv/de (Distance Learning)
           http://www.shsu.edu/~adm_www (Undergraduate Admissions)
           http://www.shsu.edu/~grs_www (Graduate Studies)

---

# San Joaquin Delta College

## DeltaOnline
Stockton, California

*San Joaquin Delta College, one of California's 106 community colleges, was founded in 1963 and is accredited by the Western Association of Schools and Colleges. The College offers courses leading to transfer to the University of California and California State University systems and to other colleges and universities. Associate degrees in arts and science and nearly seventy certificate programs are available. San Joaquin Delta College is recognized as a leader in computer applications and program development on a statewide and national level.*

*San Joaquin Delta College is committed to excellence in the provision of postsecondary education throughout the college district. This commitment is reflected in the College's comprehensive instructional programs, services to students and the public, professionalism of faculty and staff, and campus beauty and utility.*

## DISTANCE LEARNING PROGRAM

San Joaquin Delta College is committed to providing high-quality distance learning opportunities. Some 2000 students annually have enrolled in distance learning courses, which utilize interactive television and the Internet.

San Joaquin Delta College has launched its virtual campus, DeltaOnline (address listed below), for fall 2001; sixty-one course sections will be offered online.

## DELIVERY MEDIA

San Joaquin Delta College offers distance learning via a variety of media. The College offers interactive television (ITV) and online courses.

ITV students attend classes at sites located in the communities of Jackson, San Andreas, Manteca, and Tracy. ITV has two-way video and two-way audio capabilities.

Online students have access to general education and transfer elective courses as well as a variety of specialized classes via DeltaOnline. DeltaOnline students can access their

courses completely at a distance by using the Internet. Online students require access to a computer and an Internet service provider and communicate via a variety of online tools.

The online courses are offered via the eCollege.com system.

## PROGRAMS OF STUDY

Currently, the College offers courses leading to the Associate of Arts (A.A.) degree. There are nineteen courses offered online that meet the associate degree general education pattern. In addition to general education requirements, a minimum of 18 units of course work in an approved program of study plus electives must be completed for a minimum total of 60 units for the A.A. degree. Courses in business, as well as a variety of elective courses, are available online to fulfill those requirements.

## SPECIAL PROGRAMS

Certificates in business are now available online. Distance learners can acquire supervision and management and merchandising certificates through DeltaOnline. These certifi-

cate programs offer a variety of knowledge and skills for business students.

The College also provides three online courses for the attainment of an early childhood education assistant certificate. Other early childhood education courses, which apply toward early childhood education certificates, are also available.

## STUDENT SERVICES

Many of the student services available on campus are also available to distance learning students via the Internet. San Joaquin Delta College students can use the Internet to access admissions and registration as well as the Delta College Bookstore and Library. In addition, DeltaOnline students may access tutoring, guidance and counseling, financial aid, disabled student programs and services, and extended opportunity programs and services. A guidance course in job-seeking skills is also offered.

## CREDIT OPTIONS

Delta Online courses may be taken for credit and, in some cases, with a credit/no credit option. Course descriptions indicate whether the course is transferable to the California State University or University of California. Courses may also meet general education requirements for the associate degree in arts or science, California State University, or the University of California. Credits earned from accredited institutions of higher education may be transferable.

## FACULTY

Ninety-nine percent of the Delta Online faculty members are full-time instructors at San Joaquin Delta College. All faculty members have master's degrees or the equivalent in their respective disciplines.

## ADMISSION

New students must submit an application for admission, which is available from the Admissions Department on campus or on line through the Delta Online Web site or through the admissions information Web page (addresses listed below). Current high school students can apply for admission and take college courses concurrently with their high school programs.

## TUITION AND FEES

Students who are California residents are charged $11 per unit, regardless of the number of units. For example, a 3-unit course would cost $33. Nonresident students are charged $130 per unit for tuition plus an enrollment fee of $11 per unit and a fee of $307 for Internet classes. For example, a 3-unit course would cost $730. All fees are to be paid when a student registers for classes.

Active military personnel and their dependents living within the district may have tuition fees waived for classes taken during their stay in California.

## APPLYING

Students can apply on line through Delta Online or the Delta College Web site (listed below).

---

### CONTACT

For additional information, students should contact:

Kathryn Campbell
San Joaquin Delta College
5151 Pacific Avenue
Stockton, California 95207
Telephone: 209-954-5039
E-mail: kcampbell@sjdccd.cc.ca.us
Web site: http://deltaonline.org (Delta Online)
　　　　　http://www.sjdccd.cc.ca.us (admissions information)
　　　　　http://www.deltacollege.org

# Santa Monica College

## SMC Online
Santa Monica, California

*Santa Monica College (SMC), founded in 1929, is a California public community college accredited by the Western Association of Schools and Colleges. Santa Monica College was named among the top ten best community colleges in the country by Rolling Stone magazine. SMC is recognized around the world as number one in college transfers and career education. The College is the national leader in transfers to the University of California and the number one choice of international students. SMC is also well known for its award-winning programs and services.*

*The Santa Monica College vision is to change lives through excellence in education for a global community. Santa Monica College believes that individuals should develop to their full potential. Its mission is to challenge and enable students to set and achieve personal educational goals and to understand their personal relationship to the social, cultural, political, economic, technological, and natural environments. To fulfill this mission, the College provides open and affordable access to excellent programs that prepare students for successful careers, develop college-level skills, enable transfer to universities for baccalaureate and advanced graduate and professional education, and foster a personal commitment to lifelong learning. The College prepares its students to interact with and contribute to the global community.*

*Santa Monica College is representative of, and sensitive to, the racial and cultural diversity of its community. Creativity, collaboration, and the free exchange of ideas are promoted in an open, caring community of learners. Continual development of individual talents is encouraged and the critical importance of each person to the achievement of a common purpose is recognized.*

## DISTANCE LEARNING PROGRAM

The Santa Monica College distance education program, SMC Online, is committed to providing excellence in education and increasing student access to post-secondary education. All courses are developed to ensure that the classes and programs delivered sustain the quality of teaching and learning achieved in the traditional classroom.

Students must enroll in Santa Monica College to participate in the SMC Online. The College launched its virtual campus, located at http://smconline.org, in fall 1999 with an expanded number of online courses.

## DELIVERY MEDIA

Santa Monica College offers distance education courses online, utilizing the Internet. Students should log onto SMCONLINE.org to see the online course catalogue, current schedule of courses, specific course information, as well as for application and enrollment information.

Santa Monica College uses the eCollege.com delivery system for its Distance Education Program.

## PROGRAMS OF STUDY

It is the goal of the Santa Monica distance education program to offer Associate in Arts degrees and certificate programs online. While entire de-

gree and certificate programs are not yet online, various courses that meet transfer, degree, and certificate requirements are available through SMC Online.

## STUDENT SERVICES

A variety of online student services are currently available on the Web through SMC Online, the Internet campus of Santa Monica College. SMC Online students have access to advising services, admissions, library services, and registration as well as financial aid and the Santa Monica College Bookstore.

## FACULTY

The faculty members at Santa Monica College are highly qualified in their fields and dedicated to teaching and learning. All instructors at Santa Monica College either have a master's degree or Ph.D. in their subject area or hold vocational certificates. Those teaching in both the vocational and the lower-division transfer programs have had a broad range of experience in their subject areas.

## ADMISSION

Any person who has graduated from high school or who is 18 years of age or older may be admitted to Santa Monica College if he or she meets the residence requirements and can profit from the program. Each person applying for admission to a California community college is classified as either a resident or nonresident. Each new student must file a college application with information that satisfies state registration requirements and initiates the educational planning process.

## TUITION AND FEES

All students in graded credit courses must pay an academic enrollment fee of $11 per unit/credit. All students enrolled in credit courses pay a $29 nonacademic fee per semester. Students who are both citizens and residents of another country (including F-1 visa students) must pay an additional tuition fee of $150 per unit/credit. Other nonresident students must pay a tuition fee of $130 per unit/credit. These fees are in addition to the $11 per unit/credit and the $29 per semester nonacademic fee assessed to all SMC students.

## FINANCIAL AID

To aid and encourage students who need financial assistance, numerous scholarships, loans, grants, and awards are available. Applications and additional information regarding financial aid and scholarships can be obtained at the SMC Financial Aid Office at 310-434-4343 or online at http://www.fafsa.ed.gov.

## APPLYING

All students must apply to Santa Monica College if they have never attended or if they have not attended for one or more semesters. Admissions applications are available on line through SMC Online at the Web address listed below.

Local residents may pick up an application at the Santa Monica College Admissions Office. Applications are also available by mail. Students should include a self-addressed envelope with their request to the Admissions Office at the address below.

---

### CONTACT
Winniphred Stone, Dean, Distance Education
Santa Monica College
1900 Pico Boulevard
Santa Monica, California 90405
Telephone: 310-434-3761
Fax: 310-434-3769
E-mail: stone_winniphred@smc.edu
Web site: http://smconline.org

---

# Saybrook Graduate School

## Graduate Programs in Psychology, Human Science, and Organizational Systems

San Francisco, California

*Since 1971, Saybrook has been educating mid-career professionals in humanistic values relevant to the work place and the community. Saybrook Graduate School and Research Center's graduate education prepares scholar/practitioners to take effective leadership roles, develop the consciousness to realize the immense possibilities of these times, and minimize the potential for social and individual suffering. Saybrook provides a unique learning-centered environment based in an emancipatory humanistic tradition. Advanced studies in psychology, human science, and organizational systems are offered. Programs are designed for adult, mid-career professionals seeking an opportunity to engage in serious scholarly work, and who wish to develop the necessary research skills, scope of knowledge, and intervention skills to become more effective in their chosen sphere of work.*

*Approximately 425 students are currently enrolled at Saybrook, ranging in age from the mid-20s to the 60s and representing more than thirty-six states and several other countries. Saybrook is fully accredited by the Western Association of Schools and Colleges (WASC).*

## DISTANCE LEARNING PROGRAM

For thirty years, Saybrook Graduate School's mode of education has been at-a-distance learning. Because of the unique mix of mentorship, on-site residential programs, and online classes, the Saybrook model encourages close contact between faculty members and students, and among students. Programs are structured to meet the personal and professional needs of adult learners and persons not able or willing to travel to traditional classrooms.

## DELIVERY MEDIA

Learning takes place through one-on-one mentorships with faculty members in small cohort groups, courses online, and at seminars at residential conferences. Using learning guides, students complete course work which is evaluated by faculty members who communicate by phone, letter, fax, computer, or in person at conferences.

## PROGRAMS OF STUDY

Saybrook Graduate School offers programs in psychology, human science, and organizational systems. Students may pursue an M.A. or a Ph.D. in any program. Within each program, students select an area of study, which includes humanistic and transpersonal clinical inquiry and health studies, consciousness and spirituality, social transformation, and organizational systems.

Saybrook's psychology degree program prepares its graduates to be scholars and researchers in the broad domain of human experience. Saybrook is an institute providing alternative education that conscientiously challenges many of the axioms of mainstream medicalized and industrialized psychology, and offers an emancipatory alternative. While the primary focus of Saybrook's psychology program is not clinical, Saybrook offers the course work necessary to take the licensing exam in most states.

The human science program provides an opportunity for a humanistic, action-learning approach to group, family, public and private organizations, and community and global spheres of life. The Saybrook approach combines responsible action with scholarly reflection, exploring transformative change that respects human dignity and creative possibilities. The human science program consists of a set of perspectives pertaining to the human condition in historical, contextual, cross-cultural, political, and religious terms. It employs perspectives such as feminism, post-structuralism, critical theory, existential phenomenology, and postmodernism. The human sciences are a collective understanding of the common condition and contribute to the ongoing story of social improvement and consciousness evolution.

The organizational systems program is designed to develop leaders, scholars, and practitioners who are capable of addressing the challenge of building organizations and communities with greater capacity to deal with the increasing turbulence, interconnection, and diverse frameworks of interpretation of the information age/knowledge era. The mission of the organizational systems program is to educate leaders to become adept at changing and designing organizations that reflect the highest human ideals.

## STUDENT SERVICES

It is Saybrook's intent to be responsive to student and institutional needs, to provide programs and services in support of the mission, to assist students in achieving academic success, and to enhance the overall learning environment.

## FACULTY

Saybrook Graduate School and Research Center is proud to have an internationally recognized faculty of scholars and practitioners, all of whom hold a doctoral or terminal degree in their field. In addition to teaching, faculty members have extensive experience as researchers, practitioners, consultants, authors, business people, and organizational leaders. They are committed to Saybrook's ideals and values and are supportive of the students' personal and scholarly growth.

## ADMISSION

All applicants must hold a bachelor's degree from a regionally accredited institution. Applicants to the Ph.D. program must have an appropriate master's degree from a regionally accredited institution. The minimum GPA requirement is 3.0. All international students must submit recent TOEFL scores and translated transcripts.

## APPLYING

Students are admitted in September and March. For the September start date, all application materials should be received by June 1. For the March start date, all application materials should be received by December 16. Applications completed after this deadline are considered on a space-available basis or, with the applicant's permission, held for the next enrollment period.

Applicants are evaluated on writing ability, past academic record, and professional background. They should be a good match with the distance learning format, research interests, and Saybrook's mission and values. New students attend a four-day Residential Orientation Conference (ROC) held in the San Francisco Bay area.

## TUITION AND FEES

Tuition for the 2001–02 academic year is $13,800. Fees for attending two Residential Conferences (RC) per year are also required. These fees include the cost of registration, lodging, meals, conference materials, and meeting space.

## FINANCIAL AID

U.S. citizens or eligible permanent residents may borrow up to $18,500 per year through the Federal Stafford Loan Program. Saybrook offers limited tuition assistance to its continuing students.

---

### CONTACT

Mindy Myers, Vice President, Recruitment and Admissions
Saybrook Graduate School and Research Center
450 Pacific, Third Floor
San Francisco, California 94133
Telephone: 800-825-4480 Ext. 6196 (toll-free)
Fax: 415-433-9271
E-mail: mmyers@saybrook.edu
Web site: http://www.saybrook.edu

# Seton Hall University

## *SetonWorldWide*

South Orange, New Jersey

*Seton Hall University has been distinguished by a number of firsts. It is the first diocesan college in the United States, founded in 1856 by James Roosevelt Bayley, the first Bishop of Newark, and named for Elizabeth Ann Seton, the first American-born saint. Now, through SetonWorldWide, it is one of the first traditional universities to offer full online graduate degree programs. The University's mission, to provide an educational experience that imparts concrete knowledge and skills in the context of ethical values, is as timely today as in 1856, and as important on the Internet as in the classroom. At Seton Hall, timeless values intersect with cybertechnology to offer high-quality online graduate programs that serve the educational aspirations and professional needs of students from across the country and around the world. By utilizing the Internet and the latest teaching technologies, students benefit from the flexibility to fulfill course requirements at the time of day when they are at their best and from the place that is most convenient. For its ability to empower students with technology, Seton Hall has been recognized as one of "America's Most Wired Universities" by* Yahoo! Internet Life *for two consecutive years and was awarded the prestigious EDUCAUSE Award for excellence in campus networking.*

## DISTANCE LEARNING PROGRAM

SetonWorldWide's online degree programs are designed for professionals who have demonstrated significant achievement in their respective fields, and who have the ability, desire, and dedication to accept the rigors of a fast-paced, challenging curriculum, balance the demands of personal and professional commitments, and maintain high standards of integrity and productivity—both in the workplace and in academic pursuits.

As a learning team member, a student, along with his or her peers, instructional facilitators, and executive mentors, as well as noted expert practitioners, are all interrelated and interdependent. Each plays a pivotal role in the teaching and learning process. These relationships are key to a rich and dynamic online learning experience. Each participant is a vital link in the overall success of this effort, and each must acknowledge a commitment to promoting academic integrity.

A short residency at the start and middle of the program enables students to meet their classmates and instructional team members in person. During the third residencies, students are awarded their degrees. All degrees are granted by Seton Hall University, an institution fully accredited by the Middle States Association of Colleges and Schools.

## DELIVERY MEDIA

SetonWorldWide online degree programs feature electronic seminar discussions, e-mail, Internet-based audio and video, electronic research, and different types of software to enhance learning. Prior to the start of the program, students receive all the course materials, including books, articles, audiotapes, videotapes, and CD-ROMs. Computer requirements include a midrange desktop or laptop computer with Internet access.

## PROGRAMS OF STUDY

The Master of Healthcare Administration (39 credits, twenty months) provides a rigorous and thorough understanding of today's challenging health-care environment, addressing real-world strategies and skills that help managers make significant contributions to their organizations.

The Master of Strategic Communication and Leadership (36 credits, twenty months) program provides executives with the essential communication and leadership skills to achieve personal and organizational success, acknowledging the demands brought about by markets, a diverse workplace, and the explosion of electronic media technology.

The Master of Arts in Counseling (48 credits, 2½ to three years) provides students with a necessary background and preparation in counseling, and a thorough understanding of theory, skills, and models of intervention. Two 10-day residencies are part of the degree requirements.

The Master of Arts in Educational Administration And Supervision (36 credits, twenty months) program is designed to enable students to broaden their knowledge and understanding of the process of education, improve their professional techniques, or prepare for leadership positions and careers in education.

The Master of Nursing (nurse practitioner) program (43–46 credits) is designed for nurses who wish to balance graduate education with career, family, and personal responsibilities. Students are able to study the didactic portion of the program in their homes at their own convenience. The clinical practice is provided within the students' local community. Upon admission to the program, students are assigned a mentor to assist them throughout the learning process.

The Bachelor of Science in Nursing (for RNs) (33 credits, nineteen months) is designed for registered nurses who wish to obtain their Bachelor of Science degree.

## SPECIAL PROGRAMS

Corporations, nonprofit agencies, and other organizations may be eligible to sponsor a learning team composed of their employees for an online graduate program modified for their specific needs. If desired, SetonWorldWide will establish an action team consisting of senior faculty members, specialists in the field, and representatives from the sponsoring organization to conduct an organizational diagnosis and need assessment based on interviews, focus groups, and surveys. Course content may then be modified to include case studies from within the organization itself, a similar organization, or within an industry or profession. Employers are able to provide their employees with a high-quality degree program while also addressing specific organizational issues. This is part of the SetonWorldWide "value added" approach.

## STUDENT SERVICES

Students find everything they need online, including admission information, academic assistance, financial aid assistance, career guidance, and other services. The Help Desk's technical support staff is dedicated to helping students become confident and productive in the online learning environment. They understand that online classes can be challenging at first, but they have the knowledge and experience to help make every student's transition into the virtual classroom a smooth one. The Help Desk is available 24 hours a day, seven days a week. All SetonWorldWide participants also have access to Seton Hall University library resources. During orientation, students meet the librarians and technical staff members who provide assistance throughout the program. Students can use the library's ASK ME service to request and receive assistance from a fully qualified librarian.

## ADMISSION

SetonWorldWide online degree programs are designed for professionals who demonstrate significant achievement in their respective fields. Specific program admission requirements are found on SetonWorldWide's Web site.

## TUITION AND FEES

The all-inclusive tuition includes all fees, except for the application fee, and all expenses, including books and other materials and room and meals for short residencies. Computer equipment, software, Internet access, and travel expenses to the residencies are not covered. Reduced tuition can be offered to students employed by organizations that sponsor a full learning team of students as part of a customized program.

## FINANCIAL AID

Financial aid is available in the form of subsidized and unsubsidized government loan programs. Students who want to apply for Federal Direct Loans should visit http://www.fafsa.ed.gov on the Internet. For further information and guidance, students should contact SetonWorldWide at the Web site listed below.

## APPLYING

To apply, students should visit the Web site listed below and click on Apply.

---

### CONTACT

SetonWorldWide
Seton Hall University
400 South Orange Avenue
South Orange, New Jersey 07079
Telephone: 888-SETON-WW (toll-free)
Web site: http://www.setonworldwide.net

---

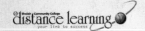

# Sinclair Community College

## Distance Learning Program

Dayton, Ohio

---

*Sinclair Community College is located on a modern, tree-lined campus in downtown Dayton, Ohio. The College has a rich history in the Dayton community, dating back to 1887. In 1966, Sinclair became a publicly funded community college, enjoying strong community support through ongoing passage of a college levy.*

*Sinclair offers more than 100 transfer and technical associate degree and certificate programs, as well as continuing education opportunities through a system of diverse resources and delivery alternatives. Sinclair enrolls about 20,000 credit students each quarter.*

*The College is fully accredited by the North Central Association of Colleges and Schools and has been authorized by the Ohio Board of Regents to grant associate degrees in arts, sciences, applied science, and individualized and technical study. The College's technical, health, and business programs are fully accredited by national and/or state-approved accrediting organizations.*

*Sinclair Community College is a proud member of the prestigious League for Innovation in the Community College and has been selected as one of twelve Vanguard Learning Colleges for developing and promoting learner-centered practices and curricula.*

## DISTANCE LEARNING PROGRAM

Over the past twenty years, the Distance Learning Program has developed into a nationally recognized, state-of-the-art entity with in-house video and online course production facilities. The program offers more than 170 distance courses, spanning all six of Sinclair's academic divisions. The program enrolled more than 4,000 credit students in fall 2000.

## DELIVERY MEDIA

Courses are delivered via the World Wide Web, videotape, interactive television, audiotape, CD-ROM, and print. Students and faculty members communicate in person or through a variety of methods, including mail, telephone, fax, and e-mail. The following may be required: audiocassette player, television, videocassette player, computer, modem, Internet access, e-mail, and CD-ROM.

## PROGRAMS OF STUDY

Two complete degree programs are available to students through distance learning. The courses are delivered through a variety of distance learning and independent study methods.

The Associate of Art in distance learning is comprised of 94 quarter-credit hours. Twenty-three of the thirty program courses can be taken solely through a distance format. The remaining courses must be taken either through independent study or include an on-campus lab. It is also possible to obtain credit for these courses through transfer.

The Associate of Science in business administration is comprised of 98 quarter-credit hours. Twenty-three of the thirty program courses can be taken solely through a distance format. The remaining courses must be taken either through independent study or include an on-campus lab. It is also possible to obtain credit for these courses through transfer.

Information about these degree programs can be accessed online by visiting the Sinclair Distance Learning Web site listed in the Contact section.

A short-term, 21-credit hour certificate in Software Applications for the Professional is available online or through CD-ROMs. This certificate provides office workers, manager, professionals, and other interested participants with the opportunity to develop and refine their skills in a variety of current personal computer software applications common in today's work environment. Software applications learned include Microsoft Word, Excel, PowerPoint, Publisher, and Access. Internet capabilities and software integration are also covered in this program. More information is available from the Business Technologies Division counselors at 937-512-3054 or on the Web site at http://www.sinclair.edu/departments/bis/biscert.htm.

## SPECIAL PROGRAMS

Sinclair Community College has a partnership with Governors State University that enables Sinclair graduates to transfer to GSU to complete a Bachelor of Arts degree via distance learning. The Governors State University B.A. degree is a generalist degree that is acceptable in almost all fields of work. It is not organized around any specific discipline or major, so it offers students the freedom to take courses that meet their educational or professional goals. Courses taken from Governors State are offered in a variety of formats: videotape, correspondence, and Internet.

## STUDENT SERVICES

Services available to Sinclair Community College distance learners include academic advising and online access to tutoring and library services. Testing by proctor for placement and course testing is also available.

## CREDIT OPTIONS

Sinclair Community College associate degrees range from 91 to 110 quarter-credit hours. Students must take the last 30 hours at Sinclair. Students may transfer credit from regionally accredited institutions for which they receive a passing grade or a letter grade of C or higher. Alternative credit assessment options are also available (portfolio, CLEP, PONSI).

## FACULTY

Sinclair Community College has more than 400 full-time and 500 part-time faculty members. More than 12 percent of the full-time faculty members hold doctoral degrees or earned advanced degrees. About 100 faculty members support the distance learning courses; most of these individuals are experienced, full-time faculty members.

## ADMISSION

Sinclair has an open door admission policy. All students are welcome. Students seeking degrees or taking math and English classes are expected to take a placement test. This testing can be done by proctor.

## TUITION AND FEES

Tuition and fees for distance learning students are the same as for other Sinclair Community College students. Students pay a one-time, nonrefundable $10 admission fee. Montgomery County (Ohio) residents pay $29.45 per credit hour, other Ohio residents pay $48.45 per credit hour, and out-of-state residents pay $81.45 per credit hour.

## FINANCIAL AID

The Sinclair Financial Aid Office administers grants and scholarships that do not have to be repaid, low-interest loans, and student employment. A need-based financial aid package may consist of one or more of the following: Federal Pell Grant, Ohio Instructional Grant, Federal Supplemental Educational Opportunity Grant, and Federal Direct Student Loans. Information about financial aid opportunities at Sinclair may be obtained online by visiting the Sinclair College main Web site (http://www.sinclair.edu).

## APPLYING

Students may apply for admission and register for classes online by visiting the Sinclair Distance Learning Web site listed below and accessing the "How Do I Get Started?" selection from the menu.

### CONTACT

Linda M. PaHud
Coordinator of Distance Learning Services
Sinclair Community College
444 West Third Street
Dayton, Ohio 45402
Telephone: 937-512-2694
Fax: 937-226-2891
E-mail: linda.pahud@sinclair.edu
Web site: http://www.sinclair.edu/distance

# Skidmore College

## Master of Arts in Liberal Studies

Saratoga Springs, New York

---

*Skidmore College is an independent, liberal arts institution with an enrollment of approximately 2,400 men and women. It is located in Saratoga Springs, New York. The College was founded by Lucy Skidmore Scribner in 1903 as a woman's college. In 1971, it became coeducational and moved to its new campus. It is accredited by the Middle States Association of Colleges and Secondary Schools.*

*While Skidmore's main focus has been on the traditional 18- to 21-year-old residential student, the undergraduate University Without Walls program and the Master of Arts in Liberal Studies (M.A.L.S.) program are extensions of Skidmore's belief in the primacy of a liberal education. The goal of these programs is to provide working adults who are outside the boundaries of the campus (average age 42) the same quality and opportunity as the College's residential population.*

## DISTANCE LEARNING PROGRAM

M.A.L.S. serves approximately 60 full-and part-time students from as near as the city of Saratoga Springs and from as far away as Europe and South America. The M.A.L.S. program does not require its students to be in residence on campus. Student programs can include graduate-level seminars, independent studies, internships, and preapproved in-class and correspondence courses from other accredited institutions. Every program includes a final project or thesis in the area of the student's focus.

## DELIVERY MEDIA

Independent study courses take place through e-mail, phone, or mail communication. Online courses are also a possibility. Such courses require a Web browser and e-mail capability.

## PROGRAMS OF STUDY

The distinctive features of the M.A.L.S. graduate program are that it is self-paced, and that the students, with the assistance of their advisers, construct their own programs of study. During the week in which they take the initial core seminar, students are assigned an adviser in their area of interest. In conjunction with this adviser and the M.A.L.S. office staff, they work out a general program of possible courses leading to the 30-semester-hour degree. These courses may be taken on the Skidmore campus or as independent studies in the student's home. Also, with prior approval from their adviser, students may take appropriate graduate courses at other institutions. These are then transferred into their Skidmore program. This program of study leads to a special topic or project that is the focus of the student's thesis.

The average student (a working adult) completes the Skidmore degree in approximately 2½ to 3 years. There is a five-year time limit on each student's program of study; no specific number of courses is required on a yearly basis.

All student programs are based in the liberal arts rather than professional areas of study and are interdisciplinary in nature. Students work within at least two liberal arts disciplines. An example of an interdisciplinary M.A.L.S. focus is environmental studies, where the student may take courses in ecology, biology, public policy, and economics.

## SPECIAL PROGRAMS

Because each student's program is self-designed, each is unique in its own right. Rather than taking a set of predetermined courses, students study what interests them. They do this within the framework of the enormous faculty and administrative support that is so central to the program.

## STUDENT SERVICES

Skidmore College believes that special advising and mentoring is essential to a student's success. M.A.L.S. staff members are happy to assist students in any way possible. Typical services include academic advising, registration assistance, financial aid counseling, and book-order assistance. All graduate students enjoy Skidmore library privileges and an e-mail account.

## CREDIT OPTIONS

Students may transfer up to 15 semester hours of credit into their graduate program, provided they are appropriate to their field of study. These may include up to 6 credits for experiential learning, as well as traditional graduate work from accredited institutions. At least 15 semester hours of the 30 necessary to complete the degree must be taken while matriculated at Skidmore.

## FACULTY

The faculty of Skidmore College is a community of scholars devoted to the highest standards of research and teaching within the liberal arts tradition. Its distinction is reflected in national surveys and numerous publications. Talented and dedicated faculty members carry out research in all of the traditional liberal arts disciplines and are engaged in interdisciplinary endeavors as well.

## ADMISSION

Admission to Skidmore College's Master of Arts in Liberal Studies program requires a completed bachelor's degree from an accredited institution of higher learning. While GRE scores are not required, applicants must appear for a personal interview, write an extensive essay concerning their interests and aspirations, and provide other required documentation.

## TUITION AND FEES

In 2001–02, there is a fee of $50, which is submitted with the application. If accepted, students pay a $500 nonrefundable deposit. This deposit is applied to the $5200 initial enrollment fee, which is reduced to $4900 in subsequent years. At the point when students begin their final project, the enrollment fee is eliminated and replaced by a one-time fee of $2000 for the remainder of the program. The cost of each three-semester-hour independent study course is $650.

## FINANCIAL AID

Students in the Skidmore M.A.L.S. program may apply for a Federal Stafford loan. In addition, the M.A. L.S. program annually grants several small scholarships to continuing students on the basis of need and academic achievement.

## APPLYING

Applications are accepted throughout the year. The application forms are available upon request or can be filled out (or downloaded) online at the M.A.L.S. Web site (listed below).

---

### CONTACT

David Glaser, Director
Master of Arts in Liberal Studies Program
Skidmore College
Saratoga Springs, New York 12866
Telephone: 518-580-5480
Fax: 518-580-5486
E-mail: mals@skidmore.edu
Web site: http://www.skidmore.edu/administration/mals/

---

# Skidmore College

## *University Without Walls*

Saratoga Springs, New York

---

*University Without Walls (UWW) is the external degree program for adults at Skidmore College. UWW was in the vanguard in establishing a program for distance learners. The program began in 1971 as an experiment in nontraditional education jointly funded by the Ford Foundation and the U.S. Department of Education. When the funding for this experiment ended in 1975, Skidmore College took over the program as its own. Over the years, UWW has evolved to serve adult students pursuing baccalaureate degrees in a variety of liberal arts, performing arts, and preprofessional fields.*

*The UWW program is characterized by its flexibility and the high quality of education students receive. The unique advising system at UWW guarantees that each program meets the student's individual needs and the high standards of Skidmore College.*

## DISTANCE LEARNING PROGRAM

UWW serves 280 full- and part-time baccalaureate students from as near as the city of Saratoga Springs and as far away as Europe, Africa, and Asia. The UWW program does not require its students to be in residence on campus. Student programs may include on-site UWW seminars, UWW online courses, independent study with Skidmore faculty members, courses at other accredited institutions, internships, and distance learning courses from major universities. Every program includes a final project in the area of the student's focus.

## DELIVERY MEDIA

Independent study courses take place through phone, mail, or e-mail communication. When possible, they may involve meetings on the Skidmore campus. At the present time, UWW's online courses are Web based and require a Web browser and e-mail capability.

## PROGRAMS OF STUDY

UWW offers Bachelor of Arts degrees in most traditional liberal arts fields, including American studies, anthropology, art history, biology, chemistry, classics, computer science, economics, English, French, geology, German, government, history, mathematics, philosophy, physics, political economy, psychology, religion, Russian, sociology, Spanish, and women's studies. Bachelor of Science degrees are available in art, business, dance, human services, exercise science, and theater. Students can also combine fields to create an interdisciplinary program, such as arts management, Asian studies, communications, environmental studies, health studies, human behavior, Latin American studies, management information systems, nonprofit management, organizational behavior, public administration, and religion and culture. Individually designed majors are welcomed.

All degrees are 120-credit programs. Programs are expected to include at least 12 credits in the humanities, 6 credits in history, 12 credits in the social sciences, and 9 credits in math or science, including laboratory experience. Professional programs must include at least 60 credits in the liberal arts. Courses taken prior to entry of UWW may be considered in satisfaction of these requirements.

## SPECIAL PROGRAMS

UWW's flexibility allows many students to take advantage of unusual learning opportunities. Recent UWW students have studied abroad in Austria, Canada, Costa Rica, the Czech Republic, Germany, Ireland, Poland, Spain, Switzerland, and Thailand, among other locations. Business students often have the opportunity to include professional management and banking seminars in satisfaction of their degree requirements.

UWW students are often able to participate in programs sponsored by Skidmore College and the Office of Special Programs, including a summer study program in Florence, the New York State Writers Institute, the Skidmore Jazz Institute, the Summer Dance Workshop, and the Siti Summer Theater Workshop. UWW students are eligible for substantial discounts on courses offered by Skidmore Summer Academic Sessions and the Summer Six Art Program.

UWW business students are eligible to apply for 3/2 M.B.A.

programs in cooperation with Rensselaer Polytechnic Institute in Troy and Rensselaer–Hartford.

## STUDENT SERVICES

UWW is a small, personal program, and the staff members are happy to assist students in any way possible. Typical services include academic advising, registration assistance, financial aid counseling, and book-order assistance. Local students also enjoy library privileges, career counseling, access to recreational facilities, access to computer labs, and an e-mail account. Some summer housing is available for special program participants.

## CREDIT OPTIONS

UWW accepts transfer credit for courses completed with a grade of C or better. There is no limit to the number of credits transferred or the age of the work, provided that the course is appropriate to a liberal arts curriculum. Credit is also available for experiential learning. In addition, students may document knowledge through CLEP, ACT-PEP, DANTES, and Regents examinations. Many college-level courses offered through the military are accepted. Credit from international universities is usually accepted.

## FACULTY

There are approximately 200 full- and part-time members of the Skidmore faculty. Most participate as advisers and instructors in the UWW program. Ninety-three percent of the Skidmore faculty members have a terminal degree.

## ADMISSION

UWW considers any applicant able to succeed at demanding college-level work. However, the program works best for students who have had some college experience. Applicants must have a high school diploma or the equivalent.

## TUITION AND FEES

Students pay an initial enrollment fee of $3800; after the first year, an annual enrollment fee of $3200 is charged. The fee for the final project is $600. All independent study courses sponsored by Skidmore are $500.

## FINANCIAL AID

Students are eligible for Federal Pell Grants, New York State TAP awards, and all federal loan programs. A small amount of scholarship assistance is available.

## APPLYING

Application forms are available from UWW or can be downloaded from the UWW Web site. All students are required to attend a personal admissions interview on the Skidmore campus.

### CONTACT

Cornel J. Reinhart, Director
University Without Walls
Skidmore College
815 North Broadway
Saratoga Springs, New York 12866
Telephone: 518-580-5450
Fax: 518-580-5449
E-mail: uww@skidmore.edu
Web site: http://www.skidmore.edu/uww

# Southern Christian University

## *Distance Learning Programs*

Montgomery, Alabama

---

*Founded in 1967, Southern Christian University (SCU) is an independent, nonsectarian, coeducational institution dedicated to the spirit of its ideals and Christian heritage. All of SCU's programs are taught from a Christian perspective. SCU is the home of one of the nation's leading universities offering distance learning programs and services to adults nationally. Adding to the prestige of this University is its recent designation as a Distance Education Demonstration Program Institution by the U.S. Department of Education. One of fifteen initial participants in the nation, SCU is partnering with the U.S. Department of Education to serve as a national model that will help chart the future of distance learning. Accredited by the Southern Association of Colleges and Schools, SCU grants bachelor's, master's, and doctoral degrees—all available via a distance learning format.*

## DISTANCE LEARNING PROGRAM

SCU programs are designed with the adult learner in mind. Eighty percent of SCU's students are employed while they are attending SCU. Courses can be taken anywhere there is Internet access and at anytime. SCU has enrolled thousands of students in distance learning courses throughout the United States and internationally.

## DELIVERY MEDIA

Utilizing state-of-the-art technologies, SCU's distance learning programs are delivered to students over the Internet. Students participate via online discussion groups, testing, e-mail, and telephone. Some courses are streamed live over the Internet, which can be viewed as the class is being taught, or at the student's convenience. The flexibility of the programs ensures continuity for students in transit (e.g., military, clergy, salesmen who must move while still in school).

## PROGRAMS OF STUDY

SCU programs are structured with the traditional program in mind. Distance education is approved by the Southern Association of Colleges and Schools and the U.S. Department of Education, ensuring that distance education students receive the same high-quality education as on-campus students. Faculty and student services for online students are available to distance learning students. SCU ensures that students have regular contact with faculty and staff members via e-mail and telephone. Residency is only required in certain programs. No residency is required for undergraduates. Undergraduate degrees include management communication, human development, liberal studies, and Bible. These degrees promote management communication skills, human development skills, knowledge in the arts, and biblical and Christian ministry skills. Graduate degrees include organizational leadership, counseling/family therapy, and religious studies. These degrees foster leadership knowledge and skills, counseling and family therapy skills, and biblical and Christian ministry skills. The counseling degrees are designed to help prepare students for licensure. Doctoral degrees include family therapy and ministry. These degrees are advanced professional degrees for community organizations and church-related vocations, with a concentration designed to prepare participants to counsel families and individuals. SCU students are fully matriculated students of Southern Christian University with full student privileges, rights, and responsibilities.

## SPECIAL PROGRAMS

In response to the adult migration into institutions of higher education, SCU has developed fully accredited programs of study to help working adults obtain their bachelor's degree in a timely manner through the EXCEL program. SCU recognizes that many adult students have lifetime experiences that should be translated into college credit. SCU's EXCEL program allows undergraduates to receive credit for lifetime learning, enabling students to complete their degree at an accelerated rate. In addition, all undergraduate courses are 4 semester hours, rather than 3. This means that a student only has to take three courses (12 semester hours) to be a full-time student and eligible for maximum financial aid benefits. Also, fewer courses are required for degree completion. Undergraduate students who enroll on a full-time basis enjoy a significant savings, receiving 50 percent off the published tuition rate.

## STUDENT SERVICES

SCU provides support for all aspects of the distance learning experience. ProQuest Religion Database and First Search library programs give students access to 65 online databases, including the Library of Congress. Students have access to the collections of 150 theological schools online. Personal academic advising is performed via phone or e-mail. Students also receive personal evaluations of their degree program.

## CREDIT OPTIONS

Fulfillment of some degree requirements is possible by passing the CLEP/DANTES tests or Regents examinations and through credit for lifetime learning and credit for military experience. Students can register for a course designed to show them how to prepare a portfolio that demonstrates prior learning. Credit is awarded by the Office of Portfolio Development for prior learning that is demonstrated through a documented learning portfolio.

## FACULTY

Instructional faculty members total 21. Sixty-seven percent of the full-time faculty members hold doctoral degrees, 100 percent hold master's degrees, and 100 percent hold terminal degrees. Faculty members are specialized in their areas and have training in distance learning delivery.

## ADMISSION

There is a rolling admission plan. Admission requirements are verification of high school graduation or GED for undergraduates and demonstrated proficiency in computer literacy. Ninety percent of applicants are accepted.

## TUITION AND FEES

Graduate tuition cost per semester hour is $390. Undergraduate tuition per semester hour is $320. Full-time undergraduates receive a 50 percent scholarship. A comprehensive fee of $400 per semester is required of all students.

## FINANCIAL AID

Aid from institutionally generated funds is provided on the basis of academic merit, financial need, or other criteria. A limited number of scholarships is available. Priority is given to early applicants. Federal funding available for undergraduates and graduates includes Pell and FSEOG grants for undergraduates, Federal Work-Study, and FFEL subsidized and unsubsidized loans for undergraduates and graduates. Eighty percent of students receive financial aid.

## APPLYING

Prospective students must submit a $50 nonrefundable fee along with the completed application for admission. During the first semester, graduate students must submit letters of recommendation, transcripts, and test scores.

---

### CONTACT

Rick Johnson
Southern Christian University
1200 Taylor Road
Montgomery, Alabama 36117
Telephone: 800-351-4040 Ext. 213 (toll-free)
E-mail: rickjohnson@southernchristian.edu
Web site: http://www.southernchristian.edu

# Southern Methodist University

## *School of Engineering*

Dallas, Texas

*Founded in 1911, SMU is a private, comprehensive university. SMU comprises six degree-granting schools: the School of Engineering, Dedman College of Humanities and Sciences, Meadows School of the Arts, the Edwin L. Cox School of Business, the Dedman School of Law, and Perkins School of Theology. Southern Methodist University is accredited by the Commission on Colleges of the Southern Association of Colleges and Schools.*

*For more than thirty years, the School of Engineering has been a national pioneer in offering distance education courses for graduate study. In 1964, the School of Engineering established one of the first two regional closed-circuit TV distance learning networks in the nation. In 1978, it instituted its own for-credit videotape program for students living outside the Dallas–Fort Worth area. Today, video-program students are enrolled nationally from coast to coast and in Europe, Asia, South America, and Canada.*

## DISTANCE LEARNING PROGRAM

The School of Engineering's distance learning programs serve more than 600 graduate students. Degree programs are offered nationally via videotape or, in the north Texas area, via a closed-circuit television network. The Master of Science in Telecommunications program is available via the National Technological University satellite network. No campus attendance is required to complete the degree programs.

## DELIVERY MEDIA

Distance learning students are enrolled in classes that are given on the SMU campus. The lectures are videotaped and sent once a week to the distance learning student. North Texas and satellite students may view the lectures live. Distance learning students interact with their professor via telephone, fax, e-mail, or the Internet. Many courses make course materials available to the student via the School of Engineering's Web site.

## PROGRAMS OF STUDY

Engineering schools have an obligation to be responsive to challenges and opportunities in a technological society. As a private university, SMU can respond quickly to engineering needs with high-quality academic programs.

The School of Engineering offers the following Master of Science degree programs via distance learning: telecommunications, software engineering, engineering management, operations research, systems engineering, environmental engineering, civil engineering, electrical engineering, mechanical engineering, environmental systems management, manufacturing systems management, facilities management, and computer science.

The Master of Science degree requires 30–36 (depending on the program) semester credit hours for completion, with a minimum 3.0 grade point average on a 4.0 scale. Distance learning students may meet the credit requirement entirely by course work or have the option of preparing a thesis for 6 semester hours of credit.

## SPECIAL PROGRAMS

The School of Engineering offers a certificate program in telecommunications. This program is designed for students who have extensive experience but do not hold a bachelor's degree or who do not wish to pursue a master's degree. Admission to the telecommunications certificate program requires 60 semester credit hours of college study with a minimum GPA of 2.0 on a 4.0 scale, three years of related work experience, and three letters of recommendation. Certificate students must complete six courses with a minimum grade of 70 percent in each course. All courses are available to the distance learning student via videotape.

## CREDIT OPTIONS

Generally speaking, up to 6 semester hours of graduate courses may be transferred from an institution approved by the School of Engineering's Graduate Division, provided that such course work was completed in the five years prior to matriculation, that the transferred courses carried graduate credit, that those courses were not used to meet the requirements of an undergraduate degree, and that grades of B– or higher were received in the courses to be transferred.

## FACULTY

Of the 485 full-time faculty members, 88 percent hold the doctorate or terminal professional degree in their fields. In addition, in the professional degree programs, the School of Engineering utilizes outstanding adjunct faculty members to bring into the classroom valuable experience from industry and government.

## ADMISSION

Admission to a Master of Science degree program requires the bachelor's degree appropriate to the program to which the student is applying, as well as a minimum grade point average of 3.0 (on a 4.0 scale) in previous undergraduate and graduate study. Scores on the Graduate Record Examinations (GRE) are required for the M.S. programs in electrical engineering, mechanical engineering, computer science, environmental engineering, and civil engineering.

## TUITION AND FEES

Tuition for distance learning students is $777 per credit hour or $2331 for a 3-credit-hour course.

## FINANCIAL AID

Financial aid opportunities are available to distance learning students, including Federal Stafford Student Loans. SMU's distance learning programs are approved for Veterans Administration educational benefits.

## APPLYING

Distance learning students must complete an application for admission to the Graduate Division of the School of Engineering and submit transcripts of all previous undergraduate and graduate work. Application deadline dates are as follows: for the fall semester, July 1; for the spring semester, November 15; and for the summer semester, April 15.

---

**CONTACT**

Stephanie Dye
Associate Director, Distance Education
School of Engineering
Southern Methodist University
P.O. Box 750335
Dallas, Texas 75275-0335
Telephone: 214-768-3232
           800-601-4040 (toll-free)
Fax: 214-768-3778
E-mail: sdye@engr.smu.edu
Web site: http://www.engr.smu.edu

---

# Southern New Hampshire University

## *Distance Education Program*

Manchester, New Hampshire

---

*Southern New Hampshire University (SNHU), founded in 1932, is a private, accredited, coeducational, professional college. The College has a total enrollment of more than 10,000 in various divisions—undergraduate day, Continuing Education, Distance Education, the Culinary Institute, and the Graduate School of Business. Southern New Hampshire University maintains Continuing Education undergraduate and graduate centers in Laconia, Manchester, Nashua, Portsmouth, and Salem, New Hampshire; Brunswick, Maine; and Roosevelt Roads, Puerto Rico.*

*Southern New Hampshire University and the Distance Education Program are accredited by the New England Association of School and Colleges. Accreditation by this association indicates that the institution has been carefully evaluated and found to meet the standards agreed upon by qualified educators. The College and the program are also accredited by the Association of Collegiate Business Schools and Programs (ACBSP), the New Hampshire Post-secondary Education Commission, and the New Hampshire State Department of Education for Teacher Certification. Southern New Hampshire University is also approved for the education of veterans and the children of veterans, approved for the rehabilitation training of handicapped students, and listed in the Department of Education's* Education Directory, Part 3, Higher Education.

## DISTANCE LEARNING PROGRAM

Established in 1932, Southern New Hampshire University is a private, nonprofit coeducational institution. The main campus rests on nearly 300 acres situated along the banks of the Merrimack River in Manchester, New Hampshire. SNHU offers certificates and programs in business, liberal arts, and hospitality, with degrees beginning at the associate level and continuing to the Ph.D. The SNHU Distance Education (DE) program offers certificates and degrees up to the M.B.A., and is one of the largest and fastest growing programs in New England. SNHU is both regionally and nationally accredited by the New England Association of Schools and Colleges, Association of Collegiate Business

Schools and Programs, and the New England Postsecondary Education Commission. SNHU is a recognized leader in asynchronous learning and 100 percent Internet-based instruction. Total enrollments exceed 7,000 for the 2001–02 academic year. Undergraduate terms are eight weeks in length and there are six terms in an academic year. Graduate terms are twelve weeks in length with four terms offered in an academic year. Distance Education has an open-enrollment policy. The undergraduate residency requirement is 30 semester hours through SNHU, including 12 hours from the major for the bachelor's degree, and 9 hours from the major for the associate degre. Each student's final 24 semester hours must be through SNHU. The graduate

program typically limits transfer credit to 6 semester hours.

## DELIVERY MEDIA

The Distance Education Program offers many advantages to students and faculty members. The classes are limited to 18 enrollemnts, providing a significant measure of faculty-student interaction not found in more traditional class environments. The average faculty-student ratio is 1:15. Blackboard CourseInfo software (a product of Blackboard, Inc.) is the standard delivery product for all SNHU online courses. To participate in distance education through Southern New Hampshire University, the student must have a computer with a modem and access to the Internet. A working knowledge of Internet use and applications is helpful.

## PROGRAMS OF STUDY

Southern New Hampshire University provides students with a solid educational foundation and professional training through programs in the Divisions of Business and Liberal Arts. Degree and certificate programs available online within the Division of Business include accounting, business administration, business studies, computer information systems/information technology, economics/finance, international business, management, advisory services, marketing, retailing, and technical management. Online degree and certificate programs offered through the Division of Liberal Arts include communication, English language and literature, humanities, psychology, and social science. The Master of Business Administration (M.B.A.), the Master of Business Education (M.B.E.), and the master's degree in international business are also offered online.

Southern New Hampshire University's online classes carry the same high level of accreditation, and provide exactly the same credit toward a degree as classes taken in SNHU's day school or through one of the University's continuing education centers. For an overview of degree requirements, students should visit the Web site at http://www.snhu.edu/.

## SPECIAL PROGRAMS

Through the College's membership in NHCUC (New Hampshire College and University Council), Southern New Hampshire University students may take advantage of academic facilities and course offerings at eleven other four-year colleges and universities in the consortium.

## CREDIT OPTIONS

Students can transfer undergraduate credits earned at other accredited postsecondary institutions to SNHU and can receive undergraduate credit by taking the College-Level Examination Program (CLEP) or other standardized tests. A maximum of 90 credits may be transferred toward a bachelor's degree, and 30 credits may be applied to an associate degree. A maximum of 6 semester hours may be transferred into any of the graduate degree programs. As a Serviceman's Opportunity College, credit is awarded for service-related education, and for completion of an associate degree through the Community College of the Air Force.

## FACULTY

Southern New Hampshire University faculty members must meet strict educational and background criteria and are considered experts in their fields. Students participating in distance education have the unique opportunity to study with the finest instructors throughout the world.

## ADMISSION

Applicants for undergraduate degrees must have graduated from high school or passed the GED test before entering. Admission to graduate programs requires a bachelor's degree from an accredited institution.

## TUITION AND FEES

The tuition for undergraduate distance education courses is $645 per course ($215 per semester hour). Tuition for distance education graduate courses is $1320 per course ($440 per semester hour). Other general expenses include textbooks, which may be ordered online, and some courses require specific software packages. Tuition rates are subject to change.

## FINANCIAL AID

All forms of tuition assistance, government loans, grants, and corporate reimbursement are accepted. Help with Federal Aid forms are provided online through the SNHU financial aid office.

## APPLYING

Distance education students may enroll in undergraduate or graduate classes on a rolling basis. Applicants must submit an application along with appropriate documentation, such as an official high school transcript, GED scores, or official transcripts from previous colleges. There is no application fee. Applicants may register for course work immediately. Students should visit the DE Web site, listed below, for online forms, applications, or information.

### CONTACT

Kim Dabilis Byrne, Assistant Director
Janet Byrne, Supervisor of Academic Advising
Distance Education Program
Southern New Hampshire University
2500 North River Road
Manchester, New Hampshire 03106-1045
Telephone: 603-645-9766
Fax: 603-645-9706
Web site: http://de.snhu.edu

# Spring Arbor University

## *School of Adult Studies*

Spring Arbor, Michigan

eCollege.com   *www.ecollege.com*

*Founded in 1873, Spring Arbor University has become a leader in the design of degree-completion programs, and the University has a network of twenty affiliate colleges that have adopted or adapted the Spring Arbor curriculum. Currently, there are more than 1,500 students enrolled in Spring Arbor University programs. Spring Arbor University is accredited by the North Central Association of Colleges and Schools. Since 1963, when the University began its four-year curricula, the Spring Arbor Concept has expressed the educational philosophy and purposes of the institution. That concept, with slight amendments, has been incorporated as the foundational statement in the new University mission statement, which was adopted in February 1996. The mission statement affirms the University's respect for tradition, heritage of innovation, and pledge to pursue excellence.*

*Spring Arbor University offers bachelor's degrees at seventeen sites across Michigan; some sites also offer master's degrees.*

## DISTANCE LEARNING PROGRAM

Spring Arbor University offers the convenience of classroom accessibility 24 hours a day, seven days a week, from anywhere in the world. Currently, the University is in the process of offering ten courses on line. Spring Arbor University also has seventeen sites across Michigan that offer four degree-completion majors, as well as graduate programs. These degrees were designed with the working adult in mind and meet one night a week.

## DELIVERY MEDIA

The online courses require students to have the following requirements: a PC or Power PC processor with Windows 95, 98, or NT; a 75-MHz Pentium or faster processor; 32 MB of RAM or more; a 28.8-kbps or faster modem; speakers; and a sound card. Mac users must have MacOs or later Quadra Level. Students must have Internet Explorer or Netscape and an Internet service provider that provides them with the software necessary for getting onto the Internet. Stu-

dents should contact their local Internet service provider to set up a personal account. All courses are conducted entirely on the Internet. A good resource for finding a service is http://thelist.internet.com.

The online courses are offered via the eCollege.com system.

## PROGRAMS OF STUDY

Spring Arbor University has designed courses to be delivered on line. These courses typically satisfy the general education requirements of most students. Further, some courses meet elective requirements for graduate students. Additionally, the Master of Arts in organizational management may be completed entirely online.

At seventeen sites across Michigan, Spring Arbor University offers bachelor's degrees; some sites also offer master's degrees. The Bachelor of Science degree in management of health services focuses on the development of management and administrative skills in the delivery of health services. Course work provides a blend of specialized knowledge, skills, and attitudes essential for effective per-

formance as a leader or manager. A gerontology certificate is available.

The Bachelor of Arts degree program in management and organizational development provides expertise in human resource management and organizational development—two of the most important aspects of business and public administration. The program takes a systems approach to the problems, principles, and practices of management, incorporating conceptual and theoretical knowledge.

The Bachelor of Arts degree program in family life education offers an applied interdisciplinary approach that focuses on the study of family dynamics and the relationships between families and the larger society. This major benefits students through frequent exposure to professionals in the field, who serve as faculty members. Students who complete the program are eligible to become certified family life educators as designated by the National Council on Family Relations. In addition, the program has been endorsed by Dr. Kenneth Ogden of Focus of the Family.

The Bachelor of Science in Nursing is a degree-completion program designed for RNs who have been state certified and have completed an associate degree or a diploma program from an American Association of Colleges of Nursing (AACN) or National League for Nursing Accrediting Commission (NLNAC) approved school. The advanced theory and practices covered in this degree are applied to the student's work setting. This degree-completion program will be available online in the spring of 2002.

## SPECIAL PROGRAMS

Online courses offer undergraduate classes. Several courses satisfy general education requirements at most colleges and universities.

Weekend classes are offered on Fridays and Saturdays at most of the University's off-campus locations. Weekend classes are also designed to meet the general education requirements.

## STUDENT SERVICES

Students have access to the Spring Arbor University library, which is connected to FirstSearch (online indexes and directories), ProQuest Direct (an index to scholarly and professional business and economics articles), and Unicorn (access to the library collection).

## CREDIT OPTIONS

Spring Arbor University has transfer agreements with most community colleges. The University follows the Michigan Association of Collegiate Registrars and Admissions Officers Official Policies, recognizes college-level exams (CLEP, DANTES, and TECEP), and offers portfolio opportunities.

## ADMISSION

Students have open enrollment for online courses. The bachelor's completion programs require student to have 60 transferable credits and an acceptable writing sample. The graduate program requires a GPA of 3.0 of higher for the last two years (four semesters) of undergraduate study and a bachelor's degree from a regionally accredited institution.

## APPLYING

Spring Arbor University starts cohort classes several times throughout the year. Students should contact the site nearest them for more details. For more information on the online classes, students should visit the Web site listed below.

---

### CONTACT

John Nemecek
Assistant Dean
School of Adult Studies
Spring Arbor University
106 East Main Street
Spring Arbor, Michigan 49283
Telephone: 517-750-1200
Web site: http://www.arbor.edu

---

# Stanford University

## Stanford Center for Professional Development

Stanford, California

Since 1969, the Stanford Center for Professional Development (SCPD) has extended the School of Engineering's academic programs beyond the boundaries of the Stanford campus to address the career-long education needs of the best engineering, computer science, and management professionals worldwide. This important link between Stanford University and industry is designed to keep technical professionals at the leading edge of their fields by offering them the same educational opportunities as full-time Stanford students.

SCPD provides a broad range of continuing education options, including graduate engineering and computer science degree programs, individual courses for credit or audit, certificate programs, noncredit short courses, research seminars, and executive education.

## DISTANCE LEARNING PROGRAM

Stanford Center for Professional Development offers more than 250 engineering courses annually, reaching more than 400 corporate sites across the nation. Industry students access courses via the Internet, television broadcast, or videotape. SCPD's delivery options bring Stanford to the student at work, at home, or while traveling.

## DELIVERY MEDIA

SCPD is one of the world's largest single-university providers of televised engineering, computer science, and technology management courses, providing hundreds of programs for technology professionals and managers. SCPD offers a wide range of delivery options, including the Internet (or company Intranet), television broadcast, two-way videoconferencing, videotape, instructional modules, multimedia, and customized courseware.

SCPD's award-winning Stanford Online program is the first service to deliver complete video-based courses over the Internet (or company Intranet), offering Stanford programs in both a live and on-demand (asynchronous) videostreaming environment. Recognized nationally as the "Most Significant Advancement in Distance Learning for 1997" by the U.S. Distance Learning Association, Stanford Online's technology enables fifteen-frames-per-second videostreaming and provides a table of contents from which students may instantly access specific lecture material. Students may access courses via Stanford Online directly from their desktop, on an independent viewing schedule.

## PROGRAMS OF STUDY

More than 5,000 students have earned graduate degrees by participating in the Honors Cooperative Program (HCP), Stanford's only part-time graduate degree program. HCP students are fully matriculated graduate students of Stanford University with full student privileges, rights, and responsibilities. Graduate degree programs are available in a range of academic areas including aeronautics, applied physics, computer science, education-learning design and technology, electrical engineering, management science and engineering, materials science and engineering, mechanical engineering, and scientific computing and computational mathematics.

The Non-Degree Option (NDO) is for those students who wish to enroll in individual Stanford University courses and receive a grade and units for their course work. Individual course credit is available from all of the academic departments listed above, as well as in bioinformatics, medical informatics, scientific computing and computational math, statistics, and structural biology. Though those enrolled in the NDO program are not matriculated graduate students, they may enroll in certificate programs in more than twenty-five topics. Certificate programs are offered in astronautics, bioinformatics, computer science, electrical engineering, and mechanical engineering. These programs require completion of astronautics, bioinformatics, computer science, electrical engineering, and engineering—economic systems and operations research.

The Audit Option is available for participants to access courses without the time commitment of a graded course.

## SPECIAL PROGRAMS

Through SCPD, Stanford also offers a wide range of noncredit short courses and customized programs to help participants expand their professional networks and advance in their fields. Short course topics include medical informatics, ecodesign, advanced computer science, emotional intelligence in technology corporations, advanced project management, and telecommunications.

## CREDIT OPTIONS

SCPD offers a range of credit options in each program. Through the Honors Cooperative Program, students may work towards a master's degree in Engineering (in selected departments) or a Ph.D. (in selected departments). Through SCPD's Non-Degree Option, students may complete a Certificate Program, earn individual course credits, or may complete up to 18 units to be transferred to HCP status. Units may also be eligible for transfer to other institutions.

## FACULTY

Stanford University has a faculty of more than 1,500 members, of whom 98.8 percent hold doctorates or professional degrees. Among these distinguished professors are 14 Nobel Laureates, 3 Pulitzer Prize winners, 19 MacArthur Fellows, a winner of the Congressional Medal of Honor, and more than 100 members of National Academies and winners of National Medals.

## ADMISSION

Traditionally, students enroll on a part-time basis while maintaining employment at an SCPD member company. However, some programs do not require SCPD membership. Both member and nonmember compa-

nies may have different procedures to authorize student participation. Each student should contact their company education coordinator or manager to determine what is required for company approval of their program of study. For more information on SCPD membership, interested students should refer to the Web site located at http://scpd.stanford.edu/overview/membership/membership.html.

## TUITION AND FEES

For both HCP and NDO students, a one-time $55 document fee will be assessed by the Stanford University Registrar on the first quarter of registration. In addition, a minimum charge of 3 units per student is assessed for every quarter of enrollment, at $1055 per unit for HCP students and $811 per unit for NDO students. Audit students pay $555 per enrollment. Prices are subject to change. Students should refer to http://scpd.stanford.edu for updated tuition and fee information.

For further details and fee information on noncredit short courses and other programs, students should refer to the SCPD Professional Education Web site at http://scpd.stanford.edu.

## APPLYING

Prospective HCP students must obtain a "Guide to Graduate Admissions" booklet and application from the Graduate Admissions Support Section of the Stanford University Registrar's Office (telephone: 650-723-4291) or from http://www.stanford.edu/home/admission/index.html. Graduate Program details from departments in the School of Engineering may be found at http://soe.stanford.edu/programs/graduate/graduate.html. In addition, students must provide GRE test scores from within the past five years (information may be obtained at http://www.gre/org or 609-771-7670) and may be required to submit subject test scores in some departments. Completed application, statement of purpose, transcripts, and letter of recommendation should be sent to the Admissions Committee of the department to which the student intends to apply.

First-time NDO students must complete the SCPD Registration Form and submit transcripts from previous universities and colleges with their application.

---

### CONTACT

Stanford Center for Professional Development
496 Lomita Mall, Durand Building, Room 300
Stanford, California 94305-4036
Telephone: 650-725-3016
E-mail: sitn-registration@stanford.edu
World Wide Web: http://scpd.stanford.edu

Stanford Graduate Admissions Office
Telephone: 650-725-4291
Web site: http://www.stanford.edu

---

# State University of New York at Oswego

## Division of Continuing Education
## B.A. in Broadcasting and Communications

Oswego, New York

The State University of New York at Oswego was founded in 1861 as the Oswego Normal School. The institution became Oswego State Teachers College and one of SUNY's charter members in 1948. While maintaining its high standards as a center for teacher education, the college began to broaden its academic perspective in 1962 when it became one of the colleges of arts and science of the State University of New York.

Today, Oswego is one of thirteen university colleges in the SUNY system. About 8,000 students enroll annually. Oswego offers more than 100 academic programs leading to bachelor's degrees, master's degrees, and certificates of advanced study. The college is accredited by the Middle States Association of Colleges and Schools and by the Commission on Higher Education.

## DISTANCE LEARNING PROGRAM

The Bachelor of Arts (B.A.) in broadcasting and mass communication is available to students with two-year degrees in appropriate disciplines. All required courses, cognates, and electives as well as courses in other disciplines to fulfill general education requirements are offered online.

## DELIVERY MEDIA

All courses are taught via the World Wide Web in asynchronous mode through facilities of the SUNY Learning Network (SLN) (http://sln.suny. edu). Students are required to have reliable access to computers connected to the Internet. Courses use texts and involve substantial writing. SLN provides a help desk and online resources to help students with research and writing assignments. Students may be required to arrange laboratory experiences with colleges or universities close to home.

## PROGRAM OF STUDY

Forty-five hours of courses within the major, electives, and cognates are required, some of which may be trans-ferred into the program through sub-stitution or through articulation agreements with two-year colleges (two-year degrees typically account for about 50 percent of the require-ments). A transfer evaluation of credit assigns previously earned credits to the appropriate program and to gen-eral education and college require-ments. Students must complete a to-tal of 122 credit hours to graduate, with a minimum of 30 credit hours taken from SUNY Oswego. At least 60 hours must be at the upper-division (300–400) level. General edu-cation requirements also apply.

A total of 24 credit hours are re-quired in the major. The courses re-quired include COM 100, Founda-tions of Communication Studies (3 hours); COM 210, Speech Communi-cation (3 hours); BRC 108, Introduc-tion to Mass Communication (3 hours); BRC 110, Introduction to Broadcasting (3 hours); BRC 220, Ra-dio Production or BRC 235, Televi-sion Production (3 hours); BRC 319, Regulation and Control (3 hours); BRC 320, Media Economics (3 hours); and BRC 321, Broadcast Sales (3 hours).

A total of 15 credit hours in electives are required. Elective courses in-clude 6 hours of COM-prefix courses and 9 hours of BRC courses, with at least 6 hours at the 300 to 400 level.

A total of 6 credit hours in cognates are required. Cognate courses in-clude CSC 101, Computers and Their Applications (3 hours) and POL 205, American Politics and Government (3 hours).

## SPECIAL PROGRAMS

Online degree program students may benefit from internship opportuni-ties arranged through the Office of Experience-Based Education. Up to 15 hours of internship credit may be applied as electives both in the major and under the general studies cur-riculum. Past students have per-formed internships in network tele-vision, local and regional media, advertising, media research, and gov-ernment. Such experiences often lead to job offers and referrals.

## STUDENT SERVICES

Some of the campus services and re-sources that are available online in-clude Penfield Library, the Registrar's Office, Bursar Office, Financial Aid Office, and the Career Services Cen-ter. Oswego State University of New York's Web site is http://www. oswego.edu. Advisement options in-clude e-mail and telephone for all stu-dents.

## CREDIT OPTIONS

Up to 62 transfer credits from a two-year school may be applied toward a degree. The College-Level Examina-tion Program (CLEP) is offered and accepted. Up to 32 credits may be earned through CLEP.

## FACULTY

Approximately 22 full-time and 5 part-time faculty members currently teach distance courses at SUNY Oswego. Of these, 78 percent have doctoral degrees.

## ADMISSION

Applicants must submit official transcripts indicating that they have graduated with a two-year degree in a program in the media fields. Students may enroll full-time or part-time and must become matriculated after completing 22 hours of study.

## TUITION AND FEES

Part-time undergraduate tuition (in-state) is $137 per credit hour. Part-time undergraduate tuition (out-of-state) is $346 per credit hour. Full-time undergraduate tuition (in-state) is $1700. Full-time undergraduate tuition (out-of-state) is $4150.

Part-time fees (in-state and out-of-state) are $14.43 per credit hour.

Tuition and fee amounts are subject to change.

## FINANCIAL AID

Students should contact the Office of Financial Aid for information regarding income, credit hours, and other guidelines. In most instances, students must be enrolled in at least 6 credit hours to be eligible for financial aid.

## APPLYING

A SUNY application and a Distance Learning Program application both need to be submitted. Students are notified in writing if and when they are accepted into the program. An orientation session is optional.

---

### CONTACT

Dr. Michael S. Ameigh, Assistant Provost and Coordinator,
 Online Degree Program
35A Lanigan Hall
State University of New York at Oswego
Oswego, New York 13126

Telephone: 315-312-3500
Fax: 315-312-3078
E-mail: ameigh@oswego.edu
Web site: http://www.oswego.edu/~ameigh/ODP.htm

---

# State University of New York
# Empire State College

## *Center for Distance Learning*

Saratoga Springs, New York

*SUNY Empire State College is an internationally recognized innovator in adult education and a pioneer in distance learning. Since 1971, the College has served students who need alternatives to campus-based education because of work, family, or other responsibilities. Providing flexible degree programs at the associate, bachelor's, and master's levels, Empire State College features a number of student-focused study methods, such as one-to-one instruction, intensive mentoring by a faculty adviser, learning "contracts" instead of traditional courses, and undergraduate credit for college-level learning gained from life experience.*

*The College currently enrolls 13,000 students per year at forty-eight locations in New York State. Through its Center for Distance Learning (CDL), the College also serves students across the nation and around the world. Empire State College was the first public, nontraditional institution to receive regional accreditation by the Middle States Association of Colleges and Schools.*

## DISTANCE LEARNING PROGRAM

More than 5,000 students are served annually by the College's Center for Distance Learning. Established in 1978, CDL offers distance courses in a variety of media, primarily print and Web. As a founding member of the SUNY Learning Network, the College was among the first in the State University of New York to offer online courses. It was also the first within the University to offer an entire degree (in business, management, and economics) online. In addition to the online business degree, students may also earn an online degree in community and human services. Through the Graduate Studies program, an M.B.A. is offered primarily via the World Wide Web.

## DELIVERY MEDIA

The Center for Distance Learning makes use of the latest distance learning technology on the World Wide Web, as well as standard mail and telecommunications. Empire State College's online distance learning courses can be accessed at any time of the day, allowing students and faculty members to share ideas and concepts at times that are convenient to them. In addition, all student services, such as registration, academic advising, career and library services, and peer support, are also available on the Web.

## PROGRAMS OF STUDY

The Center for Distance Learning offers both two- and four-year degrees: Associate in Arts, Associate in Science, Bachelor of Arts, Bachelor of Science, and Bachelor of Professional Studies. The College also offers four Master of Arts programs, with concentrations in business and policy studies, labor and policy studies, liberal studies, and social policy, in addition to an M.B.A. with online courses.

One of the strengths of the Empire State College distance learning program is that students are assigned a faculty mentor, who guides them through all phases of their degree program, from academic planning to graduation. With their adviser, under-graduate students design individualized degree programs in any of eleven areas of study: the arts; business, management, and economics; community and human services; cultural studies; educational studies; historical studies; human development; interdisciplinary studies; labor studies; science, mathematics, and technology; and social theory, social structure, and change. Within these degree programs, a number of concentrations can be developed. Some examples of these are fire service administration, criminal justice, and management of health services. A degree in interdisciplinary studies includes concentrations in the social sciences or humanities.

To earn an associate degree, a student must successfully complete 64 credits, with at least 24 earned through study with Empire State College. A bachelor's degree requires successful completion of 128 credits, with at least 32 being earned through the College.

## SPECIAL PROGRAMS

In collaboration with nationally recognized online course providers Education To Go and SkillSoft, Inc., Empire State College's Center for Workforce Advancement (http://www.esc.edu/cwa) offers a series of 250 noncredit online courses geared to adult learners in the workplace. The courses are available in two different delivery formats: more than 100 six-week, instructor-supported courses and 150 two- and three-hour independent study courses that are available to students for a three-month usage period.

## CREDIT OPTIONS

Students can transfer credits earned at other regionally accredited institutions to Empire State College and can receive credit for college-level learning gained through work and life experience and through the College-Level Examination Program (CLEP) or other standardized tests. A total of 40 prior learning credits may be granted in the associate degree program; 96 credits may be applied to a bachelor's degree program.

## FACULTY

There are 345 full- and part-time mentors at Empire State College. Eighty-five percent of full-time faculty members and nearly half of part-time faculty members have doctoral or other terminal academic degrees. To supplement the academic expertise of its residential faculty, the College makes use of adjunct faculty members.

## ADMISSION

There are two principal requirements for admission to SUNY Empire State College: possession of a high school diploma or its equivalent and the ability of the College to meet the applicant's educational needs and objectives.

## TUITION AND FEES

In 2000–01, undergraduate tuition was $113 per credit. A per-term telecommunications development and support fee of $50 was also charged, which provided access to electronic mail, computer conferencing, the Internet, and other information sources.

## FINANCIAL AID

More than $6 million in financial aid was awarded to Empire State College students in 2000–01, with more than 40 percent of the enrolled students receiving some form of financial assistance. General financial aid programs available through Empire State College include the Federal Pell Grant, Federal Supplemental Educational Opportunity Grant, Federal Perkins Loan, and the Federal Work-Study Program. New York State financial aid programs include the Tuition Assistance Program (TAP), Aid for Part-Time Study (APTS), and the SUNY Supplemental Tuition Award. The Empire State College Foundation awards more than $30,000 in scholarships and grants annually.

## APPLYING

Empire State College reviews applications in order of date received, and students may apply online. The number of new students accepted depends on available space. There are five deadlines per year posted on the Web site (address listed below). Nonmatriculated students can take up to 16 credits without applying to the College.

---

### CONTACT

Paul Trela
Center for Distance Learning
SUNY Empire State College
3 Union Avenue
Saratoga Springs, New York 12866-4391
Telephone: 800-847-3000 Ext. 300 (toll-free)
Fax: 518-587-2660
E-mail: cdl@esc.edu
Web site: http://www.esc.edu/cdl

# State University of New York Institute of Technology at Utica/Rome

## School of Management

Utica, New York

---

*State University of New York (SUNY) Institute of Technology is the newest and youngest college in the sixty-four-campus SUNY system. It is a leader in technology, innovation, and excellence. It has been ranked two years in a row as one of the 100 Most Wired Colleges by* Yahoo! Internet Life *magazine. The Institute's School of Management is a pioneer in delivering high-quality education over the Internet.*

## DISTANCE LEARNING PROGRAM

The School of Management offers a Master of Science in Accountancy (M.S.A.) degree online. For students the advantages of this program are numerous. Graduate accounting students study and take classes at any time from anywhere in the world. No classroom attendance is required. Twenty-first-century technology is employed to create a virtual college on the World Wide Web. The online M.S.A. program eliminates the constraints of time and location that colleges normally place on students as well as the problems of long commutes, child care, conflicting work schedules, handicap accessibility, and absences due to illness. The online M.S.A. program combines quality education, lifestyle flexibility, and affordable tuition.

Students utilize the Internet for career advancement. The M.S.A. is an applied program for goal-oriented individuals. Students use the program to prepare for the CPA and CMA exams. The online M.S.A. fully complies with the new AICPA education requirements and is fully accredited. CPAs and CMAs satisfy Continuing Professional Education requirements while earning a graduate degree. It is a convenient and effective way for accountants to continue their education.

## DELIVERY MEDIA

Students must have access to the following resources: a computer with at least 64 MB RAM, 33.6 kbps modem, and Pentium processor (Macintosh users must have System 7 or higher); an Internet connection to the World Wide Web; a Web browser that supports file attachments (Netscape Navigator 4.0 or Microsoft Internet Explorer 4.0 or higher); a valid, working Internet e-mail account that accepts redirected mail and does not block Internet mail messages; and the ability to print documents, such as the syllabus, course schedule, and assignments. Students need to be able to create and save documents in a common file format. SUNY-IT recommends that students have access to a word processor with the capability to save files in the Microsoft Word 6.0 (or higher) file format. Professors may require their students to use additional software such as Microsoft Office 2000 or a spreadsheet application.

## PROGRAM OF STUDY

The degree program requires a total of 33 credit hours distributed among courses in advanced income tax research, fund accounting, advanced auditing theory, advanced financial accounting theory, managerial economics, management information systems, research seminar, financial management problems, management

science, and two electives that consist of any two graduate courses from the School of Management, including advanced management accounting, independent study, internship, international marketing and trade, health-care industry policy, human resource management, portfolio management, and strategies in national and international business. Students must attain a grade point average of 3.0 for all graduate courses included in their program. No more than three C grades, regardless of overall grade point average, are counted toward graduation.

## SPECIAL PROGRAMS

The Master of Science in Accountancy offers an internship program (ACC 595, 3 credit hours). Internship placements provide students with field experience related to their academic preparation, enabling them to apply classroom instruction to the work site. Students are placed with an organization related to their major area of interest to work with experienced professionals. These opportunities cannot not be duplicated in the classroom environment and prepare students for the transition into their chosen field.

## STUDENT SERVICES

Technical support, online libraries, and transfer and career advisement are available. Placements are excellent, with students being recruited by nationally recognized accounting firms, Fortune 500 companies, government organizations, and teaching institutions.

## CREDIT OPTIONS

Students from undergraduate accounting programs that are registered as CPA preparation programs typically have no prerequisite foundation course work. Other students are required to complete course work in accounting, business law, finance, statistics, economics, general business, and liberal arts as appropriate to prepare for the M.S.A. degree course requirements. Students should consult with a graduate adviser to determine appropriate course selection. Prerequisite skills may be fulfilled in a variety of ways, including transfer courses, courses at the Institute of Technology, and College Level Entrance Program (CLEP) examinations.

## FACULTY

The faculty members have extensive experience and meet the highest standards for quality. All the faculty members who teach in the M.S.A. program have earned a doctorate in their field of expertise.

## ADMISSION

To be admitted into the program, a student's score from the GMAT (Graduate Management Admissions Test) is combined with his or her undergraduate GPA as follows:

A total of 950 points based on 200 x undergraduate GPA + GMAT score, or a total of 1,000 points based on 200 x upper division GPA + GMAT score.

SUNY Institute of Technology makes an exception to these standards in cases where the applicant has demonstrated, through exceptional performance in a management career, that his or her undergraduate grades are not indicative of his or her ability, and conditional admission may be allowed for promising candidates who do not perform well on the GMAT. Students must maintain at least a B average in the first three courses they complete in order to remain matriculated when admitted in this category.

## TUITION AND FEES

In-state students take advantage of low SUNY tuition rates, making the M.S.A. very affordable. Graduate tuition rates are $213 per credit hour for part-time New York residents, $2550 per semester for full-time New York residents, $351 per credit hour for part-time nonresidents, and $4208 per semester for full-time nonresidents. Scholarships, financial aid, and internships are available.

## APPLYING

Applications are available online or by contacting the School.

---

### CONTACT

Dr. Thomas Tribunella, Director
School of Management
P.O. Box 3050
SUNY Institute of Technology at Utica/Rome
Utica, New York 13504-3050
Telephone: 315-792-7126 (Director)
        315-792-7429 (School of Management)
        315-792-7500 (admissions)
E-mail: ftjt@sunyit.edu
        admissions@sunyit.edu
Web site: http://www.pubm.sunyit.edu

# SUNY Learning Network
## Distance Learning Program
Albany, New York

The SUNY Learning Network (SLN) is a growing consortium, currently with fifty-three campuses in the State University of New York System that have joined together to offer graduate and undergraduate online courses. Many of the SUNY campuses now offer complete online degree programs through the SUNY Learning Network. Online degree programs are available in many disciplines at the associate, baccalaureate, and graduate levels.

Courses offered through the SUNY Learning Network are fully accredited by the Middle States Association of Colleges and Schools.

The SUNY Learning Network is supported by the Alfred P. Sloan Foundation and SUNY System Administration, Office of the Provost–Advanced Learning and Information Services.

## DISTANCE LEARNING PROGRAM

Students can study, take classes, and complete entire degree programs at any time and from any place. For those who find it difficult to adjust their schedule or commute to a campus, the SUNY Learning Network offers a new approach to teaching and learning that eliminates the constraints of time and location that higher education normally places on students.

The SUNY Learning Network now offers more than 1,500 online courses with more than 25,000 statewide, national, and international student enrollments. The online courses are designed and taught by State University of New York faculty members at the fifty-three participating SUNY institutions located around the state. Online courses are available to degree-seeking students or to students who simply want to take courses for personal or professional development (nonmatriculating students). In addition to online courses, there are more than thirty-five online degree programs now available entirely through the World Wide Web. The consortium, which began in fall 1995 with just four courses, continues to evolve and expand each academic year.

## DELIVERY MEDIA

In an online college course through the SUNY Learning Network, the instructor and the students are connected to each other through the Internet. Using the Internet, students can at any time receive instruction, compose and submit assignments, ask questions of the instructor and other students, discuss issues, and actively participate in the class—all from their home, office, or the nearest campus computer lab. Depending on the faculty member and the discipline, courses may also incorporate other Web-based materials, textbooks, application software, simulations, and even learning activities outside of the Internet, such as experiments, observations, or other projects. Students are welcome to see a sample SLN course located on the SLN Web site listed below.

To participate in an SLN course, students need access to a computer having the minimum of a Pentium processor; 32 MB of RAM; a 28.8K baud modem; a PPP/SLIP Internet connection to the World Wide Web; a Web browser that supports file attach-ments, such as Netscape Navigator 4.0 or higher or Microsoft Internet Explorer 4.0 or higher; an Internet e-mail account that accepts re-directed mail and does not block Internet mail messages; and access to a word processor with the capability to save files in the Microsoft Word 6.0 (or higher) file format. Macintosh users must have System 7 or higher.

## PROGRAMS OF STUDY

Many of the SUNY campuses participating in SLN offer complete degree programs through the SUNY Learning Network. Online degree programs are available in many disciplines at the associate, baccalaureate, and graduate levels. The SUNY Learning Network is not a separate degree-granting institution. Students need to matriculate at one of the SUNY campuses and work with their adviser on their home campus to make sure they fulfill the requirements of the degree program. For more information on the more than thirty-five online degree programs offered through SLN, students should visit the SLN Web site.

Students can also earn credits by combining traditional on-campus courses and distance learning studies from the colleges participating in the SUNY Learning Network.

## SPECIAL PROGRAMS

Starting in the 2001–02 academic year, the new State University of New York General Education Requirement requires baccalaureate degree candidates to complete no fewer than 30 credit hours in ten core subject areas. Each campus creates its own set of core courses using guidelines established by the Provost's Task Force on General Education. Many courses that satisfy the General Education requirements are available through the SUNY Learning Network.

## STUDENT SERVICES

The SUNY Learning Network Helpdesk is available seven days a week to answer students' technical questions and to assist students throughout the semester as they complete their courses.

## CREDIT OPTIONS

While students should always check with their adviser, credits earned in the SLN program are typically transferable. Students can also earn credits by combining traditional on-campus courses and distance learning studies from the colleges participating in the SUNY Learning Network.

## FACULTY

Online courses offered through SLN are designed and taught by State University of New York faculty members on staff at the participating SUNY institutions located around the state of New York.

## ADMISSION

Admission into degree programs offered through the SUNY Learning Network is handled directly by the individual SUNY campus that offers the degree program. Campus contact information is available on the SLN Web site.

## TUITION AND FEES

Tuition costs vary depending on campus, course level, and residency status. For detailed information on tuition costs for the campuses participating in SLN, students should visit the SLN Web site.

## FINANCIAL AID

Students should contact the financial aid office on their home campus regarding information on financial aid before registering for an SLN course.

## APPLYING

For complete instructions on how to apply and register for courses offered through the SUNY Learning Network, students should visit the SLN Web site.

---

### CONTACT

Students should visit the SUNY Learning Network Web site at http://SLN.suny.edu for the most up-to-date information on hundreds of courses, online degree programs, semester dates, tuition, and books and materials and to view a sample SUNY Learning Network course.

For additional questions, students may also call the SLN office at 518-443-5331 or 800-875-6269 (toll-free).

# Stephens College

## School of Graduate and Continuing Education

Columbia, Missouri

*Founded in 1833, Stephens College is a private college nationally known for its innovation in education. The School of Graduate and Continuing Education is built on a history of quality education and academic service to students. Located in Columbia, Missouri, Stephens College offers distance learning programs that allow men and women to complete their degrees as quickly as their schedules allow from home or work. Stephens has generous transfer credit options, credit for prior learning, one-office registration, and individual advising and degree planning.*

*Stephens College is nationally known for excellence in education and in fostering lifelong associations with alumni. The College has more than 30,000 alumni across the world.*

*Stephens College is accredited by the North Central Association of Colleges and Schools.*

## DISTANCE LEARNING PROGRAM

The School of Graduate and Continuing Education offers graduate, undergraduate, and nondegree programs for adult learners. Flexibility is the hallmark. External Degree courses are designed for bachelor's degree candidates, and the Master of Business Administration Program is designed for graduate students seeking to complete a challenging program without relocating or leaving their current jobs.

## DELIVERY MEDIA

External Degree courses are delivered worldwide through a variety of methods, including the Internet, telephone, fax, e-mail, and regular mail. Students are strongly encouraged to have access to a computer with an Internet connection. Students in the M.B.A. Program are required to have Internet access and an e-mail address. Certain courses require specific software programs.

## PROGRAMS OF STUDY

The adult student is at the heart of Stephens' nontraditional programs.

Students are assured a quality education designed with flexibility that allows them to meet the demands of their busy lives. Faculty members, staff members, and advisers understand the complexities of returning to college and are aware of the many responsibilities adult students must manage. They offer encouragement and support as the students progress through their course work toward graduation.

Working with Stephens College faculty members, students enrolled in External Degree courses study at home or work. This program is designed to complement the student's commitments to career, family, and community, and because courses are taken by independent study, students have some flexibility in completing their courses. Working with an adviser, students plan an individual program of study for their degree completion.

Majors available to students include business administration; early childhood or elementary education; English; health care and a second area; health information administration; health science and a second area; law, philosophy, and rhetoric; and psy-

chology. Students who wish to develop an individualized major in two disciplines may combine approved guided study courses from the list of majors.

The Stephens College Master of Business Administration Program utilizes communication technology to deliver a challenging curriculum to students around the globe. With individual attention from instructors and interaction with fellow students, the Internet-based program combines theoretical and practical approaches to provide the student with a well-rounded business education at the advanced level. Emphasis areas within the M.B.A. Program include entrepreneurial studies, management, and clinical information systems management. Undergraduate core requirements for the M.B.A. Program are offered through the Stephens College External Degree courses.

## SPECIAL PROGRAMS

Prior learning credit is available for adult undergraduate students who have achieved college-level learning and experience outside the classroom. Evidence of prior learning is presented by the student in a written narrative; oral interview, with supporting materials; and the actual product or demonstrations, if applicable. No letter grades are given.

Dual-disciplinary majors are available for graduates of hospital diploma programs, two-year registered nursing programs, accredited associate degree programs in allied health, or accredited noncollegiate hospital-based programs in allied health. These students may build on their specialized training in health care to earn dual-disciplinary majors such as health care and psychology, health care and business administration, health care and history, health care and philosophy/religion, health science and business administration, health science and psychology, health science and history, and health science and philosophy/religion.

## STUDENT SERVICES

Students receive the following services from the College: an individual academic adviser, assistance with prior learning, periodic mailings from the program, course schedules, a course catalog, a student handbook, and maintenance of student records and academic transcripts. Students also may use the College bookstore, Hugh Stephens Library, computer labs, Career Services office, and the College's recreational and other facilities.

## CREDIT OPTIONS

Stephens College offers many flexible options for earning academic credit, including independent guided study courses, Internet-based courses, on-campus courses, short-format courses, contract-study courses, transfer credit, noncollegiate professional education or training, prior learning, and credit by standard examination

(CLEP tests). Stephens accepts transfer credit from regionally accredited institutions.

## FACULTY

Students are taught by experienced, qualified faculty members who are dedicated to student learning. With a low student-faculty ratio, students benefit from a high level of interaction with instructors.

## ADMISSION

The Stephens College School of Graduate and Continuing Education follows an open admission policy for women and men over 23 years of age who have earned a high school diploma or GED. Students must complete the Liberal Studies Seminar with a grade of C or better to matriculate into the undergraduate program. The M.B.A. Program admits students with a bachelor's degree from a regionally accredited institution who have met minimum GPA and GMAT requirements.

## TUITION AND FEES

Tuition for the undergraduate program is $670 per course ($515 per course for Missouri residents). After completing the first year, students are

eligible for substantial tuition discounts when enrolling in more than two courses per year. The M.B.A. Program is $710 per course. Depending on courses selected and the degree sought, other fees may apply. Students should contact the School of Graduate and Continuing Education for more information.

## FINANCIAL AID

A variety of federal, state, and private funds may be available for students who meet specific criteria. Students should call the Office of Financial Aid at 800-876-7207 (toll-free) for more information.

## APPLYING

The Stephens College School of Graduate and Continuing Education accepts applications on a rolling basis. Applicants to the undergraduate program must submit an application along with documentation such as transcripts and/or GED scores. Applicants to the M.B.A. Program must submit transcripts from an accredited college or university, GMAT scores, three references, and an essay. Students for whom English is a second language must submit a minimum TOEFL score of 550. Application fees are $50 for undergraduate applicants and $25 for graduate applicants.

---

## CONTACT

Stephens College School of Graduate and Continuing
 Education
1200 East Broadway
Columbia, Missouri 65215
Telephone: 573-876-7225
                800-388-7579 (toll-free)
Fax: 573-876-7248
E-mail: sce@stephens.edu
grad@stephens.edu
Web site: http://www.stephens.edu/gce

---

# Stevens Institute of Technology

## The Graduate School Distance Learning Programs

Hoboken, New Jersey

*Stevens Institute of Technology, one of the world's premier technical universities, offers an array of Web-based distance learning graduate programs from its WebCampus. Stevens online initiatives include telecommunications management, wireless communications, technology management, project management, elements of computer science, atmospheric and environmental science and engineering, and technology applications in science education. Students are instructed by noted Stevens faculty members delivering the same superior courses as taught on the main campus. Other off-campus courses in a variety of fields are conveniently offered at corporate locations in six states, suiting the needs of graduate students who are working professionals. Some classes are delivered using interactive video. Stevens is accredited by the Middle States Association of Colleges and Schools (MSA) Commission on Institutions of Higher Education (CIHE). Online programs are co-sponsored by the Institute for Electrical and Electronics Engineers (IEEE) and ASME International.*

## DISTANCE LEARNING PROGRAM

Graduate certificates for professionals seeking advanced knowledge in science, engineering, management, and teacher education are available online through WebCampus.Stevens. Master's degrees and graduate certificates are offered online. A wide range of off-campus graduate degree programs in engineering, management, computer science, and mathematics, among other disciplines, are taught at corporate sites.

## DELIVERY MEDIA

Stevens has been at the forefront of distance learning for a number of years, offering courses that exploit the benefits of interactive video, Internet, and other advanced instructional technologies. WebCampus. Stevens online graduate students use rich Web features such as threaded discussions, chat, bulletin boards, e-mail, file sharing, whiteboards, and work groups for in-depth online participation. Students also have online library privileges, with instant search and retrieval of important databases.

## PROGRAMS OF STUDY

Graduate students may now take Web-based courses that lead to graduate certificates in telecommunications management, wireless communications, technology management, project management, atmospheric and environmental science and engineering, elements of computer science, and technology applications in science education. Graduate certificate programs offer students the opportunity to focus on a specific area of study without having to complete a master's program. Credits earned toward a graduate certificate at Stevens may also be applied to a master's degree, should students wish to continue with their studies. In addition to offering graduate certificates, the wireless communications program also offers a master's degree.

Off campus, at corporate and other sites, graduate students who enroll as part of company-sponsored and other programs may enroll in a wide variety of other programs, some of which are delivered using interactive video. Employees at some of the nation's most progressive and prominent companies, including Lucent Technologies, AT&T, Verizon, and dozens of others, may take graduate certificate courses and master's degrees at corporate locations in a number of disciplines. These include computer engineering, computer science, electrical engineering, management, mechanical engineering, project management, technology management, and telecommunications management, among others.

WebCampus.Stevens also offers Professional e-Seminars, which are non-credit, week-long short courses in engineering, science, and management. These courses are open to all, and no special background is required.

## STUDENT SERVICES

Distance learning graduate students access the entire range of Stevens' student services, which include faculty advising, ordering books and other materials, admission, registration, and applications for financial aid, among other services, via e-mail, telephone, and by post. Graduate students also have instant online access to the School's digital library. A CyberLibrarian is available via e-mail and telephone to guide students in the use of databases and other research tools and media. Seven days per week, 24-hour technical and other help desk support services are also available online. Stevens' Student Information System allows distance learners to access course schedules, grades, account statements, and other documents entirely online.

## CREDIT OPTIONS

Nearly all graduate courses are 3 credit courses. Depending upon the program, most graduate certificates are offered after students complete four courses. To earn a master's degree in engineering and science, students are required to complete ten courses. Students are required to complete ten courses for a master's degree in management.

## FACULTY

An impressive graduate faculty teaches courses at Stevens in conventional settings, providing superior instruction online and off-campus. WebCampus.Stevens faculty members are required to participate in teaching and learning colloquia, held periodically during each semester, in order to share their experiences and to demonstrate the capabilities of online teaching and learning. Net faculty are also trained in how to exploit the technological and pedagogical benefits of Web-based courseware applications.

## ADMISSION

To be admitted to a distance learning program at Stevens Institute of Technology, students are required to satisfy the same qualifications as those who wish to enroll in Stevens' conventional courses. Prospective graduate students need to have completed an undergraduate degree at an accredited institution. Applicants may either apply by mail or complete an application form online at the Internet address listed below. Applications should be accompanied by a nonrefundable check or money order for $50, made payable to Stevens Institute of Technology. Two letters of recommendation are required unless applying to the Technology Applications in Science Education graduate

certificate program. For this program, students must submit three letters of recommendation confirming that they are experienced teachers with basic knowledge of the Internet and mathematics or science. Applicants must also provide official transcripts, in English, for each college or university attended. Transcripts translated into English must be prepared by the school attended or prepared by an official translator with a recognized seal. Applicants must also provide official confirmation of the degree earned if it was awarded by a non-U.S. institution. Name, Social Security number, and/or date of birth must be on all submitted documents. All documents must be in English or have attested English translations.

## TUITION AND FEES

Prospective students must pay a $50 application fee, which is waived for current Stevens undergraduate students, Stevens alumni, and those entering from selected corporate programs. Each semester, students are also required to pay an $80 enrollment fee. Tuition for management courses is $605 per credit hour. Tuition for engineering and science courses is $725 per credit hour. Other fees apply for late enrollment and late payment, among other services. Tuition for the Professional e-Seminars is $595 per course.

## FINANCIAL AID

Stevens has a strong commitment to assisting and investing in talented students. The school offers a number of

scholarships, many of which are made available through generous friends and successful alumni. Many graduate students receive tuition reimbursement from their companies.

## APPLYING

Before applying to either online or off-campus distance learning programs, it is recommended that students review the Graduate School Web site or the Stevens' online learning site, both listed below, where students can find information, instructions, and online application forms.

### CONTACT

Online programs:
WebCampus.Stevens
Stevens Institute of Technology
Castle Point on Hudson
Hoboken, New Jersey 07030
Telephone: 201-216-0854
          800-494-4935 (toll-free)
Fax: 201-216-8044
E-mail: webcampus@stevens-tech.edu
Web site: http://www.webcampus.stevens.edu

Off-campus programs:
The Graduate School
Stevens Institute of Technology
Castle Point on Hudson
Hoboken, New Jersey 07030
Telephone: 201-216-5234
Fax: 201-216-8044
Web site:
    http://www.stevens-tech.edu

# Strayer University

## *Strayer Online*

Newington, Virginia

*Strayer University, founded in 1892 in Baltimore, Maryland, has more than 100 years of experience educating working adults. Currently, more than 12,000 students are enrolled at Strayer, the majority of whom work full-time. Undergraduate and graduate degrees are offered in technology and business-oriented programs. Strayer has seventeen campuses located in Maryland, Virginia, and the District of Columbia and is accredited by the Middle States Association of Colleges and Schools (MSA). Strayer University is a subsidiary of Strayer Education, Inc., a publicly held corporation whose stock is traded on the NASDAQ market (STRA). Strayer Education was recognized by Forbes magazine as one of the "200 Best Small Companies in America" for the third consecutive year.*

## DISTANCE LEARNING PROGRAM

Strayer Online classes are delivered via the Internet by live audio from professors and use real-time text-based communication between students and the professors. Classes meet at the same time each week. Students need a computer and access to the Internet. All of the software needed is provided.

## DELIVERY MEDIA

The following is a list of the minimal hardware and software recommended for participation in Strayer Online classes: a 300-MHz processor (Pentium II equivalent or higher) with Windows '98, Microsoft Office '97 Professional Edition (or more recent), a 128-KB L2 Cache (laptop) or 512-KB L2 Cache (desktop), 64 MB of memory, a 4-GB hard drive, a 12.1-inch SVGA TFT display (laptop) or larger (desktop), a 1.44-MB floppy drive, 2 MBs of video memory, a 24X (laptop) or 40X (desktop) CD-ROM drive, a 56-K PCMCIA modem with fax capability, a 10/100 Ethernet network card (laptop only), and an integrated microphone and speakers.

## PROGRAMS OF STUDY

Degree programs available online include the 54-credit Master of Science (M.S.) programs in business administration, communications technology, information systems, and professional accounting; Bachelor of Science (B.S.) programs (180 credits) in accounting, business administration, computer information systems, computer networking, economics, and international business; and Associate in Arts (A.A.) programs (90 credits) in accounting, acquisition and contract management, business administration, computer information systems, computer networking, economics, general studies, and marketing. There are also 54-credit diploma programs in accounting and computer information systems.

Courses are taught on the quarter system, and each course provides 4.5 credit hours. Associate in Arts degree programs require twenty courses, or 90 hours, to complete. B.S. degrees require forty courses, or 180 hours. M.S. degrees require twelve courses, or 54 hours, to complete.

Each degree program has a business component and a major component. The undergraduate programs also have liberal arts/general studies and an elective component.

## STUDENT SERVICES

Applications for federal financial aid, the Strayer Education Loan (a low-interest loan program), and scholarships are available online. Students may register for classes through the Web site or by telephone. In addition, library resources, other learning resources, and career-development services are available online.

## CREDIT OPTIONS

Students who have attended other educational institutions may receive transfer credit or advanced standing in Strayer's degree and diploma programs. College credit may be awarded for CLEP and DANTES tests, certain training received in the military, or prior work/life learning demonstrated through portfolio preparation. The required number of credits taken in residence, online or on campus, is 36 for a master's degree, 54 for a bachelor's degree, 27 for an associate, and 31.5 for a diploma.

## FACULTY

Strayer University has 113 full-time and 237 part-time faculty members. Of these, 10 teach full-time and 50 teach part-time for Strayer Online. Approximately 50 percent of full-time faculty members have a doctoral or terminal degree in their field.

## ADMISSION

Students who apply to undergraduate degree programs must provide certification of high school graduation or the equivalent. For admission to graduate degree programs, students must have graduated from an accredited college or university with a baccalaureate degree.

## TUITION AND FEES

In the 2000–01 academic year, tuition for graduate courses was $280 per credit hour. Full-time undergraduate students (3.5 credits or more) paid $210 per credit hour, and part-time undergraduate students paid $220 per credit hour.

## FINANCIAL AID

Students may apply online for financial aid. The Free Application for Federal Student Aid (FAFSA) may be accessed through the Strayer University Web address listed below. Students may apply for the following grants, loans, and scholarships: Federal Pell Grant, Federal Supplemental Educational Opportunity Grant, Federal Perkins Loan, Federal Stafford Student Loan, Federal PLUS Loan, Federal Direct Loan Programs, Federal Work-Study Program, Strayer University Education Loan Program, and Strayer University Scholarships. Thirteen percent of students studying online receive federal financial assistance.

## APPLYING

Applications are accepted on an ongoing basis and can be accessed online at the Web site listed below. There is a $25 application fee.

### CONTACT

Strayer Online
P.O. Box 487
Newington, Virginia 22122
Telephone: 888-4-STRAYER (toll-free)
Fax: 703-339-1852
E-mail: info40@strayer.edu
Web site: http://www.strayer.edu

# Suffolk University

## *Frank Sawyer School of Management/eMBA Program*

Boston, Massachusetts

eCollege.com    *www.ecollege.com*

*Suffolk University is a dynamic urban university that enrolls more than 6,500 students in its College of Arts and Sciences, Frank Sawyer School of Management, and Law School. The University is located in the heart of Boston's business and governmental districts on Boston's historic Beacon Hill. The Sawyer School of Management was established in 1937 and enrolls more than 2,100 undergraduate and graduate students. The Sawyer School is dedicated to providing access to pragmatic management education for preprofessional and working students. Suffolk University is accredited by the New England Association of Schools and Colleges, Inc. The Sawyer School is accredited by AACSB–The International Association for Management Education and the National Association of Schools of Public Affairs and Administration (NASPAA).*

## DISTANCE LEARNING PROGRAM

The distance learning program through the eMBA Program at the Sawyer School of Management continues Suffolk University's ninety-three-year tradition of providing access to higher education. Designed to meet the needs of people who wish to avoid the constraints of taking courses at a fixed location or who prefer the computer as the learning tool of convenience, the eMBA Program provides students with the opportunity to earn an accredited M.B.A. in a flexible, convenient, rigorous learning environment.

## DELIVERY MEDIA

eMBA instruction utilizes a variety of media as appropriate to the subject matter. Media typically include slideshows and other forms of online text and streaming audio and video to provide the student with access to course material wherever and whenever desired. These media are combined with document sharing, chat rooms, e-mail, and threaded discussions to provide interaction with faculty members and among students as needed to facilitate class discussions,

group work, case evaluations, simulations, and exercises and to provide feedback.

Students require access to the Internet and a moderate level of comfort working on the World Wide Web to participate in online courses. As a minimum configuration, the School recommends a Pentium computer, a 28.8 k-baud modem, Microsoft Windows 95, and Office 97 Professional.

Suffolk University has partnered with eCollege.com to provide the virtual campus and online courses. The online courses are offered via the eCollege.com system.

## PROGRAMS OF STUDY

The Sawyer School of Management offers an M.B.A. degree in cooperation with eCollege.com. This program is accredited by AACSB–The International Association for Management Education. The eMBA Program consists of sixteen courses, or 52 credits. The curriculum includes seven required courses (a maximum of five required courses can be waived) and nine elective courses. A student with strong prior academic preparation in business or management typically completes

the M.B.A. program in eleven to thirteen courses, depending upon the waiver process.

The eMBA captures the full value of the Suffolk M.B.A. by providing an integrated core, a global perspective, and real-life business applications. The eMBA standards are the same standards that the School demands from its on-campus students.

## SPECIAL PROGRAMS

eMBA students earn the same degree as students who attend Suffolk University's campuses and work with the same faculty. eMBA students have access to special programs that are available to on-campus students. eMBA students are allowed to register for courses or transfer into the on-campus M.B.A. program with the permission of the program director. The program offers optional international seminars (one to two weeks), which are hosted by one of Suffolk's international university partners and include extensive company and government visits. In the past, students have traveled to Europe, Asia, and Latin America.

## STUDENT SERVICES

eMBA students have access to the same materials and services that are available to students on campus. Remote access to library services, online registration, academic advising, and other services are available.

## CREDIT OPTIONS

Transfer credit is granted for core courses for graduate-level courses completed at a college or university that is accredited by AACSB–The International Association for Management Education; courses must have been taken within the last seven years, with a grade of B or better, and must not be used toward another degree. Students are required to complete a minimum of 34 credit hours of Sawyer School classes.

## FACULTY

The Sawyer School faculty consists of 69 full-time and approximately 80 part-time members. Ninety-three percent of the full-time faculty members hold doctoral degrees. The senior faculty members who teach in eMBA program have been selected for their commitment to online instruction and depth of experience.

## ADMISSION

Admissions criteria include a completed application form, an application fee, a current resume, two recommendation letters, official transcripts of all prior academic work, a statement of professional goals, TOEFL scores (for international students), and official GMAT scores.

## TUITION AND FEES

For the 2001–02 academic year, the eMBA tuition is $2043 per 3-credit course. eMBA students are also assessed a $120 technology fee per 3-credit course.

## FINANCIAL AID

For information regarding financial aid options, students should contact the Financial Aid Office.

## APPLYING

Applications are accepted for the fall, spring, and summer semesters. The fall 2001 semester begins September 10. Suffolk University operates on a rolling admission basis. Students are encouraged to submit applications well in advance of the deadlines. When all the required materials have been received in the Admissions Office, students are notified of a decision within one week.

---

### CONTACT

Dr. Mawdudur Rahman, Online Program Director
Christine Maher, Assistant Director
Frank Sawyer School of Management
Suffolk University
8 Ashburton Place
Boston, Massachusetts 02108-2770
Telephone: 617-973-5383
Fax: 617-723-0139
E-mail: mrahman@acad.suffolk.edu
        cmaher@suffolk.edu
Web site: http://www.SuffolkeMBA.org

Graduate Admissions Office
Suffolk University
20 Beacon Street
Boston, Massachusetts 02108-2770
Telephone: 617-573-8302
Fax: 617-523-0116
E-mail: grad.admission@admin.suffolk.edu

# Syracuse University

## *Independent Study Degree Programs*

Syracuse, New York

---

*Founded in 1870, Syracuse University is a major private research university of 14,400 residential students and an additional 3,800 part-time adult students located in central New York State. Organized into thirteen separate schools and colleges, each offering a variety of baccalaureate, master's, and doctoral degrees, Syracuse has excellent research facilities, including sophisticated computer networks and a library containing more than 2.8 million volumes. Syracuse is ranked by* U.S. News & World Report *as one of the top fifty-two universities in the United States and is one of the select group of American and Canadian universities chosen for membership in the prestigious Association of American Universities.*

*Syracuse has a long-standing commitment to adult education. The University's innovative Independent Study Degree Programs (ISDP) are a form of nontraditional education in which Syracuse was a pioneer. Offered through nine of the University's academic units, in partnership with Syracuse's Division of Continuing Education and Summer Sessions, ISDP is one of the three oldest external degree programs in the United States. The programs have been active since 1966 and reflect the University's response to the demands for creative educational techniques and programs in a constantly changing society.*

## DISTANCE LEARNING PROGRAM

Syracuse's Independent Study Degree Programs (ISDP) have a limited-residency structure: they combine short periods of intensive on-site instruction with longer periods of home study, during which students and faculty members communicate at a distance by correspondence, telephone, fax, and computer. There are currently about 1,000 adults actively enrolled in twelve different degree programs through ISDP, approximately one sixth of whom are international students or Americans living abroad. Syracuse degrees earned through ISDP are the same as those earned by traditional Syracuse students in comparable campus programs and have the same accreditation.

## PROGRAMS OF STUDY

ISDP offers two undergraduate and ten master's programs by means of the limited-residency, distance edu-

cation format. Undergraduate degrees include an Associate of Arts and a Bachelor of Arts in Liberal Studies. The Associate of Arts degree is 60 credits. The bachelor's degree is a 120-credit program.

The master's degrees include an M.A. in either advertising design or illustration, a Master of Library Science (M.L.S), an M.S. in communications management, an M.S. in information resources management, an M.S. in telecommunications and network management, an M.S. in nursing, a Master of Social Science (M.S.Sc.) with an international relations emphasis, an M.B.A., and an M.S. in engineering management. The M.A. and M.S.Sc. degrees are 30-credit degrees; the M.L.S., M.S. in communications management, and M.S. in engineering management are 36 credits, the M.S. in information resources management and the M.S. in telecommunications and network management are 42 credits, the M.S. in nursing is 45 credits, and the M.B.A. is 54 credits.

In addition to state and regional accreditation, several of the master's programs enjoy professional accreditation appropriate to the field of study. The advertising design and illustration programs are accredited by the National Association of Schools of Art and Design, the nursing program is accredited by the National League for Nursing Accrediting Commission, the M.B.A. program is accredited by the American Association of Collegiate Schools of Business, and the M.L.S. program is accredited by the American Library Association.

Students may initially enroll in the A.A., B.A., and M.S.Sc. degrees on a nonmatriculated basis. All other degrees require matriculation prior to participation.

## SPECIAL PROGRAMS

Syracuse University Continuing Education offers a selected number of individual online credit and non-credit courses each semester. Information on these is available on the World Wide Web (http://www.suce.syr.edu/online).

## STUDENT SERVICES

ISDP students are provided with free computer accounts and have access to the Syracuse University library and mainframe computer facilities. Online students have access to a help desk for technical problems. All distance students at Syracuse have access to a full range of online student services, including academic advising, financial aid, assistance, and registration.

## CREDIT OPTIONS

The associate degree program accepts a maximum of 30 credits to be transferred from another postsecondary institution. The baccalaureate program accepts a maximum of 90 transfer credits, which may include 66 credits from a junior college. Transfer credit is granted for most courses in which a grade of C or better has been earned, provided courses are from an accredited college and fit the ISDP degree requirements. For credit to be accepted from an international institution of higher learning, the institution must be a recognized third-level institution.

A maximum of 30 credits gained through testing or through evaluation of extra-institutional or experiential learning may be applied toward an undergraduate degree program. DANTES, CLEP, and Syracuse advanced credit exams may be used for this purpose. However, credit awarded through testing or experiential evaluation does not count toward the minimum number of credits that must be taken at Syracuse in order to earn a degree. On the graduate level, there is no provision for experiential credit. However, 6 credits may be taken in transfer from other accredited graduate programs, with a grade of C or better. The M.B.A. program also allows students to waive certain core courses by means of testing or documentation of prior academic experience.

## FACULTY

ISDP courses are taught by full-time Syracuse University faculty members, who participate in the limited-residency programs in addition to their full-time campus responsibilities. In the case of the M.A. programs in advertising design and illustration, additional visiting faculty members are drawn from among the world's most recognized designers and illustrators.

## ADMISSION

Candidates for admission to the associate and baccalaureate programs should have a high school diploma or its equivalent. Transfer students must have at least a 2.0 (C) average for the liberal studies program. On the graduate level, candidates must take the GMAT for the M.B.A. program and the GRE for the communications management, information resources management, telecommunications and network management, and nursing programs. Applicants whose primary language is a language other than English must also take the TOEFL. Portfolios of related professional work must be submitted for the advertising design, illustration, and communications management programs.

Applicants for all programs must submit official transcripts of prior academic work, letters of recommendation, and a personal statement that accompanies the application form.

Applicants to the Master of Library Science, communications management, engineering management, information resources management, telecommunications and network management, and nursing programs must also have a computer with at least a 486 microprocessor, a modem, and Internet access.

## TUITION AND FEES

For 2001–02, the undergraduate tuition rate is $390 per credit, and the graduate rate is $647 per credit. Additional expenses for room and board at the on-campus residences average $72–$100 per day, depending upon the choice of facility, and book charges average $100 per course. There are additional Internet line charges each semester for programs relying upon that means of communication.

## FINANCIAL AID

ISDP students who are U.S. citizens are eligible for all the standard federal grants and loans available to part-time students. Selective institutional aid is available for several of the programs listed above; detailed information is available upon request. Syracuse University awards more than $100,000 to ISDP students each year. International students (non-U.S. citizens) are not eligible for financial aid.

## APPLYING

Applicants should request application materials from the address below. The undergraduate programs and the M.B.A. and M.S.Sc. programs admit students on a continuous basis, and students can begin in the fall, spring, or summer terms. The other master's programs require newly admitted students to begin each summer, with the exception of the nursing program, which begins every other summer. In-person interviews are not required, although they can be arranged upon request. Portfolios may be sent to the ISDP office for evaluation.

### CONTACT

Robert M. Colley
Director, Marketing Communications and Distance Education
Syracuse University Continuing Education
700 University Avenue
Syracuse, New York 13244-2530
Telephone: 315-443-4590
         800-442-0501 (toll-free)
Fax: 315-443-4174
E-mail: suisdp@uc.syr.edu
Web site:
    www.suce.syr.edu/DistanceEd

# Syracuse University

## School of Management, Independent Study M.B.A.

Syracuse, New York

---

*Founded in 1870, Syracuse University—a private, nonsectarian liberal arts institution—is one of the largest and most comprehensive independent universities in the nation. The University is one of only sixty American and Canadian universities chosen for membership in the prestigious Association of American Universities. Syracuse University enrolls more than 10,000 undergraduates and 4,800 graduate students for full-time and part-time study. The campus is located in the city of Syracuse, in an area of New York State known as "Upstate" or "Central New York." Syracuse is less than a one-half-day drive away from New York City, Boston, Philadelphia, Toronto, and Montreal. The city is served by the Hancock International Airport, a mere 10-minute drive from downtown. Hancock airport features daily nonstop flights to New York, Boston, Atlanta, Chicago, Philadelphia, Washington, D.C., and other business centers.*

*The School of Management, in existence since 1919, has offered graduate programs since 1947. The School of Management has been continuously accredited by the premier accrediting body for business schools, AACSB International–The Association to Advance Collegiate Schools of Business, since 1921. The latest reaffirmation of accreditation was achieved by the School in April, 2001. The Independent Study MBA has been offered by the School of Management since 1977.*

## DISTANCE LEARNING PROGRAM

The Independent Study M.B.A. is a limited residency distance education program. It allows successful business people, working around the world, to acquire a Master of Business Administration degree on a part-time basis while continuing to advance in their careers. The program enrolls students who reside in many cities within the United States and from about fifteen other countries. The students' employers represent numerous prominent corporations and government agencies.

## DELIVERY MEDIA

Students meet on the Syracuse University campus three times each year for a week-long residency at the beginning of the fall trimester in August, the spring trimester in January and the summer trimester in May. During these intensive weeks, stu-

dents attend classes that serve to orient the students to the demands and expectations of the curriculum. Students also establish bonds and working relationships with faculty members and fellow students. At the conclusion of each residency, students return to their homes and workplaces with a clear understanding of the course requirements as well as access to the campus resources necessary for the successful completion of their courses. Final exams, if required for the course, are taken on campus at the following residency.

## PROGRAM OF STUDY

The Independent Study M.B.A. program emphasizes a broad, strategic-management view of business, leading to the Master of Business Administration in general management. The curriculum consists of eighteen courses for a total of 54 credits. There are thirteen core courses and five electives in a student's program.

Electives are drawn from the areas of accounting, finance, marketing, and organizational management.

## SPECIAL PROGRAMS

Optional off-campus residencies are occasionally held in other cities such as London and Shanghai. The programs held in these locations are identical in format to the on-campus residencies. Students take courses in the same manner and receive credit in the same manner as if they had attended a residency at Syracuse University.

## CREDIT OPTIONS

A student who enters the program with no transfer credits or waivers will complete 54 credits for the M.B.A. degree. The normal courseload is two courses per trimester. Following this model, students typically finish the program within three years. However, the program is flexible, allowing students to skip a residency when necessary for personal or professional reasons.

The School will accept a maximum of 6 transfer credits, if earned from an AACSB-accredited school of business within five years of enrollment in the program. If a student's academic background in program areas is extensive, there is a waiver policy leading to the possible waiver of up to 18 credits. Thus, an unusually well-prepared student may complete the M.B.A. degree with a minimum of 30 credits taken through Syracuse University.

## FACULTY

The faculty members who teach in the Independent Study M.B.A. program are the same faculty members who teach in the School's full-time and part time M.B.A. programs. However, during the residency weeks they are free of teaching obligations in other programs—so that they may concentrate their efforts on their Independent Study M.B.A. students. This creates a strongly cohesive environment and provides a high degree of personal interaction in the program.

## ADMISSION

An applicant must have received a bachelor's degree or its equivalent from an accredited college or university to be considered for admission. Admission is competitive. Acceptance is based primarily upon prior academic success and career achievement. Full-time work experience of at least two years is required for this program. A full description of the admissions policy is contained in the application instructions.

## TUITION AND FEES

Tuition in 2001–02 is $647 per credit. There is an annual tuition increase beginning with the summer residency. Textbooks average about $40 per credit. Housing and meal costs depend upon the accommodations chosen by the student, usually $70 to $120 per day. There is a one-time application processing fee of $40 for the paper application or $50 for the online application.

## FINANCIAL AID

Most Independent Study M.B.A. students hold full or partial sponsorship through their employer's tuition assistance program. Government or private loan programs are available for most students who are U.S. citizens or have a U.S. cosigner.

## APPLYING

New students may begin the program at any of the three annual residencies. Applications are considered on a continuous year-round basis. The application should be completed at least six weeks prior to the intended first residency. The Graduate Management Admission Test (GMAT) is required of all applicants. The Test of English as a Foreign Language (TOEFL) is required of those for whom English is not the first language, unless the undergraduate degree was acquired in a program taught in English. Prospective students may apply online via the Web at http://Embark.com

## CONTACT
Paula C. O'Callaghan, Assistant Dean
Independent Study M.B.A. Admissions
Syracuse University School of Management
Syracuse, New York 13244-2130
Telephone: 315-443-9214
Fax: 315-443-9517
E-mail: paula@som.syr.edu
Web site: http://www.som.syr.edu/isp

# Taylor University

## College of Lifelong Learning

Fort Wayne, Indiana

---

*Taylor University is one of America's oldest evangelical Christian institutions. In 1846, it began as a women's college with the conviction that women as well as men should have an opportunity for higher education. In 1855, it became coeducational and, in 1938, it offered its first distance learning course.*

*Today, U.S. News & World Report repeatedly ranks Taylor as one of America's best regional liberal arts colleges. The Templeton Foundation has named it one of the nation's top colleges for building character in students, and Barron's has listed it as a "best buy in college education."*

*Taylor University's mission is to educate men and women for lifelong learning and for ministering the redemptive love of Jesus Christ. It is accredited by the Higher Learning Commission of the North Central Association of Colleges and Schools.*

## DISTANCE LEARNING PROGRAM

The College of Lifelong Learning is the virtual campus of Taylor University; it emphasizes the integration of faith and learning through distance education. The College offers three Associate of Arts (A.A.) degrees, two certificate programs, and more than 130 courses from most academic disciplines, and is currently developing baccalaureate degree programs. Annually, it enrolls more than 1,200 students in more than 2,000 courses.

## DELIVERY MEDIA

The College of Lifelong Learning offers courses for credit through four different learning options to meet various individual learning needs. These include mentored learning, independent study, correspondence study, and online study. Mentored learning courses are the newest modality available and are offered in both online and offline formats. Mentored learning places an emphasis on strong interaction between the student and faculty, offering continuous access to the instructor by e-mail, telephone, or postal mail.

## PROGRAMS OF STUDY

The 64-credit-hour A.A. degree in biblical studies is designed for individuals preparing for vocational or lay Christian ministry. The curriculum is designed to give the student a foundational understanding of the Bible, Christian theology, and the knowledge and skills required for serving in a church or parachurch setting. It consists of 43 credit hours of general education course work, 15 hours in the discipline, and 6 elective hours.

The 64-credit-hour A.A. degree in justice administration is designed for individuals currently serving in or seeking to enter criminal justice, courts, corrections, law enforcement, or juvenile justice. It consists of 43 credit hours of general education course work and 21 hours in the discipline. Students also select a ministry or public policy concentration.

The 64-credit-hour A.A. degree in the liberal arts (general studies) is for students who desire a breadth of knowledge. It consists of 43 credit hours of general education course work, 15 hours in the discipline, and 6 elective hours.

The two certificate programs include the 18-credit-hour Christian Worker Certificate, designed for an in-depth study of God's Word, and the 18-credit-hour Justice and Ministry Certificate, aimed at equipping individuals who work with at-risk populations and/or inmates.

## SPECIAL PROGRAMS

Mentored learning courses are the newest learning option with the College of Lifelong Learning. Available in both online and offline formats, the mentored learning modality is specifically designed for learners with busy schedules and allows the student to control the pace of learning. Courses are competency-based, and students complete them according to their timetables. Successful completion occurs when the student attains the competencies of the course.

The independent study option is specifically designed for those hard-to-find courses that are not readily available in distance learning formats. With more than 100 faculty members representing a variety of disciplines, the College of Lifelong Learning is able to work with an individual student to develop a unique, customized course that meets his or her specific needs and graduation requirements. The student works independently under the guidance of a qualified faculty mentor.

## STUDENT SERVICES

The College of Lifelong Learning staff is committed to providing qualified, efficient and responsive service in a timely manner. Online registration facilitates course enrollments at any time of the day or night. Once enrolled, students become part of the

College's virtual campus, meeting the needs of today's Internet-savvy students. Within the virtual campus, students enjoy a relational, faith-based learning environment.

## CREDIT OPTIONS

Students earn credits by completing courses. Up to 34 hours of transfer credit may be approved toward the 64-credit-hour A.A. degree programs. Only course work with a grade of C- or better is accepted.

To receive credit for work done at other accredited institutions, students should send their transcripts to the College of Lifelong Learning for review. CLEP, AP, and DANTES credit must meet Taylor's standards to be accepted as transfer credit.

## FACULTY

More than 100 highly credentialed, dedicated Christians comprise the faculty of the College of Lifelong Learning. These instructors, many of whom hold doctorates, are among the most qualified academic professionals in the field of Christian higher education.

## ADMISSION

Admission is open to all students registering for individual courses or beginning a certificate program. Degree-seeking students must meet certain minimum admission standards and complete an application, which includes a personal reference recommendation.

## TUITION AND FEES

Correspondence courses are $149 per credit hour. Mentored learning, online, and independent study courses are $169 per credit hour. Other expenses include textbooks, study guides, supplemental materials, and shipping and handling fees. Taylor's most current fee structure is maintained at the online registration center.

## FINANCIAL AID

Students who have been accepted into online degree programs and who will be registered for at least 6 credit hours in one term may apply for financial aid available through the University's Title IV agreement with the U.S. Department of Education.

The Department of Veterans Affairs has approved courses offered by the College of Lifelong Learning for those students entitled to receive veteran's educational benefits.

## APPLYING

Students may enroll at any time in courses or certificate programs offered by the College of Lifelong Learning by simply completing an enrollment form. Those who desire an A.A. degree must apply and be accepted.

---

### CONTACT

Kevin Mahaffy, M.Min.
Enrollment Manager
Taylor University College of Lifelong Learning
1025 West Rudisill Boulevard
Fort Wayne, Indiana 46807-2197
Telephone: 219-744-8750
       800-845-3149 (toll-free)
Fax: 219-744-8796
E-mail: wwcampus@tayloru.edu
Web site: http://wwcampus.tayloru.edu

---

# Teachers College, Columbia University

## *The Distance Learning Project*

New York, New York

*Founded in 1887 to provide training for teachers of poor, immigrant children in New York City, Teachers College to date has educated nearly 100,000 individuals from around the world and is consistently ranked among the top three schools of education in the country. One third of the students are in teacher preparation programs, and the rest are planning careers in administration, policy, research, and teaching across the fields of education, health, and psychology. The College's mission is a dual leadership role: first, to be a major player in policy making, ensuring that schools are reformed to welcome learning for all students regardless of their status, and second, to prepare educators who not only serve students directly but also coordinate the educational, psychological, behavioral, technological, and health initiatives to remove the barriers to learning at all ages.*

## DISTANCE LEARNING PROGRAM

Situated within the Center for Educational Outreach and Innovation, the Distance Learning Project seeks to increase access to educational opportunities at Teachers College and provide a source of research, evaluation, and innovation in computer-mediated learning. Since 1997, enrollment in online courses has steadily increased and the program currently serves approximately 275 students per semester.

## DELIVERY MEDIA

Courses are offered through password-protected Web sites with features such as a threaded discussion area, asynchronous chat, easy ways to upload and share documents, and the capacity for multimedia (audio and video) or hypertext links to supplemental materials. Most courses consist of reading and written assignments or project work with supplementary lecture notes and in-depth communication among students, the instructor, and the teaching assistant using the discussion board and e-mail.

## PROGRAMS OF STUDY

At present, Teachers College does not offer any degrees entirely via distance learning, but online courses taken for credit can be applied toward most on-campus degree programs, including the intensive M.A. in technology and education, which only requires a short summer residency. Two 15-credit certificate programs can be earned entirely via online course work and consist of four required courses and an independent study project. The Teaching and Learning with Technology certificate is designed to prepare K–12 teachers, technology coordinators, principals, superintendents, and other educational professionals to integrate technology into the classroom. The Designing Interactive Multimedia Instruction certificate provides skills in designing multimedia applications for teachers, school personnel, curriculum developers, software designers, publishing professionals, media specialists, and other educational professionals. Both programs include a combination of essential hands-on and theoretical work designed to make use of new technologies and can be taken on a

credit or noncredit basis. Admission criteria include an essay and evidence of the student's achievement and potential to benefit from the program. Both certificates have been approved by the New York State Board of Education. Students who are not enrolled in a degree or certificate program are eligible to register for any single online course, subject to the College's admissions requirements.

## STUDENT SERVICES

Online learners receive a University e-mail address and an ID and password that allow access to electronic resources and server space. The Milbank library provides access to electronic databases, full-text articles, and extensive indexes of education, psychology, and health-related Web sites. Students can order course materials through the Teachers College bookstore, and Distance Learning Project staff members are available to provide technical support.

## CREDIT OPTIONS

All courses can be taken for either credit or no credit, but only courses taken for credit can be applied to a campus-based master's or doctoral degree. Online certificates can be earned by taking courses for no credit, but in that case they are not transferable to a degree program. Credits will only be awarded for completion of online courses or independent study requirements as outlined by the instructor.

## FACULTY

There are 20 instructors who regularly teach online courses, including full-time faculty members, adjunct faculty members, and instructors.

## ADMISSION

Students taking courses for credit are subject to the same admissions requirements as the University or the degree program to which they are applying.

## TUITION AND FEES

Online courses are charged the same rate as on-campus courses, as determined annually by the trustees. For the 2001–02 academic year, tuition for all courses is $740 per credit. The rate for enrolling in courses for no credit varies from $195 to $795 per course.

## FINANCIAL AID

Students enrolled in a degree program at Teachers College are eligible for Federal Stafford Student Loans, grants, and scholarships, which can be applied towards online courses. For those not enrolled in a degree program, the only financial assistance available are personal loans, which are available through the Teachers College financial aid office.

## APPLYING

All application and registration materials for individual courses and certificate programs are available online at http://dlp.tc.columbia.edu/learner/registration.htm. Students currently taking courses at Teachers College can register for online courses through the University registration system.

---

**CONTACT**

Distance Learning Project
Teachers College, Columbia University
Telephone: 888-633-6933
Fax: 212-678-3291
E-mail: dlp@columbia.edu.
Web site: http://dlp.tc.columbia.edu

---

# Texas A&M University

## Graduate Programs Offered by Distance

College Station, Texas

---

Texas A&M University (TAMU), founded in 1876, is a public land-grant university dedicated to the development and dissemination of knowledge in many diversified academic and professional fields. While continuing to fulfill its missions, now as a land-grant/sea-grant/space-grant institution, the University is evolving and expanding its role to meet the changing needs of state, national, and international communities. Graduate education began in 1888, with doctoral programs launched in 1936. The University is fully accredited by the Commission on Colleges of the Southern Association of Colleges and Schools as well as the major professional associations within the disciplines. In addition to more than 100 bachelor's programs, TAMU offers more than 150 master's programs and eighty-seven doctorates in its twelve colleges and interdisciplinary degree programs.

## DISTANCE LEARNING PROGRAM

Texas A&M offers ten of its graduate programs through distance education. Programs developed for distance delivery are those that are important to adult learners who are place- and time-bound and who need graduate education for professional development. Delivery methods are often adjusted to the needs and locations of students.

## DELIVERY MEDIA

Delivery methods vary, depending on the program content and location of the students. Some courses can be delivered in several formats. Delivery formats are generally Web based, often with an interactive video or videotape component and perhaps some face-to-face instruction. Students and instructors interact via e-mail, online chat, bulletin board, and/or phone contact.

## PROGRAMS OF STUDY

Complete program descriptions and contact individuals for these programs can be found at the University's Web site (listed with contact information).

The Master of Science (M.S.) in educational human resource development requires 36 semester hours: 15 hours of core courses, 9 hours of specialization

courses, 6 hours of electives, and 6 hours in a supporting field outside the department.

The Master of Education (M.Ed.) in educational technology requires 40 semester hours: 28 hours of required courses, 6 hours of educational technology electives, and 6 hours in a supporting field.

The Master of Engineering in petroleum engineering program requires students to have a background as practicing petroleum engineers. The program requires 36 semester hours of courses and a project report.

Students in the M.S. in engineering systems management program must have a background in science or math. The program requires 12 semester hours of core requirements, 9 hours of electives, 3 hours of directed studies or internship, and 12 hours of additional course work outside the major field of study.

The target audience of the Master of Engineering in industrial engineering program includes students holding a bachelor's degree in engineering. Students must complete 36 semester hours of core requirements, including an internship or directed study.

Students in the Master of Agriculture program in agriculture development

must complete 12 hours of required courses, 3 hours of educational technology electives, 3 hours of advanced communication courses, 9 hours of subject matter electives, and 9 hours of independent study. Students taking the plant science concentration must complete 17 hours of required courses and 19 hours of subject matter electives. The natural resource development concentration includes 12 semester hours of required courses, 16 hours of courses from supporting fields, and 8 hours of directed studies.

The target audience of the Master of Industrial Distribution degree program is high-potential business managers who need to understand the processes that drive their organizations and those that direct suppliers' and customers' purchasing decisions. Students must have a corporate sponsor and hold a bachelor's degree in engineering technology, industrial distribution, engineering, business, or a related field. Students must complete 36 semester hours of courses.

The Doctor of Education (Ed.D.) in agricultural education is a collaborative doctoral degree with Texas Tech University in Lubbock, Texas. Its target audience is agricultural extension personnel. Program requirements include 64 semester hours: 6 hours of seminars; 21 hours of content specialization courses; 12 hours of courses on methods of research; 13 hours in a supporting field—6 hours of internship and the remainder in educational administration, science and technology, or research and statistical analysis; and 12 hours of record of study.

## SPECIAL PROGRAMS

The target audience of the Math and Science Professional Development Program for Public School and Two-Year

College Teachers is high school math and science teachers who need continuing education to prepare for teaching Advanced Placement math or science or to become qualified to teach in a two-year college math or science program.

Students may take any four of the courses listed on the roster of current offerings and receive a certificate after completing those four courses if at least a B average is maintained. Each course is designed to cover specific topics in science or math that are often taught in high school or two-year college programs. Each teacher may choose the courses that most effectively fill his or her knowledge and vocational needs.

To take these courses, a student must be admitted as a non-degree-seeking postbaccalaureate student. For a complete list of courses, students should visit the University's Web site.

## STUDENT SERVICES

TAMU distance students have access to a variety of library services, including remote access to electronic resources, document delivery services, interlibrary loan, reference and research services, electronic reserves, on-site borrowing at other libraries in Texas, and the Net Library, a Web-based library of more than 11,000 full-text popular, professional, and scholarly books that students can browse or read online.

## CREDIT OPTIONS

A maximum of 12 graduate semester hours may be transferred for credit from another university with approval of the Office of Graduate Studies. Acceptance of these credits toward a master's degree must be determined by the Office of Graduate Studies and the department hosting the degree program. Extension courses are not accepted for graduate credit.

## FACULTY

All distance education courses are taught by regular Texas A&M faculty members. Each distance course or program has the same requirements as residential courses or programs. All graduate faculty members hold terminal degrees in their fields.

## ADMISSION

To take any course at Texas A&M, the student must be admitted to the University. Students may seek admission to one of the distance master's programs by regular admission as a graduate student or by applying as a non-degree-seeking, postbaccalaureate student. As many as 12 semester hours taken in postbaccalaureate, non-degree-seeking status may be applied, upon approval by the program faculty, to the master's program once the student is fully admitted into the program. Successful completion of courses as a postbaccalaureate, non-degree-seeking student does not imply admission into the graduate program. Full admission to the master's program requires satisfactory completion of the GRE; a specific grade point average, as determined by the program; fulfillment of all additional criteria, as defined by each program; and completion of the graduate admission application.

## TUITION AND FEES

Tuition and fees for distance education vary among programs. Students should consult with the program contact person about cost. Minimum cost per semester hour is approximately $300 for in-state students. Out-of-state students pay a substantially higher cost per semester hour. Engineering programs carry a higher cost than other programs.

## FINANCIAL AID

The Office for Student Financial Aid interfaces with students at a distance through telephone, offers online advice using e-mail, and provides forms and information through its Web pages. Video technology—both desktop videoconferencing and prerecorded tape—has been used to provide scholarship and awards counseling and to assist in answering questions. Further grant and scholarship information is accessible by computer.

To qualify for financial aid, a student must be a U.S. citizen and must plan on registering for a minimum of 4 graduate semester hours per semester, which is considered 50 percent time. Nine semester hours is considered a full load for graduate students. All students who wish to apply for aid must submit a Free Application for Federal Student Aid (FAFSA). Distance students must meet the same criteria for financial aid as resident students. For financial aid information, students should contact the TAMU Office for Student Financial Aid at 979-845-3236.

## APPLYING

Applications for admission to TAMU can be found at http://www.tamu.edu/admissions/. Students should go to the University's Web site, scroll to Enrolling for Courses and Programs, and view the material under Admissions Information, Important Enrollment Information for New DE Students, and On-line Applications Undergraduate/Graduate. All applications and important information guidelines are available at these locations.

---

### CONTACT

Elizabeth Tebeaux, Director of Distance Education
Office of Distance Education
Texas A&M University
1478 TAMU
College Station, Texas 77843-1478
Telephone: 979-845-4282
Fax: 979-845-4422
Web site: http://www.tamu.edu/ode/disted/

# Texas Christian University

## Cyberlearning

Fort Worth, Texas

*Texas Christian University (TCU) is a major teaching and research university with the person-centered environment that typifies smaller colleges. The commitment that faculty members have to both effective teaching and research/scholarly work promotes learning amid an atmosphere of discovery. The University's student life programs encourage personal growth and individual achievement. TCU was founded in 1873 and today enrolls more than 7,000 students from every state and many other countries. TCU's programs lead to bachelor's, master's, and doctoral degrees. The University is accredited by the Southern Association of Colleges and Schools; many of its programs also hold separate accreditation in their area of emphasis.*

## DISTANCE LEARNING PROGRAM

Initially, the goal of the TCU online program was to compliment the residential undergraduate experience. This changed with the introduction of two online graduate programs, which were initiated in the spring of 2000. Currently, more than 800 students are served through the online curriculum, of whom approximately 250 are graduate students.

## DELIVERY MEDIA

Course materials, student-student and student-faculty discussions, and exams are all accessible through the Internet. Students need access to the Internet, with a connection and equipment that meets the minimum eCollege.com specifications. Students communicate with their colleagues and professors through threaded discussions and chat rooms. Readings and assignments are listed in an outline format. Exams are completed on line and e-mailed to the professor. In keeping with the TCU tradition of individualized attention, professors are also accessible through e-mail and telephone conversations.

All online courses are offered via the eCollege.com system.

## PROGRAMS OF STUDY

The Master of Liberal Arts program is a multidisciplinary curriculum designed for individuals seeking to further their education in the general liberal arts. The M.L.A. degree is awarded upon successful completion of ten courses, four of which must be designated "Perspectives on Society." All course work can be obtained on line. M.L.A. courses strive to introduce interesting diverse subjects and are taught by many of TCU's finest instructors.

The Master of Science in Nursing Program is designed to educate clinical nurse specialists in adult health/medical-surgical nursing. Emerging Internet resources will allow teaching methodology and curriculum content to change in response to developments in medical research and information technology. Students may enter the M.S.N. program with either an associate or bachelor's degree in nursing. Students with an associate degree in nursing are admitted to a year-round, three-year accelerated program. Students with a Bachelor of Science in Nursing degree are admitted to a year-round, two-year graduate program. This program is especially beneficial to nurses who have been unable to advance their

education because of geographical location or multiple schedules.

## SPECIAL PROGRAMS

Distance learning courses are available to residential TCU students and to TCU students who are away from the campus either for a summer session or for a study-abroad program.

The Master of Science in Nursing is specifically designed to allow registered nurses to complete their degree while working full-time.

## STUDENT SERVICES

Because all students in TCU distance education courses are "regular" TCU students, they have access to all TCU student services. Textbooks can be purchased on line at bookstore@tcu.edu.

## CREDIT OPTIONS

Credit for distance learning courses is awarded on the same basis as residential courses for TCU students.

## FACULTY

Regular TCU faculty members are utilized for online instruction. These faculty members were chosen from a larger set, all of whom volunteered. The faculty members who are involved in online instruction receive university provided professional development in teaching methodology through technology.

## ADMISSION

The M.L.A. Program requires successful completion of a bachelor's degree from an accredited college or university regardless of major or date of completion. No admission examination is required. Interested students should contact Patricia Yarbrough via e-mail at P.Yarbrough@tcu.edu.

The Master of Science in Nursing Program admits no more than 24 individuals per year; no more than 12 with an Associate of Arts degree and no more than 12 with a Bachelor of Science in Nursing degree are admitted. Interested students should e-mail Dr. Kathleen Baldwin, Director of Graduate Studies, Harris School of Nursing, at k.baldwin@tcu.edu.

## TUITION AND FEES

Tuition and fees for distance learners are the same as those charged to residential students. For the 2000–01 academic year, graduate tuition was $420 per credit hour. In addition, the University charges $65 per hour in fees.

## FINANCIAL AID

Interested students should contact the TCU Office of Scholarships and Financial Aid at www.fam.tcu.edu. Distance learners are eligible for the same aid consideration as residential students. Students in the M.L.A. Program currently receive a grant equivalent to 25 percent of the tuition for each course taken. Graduate nursing students are also eligible for tuition grants.

## APPLYING

Information regarding TCU online programs can be found at www.tcuglobal.edu. M.L.A. information can be obtained at www.mla.tcu.edu. Students interested in obtaining information regarding the Master of Science in Nursing should contact Dr. Kathleen M. Baldwin at k.baldwin@tcu.edu.

---

### CONTACT

Dr. Leo Munson
Associate Vice Chancellor for Academic Support
TCU Box 297024
Forth Worth, Texas 76129
Telephone: 817-257-7104
Fax: 817-257-7484
E-mail: l.munson@tcu.edu

---

# Texas Tech University

## *Distance Learning*

Lubbock, Texas

*Texas Tech University (TTU) is a state-supported university accredited by the Commission on Colleges of the Southern Association of Colleges and Schools to award bachelor's, master's and doctoral degrees. Created by legislative action in 1923, Texas Tech University is a four-year research university composed of eight colleges and two schools (Agricultural Sciences and Natural Resources, Architecture, Arts and Sciences, Business Administration, Education, Engineering, Honors, Human Sciences, the Graduate School, and the School of Law).*

*The mission of Texas Tech University is to provide the highest standard of excellence in higher education while pursuing continuous quality improvement, fostering the intellectual and personal development of students, stimulating the greatest degree of meaningful research, and supporting faculty and staff members in satisfying those who are served by the University.*

## DISTANCE LEARNING PROGRAM

Texas Tech University has offered courses at a distance since 1927. While the bulk of the course work historically has been print-based, Texas Tech University is actively developing courses and degree offerings for delivery via new technologies.

Offering flexibility and convenience, programs provide high-quality course work comparable to traditional on-campus courses. Texas Tech University now offers eight degree programs at a distance.

## DELIVERY MEDIA

Courses are currently delivered via the World Wide Web, ITV, audiotape, videotape, CD-ROM, and correspondence, depending on the course or degree program. E-mail, threaded discussions, chat rooms, and traditional communicative methods allow students to correspond with instructors, assistants, and peers.

## PROGRAMS OF STUDY

The external Bachelor of General Studies is offered by the College of Arts and Sciences and administered by Extended Studies. A highly flexible program, the Bachelor of General Studies degree features three core areas of concentration tailored to students' interests or professional goals.

In addition to administering the Bachelor of General Studies degree, Extended Studies works with academic departments to offer more than sixty college-credit courses, most of which are print-based. Students may enroll in these courses at any time during the year. For more information, prospective students should visit Texas Tech University's Distance Learning Web site in the Contact section listed below.

The College of Engineering offers four different Distance Learning master's degrees: the interdisciplinary Master of Engineering degree (M.En.), which allows students to take courses from a number of engineering fields while specializing in one area; the Master of Science in Systems and Engineering Management (M.S.S.E.M.) through industrial engineering; the Master of Science in Petroleum Engineering (M.S.P.E.); and the Master of Science in Software Engineering (M.S.S.E.)

through computer science. For more information, prospective students should visit the College of Engineering Web site (http://aln.coe.ttu.edu/).

The College of Arts and Sciences offers an online Master of Arts in Technical Communication (M.A.T.C.) degree through the Department of English. An accredited nonthesis program, it parallels the on-site M.A.T.C. in admission and degree requirements. Courses are offered on the semester schedule. Texas Tech University is the only university in Texas to offer degrees in technical communication at the bachelor's, master's, and doctoral levels. For more information, students should visit the Department of English distance education M.A.T.C. Web site (http://www.english.ttu.edu/distance_ed/grad_MATConline.asp).

The College of Human Sciences offers a Master of Science in restaurant/hotel and institutional management (RHIM) through the Department of Education, Nutrition, Restaurant, Hotel and Institutional Management. The Master of Science program is designed for industry professionals who work in management-level positions and features the same courses and course content as the traditional graduate program. Courses are offered on the semester schedule and are delivered via the Internet. For more information, prospective students should visit the College of Human Sciences Web site (http://www.hs.ttu.edu/ceo).

The College of Agricultural Sciences and Natural Resources, in conjunction with Texas A&M University, offers a Doctor of Education (Ed.D.) in agricultural education through the Department of Agricultural Education and Communications. Geared for midcareer professionals in agricultural education in Texas, the degree is designed around engagement of a cohort of learners. The program includes 64 semester hours and spans four years. Courses are semester-based and are taught using ITV and the Internet. For more information, students should visit the College of Agricultural Sciences and Natural Resources Web site (http://www.casnr.ttu.edu/).

## SPECIAL PROGRAMS

Customized training programs for organizations and corporations are offered through Extended Studies' Professional Development and Community Outreach office. Web-based certificate programs are also available, and most programs provide opportunities to earn continuing education credits. For more information, prospective students should contact Extended Studies (listed below).

## STUDENT SERVICES

College-assigned advisers provide information about accessing course materials online, register students for course work, disseminate course ma-

terials, and monitor students' progress through degree programs.

## CREDIT OPTIONS

Distance learning college-credit courses or courses taken for continuing education credit are recorded on Texas Tech University transcripts, depending on the particular course. Distance learning course credits may be transferable to other institutions.

## FACULTY

Courses are taught by Texas Tech University faculty members or instructors approved by the respective college. The majority of faculty members hold terminal degrees.

## ADMISSION

Prospective students should contact the Graduate or Undergraduate Admissions Office or visit the University's Web site (http://www.ttu.edu) for detailed information about admission requirements. For more detailed information about the external Bachelor of General Studies, prospective students should contact Extended Studies.

## TUITION AND FEES

Tuition and fees vary from program to program. Prospective students should contact Extended Studies to obtain more information on tuition and fees.

## FINANCIAL AID

A variety of financial aid opportunities exist for distance learning students. Prospective students should contact the Financial Aid Office for more information. Some colleges may also offer scholarships or other types of aid through the college.

## APPLYING

Some degree programs have application deadlines, but students may submit an application for the Bachelor of General Studies degree at any time. For specific information about these degrees, prospective students should visit the respective Web sites noted in Programs of Study. For general inquiries, prospective students should contact Extended Studies to obtain specific application procedures and deadlines for degree programs.

---

**CONTACT**

Mr. Ariel Fernandez
Associate Director, External Degree Program
Extended Studies
Texas Tech University
Box 42191
Lubbock, Texas 79409-2191
Telephone: 800-MY-COURSE Ext. 249 (toll-free)
E-mail: dldegrees.oes@ttu.edu
Web site: http://www.dce.ttu.edu

# Thomas Edison State College

Trenton, New Jersey

*Thomas Edison State College provides adults with access to some of the best choices in higher education. One of New Jersey's twelve senior public institutions of higher education, the College offers fifteen associate, baccalaureate, and master's degrees in 100 major areas of study. Students earn degrees through a variety of rigorous academic methods, including documenting college-level knowledge they already have and by completing independent study courses. Identified by* Forbes *magazine as one of the top twenty colleges and universities in the nation in the use of technology to create learning opportunities for adults, this public college is a national leader in the assessment of adult learning and a pioneer in the use of educational technologies. Founded in 1972, Thomas Edison State College is accredited by the Commission on Higher Education of the Middle States Association of Colleges and Schools.*

## DISTANCE LEARNING PROGRAM

Thomas Edison State College offers one of the most highly regarded, comprehensive distance learning programs in the United States. Adults can choose from 100 distance learning courses, including online classes. Students also take tests and submit portfolios to demonstrate and earn credit for college-level knowledge they already have and transfer credits earned at other accredited institutions.

## DELIVERY MEDIA

Distance education courses are provided through several options, including Thomas Edison State College courses offered through the mail, e-mail, and online and Contract Learning, a one-to-one learning experience with individual faculty members. Interactive television classrooms, with satellite downlinks and cable access, are also utilized.

## PROGRAMS OF STUDY

Thomas Edison State College offers fifteen associate, baccalaureate, and master's degrees in 100 major areas of study. Degrees offered include Associate in Applied Science; Associate in Science in Management; Associate in Science in Applied Science and Tech-

nology; Associate in Arts; Associate in Applied Science in Radiologic Technology; Associate in Science in Natural Science and Mathematics; Associate in Science in Public and Social Services; Bachelor of Arts; Bachelor of Science in Applied Science and Technology; Bachelor of Science in Business Administration; Bachelor of Science in Health Sciences, a joint degree program with the University of Medicine and Dentistry of New Jersey (UMDNJ) School of Health Related Professions (SHRP); Bachelor of Science in Human Services; and Bachelor of Science in Nursing.

In addition, the College offers two master's programs. The online Master of Science in Management (M.S.M.) degree serves employed adults with professional experience in management. The degree is designed to have broad appeal for those not served by conventional programs. The program integrates the theory and practice of management as it applies to diverse organizations. Specialized tracks in project management and management of substance abuse programs are also available. The College's online Master of Arts in Professional Studies (M.A.P.S.) degree provides working professionals an opportunity to study the liberal arts from an applied per-

spective. The M.A.P.S. program attracts a diverse student body working in positions such as museum curator, college business manager, computer networking specialist, nuclear engineer, and teacher.

## SPECIAL PROGRAMS

Thomas Edison State College's Military Degree Completion Program (MDCP) serves military personnel worldwide. The MDCP was developed to accommodate the special needs of military personnel whose location, relocation, and time constraints make traditional college attendance difficult, if not impossible. The program allows students to engage in a degree program wherever they may be stationed. The program allows for maximum credit for military training and education.

The College has a unique program designed specifically for New Jersey community college students. The Degree Pathways Program allows New Jersey community college students or graduates to complete a baccalaureate degree at home, in the workplace, or at their local two-year college. Degree Pathways lets students at community colleges make a smooth transition directly into a Thomas Edison State College baccalaureate program by transferring up to 80 credits from a community college toward the 120 credits needed for a bachelor's degree.

The program provides coordinated support in admissions, academic programming, advisement, registration, and the sharing of technologies. Once students complete their first year at a community college or a minimum of 30 credits, they are eligible for the Degree Pathways Program. Students may continue to take classes and use technologies available at their community college as they move toward completing their associate degree and/or baccalaureate degree.

Credit-earning options for nondegree students benefit individuals who would like to earn credit through examinations, portfolio assessment, and Thomas Edison State College courses. Students may do so by paying the appropriate fee for these programs. An application to the College is not required to take advantage of these nondegree, credit-earning options.

Credit Banking is for students who wish to document college-level learning. Credit Banking is for individuals who wish to consolidate college-level work into a Thomas Edison State College transcript. Credits transcribed under the Credit Banking program may or may not apply to a degree program at Thomas Edison State College.

The College grants credit for current professional licenses or certificates that have been approved for credit by the College's Academic Council. Students who have earned one of the licenses or certificates approved for credit must submit notarized copies of the license or certificate and current renewal card, if appropriate, to receive credit. A list of licenses and certificates approved for credit can be found in the College's Undergraduate Prospectus.

Thomas Edison State College has also developed a 12-credit, online e-commerce certificate program.

## STUDENT SERVICES

Academic advisement is provided to enrolled students by the College's Advisement Center, which assists students in integrating their learning style, background, and educational goals with the credit-earning methods and programs available. Students can access advisement through phone and in-person appointments or through the Advisement Phone Center; they also have 24-hour access through fax and e-mail.

## CREDIT OPTIONS

Students have the opportunity to earn degrees through traditional and nontraditional methods. These methods take into consideration personal needs and interests while ensuring both breadth and depth of knowledge within the degree program. Thomas Edison State College offers one of the most highly regarded, comprehensive distance learning programs in the United States. Students use several convenient methods of meeting degree requirements, depending upon their individual learning styles and preferences.

Each undergraduate degree requires work in general education, major area of study, and elective subjects. Students are encouraged to work in conjunction with one of the College's knowledgeable program advisers to develop a program plan that best meets individual needs, goals, and interests.

## FACULTY

There are more than 550 consulting faculty members at Thomas Edison State College. Drawn from other highly regarded colleges and universities, consulting faculty members provide many services, including assessment of prior knowledge and mentoring.

## ADMISSION

Adults seeking an associate, baccalaureate, or master's degree who are high school graduates are eligible to become a student. There are no tests required for admission. There are no on-campus requirements. A computer is not required to complete an undergraduate degree. A computer is only required to take Thomas Edison State College courses offered online and for the M.S.M. and M.A.P.S. degree programs. Once a student is enrolled in a specific degree program, an evaluator determines the number of credits the student has already earned and fits those into the degree program requirements. Orientation is not required.

## TUITION AND FEES

Because the College uses efficient distance learning technologies, Thomas Edison State College's tuition and fees are among the most affordable in the nation. Undergraduate students may choose one of two payment plans: a comprehensive fee paid annually, which includes enrollment, technology services, courses, testing, and portfolio assessment; or the per-service fee, which enables students to pay for services as they use them. A complete listing of tuition and fees is included in the College's information packet.

## FINANCIAL AID

Thomas Edison State College participates in a number of federal and state aid programs. Eligible students may receive Pell Grants or Federal Education Loans, such as the Subsidized Stafford Loan and the Unsubsidized Stafford Loan, for courses offered by the College. Eligible New Jersey residents may also tap a variety of state grant and loan programs. Students may use state aid to meet all or part of their college costs, provided they are taking at least 12 credits per semester.

Detailed information about the financial aid process can be found in the financial aid packet, which is available from the Office of Financial Aid and Veterans' Services. To receive this information, students should contact the office (E-mail: finaid@tesc.edu or phone number listed below).

## APPLYING

Students may apply to Thomas Edison State College any day of the year by mail or fax or through the College's Web site. The Office of Admissions assists potential applicants in determining whether Thomas Edison State College suits their particular academic goals.

### CONTACT

Director of Admissions
Thomas Edison State College
101 West State Street
Trenton, New Jersey 08608-1176
Telephone: 888-442-8372 (toll-free)
Fax: 609-984-8447
E-mail: info@tesc.edu
Web site: http://www.tesc.edu

# Tompkins Cortland Community College

## Distance Learning

Dryden, New York

---

Tompkins Cortland Community College (TC3) is a fully accredited public institution with a long tradition of serving the educational needs of a diverse population. Tompkins Cortland Community College was founded in 1968 by the governing bodies of Cortland and Tompkins Counties. It is accredited by the Middle States Association of Colleges and Schools and is one of thirty 2-year community colleges in the sixty-four-campus State University of New York (SUNY) system.

Tompkins Cortland Community College continues to expand its online course offerings to serve its student body, which is composed of working people who wish to add to their knowledge and students seeking a two-year degree or looking to build a foundation before transferring to a four-year college. Many of the 2,700 students have full-time jobs and families, so distance learning is crucial. Most courses are offered through the SUNY Learning Network, and the rest are offered by TC3 itself.

## DISTANCE LEARNING PROGRAM

Committed to innovative instruction for a wide range of students, TC3 has been offering courses for many years at its main campus in Dryden and its extension centers in Cortland and Ithaca. That commitment has grown to include online (asynchronous) courses: the College has more than fifty scheduled for the fall 2001 semester, a number that continues to increase. TC3 also offers several synchronous courses. The online courses span several disciplines, including English, hospitality, paralegal studies, and psychology. Most recent course offerings include several in ESOL, with live audio. Three degree programs, paralegal studies, hotel and restaurant management, and chemical dependency studies–counseling can be obtained completely on line. All online courses may be taken by themselves or in conjunction with classroom-based courses.

## DELIVERY MEDIA

Online courses are designed to offer close interaction with instructors who ask students to read equivalent course materials and write papers or do research as students do in a classroom. Students use personal computers connected to the Internet via the World Wide Web to receive course content and interact with the instructor and fellow students. They must have access to a graphic browser such as Netscape or Microsoft Internet Explorer.

Synchronous courses connect students in geographically separate classrooms with an instructor and some students at the "near" site (often the Dryden campus) by using high-speed digital phone lines, live video, and enhanced audio.

## PROGRAMS OF STUDY

Three of TC3's Associate in Applied Science (A.A.S.) degrees can be obtained completely on line through the SUNY Learning Network: the paralegal studies program, the hotel and restaurant management program, and the chemical dependency studies–counseling program.

The paralegal studies program can be completed in either two or three semesters if students have previous college credit. It involves 10 credits of English, 20–22 credits of paralegal studies (subjects include law, ethics, estate planning, and litigation procedure), 7 credits of business, and an internship and seminar of 2 to 4 credits. Students may transfer to bachelor's degree programs.

The hotel and restaurant management program involves 13 credits in business and economics, 24 credits in management studies such as food services and marketing, 7 credits of English, and a 3-credit summer cooperative work experience. This program is designed for students who wish to seek employment after earning their associate degree. Students may also transfer to a four-year degree program.

The chemical dependency studies–counseling program includes 120 hours of field work and provides the clock hours needed by the New York State Office of Alcoholism and Substance Abuse for certified counselors.

## SPECIAL PROGRAMS

TC3's Business Development and Training Center offers a selection of services for business and staff development needs, with hands-on experience in training programs for industry, government, small businesses, and nonprofit agencies. One of its features is Education To Go, which offers workshops designed to be accessed from home or office. Education To Go offerings include such topics as computer skills on either Macintosh or PC, the design of Web sites, and JavaScript. Students must enroll through Education To Go's Web site (http://www.ed2go.com/

TC3), which describes course syllabi, procedures, and contact information.

## STUDENT SERVICES

Distance learners have access to academic advising, career advising, financial aid information, and TC3's online service, IQ Student, which allows students to check their bills, grades, and course schedules and descriptions. The e-TC3 Web site provides information on the College's online offerings.

## CREDIT OPTIONS

Transfer credit is granted for course work completed with a minimum grade of 2.0 (C) at accredited colleges. Credit is accepted only for those courses applicable to the program in which a student is enrolled. TC3 accepts advanced placement credit for tests taken through the College Entrance Examination Board. The College also awards credit for tests from the College Level Examination Program (CLEP).

## FACULTY

There are 65 full-time faculty members and a varying number of part-time faculty members at TC3. Fifteen percent have doctorates or other terminal academic degrees.

## ADMISSION

The principal requirement for admission is a high school transcript and/or copies of the General Equivalency Diploma (GED) test scores. Transfer students need to provide an additional transcript from colleges attended. Students who plan to mix distance courses with on-campus courses must be immunized against measles, mumps, and rubella, by state law. Students who do not have a high school diploma or GED must meet additional criteria.

## TUITION AND FEES

For 2001–02, part-time tuition is approximately $102 per credit hour for New York State residents and $204 for out-of-state residents. Full-time tuition is $1300 per semester for state residents and $2600 for out-of-state residents. Out-of-state residents pay the lower in-state tuition rate for Web courses. All tuition and fees are subject to change.

## FINANCIAL AID

Distance learners are eligible for federal financial aid such as the Pell Grant, the Supplemental Educational Opportunity Grant, and Subsidized and Unsubsidized Stafford Loans. New York State residents enrolled full-time are eligible for the Tuition Assistance Program (TAP). State residents also qualify for the Vietnam Veterans Tuition Award program. The College offers aid and loans through the TC3 Foundation and the Service Tradition program, which honors students who are active community volunteers.

TC3 awards $8 million in aid each year through its own resources and state and federal sources. Seventy-five percent of its degree-seeking students receive financial aid.

## APPLYING

TC3 has a rolling admissions procedure. Applications are accepted in person at the main campus or extension centers by mail or by fax. An application form can be obtained by calling the Office of Admission at 607-844-6580. A course registration form can be obtained from the registrar at 607-844-6562 and submitted in person by mail or by fax. If the course is offered through SUNY Learning Network, the registration form can also be found on line at the SUNY Learning Network (http://sln.suny.edu/sln).

---

### CONTACT

Eric Machan Howd
Tompkins Cortland Community College
170 North Street
P.O. Box 139
Dryden, New York 13053-0139
Telephone: 607-844-8211 Ext. 4297
Fax: 607-844-6541
E-mail: howde@suny.tccc.edu
Web site: http://www.TC3.edu

---

# Touro University International

## Distance Learning Program

Los Alamitos, California

---

> *Touro University International (TUI) is a newly developed campus branch of Touro College, New York, which was founded in 1971. TUI is accredited by the Commission on Institutions of Higher Education (CHE) of the Middle States Association of Colleges and Schools(MSA), as part of the scope of accreditation of Touro College.*
>
> *TUI offers all of its programs via the Internet, employing the latest technology and innovative live interactive delivery methodology.*
>
> *TUI is committed to the high quality of its pedagogical model, its family, and its support services in all programs. It is a worldwide university that is open 24 hours a day, 365 days a year. No matter where in the world students are, they can learn conveniently without disrupting work or personal life.*

## DISTANCE LEARNING PROGRAM

All TUI classes are taught via the Internet with no residency requirements. The student-centered teaching model has two major elements: modular case-based learning and the cyber classroom. These essential elements are part of every module of every course.

## DELIVERY MEDIA

The cyber classroom approach includes the use of multimedia for academic transactions and interactive collaboration (live exchange with the professor and with peers). The multimedia approach includes audio and video-on-demand, Internet links, Power Point presentations, and live conferences among students and between the professors and the students. This allows students to work as a team with fellow students from around the world. The case-based learning provides real-world application to each topic.

## PROGRAM OF STUDY

TUI currently has two colleges. They are the College of Business Administration and the College of Health Sciences. The College of Business Administration offers three degrees including the Bachelor of Science in Business Administration (120 semester credits), with concentrations in international finance, Internet auditing, general management, e-commerce, information technology, health care management, hospitality and tourism, and degree completion specially designed for students with an A.A. or A.S. degree. Also offered is the Masters of Science in Business Administration (32 semester credits for students with business-related undergraduate degree) with concentrations in international finance, general management, information technology, and e-commerce. There is also the Doctor of Philosophy degree in Business Administration (40 semester credits of course work plus a research dissertation). The concentration depends on the candidate's specific research interests.

The College of Health Sciences offers three degrees. There is the Bachelor of Science in Health Sciences (124 semester credits) with concentrations in health education, health care management, and professional degree completion; the Master of Science in Health Sciences (40 semester credits) with concentrations in international health, health care management, and forensic examination. The Doctor of Philosophy in Health Sciences (40 semester credits) is offered with specializations in international health educator/researcher/practitioner, occupational therapy educator/researcher/practitioner, forensic educator/researcher, and physical therapy educator/researcher/practitioner.

## STUDENT SERVICES

Touro University International maintains five specific student services. Pre-admission advising assists potential students with preparatory academic advisement, enrollment in the best combination of classes, and addressing any other concerns of the student prior to entering Touro University International. Pre-admission English competency evaluation is provided for students whose first language is not English, who do not meet the TUI's English competency requirements, or feel that they do not possess adequate English skills. Post-admission advising assists students with selection of courses, sequencing of courses, assists with developing study habits and academic progress, and addressing any other concerns of the student. Information technology assistance provides students with any assistance necessary to insure that students will have access to all of the information technology features of Touro University International courses. The Information Technology department will also provide any installation and configuration assistance necessary for any student. Library resource assistance is provided by staff of Touro University International via e-mail, to assist all students in the use of all library facilities—especially those on the Internet.

TUI provides financial assistance under three Federal programs that are available to citizens and eligible noncitizens of the United States.

## FACULTY

All TUI faculty members hold doctoral degrees and have experience in their respective fields in addition to having sound academic teaching, research, and dissertation advisement records. These exceptional full-time faculty members teach nearly all TUI classes. TUI also has access to the highest level of faculty expertise in each field through guest lecturers and visiting faculty via the cyber classroom delivery mode.

## ADMISSION

Students enroll throughout the year at TUI. TUI offers four sessions per year with each session lasting 12 weeks. Sessions begin in March, June, September, and December. All TUI classes are four semester credits. A full courseload consists of two courses per session, which is 32 semester credits per year, enabling students to continue with family and work life.

The Office of Admissions assists potential students with determining their fit to the program on the basis of past academic performance and educational goals. For specific details on each degree program students may visit the Web site at the Internet address listed below.

## TUITION AND FEES

TUI's tuition is one of the most affordable in the nation for the educational value. Tuition is $200 per semester credit for B.S. degrees, $300 per semester credit for M.S. degrees, and $500 per semester credit for Ph.D. degrees. Scholarships, graduate assistantships, and financial aid are available. Students should contact TUI registration for details.

Active-duty military, retired military, military dependents, and civilian military employees receive special tuition rates through TUI's DANTES agreement. Students should contact their base or post educational officer for contact TUI for details.

## APPLYING

Applications are available online at the Internet address listed below. Applications are accepted year round. A complete application package is required two weeks prior to the start of the semester. TUI responds to applications within twenty-four business hours of receiving completed materials.

---

### CONTACT

College of Business Administration
10542 Calle Lee, Suite 102
Los Alamitos, California 90720
Telephone: 714-816-0366
Fax: 714-816-0367
E-mail: info@tourou.edu
Web site: http://www.tourou.edu

College of Health Sciences
4332 Cerritos Avenue, Suite 207
Los Alamitos, California 90720
Telephone: 714-226-9480
Fax: 714-226-9844
E-mail: info@tourou.edu
Web site: http://www.tourou.edu

---

# Troy State University

## Distance Learning Center

Troy, Alabama

*Since its founding in 1887, Troy State University (TSU) has been recognized for the quality of its academic programs and its focus on the individual student. The University is dedicated to the preparation of students in a variety of fields in the arts and sciences, fine arts, business, communication, applied science, nursing, and allied health sciences, as well as to its historic role in the preparation of teachers. The administrators, faculty, staff, and students of the University, through a system of shared governance, are committed to excellence in education. A major commitment exists to provide undergraduate and graduate education for the national and international community, especially for mature students, not only by traditional means of delivery but also by technological means. Additional information about the University may be found at its Web site: http://www.troyst.edu.*

## DISTANCE LEARNING PROGRAM

The distance learning program at Troy State University (TSU) is an important and growing part of the mission of the University. A variety of different courses are offered, including five complete graduate degrees that may be completed online. Along with personalized attention from faculty members, the TSU distance learning program is supported by the Distance Learning Center at Troy State University in Alabama.

## DELIVERY MEDIA

Distance Learning Center course offerings are mostly Web interactive. Students may complete course work on an anytime/anyplace basis worldwide. Additional distance learning courses at Troy State University are also provided using Internet, satellite, cable TV, videotape, and microwave delivery systems.

## PROGRAMS OF STUDY

There are currently five master's degree programs and a variety of individual courses offered by the Distance Learning Center. Complete details can be found by visiting the Center's Web site listed in the Contact section below.

The Master of Science in Criminal Justice (M.S.C.J.) program is designed to provide qualified students with an interdisciplinary graduate-level education in criminal justice. It provides students with knowledge or enhancement in the criminal justice field or leads to a terminal degree.

The Master of Science in International Relations (M.S.I.R.) program is designed to offer the graduates of diversified undergraduate programs an opportunity to obtain proficiency in international relations. Topics include foreign policy analysis, defense and security policy, comparative politics, regional and state-specific studies, international economics, and specific instruments of international affairs, such as international organizations and international law. The degree program offers a ten-course option and a twelve-course option.

The Master of Public Administration (M.P.A.) degree program offers two program options. The ten-course program option consists of seven core courses and three electives, with a comprehensive examination. There is no comprehensive examination in the twelve-course option, but there is a final "capstone" course. A number of three-course concentrations are also available.

The Master of Science in Human Resources Management (M.S.H.R.M.) is a professional degree program designed to offer graduates of diversified undergraduate programs an opportunity to obtain a proficiency in human resources management skills. The program emphasizes fundamental problem-solving, technical, and decision-making skills; communication and interpersonal competencies; and knowledge critical for success in today's and tomorrow's entrepreneurial and business organizations.

The Master of Science in Management (M.S.M.) is a professional program designed to offer the graduate of diversified undergraduate programs an opportunity to obtain proficiency in management skills and decision making that enables them to carry out managerial responsibilities in both the private and public sectors. Students complete a five-course core, a three-course concentration, and two elective courses suitable to their individual academic and employment backgrounds and specific career objectives.

## SPECIAL PROGRAMS

The Troy State Distance Learning Center is a part of University College. The University College component of TSU is unique to Alabama universities, as it provides a global focus to TSU's routine operations. University College sites span from Korea to Guantanamo Bay, Cuba, giving meaning to the phrase "the sun never sets on TSU." Additional information about the University's programs may be found at its Web site listed in the Contact section.

## STUDENT SERVICES

TSU is committed to providing a wide range of learning opportunities for a diverse student population. Students come to TSU with hopes and high expectations. Professors teach courses using the latest course materials and techniques for rich interaction between students and professors. Professors can advise students on course options and degree requirements. The staff members in the Distance Learning Center also provide advice and assistance with admissions, registration, evaluation of transfer credit, changes of program, and processing of Intents to Graduate.

## CREDIT OPTIONS

The Distance Learning Center offers credits through distance learning that are recorded on a Troy State University transcript in the same manner as credits earned in on-campus courses. Most students enroll as degree-seeking students, but there is opportunity for students to take individual courses that may apply to degrees at other institutions of higher learning. Students should contact the Student Services staff in the Distance Learning Center to learn more about transient authorizations or other credit opportunities.

## FACULTY

All distance learning faculty members meet the standards set forth by the Southern Association of Colleges and Schools, the state of Alabama, and the review agencies of the various TSU colleges. Faculty members are full-time or adjunct members of the department granting the course credit.

## ADMISSION

Admission to the distance learning degree programs at Troy State University has the same criteria as admission for any on-campus student. Interested students should access the Distance Learning Web site listed below for more information. There is a $20 admission fee.

## TUITION AND FEES

Current tuition and fees are subject to change and are published on the Web site listed below. For the 2000–01 academic year, graduate credit was $250 each term ($750 per course), offered only through the main campus in Troy, Alabama. All students who enroll in Distance Learning courses are considered in-state and pay no out-of-state tuition fee for graduate courses. Additional fees include $35 for graduation and $5 for transcripts.

## FINANCIAL AID

Troy State University offers a comprehensive program of financial assistance for students pursuing a graduate degree. Application for Financial Aid forms may be obtained by e-mailing a request to the e-mail address listed below in the Contact section. The G.I. Bill, Veterans Administration, and tuition assistance (TA) are also means by which students who are qualified for these forms of financial aid may pay for tuition.

## APPLYING

Students can submit an Application for Admission as well as register for courses using the Distance Learning Web site listed below. The Web site provides complete details regarding degree programs and application and registration requirements.

---

**CONTACT**

Student Services
Distance Learning Center
Troy State University
Troy, Alabama 36082
Telephone: 334-670-3976
Fax: 334-670-5679
E-mail: tsulearn@trojan.troyst.edu
Web site: http://tsulearn.net

---

# The Union Institute

## Distance Learning Program Opportunities

Cincinnati, Ohio

*The Union Institute's distinctive educational system is designed for adults who have the desire and ability to assume a significant measure of personal responsibility for planning and executing their degree programs. Degree programs are individualized, build upon previous learning, and employ the creative engagement of knowledge through a wide variety of learning resources, under the close guidance and evaluation of the university's highly qualified faculty.*

*The Union Institute's undergraduate program includes the Center for Distance Learning, administered from the university's headquarters in Cincinnati, Ohio, as well as undergraduate learning centers in Miami, Florida, and Sacramento and Los Angeles, California. The Graduate College functions nationally and internationally and is administered from Cincinnati, Ohio.*

*The Union Institute was founded in 1964 by 10 college presidents as a vehicle for educational research and experimentation and was accredited by the Commission on Higher Education of the North Central Association of Colleges and Schools in 1985. Known now as the Higher Learning Association of NCA, it reaccredited the university for ten years in 1999. The Union Institute is a recognized leader in the development and implementation of programs of higher education for strongly motivated adult learners. Its individualized programs adhere to the highest intellectual and academic standards. For nearly four decades, the Union Institute's programs have met the career and educational needs of men and women from all segments of society, including government, industry, business, education, service, and the health professions.*

## DISTANCE LEARNING PROGRAM

The College of Undergraduate Studies' Center for Distance Learning (CDL), founded in 1993, offers courses and complete baccalaureate degree programs accessible by personal computer and other media. Graduate College learners throughout the United States and in a number of other countries work in individually designed doctoral programs of interdisciplinary research and study. The Graduate College program includes independent, guided research and a requirement for brief face-to-face meetings and seminars, held in locations throughout the United States, while CDL offers any-time-anyplace access to learning opportunities.

## DELIVERY MEDIA

The primary instructional delivery mode for distance learners is online and faculty-guided independent study, involving a high degree of learner–faculty member interaction supported by computer conferencing. Learners enrolled in the undergraduate Center for Distance Learning are required to have access to and know how to operate a modem-equipped personal computer that is able to access the World Wide Web and e-mail.

## PROGRAMS OF STUDY

The Union Institute offers concentrations in liberal arts and sciences fields leading to the Bachelor of Arts (B.A.), Bachelor of Science (B.S.), and Doctor of Philosophy (Ph.D.) degrees. Doctoral programs are interdisciplinary. Undergraduate learners' individualized degree programs include a specific concentration in one area (major) as well as a general education requirement ensuring breadth of knowledge. Common areas of concentration include business and management, communications, criminal justice studies, education, psychology, social sciences, and a wide variety of arts and humanities. Other liberal arts and sciences concentrations may also be available.

The baccalaureate degree requires the successful completion of 128 semester credits, of which at least 32 credits must be from sponsored learning at the Union Institute. The doctoral program is non–credit-hour based, with a minimum of twenty-four months' enrollment for graduation.

## SPECIAL PROGRAMS

The Union Institute also provides educational programs designed specifically to meet the needs of particular populations of adult learners, such as programs for substance abuse counselors and criminal justice professionals. Corporate on-site programs are also possible. The Union Institute's mission is to provide innovative yet rigorous educational opportunities to traditionally underserved adult populations; specifically designed programs targeted at special populations are one way in which the university fulfills that mission.

## CREDIT OPTIONS

The College of Undergraduate Studies accepts academic course credit (grade C or better) earned at regionally accredited postsecondary institutions, when appropriate to the learner's degree plan. The College may also accept credit recommendations from the American Council on Education (ACE) and the College-Level Examination Program (CLEP). Articulation agreements lead to additional transfer credit possibilities. Matriculating learners earn credit toward the remaining degree requirements through sponsored learning or the assessment of prior experiential learning.

## FACULTY

The Union Institute employs 110 full- and part-time faculty members to work as advisers, mentors, and guides to its learners. Ninety-nine percent of the full-time faculty members and 92 percent of the part-time faculty members have a Ph.D. or the terminal degree in their field.

## ADMISSION

Applicants to the College of Undergraduate Studies program are required to have a high school diploma or equivalent. Graduate College applicants are required to hold a master's degree from a regionally accredited college or university.

Applicants are not required to submit standardized test scores, but all are required to submit narrative essays as part of the application process. Official college transcripts and recommendations are also required.

## TUITION AND FEES

For academic year 2000–01 (July 1 through June 30), undergraduate tuition was $272 per semester credit hour. Graduate tuition was $4472 per semester. Tuition rates are the same for all learners, regardless of state of residence. A one-time, nonrefundable application fee of $50 is required.

## FINANCIAL AID

General financial aid programs available through the Union Institute include the Federal Pell Grant, Federal Perkins and Stafford Student Loans, and Federal Work Study programs. Learners may also be eligible for state-based financial aid programs. Veterans' benefits are available to eligible veterans enrolled through the Cincinnati Center, the California centers, and the CDL. The Union Institute awards a limited number of scholarships to its learners each year. More than half of all learners received some form of financial assistance in 2000–01.

## APPLYING

The Union Institute accepts and reviews applications for admission on a rolling basis; admitted learners may begin the program in any semester. The Center for Distance Learning schedules orientation seminars for new learners three times a year, in October, February, and June. Graduate College learners matriculate at ten-day entry colloquia that are scheduled monthly. Orientation seminars and entry colloquia are held at locations throughout the United States.

---

### CONTACT

**College of Undergraduate Studies**
Timothy Mott
Dean, Center for Distance Learning
The Union Institute
440 East McMillan Street
Cincinnati, Ohio 45206-1925
Telephone: 513-861-6400
　　　　　800-486-3116
Fax: 513-861-9026
E-mail: dean-cdl@tui.edu
Web site: http://www.tui.edu

**Graduate College**
Admissions
440 East McMillan Street
Cincinnati, Ohio 45206-1925
Telephone: 513-861-6400
　　　　　800-486-3116
Fax: 513-861-0779
E-mail: admissions@tui.edu
Web site: http://www.tui.edu/

# United States Sports Academy

## Continuing Education and Distance Learning

Daphne, Alabama

*The United States Sports Academy (USSA) is a nonprofit, private graduate school designed to serve the nation and the world as a sport education resource, with programs of instruction, research, and service. Since 1972, the Academy has been addressing the need to provide high-quality, sport-specific programs. The Academy is accredited by the Commission on Colleges of the Southern Association of Colleges and Schools to award the Master of Sport Science degree (Level III) and the Doctor of Sport Management degree (Level V).*

## DISTANCE LEARNING PROGRAM

Learning experiences and student requirements in distance learning are similar to and equivalent with courses offered in the traditional on-campus setting. Courses are instructed by an Academy faculty member, who is responsible for advising and facilitating the learning experience during the structured offering of distance learning. The vast majority of the Academy's students are using the distance learning system for part or all of their degree program.

## DELIVERY MEDIA

Distance Learning students at USSA receive a code for the Web-based course, textbooks, and audiotapes. The USSA library and its extensive reference database can be accessed through the USSA Web site. All students are required to have access to a computer and an e-mail address at the time of starting the first course.

## PROGRAMS OF STUDY

Distance learning offers the student an opportunity to earn a master's degree through a Web-based environment. The Master of Sport Science degree is offered in the following majors: sport management, sports medicine, sport coaching, recreation man-

agement, and health and fitness management. Each major requires 33 semester hours of course work. The following courses are core curriculum and are required for each major: sport administration and finance, sport marketing, professional writing and applied research, and contemporary issues in sport.

The curriculum in sport management is designed to prepare students for a number of career and leadership opportunities in sport. The curriculum in sport medicine is designed to enhance and further develop the students' interest in athletic training and sport medicine, thus leading to greater professional development. The program in sport coaching is designed to prepare a student for leadership in the career of sport coaching. Recreation management is designed to prepare students in the leisure service industry or community and recreation programs.

Each course requires the student to complete online quizzes, assignments, a research paper, and a proctored final examination. A course is graded as follows: discussion, 10 percent; quizzes, 10 percent; written assignments, 25 percent, class paper, 25 percent; and the final exam, 30 percent.

All degree-seeking students must pass a written comprehensive examination in order to graduate. This exami-

nation is the only residential requirement for distance learning students. Students must have completed and passed all course work before taking this examination. Students at USSA have the option between a thesis and a mentorship.

## SPECIAL PROGRAMS

USSA has certification programs in several areas, including bodybuilding, coaching figure skating, conditioning and nutrition, fitness and exercise physiology, personal training, sport agency, sport coaching, sport medicine, sport and recreation management. These programs are available to people of all educational backgrounds. The cost for the continuing education program is $220 per course, which is equivalent to 4 CEU's.

## CREDIT OPTIONS

A student may transfer up to 15 semester hours from a regionally accredited graduate school as long as such courses are equivalent to courses offered in the Academy's graduate program, credit was earned in the past four calendar years, the student received a grade of B or better in the course(s), and the academic committee approves the transfer credit. For more information, contact the Office of Special Services.

## FACULTY

The Academy has more than 30 faculty members. They are located both on-site and at various locations around the country. All members have terminal degrees. The majority of them are specialized in a sport science.

## ADMISSION

For full standing admission to the graduate program, an applicant must be a graduate of a four-year regionally accredited undergraduate institution with a cumulative grade point average of 2.75 or better, obtain either a GRE score of 800 (combined), an MAT score of at least 27, or a GMAT score of at least 400. A student who has a conferred master's degree from a regionally accredited institution may waive the GRE, MAT, or GMAT requirement with an official transcript stating the date of completion of the master's degree.

## TUITION AND FEES

Master's courses are $350 per semester hour. The cost does not include additional fees, textbooks, audiotapes, or shipping. International shipping is slightly higher. Financial Aid USSA has a wide variety of financial aid programs available to qualified students. More information can be obtained from the Office of Student Services.

## APPLYING

A student applying for general admission to the graduate program is required to submit the following to the Office of Student Services: a completed application form and a $50 nonrefundable fee (for the master's degree program); an official copy of all college transcripts; three letters of recommendation; official GRE, MAT, or GMAT scores taken within the last five years; a written personal statement; and a resume.

A student applying for international student admission must submit the following to the Office of Student Services: a completed application form and a $125 nonrefundable fee; an official, certified copy (certified English translation) of all college transcripts; three letters of recommendation; TOEFL scores (a minimum of 550 on the paper test or 213 the computer test); a written personal statement; a resume; and an evaluation of foreign education credentials (ECE report) by an Academy-approved evaluator. The evaluation must state that the student has the equivalent of a bachelor's degree from an accredited institution. This service normally costs approximately $75. Contact the Office of Student Services for further information.

---

### CONTACT

United States Sports Academy
1 Academy Drive
Daphne, Alabama 36526
Telephone: 334-626-3303
Fax: 334-626-3303
Web site: http://www.ussa.edu

Monica Sainz, Coordinator of Distance Learning and Continuing Education, 334-626-3303 ext 154. E-mail: msainz@ussa.edu

Becky Cochran, Administrative Assistant of Distance Learning, 334-626-3303 ext 153. E-mail: bcochran@ussa.edu

Duane Hand, Administrative Assistant of Continuing Education, 334-626-3303 ext 151. E-mail: dhand@ussa.edu

Diana Britain, Registrar, Office of Student Services, 334-626-3303 ext 148. Diana Britain E-mail: dbritain@ussa.edu

# The University of Alabama

## College of Continuing Studies/Division of Distance Education

Tuscaloosa, Alabama

---

*The College of Continuing Studies' Division of Distance Education upholds the tradition of educational quality with world-class excellence through programs that overcome the obstacles of geography, individual schedules, and limited class sizes. By recognizing that lifelong learning and technological development are increasingly essential to the lives of individuals and organizations, the following distance learning programs have been developed.*

## DISTANCE LEARNING PROGRAM

The Division of Distance Education offers various educational formats to students limited by personal circumstances or distance who are seeking high school–, college-, or graduate-level credit. These programs include Independent Study, Quality University Extended Site Telecourses (QUEST), Intercampus Interactive Telecommunications System (IITS), National Technological University (NTU), and Global Online Academic Learning System (GOALS).

## DELIVERY MEDIA

Independent Study offers high school and undergraduate college credit through written correspondence. QUEST offers undergraduate and graduate courses, five master's degrees in engineering, and a master's degree in nursing case management, all via videotape. IITS is a network of videoconferencing rooms equipped for full student and teacher live interaction. NTU offers master's degrees in engineering through satellite instruction in ten engineering or engineering-related fields. GOALS features online high school, undergraduate, and graduate-level courses delivered over the World Wide Web directly to the student's home or corporate desktop.

## PROGRAMS OF STUDY

Through QUEST, a student may complete undergraduate- or graduate-level course work or obtain a Master of Science degree in aerospace engineering, electrical engineering, engineering, engineering with a concentration in engineering management, mechanical engineering, and nursing case management. Tapes are made of actual classes and then sent to various QUEST sites the following day to be viewed by students who complete the same requirements as students on campus. QUEST open or corporate sites are easy to establish. There is no fee to become a site. Establishing a site does require a person to serve as site coordinator and be responsible for receiving and returning tapes. Equipment needed at the site includes a television and VCR. Requirements for each degree vary. Normally, students must complete their chosen programs in six years. The following colleges offer courses through QUEST: Engineering, Commerce and Business Administration, Nursing, Human Environmental Sciences, and Education.

Master's degrees are available via IITS in health studies, rehabilitation counseling, and taxation law. Students choose one of several sites located in the state of Alabama, where they see and hear the instructor and students at all sites in real time. Courses are offered in business, communica-tions, education, engineering, foreign language, law, library studies, material science, math, and nursing, as well as in other disciplines.

Members from the College of Engineering contribute, via satellite, master's-level course work to non-profit NTU for business and government agency employees seeking advanced degrees. More than 1,200 courses are available from participating universities in the ten master's programs in engineering. Also available are undergraduate "bridging" courses in computer engineering, computer science, electrical engineering, and software engineering for students wishing to enter the master's programs.

## SPECIAL PROGRAMS

Independent Study, the University's oldest distance learning program, offers high school and college credit through written correspondence. Approximately 150 college-level and sixty high school–level courses are available. Courses may be completed in as little as six weeks and as long as one year. Independent Study is DANTES approved. Students may enroll at any time.

GOALS offers high school, undergraduate, and graduate courses on line over the World Wide Web directly to the student's home computer or corporate desktop. GOALS has been developed through today's most advanced technology to offer a simple format of study for those in pursuit of academic excellence. Electronic communication reinvents and enhances the student's learning experience. New courses are currently being developed, and these updates can be accessed on the Division of Distance Education Web site.

## CREDIT OPTIONS

Applicability of credit toward an undergraduate degree refers to the prerogative of the respective academic divisions to count specific credit toward a student's degree requirements. A maximum of 64 semester hours of two-year college credit may be applied toward graduation requirements.

At the graduate level, a maximum of 12 semester hours of work taken as a nondegree student may be applied to the credit-hour requirements for a degree.

Responsibility rests with the student to observe the limitations imposed on credit hours, course work, and transfer of credit. Procedures and forms for this type of admission will be furnished upon request.

## FACULTY

There are approximately 180 full-time and 10 part-time faculty members involved in these programs. Of this faculty group, 99 percent of the full-time faculty members and 90 percent of the part-time faculty members have doctoral or other terminal academic degrees.

## ADMISSION

All undergraduate students enrolling in the QUEST or IITS program must be admitted to the University. Admission to any undergraduate college or division of the University requires acceptable evidence of previous academic performance and scores on a recognized admission test. All graduate students enrolling in QUEST, IITS, or GOALS must also satisfy the University's Graduate School admission criteria. Formal admission is not required of students who enroll in Independent Study or undergraduate GOALS courses.

## TUITION AND FEES

Independent Study tuition is $75–$90 for a high school course, $185 for a 2-hour college course, $270 for a 3-hour college course, and $355 for a 4-hour college course. QUEST tuition is $180 per credit hour plus a $25 registration fee each term. There is an $80 technology fee for engineering courses. IITS tuition is the same as on-campus tuition. NTU tuition is $585 per credit hour. GOALS tuition is $380 per 3-hour undergraduate course. Students should contact the Distance Education Office for more information. Tuition is payable in full by check or by VISA, MasterCard, or Discover credit card. Normally, tuition increases, when applicable, occur during the fall semester. Students should contact the Division of Distance Education for current tuition rates.

## FINANCIAL AID

Loans and work-study are administered through the Office of Student Financial Services. In addition, most academic departments of the Graduate School have teaching or research assistantships that carry a stipend. Teaching and research assistants who are assigned duties of .5 FTE or more may receive a grant equal to their tuition.

## APPLYING

Information can be obtained or registration completed by contacting the Division of Distance Education at the address below.

---

### CONTACT

Division of Distance Education
College of Continuing Studies
The University of Alabama
Box 870388
Tuscaloosa, Alabama 35487-0388
Telephone: 205-348-9278
              800-452-5971 (toll-free)
Fax: 205-348-0249
E-mail: disted@ccs.ua.edu
Web site: http://bama.disted.ua.edu

---

# University of Alaska Fairbanks

## Center for Distance Education Independent Learning Program

Fairbanks, Alaska

*In 1917, just fifteen years after the discovery of gold in the heart of the Alaskan wilderness, the Alaska Agricultural College and School of Mines was created by a special act of the Alaska Territorial Legislature. In 1922, the college opened with 6 faculty members and 6 students. Today, the University of Alaska Fairbanks (UAF), whose name was changed in 1931, continues to grow, both in size and stature. In addition to the main campus in Fairbanks, UAF has branch campuses in Bethel, Dillingham, Kotzebue, Nome, and the Interior/Aleutians. UAF is the state's land-, sea-, and space-grant institution. Its College of Rural Alaska has the primary responsibility for Alaska Native education and study, and UAF remains the only university in Alaska that offers doctoral degrees. UAF's colleges and schools offer more than seventy fields of study and a wide variety of technical and vocational programs. All courses are approved and meet the accreditation standards of the Northwest Association of Schools and Colleges Commission on Colleges.*

## DISTANCE LEARNING PROGRAM

UAF developed a Correspondence Study Program in the late 1950s, but the current Center for Distance Education and Independent Learning (CDE) was created in 1987. It supports close to 200 distance-delivered courses for several certificate and degree programs through the master's level within Alaska each academic year. The Independent Learning Program serves approximately 3,000 students throughout the world each year.

Courses that fulfill teacher certification and recertification requirements for the State of Alaska Department of Education are available. Students may choose among several courses that satisfy the Alaska studies and multicultural requirement. Students have up to one year from the date of enrollment to finish course work. Extensions may be available, depending on circumstances. Students are encouraged to use e-mail to submit lessons to circumvent delays in the standard mailing process.

## DELIVERY MEDIA

Independent learning courses utilize a wide range of media, including basic written materials, audiotapes, videotapes, CD-ROMs, e-mail, and the World Wide Web. Not all modes of delivery are available for every course, and students must have access to the appropriate equipment as specified in individual course descriptions. Most interaction between students and instructors is asynchronous in nature.

## PROGRAM OF STUDY

The Center for Distance Education and Independent Learning is not a degree-granting organization; however, its approximately 100 independent learning courses can be used to fulfill degree program requirements within the University of Alaska's statewide system or at any other university that accepts the credits.

## SPECIAL PROGRAMS

The Center for Distance Education and Independent Learning participates in the Defense Activity for Non-Traditional Education Support (DANTES) programs; information is available from base personnel or education officers. Veterans' educational benefits are also applicable for independent learning courses. DANTES students must complete a UAF enrollment form as well as the DANTES form.

## STUDENT SERVICES

Students have access to the state library system and the UAF Rasmuson Library directly or through the Statewide Library Electronic Doorway (SLED). All students can obtain accounts on the University of Alaska Computer Network, which also gives access to the wider Internet and the World Wide Web. The UAF Writing Center offers free telefax tutoring for student use. Papers are faxed to the center, and a telephone appointment is made between tutor and student. Students may not schedule more than one appointment per day.

## CREDIT OPTIONS

Since the Center for Distance Education and Independent Learning is not a degree-granting organization, there is no transfer of credit or credit for prior learning available.

## FACULTY

The Independent Learning Program includes approximately 60 faculty members, about half of whom are also full-time members of the UAF faculty and who have terminal academic degrees. Adjunct faculty members and discipline professionals are hired to supplement the University's full-time faculty.

## ADMISSION

Since the Center for Distance Education and Independent Learning is not a degree-granting organization, there are no admissions requirements or procedures. Students may enroll in individual courses any time during the year and have one year to complete the course. An extension of six additional months is available if sufficient progress has been made.

## TUITION AND FEES

All students enrolled in UAF independent learning courses are charged the same tuition whether they are Alaska residents or not. Tuition for 100–200-level courses is $79 per credit, 300–400-level courses are $90 per credit, 500-level (professional graduate) courses are $100 per credit, and 600-level (academic graduate) courses are $178 per credit. The only other costs for independent learning courses are materials fees that vary by course and a $20 service fee per course. Students outside the U.S. must submit payment in U.S. dollars and are charged an extra $30 per course for additional postage charges plus actual shipping charges for materials delivery. Students who wish to receive graded lessons via fax should submit the fax number and an additional $50 per course ($100 for international students) with the enrollment form.

## FINANCIAL AID

Alaska students who are full-time (enrolled in at least 12 credits per semester) and are taking independent learning courses on a semester basis are eligible for all the types of financial aid available to other students, including Federal Pell Grants, Federal Supplemental Educational Opportunity Grants, State Educational Incentive grants, Bureau of Indian Affairs grants, Federal Stafford Student Loans, and Alaska student loans. Students enrolled in regular yearlong courses are not eligible to receive financial aid.

## APPLYING

Since the Center for Distance Education and Independent Learning is not a degree-granting organization, no application is required to take independent learning courses. Completion of a UAF enrollment form and payment of fees are all that is required of students to take courses.

---

**CONTACT**
Bob Anderl, Acting Director
Center for Distance Education and Independent Learning
P.O. Box 756700
University of Alaska Fairbanks
Fairbanks, Alaska 99775-6700
Telephone: 907-474-5353
          800-277-8060 (toll-free)
Fax: 907-474-5402
E-mail: distance@uaf.edu
Web site: http://www.dist-ed.uaf.edu/

# University of Baltimore

## *Robert G. Merrick School of Business*

Baltimore, Maryland

> The University of Baltimore (UB) was founded in 1925 as a private, coeducational institution and is now the state's only upper-division university. It became affiliated with the Maryland State System of Higher Education in 1975 and became part of the University System of Maryland in 1988. UB offers the junior and senior years of baccalaureate study and graduate programs in business, liberal arts, and law. The mission of the University is to offer an outstanding educational program that provides students with a broad foundation of knowledge and the latest skills and techniques to support productive careers in the public and private sectors.
>
> The University is accredited by the Middle States Association of Colleges and Schools and the Maryland State Board of Education. The Merrick School of Business and all its programs are accredited by AACSB International–The Association to Advance Collegiate Schools of Business.

## DISTANCE LEARNING PROGRAM

The webBachelors allows students to complete the junior and senior years of course work leading to the B.S. in business administration fully online. The webBachelors follows the success of UB's webMBA program which has the distinction of being the first AACSB-accredited M.B.A. program offered entirely on the Internet. The webBachelors is also the first AACSB-accredited program of its kind.

## DELIVERY MEDIA

To participate, students need a computer with the following capabilities: an Internet service provider (ISP), 28.8 modem or faster Internet connection, a Web browser (Netscape version 3.02 or later, Internet Explorer version 4.01 or later, or AOL version 4.0 or later), an e-mail account that supports attachments, fax access (needed occasionally), Microsoft Office 97 Suite, a printer, and VGA monitor and sound card.

Students interact online with professors, classmates, and business and professional leaders.

## PROGRAMS OF STUDY

The webBachelor's curriculum is designed for students who have completed their first two years of undergraduate study and wish to complete their B.S. degree online. The 60-credit curriculum focuses on career readiness, communication, information technology, and problem solving. Core courses cover all the major disciplines of business to ensure that students gain a comprehensive knowledge and understanding of business concepts. Elective courses further broaden the applicability of these concepts in an electronic world.

Students who earn their B.S in a business-related program may be eligible for either UB's on-site M.B.A. program or the webMBA program. Such students may be able to finish their M.B.A. with as few as ten courses.

The Merrick School's webMBA program is designed to help students develop broad managerial skills and advanced technological understanding through a series of core courses, cross-functional courses, and electives. The M.B.A. program explores business issues in a global context. Students learn through case studies, Internet and library research, teamwork, and interaction with the faculty. Students with bachelor's degrees in any discipline are eligible to apply for the program.

The seven core courses (21 credits) include Business Statistics, Financial Accounting, Financial Management, Economics, Organizational Behavior and Human Resource Management, Production and Operations Management, and Marketing. Some or all of these courses may be waived depending on the student's academic background.

The six cross-functional courses (18 credits) include Information Systems and Technology, Applied Management Science, Accounting for Managerial Decisions, Global and Domestic Business Environment, Organization Creation and Growth, and Strategic Innovation and Renewal.

Four specialization courses in information-based solutions are required (12 credits). Students can choose among the following options: Investment Analysis, Data Base Management, Internet Business Site Development, Managerial Challenges of Global Electronic Commerce, and Electronic Commerce and Supply Chain Management.

To sample an online course or to learn what others have thought about taking Merrick School courses online, students should visit the Web site http://ubonline.edu/.

Students enrolled in the webBachelors and webMBA programs may access most student service areas through the UB home page at http://www.ubalt.edu. This includes access to the University of Baltimore Langsdale Library and the University bookstore.

## CREDIT OPTIONS

The webBachelor's program consists of University requirements (6 credits), competency core (12 credits), additional core (21 credits), and electives (21 credits). These courses (3 credits each) fulfill the junior and senior year requirements for the B.S. in Business Administration.

The webMBA program consists of core courses (21 credits), cross-functional courses (18 credits), and electives (12 credits). Students can waive core courses they have taken within the last five years with a grade of B or better. Before earning 15 credits toward their MBA, graduate students may take a waiver exam for an undergraduate course that does not meet the grade or time requirements.

## FACULTY

Merrick School faculty members possess exceptional professional and academic credentials. Ninety-five percent of Merrick School faculty members have earned a doctorate in their fields. They are experienced in online teaching and committed to the benefits of online learning for career-minded students with busy lives outside the classroom.

## ADMISSION

Admission to candidacy in the webBachelor's program is open to students who hold an A.A. degree or who have at least 56 transferable college credits averaging at least a 2.0 on a 4.0 scale. These credits must be earned at institutions (junior/community colleges, four-year colleges or universities) accredited by any regional accrediting association.

## TUITION AND FEES

Graduate tuition for each 3-credit course is $294 per credit for in-state students and $438 per credit for out-of-state students. There is no full-time flat rate for graduate school.

Part-time undergraduate tuition and fees for each 3-credit course are $169 per credit for in-state students and $491 per credit for out-of-state students. In-state tuition for full-time students is charged at a flat rate $1842. Full-time out-of-state undergraduate tuition is charged at a flat rate of $5887.

The fee charged for part-time students (those taking less than 12 credits) is $30 per credit. A flat rate of $264.50 is charged for full-time students (those taking more than 12 credits). Students must buy textbooks and other learning materials.

## FINANCIAL AID

Financial aid and scholarships are available for the webBachelors and webMBA programs.

## APPLYING

Graduate applications consist of two letters of reference, a resume, GMAT scores for M.B.A. applicants, official transcripts from all colleges or universities attended, a letter of intent, and the webMBA Affirmation Form.

Students interested in graduate study should submit the application materials requested at the webMBA program's Web site, listed below. WebMBA classes begin in January and July. They are offered on the webMBA program's "4 X 10" track of four 10-week terms with an approximate three-week break between terms. Application deadlines are June 1 and December 1.

WebBachelors classes begin in September and January and follow a fifteen-week semester schedule. Students can apply at http://apply.usmd. edu, the University System of Maryland online application site.

---

## CONTACT

For information about the webBachelor's program, students should contact:

Julia Pitman
Director of Admissions
University of Baltimore
1420 North Charles Street
Baltimore, Maryland 21201
Telephone: 877-APPLY-UB (toll-free)
Fax: 410-837-4793
E-mail: admissions@ubmail.ubalt.edu
Web site: http://ubonline.edu/msb/
    webbach.nsf

For information about the webMBA program, students should contact:

Ray Frederick
Academic Programs Coodinator
Merrick School of Business
University of Baltimore
1420 North Charles Street
Baltimore, Maryland 21201
Telephone: 410-837-4953
Fax: 410-837-4899
E-mail: rfrederick@ubmail.ubalt.edu
Web site: http://www.ubonline.edu/
    webmbahome.nsf

# University of Bridgeport

## Distance Education Program

Bridgeport, Connecticut

*The University of Bridgeport (UB), founded in 1927, is one of America's most internationally diverse campuses. Situated on a quiet, urban campus on the shores of Long Island Sound, the University is just 1 hour from New York City and less than 3 hours from Boston. Students enrolled at UB come from thirty-four states and ninety-one countries. They represent a variety of interests, professions, nationalities, and ages. UB's main campus in Bridgeport and its satellite campus in Stamford are at the heart of Fairfield County, Connecticut, which is home to the headquarters of many of the world's largest corporations.*

*Accreditation for professional programs has been granted by a number of accrediting agencies, including the Commission for Engineering Accreditation of the Accreditation Board for Engineering and Technology, Inc. (ABET); National Association of Schools of Art and Design (NASAD); Commission on Dental Accreditation of the American Dental Association; and the Commission on Accreditation of the Council on Chiropractic Education (CCE). The School of Business is internationally accredited by the Association of Collegiate Business Schools and Programs (ACBSP).*

*UB offers a wide variety of graduate programs in business administration, electrical engineering, mechanical engineering, technology management, computer science, computer engineering, human nutrition, counseling and human resources (human resource development, college student personnel, community counseling), education (from the master's to the doctorate), naturopathic medicine, and chiropractic. Many programs are conveniently scheduled during the weekend to allow for maximum convenience for working adults. Students may also attend on a part-time basis. Weekend programs in business administration (twelve to eighteen months), human nutrition (eighteen months), human resource development (twenty-two months), and computer science (sixteen to eighteen months) are available.*

## DISTANCE LEARNING PROGRAM

The University of Bridgeport's distance learning programs are committed to the larger social mission of education throughout the world. Learning is a lifelong process involving the development of a range of skills for a diversity of learners, which the University provides through advancements in technology. The distance learning program was initiated in 1997 with eight courses offered as part of the Master of Science in human nutrition program.

## DELIVERY MEDIA

The online program offers a learning environment that is both convenient and instructive. With a computer, modem, and access to the Internet, a student communicates with instructors and classmates from the convenience of the home or office. The student has access to an array of online tools for use in the program, such as e-mail, newsgroups, class conferences, informal chat rooms, textbooks, and specially produced software.

## PROGRAM OF STUDY

The distance education program provides students with technical and professional training in the health sciences, beginning with the Master of Science in human nutrition. The goal of the human nutrition program is to provide a biochemical and physiological understanding of human nutrition and its role in health and disease. The curriculum, highly relevant to health care, is designed to provide up-to-date graduate-level information, which enables students to acquire an understanding of nutritional issues as applied to their areas of specialization.

## SPECIAL PROGRAMS

University of Bridgeport online courses and programs are fully equivalent to on-campus programs. They follow the same curriculum, have the same entrance and graduation requirements, and charge the same tuition and fees. All students receive a University login name and password, allowing access to library services, extensive databases, registration, and academic advising.

## STUDENT SERVICES

Distance learning students have access to the student resources of a traditional campus, the library, counselors, registration, and financial aid, through the University of Bridgeport's Virtual Campus. Library resources, including books, journals, and other publications within the University library system, are accessible to the students. The University's full-time reference librarians assist students in using resources such as Internet searchable databases and services, including special nutrition and medical databases (such as PubMed, alt-HealthWatch, and MANTIS). The reference librarians, academic advisers, and career placement counselors are available to the student through e-mail, fax, or telephone. The library also provides a free interlibrary loan service for all students and faculty members.

## CREDIT OPTIONS

Students can transfer undergraduate credits earned at other postsecondary institutions to the University of Bridgeport and can receive undergraduate credit by taking the College-Level Examination Program or other standardized tests. A maximum of 90 credits may be transferred toward a bachelor's degree, and a maximum of 6 semester hours may be transferred into any of the graduate degree programs.

## FACULTY

The faculty-student ratio in distance education is 1:20. All instructors hold doctoral or terminal degrees in their field.

## ADMISSION

Admission to the graduate programs requires a bachelor's degree from an accredited institution with a minimum GPA of 3.0.

## TUITION AND FEES

In 2000–01, tuition for the M.S. in human nutrition degree program was $385 per credit hour. There are 31 credit hours in the complete program. Other general expenses include registration fees and required textbooks, and some courses require specific software packages.

## FINANCIAL AID

Students accepted for enrollment may be eligible for Federal Stafford Student Loans. For further information, students should contact the Office of Financial Aid (telephone: 203-576-4568).

## APPLYING

Distance education students may obtain an application form and other program descriptions from the Office of Distance Education. Applicants must submit a completed application for admission, two letters of recommendation, and official transcripts of all previous college work.

---

### CONTACT

Michael Giampaoli
Office of Distance Education
University of Bridgeport
303 University Avenue
Bridgeport, Connecticut 06601
Telephone: 203-576-4851
      800-470-7307 (toll-free)
Fax: 203-576-4852
E-mail: ubonline@bridgeport.edu
Web site: http://www.bridgeport.edu

---

# University of California, Davis

## UC Davis Extension

Davis, California

---

University of California, Davis was founded in 1960 and is a state-supported university. It is accredited by the Western Association of Schools and Colleges, Inc. UC Davis Extension is the continuing education arm of UC Davis.

## DISTANCE LEARNING PROGRAM

UC Davis Extension first offered distance learning courses in 1987. In 2000–01, it offered more than seventy courses at a distance and served 1,165 students.

## DELIVERY MEDIA

Courses follow a variety of formats, including self-paced and synchronous, with most courses being conducted entirely online. Other delivery methods include videotape and CD-ROM. UC Davis Extension offers a wide variety of subject areas via distance learning, including information technology, writing, winemaking, Spanish, and brewing.

## PROGRAMS OF STUDY

UC Davis Extension offers more than seventy college- and professional-level courses as well as a specialized studies program in computer programming, a certificate program in information systems analysis, and the foundation certificate examination preparation program for brewing.

The specialized studies program in computer programming is an 11 unit program designed for those interested in gaining the skills necessary to design and code new application programs.

The certificate program in information systems analysis is a 14-unit program that prepares students to be a technically competent systems analyst.

The Institute of Brewing has selected UC Davis Extension as the world's only distance learning instructional provider for preparing to take the Foundation Certificate Examination. Earning the Foundation Certificate gives international recognition of a basic, underpinning knowledge and understanding of the principles and practices of brewing and packaging operations.

## CREDIT OPTIONS

Courses offered for academic credit may be applied toward degree programs. Students who wish to petition to apply a UC Davis Extension course toward a degree at another institution should verify acceptance of the course with that institution before enrolling. UC Davis Extension courses are not accepted as part of the residence requirements of the University and cannot be used to transfer from one University of California campus to another.

## FACULTY

Distance learning courses draw from a pool of more than 100 working professionals and UC Davis faculty members. Over one half of UC Davis Extension instructors hold advanced degrees in their field.

## ADMISSION

Enrollment in UC Davis Extension distance learning courses is open to students who have satisfied published prerequisites. Many courses have no prerequisite.

## TUITION AND FEES

Fees vary widely by subject area. Information technology courses cost an average of $252 per quarter unit of academic credit. Writing courses can be as little as $95, while winemaking courses run $550 to $1500.

## FINANCIAL AID

UC Davis Extension is an approved training institution for three loan providers: Citibank, Educational Resource Institute (TERI), and Microsoft 2000. Students interested in acquiring one of these loans have to go through an application process. The forms are available from UC Davis Extension. The student then works directly with the loan provider to secure funding.

## APPLYING

For most courses, students simply submit an enrollment form along with their payment. Some of the winemaking programs require a true application process before a student can enroll. Certificate programs require a $45 application fee. No orientation is required.

## CONTACT

Student Services
UC Davis Extension
University of California
1333 Research Park Drive
Davis, California 95616
Telephone: 530-757-8777
        800-752-0881 (toll-free)
Fax: 530-757-8558
E-mail: questions@unexmail.ucdavis.edu.
Web site: http://www.universityextension.ucdavis.edu/
    distancelearning/

# University of Central Arkansas

## *Division of Continuing Education*

Conway, Arkansas

---

*The University of Central Arkansas (UCA) was established in 1907 by the General Assembly as the Arkansas State Normal School and was charged with the responsibility of training teachers. As a statewide, comprehensive university, it sought to deliver the best undergraduate education in Arkansas as well as excellent graduate programs in selected disciplines. The University became UCA to reflect its status as a modern, comprehensive college that offers a variety of undergraduate and graduate programs in liberal and fine arts, basic sciences, and technical and professional fields in addition to its historical emphasis in the field of education.*

*The University is accredited by the North Central Association of Colleges and Schools and the National Council for the Accreditation of Teacher Education as a bachelor's, master's, and specialist's degree–granting institution. Today more than 9,000 students attend classes taught by 350 faculty members. The University's mission is expressed in its commitment to the personal, social, and intellectual growth of its students; its support for the advancement of knowledge; and its service to the community as a public institution.*

## DISTANCE LEARNING PROGRAM

The Division of Continuing Education was formed in 1975 as a special administrative unit to respond to the University's public service. The Division's mission is to provide high-quality, lifelong learning opportunities through credit courses, noncredit programs, and support services that address market needs. Its innovative team of people is dedicated to customer satisfaction. Its vision is to unite faculty members, state-of-the-art technology, and facilities to deliver comprehensive lifelong learning programs through a worldwide educational network.

## DELIVERY MEDIA

Students have the opportunity to enroll in distance education courses and extended-study courses. The distance education courses include graduate and some undergraduate-level courses offered via compressed video and Internet. Compressed video courses are open to students in Ar-

kansas. Internet courses are open to any student with access to the Internet.

The extended-study courses are open to any student and are all undergraduate-level courses. Students who enroll in extended-study courses come from all over the world. The syllabus and lessons are mailed to students after they register for a course.

Books can be purchased through Barnes & Noble by calling 501-450-3414. Lessons are sent to Continuing Education either via regular mail for paper-based extended study or via e-mail for Web-based extended-study courses. Students send in a test request form once they have completed all of their lessons. Tests are sent to an approved testing center to be administered, and the test administrator then returns the completed test to UCA's Division of Continuing Education.

## PROGRAMS OF STUDY

UCA offers more than forty undergraduate-level courses through ex-

tended study in a wide range of subject areas, including accounting, education, English language and literature, geography, German language and literature, history, family and consumer sciences, marketing, management, mathematics, political science, psychology, social sciences, curriculum and instruction, and special education.

UCA also offers various graduate classes and workshops in distance education, including administration of secondary education, academic technologies and educational leadership, business and marketing education, curriculum and instruction, educational media library science, family and consumer sciences, foreign language, physical therapy, occupational therapy, nursing, mathematics, management, health education, political science, and others.

## STUDENT SERVICES

Students in distance learning courses have access to the UCA library, academic advising, and career placement options. However, because extended-study students are not admitted into the University solely by acceptance into this program, they do not have access to the UCA library, academic advising, career placement options, computing services, tutoring, or other such services. Students may call 501-450-3118 for information concerning any continuing education courses. Course listings can be found on the Web site listed below.

## CREDIT OPTIONS

Students can earn graduate or undergraduate credit through the distance education program and undergraduate credit through extended study. While the distance education and extended-study programs do not award degrees, University credit earned through these courses may be applied toward a degree or used to achieve any other educational goal a student may have. Students should see an adviser concerning the use of course work for degree credit.

## FACULTY

The Division of Continuing Education employs approximately 60 instructors to grade the extended-study course work. The distance education area employs 62 instructors. Of these 62 faculty members, 60 percent have a doctoral degree.

## ADMISSION

Students must complete an application and be admitted into the graduate program to take graduate-level courses in the distance education program.

To be eligible for enrollment in an extended-study course, adult students must have a high school diploma or GED and satisfy course prerequisites. High school students who obtain written approval by the appropriate administrative official at their high school may enroll concurrently in extended-study courses. Students may enroll at any time of the year and take up to six months to complete each course.

## TUITION AND FEES

Tuition for distance education courses is $148.50 per credit hour for graduate courses and $115 per credit hour for undergraduate courses. Students must also pay a distance education fee of $40 per hour for compressed video and Internet courses.

Tuition for extended study is $80 per semester hour for paper-based courses. Web-based extended-study courses are $120 per semester hour. The undergraduate tuition for other asynchronous undergraduate offerings is $120 per semester hour; it is $190 per semester hour for graduate courses.

## FINANCIAL AID

Scholarships and other forms of financial aid are not accepted for extended-study courses. Distance education classes may be included in a student's course load for determining financial aid eligibility.

## APPLYING

Students may enroll in a continuing education course by submitting a completed application form by mail or fax or in person for extended-study courses. Applications are accepted at any time. Students may call for an enrollment package for distance education course work. The enrollment materials, along with payment, should be returned by mail or in person. Payment for these courses can be made by credit card, check, or money order.

Students are notified by mail once the review process is complete and they have been enrolled in their course(s). Falsification or omission of the requested application information voids enrollment.

---

**CONTACT**

Division of Continuing Education
Brewer-Hegeman Conference Center, Suite 102
University of Central Arkansas
201 Donaghey
Conway, Arkansas 72035-5003
Telephone: 501-450-3118
Fax: 501-450-5277
E-mail: sondrap@ecom.uca.edu (extended-study courses)
        rebeccar@ecom.uca.edu (distance learning courses)
Web site: http://www.uca.edu/conted

# University of Central Florida

*Center for Distributed Learning*

Orlando, Florida

> *The University of Central Florida (UCF) is a major metropolitan research university whose mission is to deliver a comprehensive program of teaching, research, and service. UCF was established in 1963 and opened in the fall of 1968. Its original name, Florida Technological University, was changed by the Florida Legislature on December 6, 1978.*
>
> *UCF proudly identifies with its geographic region while striving for national and international excellence in selected programs of teaching and research. The University of Central Florida is accredited by the Commission on Colleges of the Southern Association of Colleges and Schools to award degrees at the associate, baccalaureate, master's, and doctoral levels.*

## DISTANCE LEARNING PROGRAM

UCF delivers courses and programs over the Internet and via videotape to meet the diverse needs of a growing student population and to fulfill the general University mission.

Due to its strong technological background and resources, UCF provides this delivery for those who would not otherwise be able to attend classes on one of the four UCF campuses. In the last full academic year, UCF has served more than 5,900 students with Web-based courses and more than 1,000 students with videotaped courses.

These courses maintain a high-quality learning environment for the nontraditional student. The course materials and methods were developed by the UCF faculty to maximize the distant learner's achievement of course objectives. All distributed learning courses provide full University credit, and are subject to standard campus tuition charges and UCF policies.

## DELIVERY MEDIA

To participate in Web-based courses, students must have access to the Internet and a Pentium PC with a Windows operating system or a 60 mega-hertz 603 CPU Macintosh with OS 7.05 or later. Video-based courses and programs require similar Internet access and students must have a VCR to view VHS tapes.

## PROGRAMS OF STUDY

Distance learning courses offered by Florida's public universities are generally limited to upper-division and graduate course work. Links to UCF's baccalaureate programs are available on line at http://distrib.ucf.edu/programs.

The Web-based Bachelor's Degree in Liberal Studies is a general studies track that leads to either the Bachelor of Arts or Bachelor of Science in liberal studies degrees. The liberal arts track is an honors-linked Bachelor of Arts degree program available to students seeking an individualized, nontraditional, interdisciplinary major.

The Web-based RN to Bachelor's Degree in Nursing curriculum is available for Florida RN's seeking a Bachelor of Science in Nursing (B.S.N). Some campus attendance is required. Students may complete course work and clinical practica in five semesters or eighteen months. The School validates registered nurses' knowledge in the areas of adult health, pediatrics, and psychiatric–mental heath (28 credits).

UCF offers Web-based programs leading to a B.S., M.A., or M.Ed. degree in Vocational Education and Industry Training. These programs are for individuals with occupational course work and/or work experience who wish to teach in middle or secondary schools, correctional institutions, postsecondary technical institutes, or become technical trainers in business or industry. Courses for vocational teacher certification, curriculum development, and career and technical education are included.

The video-based Bachelor of Science in Engineering Technology (B.S.E.T.) degree program is comprised of courses that are offered via VHS videocassette, with Internet enhancement. Special arrangements are made for laboratory courses. This track provides an orientation for professional careers in technical management and operations in the manufacturing, sales, service, and construction industries. Classes are taped in a live classroom and the tapes and handouts are distributed to designated remote sites, usually within 72 hours.

The University also offers graduate study via FEEDS, the video-based Florida Engineering Education Delivery System. FEEDS is a product of the cooperative effort of the State University System (SUS) and private sector industries in Florida. FEEDS offers access to quality graduate programs and extended studies. The use of live and recorded television, telephone line–based teleconferencing, and computer-aided communication brings students and professors together.

The Web-based Master's Degree in Industrial Chemistry, Forensic Science Option program is designed for practicing professionals and full-time students who desire an advanced program of study in the forensic analysis of biological materials. The forensic science track has a strong biochemistry-DNA focus to serve the needs of supervisory (or prospective supervisory) personnel in DNA sections of crime laboratories.

Approximately 50 percent of the course work can be accessed on line and the remainder can be taken on site at UCF or other qualified institutions.

The newest Web-based program is the Master's Degree in Educational Media, designed for individuals who wish to become media specialists in schools. The program develops skills in administration, production, instructional design, technologies of instruction and information management, organization, selection, evaluation, and research that relate to school library media programs. Upon completion, students qualify for Florida certification in educational media. Students must have completed basic teaching certification course work and should have successful teaching experience.

UCF also offers Web-based graduate certificates. From the College of Health and Public Affairs, students may earn a Graduate Certificate in Nonprofit Management, designed to provide graduate-level education for individuals who are currently working in the nonprofit sector or in organizations that are in partnership with the nonprofit sector. This program provides advanced knowledge in nonprofit management, resource development, volunteer management, strategic planning, and program evaluation for these individuals and enhances their career development. From the College of Education, a Graduate Certificate for Community Colleges is offered, designed to prepare academic leaders in community colleges by strengthening their knowledge base with practical content in curriculum and instruction that can be applied immediately.

## FACULTY

UCF employs more than 900 full-time and 300 (FTE) part-time faculty members in the five distinct colleges that comprise the University. Eighty percent of the full-time faculty members have terminal or doctoral degrees. More than 200 resident faculty members have completed an eight week in-house faculty development course for Web-based instruction.

## ADMISSION

Students who plan to enroll in Web-based courses must be admitted to the University and must follow the same admission procedures as other students.

## TUITION AND FEES

The nonrefundable application fee is $20. The UCF Campus Card fee is $10. Summer 2001 semester registration fees for residents were $75.98 per credit hour for undergraduate study and $152.45 per credit hour for graduate study; nonresident fees were $320.57 for undergraduate study and $531.21 for graduate study.

## FINANCIAL AID

Information regarding financial aid is available from UCF's Office of Student Financial Assistance on line at http://pegasus.cc.ucf.edu/~finaid/.

## APPLYING

Undergraduate applicants with more than 60 credit hours or who have earned an Associate of Arts degree from a Florida public community college must submit high school transcripts and transcripts from all colleges attended. Applicants with fewer than 60 credit hours must also submit SAT or ACT scores and must meet the freshmen State University System eligibility requirements. Graduate applicants must submit official GRE (or GMAT scores for selected programs) test scores and official transcripts showing a bachelor's degree earned at a regionally accredited institution. The minimum University requirements for admission into a graduate program are a 3.0 GPA on a 4.0 scale or a score of 1000 on the combined verbal-quantitative portions of the GRE or 450 on the GMAT (for programs that require it). Requirements for specific programs are in addition to or different from the minimum University requirements.

---

### CONTACT

Dr. Steven E. Sorg
Assistant Vice President for Distributed Learning
12424 Research Parkway, Suite 256
Orlando, Florida 32826-3271
Telephone: 407-207-4910
Fax: 407-207-4911
E-mail: distrib@mail.ucf.edu
Web site: http://distrib.ucf.edu/

---

# University of Colorado at Denver

## *CU Online*

Denver, Colorado

*The University of Colorado at Denver is one of four institutions in the University of Colorado system and the only public university in the Denver metropolitan area. It is an urban, nonresidential campus located in downtown Denver. The University of Colorado at Denver was founded in 1965 and is accredited by the North Central Association of Colleges and Schools.*

## DISTANCE LEARNING PROGRAM

CU Online is the virtual campus of the University of Colorado system, with eleven collegiate and professional development programs offering more than 200 courses via the Internet and Web.

CU Online offers core curriculum and elective courses in a variety of disciplines, all the same high-quality courses taught throughout the University of Colorado system.

## DELIVERY MEDIA

CU Online courses are not self-paced. However, students enjoy a greater scheduling flexibility than in a traditional classroom by logging into class each week at the times of their choice. Instructors delivering their courses through CU Online make use of cutting-edge technology, such as streaming audio, video, and multimedia slide shows for presenting course content. A number of technologies allow students to interact with the instructor and their peers: threaded discussions in a bulletin board–type area, live discussions in an online classroom, e-mail, and collaborative workspaces.

## PROGRAMS OF STUDY

CU Online offers courses in liberal arts and sciences, arts and media,

business, education, engineering, public affairs, and architecture and planning. Complete online degree programs, including a Bachelor of Arts in sociology, and master's degrees in business administration, engineering (engineering management and geographic information systems), and public administration, with more programs under development (check the Web site for the latest developments). All of the courses may be applied to a degree program at the University of Colorado at Denver or may be transferred to a student's home institution, pending approval.

## STUDENT SERVICES

CU Online offers a vast range of student services. Students can search catalogs, register for courses, order text books and other course materials, get academic advising, and apply for financial aid, all on line.

## CREDIT OPTIONS

Students may take credit and non-credit courses through CU Online and, for some courses, CEUs. The methods of evaluation are letter grades or pass/fail.

## FACULTY

Online courses follow the same faculty governance policies as the established on-campus courses. All CU Online faculty members are approved by the department and usually teach on-campus courses as well. Many of the instructors are experts who are working in the field in which they teach and bring vast knowledge and resources from their industry to their online teaching.

## ADMISSION

Students living in the state of Colorado must be accepted to the University either as degree-seeking or non–degree-seeking students. Students living outside of the state of Colorado do not need to be admitted to take CU Online courses; however, if students wish to complete their degree through CU Online, formal admission must be made. Students may visit the CU Online Web site (listed below) and click on the registration link under the student's menu for more information regarding admissions and how to register for courses.

## TUITION AND FEES

Tuition rates vary between colleges and depending on residency status.

Most undergraduate courses cost approximately $130–$183 per credit hour for resident students. There is a $100 course fee that is added to each online course, a $4 fee for technology resources, and a $10 fee for the student information system. For specific information regarding tuition for online courses, students should visit the CU Online Web site.

## FINANCIAL AID

To be eligible for financial aid, students must be enrolled as degree-seeking students at the University of Colorado at Denver. Students may contact the financial aid office for more information (telephone: 303-556-2886; e-mail: finaid@carbon. cudenver.edu).

## APPLYING

Admission requirements vary by college and school. To find specific information about applying to the University of Colorado at Denver, students may visit the CU Online Web site (listed below) and click on the admissions link under the student's menu.

---

### CONTACT

For more information about CU Online, students should contact:

University of Colorado at Denver
Campus Box 198
P.O. Box 173364
Denver, Colorado 80217-3364
Telephone: 303-556-6505
Fax: 303-556-6530
E-mail: inquiry@cuonline.edu
Web site: http://www.cudenver.edu/cuonline/petersons

---

# University of Dallas

## Graduate School of Management
## Center for Distance Learning

Irving, Texas

*The University of Dallas, located in Irving, Texas, was founded in 1956 as an independent Catholic university dedicated to excellence in its educational programs.*

*The Graduate School of Management (GSM) is the largest M.B.A.-granting institution in the Southwest. GSM was founded in 1966 with a distinctive mission: to create a professionally sound M.B.A. program accessible to individuals who are already employed in business. More than 75 percent of GSM students work full-time. The student body is made up of Americans and international students representing more than sixty countries.*

*GSM prepares master's-level students for leadership roles in business and industry and is accredited to award M.B.A. and Master of Management degrees by the Commission on Colleges of the Southern Association of Colleges and Schools (SACS).*

## DISTANCE LEARNING PROGRAM

The Graduate School of Management Distance Learning Program offers the convenience of Internet-based courses accessible 24 hours a day, seven days a week from anywhere in the world. The distance learning programs serve more than 250 graduate students. All programs are credit bearing and lead to an M.B.A. degree, Master of Management degree, or a graduate certificate.

## DELIVERY MEDIA

The graduate degrees and graduate certificate programs are offered through the Internet and are accessible via any Web browser. The self-guided asynchronous method of teaching is instructor-led. There is no residency requirement.

Students from all over the globe communicate and exchange information with their instructor and each other electronically via the Internet, e-mail, facsimile, and telephone. This method of course-delivery provides flexibility for students to study on their own time anywhere in the world.

## PROGRAMS OF STUDY

The Graduate School of Management offers M.B.A., Master of Management, and graduate certificate programs through distance learning in information technology, telecommunications, and e-commerce management. These programs are designed with a specific focus on management. The M.B.A. degree requires the completion of sixteen courses with a one-hour lecture series requirement. The Master of Management requires the completion of ten courses, and the graduate certificate program requires the completion of five courses.

GSM is seeking corporate clients who are interested in hosting a full M.B.A. or graduate certificate program in telecommunications, health services, information technology, e-commerce, or general business for their employees.

## SPECIAL PROGRAMS

Distance education students are able to take on-campus courses as part of their overall degree or certificate program.

## STUDENT SERVICES

An academic adviser is available for assistance in course advising and registration. Professors are available for course curriculum advising and career counseling. The Graduate School of Management prides itself on providing exceptional customer service to its students. Students taking courses over the Internet may need additional advising, encouragement, and support. Therefore, GSM makes every effort to foster a strong relationship with the student.

## CREDIT OPTIONS

For the M.B.A. program, a maximum of 4 courses or 12 hours of transfer credits may be applied. A transfer course must be a 3-semester-hour (5-quarter-hour) graduate-level course from an accredited school. The transfer course must not be more than six years old. A grade of at least a B (3.0) is required. Course content must be substantially similar to that of a course required in a student's degree plan. For further information, students can contact the GSM Admissions Office at the address below.

## FACULTY

GSM's faculty provides a rare mix of competence in both the theoretical aspects of management and the applied working knowledge of its practical aspects. The faculty is organized into a relatively small resident group and a larger adjunct group. The resident faculty members are full-time instructors with extensive backgrounds in business, teaching, applied research, and consulting. The adjunct faculty consists of practicing managers, attorneys, accountants, consultants, and other professionals who teach part-time. GSM students enjoy the best of both worlds—academic and business.

## ADMISSION

Applicants for the M.B.A. program must have a bachelor's degree from an accredited university and must satisfy any two of the following criteria: an overall GPA of at least 3.0 on a 4.0 scale, a satisfactory score on the Graduate Management Admission Test (GMAT), or five years or more of effective managerial or professional work experience.

For the Master of Management degree program, a student must have an M.B.A. degree from an accredited university.

For the graduate certificate program, a student must have a bachelor's degree from an accredited university and have at least three years of professional and/or managerial experience. International students must submit a TOEFL score of at least 520. Students who complete the graduate certificate program can apply course work towards the M.B.A. or Master of Management program.

## TUITION AND FEES

Graduate tuition is $423 per credit hour ($1269 per course) in the 2001–02 academic year for residents and nonresidents.

## FINANCIAL AID

U.S. graduate students may obtain financial assistance through various loan programs. The University of Dallas Financial Aid Office (telephone: 972-721-5266) has information and application forms for loans. Student loan applications must be processed through the Financial Aid Office.

## APPLYING

Students are encouraged to contact the GSM Admissions Office at the address below or visit the Web site to receive additional information. Students can apply from anywhere in the world.

### CONTACT

Director of Admissions
Graduate School of Management
University of Dallas
1845 East Northgate Drive
Irving, Texas 75062-4736
Telephone: 972-721-5174
            800-UDAL-MBA (832-
            5622, toll-free)
Fax: 972-721-4009
E-mail: admiss@gsm.udallas.edu
Web site: http://gsm.udallas.edu

# University of Delaware

## UD Online/Distance Learning

Newark, Delaware

*A private university with public support, the University of Delaware is a land-grant, sea-grant, space-grant, and urban-grant institution with a rich 250-year history. Its main campus is located in Newark, Delaware, a suburban community situated between Philadelphia and Baltimore. The University offers more than 100 undergraduate majors and more than seventy graduate degrees. The University has been fully accredited by the Middle States Association of Colleges and Schools since 1921. There are more than 21,000 students enrolled at the University as undergraduate, graduate, or continuing education students.*

## DISTANCE LEARNING PROGRAM

The University's UD Online/Distance Learning system supports more than 2,700 registrations a year in a variety of undergraduate and graduate courses involving twenty-eight academic departments and five degree programs. In 1996, the United States Distance Learning Association gave the University the Most Outstanding Achievement in Higher Education rating for "extraordinary achievements through distance education." UD Online offers a way for busy professionals to continue their education on a schedule tailored to their needs.

## DELIVERY MEDIA

More than one hundred University of Delaware courses are available in videotape, CD-ROM, or Internet formats. Student-faculty interaction is maintained through e-mail and telephone office hours.

## PROGRAMS OF STUDY

Students can use distance learning to pursue the following degree programs:

Bachelor of Science in Nursing: Baccalaureate for the Registered Nurse major (BRN): Ten of thirteen required nursing courses are offered in distance learning format. Students are required to enroll in three 1-credit weekend courses held on the Newark, Delaware, campus. The BRN major requires 125 credits for program completion.

Master of Science in Nursing (MSN) with a concentration in health services administration: Delivered entirely on the Internet, except for one 2-day seminar which takes place on the Newark, Delaware, campus. For more information, students can visit the Internet address http://www.udel.edu/DSP/page4.html.

Bachelor of Science in Hotel, Restaurant, and Institutional Management (HRIM): The specialized HRIM core courses, as well as most of the required liberal arts and business courses, are available in distance-learning format, except for a required one-week management institute held on the Newark, Delaware, campus. For more information, students can visit the program Web site (http://www.udel.edu/ce/hrimwelc.shtml).

Master of Engineering, Mechanical (MEM): A 30-credit, non-thesis program comprised of five required courses and 15 credits of graduate electives. Popular concentration, available in distance format, is in composite materials. For more informa-

tion, students should visit the program Web site (http://www.me.udel.edu/GS/mme.html).

Master of Electrical Engineering (MEE): A non-thesis master's program requiring 30 credits of graduate courses, including 6 credits (2 "foundation" courses) chosen from signal processing, devices and materials, or optics and electromagnetics (other options to be added); 24 credits in advanced technical courses with a maximum of 6 credits outside of the department. For more information, students can visit the program Web site (http://www.udel.edu/engg/outreach/).

## SPECIAL PROGRAMS

Many individual engineering courses are available through distance learning; particularly at the graduate level, through National Technological University (NTU). To pursue a graduate degree, engineering professionals may enroll in courses for professional development or may combine distance learning courses with campus courses. A post-baccalaureate Certificate Program in composite materials is designed for engineering and science professionals who already possess a bachelor's degree. Students may access the program Web site (http://www.udel.edu/engg/outreach/composites-program.html). Additionally, the fundamentals of engineering review course is available via videotape, providing intensive review of fundamentals of engineering examination topics. Further information can be found at the Internet address http://www.udel.edu/engg/outreach/FE_video.html.

A professional Certificate Program in E-commerce with business analyst concentration is available entirely online. For more information, students can visit the program Web site (http://www.udel.edu/ce/it/ecommerce/).

The University's dietetic internship is delivered entirely online with the exception of a one-week professional orientation that takes place on the Newark, Delaware, campus. Students complete internship rotations in their local areas. This program is accredited by the Commission on Accreditation for Dietetic Education of the American Dietetic Association. For more information, students can visit the Web site (http://www.udel.edu/NTDT/internship/).

## CREDIT OPTIONS

In order to be eligible for a University of Delaware degree, students must complete either the first 90 or the last 30 credits of the degree program with the University of Delaware. A credit-by-examination option allows students to demonstrate competence obtained through professional experience. Exam requirements are determined by each University academic department.

## FACULTY

Of 998 full-time University faculty, 87 percent hold the doctoral or terminal professional degree in their field. Approximately 10 percent of the faculty participate in distance learning instruction.

## ADMISSION

An admissions committee considers all academic credentials, including high school and any previous college work. Students transferring from other schools are normally required to have at least a 2.5 grade point average to be considered for admission.

## TUITION AND FEES

Students registering at official UD Online/Distance Learning work sites may register as site participants and pay $217 per credit hour (undergraduate) or $630 per credit hour (graduate). Students may also register as individual/nonsite participants and pay resident (undergraduate, $188 per credit hour; graduate, $251 per credit hour) or nonresident (undergraduate, $553 per credit hour; graduate, $737 per credit hour) tuition plus a handling fee of $90 per videotaped course. Tuition and fees are subject to change. For current information on fees and tuition, students should visit the Web site (http://www.udel.edu/ce/udonline/).

## FINANCIAL AID

The Financial Aid Office administers grants and scholarships, which do not have to be repaid; low-interest loans; and student employment. A need-based financial aid package may include one or more of the following: Federal Pell Grant, Federal Supplemental Educational Opportunity Grant, Federal Perkins Loan, and a Federal Direct Loan. The Federal Direct Parents Loan Program is also available. Delaware residents may also be eligible for need-based funding through General Fund Scholarships and Delaware Right to Education Scholarships. Students must be matriculated and carry at least 6 credit hours per semester.

## APPLYING

A completed application consists of the Distance Learning Application for Admission, application fee, and official college and high school transcripts. Due dates for applications are no later than August 1 for fall admission and no later than December 1 for spring admission.

## CONTACT

Mary Pritchard
Director
UD Online/Distance Learning
211 John M. Clayton Hall
University of Delaware
Newark, Delaware 19716
Telephone: 800-597-1444 (toll-free)
Fax: 302-831-3292
E-mail: continuing-ed@udel.edu
Web site: http://www.udel.edu/ce/udonline/

# The University of Findlay

## Global Campus
Findlay, Ohio

The Churches of God, General Conference, and the citizens of the city of Findlay, Ohio founded the University of Findlay as Findlay College in 1882. It is accredited by the North Central Association of Colleges and Schools and the Ohio State Board of Education and has approval from a number of accrediting bodies for specific program areas. It is authorized to offer A.A., B.A., B.S., M.A., M.S., M.P.T., and M.B.A. degree programs by the Ohio Board of Regents. The institution's mission is to equip students for meaningful lives and productive careers. It creates and delivers high-quality and innovative programs for undergraduate, graduate, and continuing education for a diverse student body. Information technology has been integrated into instructional support, program enhancement, and distance learning through a separate Global Campus.

## DISTANCE LEARNING PROGRAM

The mission of distance learning at the University of Findlay is to provide high-quality, innovative learning experiences through technological means to reach students unable to take courses through traditional instructional formats. A separate online Global Campus (Web site listed below) is the vehicle for both credit and noncredit Web courses and programs as well as for all needed student support services. For the academic year 2000–01, the University served nearly 500 students via distance learning.

## DELIVERY MEDIA

The Global Campus uses Internet technologies to deliver graduate, undergraduate, and noncredit workforce development courses anywhere in the world. These courses make use of synchronous online sessions once a week, as well as e-mail, fax, and phone. Some classes use threaded discussions and group projects. Supplementary videotapes or CD-ROMs are often included. Videoconferencing is also used to deliver business and education courses to several off-campus locations in Ohio.

## PROGRAMS OF STUDY

The University had seventy-eight graduate and undergraduate courses available on the Web during 2000–01. These included two master's programs: the M.B.A. and the M.S. in Environmental, Safety, and Health Management (M.S.E.S.H.M.), which is offered through the National Center of Excellence for Environmental Management; and two degree-completion programs: the B.S. in Business Management (B.S.B.M.) and the B.S. in Environmental, Safety, and Health Management (B.S.E.S.H.M.). Students in these programs can combine on-site traditional instruction with Web courses or complete their programs entirely online. Most courses range from eight to twelve weeks in length. Entry to the M.B.A. program requires the GMAT, and a TOEFL score of 525 (if appropriate) is required for admission to the M.B.A. and M.S.E.S.H.M. programs. The B.S. B.M. and B.S.E.S.H.M. degree completion programs require the applicant to have completed 62 transferable semester hours of college-level work. All four programs require some prerequisite courses, some of which can be completed by proficiency testing.

In addition to these programs, several courses, each from the Master of Arts in Education and the undergraduate technology management program, are available online. The number of online courses in the general education area also continues to grow. Descriptions of all online courses may be accessed through the University's Global Campus Web site. Certificate courses are also available.

## SPECIAL PROGRAMS

The University of Findlay offers a variety of special programs open to distance learners. These include a partnership with Microsoft Great Plains Business Software in programs for preparing technology managers and programs designed for international students. In addition, the Community Education and Technology Center provides support for on-site as well as online workforce courses available to students across the nation.

Internships are also available with a variety of local and regional companies, including Whirlpool, Cooper Tire & Rubber Company, Microsoft Great Plains Business Software, and others. Arrangements can be made through the Office of Career Services.

## STUDENT SERVICES

The University of Findlay's Global Campus was designed with the student in mind. This portal provides online students with all of the same services on-campus students have. Students can find information about financial aid, admission, registration, advising, tuition and fees, and much more. Also available is a library with an extensive list of resources and searchable full-text databases.

## CREDIT OPTIONS

The Office of the Registrar evaluates all transfer credits, including those earned in the military, from official transcripts. Graduate students may transfer a maximum of 9 graduate semester hours. Undergraduate degree completion students must have 62 transferable semester hours of college-level work, some of which may be earned by portfolio assessment or CLEP tests. Proficiency tests may be used for required prerequisites. All degree completion program courses must be taken online or on-site from the University of Findlay. In certain circumstances, applicants may petition to transfer in equivalent credits for some degree-completion courses.

## FACULTY

Twenty-five full-time and 6 part-time faculty members taught in the distance learning programs in 2000–01. Of these, 50 percent had doctoral degrees. The emphasis on full-time faculty members provides for continuity and quality control of courses.

## ADMISSION

The University of Findlay's general policy for admission can be found at the Web site http://www.gcampus.org/Admissions; this includes information on credit transfer, transient credit work, nondegree credit, loans, grants, assistantships, and the refund policy.

## TUITION AND FEES

Depending on the program, graduate tuition and fees range from $286 to $365 per credit hour, and undergraduate from $220 to $372 per credit hour. Students should check with the appropriate program director for the most current fees. As of fall 2001, students are charged a $10-per-course technology fee.

## FINANCIAL AID

Each year more than 90 percent of students attending the University of Findlay receive some form of financial assistance. Just as there are a variety of programs, there are a variety of forms, procedures, and dates to consider. The Global Campus provides an abundance of information, from how to apply and what is considered in the admission process, to FAQs and a wide range of financial aid sources and programs.

## APPLYING

The application process for online courses is the same as it is for on-campus students. Students can complete an application form online (http://www.gcampus.org/Applications/default.asp). A downloadable transcript request form and other specific information about applying to the University can be found at the Internet address http://www.gcampus.org/Admissions/.

---

### CONTACT

Dr. Doris Salis
Dean of Adult and Continuing Education
The University of Findlay
1000 North Main Street
Findlay, Ohio 45840
Telephone: 800-558-9060 (toll-free)
Fax: 419-424-4822
E-mail: salis@mail.findlay.edu
Web site: http://www.gcampus.org

# University of Florida

## Distance Learning
## Master of Health Science Degree in Occupational Therapy

Ocoee, Florida

---

*Throughout the years, the University of Florida's Department of Occupational Therapy (part of the College of Health Professions) has enjoyed an excellent national reputation for occupational therapy (OT) education. The OT faculty, students, and alumni at the University of Florida have consistently been productive leaders in clinical service, education, scholarly work, and professional organizations.*

*The Master of Health Science program offers advanced studies in occupational therapy theory and research. It is rated tenth in the nation (Gourman, 1996). The University of Florida is accredited by the Southern Association of Colleges and Schools and is a member of the American Association of Universities.*

## DISTANCE LEARNING PROGRAM

This program is designed for occupational therapists who are seeking to upgrade and broaden their professional knowledge and competencies in occupational therapy theory, leadership, and practice. Upon completion of the program, graduates are conversant in the rationale behind clinical practice (theoretical foundations), prepared to move ahead in today's health-care industry (leadership foundations), and ready to engage in contemporary trends in practice (practice applications). In addition, increased knowledge in an area that is uniquely important to each student is afforded through the professional development capstone project.

## DELIVERY MEDIA

Fulfillment of the program's learning objectives occurs through a combination of lectures, readings, online activities, discussion sessions, and peer and professional support systems.

Students can participate in the majority of classroom-style lectures and demonstrations in their homes via multimedia presentations, such as videotapes and CD-ROMs. All relevant course information is posted on the course Web site, a centralized interaction portal for students, faculty members, and program administrators. The student's workplace can also serve as a resource for assignments involving patients, personnel, and case presentations.

A professional facilitator also mentors and guides small groups of students to build collaborative learning communities, complete learning activities, and participate in online discussions. Students meet with their cohort group and facilitator one or two times each semester (as needed) at sites established throughout the U.S.

## PROGRAMS OF STUDY

Upon completion of this program, graduates are prepared to apply theoretical foundations of occupational therapy practice, including constructs of occupation, evidence-based practice, and neuroscience; achieve leadership roles for occupational therapy with a keen sense of the dynamic U.S. health-care system; use competencies for occupational therapy consultancy and independent practice; make applications of assistive technology, social and behavioral contexts, and prevention for contemporary practice; and expand expertise in a self-selected area of professional growth.

In Theoretical Foundations (9 credits), students explore the occupation, evidence-based practice, and neuroscience. Foundations for Leadership courses (9 credits) study the U.S. health-care system, principles of management, and private practice. Students in the Practice Applications Across the Life Span courses (12 credits) learn about assistive technology, social and behavioral contexts, prevention and wellness, and topics in contemporary practice. With the Professional Development Project (6 credits), students are involved in independent design, implementation, and reporting of an independent project related to the working occupational therapist's practice specialty.

## CREDIT OPTIONS

Students enroll in two didactic courses each semester for 3 credits each. In addition, 1 credit of Professional Development during the first through fourth semesters and 2 credits during the fifth semester are required to complete and document the capstone Professional Development Project.

## FACULTY

The faculty is made up of experienced practitioners and educators in the field of occupational therapy and includes William C. Mann (Professor and Chair), Ph.D., OTR; Kay F. Walker (Professor and Distance Learning Program Director), Ph.D., OTR/L FAOTA; and Craig A.

Velozo (Associate Professor and Graduate Coordinator), Ph.D., OTR/L.

## ADMISSION

For entrance into the program, students must meet the following requirements: a bachelor's degree in occupational therapy from an AOTA-ACOTE–accredited or World Federation of Occupational Therapy (WFOT)-approved school; an undergraduate GPA of 3.0 (out of 4.0) or better in upper division course work; a combined score of 1000 or better on the verbal and quantitative sections of the Graduate Record Examination (GRE); and a copy of OTR license or certification. For applicants whose first language is not English, scores of 550 or better on the Test of English as a Foreign Language (TOEFL) are also required.

## TUITION AND FEES

The program requires a $20 application fee. Course tuition is $450 per semester credit hour; the total program is 36 credit hours.

## FINANCIAL AID

Financial aid information may be obtained by calling Mike Manafee, Assistant Director of Student Financial Affairs, University of Florida, at 352-392-6631. Financial aid for this program must be used on a reimbursement basis. All tuition must be paid by the registration deadline and cannot be deferred while awaiting financial aid.

## APPLYING

Applications should be submitted in their entirety with the following completed documents: $20 application fee payable to UF Office of Admissions and one photocopy of the student's check (students must include their social security number on the check); UF Graduate School application form and one photocopy; departmental application form and one photocopy; the Information for Residency Classification form and one photocopy; immunization form and one photocopy, *Varicella* (chicken pox) vaccination confirmation form; copy of OT certification or OT licensure; GRE report (copy); completed regional site planning form and one photocopy; a copy of TOEFL scores (international students only); and official transcripts (two official copies) from all undergraduate and graduate institutions attended. Applicants who do not hold a bachelors degree in occupational therapy must verify where and when they completed their OT education.

The student must also submit a statement of purpose that concisely expresses his or her interest in, and specific qualifications for, being a leader in the field of occupational therapy and for independence in distance education graduate work; and three letters of recommendation, one of which must be from an OTR, addressing applicant's leadership potential, ability to work independently, and potential for success in graduate work. Students should ensure that contact information, addresses, phone numbers, and e-mail addresses for these references are also provided on application forms. All letters should be current, professional, written on letterhead, and specific to the student's application to the program. Students should also cite one or two possible areas of study for their Professional Development Project.

Both conduct statements on reverse side of UF Application Form must be answered, and application must be signed in order for it to be processed. Application will be returned if these are not completed.

## CONTACT

Intelicus
2710 Rew Circle
Suite 100
Ocoee, Florida 34761
Telephone: 800-431-6687 (toll-free)
Web site: http://www.intelicus.com/ot/default.htm

# University of Florida

## Working Professional Doctor of Pharmacy Degree Program

Ocoee, Florida

---

*The University of Florida College of Pharmacy was established more than seventy-five years ago to educate students for professional pharmacy practice. The program is fully accredited by the American Council of Pharmaceutical Education (ACPE).*

## DISTANCE LEARNING PROGRAM

Students are provided with materials from the college, including a course syllabus, lecture materials, and video presentations. Students must also have access to a computer and modem with Internet access and downloading capabilities in order to interact with faculty members and other students.

## DELIVERY MEDIA

Each semester consists of three full days of group interaction; videotaped faculty lectures independently viewed by the student; competency-based clinical practice assessments; course material accessible through the Internet; and communication with faculty, professors, and fellow study group members via e-mail.

## PROGRAMS OF STUDY

The following is a list of offered courses and course descriptions: Neurological Disorders: pharmaceutical care for patients with nervous system disorders; Circulatory Disorders: pharmaceutical care for patients with circulatory system disease; Cardiology Disorders: pharmaceutical care for patients with cardiac system disorders; Renal Disorders: pharmaceutical care for patients with renal system disorders; Endocrine Disorders: pharmaceutical care for patients with endocrine system disorders; Respiratory Disorders: pharmaceutical care for pa-

tients with respiratory system disorders; Digestive Disorders: pharmaceutical care for patients with digestive system disorders; Psychiatric Disorders: pharmaceutical care for patients with psychiatric system disorders; and Protective Systems Disorders: pharmaceutical care for patients with protective systems disorders.

## SPECIAL PROGRAMS

The experiential program is flexible and integrated into home, work, and classroom activities. Students must demonstrate competency in both theoretical and actual clinical environments. Clinical practice concentration is in the areas of ambulatory care, inpatient care, and drug information. Students are required to demonstrate verbal and written communication skills. In the pharmaceutical care project, students are required to identify a pharmaceutical care service based on a need assessment at their workplace and/or other health-care setting. They design a service, evaluate it, and report to their peers, faculty members, and employer citing their findings and recommendations.

## STUDENT SERVICES

Online library services are available to all students who participate in the working professional program.

## CREDIT OPTIONS

Upon completion, a student earns 2 continuing education units or 20 con-

tact hours each semester. Each semester, certificates of credit are mailed after satisfactory completion of course work.

## FACULTY

Fifty part-time University of Florida (UF) facilitators are regionally located throughout the nation, all of whom have their Pharm.D. degree. The facilitator-to-student ratio is 1:14 per regional group. All presenting faculty members are expert clinical practitioners.

## ADMISSION

Admission is limited to pharmacists holding licensure in the U.S., with a preference at this time to graduates of B.S. in pharmacy programs that are accredited by the American Council of Pharmaceutical Education (ACPE). The successful applicant must be practicing and preferably have access to patients. To earn the Doctor of Pharmacy degree, the Admissions Committee must accept the student into the program.

Students may enroll for one semester as a non-degree-seeking student before formally applying for admission. Once students' applications have been approved, their status is automatically changed from non-degree-seeking to degree-seeking student, and any grades or credits earned are transferred.

## TUITION AND FEES

In-state tuition and fees total $18,000; this includes the application fee of $20 and a cost of $2000 per course. Out-of-State tuition and fees total $20,025; this includes the $20 application fee and $2225 per course. The Remote model is $22,500; this includes the $20 application fee and $2500 per course. Books cost approximately $350 per program.

## FINANCIAL AID

Currently, there is no federal financial aid available to students; however, there are some private lending institutions that lend money to nontraditional students to cover educational expenses. PLATO is one of these organizations.

## APPLYING

To apply for admissions, students must submit an application fee of $20 (check or money order made out to University of Florida); a completed application for admission; completed residency affidavit; completed statement of educational goals, personal profile questions, and access to patient questions; employer's letter of support; two letters of recommendation forms; resume or curriculum vitae; evidence of licensure or eligibility; copy of graduation certificate; official transcripts from all higher education institutions; mandatory immunization and health history form; and evidence of CPR certification (adult and child). International students must provide an evaluation of transcripts by Joseph Silney & Associates, Inc. (telephone: 305-666-0233).

### CONTACT

University of Florida
Intelicus
2710 Rew Circle, Suite 100
Ocoee, Florida 34761
Telephone: 800-431-6687 (toll-free)
Web site: http://www.intelicus.com

# University of Houston

## *Division of Distance and Continuing Education*

Houston, Texas

*The University of Houston (UH) is the premier urban teaching and research institution in Texas. Founded in 1927, its activities include a broad range of academic programs encompassing undergraduate, graduate, and professional education; basic and applied research; and public service programs. Its professional schools include law, optometry, pharmacy, hotel, business, engineering, architecture, education, and social work. It is the doctoral degree granting and research-oriented component of the University of Houston System.*

*Serving 32,600 students, University of Houston educational programs include full-time programs for traditional students and part-time and evening programs for employed individuals. Research laboratories and institutes work directly with area corporations and governments, while public service programs contribute to and enhance the cultural and social climate of the community. UH has placed special emphasis on outreach and access for students, both locally and internationally.*

## DISTANCE LEARNING PROGRAM

Serving more than 4,500 students annually, UH Distance Education offers junior, senior, and graduate-level credit courses each semester. UH has the highest number of upper-level and graduate enrollments in distance education courses of any university in the state of Texas. Students may complete degrees through a combination of television, videotape, online classes, or face-to-face courses at four off-campus sites in the greater Houston area. All courses include ongoing interaction with instructors. Corporate and public sites participate in the UH Professional Training Network for continuing professional education.

## DELIVERY MEDIA

UH Distance Education courses are delivered face-to-face at off-campus sites and either live/interactive (compressed video, microwave, or satellite) or asynchronously (tape, cable, or public broadcast, or on line). For online classes, students must be able to access the Internet. Students in asynchronous classes participate in scheduled, real-time sessions with the instructor and/or other class members. Special arrangements must be made for lab requirements in some degree programs. Proctored exams are arranged as needed.

## PROGRAMS OF STUDY

UH Distance Education students may complete degrees in thirteen fields of study. All degree program requirements, course work, and prerequisites are the same as for on-campus students. Courses generally carry 3 credits; the number of credits needed for degree completion varies by program. Students can obtain more detailed information through the UH Distance Education Web site.

Undergraduate Distance Education program areas include computer drafting design, English, hotel and restaurant management, industrial supervision, and psychology. Undergraduate courses are available at the junior and senior level. Freshman- and sophomore-level courses may be taken on the UH campus or transferred in from other institutions.

Graduate degree program areas available through Distance Education include computer science, education (reading and language arts), electrical engineering (computers and electronics), engineering management, hospitality management, and training and development. Most of these programs are 36-hour, nonthesis options.

Students not seeking a degree may enroll in a limited number of selected credit courses.

Additional credit courses outside of these program areas are available each semester, as are noncredit training classes in a variety of subject areas such as computers, environmental safety, food and sanitation services, health-care management, personal enrichment, professional development, and technical field updates.

## SPECIAL PROGRAMS

Corporate sites, schools, and libraries may join the University of Houston Professional Training Network to become a receive site for credit and noncredit classes delivered live/interactive. Membership includes special orientations and partnership opportunities with the University of Houston.

## STUDENT SERVICES

University of Houston's award-winning Distance Education program provides students access to excellent academic support services. Library support is provided for enrolled students through access to the UH Online Catalog, borrowing privileges, reference services, remote access to electronic databases, guides to research, mail delivery of journal articles on request, and cooperative arrangements with other libraries.

Computer support services available to all enrolled students include a (Houston-area) computer account, e-mail, and World Wide Web browser. Documentation, training, and software are also available.

Student support services for Distance Education students include admission by mail or on line; phone registration; fee payment by mail and by phone; book and videotape orders by mail, phone, fax, or on line; remote-site proctored exams; paper exchange by fax, mail, or courier (corporate and public sites); and online advising.

University of Houston is an equal opportunity institution. Accommodations on the basis of disability are available.

## CREDIT OPTIONS

Upon application for admission, students must submit transcripts from work completed at other postsecondary institutions. The amount and types of credit transferable to the University of Houston depend on the degree program.

## FACULTY

The University of Houston has 1,900 full- and part-time faculty members. All UH faculty members teaching Distance Education courses participate in special training programs and ongoing assessment.

## ADMISSION

Undergraduate admission is based on graduation from an accredited high school, college transfer, or entrance examination or through a combination of these criteria. Graduate applicants must have an earned bachelor's degree from an accredited institution. Individual programs have additional specific requirements.

## TUITION AND FEES

In 2001–02, resident tuition and fees for one 3-credit-hour undergraduate course are $401 (nonresident, $1046); for a graduate course, the resident cost is $521 (nonresident, $1166). For two courses (6 credit hours), the undergraduate cost is $710 (nonresident, $2000); the graduate cost is $950 (nonresident, $2240). Students enrolling in Distance Education courses are charged a $140 per course off-campus and electronic course fee. Students are only assessed fees for the first two off-campus courses in which they enroll each semester. Students enrolled exclusively in off-campus courses may qualify for up to $50 in fee waivers. Rates are subject to change.

## FINANCIAL AID

General financial aid programs through the University of Houston include the Texas Public Education Grant, Texas Public Educational State Student Incentive Grant, Federal Pell Grant, Federal Supplemental Educational Opportunity Grant, Federal Perkins Student Loan, Hinson-Hazlewood College Student Loan, Federal Stafford Student Loan, Federal Parent Loan Program, and other loan and scholarship opportunities based on merit or need. In 1999–2000, approximately 50 percent of all University of Houston students received some form of financial assistance.

## APPLYING

To enroll in any UH credit course, students must first be admitted to the University of Houston. Complete admission information is available through the UH Distance Education InfoLine or through the UH Distance Education Web site. An undergraduate Texas Common Application is available on the Web at http://www.applytexas.org.

---

### CONTACT

Distance Education Advisor
Distance Education
University of Houston
4242 South Mason Road
Katy, Texas 77450
Fax: 281-395-2629
E-mail: DEadvisor@uh.edu
Web site: http://www.uh.edu/uhdistance

---

# University of Idaho

## Engineering Outreach
Moscow, Idaho

*The University of Idaho, established in 1889, is the land-grant institution for the state of Idaho. The University has a student population of more than 13,000 and offers degree programs in the liberal arts, sciences, agriculture, architecture, engineering, natural resources, mining and metallurgy, and law. Extended program delivery and outreach activities are central to the University's mission. The University of Idaho is a member of the National Association of State Universities and Land-Grant Colleges and the National Commission on Accrediting. The University is accredited by the Northwest Association of Schools and Colleges. The University of Idaho's College of Engineering undergraduate programs are accredited by the Engineering Accreditation Commission of the Accreditation Board for Engineering Technology (EAC/ABET). The computer science program is accredited by the Computer Science Accreditation Commission of the Computing Sciences.*

## DISTANCE LEARNING PROGRAM

The Engineering Outreach program offers complete distance-delivered degree programs in eleven disciplines. The program has grown from its establishment in 1975 into one of the top providers of graduate off-campus engineering degree programs, delivering more than 100 courses per semester to more than 400 students in locations around the country and around the world. More than 200 students have received graduate degrees through Engineering Outreach.

## DELIVERY MEDIA

The Engineering Outreach program uses videotape, video conferencing, Internet, microwave, and satellite technology to deliver graduate-level courses to distant students. Courses do not require attendance at the University of Idaho campus. Courses are taught by University of Idaho faculty members and simultaneously video-taped in specially equipped studio classrooms. VHS videotapes are sent to students; each tape covers one 50-minute lecture. Additional course materials are provided on the World Wide Web for immediate access by students. Both live-taped and previously taped courses are typically offered during a semester.

## PROGRAMS OF STUDY

Engineering Outreach courses carry regular University of Idaho resident credit and may be used toward a degree program at the University of Idaho or transferred to other institutions that accept distance-delivered credit from the University of Idaho. By taking courses through Engineering Outreach, a student can obtain a graduate degree from the University of Idaho in biological and agricultural engineering with an emphasis in water resources and management (M.S. and M.Engr.), civil engineering (M.Engr.), computer engineering (M.S. and M.Engr.), computer science (M.S. and Ph.D.), electrical engineering (M.S., M.Engr., and Ph.D.), engineering management (M.Engr.), environmental science (M.S.), geological engineering (M.S.), mathematics (Master of Arts in Teaching), mechanical engineering (M.Engr.), and psychology with an emphasis in human factors (M.S.).

## SPECIAL PROGRAMS

The senior faculty members in the College of Engineering at the University of Idaho usually offer a jointly taught course in engineering fundamentals (Civil Engineering 411) through Engineering Outreach each semester. This course is a review of basic engineering and science material covered in the Fundamentals of Engineering exam that each engineering graduate must take to be registered as an engineer-in-training and work toward attainment of professional registration. Engineering Outreach also offers self-paced short courses in Java programming language and CMOS analog circuit design.

Engineering Outreach now provides students with the opportunity to receive certificates of completion in the following areas: power system protection and relaying, secure and dependable computing systems, communication systems, character education, advanced materials design, applied geotechnics, HVAC systems, structural engineering, and water resources engineering. Certificates of completion draw on selected courses within larger programs and are ideal for students who want to learn more about a specific subject area but are not ready to pursue a complete degree program. Students must complete a minimum of 12 credits, some required, others elective, depending on each topic area, to receive the certificate of completion. Students are strongly urged to apply for graduate school as they begin a certificate of completion study plan to ease into a graduate program at a later date. However, students may transfer up to 12 approved credits into their graduate study plan. Students should contact Engineering Outreach for complete details and an updated list of currently available certificates of completion.

## STUDENT SERVICES

Communication with faculty members is facilitated by e-mail and by use of the program's toll-free telephone number. Current information about the program and courses is available on the World Wide Web. Students may enroll via fax, phone, or mail. All students have access to the University of Idaho Library via the World Wide Web or telephone.

## CREDIT OPTIONS

All master's degree programs require a minimum of 30 to 36 credits. A combined total of 12 approved credits may be transferred toward the degree. Credits can be transferred to the University of Idaho, with the consent of the student's committee and the Vice President for Research and Graduate Studies, only from other institutions that grant similar graduate degrees.

## FACULTY

Up to 100 University of Idaho faculty members teach in the program each semester. With few exceptions, these faculty members hold advanced degrees in their fields of expertise; more than 90 percent hold doctorates.

## ADMISSION

Requirements for admission vary by department but generally include a bachelor's degree from an accredited college or university, a minimum undergraduate grade point average of 2.8, and a minimum grade point average of 2.8 in subsequent academic work.

## TUITION AND FEES

Registration fees are $410 per credit hour for students enrolled in a graduate program and for all graduate-level courses and $383 per credit hour for non-degree-seeking students in undergraduate courses. There are no additional fees for nonresidents. When calculating the total cost of a course, students should consider the cost of textbooks, software, computer expenses, and postage to send homework and return videotapes.

Fees are adjusted yearly by the State of Idaho Board of Regents. Students should contact Engineering Outreach for updated fees for the 2001–02 academic year.

## FINANCIAL AID

Engineering Outreach students may be eligible for federal financial aid. Determination of eligibility is made by the University of Idaho Student Financial Aid Office. Financial aid may include scholarships, Federal Pell Grants, and Federal Perkins Loans. Last year, more than $40,000 in financial aid was awarded to Engineering Outreach students. Approximately 5 percent of all students received this aid.

## APPLYING

Courses may be taken by non-degree-seeking students or for credit toward a graduate degree. Applications can be completed on the World Wide Web or with forms provided by Engineering Outreach. There is a $35 admission fee for graduate admissions. Students should contact the University of Idaho Graduate Admissions Office at http://www.uidaho.edu/admissions/ or call Engineering Outreach for assistance.

---

### CONTACT

Diane Bancke
Engineering Outreach
University of Idaho
P.O. Box 441014
Moscow, Idaho 83844-1014
Telephone: 800-824-2889 (toll-free)
Fax: 208-885-9249
E-mail: outreach@uidaho.edu
Web site: http://www.uidaho.edu/evo/

# University of Illinois

## University of Illinois Online

Urbana, Illinois

*As a land-grant institution chartered in 1867, the University of Illinois (U of I) provides undergraduate and graduate education in more than 150 fields of study, conducts both theoretical and applied research, and provides public service to the state and to the nation. Today, U of I educates more than 65,000 students a year at its Chicago, Springfield, and Urbana-Champaign campuses and thousands more through its public service and distance learning programs. The University is consistently ranked among the top national public universities, and many of its undergraduate and graduate programs are recognized as among the best in the nation. All three U of I campuses are accredited by the North Central Association of Colleges and Schools.*

## DISTANCE LEARNING PROGRAM

Established in winter 1997, the University of Illinois Online is a University-wide umbrella organization encompassing all of the online distance learning and public-service programs offered by three campuses of the University of Illinois. U of I Online delivers more than 300 courses and twenty-nine complete degree, certificate, and continuing education programs to location-bound and time-restricted students in Illinois, as well as to individuals across the country and throughout the world. During the 1999–2000 academic year, there were approximately 6,000 enrollments in U of I Online courses.

## DELIVERY MEDIA

All U of I Online courses are delivered primarily via the Internet, although some may also require the use of textbooks, CD-ROMs, or other offline materials. A wide range of Internet technologies are used, including fully integrated course management systems, Web-based asynchronous conferencing/discussion tools, real-time text and voice chat, streaming audio and video, Java applets, and other Web-based applications. Access to the Internet on a regular basis is essential. Technology requirements for specific courses are detailed in the U of I Online catalog.

## PROGRAMS OF STUDY

U of I Online offers the Bachelor of Arts in liberal studies; Doctor of Pharmacy (continuing curriculum option); Master of Arts in Education Leadership with a concentration in Master Teaching and Leadership; the Master of Computer Science; the Master of Education, with focus in curriculum, technology, and education reform; the Master of Education in vocational and technical education, with focus in human resource education; Master of Engineering; Master of Health Professions Education; Master of Science in Electrical Engineering; Master of Science in library and information science; Master of Science in Management Information Systems; Master of Science in Mechanical Engineering; credit and noncredit certificate programs in career specialist studies, community college teaching and learning, dairy studies, designing and implementing an anticoagulation clinic, employment specialist studies, financial engineering and risk management, French translation, health information man-

agement, math teacher link courses for math educators, nonprofit management, school nurse development studies; and the Certified Fire Fighter II program. Other programs include CME Online–Specialty Needs for Primary Care Physicians; a graduate medical education core curriculum; an M.B.A. core curriculum; and NetMath.

## STUDENT SERVICES

A full range of online and telephone-based support services are provided by each U of I campus to assist off-campus students with everything from admissions through graduation. These include academic advising, financial aid counseling, computer services (such as e-mail and Network ID) and technical support, library access and support, textbook sales and distribution, and disability services.

## CREDIT OPTIONS

Most of the courses in the U of I Online catalog are offered for undergraduate or graduate-level academic credit. The number of credit hours per course varies, but most courses are 4 semester hours. The unit of credit offered for graduate-level courses from the Urbana campus is called a graduate unit, with 1 graduate unit being equal to 4 semester hours.

In addition to courses for academic credit, the U of I Online catalog also includes noncredit and continuing education courses and programs for personal enrichment and professional development. Many of these courses offer continuing education units (CEUs) that can be applied toward certification/recertification requirements in specific disciplines.

## FACULTY

With rare exceptions, the faculty members who teach courses for academic credit through U of I Online are the same faculty members who teach the on-campus courses and they hold their online courses to the same academic standards as their classroom-based equivalents. Many of these faculty members are distinguished, nationally recognized scholars and researchers in their respective fields. For information about the teaching faculty associated with a specific program, students should visit the Web site for that program.

## ADMISSION

Application and admission procedures vary by campus and program.

General admissions information for each campus can be found in the Admissions section of the U of I Online Web site. In some cases, it is possible to be admitted as a nondegree student and then later apply the credits earned in online courses toward a particular program of study.

## TUITION AND FEES

Tuition and fees for U of I Online courses vary by campus and by program. In many cases, the costs are comparable to those for on-campus classes at the University of Illinois and range from approximately $96 per credit hour to $600 per credit hour, depending on the campus, program, and state of residence. To find out the costs for enrolling in a specific course, students should contact the person or department listed in the corresponding entry in the U of I Online catalog. Tuition rates for specific programs can often be found on their promotional Web sites, which are linked from the program descriptions in the U of I Online catalog.

## FINANCIAL AID

Students enrolled in an online program leading to a degree or certificate may be eligible for financial aid. To be considered, a current Free Application for Federal Student Aid (FAFSA) must be on file. Additional information about the financial aid requirements and services provided by each U of I campus is provided in the Student Services section of the U of I Online Web site.

## APPLYING

For information about how to apply for admission to a specific degree or certificate program, students should contact the person or department listed in the corresponding entry in the U of I Online catalog.

---

### CONTACT

University of Illinois Online
176 Henry Administration Building
506 South Wright Street, MC 353
Urbana, Illinois 61801
Telephone: 217-244-6465
        866-633-UIOL (toll-free)
E-mail: uiol-info@uillinois.edu
Web site: http://www.online.uillinois.edu/

---

# University of Illinois at Springfield

## *UIS Online*

Springfield, Illinois

*The University of Illinois at Springfield (UIS) is the newest of the University of Illinois (U of I) campuses. Formerly known as Sangamon State University, the campus joined the University of Illinois as part of a statewide reorganization of public higher education in 1995. Throughout its twenty-nine-year history, the University has consistently stressed excellent teaching, practical experience, and professional development as the most effective means to enlighten students' minds and give them the skills to prepare them for the next century. UIS is committed to addressing the needs of both traditional and nontraditional learners. UIS is fully accredited by the Commission of Institutions of Higher Education of the North Central Association of Colleges and Schools (NCA).*

## DISTANCE LEARNING PROGRAM

UIS Online is a part of the University of Illinois Online initiative, which provides leadership, coordination, and financial support in the areas of Internet-based education and public service. U of I Online offers online learning opportunities and complete degree and certificate programs to place-bound and time-restricted students in Illinois, the U.S., and around the world. U of I Online currently offers 150 classes with an enrollment of more than 5,000 students.

## DELIVERY MEDIA

UIS Online courses and programs are delivered through a wide range of technologies via the World Wide Web, on a sixteen-week or eight-week basis. Technologies utilized include synchronous and asynchronous Web delivery, CD-ROM, videotape, and streaming media. Students communicate with their instructors through e-mail, conferencing tools, telephone, mail, or fax. Access to an Internet-capable computer is essential.

## PROGRAMS OF STUDY

The Liberal Studies Online Bachelor of Arts degree at the University of Il-

linois at Springfield is a 60-hour, upper-division program offering classes at the junior and senior level. It is built on twenty-five years of experience in assisting learners in designing individualized academic experiences. Learners from throughout the country attend virtual classes and design individualized degree programs that meet their unique educational goals.

The program emphasizes the integration of eight topical learning categories with a variety of media-based instructional methods to form a well-rounded and individualized educational experience. Through this integrative process, Liberal Studies Online helps learners to acquire an understanding of the values, meaning, concerns, choices, and commitments that serve as foundations for the quality of life. Unique features of this degree program include the development of customized degree programs, working with multidisciplinary faculty members as advisers, and utilizing the latest networked information technologies. Liberal Studies Online is designed with the learners' priorities, interests, and experiences as the central focus of their degree program.

The Educational Leadership M.A. degree with a concentration in master

leadership (MTL) is a new online offering that began in fall 2000. MTL provides practicing teachers with the opportunity to earn a high quality master's degree that can be used as a step towards Illinois or National Board Certification. The program works to meet the needs of place-bound teachers, both in Illinois and nationally, who wish to take positions of leadership within their school or district. The program is an innovative collaboration between the Education Leadership and Teacher Education programs of UIS. The courses incorporate online interactive participation and an emphasis on independent project work that links the students' coursework to their professional growth needs.

The M.S. degree program in the Management Information Systems (MIS) Department at the University of Illinois at Springfield is specifically focused on providing a balance between technical skills and knowledge of business functions and processes. The MIS Online program showcases faculty members who bring real-world experience to a curriculum designed to integrate business and management concepts with information technology.

Today's organizations require a variety of new experts, such as information systems managers, systems analysts, applications programmers, database administrators, telecommunication analysts, and systems librarians. The MIS Online curriculum is designed to prepare students to fit these diverse organizational roles.

## SPECIAL PROGRAMS

UIS provides a growing number of additional courses online to meet the needs of its off-campus students. The Departments of Business, Chemistry, Biology, Communication, Human Development, English, Women's Studies, History, Art, Philosophy, Psychology, Sociology/Anthropology, Computer Science, Public Affairs, and Mathematics offer online classes as part of their programs.

## STUDENT SERVICES

Distance learners have access to UIS library services, the campus computer network, e-mail services, academic advising, career placement assistance, and bookstore and auditorium discounts. Individual departments may have additional special services which they offer to their online students. Students should contact individual departments for details. Technical assistance is provided through the UIS online help desk, the Office of Technology Enhanced Learning (OTEL), and the Illinois Virtual Campus's (IVC) 41 support centers. The Office of Disability Services provides academic assistance to students with documented disabilities.

## CREDIT OPTIONS

Students may transfer credits from another institution. In addition, credit for prior learning (CPL) enables qualified UIS students to receive academic credit for college-level learning acquired outside the classroom. A campus-wide faculty committee monitors the entire CPL process. For more information, students should contact CPL (217-206-7545).

## FACULTY

One third of UIS faculty members teach online. Distance learning faculty members are full-time or adjunct members within the department granting the course credit. They are the same professionals who teach the course on campus and are available to answer questions via telephone, online conferencing, fax, e-mail, or regular mail. In addition, most online professors maintain regular online office hours through conferencing tools.

## ADMISSION

Applicants with 45 or more semester hours and a cumulative grade point average of 2.00 or higher (on a 4.00 scale) from any regionally accredited institution of higher education may be admitted as an undergraduate. Applicants must have completed 3 semester hours of English Composition as a minimum for admission. Individuals with bachelor's degrees from regionally accredited colleges and universities are eligible to apply for admission to graduate study at UIS. A minimum undergraduate GPA of 2.50 and/or specific programs requirements must be met. Individual departments may require higher GPAs, GREs or other qualifications before admittance to a program. Enrollment in degreed programs requires formal admission to the University. Students should contact the

UIS Admissions Office at 800-252-8533 or visit the school on the Web at http://www.uis.edu/~admissions for additional information.

## TUITION AND FEES

Costs may vary depending upon program of study, number of credits taken, and course delivery. Tuition for fall 2001 is $112 per credit hour for graduate students and $99.50 for undergraduates. Tuition for out-of-state residents is higher. Online students pay a reduced student fee of $19 per credit hour. Additional fees vary by course.

## FINANCIAL AID

The Office of Financial Assistance coordinates financial aid in the form of scholarships, grants, or loans. Online students may apply for this assistance. Applications and additional information can be obtained by contacting the UIS Office of Financial Assistance Department~ via its Web site, http://www.uis.edu/financial aid/ or by calling 217-206-6724.

## APPLYING

Students may register by mail, fax, World Wide Web, or in person. Students should visit or contact the UIS Registration Office (World Wide Web: http://www.uis.edu/~enroll/reg1.html; telephone: 217-206-6174 or 800-252-6174, toll-free). The UIS Office of Financial Assistance, http://www.uis.edu/quicklist.html, provides applications and additional information.

---

**CONTACT**

Ray Schroeder, Director
Office of Technology Enhanced Learning
University of Illinois at Springfield
Springfield, Illinois 62794-9243
Telephone: 217-206-7317
Fax: 217-206-6162
E-mail: schroeder.ray@uis.edu

---

# The University of Illinois at Urbana-Champaign

## Division of Academic Outreach

Champaign, Illinois

*The University of Illinois at Urbana-Champaign (UIUC) is a comprehensive, major public university that is ranked among the best in the world. As a land-grant institution chartered in 1867, it provides undergraduate and graduate education in more than 150 fields of study, conducts both theoretical and applied research, and provides public service to the state and the nation. The campus includes 2,000 faculty members serving 26,000 undergraduates and 10,000 graduate and professional students.*

*The mission of UIUC is to provide excellence in education, research, and service. The University houses the largest public library collection in the world with more than 1 million logons from around the world to the online catalogue each week. It is ranked eighteenth of all universities in the nation on spending in research and development in science and engineering including more than eighty centers, laboratories, and institutes that perform research for government agencies, industry and campus units.*

## DISTANCE LEARNING PROGRAM

Each semester, the University of Illinois offers more than 200 different graduate-level credit courses away from the campus at locations throughout Illinois, in surrounding states, and internationally. Academic Outreach (AO) also offers noncredit courses in a variety of subject areas. The noncredit courses may be offered independently or as part of a certificate program. In addition, more than 130 undergraduate credit courses are available through correspondence study.

## DELIVERY MEDIA

Off-campus credit and noncredit courses are offered in a variety of formats, including face-to-face instruction, Web-based courses, compressed interactive video, videotape, CD-ROM, visual teleconferencing, or through a combinations of delivery systems.

## PROGRAMS OF STUDY

The College of Education offers an Online Master of Education (M.Ed.) degree designed for practicing teachers and administrators with a focus on curriculum, technology, and education reform (CTER). This online set of courses provides an opportunity to earn a coherent, high-quality master's degree online, with most of the interactions through personal computers and Internet connections at home or at local schools.

The master's degree in library and information science (LIS), known as the Library Education Experimental Program (LEEP), include teaching graduates to anticipate social and technological changes, to promote change to advance the profession, and to foster critical thinking about literature and research in LIS and related fields. The UIUC program is unique among schools of library and information science, and it provides significant advantages in a field increasingly involved in organizing and using electronic information.

The College of Engineering offers three online graduate degree programs for professional engineers via the Internet in computer science, electrical engineering, and mechanical engineering. Individuals who wish to pursue a master's degree must apply and be accepted as a degree candidate in the Graduate College. The online courses are also available to professionals who would like to update their current competencies and participate in one of the seven certificate programs offered for graduate credit. For more information, prospective students should visit the UIUC College of Engineering Web site at http://online.engr.uiuc.edu.

## SPECIAL PROGRAMS

Guided Individual Study (GIS) at the University of Illinois provides instruction on an individual basis. Individuals learn at their own pace using self-instructional course materials. Students contact instructors, submit assignments, and receive feedback on graded assignments by mail, and in some cases, by e-mail. More than 125 courses in a wide range of subject areas are available for undergraduate credit, and noncredit courses are also available. Enrollment is open to on-campus UIUC students, off-campus University of Illinois students, high school students, students enrolled at other colleges and universities, and individuals studying on their own. For further information on GIS, prospective students should contact the Division of Academic Outreach by mail, phone, or by accessing the Web site, listed below.

The French professional development online courses are designed for those interested in developing advanced language skills in French. The online format allows students to benefit from the expertise of the Department of French at the University of Illinois at Urbana-Champaign regardless of location. The courses are fully accredited by the University and may be taken for continuing education credit. A certificate of completion is available for students who complete two courses in translation and three courses on other topics.

The Department of Crop Sciences offers courses in crop and soil science at various locations throughout the state. Individual courses may be taken for personal or professional development. In addition, the department offers a master's degree in crop sciences to qualified applicants, as well as a nondegree Professional Development Certificate.

The College of Commerce and Business and Administration, Department of Finance, offers a professional development sequence in financial engineering and risk management. Students who complete three online graduate finance courses will be awarded a certificate of completion. The program is designed to bring professional persons the necessary knowledge and skills to increase their effectiveness as managers of and users of financial derivatives.

## STUDENT SERVICES

The Division of Academic Outreach includes a library located within the UIUC Main Library. The division provides library support for students enrolled in off-campus degree and certificate programs. The AO library does not have its own book or journal col-lections, but instead uses the resources available within the UIUC system. Material unavailable at UIUC can be obtained from ILCSO-member libraries or through interlibrary loan services. Community credit courses may be taken for no credit.

Students may also order their books online at http://www.uofibookstore. uiuc.edu as well as receive information from a live help desk.

For more information of services offered, students should visit the Web site (http://www.outreach.uiuc.edu/distance).

## CREDIT OPTIONS

The course work shown on University transcripts reflects all work attempted by a student at the University. Undergraduate credit is recorded in semester hours. Credit for graduate courses is measured in units. One unit is equivalent to 4 semester hours.

## FACULTY

Ninety-two percent of distance education faculty members are employed full-time at the Urbana campus of the University of Illinois; the remaining 8 percent are departmentally approved adjuncts.

## ADMISSION

Admission to the University of Illinois is required to enroll in certain online degree programs; admission is not required to enroll in correspondence-type courses. For further details on admission requirements, prospective students should visit the Web site, listed below.

## TUITION AND FEES

Tuition and fees vary by program type. For tuition rates for particular courses or programs of interest, prospective students should visit the Web at: http://www.outreach.uiuc.edu. Tuition and fees must be paid at time of enrollment unless students are eligible for financial aid. Only those admitted to a degree program and carrying a course load of 1.5 units (6 hours) per semester or .75 units (3 hours) during summer session are eligible for financial aid. A Free Application for Federal Student Aid (FAFSA) must be completed in order to apply for University-administered financial aid.

## APPLYING

For those programs requiring admission prior to enrollment, including LEEP, CTER, and Human Resources Education (HRE), an online Graduate College application form is available on the Web at http://www.oar. uiuc.edu/prospective/grad/instruct. html.

All offerings require enrollment prior to the first class session. Enrollment forms are available at the Web address or the toll-free number, listed below.

---

**CONTACT**
Division of Academic Outreach
1406 Presidential Tower
302 East John Street
Champaign, Illinois 61820
Telephone: 800-252-1360 Ext. 3-1321 (toll-free)
Web site: http://www.outreach.uiuc.edu

---

# The University of Iowa

## Center for Credit Programs

Iowa City, Iowa

*Established in 1847, the University of Iowa is a major national research university with a solid liberal arts foundation. Iowa was the first U.S. public university to admit men and women on an equal basis. It has won international recognition for its wealth of achievements in the arts, sciences, and humanities. A member of the select Association of American Universities, the University of Iowa maintains a balance between scholarly research and teaching. It places a strong emphasis on undergraduate, international, and interdisciplinary education. The University is accredited by the North Central Association of Colleges and Schools and other accrediting agencies.*

## DISTANCE LEARNING PROGRAM

In cooperation with University of Iowa academic colleges and departments, the Center for Credit Programs (CCP) of the University of Iowa's Division of Continuing Education delivers University credit courses, both in Iowa City and off campus, to nontraditional and other part-time students who seek a college degree, career advancement, or self-improvement. The CCP supports some 19,000 enrollments annually, including some 4,500 Guided Correspondence Study (GCS) registrations. Distance education courses may use interactive and broadcast television (available only within Iowa) or correspondence study and Web courses (available worldwide to English-speaking students). Approximately 160 GCS or Web-supported courses are available both at the undergraduate and graduate levels.

## DELIVERY MEDIA

University of Iowa distance education courses employ a variety of delivery media. Correspondence courses are offered in traditional print-based formats. In many cases, courses are available as Web or Web-assisted courses. Videos or CD-ROMs supplement some courses. Students interact with instructors via correspondence, fax, e-mail, or toll-free telephone. Within Iowa, degree program and other courses are offered via interactive video through the Iowa Communications Network (ICN), an advanced fiber-optic telecommunications network linking educational sites across the state.

## PROGRAMS OF STUDY

The Bachelor of Liberal Studies (B.L.S.) external degree program provides an opportunity for students to complete a bachelor's degree from the University of Iowa without attending classes on campus or without ever visiting the campus. The B.L.S. degree has no specific major. Instead, students concentrate course work in three of five distribution areas (humanities, communications and arts, natural science and math, social sciences, or professional fields).

The B.L.S. degree is a flexible degree program offering convenient, self-paced work; advisers who work with students to create an individual plan of study; the diverse preparation a liberal arts degree provides; the flexibility to match education efforts with career goals; and an undergraduate degree awarded by a nationally recognized institution. More than 600 students have graduated from the program since it was established in 1977 by the Iowa Board of Regents, and hundreds of students are currently active. For more specific information, see the CCP Web site or call the toll-free number below.

## SPECIAL PROGRAMS

The LionHawk program represents a formal partnership between Pennsylvania State University and the University of Iowa that allows students to earn both two- and four-year degrees without on-campus study. Students who complete Penn State's Extended Letters, Arts, and Sciences (ELAS) associate degree are ensured admission to the B.L.S. program. Upon admission to the B.L.S. program, all General Education Program requirements are considered satisfied except for the foreign language requirement.

## STUDENT SERVICES

Degree-seeking students receive ongoing registration, educational advising, library access, and other services. Entry into the program provides access to a listserv that connects B.L.S. students everywhere. The CCP provides extended office hours (Monday–Thursday, 8 a.m. to 7 p.m.; Friday 8 a.m. to 5 p.m., Central Time) to better accommodate nontraditional students.

## CREDIT OPTIONS

Credit for B.L.S. degree requirements may be met in several ways, including University of Iowa campus, off-campus, or evening classes (available only in Iowa); transfer credit from other institutions (a minimum number of credits from the University of Iowa are required); and other methods. B.L.S. students primarily take the GCS courses, which are available anywhere, are available for enrollment continuously, and allow for self-paced learning. GCS courses provide semester-hour credit. There is no limit on the number of GCS courses that may be applied toward the B.L.S. degree.

## FACULTY

All courses and instructors are approved by appropriate departmental and collegiate officers. Courses are taught by regular or adjunct faculty members and some advanced graduate students.

## ADMISSION

Students applying for admission to the B.L.S. degree program may request an information packet by calling the CCP toll-free number. No special admission requirements are necessary to enroll in GCS courses. Enrollment in GCS courses does not constitute admission to the University of Iowa.

## TUITION AND FEES

For 2001–02 (effective July 1, 2001, through June 30, 2002), GCS tuition is $99 per semester hour plus a $15-per-course enrollment fee. GCS tuition is the same for in-state, out-of-state, undergraduate, or graduate students. Tuition for semester-based distance learning courses is the same as University of Iowa residential tuition, or $130 per semester hour for undergraduates and $206 per semester hour for graduates for 2001–02.

## FINANCIAL AID

Registration in semester-based courses (generally available only in Iowa) may qualify students for Pell Grants or Stafford Loans. These programs are not accepted to fund GCS courses. The CCP provides limited funds for per-course tuition scholarships for qualifying students. Priority for scholarships is given to B.L.S. students. A private loan program is available to degree-seeking students enrolled in GCS courses.

## APPLYING

Students may enroll in GCS courses at any time. Enrollment forms may be found in the GCS catalog or on the CCP Web site. Students paying by credit card may enroll by phone. For information or enrollment in other CCP courses, call the toll-free number.

---

**CONTACT**

Center for Credit Programs
116 International Center
The University of Iowa
Iowa City, Iowa 52242-1802
Telephone: 800-272-6430 (toll-free)
Fax: 319-335-2740
E-mail: credit-programs@uiowa.edu
Web site: http://www.uiowa.edu/~ccp

# University of Maryland, College Park

## e-learning

College Park, Maryland

The University of Maryland is the flagship institution among the University System of Maryland's eleven state public colleges and universities. Founded in 1856 as the original land-grant institution in Maryland, the University is ranked among the country's premier research institutions. Fifty-two of its programs are ranked in the top twenty-five in the nation, with a dozen Maryland programs ranked in the top ten. The University of Maryland is accredited by the Middle States Association of Colleges and Secondary Schools and is a member of the Association of American Universities.

In 2000, the University of Maryland Office of Continuing and Extended Education introduced a University-wide e-learning strategy and launched its first programs: Master of Life Sciences and Master of Arts in ethnomusicology. Designed to enable practicing teachers to conveniently pursue an advanced degree, the Web-based Master of Life Sciences is a content-rich, interdisciplinary program that focuses on the most contemporary issues in modern science. The M.A. in ethnomusicology is a unique program that combines online course work with intensive summer studies in Spain.

## DISTANCE LEARNING PROGRAM

The University of Maryland is dedicated to increasing the visibility and reputation of its high-quality professional and graduate programs, measured not only by advances in research but by innovations in the delivery of programs to a worldwide audience. e-Learning provides the platform by which these programs can be conveniently delivered to students anywhere, at anytime.

## DELIVERY MEDIA

Courses are delivered asynchronously through the Internet using a range of technologies including chat rooms, threaded discussions, and links to campus libraries and academic resources. Faculty members are available in person, through e-mail, and by prescribed phone appointments.

## PROGRAMS OF STUDY

e-Learning at the University of Maryland offers two online graduate programs, a 30-credit Master of Life Sciences and a 36-credit Master of Arts in ethnomusicology.

The Master of Life Sciences provides in-depth knowledge of current research areas in the biological, biochemical, and biomedical sciences. Courses cover modern biology, modern molecular genetics, transmission genetics, human physiology, biodiversity and conservation biology, chemical ecology, principles of chemical biology, biochemistry, evolutionary biology and behavior, and experimental biology.

The School of Music's Master of Arts in ethnomusicology combines online courses with twenty-two-day sessions held for two consecutive summers in the Mediterranean town of Peñiscola, Spain. The course is taught in Spanish and English. Applicants should have reading comprehension skills in both languages. The program features popular music, analysis, theory and practice of flamenco, postmodern performance theory, transcultural music education, West African drumming and dance, ethnographic writing, evening performance, and interaction with local communities. In addition, students are trained in the technologies required to participate in online courses.

## STUDENT SERVICES

Through SPOC (Single Point of Contact) listed in the contact section below, students may inquire, apply for admission, register, pay their bills, and purchase textbooks. Students also have access to equipment and software specifications needed for successful completion of course work, and help-desk support 24 hours a day, seven days a week.

## FACULTY

The Master of Life Sciences program has 11 full-time University of Maryland faculty members with doctoral degrees. The Master of Arts in ethnomusicology has 4 full-time University of Maryland faculty members with doctoral degrees, 4 internationally acclaimed performance artists, and coordinators in the U.S. and Spain.

## ADMISSION

The Master of Life Sciences program requires an undergraduate degree in biological science, chemistry, biochemistry, or science education; one year of teaching experience; letters of recommendation from a school principal and a science supervisor; and successful completion of a gateway review class, LFSC510 Concepts of Modern Biology, or a grade of B or better on a preadmission exam based on LFSC510.

The Master of Arts in ethnomusicology program requires a bachelor's degree in music, history, anthropology, sociology, folklore, education, art, or theater (other majors are considered); a minimum 3.5 GPA; three letters of reference; writing samples; and GRE scores. The GRE and TOEFL are not required for international applicants.

## TUITION AND FEES

The Master of Life Sciences program costs $325 per credit hour, and there is a $60-per-term technology/distance learning fee and an admission exam fee of $20.

The Master of Arts in ethnomusicology program costs $150 per credit hour, and there is a $50-per-term technology/distance learning fee. Travel and accommodation expenses for summer studies in Spain are additional.

All graduate students pay a one-time $50 application fee.

## FINANCIAL AID

For information regarding financial assistance, students should contact the Office of Financial Aid, 0102 Lee Building, College Park, Maryland 20742 (telephone: 301-314-9000; e-mail: umfinaid@osfa.umd.edu).

**CONTACT**
SPOC (Single Point of Contact)
Mitchell Building, First Floor
University of Maryland
College Park, Maryland 20742-5231
Telephone: 301-314-3572
1-877-989-SPOC (toll-free)
Fax: 301-314-1282
E-mail: e-learning@umail.umd.edu
Web site: http://www.e-learning.umd.edu

# University of Maryland, College Park

## Reliability Engineering Program

College Park, Maryland

*The Reliability Engineering Program provides a rich offering of 29 courses of in-depth study of facets of reliability engineering. It is one of the academic programs within the School of Engineering in the University of Maryland at College Park, Maryland. The University, founded in 1862, is a leading public university. The Engineering School's graduate programs are collectively the fastest rising in the nation in the* U.S. News & World Report's *annual rating of graduate programs.*

## DISTANCE LEARNING PROGRAM

The Reliability Engineering Program administers a broad range of courses, a Certificate program, and programs leading to the Master of Engineering, Master of Science, and Doctor of Philosophy degrees. Product reliability leads to higher market share for companies and often is a necessary factor for corporate survival in this very competitive global economy. The demand for engineers equipped to deal with reliability issues has far outstripped the supply. The job market for reliability engineering graduates is excellent, with many companies competing for the few well-educated engineers in this field. The distance learning program makes these courses and degrees available to learners at their workplace or home. The program has awarded 161 degrees and the student body has grown to a current size of 145 distance learners.

## DELIVERY MEDIA

Courses are currently available in either videotape format or through Internet access. The Internet version includes streaming TV to provide class lectures. This program delivers the same courses at a distance as are available to on-campus students. All required work for the courses is the same for on-campus and off-campus students. The program delivers to distance learners the same high quality of learning experiences as available to the on-campus students. Access to the instructor is by means of telephone and e-mail. Homework assignments may be sent by fax or by overnight service.

Courses are available on the basic schedule in which they are offered on campus, with the same instructor responsible. All class activities for distance learners are nonsynchronous so that the student can carry out all activities at a time of their choosing. Thus, any chat room activities are in the form of accumulating threaded discussions without the need for students to sign on at a time selected by the instructor.

## PROGRAMS OF STUDY

The graduate program is designed to take qualified engineers and provide them with the tools needed to better understand the factors that cause components and systems to fail. There is an emphasis on the fact that most complex modern systems involve the interactions between hardware, software, and humans. Understanding the synergies of these factors is often critical.

Students take the core courses and select from elective courses to customize a program that meets their individual objectives. The electives provide clusters of courses in subjects such as software reliability, microelectronics reliability, data analysis, and human performance reliability.

All students seeking graduate degrees in reliability engineering must complete six core courses.

The Master of Science and Master of Engineering degrees require the completion of 31 semester hours of graduate education with a grade point average of 3.0 (B). These courses must include the core courses, an approved selection of elective courses which meet the particular student's objectives, and a research component for the M.S. degree. The research component consists of 6 credits of research for the thesis option or 3 credits of work on a scholarly paper for the nonthesis option. Such research activities are available, but not required, for the M.E. degree.

## SPECIAL PROGRAMS

The courses associated with the doctoral program can all be taken by distance delivery, but there is a residency requirement of one academic year for the Ph.D. degree. The principal activity of earning a Ph.D. degree is the research dissertation; the residency is needed to allow adequate interaction with the thesis adviser during the conducting of the research and the writing of the dissertation.

## CREDIT OPTIONS

Up to 6 credits of course work may be taken at another accredited institution and transferred as part of the electives for this program, with the requirement that all courses together form a coherent program. The courses to be transferred must be graduate level and have a grade of B or better.

All persons wishing to earn a certificate or degree must have official admission to the Graduate School either as a degree-seeking or non-degree-seeking student. A less formal registration can be done through the Program Coordinator for those wishing to take courses without official recognition.

## FACULTY

There are 9 full-time tenured faculty members who teach in the Reliability Engineering Program. In addition, 4 adjunct faculty members have been selected from experts in the field to teach selected special courses.

## ADMISSION

Admission to the program of study is open to all qualified applicants holding a bachelor's degree or higher from an accredited undergraduate or graduate instituion. Factors considered in evaluating applications include academic achievement in previous degree course work, scores on the GRE exam, TOEFL scores (for international students), the nature and extent of previous work experience, a statement of objectives, and letters of recommendation.

## TUITION AND FEES

For 2001–02, graduate tuition for this program is $681 per credit. The only additional fee is a one-time application fee of $50. These charges do not cover textbooks which may be obtained from the University bookstore or any other source of books.

## APPLYING

The University of Maryland reviews applications in the order of receipt of complete packets of application materials. Students are not required to attend any on-campus orientation sessions.

## CONTACT

Program Coordinator
Reliability Engineering
2100 Marie Mount Hall
University of Maryland
College Park, Maryland 20742-7531
Telephone: 301-405-8901
E-mail: relpgm@eng.umd.edu
Web site: http://www.enre.umd.edu

# University of Maryland University College

## Undergraduate and Graduate Online Programs

Adelphi, Maryland

*Founded in 1947, University of Maryland University College (UMUC) is one of eleven degree-granting institutions in the University System of Maryland; its Graduate School was founded in 1978. UMUC's principal mission is to serve adult, part-time students by providing high-quality educational opportunities in Maryland and around the world.*

*Through its online programs, UMUC offers fourteen bachelor's degrees, thirteen undergraduate certificates, five master's degrees, thirty-one graduate certificates. In 2000, UMUC's online course enrollment reached 40,000.*

*UMUC is accredited by the Commission on Higher Education of the Middle States Association of Colleges and Schools, 3624 Market Street, Philadelphia, Pennsylvania 19104 (telephone: 215-662-5606).*

## DISTANCE LEARNING PROGRAM

UMUC's online courses provide the same rigor, requirements, assignments, and tests as are available in a classroom environment. However, students are free to participate at times and from locations that are convenient to them. Online courses are highly structured and require students to log in several times a week and to participate actively in asynchronous, full-class, and small-group discussions.

## DELIVERY MEDIA

UMUC provides undergraduate and graduate online degree programs via WebTycho, its proprietary virtual campus interface, via the World Wide Web. Students taking online classes via WebTycho require a computer running a Web browser, such as Netscape Navigator or Microsoft Internet Explorer versions 4.0 or higher, connection to the Internet, and an e-mail account.

## PROGRAMS OF STUDY

Undergraduate Programs offers Bachelor of Arts (B.A.) and Bachelor of Science (B.S.) degree programs, with fourteen majors and sixteen minors available online. Majors include accounting, business administration, communication studies, computer and information science, computer studies, fire science, humanities, human resource management, management studies, legal studies, environmental management, information systems management, psychology, and social sciences. In addition, UMUC offers thirteen undergraduate certificate programs online.

The Graduate School offers fifteen online master's degree programs, including the Master of Business Administration, the Master of International Management, the Master of Software Engineering, the Master of Arts in Teaching, the Master of Education, and the Master of Distance Education. In addition, the Master of Science degree is available in the following areas: accounting and financial management, biotechnology studies, computer systems management, electronic commerce, environmental management, information technology, management, technology management, and telecommunications management. The Graduate School also offers four dual-degree programs and thirty-one certificate programs.

## STUDENT SERVICES

UMUC offers a complete range of support services on line that allow students to apply for admission, obtain pre-entry advising, register, order books and materials, search for scholarships, apply for financial aid, and obtain ongoing academic advising. Once students have been admitted, they also have access to UMUC's Interactive Student Information System (ISIS), which allows them to check their course schedules and grade reports from past and current semesters, statements of account, and unofficial transcripts; to update their personal information; and to access UMUC's career resources. Students also have access to extensive library resources online.

## CREDIT OPTIONS

UMUC offers undergraduate students a number of innovative options for earning credit, all of which are available at a distance. Through Experiential Learning (EXCEL), students can earn up to 30 credits toward a first undergraduate degree (15 credits toward a second degree) by having previous work or life experience evaluated. Through Cooperative Education (Co-op), undergraduate students can earn academic credit in the workplace for new on-the-job learning.

Graduate students can transfer up to 6 semester hours of graduate credit (3 semester hours for the Master of Business Administration) to UMUC if the credit was earned at a regionally accredited institution and is relevant to the student's area of study, subject to approval by the Graduate School.

## FACULTY

Before teaching online, UMUC faculty members must complete a five-week intensive training course and be certified. Of the more than 800 Undergraduate Programs faculty members, 35 percent have taught UMUC courses in distance formats. The undergraduate faculty is composed of full-time academic directors and adjunct faculty members who work actively in the fields in which they teach. The Graduate School's 35 full-time faculty members have terminal degrees that are relevant to the online degrees. They teach, are responsible for the design of the online curriculum, and provide leadership for the school's approximately 300 adjunct faculty members. More than 85 percent of those adjunct faculty members hold terminal degrees in their disciplines; all have years of practical experience in their fields.

## ADMISSION

Students who are applying for undergraduate admission must have graduated from a regionally accredited high school or have completed the General Educational Development (GED) exams with a total score of at least 225 and no individual score less than 40 and have a cumulative grade point average (GPA) of at least 2.0 on all college-level work attempted at other colleges and universities.

Applicants to the Graduate School must have a bachelor's degree from a regionally accredited college or university and an overall undergraduate GPA of at least 3.0 to be accepted as a degree-seeking student. Students with at least a 2.5 GPA in their major area of study can apply for provisional status. Applicants for the Master of Science in Technology Management must have a bachelor's degree in a social, biological, or physical science; business administration; or engineering from a regionally accredited college or university. Students applying for the Master of Science in Environmental Management program are required to have at least 3 undergraduate credits each in basic biology and chemistry.

## TUITION AND FEES

Undergraduate tuition per semester hour is $197 for Maryland residents and $364 for nonresidents. Graduate tuition for Maryland residents is $301 per semester hour; it is $494 per semester hour for nonresidents, except for the Master of Business Administration program, which is $3198 per 6-credit seminar. Books, certain course materials, and some fees are additional. Active-duty military personnel are eligible for a reduced undergraduate tuition rate of $148 per semester hour and for in-state graduate tuition rates. Spouses of active-duty military are eligible for in-state tuition for undergraduate and graduate courses. The undergraduate application fee is $30. The graduate application fee is $50. For both undergraduate and graduate students, schedule adjustments are $15, the late fee for withdrawal is $15, and the late registration fee is $30.

## FINANCIAL AID

UMUC offers a variety of financial aid programs to suit the needs of both undergraduate and graduate students. Students are eligible to apply for low-interest loans, state scholarship program funds, the Federal Work-Study Program, and UMUC grants and scholarships. Federal Direct Loans are available to students regardless of income. While UMUC handles most of the processes involved in delivering federal, state, and institutional funds, students are responsible for completing the Free Application for Federal Student Aid (FAFSA) and the UMUC Student Data Form and for adhering to deadlines. For more information and deadlines, students should contact UMUC via e-mail at umucinfo@umuc.edu.

## APPLYING

Students interested in applying to any of UMUC's online programs can find information from the points of contact or at the Web addresses listed below. UMUC accepts and processes applications throughout the year. Test scores such as SAT, GMAT, or GRE are not required for any UMUC bachelor's or master's programs.

---

**CONTACT**

University of Maryland University College
3501 University Boulevard East
Adelphi, Maryland 20783
Telephone: 800-581-UMUC (toll-free) or 301-985-7000
E-mail: umucinfo@umuc.edu
Web site: http://www.umuc.edu

---

# University of Massachusetts

## UMassOnline

Boston, Massachusetts

Founded in 2000, UMassOnline is the online program of the University of Massachusetts (UMass). UMass has been involved in distance learning since 1975 as one of the seven founders of the National Technological University (NTU). Drawing on the talents and resources of the campuses at Amherst, Boston, Dartmouth, Lowell, and Worcester, UMassOnline serves as a central portal for the University's online courses, certificates, degree programs, and corporate and professional education. UMassOnline does not confer degrees, but supports the campuses that do. The University of Massachusetts is accredited by the New England Association of Schools and Colleges.

## DISTANCE LEARNING PROGRAM

At UMassOnline, students of all ages have access to all the online academic resources of the University of Massachusetts system: courses, degree programs, certificates, and professional and corporate education. The programs are available to lifelong learners locally, regionally, nationally, and globally. Online courses have the same rigorous academic requirements found on site at the five campuses. Each campus is fully accredited and responsible for its own programs.

## DELIVERY MEDIA

UMassOnline courses are delivered via Internet-based programs to standard browsers on the popular platforms. The UMassOnline platform enables students to interact with instructors and each other via e-mail, chat, threaded discussions, live-online learning, telephone, fax, and surface mail. Technical requirements vary by sponsoring campus, but some prerequisites are standard. UMass also supports a comprehensive network of interactive video sites across the state.

## PROGRAMS OF STUDY

Graduate degree programs that are offered are the Master of Public Health

in public health practice (Amherst), the Master of Science (Nursing: community/school health) (Amherst), the M.B.A. Professional Program (Amherst), and the Master's Degree in Educational Administration (M.Ed.) (Lowell). Graduate Certificate Programs offered are the Graduate Certificate in Clinical Pathology (Lowell) and the Graduate Certificate in Photonics and Optoelectronics (Lowell). Undergraduate degree programs are the Bachelor of Liberal Arts (Lowell), RN to Bachelor of Science (Nursing) (Amherst), the Bachelor of Science in hotel, restaurant, and travel administration (Amherst), the Bachelor of Science in information technology (Lowell), and the Associate of Science in information technology (Lowell). Undergraduate certificates include the Certificate in Data/Telecommunications (Lowell), the Certificate in Fundamentals of Information Technology (Lowell), the Certificate in Intranet Development (Lowell), the Certificate in Multimedia Applications (Lowell), Certificate in Contemporary Communications, and the Certificate in UNIX (Lowell). Noncredit certificates include the Fundamentals of Arts Management Certificate program (Amherst) and the Online Communications Skills Certificate (Dartmouth).

In addition, hundreds of undergraduate and graduate courses are offered in more than 50 disciplines, such as

accounting, astronomy, biological sciences, business administration, chemistry, communications, community health, computing, counseling, economics, English, history, instructional design, journalism, linguistics, management, marketing, mathematics, nursing, philosophy, psychology, sociology, technical education, and women's studies.

The academic programs are fully accredited by the relevant accrediting bodies such as the New England Association of Schools and Colleges (NEASC), AACSB International–The Association to Advance Collegiate Schools of Business, ABET, NCATE, CEPH, CCNE, NLN, ACPHA, and others.

## STUDENT SERVICES

Online students benefit from the same student services as do on-campus students. The faculty and staff are dedicated to making students' online experience a positive one. Advisers are available by phone, e-mail, fax, and in person. Services provided include academic advising, academic calendar admissions, disabilities services, libraries, registration, textbooks, transcripts, transfer of credit, alumni and friends, and athletics.

## CREDIT OPTIONS

Students may request a transcript evaluation and, upon approval, transfer credits earned at other accredited postsecondary schools to UMass. Credits may also be earned through the College-Level Examination Program (CLEP) or through independent study. Credits earned through distance education are University of Massachusetts credits and are granted by each of the sponsoring campuses. UMass course credits are not automatically transferable from one campus to another.

## FACULTY

The faculty members that teach the online courses are selected by each of the sponsoring campuses, according to the standard campus practices for appointments. Online students encounter the same highly qualified faculty members as those on the physical campuses.

## ADMISSION

Any person with a high school diploma or its equivalent (such as a GED) may register for noncredit or undergraduate courses; however, students must have a bachelor's degree to be admitted to a graduate degree program. Some courses may require prerequisite college-level work. On all campuses, students may register for courses before being formally admitted into a certificate or degree program. Enroll-

ment does not imply acceptance into a degree program. Massachusetts residency is not a requirement.

## TUITION AND FEES

Tuition and fees vary according to the campus and type of course. Generally, a noncredit course costs $165–$350, while an undergraduate course costs $140–$220 per credit; graduate-level courses vary in cost from $200–$600 per credit. All students, regardless of residency, pay the same tuition. Massachusetts residency (in state or out of state) does not affect the fee structure for students enrolling in courses and degree programs offered through UMassOnline.

## FINANCIAL AID

Availability of financial aid varies depending upon course status and matriculation. Financial assistance is available from employers, continu-

ing education loans, and, under the G.I. Bill, for eligible military personnel.

## APPLYING

Application and acceptance processes are the same for on- and off-campus students. For more information about application and registration procedures for degree programs and individual courses, students can visit the UMassOnline Web site at the Internet address listed below.

### CONTACT

Dr. Jack M. Wilson
CEO, UMassOnline
One Beacon Street
Boston, Massachusetts 02108
Telephone: 617-287-7160
Fax: 617-287-7044
E-mail: info@UMassOnline.net
Web site:
    http://www.UMassOnline.net

# University of Massachusetts Amherst

## Division of Continuing Education

Amherst, Massachusetts

*The University of Massachusetts Amherst (UMass Amherst), the flagship campus of the University of Massachusetts system, was founded in 1863 under the Land-Grant College Act of 1862. Within its ten schools, colleges, and faculties, UMass Amherst offers associate degrees in six areas, bachelor's degrees in nearly ninety, master's degrees in more than seventy, and doctorates in more than fifty. The University serves approximately 34,000 students: 18,000 undergraduates and 6,000 graduates, plus 300 students at the Stockbridge School and nearly 10,000 Continuing Education students. The UMass Amherst Division of Continuing Education, founded in 1971, provides access to the academic resources of the University to part-time students, working professionals, local and national business firms, and the general community. The Division of Continuing Education administers the University's summer and winter sessions, as well as providing evening, weekend, and distance education courses. The University of Massachusetts is accredited by the New England Association of Schools and Colleges.*

## DISTANCE LEARNING PROGRAM

The Division of Continuing Education, in partnership with the University's schools and colleges, began offering distance education courses in 1995. Using the World Wide Web, students may interact with each other and the instructors from remote locations. Online courses have the same rigorous academic requirements as on-campus courses. The faculty members who develop the courses teach the courses. The University of Massachusetts Amherst is accredited by the New England Association of Schools and Colleges.

## DELIVERY MEDIA

The UMass Division of Continuing Education utilizes the Internet to deliver courses throughout New England, the nation, and the globe. Web-based courses are available twenty-four hours a day but must be completed within the standard semester. Students interact with the instructor via e-mail, chat rooms, telephone, fax, and mail. Courses include exercises, readings, projects, online discussions, chat rooms, live chat, illustrations, and video.

## PROGRAMS OF STUDY

In addition to online credit courses in accounting, marketing, English, journalism, management, marketing, philosophy, sociology, and wildlife and fisheries conservation, five online degree programs are offered.

The Master of Science (Nursing) in community/school health prepares advanced practice nurses as expert clinicians in the care of children, adolescents, and their families in diverse community and school health settings. The master's degree program consists of 42 credits and includes courses and clinical practica. Clinical practica, involving diverse clinical activities, are tailored to meet individual learning needs and can be completed in settings identified by the student. The School of Nursing is accredited by the National League for Nursing (NLN) and the Collegiate Commission on Nursing Education (CCNE).

The Master of Public Health (M.P.H.) in public health practice offers a broad-based, comprehensive, graduate level public health curriculum designed for health professionals currently working in the field. It is accredited by the Council on Education for Public Health (CEPH). Working health professional may expand their knowledge base in public health, extend and sharpen their professional skills, broaden their perspective of public health problems, and prepare to assume greater professional responsibility. The M.P.H. curriculum is designed to enable health care professionals to earn this advanced degree while engaged in professional activities. Students may complete the 36-credit program in three years.

The Professional M.B.A. program is a fully accredited (American Assembly of Collegiate Schools of Business [AACSB]), accelerated program for professionals who want to continue their education in the management field but cannot attend traditional classes because of full-time career commitments. Those individuals without an undergraduate business degree or extensive managerial experience are required to enroll in an additional introductory "Foundations of Business" course. The 37-credit program must be completed in three years.

The RN to Bachelor of Science (Nursing) is designed to meet the educational goals of Massachusetts Registered Nurses. Self-paced modules, lectures, seminars, simulated laboratory, independent study, Web-enhanced courses, and clinical practice are all used. Under faculty guidance, students provide nursing care to clients of all ages and develop skills in critical thinking, leadership, and research utilization.

The Bachelor of Science in hotel, restaurant, and travel administration

(HRTA) is for working adults, both international and domestic, who are unable to pursue a residential degree program on the Amherst Campus. The program integrates a variety of courses in the humanities and social and physical sciences, with a heavy concentration of business and hospitality/tourism courses. The UMass Amherst HRTA program is currently ranked fourth (Princeton Review's Gourman Report) among the more than 200 four-year hospitality management programs in the nation. It is one of 37 four-year hospitality management programs accredited by Accreditation Commission for Programs in Hospitality Administration (ACPHA).

The Certificate of Individual Study in arts management, a five-course series, can be earned entirely online. The courses teach strategic planning, board development, fundraising, marketing, basic financial management, and arts programming. The courses may also be taken for University of Massachusetts undergraduate credit.

## SPECIAL PROGRAMS

The certificate of individual study in arts management, a six-course series, can be earned entirely online. The certificate is a valuable professional development opportunity for arts managers as well as people employed by nonprofit organizations or agencies. The six courses teach strategic planning, board development, fundraising, marketing, basic financial management, and arts programming. The courses feature written and audio lectures, job-related field assignments, references, bulletin board, links to online resources, and chat rooms. Students communicate with each other and faculty members through e-mail, fax, mail, and telephone. The courses may also be taken for University of Massachusetts undergraduate credit.

## STUDENT SERVICES

Academic advisers are available by phone, e-mail, fax, and in person to assist students in course selection, transfer credit evaluation, and academic matters. Continuing Education has its own registration and business offices which can provide assistance with registration, transcripts, financial aid, and billings.

## CREDIT OPTIONS

Students may request a transcript evaluation and, upon approval, transfer credits earned at other accredited postsecondary schools to UMass. Credits may also be earned through the College Level Examination Program (CLEP) or through independent study. Credits earned through distance education are University of Massachusetts credits, and upon acceptance, may be transferred to other colleges and universities.

## FACULTY

The distance education faculty for graduate programs comprises UMass faculty members who hold doctorates or terminal degrees in their respective fields. Undergraduate and noncredit courses may be taught by doctorate-holding faculty members, graduate teaching assistants, or qualified adjunct faculty members.

## ADMISSION

The UMass Amherst Division of Continuing Education allows any person with a high school diploma or its equivalent to register for noncredit or undergraduate courses. Students must have a bachelor's degree to be admitted to a graduate degree program. It is possible to enroll in graduate-level courses and receive credit toward a bachelor's degree. Some courses may require prerequisite college-level work. Students may enroll in courses before being formally admitted to a degree program. Up to 6 credits may be taken as a nondegree graduate student and transferred to a degree program later. Enrollment does not imply acceptance into a degree program. For graduate degree programs, admission to the University's Graduate School is required.

## TUITION AND FEES

Fees vary depending on whether the course offered is noncredit or for credit and whether the level of that credit is undergraduate or graduate. Generally, a noncredit course costs from $200 to $350, while an undergraduate course costs from $200 to $250 per credit; graduate-level courses vary in cost from $200 to $600 per credit. All students, regardless of residency, pay the same tuition.

## FINANCIAL AID

Availability of financial aid varies depending on course status and matriculation. Financial assistance is available from employers, TERI Continuing Education loans, and for eligible military personnel under the G.I. Bill.

## APPLYING

Students can find information on application and registration procedures for degree programs and individual courses on the UMass Amherst virtual campus Web site listed below.

### CONTACT

Kevin Aiken, Director
Division of Continuing Education
University of Massachusetts
Box 31650
Amherst, Massachusetts 01003-1650
Telephone: 413-545-2111
Fax: 413-545-3351
E-mail: kaiken@admin.umass.edu
Web site: http://www.umass.edu/continued
http://UMAmherstOnline.Org

# University of Massachusetts Boston

## *Division of Corporate, Continuing and Distance Education*

Boston, Massachusetts

*The University of Massachusetts (UMass) Boston was founded in 1964 and is the second largest campus in the University of Massachusetts system, with more than 13,000 students in its undergraduate, graduate, and continuing education programs. Through its five colleges—the College of Arts and Sciences, the College of Management, the College of Nursing, the College of Public and Community Service, and the Graduate College of Education— UMass Boston offers undergraduate and graduate study in more than 150 fields, and awards the Ph.D., the Ed.D., the C.A.G.S., the M.A., M.B.A., M.Ed., M.S., B.A., and B.S. degrees, and several graduate certificates. The Division of Corporate, Continuing and Distance Education, founded in 1981, administers the University's summer, winter, and weekend course schedules; delivers courses at a number of off-campus sites, including international locations; and offers Web-based as well as interactive video distance education opportunities. The University of Massachusetts Boston is accredited by the New England Association of Schools and Colleges.*

## DISTANCE LEARNING PROGRAM

UMass Boston's distance learning programs are rapidly expanding in response to increasing demand and technological innovation. The programs fall into two categories: on-line (Web-based) courses, and classroom courses delivered to remote sites via videoconferencing technology. All courses are developed and taught by resident and adjunct UMass Boston faculty members and maintain the same high standard as all other University courses.

## DELIVERY MEDIA

UMass Boston's Web-based courses are open to students throughout the world who meet the prerequisites. Courses follow a semester-based calendar, but students "attend" when and where they wish. Students interact with the instructor via e-mail, chat rooms, telephone, fax, and mail. Courses include exercises, read-ings, projects, online discussions, chat rooms, live chat, illustrations and video. As an enrichment of the online learning experience, most classes offer optional on-campus class meetings. Students unable to attend are given alternative opportunities for enrichment.

## PROGRAMS OF STUDY

Undergraduate and graduate courses from a variety of disciplines are offered. Some are required or elective courses in the following campus-based certificate programs: adapting curriculum frameworks for all learners, communications, fundamentals of computing, instructional design, and technical writing. The University assumes that students registering for undergraduate courses can accurately assess their ability to do college-level work. It is the responsibility of students to meet prerequisites for individual courses. Certain courses, as their descriptions indicate, cannot be taken without special permission. Students who have not formally been admitted into UMass Boston graduate programs may enroll in online graduate courses, providing they hold a bachelor's degree and meet course prerequisites. Some courses also require permission from the appropriate graduate program director.

Disciplines offering online undergraduate courses in a typical semester include accounting/finance, computer science, information technology, management, and political science. Disciplines offering online graduate courses in a typical semester include applied linguistics, counseling, education, instructional design, management, nursing, and vocational/technical education.

Enrollment in online courses does not imply admission to a UMass Boston degree or certificate program. Successfully completed online courses may be applied towards a UMass Boston degree upon acceptance and credits earned in these courses are normally accepted as transfer credits by other colleges and universities.

## STUDENT SERVICES

Academic advisers are available by phone, e-mail, fax, and in person to assist students in course selection, application to a degree program, and other academic matters. The Corporate, Continuing and Distance Education Office assists students with registration, payment, and transcript issues.

## CREDIT OPTIONS

Online courses carry the same academic credit as courses offered on-campus and may, upon admission, be counted toward on-campus degree or certificate requirements or, upon acceptance, be transferred to other colleges and universities.

## FACULTY

Online courses are taught by resident and adjunct UMass Boston faculty members who also teach on campus sections of the same course. They generally hold doctorate or terminal degrees in their field and many have achieved national and international recognition.

## ADMISSION

The University assumes that students registering for undergraduate courses can accurately assess their ability to do college-level work. It is the responsibility of students to meet prerequisites for individual courses. Certain courses, as their descriptions indicate, cannot be taken without special permission. Students who have not formally been admitted into UMass Boston graduate programs may enroll in online graduate courses, providing they hold a bachelor's degree and meet course prerequisites. Some courses also require permission from the appropriate graduate program director.

Students who take courses before entering UMass Boston degree programs may apply up to 16 credits earned before matriculation, or 6 graduate credits, to UMass Boston degree requirements.

## TUITION AND FEES

Tuition for online courses for the academic year 2001–02 is $650 for a 3-credit undergraduate course and $695 for a 3-credit graduate course. There is also a $45 registration and service fee per semester. All students, regardless of residency, pay the same tuition and fees.

## FINANCIAL AID

Matriculated students enrolled in 6 or more credits per semester are eligible to apply for financial aid. UMass Boston's Financial Aid Services Office provides assistance in the processing of grants, scholarships, loans, and college work-study awards.

## APPLYING

Students can find information on registration procedures for online courses through the UMass Boston distance learning Web sites, listed below.

---

### CONTACT

Kitty Galaitsis
Division of Corporate, Continuing and Distance Education
University of Massachusetts Boston
100 Morrissey Boulevard
Boston, Massachusetts 02125-3393
Telephone: 617-287-7925
Fax: 617-287-7297
E-mail: kitty.galaitsis@umb.edu
Web site: http://www.umassbostononline.net
http://www.conted.umb.edu/dl

# University of Massachusetts Dartmouth

## CyberEd
Westport, Massachusetts

*The University of Massachusetts Dartmouth (UMass Dartmouth) is a publicly supported coeducational institution of higher learning, fully accredited by the New England Association of Schools and Colleges. There are approximately 7,500 day and evening students enrolled in graduate and undergraduate degree programs. UMass Dartmouth is part of the five-campus University of Massachusetts.*

## DISTANCE LEARNING PROGRAM

CyberEd, a pioneering Web-based learning program begun in 1995, is intended to extend the basic mission of the University to the global audience of the Internet as well as provide more flexible access to regional students. Approximately 500 students enroll annually in the CyberEd courses delivered primarily over the Internet. There are several important changes affecting CyberEd. The latest information is available at the CyberEd Web site: http://cybered.umassd.edu.

The University system has begun UMass Online which is the University's global gateway to all its online courses.

UMass Dartmouth has begun the development of academic minor and degree programs to be offered through UMass Online/CyberEd.

CyberEd now includes some courses that are taught partially on campus and partially online to provide the most accessible and best learning environment possible. Courses with such an on-campus component are clearly identified as such on the Web site.

## DELIVERY MEDIA

CyberEd courses are delivered primarily through the Internet using the World Wide Web. Students are ex-

pected to have a computer, Internet connection, e-mail, and a Web browser. With these they can access course materials from home or office, as well as communicate with instructors and other students in real-time (chat) or asynchronously through Web discussion groups and e-mail lists. While many courses make use of Web resources, textbooks are also required. In a few instances students may mail in assignments. Some courses require one or more field trips or face-to-face meetings on campus. Such cases are clearly stated in the course description on the CyberEd Web site.

The typical CyberEd student interacts from a home or office computer, following his or her own schedule but keeping up with the weekly pace of the class. In most CyberEd classes students are given assignments for a week or more at a time and the students choose when in the week they will work on the assignment.

Most communications between students and faculty members or other students is handled asynchronously; the participants are not required to be online at the same time. Thus the class e-mail list and Web discussion board are critical tools for interaction. While the class may have scheduled "chats," these are almost always optional. In some instances faculty members post virtual office hours when they will be available via chat to answer student questions.

A few courses, aimed at a regional audience, combine the flexibility of Internet-based content and interaction with relevant face-to-face meetings.

## PROGRAMS OF STUDY

CyberEd offers a variety of undergraduate and graduate level courses, as well as noncredit courses. Two programs are currently under development, an RN–B.S.N. program for nurses in the region, and a women's studies minor, and more are anticipated in the near future. In addition there are courses in such diverse areas as chemistry, history, astronomy, and professional writing.

The women's studies minor builds on an existing campus-based program, but will be available entirely over the Internet. The minor brings together the resources of the traditional academic disciplines to explore women's place in society. The minor consists of 18-credit hours taken in diverse fields. The new online version of the minor will include the critical perspective of women and cyberculture. Along with academic content, the minor will provide skills and access to technology, model its use, and teach the implications of it for women.

The RN–B.S.N. program gives registered nurses in the region the opportunity to advance their professional knowledge and receive a Bachelor of Science in Nursing degree. This program, which will be largely online, builds on the existing campus-based program in the College of Nursing. This will use a hybrid model of educational experiences. The Internet will be used for much of the instruction, but where face-to-face meetings are the best instructional choice, they will be used.

In addition to the credit offerings, CyberEd has an established Online Communications Skills noncredit certificate program. This is a series of seven-week, noncredit courses teaching the development of Web sites and related technologies. They are aimed at helping professionals in fields such as design, writing, education, and computer science expand their knowledge in Internet-based technologies.

## STUDENT SERVICES

Distance learning students have access to academic advising through e-mail and telephone.

Credit options Students should check the Web site, http://cybered.umassd.edu, for news on new credit programs.

## FACULTY

Faculty members participating in CyberEd are most often the same UMass Dartmouth faculty members who teach similar courses on campus.

Admissions Any person who has graduated from high school or holds a Certificate of General Education Development (GED) is entitled to enroll in undergraduate courses. Students may enroll in a single course or a number of courses simultaneously. All must enroll online. Anyone can enroll in a noncredit course.

## TUITION AND FEES

For three-credit courses, tuition and fees, including the registration fee are as follows: One course, undergraduate, $445; graduate, $520; two courses, undergraduate, $865; graduate, $1015; and three courses, undergraduate, $1285; graduate, $1510.

## FINANCIAL AID

A full range of financial aid programs, including grants, low-interest loans, and scholarships will be available to those enrolled in degree programs.

## APPLYING

Students should visit the Web site at the address listed below for the latest information on new programs and application procedures.

---

**CONTACT**

Greg Stone
Coordinator, CyberEd
University of Massachusetts Dartmouth
North Dartmouth, Massachusetts 02747
Telephone: 508-999-8077
E-mail: gstone@umassd.edu
Web site: http://cybered.umass.edu

---

# University of Massachusetts Lowell

## Undergraduate and Graduate
## Distance Learning Opportunities

Lowell, Massachusetts

*The University of Massachusetts Lowell (UMass Lowell) is a comprehensive university committed to providing students with the education and skills they need for continued success throughout their lives. Specializing in applied science and technology, the University conducts research and outreach activities that add great value to the entire region. The second largest of the University of Massachusetts campuses, Lowell currently offers its 13,000 undergraduate and graduate students more than 100 different degree programs in the Colleges of Arts and Sciences, Education, Engineering, Health Professions, and Management. The UMass Lowell Continuing Studies and Corporate Education (CSCE), which includes the evening and summer schools of the University, is one of the largest continuing education programs in New England. Credit courses lead to associate, baccalaureate, and graduate-level degrees and certificate programs in specialized technical or professional areas.*

## DISTANCE LEARNING PROGRAM

The University of Massachusetts Lowell utilizes a variety of interactive distance learning technologies to provide both undergraduate and graduate students with unique opportunities to pursue lifelong learning. The CyberEd program, offered through the University's Continuing Studies and Corporate Education Division, is one of New England's largest accredited online providers of undergraduate and graduate courses, degrees, and certificates to students from around the world. By accessing course materials and interacting with faculty members and classmates via the Internet and the World Wide Web, CyberEd students are able to learn at a time and location convenient to them.

The UMass Lowell Instructional Network offers a variety of programming to K–12 school districts, Massachusetts community colleges, and other universities within the UMass system. Students at remote locations can interact with the originating site instructor and students via bidirectional communications. The University is equipped with multiple state-of-the-art distance learning classrooms that can accommodate numerous teaching techniques, such as computer-generated presentations, laser discs, the Internet and World Wide Web, and CD-ROMs.

## DELIVERY MEDIA

The CyberEd program uses the World Wide Web, e-mail, chat, and other Internet resources to provide a meaningful learning experience for students and faculty members. Students access class lectures via a Web site, participate in online chats and discussion forums, and work collaboratively to fulfill course requirements.

The UML Instructional Network utilizes an array of transmission technologies to deliver programming to remote audiences, including satellite uplink, line of sight microwave, dedicated fiber-optic analog video, compressed video via ATM, ISDN, and consumer cable connections via public and educational access channels. The delivery method is dependent on the intended audience's capability and the course content.

The University is currently developing mixed-media classes, which incorporate a blend of interactive video classrooms with Internet-based chat, e-mail, and Web resources. These new courses provide opportunities for face-to-face interaction in addition to the benefits of asynchronous communication.

## PROGRAMS OF STUDY

Students who are enrolled in the CyberEd program can pursue an online associate or bachelor's degree in information systems, a Bachelor of Liberal Arts degree, or a master's degree in educational administration or choose from seven online certificate programs in Intranet Development, UNIX, Fundamentals of Information Technology, Data/Telecommunications, Multimedia Applications, Clinical Pathology (graduate level), and Photonics and Optoelectronics (graduate level). Many of the courses taken toward the certificates can also be applied toward the online degree programs. Courses are offered during the fall, spring, and summer semesters.

Graduate-level courses in education, civil engineering, and plastics engineering are also offered across the UML Instructional Network. A collaborative effort between UMass Lowell and UMass Boston now provides students on both campuses with a wider selection when choosing philosophy or communication electives to fulfill their program requirements. High school students also have the opportunity to begin accumulating college credits while fulfilling their requirements for graduation in biology, chemistry, computer science, and math.

## SPECIAL PROGRAMS

In collaboration with Nortel Networks, Continuing Studies and Corporate Education offers a customized Certificate in Data Telecommunications. Students complete the certificate by taking some courses via CyberEd and additional courses through authorized Nortel Networks global training operations. The University is also actively exploring additional corporate partnerships that will greatly increase student access to state-of-the-art programs. Corporate students in particular find that online courses offer them the convenience to complete the courses from work or home.

The UML Instructional Network is engaged in several special programs that support the development of K–12 teachers and their students. Professional development opportunities are broadcast for K–12 teachers, who are then able to attend graduate-level courses and PDP workshops from the convenience of their own school. A FIPSE Pre-service Teachers grant, Looking Into Classrooms, supports the group observation of mentor teachers via two-way television. The biannual Nuclear Reactor Irradiation Experiment allows area high school students to participate in a series of experiments, including those at the University's research reactor, from the safety of their classrooms.

## STUDENT SERVICES

Students can enroll in distance learning courses by telephone, fax, mail, or in person. The Advising Center provides online, telephone, and on-campus counseling regarding course selection, choice of majors, and other academic questions. Online library resources are available to students via the University's proxy server. All students are eligible for e-mail accounts on the University mail server, and students enrolled in programming courses are provided with additional remote access to University computing resources. The UMass Lowell bookstore provides telephone and online book ordering, and all CyberEd students have access to password-protected Web sites, chat rooms, bulletin boards, and other applicable collaborative environments.

Course descriptions, curriculum worksheets, certificate and degree programs, application forms, and a schedule of courses are all available on the UMass Lowell CSCE Web site.

## CREDIT OPTIONS

In general, the University of Massachusetts Lowell accepts semester credits with grades of C- (1.7 on a 4.0 scale) or better as shown on official transcripts on an hour-for-hour basis. In addition, other options for students include transfer credit, credit by exam, and independent study.

## FACULTY

All distance learning courses offered by the University are taught by its full- or part-time adjunct faculty members. All of the distance learning faculty members are required to attend training that instructs them how to best modify their course materials and facilitate communication and interaction among their students. Faculty biographies, contact information, and course syllabi are available for all CyberEd students at the CyberEd Web site.

## ADMISSION

Admission requirements for UMass Lowell's various programs can be found at UMass Lowell's CSCE Web site.

## TUITION AND FEES

Current information on tuition and fees for the graduate and undergraduate courses can be found at UMass Lowell's CSCE Web site.

## FINANCIAL AID

Availability of financial aid depends upon the matriculated status of the students. Further information is available at UMass Lowell's CSCE Web site.

## APPLYING

Students can find information on application and registration procedures for individual courses on UMass Lowell's CSCE Web site.

---

### CONTACT

Catherine Kendrick, Director of Corporate and Distance Market Development
Continuing Studies and Corporate Education
University of Massachusetts Lowell
Lowell, Massachusetts 01854
Telephone: 978-934-2495
E-mail: Catherine_Kendrick@uml.edu
UMass Lowell CSCE Web site: http://continuinged.uml.edu/

Mike Lucas, Coordinator of Distance Learning
UMass Lowell Instructional Network
College of Education
University of Massachusetts Lowell
255 Princeton Street
North Chelmsford, Massachusetts 01863
Telephone: 978-934-4681
E-mail: Michael_Lucas@uml.edu

For CyberEd:
Telephone: 800-480-3190 (toll-free)
E-mail: cybered@uml.edu
Web site: http://cybered.uml.edu

# University of Minnesota, Twin Cities Campus

## Independent and Distance Learning, University College

Minneapolis, Minnesota

---

*The University, with its four campuses, is one of the most comprehensive universities in the country and ranks among the top twenty universities in the United States. It is both a land-grant university with a strong tradition of education and public service and a major research institution. It was founded as a preparatory school in 1851 and was reorganized as a university in 1869, benefiting from the Morrill (or Land-Grant) Act of 1862.*

*The University of Minnesota has campuses in the Twin Cities (Minneapolis and St. Paul), Duluth, Morris, and Crookston, Minnesota. The Twin Cities campus is made up of nineteen colleges and offers 172 bachelor's degrees, 198 master's degrees, 116 doctoral degrees, and five professional degrees.*

## DISTANCE LEARNING PROGRAM

Independent and Distance Learning (IDL) offers outstanding university credit courses using mail and electronic technologies. In a recent year, the department received approximately 5,000 registrations from students throughout the United States and abroad. The 150 courses are fully accredited each year by approximately fifty different academic departments of the University. IDL is part of the College of Continuing Education (CCE), the division of the University of Minnesota that serves adult and part-time learners.

## DELIVERY MEDIA

Most courses are self-paced and available by mail for home study and mail lesson exchange with faculty members. Many faculty members provide the option of e-mail for lesson exchange. A growing number of online courses are fully interactive and take place in fixed semester terms. All students who register for college credit with Independent and Distance Learning receive an e-mail and Internet account.

## PROGRAMS OF STUDY

Approximately 150 credit courses are offered in a wide range of academic departments, including such varied subjects as applied business, child psychology, ecology, English literature and writing courses, management, math, and theater. Two science courses come with home lab kits: general biology and elementary physics. Independent and Distance Learning courses are known for their high academic quality and variety of topics. There are no degree or certificate programs available.

## STUDENT SERVICES

Student Support Services offers academic, financial aid, and career counseling. Academic advising can help students determine prerequisites and academic standing, evaluate transcripts, choose courses, and evaluate the applicability of IDL credits to University of Minnesota specific degree and certificate programs.

University of Minnesota libraries fully support distance learners with reference services, research assistance, and home delivery of documents.

If students have a disability, Independent and Distance Learning coordinates efforts to provide accommodations that remove academic and physical barriers to earning credits. Such accommodations may include more time to complete exams or an alternate format for an exam, a separate testing room, audiotaping required materials, and taped rather than written comments from an instructor. Requests for such accommodations should be made well in advance of when they are needed so that necessary documentation may be obtained and accommodations facilitated.

## FACULTY

IDL has approximately 80 faculty members. Approximately 40 percent are University of Minnesota professors, 30 percent are graduate student teaching assistants, and 30 percent are adjunct faculty members, lecturers, or others. All professors and many adjunct faculty members hold doctorates or other terminal degrees.

## ADMISSION

There are no admission requirements to register for courses through Independent and Distance Learning.

## TUITION AND FEES

All registrants, regardless of location, qualify for in-state tuition rates. Tuition for 2000–01 was $163 per semester credit. A materials/services fee of $54 per course enrollment is assessed. Course study guides are included in the fee. Texts and other materials may be purchased from the Minnesota Book Center at the University of Minnesota.

## FINANCIAL AID

Financial aid is limited. Eligibility requirements may vary, but most aid programs place restrictions on some types of IDL enrollment and require admission to a University of Minnesota, Twin Cities degree program or eligible certificate program. Non-admitted students who reside in Minnesota may be eligible for College of Continuing Education grants or scholarships, which have more flexible eligibility criteria. Employer assistance may also be an option for some students.

## APPLYING

No application is needed to register in individual courses.

## CONTACT

Student Support Services, University College
150 Wesbrook Hall
University of Minnesota
77 Pleasant Street, SE
Minneapolis, Minnesota 55455
Telephone: 612-624-4000
         800-234-6564 (toll-free)
Fax: 612-625-1511
E-mail: indstudy@umn.edu
Web site: http://www.idl.umn.edu

# University of Missouri-Columbia

## Center for Distance and Independent Study

Columbia, Missouri

Established in 1839 as the first public university west of the Mississippi River, the University of Missouri (UM) has a rich history of benefiting the state, the nation, and the world through its land-grant mission of teaching, research, and service. With a comprehensive array of majors and programs, including undergraduate, graduate, and professional degrees, many of the University's departments and schools rank among the nation's foremost. Among its four campuses in Columbia, Kansas City, Rolla, and St. Louis, the University enrolls more than 55,000 students, a growing number of whom learn at a distance. Often cited as one of the nation's best higher education values, the University is accredited by the North Central Association of Colleges and Schools as well as other leading accrediting organizations.

## DISTANCE LEARNING PROGRAM

Since 1911, the Center for Distance and Independent Study (CDIS), a unit of the University of Missouri–Columbia Extension, has demonstrated its commitment to lifelong learning by providing individually paced independent study courses to those students who cannot or choose not to enroll in traditional classes. Today, with nearly 19,000 enrollments annually, the Center is one of the largest and most respected education programs in the nation.

In addition to its graduate and undergraduate University courses, the center operates the University of Missouri–Columbia High School. The school offers approximately 150 high school courses, including a college preparatory curriculum with challenging courses for gifted students. CDIS also provides a curriculum, which covers grades three through eight, for families who desire to home school or enroll their children in supplemental course work.

## DELIVERY MEDIA

Students who enroll in a CDIS course have access to a study guide containing lessons and instructions necessary to complete the course. CDIS courses may utilize written materials (either printed or online), audiotapes, videotapes, computer disks, and/or CD-ROMs. All required course materials, which are listed as part of the course description, are available through the Center's bookstore.

Lessons for many CDIS courses are computer evaluated. Students may submit lessons by mail or via the Internet for immediate response. Faculty-evaluated courses may be submitted by mail, e-mail, fax, or online, depending on the nature of the assignment.

A growing number of courses allow students to access their study guides online. All lessons and instructions needed to complete these courses are accessible on the World Wide Web; if supplementary materials are required, they can be purchased through the Center's bookstore.

## PROGRAMS OF STUDY

Students may earn graduate or undergraduate credit, ranging from 2 to 6 hours, for each independent study course they complete. The Center for Distance and Independent Study awards the high school diploma, but does not award degrees. Other University of Missouri programs offer degrees via online study and interactive television. Students may use credit earned through independent study to achieve their specific educational goals in these and other programs.

Independent study courses have been approved by faculty members from the appropriate academic department at one of the four University of Missouri campuses. The Center offers approximately 160 University courses, graduate and undergraduate level, in a wide range of subject areas, including accountancy, animal sciences, anthropology, atmospheric science, biological and agricultural engineering, black studies, classical studies, communication, computer science, consumer and family economics, criminology and criminal justice, economics, education, engineering, English, entomology, geography, geology, German and Russian studies, health services management, history, human development and family studies, management, marketing, mathematics, military science, music, peace studies, philosophy, physical education, plant science, political science, psychology, Romance languages, rural sociology, sociology, statistics, and women's studies.

## SPECIAL PROGRAMS

The Center for Distance and Independent Study offers approximately thirty graduate and undergraduate education courses designed to provide specialized learning to teachers, counselors, and administrators. Teachers use graduate-level courses for certification and salary improvement. Twelve education courses are special-topics courses that incorporate textbook materials and videotapes. In order to successfully complete these courses, students must attend a weekend seminar conducted by the course instructor.

CDIS continues to add online courses in addition to taught courses. Twenty-four online courses are currently available at the university level and 40 at the high school level. One of the newest offerings, Teachers and the Law (589TL Special Topics in Educational Leadership), provides a comprehensive overview of education law to give teachers an understanding of the many legal issues affecting their professional lives. Topics range from school safety to employment law.

The Center has been providing courses to military personnel through the Defense Activity for Non-Traditional Education Support (DANTES) program for twenty years. Members of the U.S. Armed Forces, on active duty or in a reserve component, who desire to continue their education on a part-time basis outside of the traditional classroom environment are eligible to enroll in independent study. Information concerning enrollment is available in the DANTES Independent Study Catalog.

## STUDENT SERVICES

The Center maintains a student services office with a toll-free number (800-609-3727) for students needing distance education curriculum information. Students may access information, request a catalog, enroll, check the status of their courses, submit lessons, request a course exam, and send questions or comments via the World Wide Web at http://cdis.missouri.edu.

## CREDIT OPTIONS

It is possible for students to earn graduate or undergraduate credit,

ranging from 2 to 6 hours, for each independent study course they complete. While the Center for Distance and Independent Study does not award degrees, University credit earned through independent study can be applied toward a degree or used to achieve other educational goals a student may have.

## FACULTY

More than 3,500 faculty members are employed on the University of Missouri's four campuses. Each university-level distance education course is created by a faculty member or by an author who has been approved by the appropriate UM academic department. The Center employs approximately 70 instructors to grade its University courses; most of these instructors have doctoral or other terminal degrees.

## ADMISSION

There are no admission requirements for students enrolling in a CDIS course. Students may enroll at any time of the year and take up to nine months to complete each course. A three-month extension is available upon request.

## TUITION AND FEES

During 2001–02, tuition at the Center is $141.50 per credit hour for undergraduate credit and $179.10 per credit hour for graduate credit. Every enrollment requires payment of tuition and a nonrefundable $15 handling fee. Textbooks and audiovisual materials rental/deposit fees, sales tax, and other fees may also be included.

## FINANCIAL AID

Scholarships and other forms of financial aid are not available through

the Center for Distance and Independent Study; however, some business firms and organizations encourage employees to continue their education by paying part or all of their tuition and fees. Individuals should consult their employer to see if funding for distance education is available.

CDIS University courses are approved for veterans and other persons eligible under the provisions of the GI Bill. The Veterans Administration reimburses independent study fees to students after it receives a certificate of enrollment from the Center.

## APPLYING

Students may enroll in a Center for Distance and Independent Study course by submitting the completed application and textbook order form by mail, in person, by phone, fax, or via the World Wide Web. Payment for CDIS courses must accompany course enrollment and can be made by credit card, check, or money order.

---

### CONTACT

Terrie Nagel
Student Services Adviser
Center for Distance and
    Independent Study
136 Clark Hall
University of Missouri
Columbia, Missouri 65211-4200
Telephone: 800-609-3727 (toll-
    free)
Fax: 573-882-6808
E-mail: cdis@missouri.edu
Web site: http://cdis.missouri.edu

---

# University of Nevada, Reno

## College of Extended Studies
## Independent Learning Program

Reno, Nevada

---

Established in 1864, the University of Nevada first offered classes in 1874 in Elko, Nevada. In 1885, the campus was moved to Reno with 2 faculty members and 50 students. Today, the University of Nevada, Reno is the oldest of seven institutions in the University and Community College System of Nevada.

A land-grant university with an enrollment of approximately 12,500 students in ten schools and colleges, the University of Nevada, Reno offers a wide range of undergraduate and graduate programs, including selected doctoral and professional studies. The University emphasizes programs and activities that best serve the needs of the state, region, and nation. More than one fourth of students enrolled are pursuing advanced degrees. The University encourages and supports faculty research and its application to state and national problems and conducts more than $70 million in research grants and contracts each year.

The 255-acre campus is located just north of Interstate 80 near the majestic Sierra Nevada range and Lake Tahoe. The University of Nevada, Reno is an integral part of the thriving Reno-Sparks metropolitan area, home to about 311,000 people. With its blend of ivy-covered buildings, sweeping lawns, and functional, progressive architecture, the University's academic atmosphere is filled with rich surroundings for the cultural and intellectual development of students.

The University of Nevada, Reno is an Equal Opportunity/Affirmative Action, ADA institution. The University of Nevada, Reno is accredited by the Northwest Association of Schools and Colleges Commission on Colleges and recognized by the Council on Postsecondary Accreditation and the U.S. Department of Education.

## DISTANCE LEARNING PROGRAM

The Independent Learning Program at the University of Nevada, Reno offers an individualized method of learning and a flexible way to earn University credit. Students who are unable to attend on-campus courses due to location, scheduling conflicts, work, or other commitments can choose from more than 100 academic credit courses in twenty-nine subject areas, as well as high school and noncredit offerings. Students may enroll any day of the year and take up to one year to complete a course. Enrollment is accepted via the Web; by mail, phone, or fax; or in person.

## PROGRAM OF STUDY

The University of Nevada, Reno is the sole provider of university credit through independent study in the state of Nevada. Academic credit courses are offered from the University of Nevada, Reno and the University of Nevada, Las Vegas. Courses for high school credit, continuing education units, and noncredit are also available. Undergraduate credit courses are offered in twenty-nine subject areas, which include accounting, anthropology, Basque studies, criminal justice, curriculum and instruction, economics, educational leadership, English, environment, French, gaming management, geography, German, health science,

health-care administration, history, hotel administration, human development/family studies, Italian, journalism, managerial sciences, mathematics, nutrition, political science, psychology, sociology, Spanish, Western traditions, and women's studies. Graduate credit is available in educational leadership, human development/family studies, and Basque studies. All credit courses have been approved by departments and colleges of the University of Nevada, Reno and the University of Nevada, Las Vegas. High School credit courses meet Nevada State Department of Education approval.

## DELIVERY MEDIA

Instruction is given by means of a course syllabus, textbooks, video and audio cassettes (where appropriate), and additional reference and instructional materials. Lessons are accepted via mail, fax, and e-mail. After review by the course instructor, work is returned to students. A number of online correspondence courses are available. No classroom attendance is necessary for correspondence study courses. All courses have a final examination, which must be taken in a proctored setting; many courses have two or three progress examinations. Students who reside away from campus may take examinations using an approved proctor in their area.

## SPECIAL PROGRAMS

New online courses are a convenient way to study at home and communicate with instructors via the Internet. Some classes also include a listserv feature, so students can join a mail group, ask questions of fellow online students, and discuss course topics.

## STUDENT SERVICES

All textbooks, videotapes, and course materials are mailed directly to students anywhere in the world. Returning lessons for grading uses convenient e-mail or fax services or traditional mail and air mail. Independent Learning students who live in the Reno area can take full advantage of the many student services available on the University of Nevada, Reno campus; these services include tutoring, math centers, academic counseling, and support group information for nontraditional students. Local students can also receive library and computer lab privileges and use the library's video loan service. Each correspondence study student receives a student handbook upon enrollment with useful information, study tips, and guidelines. The Independent Learning staff is available to answer questions via phone, fax, or e-mail. Information about courses and programs is also included on the Independent Learning Web site, listed below.

## CREDIT OPTIONS

A maximum of 60 credits earned through Independent Learning may be applied toward a University of Nevada, Reno bachelor's degree. The University of Nevada, Las Vegas awards up to a maximum of 15 semester hours of credit through Independent Learning toward a degree. Students interested in transfer credit may contact the University's Transfer Center office (telephone: 775-784-6230) for more information. Grades for all completed credit courses are recorded on a University transcript, which may be ordered from the University.

## FACULTY

All instructors for Independent Learning have been approved by departments and colleges of the University of Nevada, Reno and the University of Nevada, Las Vegas. High school faculty members are certified high school teachers in Nevada high schools or are faculty members at the university or community college level.

## ADMISSION

Formal admission to the University of Nevada, Reno or the University of Nevada, Las Vegas is not required to enroll in Independent Learning courses. Likewise, enrollment in Independent Learning does not constitute admission to either of these universities. Students who wish to apply may contact the University of Nevada, Reno Office of Admissions and Records (telephone: 775-784-6865).

## TUITION AND FEES

The standard course fee for all undergraduate correspondence study courses is $85 per credit. Graduate tuition is $107 per credit. High school courses are $80 per one-half unit course. Textbook costs are not included in the course fee. Additional fees are charged for handling, stationery, syllabus, faxing, and special materials, as well as for air mail, international mail, and Internet courses.

## FINANCIAL AID

Some financial aid may be available to certain qualified individuals through the University of Nevada, Reno Financial Aid Office (telephone: 775-784-4666), where students can call for application deadlines and forms. Independent Learning courses at the University of Nevada, Reno are approved for veterans benefits and for military personnel (DANTES) within or outside the United States.

## APPLYING

Students can enroll any time and take up to one year to complete each course. Instruction by Independent Learning affords students the convenience of studying when and where they choose. Enrollment is accepted via the Web; by mail, phone, or fax; or in person.

---

### CONTACT

Independent Learning Staff
College of Extended Studies/050
University of Nevada, Reno
Reno, Nevada 89557
Telephone: 775-784-4652
        800-233-8928 Ext.
        4652 (toll-free)
Fax: 775-784-1280
E-mail: Istudy@nevada.unr.edu
Web site:
    http://www.dce.unr.edu/istudy

---

# University of New England

## *Certificate of Advanced Graduate Study in Educational Leadership*

Portland, Maine

eCollege.com  *www.ecollege.com*

---

*The University of New England (UNE) is an independent university whose mission it is to educate men and women to advance the quality of human life and the environment. The University was created in 1978 in Biddeford, Maine, by combining St. Francis College and the New England College of Osteopathic Medicine. In 1996 the University merged with Westbrook College, a small liberal arts college in Portland, Maine, giving UNE two distinctive campuses. The University now recognizes Westbrook College's 1831 charter date as the University of New England's founding date.*

*The University is accredited by the New England Association of Schools and Colleges. The Certificate of Advanced Graduate Study in Educational Leadership is approved by the Maine Board of Education to be offered in Maine and elsewhere.*

## DISTANCE LEARNING PROGRAM

Designed and developed for working professionals who aspire to administrative and leadership roles in an educational environment, the Certificate of Advanced Graduate Study (C.A.G.S.) in Educational Leadership provides an innovative and convenient program of study, leading to a post-master's professional credential. The part-time online program offers the self-directed, motivated adult learner the needed flexibility to accommodate a busy lifestyle while pursuing career goals.

Degree candidates in educational leadership join other graduate students at the University continuing their professional education in osteopathic medicine, human services, health and life sciences, management, and education. The online educational leadership program builds on a successful distance learning model—the master's degree in education for experienced teachers has hundreds of students enrolled throughout the country.

## DELIVERY MEDIA

Courses in educational leadership are offered online, so study is convenient and accessible. Students may opt to study at home or in their school environment, wherever they have access to the Internet. With technical support from the University's instructional technology partner, eCollege.com, students quickly become adept with the technology, which is simple and easy to use. There are many opportunities for interaction with faculty mentors and other students, using Internet tools developed and adapted specifically for online learners; these include threaded discussions, online class sessions, and an electronic bulletin board designed for communication from a faculty mentor to the students. Highlighting the program is the one-week residential Integration Seminar, which brings together all of the students in the program for an intensive session offered each summer.

## PROGRAM OF STUDY

The University of New England currently offers the Certificate of Advanced Graduate Study in Educational Leadership in an online format. The curriculum consists of fifteen 3-credit online courses and a one-week residential summer seminar. Five courses, including the seminar, are required; the additional five courses are available as electives. A minimum of ten 3-credit courses must be taken in the University's C.A.G.S. program to be awarded the Advanced Degree. The particular program of study chosen depends upon the existing requirements in the state where students work or seek certification as educational administrators. Students who do not wish to seek the Certificate of Advanced Graduate Study may enroll in an individual course. Up to two courses may be taken as a nonmatriculated student.

The curriculum is designed to apply as broadly as possible to requirements throughout the country; however, it is the responsibility of the candidate to confirm what course content is needed in the state in which certification is sought.

## STUDENT SERVICES

As a part of the University of New England's online campus, students are just a mouse click away from the services and support they need. The certificate program staff and faculty members are ready to advise on course work and program procedures. The graduate student affairs staff assists with student services and institutional policies. The library staff helps in locating and accessing learning materials. The eCollege.com staff members are available 24 hours a day on a helpline for technology-related assistance.

## CREDIT OPTIONS

Upon acceptance to the C.A.G.S. program, students may apply for a transfer of up to two 3-credit post-masters-level courses. For transfer credit to be considered, course work must have been taken following the completion of the master's degree; these must be graduate-level courses. To request a review of course work for transfer credit, students must provide an official transcript for each course, a course description, a syllabus, and a comprehensive student statement supporting the rationale for the transfer request. Courses transferred into the program must be equivalent to courses offered within the program. Transfer of credit is at the discretion of UNE's Department of Education. Students who have been enrolled in UNE's School Leadership program may transfer 6 credits of equivalent work. Students may also receive credit for an additional 6 credits taken in the School Leadership Program and must replace the additional 6 credits with elective courses. The Summer Seminar and Applied Research Project cannot be satisfied through transfer credit, and no credit for experiential learning in lieu of Educational Leadership courses is given.

## FACULTY

The faculty mentors for the program are University professors as well as practicing professionals. All are certified administrators, and the majority have earned an Ed.D. Faculty mentors include talented educators with extensive backgrounds as principals, superintendents, specialists in curriculum development and special services, educational consultants, and guidance supervisors.

## ADMISSION

Applications for admission into the Educational Leadership program are considered as received, and a new cohort begins online every term. Applicants are encouraged to prepare application materials carefully and completely in order to ensure timely action by the admissions committee. Admission criteria for advanced-degree candidacy are a master's degree from an accredited institution; a minimum of three years teaching and/or administrative experience; submission of official scores from the Graduate Record Exam (GRE) (administered by the Educational Testing Service) or the Miller Analogies Test (MAT) (administered by the Psychological Corporation); current employment in an educational setting or have ready access to one; ability to pursue rigorous, online graduate study; interest in continuing professional development and a role in educational leadership; and potential to improve practice through application of new knowledge and skills.

## TUITION AND FEES

Tuition is $900 for a 3-credit course. There is a one-time $150 program fee.

## FINANCIAL AID

There is currently a variety of private loan programs available to educational leadership students. For more information, students should contact the Financial Aid Office (telephone: 207-283-0170 Ext. 2342; fax: 207-282-6379; e-mail: finaid@mailbox.une. edu)

## APPLYING

The application process consists of six steps: completing the application forms (available in paper or online) no later than forty-five days prior to the start of a term (i.e., August 15, December 15, and April 15); submitting the nonrefundable application fee of $40 ($25 for graduates of the University of New England's master's in education program); submitting official transcripts of all graduate work; sending in three letters of recommendation (one must be from a supervisor); writing a personal goal statement; and demonstrating evidence of teaching or administrative experience. An abbreviated online application is required for those applying as non-matriculated students. This admission form enables students to enroll in a single course without formal admission into the University of New England.

---

**CONTACT**

Certificate of Advanced Graduate Study in Educational
   Leadership Program
University of New England
716 Stevens Avenue
Portland, Maine 04103
Telephone: 207-797-7261 Ext. 4360
Fax: 207-878-2434
E-mail: cags@mailbox.une.edu
Web site: http://www.uneonline.org
      http://www.une.edu

# University of Notre Dame, Mendoza College of Business

## *Executive Education*

Notre Dame, Indiana

---

*The University of Notre Dame was founded in 1842 by Rev. Edward F. Sorin, who envisioned a world-renowned educational institution. Achieving this vision is due, in large measure, to an unwavering commitment to research and teaching. The Mendoza College of Business (MCOB) is committed to providing relevant executive education and development.*

*Notre Dame is accredited by the North Central Association, and the Mendoza College of Business is separately accredited at the undergraduate and graduate levels by the AACSB–The International Association for Management Education. The Executive Education programs include the University's flagship Executive M.B.A. program, custom programs, and open-enrollment programs.*

*The Mendoza College of Business originated in 1913 when 6 students enrolled in a series of commercial courses. College status was achieved in 1921. The Master of Business Administration (M.B.A.) was first awarded in 1967 and the Executive M.B.A. in 1982. The distance learning program was implemented in 1995 and currently, there are five off-campus classrooms.*

*Academically, the Executive M.B.A. program provides an excellent all-around executive education experience that prepares individuals for top management and executive positions. The objectives are to provide exceptional knowledge and familiarity with all functional areas of business administration; lead to a thorough understanding of such modern management tools as quantitative methods, computers management information systems, and strategic planning; and practice the techniques of problem identification, problem analysis, and problem solving through models and study teams.*

## DISTANCE LEARNING PROGRAM

The distance learning program combines the high-quality Notre Dame education, first-rate faculty members and resources, and e-learning capabilities with the most effective technology available to deliver programs that are relevant and convenient to the students. Videoconferencing technology is utilized, including T-1 transmission lines, full-motion video, and sophisticated computer systems, to provide a complete real-time, interactive learning environment in all learning centers.

This program enables the University to offer a Notre Dame education to qualified individuals who, geographically, could not travel to the main campus, located in South Bend, Indiana, regularly over the two-year period. These five learning centers are in Motorola University, Schaumburg, Illinois; downtown Chicago, Illinois; Resorts Condominium International (RCI), Indianapolis, Indiana; Owens-Illinois, Toledo, Ohio; and KMK Consulting, L.L.C., Cincinnati, Ohio.

To date, Notre Dame has served hundreds of students who have earned the Executive M.B.A. degree and others who have participated in custom and certificate programs.

The U.S. Distance Learning Association has recognized Notre Dame's distance learning program as the nation's best distance learning program in higher education.

## DELIVERY MEDIA

The Mendoza College of Business faculty members teach all Executive M.B.A. students, using videoconferencing to simultaneously deliver the same high-quality, interactive Executive M.B.A. program offered on campus to the five off-campus classrooms. The College's videoconferencing technology affords the capability to bring students located a great distance from the campus into a "virtual classroom" to enrich the learning experience for all persons involved.

Courses are delivered via videoconferencing and other e-learning technologies. Student interaction with faculty and staff members and other students is facilitated by in-person communication, videoconferencing, audioconferencing, the World Wide Web, e-mail, telephone, fax, and mail.

Although no specific equipment is required, it is expected that individuals are able to effectively use the Internet and e-mail.

## PROGRAMS OF STUDY

The University's Mendoza College of Business offers two different Executive M.B.A.s (EMBAs) and the nondegree custom programs.

The EMBA program, originating in South Bend, is a two-year commitment pursued by managers and executives while they continue to work full-time. This program begins each August and ends with a May graduation two years later. Classes meet Fridays and Saturdays on alternating weekends for four semesters. There are some residency requirements.

The EMBA program, originating in Notre Dame's Chicago Loop, is an eighteen-month commitment pursued by emerging leaders preparing for senior-level executive responsibilities. This program begins each January and ends with graduation at the University of Notre Dame in May 1½ years later. Individuals in this program continue to work full-time. Classes meet Fridays and Saturdays on alternating weekends for three terms. There are residency requirements on the University's South Bend campus as well as courses taught by strategic partners.

In the nondegree custom programs, the College works with a variety of public- and private-sector organizations to design and deliver executive development programs that are tailored to the organization's needs and requirements. Subject areas include leadership development, ethics, change management and innovation, organizational behavior, accounting principles, financial management, e-business, strategic planning, marketing, operations management, and business legal environment.

## STUDENT SERVICES

The Executive Education team is dedicated to supporting and servicing all students—those on and off the main campus. A facilitator is present in every off-campus classroom during every class. This individual ensures a connection to Notre Dame and is responsible for providing a variety of student services. The University does all it can to facilitate the learning process and ensure that everyone has a positive Notre Dame experience. Students are provided access to University library services, the campus computer network, e-mail services, academic counseling, advising and tutoring, and the University bookstore.

## FACULTY

All Mendoza College of Business faculty members teaching in the various Executive Education programs have earned advanced degrees and, with very few exceptions, hold doctoral degrees as well.

All College faculty members teaching in the EMBA and other Executive Education programs are full-time members of the Notre Dame faculty.

## ADMISSION

An Admissions Committee in the Mendoza College of Business evaluates, qualifies, and selects participants for each EMBA class. Serious consideration is given to the following areas, and strong applicants possess at least five years of meaningful management responsibilities; an undergraduate degree; a score on the Test of English as a Foreign Language (TOEFL) for those applicants whose native language is not English; the motivation, commitment, and employer and family support necessary to attend classes, participate, and prepare assignments; and a registrar's transcript of previously completed college-level education as listed on the application form.

Applicants without an undergraduate degree are required to take the Graduate Management Admission Test (GMAT), and consideration may be given to unusual career success as a partial substitute for undergraduate work. International applicants must arrange for TOEFL scores to be reported to Notre Dame.

Applicants may be asked to take the GMAT or a specific class to demonstrate entrance qualifications.

Participants need the concurrence of their employer, since class attendance requires some time away from the job.

After the Admissions Committee has carefully examined the application, they may ask for additional information before a final decision is made.

## TUITION AND FEES

Tuition for the EMBA program is currently $29,320 per year. Tuition for corporate-sponsored non-degree–custom programs varies by program.

## FINANCIAL AID

Financial aid is available. Prospective students should contact the Executive Education office listed below.

## APPLYING

Upon completion of the application form, applicants should send it, together with a $50 nonrefundable application fee (checks should be made payable to the University of Notre Dame) and official copies of college-level transcripts, to Executive Education, 126 Mendoza College of Business, Notre Dame, Indiana 46556-5646.

Individuals interested in being considered for participation in the EMBA program are asked to complete the application. Those interested in early admission must submit their complete application and fees by March 30. Applications are accepted through June 1; however, class size is limited, and space may not be available for persons whose applications are received after June 1.

At the beginning of each fall term, students in the EMBA program are required to be in residence (on Notre Dame's main campus in South Bend, Indiana) for six days to be oriented and attend class and activities.

# The University of Oklahoma

## *College of Continuing Education*

Norman, Oklahoma

---

*The University of Oklahoma's (OU) College of Continuing Education (CCE) is a lifelong learning organization dedicated to helping individuals, businesses, groups, and communities transform themselves through knowledge. Formally organized in 1913, CCE is the outreach arm of the University of Oklahoma. Nationally recognized for its pioneering efforts in continuing education, CCE extends the educational resources of the University through more than thirty different program formats, including graduate and undergraduate degree programs, correspondence and other distance programs, on- and off-campus courses, and a wide variety of programs conducted under the auspices of federal and state grants and contracts. On the Norman campus, adult and other learners attend programs at the Oklahoma Center for Continuing Education, one of eleven W. K. Kellogg Foundation–funded, University-based residential conference centers in the world. Annually, CCE offers some 2,000 courses and activities to more than 175,000 nontraditional learners in Oklahoma and in locations all over the world.*

## DISTANCE LEARNING PROGRAM

In carrying out its mission to help nontraditional learners transform themselves through knowledge, CCE offers a variety of credit and noncredit distance learning courses and programs within the state of Oklahoma and beyond. In academic year 1999–2000, more than 21,000 students enrolled in CCE's 350 distance learning courses and programs.

## DELIVERY MEDIA

Courses are delivered via television, videotapes, videoconferencing, interactive television, audiotapes, audioconferencing, computer software, CD-ROM, computer conferencing, World Wide Web, e-mail, and print. Students and faculty members may meet in person or interact via videoconferencing, audioconferencing, mail, telephone, fax, e-mail, interactive television, or World Wide Web. The following equipment may be required: audiocassette player, fax machine, television, cable television, videocassette player, computer, modem, Internet access, e-mail, and CD-ROM.

## PROGRAMS OF STUDY

A variety of programs are available in various distance formats. Independent study courses (credit and noncredit)—some of which are offered online—are available in the following subjects: anthropology, astronomy, business administration, business communication, chemistry, Chinese, classical culture, communication, drama, economics, education, engineering, English, finance, French, geography, geology, German, Greek, health and sport sciences, history, human relations, journalism and mass communication, Latin, library and information studies, management, marketing, mathematics, modern languages, music, philosophy, political science, psychology, Russian, sociology, and Spanish. Master's degree programs in the following areas are presented onsite at military and civilian locations around the world: communication, economics, human relations (including a human resource development emphasis), education (administration, curriculum, and supervision; adult and higher education; instructional psychology and technology; and teacher education), public administration, and social work. In addition, a Ph.D. in organizational leadership is available at some overseas sites. (These programs combine onsite course delivery with online and correspondence study.) In addition, students in Oklahoma have access to telecourses and OneNet courses.

## SPECIAL PROGRAMS

CCE offers a number of distance learning special programs. Among these are the DHS/SATTRN (Satellite Training Network) programs held for Oklahoma Department of Human Services and other state employees. CCE's Independent Study Department works closely with the DANTES program and the Navy College PACE program. In addition, this department offers a number of noncredit writing courses and more than seventy-five high school courses, many of them available online.

## STUDENT SERVICES

Students enrolled in CCE's Advanced Programs have access to the facilities and resources of OU's Norman-based library. Advanced Programs students order all their textbooks online through Follett, and Independent Study offers students a complete array of bookstore services.

## CREDIT OPTIONS

CCE's Independent Study Department provides students various options to earn credit through testing.

---

Among these are the College-Level Examination Program (CLEP), DANTES, and institutionally developed advanced-standing examinations.

## FACULTY

The faculty for OU distance programs includes regular University of Oklahoma faculty members, adjunct faculty members, and instructors with special appointments. All are experienced and highly qualified instructional professionals who are knowledgeable about the needs, concerns, and capabilities of distance education students.

## ADMISSION

Admission to the University of Oklahoma is necessary for credit courses other than those offered through Independent Study. Independent Study students need not be first admitted to OU. To participate in graduate programs, admission to OU's Graduate College is required. For more information, prospective students should use the contact information below.

## TUITION AND FEES

Tuition and fees vary based on the chosen program. Prospective students are encouraged to inquire about the costs associated with the program in which they are interested. Expenses relating to continuing education courses taken to maintain and improve professional skills may be tax deductible (Treas. Reg. 1.162-5, Coughlin v. Commissioner, 203f.2d 307). A tax adviser can make this determination based on the particular facts relating to one's professional situation. All tuition and fees at the University of Oklahoma are subject to changes made by the State Regents for Higher Education.

## FINANCIAL AID

Financial aid is available for many of the semester-based programs offered through CCE. Financial aid is not available to Independent Study students. Each program has different eligibility requirements. Interested students are encouraged to use the contact information below. They will then be put in touch with the appropriate CCE department that can fully answer their financial aid questions.

## APPLYING

Distance learners interested in non-credit programs may enroll by telephone (800-522-0772 Ext. 2248) or by fax (405-325-7164). For many credit programs, distance learners may also enroll by telephone. Prospective students should use the contact information below to determine the appropriate telephone number.

---

**CONTACT**

Larry Hayes
College of Continuing Education
The University of Oklahoma
1700 Asp Avenue
Norman, Oklahoma 73072-6400
Telephone: 405-325-4414
Fax: 405-325-7196
E-mail: lhayes@ou.edu
Web site: http://www.occe.ou.edu

---

# University of Oregon

## Applied Information Management Program

Eugene, Oregon

*The interdisciplinary master's degree Applied Information Management (AIM) Program is designed to respond to rapid developments in information technologies and the resulting impact on organizations. Leading-edge faculty members and working professionals teach AIM courses. AIM is a fully accredited degree offered by the University of Oregon (UO).*

*This degree, specifically designed to serve midcareer professionals, was first offered in 1986. The AIM Program is based on the belief that information managers must have more than an understanding of new technologies. They must combine knowledge in management, business, and visual communications with an awareness of high technology and its global context in order to meet the challenges of the future. The AIM Program offers innovative graduate study in management education as an alternative to the traditional Master of Business Administration or a master's degree in information systems.*

## DISTANCE LEARNING PROGRAM

AIM Online provides the same dynamic curriculum as the AIM Onsite Program through a combination of core (seven weeks) and short (four weeks) courses. Courses run year-round with periodic short breaks in the schedule. It takes approximately 2½ years to earn the degree.

## DELIVERY MEDIA

AIM offers asynchronous courses over the Web. The eCollege.com Internet-learning platform used to deliver AIM courses includes e-mail, chat, threaded discussion, video, audio, journaling, note taking, and document-sharing functions. Courses are accessible using either a PC (Windows 95, 98, or NT) or a Mac (MacOS 8.1 or later). AIM provides students with an e-mail account to use for course-related messages. Prospective students are encouraged to visit the Web site for specific requirements (http://uoregononline.org/index.learn?action=Technical).

## PROGRAM OF STUDY

To earn the AIM degree requires 54 credits, 38 from twelve core courses and 16 from eight 2-credit short courses.

The required core courses are distributed among four components. Each component is made up of three courses. The information management component consists of data management and communications (3 credits), information systems and management (3 credits), and project management (3 credits). The business management component consists of e-business strategies (3 credits), management of organizations (3 credits), and marketing management and planning (3 credits). The information design component consists of two courses in information design and presentation (I and II, 3 credits each) and information and society (3 credits). The applied research component consists of writing for research (2 credits), research methods (3 credits), and AIM capstone (6 credits).

The required short courses consist of business ethics, conflict resolution through negotiation, electronic infor-

mation and research, information emergency management, knowledge management, learning in a virtual environment, making sense of financial data, and tools for systems thinking.

AIM offers an orientation module of courses to students in the online program. The three orientation courses are learning in a virtual environment, electronic information and research, and writing for research. Learning in a virtual environment is a prerequisite for all other AIM online courses.

## SPECIAL PROGRAMS

Students admitted to the online program may take on-site courses with permission. Students in the AIM Onsite Program may take online courses after taking learning in a virtual environment.

## STUDENT SERVICES

Academic advising is available from the AIM Program Coordinator via telephone or e-mail, listed below.

It is the student's responsibility to obtain all equipment and software necessary to access the courses. Technical support is available 24 hours a day, seven days a week from eCollege.com.

Admitted students have access to University of Oregon electronic library resources and may visit any Oregon University System library.

## CREDIT OPTIONS

Students earn credit by successfully completing offered courses. AIM offers all 3-credit core courses on a graded basis. Short courses and AIM Capstone are offered on a pass/no-pass basis. Although rarely done, AIM may accept transfer credits with approval of the AIM Academic Director. AIM offers courses for graduate credit only.

## FACULTY

AIM primarily employs tenure-track faculty members with doctoral degrees to teach core courses. Tenure-track faculty members, as well as practitioners from the field with at least a master's degree, teach short courses.

## ADMISSION

Requirements for admission to the AIM Program include an application form; a $50 application fee; official transcripts; results of the GMAT, GRE, or Miller Analogies Test; a statement of purpose; an autobiographical essay; a resume; three letters of recommendation; and, if the applicant does not have a degree from an English-speaking institution, results of the Test of English as a Foreign Language (TOEFL).

## TUITION AND FEES

The total cost for the AIM program is $20,550, which includes $18,900 for tuition, a $1,500 technology fee, a $50 application fee, and a $100 matriculation fee.

Tuition is $350 per credit (in state or out of state). There is also a technology fee of $75 per course.

Tuition and fees are subject to change at any time.

## FINANCIAL AID

Students may receive consideration for financial assistance through Federal Perkins Loans and the Stafford/Ford Loan programs. To be eligible, a student must enroll for at least 5 credits per academic quarter (half-time). Students pursuing the AIM degree may meet this minimum standard. Recipients of financial aid must be U.S. citizens or in the United States for other than temporary purposes.

For more information, prospective students should contact the UO Office of Financial Aid by telephone at 541-346-3221 or 800-760-6953 (toll-free) or via the Web (http://financialaid.uoregon.edu/).

## APPLYING

The entire application may be completed online by visiting the Web (http://www.aimdegree.com/materials.html). No in-person orientation is required. For an application to be considered, all materials, including test scores, must be received by the application deadline. The application deadlines are April 1 for summer term and October 1 for winter term.

---

### CONTACT

AIM Program Coordinator
University of Oregon
18640 Northwest Walker Road, Suite 1007
Beaverton, Oregon 97006-8927

Telephone: 800-824-2714 (toll-free)
Fax: 503-725-3067
E-mail: aim@continue.uoregon.edu
Web site: http://www.aimdegree.com/

# University of Pennsylvania

## School of Arts and Sciences, College of General Studies

Philadephia, Pennsylvania

*The College of General Studies began its life as Penn's evening division in 1892, when it first opened its doors at the University of Pennsylvania (Penn) to Philadelphia-area teachers. Today, the College of General Studies administers outreach and continuing education programs within the School of Arts and Sciences at Penn, including undergraduate and graduate degree programs for adults, postbaccalaureate programs, noncredit enrichment courses, University-wide Summer Sessions, and service programs for high school students, senior citizens, and international students.*

## DISTANCE LEARNING PROGRAM

As a natural extension of outreach and nontraditional education, the College of General Studies offers a wide range of courses in the arts and sciences to students outside the Philadelphia region via distance learning programs. The College currently serves approximately 400 distance students per year.

## DELIVERY MEDIA

Delivery media include online, Internet-based systems with lectures, faculty office hours, discussions, academic resources, and more on the course Web page. Minimum equipment requirements for all students include a computer with Internet access, Netscape Navigator or Internet Explorer 5.0 or higher, a Real Player, a 56-KB or faster modem, and at least 64 MB of RAM. Students must have Windows 95, Windows 98, or Windows NT with a 200-MHz processor or higher or Mac OS 7.5.5 or later with a 200-MHz processor.

The online courses are offered via the eCollege.com system.

## PROGRAMS OF STUDY

The College of General Studies offers a variety of credit-bearing courses in the arts and sciences for students of all ages, ranging from high school juniors and seniors to adult students. No degrees or certificates are available entirely at a distance. Prospective students must apply.

## SPECIAL PROGRAMS

In the 1998–99 academic year, Penn launched PennAdvance (http://www.advance.upenn.edu), a distributed learning program for academically talented high school students. During the 1999–2000 academic year, PennAdvance was expanded to include all students who have access to the Internet. Now, adult students and current Penn students can take classes from their home computers. Penn's distance programs are all delivered in an online environment.

## STUDENT SERVICES

All students have full access to the Penn Library System's online resources. In addition, the University Bookstore provides a "virtual bookstore" service as well as toll-free phone and fax numbers. Academic support and advising services are available for selected courses.

## CREDIT OPTIONS

Students who successfully complete an arts and sciences PennAdvance course or electronic seminar earn a grade and credit from the University of Pennsylvania. Credit for Penn liberal arts courses is generally transferable to other colleges and universities.

## FACULTY

Each year, approximately 8 full-time faculty members and 4 part-time faculty members teach distance courses. Approximately 90 percent of all distance instructors have a doctoral degree.

## ADMISSION

Prospective students must apply to the College of General Studies as nondegree students. Applications include transcripts of previous work at the high school or college level and an essay.

## TUITION AND FEES

Fall 2001 and spring 2002 tuition for one PennAdvance course is approximately $1100. Students should contact the College of General Studies for more information on tuition and fees.

## FINANCIAL AID

Financial aid is not available to PennAdvance students.

## APPLYING

Applications are processed on a rolling basis until the deadlines for the fall, spring, and summer terms are reached.

## CONTACT

Colleen Gasiorowski
3440 Market Street, Suite 100
Philadelphia, Pennsylvania 19104-3335
Telephone: 215-898-1684
Fax: 215-573-2053
E-mail: advance@sas.upenn.edu
Web site: http://www.advance.upenn.edu
            http://www.sas.upenn.edu/CGS

# University of Phoenix

## Online Campus

Phoenix, Arizona

Since its founding in 1976, the University of Phoenix has been dedicated exclusively to meeting the needs of working professionals. The University is accredited by the Higher Learning Commission and is a member of the North Central Association. The commitment to the adult learner is unequivocal; the University has awarded bachelor's and master's degrees to more than 115,000 graduates.

High academic standards, commitment to quality, and intensely focused programs have earned the University a reputation for leadership in both the academic and business communities. A distinguishing blend of proven academic practices and innovative instructional delivery systems has helped to build the largest private university in the country, with a growing network of campuses and learning centers throughout the United States. The goal is to provide all students with the means to be more effective at their jobs so that they may reap the rewards that follow.

## DISTANCE LEARNING PROGRAM

The Online program relies on computer communications to link faculty members and students from around the world into interactive learning groups. Class size is limited to 15 for maximum interaction. Degrees are completed entirely on line for the convenience of working adults who find it difficult or impossible to attend classes at fixed times and places.

Of the 22,000 students attending class from all over the world, 20 percent are executives or owners of their own businesses, 30 percent are middle managers in business and industry, and 44 percent are technical or licensed professionals. Roughly 54 percent are female, and the average student is 38 years old.

## DELIVERY MEDIA

Once enrolled in an Online degree program, students log on to the computer conferencing system five out of seven days each week to participate in class discussions focused on the topics they are studying. Students communicate and work off line

and only go on line to send and receive material to and from class groups. This is called asynchronous communication.

## PROGRAMS OF STUDY

The M.B.A. program is a classic sixteen-course program covering the complete spectrum of management science, including marketing, business law, finance, economics, and e-business. The Master of Arts in organizational management is a two-year, thirteen-course program emphasizing the skills and knowledge it takes to manage both people and projects at an advanced level. The M.B.A. in health-care management is a sixteen-course program designed for professionals seeking management positions in the health-care field. The M.B.A. in global management is a two-year, sixteen-course program designed to ingrain the abilities to identify business opportunities and threats and to develop effective courses of action within the parameters of the international environment. The M.B.A. in technology management is a highly specialized sixteen-course program that focuses

on proven methods and techniques for anticipating, managing, and marketing technology. The M.B.A. in e-business degree program prepares graduates for a leadership role in the rapidly expanding area of e-business. The M.B.A. in accounting is a sixteen-course program designed to develop or enhance the financial management skills necessary to function effectively within private businesses, nonprofit organizations, and public agencies. The M.A.Ed. program with an emphasis in curriculum and instruction requires the completion of 33 credits. The M.A.Ed. program with an emphasis in e-education requires the completion of 32 credits. The M.A.Ed. program with an emphasis on curriculum and technology requires the completion of 33 credits. The M.S.N. program, consisting of 39 credits, is designed to develop and enhance the knowledge and skills of registered nurses. The Master of Science in computer information systems program is made up of fifteen courses that provide the tools not only to understand technology but also to keep current in its many kinds of development. The Doctor of Management (D. M.) in organizational leadership provides those students with a professional master's degree a means of exploring their personal readiness to become leaders in their professions or their current organizations.

Bachelor of Science degree programs require 120 credits each. The business administration program is suited ideally to men and women who need to be familiar with every aspect of running a business. The business management program focuses on the areas necessary to manage both people and projects effectively. The business marketing program provides a foundation from which to build creative, analytical, and leadership abilities in individuals and workgroups. The accounting program promotes identification with and orientation to the accounting profession and is designed to provide the knowledge, skills, and abilities necessary to pursue a successful accounting career. The information technology program provides fundamental knowledge and practice in both the information technology function and in system development. The e-business program provides fundamental knowledge and practice in business management and information technology. The Bachelor of Science in Business Management degree program provides the knowledge and skills needed to successfully manage almost any dynamic and evolving organization. This program is ideal for community college students who have earned an associate degree. The nursing program (B.S.N.) is designed to develop the professional knowledge and skills of working registered nurses. In addition, students may study toward the Associate of Arts degree, a two-year program providing solid academic training, and apply those credits toward the Bachelor of Science in business majors.

## CREDIT OPTIONS

Graduate students are permitted to waive up to 9 credits by transferring comparable graduate-level course work taken at other accredited colleges or universities.

For undergraduate study, no more than 69 credits of lower-division courses may be applied toward the degree requirement. At least 39 of the 120 total credits must satisfy the University's general education requirement. Students can apply for credit by examination and portfolio.

## FACULTY

The Online Campus has more than 1,600 faculty members. All faculty members have extensive academic credentials (more than one third hold doctoral degrees), and all work in the fields they teach, bringing practical, "real-world" experience to bear on the needs of students who are working professionals.

## ADMISSION

Graduate students must have an undergraduate degree from a regionally accredited college or university, with a cumulative GPA of 2.5 or better (3.0 for prior graduate work). Students must also be currently employed; have a minimum of three years of full-time, post–high school work experience providing exposure to organizational systems and management processes; or have access to an organizational environment appropriate for the application of theoretical concepts learned in the classroom.

Undergraduate students must have a high school diploma or its equivalent. Students must be at least 23 years old and currently employed. Students must complete the University-proctored Comprehensive Cognitive Assessment, and non-native speakers of English must have a minimum score of 550 on the TOEFL.

## TUITION AND FEES

Graduate tuition is $495 per credit and undergraduate tuition is $400 per credit. There are an application fee of $85 and a graduate fee of $55. Textbook costs vary by course.

## APPLYING

Unless students are relying on foreign transcripts for admission, all that is needed to begin the first course is to complete an application, enrollment agreement, and disclosure form. While students are in their first three classes, academic counselors work with them to complete transcript requests, the Comprehensive Cognitive Assessment, and any other items necessary for formal registration.

---

### CONTACT

Enrollment Department
University of Phoenix Online
3157 East Elwood Street
Phoenix, Arizona 85034
Telephone: 877-611-3390 (toll-free in U.S.)
Fax: 602-387-6440
Web site: http://online.uophx.edu

---

# University of St. Francis

## Distance Learning

Joliet, Illinois

---

*As a Catholic, Franciscan institution of higher learning, the University of St. Francis reaffirms the ideal that a liberal education provides the comprehensive cultural background necessary for any profession.*

## DISTANCE LEARNING PROGRAM

The distance education programs at University of St. Francis (USF) are delivered via videoconferencing, interactive television, the Internet, and at site locations throughout the United States. As of the 1999–2000 academic year, USF offered twenty-four courses online and had 360 students enrolled.

## DELIVERY MEDIA

Online courses use computer and information technologies to link faculty members and students from around the world into interactive classes. The online courses are designed for the working professional at both the undergraduate and graduate level. St. Francis uses the WebCT program to deliver its Internet classes for online courses. The only difference between an online course and a traditional course is that with WebCT, students can "attend" courses at a time that is convenient for them. Like any class, students read a textbook, participate in class discussions, and take exams using WebCT.

## PROGRAM OF STUDY

The Health Arts program is a B.S. degree-completion program for licensed health care professionals. The program gives adult workers access to higher education and allows them to work towards the completion of their bachelor's degree through credit given for prior learning experience.

The Applied Organizational Management (B.S.) is an accelerated degree program designed so that future business and industry leaders can successfully meet the challenges and demands they face in organizational management. It offers applied knowledge and practical experiences, which enable students to favorably manage everyday work situations and problems. It is a "2+2" program that recognizes the Associate in Applied Science degree from a vocational or technical program as fulfilling the first two years of the Bachelor of Science degree in professional arts. The program also awards college credit for learning gained from certificate programs, training programs, and "life experiences."

The new world of health care challenges the knowledge and flexibility of today's nurses. USF offers a B.S. in Nursing. Registered nursing students prepare for these challenges through classroom and clinical coursework developed individually to meet the needs of each RN. After completion of prerequisites, the upper division course work may be completed in as little as one year. Courses are offered one night a week, usually in eight-week blocks, by highly qualified, dedicated faculty members. The entire BSN Fast Track program is available online, except for clinical rotations.

The Health Services Management (M.S.) degree was initiated in 1980 to prepare health-care professionals for management in the dynamic health-care field. It is the institution's goal to provide a quality program of challenging content to meet the ever-changing demands of the profession. The program is designed for students who have knowledge and experience in specific areas of health care and are seeking a broader understanding of the field. While the program is offered in a convenient format, the content is rigorous. The curriculum includes both the theories of management and their practical application in the health-care field. The graduate program emphasizes administration in general rather than a concentration within a specialty.

Students in the Master's of Business Administration program have the convenience of completing their M.B.A. any time, any place through their laptop or home or office computers and an Internet connection. This program provides a flexible, viable alternative for professionals with busy personal, work, and/or travel schedules. Students interact with faculty members, who are specially trained to offer a challenging, exciting, and meaningful online course experience.

The Management (M.S.) program is appropriate for professionals who want to remain in their specialty field (such as social work, research and development, engineering, or nursing), but who want to step into a managerial role or enhance their managerial abilities. The Master of Science in management student will gain an understanding of the social, managerial, economic, environmental, and organizational concepts that comprise the public and business fields. The program is designed for the business professional who is looking for a flexible, convenient path toward degree completion.

The Master of Science programs in Continuing Education and Training

Management/Continuing Education and Training Technology were instituted in the fall of 1995 to meet the education needs of working professionals. There is a growing need for continuing education and training programs in business and industry, higher education, continuing professional education, governmental and community agencies, community education, religious organizations, gerontology programs, and health-care delivery systems. The curriculum includes areas of adult learning theory, needs analysis, instructional design, evaluation, program planning, management, marketing, and finance. The curriculum includes both theory and application.

## STUDENT SERVICES

The goal of the University of St. Francis is to provide its online students with academic services that are equivalent to those available to on-campus students, but tailored to the special demands of the distance student body. Several new student services are still under development, including the ability to register online and obtain student account information and career development services provided through the Internet.

The University of St. Francis provides an online bookstore, from which students can order books, clothing items, hats, gifts, and other general merchandise items.

Through the Student Information Center, students receive general information on financial aid, access the University's online catalog and class schedule, request transcripts, and access their individual Banner accounts on the administrative server.

## CREDIT OPTIONS

Credit for graduate work completed at another regionally accredited institution may be accepted toward a graduate degree. Up to a total of 8 semester hours may be transferred with certain provisions. The student must complete a petition for transfer of credit; the course(s) must be appropriate to the degree program of the student and not be in conflict with credit limitations; the petition must be approved by the academic adviser and the program administrator; and the student must have earned a grade of "B" or higher in the course.

Credit will be considered for transfer only after the above conditions have been met and an official transcript of the student's record has been sent directly to the College of Graduate Studies by the appropriate institution(s). Transfer credits are not included in the computation of the student's GPA.

Petition for transfer of credit must be processed, approved, and recorded before a student is considered eligible for candidacy and comprehensive examination.

Students applying for the M.B.A. program must also request an official copy of the transcript(s) from all colleges and universities they have attended. Their transcripts must be received by the College of Graduate Studies before they may take certain courses.

## FACULTY

The online courses at the University of St. Francis are taught by the same faculty members who teach on site. Besides being experts in the content area of the course, they have received special training in both the technical skills and the instructional knowledge to provide students with an excellent online learning experience.

## ADMISSION

Students must be provisionally accepted or accepted into a program in order to register for an online course. Students should refer to guidelines for each program. Students must complete the following steps in order to register for their first online class:

The student must complete an online permit request form. In order to be successful in an online course, the student's computer must meet or exceed certain hardware and software requirements. The permit is a questionnaire about the computer and browser the student will be using for his or her online class. The student completes this questionnaire only once, before the first online class. The form must be accessed through the Web site. (Health Arts: www.stfrancis/edu/ha/permit/index2/htm; Graduate Studies: www.stfrancis.edu/grd/online/index2.htm; and Professional Arts and Nursing: www.stfranics.edu/permit.)

Next, the student must complete a registration form, including his or her e-mail address.

Finally, the student must make the payment of the online technology fee either by personal check, credit card, or financial aid.

## TUITION AND FEES

Tuition and fees vary by program. For tuition rates for particular courses or programs of interest, prospective students should visit the Web site listed below. About 95 percent of USF students receive some form of financial aid, with the average award being more than 80 percent of tuition expenses. Applicants should also plan on completing a Free Application for Federal Student Aid (FAFSA).

---

### CONTACT

University of St. Francis
500 Wilcox Street
Joliet, Illinois 60435
Telephone: 800-735-7500 (toll-free)
E-mail: admissions@stfrancis.edu
Web site:
    http://www.stfrancis.edu

# University of South Alabama

*USA Online*

Mobile, Alabama

*The University of South Alabama (USA), created in 1963, is a major public university located on the upper Gulf Coast in Mobile, Alabama. The University's mission actively embraces the functions of teaching, research, public service, and health care and vigorously pursues the preservation, discovery, communication, and application of knowledge. Degrees are available in the Colleges of Allied Health Professions, Arts and Sciences, Business, Education, Engineering, and Nursing; the Schools of Computer and Information Sciences and Continuing Education and Special Programs; and the Graduate School. USA also has an outstanding College of Medicine and clinical facilities, in addition to the USA Medical Center, USA Knollwood Park Hospital, and USA Children's and Women's Hospital. Fully accredited by the Southern Association of Colleges and Schools, USA enrolls some 11,000 students at the beautiful suburban campus in west Mobile.*

## DISTANCE LEARNING PROGRAM

The fall semester of 1999 was the beginning term for USA Online, the University's online campus. USA Online is designed to deliver courses and programs via the Internet to those who cannot attend school in the traditional manner due to family, career, and location requirements.

## DELIVERY MEDIA

USA Online offers Web-based course instruction on the Internet. The courses currently offered are designated in the course offerings list with section numbers 85–89. These courses require additional technology fees. A computer with an Internet connection and e-mail is required. For specific requirements, course information, and additional registration requirements, students may visit the University's Web site (http://usaonline.southalabama.edu).

The online courses are offered via the eCollege.com system.

## PROGRAMS OF STUDY

The College of Business offers the M.B.A. degree on line. At the end of

the program, the student completes the capstone course on campus through a series of Saturday class sessions.

The College of Education offers the M.S. degree in instructional design and development and M.Ed. degrees in education administration, education media (library media), and special education (gifted education and collaborative teacher).

The College of Nursing offers several online courses for students who are enrolled in the RN-to-B.S.N. track and the M.S.N. program. All nursing courses in the RN-to-B.S.N. track are offered on line and through distant education strategies. Several of the core courses in the M.S.N. program are offered on line, and Web technology augments many other courses.

In addition, online courses are offered by the Colleges of Allied Health and Arts and Sciences, the Schools of Computer and Information Sciences and Continuing Education and Special Programs, and the College of Engineering.

## STUDENT SERVICES

Many student services that are available to on-campus students are avail-

able to online students. The libraries, the bookstore, the student newspaper, admissions, registration, financial aid information, academic information, and advising are available at USA Online.

## CREDIT OPTIONS

For the master's degree, a minimum of 30 semester hours of credit in an approved program is required. Students should see each program for the specific number of hours and other requirements. A maximum of 9 semester hours of graduate credit obtained at another accredited institution may be approved for transfer to the University of South Alabama. Only grades of A or B may be accepted.

## FACULTY

For the fall semester of 2001, approximately 50 full-time faculty members are involved with USA Online. Approximately 90 percent have a doctoral degree.

## ADMISSION

Applicants to USA Online courses, whether they are undergraduate or graduate students, must meet the same admission requirements as all University students. Students should contact the Office of Admissions at the address listed below or visit the Web site for information about the requirements for admission.

## TUITION AND FEES

The cost for a 3-semester-hour course is $511 for undergraduates and $601 for graduate students. The total tuition charges include tuition, a registration fee, and a technology service fee.

## FINANCIAL AID

Students should see the University online bulletin for financial aid information (http://www.finaid.usouthal. edu).

## APPLYING

Deadlines for the application for admission, the nonrefundable processing fee, and the official required documents (transcripts and test scores, as appropriate) are August 10 for the fall semester (August 1 for Graduate School), December 15 for the spring semester, and May 20 for the summer semester. Students should request applications and admissions material through e-mail (admiss@usamail.usouthal.edu) or visit the University's Web site at http://www.southalabama.edu (the application form and instructions are available on the Web).

### CONTACT

Dr. Thomas L. Chilton, Associate Dean
Fax: 334-380-2748
E-mail: tchilton@usamail.
  usouthal.edu
Web site: http://usaonline.
  southalabama.edu

# University of Southern Colorado

*Continuing Education*

Pueblo, Colorado

---

*The University of Southern Colorado (USC) has served the changing needs of students for more than sixty years. USC's campus, spanning more than 275 acres, crowns the north end of Pueblo, a historically and culturally rich city of 100,000 located near the Greenhorn Mountains in the colorful Pikes Peak region of southern Colorado. Enrollment exceeds 4,000 students from throughout Colorado, the nation, and several other countries. The University of Southern Colorado is accredited at the bachelor's and master's levels by the Commission on Institutions of Higher Education of the North Central Association of Colleges and Schools.*

## DISTANCE LEARNING PROGRAM

USC has been providing degree-completion options for off-campus students for more than thirty-five years. The USC External Degree Completion Program offers Bachelor of Science degrees in social science and in sociology. At any one time there are approximately 250 individuals enrolled in the program, with many more enrolled in independent study courses.

## DELIVERY MEDIA

Upon course registration, a syllabus explaining course requirements is mailed to the student, or the student may download the syllabus from the USC Web site. Students send completed course work directly to the instructor. Some courses require proctored examinations, while others have examinations sent directly to the student. A variety of online and traditional tools are available for courses, such as e-mail, textbooks, and videotapes. Instructors are available by telephone, fax, e-mail, and correspondence.

## PROGRAM OF STUDY

USC offers Bachelor of Science degrees in social science and in sociol-

ogy. Each degree allows students to create an area of concentration tailored to meet their needs, such as law enforcement, business, criminology, and public and program administration. Requirements for the degrees are generally as follows: general education (39 semester hours), major core (36 semester hours), area of concentration (20 semester hours), and electives (33 semester hours). There are 128 semester hours required for graduation; 40 must be junior- or senior-level credits. Thirty-two credits must be completed with USC in order to receive this degree. Sixteen of the last 32 credits must be completed with USC. A maximum of 96 semester credits can be transferred. Of those credits, a maximum of 64 semester credits may be from junior/community colleges. Active student enrollment is maintained by enrolling in at least one USC course per year. Off-campus credits are nondistinguishable from those earned on campus.

Credit is accepted from accredited institutions recommended by the American Association of Collegiate Registrars and Admissions Officers. Credits from a nonaccredited institution may be petitioned for transfer after the student has completed at least 24 semester hours at USC with a

C (2.0 GPA) average or better. Courses that are not accepted in the transfer process may be petitioned.

## SPECIAL PROGRAMS

Legal certificate programs are offered without credit, including legal investigation, victim advocacy, and legal secretary studies. Noncredit enrollment cannot be applied toward academic degree programs. However, a 6-credit-hour paralegal certificate program that can be applied toward the degree programs is offered.

## STUDENT SERVICES

A free, preliminary, unofficial credit evaluation is available upon request. Unofficial transcripts are reviewed by the program adviser in an attempt to show the placement of previous college credits against the USC requirements. The unofficial evaluation is subject to change based on the official evaluation and the acceptance of transfer courses by the Admissions Office. The adviser assists admitted students with any petitions required.

## CREDIT OPTIONS

A student may earn a maximum of 30 semester hours through the College-Level Examination Program (CLEP). A maximum of 6 semester hours may be applied toward credit for life experience. A maximum of 20 semester hours of military service credit is accepted when military service credit is processed and official copies of certificates are received. Twelve credit hours of field experience can also be used to fulfill degree requirements.

## FACULTY

Approximately 60 percent of the faculty members in the External Degree Program have a Ph.D. and are full-time professors on campus at USC. The remaining 40 percent are part-time professors. All professors have experience working with distance learners.

## ADMISSION

Students must submit the program enrollment fee, the Application for External Degree Program, the Application for Undergraduate Admission, and high school transcripts with ACT/SAT I scores. Students with at least 30 transferable college credits are not required to submit ACT/SAT I scores.

## TUITION AND FEES

Tuition costs of $85 per semester hour for undergraduate credit and $95 per semester hour for graduate credit must be submitted with the registration for the course. Some courses require videotape fees of $75.

## FINANCIAL AID

Currently, students enrolled in the External Degree Program are eligible for financial aid. Company-sponsored tuition and military tuition assistance programs may be used for USC courses. Students are encouraged to seek scholarship aid from local civic groups that may sponsor such study.

USC courses are approved for the Defense Activity for Non-Traditional Educational Support (DANTES) program. Eligible military personnel should process DANTES applications through their education office.

## APPLYING

A $135 enrollment fee must be submitted with the applications for admission to the degree program. Upon acceptance, students receive an acceptance letter followed by an official transfer statement of credits. Shortly thereafter, an official evaluation is issued to the student.

---

### CONTACT

Joanna Ponce, Assistant Program Manager
Don Spano, Advisor
Continuing Education Program
University of Southern Colorado
2200 Bonforte Boulevard
Pueblo, Colorado 81001-4901
Telephone: 877-872-9653, press 3 (toll-free)
Fax: 719-549-2438
Web site: http://uscolo.edu/coned

---

# University of Tennessee

## *Distance Education and Independent Study*

### Knoxville, Tennessee

The University of Tennessee (UT) is a state-supported, land-grant university that traces its roots to Blount College, which was founded in 1794. The University of Tennessee is dedicated to excellence in undergraduate and graduate studies, research and creative activities, and public service. UT is accredited by the Southern Association of Colleges and Schools. UT participates in Southern Regional Educational Board's Academic Common Market, which allows students in Arkansas, West Virginia, and Virginia to register for the Master's in Information Science at in-state rates.

## DISTANCE LEARNING PROGRAM

Many students find that the University of Tennessee offers exactly the unique course or program of study they need to get ahead. From the Physician's Executive M.B.A. and the sign language interpreter certification to the nuclear or industrial engineering M.S. degrees and noncredit classes in the high-paying information technology fields, hundreds of students per semester find distance education and independent study can help them meet their educational goals.

UT offers Web, videotape, and correspondence courses to home school, high school, or college students. Hundreds of courses for high school credit, graduation or entrance requirements, college credit towards a degree, professional development, or personal enhancement are offered in a variety of subjects, including foreign languages, social sciences, natural sciences, engineering, business, communications, math, English, history, and many others. More information about UT Distance Education and Independent Study is available on the Web site at: http://www.anywhere.tennessee.edu.

## DELIVERY MEDIA

University Outreach and Distance Education courses are delivered through a wide range of technologies. Some courses are offered via the Web, videotape, and correspondence courses while others are offered via advanced voice/data interactive "cyberclass" technology over the Internet. Students "meet" using multimedia computers and the Internet. Correspondence courses via postal mail, e-mail, and "click-to-learn" Web delivery methods provide undergraduate credit to individuals anywhere, anytime.

## PROGRAMS OF STUDY

University Outreach offers many undergraduate, graduate distance education, and certificate programs. The industrial engineering/engineering management M.S. is available via videotape. Students must have a bachelor's degree in engineering or a related scientific or technical field. The information sciences M.S., accredited by the American Library Association, focuses on electronic and traditional print media. Available via the Internet, the program requires 42 semester graduate course hours. The nuclear engineering M.S., available via the Internet, requires 24 semester graduate course hours, and is intended for students interested in nuclear engineering, health physics, or radiological engineering careers. The three flexibly delivered Executive M.B.A. programs, offered through UT's College of Business Administration, combine Internet-delivered courses with on-campus residence periods.

Certificate programs include UT's Graduate Certificate in applied statistical strategies focusing on customized-designed course tracks for manufacturing and engineering data or a service industry and business. The Internet eLearning Institute (IEI) provides certificate programs, professional development courses, and training for Information Technology professionals interested in updating their skills and for students seeking quality Web training to pursue IT careers. Courses in the areas of e-commerce, Web databases, Web mastering, network systems engineering, administrative technology, technical sales, and instructional technology are offered via the Internet. More information on IEI is available on the Web site at http://www.iei.utk.edu.

## STUDENT SERVICES

UT's Learner Services Center, available via Web or phone, provides support for inquiries, bookstore, advising, and library services. Access to library services, academic advising, books, materials, and career placement assistance are provided through a central portal, creating a convenient and friendly environment for students.

## CREDIT OPTIONS

Students may transfer up to 6 hours of credit from an accredited university to a UT master's degree program. In the information sciences program, some elective hours may be earned through directed independent study. Credits earned in independent study courses are generally transferable to other colleges and universities toward the completion of a degree. Internet eLearning Institute courses qualify for CEU professional credit.

## ADMISSION

University admission is not required to take undergraduate correspondence or Internet eLearning Institute courses. Application to the UT Graduate School is required for credit or audit of graduate distance education courses.

## TUITION AND FEES

Undergraduate distance education and independent student tuition is $118 per semester hour ($1681 maximum) and the graduate tuition is $192 per semester hour ($2002 maximum) for in-state students. Out-of-state students pay undergraduate tuition of $431 per semester hour ($5083 maximum) and graduate tuition of $584 per semester hour ($5298 maximum). A $12 per semester hour technology fee may apply to registrations. Fees for Internet eLearning

Institute certificate courses vary according to course. As fees and tuition are subject to change, students may visit the Web site or contact the Call Center for current information.

## APPLYING

Students should visit the University Outreach Web site (www.outreach.utk.edu) or contact the Call Center for detailed application information. Students may register by mail, fax, telephone, Internet, or in person.

---

**CONTACT**
Distance Education and Independent Study
University of Tennessee
1534 White Avenue
Knoxville, Tennessee 37996-1525
Telephone: 800-325-8657 (toll-free)
Fax: 865-974-4684
Web site: http://www.outreach.utk.edu

---

# The University of Texas at Austin

## Continuing and Extended Education
## Distance Education Center

Austin, Texas

*The University of Texas at Austin (UT Austin) was founded in 1883 on 40 acres of land near the state capitol. As the academic flagship of the University of Texas system, UT Austin enrolls more than 49,000 students annually. It is home to students from county in Texas, all fifty states, and approximately 120 foreign countries. It has the distinction of awarding more doctorate degrees of any university in the nation. UT Austin is accredited by the Commission on Colleges of the Southern Association of Colleges and Schools.*

*The mission of the University is to achieve excellence in the interrelated areas of undergraduate education, graduate education, research, and public service; to provide superior and comprehensive educational opportunities at the baccalaureate through doctoral and special professional educational levels; to contribute to the advancement of society through research, creative activity, scholarly inquiry, and the development of new knowledge; to preserve and promote the arts, to benefit the state's economy, to serve the citizens through public programs, and to provide other public service.*

## DISTANCE LEARNING PROGRAM

For ninety years, Continuing and Extended Education has been providing UT Austin resources to the citizens of Texas. In 1909, the first offerings through the Distance Education Center (DEC) were college courses, but today the offerings also include programs for professional and personal development. In 2000, the DEC served more than 24,000 students from across the nation and the world.

## DELIVERY MEDIA

The Distance Education Center offers synchronous and asynchronous courses in three formats: an online format; a format that uses a blend of delivery methods, including print-based materials, Internet components, audio-conferencing, CD-ROMs, diskette, videoconferencing, audiotape, and videotape; and the traditional print-based correspondence course format. Students submit lessons through U.S. mail, e-mail, the Internet, telephone, and fax. Interaction with instructors is available over the Internet, by telephone, e-mail, U.S. mail, listserve, and through bulletin boards.

## PROGRAMS OF STUDY

The Distance Education Center college curriculum covers 30 fields of study in upper and lower division courses, including substantial writing component courses. All courses are aligned with on-campus curriculum and are developed and taught by instructors who are approved by UT Austin department chairs. Specific content areas include anthropology, art history, business, curriculum and instruction, economics, educational psychology, English, government, history, kinesiology and health education, philosophy, psychology, radio/television/film production, social work, sociology, visual arts studies, and women's studies. Science and language courses include astronomy, geography, mathematics, nursing, nutrition, physics, zoology, Czech, French, German, Latin, and Spanish. Courses are available online and in print.

DEC middle and high school courses are available online and in print to all interested individuals, anytime, anywhere. Students may select from a full range of courses, all of which comply with requirements of the Texas Essential Knowledge and Skills (TEKS). To complement the course offerings, the DEC offers the following programs:

The Credit by Exam Program and the Examination for Acceleration Program, which allow K–12 students to be awarded credit in grade levels and courses if they can demonstrate mastery of course content on comprehensive examinations.

The DEC High School Diploma Program, which is accredited by the Texas Education Agency and which requires students to pass the Texas Assessment of Academic Skills (TAAS) exit test for completion of the Program.

The Migrant Student Graduation Enhancement Program is a fully accredited high school program designed to meet the special needs of migrant students in Texas high schools. Students are required to pass the Texas Assessment of Academic Skills (TAAS) exit test for completion of the Program

The University Charter School offers enrollment to selected students in Austin area.

Several professional development courses of study are also offered through the DEC. In collaboration with the University of Texas at San Antonio, the Center offers a self-paced, eight-module purchasing management certificate program that trains participants in procurement, purchasing economics, and specification writing. Also, in cooperation with the Texas Commission on Law Enforcement Officers Standards and Education, the DEC offers continuing education courses for Texas law enforcement officers. Other professional development courses include a number of Apple ALI online computer courses as well as all of the DEC college credit courses, in which many professionals enroll on a non-credit basis for professional development.

## STUDENT SERVICES

Students may enroll online at http://www.utexas.edu/cee/dec, by mail, by telephone, by fax, or in person. The Distance Education Center strongly recommends that students talk to a DEC student services representative before enrolling in more than two DEC courses concurrently. Student services representatives can also provide information about learning at a distance and can answer questions about courses and materials. Student service representatives are available for telephone advising in the Austin are at 512-232-5000, and outside the Austin area at 888-232-4723 (toll-free).

## CREDIT OPTIONS

If a student is taking a Distance Education Center course to satisfy a requirement for a degree or diploma, he or she should contact a university adviser or school adviser to confirm that credit acquired through the DEC will transfer as the appropriate course. Earned college credit is recorded on a UT Austin transcript.

## FACULTY

More than 50 UT Austin faculty members teach for the Distance Education Center. More than 30 certified Texas teachers teach the high school courses.

## ADMISSION

Enrollment in Distance Education Center courses does not constitute admission to UT Austin. Any student can enroll in any of the programs at any time.

## TUITION AND FEES

Tuition fees vary depending on the course. In most cases, however, print-based college courses are $299, and online courses are $399. Middle and high school print-based courses are generally $99, and online courses are $299. Other fees may be applicable if the course includes additional materials.

## FINANCIAL AID

For college students completing courses in traditional semester time frames, financial aid is available.

Financial aid also is administered through governmental agencies to military personnel, veterans, and persons with specific, identified disabilities. Federal financial programs usually require that students be enrolled in programs leading to a degree, a certificate, or some other educational credential in order to be considered for assistance.

## APPLYING

Students can apply over the Web, by telephone, by fax, by mail, and in person. As soon as the application and payment have been processed, a receipt and study materials are mailed to the student.

Applications are accepted at any time.

---

### CONTACT

Olga Garza
Manager of Student Services
The University of Texas at Austin
Continuing and Extended Education
Distance Education Center
P.O. Box 7700
Austin, Texas 78713-7700
Telephone: 888-BE-A-GRAD (toll-free)
Fax: 512-475-7933
E-mail: dec@www.utexas.edu
Web site: http://www.utexas.edu/cee/dec

# The University of Texas at Dallas

## Global M.B.A. Online Program

Richardson, Texas

---

The University of Texas at Dallas (UTD) was created in September 1969. The mission of the University is to provide Texas and the nation with the benefits of educational and research programs of the highest quality. The School of Management was established in 1975. The School's mission is to meet the challenges of a rapidly changing, technology-driven, global society by partnering with the business community to deliver high-quality management education to a diverse group of undergraduate and graduate students and practicing executives, to develop and continuously improve programs advancing management education and practice, and to conduct research enhancing management knowledge. The University of Texas at Dallas is accredited by the Commission on Colleges of the Southern Association of Colleges and Schools.

## DISTANCE LEARNING PROGRAM

The Global M.B.A. Online extends delivery of UTD's part-time M.B.A. Program to students who cannot commit to regularly scheduled classes on campus. The online M.B.A. is 48 credit hours, anchored by the same 27 hours of core courses as delivered in the classroom. Electives (21 hours) emphasize international management and information technology, two of UTD's strongest academic areas. Students are not organized in distinct classes (cohort groups) but select course loads consistent with their own part-time pace.

## DELIVERY MEDIA

Faculty members engage online students using instructional resources and techniques that retain many of the classroom's dynamics, including audio streaming lectures supported by downloadable presentations, online text-based conferences, bulletin board and e-mail exchanges, and teleconferences. In addition to a confident level of computer literacy, technical requirements include a Pentium II or equivalent processor; a 28.8K or faster modem (56K recom.); 32 M system RAM; 200 MB free hard disk space memory; Internet access with Netscape 4.06 or better or MS Explorer 4.0 or better; and CD-ROM capabilities. Software requirements include Microsoft Office 97 or better and virus detection/protection software such as McAfee. "Plug-ins" may be required for specific courses.

## PROGRAM OF STUDY

A Master of Business Administration (M.B.A.) is awarded. The 27-hour basic core, consisting of eleven courses, includes accounting for managers, social and political environment of business, strategic management, financial management, global economy, business economics, introduction to marketing management, introduction to organizational behavior, introduction to operations research, operations management, and applied statistics for management science. Electives (21 hours) emphasize international management and information technology. Electives in international management include multinational firm, international corporate finance, international marketing, and cross-cultural management. Breadth electives include strategic cost management and advanced financial management. Electives in information technology include the information age enterprise, economics of information goods, Internet business models, and database management systems.

## CREDIT OPTIONS

Some of UTD's core course equivalents are offered through the UT-System TeleCampus M.B.A. Online, and 18 hours are transferable to the Global M.B.A. Online. Transfer credit requests are initiated by students after admission. Prospective transfers from other UT-System components participating in the TeleCampus M.B.A. will be pre-approved if identified on degree plan.

## FACULTY

The University of Texas at Dallas School of Management has strong, committed faculty members who teach all of the master's programs. All faculty members have extensive experience in master's education, consulting, and/or practical experience both domestically and internationally. Some are leading scholars. Many serve as editors of professional journals. Others have received awards for teaching excellence. At times, faculty members join together to team teach selected courses.

## ADMISSION

Admission requirements and tuition are the same as those for the traditional M.B.A. Prospective students use the online graduate application form and submit a GMAT score and undergraduate degree transcript(s). Prerequisites for the Global M.B.A. Online include the knowledge of calculus (equivalent to UTD's Math 5304,

Applied Mathematical Analysis for Non-Majors, with grade of B or better) and competence in personal computing (equivalent to UTD's BA 3351). Deficiencies must be remedied within the first 12 hours of graduate work. Currently, these prerequisite courses are not offered online.

## TUITION AND FEES

Tuition and fees are approximately $679 for a 3-credit-hour course for Texas residents and $1336 for non-residents. Included are UTD fees associated with distance learning delivery and School of Management fees. Excluded are some fees associated with campus programs (e.g., student union, physical instruction facility, and medical services).

## FINANCIAL AID

Students may access the University of Texas at Dallas financial aid department for information and applications via http://www.utdallas.edu.

## APPLYING

Like the campus-based program, courses are offered during the three regular semesters starting in August/ September, January, and May. Application deadlines for each semester are the same as for the regular M.B.A. program.

---

**CONTACT**

Mr. George Barnes, Director
Global M.B.A. Online
School of Management
The University of Texas at Dallas
P. O. Box 830688, JO51
Richardson, Texas 75083-0688
Telephone: 972-883-2783
Fax: 972-883-2799
E-mail: gbarnes@utdallas.edu
Web site: http://som.utdallas.edu/globalmba

# The University of Texas at Dallas

## School of Management
## M.I.M.S. Global Leadership Executive Programs

Richardson, Texas

---

*The University of Texas at Dallas was created in September 1969. The mission of the University is to provide Texas and the nation with the benefits of educational and research programs of the highest quality. The School of Management was established in 1975. The School's mission is to meet the challenges of a rapidly changing, technology-driven, global society by partnering with the business community to deliver high quality management education to a diverse group of undergraduate and graduate students and practicing executives; to develop and continuously improve programs advancing management education and practice; and to conduct research enhancing management knowledge. The University of Texas at Dallas is accredited by the Commission on Colleges of the Southern Association of Colleges and Schools.*

## DISTANCE LEARNING PROGRAM

The Master's in International Management Studies Program (M.I.M.S.) at the University of Texas at Dallas (UTD) School of Management offers two Global Leadership graduate executive programs via distance education, one leading to an M.B.A. degree; the other to a Master of Arts degree, an ideal second management degree for those already holding an M.B.A. The degree programs are designed for experienced midcareer managers and senior professionals who wish to develop global leadership knowledge and skills and who require a flexible, convenient learning environment.

## DELIVERY MEDIA

M.I.M.S. distance learning design combines a variety of learning and delivery methods. Curriculum is delivered sequentially, one course at a time, over the Internet through a variety of technologies including text, audio, teleconference, and groupware. Students join a cohort group and study both independently and in virtual teams. Students are required to participate in a ten-day foreign study tour and in quarterly weekend retreats (four retreats for the M.A.; six retreats for the M.B.A.). Retreats are normally held in Dallas, Texas.

## PROGRAMS OF STUDY

The Master in International Management Studies Program (M.I.M.S.) at the University of Texas at Dallas offers two graduate executive programs via distance education. The 48-credit-hour Global Leadership program leading to an M.B.A. degree (GLEMBA) can be completed in thirty-two months and a 36-credit-hour Master of Arts degree in international management can be completed in twenty-eight months. Students already holding an M.B.A. may, under some circumstances, complete the M.A. in seventeen months.

The comprehensive, integrated curriculum, focused on developing global leaders, is designed to build knowledge, competencies, and skills required by contemporary multinational companies. Key areas of learning encompass environmental intelligence, international business best practices, systems and interfunctional thinking, and global mindset and intercultural savvy.

Curriculum is organized into two tracks: Business Core and Global Leadership. Students begin the program in the Business Core track the first year, then take the Global Leadership track in the second year. The third year combines courses from the Business Core and the Global Leadership tracks.

## STUDENT SERVICES

Students join a cohort class and receive benefit from group interaction and support throughout the program. Class sizes are limited to allow for frequent communication and feedback among students and faculty members.

M.I.M.S. uses a groupware system to post all administrative information and course materials. Faculty members and students use e-mail and group conferencing. Students access electronic libraries for search and document retrieval. M.I.M.S. administration arranges all course registration, billing services, and reservations for quarterly retreat accommodations and the international study tour travel.

## CREDIT OPTIONS

Students who have successfully completed graduate work at an accredited institution within the past six years may petition for transfer of credits into the M.I.M.S. program. All petitions for transfer of credit must be accompanied by an official transcript and an official explanation of the course numbering at the school where the credit was earned. To qualify for transfer of credit, the grade earned in the course must be a B or better from an accredited college or university, and the course must not be a correspondence or extension course. Also, the transfer credit is not awarded for experiential learning, performance, or experience that occurs prior to enrollment. The total number of credit transfers toward the completion of a master's degree cannot exceed twelve hours toward the M.A. and fifteen towards the M.B.A. degree.

## FACULTY

The M.I.M.S. faculty is composed of professors who teach in the University of Texas at Dallas School of Management, as well as distinguished faculty and experts from national and international universities.

## ADMISSION

Applicants into the M.I.M.S. Global Leadership Executive Programs must have a bachelor's degree from an accredited university with a grade point average of 3.0 or better on a 4.0 scale, work experience of at least seven years in a managerial or professional position, proficient computer and Internet skills, and fluency in written and spoken English.

## TUITION AND FEES

Program fees of $28,500 for the M.A. and $37,150 for the M.B.A. are inclusive of tuition, texts, specialized software, retreats, and travel and hotel costs for the international study tour. Travel and living expenses associated with retreat attendance is not included in the tuition.

## FINANCIAL AID

Students may access the University of Texas at Dallas financial aid department for information and applications via the University's Web site at www.utdallas.edu.

## APPLYING

The M.I.M.S. program accepts and reviews applications for admission on a rolling basis. Enrollments in the Business Core track is three times a year (January, May, and August). The Global Leadership track begins each January.

---

**CONTACT**

Dr. Stephen Guisinger, Director
M.I.M.S. Global Leadership Executive Programs
School of Management
University of Texas at Dallas
P.O. Box 830688
Richardson, Texas 75083-0688
Telephone: 972-883-MIMS
Fax: 972-883-6164
E-mail: glemba@utdallas.edu
Web site: http://www.utdallas.edu/mims

# The University of Texas System

## UT TeleCampus, Online Degrees, Courses, and Support

Austin, Texas

---

*The University of Texas (UT) System offers several fully online degree programs and courses via the award-winning UT TeleCampus. The UT TeleCampus is the central support unit for distance education among the UT System's fifteen campuses and research facilities. Students find expert faculty members, virtual classrooms, links to University services and offices, extensive digital libraries and hundreds of learning resources, tutorials, and other service features. Launched in May 1998, the UT TeleCampus gives students the assurance of accredited universities and quality online education, along with the support services they need to succeed. All UT campuses participating in UT TeleCampus–based degrees are SACS (Southern Association of Colleges and Schools) accredited. To learn more about online degrees or courses, prospective students should go to the Web site or call the TeleCampus office toll-free number listed below.*

## DISTANCE LEARNING PROGRAM

UT TeleCampus–based programs and courses are comprised of the same rigorous content found on-site at its fifteen campuses and research facilities. From application to graduation processes, students face the same general expectations and receive the same high-quality courses on-site or online. Online courses run semester to semester, allowing flexibility during the week for study and participation in group Web-based discussions. An online syllabus identifies when tests and projects are due.

An academic advisory committee oversees each online master's program. These committees are composed of deans and faculty members from participating schools, and together they ensure accreditation standards and the integrity of courses are upheld as they transfer from classroom to the Internet. Students receive the same academic credit for the courses listed with online degree programs as they would for similar courses offered on-site.

## DELIVERY MEDIA

The TeleCampus uses Internet technologies for course delivery and student support via the World Wide Web. Courses may also utilize additional distance education tools, including CDs, audiotapes and videotapes, streaming video and audio, e-mail, and chat rooms. Faculty members maintain interaction with students in a variety of ways, including timely responses to individual e-mail inquiries.

## PROGRAMS OF STUDY

The University of Texas System offers eight fully online master's degrees, undergraduate curriculum, nursing and health-care courses, and various certification programs. Courses and support services are delivered to the student online via the UT TeleCampus.

The M.B.A. in general management is a 48-hour program that received the U.S. Distance Learning Association's Excellence for Distance Learning Programming award.

The 36-hour M.Ed. in educational technology is designed for teachers, technology coordinators, and administrators who want to excel at integrating technology into the school curriculum.

A master's degree in curriculum and instruction with a reading specialization offers different tracks, including opting for a short, four-course English as a Second Language Endorsement Program.

Physical educators, athletic directors, and coaches can earn their master's degree in kinesiology online from their choice of four UT campuses.

Telecommunications professionals can select from three degrees: electrical engineering, computer science, or computer science and engineering as part of the CSEE program. All three degrees are conferred with the Graduate Telecommunications Engineering Certificate.

Other areas of study include most general undergraduate curriculum required in Texas, nursing courses and an innovative Chess in Education Program. Launching in spring 2002 are a bachelor's completion program in criminal justice and an undergraduate minor in management and information systems for business majors. Prospective students should visit the Web site, listed below, for updates and details.

## SPECIAL PROGRAMS

Faculty members from within University of Texas institutions develop all academic courses within the TeleCampus. Students receive the same academic credit from distance learning courses as they do for traditional, on-site instruction. In addition, students who are enrolled in courses from the TeleCampus receive identification that allows them to utilize the digital library and other password protected campus services. The TeleCampus has worked closely with registrars from each component in the UT System so that students enrolled in TeleCampus courses need only be admitted to one UT component to take courses across the system, rather than following traditional admissions procedures at every campus offering TeleCampus courses.

## STUDENT SERVICES

The UT TeleCampus was designed with the student in mind, providing all of the services students expect to find on a traditional campus, including admission, registrar, financial aid, bookstores, transcripts, veterans' resources, and student centers. In addition, important services for online students include a free online tutorial service, extensive digital libraries, searchable databases for use in research projects, chat rooms, academic computing, media, various resource links, and more.

## CREDIT OPTIONS

Transfer credit toward online courses and programs is generally the same as comparable on-site programs. Stu-dents should contact the program advisers listed inside the TeleCampus for specifics.

## FACULTY

The same nationally recognized faculty that teaches on-campus courses at the University of Texas campuses teaches online courses offered through the UT TeleCampus. Courses are designed and developed by these faculty members with production support and faculty development provided by the UT TeleCampus.

## ADMISSION

Admission criteria and processes for online offerings are approximately the same as on-site courses. It is advisable to start the initial application process 90 days prior to the beginning of a semester. Applications may be downloaded from links within the TeleCampus. Students may use e-mail, fax, and phone to facilitate the process in most cases.

## TUITION AND FEES

Tuition and fees vary slightly from program to program. Generally, graduate-level courses within the TeleCampus are approximately $200 per credit hour and $600 per 3-hour course for in-state tuition. Undergraduate courses average $100 per credit hour and $300 per 3-hour course. Students should access the UT TeleCampus Web site for specific details or call the TeleCampus office at the toll-free number listed below.

## FINANCIAL AID

Financial aid opportunities are available for students enrolled in TeleCampus courses. Links to financial aid offices are found by clicking on Student Services from within the TeleCampus. Students apply for financial aid via their home campus.

## APPLYING

Application processes for online courses are the same for on-site courses, although they can be completed without going to the campus. Calendars can be referenced from within the TeleCampus. Registration can also be completed from a distance, and the TeleCampus has detailed instructions. For collaborative online programs, a special form allows easy cross-campus registration when desired.

---

## CONTACT

Darcy W. Hardy, Director
UT TeleCampus
The University of Texas System
210 West Sixth Street, Suite 2100
Austin, Texas 78701
Telephone: 888-TEXAS-16 (toll-free)
Fax: 512-499-4715
E-mail: telecampus@utsystem.edu
Web site: http://www.telecampus.utsystem.edu

# The University of the Incarnate Word

## Universe Online
San Antonio, Texas

*The University of the Incarnate Word (UIW) was founded in 1881 as an outgrowth of the original mission of the Sisters of Charity of the Incarnate Word who settled in San Antonio, Texas, in 1869. The school maintains the mission of the founders by providing quality educational opportunities to all students, developing graduates who are concerned, and enlightening citizens. UIW is accredited by a variety of regional and national associations, but most notably by the regional accrediting body of the Commission on Colleges of the Southern Association of Colleges and Schools. Through its College of Professional Studies, UIW is nationally accredited by the Association of Collegiate Business Schools and Programs.*

## DISTANCE LEARNING PROGRAM

Universe Online is a natural extension of the mission and the entrepreneurial nature of UIW. By utilizing personal computers and asynchronous instruction, the program addresses the changing needs of adult learners. Maintaining the quality for which it is known, UIW allows students to complete a degree program totally online.

## DELIVERY MEDIA

Students accepted in the program use computer-conferencing software that allows for asynchronous interaction in an eight-week term format. Students will interact five out of seven days each week in both private and group discussion. Students are required to have an Internet Service Provider (ISP) to connect and upload/download assignments.

## PROGRAMS OF STUDY

Universe Online offers a variety of undergraduate degree programs and graduate programs.

The Bachelor of Business Administration prepares the student for today's changing business climate. The required core and choice of special- ization prepare students for positions of leadership in the business world. Areas of specialization include accounting, marketing, management, international business, and information systems.

The Bachelor of Arts in psychology of organizations and development is an interdisciplinary major that combines the findings and methods of psychology with business and specialized human resources courses.

The Master of Business Administration (M.B.A.) degree program seeks to develop in each student a broad understanding of how the elements and processes of business organizations relate to one another and to the external environment. Degree requirements are designed to develop students' proficiency and confidence in all of the functional areas of business.

The Master of Arts in Administration/Organizational Development (M.A.A. O.D.) degree program provides participants with the knowledge and skills required for managers, administrators, and supervisors to function more effectively in all types of organizations, plus the specialized managerial expertise needed for management positions within or related to the organizational development profession.

Students must complete both course work in their major field of study and the University's general studies core as required in all courses. A minimum of 128 credits of course work is required to graduate in all undergraduate programs. All classes, including graduate classes, are 3 credits (semester hours). Students must complete 36 semester hours to graduate from the graduate programs.

## STUDENT SERVICES

All students at UIW, including Universe Online students, have a wide variety of student service options. Online students have access to academic and financial aid advising, library and bookstore services, and online admission application and registration. In addition, students have access to career planning services.

## CREDIT OPTIONS

Universe Online welcomes transfer students. UIW accepts a maximum of 66 transferable hours from accredited two-year schools. These courses will be used to fulfill only lower-level division requirements. UIW will accept a total of 92 semester hours from senior colleges (or a combination of colleges).

Upon acceptance as a degree-seeking student at the University, a student must obtain prior written approval to transfer any additional credits from other institutions.

## FACULTY

Given the stringent requirements of national/regional accreditation, faculty members must meet a very exacting set of requirements; this has led to a high-quality educational program delivered by a highly credentialed and dedicated faculty.

## ADMISSION

Undergraduate students must possess a high school diploma or its equivalent. Students having previous college work must have a 2.5 GPA or better. Students must have worked for three years prior to application, in or outside of the home. Students who have not completed English composition I and II and college algebra must take these courses and may be tested for level.

Nonnative speakers of English must have a minimum score of 560 on the TOEFL. International student transcripts and course descriptions must be translated.

## TUITION AND FEES

Undergraduate tuition is $330 per credit and graduate tuition is $445 per credit. There is an application fee of $20 and a one-time transcript fee of $30.

## FINANCIAL AID

Financial aid and payment plans are available for all qualified students. Military benefits, as well as employer reimbursement benefits, may be used for online courses.

## APPLYING

To apply for admission, students can fill out an application for admission through the Web site listed below. In order to be considered for admission, students must fill out an application, remit a $20 nonrefundable application fee, and submit official high school or postsecondary school transcripts from all institutions attended. Students will be notified of application decisions via e-mail and U.S. mail.

---

**CONTACT**

Universe Online
University of the Incarnate Word
CPO #324
4301 Broadway
San Antonio, Texas 78209
Telephone: 877-827-2702 (toll-free)
Fax: 210-829-2756
E-mail: virtual@universe.uiwtx.edu
Web site: http://www.uiw.edu/online

---

# University of Tulsa

## *Internet-mediated MBA (iMBA™)*

Tulsa, Oklahoma

*The University of Tulsa is a private institution that was founded in 1894 in Indian Territory. The College of Business Administration was established in 1935 and is fully accredited by AACSB International - The Association to Advance Collegiate Schools of Business at both the graduate and undergraduate levels. As faculty members in the College of Business have sought to provide programs that are on the leading edge of technology, they have acted on the need to address new ways of delivering advanced education. The Internet-mediated MBA (iMBA™) was their response to professionals whose schedules simply would not permit regular classroom attendance. Interaction between student and professor is emphasized and encouraged in the iMBA. Graduates of the program receive the fully-accredited University of Tulsa M.B.A. degree. The iMBA program prepares graduates to be the successful managers businesses have come to expect from the University of Tulsa.*

## DISTANCE LEARNING PROGRAM

The iMBA makes graduate business education accessible to the motivated professional who would wish to earn an M.B.A., but cannot put his or her career on hold to get the degree. Students in classes of no more than 50 people enjoy more options for interaction with their professors and classmates than ever before.

## DELIVERY MEDIA

This technology-based online program requires students to have a computer with Internet access; Windows 95, 98, or NT; Office 2000; Netscape; speakers; and a sound card. All courses have been developed utilizing WebCT. Students are able to access chat rooms, e-mail, online forums, and bulletin boards . To access a sample course, visitors may visit the Web site at http://www.imba.utulsa.edu.

## PROGRAMS OF STUDY

The University of Tulsa designed an entire M.B.A. curriculum to be delivered online. This program, known as the iMBA, encompasses a solid M.B.A. curriculum with an added emphasis on information technology. It consists of two courses per term, three terms per year, and two years for completion. This is a part-time, 48-hour program in which 12 hours may be waived depending on the student's undergraduate degree and grades. Persons applying for this program must have at least two years of working experience following completion of their Baccalaureate degree. Students earn a high-quality M.B.A. from an internationally recognized and AACSB International–accredited university, the University of Tulsa.

Interactivity is a key component of the iMBA. Chat rooms, e-mail, and online forums provide a powerful arena for discussion, analysis, and collaboration. Students come to campus for one two-day session each term to meet their professors and classmates, receive orientation materials, and take their final exams.

By fall 2002, the University of Tulsa will begin offering the Master of Taxation program online. This 30-hour specialized program will bring graduate education to tax professionals whose schedules make class attendance nearly impossible or those who do not have local access to a Master of Taxation program.

## SPECIAL PROGRAMS

Because the majority of the graduate business students at the University of Tulsa have full-time jobs, all on-campus graduate business courses are offered in the evening. These include both foundation and advanced curriculum courses.

## STUDENT SERVICES

All students in the online programs receive training in the use of WebCT, the software in which all of the distance education courses reside. Students have an e-mail address within WebCT for communicating directly with classmates and faculty members in their respective classes. In addition, all students enrolled at the University of Tulsa are assigned a universal e-mail account. With the establishment of the university e-mail account, students may access McFarlin Library electronically. Both part-time and full-time students and alumni of the University of Tulsa may access Career Services.

## CREDIT OPTIONS

University policy allows for transfer of up to 6 credit hours at the master's level. Any such graduate credit must have been earned at an accredited graduate school and have been completed within the last six years. The graduate adviser is responsible for determining the applicability of transfer work to the student's program, subject to final approval by the Dean of Research and Graduate Studies.

## FACULTY

All faculty members who teach in the iMBA and the Master of Taxation programs have obtained a Ph.D. and/or a J.D.

## ADMISSION

Enrollment in the iMBA is limited to the fall term. Students must have a baccalaureate degree, two years work experience, preferably a 3.0 or better GPA, an acceptable GMAT score, and three letters of reference.

## TUITION AND FEES

The iMBA costs $25,000 for the entire six terms of advanced work. Foundation work is $530 per credit hour. Graduate student fees are $3 per credit hour and $100 additional fee for international students.

## FINANCIAL AID

Students are eligible to apply for Stafford loans (subsidized and unsubsidized) as well as other funded loans. Graduate students can normally apply year round for these loans. Students who are residents of the State of Oklahoma may apply for Oklahoma Tuition Aid Grants. The annual deadline for these grants is March 1. Students receiving reimbursement from their employers may arrange to defer tuition to match their reimbursement.

## APPLYING

For more detailed information on the iMBA or to apply online, students should visit the Web site at the address listed below. Students who want additional details on the Master of Taxation should go to the Web site and click on Graduate Business.

---

### CONTACT

Rebecca Holland, Ph.D.
Director of Graduate Business Programs
University of Tulsa
BAH 217, 600 S. College Avenue
Tulsa, Oklahoma 74104-3189
Telephone: 918-631-2680
Fax: 918-631-2142
E-mail: Graduate-Business@utulsa.edu
Web site: http://www.cba.utulsa.edu

# University of Utah

## Academic Outreach and Continuing Education
## Distance Education

Salt Lake City, Utah

---

> *Founded in 1850, the University of Utah is the premier research and teaching institution in the Intermountain West. Located just east of downtown Salt Lake City, the University is an urban campus serving more than 20,000 undergraduate and 5,000 graduate students. Students can choose from seventy-three majors at the undergraduate level and more than ninety-four major fields of study at the graduate level, as well as more than fifty teaching majors and minors.*
>
> *Utah offers students a huge array of outdoor activities to complement their academic studies on campus, which is minutes from the Wasatch Mountains and some of the best skiing in the world. The University will host athletes and serve as a venue for the opening and closing ceremonies of the 2002 Winter Olympic Games.*
>
> *The University of Utah is a member of the Northwest Association of Schools and Colleges.*

## DISTANCE LEARNING PROGRAM

The University of Utah's extension program, now called Academic Outreach and Continuing Education (AOCE), was established in 1913. The mission of today's AOCE is to extend the University's educational resources beyond its campus boundaries. This requires creative, flexible delivery routes, and ULEARN (formerly Independent Study and U-Online) is one of them. ULEARN is divided into two programs: Term Specific and Open Enrollment courses. Term Specific courses follow the semester system, while Open Enrollment courses follow an open-enrollment system that accepts registrations throughout the year; students have up to nine months to complete courses. ULEARN currently serves more than 2,800 students, offers a high level of communication with faculty members, and makes undergraduate credit courses available to students throughout the world.

## DELIVERY MEDIA

Assignments can be submitted by e-mail, fax, or postal mail. To take an online course, students need a computer (system requirements differ for each course and are listed in the course descriptions on the ULEARN Web site); an Internet connection and a browser (preferably 4.0 or higher; newer browsers work with plug-ins or media enhancements); and an e-mail address.

Exams for ULEARN courses must be proctored. This can take place at a university or college testing center. Students who cannot locate such a facility can take exams under the supervision of an approved proctor, such as a school district superintendent, the head librarian at a city or county library, a high school principal, or the town sheriff.

## PROGRAMS OF STUDY

ULEARN currently offers seventy-four courses from twenty academic departments. Thirteen educational studies courses from the Department of Teaching and Learning are offered, many of which can be applied toward the continuing education requirements of state education boards all over the United States. ULEARN offers general education courses in behavioral science, fine arts, science, humanities, and American history. These courses meet many of the graduation requirements for the University of Utah's general education program and may meet similar requirements at other institutions.

## CREDIT OPTIONS

The University of Utah does not currently offer an external degree. Courses earn regular college credit. There is no limit on credit hours that can be applied to a baccalaureate degree from Term Specific courses. Open Enrollment course credits may transfer to other schools; however, limits on the number of Open Enrollment course credit hours that may be applied toward a degree vary from one institution to another. University of Utah students may apply up to 30 semester units toward a bachelor's degree. Before enrolling in any Open Enrollment course, students are encouraged to contact their academic adviser to confirm that Open Enrollment course credit hours will be accepted. ULEARN courses may also be audited (students submit assignments for instructor's comments but take no exams; fees remain the same) or courses may be taken for credit/noncredit.

Military personnel should consult with their education officer, and teachers seeking endorsements and lane-change credit should speak with their school district or state board of education recertification specialist regarding Open Enrollment credit prior to enrolling in any Open Enrollment course.

## FACULTY

ULEARN courses are developed and taught by faculty members approved by the appropriate academic department at the University of Utah.

## ADMISSION

There are no admission requirements for ULEARN courses unless you are a matriculated (degree-seeking) University of Utah student. However, there are different registration procedures for matriculated and nonmatriculated students. The enrollment period options for each online course are listed in the course description on the University's Web site (listed below). All Term Specific courses begin and end at the same time as a traditional semester. All Open Enrollment courses operate under an open enrollment policy and have nine-month terms. There are no admission requirements. Enrollment in a ULEARN course does not constitute admission to the University of Utah.

## TUITION AND FEES

Students taking Term Specific courses pay regular campus tuition. (See the University's Web site for current costs.) Students taking Open Enrollment courses (nine-month term) pay $95 per semester unit of credit. This same tuition structure applies to credit/noncredit or audited courses. Required and optional textbooks and supplemental materials costs for ULEARN courses are listed in each course description. Textbooks can usually be purchased at neighborhood bookstores or through an online bookstore, including the University of Utah Bookstore. Open Enrollment course manuals cost approximately $15. All textbooks and any supplemental course materials, such as videotapes and computer disks for Open Enrollment courses, are purchased through Specialty Books and their costs vary. All fees are subject to change without notice, and payment for all fees and materials is due at the time of enrollment.

## FINANCIAL AID

Students should contact the financial aid office for details on distance education financial aid issues. Some companies pay all or part of tuition, fees, and books for employees. Students should consult their employers to see if funding for continuing education is available.

## APPLYING

A complete list of available ULEARN courses is located at the Web site listed below. To request a catalog of ULEARN courses, students should contact the University via any of the methods listed below. Once students have selected a course, they can enroll by mail, e-mail, fax, or phone.

---

### CONTACT

ULEARN
Academic Outreach and Continuing Education
Room 1215
1901 East South Campus Drive
University of Utah
Salt Lake City, Utah 84112-9359
Telephone: 801-581-8801
        800-467-8839 (toll-free)
Fax: 801-581-6267
E-mail: ulearn@aoce.utah.edu
Web site: http://www.ulearn.utah.edu

# University of Vermont

## *Distance Learning Network*

Burlington, Vermont

*The University of Vermont (UVM) is a state-supported university. It is accredited by the New England Association of Schools and Colleges. It first delivered courses via distance learning technologies in 1990. In 2000–01, it offered sixty courses at a distance to 750 students.*

## DISTANCE LEARNING PROGRAM

The University of Vermont's Distance Learning Network (DLN) works with academic departments to originate and support Web-based and interactive video courses to a variety of local, statewide, and national audiences.

## DELIVERY MEDIA

Courses are delivered to students nationally and internationally via the Internet, and to corporate sites, health-care facilities, high schools, interactive television locations, and to UVM regional centers in Brattleboro, Montpelier, and Rutland through a variety of media. Interactive video courses employ various other support technologies, based on the instructional goals of each course and the audience's geographic location and access to technology.

## PROGRAMS OF STUDY

The University of Vermont delivers courses and programs to students who are interested in part-time undergraduate, graduate, or professional studies, and to non-degree-seeking or continuing education students.

The Learning by Degrees: R.N.-B.S.-M.S. On-Line program is a fully accredited program that is designed for registered nurses who are interested in earning a bachelor's or master's degree at a distance. This degree completion program offers flexibility, accessibility, and personalized contact with advisers, colleagues, and faculty members. The online course format offers nurses the opportunity to work at their own pace and around their own schedules.

The Cyber Summer program offers degree-seeking and non-degree-seeking students the opportunity to study online from anywhere during the summer. More than twenty online courses were offered in summer 2001 to almost 500 students who chose to study online to explore the UVM curriculum, to make up a course, or to get ahead prior to the start of the fall semester.

In addition to the Cyber Summer curriculum, UVM offers Cyber Courses Year Round in mathematics, the liberal arts, engineering, and computer science, available in the fall and spring semesters.

The Certificate in Gerontology program is a series of courses that provide information that is required to work effectively in a number of fields related to aging. Studies include special topics in sociology, psychology, biology, policy and consumer affairs, nursing, and other issues related to elder care. This 18-credit-hour program may be completed in two to three years while working full-time. Courses are delivered to UVM regional centers, Vermont Interactive Television sites, and health-care facilities.

The School Library Media Studies Sequence prepares teachers and others for licensure as school library media specialists. Courses provide essential competencies required by the State of Vermont. All courses are at the upper/graduate level. Library professionals may find individual courses particularly useful for professional development, and some courses may be appropriate to degree programs in education. Courses are delivered via the Internet and interactive television.

The Master's Degree/Certificate of Advanced Studies in Educational Leadership program is a field-based graduate program that prepares leaders to serve with vision and integrity to make a positive difference in the lives of young people, adults, and families. A wide-ranging curriculum encourages students to think and act creatively, responsibly, and effectively in leadership roles. The program also prepares qualified individuals to earn Vermont Administrative Endorsement. Courses are delivered to UVM regional centers via interactive television.

The interdisciplinary Master of Public Administration program offers opportunities for specialization in fields such as health care, environmental issues, economic policy, and institutional finance. Students prepare for public service by learning or enhancing the leadership, analytical, and management skills that are essential to effective public administration and policy making. The curriculum is designed for those currently working in or seeking to work in nonprofit, government, or private sector organizations. Courses are delivered to UVM regional centers.

The Master of Social Work program, nationally accredited by the Council on Social Work Education (CSWE), prepares students for the multiple-role demands and organizationally based settings that are characteristic of social work in Vermont and the current era of social work in the U.S. This part-time program is designed for working professionals. Courses are delivered to UVM regional centers, Vermont Interactive Television sites, and health-care facilities, and utilize Web-based document delivery and other supports.

The Graduate Nursing program is a fully-accredited program that focuses on specialization and prepares professional nurses to assume leadership roles. Part-time study is available in adult health nursing, advanced population-focused nursing, and primary care nursing (nurse practitioner studies or nurse midwifery). Courses are delivered to UVM regional centers, Vermont Interactive Television sites, and health-care facilities.

The Bridge Plan toward the Bachelor of Science in Electrical Engineering is a series of courses that are available to prepare technical staff members of area industries to enter UVM's Bachelor of Science in Electrical Engineering program. Courses are delivered to selected corporate sites throughout Vermont, New Hampshire, and New York, through a variety of media.

## SPECIAL PROGRAMS

UVM's award-winning Advanced Placement program delivers courses to high schools and home-schooled students in Vermont, the New England region, and throughout the U.S. Designed and executed in consultation with the College Board, these courses follow a rigorous curriculum to prepare students for the annual AP exams. Courses are delivered from September to mid-May. English literature and composition and environmental science were available as of fall 2001 and are delivered using the Internet, video, satellite, or interactive television. Courses are offered tuition-free to Vermont high school students.

## STUDENT SERVICES

By using the World Wide Web and e-mail, students can gain access to the many resources available at the University of Vermont. Online library catalogs, journal indexes, searchable databases and other resources are available from the UVM libraries through the Web. Course text books and materials can be purchased through the UVM Bookstore via the Internet.

Students can establish e-mail accounts on the University computer system via the Web. In addition, students can contact a student adviser via e-mail at onlineadvisor@ced.uvm.edu.

## CREDIT OPTIONS

All courses in the programs listed above are for University credit, with the exception of the Advanced Placement courses for high school students.

## FACULTY

Eighty-nine percent of the 900 full-time faculty members hold the doctoral or terminal degree in their field. During the past academic year, 12 percent of the faculty participated in distance learning activities.

## ADMISSION

Admission in the programs listed above are dependent on the requirements of University schools and departments. Students should visit the Web site (listed below) and the UVM home page (http://www.uvm.edu) to determine admission requirements for each program.

## TUITION AND FEES

Tuition (summer 2001 to spring 2002) for courses delivered via distance technologies (i.e., the Internet, interactive television, or a combination of distance technologies) is $281 for non-degree-seeking and graduate students (Vermont residents and non-residents). Some courses may have additional fees for program materials or labs.

## FINANCIAL AID

Continuing Education (non-degree-seeking) students are eligible to apply for federal financial aid through the UVM Financial Aid Office and the Vermont Student Assistance Corporation (VSAC). The Stafford Loan Program, the VSAC Non-Degree Grant, and private sector loans and scholarships are available to qualified non-degree-seeking students.

---

### CONTACT

University of Vermont
Division of Continuing Education
322 South Prospect Street
Burlington, Vermont 05405
Telephone: 800-639-3210 (toll-free)
E-mail: eveninguniversity@uvm.edu
Web site: http://cybercourses.uvm.edu

# The University of Wyoming

## The Outreach School

Laramie, Wyoming

*The University of Wyoming (UW), a land-grant university founded in 1886, is accredited by the North Central Association of Colleges and Schools. The University of Wyoming was the first university west of the Missouri River to offer correspondence courses. In its outreach mission, the University of Wyoming is guided by the following vision: the state of Wyoming is the campus of the University of Wyoming. The University has one faculty and staff, one student body, and one set of academic programs. Teaching, research, and service are the mission of the University, regardless of location. The University recognizes that its "one student body" is composed of a wide variety of students whose needs differ.*

## DISTANCE LEARNING PROGRAM

The Outreach School delivers the University's distance learning programs. The mission of the Outreach School is to extend the University of Wyoming's educational programs and services to the state of Wyoming and beyond. The School delivers more than 300 courses and complete degree and certificate programs to approximately 3,000 students per semester, or 6,000 each year.

## DELIVERY MEDIA

The School launched Online UW, the University of Wyoming's virtual campus, in the spring of 1999 in cooperation with eCollege. In addition, the School delivers programs via Flexible Enrollment (correspondence study), audio-teleconference, and compressed video. Currently being offered through Online UW are bachelor's degrees in business administration and family and consumer sciences; an RN/B.S.N. completion degree in nursing; a master's degree in nursing with advanced practice in rural health, with clinical concentrations in community health clinical specialist and nurse educator; real estate certification; a master's degree in instructional technology; and an early childhood program director's

certificate. For more information, students can access the Online UW Web site (http://online.uwyo.edu). All flexible enrollment courses, a limited number of audio-teleconference courses, and all Online UW courses are available to students outside the state of Wyoming. Online UW generated over 1,000 enrollments in 1999-2000.

## PROGRAMS OF STUDY

Degrees and certificates are available to students outside Wyoming. Certificate programs include land surveying (offered nationwide through audio-teleconference with videotaped lectures), real estate certification (available online), and family and consumer sciences/early childhood program director's certificate (available online). Graduate programs include an M.S. in speech-language pathology (available nationwide through audio-tele-conference with videotaped lectures) and an M.S. in education with specialization in instructional technology (available online). Other available distance degrees are bachelor's degrees in business administration (online); criminal justice, psychology, and social science; an RN/B.S.N. completion program (available online); an M.S. in nursing with advanced practice in rural health/nurse educator option or community health clinical specialist

option (both online); an M.B.A. (available statewide via compressed video); an M.S. in kinesiology and health; an M.S.W. in social work; an M.P.A. (available through audio-teleconference and compressed video); and master's degrees in education, with specialization options in special education, adult and postsecondary education, and teaching and learning.

## SPECIAL PROGRAMS

The University of Wyoming's virtual campus, Online UW, currently offers more than eighty courses and seven degrees completely online. Courses are available worldwide via http://online.uwyo.edu. Online courses are available in the areas of adult learning, astronomy, biochemistry, business administration, child development, directing preschool and day-care programs, economics, education, engineering, family and consumer sciences, human resources management, instructional technology, nutrition, physics, psychology, real estate, religion, statistics, and Western integrated resource education.

## STUDENT SERVICES

All student services (such as admission, enrollment, tuition payment, grade reporting, financial aid, and bookstore and library outreach) are available through the Outreach School.

## CREDIT OPTIONS

Students may transfer courses from accredited institutions of higher education. Credit is also available through AP, CLEP, portfolio assessment, and departmental examinations. Degrees require a minimum of 48 hours of upper-division credit, with a minimum of 30 credits from the University of Wyoming. Most degree programs require 120–124 credits for graduation.

## FACULTY

The majority of those who teach in the Outreach School are full-time faculty members at the University of Wyoming. A limited number of adjunct faculty members, who are approved by the academic departments, offer distance learning courses. The programs offered via distance learning are the same programs offered on the main University campus in Laramie, Wyoming. In any given semester, approximately 75 regular full-time faculty members and 15 part-time adjunct faculty members teach distance learning courses for the Outreach School.

## ADMISSION

Students not seeking a University of Wyoming degree may enroll in distance learning courses without being admitted to the University. Students can apply a maximum of 12 credit hours toward the requirements for a UW undergraduate degree prior to

admission to the University. Degree-seeking students should apply to the Admissions Office. Undergraduate admission generally requires completion of at least 13 high school units in a precollege curriculum, a cumulative high school grade point average of at least 2.75, an ACT score of at least 20, or an SAT score of at least 960. Conditional admission is available for adult learners who do not meet these criteria. Graduate programs require a Graduate Record Exam (GRE) combined verbal and quantitative score of at least 900. The University offers GRE testing through the University of Wyoming Testing Center. For more information, students can visit the Web site (http://www.uwyo.edu/ucc/utc/).

## TUITION AND FEES

All outreach students are charged tuition at an in-state rate. Undergraduate tuition for outreach courses is $96.50 per credit hour with a $10-per-credit-hour delivery fee or a $40-per-credit-hour delivery fee for Online UW courses. Graduate tuition for outreach courses is $160.85 per credit hour with a $10-per-credit-hour delivery fee or a $40-per-credit-hour de-

livery fee for Online UW courses. Tuition for the Master of Social Work degree program is $349.70 per credit hour with a $10-per-credit-hour fee. Delivery fees are nonrefundable. Tuition for the M.B.A. program is $206.75 per credit hour and tuition for the land surveying program is $175.00 per credit hour.

## FINANCIAL AID

All forms of federal financial aid and other scholarship aid are available to Outreach students. The Outreach School also has a number of $1000 scholarships available to Outreach students. Information describing available aid and award criteria is available from the Office of Student Financial Aid, P.O. Box 3335, University of Wyoming, Laramie, Wyoming 82071.

## APPLYING

Non-degree-seeking students may apply through the Office of Outreach Credit Programs. Degree-seeking students should apply through the Admissions Office (telephone: 307-766-2287) or Graduate Admissions (telephone: 307-766-2118). For more information, students can visit the Web site (http://www.uwyo.edu).

---

**CONTACT**

The Outreach School
Office of Outreach Credit Programs
University of Wyoming
P.O. Box 3274
Laramie, Wyoming 82071-3274
Telephone: 307-766-4300
       800-448-7801 (toll-free)
Fax: 307-766-3445
E-mail: occ@uwyo.edu
Web site: http://outreach.uwyo.edu

---

# University System of Georgia Independent Study

## University of Georgia Center for Continuing Education

Athens, Georgia

---

> University System of Georgia Independent Study (USGIS) is an academic department of the University of Georgia Center for Continuing Education. The mission of University System of Georgia Independent Study is to offer University System academic credit courses to University System students and individuals who are interested in earning academic credit through distance learning methods and technologies.

## DISTANCE LEARNING PROGRAM

University System of Georgia Independent Study offers undergraduate academic credit courses through senior institutions of the University System of Georgia, including Armstrong Atlantic State University, Georgia College and State University, Georgia Southern University, North Georgia College and State University, the University of Georgia, and Valdosta State University. USGIS allows flexibility of registration, permitting students to register at any time and to take several courses simultaneously, with up to one year to complete each course (students may purchase a three-month extension). Academic credit is recorded on the student's permanent record in the University of Georgia Registrar's Office and may be used for degree requirements according to the regulations of the institution from which the student plans to graduate. Approximately 5,000 students enroll in 6,000 USGIS courses annually. USGIS recommends that students enrolled in degree programs consult with their academic adviser prior to enrollment in a USGIS course. (While USGIS has added a certification, it does not yet offer an entire degree program.)

When students enroll in an Independent Study course, they receive a course guide and packet with materials necessary for course completion. Students must purchase required textbooks and materials. Each course consists of readings, written lesson assignments, and a final examination (some courses have midterm examinations). Students complete the lessons and submit assignments at their own pace. Midterm and final examinations must be taken under the supervision of an approved test site (such as an accredited college or university). Students must pass the final examination to pass the course. Technology enrollment options (described below) are available for selected courses.

## DELIVERY MEDIA

All USGIS courses are available in the traditional print version of the course guide, allowing submission of lessons via the U.S. Postal Service. Technology enrollment options are described below. Students may choose these technology enrollment options for selected courses on the registration form.

Web courses are taken completely on line, with the exception of the course midterm and/or final examinations (all USGIS examinations must be taken at an approved test site). Web courses offer a variety of online features, such as course guides, lesson submission, World Wide Web resources, and e-mail links to Independent Study.

An e-mail lesson submission course has the same requirements and follows the same process as the traditional print-based version, with one exception: lessons are delivered to Independent Study via e-mail rather than through the U.S. Postal Service. Students receive a print-based course guide or Electronic Course Guide (E-Guide) on diskette containing the same information. All e-mail lessons are submitted to Independent Study for forwarding to the instructor for grading. Once graded, lessons are returned via e-mail to students.

Many University System of Georgia Independent Study courses are available as E-Guides. This version offers the course guide and written assignments for the course in electronic format on diskette. E-Guides are created using Adobe Portable Document Format (PDF) technology. PDF files are universally readable by both IBM and Macintosh computers through the use of the Adobe Acrobat Reader, which is available as a free download (http://www.adobe.com).

Lesson submission via fax is available for all courses, except those lessons requiring audiotape or project submissions. There is no charge for submission of ungraded lessons by fax. There is a fee to have graded lessons returned to the student via fax.

## PROGRAMS OF STUDY

Approximately 120 courses are offered in the areas of agricultural and environmental sciences, arts and sciences, business, education, family and consumer sciences, forestry, and journalism and mass communication.

## TUITION AND FEES

USGIS nonresident credit tuition is $104 per semester hour ($312 for a 3-semester-hour course). Tuition is payable in full by check, money orders drawn on United States banks or international banks with affiliate branches in the U.S., international money order, or credit card (MasterCard, Visa, and Discover). USGIS accepts authorization invoices to bill from an outside agency. Special fees such as drop/add, extension, special airmail/handling, and return of graded lessons via fax are described in the catalog and on the Web site listed below. USGIS does not provide financial aid or scholarship services.

## APPLYING

Students must submit a completed registration form, which may be obtained from an Independent Study Bulletin, with appropriate fees. Students have the option of enrolling on line from the USGIS Web site with credit card payment. Registration for a USGIS course does not require admission tests, transcripts of previous high school or college work, or enrollment in a college or university. High school and home school students enrolled in a college early admission or joint-enrollment program may enroll in USGIS courses. Enrollment is effective for one year and may be extended for an additional three months if the extension fee is received prior to the course expiration date. Students should contact USGIS for more information.

---

### CONTACT

Melissa Pettigrew or a Student Representative
University System of Georgia Independent Study
University of Georgia Center for Continuing Education
Athens, Georgia 30602-3603
Telephone: 706-542-3243
          800-877-3243 (toll-free)
Fax: 706-542-6635
E-mail: usgis@arches.uga.edu
Web site: http://www.gactr.uga.edu/usgis

---

# Upper Iowa University

## Extended University

Fayette, Iowa

*Upper Iowa University (UIU) was established in 1857 and has since become the second-largest private university in the state of Iowa. Unlike some of the newer schools offering distance learning programs, UIU has a beautiful residential campus on 90 acres with seven academic buildings and three residence halls. Upper Iowa also has seventeen sports teams, known as the Peacocks, who compete in the NCAA Division III. As a nonprofit, rapidly growing, four-year liberal arts institution of higher learning, UIU offers a wide range of high-quality degree programs to more than 4,500 students worldwide. Its vision is to become a distinctively entrepreneurial university that meets the educational needs of learners worldwide. Upper Iowa University is accredited by the Higher Learning Commission and is a member of the North Central Association (Web: http://www.ncahigherlearningcommission.org; telephone: 312-263-0456.*

## DISTANCE LEARNING PROGRAM

The Extended University's distance learning programs are offered through two primary modes of delivery. Its External Degree program offers Associate of Arts and Bachelor of Science degree programs with nine majors through independent study/correspondence, and its Online program currently offers a Bachelor of Science (B.S.) with four business majors and a Master of Business Administration (M.B.A.). Courses offered through both External Degree and Online formats meet the same standards as courses offered through the residential University in Fayette, Iowa. The External Degree program, which began in 1972, has been successfully delivered to more than 10,000 learners. Upper Iowa's External Degree program was one of the first and most successful in the United States. Both the External Degree and Online programs continue to be vital components in serving both civilian and military learners worldwide.

## DELIVERY MEDIA

In the External Degree program, students communicate with instructors via e-mail, fax, and regular mail. Classes are self-paced with no minimum completion time. Upper Iowa's Online program is noted for its e-mail–like feel. Online students log on (via the Internet) just long enough to send and receive materials, anytime, anywhere, day or night. Most work is accomplished off-line, or through asynchronous communication. Online students may also communicate with their instructors through course software, e-mail, fax, or phone.

## PROGRAMS OF STUDY

Upper Iowa University has a long history of offering high-quality degree programs through distance learning. In the External Degree program, associate and bachelor's degree programs are available in a wide range of academic areas including accounting, business, human resources management, human services, management, marketing, psychology, public administration (general, law enforcement, or fire science), social science, and technology and information management. Upper Iowa's Online program offers a Bachelor of Science degree with four majors to choose from:

accounting, management, marketing, and technology and information management. The M.B.A. offers four areas of emphasis: accounting, human resources management, quality, and organizational development. The course work focuses on the theories and skills that will be the foundation for tomorrow's organizations, including organizational design, total quality management, self-managed teams, employee empowerment, change management, facilitation skills, high-performance work systems, and more.

## SPECIAL PROGRAMS

Each summer the external degree program sponsors the Institute for Experiential Learning (IEXL) for undergraduate students. During an intensive week-long session held on the Fayette campus, students have the opportunity to earn 3 semester hours of undergraduate credit while visiting the residential campus and networking with other learners from around the world.

## STUDENT SERVICES

External degree and online students are provided with one-on-one academic advising via U.S. mail, e-mail, telephone, fax communication, and through use of a special software/courseware package (for online program students). In addition to local university libraries, undergraduate and graduate students and faculty members have access to the Henderson Wilder Library holdings through Upper Iowa University's Web site (listed below).

## CREDIT OPTIONS

Full credit is given for college-level courses completed at regionally accredited colleges and universities. Students can transfer a maximum of 45 semester hours for an associate degree, 90 semester hours for a bachelor's degree, and 12 semester hours for a master's degree. Other sources of credit include the American Council on Education (ACE), the College-Level Examination Program (CLEP), Defense Activity for Nontraditional Education support (DANTES) subject exams, and experiential learning.

## FACULTY

Upper Iowa University has more than 100 faculty members, all of whom have doctorates or terminal degrees. Nearly 70 percent are adjunct faculty members who are involved in distance learning programs.

## ADMISSION

Admissions criteria for undergraduate degrees include graduation from an accredited public or private high school or completion of the GED test or its equivalent. For the graduate program, prospective students must hold an undergraduate degree from a regionally accredited college or university. More information regarding grade point requirements, TOEFL scores for international students, and tranfer credit is available upon request or on the UIU Web site (listed below).

## TUITION AND FEES

Associate- and baccalaureate-level tuition for courses taken through External Degree (independent study/correspondence) or at off-campus learning centers (classroom) for 2001–02 is $498 per 3–semester credit course. Undergraduate and graduate online (Internet-based) courses are $648 and $870 respectively per 3-semester credit course.

## FINANCIAL AID

Financial aid in the form of Federal Stafford Loan or PELL Grants, Iowa Tuition Grants (Iowa residents only), Veterans Assistance, and Military Tuition Assistance is available. Last year, a total of $273,420 in financial aid was disbursed to 21 percent of Upper Iowa University's distance learning students.

## APPLYING

Students may enroll in UIU distance learning programs at any time. In the External Degree program, students may start courses at any time. In the Online program, eight-week terms begin six times a year. Students should send official transcripts (including CLEP, DANTES, or DD-214), GRE/GMAT score reports (if required), and a completed Application for Admission form (available online or by contacting the school via telephone or e-mail) directly to Upper Iowa University at the address below.

---

### CONTACT

Extended University
Upper Iowa University
605 Washington Street, P.O. Box 1857
Fayette, Iowa 52142-1857
Telephone: 877-366-0581
Fax: 319-425-5771
E-mail: moreinfo@uiu.edu
Web site: http://www.uiu.edu

---

# Utah State University

## Independent and Distance Education

Logan, Utah

---

> Utah State University (USU) was founded in 1888 as part of the public educational system of Utah and operates under the constitution and laws of the state. It belongs to the family of institutions known as land-grant universities, which had their origin in 1862. USU is governed by the State Board of Regents and accredited by Northwest Association of Schools and Colleges.
>
> USU integrates teaching, research, extension, and service to meet its unique role as Utah's land-grant university. Students are the focus of the University as they seek intellectual, personal, and cultural development.

## DISTANCE LEARNING PROGRAM

USU Extension Services is an integral part of USU's outreach mission. USU Independent & Time Enhanced Learning is part of University Extension Services and is comprised of video-streamed degree programs offered over a state-of-the-art satellite system in partnership with the Utah Education Network (UEN), a graduate-level online program, and correspondence courses. Enrollments through Independent & Time Enhanced Learning average 3,000 each semester.

## DELIVERY MEDIA

USU Independent & Time Enhanced Learning employs several medias for delivery of courses and degrees. Video-streamed programs originate at USU and are taught at specific Mountain times. Students who register for video-streamed classes may interact with their instructors via e-mail. Online courses are designed for access and time of day or night. Online students submit assignments electronically and interact with their instructors via e-mail and online discussions. Students who register for print-based (correspondence) courses receive a course outline at registration, mail-in assignments, and take proctored examinations. Correspondence students may contact their instructors by phone or e-mail.

## PROGRAMS OF STUDY

USU Independent & Time Enhanced Learning offers four undergraduate degrees and two graduate degrees via a video-streaming option, and an online Master of Science in English degree with a specialization in technical writing. The graduate technical writing degree is designed primarily for nontraditional students—working technical/professional communicators who want to enhance their credentials and build a strong theoretical understanding of their profession. However, the program also accepts some traditional students who have just finished their undergraduate studies, or working professionals from other fields who are seeking to become technical/professional communicators. Applicants must be admitted to the program prior to registering for online courses in technical writing.

## SPECIAL PROGRAMS

USU Independent & Time Enhanced Learning video streaming option offers bachelor's and master's degrees to students with the required computer hardware and software. Bachelor's degrees offered include accounting, business administration, business information systems, and psychology. Master's degrees are offered in business information systems and human environments.

The Bachelor of Science in accounting degree is designed to prepare students for accounting and business careers in industry and government and prepares students for graduate study in such areas as accounting, business, and law.

The Bachelor of Science in business administration degree is a general business major that covers all major business functions and is designed to prepare students for administrative positions in business and government.

The Bachelor of Science in business information systems is designed for students who want to qualify for positions as information specialists, systems analysts, network managers, Internet support personnel, information managers, and end-user computing specialists in business and industry.

The Bachelor of Science in psychology degree is designed to provide students with knowledge in the broad discipline areas of psychology to prepare for employment in private/public education, human services, government, and corporations.

The Master of Science in business information systems and education is designed for candidates who want to work in system analysis and design, as information and computer specialists in business and industry, and for candidates who plan to teach in business or marketing.

The Master of Science in human environments places emphasis on teaching and curriculum/program development and/or extension. It prepares students for community professions in secondary teaching, urban and rural extension, social sciences, and business.

## STUDENT SERVICES

Student services available to distance learners include access to the University bookstore, Library Support System for Distance Learners, Online Book Exchange, and writing and researching resources. For more information on student services available to distance learners, prospective students should visit the Web site http://online.usu.edu/student_resources/.

## CREDIT OPTIONS

Credit earned through USU Independent & Time Enhanced Learning is measured in semester units and is transferable to most colleges and universities in the U.S. Students who plan to transfer credit should make arrangements with the transfer institution prior to registration.

## FACULTY

Ninety percent of Independent & Time Enhanced Learning instructors are USU faculty members; many are leading researchers in their field. Independent & Time Enhanced Learning faculty members recognize that the needs of individuals are of major importance; programs have been established to give students optimal individual attention.

## ADMISSION

Admission requirements are program specific and may be obtained by contacting the Admissions Office at 435-797-1079. Prospective students may complete an application for admission online at http://www.usu.edu/~registra/admrec.

## TUITION AND FEES

Tuition for classes in the graduate technical writing degree program is $200 per credit.

## FINANCIAL AID

Financial aid is available for distance education students. Utah State University participates in the following financial aid programs: Federal Pell Grants, Federal Supplemental Educational Opportunity Grants (FSEOG), LEAAP Grants, Federal Perkins Loans, Federal Work-Study, Federal Stafford Loans, Plus Loans, scholarships, and emergency loans. For more information, prospective students should contact the financial aid office at 435-797-0173 or visit the Web site at http://www.usu.edu/~finaid/.

## APPLYING

Students working toward any of the degree programs offered through Independent & Time Enhanced Learning must be admitted to the University. Prospective students may complete an application for admission online at http://www.usu.edu/~registra/admrec or request a printed application by contacting the Admissions Office at 435-797-1079.

## CONTACT

Independent & Time Enhanced Learning
3080 Old Main Hill
Utah State University
Logan, Utah 84322-3080
Telephone: 800-233-3137 (toll-free)
Fax: 435-797-1399
E-mail: de-info@ext.usu.edu
Web site: http://extension.usu.edu
http://online.usu.edu/

# Virginia Polytechnic Institute and State University

## *Institute for Distance and Distributed Learning*

Blacksburg, Virginia

*For more than a century, Virginia Tech has been a leader in providing high-quality undergraduate, graduate, and continuing education and an innovator in instructional methods and delivery modes. Founded in 1872 as the state's land-grant university, Virginia Tech is dedicated to instruction, research, and outreach. The University offers more than 200 degree programs and, with an enrollment of approximately 25,000 students, is the largest university in Virginia. A comprehensive land-grant university with seven undergraduate colleges, a graduate school, and a veterinary college, Virginia Tech is also one of the nation's leading research institutions. Virginia Tech is committed to the creation of new knowledge and the transfer and dissemination of that knowledge to serve Virginia, the nation, and the international community. The University has a long and successful history of providing distance learning programming and opportunities. In recent years, the University has gained national recognition for its creative initiatives in faculty development, instructional technology, and networking. The University continues to break the barriers of time and space by providing quality learning opportunities anywhere and anytime. Using advanced technologies, Virginia Tech is creating more responsive teaching and learning environments while meeting the changing needs, resources, and expectations of its students. Through Virginia Tech's open and extended campus environment, the University is meeting the changing needs of undergraduate and graduate students, assisting in the training efforts of employers, and supporting lifelong learning. Virginia Tech is accredited by the Commission on Colleges of the Southern Association of Colleges and Schools.*

## DISTANCE LEARNING PROGRAM

The Institute for Distance and Distributed Learning provides leadership, coordination, and support to the growing distance and distributed learning activities of Virginia Tech. The Institute takes a holistic approach to distance learning where all aspects of a student's educational experience are considered. Through distance and distributed learning, Virginia Tech extends its campus to communities throughout the commonwealth and provides an open campus environment that allows individuals to engage in learning anytime, anywhere. In addition, Virginia Tech shares the practical application of the University's knowledge and expertise in support of economic development, increases the University's access to the world and the world's access to the University, and researches new teaching and learning environments through the application of technology. More than 7,300 enrollments were accounted for in more than 200 different courses and fourteen master's degrees and six certificate programs. Virginia Tech actively participates in the Electronic Campus of Virginia and the Southern Region Electronic Campus and collaboratively delivers courses and degree programs at a distance with other Virginia colleges and universities through the Commonwealth Graduate Engineering Program and the Virginia Consortium of Engineering and Science Universities.

## DELIVERY MEDIA

Faculty members utilize multiple methods of instructional delivery and student interaction to provide an engaging, high-quality learning environment. Virginia Tech delivers distance learning courses via the Internet, videoconferencing, satellite, archived video, and desktop computer audio-graphics. Net.Work.Virginia is a statewide, high-speed, broadband ATM network that uses cutting-edge technology. The network is used to support different types of teaching and learning activities and allows faculty members to customize their courses to meet the needs of their students. Through Net.Work.Virginia, Virginia Tech provides electronically delivered two-way interactive video courses to its four extended campuses (Northern Virginia Center, Roanoke Graduate Center, Southwest Virginia Higher Education Center, Hampton Roads Graduate Center, and Richmond Center) and numerous other higher education, government, business, and industry sites located in Virginia and several other states. The University uses the Internet to provide a variety of learning opportunities through online assignments, chat rooms, threaded discussions, e-mail, and audio and computer conferencing.

## PROGRAMS OF STUDY

Virginia Tech provides working professionals with the opportunity to obtain a master's degree in fourteen different programs through distance and distributed learning. These programs include a Master of Business Administration; Master of Science degrees in Aerospace Engineering, Civil Engineering, Electrical and Computer Engineering, Industrial and Systems Engineering, Instructional Technology, Materials Science and Engineering, Ocean Engineering, Physical Education, and Systems Engineering; a Master of Arts in Political Science; and a career and technical education master's degree. Virginia Tech also offers certificate programs in administration of community-based services for older adults, career and technical education licensure, computer engineering, networking, software development, and information policy and society studies.

A wide variety of credit and noncredit courses is also offered through distance learning in the areas of accounting, architecture, art, biology, black studies, building construction, communications, computer science, economics, education, engineering, English, entomology, finance, geography, hotel management, information science, landscape architecture, management, marketing, math, philosophy, physics, psychology, science and technology, sociology, Spanish, statistics, and women's studies.

## STUDENT SERVICES

Virginia Tech distance learners have the ability to register on line and to access student information and services. The Virginia Tech Online Writing Lab (VT OWL) offers an electronic tutoring environment. Online tutoring sessions are individually scheduled between tutor and client, so there are no fixed hours. The OWL also includes a self-help area and a grammar hotline. The self-help area contains handouts and exercises to provide any person with 24-hour access to writing assistance. The grammar hotline (gram@vt.edu) is an e-mail-based service available to students and nonstudents alike; its main purpose is to provide assistance to students with writing questions that can be answered immediately.

Virginia Tech also provides extensive access to library services. Addison, the online library catalog, is available as a Web or telnet interface. Electronic reference assistance is easily accessed through the library's AskUs request form. Students may also contact the University's distance education librarian. Distance learners have access to Virginia Tech's full-text electronic resources and databases plus document delivery services.

## CREDIT OPTIONS

Distance learners can transfer credits earned at other accredited postsecondary institutions to Virginia Tech following the established University policies. Students admitted to the University who have been certified by the Virginia Community College System or Richard Bland College as completing the transfer module will be deemed to have completed the University core curriculum components and will receive 35 total credits for the module.

## FACULTY

The faculty is the foundation of Virginia Tech's distance learning programs and assures its academic excellence. Virginia Tech has 1,425 full-time instructional faculty members, more than 160 of whom taught distance learning courses in 2000–01.

## ADMISSION

To become undergraduate or graduate degree candidates at Virginia Tech, students must apply formally for admission. Students' records at Virginia Tech and all other colleges and universities attended are reviewed within the context of current admission policies.

As a member of the Electronic Campus of Virginia, Virginia Tech allows qualified students at other Virginia universities and colleges to enroll in its courses as transient students. For more information on undergraduate admissions, students should refer to the Admissions Web site at http://www.admiss.vt.edu; those interested in graduate programs should see Graduate Admission's Web site at http://www.rgs.vt.edu.

## TUITION AND FEES

Tuition for undergraduate courses for in-state residents is $349.50 for one 3-credit-hour course; it is $1452 for one 3-credit-hour course for out-of-state residents. Tuition for graduate courses for in-state residents is $724.50 for one 3-credit-hour course; it is $1219.50 for one 3-credit-hour course for out-of-state residents. Tuition for noncredit courses varies. Complete information on tuition and fees can be found on the World Wide Web at http://www.bursar.vt.edu/tuit_fees_2001-2002.htm.

## FINANCIAL AID

Virginia Tech is a direct lending institution and awards financial aid from federally funded and state-funded programs as well as privately funded sources. Financial aid sources include the Federal Direct Stafford Loan, Federal Perkins Loan, Federal Direct PLUS Loan, Federal Pell Grant, Federal Work-Study, Virginia Guaranteed Assistance program, Commonwealth Award, and the College Scholarship Assistance Program.

## APPLYING

Students applying for undergraduate admission can access current information at http://www.admiss.vt.edu. Students applying for graduate admission can access current information at http://www.rgs.vt.edu. Students can register for Internet-based courses at http://www.vto.vt.edu. There is a nonrefundable $25 processing fee for non–Virginia Tech, non–program bound undergraduate students.

### CONTACT

Cate Mowrey
Institute for Distance and
    Distributed Learning
Virginia Polytechnic Institute and
    State University
Blacksburg, Virginia 24061-0445
Telephone: 540-231-9584
Fax: 540-231-2079
E-mail: vtwebreg@vt.edu
Web site: http://www.iddl.vt.edu
            http://www.vto.vt.edu
            (online catalog)

# Walden University

*Graduate Distance Education*

Minneapolis, Minnesota

---

*Academic programs at Walden University combine high-quality curriculum and innovative distance delivery models. The result is a collection of highly applied, rigorous programs that are flexible. These programs are ideally suited to adult learners who wish to pursue an advanced degree without the professional and personal sacrifices associated with traditional, campus-based programs.*

*Four academic divisions make up Walden University: the Management Division, the Education Division, the Health and Human Services Division, and the Psychology Division. Walden students complete much of their work on line. Both doctoral and master's degrees are offered.*

*A pioneer in distance delivery, Walden has been serving the needs of adult learners since the University's founding in 1970. Walden University is accredited by the North Central Association of Colleges and Schools.*

## DISTANCE LEARNING PROGRAM

Walden University enrolls nearly 1,600 students from all fifty states and thirty other countries. One half of the University's students are members of minority groups. The University offers programs that allow busy adults to complete a master's or Ph.D. degree from home or work on their own schedules.

## DELIVERY MEDIA

Depending on the program in which they are enrolled, Walden students complete much of their degree requirements through online interaction, instruction, and submission of work. Individual mentoring, online courses, and progress based on demonstrations of knowledge are among the ingredients found in Walden's delivery system. Students enrolling in a Walden program should be comfortable using a personal computer, a word processor, and e-mail.

## PROGRAMS OF STUDY

Ph.D. programs are offered in applied management and decision sci-

ences, education, health services, human services, and psychology. Master of Science degrees are offered in education, psychology, and public health.

The Ph.D. in applied management and decision sciences program comprises 128 quarter credit hours. Students may elect a broad program or a self-designed specialization or specialize in engineering management, finance, information systems management, leadership and organizational change, or operations research.

The Ph.D. in education program comprises 128 quarter credit hours. Enrollment options include a general program, an educational technology specialization, a higher education specialization, a K–12 educational leadership specialization, an early childhood specialization, an adult education leadership specialization offered in collaboration with Indiana University, and a self-designed specialization.

The Ph.D. in health services program comprises 128 quarter credit hours. General study is available, as are a self-designed specialization and spe-

cializations in community health, health administration, and health and human behavior.

The Ph.D. in human services program comprises 128 quarter credit hours. Students may design a specialization or specialize in clinical social work, counseling, criminal justice, family and intervention strategies, or social policy analysis and planning.

The course-based Ph.D. in professional psychology program comprises 127 quarter credit hours. Specializations offered include academic psychology, clinical psychology, counseling psychology, health psychology, and organizational psychology.

The course-based, online M.S. in psychology program comprises 45 quarter credit hours.

The M.S. in education program comprises 45 quarter credit hours and has specializations in classroom education, educational change and innovation, educational technology, and middle-level education.

The M.S. in public health program comprises 50 quarter credit hours and has a focus on community health.

## SPECIAL PROGRAMS

Walden University offers a limited number of National Service Fellowships to enrolled doctoral students. These fellowships are available to students who have dedicated their careers to public service. National Service Fellowships are competitive among enrolled students who have completed at least one full academic quarter. Each fellowship includes an annual (twelve-month) remission of tuition and fees of $1500 per academic year, renewable up to three years.

Through its Higher Education Professional Development Fellowship program, Walden University offers other educational institutions a way to help faculty and staff members upgrade academic credentials. A minimum of 2 participants from an institution is required for participation in this fellowship, which provides waiver of the application, orientation materials, and commencement fees and reduces tuition by 10 percent.

School- and school district–based cohort groups in education are welcome and receive a tuition discount and learner support groups.

## STUDENT SERVICES

Student services include academic counseling, financial aid services, an information technology help desk, orientation programming, and dissertation editing.

Walden University's partnership with the Indiana University library provides students with access to a collection of more than 4 million journals. Walden's full-time staff at the Indiana University–Bloomington graduate library provides reference, search, catalog, and distribution services.

## CREDIT OPTIONS

For the M.S. programs in education and psychology, up to 16 quarter credit hours are accepted in transfer. Up to 36 quarter credit hours may be transferred into the Ph.D. in psychology program. For the Ph.D. in education program, up to 42 quarter credit hours are transferable. The Ph.D. in applied management and decision sciences allows for the transfer of up to 20 quarter credit hours into the finance, leadership and organizational change, and operations research specializations.

## FACULTY

Walden University has 200 faculty members. Risky students have a faculty mentor who provides individualized attention as they pursue their degree.

## ADMISSION

For admission, a bachelor's or master's degree from a regionally accredited institution and two to three years of professional experience are required, depending on the program of study.

## TUITION AND FEES

Tuition for doctoral programs is $3245 per quarter. For psychology (Ph.D.

and M.S.) and master's in public health students, tuition is $310 per credit hour. For the M.S. in education, tuition is $235 per credit hour.

## FINANCIAL AID

Walden University offers prospective students a variety of options to assist in funding their educational expenses. Approximately 64 percent of Walden students receive some form of financial assistance. Many receive 100 percent assistance in the payment of tuition and fees. Options available include federal financial assistance programs, veterans' education benefits, and institutional fellowships. Discounts are also available for group/spousal enrollment. In addition, Walden can assist students in securing private scholarships, employer tuition benefits, and loans from private lenders.

## APPLYING

Submission of a completed and signed application, a $50 application fee, and a personal/professional statement of purpose is required. Applicants must also send a resume, official transcripts (from the institution that conferred the bachelor's or master's degree), and two required recommendation forms. Students can also apply on the Web at the address listed below.

---

### CONTACT

Walden University
155 Fifth Avenue South
Minneapolis, Minnesota 55401
Telephone: 800-444-6795 (toll-free)
Fax: 941-498-4266
E-mail: info@waldenu.edu
Web site: http://www.waldenu.edu

---

 # Washington State University

## *Distance Degree Programs*

Pullman, Washington

---

*Washington State University (WSU), the state's land-grant institution, is dedicated to the preparation of students for productive lives and professional careers, to basic and applied research, and to the dissemination of knowledge. Founded in 1890, the University is a statewide institution with a main campus in Pullman, three branch campuses, eleven community learning centers, and numerous Cooperative Extension and research facilities throughout the state. WSU is accredited by the Northwest Association of Schools and Colleges.*

*In addition, the University is an acknowledged leader in developing and delivering distance education programs. Since 1992, WSU's Office of Distance Degree Programs (DDP) has been serving students in Washington and across the nation. The University's undergraduate core curriculum, including world civilization courses and expanded writing requirements, is nationally recognized. Money magazine has called WSU a "public ivy" and rated the honors program as one of the nation's best, and in 1998, Yahoo! Internet Life magazine rated WSU as the top most wired college in the nation.*

## DISTANCE LEARNING PROGRAM

WSU's Office of Distance Degree Programs offers degree-completion programs leading to a Bachelor of Arts in social sciences, business administration, criminal justice, or human development and a Bachelor of Science in agriculture or nursing. These programs are designed primarily for students who have completed the equivalent of the first two years of college. They are delivered directly to students' homes through a variety of distance learning technologies. They are the same degrees offered on three WSU campuses; requirements are the same as those for completing degrees on campus; however, students can complete their degrees without attending WSU in person.

For more information about the degrees WSU has to offer, visit the Web site or call the toll-free number (listed on the next page).

## DELIVERY MEDIA

Courses are delivered by the Internet, videotape (available for rent), satellite, cable television, and print materials. As computers become more common, most courses will have World Wide Web requirements.

## PROGRAMS OF STUDY

WSU's Bachelor of Arts in social sciences is a liberal arts degree that offers students multiple options and emphases in the social sciences and provides a broad background applicable to a variety of careers. It emphasizes an interdisciplinary approach with possible major and/or minor course concentrations in anthropology, criminal justice, history, human development, political science, psychology, sociology, and women's studies. A formal minor in business administration is also available.

A Bachelor of Arts in human development is also available with an asynchronous distance format from WSU. The human development degree is especially effective for individuals who work in child- or elder-care programs or in direct service roles with a variety of special-needs clients. The degree program includes an internship component supervised by a WSU faculty member.

The Bachelor of Arts in Business Administration is designed to provide a broad foundation for employment in the world of business, either at a large corporation or in a small private company. A set curriculum, fully accredited by AACSB–The International Association for Management Education, leads students through courses in finance, management, information systems, marketing, international business, business law, and economics.

WSU's Bachelor of Arts in Criminal Justice degree prepares students for positions in the criminal justice system, other government agencies, and the private sector. A completion degree, the distance B.A. in Criminal Justice offers a policy-focused curriculum which provides students with broad exposure in the social sciences preferred by governmental and private agencies. The curriculum is based on 12 credit hours of criminal justice core courses, 12 credit hours of criminal justice electives, and 24 or 25 credit hours of collateral electives in sociology and psychology; most courses are available through distance learning options.

The Tri-State Agricultural Distance Delivery Alliance (TADDA) is a cooperative distance delivery program developed by the land-grant universities of the University of Idaho (UI), Oregon State University (OSU), and Washington State University (WSU). Combining resources from all three universities, TADDA enables students throughout the world to obtain a variety of bachelor's degrees in general agriculture. Courses from a variety of agricultural disciplines are offered through participating community colleges and learning centers.

To earn a bachelor's degree, WSU generally requires the completion of at least 120 semester credits, 40 at the upper-division level. At least 30 of the 120 credits must be taken through WSU. The 120 credits must include courses that meet WSU General Education Requirements (GER). To learn about requirements for each degree, students should speak to a DDP adviser.

More than eighty video courses and nearly 100 correspondence courses are available to students. Courses are also available from the National Universities Degree Consortium (NUDC), a group of nine land-grant and state universities formed to address the needs of adult and part-time learners.

## STUDENT SERVICES

Academic advising is available to all prospective and currently enrolled degree-seeking students through toll-free telephone or electronic mail. The WSU Office of Admissions prepares an official evaluation of a student's transcript when he or she is admitted to the University. A DDP adviser assists DDP students in developing a study plan based on the program options and University requirements. A student services coordinator is available to help students with logistical details.

Students may register on line via toll-free telephone, fax, or e-mail. Videotapes, lab kits, and other supplementary materials are available through the DDP office. Students may order textbooks and course guides from the WSU Students Book Corporation on line via toll-free telephone.

All DDP students have access to the WSU libraries. The DDP librarian is available via toll-free telephone to as-sist students with database searches, in checking out materials, and in copying articles.

## CREDIT OPTIONS

Students may transfer to WSU a maximum of 60 semester credits of lower-division credit and up to 30 more credits from other four-year institutions. The exact number of transfer credits accepted by WSU may vary depending upon an individual's choice of degree.

WSU recognizes there are alternative ways students may gain knowledge and credit. The University has developed a method of accepting credit by examination, including Advanced Placement (AP), College-Level Examination Program (CLEP), DANTES, and American Council on Education (ACE). Interested students should check with their advisers for details.

## FACULTY

There are 1,206 full-time and 187 part-time faculty members in the Washington State University system. Ninety-three percent of the faculty members have terminal academic degrees.

## ADMISSION

Admission to the Distance Degree Program requires at least 27 semester or 40 quarter credits of transferable college course work from an accredited community or four-year college, with at least a 2.0 cumulative GPA.

## TUITION AND FEES

In 2001–02, undergraduate tuition (semester-based) is $183 per semester credit for Washington residents and $274 per semester credit for non-residents. Videotape rental averages $60 per course. Correspondence (flexible enrollment) course tuition is $130 per credit. Payment options for full-time students are available as well.

## FINANCIAL AID

A financial aid adviser is available to all DDP students. Washington State University students receive aid from all federal programs, such as the Federal Pell Grants and Federal Supplemental Educational Opportunity Grants (FSEOG) and the Federal Perkins, Federal Stafford Student, and Federal PLUS Loans. Washington residents are eligible for institutional and state need grants. In 1999–2000, WSU awarded more than $70 million in financial aid. Approximately 50 percent of all WSU students and 52 percent of distance degree students receive financial aid.

## APPLYING

WSU degree-seeking students must be admitted to the University. Admission requires that a student submit an admissions form, have official copies of his or her transcript(s) sent directly from the postsecondary institution(s) attended to WSU's Office of Admissions, and pay the $35 application fee.

---

### CONTACT

Cheri Curtis
Program Coordinator
Distance Degree Programs
Van Doren 204
Washington State University
P.O. Box 645220
Pullman, Washington 99164-5220
Telephone: 509-335-3557
                800-222-4978 (toll-free)
Fax: 509-335-4850
E-mail: edp@wsu.edu
Web site:
     http://www.eus.wsu.edu/edp/

# Weber State University

## Distance Learning

Ogden, Utah

Weber State University (WSU) provides lifelong opportunities for diverse learners on and off campus. It offers degrees through seven colleges and forty departments via distance learning. Students may receive specialized training in health professions, criminal justice, and manufacturing. WSU's academic programs prepare students for immediate employment or further study and equip them with liberal education concepts and skills to support their lifelong learning.

WSU serves as Utah's premier public undergraduate university. The institution was founded in 1889, became a state junior college in 1933, and added upper-division courses and began bachelor's degree programs in 1959. On January 1, 1991, Weber State further expanded its offerings and was granted university status.

Weber State University is accredited by the Northwest Association of Schools and Colleges. In addition, professional agencies such as the Commission on Accreditation for Allied Health Education Programs and the Association of University Programs in Health Administration accredit specific disciplines.

## DISTANCE LEARNING PROGRAM

The WSU Distance Learning Program serves students who cannot attend college classes in person. During the 2000–01 academic year, more than 7,000 students enrolled in print- and Internet-based courses. Students use distance learning to earn general education credits, as well as degrees and professional credentials in manufacturing, criminal justice, and health science areas.

## DELIVERY MEDIA

Students follow study guides, read textbooks, view videotapes, hear cassettes, and/or participate in online courses. They interact with other students, instructors, and advisers by using mail, telephone, e-mail, and online discussion groups. Exams are delivered online or through the mail and are administered by approved proctors. Access to a videocassette player, audiocassette player, word processor, or a computer with browser software and an Internet service provider may be required.

## PROGRAMS OF STUDY

The WSU Distance Learning degree program evolved from a commitment to providing education for health-care professionals and other working adults regardless of location. Combining independent study with Internet courses, a bachelor's degree requires 120 semester hours (40 upper-division, 30 through WSU) with a minimum GPA of at least a 2.0 (or C).

Bachelor's degrees are available in clinical laboratory science, health administrative services (emphases in health information management, health promotion, and health services administration), radiologic science (emphases in computed tomography, magnetic resonance imaging, cardio-vascular-interventional technology, advanced radiography, mammography, quality management, nuclear medicine, radiation therapy), diagnostic medical sonography (medical-vascular), respiratory therapy, computer engineering technology, and electronics engineering technology.

Associate of Applied Science and Associate of Science degrees in respiratory therapy require 20 credits taken in residence at WSU, completion of the requirements for a major in respiratory therapy, and an overall GPA of at least 2.0.

The associate degree in general studies serves the needs of students who want to individualize the first two years of their academic programs, students who want to obtain a broad liberal education, and students who want to lay broad foundations for continued higher education.

The Weber State University Distance Learning associate of science degree program in criminal justice and the professional certificate programs in production and inventory management are designed for professionals whose work and travel schedules and far-flung locations make it difficult for them to participate in campus classwork.

Law enforcement and security professionals register online with Weber State University or one of its six collaborating institutions, and take their training on their home or work computers.

Weber State University works in partnership with APICS, the 70,000-member Educational Society for Resource Management, to offer its certification program through WSU Online for people who work in production and resource management.

WSU certificate programs include health-care coding and classification, radiologic sciences and respiratory therapy (entry-level respiratory care practitioner or registered respiratory therapist). Radiologic sciences classes can be used toward continuing education units (CEU).

## SPECIAL PROGRAMS

WSU Online, the award-winning extension of the University on the Internet, allows students to take online courses, use online support services, and participate in online discussions and activities with faculty and staff members and other students. WSU Online makes it possible for students with busy schedules and/or long commutes to take advantage of the convenience of online courses with support services and interpersonal experiences that are essential to their success. For current course listings and additional information, students can visit the WSU Web site at http://wsuonline.weber.edu.

Courses from a wide range of academic disciplines are available through Weber State University's independent study program, allowing students to complete their course work at their convenience. Each year, more than 2,000 students enroll in these print-based courses and take advantage of this self-paced, individualized mode of study.

## STUDENT SERVICES

WSU recognizes that most of its students have work, family, and other responsibilities that limit their participation in traditional-classroom college courses; therefore, convenience is a major factor in the design of the Distance Learning Program.

Students receive guidance from distance learning staff and faculty members. Degree-seeking students are assigned academic advisers who review transcripts and past learning experiences. This information is used to design individualized programs of study.

Students may access Stewart Library's catalog, interlibrary loan, reference help, document delivery, and other services electronically at http://library.weber.edu. Textbooks can be purchased directly from the WSU bookstore, by mail or online for a small handling charge (telephone: 800-848-7770 Ext. 6352).

Credit Options WSU may grant credit for active military, National Guard, or reserve experience; 38 or more credits to registered radiographers; a maximum of 45 credits to diploma nursing school graduates; and varying credits to registered respiratory therapy technicians and graduates of accredited therapy/specialty programs. Official transcripts should be sent directly from universities and colleges attended. WSU also recognizes College-Level Examination Program (CLEP) credits.

## FACULTY

WSU Distance Learning currently employs 111 full-time university faculty members and 14 adjunct faculty members. Nearly all faculty members hold terminal degrees in their respective fields.

## ADMISSION

Degree-seeking Distance Learning applicants must meet WSU admission requirements. The programs in health professions require separate applications and information specific to their academic areas. Students not seeking to complete a degree at WSU may be eligible for simplified, nonmatriculated admission.

## TUITION AND FEES

Distance Learning tuition averages $99 per semester hour. Additional materials may include course study guides ($3–$40) and audiotape or videotape deposits of $60, with a $40 refund upon their return.

Tuition fees for online courses are based on the WSU tuition table; students may contact staff members for information. All fees are subject to change. Students can consult the current catalog or visit the Web site at http://www.weber.edu/ce/dl/ for more information.

## FINANCIAL AID

Eligible students may apply for federal financial aid such as Pell Grants, Supplemental Educational Opportunity Grants (SEOG), Perkins Loans, and Stafford Loans. Students can contact the office of financial aid toll-free at 800-848-7770 Ext. 7569.

Veterans may also be considered for VA educational benefits (office of Veteran Affairs telephone: 800-848-7770 Ext. 6039, toll-free). Health professions degree programs are approved by DANTES.

## APPLYING

Students should send an admissions application; an individual program application, if required; official transcripts from previous colleges; and an application fee of $30 to the contact address listed below. Students may also apply online at http://catsis.weber.edu/admissions/. Distance Learning students need not attend an orientation.

---

### CONTACT

Office of Distance Learning
Weber State University
4005 University Circle
Ogden, Utah 84408-4005
Telephone: 801-626-6785
　　　　　800-848-7770 Ext.
　　　　　6785 (toll-free)
Fax: 801-626-8035
E-mail: dist-learn@weber.edu
Web site: http://wsuonline.
　　　weber.edu
　　　http://catsis.weber.edu/
　　　ce/dl/

# Western Baptist College

## *Adult Studies Online Programs*

Salem, Oregon

---

*Western Baptist College is an independent, Christian liberal arts college and is accredited by the Northwest Association of Schools and Colleges. Its core purpose is to educate Christians who will make a difference in the world for Jesus Christ.*

*The College offered its first distance learning program in 1994, which developed into a uniquely online format in 1997. It now offers two online degree completion programs for Christian students in the areas of management and communication and family studies.*

## DISTANCE LEARNING PROGRAM

Western's online degree completion programs are specifically and conveniently formatted for the Christian student who has two years of college credit and desires a Christian college education but is unable to attend on-campus classes. With only a three-day residency orientation, the entirety of the sixteen-month program is completed from home via computer.

## DELIVERY MEDIA

Online course work requires an IBM-compatible computer system, Internet access, and completion of an initial orientation held on campus. Complete precourse training is provided for all students via self-paced tutorials, hands-on workshops, and follow-up technical support. Course instruction is accomplished by utilizing facilitated discussion forums, live chat conferences, and collaborative project reports, which are supported by Internet course-management software, audio-video and keyboard conferencing programs, e-mail, and telephone.

## PROGRAMS OF STUDY

Western Baptist offers two degree completion programs entirely online.

Individual online courses are also offered to assist students in completing general education requirements. The online degree completion programs lead to a B.S. or B.A. degree. Students enrolling in the degree completion program must have completed 60 semester hours of transferable credit. A total of 128 semester hours is required for the bachelor's degree.

Both online degree completion programs in management and communication and family studies are excellent preparation for graduate study. The Management and Communication online degree completion program is 37 semester hours. The curriculum is structured to develop leadership, analytical, and problem-solving skills with a Christian perspective. Course work provides expertise in management, organization development, and communication—three of the most important aspects of business and public administration. The Family Studies online degree completion program is 44 semester hours. It is an applied interdisciplinary approach, focusing on the study of family dynamics and the relationships between families and the society at large. The curriculum is integrated with biblical principles and is taught by Christian professionals. Students completing the program are eligible for certification as family life educators through the National Council on Family Relations.

## SPECIAL PROGRAMS

Students are given the opportunity to earn college credit for prior learning through the Prior Learning Assessment program. Students learn how to identify, document, and describe appropriate prior learning experiences. Weekend classes are offered both online as well as on-campus and are designed to meet general education requirements. The course offerings vary in length. Internships and research projects are required in the online degree completion programs. They are generally completed within the workplace or in a related local business or agency.

## STUDENT SERVICES

Online students enjoy complete access to the same College services as campus students via Web-based communication, fax, or telephone. In addition to academic advising and project mentoring, financial aid, registrar's office, technical support, campus bookstore, and library services are available. Online library resources include EBSCOhost, ERIC, Academic Universe, ProQuest Direct, and other comprehensive databases.

## CREDIT OPTIONS

Qualifying college credit may be transferred subject to the approval of the College registrar. Students may earn a maximum of 32 semester hours of credit through college-level exams (CLEP, DANTES) and 30 semester hours of credit through the Prior Learning Assessment program.

## ADMISSION

Enrollment in the online degree completion program requires applicants to have a minimum of 60 semester hours of transferable college credit as well as profession of a personal faith in Jesus Christ.

## TUITION AND FEES

The 2001 tuition for the online degree completion program is $12,300. Tuition includes all textbooks and graduation fees.

## FINANCIAL AID

Financial aid is available through federal and state financial aid programs. For further information, students should contact the financial aid office at 800-845-3005 (toll-free) or via e-mail at aid@wbc.edu.

## APPLYING

Applicants for online degree completion programs must complete an application and submit transcripts, two references, an acceptable writing sample, and a profession of faith in Jesus Christ.

---

### CONTACT

Adult Studies Online Program
Western Baptist College
5000 Deer Park Drive, SE
Salem, Oregon 97301
Telephone: 800-764-1383 (toll-free)
Fax: 503-375-7583
E-mail: asd@wbc.edu
Web site: http://www.wbc.edu

# Western Governors University

*Distance Learning Program*

Salt Lake City, Utah

*WGU is a degree-granting, competency-based, online, distance education institution. By visiting the University's Web site at www.wgu.edu, a student can find everything that is needed to advance his or her educational goals, including competency-based degree programs, an online catalog of high-quality distance learning courses, an online library, bookstore, and one-on-one access to a personal WGU mentor, who guides the student through his or her customized degree program from beginning to end. As one of the most ambitious higher education initiatives of its time, WGU was founded and is supported by nineteen states and governors and is a leader in the movement to increase access to educational opportunities for today's adult, lifelong learner and to provide students with recognition for the skills and knowledge they already possess. With candidacy for accreditation status, WGU is using technology to provide accessibility, flexibility, and the opportunity for every type of student to achieve his or her educational goals.*

## DISTANCE LEARNING PROGRAM

Every course and program offered through or by WGU is distance delivered. WGU's campus is its Web site, which provides access to high-quality, distance-delivered educational opportunities to students no matter where they are.

## DELIVERY MEDIA

The courses available through WGU from its affiliated education providers are delivered via a wide variety of methods—everything from postal correspondence to desktop video and e-mail. Interaction between faculty members and students is also conducted via many different methods. A description of the delivery methods for each course and any equipment students will need is included in WGU's online catalog as well as the syllabi for each course selected.

## PROGRAMS OF STUDY

WGU currently offers three certificates and seven degrees in various areas of study, with additional programs scheduled for 2001. The general education Associate of Arts provides students with a broad academic background in the major disciplines. The general education Associate of Arts provides students with a broad academic background in the major disciplines. The Associate of Science in business is a degree that prepares students for a career in business, industry, or government or can be used as a stepping-stone to a bachelor's degree in business. The Associate of Science in information technology helps students get ready for a job in customer support, software testing, or other entry-level IT and business positions. The Associate of Applied Science in information technology with a Certified Novell Engineer (CNE) emphasis allows students to receive recognition for their CNE while earning an associate degree that could serve as a stepping-stone to a bachelor's degree or to a better job. The Associate of Applied Science in information technology network administration is awarded to individuals who demonstrate their competence in occupations directly related to conceiving, building, monitoring, and managing network architecture. The Bachelor of Science with an information technology management emphasis is great preparation for a career as an IT project manager, MIS manager/director, data center manager/director, or manager/director of customer service and is a natural follow-up to WGU's business associate degree. Finally, the Master of Arts in learning and technology is a degree that enhances teaching talents with cutting-edge technology skills to improve education and training results in the classroom.

To earn a WGU degree or certificate, students must successfully complete a series of assessments that demonstrate mastery of WGU competencies. Most degree programs also include a portfolio requirement.

## SPECIAL PROGRAMS

All of WGU's programs of study are entirely competency-based and distance-delivered, and they are designed with the working adult in mind. Each program is made up of a number of domains. Each domain roughly covers a subject area, such as mathematics and quantitative skills. The student, in close consultation with his or her mentor—an expert in the student's field of study—prepares for each domain assessment battery via whatever means appropriate; that may include taking distance-delivered classes or conducting self-study activities. The student who is well prepared for the domain assessment due to his or her life or work experience is not required to take any classes prior to the assessment. This system allows a student to capitalize on his or her strengths and receive recognition for prior learning, thus decreasing the overall time it takes to complete the degree program.

## STUDENT SERVICES

WGU's goal is to provide distance learning students with all the student services they need to succeed. WGU offers an online bookstore, an online library, and one-on-one advising with a WGU mentor. Every student enrolled in a WGU degree or certificate program is assigned a mentor who helps the student develop an Academic Action Plan (AAP) and select appropriate courses and generally advises the student throughout his or her academic program.

## CREDIT OPTIONS

As a competency-based institution, WGU does not issue or accumulate credits. There are no required classes for a WGU degree. Instead, a student earns a WGU degree or certificate by successfully demonstrating his or her competency through a series of WGU assessments. Though WGU does not accept transfer credits, students with previous college experience may transfer their previous learning by proceeding on a fast track through their WGU degree and moving directly to the appropriate assessments.

## FACULTY

Teaching faculty members associated with WGU students are located at WGU-affiliated institutions that offer courses through the WGU online catalog. WGU faculty members include council members who develop WGU competencies and identify and approve assessments, as well as the WGU mentors who work directly with students regarding their competency-based degree progress.

## ADMISSION

Applicants must be at least 16 years old and must demonstrate an ability to benefit from WGU degree programs. A high school diploma or its equivalent is required for entry into all college-level degree programs. An associate degree or transcripts from all previous college work must be submitted for evaluation and entrance into a bachelor's degree program. A bachelor's degree is required for admission to the master's degree program.

## TUITION AND FEES

WGU makes no distinction between in-state and out-of-state students. Tuition for an associate degree is $3250, for a bachelor's degree is $3650, and for a master's degree is $3850. Optional classes are extra. (Students should refer to the WGU online catalog for specific course tuition.)

## FINANCIAL AID

WGU was one of the first institutions to make federal financial aid available to distance education students. Aid available through WGU includes Federal Pell Grants and Federal Direct Loans (both subsidized and unsubsidized).

## APPLYING

Students may apply to WGU via an online application form that is available at the WGU Web site. There is a $100 application fee. Applicants are contacted within a few business days regarding the status of their application and information regarding next steps for their academic progress.

---

### CONTACT

WGU Student Information Center
Western Governors University
2040 East Murray Holladay Road, Suite 106
Salt Lake City, Utah 84117
Telephone: 877-HELP-WGU (toll-free)
Fax: 801-274-3305
E-mail: info@wgu.edu
Web site: http://www.wgu.edu

---

# Western Washington University

## *Extended Education and Summer Programs*

Bellingham, Washington

*Now over 101 years old, Western Washington University (WWU) began its history as a school for the education of rural teachers. Western evolved into a degree-granting institution in 1933, a college of education in 1937, a state college in 1961, and a university in 1977. The institution now enrolls more than 11,000 students and is organized into a graduate school and six undergraduate colleges: College of Arts and Science, College of Business and Economics, College of Fine and Performing Arts, Fairhaven College, Huxley College of Environmental Studies, and Woodring College of Education. The University is large enough to offer a wide range of high quality programs and small enough to focus its resources on individual students. Located in the northwestern corner of the state near the Canadian border, Western enjoys proximity to scenic attractions as well as a campus that blends both art and natural beauty.*

## DISTANCE LEARNING PROGRAM

Although students at Western primarily attend class on campus, distance education is used to supplement traditional programs both on the main campus and at satellite branches in the Puget Sound area. Approximately 1500 students are served through programs at other locations and distance education.

## DELIVERY MEDIA

Distance learning is provided through a variety of media. More than 80 correspondence courses are offered with enrollment open to all. Almost 50 additional courses with a focus on educators and human service professionals can be utilized online or through computer-mediated instruction. Courses at sites other than the main campus may be taught by satellite, face-to-face, or online.

## PROGRAMS OF STUDY

Western offers one degree program, a Bachelor of Arts in human services, entirely through distance education. The program is a two-year, upper-division program with the Woodring College of Education. Admission to the program requires a transferable Associate of Arts degree or 90 credits that include WWU's General University Requirements and a minimum transferable GPA of 2.50.

## SPECIAL PROGRAMS

Of additional interest to distance learners is Western's certificate program in Teaching English as a Second Language (TESL). Formal admission is required and limited to students who have completed a bachelor's degree or higher. The TESL program runs both as a traditional on-campus program and also as a program with a significant distance component. Students at a distance are required to attend classes on campus in an intensive summer format, but may complete some requirements through online and correspondence courses.

## STUDENT SERVICES

During the quarter enrolled, students at a distance may check their grades and transcripts online. Various library services are available. Extended Programs staff members are available for advising and student help from 8 to 5 (PDT), Monday through Friday, by telephone or e-mail.

## FACULTY

About 86.5 percent of Western's faculty members have earned a full or terminal advanced degree. Most distance learning courses are designed and taught by the same faculty members who teach the class on campus. The majority of faculty members are available for student interaction through voice mail or e-mail.

## TUITION AND FEES

Tuition varies from program to program and is subject to change upon action of the Board of Trustees and the Washington State Legislature. At the time of publication, tuition is as follows: correspondence courses, $80 per credit; human service degree program, $137 per credit; TESL program, $126 per credit. Other fees may apply for admission, registration, online courses, and materials.

## FINANCIAL AID

Financial aid is available only for programs that require formal admission to the University. In general, financial aid is not available to students who enroll in only distance education courses except for the degree program in human services.

## ADMISSION

Application for formal admission is made through the Office of Admissions for degree and certificate programs. An application form and transcripts are required for such programs. For information and application forms, students should contact the Office of Admissions at 360-650-3440 or admit@wwu.edu.

Admission is not required for correspondence courses or distance learning courses for professionals in human service and education.

**CONTACT**

Extended Education and Summer Programs
MS 5293
Western Washington University
516 High Street
Bellingham, Washington 98225-5293
Telephone: 360-650-2841
Fax: 360-650-6858
E-mail: extendedprograms@wwu.edu
Web site: http://www.wwu.edu/~extended

# Wheaton College Graduate School

## *Distance Learning*

Wheaton, Illinois

*The Wheaton College Graduate School was established in 1937 as part of Wheaton College (founded in 1860). Its mission is to provide academic and professional preparation that will enable the committed Christian student to formulate and articulate a biblical and global understanding of life and ministry and apply it to service for Christ and His Kingdom. The emphasis of the Graduate School throughout its history has been on practical scholarship—scholarship totally rooted in the final authority of the Scriptures but practical so that educated and trained Christian leaders are equipped to relate to the real needs of people today. Wheaton College is accredited by the North Central Association of Colleges and Schools.*

## DISTANCE LEARNING PROGRAM

As part of the Graduate School, Distance Learning shares in its mission of scholarship committed to servanthood. The program is also committed to making this education accessible to those who are unable to relocate. Distance Learning courses enable students to pursue graduate study without leaving their place of ministry or employment.

## DELIVERY MEDIA

Distance Learning courses employ a variety of media. Traditional independent study courses consist of audiocassettes, instruction manuals, and textbooks. Most Web-based courses include streaming audio and video and interactive asynchronous discussion with faculty members and other students. These courses require a PC or a Mac with a standard Internet connection (with a minimum modem speed of 28.8 KB per second), an e-mail account, and a Java-capable browser.

Wheaton College has partnered with eCollege.com to provide its Web-based courses.

## PROGRAMS OF STUDY

The Certificate of Advanced Biblical Studies–Distance Learning Option may be taken entirely at a distance. It is designed for people who desire advanced training in biblical and theological studies to better equip them for personal Christian living and service in the church. The certificate program provides professional development opportunities for pastors, teachers in Christian schools, missionaries, and other Christian workers. It also provides a way for those working in other vocations and disciplines to attain a theological and biblical foundation necessary for the integration of faith, learning, and living.

Students who are interested in this 24-hour program must meet the general requirements for admission to Wheaton College Graduate School, including the biblical and theological proficiency requirements (which can also be fulfilled through non-credit distance learning courses). Required courses include Foundations for Biblical Interpretation and Christian Theology. Additional hours are worked out in consultation with a faculty adviser. Students may choose to combine on-campus study with courses offered at a distance.

Wheaton College Graduate School also offers two special Master of Arts degree programs that combine Distance Learning courses with short intensive courses and one semester of residential study.

## SPECIAL PROGRAMS

Wheaton College Graduate School offers two special Master's Programs for People in Ministry or the Marketplace (MPPM). These flexible programs combine Distance Learning courses with on-campus intensive courses and a final semester in residence. They lead to an M.A. degree in Biblical and Theological Studies (36 hours) or Missions and Intercultural Studies (40 hours). Up to 16 hours may be taken through distance learning for these programs.

Prospective students should contact the School for additional information about abbreviated summer school courses and the Institute for Cross-Cultural Training.

## CREDIT OPTIONS

No transfer credit can be accepted in the MPPM programs or in the Certificate of Advanced Biblical Studies–Distance Learning Option. Students who are prematriculated in other programs may apply up to 8 to 10 semester hours of Distance Learning courses or transfer credit to a degree program, provided the courses meet degree requirements.

## FACULTY

Four full-time faculty members and 1 part-time faculty member currently teach distance learning courses. All have earned doctorates. Additional support is provided by course development staff in Media Resources, Library Services, and Distance Learning.

## ADMISSION

Applicants must have a bachelor's degree from a regionally accredited college or university at a level indicative of high-quality scholarship (a 2.75 minimum grade point average on a 4.0 scale). Each academic department maintains additional requirements. Prospective students should see the course catalog for a full list of requirements and recommendations for optimal preparation.

## TUITION AND FEES

Tuition for Web-based and self-paced audiocassette/print courses is $272 per semester hour in 2001–02. The cost of textbooks is variable.

## FINANCIAL AID

No financial aid is available for distance learning students at this time. Veterans with educational benefits who plan to complete a degree on campus should contact the program before enrolling in distance learning courses.

## APPLYING

While no application fee is required to enroll in an individual distance learning course, an official undergraduate transcript must be submitted. A one-time $30 nonrefundable application fee is required for admission to the Certificate of Advanced Biblical Studies–Distance Learning Option or the MPPM programs. Students admitted to either the certificate or MPPM programs are given priority in registering for a course.

---

### CONTACT

Doug Milford, Director
Distance Learning
501 College Avenue
Wheaton, Illinois 60187-5593
Telephone: 630-752-5944
          800-888-0141 (toll-free)
Fax: 630-752-5935
E-mail: distance.learning@wheaton.edu
Web site: http://www.wheaton.edu/distancelearning/

# Worcester Polytechnic Institute

## Advanced Distance Learning Network

Worcester, Massachusetts

*Founded in 1865, Worcester Polytechnic Institute (WPI) has long been a pioneer in technological higher education. Three decades after it was created, the university's distinctive outcomes-oriented approach to education is being viewed as a model for reform at the national level, and WPI is recognized as the leader in global technological education. WPI is fully accredited by the New England Association of Schools and Colleges.*

*WPI awarded its first advanced degree in 1893. Today, most of its academic departments offer master's and doctoral programs and support leading-edge research in a broad range of fields. Through the years, WPI has earned a reputation for its academic excellence, its responsiveness to the needs of the marketplace, and for its faculty of renowned academicians and industry experts who are practitioners in their fields.*

## DISTANCE LEARNING PROGRAM

In 1979, WPI's commitment to active, lifelong learning prompted the creation of the Advanced Distance Learning Network (ADLN), a partnership between several academic departments and WPI's Instructional Media Center. ADLN programs empower working professionals to continue to grow within their chosen field without having to take classes on campus. There is no residency requirement.

## DELIVERY MEDIA

ADLN courses consist of the same content and materials as on-campus class meetings. Courses originate in one of WPI's studio classrooms and are delivered to ADLN students via interactive compressed video, expressed-mail videotapes, or the Internet, depending on the best method for course content. Materials such as books, handouts, and supplemental readings are sent by express mail, fax, or e-mail or are posted on the Internet. An e-mail account and access to the Internet are required for participation in an ADLN course.

## PROGRAMS OF STUDY

ADLN offers a Master of Business Administration (M.B.A.) in technology organizations, a Master of Science (M.S.) in fire protection engineering, and a Master of Science (M.S.) in civil and environmental engineering. In addition to these degree options, WPI's ADLN also offers numerous graduate certificate programs in these areas.

The M.B.A. program focuses on the management of technology and features a highly integrative curriculum that emphasizes leadership, ethics, communication, and a global perspective. Concentration areas include MIS, technology marketing, technological innovation, entrepreneurship, operations management, and management of technology. This 49-credit M.B.A. program may be reduced to as few as 31 credits with an appropriate academic background. A customized 15-credit graduate certificate program in management is also available.

The Fire Protection Engineering (FPE) program is oriented toward developing a well-rounded professional who can be successful in a competitive career environment. The curriculum is designed to teach students current standards of practice and expose them to state-of-the-art research literature that will support future practices. In addition to the ten-course (30-credit) M.S. option, professionals with a B.S. degree in an engineering, engineering technology, or science field who complete four thematically related FPE courses can receive a graduate certificate in FPE. Master's degree holders may instead opt to complete five thematically related courses for an advanced certificate in FPE.

The Civil and Environmental Engineering programs are arranged to meet the interests and objectives of individual students and their employers. The curriculum focuses on today's environmental issues and their relationship to engineering, business, and law. The 33-credit Master of Science degree is a professional practice–oriented degree designed to meet the continuing challenges faced by practicing environmental engineers. A four-course graduate certificate is also available through ADLN.

Credits earned in any WPI certificate program can later be applied toward an advanced degree, contingent upon formal admission to graduate study. A maximum of two courses taken at WPI as a nondegree-seeking student may be applied for credit to the M.B.A. program; a maximum of four courses taken at WPI as a nondegree-seeking student may be applied for credit to an M.S. in fire protection engineering or an M.S. in civil and environmental engineering.

## SPECIAL PROGRAMS

ADLN and appropriate academic personnel are always willing to consider the addition of new programs for which there is sufficient interest.

## STUDENT SERVICES

Academic advisers are assigned upon admission. Online library services are free, and reference services are available by phone or e-mail. Dial-up UNIX accounts (for e-mail, etc.) and career placement and counseling are available for matriculated students. Books can be ordered toll-free from the WPI bookstore (888-WPI-BOOKS) and are typically delivered one to three days after ordering.

## CREDIT OPTIONS

The M.B.A. program allows 18 foundation-level credits to be waived for those with appropriate academic backgrounds, either via straight waivers for those with appropriate course work completed within the past six years with a grade of B or better or via waiver exams. The M.B.A. program, the M.S. in fire protection engineering, and the M.S. in civil and environmental engineering allow students to transfer up to 9 credits from graduate-level course work at other schools. Graduate and Advanced Certificate programs require all credits to come from WPI.

## FACULTY

Management has 26 faculty members (20 full-time members and 6 part-time members), 24 of whom have Ph.D. degrees. Fire protection engineering has 6 full-time faculty members, all with Ph.D. degrees, and 2 part-time professors. Civil and environmental engineering has 13 full-time faculty members, all with Ph.D. degrees, and 8 part-time professors.

## ADMISSION

To be considered for admission to the M.B.A. program or a graduate certificate in management, an applicant must hold a B.S. degree and possess the analytic aptitude necessary to complete a technology-oriented program. Admission to WPI's M.S. programs or graduate certificate options in fire protection engineering or civil and environmental engineering require an applicant to hold a B.S. degree in an appropriate field of engineering, engineering technology, or science and meet department-specific admission standards. Conditional admission is available if all requirements are not met at the time of application.

## TUITION AND FEES

Tuition is $752 per credit hour ($2256 per 3-credit course) for all programs in the 2001–02 academic year. Students wishing to earn Continuing Education Units (CEU) instead of graduate credit may opt to audit courses at half tuition.

## FINANCIAL AID

Loan-based aid is available only through special arrangements. Students must be registered on at least a half-time basis (two courses per semester).

## APPLYING

All departments require standard forms, official transcripts, and a $60 application fee. Management degree programs also require three letters of recommendation and GMAT scores. All international applicants must submit TOEFL scores. GRE scores are not required but may be substituted for the GMAT scores when applying for a graduate certificate in management.

### CONTACT

Pamela Shelley, Assistant Director
Advanced Distance Learning
 Network
Worcester Polytechnic Institute
100 Institute Road
Worcester, Massachusetts 01609-
 2280
Telephone: 508-831-5810
Fax: 508-831-5881
E-mail: adln@wpi.edu
Web site: http://www.wpi.edu/
 Academics/ADLN

# CONSORTIUM DESCRIPTIONS

The organizations listed in this section represent consortia of institutions offering Distance Learning programs. Each consortia has been formed so that an expanded set of distance learning options can be offered beyond the resources available through any single member institution.

The following consortia do not have a central application process and/or do not directly award credits and degrees. The application process, credits, or conferred degrees are awarded through one of the member institutions. Further, consortia generally are not directly granted accreditation; rather, credits and degrees reflect the accreditation of the awarding institution. The reader should obtain specific information directly from the consortia itself.

 # Kentucky Virtual University

Frankfort, Kentucky

*The Kentucky Virtual University (KYVU) is a program of the Kentucky Council on Postsecondary Education. Created by the Kentucky General Assembly in 1997, the virtual University is part of sweeping higher education reforms designed to raise education achievement. KYVU strategically coordinates the anywhere, any-time delivery of online courses, degrees, and certificates in a learner-friendly system.*

*Kentucky's virtual University is in partnership with the state's four-year and two-year public and independent colleges and universities. For the fall 2001 term, the following Kentucky colleges and universities offer courses and/or programs through KYVU: Eastern Kentucky University, Kentucky State University, Morehead State University, Murray State University, Northern Kentucky University, Sullivan University, University of Kentucky, University of Louisville, Western Kentucky University, and Lexington Community College. In addition, the colleges within the Kentucky Community and Technical College System participating include Ashland Community College, Central Kentucky Technical College, Elizabethtown Community College, Elizabethtown Technical College, Hazard Community College, Henderson Community College, Hopkinsville Community College, Jefferson Community College, Madisonville Community College, Maysville Community College, Owensboro Community College, Paducah Community College, Prestonsburg Community College, Somerset Community College, and Southeast Community College.*

## DISTANCE LEARNING PROGRAM

KYVU is a student-centered, technology-based system for the delivery of postsecondary education. Created by the Kentucky General Assembly as part of Governor Paul Patton's historic higher education reforms, KYVU addresses the needs of Kentuckians who want to learn longer but, due to barriers such as time and distance, are unable to access traditional, on-campus education. KYVU serves as a clearinghouse for quality distance learning opportunities offered by Kentucky postsecondary education institutions and provides competency based credentialing and a single point of access to student, library, and academic support services.

All KYVU courses and programs are offered by existing, fully-accredited institutions that will confer the diploma, certificate, or degree. All

courses are transferable and taught by Kentucky faculty members.

KYVU has experienced tremendous growth since its inaugural fall 1999 semester, when it offered 30 courses in nine pilot programs and registered 235 students. In spring 2001, KYVU registered more than 3,200 students.

A survey of students revealed high satisfaction levels of online learning through the virtual University. Students also reported high levels of student-faculty member interaction and student-to-student interaction.

In addition to its role of enhancing and encouraging lifelong learning for all Kentuckians, KYVU is also an important economic development driver for providing knowledge workers for Kentucky business and industry and providing upward-mobility opportunities for citizens.

## DELIVERY MEDIA

Courses and programs offered through KYVU rely on Web-based, asynchronous instruction platforms through a high-speed ATM network, the Kentucky Information Highway (KIH), supported in substantial part by the KYVU.

## PROGRAMS OF STUDY

KYVU is rapidly gaining popularity among students looking for convenience, value, and quality in their higher education pursuits. Currently, students can enroll in these college credit programs: Associate in Applied Science (network and information system technology (NIST)), Associate in Arts (business transfer framework), Associate in Applied Science (MCSE), Bachelor of Independent Studies, Bachelor of Science in Business Administration in Hospitality Management, Bachelor of Science in Human Resources Leadership, Certificate (office systems technology), Library Science, Master of Business Administration, Master of Science Managing Information Technology, Master of Science (communication disorders), Teacher Certificate (Special Education: Moderate and Severe Disabilities), TESOL-English as a Second Language Certificate, Master of Public Administration, and Master of Education in Human Resource Education.

Professional training programs include Certified Public Accounting, Firefighters Certificate, Certified Internet Webmaster, Cisco Certified Network Associate 2.0, Comp TIA Certifications, End User Training in Lotus Notes and Lotus Domingo RF, SAIR Linux Certification, Windows 2000 MCSE, Windows 2000 MCSE Upgrade, Paralegal and Legal Assistant Training, Public Safety Communications Training, and Travel and Tourism Training.

In addition to these programs, KYVU offers more than 300 courses that apply to college degree programs and professional development programs. Subject areas range from general education core courses to specialized science and humanities courses, in addition to a wide variety of information technology courses.

## STUDENT SERVICES

The KYVU offers a wide range of one-stop services to students, faculty members, and the public. Through the Call Center and Web page, KYVU provides a course catalog and schedule, general advising and referral of students, expedited admission and online registration, an online bookstore, and technical assistance.

The Kentucky Virtual Library (KYVL) is a fundamental and vital component of KYVU. Open seven days a week, 24 hours a day, the virtual library serves all the citizens of Kentucky, in addition to KYVU students and faculty members. KYVL provides quality library and information resources and trained, professional staff to help support the research and lifelong learning needs of students and Kentuckians. Services include access to more than thirty electronic databases through a single gateway, inter-library document delivery service,

Internet/fax/e-mail transmission of journal articles, a single point of service for technical and reference assistance, and an information literacy tutorial program. Students may visit the library at http://www.kyvl.org.

## CREDIT OPTIONS

All KYVU courses are fully transferable and may be applied to the student's program degree or skill certification at any of the partnering institutions and, because all courses for academic credit are offered by accredited institutions, should be transferable to other institutions.

## FACULTY

Faculty members of the partnering institutions provide instruction for all KYVU courses. KYVU supports faculty development through continuous improvement programs and delivery software and course publishing training.

## STUDENT PROFILE

Given the charge to increase access to and attainment of postsecondary education opportunities, KYVU primarily targets place- and time-bound students, employers, and employees in business, government, and industry, and P–12 students, teachers, and administrators. However, the nature of electronic delivery systems is such that potential users/clients are essentially unlimited and include tradi-

tional residential students and students in other states and countries. All are welcome.

## ADMISSION

All students can apply for admission to an institution through KYVU, but admissions decisions ultimately are made by the institutions. KYVU facilitates the process.

## TUITION AND FEES

The 2000–01 tuition for public community colleges was $52 per credit hour for Kentucky residents. The public university rate for residents ranged from $85 to $124 per credit hour. Nonresident tuition is approximately three times the resident rate.

## FINANCIAL AID

Financial aid for KYVU students is governed by the rules of the institutions offering the course or courses. The KYVU Call Center staff assists in this process.

## APPLYING

Students may apply for admission through the KYVU with the final admissions decisions made by the institutions providing the courses. Students and prospective students may call the KYVU Call Center toll-free at 877-740-4357 to register for courses by telephone or for assistance needed in the online registration process. Students may also register for classes online at the Web site listed below.

## CONTACT

Kentucky Virtual University
1024 Capital Center Drive, Suite 320
Frankfort, Kentucky 40601
Telephone: 877-740-4357 (toll-free) (KCVU Call Center)
Fax: 502-573-0222
E-mail: kyvu@kyvu.org
Web site: http://www.kyvu.org

# National Universities Degree Consortium

*The National Universities Degree Consortium (NUDC), established in 1991, is a consortium of regionally accredited universities across the United States that offer courses, certificates, and degrees through distance education. NUDC members include Colorado State University, Kansas State University, Mississippi State University, Oklahoma State University, University of Alabama, University of Houston System, University of Maryland University College, University of New Orleans, University of South Carolina, Washington State University, and Weber State University.*

## DISTANCE LEARNING PROGRAM

NUDC was established in response to widespread requests from potential, nontraditional-age students for integrated, external degree programs that are delivered in a flexible, off-campus format and readily available to adults and part-time students. In many cases, these students are one to two years away from completing their undergraduate degrees. The member institutions of the consortium develop and manage the operations of the consortium and ensure high-quality programs with the ultimate goal of providing university-credit courses that lead to external degrees. NUDC serves as a vehicle for the development and promotion of undergraduate courses and programs, graduate degree programs, certificate programs (credit and noncredit), and noncredit courses in a variety of subject areas.

## DELIVERY MEDIA

More than 1,000 courses are offered through a variety of distance learning formats. These courses include traditional print-based correspondence courses, Internet courses, and courses that include other media components, such as audiotapes, videotapes, computer disks, CD-ROM, e-mail, and more. Many courses feature technology-mediated interaction between students and faculty members. Students are encouraged to contact the offering university to find out the format for the course or courses of choice.

## PROGRAMS OF STUDY

Through NUDC, each member of the consortium offers courses through a variety of distance education formats. Some institutions offer external degree completion programs. The NUDC Web site lists the programs offered by each institution.

Bachelor's degrees are available in accounting, administrative sciences, animal sciences and industry, applied sciences, behavioral and social sciences, business and management, communication, communication studies, computer and management information science, computer studies, criminal justice, English, fire science, food science and industry, general business, human development, human services, humanities, interdisciplinary social sciences, liberal arts, management, management studies, natural sciences, paralegal studies, social sciences, and technology and management.

Master's degrees are available in agribusiness, business administration, business management, computer science, computer systems management, engineering (aerospace, biosystems, chemical and bioresource, chemical, civil, control systems, electrical, electrical and computer, environmental, industrial, mechanical, software, and systems and optimization), engineering and technology management, engineering with a concentration in engineering management, engineering management, fire and emergency management administration, general administration, health education/health promotion, health studies, human resource development, industrial/organizational psychology, international management, library science, natural and applied sciences with a specialization in gerontology, statistics, technology management, and telecommunications management.

The Education Specialist degree is available in educational leadership and policy studies.

Doctoral degrees are available in electrical engineering, industrial engineering, and mechanical engineering.

Credit and noncredit certificate programs are available in bail bonds management, broadcast meteorology, criminal justice, fire protection technology, food science, operational meteorology, and technical and professional writing.

## SPECIAL PROGRAMS

Members of NUDC offer special services such as academic advising and external library resources to their distance students. To learn more about distinctive programs available to students through NUDC member institutions, students should contact the institution of choice directly.

## CREDIT OPTIONS

NUDC members have agreed to accept credits from other member institutions toward completion of the external degree programs. A student wishing to complete a degree must verify transfer credits with the degree-granting institution.

## FACULTY

Each university member of NUDC is an accredited institution that maintains the highest standards for all faculty members. These standards are reflected in the high quality of instruction offered to the distance learner.

## STUDENT PROFILE

The students who are interested in degree completion via distance learning are typical of all distance students. They often are not able to attend courses on a campus during the day due to work or family obligations, geographic location, or other inhibitors. Most distance students are 23 years old or older. For profiles distinctive to a particular university, students should contact the institution directly.

## ADMISSION

Degree-seeking students must follow the admission and graduation requirements of the particular institution whose degree they are pursuing. The student may choose from more than 1,000 courses offered by the consortium members to complete the degree program of a particular institution. Formal admission is not required for students not interested in a degree.

## TUITION AND FEES

NUDC does not have a tuition and fee standard for participants. Each institution sets tuition and fees according to its own schedule.

## FINANCIAL AID

The rules for financial aid vary by program. Students should contact the financial aid office at the institution offering the courses of interest for specific information. Courses taken in a non-degree-granting program may not be eligible for federal grants.

## APPLYING

Each NUDC member has its own application requirements and deadlines. Students should contact the institution offering the course or program of interest for specific information.

---

### CONTACT

For more information regarding any NUDC program or course offering, students should contact the offering institution.

For general information about the National Universities Degree Consortium or to view the NUDC catalog, students should visit the NUDC Web site: http://www.nudc.org.

# The New Jersey Virtual Community College Consortium

## *A Partnership of New Jersey's Nineteen Community Colleges*

Trenton, New Jersey

---

New Jersey's community colleges have formed a consortium to share online courses. The New Jersey Virtual Community College Consortium's (NJVCCC) mission is to increase access to postsecondary education for all New Jerseyans regardless of geographic or time constraints. The NJVCCC was developed as a companion to the New Jersey Virtual University, which was launched in January 1999. The NJVCCC began offering distance learning courses via the Internet in fall 1999. In spring 2000, more than 200 distance learning courses were offered to community college students throughout the state of New Jersey. The NJVCCC is not a separate degree-granting college.

## DISTANCE LEARNING PROGRAM

A New Jersey community college serves as either a host for a course, a provider of a course, or both. One college develops or provides the course, while the other colleges subscribe to the course to offer or host it to their students locally.

The NJVCCC provides high-tech college-level courses with the "high-touch" services students have come to expect from their local community colleges, such as tutoring, advisement, and counseling.

The NJVCCC served several hundred students across New Jersey during its first year of operation in 1999–2000.

## DELIVERY MEDIA

All NJVCCC courses are offered using the Internet. Students enrolled in NJVCCC courses correspond with professors via e-mail, bulletin boards, and the World Wide Web. Online courses require a computer with a graphical user interface (Mac or Windows), a modem (28.8 kbps or higher), and connection to an Internet service provider (ISP), and students need to know how to download software from the Internet and install and configure software.

## PROGRAMS OF STUDY

The NJVCCC does not grant degrees. However, three New Jersey community colleges offer online degrees.

Atlantic Cape Community College (ACCC) in Mays Landing, New Jersey, offers online Associate in Arts degrees in liberal arts, history, and social science. ACCC offers online Associate in Science degrees in general studies and business administration. For more information on ACCC's online degree offerings, students should visit the College's Web site at http://www.atlantic.edu.

Burlington County College (BCC) in Pemberton, New Jersey, offers an online Associate in Science degree in business administration and an online Associate in Arts degree in liberal arts. For more information on BCC's online degree offerings, students should visit the College's Web site at http://www.bcc.edu.

Mercer County Community College (MCCC) in Trenton, New Jersey, offers an online Associate in Applied Science degree in general business and an online Associate in Arts degree in humanities and social sciences. For more information on MCCC's online degree offerings, students should visit the College's Web site at http://www.mccc.edu.

## SPECIAL PROGRAMS

All nineteen NJVCCC member community colleges are accredited by the Commission of Higher Education, Middle States Association of Colleges and Schools. All New Jersey community colleges offer credit courses that lead to various associate degrees. Separate from the NJVCCC, many New Jersey community colleges offer other distance learning credit and noncredit courses using television, video, CD-ROM, and radio.

## STUDENT SERVICES

Students who take NJVCCC courses are entitled to all services offered by their local community college, such as tutoring, library services, proctored testing, advisement, counseling, registration, and access to computer labs.

## CREDIT OPTIONS

Many of the courses offered by the NJVCCC are 3-credit college-level courses. NJVCCC courses can be used to fulfill partial requirements of a degree program at one of New Jersey's community colleges. Degrees earned at community colleges can be used to transfer to four-year institutions, or students can enter the workforce directly.

## FACULTY

All of New Jersey's community college faculty members who teach NJVCCC courses are highly skilled instructors with extensive distance learning experience. Many NJVCCC teachers hold doctorates, master's degrees, or other terminal degrees.

## ADMISSION

The principal requirement for admission is the applicant's possession of a high school diploma or its equivalent.

## TUITION AND FEES

NJVCCC courses cost $80 per credit, with no service fees, for in-state and out-of-state students. The only fee a student may pay is a registration fee.

## FINANCIAL AID

Financial aid is available to distance learners who are enrolled as full- or part-time students in degree programs at any of New Jersey's nineteen community colleges. General financial aid programs include state Tuition Aid Grants, Federal Pell Grants, state Educational Opportunity Fund Grants, and the Federal Direct Student Loan Program.

## APPLYING

To register for NJVCCC courses, students should visit the Consortium's Web site (listed below). Full registration instructions are provided online.

---

### CONTACT

Jacob C. Farbman
Public Relations Officer
New Jersey Council of County Colleges
330 West State Street
Trenton, New Jersey 08618
Phone: 609-392-3434
Fax: 609-392-8158
E-mail: farbmanj@aol.com
Web site: http://www.njvccc.cc.nj.us (NJVCCC courses and registration)
http://www.njccc.org (New Jersey community colleges information)

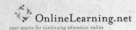

# OnlineLearning.net

## *Distance Learning Program*

Los Angeles, California

*OnlineLearning.net is the leading online supplier of continuing education, providing busy professionals with the tools needed to pursue their lifelong learning objectives. Combining technological innovation with extraordinary customer service, OnlineLearning.net is committed to helping adult learners around the world access the best in educational resources—anytime, anywhere, at any stage in life. Since September 1996, OnlineLearning.net has offered more than 1,700 online courses to more than 20,000 students in all fifty states. Founded in 1994, OnlineLearning.net delivers online instructor-led and self-paced courses from leading accredited universities and established partners, including UCLA Extension, the nation's largest single-campus continuing education program; the University of San Diego; Houghton Mifflin Company, the leading publisher of textbooks and reference manuals; and the California CPA Education Foundation, providing education and information to CPAs and related professionals.*

## DISTANCE LEARNING PROGRAM

OnlineLearning.net offers more than 250 online classes each quarter in five areas of interest, including business and management, computer and information systems, education, general interest, and writing. Instructor-led online courses mirror traditional classroom-style courses in that they are interactive, feature specific start and end dates, require textbooks, and provide the same levels of academic/professional credit. Students enrolled in any instructor-led course with Online Learning.net have access to 24-hour customer service and technical support through the company's Concierge Service, a unique course management service that helps to ease the transition to learning online. Online self-paced courses are also offered through OnlineLearning.net.

OnlineLearning.net has an unparalleled history of student satisfaction. Eighty-five percent of students surveyed rate online courses distributed by OnlineLearning.net as "as good as or better than face-to-face learning." Ninety percent say they are likely to take additional online courses distributed by OnlineLearning.net. Nearly 90 percent of the students successfully completed their online courses.

## DELIVERY MEDIA

Any PC or Macintosh with reliable access to the Internet is sufficient. During instructor-led courses, interaction is asynchronous, with instructors delivering lectures, assignments, and feedback, all online. Prior to the start of the courses, students participate in an interactive online orientation designed to maximize their comfort level with the online format. Course managers are assigned to each course to assist students in their online experience. Access to a free course demonstration is available at http://www.OnlineLearning.net/demo.

## PROGRAMS OF STUDY

OnlineLearning.net delivers certificate programs and professional sequences in addition to individual courses. In the teacher education community, students can earn professional development credits online. Students can also choose courses for credential clearing, online teaching, instructional technology, CLAD, TESOL, TEFL, a certificate in college counseling, and a certificate in character education.

In the computer community, courses range from Web technology and production to Microsoft Office and applications programming. OnlineLearning.net offers self-paced courses in Microsoft (MCSE), A+, Linux, Cisco (CCNA), and more.

In the business community, students can take courses in accounting, human resources, investing, e-commerce, and more. UCLA Extension offers a number of professional designations and awards online, including an Award in General Business Studies and a professional designation in personal financial planning.

In the writing community, UCLA Extension's online writing courses (the nation's largest online writing program) help students achieve goals in creative writing, screenwriting, public relations, and journalism. In the general education community, students can enrich their knowledge in history, political science, writing, philosophy, and more.

## SPECIAL PROGRAMS

OnlineLearning.net offers the following special programs:

The certificate program in college counseling includes six courses and a 65-hour practicum completed at a convenient school venue.

The certificate in character education, the first of its kind in the nation.

The online teaching program is the most comprehensive program of its type.

CLAD/TEFL programs satisfy the state-issued CLAD certificate. Credential-clearing courses for educators fulfill the professional clear credential requirements.

Professional designations in applications programming.

Estate planning, California tax series, and Federal tax series certificates provided by the California CPA Education Foundation.

Through the Award in General Business Studies, students can choose to concentrate their studies in technical communication, accounting, human resources, marketing, or personal financial planning.

The professional designation in personal financial planning satisfies the Certified Financial Planner Board of Standards for pursuing the CFP designation.

## CREDIT OPTIONS

The transfer of course work is evaluated on a case-by-case basis by each university. UCLA Extension offers transferable degree credit courses online. Courses numbered X 1 to X 199 carry undergraduate-level credit; Courses numbered X 300 to X 499 are professional credit courses. Educators are advised to gain prior approval from their school district, college, or university for credit approval.

## FACULTY

All instructors are trained by OnlineLearning.net to be more effective teachers online. Many are experts in their fields.

## ADMISSION

A college degree is not required to enroll in an online course presented by OnlineLearning.net. Some courses have prerequisites, but most only require the desire to learn.

## TUITION AND FEES

Costs vary depending on the number of credit units and course materials.

An early-bird discount and returning student discount are available, as specific association discounts, including a $75 or 15 percent discount (whichever is greater) on any instructor-led course for members of the National Education Association and the California Teachers Association. For additional information, students should visit the OnlineLearning.net Web site (http://www.OnlineLearning.net/specialoffers).

## FINANCIAL AID

Financial aid may be available through the appropriate university for the program desired.

## APPLYING

Class size is limited in all online instructor-led courses. Orientation is mandatory for new students. Students may enroll either online or by phone. To enroll online, students should visit the Web site http://www.OnlineLearning.net/enroll. Enrollment by phone is available at the toll-free number listed below.

---

### CONTACT

OnlineLearning.net
555 South Flower Street
Suite 2850
Los Angeles, California 90071
Telephone: 213-689-4656
          800-784-8436 (toll-free)
Fax: 213-689-4657
E-mail: info@OnlineLearning.net
Web site: http://www.OnlineLearning.net

---

# SREB Southern Regional Education Board

## Electronic Campus

Atlanta, Georgia

---

*The Electronic Campus of the Southern Regional Education Board (SREB) is a marketplace of distance learning courses, programs, and services available from colleges and universities across the South.*

*Founded in January 1998, the Electronic Campus has grown from 104 courses to almost 4,000 courses and 175 degree programs from more than 325 colleges and universities throughout the South. The campus includes courses and programs from all sixteen SREB member states, and participating colleges, courses, and programs are added continually. The SREB's member states are Alabama, Arkansas, Delaware, Florida, Georgia, Kentucky, Louisiana, Maryland, Mississippi, North Carolina, Oklahoma, South Carolina, Tennessee, Texas, Virginia, and West Virginia.*

*The Southern Regional Education Board, the nation's first interstate compact for education, was created in 1948 at the request of Southern business, education, and governmental leaders. It was designed to help leaders in government and education work together to advance education and to improve the region's social and economic life.*

## DISTANCE LEARNING PROGRAM

The Electronic Campus provides detailed and common information about distance learning courses and programs offered by participating colleges and universities. The Electronic Campus' goal is to provide enhanced educational opportunities for traditional and nontraditional students in a method that removes many of the barriers that long have hindered access to higher education.

## DELIVERY MEDIA

Courses and programs are available in a variety of delivery formats. The predominant delivery method is the World Wide Web. Courses and programs are available via the Web in both synchronous and asynchronous modes. Other delivery formats are the Internet, videotapes, satellite, CD-ROMs, compressed video, and open broadcast. Information on the delivery formats for each course and program is available on the Web site, listed below.

## PROGRAMS OF STUDY

The Electronic Campus provides access to regionally accredited academic degree programs in higher education. Certificate, associate, bachelor's, master's, and doctoral programs and credit courses are offered electronically.

Courses and programs must meet the following requirements: the course or program provides for appropriate interaction between faculty members and students and among students; quality faculty members provide appropriate supervision of the program or course that is offered electronically; academic standards for all programs or courses offered electronically are the same as those for other courses or programs delivered at the institution where they originate; each course listed meets the Principles of Good Practice, the cornerstone of this electronic marketplace; and all courses and programs have been reviewed against the Principles of Good Practice.

## SPECIAL PROGRAMS

The Electronic Campus offers a variety of special programs, and that number continues to grow. More information on these special programs can be found on the Web site. Students taking courses through the Electronic Campus have access to the nationally recognized GALILEO virtual library. A student easily can access a database of more than 3,800 publications, more than 1,500 of which are available in full text. The disciplines are varied and include social sciences, general sciences, business, and education. All of these publications can be searched easily and quickly using GALILEO's powerful search engines.

## FACULTY

Many of the SREB region's most respected professors have courses and programs on the Electronic Campus. The faculty members respond to students' questions and often list times that they can be reached by telephone in their campus offices.

Students often say communication with the professors through the Electronic Campus is as effective as or even more effective than in a classroom setting.

## ADMISSION

The offering college or university handles admission to degree programs. Students can access this information from the Electronic Campus Web site. Many institutions allow potential students to complete the application for admission on line. Students who wish to enroll in courses may be able to do so without formal application and admission. The enrollment procedures and requirements are outlined on the Electronic Campus Web site.

## TUITION AND FEES

The college or university offering the courses and programs sets tuition and fees. Tuition and fees are available at the Electronic Campus Web site.

SREB is promoting the establishment of an "electronic tuition rate" by college and universities participating in the Electronic Campus. This rate would apply to in-state and out-of-state students.

Through a pilot project, residents of SREB states will have access to selected degree programs at in-state rates. This arrangement adds electronically delivered programs to SREB's 25-year-old Academic Common Market.

## FINANCIAL AID

Participating colleges and universities coordinate financial aid. Specific information on financial aid is available from the colleges and universities; general information is available on the Electronic Campus Web site.

## APPLYING

Anyone with Internet access may search the courses and programs available through the Electronic Campus marketplace. There is no charge for this service, and application and registration are not required.

---

### CONTACT

Mary Larson
Coordinator, Program Services
Southern Regional Education Board
592 10th Street, NW
Atlanta, Georgia 30318-5790
Telephone: 404-875-9211
Fax: 404-872-1477
E-mail: mary.larson@sreb.org
Web site: http://www.electroniccampus.org

Bruce Chaloux
Director, Electronic Campus
Southern Regional Education Board
E-mail: bruce.chaloux@sreb.org

---

**Colorado Consortium for Independent Study**

www.colorado.edu/ccis

# University of Northern Colorado

## *Colorado Consortium for Independent Study*

Greeley, Colorado

eCollege.com   *www.ecollege.com*

*The Colorado Consortium for Independent Study, founded in the 1970s under the auspices of the Colorado Commission on Higher Education, comprises the Independent Study programs of seven public colleges and universities in Colorado. Members of the Consortium are committed to removing boundaries and to providing access to courses, programs and services of their respective institutions.*

*Guided instruction offered by the institutions is supported through a variety of technologies and media. To learn more, students should visit http://www. colorado.edu/ccis.*

*Member institutions are accredited by the North Central Association. Credit courses and instructors are approved by academic divisions at the institution offering a specific course. Appropriate departments of the institution and state regulating or accrediting agencies have approved noncredit and certificate courses.*

## DISTANCE LEARNING PROGRAM

Distance learning through the members of the Consortium ranges from individual courses through complete degree programs. Concise descriptions of each are available via the respective Web sites. Students may begin at http://www.colorado.edu/ccis or go directly to one of the following:
Adams State College: http://www.adams.edu/exstudies/index.html
Colorado State University: http://www.learn.colostate.edu
Metropolitan State College of Denver: http://clem.mscd.edu/~options
University of Colorado at Boulder: http://www.colorado.edu/cewww
University of Colorado at Colorado Springs: http://www.uccs.edu
University of Northern Colorado: http://www.unco.edu/center/oes/
University of Southern Colorado http://coned.uscolo.edu

During the past year the Consortium has served approximately 6,500 individuals, processing more than 8,000 enrollments in Independent Study alone. Hundreds more are enrolled in the degree programs.

## DELIVERY MEDIA

Students enrolled in an Independent Study (correspondence) course receive a course syllabus and/or study guide and may be directed to purchase a textbook or other printed material. Students complete assignments, then mail, e-mail, or fax them as instructed for grading. The courses may also be delivered or supplemented by audio- and videotapes, slides, CDs, and a variety of computer technologies.

## PROGRAMS OF STUDY

For details concerning the degree programs, students should contact the school offering the program in which they are interested. Degree programs offered through distance technology are designed specifically to serve adult learners and do not require on-campus attendance for orientation or classes.

Colorado State University offers bachelor's, master's, and doctoral degree programs in agriculture, engineering, business, computer science, statistics, human resource development, and other fields. Students may visit its Web site listed above.

University of Northern Colorado offers a bachelor's degree in nursing (for RNs only) and master's degrees in communication disorders and special education. Students may visit its Web site listed above.

University of Southern Colorado offers a bachelor's degree completion program in social science, sociology, and sociology/criminology. Students may visit its Web site listed above.

## SPECIAL PROGRAMS

Other programs for non–degree-seeking students may lead to certificates or other formal recognition. For more detail, students should visit the Consortium members' Web sites. These programs, too, are designed to assure convenience for the adult learner.

Adams State College participates in the StarNet, a service to educators whose districts participate in the StarNet Professional Development Program. Students may visit its Web site listed above.

Colorado State University features a number of professional development online courses at its Web site listed above.

University of Colorado-Boulder offers advanced training to individuals and companies through its Center for Advanced Training in Engineering and Computer Science (CATECS). UC-Boulder also offers high school independent learning. Students may visit its Web site listed above.

University of Northern Colorado has a dietetic internship program to assist individuals seeking to become registered dietitians and offers a graduate certificate in gerontology. Students may visit its Web site listed above.

University of Southern Colorado features a number of online interactive courses. Students may visit its Web site listed above.

## STUDENT SERVICES

**Advising:** Colorado State University, University of Colorado-Boulder and University of Southern Colorado provide the services of academic advisers to their continuing education students.

**Textbooks:** Books may be purchased at many bookstores, but to ensure getting the correct edition, students should order them from the bookstore of the institution offering the course. Each bookstore stocks books required for only those courses offered by that institution. Students who wish to know textbook costs prior to enrollment should contact the appropriate bookstore.

**Library Services:** Students are encouraged to use local libraries to order materials that are not locally available through interlibrary loan. Some materials may also be available through Internet connections with public libraries, and there may be special services available from the institution in whose course or program the students are enrolled.

**Special Services for the Disabled:** Students who are disabled and require special services should contact the institution offering the course or program in which they are interested to find out what services and assistance are available.

## CREDIT OPTIONS

Academic semester-hour credit is awarded by the institution offering the course. Students who wish to apply Independent Study courses toward degree requirements or for certification or licensing should contact their adviser or the certification/licensing agency before registering to make sure a course will meet their requirements.

Applicability of credits transferred or earned through challenge exams and other alternative forms of learning may be applicable to a degree program. Students should check with the school from which they intend to earn a degree.

## FACULTY

The number of faculty members from the Consortium's member institutions who are involved in distance learning runs into the hundreds. The Independent Study courses alone involve nearly 150 faculty members, and an average of 69 percent of all courses (regardless of undergraduate or graduate level) are taught by faculty members with doctoral or terminal (professional) degrees. Among member schools with graduate program offerings, the range of those with advanced degrees runs to 89 percent.

## ADMISSION

Enrollment in Independent Study courses does not constitute admission to any of the Colorado Consortium institutions. Metropolitan State requires additional information at the time of enrollment in an Independent Study course. Degree students at University of Colorado at Boulder (except those in Arts and Sciences) and at Adams State must have their dean's signature approval to register for Independent Study courses.

Students currently enrolled in a degree program should check with the appropriate official at their degree-granting institution to make certain the course will apply to their degree program.

Admissions to degree programs must be completed through the Admissions Office or Graduate Studies Office of the institution from which students intend to earn a degree.

Students should inquire in advance as to the technology requirements of the course or program in which they plan to enroll.

## TUITION AND FEES

These vary from program to program, even within the same institution. Students should inquire of the institution(s) whose courses or programs they are considering.

## FINANCIAL AID

Federal grants may not be applied to Independent Study correspondence courses. Students are encouraged to seek scholarship aid from organizations and local civic groups that may sponsor such study. For information concerning VA benefits, students should contact the VA office at the institution in which they plan to enroll.

Colorado State University and University of Southern Colorado courses are approved for the DANTES program. Eligible military personnel should process DANTES applications through their education office.

Students accepted into distance degree programs may be eligible for student loans. Applicants should contact the Financial Aid Office of the institution to which they are seeking admission.

## APPLYING

Application procedures vary by institution. For credit programs, the process and criteria may be expected to be consistent with the requirements for on-campus admissions. Most programs do not require on-campus attendance at any point during admissions, orientation, instruction, or testing.

---

### CONTACT
Interested applicants should visit the Colorado Consortium for Independent Study Web site at www.colorado.edu/ccis. E-mail: indeps.desk@unco.edu

---

# Utah Electronic College

## *Utah System of Higher Education*

Salt Lake City, Utah

*The Utah Electronic College (UEC) is a gateway to distance-delivered courses and programs offered by Utah's nine community and state colleges and universities. Students can take individual classes or earn full certificates or degrees. The UEC does not confer degrees; rather, it supports the member institutions that do. Each of the member schools is fully accredited.*

*The UEC was established fall 1998 to serve as a portal for Utah's distance-delivered courses and programs. The UEC centrally coordinates key student services. A single application entitles students to enroll in the distance learning courses from all the partner colleges. A single tuition rate applies to the five two-year schools and a second rate applies to the universities. UEC Service Center staff coordinate with designated campus coordinators to ensure students gain access to campus services including academic advising, financial aid counseling, library resources, and the bookstore. When a student applies for admission, he or she selects a home college. This school provides the student with the services mentioned above. Detailed information is available at the Web site at http://uec.org.*

## DISTANCE LEARNING PROGRAM

As students apply for admission through the Utah Electronic College, they must select a "home college." The home college is the school most likely to confer a certificate or degree. This institution provides student services such as financial aid and advising and the student must abide by the home college's graduation requirements.

The UEC admits students to take the distance-delivered offerings of all partner schools, registers students in these classes, and acts as the Income Accounting office. UEC is the front door: there is one Web site and one central catalog listing all member schools' distance offerings. The UEC Service Center staff members work closely with numerous admissions, registration, and student services offices at member institutions.

## DELIVERY MEDIA

In the UEC catalog is a listing of hundreds of distance learning courses delivered using innovative technologies, designed to fit the busy schedules of adult learners. The online course catalog provides detailed information on course and program offerings including faculty contact information. Students are encouraged to contact the faculty member before enrolling. Some courses require students to "attend" class at a certain time or location. Others allow students to determine when and where they want to "go to class."

Internet/Online: The "classroom" is the Internet. It is always open. Some online courses are delivered entirely on the Internet. Others require face-to-face meetings or videos to supplement online content. Generally, students access lectures and assignments online and chat with or send e-mail to instructors and fellow students. Students need access to a computer with a browser, Internet access, and e-mail.

Live/Two-Way Interactive/EdNet: Teleconferencing and satellite technologies deliver courses to "receive" sites such as high schools and colleges located around the state. Students use microphones to interact with the instructor and with fellow students at other sites. These are "real time" classes: students must be at the receive site while the course is delivered.

Broadcast/Telecourse: Students watch class at home on public television. Many set the VCR to record class lectures to watch later. On-campus discussion sessions are often scheduled. Tests are proctored at approved testing sites. Generally, students communicate with the instructor by telephone, fax, e-mail, or during the discussion sessions. Students need access to a television and to KULC or one of its translators.

Videocassette/Video Check Out: Some telecourses are available for home viewing. These classes have the same format as a telecourse, but students check out videos of the broadcast portion to view at home. Students need a television and a VCR.

Print/Independent Study: Course content is delivered with extended syllabi, study guides, and textbooks. Course work is submitted by mail, fax, or e-mail. Tests are proctored at approved testing sites. Generally, students use telephone, fax, or e-mail to correspond with the instructor. Students do not need special equipment to complete the course.

Multimedia: Many classes use a combination of the delivery modes listed above. Students should check the catalog entry to ensure the class in which they are interested comes in a delivery format they like.

## PROGRAMS OF STUDY

Many courses found in the UEC class catalog fill general education or graduation requirements at Utah schools. Often, these general education classes are accepted at colleges in other states. In spring 2001 students could earn six different associate's degrees and two certificates through the UEC: A.A./A.S. in aviation mechanics, aviation science, business, criminal justice, and psychology as well as a general transfer associate's degree; certificates in railroad operations and paraeducation. Bachelor's degrees in aviation science and business should be available in spring 2002.

As the UEC involves the universities within the Utah System of Higher Education beginning in fall 2001, the number of technology delivered certificates and degrees will expand greatly. Current information is available on the Web site listed below.

## STUDENT SERVICES

The UEC is committed to servicing students. UEC Service Center staff members answer general questions about distance and higher education and direct students to appropriate school and class contacts for detailed information. Students may contact the program by toll-free phone, fax, and e-mail. Representatives are available Monday through Friday, 8 a.m. to 5 p.m. MST, with extended hours Tuesday and Thursday until 7 p.m. MST.

The school a student designates as his or her home college provides such services as financial aid counseling and academic advising. Each school has a campus coordinator who can provide directions to student services staff (information is available at Campus Resources on the UEC Web site). Each class listed in the UEC catalog includes contact information for the instructor and for the distance education program administrator. This network of support ensures a positive UEC experience.

## CREDIT OPTIONS

Students may audit classes or take classes for a letter grade or credit/no

credit. Utah's nine colleges and universities accept transfer credit for college-level courses from any other public Utah college as long as minimum grades were earned. However, accepting transfer credit does not automatically mean the credits a student earned at his or her first school will count toward degree requirements at his or her second school. Students are strongly advised to check with their college's advisers to ensure the class they take at another school will not only transfer, but will also count toward graduation or the requirements of their major.

## FACULTY

Courses found in the UEC catalog are developed and taught by the same faculty members that teach courses on the campuses of Utah's colleges and universities. Students should expect the same attention from an instructor of a distance-delivered class as they would receive in a campus-based class. Faculty members respond to student inquiries by telephone, fax, and e-mail. In instances where contacting the faculty member is problematic, the UEC Service Center staff members will help.

## ADMISSION

Admissions requirements are the same as the requirements for on-campus programs. Most UEC partner schools have an open admissions policy. Applicants simply complete the application, pay a $35 processing fee, and provide documentation of their high school graduation. Placement and/or college entrance test scores are used only to place students in appropriate entry-level college classes. Students are notified electronically if additional documentation is required to complete the admissions process.

## TUITION AND FEES

There is one UEC tuition rate that covers both Utah residents and nonresi-

dents. Tuition and fees range from $69 to $100 per semester credit hour, depending on the provider institution. Member schools may charge additional technology fees per class. The UEC class catalog has specific course costs. UEC tuition and fees are subject to change without notice.

## FINANCIAL AID

Students enrolling through the UEC can apply for financial aid through the school they designate as the home college. Each financial aid office has a UEC contact (contact information is available through Campus Resources on the UEC Web site for contact information).

## APPLYING

The UEC admissions form is available online at http://uec.org under the "Admissions and Registration" section. The UEC online admissions form has eight sections and may take five to ten minutes to complete. Students provide specific information such as birth city and county, driver's license number, and high school GPA and graduation year. Common contact information can be corrected later using an "update" screen.

---

### CONTACT

Utah Electronic College Service Center
101 Wasatch Drive
Salt Lake City, Utah 84112
Telephone: 801-581-UTAH (8824)
877-533-9235 (toll-free)
Fax: 801.58LEARN (575.3276)
E-mail: help@uec.org
Web site: http://uec.org

---

# INDEXES

# INDEX OF INSTITUTIONS OFFERING DEGREE AND CERTIFICATE PROGRAMS

**(BAS) Resources Management**
Troy State University-Florida Region (B)

**3 Year General**
University of Manitoba (B)

**Academic Certificate Program in Community Employment Services**
Auburn University (UC)

**Accountancy**
Davenport University Online (B)
State University of New York Institute of Technology at Utica/Rome (M)

**Accounting**
Alaska Pacific University (A, B)
Athabasca University (UC)
Brenau University (M)
Caldwell College (B)
Champlain College (A, UC)
Coastline Community College (A)
Colorado Electronic Community College (A)
Davenport University Online (M, A)
Excelsior College (B)
Fayetteville Technical Community College (A)
Golden Gate University (GC)
Graceland University (B)
Indiana Higher Education Telecommunication System (A)
Indiana Institute of Technology (B)
Ivy Tech State College-Wabash Valley (A)
Lakeland College (B)
Marywood University (B)
Northampton County Area Community College (A)
Northwest Missouri State University (B)
Nova Southeastern University (M)
Robert Morris College (B)
Saint Leo University (B)
Saint Mary-of-the-Woods College (A, B)
Southern New Hampshire University (UC)
Strayer University (A, B, UC)
Thomas Edison State College (A, B)

The University Alliance (B)
University of Northwestern Ohio (A, B)
University of Phoenix (M)
University of Sarasota (M)
Upper Iowa University (B)

**Accounting ASB**
Harcourt Learning Direct Center for Degree Studies (A)

**Accounting Information Systems**
Saint Mary-of-the-Woods College (B)

**Accounting Procedures**
Davenport University Online (UC)

**Accounting/Finance**
Keller Graduate School of Management (M)

**Accounting: Advanced**
College of Southern Maryland (UC)

**Accounting: Basic**
College of Southern Maryland (UC)

**Acquisition and Contract Management**
Florida Institute of Technology (M)
Strayer University (A)

**Action for a Viable Future**
Sonoma State University (M)

**Add-on Teacher Licensure in Special Education**
The University of North Carolina at Greensboro (UC)

**Addiction Studies**
Bethany College of the Assemblies of God (B)
University of Cincinnati (B)

**Administration**
Athabasca University (UC)

**Administration of Justice**
Maui Community College (A)
Thomas Edison State College (A)

**Administrative Manager Certificate**
Pitt Community College (UC)

**Administrative Office Management**
Thomas Edison State College (A, B)

**Administrative Office Technology— Office Software Specialist**
Vincennes University (UC)

**Administrative Studies**
Southwest Missouri State University (M)
York University (B)

**Administrative/Management Studies**
Excelsior College (A)

**Adult and Vocational Education**
Valdosta State University (M, B)

**Adult Degree Completion Program**
Prescott College (B)

**Adult Development and Aging Services**
The Pennsylvania State University University Park Campus (UC)

**Adult Education**
Brock University (B, UC)
Indiana Higher Education Telecommunication System (M)
Indiana University System (M)
Newman University (M)
North Carolina Agricultural and Technical State University (M)
Northwestern State University of Louisiana (M)
The Pennsylvania State University University Park Campus (M)
University of New Brunswick (M, B, UC)

**Adult Liberal Studies**
University of Toledo (B)

**Advanced Accounting**
Athabasca University (UC)

**Advanced Business Management**
The Pennsylvania State University University Park Campus (UC)

**Advanced Electronics**
Illinois Institute of Technology (GC)

**Advanced Management**
The American College (GC)

**Advanced Material Design**
University of Idaho (UC)

**Advanced Nursing Practice**
Athabasca University (GC)

**Advanced Professional Certificate**
Suffolk University (UC)

**Advanced Programs**
University of Oklahoma (M)

**Advanced Respiratory Therapy**
Weber State University (B)

**Adventure Education**
Prescott College (M)

**Advertising Design**
Syracuse University (M)

**Advertising Management**
Thomas Edison State College (B)

**Aeronautical Science**
Embry-Riddle Aeronautical University (M)

**Aerospace Engineering**
Auburn University (M)
Stanford University (M)
The University of Alabama (M)
University of Colorado at Boulder (M)
The University of Texas at Arlington (M)

**African American Ministry Leadership**
Defiance College (UC)

**Agribusiness**
Kansas State University (M)
University of Northwestern Ohio (A)

**Agribusiness Management**
Purdue University (M)

**Agricultural Business**
Colorado Community College Online (A)
Pueblo Community College (UC)

**Agricultural Development, Plant Science, or Natural Resource Development**
Texas A&M University (M)

**Agricultural Education**
Oklahoma State University (M)
Texas Tech University (D)
University of Florida (M)

**Agricultural Sciences**
Colorado State University (M)

**Agriculture**
Iowa State University of Science and Technology (M)
Washington State University (M)

**Agronomy**
Iowa State University of Science and Technology (M)

**Air Traffic Control**
Thomas Edison State College (A, B)

**Allied Health**
California College for Health Sciences (A)

**American Indian Studies**
University of Denver (GC)

**American Studies**
Saint Joseph's College (B, UC)

**Animal Science and Industry**
Kansas State University (B)

**Applied Arts and Science**
Rochester Institute of Technology (B)

**Applied Arts and Sciences**
Midwestern State University (B)

**Applied Computer Science**
Columbus State University (M)

**Applied Computer Science ASB**
Harcourt Learning Direct Center for Degree Studies (A)

**Applied Geotechnics**
University of Idaho (UC)

**Applied Gerontology**
University of North Texas (GC, M)

**Applied Health Studies**
Pennsylvania College of Technology (B)

**Applied Information Management**
University of Oregon (M)

**Applied Management**
National American University (A, B)

**Applied Management and Decision Sciences**
Walden University (D)

**Applied Professional Studies**
Bethany College of the Assemblies of God (B)

**Applied Psychology**
St. Cloud State University (M)

**Applied Social Sciences**
Maui Community College (B)

**Applied Statistical Quality**
Rochester Institute of Technology (M)

**Applied Statistics**
The University of Tennessee (GC)

**Applied Technology**
Rogers State University (A, B)

**APSU Regents Online Degree Program**
Austin Peay State University (B)

**Art Therapy**
Norwich University (M)
Saint Mary-of-the-Woods College (M)

**Arts**
Athabasca University (UC)
Honolulu Community College (A)
Thomas Edison State College (A)

**Arts Administration**
Goucher College (M)

**Arts and Humanities**
Ohio University (A)

**Arts and Sciences**
Clarion University of Pennsylvania (A)
College of Southern Maryland (A)
Hawkeye Community College (A)
Rowan-Cabarrus Community College (A)

**Arts and Sciences: Arts and Humanities**
College of Southern Maryland (A)

# Index of Institutions Offering Degree and Certificate Programs

**Arts Management**
University of Massachusetts Amherst (UC)
University of Massachusetts System (UC)

**AS400 Operations**
Alexandria Technical College (UC)

**AS400 Programming**
Alexandria Technical College (UC)

**Asset Management**
The American College (GC)

**Assistive Technology**
California State University, Dominguez Hills (UC)

**Associate in Arts Degree (Business Transfer Framework)**
Prestonsburg Community College (A)

**Associate of Arts—Pre-Baccalaureate**
North Iowa Area Community College (A)

**Associate of Arts Programs**
Kirkwood Community College (A)

**Associate of General Education (AGE)**
Craven Community College (A)

**Atmospheric and Environmental Science and Engineering**
Stevens Institute of Technology (GC)

**Audiology**
Central Michigan University (GC)
University of Florida (M)

**Autism/Assistive Technology**
University of Louisville (M)

**Automated Accounting Technology**
Davenport University Online (A)

**Automotive Engineering**
University of Michigan (M)

**Automotive Management**
University of Northwestern Ohio (A)

**Automotive Technology**
Pennsylvania College of Technology (B)

**Automotive Technology and HVAC Technology**
Sequoia Institute (A)

**Aviation Flight Technology**
Thomas Edison State College (A, B)

**Aviation Maintenance Technology**
Thomas Edison State College (A, B)

**Aviation Studies**
Excelsior College (A)
University of Nebraska at Omaha (B)

**Aviation Technology**
Mountain State University (A, UC)

**Baccalaureate Nursing**
University of South Carolina Spartanburg (B)

**Bachelor of Administration (with Concentration)**
Athabasca University (B)

**Bachelor of Administration Post Diploma (with Concentration)**
Athabasca University (B)

**Bachelor of Arts (3 year)**
Athabasca University (B)

**Bachelor of Arts (3 year) with Concentration**
Athabasca University (B)

**Bachelor of Arts (4 year) General or with Major**
Athabasca University (B)

**Bachelor of Commerce (4 year)**
Athabasca University (B)

**Bachelor of General Studies with Designation (Arts/Science or Applied Studies)**
Athabasca University (B)

**Bachelor of Liberal Arts Degree (BLA)**
University of Massachusetts Lowell (B)

**Bachelor of Nursing—Post R.N.**
Athabasca University (B)

**Bachelor of Professional Arts with Major (4 year)**
Athabasca University (B)

**Bachelor of Religious Education**
Master's Pentecostal Bible College (A)

**Bachelor of Science**
Touro University International (B)

**Bachelor of Science (4 year)**
Athabasca University (B)

**Bachelor of Science—Post Diploma**
Athabasca University (B)

**Bachelor of Science in Nursing for Registered Nurses**
Northeastern State University (B)

**Bachelor of Theology**
Master's Pentecostal Bible College (B)

**Banking**
Mercy College (M)
Thomas Edison State College (A, B)

**Banking and Finance**
Mountain State University (A)

**Basic Accounting Certification**
Pitt Community College (UC)

**Basic Quality Management**
Rochester Institute of Technology (UC)

**Basic Supervisory Leadership**
The Pennsylvania State University University Park Campus (UC)

**Beam Physics**
Michigan State University (D, M)

**Behavior Analysis**
University of North Texas (GC)

**Behavioral and Social Sciences**
University of Maryland University College (B)

**Behavioral Science**
Lynn University (B)

**Behavioral Science (External Degree Program)**
University of Maine at Machias (B)

**Behavioral Sciences**
Vincennes University (A)

**Bible**
Briercrest Bible College (UC)
North Central University (UC)
Prairie Bible College (UC)

**Bible and Theology**
Global University of the Assemblies of God (M, A, B)

**Biblical and Theological Studies**
Bethany College of the Assemblies of God (B)

## Biblical Studies
The Baptist College of Florida (B)
Indiana Higher Education
    Telecommunication System (A)
LIFE Bible College (A)
Moody Bible Institute (A, B, UC)
Southern Christian University (M, B)
Taylor University, World Wide Campus (A)
Tennessee Temple University (A, B)

## Biblical Studies, Urban Ministry, Marketplace Leadership
Beulah Heights Bible College (B)

## Bilingual Education
Northern Arizona University (UC)

## Bilingual/Multicultural Education
Northern Arizona University (M)

## Bioinformatics
Rensselaer Polytechnic Institute (UC)

## Biological and Agricultural Engineering
University of Idaho (M)

## Biology
Northern Arizona University (B)

## Bioresources and Agricultural Engineering
Colorado State University (M)

## Birth-Kindergarten Teacher Licensure
The University of North Carolina at
    Greensboro (B)

## Broadcast Meteorology
Mississippi State University (UC)

## Building Code Enforcement
Red Rocks Community College (A)

## Building Leadership
Newman University (M)

## Business
Alaska Pacific University (A)
Bellevue Community College (A)
Buena Vista University (B)
Caldwell College (B)
California College for Health Sciences (M)
Cedar Crest College (B)
Champlain College (A, UC)
Coastline Community College (A)
Colorado Community College Online (A)
Colorado Electronic Community College (A)
Dallas Baptist University (M, B)
Drexel University (M)
East Tennessee State University (B)

Excelsior College (A)
Fayetteville Technical Community College
    (A)
Florence-Darlington Technical College (A)
Judson College (B)
Kennesaw State University (M)
Lansing Community College (A)
Liberty University (B)
Lynn University (B)
Maui Community College (UC)
Maysville Community College (A)
Missouri Southern State College (B)
New York Institute of Technology (M)
Pueblo Community College (A)
Purdue University (M)
Red Rocks Community College (A)
Salve Regina University (B)
Southern New Hampshire University (A)
Southwestern Assemblies of God University
    (B)
Troy State University (A)
The University Alliance (A)
University of Alaska Southeast, Ketchikan
    Campus (A, UC)
University of Houston-Victoria (M)
University of St. Francis (M)
The University of Texas at Dallas (M)
Upper Iowa University (A, B)
Walsh College of Accountancy and Business
    Administration (M)
Western Governors University (A)

## Business Accounting
University of Phoenix (B)

## Business Administration
Acadia University (UC)
Adirondack Community College (A)
Alaska Pacific University (B)
Anne Arundel Community College (A)
Arizona State University West (M)
Atlantic Cape Community College (A)
Auburn University (M)
Baker College of Flint (M, A, B)
Ball State University (M)
Bellevue University (M)
Bucks County Community College (A)
California National University for Advanced
    Studies (M, B)
Catawba Valley Community College (UC)
Cayuga County Community College (A)
Central Community College (A)
College of Southern Maryland (A)
College of The Albemarle (A)
Colorado Christian University (M)
Colorado State University (M)
Concordia University Wisconsin (M)
Craven Community College (A)

DeVry Online (B)
Eastern New Mexico University (M, B)
Eastern Oregon University (B)
East Tennessee State University (M)
Florida Gulf Coast University (M)
Forsyth Technical Community College (A)
Franklin University (B)
Gardner-Webb University (M)
Golden Gate University (M)
Graceland University (B)
Indiana Higher Education
    Telecommunication System (M)
Indiana Institute of Technology (A)
Indiana State University (B)
Indiana University System (M)
Indiana Wesleyan University (M)
ISIM University (M)
Ivy Tech State College-Wabash Valley (A)
Jones International University (M)
Lakeland College (B)
Lehigh University (M)
Liberty University (M)
Limestone College (A, B)
Marist College (M)
Marylhurst University (M)
Marywood University (B)
Maui Community College (M, B)
Memorial University of Newfoundland (B,
    UC)
Mercy College (M, B)
Morehead State University (M)
Mountain Empire Community College (A)
Mount Saint Vincent University (B, UC)
Mount Wachusett Community College (A)
National American University (A, B)
National Technological University (M, M)
National University (M, B)
New York Institute of Technology (B)
Northampton County Area Community
    College (A)
Northcentral University (D, M, B)
Northern Arizona University (B)
Northern Virginia Community College (A)
Nova Southeastern University (M)
Oklahoma State University (M)
Old Dominion University (B)
Open Learning Agency (B)
Oral Roberts University (B)
Ottawa University (M)
Parkland College (A)
Peirce College (A, B)
The Pennsylvania State University University
    Park Campus (A)
Pitt Community College (A)
Rogers State University (A)
Rowan-Cabarrus Community College (A)
Saint Joseph's College (A, B, UC)
Saint Leo University (B)

**Business Administration** *(continued)*

Saint Mary-of-the-Woods College (B)

Salve Regina University (M)

Sinclair Community College (A)

Southeast Community College, Beatrice Campus (A)

Southeast Community College, Lincoln Campus (A)

Southern New Hampshire University (M, B, UC)

Southwest Missouri State University (M)

Stephens College (B)

Strayer University (M, A, B)

Suffolk University (M)

Syracuse University (M)

Tiffin University (M)

Touro University International (D, M)

Troy State University (M)

Troy State University-Florida Region (A)

Troy State University Montgomery (A, B)

Tyler Junior College (A)

United States Open University (M, B)

The University Alliance (B)

University of Baltimore (M, B)

University of Colorado at Denver (M)

The University of Findlay (M)

University of Florida (M)

University of Great Falls (B)

University of Massachusetts Amherst (M)

University of Massachusetts System (M)

University of Missouri-St. Louis (M)

The University of Montana-Missoula (M)

University of North Dakota (M)

University of Northwestern Ohio (A, B)

University of Phoenix (M, B)

University of Pittsburgh (M)

University of Sarasota (M, B)

University of South Carolina (M)

The University of Tennessee at Martin (M)

The University of Texas of the Permian Basin (M)

University of Tulsa (M)

University of Wisconsin-Platteville (B)

University of Wyoming (M, B)

Utah State University (B)

Valdosta State University (M)

Vincennes University (A)

Virginia Polytechnic Institute and State University (M)

Virginia Western Community College (A)

Washington State University (B)

Western Piedmont Community College (A)

West Virginia University (M)

Worcester Polytechnic Institute (M)

## Business Administration (Management and Marketing Specialties)

Indiana Higher Education Telecommunication System (A)

## Business Administration (Management Option)

Indiana Higher Education Telecommunication System (A)

## Business Administration and Accounting

The University Alliance (B)

## Business Administration and Management

Lehigh Carbon Community College (A)

The University Alliance (B)

The University of Texas System (M)

Valdosta State University (B)

## Business Administration in Aviation

Embry-Riddle Aeronautical University (M)

## Business Administration, Public Sector Management Option

Open Learning Agency (B)

## Business Administration: Accounting

Mountain State University (A, B)

## Business Administration: Business Law

Mountain State University (A, B)

## Business Administration: General Business

Mountain State University (A, B)

## Business Administration: Management

Mountain State University (A, B)

## Business Administration: Office Management

Mountain State University (A, B)

## Business and Economics

Eastern Oregon University (B)

## Business Areas

University of Sarasota (UC)

## Business Communication

Jones International University (M, B)

## Business Education

Parkland College (A)

Southern New Hampshire University (M)

## Business Environmental Management

University of Denver (GC)

## Business in Real Estate

Open Learning Agency (B)

## Business Information Systems

Bellevue University (B)

Indiana Wesleyan University (B)

## Business Management

Anne Arundel Community College (A)

Burlington County College (A)

Hawkeye Community College (A)

Newman University (B)

Northampton County Area Community College (A)

Northern Virginia Community College (A)

Northwest Missouri State University (B)

Parkland College (A)

The Pennsylvania State University University Park Campus (UC)

Roger Williams University (B)

Tyler Junior College (A)

The University of Findlay (B)

University of Phoenix (B)

University of St. Francis (M)

## Business Management and Administration

Barclay College (B)

## Business Management ASB

Harcourt Learning Direct Center for Degree Studies (A)

## Business Management Technology

University of Toledo (A, UC)

## Business Management, Public Management Specialization

Northern Virginia Community College (A)

## Business Marketing

University of Phoenix (B)

## Business Military Management

Barton County Community College (A)

## Business Online

Bryant and Stratton Online (A)

## Business Operations—Accounting

Arizona Institute of Business & Technology (A)

## Business Operations—Business Technology

Arizona Institute of Business & Technology (A)

**Business Studies**
Southern New Hampshire University (B)
Vincennes University (A)

**Business Succession Planning**
The American College (GC)

**Business Transfer**
Middlesex Community College (A)

**Business, History, Political Science, Psychology, Social Science, Child Care**
Troy State University Montgomery (A)

**Business, IT Management**
Western Governors University (B)

**Business, Management and Economics**
State University of New York Empire State College (A, B)

**C++/Unix Programming**
Northeastern University (UC)

**Canadian Studies**
University of Waterloo (B)

**Career and Technical Education**
Virginia Polytechnic Institute and State University (M)

**Career Development**
Athabasca University (UC)
Memorial University of Newfoundland (UC)

**Career Master of Public Health Program**
Emory University (M)

**CDA in Early Childhood Education**
University of Alaska Southeast, Sitka Campus (UC)

**Certificat en Gérontologie**
Universite de Montreal (UC)

**Certificate in Bible**
Northwestern College (UC)

**Certificate in Interdisciplinary Palliative Care**
Lakehead University (UC)

**Certificate Program in Environmental Management**
Lakehead University (UC)

**Certification Program in Addiction Counseling**
Bethany College of the Assemblies of God (UC)

**CFP(tm) Educational Curriculum**
The American College (UC)

**Character Education**
University of Idaho (UC)

**Chartered Financial Consultant (ChFC) Designation**
The American College (UC)

**Chartered Leadership Fellow (CLF) Designation**
The American College (UC)

**Chartered Life Underwriter (CLU) Designation**
The American College (UC)

**Chemical Dependency Studies Counseling**
Tompkins Cortland Community College (A)

**Chemical Engineering**
Auburn University (M)
Illinois Institute of Technology (M)
Kansas State University (M)
Lehigh University (M)
Michigan State University (GC)
Mississippi State University (D, M)
National Technological University (M, UC)
University of North Dakota (B)
University of South Carolina (D, M)

**Chemistry**
Illinois Institute of Technology (GC, M)
Lehigh University (M)
Thomas Edison State College (B)

**Chess and Education Online**
The University of Texas System (UC)

**Child Development**
Concordia University (B)

**Child Development Services**
Thomas Edison State College (A)

**Children, Youth and Family Services**
The Pennsylvania State University University Park Campus (UC)

**Christian Care and Counseling**
Oral Roberts University (B)

**Christian Education**
North Central University (A, B, UC)

**Christian Ministries**
Crown College (A)

**Christian Ministry**
Crown College (B)
Southern Christian University (D, M)

**Christian Ministry Leadership**
Barclay College (B)

**Christian School Administration**
Oral Roberts University (M)

**Christian School Administration (Post-secondary)**
Oral Roberts University (D)

**Christian School Administration (PK-12)**
Oral Roberts University (D)

**Christian School Curriculum**
Oral Roberts University (M)

**Christian School Post-secondary Administration**
Oral Roberts University (M)

**Christian School Teaching**
Oral Roberts University (M)

**Christian Studies**
Briercrest Bible College (A, B)
North Central University (B)

**Christian Tradition**
Saint Joseph's College (B, UC)

**Christian Worker**
Taylor University, World Wide Campus (UC)

**Church Business Management**
Griggs University (B)

**Church Education**
Defiance College (UC)

**Church Leadership**
Bethany College of the Assemblies of God (B)
Crown College (M)

**Church Ministries**
Bethany College of the Assemblies of God (A)
North Central University (B, UC)
Oral Roberts University (B)
Southwestern Assemblies of God University (B)

**Church Ministry**
Warner Southern College (A, B, UC)

**Cinema Studies and Film Production**
Burlington College (B)

**Civil and Environmental Engineering**
University of South Carolina (M)
Virginia Polytechnic Institute and State
  University (M)

**Civil Engineering**
Auburn University (M)
Colorado State University (M)
Kansas State University (M)
Mississippi State University (D, M)
Purdue University (M)
Southern Methodist University (M)
The University of Alabama (M)
University of Idaho (M)
The University of Texas at Arlington (M)
Worcester Polytechnic Institute (M)

**Civil Engineering Technology**
Old Dominion University (B)

**Civil Infrastructure Engineering**
Virginia Polytechnic Institute and State
  University (M)

**CJA**
Taft College (A)

**CLAD Multiple or Single Subject
Certificate**
National University (UC)

**Classical Studies**
University of Waterloo (B)

**Clinical Health Sciences**
The George Washington University (M)

**Clinical Information Systems
Management**
Stephens College (M)

**Clinical Laboratory Sciences**
Weber State University (B)

**Clinical Laboratory Technician**
Weber State University (A)

**Clinical Management and Leadership**
The George Washington University (M)

**Clinical Nurse Specialist—Family
Nursing**
Graceland University (M)

**Clinical Pathology**
University of Massachusetts System (GC)

**Clinical Psychology**
Fielding Graduate Institute (D)

**Clinical Research Administration**
The George Washington University (M)

**Clinical Vision Research**
Nova Southeastern University (M)

**Coding and Reimbursement Specialist**
State University of New York College of
  Technology at Alfred (UC)

**Cognitive Retraining**
Coastline Community College (UC)

**College Transfer**
Caldwell Community College and Technical
  Institute (A)
Forsyth Technical Community College (A)

**Commerce (General)**
Memorial University of Newfoundland (B)

**Communication**
Southern New Hampshire University (B)

**Communication Arts**
Caldwell College (B)

**Communication Disorders, Speech-
Language Pathology**
University of Northern Colorado (M)

**Communication Studies**
University of Maryland University College
  (B)

**Communication Systems**
University of Idaho (UC)

**Communication/Organizational
Communications/Mass
Communication/Public Relations**
Montana State University-Billings (B)

**Communications**
State University of New York at Oswego (B)
Thomas Edison State College (B)
University of Florida (M)
University of Southern Indiana (A)

**Communications Management**
Syracuse University (M)

**Communications Technology**
Strayer University (M)

**Communicative Disorders**
Eastern New Mexico University (M)

**Community and Human Services**
State University of New York Empire State
  College (A, B)

**Community College Leadership**
Mississippi State University (D)

**Community Development**
Central Michigan University (B)

**Community Health**
University of Alaska Fairbanks (A, UC)

**Community Health Education**
The University of North Carolina at
  Greensboro (B)

**Community Mental Health**
New York Institute of Technology (B)

**Community Rehabilitation**
Vincennes University (UC)

**Community Services**
Thomas Edison State College (A)

**Completion in Mechanical Technology**
Indiana State University (B)

**Completion in Vocational Trade-
Industrial-Technical Area Major/
Career and Technology Education**
Indiana State University (B)

**Completion Program in Vocational
Trade-Industrial-Technical Area**
Indiana Higher Education
  Telecommunication System (B)

**Comprehensive Business Skills**
Marywood University (UC)

**Computer and Information Sciences**
Florida State University (B)
Knowledge Systems Institute (M, UC)
University of Maryland University College
  (B)

**Computer and Information Systems**
Capital Community College (A)

**Computer and Systems Engineering**
Rensselaer Polytechnic Institute (M)

**Computer Applications**
Mississippi State University (UC)

**Computer Drafting Design**
University of Houston (B)

**Computer Education and Cognitive Systems**
University of North Texas (M)

**Computer Education and Technology**
Dakota State University (M)

**Computer Engineering**
Illinois Institute of Technology (GC)
Iowa State University of Science and Technology (M)
National Technological University (M, UC)
University of Idaho (M)
University of South Carolina (D, M)
University of Wisconsin-Madison (M)
Virginia Polytechnic Institute and State University (M)

**Computer Graphics and Data Visualization**
Rensselaer Polytechnic Institute (UC)

**Computer Information and Office Systems**
University of Alaska Southeast, Sitka Campus (UC)

**Computer Information Office Systems**
University of Alaska Southeast, Sitka Campus (A)

**Computer Information Systems**
Atlantic Cape Community College (A)
Caldwell College (B)
Champlain College (B)
Davenport University Online (A)
Excelsior College (B)
Moberly Area Community College (A)
Saint Leo University (B)
Saint Mary-of-the-Woods College (B)
Southern New Hampshire University (UC)
Southwest Missouri State University (M)
Strayer University (A, B, UC)
The University Alliance (B)
University of Denver (M)
University of Phoenix (M)
Western Governors University (B)

**Computer Information Technology**
Mountain State University (A)

**Computer Network Professional**
East Carolina University (GC)

**Computer Networking**
Colorado Community College Online (A)
Colorado Electronic Community College (A)
Mountain State University (B)
New Jersey Institute of Technology (UC)

Strayer University (A, B)

**Computer Networking and Telecommunications**
Illinois Institute of Technology (GC)

**Computer Networking Technology**
Mountain State University (A)

**Computer Networks**
Rensselaer Polytechnic Institute (UC)

**Computer Occupations Technology**
Mott Community College (A)

**Computer Programming**
Pitt Community College (A)

**Computer Science**
Acadia University (UC)
American College of Computer & Information Sciences (M, B)
California National University for Advanced Studies (B)
California State University, Chico (M, B)
Colorado State University (M)
Columbia University (D, M)
Franklin University (B)
Grantham College of Engineering (A, B)
Illinois Institute of Technology (M)
Indiana Higher Education Telecommunication System (M)
Jamestown Community College (A)
Lakeland College (B)
Marycrest International University (M)
Maui Community College (B)
Mercy College (B)
National Technological University (M, UC)
New Jersey Institute of Technology (B)
Oklahoma State University (M)
Old Dominion University (B)
Rensselaer Polytechnic Institute (M, UC)
Rogers State University (A)
Southern Methodist University (M)
Stanford University (M)
Stevens Institute of Technology (M)
Thomas Edison State College (A)
Troy State University-Florida Region (B)
University of California, Santa Barbara (M)
University of Colorado at Boulder (M)
University of Houston (M)
University of Houston-Victoria (B)
University of Idaho (D, M)
University of Massachusetts Amherst (M)
The University of Texas System (M)

**Computer Science and Engineering**
Auburn University (M)
The University of Texas at Arlington (M)

The University of Texas System (M)

**Computer Science Internet Management**
Limestone College (A, B)

**Computer Science Management Information Systems**
Limestone College (A, B)

**Computer Science Programming**
Limestone College (A, B)

**Computer Science Technology**
Thomas Edison State College (A, B)

**Computer Skills for Managers**
College of Southern Maryland (UC)

**Computer Software**
Excelsior College (A, B)

**Computer Software Applications Certificate**
Pitt Community College (UC)

**Computer Systems Management**
University of Maryland University College (M)

**Computer Technology**
Excelsior College (B)
Northern Arizona University (B)

**Computer-Aided Design (CAD) Technologies**
Michigan State University (UC)

**Computers and Management Information Systems**
Athabasca University (UC)

**Computing**
Open Learning Agency (B)
United States Open University (M, B)

**Computing and Information Systems**
Athabasca University (UC)

**Computing and Information Systems (4 year)**
Athabasca University (B)

**Computing and Information Systems— Post Diploma**
Athabasca University (B)

**Concentration in Information Security**
James Madison University (M)

# Index of Institutions Offering Degree and Certificate Programs

**Concurrent Engineering**
Stevens Institute of Technology (GC)

**Conflict Analysis and Management**
Royal Roads University (M)

**Conflict Resolution**
Antioch University McGregor (M)

**Construction Management**
Illinois Institute of Technology (GC)
Northern Arizona University (B)

**Construction Science and Management**
Clemson University (M)

**Construction Technology**
Colorado Electronic Community College (A)

**Construction Technology—Construction Electrician emphasis**
Colorado Community College Online (A)

**Construction Technology—Emphasis in Construction Electrician**
Red Rocks Community College (A)

**Construction Technology—Emphasis in Power Technology**
Red Rocks Community College (A)

**Contemplative Education**
Naropa University (M)

**Contemporary Communications**
University of Massachusetts Lowell (UC)
University of Massachusetts System (UC)

**Continuing Curriculum Option (CCO) Pathway to PharmD Degree**
University of Illinois at Chicago (D)

**Continuing Education Certificate in Body Building**
United States Sports Academy (UC)

**Continuing Education Certificate in Coaching Figure Skating**
United States Sports Academy (UC)

**Continuing Education Certificate in Conditioning and Nutrition**
United States Sports Academy (UC)

**Continuing Education Certificate in Fitness and Exercise Physiology**
United States Sports Academy (UC)

**Continuing Education Certificate in Mental Skills in Sports**
United States Sports Academy (UC)

**Continuing Education Certificate in Personal Training**
United States Sports Academy (UC)

**Continuing Education Certificate in Sport Recreation Management**
United States Sports Academy (UC)

**Continuing Education Certificate in Sports Agency**
United States Sports Academy (UC)

**Continuing Education Certificate in Sports Coaching**
United States Sports Academy (UC)

**Continuing Education Certificate in Sports Medicine**
United States Sports Academy (UC)

**Control Systems**
Illinois Institute of Technology (GC)

**Control Systems Engineering**
Oklahoma State University (M)

**Convergent Technologies**
Colorado Electronic Community College (A)

**Convergent Technology**
Colorado Community College Online (A)

**Corporate Communication**
Austin Peay State University (M)

**Corrections**
Indiana Higher Education Telecommunication System (UC)
Indiana State University (UC)

**Corrections Pre-certification**
Tunxis Community College (UC)

**Counseling**
Liberty University (M)
Northern Arizona University (M)
Seton Hall University (M)

**Counseling and Psychology**
Prescott College (M)

**Counseling Psychology**
University of Sarasota (D)

**Counseling Women**
Athabasca University (UC)

**Counseling/Family Therapy**
Southern Christian University (M)

**Counseling/Human Relations**
Northern Arizona University (M)

**Counseling/School Counseling**
Northern Arizona University (M)

**Counselor Education**
Mississippi State University (M)
The University of Montana-Missoula (M)

**Counselor Education with a concentration in rehabilitation counseling**
Mississippi State University (M)

**Counselor Education-Chemical Dependency**
The Pennsylvania State University University Park Campus (UC)

**Court and Real-Time Reporting**
State University of New York College of Technology at Alfred (A)

**Creative Nonfiction**
Goucher College (M)

**Creative Writing**
Goddard College (M)

**Criminal Justice**
American Military University (M)
Bismarck State College (A)
Caldwell College (B)
Central Missouri State University (M)
Clovis Community College (A)
College for Professional Studies (B)
Colorado Electronic Community College (A)
Colorado Northwestern Community College (A)
Concordia University (B)
Florence-Darlington Technical College (A)
Florida Gulf Coast University (B)
Iowa Western Community College (A)
Judson College (B)
Loyola University New Orleans (M)
Lynn University (B)
Mansfield University of Pennsylvania (A)
Michigan State University (GC, M)
Missouri Southern State College (B)
Mountain State University (A, B)
National University (B)
New York Institute of Technology (B)
North Carolina Central University (B)
Northern Arizona University (B)
Northern Michigan University (M)
Northwestern State University of Louisiana (A)
Old Dominion University (B)

Roger Williams University (B)
Saint Joseph's College (A, B, UC)
Tiffin University (M)
Troy State University (M)
Tunxis Community College (A)
University of Baltimore (B)
University of Great Falls (B)
University of North Texas (M)
The University of Texas of the Permian Basin (B)
University of Wisconsin-Platteville (GC, M)
University of Wyoming (B)
Valdosta State University (B)
Washington State University (B)
Weber State University (A)

**Criminal Justice (Police Science)**
Adirondack Community College (A)

**Criminal Justice—Completion Degree**
The University of Texas System (B)

**Criminal Justice Administration**
Bellevue University (B)
The University of Findlay (B)

**Criminal Justice Diploma Program**
College for Professional Studies (UC)

**Criminal Justice Specialized Associate Degree Program**
College for Professional Studies (A)

**Criminal Justice Technology**
Fayetteville Technical Community College (A)

**Criminal Justices**
Mount Wachusett Community College (A)

**Criminology**
Danville Area Community College (A)
Indiana Higher Education Telecommunication System (M)
Indiana State University (M, B)
Memorial University of Newfoundland (UC)
The University Alliance (B)

**Criminology/Criminal Justice**
Florida State University (M)

**Cross Cultural Education with Credential Options**
National University (M)

**Cross Disciplinary Professional Studies**
Rochester Institute of Technology (M)

**CSU Consortial Jewish Studies Major**
San Diego State University (B)

**Cultural Studies**
State University of New York Empire State College (A, B)

**Curriculum and Instruction**
The College of St. Scholastica (M)
College of the Southwest (M)
Concordia University Wisconsin (M)
Florida Gulf Coast University (M)
The University of North Carolina at Greensboro (M)
The University of Texas System (M)

**Curriculum and Instruction-Health Promotion Emphasis**
Virginia Polytechnic Institute and State University (M)

**Curriculum and Instruction-Instructional Technology Emphasis**
Virginia Polytechnic Institute and State University (M)

**Curriculum and Instruction-Physical Education Emphasis**
Virginia Polytechnic Institute and State University (M)

**Curriculum and Instructional Technology**
Valdosta State University (D)

**Curriculum Studies**
The University of Montana-Missoula (M)

**Customer Relationship Management**
The Pennsylvania State University University Park Campus (UC)

**Data Entry Applications Certificate**
Pitt Community College (UC)

**Data/Telecommunications**
University of Massachusetts Lowell (UC)
University of Massachusetts System (UC)

**Database Applications**
Loyola University Chicago (UC)

**Database Management**
University of Hawaii at Manoa (UC)

**Database Systems Design**
Rensselaer Polytechnic Institute (UC)

**Degree Completion**
Duquesne University (B)

**Degree Completion in Mechanical Technology**
Indiana Higher Education Telecommunication System (B)

**Degree Completion Program in Nursing**
Indiana Higher Education Telecommunication System (B)

**Dental Hygiene**
Pennsylvania College of Technology (B)
Virginia Western Community College (A)

**Dental Hygiene Completion Program**
Northern Arizona University (B)

**Design**
Ivy Tech State College-Wabash Valley (A)
Open Learning Agency (B)

**Design Technology (Architecture Specialty)**
Indiana Higher Education Telecommunication System (A)

**Designing Interactive Multimedia Instruction**
Teachers College, Columbia University (UC)

**Dietary Management**
Auburn University (UC)
Barton County Community College (UC)

**Dietary Manager**
The Pennsylvania State University University Park Campus (UC)

**Dietetic Food Systems Management**
The Pennsylvania State University University Park Campus (A)

**Dietetics**
Eastern Michigan University (B)
Kansas State University (B)
University of Northern Colorado (UC)

**Dietetics and Aging**
The Pennsylvania State University University Park Campus (UC)

**Digital Arts: Computer Graphics**
Rochester Community and Technical College (UC)

**Digital Communication**
Franklin University (B)

**Digital Communication Technology**
East Carolina University (M)

# Index of Institutions Offering Degree and Certificate Programs

**Digital Design**
The Art Institutes International (UC)

**Digital Imaging and Publishing**
Rochester Institute of Technology (UC)

**Digital Media Communication**
Saint Mary-of-the-Woods College (B)

**Digital Signal Processing**
Indiana Higher Education
   Telecommunication System (UC)

**Digital Technologies Management**
Royal Roads University (M)

**Diploma**
Indiana University System (UC)

**Direct Marketing**
Mercy College (M)

**Disaster and Emergency Management**
Rochester Institute of Technology (UC)

**Distance Education**
Indiana Higher Education
   Telecommunication System (UC)
Indiana University System (UC)
University of Wisconsin-Madison (UC)

**Distance Education Technology**
Athabasca University (GC)

**Distance Learning**
University of Maryland, Baltimore County
   (GC)

**Distributed Learning**
Royal Roads University (M)

**Divinity**
Liberty University (M)
Oral Roberts University (M)

**Driver Education**
Indiana State University (UC)

**E-Business**
Bellevue University (B)
Rensselaer Polytechnic Institute (UC)
University of Phoenix (M, B)

**E-Business and Commerce**
Champlain College (A, UC)

**E-Business Management**
Lehigh Carbon Community College (A)

**E-Business Technology**
Owens Community College (A)

**E-Commerce**
Dallas Baptist University (UC)
Golden Gate University (M)
New Jersey Institute of Technology (UC)

**E-Commerce (Bachelor of Applied Science—BAS)**
Davenport University Online (B)

**E-Commerce Management**
University of Dallas (GC, M)

**E-Commerce Professional**
National American University (UC)

**E-Commerce(MBAeC)**
Golden Gate University (M)

**Early Child Development**
Bethany College of the Assemblies of God
   (A, B)

**Early Childhood**
Concordia University (M)

**Early Childhood Development**
University of Alaska Fairbanks (A, UC)

**Early Childhood Education**
Brenau University (M)
California College for Health Sciences (A)
Ivy Tech State College-Central Indiana (A)
Ivy Tech State College-Columbus (A)
Ivy Tech State College-Eastcentral (A)
Ivy Tech State College-Kokomo (A)
Ivy Tech State College-Lafayette (A)
Ivy Tech State College-North Central (A)
Ivy Tech State College-Northeast (A)
Ivy Tech State College-Northwest (A)
Ivy Tech State College-Southcentral (A)
Ivy Tech State College-Southeast (A)
Ivy Tech State College-Southwest (A)
Ivy Tech State College-Wabash Valley (A)
Ivy Tech State College-Whitewater (A)
Kean University (M)
Northern Arizona University (M, UC)
Oral Roberts University (M)
Pacific Oaks College (M)
Saint Mary-of-the-Woods College (A, B)
University of Alaska Southeast, Sitka
   Campus (A)
Valdosta State University (M)

**Early Childhood Education Assistant**
San Joaquin Delta College (UC)

**Early Childhood Professions Program**
Pueblo Community College (UC)

**Earth and Environmental Engineering**
Columbia University (M)

**Earth Literacy**
Saint Mary-of-the-Woods College (M)

**Economics**
Foothill College (A)
Strayer University (A, B)
Thomas Edison State College (B)
University of Waterloo (B)

**Ecopsychology**
Naropa University (GC)

**Ecotourism Management**
University of Denver (GC)

**Education**
Alaska Pacific University (A, B)
Buena Vista University (B)
Casper College (A)
Eastern New Mexico University (M, B)
Florida Gulf Coast University (B)
Graceland University (M)
Hamline University (M)
Indiana Wesleyan University (M)
Liberty University (D, M)
Michigan State University (M)
Montana State University-Bozeman (M)
Mountain Empire Community College (A)
Mount Saint Vincent University (M)
Norwich University (M)
Olivet Nazarene University (M)
Prescott College (M)
Saint Joseph's College (M)
Southwestern Assemblies of God University
   (B)
Stephens College (B, UC)
University of Alaska Southeast, Ketchikan
   Campus (M, B)
The University of British Columbia (M)
University of Central Florida (B)
University of Houston-Victoria (M)
University of Manitoba (GC)
University of Sarasota (M)
The University of Tennessee at Martin (M)
Valdosta State University (M, B)
Walden University (D, M)

**Education (Human Resource Development)**
Colorado State University (M)

**Education—Adult and Post-Secondary Education**
University of Wyoming (M)

**Education—Instructional Technology**
University of Wyoming (M)

**Education—Middle Grades**
Valdosta State University (B)

**Education—Pre K Through 6**
Old Dominion University (M)

**Education—Special Education**
University of Wyoming (M)

**Education—Teaching and Learning**
University of Wyoming (M)

**Education -Teacher Preparation**
Old Dominion University (B)

**Education Administration**
Cleveland College of Jewish Studies (M)
Concordia University Wisconsin (M)

**Education contemporaine**
Universite du Quebec a Rimouski (UC)

**Education Counseling**
Concordia University Wisconsin (M)

**Education Law**
Franklin Pierce Law Center (GC, M)

**Education Leadership**
San Diego State University (M)
University of North Dakota (M)
University of Vermont (M)

**Education Technology**
San Diego State University (UC)

**Education/Curriculum and Instruction**
University of Phoenix (M)

**Education/Curriculum and Technology**
University of Phoenix (M)

**Education/E-Education**
University of Phoenix (M)

**Educational Administration**
Buena Vista University (M)
Maui Community College (M)
National University (M)
St. Cloud State University (M)
Texas A&M University-Texarkana (M)
University of Massachusetts System (M)
University of South Alabama (UC)

**Educational Administration and Counseling**
College of the Southwest (M)

**Educational Administration and Supervision**
Ball State University (M)
Indiana Higher Education
    Telecommunication System (M)
Seton Hall University (M)

**Educational Administration Focus**
MU Direct: Continuing and Distance
    Education (M)

**Educational Foundations**
Maui Community College (M)

**Educational Human Resource Development**
Texas A&M University (M)

**Educational Leadership**
Northern Arizona University (D, M)
State University of West Georgia (M)
The University of Montana-Missoula (D, M)
University of South Alabama (M)

**Educational Leadership and Change**
Fielding Graduate Institute (D)

**Educational Media**
University of Central Florida (M)

**Educational Media (Library Media)**
University of South Alabama (M)

**Educational Media and Technology**
The College of St. Scholastica (M)

**Educational Organization and Administration**
Dallas Baptist University (M)

**Educational Studies**
State University of New York Empire State
    College (A, B)

**Educational Technology**
Boise State University (M)
National University (M)
Northern Arizona University (M, UC)
Northwestern State University of Louisiana
    (M)
Pepperdine University (D, M)
Texas A&M University (M)
The University of Texas System (M)

**Educational Technology Focus**
MU Direct: Continuing and Distance
    Education (M)

**Educational Technology Integration**
The Pennsylvania State University University
    Park Campus (UC)

**Educational Technology Leadership**
The George Washington University (M)

**EEG Technology**
California College for Health Sciences (A)

**Electric Power Engineering**
Rensselaer Polytechnic Institute (M, UC)

**Electrical and Computer Engineering**
Colorado State University (M)
Illinois Institute of Technology (M)
Indiana Higher Education
    Telecommunication System (M)
Mississippi State University (D, M)
Northeastern University (M)
Purdue University (M)
University of California, Santa Barbara (M)
University of Colorado at Boulder (M)
University of Massachusetts Amherst (M)
Virginia Polytechnic Institute and State
    University (M)

**Electrical and Mechanical Engineering Technology**
Rochester Institute of Technology (B)

**Electrical Engineering**
Arizona State University (M)
Bradley University (M)
California State University, Northridge (M)
Clemson University (M)
Colorado State University (D, M)
Columbia University (D, M)
Georgia Institute of Technology (M)
Illinois Institute of Technology (M)
Iowa State University of Science and
    Technology (M)
Kansas State University (M)
Michigan Technological University (D, M)
National Technological University (M, UC)
Oklahoma State University (M)
Rensselaer Polytechnic Institute (M)
Southern Methodist University (M)
Stanford University (M)
The University of Alabama (M)
University of Houston (M)
University of Idaho (D, M)
University of North Dakota (B)
University of South Carolina (D, M)
The University of Texas at Arlington (M)
The University of Texas System (M)
University of Wisconsin-Madison (M)

# Index of Institutions Offering Degree and Certificate Programs

**Electrical Engineering Technology**
Old Dominion University (B)

**Electrical Technology**
Thomas Edison State College (A)

**Electricity Markets**
Illinois Institute of Technology (GC, M)

**Electronic Commerce**
National University (M, UC)

**Electronic Commerce Management**
Capitol College (M)

**Electronics and Computer Control Systems**
Wayne State University (M)

**Electronics Engineering Technology**
Cleveland Institute of Electronics (B)
Grantham College of Engineering (A, B)
Thomas Edison State College (B)

**Electronics Technology**
Excelsior College (A, B)
Indiana State University (B)

**Elementary Education**
Ball State University (M)
Fort Hays State University (B)
Graceland University (B)
Indiana Higher Education
    Telecommunication System (M)
Maui Community College (B)
Mississippi State University (B)
Northern Arizona University (M, B)
Northern Michigan University (B)
Saint Mary-of-the-Woods College (B)
Southwest Missouri State University (M, B)
Stephen F. Austin State University (UC)
University of North Dakota (M)
University of Pittsburgh (M)

**Elementary Education with Certification**
Oral Roberts University (B)

**Elementary Education/Special Education**
Maui Community College (B)

**Elementary Teacher Preparation**
Mountain State University (A)

**Elements of Computer Science**
Stevens Institute of Technology (GC)

**EMBA (Chicago-based)**
University of Notre Dame (M)

**EMBA (South Bend-based)**
University of Notre Dame (M)

**Emergency Administration and Management**
Central Carolina Technical College (UC)

**Emergency Disaster Management**
Thomas Edison State College (A)

**Emergency Health Services**
The George Washington University (M)
University of Maryland, Baltimore County
    (M)

**Emergency Management**
Colorado Electronic Community College (A)
Jacksonville State University (M)

**Emergency Management and Planning**
Colorado Community College Online (A)
Red Rocks Community College (A)

**Emergency Medical Service Professions [Paramedic Option]**
Tyler Junior College (A)

**Emergency Medical Services**
American College of Prehospital Medicine
    (A, B)

**Emergency Preparedness Technology**
Caldwell Community College and Technical
    Institute (A)

**Emerging Technologies for Educators**
Pitt Community College (UC)

**Emotional Disturbance**
Indiana State University (UC)

**Energy Management**
New York Institute of Technology (M)

**Engineering**
Arizona State University (M)
California National University for Advanced
    Studies (M, B)
Eastern Michigan University (M)
Kettering University (M)
Michigan Technological University (B)
North Carolina Agricultural and Technical
    State University (M)
Northern Arizona University (M)
Northern Virginia Community College (A)
Purdue University (M)
Texas Tech University (M)
The University of Alabama (M)
The University of Arizona (M)
University of Illinois at Chicago (M)

University of Wisconsin-Madison (M)
University of Wisconsin-Platteville (M)

**Engineering Administration**
Virginia Polytechnic Institute and State
    University (M)

**Engineering and Management Systems**
Columbia University (M)

**Engineering Design**
Michigan Technological University (UC)

**Engineering Management**
California State University, Northridge (B)
Colorado State University (M)
Kansas State University (M)
National Technological University (M, UC)
Old Dominion University (M)
Southern Methodist University (M)
Syracuse University (M)
The University of Alabama (M)
University of Colorado at Boulder (M, UC)
University of Colorado at Denver (M)
University of Houston (M)
University of Idaho (M)
University of Massachusetts Amherst (M)
University of Missouri-Rolla (M)

**Engineering Science**
Broome Community College (A)
Rensselaer Polytechnic Institute (M)

**Engineering Systems Management**
Texas A&M University (M)

**Engineering Technology**
Michigan Technological University (A)
University of Central Florida (B)
The University of North Carolina at
    Charlotte (B)

**Engineering Technology AST**
Harcourt Learning Direct Center for Degree
    Studies (A)

**Engineering Technology Management**
Oklahoma State University (M)

**Engineering/Industrial Management**
New Jersey Institute of Technology (M)

**English**
Caldwell College (B)
Eastern New Mexico University (M)
Judson College (B)
Maui Community College (B)
Mount Allison University (B)
Northern Arizona University (M, B)
Saint Mary-of-the-Woods College (B)

Stephens College (B)
Thomas Edison State College (B)
Troy State University Montgomery (B)
United States Open University (B)
University of Houston (B)
University of Waterloo (B)

**English as a Second Language**
Hamline University (M)
Northern Arizona University (M, UC)

**English as a Second Language (ESL)**
The University of Texas System (UC)

**English for Speakers of Other Languages**
Florida Gulf Coast University (UC)

**English Language Studies**
Athabasca University (UC)

**Enterprise in Society**
Northern Arizona University (B)

**Entrepreneurial Management**
Royal Roads University (B)

**Entrepreneurial Studies**
Stephens College (M)

**Entrepreneurship**
Bucks County Community College (UC)
Davenport University Online (A, B)

**Environment and Management**
Royal Roads University (M)

**Environmental Management**
University of Maryland University College (M)

**Environmental Assessment**
Lakehead University (UC)

**Environmental Engineering**
Colorado State University (M)
Georgia Institute of Technology (M)
Illinois Institute of Technology (M)
Southern Methodist University (M)
The University of Alabama (M)
Worcester Polytechnic Institute (GC, M)

**Environmental Health and Safety Management**
Rochester Institute of Technology (M)
University of Denver (GC)

**Environmental Management**
Rochester Institute of Technology (B)
University of Denver (GC)

The University of Findlay (M, B)

**Environmental Management Science**
Rochester Institute of Technology (UC)

**Environmental Policy and Management**
University of Denver (M)

**Environmental Regulatory Compliance**
University of Denver (GC)

**Environmental Resource Management**
California State University, Bakersfield (B, UC)

**Environmental Science**
Royal Roads University (B)
University of Idaho (M)

**Environmental Science/Management**
Oklahoma State University (M)

**Environmental Sciences**
Northern Arizona University (B)
Oregon State University (B)
Thomas Edison State College (B)

**Environmental Studies**
Mountain State University (A)
Prescott College (M)

**Environmental Systems Management**
National Technological University (M)
Southern Methodist University (M)

**Environmental Technology**
University of Alaska Southeast, Sitka Campus (A, UC)

**Environmental Technology Management**
Arizona State University East (M)

**Equine Business Management**
Saint Mary-of-the-Woods College (B)

**Estate Planning and Taxation**
The American College (GC)

**European Studies**
United States Open University (B)

**Event Management**
The George Washington University (UC)

**Executive Business Administration**
University of North Alabama (M)

**Executive Development and Public Service**
Indiana Higher Education Telecommunication System (M)

**Executive Development for Public Service**
Ball State University (M)

**Executive Management**
Royal Roads University (M)

**Executive Program in Health Informatics**
MU Direct: Continuing and Distance Education (M)

**Executive Program in Health Services Management**
MU Direct: Continuing and Distance Education (M)

**Facilities Management**
Southern Methodist University (M)

**Facility Management**
Michigan State University (GC)

**Family and Consumer Sciences (Early Childhood Program Director's Certificate)**
University of Wyoming (UC)

**Family and Consumer Sciences (Professional Child Development Option)**
University of Wyoming (B)

**Family and Financial Planning**
Montana State University-Bozeman (M)

**Family Financial Planning**
Kansas State University (M)

**Family Life Studies and Human Sexuality**
Laurentian University (UC)

**Family Nurse Practitioner**
Clarion University of Pennsylvania (M)
Clarkson College (GC)
Graceland University (M)
Western University of Health Sciences (UC)

**Family Nurse Practitioner Graduate Program**
Slippery Rock University of Pennsylvania (M)

# Index of Institutions Offering Degree and Certificate Programs

**Family Therapy**
Southern Christian University (D, M)

**Fashion Merchandising Management**
Fashion Institute of Technology (A)

**Finance**
Excelsior College (B)
Golden Gate University (GC, M)
Thomas Edison State College (A)

**Finance(Undergraduate)**
Golden Gate University (UC)

**Financial Engineering**
Columbia University (UC)

**Financial Planning**
Golden Gate University (GC, M)

**Financial Planning(Undergraduate)**
Golden Gate University (UC)

**Financial Planning/Graduate School**
The American College (UC)

**Financial Services**
The American College (M)
Nipissing University (B)

**Fine and Applied Arts**
Coastline Community College (A)

**Fine Arts**
Burlington College (B)
Open Learning Agency (B)

**Finite Element Method/Computational Fluid Dynamics**
Columbia University (UC)

**Fire and Emergency Management Administration**
Oklahoma State University (M)

**Fire Protection Engineering**
Worcester Polytechnic Institute (GC, M)

**Fire Science**
University of Maryland University College (B)
The University of North Carolina at Charlotte (B)

**Fire Science Administration**
University of Cincinnati (B)

**Fire Science Management and Training**
Colorado State University (B)

**Fire Science Technology**
Pikes Peak Community College (A)

**Fire Services Administration**
Eastern Oregon University (B)
Western Oregon University (B)

**Folklore et Ethnologie de l'amerique Francaise**
Laurentian University (B, UC)

**Food and Agricultural Business**
Indiana Higher Education Telecommunication System (M)

**Food and Resource Economics**
University of Florida (M)

**Food Science**
Kansas State University (UC)
University of Guelph (UC)

**Food Science and Industry**
Kansas State University (B)

**Food Service Training Program**
Southeast Community College, Beatrice Campus (UC)

**For registered nurses**
Laurentian University (B)

**Foreign Language**
Caldwell College (B)

**Forensic Chemistry**
University of Central Florida (M)

**Forensic Sciences**
National University (M)

**Forensic Toxicology**
University of Florida (GC)

**French**
Mount Saint Vincent University (UC)
University of Waterloo (B)

**French Language Proficiency**
Athabasca University (UC)

**Fundamentals of Information Technology**
University of Massachusetts Lowell (UC)
University of Massachusetts System (UC)

**General**
Central Carolina Community College (A)
Howard Community College (A)
Indian River Community College (A)
Pensacola Junior College (A)

St. Louis Community College System (A)
St. Petersburg College (A)
Spokane Falls Community College (A)
Spoon River College (A)
University of South Alabama (M)
Western Wyoming Community College (A)

**General Administration**
Central Michigan University (M)

**General Agriculture**
Oregon State University (B)
Washington State University (B)

**General and Military Studies**
Barton County Community College (A)

**General Arts**
Ball State University (A)
Indiana Higher Education Telecommunication System (A)

**General Aviation Flight Technology**
Indiana Higher Education Telecommunication System (A)
Indiana State University (A)

**General Business**
Excelsior College (B)
Kansas State University (B)
Mott Community College (A)
Mountain State University (UC)
The Pennsylvania State University University Park Campus (UC)
Saint Mary-of-the-Woods College (A)

**General Certificate**
Arizona Western College (UC)

**General Christian Studies**
Hobe Sound Bible College (B)

**General Education**
Colorado Community College Online (A)
Fayetteville Technical Community College (A)
Pueblo Community College (A)
Troy State University (A)
Troy State University-Florida Region (A)
Troy State University Montgomery (A)
Western Governors University (A)

**General Education Studies**
National American University (A)

**General Education Transfer Degree**
Northwestern Michigan College (A)

**General Industrial Technology**
Indiana State University (B)

**General Liberal Arts**
Iowa Lakes Community College (A)

**General Management**
Thomas Edison State College (A, B)

**General Ministries**
Bethany College of the Assemblies of God (B)

**General Preventive Medicine**
Medical College of Wisconsin (M)

**General Program**
Open Learning Agency (B)

**General Science, Non-Major**
University of Waterloo (B)

**General Studies**
Anne Arundel Community College (A)
Athens Technical College (A)
Atlantic Cape Community College (A)
Barton County Community College (A)
Bellevue Community College (A)
Bethany College of the Assemblies of God (A)
Brevard Community College (A)
Burlington College (A)
Capital Community College (A)
Central Texas College (A)
Central Wyoming College (A)
Charter Oak State College (A, B)
College of Southern Maryland (A)
Copiah-Lincoln Community College (A)
Dallas County Community College District (A)
Fort Hays State University (B)
Green River Community College (A)
Harford Community College (A)
Howard Community College (A)
Indiana Higher Education Telecommunication System (UC)
Indiana University System (A, B)
Iowa Western Community College (A)
Johnson County Community College (A)
John Wood Community College (A)
Lakehead University (B)
Liberty University (A)
Missouri Southern State College (A, B)
Montgomery County Community College (A)
Mountain Empire Community College (A)
Mountain State University (A)
Mount Wachusett Community College (A)
Northampton County Area Community College (A)
Northern Virginia Community College (A)
North Seattle Community College (A)

Northwestern State University of Louisiana (A)
Open Learning Agency (A, B)
Parkland College (A)
Pima Community College (A)
Portland Community College (M, A)
Pratt Community College and Area Vocational School (A)
Quinebaug Valley Community College (A)
Rappahannock Community College (A)
Rio Salado College (A)
Saint Joseph's College (B)
Strayer University (A)
Tarrant County College District (A)
Texas Tech University (B)
Tyler Junior College (A)
University of Alaska Fairbanks (A)
University of Alaska Southeast, Sitka Campus (A)
University of South Dakota (A)
Valdosta State University (A, B)
Vincennes University (A, UC)
Virginia Western Community College (A)
Weber State University (A)
Yuba College (A)

**General Studies (for transferring)**
Mott Community College (A)

**General Studies (Secondary Education)**
University of North Dakota (M)

**General Studies (University Parallel)**
Columbia State Community College (A)

**General Studies Degree**
Frederick Community College (A)

**General Studies Surgical Technology Degree Completion**
Vincennes University (A)

**General Studies, Non-Major**
University of Waterloo (B)

**General Studies/Liberal Arts**
Tunxis Community College (A)

**General Studies/Social Science**
Foothill College (A)

**General Studies; Business Administration**
Georgia Perimeter College (A)

**Genomic Engineering**
Columbia University (UC)

**Geographic Information Systems**
The Pennsylvania State University University Park Campus (UC)
University of Denver (GC)

**Geographic Information Systems (GIS)**
University of Colorado at Denver (M)

**Geography**
University of Waterloo (B)
Wilfrid Laurier University (B)

**Geological Engineering**
University of Idaho (M)

**Geoscience**
Mississippi State University (M)

**Geoscience, Broadcast Meteorology**
Mississippi State University (B)

**Geotechnical Engineering**
Illinois Institute of Technology (M)

**Gerontology**
Arizona State University (GC)
Arizona State University West (GC)
Colorado State University (UC)
Florida Gulf Coast University (UC)
Laurentian University (B, UC)
Mount Saint Vincent University (UC)
Saint Mary-of-the-Woods College (A, B, UC)
Thomas Edison State College (A)
University of Northern Colorado (GC)

**Gifted and Talented Education**
University of North Texas (UC)

**Gifted Education**
Northern Arizona University (UC)

**Gifted Education Focus**
MU Direct: Continuing and Distance Education (M)

**Global Business Management**
Bellevue University (B)

**Global Leadership Executive MBA**
MIMS Global Leadership Executive Program (M)

**Global Management**
Michigan State University (GC)
University of Phoenix (M)

**Global Networks and Telecommunications**
Champlain College (A, UC)

**Health Sciences**
Mercy College (M)
Touro University International (D, M)
University of Medicine and Dentistry of
New Jersey (B)

**Health Services**
University of St. Francis (M)
Walden University (D)

**Health Services Administration**
Florida Gulf Coast University (M, B, UC)
Medical College of Wisconsin (M)
Saint Joseph's College (M)
State University of New York Institute of
Technology at Utica/Rome (M)
University of Delaware (M)
University of Florida (M)

**Health Services Management**
University of Dallas (GC, M)

**Health Services/Community Health**
California College for Health Sciences (M)

**Health Services/Respiratory Care**
California College for Health Sciences (B)

**Health Services/Wellness Promotion**
California College for Health Sciences (M)

**Health Systems Administration**
Rochester Institute of Technology (M, UC)

**Health Technology Management—
Medical Assistant**
Arizona Institute of Business & Technology
(A)

**Health Technology Management—
Patient Care Technician**
Arizona Institute of Business & Technology
(A)

**Health-Related Sciences**
Virginia Commonwealth University (D)

**Healthcare Administration**
Seton Hall University (M)

**Healthcare Leadership and
Management**
Pitt Community College (UC)

**Hearing Disorders**
North Carolina Central University (M)

**Heating, Ventilation, and Air
Conditioning (HVAC) Systems**
University of Idaho (UC)

**Hebrew language and literature**
Cleveland College of Jewish Studies (M)

**Higher Education**
University of North Dakota (D)

**Higher Education Administration**
University of Sarasota (D)

**Himalayan Studies**
University of Connecticut (UC)

**Historic Preservation**
Goucher College (M)

**Historical Studies**
State University of New York Empire State
College (A, B)

**History**
Arizona State University (B)
Atlantic Cape Community College (A)
Caldwell College (B)
Foothill College (A)
Judson College (B)
Mount Allison University (B)
Thomas Edison State College (B)
Troy State University Montgomery (A, B)
University of Houston (B)
University of Waterloo (B)

**History (in development)**
Laurentian University (B)

**History and Political Studies**
Saint Mary-of-the-Woods College (B)

**Histotechnology**
Indiana Higher Education
Telecommunication System (A)
Indiana University System (A)

**Home Health Nursing**
Athabasca University (UC)

**Home Office Computing**
Pitt Community College (UC)

**Home-based Early Childhood
Education**
Northampton County Area Community
College (UC)

**Hospital Health Care Administration**
Thomas Edison State College (B)

**Hospitality Management**
New York Institute of Technology (B)
University of Houston (M)
University of North Texas (M)

**Hospitality Management ASB**
Harcourt Learning Direct Center for Degree
Studies (A)

**Hotel Administration**
University of Nevada, Las Vegas (M)

**Hotel and Restaurant Management**
Auburn University (M)
Northern Arizona University (B)
Tompkins Cortland Community College (A)
University of Houston (B)

**Hotel, Restaurant, and Institutional
Management**
The Pennsylvania State University University
Park Campus (A)
University of Delaware (B)

**Hotel/Motel/Restaurant Management**
Thomas Edison State College (A, B)

**HRTA**
University of Massachusetts Amherst (B)
University of Massachusetts System (B)

**Human and Organizational
Development**
Fielding Graduate Institute (D)

**Human Development**
Pacific Oaks College (M, B)
Salve Regina University (M)
Southern Christian University (B)
State University of New York Empire State
College (A, B)
Washington State University (B)

**Human Development and Family
Studies**
The Pennsylvania State University University
Park Campus (A)

**Human Nutrition**
University of Bridgeport (M)

**Human Resource Development**
Clemson University (M)
Indiana State University (M, B)
Limestone College (B)
University of Arkansas (B)

**Human Resource Management**
California National University for Advanced
Studies (A)
Davenport University Online (B, UC)
Saint Mary-of-the-Woods College (B)
Thomas Edison State College (A)
Troy State University (M)

# Index of Institutions Offering Degree and Certificate Programs

**Human Resource Management Practice**
California National University for Advanced Studies (UC)

**Human Resources**
Indiana Institute of Technology (B)
Ottawa University (M)
The Pennsylvania State University University Park Campus (UC)

**Human Resources Management**
Florida Institute of Technology (M)
Royal Roads University (M)
Southern New Hampshire University (UC)
Thomas Edison State College (B)
Upper Iowa University (B)

**Human Science**
Saybrook Graduate School and Research Center (D, M)

**Human Science—Post Diploma**
Athabasca University (B)

**Human Science Major**
Athabasca University (B)

**Human Services**
Alaska Pacific University (A, B)
Burlington College (B)
Concordia University (B)
Mount Wachusett Community College (A)
Saint Mary-of-the-Woods College (B)
Upper Iowa University (B)
Walden University (D)
Western Washington University (B)

**Human Services—Family Studies**
Concordia University (M)

**Human Services—Leadership**
Concordia University (M)

**Human Services Counseling**
Old Dominion University (B)

**Human Services Technology**
University of Alaska Fairbanks (A)

**Human-Computer Interaction**
Rensselaer Polytechnic Institute (UC)

**Humanitarian Studies—MA pending approval**
University of Connecticut (GC)

**Humanities**
Atlantic Cape Community College (A)

California State University, Dominguez Hills (M)
Coastline Community College (A)
Prescott College (M)
Saint Mary-of-the-Woods College (A, B)
Thomas Edison State College (B)
United States Open University (B)
University of Maryland University College (B)
University of Pittsburgh (B)
University of Waterloo (B)

**Illustration**
Syracuse University (M)

**Imaging Science**
Rochester Institute of Technology (M)

**iMBA**
The Pennsylvania State University University Park Campus (M)

**Inclusive Education**
Athabasca University (UC)

**Individualized Liberal and Professional Studies**
Antioch University McGregor (M)

**Individualized Major/Interdisciplinary Studies**
Burlington College (B)

**Individualized Ph.D., Advanced Standing Doctoral Students**
Saybrook Graduate School and Research Center (D)

**Individualized Ph.D., Post Masters**
Saybrook Graduate School and Research Center (D)

**Individualized Studies**
Goddard College (B)
Governors State University (B)
Ohio University (A)
Skidmore College (B)

**Individualized Study in the Liberal Arts**
Goddard College (M)

**Individualized Transfer Studies**
Northampton County Area Community College (A)

**Individually Designed Focus Area**
DePaul University (B)

**Indoor Air Quality**
Illinois Institute of Technology (GC)

**Industrial and Management Engineering**
Rensselaer Polytechnic Institute (M)

**Industrial and Systems Engineering**
Auburn University (M)
Georgia Institute of Technology (M)

**Industrial Engineering**
Colorado State University (D, M)
Columbia University (UC)
Indiana Higher Education Telecommunication System (M)
Mississippi State University (D, M)
Purdue University (M)
The University of Tennessee (M)
The University of Texas at Arlington (M)

**Industrial Environmental Management**
Rochester Institute of Technology (UC)

**Industrial Management**
Central Missouri State University (M)
Davenport University Online (B)

**Industrial Relations and Human Resources**
Athabasca University (UC)

**Industrial Supervision**
Indiana State University (B)

**Industrial Systems Technology**
Indiana University System (M)

**Industrial Technology**
Central Community College (A)
East Carolina University (M, B)
Roger Williams University (B)

**Industrial/Organizational Psychology**
Kansas State University (M)

**Information and Computer Science**
University of Hawaii at Manoa (M, B)

**Information and Computer Sciences**
Maui Community College (M, B)

**Information and Telecommunication Systems Management**
Capitol College (M)

**Information Architecture**
Capitol College (M)

**Information Management**
ISIM University (M)

**Information Processing and Communications**
Montana State University-Billings (M)

**Information Processing Specialist**
Bismarck State College (UC)

**Information Resource Management**
Syracuse University (M)

**Information Science**
North Carolina Central University (M)

**Information Sciences**
University of North Texas (M)
The University of Tennessee (M)

**Information Services Technology**
College of Southern Maryland (A, UC)

**Information Studies**
Florida State University (B)

**Information Systems**
American College of Computer & Information Sciences (B)
Athabasca University (M)
Columbia University (UC)
Dakota State University (M)
Golden Gate University (GC, M)
Keller Graduate School of Management (A)
National Technological University (M)
New Jersey Institute of Technology (B)
Northeastern University (M)
Robert Morris College (B)
Strayer University (M)
University of Great Falls (M)
University of Maryland, Baltimore County (M)
University of Sarasota (M)

**Information Systems Generalist**
Pitt Community College (A)

**Information Systems Management**
United States Open University (M)

**Information Systems Networking Technologies [Novell]**
Tyler Junior College (A)

**Information Systems Technology**
Northern Virginia Community College (A)
University of Northwestern Ohio (A)

**Information Systems Technology Certificate**
Pitt Community College (UC)

**Information Systems, Design, and Development**
New Jersey Institute of Technology (UC)

**Information Technologies**
East Carolina University (B)

**Information Technology**
Columbia State Community College (A)
DeVry Online (B)
Graceland University (B)
Indiana Higher Education Telecommunication System (UC)
Indiana University System (UC)
National American University (A, B)
New Jersey Institute of Technology (M)
Peirce College (A, B)
Rensselaer Polytechnic Institute (M, UC)
Rochester Institute of Technology (M)
Rogers State University (B)
United States Open University (B)
University of Charleston (A)
University of Connecticut (UC)
University of Dallas (GC, M)
University of Massachusetts Lowell (A, B)
University of Massachusetts System (A, B)
University of Phoenix (B)
Western Governors University (A)

**Information Technology Management**
Athabasca University (M)
Mount Saint Vincent University (UC)

**Information Technology Online**
Bryant and Stratton Online (A)

**Information Technology with Business Minor**
University of Massachusetts Lowell (B)

**Information Technology, CNE Emphasis**
Western Governors University (A)

**Information Technology, Network Administration**
Western Governors University (A, UC)

**Inquiry and Applied Research for Educational Change**
St. Norbert College (M)

**Instructional and Performance Technology**
Boise State University (M)

**Instructional Design**
Western Governors University (GC)

**Instructional Design and Development**
University of South Alabama (M)

**Instructional Services Technology— Library Technical Assistant**
Indian River Community College (A)

**Instructional Systems Technology**
Indiana University System (M)

**Instructional Systems/Open and Distance Learning**
Florida State University (M)

**Instructional Technology**
East Carolina University (M)
National University (M)
North Carolina Agricultural and Technical State University (M)
University of Nevada, Las Vegas (GC)

**Insurance**
Indiana State University (B)
Thomas Edison State College (A, B)

**Integrated Health Systems, Health Systems Finance**
Rochester Institute of Technology (GC)

**Integrated Marketing Communications Program**
West Virginia University (UC)

**Integrated Studies**
Athabasca University (M)

**Intelligent Information Systems**
Illinois Institute of Technology (GC)

**Intelligent Systems**
Columbia University (UC)

**Interactive Marketing**
Walsh College of Accountancy and Business Administration (UC)

**Intercultural Ministries**
Northwestern College (B)

**Interdepartmental Studies—Judaic Studies**
Jewish Theological Seminary of America (M)

**Interdisciplinary Arts**
Goddard College (M)

**Interdisciplinary Engineering**
Indiana Higher Education Telecommunication System (M)

**Interdisciplinary Humanities**
Burlington College (B)

# Index of Institutions Offering Degree and Certificate Programs

**Interdisciplinary Social Science**
Florida State University (B)

**Interdisciplinary Social Sciences**
Kansas State University (B)

**Interdisciplinary Studies**
New York Institute of Technology (B)
State University of New York Empire State
    College (A, B)
The Union Institute (D)

**Interdisciplinary Studies in Vicksburg
(3rd and 4th year program)**
Mississippi State University (B)

**Interdisciplinary Studies: Biology**
Mountain State University (B)

**Interdisciplinary Studies:
Environmental Studies**
Mountain State University (B)

**Interdisciplinary Studies: Health
Services Management**
Mountain State University (B)

**Interdisciplinary Studies: Natural
Sciences**
Mountain State University (B)

**Interdisciplinary Studies: Pre-Medicine**
Mountain State University (B)

**Interdisciplinary Studies: Psychology**
Mountain State University (B)

**Interdisciplinary Studies: Social and
Behavioral Sciences**
Mountain State University (B)

**Interior Design**
Northern Arizona University (B)

**International Business**
Caldwell College (B)
Champlain College (A, UC)
Davenport University Online (UC)
Excelsior College (B)
Schiller International University (M)
Southern New Hampshire University (M,
    UC)
Strayer University (B)
Thomas Edison State College (A, B)
University of Sarasota (M)

**International Construction
Management**
University of Florida (M)

**International Development**
Hope International University (M)

**International Food Laws**
Michigan State University (UC)

**International Public Health–Community
Oriented Primary Care Option**
The George Washington University (UC)

**International Relations**
Salve Regina University (M)
Troy State University (M)

**International Studies**
Montgomery County Community College
    (UC)
United States Open University (B)

**International Tourism Management**
Northern Arizona University (UC)

**Internet**
Illinois Institute of Technology (GC)

**Internet and E-Commerce**
Mountain State University (B)

**Internet Applications Development**
New Jersey Institute of Technology (UC)

**Internet Business Systems**
Mercy College (M)

**Internet Database Mastery**
The University of Tennessee (UC)

**Internet Systems Engineering**
New Jersey Institute of Technology (UC)

**Internet Technologies**
University of Wisconsin-Milwaukee (UC)

**Intranet Development**
University of Massachusetts Lowell (UC)
University of Massachusetts System (UC)

**Jewish Education**
Jewish Theological Seminary of America (M)

**Jewish Studies**
California State University, Chico (B)
Cleveland College of Jewish Studies (M)

**Journalism**
Saint Mary-of-the-Woods College (B)

**Journalism–Media Management**
MU Direct: Continuing and Distance
    Education (M)

**Justice Administration**
Arizona Institute of Business & Technology
    (A)

**Justice Administration (Ministry
Concentration)**
Indiana Higher Education
    Telecommunication System (A)

**Justice Administration–Ministry
Concentration**
Taylor University, World Wide Campus (A)

**Justice Administration–Public Policy
Concentration**
Taylor University, World Wide Campus (A)

**Justice and Ministry**
Indiana Higher Education
    Telecommunication System (UC)
Taylor University, World Wide Campus
    (UC)

**Justice Systems and Policy Planning**
Northern Arizona University (B)

**Kinesiology**
The University of Texas of the Permian
    Basin (M)
The University of Texas System (M)

**Kinesiology and Health**
University of Wyoming (M)

**Labor Studies**
Indiana University System (A, B, UC)
State University of New York Empire State
    College (A, B)
Thomas Edison State College (B)

**Labour Studies**
Athabasca University (UC)

**Land Surveying**
University of Wyoming (UC)

**Language Education**
Indiana Higher Education
    Telecommunication System (M)
Indiana University System (M)

**Langue et Linguistique (en
developpement)**
Laurentian University (B)

**Law and Justice (in development)**
Laurentian University (B, UC)

**Law Enforcement**
Indiana Higher Education
Telecommunication System (A, UC)
Indiana State University (UC)
Missouri Southern State College (A)

**Law Enforcement Studies**
Vincennes University (A)

**Law Office Management Specialty**
College for Professional Studies (UC)

**Law, Philosophy and Rhetoric**
Stephens College (B)

**Leadership**
Bellevue University (M)
Davenport University Online (UC)

**Leadership and Human Performance
Certificate and Human Resource
Management Certificate**
University of Wisconsin-Platteville (UC)

**Leadership and Training**
Royal Roads University (M)

**Leadership Certificate**
Pitt Community College (UC)

**Leadership Development**
Brenau University (M)

**Leadership in Nursing and Health Care
Systems**
Old Dominion University (M)

**Leadership Studies**
Sacred Heart University (B)

**Leadership-Christian**
Global University of the Assemblies of God
(M)

**Learning and Pedagogy**
Northern Arizona University (B)

**Learning and Technology**
Western Governors University (M)

**Legal Administration**
Eastern Michigan University (GC)

**Legal Assisting**
University of Northwestern Ohio (A)

**Legal Issues for Business Professionals**
The Pennsylvania State University University
Park Campus (UC)

**Legal Issues for Those Dealing with the
Elderly**
The Pennsylvania State University University
Park Campus (UC)

**Legal Nurse**
Saint Mary-of-the-Woods College (UC)

**Legal Nurse Consultant Paralegal
Diploma Program**
College for Professional Studies (UC)

**Legal Research Specialty**
College for Professional Studies (UC)

**Legal Services**
Thomas Edison State College (A)

**Legal Studies**
Brevard Community College (A)
Sussex County Community College (UC)

**Letters, Arts, and Sciences**
The Pennsylvania State University University
Park Campus (A, B)

**Liberal Arts**
Atlantic Cape Community College (A)
Bethany College of the Assemblies of God
(B)
Bucks County Community College (A)
Citrus College (A)
Clovis Community College (A)
Colorado Electronic Community College (A)
Duquesne University (M)
Eastern Illinois University (B)
Excelsior College (A, B)
Florence-Darlington Technical College (A)
Goddard College (B)
Hawkeye Community College (A)
Kirkwood Community College (A)
Maui Community College (A)
Metropolitan Community College (A)
Minnesota West Community and Technical
College-Worthington Campus (A)
Mountain Empire Community College (A)
New Hampshire Community Technical
College, Nashua/Claremont (A)
New School University (B)
Northern Virginia Community College (A)
Norwich University (M, B)
Rogers State University (A, B)
St. Cloud State University (A)
Schoolcraft College (A)
Seattle Central Community College (A)
Sinclair Community College (A)
Southern New Hampshire University (A, B)
Southwestern Community College (A)
Syracuse University (A)

Ulster County Community College (A)
United States Open University (B)
The University Alliance (A)
University of Alaska Southeast, Sitka
Campus (B)
University of Massachusetts System (B)
University of Wisconsin Colleges (A)
Upper Iowa University (A)

**Liberal Arts (General Studies)**
Taylor University, World Wide Campus (A)

**Liberal Arts—Social Science**
Colorado State University (B)

**Liberal Arts and General Studies**
Dallas County Community College District
(A)
Mount Saint Vincent University (B)

**Liberal Arts and Humanities**
Cayuga County Community College (A)

**Liberal Arts and Science**
San Joaquin Delta College (A)

**Liberal Arts and Sciences**
Burlington County College (A)
Mercy College (A)
Rockland Community College (A)
The Union Institute (B)
Wenatchee Valley College (A)

**Liberal Arts Transfer**
Western Iowa Tech Community College (A)

**Liberal Science (in development)**
Laurentian University (B)

**Liberal Studies**
Alaska Pacific University (A, B)
California State University, Chico (B)
College of San Mateo (A)
Eastern Oregon University (B)
Excelsior College (M, B)
Fort Hays State University (M)
Graceland University (B)
Limestone College (A, B)
Maui Community College (B)
Middlesex Community College (A)
Middle Tennessee State University (B)
Montgomery County Community College
(A)
Oral Roberts University (B)
Oregon State University (B)
Salve Regina University (B)
Skidmore College (M)
Sonoma State University (B)
Southern Christian University (B)

*Liberal Studies (continued)*

Stony Brook University, State University of
New York (M)
Syracuse University (B)
Thomas Edison State College (B)
University of Central Florida (B)
University of Illinois at Springfield (B)
The University of Iowa (B)
University of Maryland University College
(B)
The University of Montana-Missoula (B)
The University of North Carolina at
Greensboro (M)
University of Northern Iowa (B)
University of Toledo (M)

**Liberal Studies with Concentration in
Management and Communication**
Montana State University-Billings (B)

**Liberal Studies—Human Resource
Management**
University of Hawaii at Manoa (B)

**Liberal Studies—Information Resource
Management**
University of Hawaii at Manoa (B)

**Library and Information Science**
Maui Community College (M)
MU Direct: Continuing and Distance
Education (M)
University of Wisconsin-Milwaukee (M)

**Library and Information Sciences**
Louisiana State University and Agricultural
and Mechanical College (M)
University of North Texas (UC)
University of South Carolina (M)

**Library and Information Studies**
Florida State University (M)
The University of North Carolina at
Greensboro (M)

**Library Information Technology**
Central Missouri State University (M)

**Library Media**
The University of Montana-Missoula (UC)

**Library Media Teaching**
Azusa Pacific University (UC)

**Library Science**
Clarion University of Pennsylvania (M)
Connecticut State University System (M)
East Carolina University (M)
North Carolina Central University (M)

Southern Connecticut State University (M)
Syracuse University (UC)
Texas Woman's University (M)
University of North Texas (M)

**Library Studies**
Memorial University of Newfoundland (UC)

**Library Technical Assistant**
Northampton County Area Community
College (UC)

**Library Technician**
Colorado Community College Online (A)
Colorado Electronic Community College (A)
Pueblo Community College (A, UC)

**Library/Media Services**
Indiana Higher Education
Telecommunication System (GC, UC)
Indiana State University (GC, UC)

**Literacy Focus**
MU Direct: Continuing and Distance
Education (M)

**Literature**
Atlantic Cape Community College (A)

**Litigation Assistantship Specialty**
College for Professional Studies (UC)

**Logistics and Supply Chain
Management**
The Pennsylvania State University University
Park Campus (UC)

**Logistics Management**
Florida Institute of Technology (M)

**Long-Term Care Administration**
Saint Joseph's College (B, UC)

**LUTC Fellow Designation**
The American College (UC)

**Major in Administration**
Central Michigan University (B)

**Major Program**
Open Learning Agency (B)

**Management**
American Military University (M, B)
Athabasca University (GC)
Bellevue University (B)
Bucks County Community College (A)
Caldwell College (B)
Champlain College (A, UC)
Davenport University Online (A, B)

Florida Institute of Technology (M)
Hope International University (M)
Indiana Institute of Technology (B)
Indiana Wesleyan University (B)
Marylhurst University (B)
Northern Arizona University (M)
Northern Michigan University (B)
Rensselaer Polytechnic Institute (M)
Robert Morris College (B)
Salve Regina University (M, UC)
Stephens College (M)
Thomas Edison State College (M)
Troy State University-Florida Region (B)
University of Maryland University College
(M, B)
University of Phoenix (B)
University of Sarasota (M)
Upper Iowa University (B)
Valdosta State University (B)
Worcester Polytechnic Institute (GC)

**Management—Entrepreneurial
Specialty**
Davenport University Online (M)

**Management—Strategic Management
Specialty**
Davenport University Online (M)

**Management and Correctional
Administration**
Salve Regina University (UC)

**Management and Leadership**
Judson College (B)

**Management and Technology**
Rensselaer Polytechnic Institute (M, UC)

**Management Application and
Principles Certificate**
Pitt Community College (UC)

**Management Communication**
Southern Christian University (B)

**Management Development**
College of Southern Maryland (A)

**Management Information Sciences**
Franklin University (B)

**Management Information Systems**
Bellevue University (B)
Excelsior College (B)
University of Illinois at Springfield (M)

**Management of Hazardous Materials**
University of Denver (GC)

**Management of Health Services**
Ottawa University (B)

**Management of Human Resources**
Bellevue University (B)
Excelsior College (B)

**Management of Technical Operations**
Embry-Riddle Aeronautical University (B)

**Management of Technology**
National Technological University (M)

**Management Science and Engineering**
Stanford University (M)

**Manufacturing**
East Carolina University (M)

**Manufacturing Engineering**
Boston University (M)
Columbia University (UC)
Illinois Institute of Technology (M)
University of Michigan (M)

**Manufacturing Management**
Kettering University (M)

**Manufacturing Systems Engineering**
National Technological University (M, UC)
Rensselaer Polytechnic Institute (UC)

**Manufacturing Systems Management**
Southern Methodist University (M)

**Marine Science**
Maui Community College (B)

**Marketing**
American Military University (B)
Bucks County Community College (A)
Caldwell College (B)
Davenport University Online (A, B)
Excelsior College (B)
Golden Gate University (GC, M)
Indiana Institute of Technology (B)
Lakeland College (B)
Mountain State University (A, B)
St. Cloud State University (M)
Saint Mary-of-the-Woods College (B)
Southern New Hampshire University (B)
Strayer University (A)
Thomas Edison State College (A, B)
University of Northwestern Ohio (A)
University of Sarasota (M)
Upper Iowa University (B)

**Marketing Certificate**
Pitt Community College (UC)

**Marketing Management**
The Pennsylvania State University University Park Campus (UC)

**Marketing, Management and Technology**
University of Northwestern Ohio (A)

**Mass Communication: Advertising/ Public Relations**
Parkland College (A)

**Mass Communications (Journalism)**
Parkland College (A)

**Master in Teaching Leadership Degree Concentration**
University of Illinois at Springfield (M)

**Master of Accountancy**
Gardner-Webb University (M)
Golden Gate University (M)

**Master of Acquisition Management**
American Graduate University (M)

**Master of Applied Science Management Science, Technology Management**
University of Waterloo (M)

**Master of Business Administration**
Athabasca University (M)

**Master of Business Administration at Columbus Air Force Base**
Mississippi State University (M)

**Master of Distance Education**
Athabasca University (M)

**Master of Health Studies**
Athabasca University (M)

**Master of Human Resources Management (MHRM)**
Keller Graduate School of Management (M)

**Master of Information Systems Management (MISM)**
Keller Graduate School of Management (M)

**Master of Information Technology**
Virginia Polytechnic Institute and State University (M)

**Master of Project Management**
American Graduate University (M)

**Master of Public Policy and Administration**
Mississippi State University (M)

**Master of Science in Elementary Education**
Mississippi State University (M)

**Master of Science in Radiologic Sciences, Education or Administration Major**
Midwestern State University (M)

**Master Reading Teacher**
The University of Texas System (UC)

**Master's Degree in Educational Administration**
University of Massachusetts Lowell (M)

**Masters in Nursing**
University of Pennsylvania (M)

**Materials Engineering**
Auburn University (M)

**Materials Science and Engineering**
Columbia University (M, UC)
National Technological University (M, UC)
Stanford University (M)
Virginia Polytechnic Institute and State University (M)

**Materiel Acquisition Management**
Florida Institute of Technology (M)

**Math Education**
Northern Arizona University (UC)

**Mathematics**
Middle Tennessee State University (M)
Montana State University-Bozeman (M)
Ohio University (A)
Saint Mary-of-the-Woods College (B)
Thomas Edison State College (A)
University of Houston-Victoria (B)

**Mathematics/Statistics**
Northern Arizona University (B)

**Mechanical and Aerospace Engineering**
Illinois Institute of Technology (M)

**Mechanical Engineering**
Auburn University (M)
Bradley University (M)
Colorado State University (D, M)
Columbia University (D, M)
Florida State University (M)

*Mechanical Engineering (continued)*
Georgia Institute of Technology (M)
Iowa State University of Science and
 Technology (M)
Michigan Technological University (D, M)
Mississippi State University (D, M)
National Technological University (M)
Purdue University (M)
Rensselaer Polytechnic Institute (M)
Southern Methodist University (M)
Stanford University (M)
The University of Alabama (M)
University of Delaware (M)
University of Idaho (M)
University of North Dakota (B)
University of South Carolina (D, M)
The University of Texas at Arlington (M)
University of Wisconsin-Madison (M)

**Mechanical Engineering Technology**
Old Dominion University (B)
Thomas Edison State College (A)

**Media and Technology**
State University of West Georgia (M)

**Media Studies**
New School University (M)

**Medical Assistant Technology**
University of Northwestern Ohio (A)

**Medical and Dental Practice
Administration**
Saint Joseph's College (UC)

**Medical Assisting**
Mountain State University (A)
Portland Community College (UC)

**Medical Coding**
Northwestern Technical College (UC)

**Medical Engineering Technology**
Thomas Edison State College (B)

**Medical Imaging**
Clarkson College (B)
Thomas Edison State College (A, B)

**Medical Laboratory Technology**
Central Virginia Community College (A)

**Medical Office Administration
Certificate**
Pitt Community College (UC)

**Medical Transcription**
California College for Health Sciences (A)

State University of New York College of
 Technology at Alfred (UC)

**Medicine**
Saint Francis University (M)

**Mental Health and Rehabilitation
Services**
Thomas Edison State College (A)

**Mental Health and Rehabilitative
Services**
Thomas Edison State College (B)

**Merchandising**
San Joaquin Delta College (UC)
University of North Texas (M)

**Metallurgical and Materials
Engineering**
Illinois Institute of Technology (M)

**Microcomputer and Network
Technology**
Northwest Technical College (A)

**Microcomputer Applications**
Davenport University Online (UC)

**Microcomputer Network Systems**
Arizona Institute of Business & Technology
 (A)

**Microcomputer Support Specialist**
University of Alaska Fairbanks (A, UC)

**Microelectronics Manufacturing
Engineering**
Rensselaer Polytechnic Institute (UC)

**Microelectronics Technology and
Design**
Rensselaer Polytechnic Institute (UC)

**Microsoft Certified System Engineers**
Western Washington University (UC)

**Microsoft Office**
Bucks County Community College (UC)

**Microsoft Officer User Specialist**
Northwestern Technical College (UC)

**Middle School Education**
Northern Arizona University (UC)

**Midwifery**
Philadelphia University (M)

**Military History, Military Management,
Intelligence Studies**
American Military University (M, B)

**Military Studies**
American Military University (M, A)

**Ministry**
Mid-America Bible College (M)
Oral Roberts University (D)
Prairie Bible College (B)

**Ministry Studies**
Judson College (B)

**Ministry/Bible**
Southern Christian University (B)

**Missions**
Global University of the Assemblies of God
 (M, A, B)

**Moderate/Severe Disabilities**
University of Louisville (M)

**Molecular Biology**
Lehigh University (M)

**Molecular Laboratory Diagnostics**
Michigan State University (GC)

**Multidisciplinary Studies**
Liberty University (B)

**Multidisciplinary Study**
Johnson County Community College (A)

**Multimedia Applications**
University of Massachusetts Lowell (UC)
University of Massachusetts System (UC)

**Multimedia Networking**
Columbia University (UC)

**Municipal Administration**
Memorial University of Newfoundland (UC)

**Music**
Judson College (B)

**Music Education**
Duquesne University (M)

**Music Technology**
Indiana University System (M)

**Music Therapy**
Open Learning Agency (B)
Saint Mary-of-the-Woods College (M)

**Music, Jazz Studies**
Open Learning Agency (B)

**Music, Performance**
Open Learning Agency (B)

**Native Human Services**
Laurentian University (B)

**Native Studies**
Laurentian University (B)

**Natural Resource Management**
University of Denver (GC)

**Natural Resources**
Oregon State University (B)

**Natural Resources and the Environment**
Colorado State University (UC)

**Natural Science**
Ohio University (A)

**Natural Sciences, Social Science, and Humanities**
College of San Mateo (A)

**Natural Sciences/Mathematics**
Thomas Edison State College (B)

**Negotiation and Conflict Management**
California State University, Dominguez Hills (M)

**Network Administration**
Northwestern Michigan College (UC)

**Network Analysis and Design**
University of Denver (GC)

**Network Security**
Capitol College (M)

**Networking and Systems**
Columbia University (UC)

**Networks and Telecommunications**
Loyola University Chicago (UC)

**Neuropsychology**
Fielding Graduate Institute (UC)

**New Media Engineering**
Columbia University (UC)

**New Testament**
Johnson Bible College (M)

**Newfoundland Studies**
Memorial University of Newfoundland (UC)

**Noise Control Engineering**
The Pennsylvania State University University Park Campus (UC)

**Non-Profit Management**
Hope International University (M)
Oral Roberts University (M, UC)

**Nontraditional**
Duquesne University (D)

**Not for Profit: Child Care Administration**
Saint Mary-of-the-Woods College (B)

**Not for Profit: Financial Administration**
Saint Mary-of-the-Woods College (B)

**Not for Profit: Human Services**
Saint Mary-of-the-Woods College (B)

**Not for Profit: Public Relations**
Saint Mary-of-the-Woods College (B)

**Nuclear Criticality Safety**
The University of Tennessee (GC)

**Nuclear Engineering**
The University of Tennessee (M)

**Nuclear Engineering Technology**
Thomas Edison State College (A, B)

**Nuclear Medicine**
Thomas Edison State College (A, B)
Weber State University (UC)

**Nuclear Technology**
Excelsior College (A, B)

**Nurse Practitioner**
Seton Hall University (M)

**Nursing**
Ball State University (M, B)
California State University, Chico (B)
California State University, Dominguez Hills (M)
Clarkson College (B)
Clemson University (M, B)
Concordia University Wisconsin (M)
Duquesne University (D, M, B)
Eastern New Mexico University (B)
Excelsior College (M, A, B)
Ferris State University (B)
Florida State University (B)
Fort Hays State University (B)

Husson College (B)
Illinois State University (B)
Indiana State University (M, B)
Indiana University System (M)
Lakehead University (B)
Loyola University New Orleans (M, B)
Maui Community College (M)
Montana State University-Bozeman (M)
National University (M, B)
Newman University (B)
North Carolina Central University (B)
Northern Arizona University (B)
Northern Michigan University (M)
Northwestern Michigan College (A)
Northwestern State University of Louisiana (B)
Old Dominion University (B)
Oregon Health & Science University (B)
Plattsburgh State University of New York (B)
Sacred Heart University (B)
Saint Joseph's College (M, B)
Saint Louis University (M, GC, M)
Samuel Merritt College (M)
Southwest Missouri State University (B)
Syracuse University (M)
Texas Christian University (M)
Texas Woman's University (D)
Thomas Edison State College (B)
The University Alliance (B)
University of Central Florida (B)
University of Delaware (B)
University of Manitoba (B)
University of Massachusetts Amherst (M)
University of Massachusetts System (M)
University of Missouri-St. Louis (M, B)
University of Nebraska Medical Center (B)
University of New Brunswick (M, B)
University of New Mexico (B)
The University of North Carolina at Greensboro (M, B)
University of Phoenix (M, B)
University of Saint Francis (M)
University of South Alabama (B)
University of South Carolina Spartanburg (M)
University of Southern Indiana (M, B)
The University of Texas at Tyler (B)
University of Vermont (M)
University of Wisconsin-Madison (B)
University of Wisconsin-Milwaukee (D)
Valdosta State University (M, B)
Western University of Health Sciences (M)
West Virginia University (M)
West Virginia Wesleyan College (B)

**Nursing (Community Health Clinical Specialist)**
University of Wyoming (M)

## Nursing (Nurse Educator Option)
University of Wyoming (M)

## Nursing (Post-Basic RN)
Memorial University of Newfoundland (B)

## Nursing (RN to BS)
University of Massachusetts Amherst (B)
University of Massachusetts System (B)

## Nursing (RN to BSN)
University of Northern Colorado (B)

## Nursing—Mental Health Nurse Practitioner
MU Direct: Continuing and Distance Education (M)

## Nursing—Pediatric Nurse Practitioner
MU Direct: Continuing and Distance Education (M)

## Nursing—Public Health or School Health
MU Direct: Continuing and Distance Education (M)

## Nursing Administration
Texas A&M University-Corpus Christi (M)
University of New Mexico (M)

## Nursing Bachelor's Completion Program
MU Direct: Continuing and Distance Education (B)

## Nursing Case Management
The University of Alabama (M)

## Nursing Degree Completion Program
University of Wisconsin-Eau Claire (B)

## Nursing Home Administration
Southeast Community College, Beatrice Campus (UC)

## Nursing, Completion Program
California State University, Dominguez Hills (B)

## Nursing, Major in Administration
Clarkson College (M)

## Nursing, Major in Education
Clarkson College (M)

## Nursing, Major in Family Nurse Practitioning
Clarkson College (M)

## Nursing, RN to BSN
University of Wyoming (B)

## Nursing-RN-BSN Completion
Saint Louis University (B)

## Nutrition
American Academy of Nutrition, College of Nutrition (A)

## Nutrition and Dietetics
East Carolina University (M)

## Nutrition and Food Management
Oregon State University (M)

## Object Oriented Programming Certificate
Pitt Community College (UC)

## Object-Oriented Design
New Jersey Institute of Technology (UC)

## Occupational and Technical Studies
Old Dominion University (M, B)

## Occupational Medicine
Medical College of Wisconsin (M)

## Occupational Safety
East Carolina University (M)

## Occupational Safety and Health
Colorado Electronic Community College (A)
Montana Tech of The University of Montana (B)
North Carolina Agricultural and Technical State University (B)

## Occupational Safety and Health Program
University of Connecticut (UC)

## Occupational Safety and Health Technology
Colorado Community College Online (A)

## Occupational Safety Management
Indiana State University (M)

## Occupational Therapy
University of Florida (M)

## Occupational Therapy Applications
Saint Mary-of-the-Woods College (B)

## Occupational Therapy, Post Professional Masters
Belmont University (M)

## Ocean Engineering
Virginia Polytechnic Institute and State University (M)

## Office Administration
Delaware Technical & Community College, Jack F. Owens Campus (A)
Marywood University (UC)

## Office Management Technology
University of Alaska Southeast, Ketchikan Campus (A)

## Office Technology: Secretarial Skills
Mountain State University (UC)

## Office Technology: Word Processing
Mountain State University (UC)

## Omnibus
Schoolcraft College (M)

## One Year Bible Certificate
Eugene Bible College (UC)

## Online Communications Skills
University of Massachusetts System (UC)

## Online MBA
Franklin University (M)

## Online Teaching
Cerro Coso Community College (UC)

## Operational Meteorology
Mississippi State University (B)

## Operations Management
Excelsior College (B)
Kettering University (M)
Thomas Edison State College (B)

## Operations Research
Columbia University (UC)
Florida Institute of Technology (M)
Southern Methodist University (M)

## Optical Science
National Technological University (M)

## Optical Sciences
The University of Arizona (M)

## Oregon Transfer Degree
Central Oregon Community College (A)

## Organizational Communications
Marylhurst University (B)

## Organizational Leadership
Austin Peay State University (B)
Southern Christian University (M)

## Organizational Management
Dallas Baptist University (M)
Spring Arbor University (M)
Thomas Edison State College (B)
University of Phoenix (M)

## Organizational Management; Organizational Development
Fielding Graduate Institute (M)

## Organizational Studies
Saybrook Graduate School and Research Center (D)

## Organizational Systems
Saybrook Graduate School and Research Center (M)

## Orientation and Mobility
University of Louisville (M)

## Packaging
Michigan State University (M)

## Paralegal
The Paralegal Institute, Inc. (A)

## Paralegal Diploma Program
College for Professional Studies (UC)

## Paralegal Program
The Pennsylvania State University University Park Campus (UC)

## Paralegal Specialized Associate Degree
College for Professional Studies (A)

## Paralegal Studies
College for Professional Studies (B)
Grambling State University (UC)
Saint Mary-of-the-Woods College (A, B, UC)
Tompkins Cortland Community College (A)
University of Great Falls (B)
University of Maryland University College (B)
University of Southern Colorado (UC)
Western Piedmont Community College (A)

## Parish Education
Concordia University (M)

## Parish Nursing
Saint Joseph's College (UC)

## Park and Resource Management
Slippery Rock University of Pennsylvania (M)

## Parks and Recreation Management
Northern Arizona University (B, UC)

## Particle Processing
Illinois Institute of Technology (GC)

## Pastoral Community Counseling
University of Sarasota (D)

## Pastoral Ministry
Mid-America Bible College (B)
Newman University (B)

## Pastoral Studies
Saint Joseph's College (M, UC)

## Pastoral Theology
Saint Mary-of-the-Woods College (M)

## Personal Financial Planning
College for Financial Planning (M)
Kansas State University (UC)

## Personal Ministries
Griggs University (A)

## Petroleum Engineering
Texas A&M University (M)
Texas Tech University (M)

## Pharmaceutical Chemistry
Lehigh University (M)

## Pharmaceutical Processing
Illinois Institute of Technology (GC)

## Pharmacy
Ohio Northern University (D)
University of Colorado at Denver (D)
University of Florida (D)
The University of Montana-Missoula (D)
University of Wisconsin-Madison (D)

## Philosophy
Thomas Edison State College (B)
University of Waterloo (B)

## Philosophy and Religious Studies
Christopher Newport University (B)

## Philosophy, Politics and Economics
Eastern Oregon University (B)

## Photonics and Optoelectronics
University of Massachusetts System (GC)

## Physical Education
Mississippi State University (M)
North Carolina Agricultural and Technical State University (M)

## Physical Education—Emphasis in Health Education/Health Promotion
Mississippi State University (M)

## Physical Education/Health
Eastern Oregon University (B)

## Physician Executive MBA
The University of Tennessee (M)

## Physiotherapy
Open Learning Agency (B)

## Plastics Engineering Technology
University of Massachusetts Lowell (UC)

## Political Science
Caldwell College (B)
Thomas Edison State College (B)
Troy State University Montgomery (A, B)
Valdosta State University (B)
Virginia Polytechnic Institute and State University (M)

## Polymer Operations Management
Illinois Institute of Technology (GC)

## Polymer Science and Engineering
Lehigh University (M)

## Post-BSN
Duquesne University (UC)

## Post-Master's
Duquesne University (UC)

## Post-Secondary Teaching
Colorado State University (GC)

## Postdegree Elementary Education
Northern Arizona University (UC)

## Postdegree Secondary Education
Northern Arizona University (UC)

## Postdegree Special Education
Northern Arizona University (UC)

## Power Electronics
University of Colorado at Boulder (UC)

## Power Engineering
Illinois Institute of Technology (GC)

## Power Plant Technology
Bismarck State College (A, UC)

# Index of Institutions Offering Degree and Certificate Programs

**Power System Protection and Relaying**
University of Idaho (UC)

**Practical Theology**
Oral Roberts University (M)

**Practice of Technology Communications**
New Jersey Institute of Technology (UC)

**Preliminary and Professional Clear Multiple Subject Teaching with CLAD/BCLAD emphasis**
National University (UC)

**Preliminary and Professional Clear Single Subject Teaching Credential with CLAD or BCLAD emphasis**
National University (UC)

**Preliminary Level 1 Education Specialist: Mild/Moderate Disabilities with Concurrent CLD/BCLAD**
National University (UC)

**Principalship**
Northern Arizona University (UC)

**Private Security**
Indiana Higher Education Telecommunication System (UC)
Indiana State University (UC)

**Process Plant Technology**
Bismarck State College (A, UC)

**Production and Inventory Control**
California State University, Dominguez Hills (UC)

**Production and Inventory Management—APICS**
Weber State University (UC)

**Professional Accounting**
Strayer University (M)

**Professional Aeronautics**
Embry-Riddle Aeronautical University (A, B)

**Professional Agriculture**
Iowa State University of Science and Technology (B)

**Professional and Technical Communications**
New Jersey Institute of Technology (M)

**Professional Arts**
Saint Joseph's College (B)
University of St. Francis (B)

**Professional Certificate in Computer Science**
Loyola University Chicago (UC)

**Professional Certificate in Criminal Justice**
National University (UC)

**Professional Communication**
East Carolina University (GC)
East Tennessee State University (M)

**Professional Communications**
Marywood University (UC)

**Professional Counseling**
Liberty University (M)

**Professional Development**
Amberton University (M, B)

**Professional Graduate Certificate in Systems Engineering**
The University of Arizona (UC)

**Professional Master of Business Administration**
Florida Institute of Technology (M)

**Professional Nursing**
Graceland University (B)

**Professional Practice**
University of Wisconsin-Madison (M)

**Professional Psychology**
Walden University (D)

**Professional Studies**
Champlain College (B)
Metropolitan Community College (A)
Saint Joseph's College (UC)
Southwestern Assemblies of God University (B)
Thomas Edison State College (M)

**Professional Studies, Concentration in Information Technology**
Middle Tennessee State University (B)

**Professional Studies, Concentration in Organizational Leadership**
Middle Tennessee State University (B)

**Professional Tier I Administrative Services**
National University (UC)

**Professional Writing**
Saint Mary-of-the-Woods College (B)

**Programmer/Analyst**
Wisconsin Indianhead Technical College, New Richmond Campus (A)

**Programming Environmental Tools**
New Jersey Institute of Technology (UC)

**Project Engineering and Management**
Montana Tech of The University of Montana (M)

**Project Management**
Florida Institute of Technology (M)
The George Washington University (M)
Keller Graduate School of Management (M)
National Technological University (M)
New Jersey Institute of Technology (UC)
Stevens Institute of Technology (GC)
University of Wisconsin-Platteville (M, UC)
Western Carolina University (M)

**Psychiatric Nursing**
Open Learning Agency (B)

**Psychologie**
Laurentian University (B)

**Psychology**
Atlantic Cape Community College (A)
Bethany College of the Assemblies of God (B)
Burlington College (B)
Caldwell College (B)
Foothill College (A)
Judson College (B)
Laurentian University (B)
Liberty University (B)
Limestone College (B)
Mercy College (B)
New York Institute of Technology (B)
Northcentral University (D, M, B)
Northern Arizona University (B)
Pacific Graduate School of Psychology (M)
Parkland College (A)
Saint Mary-of-the-Woods College (B)
Saybrook Graduate School and Research Center (D, M)
Stephens College (B)
Thomas Edison State College (B)
Troy State University Montgomery (A, B)
University of Baltimore (B)
University of Great Falls (B)

University of Houston (B)
University of Idaho (M)
University of Waterloo (B)
University of Wyoming (B)
Walden University (M)

**Psychology and Counseling**
Goddard College (M)

**Psychology Licensure**
Saybrook Graduate School and Research Center (M)

**Psychology/Family Counseling**
Barclay College (B)

**Psychology/Sociology**
Western Baptist College (B)

**Public Administration**
Athabasca University (UC)
Colorado Electronic Community College (A)
Florida Gulf Coast University (M)
Florida Institute of Technology (M)
Golden Gate University (M)
Indiana Higher Education Telecommunication System (GC)
Indiana State University (UC)
Marist College (M)
Memorial University of Newfoundland (UC)
Northern Michigan University (M)
Nova Southeastern University (M)
Pueblo Community College (A)
Roger Williams University (B)
Troy State University (M)
University of Colorado at Denver (M)
University of La Verne (B)
University of Nebraska at Omaha (M)
University of North Dakota (M)
University of Wyoming (M)
Utah State University (M)
Valdosta State University (M)

**Public Administration (General)**
Upper Iowa University (B)

**Public Administration (Law Enforcement/Fire Science)**
Upper Iowa University (B)

**Public Health**
California College for Health Sciences (M)
Walden University (M)

**Public Health Practice**
University of Massachusetts Amherst (M)
University of Massachusetts System (M)

**Public Relations and Communication Management**
Royal Roads University (M)

**Public Safety Management**
Franklin University (B)

**Public School Administration**
Oral Roberts University (D)

**Public Service Studies**
York University (B)

**Public Works**
Illinois Institute of Technology (M)

**Purchasing**
California State University, Dominguez Hills (UC)

**Quality and Reliability**
Rensselaer Polytechnic Institute (UC)

**Quality Assurance**
California State University, Dominguez Hills (M, UC)

**Quality Assurance Science**
California National University for Advanced Studies (B)

**Quality Engineering**
Lehigh University (M)

**Quality Leadership**
Davenport University Online (UC)

**Radiation Protection**
Thomas Edison State College (A, B)

**Radiation Therapy**
Thomas Edison State College (A, B)
Weber State University (UC)

**Radiologic Sciences**
Midwestern State University (B)

**Radiologic Sciences Bachelor's Completion Program—Radiography**
MU Direct: Continuing and Distance Education (B)

**Radiologic Technology**
Northwestern State University of Louisiana (B)

**Radiologic Technology Continuing Education**
Sinclair Community College (UC)

**Radiologic Technology Program**
Southeast Community College, Beatrice Campus (A)

**Radiological Sciences**
Saint Joseph's College (B)
Weber State University (B, UC)

**Radiological Technology**
Southeast Community College, Lincoln Campus (A)

**Reading**
Concordia University Wisconsin (M)

**Reading Specialist**
Northern Arizona University (UC)
The University of Texas System (UC)

**Real Estate**
Thomas Edison State College (A)
University of Wyoming (UC)

**Real Estate Law Specialty**
College for Professional Studies (UC)

**Records and Information Management**
Memorial University of Newfoundland (UC)

**Records Management**
The George Washington University (UC)

**Recreation Management**
North Carolina Central University (UC)

**Recreation Management—Therapeutic Option**
Vincennes University (A)

**Recreation Resources Management**
George Mason University (M)

**Recreation Services**
Thomas Edison State College (A)

**Recreational Management**
United States Sports Academy (M)

**Registered Employee Benefits Consultant (REBC) Designation**
The American College (UC)

**Registered Health Underwriter (RHU) Designation**
The American College (UC)

**Rehabilitation Counseling**
Auburn University (GC)
University of Arkansas at Little Rock (M)

**Service Social**
Laurentian University (B)

**Service Systems**
Rensselaer Polytechnic Institute (UC)

**Ships Systems Design Technology**
Maine Maritime Academy (A)

**Signal Processing**
Illinois Institute of Technology (GC)

**Small Business Management**
Davenport University Online (UC)
The Pennsylvania State University University
    Park Campus (UC)

**Small Business
Management/Entrepreneurship**
Thomas Edison State College (A, B)

**Social Development Studies**
University of Waterloo (B)

**Social Ecology**
Goddard College (M, B)

**Social Science**
Bethany College of the Assemblies of God
    (B)
Virginia Western Community College (A)

**Social Science Studies**
University of Nevada, Las Vegas (B)

**Social Science/History**
Saint Mary-of-the-Woods College (B)

**Social Science/Sociology**
Northern Michigan University (B)

**Social Sciences**
Buena Vista University (B)
California State University, Chico (B)
Ohio University (A)
Syracuse University (M)
Troy State University Montgomery (A, B)
United States Open University (B)
University of Pittsburgh (B)
University of Southern Colorado (B)
University of Waterloo (B)
University of Wyoming (B)
Upper Iowa University (B)
Washington State University (B)

**Social Sciences/History**
Thomas Edison State College (B)

**Social Studies Focus**
MU Direct: Continuing and Distance
    Education (M)

**Social Theory, Social Structure and
Change**
State University of New York Empire State
    College (A, B)

**Social Work**
Lakehead University (B)
Maui Community College (M)
Michigan State University (GC)
Northern Arizona University (B)
Northern Michigan University (B)
Southwest Missouri State University (M)
University of Alaska Fairbanks (B)
University of Alaska Southeast, Ketchikan
    Campus (M, B)
University of Manitoba (B)
University of North Dakota (M)
University of Vermont (M)
University of Wyoming (M)
Valdosta State University (M)

**Social Work (as a 2nd degree)**
Memorial University of Newfoundland (B)

**Sociology**
Caldwell College (B)
California State University, Chico (B)
Graceland University (B)
Laurentian University (B)
New York Institute of Technology (B)
Northern Arizona University (B)
Thomas Edison State College (B)
University of Colorado at Denver (B)
University of Great Falls (B)
University of Waterloo (B)
Wilfrid Laurier University (B)

**Software Applications for the
Professional**
Sinclair Community College (UC)

**Software Development**
Champlain College (A, UC)

**Software Development and
Management**
Rochester Institute of Technology (M)

**Software Engineering**
Carnegie Mellon University (M)
Champlain College (B)
Illinois Institute of Technology (GC)
Kansas State University (M)
National Technological University (M, UC)
Rensselaer Polytechnic Institute (UC)

**Southern Methodist University (M)**
Texas Tech University (M)
West Virginia University (M)

**Space Studies**
University of North Dakota (M)

**Spanish**
Northern Arizona University (B)

**Special and Elementary Education**
Northern Arizona University (B)

**Special Education**
Ball State University (M)
Eastern New Mexico University (M)
Indiana Higher Education
    Telecommunication System (M)
Northern Arizona University (M, UC)
Old Dominion University (M)
Saint Mary-of-the-Woods College (B)
University of Louisville (M)
University of North Dakota (M)
West Virginia University (M)

**Special Education (Cross-Categorical
Emphasis)**
The University of North Carolina at
    Greensboro (M)

**Special Education (Gifted)**
University of South Alabama (M)

**Special Education with Credential
Options**
National University (M)

**Special Education, Moderate Needs
Emphasis**
University of Northern Colorado (M)

**Special Education, Severe Needs
Vision Emphasis**
University of Northern Colorado (M)

**Special Majors**
National Technological University (M)

**Specialized Studies**
Ohio University (M)

**Speech Communication**
St. Cloud State University (M)

**Speech Language and Auditory
Pathology**
East Carolina University (M)

**Speech Pathology**
California State University, Northridge (M)

# Index of Institutions Offering Degree and Certificate Programs

**Speech-Language Pathology**
Texas Woman's University (M)
University of Wyoming (M)

**Sport Art**
United States Sports Academy (M)

**Sports Coaching**
United States Sports Academy (M)

**Sports Management**
United States Sports Academy (M)
University of Dallas (M)

**Sports Medicine**
United States Sports Academy (M)

**Starting Your Own Business**
Pitt Community College (UC)

**State and Local Taxation**
University of Wisconsin-Milwaukee (UC)

**Statistical Quality**
Rochester Institute of Technology (GC)

**Statistics**
Colorado State University (M)
Iowa State University of Science and
    Technology (M)

**Strategic Communication and
Leadership**
Seton Hall University (M)

**Structural Design**
Rochester Institute of Technology (UC)

**Structural Engineering**
Illinois Institute of Technology (M)
University of Idaho (UC)

**Student Affairs Administration**
Indiana Higher Education
    Telecommunication System (M)
Indiana State University (M)

**Substance Abuse**
Maui Community College (UC)

**Superintendency**
Northern Arizona University (UC)

**Supervision**
Bucks County Community College (UC)
Owens Community College (UC)

**Supervision and Management**
San Joaquin Delta College (UC)

**Supervisory**
Northern Arizona University (UC)

**Supervisory Management**
Western Wisconsin Technical College (A)

**Surgical Technology**
Southeast Community College, Beatrice
    Campus (A)
Southeast Community College, Lincoln
    Campus (A)

**Surgical Technology Accelerated
Option, Certificate of Graduation**
Vincennes University (GC)

**Surveying**
Michigan Technological University (B)

**Systems Analysis and Application
Development**
Davenport University Online (A)

**Systems and Engineering Management**
Texas Tech University (M)

**Systems Engineering**
Colorado State University (D, M)
Iowa State University of Science and
    Technology (M)
National Technological University (M)
Southern Methodist University (M)
University of Missouri-Rolla (M)
Virginia Polytechnic Institute and State
    University (M)

**Systems Management**
Mississippi State University (M)

**Taxation**
Golden Gate University (GC, M)
Old Dominion University (M)

**Teacher Education**
Goddard College (M)
Lehigh Carbon Community College (A)
Newman University (B)

**Teaching**
Grand Canyon University (M)

**Teaching and Learning with
Technology**
Teachers College, Columbia University (UC)

**Teaching Effectiveness**
Buena Vista University (M)

**Teaching English as a Second
Language**
Seattle Central Community College (UC)

**Teaching English as a Second
Language (TESL)**
Oral Roberts University (M)

**Teaching Mathematics**
University of Idaho (M)

**Teaching/Education with Credential
Options**
National University (M)

**Technical Communication**
Texas Tech University (M)

**Technical Communications**
Rensselaer Polytechnic Institute (M)
Rochester Institute of Technology (UC)
The University of Findlay (B)

**Technical Japanese**
National Technological University (UC)
University of Wisconsin-Madison (M)

**Technical Management**
Franklin University (B)

**Technical Studies**
Excelsior College (A)

**Technical Studies in Information
Systems**
Fairmont State College (A)

**Technology**
Excelsior College (A, B)

**Technology and Information
Management**
Upper Iowa University (B)

**Technology Applications in Science**
Stevens Institute of Technology (GC)

**Technology Apprenticeship**
Vincennes University (A)

**Technology Education**
North Carolina Agricultural and Technical
    State University (M)

**Technology in Education**
Lesley University (M)

**Technology Leadership and
Supervision**
University of Houston (B)

**Technology Management**
Central Missouri State University (D)
Indiana State University (D)
Open Learning Agency (B)
Pennsylvania College of Technology (B)
Stevens Institute of Technology (GC)
University of Phoenix (M)

**Technology Management (Undergraduate)**
Golden Gate University (UC)

**Technology Proficiency**
Western Governors University (GC)

**Technology Studies**
Austin Peay State University (B)

**Tele-Learning**
East Carolina University (GC)

**Telecommunication and Information Resource Management**
Maui Community College (GC)

**Telecommunications**
Columbia University (UC)
Keller Graduate School of Management (M)
National Technological University (M)
Rochester Institute of Technology (B)
Southern Methodist University (M)
University of Colorado at Boulder (M)
University of Denver (GC, M)
University of Pennsylvania (M)

**Telecommunications and Software Engineering**
Illinois Institute of Technology (M)

**Telecommunications Management**
Golden Gate University (M)
New York Institute of Technology (B)
Oklahoma State University (M)
Stevens Institute of Technology (GC, M)
University of Dallas (GC, M)

**Telecommunications Network Management**
Rochester Institute of Technology (UC)
Syracuse University (M)

**Telecommunications Networking**
New Jersey Institute of Technology (UC)

**Telelearning and Rural School Teaching**
Memorial University of Newfoundland (UC)

**Textile & Apparel Marketing**
Philadelphia University (M)

**Textile Off-Campus Televised Education (TOTE)**
North Carolina State University (M)

**The Arts**
State University of New York Empire State College (A, B)

**The Duke MBA—Global Executive**
Duke University (M)

**The Executive Master of Business Administration Program (EMB)**
Krannert Graduate School of Management (M)

**Theological Studies**
Griggs University (B)
Lincoln Christian College (UC)
Prairie Bible College (GC)

**Theology**
Caldwell College (B)
Covenant Theological Seminary (GC, M)
Franciscan University of Steubenville (M)
North Central University (A)
Oral Roberts University (UC)
Saint Mary-of-the-Woods College (B, UC)

**Therapeutic Recreation**
Indiana University System (M)

**Tourism and Hospitality Management**
Mount Saint Vincent University (B)

**Tourism Management**
Open Learning Agency (B)

**Training and Development**
North Carolina State University (UC)
University of Houston (M)

**Transfer Degree**
Bellevue Community College (A)

**Transitional Doctor of Physical Therapy**
University of St. Augustine for Health Sciences (D)

**Transpersonal Psychology**
Burlington College (B)
Naropa University (M)

**Transpersonal Studies**
Atlantic University (M)

**Transportation Engineering**
Illinois Institute of Technology (M)

**Transportation Systems Engineering**
National Technological University (UC)

**Transportation/Distribution Management**
Thomas Edison State College (A, B)

**Travel**
Mountain State University (A)

**Travel and Tourism**
Mountain State University (UC)

**Travel Management**
University of Northwestern Ohio (A)

**Turfgrass Management**
The Pennsylvania State University University Park Campus (UC)

**Undergraduate Endorsement in Driver Education**
Indiana Higher Education Telecommunication System (UC)

**Universal Degree**
Lorain County Community College (A)

**University Studies**
Eastern New Mexico University (B)

**UNIX**
University of Massachusetts Lowell (UC)
University of Massachusetts System (UC)

**Various**
DePaul University (B)

**Various Concentrations**
Keller Graduate School of Management (M)

**Veterinary Technology**
St. Petersburg College (A)

**Video-Based Engineering Education**
North Carolina State University (M)

**Virtual Reality in Education and Training**
East Carolina University (GC)

**Visual Art**
Norwich University (M)

**Visual Impairment**
University of Louisville (M)

**Visual Impairment and Blindness**
Illinois State University (UC)

**Vocational Education**
Northern Arizona University (M, B)

# Index of Institutions Offering Degree and Certificate Programs

**Vocational Technological Education**
Northern Arizona University (UC)

**Vocational-Technical Licensure**
Mississippi State University (M)

**Voice Communications**
Rochester Institute of Technology (UC)

**Votech/Technology**
Iowa Western Community College (A)

**Water and Wastewater Treatment**
Illinois Institute of Technology (GC)

**Water Resources Engineering**
University of Idaho (UC)

**Water/Wastewater Specialization**
Mountain Empire Community College (A)

**Watershed Management**
Michigan State University (UC)

**Web Authoring**
Bellevue Community College (A, UC)

**Web Designer**
Bucks County Community College (UC)

**Web Developer**
College of Southern Maryland (UC)
National American University (UC)

**Web Development**
Loyola University Chicago (UC)
Northwestern Michigan College (UC)

**Web Development and Management**
Alexandria Technical College (UC)

**Web Devolper**
Middlesex Community College (UC)

**Web Page Design**
Wytheville Community College (UC)

**Web Site Development and Management**
Champlain College (A, UC)

**Webmaster**
The Pennsylvania State University University Park Campus (UC)

**Website Developer**
East Carolina University (GC)

**Wireless and Mobile Communications**
Columbia University (UC)

**Wireless Communications**
Illinois Institute of Technology (GC)
Stevens Institute of Technology (GC, M)
Worcester Polytechnic Institute (GC)

**Wisconsin Credential Program for Child Care Administrators**
University of Wisconsin-Milwaukee (UC)

**Women's Health**
Texas Woman's University (UC)

**Women's Studies**
Laurentian University (B)

**Wood and Paper Science**
North Carolina State University (M)

**Word Processing-Administrative Support**
University of Northwestern Ohio (A)

**WordProcessing/Transcription Certificate**
Pitt Community College (UC)

**Working Professional Doctor of Pharmacy Program**
University of Florida (D)

**Writing**
Norwich University (M)

**Writing and Literature**
Burlington College (B)

**Writing Social Commentary**
The Pennsylvania State University University Park Campus (UC)

**Youth Development**
Concordia University (M, B)

**Youth Ministry Leadership**
Defiance College (UC)

# INDIVIDUAL COURSES INDEX

*Index of individual courses offered by institutions, arranged by subject. U=Undergraduate; G=Graduate; N=Noncredit*

## Accounting

Acadia University (U)
Adams State College (U)
Adirondack Community College (U)
Alexandria Technical College (U)
American College of Computer & Information Sciences (U)
American Graduate University (G)
Andrew College (U)
Anne Arundel Community College (U)
Antelope Valley College (U)
Aquinas College (G)
Arizona State University (U)
Arizona Western College (U)
Athens Technical College (U)
Bakersfield College (U)
Bellevue Community College (U)
Berkeley College (U)
Blinn College (U)
Blue River Community College (U)
Boise State University (U)
Brenau University (U, G)
Brevard Community College (U)
Brigham Young University (U)
Bristol Community College (N, U)
Broward Community College (U)
Bryant and Stratton Online (U)
Bucks County Community College (U)
Caldwell Community College and Technical Institute (U)
California National University for Advanced Studies (U, G)
California State University, Chico (U)
Calvin College (U)
Cape Fear Community College (U)
Carl Albert State College (U)
Carleton University (U)
Casper College (U)
Catawba Valley Community College (U)
Central Carolina Community College (U)
Central Carolina Technical College (U)
Central Community College (U)
Central Michigan University (U)
Central Texas College (U)
Central Washington University (U)
Central Wyoming College (U)

Century Community and Technical College (N)
Chadron State College (U, G)
Champlain College (U)
Chesapeake College (U)
Cincinnati State Technical and Community College (U)
Clackamas Community College (U)
Clarkson College (U)
Cleveland State Community College (U)
College for Financial Planning (N)
College of DuPage (U)
College of Southern Maryland (U)
College of The Albemarle (U)
College of the Southwest (U)
Colorado Christian University (G)
Colorado Community College Online (U)
Colorado Northwestern Community College (U)
Colorado State University (N)
Columbia Basin College (U)
Columbia College (U)
Community College of Vermont (U)
Connecticut State University System (U, G)
Copiah-Lincoln Community College-Natchez Campus (U)
Corning Community College (U)
Craven Community College (U)
Dallas County Community College District (U)
Danville Area Community College (U)
Danville Community College (U)
Davenport University Online (U, G)
Delaware Technical & Community College, Jack F. Owens Campus (U)
Des Moines Area Community College (U)
Drake University (U)
Duke University (G)
East Carolina University (G)
Eastern New Mexico University (U, G)
Eastern Oregon University (U)
East Los Angeles College (U)
Edison State Community College (U)
EduKan (U)
Elgin Community College (U)
Elizabeth City State University (U)

Elizabethtown College (U)
Erie Community College, North Campus (U)
Erie Community College, South Campus (U)
Evergreen Valley College (U)
Fayetteville Technical Community College (U)
Florence-Darlington Technical College (N)
Florida Community College at Jacksonville (U)
Florida Gulf Coast University (U)
Florida Institute of Technology (G)
Foothill College (U)
Forrest Junior College (U)
Forsyth Technical Community College (U)
Franklin University (U)
Frank Phillips College (U)
Frederick Community College (N)
Frostburg State University (U)
Fullerton College (U)
Gardner-Webb University (G)
Gaston College (U)
Genesee Community College (U)
Georgia Southern University (U, G)
Georgia State University (G)
Glendale Community College (U)
Gogebic Community College (U)
Golden Gate University (U, G)
Governors State University (U)
Graceland University (U)
Grand Valley State University (U, G)
Hamilton College (U)
Harcourt Learning Direct Center for Degree Studies (N)
Harrisburg Area Community College (U)
Heartland Community College (U)
Hibbing Community College (N, U)
Holmes Community College (U)
Hope International University (U, G)
Horry-Georgetown Technical College (U)
Illinois Valley Community College (U)
Indiana State University (U)
Indiana University System (N)
Iowa Wesleyan College (U)

# Individual Courses Index

State University of New York College at Fredonia (U)

State University of New York College of Agriculture and Technology at Morrisville (U)

State University of New York Empire State College (U)

State University of New York Institute of Technology at Utica/Rome (U, G)

State University of West Georgia (U, G)

Stephens College (U, G)

Strayer University (U, G)

Suffolk County Community College (U)

Suffolk University (U, G)

Syracuse University (U, G)

Taft College (U)

Tarrant County College District (U)

Temple University (G)

Texas A&M University-Texarkana (U)

Texas Tech University (U)

Thomas Edison State College (U)

Tidewater Community College (U)

Tompkins Cortland Community College (U)

Trident Technical College (U)

Tri-State University (U)

Triton College (U)

Troy State University (U)

Troy State University Montgomery (U)

Tulsa Community College (U)

Tyler Junior College (N, U)

The University Alliance (U)

University College of the Fraser Valley (U)

The University of Akron (U)

The University of Alabama (U, G)

University of Alaska Anchorage (U)

University of Alaska Southeast, Ketchikan Campus (U)

University of Alaska Southeast, Sitka Campus (U)

University of Baltimore (G)

University of California, Berkeley (U)

University of California, Santa Barbara (N)

University of Colorado at Denver (N, U, G)

University of Connecticut (U, G)

University of Dallas (G)

The University of Findlay (N, U, G)

University of Great Falls (U)

University of Houston-Downtown (U)

University of Idaho (U)

University of Illinois at Springfield (U)

University of Maine (U)

University of Massachusetts Amherst (U, G)

University of Massachusetts System (U, G)

University of Michigan-Flint (U, G)

University of Minnesota, Twin Cities Campus (U)

University of Missouri-Columbia (U)

University of Missouri-Rolla (G)

University of Nevada, Reno (U)

University of New Brunswick (U)

The University of North Carolina at Chapel Hill (U)

University of North Dakota (U)

University of Northern Iowa (U)

University of Northwestern Ohio (U)

University of Notre Dame (N, G)

University of Phoenix (U, G)

University of South Alabama (G)

University of South Carolina (U)

University of South Dakota (U)

University of Southern Mississippi (U)

The University of Tennessee (U)

The University of Tennessee at Martin (U, G)

The University of Texas at Tyler (U)

The University of Texas System (U)

University of Tulsa (G)

University of Washington (U)

University of Waterloo (U)

University of Wisconsin-Eau Claire (N)

University of Wisconsin-Milwaukee (U, G)

University of Wisconsin-Parkside (G)

University of Wisconsin-Platteville (U)

University of Wisconsin-River Falls (U)

Upper Iowa University (N, U)

Victoria College (U)

Villanova University (U, G)

Vincennes University (U)

Virginia Polytechnic Institute and State University (G)

Virginia Western Community College (U)

Volunteer State Community College (U)

Walla Walla Community College (U)

Walsh College of Accountancy and Business Administration (G)

Washington State University (U)

Wayland Baptist University (G)

Weber State University (U)

Western Governors University (U)

Western Illinois University (U)

Western Nevada Community College (U)

Western Piedmont Community College (U)

Western Wisconsin Technical College (N)

Western Wyoming Community College (U)

West Los Angeles College (U)

West Virginia Northern Community College (U)

West Virginia University Institute of Technology (U)

West Virginia Wesleyan College (U)

Wichita State University (U)

Wilfrid Laurier University (U)

William Jewell College (U)

William Paterson University of New Jersey (U)

William Rainey Harper College (U)

Wisconsin Indianhead Technical College, New Richmond Campus (U)

Worcester Polytechnic Institute (G)

Wytheville Community College (U)

York College of Pennsylvania (N, U)

York Technical College (U)

York University (N, U)

## Administrative and secretarial services

Alexandria Technical College (U)

Alvin Community College (U)

Athens Technical College (U)

Atlantic Cape Community College (N)

Blackhawk Technical College (U)

Bristol Community College (N)

Brunswick Community College (U)

Carl Albert State College (U)

Carroll Community College (N)

Central Carolina Technical College (U)

Central Community College (U)

Central Virginia Community College (U)

Cincinnati State Technical and Community College (U)

Clackamas Community College (U)

Coastline Community College (U)

College of the Canyons (U)

Community College of Philadelphia (U)

Copiah-Lincoln Community College-Natchez Campus (U)

Craven Community College (U)

Del Mar College (U)

East Carolina University (U)

Eastern New Mexico University-Roswell (U)

East Los Angeles College (U)

Edison State Community College (U)

Elgin Community College (U)

Fayetteville Technical Community College (U)

Florence-Darlington Technical College (N, U)

Forrest Junior College (U)

Hamilton College (U)

Harcourt Learning Direct Center for Degree Studies (N)

Horry-Georgetown Technical College (U)

James Sprunt Community College (U)

J. Sargeant Reynolds Community College (U)

Kansas City Kansas Community College (U)

Lakeland Community College (N)

Lake Superior College (U)

Lehigh Carbon Community College (U)

Lewis and Clark Community College (U)

Lewis-Clark State College (U)

Lincoln Land Community College (U)

Maranatha Baptist Bible College (U)

Marywood University (U)

Meridian Community College (U)

# Individual Courses Index

North Carolina State University (G)
Sheridan College (U)
University of Connecticut (U)
University of Saskatchewan (N)
Washington State University (G)

## Agricultural economics
Connors State College (U)
Iowa State University of Science and
    Technology (G)
Murray State University (U)
Oklahoma State University (U)
Oregon State University (U)
Palo Alto College (U)
Texas Tech University (N, U)
The University of British Columbia (U)
University of Northwestern Ohio (U)
The University of Tennessee (U)

## Agricultural engineering
University of Idaho (U, G)
University of Missouri-Columbia (U)
Washington State University (G)

## Agricultural mechanization
Southern Illinois University Carbondale (U)

## Agricultural production workers and managers
Minnesota West Community and Technical
    College-Worthington Campus (U)
York College of Pennsylvania (N)

## Agricultural supplies and related services
Washington State University (G)

## Agriculture/agricultural sciences
Butte College (U)
Central Carolina Technical College (U)
Colorado State University (U)
Delaware Technical & Community College,
    Jack F. Owens Campus (U)
Horry-Georgetown Technical College (U)
Illinois Valley Community College (U)
Iowa State University of Science and
    Technology (U, G)
Kansas State University (U)
Louisiana State University and Agricultural
    and Mechanical College (G)
North Carolina State University (G)
NorthWest Arkansas Community College
    (U)
Oregon State University (U, G)
Purdue University (N)
Seward County Community College (U)
Stephen F. Austin State University (U)
Texas A&M University (G)
Texas Tech University (U, G)

University College of the Fraser Valley (U)
The University of British Columbia (U)
University of California, Berkeley (U)
University of Minnesota, Twin Cities
    Campus (U)
The University of North Carolina at
    Pembroke (U)
University of Saskatchewan (U)
University of Wisconsin-River Falls (N, U)
Walla Walla Community College (U)
Washington State University (G)

## Agriculture/agricultural sciences, other
Brigham Young University (U)
Danville Area Community College (U)
James Sprunt Community College (U)
Kansas State University (U)
Oklahoma State University (U)
Oregon State University (U)
University of California, Riverside (N)
University of Minnesota, Twin Cities
    Campus (U)

## Air transportation workers
Embry-Riddle Aeronautical University (G)
York University (N)

## Alcohol/drug abuse counseling
Central Michigan University (U, G)
Central Texas College (U)
The Pennsylvania State University University
    Park Campus (G)
Pitt Community College (U)
Southwest Missouri State University (N, U)
Tompkins Cortland Community College (U)
University of Cincinnati (U)

## American (United States) history
Anne Arundel Community College (U)
Bossier Parish Community College (U)
Brigham Young University (U)
Broward Community College (U)
Bucks County Community College (U)
Burlington County College (U)
Central Arizona College (U)
Central Methodist College (U)
Central Texas College (U)
Clackamas Community College (U)
Clovis Community College (U)
Coastline Community College (U)
College of DuPage (U)
Colorado Northwestern Community College
    (U)
Community College of Vermont (U)
Concordia University at Austin (N, U)
Delaware Technical & Community College,
    Jack F. Owens Campus (U)
Delaware Technical & Community College,
    Stanton/Wilmington Campus (U)

Del Mar College (U)
Delta College (U)
Eastern Kentucky University (U)
Eastern Michigan University (U)
Elizabethtown Community College (U)
Florida Community College at Jacksonville
    (U)
Floyd College (U)
Forsyth Technical Community College (N)
Frank Phillips College (U)
Fullerton College (U)
Graceland University (U)
Ivy Tech State College-Whitewater (U)
Jefferson College (U)
Johnson County Community College (U)
John Wood Community College (U)
Kansas State University (U)
Kellogg Community College (U)
Lehigh Carbon Community College (U)
Lewis and Clark Community College (U)
Manatee Community College (U)
Manchester Community College (U)
Marylhurst University (U)
Maysville Community College (U)
Mercy College (U)
Mountain Empire Community College (U)
Mountain State University (U)
Mount Allison University (U)
Mount Wachusett Community College (U)
Murray State University (U)
Northern Virginia Community College (U)
Northwestern Michigan College (U)
Northwest Missouri State University (U)
Oklahoma State University (U)
Oregon State University (U)
Palo Alto College (U)
Parkland College (U)
Park University (U)
Patrick Henry Community College (U)
The Pennsylvania State University University
    Park Campus (U)
Portland Community College (U)
Prairie Bible College (G)
Roosevelt University (U)
Saddleback College (U)
St. Petersburg College (U)
St. Petersburg College (U)
Sam Houston State University (U)
San Diego State University (U)
Sauk Valley Community College (U)
Southeast Community College, Lincoln
    Campus (U)
Southwest Missouri State University (U)
State University of New York Empire State
    College (U)
State University of West Georgia (U, G)
Suffolk County Community College (U)
Texas Christian University (U)

## American (United States) history (continued)

Texas Tech University (U)
Thomas Edison State College (U)
Triton College (U)
Tyler Junior College (U)
University of Alaska Southeast, Ketchikan Campus (U)
University of Arkansas (U)
University of Colorado at Denver (U)
University of Delaware (U)
The University of Iowa (U, G)
University of Minnesota, Twin Cities Campus (U)
University of Nevada, Reno (U)
University of North Alabama (U)
The University of North Carolina at Chapel Hill (U)
The University of North Carolina at Greensboro (U)
University of Northwestern Ohio (U)
The University of Tennessee (U)
University of Waterloo (U)
University of Wisconsin-Stevens Point (U, G)
Upper Iowa University (N, U)
Virginia Polytechnic Institute and State University (U)
Washington State University (U)
Weber State University (U)
Western Washington University (U)
West Virginia Northern Community College (U)
West Virginia Wesleyan College (U)
Wytheville Community College (U)

## American literature (United States)

Alvin Community College (U)
Amarillo College (U)
Arizona State University (U)
Ashland Community College (U)
Brigham Young University (U)
Calvin College (U)
Columbia College (U)
Copiah-Lincoln Community College-Natchez Campus (U)
Delaware Technical & Community College, Stanton/Wilmington Campus (U)
Del Mar College (U)
Drake University (U)
Elgin Community College (U)
Elizabethtown College (U)
Fayetteville Technical Community College (U)
Ferris State University (U)
Gaston College (U)
Harrisburg Area Community College (U)
Heartland Community College (U)
Horry-Georgetown Technical College (U)

Jacksonville State University (U)
Kansas City Kansas Community College (U)
Lehigh Carbon Community College (U)
McLennan Community College (U)
Mendocino College (U)
Meridian Community College (U)
Middle Tennessee State University (U)
Minot State University (U)
Mohawk Valley Community College (U)
Mt. Hood Community College (U)
Naropa University (U)
North Carolina State University (U)
Northeastern State University (U)
North Idaho College (U)
North Seattle Community College (U)
Northwest Iowa Community College (U)
Ohio University (U)
Oklahoma City Community College (U)
Oregon State University (U)
Palo Alto College (U)
Park University (U)
Pulaski Technical College (U)
Rappahannock Community College (U)
Raritan Valley Community College (U)
Rowan-Cabarrus Community College (U)
San Jacinto College North Campus (U)
San Joaquin Delta College (U)
Santa Barbara City College (U)
Seward County Community College (U)
Taylor University, World Wide Campus (U)
Texas Tech University (U)
Tulsa Community College (U)
Tyler Junior College (U)
The University of Alabama (U)
University of Alaska Fairbanks (U)
University of Colorado at Denver (N, U)
University of Connecticut (U)
University of Illinois at Urbana-Champaign (U)
University of Maine at Machias (U)
University of Massachusetts System (U)
University of Missouri-Columbia (U)
University of South Carolina Sumter (U)
University of Washington (U)
University of Waterloo (U)
Villanova University (U)
Virginia Western Community College (U)
Walters State Community College (U)
Western Washington University (U)
William Paterson University of New Jersey (U)
Yuba College (U)

## American studies/civilization

Bellevue Community College (U)
Marylhurst University (U)
Seattle Central Community College (U)
Southwestern Community College (U)

University of Denver (U, G)
The University of Iowa (U)
University of Minnesota, Twin Cities Campus (U)
University of Nevada, Reno (U)
University of North Alabama (U, G)
The University of North Carolina at Chapel Hill (U)
Washington State University (U)

## Analytical chemistry

Illinois Institute of Technology (G)

## Anatomy

American Academy of Nutrition, College of Nutrition (U)
Central Arizona College (U)
Central Methodist College (U)
Century Community and Technical College (N)
Coastline Community College (U)
Community Hospital of Roanoke Valley-College of Health Sciences (U)
Florida Community College at Jacksonville (U)
Floyd College (U)
Forsyth Technical Community College (N)
Hocking College (U)
John Wood Community College (U)
Mountain State University (U)
Parkland College (U)
St. Petersburg College (U)
Southern Illinois University Carbondale (U)
Southwestern Community College (U)
Tyler Junior College (U)
West Virginia Wesleyan College (U)

## Animal sciences

Auburn University (U)
Calvin College (U)
Colorado State University (U)
James Sprunt Community College (U)
Kansas State University (U)
Manor College (U)
Minnesota West Community and Technical College-Worthington Campus (U)
Mississippi State University (U)
Oklahoma State University (U)
The Pennsylvania State University University Park Campus (U)
Sampson Community College (U)
State University of New York College of Technology at Canton (U)
Texas Tech University (G)
The University of British Columbia (U)
University of Connecticut (U)
University of Delaware (U)
University of Maine (G)

University of Missouri-Columbia (U, G)
University of Vermont (U)

## Anthropology

Anne Arundel Community College (U)
Bellevue Community College (U)
Blinn College (U)
Bridgewater State College (U)
Brigham Young University (U)
Bristol Community College (U)
Broward Community College (U)
Burlington County College (U)
Butte College (U)
California State University, Chico (U)
Calvin College (U)
Carleton University (U)
Central Arizona College (U)
Central Texas College (U)
Central Wyoming College (U)
Cerro Coso Community College (U)
Chaminade University of Honolulu (U)
Charter Oak State College (U)
Citrus College (U)
Clackamas Community College (U)
Coastline Community College (U)
College of DuPage (U)
College of San Mateo (U)
College of the Canyons (U)
Colorado Community College Online (U)
Colorado Electronic Community College (U)
Colorado Northwestern Community College (U)
Columbia Basin College (U)
Columbia International University (N, G)
Community College of Philadelphia (U)
Concordia University (U)
Concordia University Wisconsin (U)
Connecticut State University System (U, G)
Cumberland County College (U)
Cuyamaca College (U)
Danville Area Community College (U)
Eastern Kentucky University (U)
Eastern Oregon University (U)
Edison State Community College (U)
EduKan (U)
Elgin Community College (U)
Elizabethtown College (U)
Everett Community College (U)
Evergreen Valley College (U)
Ferris State University (U)
Florida Community College at Jacksonville (U)
Florida Keys Community College (U)
Foothill College (U)
Forsyth Technical Community College (U)
Genesee Community College (U)
Glendale Community College (U)

Governors State University (U, G)
Grand Rapids Community College (U)
Hamline University (U)
Harrisburg Area Community College (U)
Haywood Community College (U)
Honolulu Community College (U)
Hope International University (U)
Indiana Higher Education Telecommunication System (U)
Indian River Community College (U)
Iowa Wesleyan College (U)
Jacksonville State University (U)
Johnson County Community College (U)
John Wood Community College (U)
Kansas City Kansas Community College (U)
Kapiolani Community College (U)
Kellogg Community College (U)
Kentucky State University (U)
Lehigh Carbon Community College (U)
Long Beach City College (U)
Marshall University (U)
Mary Baldwin College (U)
Marylhurst University (U)
Mendocino College (U)
Metropolitan State University (U)
Montgomery County Community College (U)
Mott Community College (U)
Mt. San Antonio College (U)
Murray State University (U)
Naropa University (U, G)
Nassau Community College (U)
New School University (U)
New York Institute of Technology (U)
Northampton County Area Community College (U)
North Arkansas College (U)
North Carolina State University (U)
North Central Michigan College (U)
North Country Community College (U)
Northeastern State University (U)
Northern Kentucky University (U)
North Idaho College (U)
North Seattle Community College (U)
Northwestern Michigan College (U)
Ohio University (U)
Ohlone College (U)
Oklahoma State University (U)
Olympic College (U)
Oregon State University (U)
Parkland College (U)
Pasco-Hernando Community College (U)
The Pennsylvania State University University Park Campus (U)
Pierce College (U)
Pikes Peak Community College (U)
Plattsburgh State University of New York (U)

Portland Community College (U)
Prairie Bible College (U, G)
Randolph Community College (U)
Raritan Valley Community College (U)
Rend Lake College (U)
The Richard Stockton College of New Jersey (U)
Rio Hondo College (U)
Roger Williams University (U)
Saddleback College (U)
Saint Charles Community College (U)
St. Cloud State University (U)
St. Petersburg College (U)
Sam Houston State University (U)
Santa Rosa Junior College (U)
Seattle Central Community College (U)
Seminole Community College (U)
Shawnee State University (U)
Southeast Arkansas College (U)
Southeast Community College, Lincoln Campus (U)
South Puget Sound Community College (U)
Southwestern College (U)
Southwest Missouri State University (U)
State University of New York College at Fredonia (U)
Strayer University (U)
Syracuse University (U)
Tacoma Community College (U)
Temple University (U)
Texas Tech University (U)
Thomas Edison State College (U)
Triton College (U)
University College of the Fraser Valley (U)
University of Alaska Fairbanks (U)
University of Alaska Southeast, Ketchikan Campus (U)
University of Arkansas at Little Rock (U)
University of California, Berkeley (U)
University of Colorado at Denver (N, U)
University of Connecticut (U, G)
University of Guelph (U)
University of Houston (U)
University of Idaho (U)
University of Illinois at Urbana-Champaign (U)
The University of Iowa (U, G)
University of Kansas (U)
University of La Verne (U)
University of Maine (G)
University of Manitoba (U)
University of Minnesota, Twin Cities Campus (U)
University of Missouri-Columbia (U)
University of Nevada, Reno (U)
University of New Mexico (U)
The University of North Carolina at Chapel Hill (U)

*Anthropology (continued)*
University of North Texas (U)
University of Oklahoma (U)
University of Pennsylvania (U)
University of Pittsburgh (U)
University of Saskatchewan (U)
University of Southern Mississippi (U)
The University of Tennessee (U)
The University of Texas at Tyler (U)
University of Utah (U)
University of Waterloo (U)
University of Wisconsin-Stevens Point (U)
Walla Walla Community College (U)
Walters State Community College (U)
Washington State University (U)
Weber State University (U)
Western Connecticut State University (U)
Western Michigan University (U)
Western Washington University (U)
Western Wyoming Community College (U)
Wichita State University (U)
Wilfrid Laurier University (U)
William Paterson University of New Jersey (U)
Yuba College (U)

## Apparel and accessories marketing operations
Kean University (U)
Stephen F. Austin State University (U)
University of Connecticut (U)
University of North Texas (U, G)

## Applied mathematics
Alvin Community College (U)
American College of Computer & Information Sciences (U)
Bossier Parish Community College (U)
Butte College (U)
California Polytechnic State University, San Luis Obispo (U)
Calvin College (U)
Central Virginia Community College (U)
Century Community and Technical College (N)
Columbia University (N, G)
Danville Area Community College (U)
Elgin Community College (U)
Embry-Riddle Aeronautical University (U)
Eugene Bible College (U)
Garland County Community College (U)
Grand Rapids Community College (U)
Harrisburg Area Community College (U)
Hibbing Community College (U)
Jacksonville State University (U)
Judson College (U)
Kennesaw State University (U)
Lakeland Community College (U)

Lord Fairfax Community College (U)
Lynn University (U)
Mary Baldwin College (U)
Meridian Community College (U)
Mississippi State University (N, U)
Pierce College (U)
Raritan Valley Community College (U)
Red Rocks Community College (U)
The Richard Stockton College of New Jersey (U)
San Jacinto College North Campus (U)
Santa Barbara City College (U)
Southeast Community College, Lincoln Campus (U)
Stanly Community College (U)
Tacoma Community College (U)
Taft College (U)
Tarleton State University (U)
University of Connecticut (U)
University of Waterloo (U)
Volunteer State Community College (U)
Western Governors University (U)
Western Wyoming Community College (U)
William Paterson University of New Jersey (U)
York College of Pennsylvania (N)

## Archaeology
Beulah Heights Bible College (U)
Elgin Community College (U)
Foothill College (U)
Northwestern College (U)
University of California, Los Angeles (G)
University of Saskatchewan (U)

## Architectural engineering
Boston Architectural Center (N, U, G)

## Architectural environmental design
The Pennsylvania State University University Park Campus (N, G)

## Architecture and related programs, other
Calvin College (U)

## Architecture
Boston Architectural Center (N, U, G)
Louisiana Tech University (U)
Temple University (U)
Texas Tech University (N, G)
Universite de Montreal (U)
University of California, Berkeley (U)
University of Colorado at Denver (N)
Virginia Polytechnic Institute and State University (N)

## Area studies
Taylor University, World Wide Campus (U)

## Area, ethnic and cultural studies, other
Antioch University McGregor (G)
California State University, Chico (U)
Central Wyoming College (U)
Drake University (U)
Elgin Community College (U)
Foothill College (U)
Hibbing Community College (U)
John F. Kennedy University (U, G)
Middle Tennessee State University (U)
Naropa University (U, G)
North Idaho College (U)
North Seattle Community College (U)
Oregon State University (U)
Plattsburgh State University of New York (U)
Providence College and Theological Seminary (G)
Raritan Valley Community College (U)
Seminole Community College (U)
State University of New York College at Cortland (U)
State University of New York College at Fredonia (U)
Strayer University (U)
Temple University (U)
University of Colorado at Denver (N)
University of Connecticut (U)
University of Massachusetts Boston (U)
University of Missouri-Columbia (U)
University of Utah (U)
University of Waterloo (U)
Vincennes University (U)
Western Connecticut State University (U)
Western Governors University (U)

## Army R.O.T.C.
John Wood Community College (U)
North Georgia College & State University (U)
University of Wyoming (U)

## Art history, criticism and conservation
Acadia University (U)
Arizona State University (G)
Atlantic University (N, G)
Bellevue Community College (U)
Blinn College (U)
Bossier Parish Community College (U)
Brigham Young University (U)
Bucks County Community College (U)
Burlington County College (U)
Central Arizona College (U)
Central Texas College (U)
Charter Oak State College (U)
Clovis Community College (U)
College of Southern Maryland (U)
College of The Albemarle (U)

Colorado Northwestern Community College (U)
Columbia Basin College (U)
Columbia College (U)
Concordia University Wisconsin (U)
Connors State College (U)
Duquesne University (U)
Eastern Kentucky University (U)
Edison State Community College (U)
Foothill College (U)
Genesee Community College (U)
Governors State University (U, G)
Illinois Eastern Community Colleges, Wabash Valley College (U)
John Wood Community College (U)
Lakeland Community College (U)
Lehigh Carbon Community College (U)
Lewis and Clark Community College (U)
Manatee Community College (U)
Marywood University (U)
Mayland Community College (U)
Mercy College (U)
Metropolitan Community College (U)
Montana State University-Billings (U)
Mott Community College (U)
Mountain Empire Community College (U)
Mountain State University (U)
North Arkansas College (U)
North Country Community College (U)
Northern Arizona University (U)
Northern Virginia Community College (U)
Parkland College (U)
Patrick Henry Community College (U)
Pennsylvania College of Technology (U)
The Pennsylvania State University University Park Campus (U)
Red Rocks Community College (U)
Richland Community College (U)
St. Petersburg College (U)
Sinclair Community College (U)
Southwestern Community College (U)
Southwest Texas State University (U)
State University of West Georgia (U)
Suffolk County Community College (U)
Texas Christian University (U)
Thomas Edison State College (U)
Triton College (U)
Tyler Junior College (U)
University of Alaska Fairbanks (U)
University of Alaska Southeast, Ketchikan Campus (U)
University of Central Oklahoma (U, G)
University of Minnesota, Twin Cities Campus (U)
The University of North Carolina at Chapel Hill (U)
University of North Texas (U)
University of South Dakota (U)

The University of Texas of the Permian Basin (U)
University of Utah (U)
Upper Iowa University (N, U)
Virginia Polytechnic Institute and State University (U)
Weber State University (U)

## Asian studies
Connecticut State University System (U, G)
Mount Allison University (U)
Seattle Central Community College (U)
Suffolk County Community College (U)
Thomas Edison State College (U)
University of Illinois at Urbana-Champaign (U)
The University of Iowa (U, G)
University of Maine (U)
Washington State University (U)
Western Washington University (U)

## Astronomy
Acadia University (U)
Amarillo College (U)
Bakersfield College (U)
Brigham Young University (U)
Calvin College (U)
Carroll Community College (U)
Central Michigan University (U)
Central Virginia Community College (U)
Coastline Community College (U)
College of Southern Maryland (U)
College of the Canyons (U)
Colorado Community College Online (U)
Cuyamaca College (U)
Danville Area Community College (U)
EduKan (U)
Elgin Community College (U)
Evergreen Valley College (U)
Florida Keys Community College (U)
Georgia Perimeter College (U)
Grand Rapids Community College (U)
Honolulu Community College (U)
Horry-Georgetown Technical College (U)
Illinois Eastern Community Colleges, Frontier Community College (U)
Illinois Eastern Community Colleges, Lincoln Trail College (U)
Illinois Eastern Community Colleges, Olney Central College (U)
Illinois Eastern Community Colleges, Wabash Valley College (U)
Indiana Higher Education Telecommunication System (U)
Indian River Community College (U)
John Wood Community College (U)
Judson College (U)
Lehigh Carbon Community College (U)

Lewis and Clark Community College (U)
Long Beach City College (U)
Lord Fairfax Community College (U)
Middle Tennessee State University (U)
Mineral Area College (U)
Mississippi State University (U)
Moraine Valley Community College (U)
Mountain State University (U)
Mt. Hood Community College (U)
Nassau Community College (U)
National American University (U)
Northampton County Area Community College (U)
Northeast State Technical Community College (U)
North Seattle Community College (U)
Northwestern College (U)
Oklahoma City Community College (U)
Pierce College (U)
Pueblo Community College (U)
Quinebaug Valley Community College (U)
Rowan-Cabarrus Community College (U)
St. Clair County Community College (U)
Schenectady County Community College (U)
Seminole Community College (U)
Southwestern College (U)
Spokane Falls Community College (U)
Tidewater Community College (U)
Tyler Junior College (U)
Universite de Montreal (U)
The University of Alabama (U)
University of California, Berkeley (U)
University of Great Falls (U)
University of Massachusetts Dartmouth (U)
University of Massachusetts System (U)
University of Minnesota, Twin Cities Campus (U)
University of Missouri-Columbia (U)
University of Nebraska at Omaha (U)
University of New Mexico (U)
The University of North Carolina at Greensboro (U)
University of Oklahoma (U)
University of Oregon (U)
University of South Carolina (U)
University of Waterloo (U)
University of Wisconsin-River Falls (U)
University of Wyoming (U)
Volunteer State Community College (U)
Wichita State University (U)
William Rainey Harper College (U)

## Atmospheric sciences and meteorology
Iowa State University of Science and Technology (U, G)
Jacksonville State University (U)
Miami-Dade Community College (U)

# Individual Courses Index

Oklahoma City Community College (U)
Ozarks Technical Community College (U)
The Pennsylvania State University University
    Park Campus (U)
Sandhills Community College (U)
Santa Barbara City College (U)
Shasta College (U)
Southern Arkansas University Tech (U)
Southwest Baptist University (U)
Spokane Falls Community College (U)
State University of New York College of
    Technology at Alfred (U)
Taft College (U)
Taylor University, World Wide Campus (U)
The University of Alabama (U)
University of Connecticut (U, G)
University of Massachusetts System (G)
University of Pennsylvania (U)
University of Vermont (N)
University of Waterloo (U)
University of Wisconsin Colleges (U)
Volunteer State Community College (U)
Western Wyoming Community College (U)

## Biological sciences/life sciences, other

Athens Technical College (U)
Bossier Parish Community College (U)
Calvin College (U)
Capital Community College (U)
Central Community College (U)
Coastline Community College (U)
Columbia College (U)
Concordia University (U)
Danville Area Community College (U)
EduKan (U)
Ferris State University (U)
Gaston College (U)
Illinois Institute of Technology (U, G)
Immaculata College (U)
Indiana State University (G)
John F. Kennedy University (G)
Lewis and Clark Community College (U)
Louisiana Tech University (U)
Lynn University (U)
Meridian Community College (U)
Mineral Area College (U)
Northampton County Area Community
    College (U)
Northern Kentucky University (U)
Southeast Community College, Beatrice
    Campus (U)
Southwest Texas State University (U)
State University of New York College of
    Technology at Alfred (U)
University College of the Fraser Valley (U)
University of Connecticut (U)
University of Waterloo (U)
University of Wisconsin-Parkside (U)

Villanova University (U)
West Virginia Wesleyan College (U)

## Biology, general

Acadia University (U)
Alvin Community College (U)
Amarillo College (U)
American Academy of Nutrition, College of
    Nutrition (U)
American College of Computer &
    Information Sciences (U)
American College of Prehospital Medicine
    (U)
American River College (U)
Anne Arundel Community College (U)
Bellevue Community College (U)
Blinn College (U)
Blue River Community College (U)
Brevard Community College (U)
Brigham Young University (U)
Broward Community College (U)
Bucks County Community College (U)
Burlington County College (U)
Butte College (U)
Caldwell Community College and Technical
    Institute (U)
California State University, Bakersfield (U)
Calvin College (U)
Capital Community College (U)
Carleton University (U)
Carroll Community College (U)
Cayuga County Community College (U)
Cedarville University (U)
Central Methodist College (U)
Central Texas College (U)
Central Virginia Community College (U)
Central Wyoming College (U)
Charter Oak State College (U)
Chattanooga State Technical Community
    College (U)
Clackamas Community College (U)
Clovis Community College (U)
Coastline Community College (U)
College of DuPage (U)
College of Mount St. Joseph (U)
The College of St. Scholastica (U)
College of Southern Maryland (U)
College of the Southwest (U)
Colorado Community College Online (U)
Colorado Electronic Community College
    (U)
Colorado Northwestern Community College
    (U)
Community College of Philadelphia (U)
Concordia University at Austin (N, U)
Copiah-Lincoln Community College (U)
Copiah-Lincoln Community College-
    Natchez Campus (U)

Craven Community College (U)
Cumberland County College (U)
Dallas County Community College District
    (U)
Dawson Community College (U)
Delaware Technical & Community College,
    Jack F. Owens Campus (U)
Del Mar College (U)
Delta College (U)
East Central College (U)
Eastern Kentucky University (U)
Eastern New Mexico University-Roswell (U)
Eastern Oregon University (U)
Eastern Wyoming College (U)
Edison State Community College (U)
Elgin Community College (U)
Erie Community College, North Campus
    (U)
Eugene Bible College (U)
Ferris State University (U)
Finger Lakes Community College (U)
Florence-Darlington Technical College (U)
Florida Community College at Jacksonville
    (U)
Frank Phillips College (U)
Fullerton College (U)
Garland County Community College (U)
Genesee Community College (U)
Graceland University (U)
Griggs University (U)
Harvard University (N, U, G)
Hillsborough Community College (U)
Indian River Community College (U)
Iowa State University of Science and
    Technology (U)
Iowa Western Community College (U, G)
Ivy Tech State College-North Central (U)
Jefferson College (U)
Johnson County Community College (U)
J. Sargeant Reynolds Community College
    (U)
Kansas City Kansas Community College (U)
Kapiolani Community College (U)
Lakeland Community College (U)
Lake Michigan College (U)
Lehigh Carbon Community College (U)
LeTourneau University (U)
Lewis and Clark Community College (U)
Liberty University (U)
Long Beach City College (U)
Longview Community College (U)
Lord Fairfax Community College (U)
Loyola University Chicago (U)
Lynn University (U)
Malone College (U)
Manatee Community College (U)
Maple Woods Community College (U)
Mary Baldwin College (U)

*Biology, general (continued)*

Marylhurst University (U)
Maui Community College (U)
Maysville Community College (U)
Memorial University of Newfoundland (U)
Mercy College (U)
Metropolitan Community College (U)
Miami-Dade Community College (U)
Minnesota West Community and Technical
   College-Worthington Campus (U)
MiraCosta College (U)
Mississippi State University (U)
Missouri Southern State College (U)
Missouri Western State College (U)
Montana State University-Billings (U)
Montana State University-Bozeman (G)
Montcalm Community College (U)
Montgomery County Community College
   (U)
Mott Community College (U)
Mountain Empire Community College (U)
Mountain State University (U)
Mt. San Antonio College (U)
Mount Wachusett Community College (U)
New Mexico Institute of Mining and
   Technology (U)
Northampton County Area Community
   College (U)
Northeastern State University (U)
Northern Arizona University (U)
Northern Virginia Community College (U)
North Idaho College (U)
North Iowa Area Community College (U)
Northwestern Michigan College (U)
Ohio University (U)
Okaloosa-Walton Community College (U)
Oklahoma City Community College (U)
Oregon State University (U)
Palo Alto College (U)
Parkland College (U)
Park University (U)
Pasco-Hernando Community College (U)
Pennsylvania College of Technology (U)
The Pennsylvania State University University
   Park Campus (U)
Penn Valley Community College (U)
Pierce College (U)
Pitt Community College (U)
Portland Community College (U)
Pueblo Community College (U)
Pulaski Technical College (U)
Rochester Community and Technical
   College (U)
Roger Williams University (U)
Saint Charles Community College (U)
St. Cloud State University (U)
St. Petersburg College (U)
Sauk Valley Community College (U)

Seward County Community College (U)
Shawnee State University (U)
Shippensburg University of Pennsylvania (U)
Skidmore College (U)
Southeast Missouri State University (U)
Southern Illinois University Carbondale (U)
Southern University and Agricultural and
   Mechanical College (U)
South Piedmont Community College (U)
Southwestern Assemblies of God University
   (U)
Southwestern Community College (U)
Southwest Missouri State University (U)
Southwest Texas State University (U)
Spoon River College (U)
Stanly Community College (U)
State University of New York College at
   Fredonia (U, G)
State University of New York College of
   Technology at Alfred (U)
State University of New York Empire State
   College (U)
Stephens College (U)
Tacoma Community College (U)
Tarrant County College District (U)
Taylor University, World Wide Campus (U)
Tennessee Temple University (U)
Texas Christian University (U)
Thomas Edison State College (U)
Treasure Valley Community College (U)
Triton College (U)
Tyler Junior College (U)
The University of Akron (U)
The University of Alabama (U)
University of Alaska Anchorage (U)
University of Alaska Fairbanks (U)
University of Alaska Southeast, Sitka
   Campus (U)
University of California, Berkeley (U)
University of Colorado at Boulder (N)
University of Colorado at Denver (N, U)
University of Connecticut (U, G)
University of Delaware (U)
University of Florida (U)
University of Guelph (U)
University of Idaho (U)
University of Illinois at Springfield (U)
University of Kansas (U)
University of La Verne (U)
University of Maine (U)
University of Massachusetts Dartmouth (U)
University of Massachusetts System (U)
The University of Memphis (U)
University of Minnesota, Twin Cities
   Campus (U)
University of New Brunswick (U)
The University of North Carolina at Chapel
   Hill (U)

University of North Dakota (U)
University of Northern Colorado (U)
University of South Dakota (U)
University of Southern Indiana (U)
University of Southern Mississippi (U)
The University of Texas at Arlington (U)
The University of Texas at Tyler (U)
The University of Texas System (U)
University of Utah (U)
University of Waterloo (U)
University of Wisconsin Colleges (U)
University of Wisconsin-Extension (U)
University of Wisconsin-Parkside (U)
Upper Iowa University (N, U)
Virginia Polytechnic Institute and State
   University (U)
Volunteer State Community College (U)
Walla Walla Community College (U)
Washington State University (U)
Western Governors University (U)
Western Illinois University (G)
Western Nevada Community College (U)
Western Washington University (U)
West Shore Community College (U)
West Virginia Northern Community College
   (U)
West Virginia University (G)
Wichita State University (U)
Wilfrid Laurier University (U)
Wytheville Community College (U)

## Botany

Arizona State University (U)
Brigham Young University (U)
Calvin College (U)
Eastern Oregon University (U)
Elgin Community College (U)
Florence-Darlington Technical College (U)
Mississippi State University (U)
Mountain State University (U)
Oregon State University (U)
University of California, Berkeley (U)
University of Massachusetts System (U)
University of Saskatchewan (N)
Weber State University (U)
William Paterson University of New Jersey
   (U)

## Business administration and management

Adirondack Community College (U)
Albuquerque Technical Vocational Institute
   (U)
Alvin Community College (U)
The American College (U, G)
American College of Computer &
   Information Sciences (U)
American Graduate University (G)

## Business and personal services marketing operations

University of Colorado at Denver (N, G)
The University of Findlay (N)
The University of North Carolina at Pembroke (U)
Walla Walla Community College (N)

## Business communications

Adirondack Community College (U)
Alvin Community College (U)
American Graduate University (G)
American River College (U)
Aquinas College (U)
Atlantic Cape Community College (N)
Berkshire Community College (N)
Bridgewater State College (U)
Bristol Community College (N)
Bryant and Stratton Online (U)
Caldwell Community College and Technical Institute (U)
California National University for Advanced Studies (U)
Chadron State College (U)
Champlain College (U)
Clackamas Community College (U)
Coastline Community College (U)
College of Southern Maryland (U)
College of the Canyons (U)
Colorado Christian University (U)
Concordia College (U)
East Carolina University (U)
Edison State Community College (U)
Elgin Community College (U)
Elizabeth City State University (U)
Fairmont State College (U)
Finger Lakes Community College (U)
Forrest Junior College (U)
Frederick Community College (N)
Gannon University (U)
George Mason University (U)
Grand Rapids Community College (U)
Holmes Community College (U)
Honolulu Community College (U)
Hope International University (U, G)
Horry-Georgetown Technical College (U)
Illinois Valley Community College (U)
Jacksonville State University (G)
James Sprunt Community College (U)
Jones College (U)
Judson College (U)
Lakeland Community College (N)
Lake Superior College (U)
Lehigh Carbon Community College (U)
Liberty University (G)
Lord Fairfax Community College (N)
Lynn University (U)
Manchester Community College (U)
Meridian Community College (U)
Middle Tennessee State University (U)

Midwestern State University (U)
Mississippi State University (N)
Montana State University-Billings (U)
Morehead State University (U)
Northampton County Area Community College (U)
North Arkansas College (U)
North Carolina Community College System (U)
North Country Community College (U)
Northern Essex Community College (U)
NorthWest Arkansas Community College (U)
Northwestern Michigan College (U)
Okaloosa-Walton Community College (U)
Oklahoma City Community College (U)
Oklahoma State University (U)
Old Dominion University (U)
Olympic College (U)
Pasco-Hernando Community College (N)
The Pennsylvania State University University Park Campus (N, U)
Pierce College (U)
Pikes Peak Community College (U)
Prairie State College (U)
Radford University (G)
Rappahannock Community College (U)
Richland Community College (U)
Rockingham Community College (N)
Roosevelt University (U)
Royal Roads University (G)
St. Clair County Community College (U)
San Jacinto College North Campus (U)
Santa Rosa Junior College (U)
Schiller International University (U)
Southeast Arkansas College (U)
Southeast Missouri State University (U)
Spring Arbor University (G)
Tompkins Cortland Community College (U)
Tyler Junior College (U)
University College of the Fraser Valley (U)
University of Colorado at Denver (N, G)
University of Connecticut (U)
The University of Findlay (G)
University of Massachusetts Lowell (U)
University of Massachusetts System (U)
University of Nevada, Reno (N)
The University of North Carolina at Chapel Hill (U)
University of Notre Dame (N, G)
University of Oklahoma (U)
University of Phoenix (N)
University of Washington (U)
University of Wisconsin-Extension (U)
University of Wisconsin-Stevens Point (N, G)
Vermont Technical College (U)
Western Governors University (N, U)

West Virginia Wesleyan College (U)
William Paterson University of New Jersey (N)
William Rainey Harper College (U)
York University (U)

## Business information and data processing services

Albuquerque Technical Vocational Institute (U)
Bevill State Community College (U)
Blinn College (U)
Bristol Community College (N, U)
Carl Albert State College (U)
Centralia College (N, U)
Central Washington University (U)
Chadron State College (U, G)
Cincinnati State Technical and Community College (U)
Clackamas Community College (U)
Coastal Carolina Community College (N)
Coastline Community College (U)
Community College of Rhode Island (U)
Danville Area Community College (U)
Drake University (U)
East Los Angeles College (U)
Edison State Community College (U)
Elgin Community College (U)
Forrest Junior College (U)
Fresno City College (U)
Fullerton College (U)
Haywood Community College (U)
Hope International University (G)
Jacksonville State University (U, G)
Jones College (U)
Lakeland Community College (N)
Lewis-Clark State College (U)
Lord Fairfax Community College (N)
Marion Technical College (U)
Meridian Community College (U)
Minot State University (U, G)
Mississippi State University (N)
Mount Wachusett Community College (U)
New York Institute of Technology (G)
North Arkansas College (U)
North Carolina Central University (U)
Northcentral University (U, G)
Northern Essex Community College (N)
Northern Kentucky University (U)
Northwestern Michigan College (U)
Old Dominion University (U)
Owens Community College (U)
Patrick Henry Community College (U)
Rockingham Community College (N)
Roosevelt University (U)
Royal Roads University (G)
Saddleback College (U)
San Jacinto College North Campus (U)

## Business quantitative methods and management science

## Business

# Individual Courses Index

University of Alaska Fairbanks (U)
University of California, Berkeley (U)
University of Cincinnati (N, U)
University of Colorado at Denver (N, G)
The University of Findlay (N, U, G)
University of Idaho (U)
University of Illinois at Chicago (G)
University of Maine (G)
University of Maine at Machias (U)
University of Massachusetts Lowell (U)
University of Massachusetts System (U)
University of New Hampshire (N)
The University of North Carolina at Pembroke (U, G)
University of Notre Dame (N, G)
University of Pennsylvania (N)
University of Phoenix (N)
University of St. Francis (U)
University of South Carolina Spartanburg (U)
The University of Tennessee at Martin (U, G)
The University of Texas at Tyler (U)
University of Tulsa (G)
University of Wisconsin-Extension (U)
University of Wisconsin-Madison (G)
University of Wisconsin-Parkside (G)
University of Wisconsin-Platteville (G)
University of Wisconsin-River Falls (N, U)
Valdosta State University (U)
Vanguard University of Southern California (U)
Volunteer State Community College (U)
Wake Technical Community College (U)
Walla Walla Community College (U)
Walters State Community College (U)
Wayne Community College (U)
Weber State University (U)
Western Governors University (N, U)
Western Illinois University (U)
Western Iowa Tech Community College (N, U)
Western Piedmont Community College (U)
Western Wyoming Community College (U)
West Los Angeles College (U)
Worcester State College (N)
York Technical College (U)

## Business/managerial economics

American Graduate University (G)
American River College (U)
Anne Arundel Community College (U)
Berkeley College (U)
Bridgewater State College (U)
California National University for Advanced Studies (U)
Chadron State College (U, G)
Corning Community College (U)

Drake University (U)
Elgin Community College (U)
Elizabeth City State University (U)
Florida Institute of Technology (G)
Forrest Junior College (U)
Frederick Community College (N)
Gardner-Webb University (G)
Harrisburg Area Community College (U)
Hope International University (U, G)
Jacksonville State University (U, G)
Kean University (U)
Lakeland Community College (N)
Lewis and Clark Community College (U)
Lincoln Christian College (U)
Lord Fairfax Community College (N)
Mississippi State University (N)
Mohawk Valley Community College (U)
Morehead State University (U)
Northampton County Area Community College (U)
North Carolina Community College System (U)
Northwest Iowa Community College (U)
Oklahoma City Community College (U)
Old Dominion University (U)
Olympic College (U)
The Pennsylvania State University University Park Campus (G)
Radford University (G)
Rockingham Community College (N)
Rowan-Cabarrus Community College (U)
Schiller International University (U, G)
Sheridan College (U)
Southeast Arkansas College (U)
Spring Arbor University (G)
State University of New York at Oswego (U)
Tarleton State University (U)
Taylor University, World Wide Campus (U)
Trident Technical College (U)
University of Colorado at Denver (N, G)
University of Connecticut (U)
The University of Findlay (U, G)
University of Great Falls (U)
University of Missouri-Columbia (U)
University of Notre Dame (N, G)
University of Tulsa (G)
University of Wisconsin-Parkside (G)
Villanova University (U, G)
Western Piedmont Community College (U)
York University (U)

## Canadian studies

Carleton University (U)
Memorial University of Newfoundland (U)
The University of British Columbia (U)
University of Waterloo (U)
Western Washington University (U)

## Carpenters

Florence-Darlington Technical College (N, U)

## Cell and molecular biology

Calvin College (U)
Illinois Institute of Technology (U)
Oregon State University (U)
University of Connecticut (U)
University of Massachusetts Boston (U)
University of Pennsylvania (U)
University of Waterloo (U)
University of Wisconsin-Parkside (U)

## Cell biology

Edison State Community College (U)
University of Colorado at Denver (U)
University of Guelph (U)

## Chemical engineering

Arizona State University (U, G)
Brevard Community College (U)
Brigham Young University (U)
Calvin College (U)
Colorado State University (G)
Illinois Institute of Technology (G)
Kansas State University (G)
Michigan State University (N, U, G)
Mississippi State University (G)
New Jersey Institute of Technology (G)
New Mexico Institute of Mining and Technology (U, G)
North Carolina State University (G)
Oklahoma State University (U, G)
Texas Tech University (G)
The University of Alabama (G)
The University of Arizona (G)
University of Connecticut (U, G)
University of Delaware (U, G)
University of Idaho (U, G)
University of Massachusetts Amherst (N, G)
University of New Mexico (U, G)
University of North Dakota (U)
Virginia Polytechnic Institute and State University (U)

## Chemistry

Acadia University (U)
Bevill State Community College (U)
Brigham Young University (U)
Brunswick Community College (U)
Calvin College (U)
Cape Fear Community College (U)
Central Oregon Community College (U)
Central Virginia Community College (U)
Central Washington University (U)
Central Wyoming College (U)
Clackamas Community College (U)
Coastline Community College (U)

*Chemistry (continued)*

College of the Canyons (U)
Colorado Community College Online (U)
Colorado Electronic Community College (U)
Community College of Philadelphia (U)
Eastern Oregon University (U)
Edison State Community College (U)
EduKan (U)
Elgin Community College (U)
Erie Community College, North Campus (U)
Fayetteville Technical Community College (U)
Ferris State University (U)
Fresno City College (U)
Gaston College (U)
George C. Wallace Community College (U)
Georgia Perimeter College (U)
Illinois Institute of Technology (G)
Indiana University of Pennsylvania (U)
Indian River Community College (U)
Iowa Western Community College (U, G)
Jamestown Community College (U)
Johnson County Community College (U)
J. Sargeant Reynolds Community College (U)
Kennesaw State University (U)
Los Angeles Pierce College (U)
Mary Baldwin College (U)
Maysville Community College (U)
Mississippi State University (U)
Missouri Western State College (U)
Montana State University-Bozeman (G)
Mountain State University (U)
Mt. Hood Community College (U)
North Carolina State University (U)
Northeast State Technical Community College (U)
Northern Arizona University (U)
Northern State University (U)
North Idaho College (U)
North Iowa Area Community College (U)
North Seattle Community College (U)
NorthWest Arkansas Community College (U)
Northwestern College (U)
Northwestern State University of Louisiana (U)
Ohio University (U)
Okaloosa-Walton Community College (U)
Oregon State University (U)
Palo Alto College (U)
The Pennsylvania State University University Park Campus (U)
Portland State University (U)
Pueblo Community College (U)
Sacred Heart University (U)

St. Clair County Community College (U)
Santa Barbara City College (U)
Seward County Community College (U)
Shawnee State University (U)
State University of New York College at Fredonia (U, G)
State University of New York College of Technology at Alfred (U)
Treasure Valley Community College (U)
University of Connecticut (U)
University of Delaware (U)
The University of Findlay (U)
University of Florida (U)
University of Illinois at Springfield (U)
University of La Verne (U)
University of Massachusetts Dartmouth (U)
University of Massachusetts System (U)
The University of North Carolina at Chapel Hill (U)
The University of North Carolina at Greensboro (U)
University of North Dakota (U)
University of North Texas (G)
University of Oklahoma (U)
The University of Texas System (U)
University of Utah (U)
University of Vermont (U)
University of Washington (U)
University of Waterloo (N, U)
University of Wisconsin-Extension (U)
Victoria College (U)
Vincennes University (U)
Volunteer State Community College (U)
Western Governors University (U)
Western Wyoming Community College (U)
West Virginia University (G)

## Child care and guidance workers and managers

Amarillo College (U)
Athens Technical College (U)
Bevill State Community College (U)
Blue River Community College (U)
Caldwell Community College and Technical Institute (U)
Catawba Valley Community College (U)
College of Southern Maryland (U)
Danville Community College (U)
Edison State Community College (U)
Elgin Community College (U)
Everett Community College (U)
Fayetteville Technical Community College (U)
Florence-Darlington Technical College (U)
Harcourt Learning Direct Center for Degree Studies (N)
Heartland Community College (U)
Isothermal Community College (U)

Ivy Tech State College-Eastcentral (U)
Ivy Tech State College-Lafayette (U)
Ivy Tech State College-Southcentral (U)
Ivy Tech State College-Whitewater (U)
Jacksonville State University (U)
J. Sargeant Reynolds Community College (U)
Kansas State University (U)
Lehigh Carbon Community College (U)
Lewis-Clark State College (U)
Long Beach City College (U)
Longview Community College (U)
Maple Woods Community College (U)
Maranatha Baptist Bible College (U)
Mayville State University (U)
Moberly Area Community College (U)
Mt. Hood Community College (U)
Northampton County Area Community College (U)
Northeastern Oklahoma Agricultural and Mechanical College (U)
North Idaho College (U)
North Iowa Area Community College (N)
North Seattle Community College (U)
Oklahoma City Community College (U)
Olympic College (U)
Owens Community College (U)
Penn Valley Community College (U)
Rochester Community and Technical College (U)
Rowan-Cabarrus Community College (U)
St. Cloud Technical College (N)
San Joaquin Delta College (U)
Southeast Community College, Lincoln Campus (N)
Southwestern College (U)
Southwestern Community College (U)
Spoon River College (U)
Stanly Community College (U)
Taft College (U)
University College of the Fraser Valley (U)
University of Wisconsin-Milwaukee (G)
Victoria College (U)
Walla Walla Community College (U)

## Chinese language and literature
College of San Mateo (U)

## City/urban, community and regional planning
Arizona State University (U)
Florence-Darlington Technical College (N)
New School University (U)
University of Missouri-Columbia (N)

## Civil engineering
Brigham Young University (U)
Calvin College (U)

Columbia University (N, G)
Illinois Institute of Technology (G)
Kansas State University (G)
North Carolina State University (G)
Southern Methodist University (G)
Texas Tech University (G)
The University of British Columbia (U)
University of Colorado at Boulder (N, U, G)
University of Colorado at Denver (N, U)
University of Connecticut (U)
University of Delaware (U, G)
University of Idaho (U)
University of Maine (G)
University of New Mexico (U, G)
University of Wisconsin-Madison (U, G)
University of Wisconsin-Platteville (G)
Villanova University (G)

### Civil engineering/civil technology
Florence-Darlington Technical College (U)
Lake Superior College (U)
University of Colorado at Denver (N)
University of New Hampshire (N)

### Classical and ancient Near Eastern languages and literatures
Moody Bible Institute (U)
University of Minnesota, Twin Cities Campus (U)

### Clinical psychology
Elgin Community College (U)
Ferris State University (U)
John F. Kennedy University (G)
Naropa University (U)
Northcentral University (G)

### Clothing, apparel and textile workers and managers
North Carolina Central University (U)

### Clothing/apparel and textile studies
North Carolina Central University (U)
North Carolina State University (U)
University of North Texas (U, G)

### Cognitive psychology and psycholinguistics
Elgin Community College (U)
Horry-Georgetown Technical College (U)
Saybrook Graduate School and Research Center (G)
Tarleton State University (U)
Teachers College, Columbia University (U)
University of Connecticut (U)
University of Southern Mississippi (G)
University of Washington (U)

### Communication disorders sciences and services
Bridgewater State College (U)
Brigham Young University (U)
Calvin College (U)
East Carolina University (G)
Lakeland Community College (N)
North Carolina Central University (G)
Northern Arizona University (U)
Oklahoma State University (U)
State University of New York College at Fredonia (U, G)
University of Connecticut (U)
University of Kansas (U)
University of Northern Colorado (U)
University of Vermont (U, G)

### Communications technologies
Colorado Community College Online (U)
Elgin Community College (U)
Foothill College (U)
Lakeland Community College (N)
Montana State University-Billings (U)
Northeastern University (N)
North Georgia College & State University (N)
Rockingham Community College (N)
Santa Rosa Junior College (U)
Southern Illinois University Carbondale (U)
Temple University (U, G)
Tuskegee University (N)
University College of the Fraser Valley (U)
The University of Akron (N)
University of California, Berkeley (U)
University of Massachusetts Boston (U)
University of Massachusetts Dartmouth (N)
University of North Texas (G)
University of Wisconsin-Stevens Point (U)
Worcester Polytechnic Institute (G)

### Communications, general
Abilene Christian University (U)
Albuquerque Technical Vocational Institute (U)
Amarillo College (U)
Beulah Heights Bible College (U)
Bradley University (U)
Brenau University (U)
Bridgewater State College (U)
Brigham Young University (U)
Bristol Community College (N)
Calvin College (U)
Cape Fear Community College (U)
Central Methodist College (N)
Central Oregon Community College (U)
Central Washington University (U)
Century Community and Technical College (N)

Chaminade University of Honolulu (U)
Champlain College (U)
Citrus College (U)
Clarion University of Pennsylvania (U)
Cleveland Institute of Electronics (U)
Coastline Community College (U)
College of DuPage (U)
College of Southern Maryland (U)
Concordia University (U)
Connecticut State University System (U)
Craven Community College (U)
Danville Community College (U)
Dawson Community College (U)
Drake University (U)
Eastern New Mexico University-Roswell (U)
EduKan (U)
Elgin Community College (U)
Frederick Community College (N)
Gaston College (U)
Georgia Perimeter College (U)
Grand Valley State University (G)
Griggs University (U)
Hamilton College (U)
Heartland Community College (U)
Hocking College (U)
Hutchinson Community College and Area Vocational School (U)
Ivy Tech State College-Central Indiana (U)
Ivy Tech State College-Columbus (U)
Ivy Tech State College-Eastcentral (U)
Ivy Tech State College-Kokomo (U)
Ivy Tech State College-Lafayette (U)
Ivy Tech State College-North Central (U)
Ivy Tech State College-Northeast (U)
Ivy Tech State College-Northwest (U)
Ivy Tech State College-Southcentral (U)
Ivy Tech State College-Southeast (U)
Ivy Tech State College-Southwest (U)
Ivy Tech State College-Wabash Valley (U)
Ivy Tech State College-Whitewater (U)
Judson College (U)
Kennesaw State University (U)
Lakeland Community College (N)
Lake Superior College (U)
LeTourneau University (U)
Lewis and Clark Community College (U)
Lewis-Clark State College (U)
Long Island University, Southampton College (U)
Lord Fairfax Community College (N)
Louisiana State University and Agricultural and Mechanical College (U)
Malone College (U)
Marshall University (U)
Mary Baldwin College (U)
Marywood University (U)
Maysville Community College (U)
Meridian Community College (U)

# Individual Courses Index

University of Connecticut (U)
University of Massachusetts System (U)
University of South Dakota (U)
The University of Texas System (U)
Walla Walla Community College (U)
Wichita State University (U)

## Computer and information sciences, general

Albuquerque Technical Vocational Institute (U)
Alvin Community College (U)
Amarillo College (U)
American College of Computer & Information Sciences (U)
American River College (U)
Andrew College (U)
Anne Arundel Community College (U)
Antelope Valley College (U)
Arizona Western College (U)
Armstrong Atlantic State University (U)
Berkshire Community College (N)
Bevill State Community College (U)
Blackhawk Technical College (U)
Blinn College (U)
Bloomfield College (U)
Bossier Parish Community College (U)
Bristol Community College (N, U)
Bucks County Community College (U)
Caldwell Community College and Technical Institute (U)
California National University for Advanced Studies (U, G)
Calvin College (U)
Capital Community College (N)
Capitol College (U, G)
Carl Albert State College (U)
Carroll Community College (U)
Centralia College (N, U)
Central Methodist College (U)
Central Oregon Community College (U)
Central Virginia Community College (U)
Central Wyoming College (U)
Century Community and Technical College (N)
Champlain College (U)
Chesapeake College (U)
Cincinnati State Technical and Community College (U)
Cleveland State Community College (U)
Clovis Community College (U)
Coastline Community College (U)
College of the Canyons (U)
Colorado Christian University (U)
Colorado Community College Online (U)
Colorado Electronic Community College (U)
Columbia College (U)

Community College of Rhode Island (U)
Cosumnes River College (U)
County College of Morris (N)
Craven Community College (N)
Dakota State University (U)
Davenport University Online (U)
Del Mar College (U)
Drake University (U)
East Central College (U)
Eastern Connecticut State University (U, G)
Eastern Wyoming College (U)
East Los Angeles College (U)
Edison State Community College (U)
EduKan (U)
Elgin Community College (U)
Erie Community College, North Campus (U)
Eugene Bible College (U)
Everett Community College (U)
Fayetteville Technical Community College (U)
Ferris State University (U, G)
Florence-Darlington Technical College (N)
Florida Institute of Technology (N)
Foothill College (U)
Forrest Junior College (N, U)
Frederick Community College (N)
Fresno City College (U)
Garland County Community College (N)
Gaston College (U)
George C. Wallace Community College (U)
Georgia Perimeter College (U)
Great Basin College (U)
Hamilton College (U)
Harford Community College (N, U)
Haywood Community College (U)
Hibbing Community College (N, U)
Honolulu Community College (U)
Illinois Eastern Community Colleges, Lincoln Trail College (U)
Illinois Eastern Community Colleges, Olney Central College (U)
Indiana Wesleyan University (U)
Isothermal Community College (U)
Ivy Tech State College-Central Indiana (U)
Ivy Tech State College-Columbus (U)
Ivy Tech State College-Eastcentral (U)
Ivy Tech State College-Kokomo (U)
Ivy Tech State College-Lafayette (U)
Ivy Tech State College-North Central (U)
Ivy Tech State College-Northeast (U)
Ivy Tech State College-Southcentral (U)
Ivy Tech State College-Southeast (U)
Ivy Tech State College-Southwest (U)
Ivy Tech State College-Wabash Valley (U)
Ivy Tech State College-Whitewater (U)
Jacksonville State University (U, G)
John Wood Community College (U)

Jones College (U)
Kansas City Kansas Community College (U)
Kean University (N)
Kellogg Community College (U)
Kentucky State University (U)
Kirkwood Community College (N)
Lakeland Community College (N, U)
Lake Superior College (U)
Lehigh Carbon Community College (U)
Lewis and Clark Community College (U)
Lewis-Clark State College (U)
Lincoln Land Community College (U)
Long Beach City College (U)
Long Island University, Southampton College (U)
Lord Fairfax Community College (N)
Macon State College (U)
Manchester Community College (U)
Manor College (U)
Marion Technical College (U)
Marshall University (U, G)
Mary Baldwin College (U)
Maysville Community College (U)
McLennan Community College (U)
Mendocino College (U)
Meridian Community College (U)
Michigan State University (N, U)
Mid-Plains Community College Area (U)
Mohawk Valley Community College (U)
Montcalm Community College (N)
Morehead State University (U)
Mt. Hood Community College (U)
Mt. San Antonio College (U)
Nash Community College (N, U)
National American University (U)
New York Institute of Technology (N)
North Country Community College (U)
Northeast State Technical Community College (U)
Northern Arizona University (U)
Northern Kentucky University (U)
Northern State University (U)
North Georgia College & State University (N, U)
North Seattle Community College (U)
Northwestern Michigan College (U)
Northwestern State University of Louisiana (U)
Okaloosa-Walton Community College (U)
Old Dominion University (U)
Olympic College (U)
Ouachita Technical College (U)
Owens Community College (U)
Palo Alto College (U)
Park University (U)
Pasco-Hernando Community College (N)
Passaic County Community College (U)
Pierce College (U)

## Computer science

# Individual Courses Index

Oklahoma State University (U)
Providence College and Theological
   Seminary (G)
Saybrook Graduate School and Research
   Center (G)
Slippery Rock University of Pennsylvania
   (G)
Tarleton State University (U)
Taylor University, World Wide Campus (U)
University of California, Berkeley (U)
University of Connecticut (U)
University of Great Falls (U)
University of Illinois at Urbana-Champaign
   (U)
University of Massachusetts System (U, G)
University of Missouri-Columbia (G)
Wayne State College (G)
Weber State University (U)
Western Illinois University (U)

## Crafts, folk art and artisanry
Kentucky State University (N)

## Criminal justice and corrections
Adirondack Community College (U)
Albuquerque Technical Vocational Institute
   (U)
Alpena Community College (U)
American Military University (G)
Angelina College (U)
Arizona Western College (U)
Bakersfield College (U)
Bemidji State University (U)
Blue River Community College (U)
Brenau University (U)
Brunswick Community College (U)
Calvin College (U)
Carl Albert State College (U)
Carroll Community College (U)
Central Carolina Technical College (U)
Central Community College (U)
Central Missouri State University (U, G)
Central Oregon Community College (U)
Central Virginia Community College (U)
Central Washington University (U)
Central Wyoming College (U)
Cerro Coso Community College (U)
Chaminade University of Honolulu (U)
Charter Oak State College (U)
Chesapeake College (U)
Clackamas Community College (U)
Clovis Community College (U)
College for Professional Studies (U)
College of DuPage (U)
College of Southern Maryland (U)
College of the Southwest (U)
Colorado Community College Online (U)

Colorado Electronic Community College
   (U)
Columbia College (U)
Community College of Philadelphia (U)
Connecticut State University System (U)
Craven Community College (U)
Danville Area Community College (U)
Delaware Technical & Community College,
   Jack F. Owens Campus (U)
Eastern Connecticut State University (G)
Elgin Community College (U)
Florence-Darlington Technical College (U)
Florida Gulf Coast University (U)
Gannon University (U)
Gaston College (U)
George Mason University (U)
Grand Rapids Community College (U)
Grand Valley State University (U)
Harrisburg Area Community College (U)
Horry-Georgetown Technical College (U)
Indiana Higher Education
   Telecommunication System (U)
Indian River Community College (U)
Isothermal Community College (U)
James Sprunt Community College (U)
Jefferson Davis Community College (U)
John Wood Community College (U)
Judson College (U)
Kean University (U)
Lake Superior State University (U)
Lewis and Clark Community College (U)
Lincoln Land Community College (U)
Longview Community College (U)
Loyola University Chicago (N)
Lynn University (U, G)
Maple Woods Community College (U)
Meridian Community College (U)
Michigan State University (G)
Middle Tennessee State University (U)
Minot State University (U)
Missouri Western State College (U)
Mitchell Community College (U)
Mohawk Valley Community College (U)
Monmouth University (G)
Montcalm Community College (U)
Mountain State University (U)
Mount Wachusett Community College (U)
Nash Community College (U)
New Jersey City University (U)
North Carolina Central University (U)
North Carolina Community College System
   (U)
Northcentral University (U, G)
Northeastern Oklahoma Agricultural and
   Mechanical College (U)
Northeastern State University (U)
Northern Arizona University (U)
Northern Michigan University (U)

Northwestern Michigan College (U)
Northwestern State University of Louisiana
   (U)
Okaloosa-Walton Community College (U)
Old Dominion University (U)
Orangeburg-Calhoun Technical College (U)
Palo Alto College (U)
Park University (U)
The Pennsylvania State University University
   Park Campus (U)
Penn Valley Community College (U)
Pikes Peak Community College (U)
Portland State University (U)
Rappahannock Community College (U)
Roger Williams University (U)
Rowan-Cabarrus Community College (U)
Saint Charles Community College (U)
San Jacinto College North Campus (U)
Santa Rosa Junior College (U)
Sauk Valley Community College (U)
Seminole Community College (U)
Shippensburg University of Pennsylvania (U)
Simpson College (U)
Southeast Missouri State University (U)
Southern Illinois University Carbondale (U)
Southwestern Community College (U)
Southwest Texas State University (U)
Stanly Community College (U)
State University of New York College at
   Fredonia (U)
State University of New York College of
   Technology at Canton (U)
Stephen F. Austin State University (U)
Sussex County Community College (U)
Taft College (U)
Taylor University, World Wide Campus (U)
Trident Technical College (U)
Tyler Junior College (U)
The University of Alabama (U)
University of Arkansas at Little Rock (U)
University of Cincinnati (U)
University of Delaware (U)
University of Great Falls (U)
University of Houston-Downtown (U)
University of Massachusetts Amherst (U)
The University of Memphis (U)
University of Missouri-Columbia (U, G)
University of Nevada, Reno (U)
University of North Texas (U, G)
University of South Dakota (U, G)
University of Southern Mississippi (G)
The University of Texas at Tyler (U)
The University of Texas of the Permian
   Basin (G)
University of Wisconsin-Extension (U)
University of Wisconsin-Parkside (U)
University of Wisconsin-Platteville (G)

# Individual Courses Index

Portland Community College (U)
St. Petersburg College (U)
Southeast Community College, Lincoln
　Campus (U)
Suffolk County Community College (U)
Thomas Edison State College (U)
The University of Iowa (U, G)
University of Nevada, Reno (U)
University of Waterloo (U)
Upper Iowa University (U)
Vincennes University (U)

## East and Southeast Asian languages and literatures

Amarillo College (U)
Elgin Community College (U)
Mary Baldwin College (U)
Naropa University (G)
Southern Illinois University Carbondale (U)
University of Kansas (U)
Western Washington University (U)

## East European languages and literatures

Cerro Coso Community College (U)
Elgin Community College (U)
Mary Baldwin College (U)
Missouri Western State College (U)
Tennessee Temple University (U)
University of Manitoba (U)
University of Washington (U)
University of Wisconsin-Extension (U)

## Ecology

Burlington County College (U)
Coastline Community College (U)
Edison State Community College (U)
Gogebic Community College (U)
Mountain State University (U)
Oregon State University (U)
University of Guelph (U)
University of Minnesota, Twin Cities
　Campus (U)
University of Waterloo (U)

## Economics

Acadia University (U)
American College of Computer &
　Information Sciences (U)
Andrew College (U)
Anne Arundel Community College (U)
Ashland Community College (U)
Avila College (U)
Bemidji State University (U)
Blue River Community College (U)
Brigham Young University (U)
Broward Community College (U)
Butte College (U)

California National University for Advanced
　Studies (U)
Calvin College (U)
Carroll Community College (U)
Catawba Valley Community College (U)
Cayuga County Community College (U)
Central Carolina Community College (U)
Central Carolina Technical College (U)
Central Methodist College (U)
Central Michigan University (U)
Central Virginia Community College (U)
Central Washington University (U)
Central Wyoming College (U)
Chadron State College (U)
Champlain College (U)
Charter Oak State College (U)
Clarkson College (U)
Clovis Community College (U)
Coastline Community College (U)
College of DuPage (U)
The College of St. Scholastica (U)
College of Southern Maryland (U)
College of the Canyons (U)
Colorado State University (N, U)
Columbia Basin College (U)
Columbia State Community College (U)
Community College of Philadelphia (U)
Concordia University (U)
Connecticut State University System (U)
Copiah-Lincoln Community College-
　Natchez Campus (U)
Craven Community College (U)
Cuyamaca College (U)
Cypress College (U)
Dakota State University (U)
Danville Area Community College (U)
Delaware Technical & Community College,
　Jack F. Owens Campus (U)
Delaware Technical & Community College,
　Stanton/Wilmington Campus (U)
Des Moines Area Community College (U)
Drake University (U, G)
East Central College (U)
Eastern Connecticut State University (U)
Eastern Oregon University (U)
Eastern Wyoming College (U)
Edison State Community College (U)
EduKan (U)
Elgin Community College (U)
Embry-Riddle Aeronautical University (U)
Erie Community College, North Campus
　(U)
Erie Community College, South Campus
　(U)
Fairmont State College (U)
Finger Lakes Community College (U)
Florence-Darlington Technical College (U)
Foothill College (U)

Gannon University (U)
George C. Wallace Community College (U)
Grand Rapids Community College (U)
Grand View College (U)
Hamilton College (U)
Harrisburg Area Community College (U)
Haywood Community College (U)
Hibbing Community College (U)
Holmes Community College (U)
Hope International University (U)
Humboldt State University (U)
Illinois State University (U)
Indiana Higher Education
　Telecommunication System (U)
Indiana State University (U)
Indian River Community College (U)
Iowa State University of Science and
　Technology (U)
Iowa Western Community College (G)
Isothermal Community College (U)
Ivy Tech State College-Central Indiana (U)
Ivy Tech State College-Columbus (U)
Ivy Tech State College-Eastcentral (U)
Ivy Tech State College-Kokomo (U)
Ivy Tech State College-Lafayette (U)
Ivy Tech State College-North Central (U)
Ivy Tech State College-Northeast (U)
Ivy Tech State College-Northwest (U)
Ivy Tech State College-Southcentral (U)
Ivy Tech State College-Southeast (U)
Ivy Tech State College-Southwest (U)
Ivy Tech State College-Wabash Valley (U)
Ivy Tech State College-Whitewater (U)
Jacksonville State University (U, G)
Jefferson Community College (U)
Jefferson Davis Community College (U)
Johnson County Community College (U)
John Wood Community College (U)
J. Sargeant Reynolds Community College
　(U)
Kansas City Kansas Community College (U)
Lakeland Community College (U)
Lehigh Carbon Community College (U)
Lewis and Clark Community College (U)
Liberty University (U)
Longview Community College (U)
Lord Fairfax Community College (U)
Maple Woods Community College (U)
Mary Baldwin College (U)
Marywood University (U)
Maysville Community College (U)
McLennan Community College (U)
Meridian Community College (U)
Michigan State University (U)
Middle Tennessee State University (U, G)
Millersville University of Pennsylvania (U)
MiraCosta College (U)
Missouri Western State College (U)

## Education administration and supervision

MU Direct: Continuing and Distance Education (G)

New Jersey City University (G)

North Carolina Central University (U)

North Carolina State University (G)

Northeastern State University (U, G)

Northern Arizona University (G)

North Georgia College & State University (G)

Northwestern State University of Louisiana (G)

Oregon State University (G)

The Pennsylvania State University University Park Campus (G)

Pittsburg State University (G)

Radford University (G)

Royal Roads University (G)

Southern Illinois University Carbondale (U)

Southern University and Agricultural and Mechanical College (U)

South Piedmont Community College (U)

Southwestern Baptist Theological Seminary (G)

Southwest Missouri State University (G)

State University of New York College at Cortland (G)

State University of New York College at Fredonia (G)

Tarleton State University (U)

Temple University (G)

Texas A&M University (G)

Texas A&M University-Kingsville (G)

Texas A&M University-Texarkana (G)

Texas Tech University (G)

University College of the Fraser Valley (U)

University of Alaska Fairbanks (G)

University of Central Oklahoma (U, G)

University of Connecticut (U, G)

University of Manitoba (U, G)

University of Massachusetts Amherst (G)

University of Massachusetts Lowell (G)

University of Massachusetts System (G)

University of Missouri-Columbia (G)

University of New Mexico (U)

University of North Texas (G)

University of Oklahoma (G)

University of Sioux Falls (G)

University of South Alabama (G)

University of South Carolina Sumter (U)

University of South Dakota (G)

The University of Tennessee at Martin (U, G)

The University of Texas of the Permian Basin (G)

University of Wisconsin-Milwaukee (G)

Wayne State College (G)

Western Governors University (G)

Western Illinois University (U)

Western Washington University (U)

## Education of the speech impaired

St. Cloud State University (U)

## Education, general

Acadia University (U)

Adams State College (G)

Armstrong Atlantic State University (U)

Bemidji State University (G)

Blue River Community College (U)

Bossier Parish Community College (U)

Brenau University (U, G)

Bridgewater State College (U)

Brigham Young University (U)

Bucks County Community College (U)

Cabrini College (U, G)

California Polytechnic State University, San Luis Obispo (G)

California State University, Chico (U)

California State University, San Marcos (U)

Calvin College (U, G)

Casper College (U)

Central Washington University (U)

Chadron State College (U, G)

Chaminade University of Honolulu (U, G)

Chapman University (N)

Clarion University of Pennsylvania (G)

College of Southern Maryland (N)

Columbia College (U)

Corning Community College (U)

Drake University (U, G)

East Carolina University (U, G)

Eastern Connecticut State University (U, G)

East Tennessee State University (U, G)

Elgin Community College (U)

Elizabeth City State University (U)

Eugene Bible College (U)

Fairmont State College (U)

Ferris State University (U)

Florida Community College at Jacksonville (U)

Florida Keys Community College (U)

Franklin Pierce Law Center (G)

Genesee Community College (U)

The George Washington University (N, G)

Goucher College (G)

Grand Valley State University (G)

Green River Community College (U)

Griggs University (U)

Hamline University (N, G)

Haywood Community College (U)

Hobe Sound Bible College (N)

Humboldt State University (U)

Immaculata College (G)

Indiana State University (U)

Indian River Community College (U)

Jacksonville State University (U, G)

John F. Kennedy University (U)

Judson College (U)

Kean University (N)

Kennesaw State University (U)

Lesley University (G)

LeTourneau University (U)

Lewis-Clark State College (U)

Liberty University (U)

Longview Community College (U)

Lynn University (G)

Maple Woods Community College (U)

Maranatha Baptist Bible College (U)

Mary Baldwin College (U)

Maysville Community College (U)

McDowell Technical Community College (U)

Michigan State University (G)

Middle Tennessee State University (U)

Midwestern State University (U)

Millersville University of Pennsylvania (G)

Minot State University (U)

Mississippi State University (N, U, G)

Missouri Western State College (U)

Mohawk Valley Community College (U)

Monmouth University (U, G)

Montana State University-Billings (U, G)

MU Direct: Continuing and Distance Education (G)

Naropa University (G)

Northampton County Area Community College (U)

North Carolina Central University (U)

Northeastern Oklahoma Agricultural and Mechanical College (U)

Northeastern State University (U)

Northeast State Technical Community College (U)

Northern State University (G)

North Seattle Community College (U)

Oregon State University (U, G)

Penn Valley Community College (U)

Roosevelt University (U, G)

Sacred Heart University (G)

St. Norbert College (N, G)

San Diego State University (N)

Seminole Community College (U)

Shawnee State University (U)

Slippery Rock University of Pennsylvania (U, G)

Southwest Missouri State University (G)

Spoon River College (U)

State University of New York College at Fredonia (U, G)

Stephens College (U)

Stony Brook University, State University of New York (G)

Taylor University, World Wide Campus (U)

Temple University (U)

# Individual Courses Index

Oklahoma State University (G)

The Pennsylvania State University University Park Campus (U)

Southwestern Baptist Theological Seminary (G)

University College of the Fraser Valley (U)

The University of Akron (G)

University of Colorado at Colorado Springs (G)

University of Connecticut (G)

University of Missouri-Columbia (U, G)

University of North Texas (G)

University of Sioux Falls (G)

University of South Carolina Sumter (U)

University of Southern Mississippi (G)

Western Governors University (G)

## Educational psychology

American College of Computer & Information Sciences (U)

Arizona State University (G)

Brigham Young University (U)

Burlington College (U)

Central Methodist College (U, G)

Chadron State College (U, G)

College of DuPage (U)

College of Southern Maryland (U)

College of the Southwest (U, G)

Colorado Northwestern Community College (U)

Colorado State University (U)

Columbia International University (N)

Columbia State Community College (U)

Columbus State University (G)

Concordia University (G)

Dakota State University (U)

Duquesne University (U)

East Carolina University (U)

Eastern Kentucky University (U, G)

East Tennessee State University (U, G)

Elizabeth City State University (U)

Eugene Bible College (U)

Graceland University (U, G)

Grand Valley State University (U, G)

Indiana State University (G)

Indiana Wesleyan University (G)

Jacksonville State University (U, G)

John Wood Community College (U)

Liberty University (U)

Marshall University (U, G)

Marylhurst University (U)

Memorial University of Newfoundland (U)

Michigan State University (G)

Middle Tennessee State University (U)

Mississippi State University (U, G)

Mohawk Valley Community College (U)

Moody Bible Institute (U)

National University (G)

North Central University (N, U)

Northern Arizona University (G)

Northern State University (U, G)

Northwestern State University of Louisiana (G)

Northwest Iowa Community College (U)

Ohio University (U)

Okaloosa-Walton Community College (U)

Oklahoma State University (U)

Slippery Rock University of Pennsylvania (G)

Southeastern Illinois College (U)

Southwestern Assemblies of God University (U)

Southwestern Baptist Theological Seminary (G)

State University of West Georgia (U, G)

Stephen F. Austin State University (U, G)

Tarleton State University (G)

Taylor University, World Wide Campus (U)

Texas Tech University (U)

Triton College (U)

Troy State University (G)

University of Alaska Fairbanks (U, G)

University of Arkansas (U)

University of California, Santa Barbara (U)

University of Colorado at Denver (G)

University of Connecticut (G)

University of Houston (U, G)

University of Maine (U)

University of Missouri-Columbia (U, G)

University of New Brunswick (U, G)

University of Northern Iowa (U, G)

University of North Texas (G)

University of Oklahoma (G)

University of Pittsburgh (U)

University of South Alabama (G)

University of Southern Indiana (U)

The University of Texas of the Permian Basin (G)

The University of Texas System (G)

University of Utah (U)

University of Washington (U)

University of Waterloo (U)

University of Wyoming (G)

Volunteer State Community College (U)

Walden University (G)

Western Washington University (U)

## Educational/instructional media design

Arizona State University (U)

Arizona State University West (G)

Azusa Pacific University (G)

Bemidji State University (G)

Boise State University (U, G)

Chadron State College (G)

The College of St. Scholastica (G)

Connecticut State University System (G)

Dakota State University (G)

Delaware Technical & Community College, Stanton/Wilmington Campus (U)

Duquesne University (G)

East Carolina University (G)

Elizabeth City State University (U)

Hamline University (N, G)

Jacksonville State University (G)

Lesley University (G)

MU Direct: Continuing and Distance Education (G)

New Jersey City University (G)

New York Institute of Technology (G)

Northeastern State University (U)

Northern Arizona University (G)

North Georgia College & State University (N)

Northwestern State University of Louisiana (U, G)

The Pennsylvania State University University Park Campus (G)

San Diego State University (U, G)

Southeast Missouri State University (U)

Southern Illinois University Carbondale (G)

Southwestern Baptist Theological Seminary (G)

Taylor University, World Wide Campus (U)

Teachers College, Columbia University (U)

Temple University (U)

Texas A&M University (G)

Texas Tech University (G)

Tyler Junior College (N)

The University of Akron (U, G)

University of Bridgeport (U, G)

University of Connecticut (G)

The University of Findlay (G)

University of Maryland, Baltimore County (G)

University of Massachusetts System (G)

University of North Texas (U, G)

University of Pennsylvania (G)

University of Saskatchewan (N)

University of South Alabama (G)

University of South Dakota (U)

The University of Texas System (U, G)

Wayne State College (G)

Western Governors University (G)

William Paterson University of New Jersey (G)

## Electrical and electronic engineering-related technology

Albuquerque Technical Vocational Institute (U)

Alexandria Technical College (U)

Arizona State University (U)

Arizona State University West (G)

Bristol Community College (N)

# Individual Courses Index

Elgin Community College (U)
Harrisburg Area Community College (U)
Kansas State University (G)
Longview Community College (U)
Louisiana State University and Agricultural and Mechanical College (U)
Maple Woods Community College (U)
Mercer University (N)
North Carolina State University (G)
Northern Arizona University (U)
Penn Valley Community College (U)
Purdue University (N, G)
Temple University (G)
Texas Tech University (G)
The University of Arizona (N)
University of Colorado at Denver (N, U, G)
University of Connecticut (U, G)
University of Illinois at Chicago (G)
University of Maryland, College Park (U, G)
University of Missouri-Rolla (G)
University of Oklahoma (U)
University of South Carolina Sumter (U)
University of Wisconsin-Extension (U)
University of Wisconsin-Madison (G)

### Engineering, other
Kansas State University (G)
Lakeland Community College (N)
Michigan State University (G)
Moraine Valley Community College (U)
National Technological University (U, G)
North Georgia College & State University (U)
Texas Tech University (G)
University of Alaska Anchorage (G)
University of Colorado at Colorado Springs (G)
University of Colorado at Denver (N, G)
University of Maryland, College Park (U, G)
University of Wisconsin Colleges (U)

### Engineering-related technologies, other
Bristol Community College (N)
Elgin Community College (U)
Great Basin College (U)
Haywood Community College (U)
Indiana University of Pennsylvania (U, G)
Kentucky State University (U)
Missouri Western State College (U)
Old Dominion University (U)
Southern Illinois University Carbondale (U)
Texas A&M University (G)
University of Colorado at Colorado Springs (G)
University of Colorado at Denver (N, G)
University of Connecticut (U)
University of Maryland, College Park (U, G)
University of North Texas (U)

### Engineering/industrial management
Alexandria Technical College (N)
Arizona State University (G)
Boston University (G)
Bristol Community College (N)
Central Missouri State University (U, G)
Colorado State University (G)
Columbia University (N, G)
East Carolina University (U)
Edison State Community College (U)
Elgin Community College (U)
Florida Institute of Technology (G)
Kansas State University (G)
Lake Superior State University (U)
Mississippi State University (G)
Montana Tech of The University of Montana (G)
MU Direct: Continuing and Distance Education (N)
New Jersey Institute of Technology (G)
Northcentral University (G)
Northeastern University (G)
Old Dominion University (G)
Rochester Institute of Technology (U)
Roger Williams University (U)
Southern Methodist University (G)
Stanford University (N, G)
Texas A&M University (G)
The University of Arizona (G)
University of Colorado at Boulder (N, U, G)
University of Colorado at Denver (N, G)
University of Dallas (G)
University of Idaho (U, G)
University of Massachusetts Amherst (N, G)
University of Michigan (N)
University of Missouri-Rolla (G)
University of Waterloo (G)
Virginia Polytechnic Institute and State University (U, G)
Western Michigan University (U)
Worcester Polytechnic Institute (G)

### English as a second language
Albuquerque Technical Vocational Institute (N)
Butte College (U)
Central Missouri State University (U, G)
Clackamas Community College (U)
Coastline Community College (N)
College of DuPage (U)
College of San Mateo (U)
College of the Southwest (U)
Contra Costa College (U)
Dallas County Community College District (U)
Elgin Community College (U)
Fashion Institute of Technology (U)

Florida Gulf Coast University (U, G)
Foothill College (U)
Fullerton College (U)
Glendale Community College (U)
Hamline University (N, G)
Hartnell College (U)
Honolulu Community College (U)
Lorain County Community College (U)
Lord Fairfax Community College (N)
Miami-Dade Community College (U)
MiraCosta College (N, U)
Mississippi State University (N, U)
Mt. San Antonio College (U)
New School University (N, U, G)
North Carolina Central University (N, U)
North Seattle Community College (U)
Ohlone College (U)
Plattsburgh State University of New York (U)
Red Rocks Community College (U)
St. Cloud State University (G)
St. Norbert College (N)
Schenectady County Community College (N)
Shawnee State University (U)
Sinclair Community College (U)
Southeast Missouri State University (U)
Southwestern College (N, U)
State University of West Georgia (U)
Texas A&M University-Kingsville (G)
Tompkins Cortland Community College (U)
University of California, Santa Barbara (N)
University of Central Oklahoma (U, G)
University of Florida (U)
University of Maine (U)
University of Nevada, Las Vegas (U)
The University of North Carolina at Chapel Hill (U)
The University of North Carolina at Greensboro (G)
University of Saskatchewan (N)
The University of Texas of the Permian Basin (U, G)
University of Washington (N)
Western Governors University (G)

### English composition
Adams State College (U)
Adirondack Community College (U)
Albuquerque Technical Vocational Institute (N, U)
Alvin Community College (U)
Amarillo College (U)
American River College (U)
Andrew College (U)
Angelina College (U)
Anne Arundel Community College (U)
Antelope Valley College (U)

# Individual Courses Index

Oklahoma State University (U)
Olympic College (U)
Oregon State University (U)
The Paralegal Institute, Inc. (U)
Park University (U)
The Pennsylvania State University University Park Campus (U)
Pierce College (U)
Pitt Community College (N)
Portland Community College (N, U)
Pulaski Technical College (U)
Raritan Valley Community College (U)
Richland Community College (U)
Saddleback College (U)
St. Petersburg College (U)
Sam Houston State University (U)
San Diego State University (N)
San Jacinto College North Campus (U)
Santa Rosa Junior College (N)
Schenectady County Community College (N)
Seton Hill College (G)
Sheridan College (U)
Skidmore College (U)
Southern New Hampshire University (U)
Southwestern Assemblies of God University (U)
Southwestern Community College (U)
Southwest Texas State University (U)
Spring Arbor University (U)
State University of New York College at Cortland (U)
State University of New York College of Agriculture and Technology at Morrisville (U)
State University of West Georgia (U)
Stephens College (U)
Suffolk County Community College (U)
Syracuse University (U)
Taft College (U)
Tarleton State University (U)
Tarrant County College District (U)
Tuskegee University (N)
Tyler Junior College (U)
University of Alaska Fairbanks (U)
University of Alaska Southeast, Sitka Campus (U)
University of Arkansas at Little Rock (U)
University of Baltimore (U)
University of California, Santa Barbara (N, U)
University of Central Arkansas (U)
University of Colorado at Denver (N, U)
University of Denver (G)
University of Houston (U)
University of La Verne (U)
University of Maine (U)
University of Maine at Machias (U)

University of Minnesota, Twin Cities Campus (U)
University of Missouri-Columbia (U)
The University of Montana-Missoula (U)
University of New Brunswick (N)
University of New Mexico (U, G)
The University of North Carolina at Chapel Hill (U)
The University of North Carolina at Greensboro (N)
University of Pennsylvania (N, U)
University of Southern Mississippi (U)
The University of Tennessee (N)
The University of Texas System (U)
University of Utah (U)
University of Vermont (U)
University of Washington (N, U)
University of Wisconsin-Stevens Point (N)
Vincennes University (U)
Virginia Commonwealth University (U)
Virginia Polytechnic Institute and State University (U)
Volunteer State Community College (U)
Walla Walla Community College (N)
Walters State Community College (U)
Washington State University (U)
Weber State University (U)
Western Washington University (U)
West Los Angeles College (U)
West Virginia University (U)
William Paterson University of New Jersey (U)

## English language and literature, general
Acadia University (U)
Adirondack Community College (U)
Alvin Community College (U)
Amarillo College (U)
Arizona State University (U)
Arizona Western College (U)
Beulah Heights Bible College (U)
Blinn College (U)
Briercrest Bible College (U)
Caldwell Community College and Technical Institute (U)
California State University, Bakersfield (U)
Calvin College (U)
Catawba Valley Community College (U)
Cayuga County Community College (U)
Central Carolina Community College (U)
Central Carolina Technical College (U)
Central Community College (U)
Central Virginia Community College (U)
Central Washington University (U)
Cerro Coso Community College (U)
Chadron State College (G)
Chaminade University of Honolulu (U)

Champlain College (U)
Charter Oak State College (U)
Cincinnati State Technical and Community College (U)
Coastline Community College (U)
Colorado Community College Online (U)
Colorado Electronic Community College (U)
Columbia College (U)
Columbia State Community College (U)
Concordia University (U)
Contra Costa College (U)
Craven Community College (U)
Cuyamaca College (U)
Dakota State University (U)
Drake University (G)
Eastern Oregon University (U)
Elgin Community College (U)
Elizabethtown College (U)
Embry-Riddle Aeronautical University (U)
Erie Community College, South Campus (U)
Ferris State University (U)
Florence-Darlington Technical College (U)
Fresno City College (U)
Fullerton College (U)
Gaston College (U)
Georgia Perimeter College (U)
Griggs University (U)
Hamilton College (U)
Harrisburg Area Community College (U)
Haywood Community College (U)
Hocking College (U)
Honolulu Community College (U)
Husson College (U)
Illinois State University (U)
Illinois Valley Community College (U)
Indiana Higher Education Telecommunication System (U)
Indian River Community College (U)
Iowa Western Community College (U, G)
Jacksonville State University (U)
Jones College (U)
Judson College (U)
Kansas City Kansas Community College (U)
Kansas State University (U)
Kapiolani Community College (U)
Kentucky State University (U)
LeTourneau University (U)
Lincoln Land Community College (U)
Los Angeles Pierce College (U)
Louisiana State University and Agricultural and Mechanical College (U)
Louisiana Tech University (G)
Lynn University (U)
Manchester Community College (U)
Mary Baldwin College (U)
Maysville Community College (U)

# Individual Courses Index

## English technical and business writing

Adirondack Community College (U)
Alexandria Technical College (N, U)
Amarillo College (U)
Arizona State University (U)
Arizona State University West (U)
Armstrong Atlantic State University (U)
Atlantic Cape Community College (N)
Bridgewater State College (U)
Bristol Community College (U)
Caldwell Community College and Technical Institute (U)
California State University, Bakersfield (U)
Cape Fear Community College (U)
Carroll Community College (N, U)
Central Virginia Community College (U)
Chadron State College (U)
Chattanooga State Technical Community College (U)
Cincinnati State Technical and Community College (U)
Clackamas Community College (U)
College of Southern Maryland (U)
Colorado Community College Online (U)
Community Hospital of Roanoke Valley-College of Health Sciences (U)
Dakota County Technical College (U)
Delaware Technical & Community College, Stanton/Wilmington Campus (U)
East Carolina University (G)
Elgin Community College (U)
Embry-Riddle Aeronautical University (U)
Florence-Darlington Technical College (U)
Frederick Community College (N)
George Mason University (U)
Harrisburg Area Community College (U)
Haywood Community College (U)
Hocking College (U)
Jefferson Community College (U)
Johnson County Community College (U)
Judson College (U)
Lake Superior College (U)
Lehigh Carbon Community College (U)
Lord Fairfax Community College (N)
Louisiana Tech University (U)
Montana Tech of The University of Montana (U)
Mt. Hood Community College (U)
North Arkansas College (U)
North Carolina State University (U)
Northeastern State University (U)
Northern Arizona University (U)
Northern Essex Community College (U)
Northern Michigan University (U)
Northwestern Michigan College (U)
Northwestern State University of Louisiana (U)
Ohio University (U)

Oklahoma State University (N, U)
Orangeburg-Calhoun Technical College (U)
Oregon State University (U)
Pasco-Hernando Community College (N)
The Pennsylvania State University University Park Campus (U)
Pikes Peak Community College (U)
Portland Community College (N)
Salve Regina University (U)
Sandhills Community College (U)
San Jacinto College North Campus (U)
Schenectady County Community College (U)
Seminole Community College (U)
Sinclair Community College (U)
Southeast Community College, Beatrice Campus (U)
State University of New York College of Agriculture and Technology at Morrisville (U)
Stephen F. Austin State University (U)
Tarleton State University (U)
Texas Tech University (U, G)
Trident Technical College (U)
Tulsa Community College (U)
Tuskegee University (N)
The University of Akron (U)
University of Alaska Fairbanks (U)
University of California, Los Angeles (G)
University of Colorado at Denver (N, U)
University of Great Falls (U)
University of Massachusetts Boston (U)
University of Massachusetts Dartmouth (U, G)
University of Missouri-Columbia (U)
University of North Texas (U)
University of South Carolina (U)
University of the Sciences in Philadelphia (G)
University of Washington (U)
University of Wisconsin-Stevens Point (U, G)
West Los Angeles College (U)
West Virginia University (U)
William Paterson University of New Jersey (G)
Wisconsin Indianhead Technical College, New Richmond Campus (U)

## Enterprise management and operation

Columbia College (U)
Hope International University (U)
Lakeland Community College (N)
Lord Fairfax Community College (N)
Michigan State University (G)
Nash Community College (N)
Northern Essex Community College (N)

The Pennsylvania State University University Park Campus (U)
Schenectady County Community College (U)
University of Tulsa (G)
Walla Walla Community College (N)
William Paterson University of New Jersey (N)

## Entomology

Iowa State University of Science and Technology (U)
University of Missouri-Columbia (U)

## Entrepreneurship

American River College (U)
Bridgewater State College (U)
Broward Community College (U)
Champlain College (U)
Coastal Carolina Community College (N)
Cuyamaca College (U)
Lakeland Community College (N, U)
Nassau Community College (U)
Northern Essex Community College (N)
Northern Kentucky University (U)
Owens Community College (U)
Plattsburgh State University of New York (G)
Rockingham Community College (N)
Spokane Falls Community College (U)
Stephens College (G)
Syracuse University (U)
The University of Findlay (N)
University of Southern Indiana (N)
University of Tulsa (G)
Walla Walla Community College (N)
William Paterson University of New Jersey (N)

## Environmental control technologies

Arizona State University East (U, G)
Cincinnati State Technical and Community College (U)
Clackamas Community College (U)
Cosumnes River College (U)
Florence-Darlington Technical College (N, U)
Immaculata College (U)
Jacksonville State University (U)
Judson College (U)
Lakeland Community College (N)
Mississippi State University (N)
The Pennsylvania State University University Park Campus (G)
Shawnee State University (U)
The University of British Columbia (U)
The University of Findlay (N, G)
University of Kansas (U)

# Individual Courses Index

## Environmental health
American Academy of Nutrition, College of Nutrition (U)
Central Michigan University (U)
Great Basin College (U)
Medical College of Wisconsin (G)
Mountain State University (U)
North Seattle Community College (U)
Skidmore College (U)
The University of Iowa (U, G)
University of Maine (U)
University of Massachusetts Amherst (G)

## Environmental science/studies
Adams State College (U)
Bellevue Community College (U)
Bristol Community College (U)
California State University, Bakersfield (U)
Community College of Vermont (U)
Duquesne University (U, G)
Ivy Tech State College-Northwest (U)
Johnson County Community College (U)
Maysville Community College (U)
Mercy College (U)
Mountain Empire Community College (U)
Mountain State University (U)
North Country Community College (U)
Northern Arizona University (U)
Oregon State University (U)
Ouachita Technical College (U)
The Pennsylvania State University University Park Campus (U)
Rochester Institute of Technology (U)
St. Cloud State University (U)
Seattle Central Community College (U)
Southwestern Community College (U)
Thomas Edison State College (U)
Tyler Junior College (U)
University of Alaska Southeast, Sitka Campus (U)
University of Arkansas (U)
University of Guelph (U)
The University of North Carolina at Chapel Hill (U)
University of Southern Indiana (U)
University of Waterloo (U)
Western Washington University (U)
Wilfrid Laurier University (U)

## Environmental/environmental health engineering
Arizona State University (G)
Blue River Community College (U)
California National University for Advanced Studies (U, G)
Central Carolina Technical College (U)
Colorado State University (G)
Columbia University (N, G)

Danville Area Community College (U)
Florida Gulf Coast University (U)
Georgia Institute of Technology (N, G)
Harvard University (N, U, G)
Illinois Institute of Technology (G)
Lac Courte Oreilles Ojibwa Community College (U)
Lakeland Community College (N)
Longview Community College (U)
Mississippi State University (N, G)
New Jersey Institute of Technology (G)
New Mexico Institute of Mining and Technology (U, G)
Northern Arizona University (U)
Oklahoma State University (G)
Old Dominion University (G)
Oregon State University (G)
Owens Community College (U)
Southern Methodist University (G)
Texas A&M University-Kingsville (G)
Texas Tech University (G)
The University of Alabama (G)
University of Idaho (G)
University of Pennsylvania (G)
The University of Texas at Arlington (G)
University of Wisconsin-Stevens Point (N, U)
Virginia Polytechnic Institute and State University (U, G)
William Paterson University of New Jersey (U)
Worcester Polytechnic Institute (G)
York Technical College (U)

## Ethnic and cultural studies
American Military University (G)
Aquinas College (U)
Beulah Heights Bible College (U)
Bridgewater State College (U)
Burlington College (U)
Covenant Theological Seminary (G)
Drake University (U)
EduKan (U)
Elgin Community College (U)
John F. Kennedy University (U, G)
Lac Courte Oreilles Ojibwa Community College (U)
Lehigh Carbon Community College (U)
Minnesota State University Moorhead (U)
Naropa University (U)
North Seattle Community College (U)
Northwestern College (U)
The Pennsylvania State University University Park Campus (U)
Plattsburgh State University of New York (U)
Santa Barbara City College (U)
Tuskegee University (N)

University of Alaska Fairbanks (U)
University of California, Berkeley (U)
University of Colorado at Denver (N, U)
University of Connecticut (U)
The University of Findlay (U)
University of Kansas (G)
University of Massachusetts Lowell (U)
The University of North Carolina at Greensboro (N)
University of Washington (U)
University of Waterloo (U)
University of Wisconsin-Extension (U)
University of Wyoming (U)
Western Wyoming Community College (U)

## European history
Bellevue Community College (U)
Bossier Parish Community College (U)
Brigham Young University (U)
Bristol Community College (U)
Broward Community College (U)
Bucks County Community College (U)
Burlington County College (U)
Clackamas Community College (U)
College of San Mateo (U)
College of The Albemarle (U)
Concordia University Wisconsin (U)
Elizabethtown Community College (U)
Florida Community College at Jacksonville (U)
Floyd College (U)
Genesee Community College (U)
Jefferson College (U)
Maysville Community College (U)
Mercy College (U)
Mountain State University (U)
Mount Allison University (U)
Northwestern Michigan College (U)
Oregon State University (U)
Prairie Bible College (U)
Randolph Community College (U)
Richland Community College (U)
St. Petersburg College (U)
Southeast Community College, Lincoln Campus (U)
State University of New York at Oswego (U)
State University of West Georgia (U, G)
Suffolk County Community College (U)
Texas Tech University (U)
University of Alaska Southeast, Ketchikan Campus (U)
The University of Iowa (U, G)
University of Minnesota, Twin Cities Campus (U)
University of Nevada, Reno (U)
The University of North Carolina at Chapel Hill (U)
The University of Tennessee (U)

University of Waterloo (U)
Washington State University (U)
Weber State University (U)
Western Washington University (U)
West Virginia Wesleyan College (U)

## Experimental psychology
Burlington College (U)
Naropa University (U)

## Family and community studies
Arizona State University (U)
Beulah Heights Bible College (U)
Burlington College (U)
Cabrini College (U)
California State University, Chico (U)
Chadron State College (U)
Clackamas Community College (U)
Delaware Technical & Community College, Stanton/Wilmington Campus (U)
Elgin Community College (U)
Hunter College of the City University of New York (U, G)
Hutchinson Community College and Area Vocational School (U)
Jacksonville State University (G)
Kean University (U)
Kentucky State University (U)
Lakeland Community College (N)
North Seattle Community College (U)
Oklahoma State University (U)
Raritan Valley Community College (U)
Santa Rosa Junior College (U)
Seminole Community College (U)
Southeast Community College, Lincoln Campus (N)
South Piedmont Community College (U)
Southwestern Baptist Theological Seminary (G)
Troy State University-Florida Region (U)
University of Alaska Fairbanks (U)
University of Connecticut (G)
University of Missouri-Columbia (U, G)
University of New Mexico (U, G)
The University of North Carolina at Greensboro (U)
University of North Texas (U, G)
University of Southern Mississippi (G)
University of Waterloo (U)
University of Wisconsin-Extension (U)
University of Wisconsin-Madison (U, G)
Western Wisconsin Technical College (N)
Yuba College (U)

## Family and marriage counseling
Central Wyoming College (U)
College of San Mateo (U)
Eastern Kentucky University (U)

Mountain State University (U)
Mount Wachusett Community College (U)
St. Petersburg College (U)
Thomas Edison State College (U)

## Family/consumer resource management
Central Community College (U)
East Los Angeles College (U)
Iowa State University of Science and Technology (G)
Lakeland Community College (N)
Pasco-Hernando Community College (N)
Sam Houston State University (U)
Texas Tech University (G)
University of Missouri-Columbia (U)
University of North Texas (U, G)
Wichita State University (U)

## Film/cinema studies
Bellevue Community College (U)
Brigham Young University (U)
Burlington County College (U)
College of San Mateo (U)
Columbia Basin College (U)
Foothill College (U)
Fullerton College (U)
Genesee Community College (U)
Kansas State University (U)
Marylhurst University (U)
Mayland Community College (U)
Metropolitan Community College (U)
MiraCosta College (U)
Moraine Valley Community College (U)
Northern Virginia Community College (U)
Sandhills Community College (U)
Seattle Central Community College (U)
Southwest Missouri State University (U)
University at Buffalo, The State University of New York (U)
University of Alaska Fairbanks (U)
The University of British Columbia (U)
University of California, Berkeley (U)
University of Houston (U)
University of Illinois at Urbana-Champaign (U)
University of Kansas (U)
University of South Dakota (U)

## Film/video and photographic arts
Auburn University (U)
Bossier Parish Community College (U)
Butte College (U)
Calvin College (U)
Chapman University (U)
Charter Oak State College (U)
Elgin Community College (U)
Fullerton College (U)

Grand Rapids Community College (U)
Lakeland Community College (N, U)
Long Beach City College (U)
Nassau Community College (U)
New School University (U)
Northeastern Oklahoma Agricultural and Mechanical College (U)
North Seattle Community College (U)
Pueblo Community College (U)
The Richard Stockton College of New Jersey (U)
Temple University (U)
University of California, Los Angeles (G)
Walla Walla Community College (N)

## Finance, general
Adams State College (U)
The American College (U)
Anne Arundel Community College (U)
Bakersfield College (U)
California National University for Advanced Studies (U)
Carleton University (U)
Central Michigan University (U)
Chaminade University of Honolulu (U)
College for Financial Planning (G)
Colorado State University (G)
Duke University (G)
Florida Community College at Jacksonville (U)
Forsyth Technical Community College (U)
Golden Gate University (U, G)
Graceland University (U)
Hillsborough Community College (U)
Kansas State University (U)
Keller Graduate School of Management (G)
Lehigh Carbon Community College (U)
Marylhurst University (U, G)
Marywood University (U)
Maysville Community College (U)
Medical College of Wisconsin (G)
Mercy College (U)
Metropolitan Community College (U)
Milwaukee School of Engineering (N, G)
Mountain State University (U)
New York Institute of Technology (U)
Northern Illinois University (G)
Northern Virginia Community College (U)
Oklahoma State University (U)
Old Dominion University (U, G)
Park University (U)
Pennsylvania College of Technology (U)
The Pennsylvania State University University Park Campus (U)
Pitt Community College (N)
Randolph Community College (U)
Robert Morris College (U)
Roosevelt University (U)

University of Massachusetts Dartmouth (U)
University of Massachusetts System (U)
The University of North Carolina at
    Greensboro (U, G)
University of Pennsylvania (U, G)
University of Sioux Falls (U)
The University of Tennessee at Martin (U)
The University of Texas System (U)
University of Wisconsin Colleges (U)
Victoria College (U)
Virginia Western Community College (U)
Western Piedmont Community College (U)
West Virginia Wesleyan College (U)
Wilfrid Laurier University (U)
York University (U)

**Fire protection**
Arizona Western College (U)
Blue River Community College (U)
Caldwell Community College and Technical
    Institute (U)
Elgin Community College (U)
Georgia Perimeter College (U)
Ivy Tech State College-Columbus (U)
Jacksonville State University (G)
Longview Community College (U)
Maple Woods Community College (U)
Meridian Community College (U)
Northern Essex Community College (N)
Oklahoma State University (N)
Pikes Peak Community College (U)
Rio Hondo College (U)
Rockingham Community College (N)
Schenectady County Community College
    (U)
Tyler Junior College (U)
University of Maryland, College Park (U, G)
University of Missouri-Columbia (N)
Western Wisconsin Technical College (N)

**Fire science/firefighting**
Bakersfield College (U)
Berkshire Community College (U)
Bossier Parish Community College (U)
Chattanooga State Technical Community
    College (U)
Honolulu Community College (U)
Ivy Tech State College-Central Indiana (U)
Ivy Tech State College-Northwest (U)
Oklahoma State University (U, G)
Penn Valley Community College (U)
Portland Community College (U)
St. Petersburg College (U)
University of Cincinnati (U)
Vincennes University (U)
Worcester Polytechnic Institute (G)

**Fire services administration**
Coastal Carolina Community College (U)
St. Petersburg College (U)
State University of New York Empire State
    College (U)
The University of Memphis (U)

**Fishing and fisheries sciences and
management**
Oregon State University (U, G)

**Floristry marketing operations**
Lakeland Community College (N)

**Food products retailing and
wholesaling operations**
North Carolina Central University (G)
North Georgia College & State University
    (N)
Sheridan College (U)
University of North Texas (U)

**Food sciences and technology**
Bossier Parish Community College (U)
Brigham Young University (U)
Elgin Community College (U)
Illinois Institute of Technology (G)
Iowa State University of Science and
    Technology (U, G)
J. Sargeant Reynolds Community College
    (U)
Kansas State University (N, U)
Michigan State University (U)
Middle Tennessee State University (U)
Mississippi State University (N)
North Georgia College & State University
    (N)
Texas Tech University (U)
University of California, Davis (U)
University of North Texas (U, G)
University of Wisconsin-Madison (U)

**Foods and nutrition studies**
Acadia University (U)
Auburn University (N)
Central Oregon Community College (U)
Clackamas Community College (U)
Clemson University (G)
Colorado State University (U)
Danville Community College (U)
East Carolina University (G)
East Los Angeles College (U)
Elgin Community College (U)
Elizabethtown Community College (U)
Fairmont State College (U)
Florida Community College at Jacksonville
    (U)
Griggs University (U)
Hamilton College (U)

Harcourt Learning Direct Center for Degree
    Studies (N)
Harrisburg Area Community College (U)
Heartland Community College (U)
Hibbing Community College (U)
Honolulu Community College (U)
Husson College (U)
Illinois Eastern Community Colleges,
    Frontier Community College (U)
Illinois Eastern Community Colleges,
    Lincoln Trail College (U)
Illinois Eastern Community Colleges, Olney
    Central College (U)
Illinois Eastern Community Colleges,
    Wabash Valley College (U)
Immaculata College (U)
Indiana University of Pennsylvania (U)
Kansas State University (U)
Long Beach City College (U)
Louisiana Tech University (G)
Meridian Community College (U)
Mississippi State University (U)
Mohawk Valley Community College (U)
North Georgia College & State University
    (N)
Ohlone College (U)
Oklahoma State University (U)
Orange Coast College (U)
Oregon State University (G)
The Pennsylvania State University University
    Park Campus (U)
San Jacinto College North Campus (U)
Southwest Baptist University (U)
Texas Tech University (U)
University of Massachusetts Amherst (U)
University of Massachusetts System (U)
University of Minnesota, Twin Cities
    Campus (U)
University of New Hampshire (G)
University of Utah (U)
Weber State University (U)
Western Wyoming Community College (U)
West Virginia Wesleyan College (U)
William Paterson University of New Jersey
    (U)

**Foreign languages and literatures**
Arizona State University (U)
Brenau University (U)
Butte College (U)
Calvin College (U)
Capital Community College (U)
Cincinnati State Technical and Community
    College (U)
Coastline Community College (U)
Colorado Community College Online (U)
Community College of Philadelphia (U)
Cumberland County College (U)

*Foreign languages and literatures (continued)*

EduKan (U)
Elgin Community College (U)
Foothill College (U)
Fullerton College (U)
Georgia Perimeter College (U)
Hebrew College (N, U, G)
Hutchinson Community College and Area
    Vocational School (U)
Illinois State University (U)
Indiana Higher Education
    Telecommunication System (U)
J. Sargeant Reynolds Community College
    (U)
Judson College (U)
Kansas City Kansas Community College (U)
Kapiolani Community College (U)
Kentucky State University (U)
Maysville Community College (N)
Millersville University of Pennsylvania (U,
    G)
Morehead State University (U)
New Hampshire Community Technical
    College, Nashua/Claremont (U)
New School University (U)
North Carolina Central University (N)
Northeastern State University (U)
Northern State University (U)
North Georgia College & State University
    (U)
Northwest Iowa Community College (U)
Ohio University (U)
Ohlone College (U)
Oklahoma State University (U)
Owens Community College (U)
The Pennsylvania State University University
    Park Campus (U)
Pueblo Community College (U)
St. Norbert College (N, G)
Santa Barbara City College (U)
Southeast Missouri State University (U)
Southwestern Baptist Theological Seminary
    (G)
Southwestern Community College (U)
Spokane Falls Community College (U)
Strayer University (U)
Tulsa Community College (U)
The University of Alabama (U)
University of Alaska Anchorage (U)
University of Alaska Fairbanks (U)
University of California, Davis (N)
University of Colorado at Denver (N, U)
University of Connecticut (U)
University of Minnesota, Twin Cities
    Campus (U)
The University of North Carolina at Chapel
    Hill (N)
University of South Carolina (U)

University of Southern Indiana (U)
The University of Texas System (U)
University of Waterloo (U)
University of Wisconsin-Madison (U)
University of Wisconsin-Parkside (U)
University of Wisconsin-Stevens Point (U)
Virginia Commonwealth University (U)
Wayne State College (U)
Western Governors University (U)

## Foreign languages and literatures, other

Central Wyoming College (U)
Coastline Community College (U)
Colorado Electronic Community College
    (U)
Elgin Community College (U)
Mississippi State University (U)
Santa Rosa Junior College (U)
Shawnee State University (U)
University of California, Los Angeles (G)
University of Missouri-Columbia (U)
Yuba College (U)

## Forest production and processing

Mississippi State University (N, U)

## Forestry and related sciences

Central Carolina Technical College (U)
George Mason University (G)
Humboldt State University (U)
Mississippi State University (N, U)
North Carolina State University (U)
Northern Arizona University (U)
Oregon State University (U)
The University of British Columbia (G)
The University of North Carolina at
    Pembroke (U)
University of Wisconsin-Stevens Point (N)

## Forestry, general

Clemson University (U)
Oregon State University (U)
The University of British Columbia (U)
The University of Montana-Missoula (U)
The University of Tennessee (U)

## French language and literature

Burlington County College (U)
Coastline Community College (U)
College of San Mateo (U)
Eastern Michigan University (U)
Florida Community College at Jacksonville
    (U)
Jefferson College (U)
Lehigh Carbon Community College (U)
Marywood University (U)
Metropolitan Community College (U)
Mount Saint Vincent University (U)

Nassau Community College (U)
Northern Virginia Community College (U)
Oklahoma State University (U)
The Pennsylvania State University University
    Park Campus (U)
Pierce College (U)
St. Petersburg College (U)
Skidmore College (U)
University of Arkansas (U)
The University of British Columbia (U)
University of Guelph (U)
University of Illinois at Urbana-Champaign
    (U)
The University of Iowa (U)
University of Kansas (U)
University of Minnesota, Twin Cities
    Campus (U)
University of Missouri-Columbia (U)
University of Nevada, Reno (U)
The University of North Carolina at Chapel
    Hill (U)
The University of North Carolina at
    Greensboro (G)
The University of Tennessee (U)
University of Waterloo (U)
University of Wisconsin-Extension (U)
Washington State University (U)
Weber State University (U)
Western Washington University (U)
Wilfrid Laurier University (U)

## Funeral services and mortuary science

Mt. Hood Community College (U)
University of Central Oklahoma (U, G)

## Gaming and sports officiating services

North Idaho College (U)

## General retailing and wholesaling operations and skills

Chadron State College (U)
Lakeland Community College (N)
Okaloosa-Walton Community College (U)
Walla Walla Community College (N)

## General teacher education

Armstrong Atlantic State University (G)
Bemidji State University (U)
Brenau University (U)
Calvin College (U)
Chadron State College (U)
Concordia University (G)
Elgin Community College (U)
Fairmont State College (U)
Georgia Perimeter College (U)
Hamline University (G)
Isothermal Community College (U)
John F. Kennedy University (G)
Maranatha Baptist Bible College (U)

Minot State University (U)
Mississippi State University (U)
North Carolina Agricultural and Technical
State University (G)
North Georgia College & State University
(N, U, G)
Northwestern State University of Louisiana
(U)
Pasco-Hernando Community College (U)
Radford University (G)
St. Clair County Community College (U)
Southeast Missouri State University (U)
State University of New York College at
Fredonia (U)
Stephen F. Austin State University (G)
The University of Akron (U)
University of Southern Indiana (U)
The University of Texas of the Permian
Basin (G)
Western Washington University (U)
Western Wyoming Community College (U)

**Geography**

Alvin Community College (U)
Anne Arundel Community College (U)
Arizona State University (U)
Bellevue Community College (U)
Bemidji State University (U)
Blinn College (U)
Blue River Community College (U)
Boise State University (U)
Bridgewater State College (U)
Brigham Young University (U)
Bristol Community College (U)
Broward Community College (U)
California State University, Bakersfield (U)
Calvin College (U)
Carleton University (U)
Carroll Community College (U)
Central Michigan University (U)
Central Oregon Community College (U)
Central Wyoming College (U)
Chadron State College (U)
Champlain College (U)
Charter Oak State College (U)
Chattanooga State Technical Community
College (U)
College of Southern Maryland (U)
Colorado Community College Online (U)
Colorado Electronic Community College
(U)
Columbia Basin College (U)
Community College of Philadelphia (U)
Concordia University Wisconsin (U)
Connors State College (U)
Copiah-Lincoln Community College-
Natchez Campus (U)
Danville Area Community College (U)

Eastern Kentucky University (U)
Eastern Oregon University (U)
EduKan (U)
Elgin Community College (U)
Erie Community College, City Campus (U)
Erie Community College, North Campus
(U)
Fairmont State College (U)
Flathead Valley Community College (U)
Florence-Darlington Technical College (U)
Florida Community College at Jacksonville
(U)
Fullerton College (U)
George Mason University (U)
Georgia Perimeter College (U)
Governors State University (U)
Grand Rapids Community College (U)
Great Basin College (U)
Griggs University (U)
Harrisburg Area Community College (U)
Hunter College of the City University of
New York (U, G)
Illinois Valley Community College (U)
Indiana Higher Education
Telecommunication System (U)
Indiana State University (U)
Indian River Community College (U)
Jacksonville State University (U)
Kapiolani Community College (U)
Labette Community College (U)
Lakeland Community College (U)
Lehigh Carbon Community College (U)
Long Beach City College (U)
Longview Community College (U)
Maple Woods Community College (U)
Marshall University (U)
Maysville Community College (U)
Meridian Community College (U)
Michigan State University (U)
Moberly Area Community College (U)
Montana State University-Billings (U)
Moraine Valley Community College (U)
Mountain State University (U)
Mount Allison University (U)
Murray State University (U)
Northampton County Area Community
College (U)
North Country Community College (U)
Northeastern Oklahoma Agricultural and
Mechanical College (U)
Northern Arizona University (U)
Northern Kentucky University (U)
Northern Michigan University (U)
Northern Oklahoma College (U)
Northern Virginia Community College (U)
North Iowa Area Community College (U)
Northwest Missouri State University (U)
Ohio University (U)

Ohlone College (U)
Oklahoma City Community College (U)
Oklahoma State University (U)
Park University (U)
The Pennsylvania State University University
Park Campus (N, U)
Penn Valley Community College (U)
Portland Community College (U)
Portland State University (U)
Pueblo Community College (U)
Red Rocks Community College (U)
Roosevelt University (U)
Sam Houston State University (U)
Sandhills Community College (U)
Seattle Central Community College (U)
Seminole Community College (U)
Seward County Community College (U)
Shawnee State University (U)
Shippensburg University of Pennsylvania (U)
Skidmore College (U)
Southeast Arkansas College (U)
Southeast Community College, Lincoln
Campus (U)
Southern Illinois University Carbondale (U)
Southern Illinois University Edwardsville (G)
Southwestern Community College (U)
Southwest Texas State University (U, G)
Spokane Falls Community College (U)
Syracuse University (U)
Tacoma Community College (U)
Taylor University, World Wide Campus (U)
Texas A&M University-Kingsville (U)
Troy State University Montgomery (U)
Tulsa Community College (U)
University College of the Fraser Valley (U)
The University of Akron (U)
The University of Alabama (U)
University of Alaska Anchorage (U)
University of Alaska Fairbanks (U)
University of Arkansas (U)
University of Arkansas at Little Rock (U)
University of Central Arkansas (U, G)
University of Cincinnati (U)
University of Colorado at Denver (N, U)
University of Connecticut (U, G)
University of Guelph (U)
University of Idaho (U)
University of Illinois at Urbana-Champaign
(U)
The University of Iowa (U, G)
University of Kansas (U)
University of Manitoba (U)
University of Minnesota, Twin Cities
Campus (U)
University of Missouri-Columbia (U)
University of Nevada, Reno (U)
University of North Alabama (U)

# Individual Courses Index

*Health and physical education/fitness* (continued)

Jacksonville State University (U)
Jefferson Davis Community College (U)
John Wood Community College (U)
J. Sargeant Reynolds Community College (U)
Kean University (U)
Kennesaw State University (U)
Kentucky State University (U)
Labette Community College (U)
Lakeland Community College (N, U)
Lehigh Carbon Community College (U)
Lincoln Land Community College (U)
Louisiana State University in Shreveport (U)
Malone College (U)
Meridian Community College (U)
Middle Tennessee State University (U)
Mississippi State University (U, G)
Missouri Western State College (U)
Montana State University-Bozeman (G)
Nassau Community College (U)
Northampton County Area Community College (U)
North Carolina State University (U)
Northern State University (U)
Oklahoma State University (U)
Palo Alto College (U)
The Pennsylvania State University University Park Campus (U)
Plattsburgh State University of New York (U)
Rappahannock Community College (U)
Sacred Heart University (U)
Saint Charles Community College (U)
Shawnee State University (U)
Southeast Arkansas College (U)
Spokane Falls Community College (U)
Tarleton State University (U)
University of California, Los Angeles (G)
The University of Memphis (U)
University of Missouri-Columbia (U)
University of North Texas (U)
University of Oklahoma (U)
University of Sioux Falls (U)
University of Southern Mississippi (G)
The University of Texas of the Permian Basin (U, G)
Valdosta State University (U)
Walters State Community College (U)
Weber State University (U)
West Virginia Wesleyan College (U)
Wytheville Community College (U)

## Health products and services marketing operations

Lakeland Community College (N)
Pasco-Hernando Community College (N)

## Health professions and related sciences, other

Adirondack Community College (U)
American Academy of Nutrition, College of Nutrition (N)
Athens Technical College (U)
Brenau University (G)
Brunswick Community College (U)
California College for Health Sciences (U)
Calvin College (U)
Central Methodist College (N)
Chattanooga State Technical Community College (U)
Clarkson College (U, G)
College of Southern Maryland (N)
Columbia Basin College (N)
Community Hospital of Roanoke Valley-College of Health Sciences (U)
Danville Area Community College (U)
Delaware Technical & Community College, Stanton/Wilmington Campus (U)
Drake University (U, G)
East Central College (U)
Eastern New Mexico University-Roswell (U)
Elgin Community College (U)
Excelsior College (N)
Florence-Darlington Technical College (U)
Forrest Junior College (N)
The George Washington University (U, G)
Illinois State University (U)
Jacksonville State University (U, G)
Kean University (U)
Lakeland Community College (N)
Lorain County Community College (N)
Miami-Dade Community College (N)
Midwestern State University (U, G)
Mississippi State University (N, U, G)
Montana Tech of The University of Montana (U, G)
Montcalm Community College (N)
Moraine Valley Community College (U)
Morehead State University (U)
MU Direct: Continuing and Distance Education (U)
Northern Arizona University (U)
North Georgia College & State University (N)
Nova Southeastern University (G)
Passaic County Community College (U)
Pine Technical College (U)
Portland Community College (N, U)
Pueblo Community College (U)
Purdue University (U)
Radford University (G)
The Richard Stockton College of New Jersey (U)
Rockland Community College (U)
Sandhills Community College (U)

San Jacinto College North Campus (U)
Sinclair Community College (N)
Southeast Community College, Beatrice Campus (U)
Southeast Community College, Lincoln Campus (N)
Southeastern Illinois College (U)
South Piedmont Community College (U)
Spoon River College (U)
State University of New York College at Brockport (U)
State University of New York College of Technology at Alfred (U)
State University of New York Institute of Technology at Utica/Rome (U, G)
Tacoma Community College (U)
Temple University (G)
Universite de Montreal (U)
University of Arkansas at Little Rock (U)
University of Connecticut (N, U, G)
University of Delaware (G)
University of Illinois at Chicago (G)
University of Illinois at Urbana-Champaign (U)
University of Massachusetts Lowell (G)
University of New Hampshire (G)
University of Northern Colorado (U)
University of North Florida (U, G)
University of St. Augustine for Health Sciences (N)
University of St. Francis (U)
University of South Carolina (U)
University of Southern Indiana (G)
The University of Texas at Tyler (G)
The University of Texas Medical Branch at Galveston (U)
The University of Texas System (G)
University of the Sciences in Philadelphia (G)
Virginia Commonwealth University (G)
Weber State University (U)
Western Connecticut State University (U)
Wytheville Community College (U)

## Health system/health services administration

Central Michigan University (U)
Dakota State University (U)
Franklin University (U)
Golden Gate University (G)
Ivy Tech State College-Wabash Valley (U)
Keller Graduate School of Management (G)
Medical College of Wisconsin (G)
Montana State University-Billings (G)
Mountain State University (U)
Oregon State University (U, G)
Ottawa University (U)
Park University (U)

The Pennsylvania State University University Park Campus (U)
Seton Hall University (G)
Southwest Texas State University (U)
University of Central Florida (U, G)
University of Dallas (G)
University of Missouri-Columbia (U)
The University of North Carolina at Chapel Hill (U)
University of St. Francis (G)
University of Sarasota (G)
University System College for Lifelong Learning (U)
Virginia Commonwealth University (G)
Walden University (G)
Weber State University (U)

## Heating, air conditioning and refrigeration mechanics and repairers
Blue River Community College (U)
Elgin Community College (U)
Florence-Darlington Technical College (N, U)
Lakeland Community College (N)
Longview Community College (U)
Minnesota West Community and Technical College-Worthington Campus (U)

## Hebrew language and literature
Brigham Young University (U)
Cleveland College of Jewish Studies (N, U, G)
Lincoln Christian College (N, U, G)
North Central University (N, U)
University of Waterloo (U)
University of Wisconsin-Extension (U)

## Historic preservation, conservation and architectural history
Lakeland Community College (N)
Mary Baldwin College (U)
Randolph Community College (U)
The University of North Carolina at Greensboro (G)

## History and philosophy of science and technology
Bellevue Community College (U)
Colorado Electronic Community College (U)
Northern Michigan University (U)
Oregon State University (U)
Pennsylvania College of Technology (U)
Roger Williams University (U)
University of North Texas (U)

## History
Acadia University (U)
Adirondack Community College (U)

Alvin Community College (U)
American College of Computer & Information Sciences (U)
Andrew College (U)
Anne Arundel Community College (U)
Arizona State University (U)
Assemblies of God Theological Seminary (G)
Azusa Pacific University (U)
Bemidji State University (U)
Bevill State Community College (U)
Blinn College (U)
Blue River Community College (U)
Brenau University (U)
Briercrest Bible College (U)
Brigham Young University (U)
Bristol Community College (U)
Broome Community College (U)
Bucks County Community College (U)
Burlington College (U)
Butte College (U)
Cabrini College (U)
Caldwell Community College and Technical Institute (U)
California State University, Chico (U)
California State University, San Marcos (U)
Calvin College (U)
Canadian Bible College (U, G)
Cape Fear Community College (U)
Carl Albert State College (U)
Carroll Community College (U)
Catawba Valley Community College (U)
Cayuga County Community College (U)
Central Carolina Community College (U)
Central Missouri State University (U)
Central Oregon Community College (U)
Central Wyoming College (U)
Chadron State College (U, G)
Chaminade University of Honolulu (U)
Champlain College (U)
Chapman University (U)
Charter Oak State College (U)
Chattanooga State Technical Community College (U)
Citrus College (U)
Cleveland State Community College (U)
Coastline Community College (U)
College of DuPage (U)
College of Southern Maryland (U)
College of the Canyons (U)
Colorado Christian University (U)
Colorado Community College Online (U)
Colorado Electronic Community College (U)
Colorado State University (U)
Columbia Basin College (U)
Columbia College (U)
Community College of Philadelphia (U)
Concordia University (U)

Copiah-Lincoln Community College-Natchez Campus (U)
Corning Community College (U)
County College of Morris (U)
Craven Community College (U)
Cuyamaca College (U)
Cypress College (U)
Danville Area Community College (U)
Delaware Technical & Community College, Stanton/Wilmington Campus (U)
Des Moines Area Community College (U)
Drake University (U, G)
East Central College (U)
Eastern New Mexico University-Roswell (U)
East Los Angeles College (U)
Elgin Community College (U)
Elizabeth City State University (U)
Elizabethtown College (U)
Erie Community College, North Campus (U)
Eugene Bible College (U)
Everett Community College (U)
Evergreen Valley College (U)
Fairmont State College (U)
Fayetteville Technical Community College (U)
Florence-Darlington Technical College (U)
Florida Gulf Coast University (U)
Foothill College (U)
Fullerton College (U)
Garland County Community College (U)
Gogebic Community College (U)
Grace University (U)
Grand Rapids Community College (U)
Harrisburg Area Community College (U)
Haywood Community College (U)
Heartland Community College (U)
Holmes Community College (U)
Honolulu Community College (U)
Hope International University (U, G)
Horry-Georgetown Technical College (U)
Hutchinson Community College and Area Vocational School (U)
Illinois Eastern Community Colleges, Frontier Community College (U)
Illinois Eastern Community Colleges, Lincoln Trail College (U)
Illinois Eastern Community Colleges, Wabash Valley College (U)
Illinois State University (U)
Immaculata College (U)
Indiana Higher Education Telecommunication System (U)
Indiana State University (U)
Indiana Wesleyan University (U)
Indian River Community College (U)
Iowa Western Community College (U, G)
Isothermal Community College (U)

*History (continued)*

Ivy Tech State College-Columbus (U)
Ivy Tech State College-Eastcentral (U)
Ivy Tech State College-Kokomo (U)
Ivy Tech State College-North Central (U)
Ivy Tech State College-Northeast (U)
Ivy Tech State College-Southeast (U)
Ivy Tech State College-Wabash Valley (U)
Ivy Tech State College-Whitewater (U)
Jacksonville State University (U)
James Sprunt Community College (U)
Jefferson Community College (U)
J. Sargeant Reynolds Community College (U)
Judson College (U)
Kansas City Kansas Community College (U)
Kapiolani Community College (U)
Labette Community College (U)
Lakeland Community College (N, U)
Lehigh Carbon Community College (U)
LeTourneau University (U)
Lewis and Clark Community College (U)
Lincoln Land Community College (U)
Long Beach City College (U)
Longview Community College (U)
Lord Fairfax Community College (U)
Louisiana State University and Agricultural and Mechanical College (U)
Louisiana State University in Shreveport (U)
Malone College (U)
Maple Woods Community College (U)
Mary Baldwin College (U)
Marywood University (U)
Maysville Community College (U)
McLennan Community College (U)
Meridian Community College (U)
Millersville University of Pennsylvania (U)
Mineral Area College (U)
Minnesota State University Moorhead (U)
Minot State University (U)
MiraCosta College (U)
Mississippi State University (U)
Moberly Area Community College (U)
Montana State University-Billings (U)
Moraine Valley Community College (U)
Mountain State University (U)
Nash Community College (U)
Nassau Community College (U)
New Hampshire Community Technical College, Nashua/Claremont (U)
New School University (U)
North Arkansas College (U)
North Carolina State University (U)
North Central Michigan College (U)
Northeastern Oklahoma Agricultural and Mechanical College (U)
Northeast State Technical Community College (U)

Northern Arizona University (U)
Northern Kentucky University (U)
Northern Michigan University (U)
North Iowa Area Community College (U)
NorthWest Arkansas Community College (U)
Northwestern College (U)
Northwestern Michigan College (U)
Northwestern State University of Louisiana (U)
Northwest Iowa Community College (U)
Ohio University (U)
Oklahoma City Community College (U)
Oklahoma State University (U)
Olympic College (U)
Orangeburg-Calhoun Technical College (U)
Oregon State University (U)
Owens Community College (U)
Ozarks Technical Community College (U)
Pasco-Hernando Community College (U)
The Pennsylvania State University University Park Campus (U)
Penn Valley Community College (U)
Piedmont College (U)
Pierce College (U)
Pikes Peak Community College (U)
Portland State University (U)
Prestonsburg Community College (U)
Quinebaug Valley Community College (U)
Randolph Community College (U)
Rappahannock Community College (U)
Raritan Valley Community College (U)
Red Rocks Community College (U)
Rio Hondo College (U)
Robert Morris College (U)
Rockhurst University (U)
Roosevelt University (U)
Rowan-Cabarrus Community College (U)
Sacred Heart University (U)
Saddleback College (U)
Saint Charles Community College (U)
Sandhills Community College (U)
San Joaquin Delta College (U)
Santa Barbara City College (U)
Schenectady County Community College (U)
Schiller International University (U)
Seminole Community College (U)
Seton Hill College (U)
Seward County Community College (U)
Shasta College (U)
Shawnee State University (U)
Sinclair Community College (U)
Southeast Arkansas College (U)
Southeast Community College, Beatrice Campus (U)
Southeastern Illinois College (U)
Southeastern Oklahoma State University (U)

Southeast Missouri State University (U)
Southern Arkansas University Tech (U)
Southern Illinois University Carbondale (U)
South Puget Sound Community College (U)
Southwestern College (U)
Southwestern Community College (U)
Southwest Texas State University (U)
Spokane Falls Community College (U)
Spring Arbor University (U)
State University of New York College at Fredonia (U)
State University of West Georgia (U)
Stephens College (U)
Strayer University (U)
Taft College (U)
Tarleton State University (U, G)
Taylor University, World Wide Campus (U)
Texas Tech University (U)
Trident Technical College (U)
Tri-State University (U)
Troy State University Montgomery (U)
Tulsa Community College (U)
University College of the Fraser Valley (U)
The University of Alabama (U)
University of Alaska Anchorage (U, G)
University of Alaska Fairbanks (U)
University of Arkansas at Little Rock (U)
The University of British Columbia (U)
University of Cincinnati (U)
University of Colorado at Colorado Springs (U)
University of Colorado at Denver (N, U)
University of Great Falls (U)
University of Houston-Downtown (U)
University of Idaho (U)
University of Illinois at Urbana-Champaign (U)
University of Kansas (U, G)
University of La Verne (U)
University of Manitoba (U)
The University of Memphis (U)
University of Minnesota, Twin Cities Campus (U)
University of Missouri-Columbia (G)
University of Nebraska at Omaha (U)
University of New Mexico (U)
The University of North Carolina at Chapel Hill (U)
University of North Texas (U)
University of Oklahoma (U)
University of Saskatchewan (U)
University of Sioux Falls (U)
University of South Carolina (U)
University of South Carolina Sumter (U)
University of South Dakota (U)
The University of Texas at Tyler (U)
The University of Texas of the Permian Basin (U)

College of Southern Maryland (U)
Colorado Community College Online (U)
Connecticut State University System (U)
Dakota State University (U, G)
Eastern Connecticut State University (G)
Elgin Community College (U)
Fairmont State College (U)
Florida Institute of Technology (N, G)
Gardner-Webb University (G)
Gaston College (U)
George Mason University (G)
Haywood Community College (U)
Hibbing Community College (U)
Indiana University System (N)
Jacksonville State University (U, G)
J. Sargeant Reynolds Community College (U)
Keller Graduate School of Management (G)
Knowledge Systems Institute (G)
McDowell Technical Community College (U)
Minnesota State University Moorhead (G)
MU Direct: Continuing and Distance Education (G)
National American University (U)
Northeastern University (G)
Northern Kentucky University (U)
North Seattle Community College (U)
The Pennsylvania State University University Park Campus (U)
San Jacinto College North Campus (U)
Strayer University (U, G)
Taylor University, World Wide Campus (U)
Tidewater Community College (N)
Tunxis Community College (N)
Tyler Junior College (N)
The University of Akron (N)
University of Charleston (U)
University of Connecticut (U)
University of Massachusetts Lowell (U)
University of Nebraska at Omaha (U)
The University of North Carolina at Greensboro (G)
University of North Texas (G)
University of Oregon (G)
The University of Tennessee (N)
University of Tulsa (G)
University of Wisconsin-Eau Claire (N)
University of Wisconsin-Milwaukee (U)
Western Governors University (U)

## Inorganic chemistry
Illinois Institute of Technology (G)
Sam Houston State University (U)

## Institutional food workers and administrators
Elgin Community College (U)

North Georgia College & State University (N)
The Pennsylvania State University University Park Campus (U)
Southeast Community College, Beatrice Campus (U)

## Insurance and risk management
The American College (U, G)
Indiana State University (U)
Ivy Tech State College-North Central (U)
John Wood Community College (N)
Mountain State University (U)
Roger Williams University (U)
Sam Houston State University (U)
University of Dallas (G)
University of Waterloo (U)
Washington State University (U)

## Insurance marketing operations
State University of New York College of Technology at Canton (U)
University of Connecticut (N)

## Interior design
Eastern Michigan University (U)
New York Institute of Technology (U)
San Joaquin Delta College (U)
Weber State University (U)

## International and comparative education
North Georgia College & State University (U, G)

## International business
Arizona State University (G)
Berkeley College (U)
Brenau University (G)
California National University for Advanced Studies (U)
Calvin College (U)
Central Michigan University (U)
Champlain College (U)
Coastline Community College (U)
College of Southern Maryland (U)
Duke University (G)
Florence-Darlington Technical College (U)
Gardner-Webb University (G)
Indiana State University (U)
Keller Graduate School of Management (G)
Kellogg Community College (U)
Long Beach City College (U)
Marywood University (U)
Mercy College (U)
Milwaukee School of Engineering (N, G)
Montcalm Community College (U)
Mountain State University (U)
National American University (U)

Northcentral University (G)
North Seattle Community College (N, U)
Pennsylvania College of Technology (U)
Pitt Community College (U)
Rio Hondo College (U)
Rockingham Community College (N)
Sacred Heart University (U)
Sauk Valley Community College (U)
Schiller International University (U, G)
School for International Training (N)
Southern New Hampshire University (U, G)
Spring Arbor University (G)
State University of New York Empire State College (U)
Strayer University (U)
Suffolk University (G)
Tompkins Cortland Community College (U)
University of California, Berkeley (U)
University of Dallas (G)
The University of Findlay (U)
University of Houston-Downtown (U)
University of Northwestern Ohio (U)
University of Phoenix (N, G)
University of Sarasota (G)
University of Tulsa (G)
University of Washington (U)
Upper Iowa University (N, U)
Washington State University (U)
Western Iowa Tech Community College (U)
Worcester Polytechnic Institute (G)

## International relations and affairs
American Military University (U, G)
Drake University (U)
Miami-Dade Community College (U)
New Jersey City University (U)
North Georgia College & State University (U)
North Seattle Community College (N)
University of Massachusetts Boston (U)
University of South Carolina (U)
West Los Angeles College (U)

## Internet and World Wide Web
Alexandria Technical College (N)
Alvin Community College (U)
Barton College (U)
Bristol Community College (N)
Bryant and Stratton Online (U)
Cape Fear Community College (U)
Capital Community College (U)
Capitol College (U, G)
Central Community College (U)
Centralia College (N, U)
Champlain College (U)
Coastal Carolina Community College (N)
Coastline Community College (U)
Columbia Basin College (U)

Shawnee State University (U)
Southern Illinois University Carbondale (G)
Spokane Falls Community College (U)
Taylor University, World Wide Campus (U)
Temple University (U, G)
Texas Tech University (U)
The University of Alabama (U)
University of Alaska Fairbanks (U)
University of Arkansas at Little Rock (U)
University of Massachusetts Amherst (U)
University of Massachusetts System (U)
The University of Memphis (U)
The University of North Carolina at Chapel Hill (U)
University of North Texas (U)
University of Oklahoma (U)
University of Southern Indiana (U)
The University of Texas of the Permian Basin (U)
University of Washington (U)
University of Wisconsin Colleges (U)
Virginia Western Community College (U)
West Virginia University (U)
Yuba College (U)

## Journalism
Brevard Community College (U)
Central Michigan University (U)
Columbia University (N, G)
Corning Community College (U)
Delaware Technical & Community College, Jack F. Owens Campus (U)
Gogebic Community College (U)
Illinois Eastern Community Colleges, Wabash Valley College (U)
Indiana State University (U)
Lehigh Carbon Community College (U)
Marshall University (U)
Mt. San Antonio College (U)
Murray State University (U)
New Jersey Institute of Technology (G)
New School University (N, U)
North Central University (N, U)
Northern Kentucky University (U)
Northern Virginia Community College (U)
Ohio University (U)
Oklahoma State University (U)
Old Dominion University (U)
Parkland College (U)
Park University (U)
The Pennsylvania State University University Park Campus (U)
St. Petersburg College (U)
Seattle Central Community College (U)
Skidmore College (U)
Southwestern Community College (U)
University of Alaska Fairbanks (U)

University of Alaska Southeast, Sitka Campus (U)
University of Arkansas (U)
The University of Iowa (U, G)
University of Massachusetts Lowell (U)
The University of Memphis (G)
University of Minnesota, Twin Cities Campus (U)
University of Nevada, Reno (U)
The University of North Carolina at Chapel Hill (U)
University of Southern Indiana (U)

## Labor/personnel relations and studies
Kansas State University (U, G)
Mountain State University (U)
Ouachita Technical College (U)
Park University (U)
The Pennsylvania State University University Park Campus (U)
State University of New York Empire State College (U)
University of Wyoming (U, G)
Upper Iowa University (N, U)

## Landscape architecture
The University of British Columbia (U)
University of Connecticut (G)
University of Saskatchewan (N)

## Latin American studies
Florida Community College at Jacksonville (U)
Rend Lake College (U)
Triton College (U)

## Latin language and literature (ancient and medieval)
University of Alaska Fairbanks (U)
University of Arkansas (U)
University of Colorado at Denver (U)
University of Illinois at Urbana-Champaign (U)
The University of Iowa (U)
University of Minnesota, Twin Cities Campus (U)
The University of North Carolina at Chapel Hill (U)
The University of North Carolina at Greensboro (G)
University of Waterloo (U)

## Law and legal studies
American Institute for Paralegal Studies, Inc. (U)
Arizona State University (U)
Arizona State University West (U)
Athens Technical College (U)
Bemidji State University (U)

Brenau University (U)
Bristol Community College (N)
California State University, San Marcos (N)
Cape Fear Community College (U)
Central Carolina Technical College (U)
Central Community College (U)
Chadron State College (U)
College for Professional Studies (U)
Colorado State University (N)
Columbia College (U)
Community College of Philadelphia (U)
Drake University (G)
Elgin Community College (U)
Finger Lakes Community College (U)
Forrest Junior College (U)
Franklin Pierce Law Center (G)
Gannon University (U)
Gaston College (U)
Hamilton College (U)
Iowa Western Community College (U)
John F. Kennedy University (G)
Jones College (U)
Lord Fairfax Community College (U)
Manchester Community College (U)
Manor College (U)
Maysville Community College (N)
Missouri Western State College (U)
North Carolina Community College System (U)
Northeastern State University (U)
Northwestern Michigan College (U)
Raritan Valley Community College (U)
Rockingham Community College (N)
Roosevelt University (U)
Schenectady County Community College (U)
Shawnee State University (U)
State University of New York College of Technology at Alfred (U)
Stephens College (U)
Strayer University (U, G)
Texas Tech University (U)
Tompkins Cortland Community College (U)
Tri-State University (U)
Tulsa Community College (U)
University at Buffalo, The State University of New York (U)
University of Great Falls (U)
University of Tulsa (G)
University of Wisconsin-Extension (U)
University of Wisconsin-Parkside (N)
Victoria College (U)
Walla Walla Community College (N)
West Los Angeles College (U)

## Law and legal studies, other
Adams State College (U)
Anne Arundel Community College (U)

State University of New York College of Technology at Alfred (U)
Stony Brook University, State University of New York (G)
Tarrant County College District (U)
Taylor University, World Wide Campus (U)
Tennessee Temple University (U)
Texas Tech University (U)
Tri-State University (U)
Tulsa Community College (U)
Tyler Junior College (U)
Ulster County Community College (U)
University of Arkansas at Little Rock (U)
University of California, Los Angeles (G)
University of Colorado at Denver (N, U)
University of Connecticut (U, G)
University of Great Falls (U)
University of Houston-Downtown (U)
University of Maine (G)
University of Massachusetts Lowell (U)
The University of North Carolina at Greensboro (N, G)
University of Pennsylvania (U)
The University of Texas System (U)
University of Waterloo (U)
University of Wisconsin-Milwaukee (N)
University of Wisconsin-River Falls (U)
University of Wyoming (U)
University System College for Lifelong Learning (U)
West Virginia Wesleyan College (U)
York University (U)

### Library assistant
Colorado Community College Online (U)
Indian River Community College (U)
Northampton County Area Community College (U)
Pueblo Community College (U)
University College of the Fraser Valley (U)

### Library science, other
Central Carolina Community College (U)
Central Missouri State University (U, G)
Chadron State College (U)
Coastline Community College (U)
Colorado Community College Online (U)
Colorado Electronic Community College (U)
Contra Costa College (U)
Everett Community College (U)
Florida Keys Community College (U)
MU Direct: Continuing and Distance Education (G)
North Seattle Community College (U)
Northwestern State University of Louisiana (U)
Ohlone College (U)

Plattsburgh State University of New York (U)
Rio Hondo College (U)
Saddleback College (U)
Seminole Community College (U)
Tacoma Community College (U)
The University of British Columbia (U)
University of Idaho (U, G)
The University of Montana-Missoula (G)
The University of North Carolina at Greensboro (N, G)
University of North Dakota (U)
University of North Texas (U, G)
University of Oklahoma (U)
University of Wisconsin-Eau Claire (U)
University of Wisconsin-Milwaukee (G)

### Library science/librarianship
Clarion University of Pennsylvania (U, G)
East Carolina University (G)
Foothill College (U)
Louisiana State University and Agricultural and Mechanical College (G)
Louisiana State University in Shreveport (G)
MU Direct: Continuing and Distance Education (G)
North Carolina Central University (G)
Northern State University (U)
Santa Rosa Junior College (U)
University of Alaska Fairbanks (U)
The University of Arizona (G)
University of Central Oklahoma (U, G)
University of North Texas (U, G)
University of Vermont (G)
University of Washington (U)
University of Wisconsin-Milwaukee (G)

### Management information systems and business data processing, general
Adams State College (U)
Bellevue Community College (U)
California National University for Advanced Studies (U, G)
Capitol College (G)
Connecticut State University System (U, G)
Fashion Institute of Technology (U)
Forsyth Technical Community College (N)
Golden Gate University (U, G)
Kansas State University (U)
Lincoln Christian College (N, U)
Manatee Community College (U)
Marshall University (U)
Marywood University (U)
Mercy College (U, G)
Metropolitan State University (U, G)
Mountain State University (U)
Northern Illinois University (G)
Northern Virginia Community College (U)

Oklahoma State University (U)
Old Dominion University (U, G)
Otero Junior College (U)
The Pennsylvania State University University Park Campus (U)
Robert Morris College (U)
State University of New York Empire State College (U)
State University of West Georgia (U)
Stevens Institute of Technology (G)
Suffolk University (G)
University of Colorado at Denver (G)
University of Dallas (G)
University of Houston-Downtown (U)
University of Illinois at Springfield (G)
University of Minnesota, Twin Cities Campus (U)
University of Oregon (G)
University of Phoenix (G)
University of Sarasota (G)
University of Southern Mississippi (U)
University of Waterloo (G)
University System College for Lifelong Learning (U)
Upper Iowa University (N, U)
Virginia Polytechnic Institute and State University (G)
Walden University (G)
Wayland Baptist University (U, G)
Weber State University (U)
West Virginia Northern Community College (U)
West Virginia University Institute of Technology (U)
Worcester Polytechnic Institute (G)

### Management science
Stevens Institute of Technology (G)
University of Wisconsin-Platteville (G)
Western Nevada Community College (U)

### Marketing management and research
Alexandria Technical College (N)
Aquinas College (G)
Arizona State University (U)
Athens Technical College (U)
Brenau University (G)
Bristol Community College (N)
Caldwell Community College and Technical Institute (U)
Calvin College (U)
Carroll Community College (U)
Central Carolina Community College (U)
Central Carolina Technical College (U)
Chadron State College (U, G)
Clackamas Community College (U)
Colorado Community College Online (U)

Colorado Community College Online (U)

Colorado Electronic Community College (U)

Colorado Northwestern Community College (U)

Community Hospital of Roanoke Valley-College of Health Sciences (U)

Connecticut State University System (U, G)

Danville Area Community College (U)

Delaware Technical & Community College, Jack F. Owens Campus (U)

Delaware Technical & Community College, Stanton/Wilmington Campus (U)

Delta College (U)

Duke University (G)

Edison State Community College (U)

Elgin Community College (U)

Grand Rapids Community College (U)

Harrisburg Area Community College (U)

Husson College (U)

Illinois Eastern Community Colleges, Frontier Community College (U)

Illinois Eastern Community Colleges, Lincoln Trail College (U)

Illinois Eastern Community Colleges, Olney Central College (U)

Illinois Eastern Community Colleges, Wabash Valley College (U)

Indiana State University (U)

Iowa State University of Science and Technology (G)

Iowa Wesleyan College (U)

Jefferson Davis Community College (U)

Kansas State University (U)

Lakeland Community College (U)

Lehigh Carbon Community College (U)

Loyola University Chicago (U)

Loyola University New Orleans (U)

Manatee Community College (U)

Marylhurst University (U, G)

Marywood University (U)

Maysville Community College (U)

Mercy College (U)

Montana State University-Billings (U)

Montana State University-Bozeman (G)

Montgomery County Community College (U)

Mountain State University (U)

Mount Allison University (U)

Mount Wachusett Community College (U)

Nassau Community College (U)

New York Institute of Technology (U)

North Carolina Community College System (U)

North Dakota State University (U)

Northern Arizona University (G)

Northern Michigan University (U)

Northern Virginia Community College (U)

Northwest Iowa Community College (U)

Oklahoma City Community College (U)

Oklahoma State University (U)

Oregon State University (U)

Parkland College (U)

Park University (U)

Passaic County Community College (U)

Pennsylvania College of Technology (U)

The Pennsylvania State University University Park Campus (U, G)

Plattsburgh State University of New York (U)

Portland Community College (U)

Portland State University (U)

Presentation College (U)

Prestonsburg Community College (U)

Purdue University North Central (U)

St. Ambrose University (G)

St. Petersburg College (U)

Schiller International University (G)

Seattle Central Community College (U)

Seward County Community College (U)

Shawnee State University (U)

Southern New Hampshire University (U, G)

State University of New York at Oswego (U)

State University of New York Empire State College (U)

Stephens College (G)

Taft College (U)

Teachers College, Columbia University (U)

Texas A&M University-Corpus Christi (U)

Texas Tech University (G)

Triton College (U)

University of Alaska Fairbanks (U)

University of Central Florida (U, G)

University of Colorado at Denver (U)

The University of Findlay (U)

University of Guelph (U)

University of Houston-Downtown (U)

University of Idaho (U, G)

University of Illinois at Springfield (U)

The University of Iowa (U, G)

University of Maine at Machias (U)

University of Minnesota, Morris (U)

University of Missouri-Columbia (U)

University of New Brunswick (U)

University of New Hampshire (G)

The University of North Carolina at Chapel Hill (U)

University of Northwestern Ohio (U)

University of Notre Dame (N, G)

University of Pennsylvania (U)

University of Pittsburgh (U)

University of South Dakota (U)

University of Southern Mississippi (G)

The University of Tennessee (U)

The University of Texas of the Permian Basin (G)

The University of Texas System (U)

University of Toledo (U)

University of Utah (U)

University of Washington (U)

University of Waterloo (U)

University of Wisconsin Colleges (U)

University of Wisconsin-Extension (U)

University of Wisconsin-Parkside (G)

University of Wisconsin-Stevens Point (U, G)

University of Wyoming (U)

Upper Iowa University (N, U)

Villanova University (U)

Virginia Polytechnic Institute and State University (G)

Washington State University (U)

Weber State University (U)

Western Washington University (U)

William Paterson University of New Jersey (G)

Yuba College (U)

## Mathematics and computer science

Alvin Community College (U)

American College of Computer & Information Sciences (U)

Bank Street College of Education (G)

Calvin College (U)

Chadron State College (U, G)

Champlain College (U)

Colorado Community College Online (U)

Columbia College (U)

Concordia University (U)

Drake University (U)

Edison State Community College (U)

Elgin Community College (U)

Florence-Darlington Technical College (U)

Georgia Perimeter College (U)

Harrisburg Area Community College (U)

Haywood Community College (U)

Jacksonville State University (U)

Kapiolani Community College (U)

North Seattle Community College (U)

San Jacinto College North Campus (U)

Shippensburg University of Pennsylvania (G)

Southwest Texas State University (U)

Tuskegee University (N)

University of Connecticut (G)

University of Massachusetts Lowell (U)

Walla Walla Community College (U)

## Mathematics

Acadia University (N)

Adirondack Community College (U)

Albuquerque Technical Vocational Institute (U)

Alvin Community College (U)

Amarillo College (U)

# Individual Courses Index

Ohio University (U)
Oklahoma City Community College (U)
Olympic College (U)
Orangeburg-Calhoun Technical College (U)
Ouachita Technical College (U)
Owens Community College (U)
Ozarks Technical Community College (U)
Palo Alto College (U)
The Paralegal Institute, Inc. (U)
The Pennsylvania State University University Park Campus (U)
Penn Valley Community College (U)
Piedmont College (U)
Prestonsburg Community College (U)
Pueblo Community College (U)
Rappahannock Community College (U)
Raritan Valley Community College (U)
Red Rocks Community College (U)
Rend Lake College (U)
Rio Hondo College (U)
St. Clair County Community College (U)
San Jacinto College North Campus (U)
Schenectady County Community College (U)
Schiller International University (U)
Seward County Community College (U)
Shawnee State University (U)
Shippensburg University of Pennsylvania (U, G)
Sinclair Community College (U)
Southeast Arkansas College (U)
Southeast Community College, Beatrice Campus (N, U)
Southeastern Illinois College (U)
Southeastern Oklahoma State University (U)
Southeast Missouri State University (U)
Southern Illinois University Carbondale (U)
Southwestern Community College (U)
Southwest Texas State University (U, G)
Spokane Falls Community College (U)
State University of New York College at Fredonia (U)
State University of New York College of Agriculture and Technology at Morrisville (U)
Stephens College (U)
Strayer University (U, G)
Sussex County Community College (U)
Taft College (U)
Taylor University, World Wide Campus (U)
Temple University (U)
Tennessee Temple University (U)
Texas Tech University (G)
Tidewater Community College (U)
Tompkins Cortland Community College (U)
Trident Technical College (U)
Troy State University-Florida Region (U)
Tulsa Community College (U)

The University Alliance (U)
The University of Akron (U)
The University of Alabama (U)
University of Alaska Fairbanks (U)
University of Arkansas at Little Rock (U)
University of California, Los Angeles (G)
University of Colorado at Denver (N)
University of Connecticut (U)
The University of Findlay (U)
University of Great Falls (U)
University of Idaho (U)
University of Illinois at Springfield (U)
University of Illinois at Urbana-Champaign (U)
University of Kansas (U)
University of Manitoba (U)
University of Massachusetts System (U)
University of Minnesota, Morris (U)
University of Minnesota, Twin Cities Campus (U)
University of New Mexico (U)
University of Northern Colorado (U)
University of North Texas (U)
University of Oklahoma (U)
University of Pennsylvania (U)
University of South Carolina (U)
The University of Texas at Tyler (U)
The University of Texas of the Permian Basin (U)
The University of Texas System (U)
University of Utah (U)
University of Washington (U)
University of Waterloo (U)
University of Wisconsin Colleges (U)
University of Wisconsin-Extension (U)
University of Wisconsin-Parkside (U)
University of Wisconsin-Platteville (U, G)
University of Wisconsin-Stevens Point (U)
Valdosta State University (U)
Victoria College (U)
Vincennes University (U)
Virginia Western Community College (U)
Volunteer State Community College (U)
Walla Walla Community College (U)
Walters State Community College (U)
Wayne State College (U)
Weber State University (U)
Western Governors University (U)
Western Washington University (U)
West Virginia University (U)
West Virginia University Institute of Technology (U)
Worcester State College (U)
York College of Pennsylvania (N)
York Technical College (U)
York University (U)
Yuba College (U)

## Mathematics, other

Alvin Community College (U)
Amarillo College (U)
Anne Arundel Community College (U)
Bank Street College of Education (N, G)
Bellevue Community College (U)
Blinn College (U)
Bossier Parish Community College (U)
Brigham Young University (U)
Bristol Community College (U)
Broward Community College (U)
Central Arizona College (U)
Central Community College (U)
Central Methodist College (U)
Central Texas College (U)
Chadron State College (G)
Clovis Community College (U)
Coastline Community College (U)
College of Southern Maryland (U)
College of The Albemarle (U)
Colorado Community College Online (U)
Colorado Electronic Community College (U)
Colorado Northwestern Community College (U)
Columbia Basin College (U)
Copiah-Lincoln Community College (U)
Dallas County Community College District (U)
Delaware Technical & Community College, Stanton/Wilmington Campus (U)
Delta College (U)
Eastern Kentucky University (U)
Elgin Community College (U)
Florida Community College at Jacksonville (U)
Floyd College (U)
Forsyth Technical Community College (N)
Frank Phillips College (U)
Genesee Community College (U)
Grand Rapids Community College (U)
Grantham College of Engineering (U)
Great Basin College (U)
Hope International University (G)
Horry-Georgetown Technical College (U)
Illinois Eastern Community Colleges, Wabash Valley College (U)
Indiana State University (U)
Jefferson College (U)
Jefferson Community College (U)
Kellogg Community College (U)
Kentucky State University (U)
Lansing Community College (U)
Manatee Community College (U)
Marlhurst University (U)
Marywood University (U)
Mercy College (U)
Mountain State University (U)

Seattle Central Community College (U)
Taylor University, World Wide Campus (U)
The University of British Columbia (U)
University of Waterloo (U)
Virginia Polytechnic Institute and State
 University (U)
Western Washington University (U)

## Mental health services
Elgin Community College (U)
MU Direct: Continuing and Distance
 Education (G)

## Microbiology/bacteriology
Brigham Young University (U)
Calvin College (U)
Delta College (U)
Garland County Community College (U)
Graceland University (U)
Harrisburg Area Community College (U)
Iowa State University of Science and
 Technology (U, G)
Iowa Western Community College (U)
Manatee Community College (U)
Montana State University-Bozeman (G)
Mountain State University (U)
Rend Lake College (U)
St. Petersburg College (U)
Skidmore College (U)
University of Arkansas (U)
University of Guelph (U)
University of Idaho (U)
University of Manitoba (U)
University of New Brunswick (U)
University of Waterloo (U)
Virginia Polytechnic Institute and State
 University (U)
West Virginia Northern Community College
 (U)

## Middle Eastern languages and literatures
Elgin Community College (U)
Hebrew College (N, U, G)

## Military studies
American Military University (G)
Georgia Southern University (U)
Mary Baldwin College (U)
North Georgia College & State University
 (N, U)

## Military technologies
American Military University (G)
Eastern Michigan University (U)

## Miscellaneous engineering-related technologies
Bristol Community College (N)
Florence-Darlington Technical College (U)

University of North Texas (U)

## Miscellaneous health aides
California College for Health Sciences (N)
Elgin Community College (U)
Erie Community College, North Campus
 (U)
Forrest Junior College (U)
Western Wisconsin Technical College (N)

## Miscellaneous health professions
Alexandria Technical College (N, U)
Alvin Community College (U)
Amarillo College (U)
Armstrong Atlantic State University (U)
Brenau University (U, G)
California College for Health Sciences (N,
 U)
Chattanooga State Technical Community
 College (U)
Cincinnati State Technical and Community
 College (U)
Community Hospital of Roanoke Valley-
 College of Health Sciences (U)
Elgin Community College (U)
Florence-Darlington Technical College (U)
Forrest Junior College (U)
Jacksonville State University (G)
J. Sargeant Reynolds Community College
 (U)
Kentucky State University (U)
Lackawanna Junior College (N, U)
MU Direct: Continuing and Distance
 Education (U)
Northern Arizona University (U)
North Georgia College & State University
 (N)
Portland Community College (N)
Radford University (G)
Sinclair Community College (U)
Southeast Community College, Beatrice
 Campus (U)
State University of New York College of
 Technology at Alfred (U)
University of Connecticut (N, U, G)
University of Phoenix (N)

## Miscellaneous mechanics and repairers
Elgin Community College (U)
Erie Community College, South Campus
 (U)
Florence-Darlington Technical College (N,
 U)

## Miscellaneous physical sciences
Elgin Community College (U)
Lord Fairfax Community College (U)
University of Massachusetts System (U)
University of Waterloo (U)

## Missions/missionary studies and missiology
Assemblies of God Theological Seminary (G)
Briercrest Bible College (U)
Columbia International University (N, U,
 G)
Covenant Theological Seminary (G)
Dallas Theological Seminary (G)
Eugene Bible College (U)
Hobe Sound Bible College (N, U)
Northwestern College (U)
Providence College and Theological
 Seminary (G)
Southern Christian University (N, U, G)
Taylor University, World Wide Campus (U)

## Multi/interdisciplinary studies, other
Burlington College (U)
Butte College (U)
Columbia College (U, G)
Fairmont State College (U)
Hibbing Community College (U)
Mary Baldwin College (U)
Naropa University (U, G)
North Carolina State University (U)
Taylor University, World Wide Campus (U)
Temple University (U)
University of Connecticut (U, G)
The University of Memphis (U)
The University of North Carolina at
 Greensboro (N)
University of Waterloo (U)

## Museology/museum studies
Brenau University (U)
Harvard University (N, U, G)
John F. Kennedy University (G)

## Music
Acadia University (N)
Amarillo College (U)
Bridgewater State College (U)
Brigham Young University (U)
Bucks County Community College (U)
Caldwell Community College and Technical
 Institute (U)
California State University, Chico (U)
Calvin College (U)
Catawba Valley Community College (U)
Central Michigan University (U)
Cerro Coso Community College (U)
Chaminade University of Honolulu (U)
Cleveland State Community College (U)
College of DuPage (U)
College of the Canyons (U)
Colorado Community College Online (U)
Colorado State University (N)
Dakota State University (U)

Illinois State University (G)

Indiana Higher Education Telecommunication System (U)

Indiana State University (G)

Iowa Western Community College (U)

Ivy Tech State College-Northeast (U)

Ivy Tech State College-Northwest (U)

Ivy Tech State College-Southcentral (U)

Ivy Tech State College-Southwest (U)

Jacksonville State University (U)

J. Sargeant Reynolds Community College (U)

Kean University (U)

Kellogg Community College (U)

Kennesaw State University (U)

Lac Courte Oreilles Ojibwa Community College (U)

Lake Superior State University (U)

Lakeview College of Nursing (U)

Lewis-Clark State College (N)

Lincoln Land Community College (U)

Long Beach City College (U)

Lord Fairfax Community College (U)

Loyola University Chicago (G)

Macon State College (U)

Maranatha Baptist Bible College (U)

Marshall University (U)

Marycrest International University (U)

Maysville Community College (U)

Memorial University of Newfoundland (G)

Metropolitan State University (U)

Michigan State University (G)

Middle Tennessee State University (U, G)

Midwestern State University (G)

Minot State University (U)

Mississippi University for Women (G)

Missouri Western State College (U)

Mohawk Valley Community College (U)

Montana Tech of The University of Montana (U)

Morehead State University (U)

Mountain State University (U)

MU Direct: Continuing and Distance Education (U, G)

Northeastern State University (U)

Northeastern University (G)

Northern Arizona University (U)

Northern Kentucky University (U, G)

North Georgia College & State University (U, G)

North Iowa Area Community College (N)

Northwestern Michigan College (U)

Northwestern State University of Louisiana (U)

Old Dominion University (U, G)

Plattsburgh State University of New York (U)

Presentation College (U)

Radford University (N, G)

Raritan Valley Community College (U)

Rend Lake College (U)

The Richard Stockton College of New Jersey (U)

Rockland Community College (U)

Sacred Heart University (U)

St. Clair County Community College (U)

Salve Regina University (U)

San Joaquin Delta College (U)

Shawnee State University (U)

Slippery Rock University of Pennsylvania (U)

Southeastern Oklahoma State University (U)

Southeast Missouri State University (U)

Southern Illinois University Edwardsville (G)

Southern University and Agricultural and Mechanical College (G)

Southwest Missouri State University (U)

Stanly Community College (U)

State University of New York Institute of Technology at Utica/Rome (U, G)

Syracuse University (G)

Tarleton State University (U)

Temple University (U)

Universite de Montreal (U)

The University of Akron (U, G)

The University of Alabama (G)

University of Alaska Anchorage (U)

University of Colorado at Denver (G)

University of Connecticut (U)

University of Delaware (U, G)

University of Illinois at Chicago (N, G)

The University of Iowa (U)

University of Kansas (N)

University of Manitoba (U)

University of Massachusetts Boston (U)

University of Massachusetts Dartmouth (U)

University of Massachusetts System (G)

The University of Memphis (U)

University of Michigan-Flint (U)

University of Minnesota, Twin Cities Campus (U)

University of New Mexico (U, G)

The University of North Carolina at Chapel Hill (N)

University of Northern Colorado (U)

University of North Florida (U)

University of Pennsylvania (G)

University of Pittsburgh at Johnstown (G)

University of Saint Francis (U, G)

University of South Carolina Spartanburg (U)

University of South Dakota (U)

University of Southern Indiana (U, G)

University of Southern Mississippi (G)

The University of Texas at Tyler (G)

The University of Texas Medical Branch at Galveston (U, G)

The University of Texas System (G)

University of Vermont (U, G)

University of Wisconsin-Eau Claire (N, U)

University of Wisconsin-Madison (U, G)

University of Wisconsin-Parkside (U)

Victoria College (U)

Villanova University (U, G)

Walters State Community College (U)

Weber State University (U)

Western Nevada Community College (U)

Western University of Health Sciences (N, G)

West Virginia University Institute of Technology (U)

West Virginia Wesleyan College (U)

William Paterson University of New Jersey (G)

York Technical College (U)

York University (U)

Yuba College (U)

## Occupational therapy

Manchester Community College (U)

St. Ambrose University (G)

University of Central Arkansas (G)

University of Minnesota, Twin Cities Campus (U)

University of St. Augustine for Health Sciences (U)

Western Michigan University (U)

## Ocean engineering

University of Connecticut (G)

William Paterson University of New Jersey (U)

## Oceanography

Anne Arundel Community College (U)

Bellevue Community College (U)

Coastline Community College (U)

College of Southern Maryland (U)

Fullerton College (U)

Johnson County Community College (U)

Oregon State University (U)

Portland Community College (U)

Saddleback College (U)

St. Petersburg College (U)

Seattle Central Community College (U)

The University of British Columbia (U)

The University of North Carolina at Chapel Hill (U)

University of Oregon (U)

## Ophthalmic/optometric services

Wytheville Community College (U)

# Individual Courses Index

## Optometry (O.D.)
Wytheville Community College (U)

## Organic chemistry
American Academy of Nutrition, College of Nutrition (U)
Illinois Institute of Technology (G)
Mountain State University (U)
The Pennsylvania State University University Park Campus (U)
Sam Houston State University (U)
University of Utah (U)
University of Waterloo (U)

## Organizational behavior studies
Brigham Young University (U)
California National University for Advanced Studies (U, G)
Central Michigan University (U, G)
Connecticut State University System (U, G)
Duke University (G)
Fielding Graduate Institute (G)
Kansas State University (U)
Medical College of Wisconsin (G)
Milwaukee School of Engineering (N, G)
Montana State University-Billings (U)
Mountain State University (U)
Northern Virginia Community College (U)
Oklahoma State University (U)
Park University (U)
Pennsylvania College of Technology (U)
The Pennsylvania State University University Park Campus (U)
Sacred Heart University (U)
Southern Christian University (N, U, G)
Southern New Hampshire University (U, G)
State University of New York Empire State College (U)
Suffolk University (G)
Thomas Edison State College (U)
Troy State University-Florida Region (U)
Troy State University Montgomery (U)
The Union Institute (G)
University of Dallas (G)
University of Delaware (U)
University of Missouri-Columbia (G)
University of New Brunswick (U)
University of Phoenix (G)
University of Waterloo (U)
University of Wisconsin-Madison (U, G)
University of Wisconsin-Milwaukee (U)
Virginia Polytechnic Institute and State University (G)
Weber State University (U)
Worcester Polytechnic Institute (G)

## Paralegal/legal assistant
Anne Arundel Community College (U)
Coastline Community College (U)

College of Mount St. Joseph (U)
Johnson County Community College (U)
Manatee Community College (U)
The Pennsylvania State University University Park Campus (N)
Tyler Junior College (U)

## Parks, recreation and leisure facilities management
George Mason University (G)
Mary Baldwin College (U)
North Carolina Central University (G)
North Carolina State University (U)
Northern Arizona University (U)
United States Sports Academy (U)

## Parks, recreation and leisure studies
Kean University (U)
Southern Illinois University Carbondale (U)
The University of North Carolina at Chapel Hill (U)

## Parks, recreation, leisure and fitness studies, other
State University of New York College at Brockport (G)
State University of New York College at Cortland (U, G)
University of Southern Mississippi (G)

## Pastoral counseling and specialized ministries
Assemblies of God Theological Seminary (G)
Beulah Heights Bible College (U)
Calvary Bible College and Theological Seminary (U, G)
Hobe Sound Bible College (N, U)
Liberty University (G)
Maranatha Baptist Bible College (U, G)
Providence College and Theological Seminary (G)
Southern Christian University (N, U, G)
Southwestern Baptist Theological Seminary (G)
Taylor University, World Wide Campus (U)
Tennessee Temple University (U)

## Peace and conflict studies
Antioch University McGregor (G)
Arizona State University (U)
Drake University (U, G)
John F. Kennedy University (G)
Naropa University (U)
Saybrook Graduate School and Research Center (G)
Taylor University, World Wide Campus (U)
University of California, Berkeley (U)
University of Missouri-Columbia (U)
University of Waterloo (U)

University of Wisconsin-Extension (U)

## Personal and miscellaneous services, other
Central Community College (U)
Kean University (N)
Lewis-Clark State College (N)
Walla Walla Community College (N)
Western Iowa Tech Community College (N)

## Petroleum engineering
Texas A&M University (G)
Texas Tech University (G)

## Pharmacy
Albany College of Pharmacy of Union University (G)
Drake University (U, G)
Manchester Community College (U)
Ohio Northern University (G)
San Jacinto College North Campus (U)
University of Connecticut (U, G)
University of Illinois at Chicago (G)
University of New Mexico (U)
University of Washington (U)
University of Wisconsin-Madison (G)

## Philosophy and religion
Assemblies of God Theological Seminary (G)
Atlantic University (N, G)
Bemidji State University (U)
Brigham Young University (U)
Broward Community College (U)
Bucks County Community College (U)
Calvin College (U)
Carleton University (U)
Catawba Valley Community College (U)
Chadron State College (U)
Chaminade University of Honolulu (U)
Chattanooga State Technical Community College (U)
Coastline Community College (U)
College of DuPage (U)
College of San Mateo (U)
College of Southern Maryland (U)
Colorado Electronic Community College (U)
Columbia College (U)
Community College of Vermont (U)
Covenant Theological Seminary (G)
Crown College (U, G)
Delta College (U)
Denver Seminary (N, G)
Duquesne University (U, G)
East Carolina University (U)
Eastern Kentucky University (U)
Edison State Community College (U)
Elgin Community College (U)

Florida Community College at Jacksonville (U)
Hebrew College (N, U, G)
Hobe Sound Bible College (N, U)
Indiana Wesleyan University (U)
Iowa Western Community College (U)
John F. Kennedy University (U, G)
John Wood Community College (U)
Kellogg Community College (U)
LIFE Bible College (U)
Manatee Community College (U)
Mary Baldwin College (U)
Marylhurst University (U, G)
Marywood University (U)
Maysville Community College (U)
Mendocino College (U)
Metropolitan Community College (U)
Mohawk Valley Community College (U)
Moody Bible Institute (U)
Moraine Valley Community College (U)
Mountain State University (U)
Murray State University (U)
Naropa University (U)
New York Institute of Technology (U)
North Central University (N, U)
Northern Arizona University (U)
Northern Virginia Community College (U)
North Seattle Community College (U)
Ohio University (U)
Oklahoma City Community College (U)
Oregon State University (U)
Park University (U)
Pennsylvania College of Technology (U)
Pierce College (U)
Pitt Community College (U)
Prairie Bible College (U)
Randolph Community College (U)
Rockhurst University (U)
Roger Williams University (U)
Rowan-Cabarrus Community College (U)
St. Petersburg College (U)
Salve Regina University (U)
San Joaquin Delta College (U)
Santa Barbara City College (U)
Seattle Central Community College (U)
Southeast Community College, Lincoln Campus (U)
Southeast Missouri State University (U)
Southern Christian University (N, U, G)
Southwestern Baptist Theological Seminary (G)
Southwestern Community College (U)
Spoon River College (U)
Suffolk County Community College (U)
Syracuse University (U)
Taylor University, World Wide Campus (U)
Thomas Edison State College (U)
Triton College (U)

Troy State University Dothan (U)
University College of the Fraser Valley (U)
The University of Alabama (U)
University of Alaska Fairbanks (U)
University of Arkansas (U)
University of California, Los Angeles (G)
University of Cincinnati (U)
University of Colorado at Denver (U)
University of Delaware (U)
The University of Findlay (U)
University of Great Falls (U)
University of Idaho (G)
University of Kansas (U)
The University of North Carolina at Chapel Hill (U)
University of Northwestern Ohio (U)
University of Pittsburgh (U)
University of Southern Mississippi (U)
The University of Tennessee (U)
The University of Texas of the Permian Basin (U)
University of Toledo (U)
University of Waterloo (U)
University of Wisconsin-Extension (U)
Western Governors University (U)

**Philosophy**
Alpena Community College (U)
Belmont University (U)
Bemidji State University (U)
Beulah Heights Bible College (U)
Blinn College (U)
Blue River Community College (U)
Brigham Young University (U)
Broward Community College (U)
Burlington College (U)
Butte College (U)
Calvin College (U)
Carroll Community College (U)
Central Methodist College (U, G)
Chadron State College (U)
Chaminade University of Honolulu (U)
Charter Oak State College (U)
Clackamas Community College (U)
Clarkson College (U)
Coastline Community College (U)
College of Southern Maryland (U)
College of the Canyons (U)
Colorado Community College Online (U)
Colorado Electronic Community College (U)
Columbia State Community College (U)
Community College of Philadelphia (U)
Community Hospital of Roanoke Valley-College of Health Sciences (U)
Connecticut State University System (U)
Corning Community College (U)
Eastern Oregon University (U)

East Los Angeles College (U)
Edison State Community College (U)
Elgin Community College (U)
Erie Community College, South Campus (U)
Finger Lakes Community College (U)
Florence-Darlington Technical College (U)
Franciscan University of Steubenville (N, U)
Gannon University (U)
Grand Rapids Community College (U)
Harrisburg Area Community College (U)
Harvard University (N, U, G)
Horry-Georgetown Technical College (U)
Husson College (U)
Indiana Higher Education Telecommunication System (U)
Iowa Western Community College (G)
Ivy Tech State College-Southeast (U)
Jamestown Community College (U)
Kansas City Kansas Community College (U)
Lehigh Carbon Community College (U)
Liberty University (U)
Long Beach City College (U)
Longview Community College (U)
Loyola University Chicago (U)
Malone College (U)
Maple Woods Community College (U)
Mary Baldwin College (U)
Metropolitan State University (U)
Minot State University (U)
MiraCosta College (U)
Mississippi State University (U)
Monmouth University (U)
Moody Bible Institute (U)
Mountain State University (U)
Mt. San Antonio College (U)
New School University (U)
Northampton County Area Community College (U)
North Carolina State University (U)
North Central Michigan College (U)
Northern Arizona University (U)
Northern Essex Community College (U)
North Idaho College (U)
North Iowa Area Community College (U)
North Seattle Community College (U)
Northwestern Michigan College (U)
Okaloosa-Walton Community College (U)
Oklahoma City Community College (U)
Oklahoma State University (U)
Old Dominion University (U)
Oregon State University (U)
Ouachita Technical College (U)
Owens Community College (U)
The Pennsylvania State University University Park Campus (U)
Penn Valley Community College (U)
Pueblo Community College (U)

# Individual Courses Index

Florence-Darlington Technical College (U)
Georgia Perimeter College (U)
Holmes Community College (U)
Indiana Higher Education
    Telecommunication System (U)
Indiana University of Pennsylvania (U, G)
Ivy Tech State College-Central Indiana (U)
Ivy Tech State College-Eastcentral (U)
Ivy Tech State College-Kokomo (U)
Ivy Tech State College-Lafayette (U)
Ivy Tech State College-North Central (U)
Ivy Tech State College-Wabash Valley (U)
Ivy Tech State College-Whitewater (U)
Jamestown Community College (U)
Loyola University Chicago (U)
Mississippi State University (U)
Missouri Western State College (U)
Montana State University-Billings (U)
Montana State University-Bozeman (G)
Moraine Valley Community College (U)
Mountain State University (U)
New Jersey City University (U)
North Seattle Community College (U)
The Pennsylvania State University University
    Park Campus (U)
Pierce College (U)
Pueblo Community College (U)
Shippensburg University of Pennsylvania (U)
State University of New York College at
    Fredonia (U)
Temple University (U)
University of Colorado at Denver (N, U)
University of Idaho (U)
The University of North Carolina at Chapel
    Hill (U)
University of North Dakota (U)
University of Oregon (U)
University of Pennsylvania (U)
The University of Tennessee (U)
The University of Texas System (U)
University of Utah (U)
University of Waterloo (N, U)
University of Wisconsin-Extension (U)
Virginia Commonwealth University (U)
Western Governors University (U)
Wytheville Community College (U)

## Physiological psychology/psychobiology
Lord Fairfax Community College (U)
Southeastern Oklahoma State University (U)

## Physiology, human and animal
American Academy of Nutrition, College of
    Nutrition (U)
Central Methodist College (U)
Floyd College (U)
Mountain State University (U)

The Pennsylvania State University University
    Park Campus (U)
San Diego State University (U)
University of Utah (U)
University of Waterloo (U)
West Virginia Wesleyan College (U)

## Plant sciences
Arizona State University (U)
Butte College (U)
Elgin Community College (U)
Mississippi State University (U)
Oregon State University (U)
Texas A&M University (G)
Texas Tech University (G)
University of California, Berkeley (U)
University of Connecticut (U, G)
Walla Walla Community College (U)

## Podiatry (D.P.M., D.P., Pod.D.)
Temple University (G)

## Political science and government
Acadia University (U)
Adirondack Community College (U)
Albertus Magnus College (U)
Andrew College (U)
Blinn College (U)
Brenau University (U)
Bridgewater State College (U)
Brigham Young University (U)
California State University, Bakersfield (U)
Calvin College (U)
Carl Albert State College (U)
Cayuga County Community College (U)
Central Washington University (U)
Central Wyoming College (U)
Charter Oak State College (U)
Clarkson College (U)
Coastline Community College (U)
College of Southern Maryland (U)
College of the Canyons (U)
Colorado Community College Online (U)
Colorado Electronic Community College
    (U)
Columbia College (U)
Community College of Philadelphia (U)
Connors State College (U)
Cuyamaca College (U)
Cypress College (U)
Delaware Technical & Community College,
    Stanton/Wilmington Campus (U)
Drake University (U, G)
Eastern Oregon University (U)
Eastern Wyoming College (U)
Elgin Community College (U)
Erie Community College, North Campus
    (U)

Frostburg State University (U)
Fullerton College (U)
Gateway Community College (U)
George Mason University (U)
Grand Rapids Community College (U)
Great Basin College (U)
Griggs University (U)
Haywood Community College (U)
Illinois Valley Community College (U)
Indiana University of Pennsylvania (U)
Iowa Western Community College (U)
Isothermal Community College (U)
Ivy Tech State College-Southeast (U)
Ivy Tech State College-Wabash Valley (U)
Jacksonville State University (U)
J. Sargeant Reynolds Community College
    (U)
Judson College (U)
Lehigh Carbon Community College (U)
Lincoln Land Community College (U)
Long Beach City College (U)
Los Angeles Pierce College (U)
Louisiana State University and Agricultural
    and Mechanical College (U)
Malone College (U)
Mary Baldwin College (U)
Metropolitan Community College (U)
Miami-Dade Community College (U)
Middle Tennessee State University (U)
Mississippi State University (U)
New Jersey City University (U)
North Carolina State University (U)
North Central Michigan College (U)
North Central Texas College (U)
Northern Arizona University (U)
Northern Kentucky University (U)
North Idaho College (U)
North Seattle Community College (U)
Okaloosa-Walton Community College (U)
Oklahoma City Community College (U)
Oklahoma State University (U)
Olympic College (U)
Oregon State University (U)
Ozarks Technical Community College (U)
Palo Alto College (U)
The Pennsylvania State University University
    Park Campus (U)
Pikes Peak Community College (U)
Plattsburgh State University of New York
    (U)
Prestonsburg Community College (U)
Rio Hondo College (U)
Saddleback College (U)
Saint Charles Community College (U)
Sandhills Community College (U)
Seton Hill College (U)
Shawnee State University (U)
Southeastern Illinois College (U)

*Psychology (continued)*

Roosevelt University (U)
Rowan-Cabarrus Community College (U)
Saint Charles Community College (U)
Sandhills Community College (U)
San Jacinto College North Campus (U)
San Joaquin Delta College (U)
Santa Barbara City College (U)
Santa Rosa Junior College (U)
Sauk Valley Community College (U)
Saybrook Graduate School and Research Center (G)
Seminole Community College (U)
Seward County Community College (U)
Shawnee State University (U)
Shippensburg University of Pennsylvania (U)
Sinclair Community College (U)
Slippery Rock University of Pennsylvania (U)
Southeast Arkansas College (U)
Southeast Community College, Beatrice Campus (U)
Southeastern Illinois College (U)
Southeast Missouri State University (U)
South Plains College (U)
Southwestern Baptist Theological Seminary (G)
Southwestern College (U)
Southwestern Community College (U)
Southwest Texas State University (U)
Spring Arbor University (U)
Stanly Community College (U)
Stephens College (U)
Strayer University (U)
Sussex County Community College (U)
Syracuse University (U, G)
Tacoma Community College (U)
Taft College (U)
Taylor University, World Wide Campus (U)
Temple University (U)
Tennessee Temple University (U)
Texas Tech University (U)
Tidewater Community College (U)
Tompkins Cortland Community College (U)
Treasure Valley Community College (U)
Trident Technical College (U)
Tulsa Community College (U)
Tyler Junior College (U)
The University Alliance (U)
University at Buffalo, The State University of New York (U)
University College of the Fraser Valley (U)
The University of Akron (U)
University of Alaska Fairbanks (U)
University of Arkansas at Little Rock (U)
University of California, Berkeley (U)
University of California, Los Angeles (G)
University of Colorado at Denver (N, U)

University of Connecticut (G)
University of Great Falls (U)
University of Idaho (U, G)
University of Illinois at Springfield (U)
University of Kansas (U, G)
University of Maine at Machias (U)
University of Manitoba (U)
University of Massachusetts Amherst (U)
University of Massachusetts System (U)
The University of Memphis (U)
University of Minnesota, Morris (U)
University of Minnesota, Twin Cities Campus (U)
University of Missouri-Columbia (U)
University of Nebraska at Omaha (U)
University of New Mexico (U)
University of Pennsylvania (U)
University of Saskatchewan (U)
University of South Carolina (U)
University of Southern Indiana (U)
The University of Texas of the Permian Basin (U)
The University of Texas System (U)
University of Utah (U)
University of Vermont (G)
University of Washington (U)
University of Waterloo (U)
University of Wisconsin Colleges (U)
University of Wisconsin-Extension (U)
University of Wisconsin-Platteville (G)
Upper Iowa University (N, U)
Valdosta State University (U, G)
Vanguard University of Southern California (U)
Victoria College (U)
Vincennes University (U)
Virginia Commonwealth University (U)
Virginia Western Community College (U)
Volunteer State Community College (U)
Wake Technical Community College (U)
Walters State Community College (U)
Weber State University (U)
Western Connecticut State University (U)
Western Governors University (U)
Western Piedmont Community College (U)
Western Washington University (U)
Wichita State University (U)
William Rainey Harper College (U)
York Technical College (U)

## Psychology, other

Alvin Community College (U)
Aquinas College (G)
Atlantic University (N, G)
Bristol Community College (U)
Central Community College (U)
Chadron State College (U, G)
Cincinnati Bible College and Seminary (U)

Cumberland County College (U)
Elgin Community College (U)
Garland County Community College (U)
Hope International University (U)
Husson College (U)
Illinois School of Professional Psychology, Chicago Northwest Campus (N)
Illinois Valley Community College (U)
Kentucky State University (U)
Lynn University (U)
Midwestern State University (U)
Naropa University (G)
Nassau Community College (U)
Northwestern Michigan College (U)
Northwest Iowa Community College (U)
Olympic College (U)
San Jacinto College North Campus (U)
Southwestern Baptist Theological Seminary (G)
Tarleton State University (U)
Tompkins Cortland Community College (U)
University of Missouri-Columbia (U)
University of North Texas (U)
Wisconsin Indianhead Technical College, New Richmond Campus (U)
York University (U)
Yuba College (U)

## Public administration and services, other

Drake University (G)
George Mason University (G)
Georgia Southern University (G)
Hamline University (N, G)
Jacksonville State University (G)
Northern Arizona University (G)
North Georgia College & State University (G)
Royal Roads University (G)
San Jacinto College North Campus (U)
University of Colorado at Denver (N, G)
York University (U)

## Public administration

Colorado Community College Online (U)
Drake University (G)
Elizabeth City State University (U)
Florida Gulf Coast University (U, G)
Florida Institute of Technology (G)
Grand Valley State University (G)
Hamline University (N)
Indiana State University (G)
Jacksonville State University (U, G)
Kansas State University (G)
Long Island University, Southampton College (U)
Midwestern State University (U)
Mississippi State University (G)

Northern Arizona University (G)
Northern Kentucky University (U, G)
North Georgia College & State University (G)
Roger Williams University (U)
San Jacinto College North Campus (U)
Southeastern University (U, G)
Southern University and Agricultural and Mechanical College (G)
State University of New York College at Brockport (G)
State University of West Georgia (N)
The University of Akron (U)
University of Colorado at Denver (N, G)
University of Delaware (G)
The University of Findlay (G)
University of Illinois at Springfield (U)
University of Massachusetts System (N)
The University of Memphis (U)
University of New Mexico (G)
University of North Texas (U)
University of Oklahoma (G)
University of South Carolina Sumter (U)
The University of Texas at Tyler (G)
University of Vermont (G)
Upper Iowa University (N, U)
Valdosta State University (G)

## Public health

Community Hospital of Roanoke Valley–College of Health Sciences (U)
Drake University (G)
Elgin Community College (U)
Emory University (G)
Harrisburg Area Community College (U)
Medical College of Wisconsin (G)
Minnesota State University Moorhead (U)
New Jersey City University (U, G)
Northern Arizona University (G)
North Iowa Area Community College (N)
Oregon State University (U)
Radford University (N)
Rockingham Community College (N)
University of Illinois at Chicago (G)
University of Minnesota, Twin Cities Campus (U, G)
University of South Carolina Sumter (U)
University of Southern Mississippi (G)
West Virginia University (G)
William Paterson University of New Jersey (U)

## Public policy analysis

California State University, Bakersfield (U)
Elizabeth City State University (U)
Mississippi State University (G)
Saybrook Graduate School and Research Center (G)

University of Colorado at Denver (N, G)

## Public relations and organizational communications

Frederick Community College (N)
Marywood University (U)
Royal Roads University (G)
Universite de Montreal (U)
University at Buffalo, The State University of New York (U)
University of Massachusetts Amherst (N)
University of Massachusetts System (N)
University of Southern Indiana (U)

## Quality control and safety technologies

California National University for Advanced Studies (U)
Colorado Community College Online (U)
Craven Community College (U)
East Carolina University (G)
Elgin Community College (U)
Grand Rapids Community College (N)
Jacksonville State University (U, G)
Kansas State University (G)
Lakeland Community College (N)
Okaloosa-Walton Community College (U)
Trident Technical College (U)
University of Manitoba (N)
University of Wisconsin-Extension (U)
Walla Walla Community College (N)
Western Iowa Tech Community College (N)

## Radio and television broadcasting

Adams State College (U)
Butte College (U)
Eastern Kentucky University (U)
Elgin Community College (U)
Foothill College (U)
Illinois Eastern Community Colleges, Wabash Valley College (U)
Middle Tennessee State University (U)
Missouri Southern State College (U)
MU Direct: Continuing and Distance Education (G)
Murray State University (U)
Olympic College (U)
Pikes Peak Community College (N, U)
State University of New York at Oswego (U)
Suffolk County Community College (U)
University of Alaska Fairbanks (U)
University of Arkansas at Little Rock (U)
University of Missouri-St. Louis (U)
University of Southern Indiana (U)

## Real estate

Amarillo College (U)
Chadron State College (U)
Clarion University of Pennsylvania (N, U)
Columbia Basin College (N)

Del Mar College (U)
Elgin Community College (U)
Florence-Darlington Technical College (N)
Frederick Community College (N)
Hibbing Community College (N)
Johnson County Community College (N)
Lakeland Community College (N)
Maysville Community College (U)
MiraCosta College (U)
Mississippi State University (N, U)
Mt. San Antonio College (U)
MU Direct: Continuing and Distance Education (N, G)
Oklahoma State University (N)
San Jacinto College North Campus (U)
Santa Rosa Junior College (U)
Southern Illinois University Carbondale (U)
Tuskegee University (N)
The University of Alabama (U)
University of Alaska Fairbanks (U)
University of Connecticut (N)
University of South Dakota (N)
Walters State Community College (U)
Western Wisconsin Technical College (N)

## Rehabilitation/therapeutic services

Brenau University (G)
Kentucky State University (U)
Southern Illinois University Carbondale (U, G)
The University of British Columbia (N, U, G)
University of Northern Colorado (U)
University of North Texas (G)
Vincennes University (U)

## Religion/religious studies

Assemblies of God Theological Seminary (G)
Atlantic University (N, G)
Azusa Pacific University (U)
Briercrest Bible College (U, G)
Brigham Young University (U)
Calvary Bible College and Theological Seminary (U, G)
Calvin College (U)
The Catholic Distance University (N, U)
Central Michigan University (U)
Central Wyoming College (U)
Chaminade University of Honolulu (U)
Cleveland State Community College (U)
College of Mount St. Joseph (N, U)
Columbia College (U)
Columbia International University (N, G)
Concordia University at Austin (N, U)
Covenant Theological Seminary (G)
Elgin Community College (U)
Eugene Bible College (U)
Gannon University (U)

# Individual Courses Index

Elgin Community College (U)
Elizabethtown Community College (U)
Grand Rapids Community College (U)
Grand Valley State University (U, G)
Illinois Valley Community College (U)
Ivy Tech State College-Wabash Valley (U)
John Wood Community College (U)
Lake Superior College (U)
Lansing Community College (U)
Liberty University (U)
Long Beach City College (U)
Lorain County Community College (U)
Lord Fairfax Community College (U)
Maui Community College (U)
Memorial University of Newfoundland (U)
Mercy College (U)
Missouri Southern State College (U)
Montgomery County Community College (U)
Mountain State University (U)
New Jersey Institute of Technology (U)
New School University (N, U)
New York Institute of Technology (U)
Northwest Iowa Community College (U)
Old Dominion University (U)
Otero Junior College (U)
Parkland College (U)
Park University (U)
Pensacola Junior College (U)
Pikes Peak Community College (N, U)
Red Rocks Community College (U)
Richland Community College (U)
Roosevelt University (U)
St. Petersburg College (U)
San Jacinto College North Campus (U)
Saybrook Graduate School and Research Center (G)
Seminole Community College (U)
Southeast Community College, Beatrice Campus (U)
Southeast Missouri State University (U)
Southwestern Assemblies of God University (U)
State University of New York Empire State College (U)
Tarrant County College District (U)
Taylor University, World Wide Campus (U)
Texas Tech University (U)
Thomas Edison State College (U)
Tompkins Cortland Community College (U)
Triton College (U)
University of Alaska Southeast, Sitka Campus (U)
University of California, Santa Barbara (N)
University of Colorado at Denver (U)
University of Guelph (U)
University of Houston (U)

University of Illinois at Urbana-Champaign (U)
University of Kansas (U)
University of Maine (U)
University of Missouri-Columbia (U)
University of Northern Iowa (U)
The University of Tennessee (U)
University of Utah (U)
University of Washington (U)
University of Waterloo (U)
University of Wyoming (U)
Volunteer State Community College (U)
Walden University (G)
Washington State University (U)
Wayne State University (U)
Weber State University (U)
Western Oregon University (U)

## Social sciences and history, other

Anne Arundel Community College (U)
Berkeley College (U)
Bristol Community College (U)
Chadron State College (U)
Cleveland Institute of Electronics (U)
Coastline Community College (U)
College of DuPage (U)
Colorado Community College Online (U)
Columbia College (U)
Concordia University (U)
Copiah-Lincoln Community College (U)
Drake University (U)
Elgin Community College (U)
Erie Community College, South Campus (U)
J. Sargeant Reynolds Community College (U)
Malone College (U)
Mineral Area College (U)
Mountain State University (U)
North Seattle Community College (U)
Northwest Iowa Community College (U)
Oregon State University (U)
Pasco-Hernando Community College (U)
Saddleback College (U)
State University of New York College at Cortland (U)
Taylor University, World Wide Campus (U)
Troy State University-Florida Region (U)
University of Alaska Anchorage (U)
University of Alaska Fairbanks (U)
University of Massachusetts Lowell (U)
The University of Texas System (U)
University of Waterloo (U)
Vermont Technical College (U)

## Social sciences, general

Borough of Manhattan Community College of the City University of New York (U)

Bucks County Community College (U)
Caldwell Community College and Technical Institute (U)
California State University, Chico (U)
Cedarville University (U)
Central Community College (U)
Central Wyoming College (U)
Chadron State College (U)
Charter Oak State College (U)
College of DuPage (U)
Colorado Community College Online (U)
Delaware Technical & Community College, Stanton/Wilmington Campus (U)
EduKan (U)
Elgin Community College (U)
Embry-Riddle Aeronautical University (U)
Erie Community College, City Campus (U)
Erie Community College, North Campus (U)
Everett Community College (U)
Foothill College (U)
Frank Phillips College (U)
Georgia Perimeter College (U)
Great Basin College (U)
Green River Community College (U)
Hocking College (U)
Iowa Lakes Community College (U)
Jacksonville State University (U, G)
Jones College (U)
Lewis-Clark State College (U)
Marywood University (U)
Maysville Community College (U)
Miami-Dade Community College (U)
Michigan State University (U)
Middlesex Community College (U)
Middle Tennessee State University (U)
Missouri Western State College (U)
Mohawk Valley Community College (U)
Mountain State University (U)
New School University (U)
Northampton County Area Community College (U)
Northeast State Technical Community College (U)
Northern Arizona University (U)
Northern Kentucky University (G)
Northern Michigan University (U)
Northwest Iowa Community College (U)
Oklahoma City University (U)
Portland Community College (U)
Rockhurst University (U)
Roosevelt University (U)
St. Clair County Community College (U)
Seminole Community College (U)
Shasta College (U)
Spokane Falls Community College (U)
State University of West Georgia (U)
Stephens College (U)

Copiah-Lincoln Community College-Natchez Campus (U)

Corning Community College (U)

County College of Morris (U)

Craven Community College (U)

Cumberland County College (U)

Cuyamaca College (U)

Cypress College (U)

Dakota County Technical College (U)

Dakota State University (U)

Dallas County Community College District (U)

Danville Area Community College (U)

Dawson Community College (U)

Delaware Technical & Community College, Jack F. Owens Campus (U)

Delaware Technical & Community College, Stanton/Wilmington Campus (U)

Del Mar College (U)

Delta College (U)

Des Moines Area Community College (U)

Drake University (U)

Eastern Kentucky University (U)

Eastern Michigan University (U)

Eastern New Mexico University (U, G)

Eastern Wyoming College (U)

Edison State Community College (U)

EduKan (U)

Elaine P. Nunez Community College (U)

Elgin Community College (U)

Erie Community College, North Campus (U)

Erie Community College, South Campus (U)

Eugene Bible College (U)

Everett Community College (U)

Evergreen Valley College (U)

Fairmont State College (U)

Ferris State University (U)

Finger Lakes Community College (U)

Flathead Valley Community College (U)

Florence-Darlington Technical College (U)

Florida Community College at Jacksonville (U)

Florida Keys Community College (U)

Floyd College (U)

Foothill College (U)

Forsyth Technical Community College (U)

Frostburg State University (U)

Fullerton College (U)

Garland County Community College (U)

Genesee Community College (U)

Georgia Southern University (U, G)

Glendale Community College (U)

Gogebic Community College (U)

Governors State University (U, G)

Graceland University (U)

Grand Rapids Community College (U)

Grand Valley State University (U, G)

Grand View College (U)

Great Basin College (U)

Griggs University (U)

Hamilton College (U)

Harrisburg Area Community College (U)

Haywood Community College (U)

Hillsborough Community College (U)

Holmes Community College (U)

Horry-Georgetown Technical College (U)

Humboldt State University (N, U)

Hutchinson Community College and Area Vocational School (U)

Illinois Valley Community College (U)

Indiana State University (U, G)

Indian River Community College (U)

Iowa Wesleyan College (U)

Iowa Western Community College (U, G)

Isothermal Community College (U)

Ivy Tech State College-Central Indiana (U)

Ivy Tech State College-Columbus (U)

Ivy Tech State College-Kokomo (U)

Ivy Tech State College-North Central (U)

Ivy Tech State College-Northeast (U)

Ivy Tech State College-Northwest (U)

Ivy Tech State College-Southcentral (U)

Ivy Tech State College-Southeast (U)

Ivy Tech State College-Wabash Valley (U)

Ivy Tech State College-Whitewater (U)

Jacksonville State University (U, G)

James Sprunt Community College (U)

Jamestown Community College (U)

Jefferson College (U)

Jefferson Community College (U)

Johnson County Community College (U)

John Wood Community College (U)

J. Sargeant Reynolds Community College (U)

Judson College (U)

Kansas City Kansas Community College (U)

Kansas State University (U)

Kean University (U)

Kellogg Community College (U)

Kentucky State University (U)

Labette Community College (U)

Lakeland Community College (U)

Lake Michigan College (U)

Lake Superior College (U)

Lansing Community College (U)

Lehigh Carbon Community College (U)

Lincoln Land Community College (U)

Long Beach City College (U)

Longview Community College (U)

Lorain County Community College (U)

Lord Fairfax Community College (U)

Louisiana State University and Agricultural and Mechanical College (U)

Louisiana State University in Shreveport (U)

Loyola University New Orleans (U)

Lynn University (U)

Macon State College (U)

Malone College (U)

Manatee Community College (U)

Manchester Community College (U)

Manor College (U)

Maple Woods Community College (U)

Marshall University (U, G)

Mary Baldwin College (U)

Marywood University (U)

Maui Community College (U)

Maysville Community College (U)

Memorial University of Newfoundland (U)

Mendocino College (U)

Mercy College (U)

Meridian Community College (U)

Metropolitan Community College (U)

Middle Tennessee State University (U)

Mid-Plains Community College Area (U)

Midwestern State University (U)

Minnesota State University Moorhead (U)

Minnesota West Community and Technical College-Worthington Campus (U)

Minot State University (U)

Missouri Southern State College (U)

Moberly Area Community College (U)

Mohawk Valley Community College (U)

Montgomery County Community College (U)

Moraine Valley Community College (U)

Mott Community College (U)

Mountain Empire Community College (U)

Mountain State University (U)

Mount Saint Vincent University (U)

Mt. San Antonio College (U)

Mount Wachusett Community College (U)

Murray State University (U)

Nassau Community College (U)

New Hampshire Community Technical College, Nashua/Claremont (U)

New School University (N, U)

New York Institute of Technology (U)

Northampton County Area Community College (U)

North Carolina State University (U)

North Central University (N, U)

North Country Community College (U)

Northeastern State University (U)

Northern Arizona University (U)

Northern Kentucky University (U)

Northern Michigan University (U)

Northern New Mexico Community College (U)

Northern Oklahoma College (U)

Northern State University (U)

Northern Virginia Community College (U)

Vincennes University (U)
Virginia Polytechnic Institute and State University (U)
Virginia Western Community College (U)
Volunteer State Community College (U)
Wake Technical Community College (U)
Walla Walla Community College (U)
Walters State Community College (U)
Washington State University (U)
Wayne State University (U)
Weber State University (U)
Western Connecticut State University (U)
Western Governors University (U)
Western Michigan University (U)
Western Nebraska Community College (U)
Western Nevada Community College (U)
Western Piedmont Community College (U)
Western Washington University (U)
West Shore Community College (U)
West Virginia Northern Community College (U)
West Virginia University Institute of Technology (U)
West Virginia Wesleyan College (U)
Wichita State University (U)
Wilfrid Laurier University (U)
William Rainey Harper College (U)
York Technical College (U)
York University (U)

## Soil sciences
Lakeland Community College (N)
North Carolina State University (U)
Oregon State University (U)
University of Saskatchewan (N)
Walla Walla Community College (U)

## South Asian languages and literatures
Elgin Community College (U)
Lakeland Community College (N)
North Carolina State University (U)
Piedmont College (U)

## Spanish language and literature
Boise State University (U)
Brigham Young University (U)
Broward Community College (U)
Bucks County Community College (U)
Burlington County College (U)
Central Arizona College (U)
Central Michigan University (U)
Clovis Community College (U)
Coastline Community College (U)
College of DuPage (U)
College of San Mateo (U)
College of Southern Maryland (U)
Colorado Northwestern Community College (U)

Concordia University Wisconsin (U)
Connors State College (U)
Delaware Technical & Community College, Jack F. Owens Campus (U)
Delta College (U)
Eastern Kentucky University (U)
Evergreen Valley College (U)
Jefferson College (U)
Kellogg Community College (U)
Lehigh Carbon Community College (U)
Marywood University (U)
Metropolitan Community College (U)
Montgomery County Community College (U)
Mountain Empire Community College (U)
Nassau Community College (U)
Northern Virginia Community College (U)
Oklahoma State University (U)
Oregon State University (U)
The Pennsylvania State University University Park Campus (U)
St. Petersburg College (U)
Seattle Central Community College (U)
Sheridan College (U)
Southeast Community College, Lincoln Campus (U)
Southwest Missouri State University (U)
Southwest Texas State University (U)
Texas Tech University (N, U)
Thomas Edison State College (U)
Triton College (U)
Troy State University Montgomery (U)
Tyler Junior College (U)
University of Arkansas (U)
University of Houston (U, G)
The University of Iowa (U)
University of Kansas (U)
University of Minnesota, Twin Cities Campus (U)
University of Missouri-Columbia (U)
University of Nevada, Reno (U)
The University of North Carolina at Chapel Hill (U)
The University of North Carolina at Greensboro (G)
The University of Tennessee (U)
University of Waterloo (U)
University of Wisconsin-Extension (U)
Virginia Polytechnic Institute and State University (U, G)
Walters State Community College (U)
Washington State University (U)
Western Nevada Community College (U)
Yuba College (U)

## Special education
Arizona State University (U)
Arizona State University West (U, G)

Bridgewater State College (U, G)
Brigham Young University (U)
Calvin College (U)
Cedarville University (U)
Central Missouri State University (U, G)
Chadron State College (U, G)
Clemson University (G)
Coastline Community College (U)
East Carolina University (G)
Elgin Community College (U)
Elizabeth City State University (U)
Franklin Pierce Law Center (G)
Grand Canyon University (U, G)
Grand Valley State University (G)
Hamline University (G)
Illinois State University (G)
Indiana State University (U, G)
Jacksonville State University (U, G)
Kean University (U)
Lakeland Community College (N)
Millersville University of Pennsylvania (G)
Minot State University (U, G)
Mohawk Valley Community College (U)
Montana State University-Billings (U)
Morehead State University (U, G)
New Jersey City University (G)
North Carolina Central University (G)
Northeastern State University (U)
Northern Arizona University (U)
Northwestern State University of Louisiana (G)
Oklahoma State University (N)
St. Ambrose University (G)
Slippery Rock University of Pennsylvania (G)
Southern University and Agricultural and Mechanical College (N, U, G)
State University of West Georgia (N)
University of Louisville (G)
University of Missouri-Columbia (G)
The University of North Carolina at Greensboro (G)
University of Northern Colorado (U)
University of North Florida (G)
University of North Texas (U, G)
University of South Alabama (G)
University of Southern Mississippi (G)
The University of Tennessee at Martin (U, G)
Virginia Polytechnic Institute and State University (N)
Wayne State College (U)

## Speech and rhetorical studies
Brigham Young University (U)
Cerro Coso Community College (U)
Chattanooga State Technical Community College (U)

*Speech and rhetorical studies (continued)*

Clackamas Community College (U)
Cleveland State Community College (U)
Colorado Community College Online (U)
Colorado Electronic Community College (U)
Drake University (U)
East Central College (U)
East Los Angeles College (U)
EduKan (U)
Elgin Community College (U)
Eugene Bible College (U)
Honolulu Community College (U)
Husson College (U)
Iowa Lakes Community College (U)
Iowa Western Community College (G)
Johnson County Community College (U)
Lewis and Clark Community College (U)
Moberly Area Community College (U)
Northeast State Technical Community College (U)
Northern New Mexico Community College (U)
North Iowa Area Community College (U)
North Seattle Community College (U)
Northwest Iowa Community College (U)
Ohlone College (U)
The Pennsylvania State University University Park Campus (U)
Southeast Community College, Beatrice Campus (U)
Southeast Missouri State University (U)
Taylor University, World Wide Campus (U)
Trident Technical College (U)
University of La Verne (U)
The University of Memphis (U)
University of Minnesota, Twin Cities Campus (U, G)
University of Southern Indiana (U)
University of Washington (U)
University of Wisconsin-Platteville (U)
Vincennes University (U)
Wichita State University (U)

### Student counseling and personnel services
Drake University (U)
Indiana State University (G)
Jacksonville State University (U)
University of Massachusetts Boston (U)

### Surveying
Michigan Technological University (U)
University of Maine (U)

### Systems engineering
Bristol Community College (N)
Capitol College (U, G)

Florida Institute of Technology (G)
Southern Methodist University (G)
The University of Arizona (N)
University of Pennsylvania (N, G)

### Systems science and theory
Capitol College (G)
Concordia University (U)

### Taxation
Brenau University (G)
Gardner-Webb University (G)
Jones College (U)
Lakeland Community College (N)
Liberty University (U)
Marywood University (U)
State University of New York Institute of Technology at Utica/Rome (G)
University of Connecticut (U, G)
University of Notre Dame (N, G)
University of Wisconsin-Milwaukee (G)
Western Piedmont Community College (U)

### Teacher assistant/aide
Elgin Community College (U)
Harcourt Learning Direct Center for Degree Studies (N)
Lewis and Clark Community College (U)
Tuskegee University (N)
The University of Texas System (G)

### Teacher education, specific academic and vocational programs
Aquinas College (U)
Azusa Pacific University (G)
Bemidji State University (U)
Boise State University (U)
Bucks County Community College (U)
Calvin College (U)
Central Wyoming College (U)
Chadron State College (U, G)
EduKan (U)
Elgin Community College (U)
Elizabeth City State University (U)
Gaston College (U)
Great Basin College (U)
Hamline University (N, G)
Jacksonville State University (U, G)
Kean University (G)
Louisiana State University and Agricultural and Mechanical College (G)
Maranatha Baptist Bible College (U)
Mississippi State University (N)
Missouri Baptist College (U, G)
Montana State University-Bozeman (U, G)
Morehead State University (G)
MU Direct: Continuing and Distance Education (G)

New Mexico Institute of Mining and Technology (U, G)
New School University (U, G)
North Carolina Agricultural and Technical State University (U, G)
Northeastern State University (U)
Northern Kentucky University (G)
North Georgia College & State University (N, U, G)
San Diego State University (U)
School for International Training (N)
Seminole Community College (U)
Shippensburg University of Pennsylvania (U)
South Piedmont Community College (U)
Southwest Texas State University (U)
State University of West Georgia (N)
University of Massachusetts Lowell (N, G)
University of Minnesota, Morris (U)
The University of Tennessee at Martin (U, G)
The University of Texas of the Permian Basin (G)
The University of Texas System (U, G)
University of Wisconsin-Extension (U)
University of Wisconsin-River Falls (N, U, G)
Western Governors University (G)
Western Washington University (U)

### Teaching English as a second language/foreign language
Briercrest Bible College (U)
Elgin Community College (U)
Hamline University (N, G)
Lewis-Clark State College (U)
Lincoln Christian College (U, G)
School for International Training (N)
University College of the Fraser Valley (U)
University of Massachusetts Boston (U)
The University of North Carolina at Greensboro (G)
University of Saskatchewan (N)
The University of Texas System (G)
Western Governors University (G)
Western Washington University (U)

### Technology education/industrial arts
Brigham Young University (U)
Bristol Community College (N)
Central Missouri State University (U, G)
Chadron State College (G)
Grand Rapids Community College (U)
Lesley University (G)
Michigan State University (U)
Millersville University of Pennsylvania (U, G)
Mississippi State University (U, G)
Morehead State University (U)

MU Direct: Continuing and Distance Education (G)
North Carolina Agricultural and Technical State University (U, G)
Pittsburg State University (U)
University of South Dakota (G)
University of Wisconsin-Stevens Point (G)
West Virginia University (G)

## Telecommunications
Alexandria Technical College (U)
American River College (U)
Bristol Community College (N)
Capitol College (U, G)
Carl Albert State College (U)
Cayuga County Community College (U)
Champlain College (U)
Colorado Community College Online (U)
Elgin Community College (U)
Illinois Institute of Technology (G)
Keller Graduate School of Management (G)
Lord Fairfax Community College (N)
Michigan State University (U, G)
Mississippi State University (N, G)
Northeastern State University (U)
Northeastern University (N)
Southern Illinois University Carbondale (G)
Southern Methodist University (G)
Temple University (G)
Trident Technical College (U)
Tulsa Community College (U)
The University of Alabama (U)
University of Colorado at Boulder (N, U, G)
University of Massachusetts Lowell (U)
University of Massachusetts System (U)
University of Nebraska at Omaha (U)
University of Pennsylvania (N, G)
University of Tulsa (G)

## Textile sciences and engineering
North Carolina State University (U, G)
Syracuse University (N, U)
Texas Tech University (G)

## Theological and ministerial studies
Assemblies of God Theological Seminary (G)
Azusa Pacific University (G)
The Baptist College of Florida (U)
Briercrest Bible College (U, G)
Calvary Bible College and Theological Seminary (U, G)
Calvin College (U)
Canadian Bible College (U, G)
Columbia International University (N, U, G)
Covenant Theological Seminary (G)
Dallas Theological Seminary (G)

Eastern Mennonite University (G)
Franciscan University of Steubenville (N, U, G)
Fuller Theological Seminary (N, G)
Grand Rapids Baptist Seminary (N)
Griggs University (U)
Liberty University (G)
Lincoln Christian College (N, U, G)
Moody Bible Institute (U)
Nazarene Theological Seminary (G)
North Park University (N, G)
Oral Roberts University (N)
Princeton Theological Seminary (N)
Providence College and Theological Seminary (G)
Providence College and Theological Seminary (G)
Seabury-Western Theological Seminary (N, G)
Southern Christian University (N, U, G)
Southwestern Baptist Theological Seminary (U, G)
Taylor University, World Wide Campus (U)
Trinity International University (G)
Warner Southern College (U)
Western Seminary (N, G)
Wheaton College (N, G)

## Theological studies and religious vocations, other
Assemblies of God Theological Seminary (G)
Avila College (U)
Briercrest Bible College (U, G)
Calvary Bible College and Theological Seminary (U, G)
Cincinnati Bible College and Seminary (U)
Columbia International University (N, U, G)
Covenant Theological Seminary (G)
Gannon University (U)
Grand Rapids Baptist Seminary (G)
Hope International University (U)
Liberty University (U)
Lincoln Christian College (U)
Moody Bible Institute (U)
Providence College and Theological Seminary (G)
Southwestern Baptist Theological Seminary (G)
Taylor University, World Wide Campus (U)
Western Seminary (N, G)
Wheaton College (G)

## Tourism and travel services marketing operations
Arizona State University (U)
Arizona State University West (U, G)
Chesapeake College (U)

Colorado Community College Online (U)
Colorado Electronic Community College (N)
Colorado State University (N)
Del Mar College (U)
Elgin Community College (U)
Finger Lakes Community College (U)
Lakeland Community College (N)
National American University (U)
Ohio University (U)
Rowan-Cabarrus Community College (N)
Schiller International University (G)
Texas Tech University (U)
University of Southern Mississippi (N)
West Los Angeles College (U)

## Transportation and materials moving workers, other
The Pennsylvania State University University Park Campus (G)
University of Wisconsin-Milwaukee (N)

## Urban affairs/studies
Beulah Heights Bible College (U)
Hamline University (N)
Taylor University, World Wide Campus (U)
The University of British Columbia (U)
University of Connecticut (U, G)
University of Delaware (U, G)
University of Nebraska at Omaha (U)
The University of Texas at Arlington (G)
University of Washington (U)

## Vehicle and equipment operators
Bristol Community College (N)
Frederick Community College (N)

## Vehicle and mobile equipment mechanics and repairers
Alexandria Technical College (U)
Bristol Community College (N)

## Veterinary clinical sciences (M.S., Ph.D.)
Lakeland Community College (N)
Purdue University (U)

## Veterinary medicine (D.V.M.)
Morehead State University (U)
Yuba College (U)

## Visual and performing arts
Aquinas College (U)
Brigham Young University (U)
Coastline Community College (U)
East Los Angeles College (U)
Elgin Community College (U)
Illinois State University (U)
John F. Kennedy University (G)

# GEOGRAPHIC INDEX

## UNITED STATES

### Alabama

American College of Computer & Information Sciences, 29, **292**
Auburn University, 36, **298**
Bevill State Community College, 41
George C. Wallace Community College, 99
Jacksonville State University, 120
Jefferson Davis Community College, 122
Judson College, 124
Southern Christian University, 207, **502**
Troy State University, 226, **548**
Troy State University Dothan, 226
Troy State University Montgomery, 227
Tuskegee University, 228
United States Sports Academy, 229, **552**
The University of Alabama, 231, **554**
University of North Alabama, 254
University of South Alabama, 261, **628**

### Alaska

Alaska Pacific University, 27
University of Alaska Anchorage, 231
University of Alaska Fairbanks, 231, **556**
University of Alaska Southeast, Ketchikan Campus, 231
University of Alaska Southeast, Sitka Campus, 232

### Arizona

Arizona Institute of Business & Technology, 32
Arizona School of Professional Psychology, 33
Arizona State University, 33
Arizona State University East, 33
Arizona State University West, 33
Arizona Western College, 34
Central Arizona College, 56
Grand Canyon University, 103
Northcentral University, 163, **434**
Northern Arizona University, 165, **440**
The Paralegal Institute, Inc., 178
Pima Community College, 182
Prescott College, 184, **462**
Rio Salado College, 189, **470**
The University of Arizona, 232

University of Phoenix, 258, **624**

### Arkansas

Garland County Community College, 98
North Arkansas College, 161
NorthWest Arkansas Community College, 169
Ouachita Technical College, 176
Pulaski Technical College, 185
Southeast Arkansas College, 206
Southern Arkansas University Tech, 207
University of Arkansas, 232
University of Arkansas at Little Rock, 233
University of Central Arkansas, 235, **564**

### California

Alliant International University, 28, **290**
American Graduate University, 29
American River College, 30
American School of Professional Psychology, San Francisco Bay Area Campus, 31
Antelope Valley College, 32
Azusa Pacific University, 37
Bakersfield College, 37
Bethany College of the Assemblies of God, 40
Butte College, 48
California College for Health Sciences, 49
California Lutheran University, 50
California National University for Advanced Studies, 50
California Polytechnic State University, San Luis Obispo, 50
California State University, Bakersfield, 50
California State University, Chico, 51
California State University, Dominguez Hills, 51, **312**
California State University, Northridge, 51
California State University, San Marcos, 51
Cerro Coso Community College, 59
Chapman University, 61
Citrus College, 62
Coastline Community College, 65
College of San Mateo, 66
College of the Canyons, 67
Concordia University, 73
Contra Costa College, 74
Cosumnes River College, 75

Cuyamaca College, 77
Cypress College, 77
East Los Angeles College, 86
Evergreen Valley College, 90
Feather River Community College District, 91
Fielding Graduate Institute, 92
Foothill College, 94
Fresno City College, 96
Fuller Theological Seminary, 97
Fullerton College, 97
Glendale Community College, 100
Golden Gate University, 102
Hartnell College, 106
Hope International University, 109
Humboldt State University, 110
John F. Kennedy University, 122
LIFE Bible College, 133
Long Beach City College, 134
Los Angeles Pierce College, 135
Mendocino College, 143
MiraCosta College, 149
Mt. San Antonio College, 156
National University, 158
Ohlone College, 172
Orange Coast College, 175
Pacific Graduate School of Psychology, 177
Pacific Oaks College, 177
Pepperdine University, 181
Rio Hondo College, 189
Saddleback College, 193
Samuel Merritt College, 198
San Diego State University, 199
San Joaquin Delta College, 199, **488**
Santa Barbara City College, 199
Santa Monica College, 200, **490**
Santa Rosa Junior College, 200
Saybrook Graduate School and Research Center, 200, **492**
Sequoia Institute, 203
Shasta Bible College, 203
Shasta College, 204
Sonoma State University, 206
Southwestern College, 211
Stanford University, 214, **510**

**NOTES**

# Need Help Paying for School?
# We'll Show You the Money!

**Peterson's** offers students like you a wide variety of comprehensive resources to help you meet all your financial planning needs.

### Scholarships, Grants & Prizes 2002
ISBN 0-7689-0695-4, with CD,
$26.95 pb/$39.95 CAN/£18.99 UK,
August 2001

### College Money Handbook 2002
ISBN 0-7689-0694-6,
$26.95 pb/$39.95 CAN/£18.99 UK,
August 2001

### Scholarship Almanac 2002
ISBN 0-7689-0692-X
$12.95 pb/$18.95 CAN/£9.99 UK,
August 2001

### The Insider's Guide to Paying for College
ISBN 0-7689-0230-4,
$9.95 pb/$14.95 CAN/£11.99 UK,
1999

### Scholarships and Loans for Adult Students
ISBN 0-7689-0296-7,
$19.95 pb/$29.95 CAN/£16.99 UK,
1999

### Grants for Graduate & Postdoctoral Study
ISBN 0-7689-0019-0,
$32.95 pb/$45.95 CAN/£25 UK,
1998

### Scholarships for Study in the USA & Canada
ISBN 0-7689-0266-5,
$21.95 pb/$32.95 CAN/£16.99 UK,
1999

**PETERSON'S**
**THOMSON LEARNING**

# PETERSON'S

™

## HERE'S YOUR GUIDE TO DISTANCE LEARNING COMPANION CD!

- Link to an online database of even more distance learning degree and certificate programs.
- FREE access to an online self assessment.

**The CD above is subject to the terms of a License Agreement embedded in the CD.**

**To Install: 1.** Insert the CD into your CD-ROM drive. **2.** For Windows® 95/98 or NT: The CD will start automatically. If the CD does not autostart, double-click the My Computer icon, then the DL2002 CD-ROM icon, then DL2002.exe. For Macintosh: The CD will start automatically. If the CD does not autostart, click the DL2002 CD-ROM icon on your desktop, then DL2002. **3.** Follow the instructions on the screen.

## Minimum System Requirements:

**Best viewed at 16-bit high color mode (65536 colors).**
**Internet access required.**

**Windows:**
Pentium 133
2x CD-ROM drive
32 MB RAM and color monitor

**Macintosh:**
68030 processor with System 7.1
2x CD-ROM drive
32 MB RAM and color monitor

**Call 800-338-3282, Ext. 5660 if the CD is missing from this book.**